THE
AMERICAN
PROMISE

A HISTORY OF THE UNITED STATES

CANADA

MINNESOTA

St. Paul ★
Minneapolis ●

WISCONSIN

Lake Superior

MICHIGAN

Lansing ★

Milwaukee ●
Madison ●

Chicago ●

IOWA

Des Moines ★

Lake Michigan

Lake Huron

Detroit ●

Cleveland ●

OHIO

Columbus ★

Lake Erie

Lake Ontario

Buffalo ●

ILLINOIS

Springfield ★

INDIANA

Indianapolis ★

Cincinnati ●

Frankfort ★

Louisville ●

KENTUCKY

Ohio River

WEST
VIRGINIA

Charleston ●

Pittsburgh ●

Wheeling ●

PENNSYLVANIA

Harrisburg ●

Philadelphia ★

Albany ★

NEW
YORK

Hudson River

St. Lawrence River

VERMONT

Burlington ●

Montpelier ★

Mt. Washington
(6,288 ft.; 1,917 m)

MAINE

Augusta ★

Portland ●

Concord ★

NEW
HAMPSHIRE

Manchester ●

Boston ★

MASS.

Providence ★

Hartford ★

RHODE ISLAND

CONNECTICUT

New York ●

Trenton ★

NEW JERSEY

Dover ★

DELAWARE

Baltimore ●

Annapolis ★

WASHINGTON, D.C.

MARYLAND

Chesapeake
Bay

Potomac
River

Richmond ★

Norfolk ●

VIRGINIA

ATLANTIC
OCEAN

Kansas City ●

opeka ★

Jefferson
City ★

St. Louis ●

MISSOURI

chita ●

Cumberland River

Mississippi River

Knoxville ●

Nashville ★

TENNESSEE

Tennessee River

Memphis ●

Mt. Mitchell
(6,684 ft.; 2,037 m)

NORTH CAROLINA

Raleigh ★

Charlotte ●

SOUTH CAROLINA

Columbia ★

APPALACHIAN MOUNTAINS

TIDEWATER

Tulsa ●

LAHOMA

ahoma City ●

Little Rock ★

ARKANSAS

MISSISSIPPI

Jackson ★

ALABAMA

Montgomery ★

Birmingham ●

Atlanta ★

GEORGIA

Charleston ●

Dallas ●

ort Worth ●

LOUISIANA

Alabama River

stin ●

Baton Rouge ★

New Orleans ●

Houston ●

Jacksonville ●

Tallahassee ★

Orlando ●

FLORIDA

Lake
Okeechobee

Gulf of Mexico

Miami ●

BAHAMAS

THE
UNITED STATES
OF AMERICA

Elevation

Feet	Meters
Over 13,001	Over 3,001
6,561–13,000	2,001–3,000
3,281–6,560	1,001–2,000
1,641–3,280	501–1,000
661–1,640	201–500
0–660	0–200
Below sea level	Below sea level

ATLANTIC
OCEAN

VIRGIN
ISLANDS

San Juan ★

PUERTO RICO

Caribbean Sea

	50	100 miles
0		
0	50	100 kilometers

CUBA

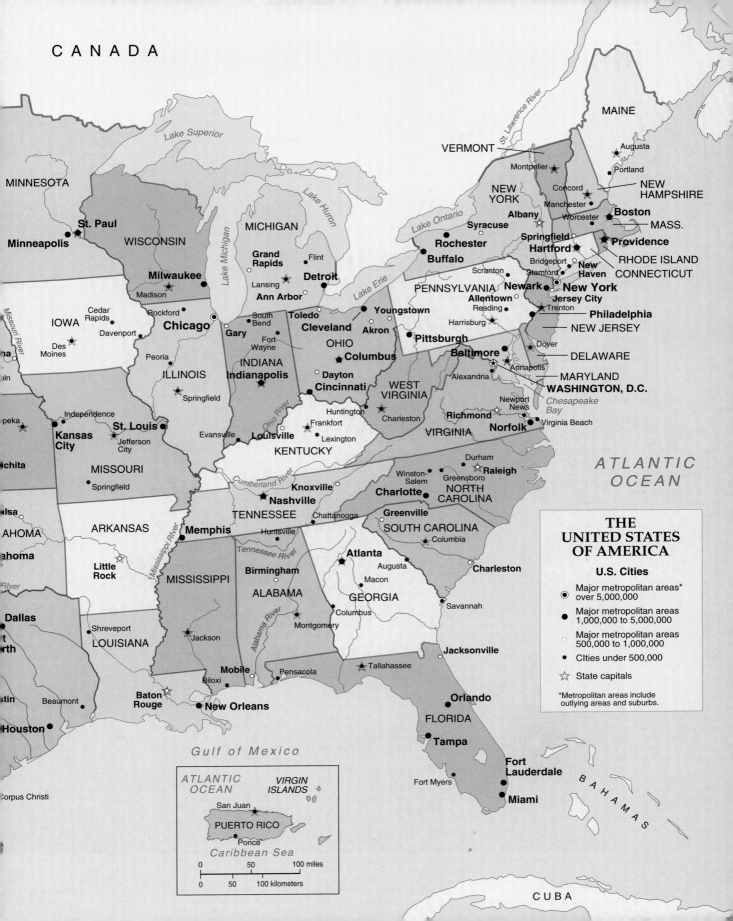

SIOUX CITY IOWA *by Grant Wood, 1930. Joslyn Art Museum.*

THE AMERICAN PROMISE

A HISTORY OF THE UNITED STATES

Volume II: From 1865

JAMES L. ROARK
Emory University

MICHAEL P. JOHNSON
Johns Hopkins University

PATRICIA CLINE COHEN
University of California at Santa Barbara

SARAH STAGE
University of Arizona, West

ALAN LAWSON
Boston College

SUSAN M. HARTMANN
The Ohio State University

BEDFORD BOOKS 〜 Boston

For Bedford Books

President and Publisher: Charles H. Christensen
General Manager and Associate Publisher: Joan E. Feinberg
History Editor: Katherine E. Kurzman
Project Manager: Tina Samaha
Developmental Editors: Louise D. Townsend and Barbara Muller
Editorial Assistant: Thomas Pierce
Managing Editor: Elizabeth M. Schaaf
Production Assistants: Ellen C. Thibault and Deborah A. Baker
Copyeditor: Barbara G. Flanagan
Proofreaders: Mary Lou Wilshaw and Lisa Wehrle
Text Design: Wanda Kossak
Photo Researcher: Pembroke Herbert/Sandi Rygiel, Picture Research Consultants & Archives, Inc.
Cartography: Mapping Specialists Limited
Page Layout: DeNee Reiton Skipper
Indexer: Steve Csipke
Cover Design: Wanda Kossak
Cover Art: Colbar Art, Incorporated, Long Island City, New York
Composition: York Graphics Services, Inc.
Printing and Binding: R. R. Donnelley & Sons

Library of Congress Catalog Card Number: 97–72376

Manufactured in the United States of America.

2 1 0 9 8 7
f e d c b a

For information, write: Bedford Books, 75 Arlington Street, Boston, MA 02116 (617–426–7440)

ISBN: 0-312-09525-2 (hardcover)
ISBN: 0-312-11196-7 (paperback Vol. 1)
ISBN: 0-312-11197-5 (paperback Vol. 2)

Cover art: Statue of Liberty souvenir bust (1997), manufactured by Colbar Art, Incorporated.

CONTENTS

A NOTE FROM THE PUBLISHER
PRESENTING *THE AMERICAN PROMISE*

YOU ARE HOLDING IN YOUR HANDS an innovative new text for the American history survey course. Carefully developed with the needs of students foremost in mind, *The American Promise* deftly wraps the inherently interesting but loose strands of social history around the more formal structure of political history. It is born of two convictions: (1) faced with an overwhelming amount of information, students need help determining what's important and (2) students won't get anything out of a textbook unless it's interesting and enjoyable. The design and art program represents an attempt to rethink the "look" of a textbook, fashioning every element from running-heads to captions to serve a pedagogical function or to further the narrative.

The next few pages offer an overview of the book and introduce its student-focused features. We urge you to take a few minutes to see how we've tried to improve on what has come before us. When you're finished, we hope you'll agree with us that *The American Promise* does more for students than any other survey of American history.

EASY-TO-FOLLOW CHAPTER STRUCTURE

The authors have sought to avoid an encyclopedic approach to American history in favor of building understanding through extensive examination of only the most important events and developments. The architecture of individual chapters is carefully designed to present information in a logical and ordered fashion that emphasizes major themes in history while incorporating individual accounts to maintain students' interest. Common to each chapter is a set of features—vignette, call-outs, conclusion, chronology, and bibliography—that provide useful guides to the narrative.

Opening vignettes

Every chapter begins with an engaging anecdote that eases readers into its major themes while immersing them in a specific historical moment.

(The complete example is found on page 605.)

(The complete example is found on page 605.)

CHAPTER

RECONSTRUCTION, 16
1863-1877

W HEN THE WAR WAS OVER, swarms of northern journalists and government officials rushed to the South to see what four years of fighting had accomplished. Ugly stories of stiff-necked defiance toward Yankees and brutal violence toward ex-slaves had drifted northward. Andrew Johnson, Abraham Lincoln's successor in the White House, asked General Carl Schurz to undertake a special fact-finding tour to assess conditions in the ex-Confederate states. Schurz, a leading antislavery lecturer and Union general, arrived in Charleston, South Carolina, the "Queen City of the South," in July 1865.

Charleston greeted the visitor with an empty harbor, rotting wharves, and gutted buildings. The city looked, Schurz observed, as if it had been struck with "the sudden and irresistible force of a thunderbolt." Cattle grazed in its weed-filled streets. Schurz met former cotton kings and rice barons who could not afford to buy breakfast. Ex-slaves, now Union soldiers, patrolled the city's streets. Schools overflowed with African American children whom it was formerly considered a crime to educate. The Citadel, the state's military school, where once "the chivalric youth of South Carolina was educated for the task of perpetuating slavery by force of arms," now ho⸺d the Fifty-fourth Massachusetts Colored Regiment.

Two-tiered running heads

Double bars at the top of every page let students know where they are in the book, and where they are in the chronology of American history.

Call-outs

Throughout each chapter, occasional brief passages have been pulled from the main text to highlight important points, focus readers' attention, and convey the liveliness of the narrative.

While northern resolve to defend black freedom withered, southern commitment to white supremacy intensified.

Conclusions

Each chapter ends with a brief conclusion that summarizes the narrative's main points, analyzes their significance, and discusses their consequences.

(The complete example is found on page 639.)

Conclusion: "A Revolution but Half-Accomplished"

In 1865, when General Carl Schurz visited the South at President Andrew Johnson's behest, he discovered "a revolution but half-accomplished." Defeat had not prepared the South for an easy transition from slavery to free labor, from white racial despotism to equal justice, and from white political monopoly to biracial democracy. The old elite wanted to get "things back as near to slavery as possible," while ex-slaves and whites who had lacked power in the slave regime were eager to exploit the revolutionary implications of defeat and emancipation.

Chronologies

A chronology at the close of each chapter provides a handy review of the most important dates and events.

(For the complete chronology, see pages 640–641.)

CHRONOLOGY

1863   **December.** Lincoln issues Proclamation of Amnesty and Reconstruction.

1864   **July.** Congress offers more stringent plan for reconstruction, Wade-Davis bill.

1865   **January.** General William T. Sherman sets aside land in South Carolina for black settlement.

     March 4. Lincoln sworn in for second term as president of United States.

     March. Congress establishes Freed-

April 14. Linc
15, is succeed
Andrew John

Fall. Southern
criminatory b

December. T
ment abolishi
of U.S. Const

1866   **April.** Congr
Amendment
blacks Ameri

Bibliographies

Each chapter includes an up-to-date list of recommended works of scholarship. These bibliographies begin with general references for the period with the remainder of the titles organized under subheadings that closely correspond to the chapter's major sections.

(For the complete bibliography, turn to page 641.)

BIBLIOGRAPHY

GENERAL WORKS

W. E. B. Du Bois, *Black Reconstruction in America* (1935).

Eric Foner, *Reconstruction: America's Unfinished Revolution, 1863–1877* (1988).

John Hope Franklin, *Reconstruction after the Civil War* (1961).

James M. McPherson, *Ordeal by Fire: The Civil War and Reconstruction* (1982).

Rembert W. Patrick, *The Reconstruction of the Nation* (1967).

J. G. Randall and David Donald, *The Civil War and Reconstruction* (1967).

WARTIME RECONSTR

Richard H. Abbott, *The
lican Party and the Sc*

Herman Belz, *Emancip
Constitutionalism in t*

Ira Berlin et al., eds.,
Emancipation, 1861–

Louis S. Gerteis, *From
icy toward Southern I*

Peyton McCrary, *Abra*
Louisiana Experiment

STRIKING VISUAL FEATURES

Beautifully designed and illustrated, *The American Promise* is replete with visual elements that expand upon—rather than merely decorate—the narrative. Every image has been chosen for its ability to enhance an understanding of the past.

Comprehensive illustration program with extensive captions

Hundreds of fresh images (many of them published in a survey text for the first time) dramatize and extend the story in the text. Unusually full captions—many of which include quotations, questions, or comparisons with other images—draw readers into active engagement with this visual material.

(For this photo, see page 1154.)

Chapter-opening artifacts

To emphasize the importance of material culture in studying the past, each chapter opens with a full-page reproduction of a contemporary cultural artifact, such as clothing, books, musical instruments, or political emblems. Informative captions provide background information and invite readers to consider the artifact's historical implications.

(For the complete example of a chapter-opening artifact, turn to page 688.)

FIGHTING THE CLIMATE AND GEOGRAPHY
Steamy tropical conditions and an inhospitable terrain were among the nonhuman enemies U.S. troops faced in Vietnam. Soldiers li̶ ̶ ̶ ̶ ̶ ̶ king their ̶ ̶

CAMPAIGN LANTERN
Political parties gave out novelty items like this paper lantern from Republican Benjamin Harrison's 1888 presidential campaign. The log cabin, a staple political icon, celebrates the candidate's humble origins, while the reference to Tippecanoe highlights his relationship to President William Henry Harrison, his grandfather, the victor of the Battle of Tippecanoe in 1811. "Protection" in bold letters underscores the Republican Party's perennial support for a tariff̶ ̶ ̶ ̶ ̶ ̶ ̶ ̶ ̶ ̶ ̶ the count̶ ̶ ̶ ̶ ̶ ̶ ̶ ̶ ̶ ̶ from foreign c̶ ̶

The Rise of the Sun Belt, 1940–1960

Extensive map and graphics program

The American Promise includes numerous four-color maps that provide a visual representation of historical data. Attractively designed tables, charts, and graphs throughout the book reinforce and expand on information in the text. An accompanying workbook — available free of charge with copies of the text — provides additional opportunities to expand on themes relating to the historical significance of geography using maps from the textbook.

(This map is found on page 1079; turn to page 729 for this graph.)

The U.S. Business Cycle, 1870–1890

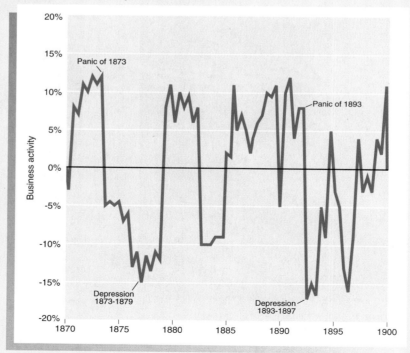

The narrative in *The American Promise* is augmented with three kinds of special features to highlight the kinds of evidence and issues that fascinate even the casual reader. Providing students a moment to pause in the great sweep of coverage, these documents and mini-essays allow a focus that is not possible within the main narrative.

TEXTS IN HISTORICAL CONTEXT

Japanese Internment

*A*ngrily determined that the bombing of Pearl Harbor would not be followed by more sneak attacks, military and political leaders on the West Coast targeted persons of Japanese descent—alien and citizen alike—as potential saboteurs. Early in 1942, General John DeWitt, commander of the Western Defense Command, persuaded President Franklin Roosevelt to issue an executive order authorizing the removal of the Japanese. Subsequently, some 110,000 Japanese Americans were confined to relocation camps in remote areas, surrounded by barbed wire and armed guards. DeWitt's recommendation expressed concern for military security within racist conceptions long used to curb Asian immigration.

DOCUMENT 1. Final Recommendations of the Commanding General, Western Defense Command and Fourth Army, Submitted to the Secretary of War

February 14, 1942

Memorandum for the Secretary of War.

Subject: Evacuation of Japanese and Other Subversive Persons from the Pacific Coast.

1. In presenting a recommendation for the evacuation of Japanese and other subversive persons from the Pacific Coast, the following facts have been considered:

Missi... of the Western Defense Com-

particula...

througho...

Hosti...
enemy ag...
vicinity t...
sisting er...

In the...
affinities...
race is an...
third gen...
possessed...
"America...
conclude...
of white...
affinity a...
to fight a...
against t...

It, the...
Coast ov...
extraction...
that thes...
action at...
no sabot...
and conf...
taken. . .

*I*mpriso...
*Japanes...
Looking b...
her confin...

Texts in Historical Context

A variety of primary documents —letters, diaries, speeches, memoirs and testimony—bring students into direct contact with the human impact of major historical events and issues. Headnotes provide background and context.

(For this complete Texts in Historical Context, turn to pages 1000–1001.)

Historical Question

These interpretive essays address specific historical questions likely to be of intrinsic interest to students. Among the topics discussed are: How Could a Vice President Get Away With Murder?, and Why Did the Allies Refuse to Bomb the Death Camps? Historical Questions single out issues of ongoing interest, providing answers in greater detail than possible in the narrative.

(For this complete Historical Question, turn to pages 952–953.)

Technology in America

Recognizing that the impact of technologies is of particular interest and relevance today, these brief (150–300 words) illustrated essays examine the ramifications —positive and negative—of specific technological changes.

(For this complete Technology in America, turn to page 1010.)

HISTORICAL QUESTION

Huey Long: Demagogue or Champion of the Dispossessed?

FROM THE TIME HE HAD BEEN A SMALL CHILD, Huey P. Long was what one exasperated neighbor called a "pesterance." Defiant at school, artful at avoiding any disagreeable chores, ruthlessly driven to be the center of attention, Long had gotten ahead through the shrewdness of his extraordinary intelligence and brash willingness to flout conventional rules. Though he spent only brief periods at the University of Oklahoma and Tulane University, he cajoled a judge to convene a special bar examination, which he passed easily at the age of twenty-one. Declaring that he came out of that examination

that you ha
have never
ways that y
are the ins
abled?" W
Louisiana
side the cit
the country
cent of tho
by 1920, th
including

Long a
poor peopl
ruthlessly.
in 1929, Lo
used to try
he said. "
miter. I dy
Long comj
around the
dictator of
his power.
ume in his

TECHNOLOGY IN AMERICA
Penicillin

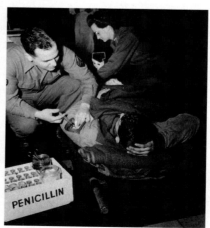

National Archives.

The antibacterial drug, penicillin, shown being injected into a soldier, did more than any other medical advance to save lives on the battlefield during World War II.

to fruition just in time to meet the de
need for drugs to fight infection. In
lish biochemist, Alexander Fleming,
discovered that mold left on laborat
plates could kill bacteria. Subsequer
using the organic form of arsenic ex
the mold, which Fleming called pen
highly effective against a wide varie
infections. These experiments succee
just as the Battle of Britain against t
bombing blitz was reaching its clim.
lifesaving use of penicillin on woun
later on soldiers in North Africa, a t
researchers rushed to the United St.
urge mass production of the drug. T
came to a dramatic conclusion wher
bor bombing ended a conference on
medicine being held in Honolulu th
the British team was to present its ca
American authorities moved cautioi
use of the new wonder drug. By Aj
than 500 men had received penicilli
its astonishingly successful results c
authorities early in 1944 to urge all
nel to use penicillin "without hesita
final tally of the war's damage, dea
tle were half those of World War I,
cause of penicillin, mortality

INNOVATIVE APPENDICES

A three-part appendix serves as a convenient repository of important documents, historical data, and research resources. As with every other part of *The American Promise*, we have endeavored to enhance the usefulness of this critical material in new ways.

Documents

In addition to the complete texts of the Declaration of Independence and the Constitution, this section features unique annotations that provide appropriate background to the twenty-seven constitutional amendments—plus six that didn't make it into the final document.

(The annotated amendments are on pages A-10–A-23.)

Amendment IV

The right of the people to be secure in their persons, houses, papers, and effects, against unreasonable searches and seizures, shall not be violated, and no warrants shall issue but upon probable cause, supported by oath or affirmation, and particularly describing the place to be searched, and the persons or things to be seized.

◆ ◆ ◆

In the years before the Revolution, the houses, barns, stores, and warehouses of American colonists were ransacked by British authorities under "writs of assistance" or general warrants. The British, thus empowered, searched for seditious material or smuggled goods that could then be used as evidence against colonists who were charged with a crime only after the items were found.

Facts and Figures

This uniquely abundant collection of political, economic, and demographic information supplements the statistical data in the text on everything from population to education. It also includes summaries of twenty-four significant Supreme Court cases.

(For Facts and Figures, see pages A-24–A-26.)

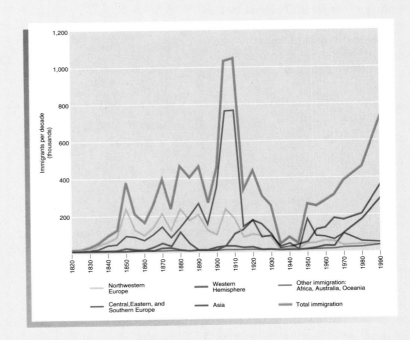

Research Resources in U.S. History

Located on pages A-67–A-69, this annotated list of reference materials and Internet offerings provides a handy starting point for research papers, with extensive suggestions for locating many kinds of primary and secondary sources.

American Memory: Historical Collection from the National Digital Library Program. <http://rs6.loc.gov/amhome.html> An Internet site that features digitized primary source materials from the Library of Congress, among them African American pamphlets, civil war photographs, documents from the Continental Congress and the Constitutional Convention of 1774–1790, materials on woman suffrage, and oral histories.

Directory of Scholarly and Professional Electronic Conferences. <http://n2h2.com/KOVAKS/>. A good place to find out what electronic conversations are going on in a scholarly discipline. Includes a good search facility and instructions on how to connect to e-mail discussion lists, newsgroups, and interactive chat sites with academic content. Once identified, these conferences are good places to raise ques... find out what controversies are currently ...

User-friendly Index

Knowing that students use indexes primarily as study aids, the index in *The American Promise* is designed to make people, events, topics, and concepts as easy to locate as possible. Page numbers for a topic's main coverage are indicated in boldface; entries for significant people and events include dates; listings of important images, maps, and graphics are provided; and cross-references highlight related subjects.

NOTE TO INSTRUCTORS

The American Promise is accompanied by an unusually full complement of ancillaries. Available for student purchase are a documents reader, a study guide, and titles from the Bedford Series in History and Culture. For teachers, we offer an instructor's manual, a testbank, a guide for teaching assistants, and a large transparency set that includes images not found in the text and a guide with teaching suggestions. Also available to be packaged free with the textbook is a two-volume map workbook with exercises based on maps drawn from every chapter in the text. For complete descriptions of each of these ancillaries, please refer to the Preface for Instructors.

PREFACE FOR INSTRUCTORS

WE SET OUT TO WRITE *The American Promise* because, as longtime teachers of the survey course, we felt that other texts simply didn't reflect what works in our classrooms. Most survey texts emphasize either a social or a political approach to history; by focusing on one, they inevitably slight the other. In our classrooms, students need *both* the structure a political narrative provides and the insights gained from examining social and cultural experiences. In our view, the story of politics is an account not merely of parties and presidents but also of the public arena in which issues of power, interest, culture, ideology, and identity are contested. In our effort to write a comprehensive account of American history, we have focused on the public arena—as the place where politics comes together with social and cultural events—to show how Americans lived within their political culture and confronted the major issues of their times.

We have worked to keep our writing clear, direct, and interesting, never losing sight of our obligation to engage our readers and offer them guidance. Because students in the introductory course often complain that they have difficulty figuring out what they need to know and why they need to know it, we deliberately avoided unnecessary detail so that we could offer more fully developed discussions of the major political, social, cultural, and economic changes that students should understand and remember when they've completed the course.

In our view, history is the story of human agency. To show students that history was made by *people*, we have included the voices of contemporaries who confronted the issues and events of their day. Every chapter includes numerous quotations from the famous and forgotten, taken from their journals, speeches, and letters. Vignettes open every chapter, spotlighting individuals like Benjamin Franklin, Frederick Douglass, and Jane Addams who worked for change in their day and whose efforts still affect our lives. More than a dozen document features demonstrate the impact of major historical events on individuals.

The American Promise also aims to demonstrate that history is both a body of knowledge and an ongoing process of investigation. Too many beginning students believe that historians simply gather facts and string them together into a chronological narrative: that what historians write, students must memorize. To show that the story of history is a reflection of questions historians consciously pose of the past, recurring interpretive essays illustrate how contemporary curiosity shapes historical inquiry and introduce students to a more textured understanding of the discipline.

Features

The narrative in *The American Promise* is buttressed by a number of features that address the concerns most frequently voiced by teachers: that students often find history boring and difficult. Every feature has been conceived and developed with one of these two elemental problems in mind.

We have tried to make American history as accessible as possible for students. In addition to stressing the most important historical developments, each chapter is clearly structured to reinforce the essential people, events, and themes of the period. Innovative **call-outs**—attention-grabbing passages pulled from the main narrative and set in larger type—help students focus. At the close of each chapter, **conclusions** summarize the main themes and events and provide a bridge to upcoming material, **chronologies** provide a handy review of significant events and dates, and extensive **bibliographies** provide an up-to-date listing of recommended works of scholarship for additional reading and research.

Because students learn more when they're interested in the subject matter, we've made a special effort to incorporate features that bring American history to life. **Chapter-opening vignettes** invite students into the narrative with a compelling account of a person or event that embodies some of the chapter's main themes. **Historical Questions** pose and investigate specific questions of continuing interest to demonstrate to students the depth and variety of possible answers. **Texts in Historical Context** reprint primary documents that illustrate the social impact of major events and issues, and **Technology in America** highlights the ramifications that new inventions and processes—most of which we now take for granted—had when they were introduced.

Finally, we are especially proud of our art program. The publisher has provided **an impressive collection of illustrations**—many of them never published before in a survey text—that supplement the narrative, drawing students in and encouraging them to engage the visual material. Rather than leave students to make what they can from these illustrations, we offer a lot of guidance. **Comprehensive captions** unpack the layers of meaning in the pictures, supplement the information in the chapter, raise questions that challenge students to use their historical imaginations, and help students view the images analytically.

Our title, *The American Promise*, reflects our conviction that American history is an unfinished story. From the beginning, Americans have differed profoundly over the meaning of the nation's promise. Yet few doubted that unusual opportunities beckoned in America. In many ways, these potential opportunities intensified conflict over the direction of change, as Americans sought to realize a measure of the promise they sensed around them. For millions, the nation held out the promise of a better life, unfettered worship, representative government, democratic politics, and other freedoms seldom found elsewhere on the globe. But none of these promises came with guarantees. And promises fulfilled for some meant promises denied to others. As we see it, much of American history is a continuing struggle over the definition and realization of the nation's promise. Abraham Lincoln, in the midst of what he termed the "fiery trial" of the Civil War, pronounced the nation "the last best hope of Earth." That hope, kept alive by countless sacrifices, has been marred by compromises, disappointments, and denials, but it lives still. Ideally, *The American Promise* will help students become aware of the legacy of hope bequeathed to them by previous generations of Americans stretching back nearly four centuries, a legacy that is theirs to preserve and to build upon.

Supplements

A comprehensive collection of supplements, every one of them created specifically to accompany *The American Promise*, provides an integrated support system for classroom success. All of the expected elements are included, but in every case we have tried to raise the bar a notch higher, adding new features to help instructors teach and students learn American history. We've also provided some new items: a guide for teaching assistants, an unusually full set of transparencies accompanied by teaching suggestions, and a map workbook that provides in-depth exercises on maps in the text.

For Students

Reading the American Past: Selected Historical Documents. This affordable two-volume collection of primary sources—selected and edited by Michael P. Johnson (Johns Hopkins University) specifically to accompany *The American Promise*—permits students to go beyond the textbook narrative and puzzle out the meanings of historical documents. Paralleling the organization of the text, each chapter includes substantial passages from several documents—including presidential speeches, court records, estate inventories, private diaries, personal letters, and oral histories. Each document is introduced by a brief headnote and followed by questions that help students understand both what the document says and what its historical significance is.

Making the Most of THE AMERICAN PROMISE: A Study Guide. This essential supplement for students, prepared by John Moretta and David Wilcox (both of Houston Community College), provides practice opportunities to reinforce the main themes and ideas from the text's narrative. For each chapter in *The American Promise*, a corresponding chapter in the study guide includes learning objectives, a brief summary, a timeline with questions on important dates, a glossary of terms, map exercises with location and analysis questions, multiple-choice questions, and essay questions. An answer key allows students to test themselves.

Mapping THE AMERICAN PROMISE: Historical Geography Workbook. Prepared by Mark Newman (University of Illinois, Chicago), this stand-alone supplement provides additional exercises using maps drawn from *The American Promise*. Because a knowledge of geography is crucial to understanding the way our country has grown over five hundred years, we make this supplement available to students free with the purchase of the text. Each exercise asks students to label landmarks on the American continent and then analyze the significance of geography in the unfolding of historical events.

Working to suggest the implications of geography for history, these exercises also reinforce basic place names in a way that helps students remember them and understand why they should.

The Bedford Series in History and Culture. Any of the volumes from this highly acclaimed series of brief, inexpensive, document-based supplements can be packaged with *The American Promise* at a reduced price. More than forty titles include *The Sovereignty and Goodness of God, The Interesting Narrative of the Life of Olaudah Equiano, The Autobiography of Benjamin Franklin, Narrative of the Life of Frederick Douglass, The Souls of Black Folk, Plunkitt of Tammany Hall,* and many more.

For Instructors

Teaching THE AMERICAN PROMISE: A Hands-On Guide for Instructors. Written by Michael Gagnon (Emory University) and Sarah E. Gardner (Mercer University), this practical two-volume guide provides myriad suggestions and resources for teaching *The American Promise.* Each of its thirty-two chapters includes an outline (in the form of questions) of the text's narrative, three lecture strategies, multiple-choice questions, a list of video and film resources, and suggestions for incorporating sources from READING THE AMERICAN PAST or from the Bedford Series in History and Culture. A particularly useful new feature for first-time teachers anticipates some of the most common misconceptions undergraduates have about each chapter's topics.

Testbank to Accompany THE AMERICAN PROMISE. Written by two longtime teachers of the American history survey, John Moretta and David Wilcox (both of Houston Community College), this set provides 70–80 multiple-choice, true/false, short-answer, identification, and essay questions for each of the thirty-two chapters in *The American Promise.* The testbank is available either on disk (Macintosh and Windows), with a function that allows users to customize the exams, or in booklet form.

Discussing THE AMERICAN PROMISE: A Survival Guide for First-Time Teaching Assistants. Tied directly to *The American Promise,* this unique resource provides a wealth of practical suggestions to help first-time teaching assistants develop their skills and succeed in the classroom. Written by experienced TA adviser Michael A. Bellesiles (Emory University), this brief supplement offers concrete advice on teaching from *The American Promise,* working with professors, dealing with difficult students, running discussion sections, designing assignments, grading tests and papers, relating research to classroom experience, overcoming common problems, and more.

Transparencies to Accompany THE AMERICAN PROMISE (with Teaching Suggestions). More than 150 images are available as full-color acetates to adopters of *The American Promise.* For each chapter a set of five transparencies has been assembled to highlight the chapter-opening artifacts, important maps and graphs, and striking illustrations. We have also selected additional illustrations that are not included in the text. To assist teachers in presenting these images, a guide provides background and elaborates on teaching possibilities.

Acknowledgments

We owe a great debt to the community of scholars who took time away from their own teaching and research to help us complete *The American Promise*. Many people have read chapters and offered valuable criticism; others have listened patiently and provided important advice. The authors would like to express their gratitude to:

Katherine G. Aiken, University of Idaho
Todd Beekley
Kathleen Christine Berkeley, University of North Carolina—Wilmington
John C. Burnham, The Ohio State University
Vernon Burton, University of Illinois, Urbana
Victoria Byerly
Victor Chen
Peter Coclanis, University of North Carolina at Chapel Hill
Joseph Cugini
Leonard Dinnerstein, University of Arizona, Tucson
Laura F. Edwards, University of South Florida
Joseph J. Ellis, Mount Holyoke College
Lancelot Farrar
Elizabeth Feder, Rhodes College
Dan Feller, University of New Mexico
Alan Gallay, Western Washington University
Mark Gelfand, Boston College
William Graebner, State University of New York, Buffalo at Fredonia
Michael D. Green, University of Kentucky
Jack Greene, Johns Hopkins University
Thomas Hartshorne, Cleveland State University
Ronald Howard, Mississippi College
George Juergens, Indiana University
Wilma King, Michigan State University
Barbara Loomis, San Francisco State University
George McJimsey, Iowa State University
Melinda McMahon, University of California, Santa Barbara
John Moon, Fitchburg State University
Roger L. Nichols, University of Arizona, Tucson
Donald K. Pickens, University of North Texas
John O. Pohlman
Theda Perdue, University of Kentucky
David Rankin, University of California, Irvine

Herbert Rissler, Indiana State University
Dave Roediger, University of Minnesota
Carole Srole, California State University, Los Angeles
Thomas Terrill, University of South Carolina
Daniel H. Usner, Jr., Cornell University

A project as large and as complex as this requires the talents of many individuals. The authors would like to thank Pembroke Herbert and Sandi Rygiel of Picture Research Consultants, Inc., whose research and imagination are responsible for the fine illustrations. Thanks are also due to Barbara Muller, whose accomplished editing and sage advice improved volume 1 in countless ways, and to Lynne Weiss for her extensive work on the appendix materials. Michael Gagnon of Emory University and Sarah Gardner of Mercer University drew deeply on their own experience to write the Instructor's Manual, and Michael Bellesiles of Emory University turned his talents to the TA guide. John Moretta and David Wilcox of Houston Community College combined their skills to produce the study guide and testbank. Mark Newman of the University of Illinois at Chicago developed the very useful map workbook. Thanks also to Gerry McCauley, who represents us as literary agent.

Finally, we would like to thank the many people at Bedford Books who have been crucial to this project. We are grateful to Katherine Kurzman and to Ellen Kuhl for their tireless efforts marketing the book, and to Charisse Kiino, who worked on the ancillary program. No one has carried more of the burden than our editor, Louise Townsend. Her skill, composure, and endurance brought the project from an incomplete draft to a finished work. With great skill and professionalism, Tina Samaha, our project manager, pulled all the pieces together. She kept her head when the rest of us were in danger of losing ours. Managing Editor Elizabeth Schaaf oversaw production of the book, while Ellen Thibault, Deborah Baker, and Thomas Pierce helped out on myriad editorial tasks. Copyeditor Barbara Flanagan's sharp eye improved our best efforts and made the entire book better. Charles Christensen, publisher, and Joan Feinberg, general manager, have taken a personal interest in this project from the first and have guided it through every stage of development.

THE
AMERICAN
PROMISE

A HISTORY OF THE UNITED STATES

ba be bi bo bu	ra re ri ro ru
da de di do du	sa se si so su
fa fe fi fo fu	ta te ti to tu
ka ke ki ko ku	va ve vi vo vu

Top.   Hen and chickens.   Drum.

la le li lo lu	ya ye yi yo yu
na ne ni no nu	*ca ce ci co cu
pa pe pi po pu	ga ge gi go gu

Bugle.

ab eb ib
ab ed id
af ef if
ag eg i

Zebra.   Hobby-horse.

Fire Engine.   Snake.

Turkey.   Hoopoe

Squirrel.

AMERICAN
ONE CENT
PRIMER.

NEW YORK:
KIGGINS & KELLOGG, PUBLISHERS,
Nos. 123 & 125 WILLIAM STREET,
Between John & Fulton.

ONE-CENT PRIMER

"The people are hungry and thirsty after knowledge," a former slave from South Carolina observed after the Civil War. Future African American leader Booker T. Washington remembered "a whole race trying to go to school. Few were too young, and none too old, to make the attempt to learn." Inexpensive elementary textbooks (this humble eight-page primer cost a penny) offered poor ex-slaves the basic elements of literacy — the letters of the alphabet and the sounds they make. For people who had been forbidden to learn to read and write as slaves, literacy symbolized freedom. It also meant that deeply religious people could experience the joy of reading the Bible. Literacy provided a crucial tool for negotiating the hostile world of the postwar South. Reading and writing permitted African Americans to understand labor agreements, sign contracts, and participate knowledgeably in politics.

The William Gladstone Collection.

RECONSTRUCTION, 1863-1877 16

WHEN THE WAR WAS OVER, swarms of northern journalists and government officials rushed to the South to see what four years of fighting had accomplished. Ugly stories of stiff-necked defiance toward Yankees and brutal violence toward ex-slaves had drifted northward. Andrew Johnson, Abraham Lincoln's successor in the White House, asked General Carl Schurz to undertake a special fact-finding tour to assess conditions in the ex-Confederate states. Schurz, a leading antislavery lecturer and Union general, arrived in Charleston, South Carolina, the "Queen City of the South," in July 1865.

Charleston greeted the visitor with an empty harbor, rotting wharves, and gutted buildings. The city looked, Schurz observed, as if it had been struck with "the sudden and irresistible force of a thunderbolt." Cattle grazed in its weed-filled streets. Schurz met former cotton kings and rice barons who could not afford to buy breakfast. Ex-slaves, now Union soldiers, patrolled the city's streets. Schools overflowed with African American children whom it was formerly considered a crime to educate. The Citadel, the state's military school, where once "the chivalric youth of South Carolina was educated for the task of perpetuating slavery by force of arms," now housed the Fifty-fourth Massachusetts Colored Regiment.

Some whites openly expressed their hatred for the new order. Schurz came across defiant young men still "in a swearing mood" who wanted to "fight the war over again." Women in particular, he discovered, remained as "vindictive and defiant as ever." Schurz witnessed one incident in a hotel. "A day or two ago a Union officer, yielding to an impulse of politeness, handed a dish of pickles to a Southern lady at the dinner-table," he said. "A look of unspeakable scorn and indignation met him. 'So you think,' said the lady, 'a Southern woman will take a dish of pickles from a hand that is dripping with the blood of her countrymen?'"

As Schurz slowly made his way across the South to New Orleans, he concluded that most whites "accept things as they are," but he meant only that they recognized that the Confederacy was dead and legal slavery was gone. More than that, they refused to grant. When they professed loyalty to the Union, they did so with a scowl. Moreover, they had not changed their minds about slavery. "The nigger is free, to be sure," ex-slaveholders told him repeatedly, "but he will not work unless compelled to work; we must make him work somehow." Former masters "study not how to build up and develop a true system of free labor," Schurz observed, "but how to avoid it." Where there were no federal troops to stop them, they resorted to the "bowie-knife and revolver, to keep the negroes in their former subjection."

But Schurz found little evidence of black-initiated violence. "Another race . . . would probably have proceeded to cut the throats of those who were in the habit

RUINS OF PINCKNEY HOUSE, CHARLESTON, SOUTH CAROLINA
Northerners had a special hatred for Charleston. According to one inhabitant, Northerners promised: "The rebellion commenced where Charleston is, and shall end, where Charleston was." A devastating fire and three years of Yankee bombardment had almost fulfilled the promise. But in 1865, other consequences of the war alarmed white Charlestonians even more than the physical destruction. Henry Middleton told his sister in Philadelphia that no one could imagine "the utter topsy-turveying of all our institutions."
Library of Congress.

of whipping wives and mothers," he thought, but freedmen simply stood up "a little more independently before their former owners." As for former slaves' performance as free laborers, Schurz deemed it only "middling-fair." He believed he knew why. "The idea has got into the heads of the negroes that the land belongs to them," he declared. They were in no hurry, consequently, to work for whites who claimed to be landlords. Still, he concluded, "the colored man will learn sooner what he has to do as a free laborer than the white man in these parts will learn how to treat a free laborer."

Two months in the South convinced Schurz that withdrawing federal troops and restoring self-government would be a fatal error. He called the Civil War a "revolution but half accomplished." Military victory had destroyed slavery, but it had not erased proslavery ideas. Left to themselves, ex-Confederates would "introduce some new system of forced labor, not perhaps exactly slavery in its old form but something similar to it." To defend themselves, blacks would need land of their own and voting rights, Schurz concluded. Until whites "cut loose

from the past," he declared, "it will be a dangerous experiment to put Southern society upon its own legs."

As Schurz discovered, the end of the war did not mean the beginning of peace. Instead, the nation entered one of its most chaotic and conflicted eras—Reconstruction. It was not that the Civil War failed to resolve anything. Northern victory had determined once and for all the fates of secession and slavery, but out of the war emerged two new divisive questions. First, what was the status of the defeated South within the Union? Would the eleven ex-Confederate states be quickly and forgivingly welcomed back, or would they be held at arm's length and required to reform before resuming their former places? Second, what would freedom mean for ex-slaves? Would they be left to make their place in the South on their own, or would the federal government guarantee full citizenship, free labor, and equality?

Throughout Reconstruction, little was fixed, and the pace of change was swift. What seemed an unlikely possibility at one moment found majority support the next. In the months after the war, calls to extend the ballot and full citizenship to freedmen generated hysteria, but the proposals quickly became standard Republican policy and the law of the land. "These are no times of ordinary politics," Boston lawyer and reformer Wendell Phillips declared in 1867. "These are formative hours; the national purpose and thought grows and ripens in thirty days as much as ordinary years bring it forward."

In one way or another, everyone agreed that the central issue in reconstruction was the place of African Americans in American society. North and South divided over the issue, but neither region spoke with a single voice. Still, a majority of southern whites rejected black rights. Southern intransigence in turn helped northern Republicans to close ranks and shifted the party's center toward more radical definitions of black freedom. It was never simply a debate between whites, however. Blacks emerged from slavery with their own ideas, and they became active agents in the struggle to define freedom.

The political part of that struggle took place in the nation's capital and in the state legislatures and county seats of the South. But the struggle also engaged the economic and social consequences of emancipation. In masters' kitchens and in plantation fields, ex-slaves strove to leave slavery behind and to become free laborers and free people. Many whites, as Carl Schurz learned, resisted letting go of the Old South. Nevertheless, emancipation and the developments of Reconstruction had profound consequences for blacks and whites in the South and for the nation as a whole.

Wartime Reconstruction

Reconstruction did not wait for the end of war. As the odds of a northern victory increased, thinking about reunification quickened. Immediately, a question arose: Who had authority to devise a plan of reconstruction? The Founders had not anticipated such a problem, and so the Constitution stood silent. Lincoln believed firmly that reconstruction was a matter of executive responsibility. Congress just as firmly asserted its jurisdiction. Fueling the argument about who had authority to set the terms of reconstruction were significant differences about the terms themselves. Lincoln's primary aim was the restoration of national unity, which he sought through a program of speedy, forgiving political

reconciliation. Congress feared that the president's lenient program amounted to restoring the old southern ruling class to power. It wanted greater assurances of white loyalty and greater guarantees of black rights. Rival plans emerged during the war, but Lincoln and Congress managed to bridge their differences. Only continued cooperation would achieve victory over the South and abolition of slavery.

In their eagerness to formulate a plan for political reunification, neither Lincoln nor Congress gave much attention to the South's land and labor problems. But war was rapidly eroding slavery and traditional plantation agriculture, and Yankee military commanders in the Union-occupied areas of the Confederacy had no choice but to oversee the emergence of a new labor system. With little guidance from Washington, northern officials felt their way along, bumping heads with both planters and freedmen. Although hastily assembled and improvised, their labor system ultimately had more staying power than any reconstruction policy formulated in wartime Washington.

"To Bind Up the Nation's Wounds"

On March 4, 1865, President Abraham Lincoln delivered his second inaugural address. His words blazed with religious imagery as he surveyed the history of the long, deadly war and then looked ahead to peace. "With malice toward none; with charity for all; with firmness in the right, as God gives us to see the right," Lincoln said, "let us strive on to finish the work we are in; to bind up the nation's wounds . . . to do all which may achieve and cherish a just, and a lasting peace." Lincoln had contemplated reunion for nearly two years. Deep compassion for the enemy guided his thinking about peace. But kindness is not the key to understanding Lincoln's program. His reconstruction plan aimed primarily at shortening the war and ending slavery.

Lincoln believed firmly that reconstruction was a matter of executive responsibility. Congress just as firmly asserted its jurisdiction.

In his Proclamation of Amnesty and Reconstruction, issued in December 1863, when Union forces had finally gained the upper hand on the battlefield, Lincoln offered a full pardon to rebels willing to renounce secession and to accept the abolition of slavery. (Pardons were valuable because they restored all property, except slaves, and full political rights.) His offer excluded several groups of Confederates, such as high-ranking civilian and military officers, but the plan called for no mass arrests, no trials for treason, and no executions. Instead, when only 10 percent of men who had been qualified voters in 1860 had taken an oath of allegiance, they could organize a new state government. Lincoln hoped that war-sick rebels would embrace the easy terms of reunification, renew their allegiance to the Union, and abandon both slavery and secession. His plan did not require that ex-rebels extend social or political rights to ex-slaves, nor did it anticipate a program of long-term federal assistance to freedmen. Clearly, the president sought to restore the broken Union, not to reform it.

Lincoln's easy terms enraged abolitionists like Wendell Phillips, who charged that the president "makes the negro's freedom a mere sham." He "is willing that the negro should be free but seeks nothing else for him," Phillips declared. He compared Lincoln unfavorably to the most passive of the Civil War generals: "What McClellan was on the battlefield—'Do as little hurt as possible!'—Lincoln is in civil affairs—'Make as little change as possible!'" Phillips and other radicals called instead for revolutionary change, for a thoroughgoing overhaul of southern society. Their ideas proved to be too drastic for most Republicans during the war years, but Congress agreed that Lincoln's plan was inadequate. In July 1864, Congress put forward a plan of its own.

As General William T. Sherman was marching on Atlanta, Congressman Henry Winter Davis of Maryland and Senator Benjamin Wade of Ohio jointly sponsored a bill that threw out Lincoln's "10 percent plan" and demanded that a majority of voters in a conquered rebel state take the oath of allegiance before reconstruction could begin. Moreover, the Wade-Davis bill banned ex-Confederates from participating in the drafting of new state constitutions. Finally, the bill guaranteed the equality of freedmen before the law. Congress's reconstruction would be neither as quick nor as forgiving as Lincoln's. Still, the Wade-Davis bill angered radicals because it did not include a provision for black suffrage. When Lincoln exercised his right not to sign the bill and let it die instead, Wade and Davis published a manifesto charging the president with usurpation of power. They warned Lincoln to confine himself to "his executive duties—to obey and execute, not make the laws—to suppress by arms armed rebellion, and leave political organization to Congress."

Undeterred, Lincoln continued to nurture the formation of loyal state governments under his own plan. Four states—Louisiana, Arkansas, Tennessee, and Virginia—fulfilled the president's requirements. Lincoln acknowledged that a government based on only 10 percent was not ideal, but he argued that it would be a "rallying point" for lukewarm rebels. "We shall sooner have the fowl by hatching the egg than by smashing it," Lincoln told Charles Sumner. "The eggs of crocodiles can produce only crocodiles," the Massachusetts senator retorted. Congress refused to seat representatives from the "Lincoln states." In his last public address in April 1865, Lincoln defended his plan but stressed his willingness to be flexible. For the first time he expressed publicly his endorsement of suffrage for southern blacks, at least "the very intelligent, and . . . those who serve our cause as soldiers." The announcement demonstrated that Lincoln's thinking about reconstruction was still evolving. Four days later, he was dead.

Land and Labor

Of all the problems raised by emancipation, none proved more critical than the transition from slave to free labor. Slavery had been, at bottom, a labor system, and while Republicans agreed that free labor would replace forced labor, they disagreed about what free labor would mean in the South. As Yankee armies proceeded to invade and occupy the Confederacy during the war, hundreds of thousands of slaves became free workers. Moreover, Yankee occupation meant that Union armies controlled vast territories where legal title to land had become unclear. The wartime Confiscation Acts punished "traitors" by confiscating their property. What to do with federally occupied land and how to organize labor on it engaged former slaves, former slaveholders, Union military commanders, and federal government officials long before the war ended.

From Virginia's tidewater to Louisiana's bayous, a variety of wartime labor experiments arose. The system that developed in the Mississippi valley proved to be a preview of postwar southern labor relations. Up and down the Mississippi, occupying federal troops ended slavery, which had already begun to fall apart because of slaves' resistance, and announced a new labor code. It required

THE EXECUTION OF BOOTH'S CO-CONSPIRATORS
Union troops tracked down and killed Lincoln's assassin, John Wilkes Booth, on April 26,
1865. Eight others were convicted of conspiring in the murder. On July 7, four were hanged,
including Mary Surratt. Although Surratt knew Booth and had clearly been a Confederate
sympathizer, there was no concrete evidence that she had participated in the murder plot.
Meserve-Kunhardt Collection.

planters to sign contracts with their laborers and to pay wages. The code also obligated employers to provide food, housing, and medical care. It outlawed whipping and other forms of physical punishment, but it reserved to the army the right to discipline blacks who refused to work. The code required black laborers to enter into contracts, work diligently, and remain subordinate and obedient. While the military took aim at slavery, it clearly had no intention of fomenting a social or economic revolution. Instead, it sought to restore plantation agriculture with wage labor. The effort resulted in a hybrid system of "compulsory free labor" that satisfied no one. Depending on one's point of view, it either provided too little or too much of a break with the past.

Planters complained because the new system fell short of slavery. A Louisiana sugar planter predicted that the military's plan would fail because Northerners did "not understand the Negro." Ex-slaves could not be "transformed by proclamation," he warned. Yet under the new system, blacks "are expected to perform their new obligations without coercion, & without the fear of punishment which is essential to stimulate the idle and correct the vicious." Without the right to whip, he concluded, the new labor system did not have a chance.

African Americans also criticized the new regime. They found it too reminiscent of slavery to be called "free labor." Of its many shortcomings, none disappointed ex-slaves more than the failure to provide them land of their own. "What's the use of being free if you don't own land enough to be buried in?" one man asked. "Might just as well stay a slave all your days." Freedmen were determined to become independent, and that required land. They believed they had a moral right to land because they and their ancestors had worked it without compensation for more than two centuries. Moreover, several wartime developments seemed to indicate that the federal government planned to link black freedom and landownership.

In January 1865, General Sherman had set aside for black settlement the Sea Islands off the South Carolina coast and part of the coast south of Charleston. He devised the plan to relieve himself of the burden of thousands of impoverished blacks who trailed desperately after his army. By June 1865, some 40,000 freedmen sat on 400,000 acres of "Sherman land." In addition, in March 1865, Congress established the Bureau of Refugees, Freedmen, and Abandoned Lands. The Freedmen's Bureau, as it was called, distributed food and clothing to destitute Southerners and eased the transition of blacks from slaves to free persons. But Congress also authorized the agency to divide abandoned and confiscated land into forty-acre plots, to rent them to freedmen, and eventually to sell them "with such title as the United States can convey." By June 1865, the bureau had situated nearly 10,000 black fami-

lies on a half million acres that had been abandoned by fleeing South Carolina and Georgia planters. Hundreds of thousands of other ex-slaves eagerly anticipated getting farms of their own.

Despite the flurry of activity, wartime reconstruction had settled nothing. Two years of controversy had failed to produce agreement about whether the president or Congress had the authority to devise and direct policy or what proper policy should be. Lincoln had organized several new state governments, but Congress had not readmitted a single "reconstructed" state into the Union. There were hints that the price of defeat for the South would be a revolution in landholding, but the "compulsory free labor" system that emerged on plantations in the Mississippi valley suggested more continuity with antebellum traditions. Clearly, the nation faced dilemmas and difficulties almost as burdensome as those of the war.

The African American Quest for Autonomy

Although white politicians had difficulty agreeing, ex-slaves never had any doubt about what they wanted freedom to mean. They had only to contemplate what they had been denied as slaves. Slaves had to remain on their plantations; freedom

AN INDEPENDENT BLACK CHURCH
Poor freedmen found that one of the sweetest fruits of emancipation was the opportunity to worship in churches of their own. White observers characterized black worship as nothing but "visions and trances," but independent black churches did more than permit members to dance and shout if they wanted. They also promoted black education, extended relief to freedmen who could not provide for themselves, and engaged in Republican politics.
South Carolina Historical Society.

allowed blacks to go wherever they pleased. Thus, in the first heady weeks after emancipation, freedmen often abandoned their plantations just to see what was on the other side of the hill and to feel freedom under their feet. Slaves had to be at work in the fields by dawn; freedom permitted blacks to taste the forbidden pleasure of sleeping through a sunrise. Slaves had to defer to whites; freedom saw them test the etiquette of racial subordination. "Lizzie's maid passed me today when I was coming from church *without speaking to me*," huffed one plantation mistress. When she asked her own house servant to scour some kettles, the black woman snapped, "You better do it yourself. Ain't you smarter than me? You think you is—why don't you scour them yourself."

To whites, it looked like pure anarchy. Without the discipline of slavery, they said, blacks had reverted to their natural condition: lazy, irresponsible, and wild. Actually, former slaves were experimenting with freedom, in both trivial and profound ways. But poor black people could not long afford to roam the countryside, neglect work, and casually provoke whites. Soon, most were back on plantations, at work in the fields and kitchens.

But other items on ex-slaves' agenda of freedom endured. Freedmen did not easily give up their quest for economic independence. In addition, slavery had deliberately kept blacks illiterate, and freedmen emerged from bondage eager to read and write. Moreover, bondage had denied slaves secure family lives and the ability to worship openly as they saw fit. Consequently, families and religion became areas of persistent black aspiration.

Although slave marriages and family relations had existed only at the master's whim, slaves had nevertheless managed to create deep, enduring family bonds. Still, slave sales had often severed family ties. As a consequence, thousands of black men and women took to the roads in 1865 to look for relations who had been sold away. One northern newspaperman encountered a ragged freedman who had walked six hundred miles to North Carolina, where he had *heard* that his wife and children had been sold. Couples who emerged from slavery with their marriages intact often rushed to northern military chaplains to legalize their unions. (See Texts in Historical Context, page 612.)

The end of slavery saw families abandon the slave quarters and scatter over plantations, building separate cabins on the patches of land they rented. In independent households, far from whites, black families escaped white intrusion. Parents no

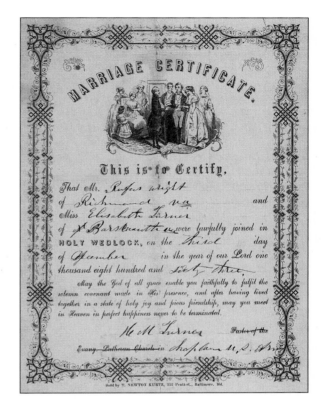

MARRIAGE CERTIFICATE
During the Civil War, blacks serving in the Union army married under military authority. Henry M. Turner, a black chaplain, officiated at the wedding of Elisabeth Turner and Rufus Wright. After the war, thousands of ex-slaves whose marriages had no legal standing under slavery rushed to formalize their unions.
National Archives.

longer had to endure interference in the raising of their children. Women were less vulnerable to violation by masters and their sons. Some wives were able to exchange field labor for housework. Whites claimed that they were "acting the lady," but what whites meant was that black women were not acting like slaves. Instead, they behaved like mothers and housewives, occupied with the same arduous domestic chores as poor white women. Extreme poverty eventually forced most black women back into the cotton fields (at least at picking time) or into white kitchens. Nevertheless, safe and secure families came high on every ex-slave's list of freedom's blessings.

Another hunger that freedom permitted African Americans to satisfy was independent worship. Under slavery, blacks had often, like it or not,

The Meaning of Freedom

On New Year's Day 1863, President Abraham Lincoln issued the Emancipation Proclamation. It stated that "all persons held as slaves" within the states still in rebellion "are, and henceforward shall be, free." Although it did not in and of itself free any slaves, it transformed the character of the war. Despite often intolerable conditions, black people focused on the possibilities of freedom.

John Q. A. Dennis, formerly a slave in Maryland, wrote to Secretary of War Edwin M. Stanton to ask his help in reuniting his family.

DOCUMENT 1. Letter from John Q. A. Dennis to Edwin M. Stanton

Boston July 26th 1864

Dear Sir I am Glad that I have the Honour to Write you afew line I have been in troble for about four yars my Dear wife was taken from me Nov 19th 1859 and left me with three Children and I being a Slave At the time Could Not do Anny thing for the poor little Children for my master it was took me Carry me some forty mile from them So I Could Not do for them and the man that they live with half feed them and half Cloth them & beat them like dogs & when I was admitted to go to see them it use to brake my heart & Now I say agian I am Glad to have the honour to write to you to see if you Can Do Anny thing for me or for my poor little Children I was keap in Slavy untell last Novr 1863. then the Good lord sent the Cornel borne [William Birney?] Down their in Marland in worsester Co So as I have been recently freed I have but letle to live on but I am Striveing Dear Sir but what I went too know of you Sir is is it possible for me to go & take my Children from those men that keep them in Savery if it is possible will you pleas give me a permit from your hand then I think they would let them go. . . .

Hon sir will you please excuse my Miserable writeing & answer me as soon as you can I want get the little Children out of Slavery, I being Criple would like to know of you also if I Cant be permited to rase a Shool Down there & on what turm I Could be admited to Do so No more At present Dear Hon Sir

Freedom also prompted ex-slaves to seek legal marriages, which under slavery had been impossible. On February 28, 1865, in Little Rock, Arkansas, A. B. Randall, the white chaplain of a black regiment, in a report to the adjutant general of the Union army, confirmed the importance of marriage to freed slaves and emphasized their conviction that emancipation was just the first step toward full freedom.

DOCUMENT 2. Report from Reverend A. B. Randall

Weddings, just now, are very popular, and abundant among the Colored People. They have just learned, of the Special Order No' 15. of Gen Thomas [Adjutant General Lorenzo Thomas] by which, they may not only be lawfully married, but have their Marriage Certificates, *Recorded*; in a *book furnished by the Government*. This is most desirable. . . . Those who were captured . . . at Ivy's Ford, on the 17th of January, by Col Brooks, had their Marriage Certificates, taken from them; and destroyed; and then were roundly cursed, for having such papers in their posession. I have married, during the month, at this Post; Twenty five couples; mostly, those, who have families; & have been living together for years. I try to dissuade single men, who are soldiers, from marrying, till their time of enlistment is out: as that course seems to me, to be most judicious.

The Colord People here, generally consider, this war not only; their *exodus*, from bondage; but the road, to Responsibility; Competency; and an honorable Citizenship—God grant that their hopes and expectations may be fully realized.

Early efforts at political reconstruction prompted petitions from former slaves demanding civil and political rights. In January 1865, black Tennesseans petitioned a convention of white unionists debating the reorganization of state government.

DOCUMENT 3. Petition "to the Union Convention of Tennessee Assembled in the Capitol at Nashville, January 9th, 1865"

We the undersigned petitioners, American citizens of African descent, natives and residents of Tennessee, and devoted friends of the great National cause, do most respectfully ask a patient hearing of your honorable body in regard to matters deeply affecting the future condition of our unfortunate and long suffering race.

First of all, however, we would say that words are too weak to tell how profoundly grateful we are to the Federal Government for the good work of freedom which it is gradually carrying forward; and for the Emancipation Proclamation which has set free all the slaves in some of the rebellious States, as well as many of the slaves in Tennessee. . . .

We claim freedom, as our natural right, and ask that in harmony and co-operation with the nation at large, you should cut up by the roots the system of slavery, which is not only a wrong to us, but the source of all the evil which at present afflicts the State. For slavery, corrupt itself, corrupted nearly all, also, around it, so that it has influenced nearly all the slave States to rebel against the Federal Government, in order to set up a government of pirates under which slavery might be perpetrated.

In the contest between the nation and slavery, our unfortunate people have sided, by instinct, with the former. We have little fortune to devote to the national cause, for a hard fate has hitherto forced us to live in poverty, but we do devote to its success, our hopes, our toils, our whole heart, our sacred honor, and our lives. We will work, pray, live, and, if need be, die for the Union, as cheerfully as ever a white patriot died for his country. The color of our skin does not lessen in the least degree, our love either for God or for the land of our birth. . . .

We know the burdens of citizenship, and are ready to bear them. We know the duties of the good citizen, and are ready to perform them cheerfully, and would ask to be put in a position in which we can discharge them more effectually. We do not ask for the privilege of citizenship, wishing to shun the obligations imposed by it. . . .

This is a democracy—a government of the people. It should aim to make every man, without regard to the color of his skin, the amount of his wealth, or the character of his religious faith, feel personally interested in its welfare. Every man who lives under the Government should feel that it is his property, his treasure, the bulwark and defence of himself and his family, his pearl of great price, which he must preserve, protect, and defend faithfully at all times, on all occasions, in every possible manner.

This is not a Democratic Government if a numerous, law-abiding, industrious, and useful class of citizens, born and bred on the soil, are to be treated as aliens and enemies, as an inferior degraded class, who must have no voice in the Government which they support, protect and defend, with all their heart, soul, mind, and body, both in peace and war. . . .

. . . The nation is fighting for its life, and cannot afford to be controlled by prejudice. Had prejudice prevailed instead of principle, not a single colored soldier would have been in the Union army to-day. But principle and justice triumphed, and now near 200,000 colored patriots stand under the folds of the national flag, and brave their breasts to the bullets of the rebels. As we are in the battlefield, so we swear before heaven, by all that is dear to men, to be at the ballot-box faithful and true to the Union.

The possibility that the negro suffrage proposition may shock popular prejudice at first sight, is not a conclusive argument against its wisdom and policy. No proposition ever met with more furious or general opposition than the one to enlist colored soldiers in the United States army. The opponents of the measure exclaimed on all hands that the negro was a coward; that he would not fight; that one white man, with a whip in his hand could put to flight a regiment of them; that the experiment would end in the utter rout and ruin of the Federal army. Yet the colored man has fought so well, on almost every occasion, that the rebel government is prevented, only by its fears and distrust of being able to force him to fight for slavery as well as he fights against it, from putting half a million of negroes into its ranks.

The Government has asked the colored man to fight for its preservation and gladly has he done it. It can afford to trust him with a vote as safely as it trusted him with a bayonet.

Document 1. Ira Berlin, Joseph P. Reidy, and Leslie S. Rowland, eds., *Freedom: A Documentary History of Emancipation, 1861–1867.* Series I, Volume I, *The Destruction of Slavery* (Cambridge University Press, 1985), 386.

Document 2. Ira Berlin, Joseph P. Reidy, and Leslie S. Rowland, eds., *Freedom: A Documentary History of Emancipation, 1861–1867.* Series II, *The Black Military Experience* (Cambridge University Press, 1982), 712.

Document 3. Ibid., 811–816.

prayed with whites in biracial churches. Full expression of black spirituality could be found only in the dead of night in secret religious services. Intent on religious independence, blacks greeted freedom with a mass exodus from white churches. Some joined the newly established southern branches of all-black northern churches, such as the African Methodist Episcopal Church. Others formed black versions of the major southern denominations, Baptists and Methodists. On the eve of the war, 42,000 blacks had worshiped in biracial Methodist churches in South Carolina; by 1870, all but 600 had left. Slaves had viewed their tribulations through the lens of their deeply felt Christian faith, and freedmen comprehended the events of the Civil War and Reconstruction as people of faith. It was not surprising that ex-slaves claimed Abraham Lincoln as their Moses.

Presidential Reconstruction

Abraham Lincoln died on April 15, 1865, just hours after John Wilkes Booth had shot him at a Washington, D.C., theater. Chief Justice Salmon P. Chase immediately administered the oath of office to Vice President Andrew Johnson. Lincoln's assassination thrust the Tennessean into responsibility at a time of grave national crisis. Moreover, Congress had adjourned in March, which meant that legislators were away from Washington when Lincoln was killed. They would not reconvene until December unless the new president called Congress back into special session. But Johnson preferred to have Washington to himself while he made critical decisions about the future of the South. Like Lincoln, he believed that responsibility for restoring the Union lay with the president. Throughout the summer and fall, therefore, the "accidental president" presided over the nation without a sitting Congress. With dizzying speed, Johnson drew up and executed a plan of reconstruction.

Congress returned to the capital in December to find that, as far as the president and former Confederates were concerned, Reconstruction was over. Appalled by what they saw, members of Congress challenged the president's prerogative and policies. To most Republicans, Johnson's modest demands of ex-rebels made a mockery of the sacrifice of Union soldiers. In an 1863 speech dedicating the cemetery at Gettysburg, Lincoln had spoken of the "great task remaining before us . . . that we here highly resolve

that these dead shall not have died in vain—that this nation, under God, shall have a new birth of freedom." Instead, Johnson had acted as midwife to the rebirth of the Old South. He had achieved political reunification at the cost of black liberty. To let his program stand, Republican legislators said, would mean that the North's dead had indeed died in vain.

Johnson's Program of Reconciliation

Born in 1808 in Raleigh, North Carolina, Andrew Johnson was the son of very poor, illiterate parents. Unable to afford to send her son to school, Johnson's widowed mother apprenticed him to a tailor. Self-educated and ambitious, the young man ran away before completing his indenture and headed for Tennessee. There he worked as a tailor, accumulated a fortune in land, acquired five slaves, and built a career in politics championing the South's common white people and assailing its "illegitimate, swaggering, bastard, scrub aristocracy." According to an old political foe, "If Johnson were a snake, he would lie in the grass to bite the heels of rich men's children." The only senator from a Confederate state to remain loyal to the Union, Johnson held no grudge against the South's rebel yeomen. He believed that they had been hoodwinked by slaveholding secessionists. Less than two weeks before he became president, he made it clear what he would do to the rascals if he ever had the chance: "I would arrest them—I would try them—I would convict them and I would hang them."

Throughout the summer and fall, the "accidental president" presided over the nation without a sitting Congress. With dizzying speed, Johnson drew up and executed a plan of reconstruction.

No wonder the South's elite trembled when Lincoln died. Republicans who looked forward to drastic changes in the South celebrated their powerful new ally in the White House. In reality, however, Johnson was no friend. Indeed, he was no Republican. A Democrat all his life, Johnson occupied the White House only because the Republican Party in 1864 had needed to broaden its appeal to loyal, Union-supporting Democrats. As a Tennessee congressman and senator, Johnson had championed traditional Democratic causes, vigorously defending states' rights (but not secession) and opposing Republican efforts to expand the power of the federal government, especially in the economic realm. He had voted against almost every federal appropriation, including a bill to pave the streets of Washington.

Moreover, Johnson had been a steadfast defender of slavery. He had owned slaves until 1862, when Tennessee rebels, angry at his Unionism, confiscated them. He only grudgingly accepted emancipation. When he did, it was more because of his hatred for slaveholders than sympathy for slaves. "Damn the negroes," he said. "I am fighting those traitorous aristocrats, their masters." At a time when the nation faced its moment of truth regarding black Americans, the new president harbored unshakable racist convictions. Africans, he said, were "inferior to the white man in point of intellect —better calculated in physical structure to undergo drudgery and hardship." On the eve of his inauguration as vice president, he had reiterated his belief in a white man's government.

One month after becoming president, Johnson announced his plan of reconstruction. He presented it as a continuation of Lincoln's plan, and in some ways it was. Like Lincoln, he stressed reconciliation between the Union and the defeated Confederacy and rapid restoration of civil government in the South. He offered to pardon most ex-rebels who promised future loyalty to the Union. Like Lincoln, Johnson excluded high-ranking ex-Confederates, but he also excluded all ex-rebels with property worth more than $20,000. The Tennessee tailor was apparently taking aim at his old enemy, the planter aristocrats. Wealthy individuals would have to apply directly to the president for pardons. Johnson recognized the state governments created by Lincoln and set out his own requirements for restoring the rebel states to the Union. All that the citizens of a state had to do was to renounce the right of secession, deny that the debts of the Confederacy were legal and binding, and ratify the Thirteenth Amendment abolishing slavery, which had become part of the Constitution in December 1865. Johnson's plan ignored Lincoln's acceptance near the end of his life of some form of limited black voting.

Johnson's eagerness to normalize relations with southern states and his lack of sympathy for blacks also led him to instruct military and government officials to return to pardoned ex-Confederates all confiscated and abandoned land, even if it was in the hands of freedmen. Reformers were shocked.

They had expected the president's vendetta against planters to mean the permanent confiscation of the South's plantations and the distribution of the land to loyal freedmen. Instead, his instructions canceled the promising beginnings made by General Sherman and the Freedmen's Bureau to settle blacks on land of their own. As one freedman observed, "things was hurt by Mr. Lincoln getting killed."

Johnson's reconstruction envisioned a quick and easy political reconciliation between North and South and demonstrated almost no concern for freedmen. Predictably, Republicans who sought a drastic overhaul of southern society denounced the plan. "Is there no way to arrest the insane course of the President?" asked Congressman Thaddeus Stevens. It appeared that the president was committed to surrendering blacks and the Republican Party to the "tender mercies of the rebels."

Southern Resistance and Black Codes

In the summer of 1865, delegates across the South gathered to draw up the new state constitutions required by Johnson's plan of reconstruction. They revealed that while they had been defeated, they had not been subdued. Rather than take their medicine, they choked on even the president's mild requirements. Refusing to declare their secession ordinances null and void, the South Carolina and Georgia conventions merely "repudiated" their ordinances, preserving in principle their right to secede. In addition, every state convention wrangled over the precise wording of the constitutional amendment ending slavery. In the end, Mississippi rejected the Thirteenth Amendment outright, and Alabama rejected it in part. Finally, South Carolina and Mississippi refused to repudiate their Confederate war debts. These defiant acts provoked only mild responses from Andrew Johnson. He recommended, suggested, and even pleaded, but he did not demand that Southerners comply with his lenient terms.

White Southerners learned dangerous lessons from this initial experience. By failing to draw a hard line, Johnson rekindled southern resistance. White Southerners began to think that, by standing up for themselves, they—not victorious Northerners—would shape the transition from slavery to freedom. In the fall of 1865, newly elected southern legislators set out to reverse the "retreat into barbarism" that followed emancipation.

Under the mantle of protectors of the freedmen, state governments across the South adopted a se-

THE BLACK CODES
Entitled Selling a Freeman to Pay His Fine at Monticello, Florida, *this 1867 drawing from a northern magazine equates the black codes with the reinstitution of slavery. The laws stopped short of reenslavement, but they did sharply restrict blacks' freedom. In Florida, as in other southern states, certain acts, such as breaking a labor contract, were made criminal offenses, the penalty for which could be involuntary plantation labor for a year.*
Library of Congress.

ries of laws known as the black codes. Rejecting the principle of legal equality, legislators argued that ex-slaves required special laws. While emancipation had brought freedmen important rights that they had lacked as slaves—to own property, to make contracts, to marry legally, and to sue and be sued in court—the black codes made a travesty of freedom. They sought to keep blacks subordinate to whites. Scores of laws subjected blacks to every sort of discrimination. Mississippi made insulting gestures and language a criminal offense. Several states made it illegal for blacks to own a gun. Blacks were barred from jury duty. Not a single southern state granted any black—no matter how educated, wealthy, or refined—the right to vote.

At the core of the black codes, however, lay the matter of labor. Faced with the death of slavery and the disintegration of plantations, legislators sought to channel freedmen back into traditional tasks. South Carolina attempted to limit blacks to either farmwork or domestic service by requiring them to pay annual taxes of $10 to $100 to work in any other occupation. Mississippi demanded that by January of each year blacks possess written evidence of employment. An offender could be declared a vagrant and be subject to fine or involuntary plantation labor. Most states allowed judges to bind black children—orphans and others whose parents they

deemed unable to support them—to white employers. Under these so-called apprenticeship laws, courts bound out thousands of black children to planter "guardians," often over the protests of their parents. Legislators bent every effort to resuscitate the traditional plantation economy and resurrect as nearly as possible the old regime.

Johnson refused to intervene decisively. A staunch defender of states' rights, he believed that the citizens of every state—even those citizens who had attempted to destroy the Union—should be free to write their own constitutions and laws. Moreover, since he shared other white Southerners' eagerness to restore white supremacy and black subordination, the black codes did not particularly offend him or seem excessive. Besides, he could point proudly to the fact that by December 1865, enough states had approved the Thirteenth Amendment to make it a part of the Constitution.

But Johnson also followed the path he believed offered him the greatest political return. A conservative Tennessee Democrat at the head of a northern Republican Party, he began to look southwards for political allies. Despite tough talk about punishing traitors, he issued more than 14,000 special pardons to wealthy or high-ranking ex-Confederates. He no doubt enjoyed the sight of former aristocrats lining up humbly to beg his pardon, but

Johnson recognized that these supplicants could also be useful politically. By pardoning planters and Confederate officials, by acquiescing in the South's black codes, and by accepting the new southern governments even when they failed to satisfy his minimal demands, he won useful allies.

If Northerners had any doubts about the mood of the South, they evaporated in the elections of 1865. To represent them in Congress, white Southerners chose former Confederates, not loyal Unionists. Of the eighty senators and representatives they sent to Washington, fifteen had served in the Confederate army, ten of them as generals. Another sixteen had served in civil and judicial posts in the Confederacy. Nine others had served in the Confederate Congress. One—Alexander Stephens—had been vice president of the Confederacy. Some had not yet even received pardons, but Johnson granted immediate clemency so that they could take office. In December, this remarkable group arrived on the steps of the nation's Capitol to be seated in Congress. As one Georgian later remarked: "It looked as though Richmond had moved to Washington."

Expansion of Black Rights and Federal Authority

Southerners had blundered monumentally. They had assumed that what Andrew Johnson was willing to accept, the northern public and Congress would accept as well. But southern intransigence compelled even moderate Republicans to conclude that ex-rebels were a "generation of vipers," still dangerous, still untrustworthy. Northerners sought evidence of a change of heart, but they searched in vain for remorse for slavery, secession, or waging a devastating war. Since white Southerners denied that they were sinners, they refused to repent. Without repentance, Northerners could not forgive.

The black codes in particular soured moderate Republicans on the South's efforts at reconstruction. The codes became a symbol of southern intentions not to accept the verdict of the battlefields, but instead to "restore all of slavery but its name." Northerners were hardly saints when it came to racial justice, but black freedom had become a hallowed war aim. The deaths of Union soldiers had sanctified it. "We tell the white men of Mississippi," the *Chicago Tribune* roared, "that the men of the North will convert the State of Mississippi into a frog pond before they will allow such laws to disgrace one foot of the soil in which the bones of our soldiers sleep and

THE LOST CAUSE
While politicians in Washington, D.C., debated the future of the South, white Southerners were coming to grips with their emotions and history. They began to refer to their failure to secede from the Union as the "Lost Cause." They enshrined the memory of certain former Confederates, especially Robert E. Lee. Lee's nobility and courage represented the white South's image of itself. This quilt from about 1870, with Lee stitched in the center, illustrates how common whites incorporated the symbols of the Lost Cause into their daily lives. The unknown maker of the quilt also included miniature Confederate flags and memorial ribbons.
Valentine Museum, Cook Collection.

over which the flag of freedom waves." Moderate Republicans generally agreed that the "first fruits of reconstruction promise a most deplorable harvest, and the sooner we gather the tares [weeds], plow the ground again and sow new seed, the better."

Moderates represented the mainstream of the Republican Party and wanted only assurance that slavery and treason were dead. They did not seek a revolution of the entire southern social order. They did not champion black equality or the confiscation of plantations or black voting, as did the Radicals, a minority faction within the Republican Party. In December 1865, however, when Congress convened in Washington, it became clear that events in the

South had succeeded in forging unity (at least temporarily) among Republican factions. Exercising Congress's right to determine the qualifications of its members, the moderate majority and the Radical minority came together to refuse to seat the southern representatives. Rather than accept Johnson's claim that the "work of restoration" was done, Congress countered his executive power. Congressional Republicans enjoyed a three-to-one majority over the Democrats, and if they could agree on a program of reconstruction, they could easily pass legislation and even override presidential vetoes.

The moderates took the initiative. Senator Lyman Trumbull of Illinois declared that the president's policy of trusting southern whites proved that the ex-slave would "be tyrannized over, abused, and virtually reenslaved without some legislation by the nation for his protection." Early in 1866, the moderates produced two bills that strengthened the federal shield. The first, the Freedmen's Bureau bill, prolonged the life of the agency established by the previous Congress. Since the end of the war, it had distributed food, supervised labor contracts, and sponsored schools for freedmen. To the cheers of southern whites and the dismay of Republican moderates, President Johnson vetoed the Freedmen's Bureau bill. The Constitution, he argued, never contemplated a "system for the support of indigent persons." Congress failed by a narrow margin to override the president's veto.

Johnson's shocking veto galvanized nearly unanimous Republican support for the moderates' second measure, the Civil Rights Act. Designed to nullify the black codes, it affirmed the rights of blacks to enjoy "full and equal benefit of all laws and proceedings for the security of person and property as is enjoyed by white citizens." Modest on its surface, the act boldly required the end of legal discrimination in state laws and represented an extraordinary expansion of black rights and federal authority. The president argued that the civil rights bill amounted to an "unconstitutional invasion of states' rights" and vetoed it. In essence, he denied that the federal government possessed authority to protect the civil rights of blacks. Had Johnson's veto stood, reconstruction would have been over, and the president would have had the final word. But in April 1866, a thoroughly aroused Republican Party again pushed a civil rights bill through Congress and overrode another presidential veto. Then in July, it sustained another Freedmen's Bureau Act. For the first time in American history, Congress had overridden presidential vetoes of major legislation.

Johnson's vetoes represented a decisive moment in reconstruction. Even moderate Republicans who wanted to avoid a break with the president concluded that he had declared war on the freedmen and the Republican Party. Jettisoning his moderate Republican political allies, he had snuggled up to conservative Democrats. Moreover, he had compounded the harm with vulgar racist statements (suggesting that a logical consequence of congressional policy would be interracial marriage), with inflammatory personal attacks (comparing certain Republicans to Judas and himself to Christ), and in general exhibiting a pugnacious, nasty temperament that made compromise and cooperation impossible. As a worried South Carolinian observed in the spring of 1866, Johnson had succeeded in uniting the Republicans and probably touched off "a fight this fall such as has never been seen."

Congressional Reconstruction

By the summer of 1866, President Andrew Johnson and Congress had dropped their gloves and stood toe to toe in a bare-knuckled contest unprecedented in American history. Johnson had made it clear that he would not budge on either constitutional questions or policy. Moderate Republicans made a major effort to resolve the dilemma of reconstruction by amending the Constitution, but the obstinacy of Johnson and white Southerners pushed Republican moderates steadily closer to the Radicals and to acceptance of additional federal intervention in the South. Each escalation of federal power brought forth new charges of congressional tyranny from the White House. Each new law produced fresh obstruction. Finally, Congress sought to end presidential interference with its prerogatives by impeaching Andrew Johnson.

Congressional reconstruction evolved haltingly and unevenly, but through it all black suffrage acted like a powerful magnet that steadily drew discussion its way. In time, white men in Congress debated whether to give the ballot to black men. Outside of Congress, blacks raised their voices on behalf of color-blind voting rights, while women argued that it was time to make voting sex-blind as well as color-blind.

The Fourteenth Amendment and Escalating Violence

In April 1866, Republican moderates introduced the Fourteenth Amendment to the Constitution, which both houses of Congress approved in June by the necessary two-thirds majority. The amendment then went to the states for ratification. Although it took two years to gather approval from the required three-fourths of the states, the Fourteenth Amendment had immediate consequences.

The most important provisions of this complex amendment made all native-born or naturalized persons American citizens and prohibited states from abridging the "privileges and immunities" of citizens, depriving them of "life, liberty, or property without due process of law," and denying them "equal protection of the laws." Lawyers have battled ever since about the meaning of this broad language, but by making blacks national citizens the amendment nullified the *Dred Scott* decision of 1857 and provided a national guarantee of equality before the law. In essence, it protected the rights of citizens against violation by their own state governments.

The Fourteenth Amendment also dealt with voting rights. Republicans revealed that while genuinely committed to black freedom, they were also alert to partisan advantage. Rather than explicitly granting the vote to blacks, as Radicals wanted, the amendment gave Congress the right to reduce the congressional representation of states that withheld suffrage from some of its adult male population. In other words, white Southerners could either allow their former slaves to vote or see their representation in Washington slashed.

Moderate Republicans soft-pedaled the voting issue because they feared that Northerners would reject any amendment that forced them to enfranchise northern blacks. At that time, only five New England states permitted black men to vote. But without the extension of voting rights to blacks, the return of the southern states to Congress would mean renewed ascendancy for the Democratic Party in the South (most southern whites were Democrats, while southern blacks could be counted on to support the party of Lincoln) and perhaps in the nation as a whole. Ironically, abolition had increased the South's representation in Congress because it had effectively ended the three-fifths compromise (a constitutional provision that had based representation on all free persons and three-fifths of all slaves). Now African Americans were free and thus whole persons in the eyes of the Constitution. Understandably, Republicans refused to sit idle while ex-rebels denied freedmen the vote and simultaneously increased by some twenty seats their power in the House of Representatives.

The Republicans drafted the Fourteenth Amendment in such a way that they could not lose. If southern whites caved in and granted voting rights to freedmen, the Republican Party, entirely a northern party since its birth, would gain valuable black votes, establish a wing in the South, and secure its national power. But if whites refused, southern representation in Congress would plunge, and Republicans would still gain immunity from southern Democratic political power. Of course, the Fourteenth Amendment's voting provision included northern states, where whites were largely hostile to black suffrage. But northern states could continue to withhold suffrage and not suffer in Washington, for their black populations were too small to count in figuring representation. Radicals labeled the Fourteenth Amendment's voting provision "hypocritical" and a "swindle," but they understood that it was the best they could get at the time.

By the summer of 1866, President Andrew Johnson and Congress had dropped their gloves and stood toe to toe in a bare-knuckled contest unprecedented in American history.

Tennessee approved the Fourteenth Amendment in July, and Congress promptly welcomed its representatives and senators back. Had Johnson counseled other southern states to ratify this relatively mild amendment and warned them that they faced the fury of an outraged Republican Party if they refused, they might have listened. Instead, Johnson advised Southerners to reject the Fourteenth Amendment and to rely on him to trounce the Republicans in the fall congressional elections.

Johnson had decided to make the Fourteenth Amendment the overriding issue of the 1866 congressional elections and to gather its white opponents into a new conservative party, the National Union Party. In August, his supporters met in Philadelphia. Democrats came, but the poor Republican turnout made it clear that rather than drawing disgruntled party members to him, Johnson had united nearly the entire Republican Party against him.

The president's strategy had already suffered a setback two weeks earlier when whites in several southern cities went on rampages against blacks. It was less an outbreak of violence than an escalation of the violence that had never ceased. In New Orleans, a mob assaulted delegates to a black suffrage convention, and thirty-four blacks died. In Memphis, white mobs hurtled through the black sections of town and killed at least forty-six people. The slaughter shocked Northerners and renewed skepticism about Johnson's claim that southern whites could be trusted. "Who doubts that the Freedmen's Bureau ought to be abolished forthwith," a New York observer declared sarcastically, "and the blacks remitted to the paternal care of their old masters, who 'understand the nigger, you know, a great deal better than the Yankees can.'"

In a last-ditch effort, Johnson took his case directly to the people. In August, he made an ill-fated "swing around the circle," which took him from Washington to Chicago and St. Louis and back to Washington. However, the president embarrassed himself and his office. When hostile crowds hurled insults, he gave as good as he got. It was Johnson at his worst—intemperate, crude, undignified. Even a friend agreed that he had "made an ass of himself." Johnson's reception on the campaign trail foretold the fate of the National Union movement in the elections. Rather than witnessing the birth of a new conservative party, the elections pitted traditional rivals: Democrats (who lined up with Johnson) against Republicans (who lined up against him). The result was an overwhelming Republican victory in which the party retained its three to one congressional majority.

Johnson had bet that Northerners would not support federal protection of black rights. He expected a racist backlash to defeat the Fourteenth Amendment and blast the Republican Party. But the cautious (and ingenious) amendment was not radical enough to drive Republican voters into Johnson's camp. Besides, the war was still fresh in northern minds. As one Republican explained, southern whites "with all their intelligence were traitors, the blacks with all their ignorance were loyal."

Radical Reconstruction and Military Rule

The elections of 1866 should have taught southern whites the folly of relying on Andrew Johnson as a guide through the thicket of reconstruction. But when Johnson continued to urge Southerners toward rejection of the Fourteenth Amendment, one by one every southern state except Tennessee voted it down. "The last one of the sinful ten," thundered Representative James A. Garfield of Ohio, "has flung back into our teeth the magnanimous offer of a generous nation." In the void created by the South's rejection of the moderates' program, the Radicals seized the initiative.

Each act of defiance by southern whites had boosted the standing of the Radicals within the Republican Party. At the core was a small group of men who had cut their political teeth on the antebellum campaign against slavery, who had goaded Lincoln toward making the war a crusade for freedom, and who had carried into the postwar period the conviction that only federal power could protect the rights of the freedmen. Except for freedmen themselves, no one did more to make freedom the "mighty moral question of the age." Men like Senator Charles Sumner, that pompous but sincere Massachusetts crusader, and Thaddeus Stevens, the caustic, cadaverous representative from Pennsylvania, did not speak with a single voice, but they united in calling for civil and political equality. They insisted on extending to ex-slaves the same opportunities that northern working people enjoyed under the free-labor system. The southern states were "like clay in the hands of the potter," Stevens declared in January 1867, and he called on Congress to have "the courage to do its duty." Stevens urged that reconstruction begin all over again, that the nation return to "the point where Grant left off the work, at Appomattox Court-House."

In March 1867, after exhaustive debate, moderates joined the Radicals to overturn the Johnson state governments and initiate military rule of the South. The Military Reconstruction Act (and three subsequent acts) divided the ten unreconstructed Confederate states into five military districts. Congress placed a Union general in charge of each district and instructed him to "suppress insurrection, disorder, and violence" and to begin political reform. After the military had completed voter registration, which would include black men and exclude all those barred by the Fourteenth Amendment from holding public office, voters would elect delegates to conventions that would draw up new state constitutions. Each constitution would guarantee black suffrage. When the voters of each state had approved the constitution and the first legislature had ratified the Fourteenth Amendment, the state could submit its work to Congress. If Congress approved, the state's senators and representatives could be seated and political reunification would be accomplished.

Radicals proclaimed the provision for black suffrage "a prodigious triumph." The doggedness of the Radicals and of African Americans, along with the pigheadedness of Johnson and the white South, had swept the Republican Party far beyond the timid suffrage provisions of the Fourteenth Amendment. Republicans finally agreed with Sumner that only the voting power of ex-slaves could bring about a permanent revolution in the South. Indeed, suffrage provided blacks with a powerful instrument of change and self-protection. When combined with the disfranchisement of thousands of ex-rebels, it promised to cripple any neo-Confederate resurgence and guarantee Republican governments in the South.

Despite its bold suffrage provision, the Military Reconstruction Act of 1867 disappointed those who

advocated the confiscation and redistribution of southern plantations. No one in Washington was more distressed than Thaddeus Stevens. Unlike Sumner, who conceived of Reconstruction primarily in political terms, Stevens believed it was at bottom an economic problem. He agreed wholeheartedly with the ex-slave who said, "Give us our own land and we take care of ourselves, but without land, the old masters can hire us or starve us, as they please." Stevens envisioned confiscating the estates of traitors, breaking them up into small farms, and distributing them widely to create a loyal black yeomanry. But Johnson's offers of amnesty and pardon had reversed the small program of land transfer begun during the war. By early 1867, nearly all of the land had been returned to its ex-Confederate owners.

Congress steadfastly refused to put land into the hands of ex-slaves. Most Republicans believed

BLACK POLITICS

The Reconstruction Act of 1867 revolutionized southern politics. It also galvanized the region's African American population. One black minister remembered, "Politics got in our midst and our revival or religious work for a while began to wane." While Congress enfranchised only black men, black women participated in the debates that sprang up everywhere. Political rights meant that freedmen had access to the power of the state to advance their interests, and women, as well as men, recognized the unprecedented opportunity.

Library of Congress.

that they had already provided blacks with the critical tools: equal legal rights and the ballot. Besides, confiscation was too radical, even for some Radicals. Confiscating private property in the South, declared the *New York Times*, "strikes at the root of all property rights in both sections. It concerns Massachusetts quite as much as Mississippi." Moreover, giving land to blacks amounted to "government paternalism," most Republicans argued. In the end, it would undermine, not strengthen, black independence. Civil and political equality, a majority of Republicans believed, gave blacks "a perfectly fair chance." If they were to get forty acres, they would have to gain it themselves.

Declaring that he would rather sever his right arm than sign such a formula for "anarchy and chaos," Andrew Johnson vetoed the Military Reconstruction Act. Congress overrode his veto the very same day, dramatizing the shift in power from the executive to the legislative branch of government. With the passage of the Reconstruction Acts of 1867, congressional reconstruction was virtually completed. Congress had left white folks owning most of the South's land, but in a radical departure it had given black folks the ballot. More than any other provision, black suffrage justifies the term "radical reconstruction." In 1867, the nation began an unprecedented experiment in interracial democracy—at least in the South, for Congress's plan did not touch the North. Soon the former Confederate states would become the primary theater for political struggle. But before the spotlight swung away from Washington, the president and Congress had one more scene to play.

Impeaching a President

Although Johnson had lost the support of the northern people and faced a hostile Republican majority in Congress, he had no intention of yielding control of reconstruction. Ever defiant, he fought a guerrilla campaign to obstruct and delay implementation of Republican policies in the South. As president, he was responsible for enforcing the laws that Congress enacted. As commander in chief, he oversaw the military rule of the South that Congress instituted. Yet in a dozen ways he sabotaged Congress's will and encouraged white belligerence and resistance. He issued a flood of pardons to undermine efforts at political and economic change. He waged war against the Freedmen's Bureau by removing officers who sympathized too fully with ex-slaves. And he replaced Union generals eager to enforce

ANDREW JOHNSON, WITH ADDITIONS
This dignified 1868 portrait by Currier and Ives of President Andrew Johnson was apparently amended by a disgruntled citizen. Johnson's vetoes of several reconstruction measures passed by Congress caused his opponents to charge him with arrogant monarchical behavior.
Museum of American Political Life.

Congress's Reconstruction Acts with conservative men who were eager to defeat them. Johnson believed that Congress had exceeded its authority when it launched military rule and imposed black suffrage, and he claimed that he was merely defending the "violated Constitution." At bottom, however, he subverted congressional reconstruction to protect southern whites from what he considered the horrors of "Negro domination."

When Congress learned that overriding Johnson's vetoes did not assure victory, it attempted to tie the president's hands. Congress required that all orders to field commanders pass through the General of the Army, Ulysses S. Grant, who Congress believed was sympathetic to southern freedmen, Unionists, and Republicans. It also enacted the

Tenure of Office Act, which required the approval of the Senate for the removal of any government official who had been appointed with Senate consent. Republicans were seeking to protect Secretary of War Edwin M. Stanton, the lone cabinet officer who supported congressional policies. Some Republicans, however, claimed that efforts to subdue Johnson were useless. Nothing less than removing him from office could save reconstruction, they claimed, and they initiated a crusade to impeach the president. According to the Constitution, the House of Representatives can impeach and the Senate can try any federal official for "Treason, Bribery, or other high Crimes and Misdemeanors."

As long as Johnson refrained from breaking a law, however, impeachment languished. Moderates interpreted "high Crimes and Misdemeanors" to mean violation of criminal statutes, and they did not believe that the president had committed an actual crime. Radicals denounced the moderates' interpretation as excessively narrow and argued that Johnson's abuse of constitutional powers and his failure to fulfill constitutional obligations were impeachable offenses. But in August 1867, Johnson suspended Secretary of War Stanton from office. As required by the Tenure of Office Act, he requested the Senate to consent to dismissal. When the Senate balked, the president removed Stanton anyway. "Is the President crazy, or only drunk?" asked a dumbfounded Republican moderate. "I'm afraid his doings will make us all favor impeachment."

News of Johnson's open defiance of the law did indeed convince every Republican in the House to vote for a resolution impeaching the president. Chief Justice Salmon Chase presided over the Senate trial, which lasted from March until May 1868. Chase refused to allow Johnson's opponents to raise the broad issues of misuse of power, his "great crimes," and forced them to argue their case exclusively on the narrow legal grounds of Johnson's removal of Stanton. Johnson's lawyers argued that he had not committed a criminal offense, that the Tenure of Office Act was unconstitutional, and that in any case it did not apply to Stanton, who had been appointed by Lincoln. When the critical vote came, seven moderate Republicans broke with their party and joined the Democrats in voting "not guilty." With thirty-five in favor and nineteen opposed, the impeachment forces fell one vote short of the two-thirds needed to convict.

Republicans had put Johnson on trial because he threatened their efforts to remake the South. But some, including Chief Justice Chase, feared that im-

peachment for insufficient cause would permanently weaken the office of president. Others shied away from conviction because they feared Benjamin Wade, president pro tem of the Senate, the man who would take Johnson's place in the White House. A crusty old Ohio Radical, Wade professed ideas about monetary policy, the rights of workingmen, and female suffrage that frightened moderates. So Johnson survived, but he did not come through the ordeal unscathed. After his trial he called a truce, and for the remaining ten months of his term reconstruction proceeded unhindered by presidential interference.

The Fifteenth Amendment and Women's Demands

In February 1869, Republicans passed their last major piece of reconstruction legislation: the Fifteenth Amendment to the Constitution. The amendment prohibited states from depriving any citizen of the right to vote because of "race, color, or previous condition of servitude." The Reconstruction Acts of 1867 had already required black suffrage in the South, but the Fifteenth Amendment extended black voting to the entire nation. Some Republicans felt morally obligated to do away with the double standard between North and South. (Eleven northern states and five border states had stubbornly resisted enfranchising blacks.) Others believed that the freedman's ballot required the extra armor of a constitutional amendment to protect it from white counterattack. But partisan advantage also played an important role in the amendment's passage. Gains by northern Democrats in the 1868 elections worried Republicans, and black voters now represented the balance of power in several northern states. By giving ballots to northern blacks, Republicans could lessen their political vulnerability. As one Republican congressman observed, "party expediency and exact justice coincide for once."

Some Republicans, however, found the final wording of the Fifteenth Amendment "lame and halting." Rather than absolutely guaranteeing the right to vote, the amendment merely prohibited exclusion on grounds of race. The distinction would prove to be significant. In time, inventive white Southerners would devise tests of literacy and property and other apparently nonracial measures that would effectively disfranchise blacks and yet not violate the Fifteenth Amendment. But an amendment that guaranteed the right to vote courted defeat in the North. Rising antiforeign sentiment—against the Chinese in California and against European immigrants in the Northeast—caused states to resist giving up control of suffrage requirements. In March 1870, after three-fourths of the states had ratified it, the Fifteenth Amendment became part of the Constitution. Republicans generally breathed a sigh of relief, confident that black suffrage had been "the last great point that remained to be settled of the issues of the war."

But the Republican Party's reappraisal of suffrage had ignored completely the band of politicized and energized women who had emerged from the war demanding "the ballot for the two disenfranchised classes, negroes and women." Founding the Equal Rights Association in 1866, Susan B. Anthony and Elizabeth Cady Stanton lobbied for "a government by the people, and the whole people; for the people and the whole people." They felt betrayed when their old antislavery allies, who now occupied positions of national power, proved to be fickle and would not work for their goals. "It was the Negro's hour," Frederick Douglass later explained. The Republican Party had to avoid anything that might jeopardize black gains, Charles Sumner declared. He suggested that woman suffrage could be "the great question of the future."

It was not the first time women's expectations had been dashed. The Fourteenth Amendment had provided for punishment of any state that excluded voters on the basis of race but not on the basis of sex. It had also introduced the word *male* into the Constitution when it referred to a citizen's right to vote. Stanton had predicted that "if that word 'male' be inserted, it will take us a century at least to get it out." The Fifteenth Amendment proved to be no less disappointing. Although women fought hard to include the word *sex*, the amendment denied states the right to forbid suffrage only on the basis of race. Stanton and Anthony condemned the Republicans' "negro first" strategy and concluded that woman "must not put her trust in man."

On the eve of the Civil War, individuals who had advocated black suffrage risked ridicule in the North and their lives in the South. A decade later, in William Lloyd Garrison's words, blacks had progressed from "the auction-block to the ballot-box." Most Republicans believed that the Fifteenth Amendment completed reconstruction. "The Fifteenth Amendment," Congressman James A. Garfield of Ohio proclaimed, "confers upon the African race the care of its own destiny. It places their fortunes in their own hands." Even Wendell Phillips, that uncompromising crusader for equal-

SUSAN B. ANTHONY
Like many outspoken suffragists, Anthony, depicted here around 1850, had begun her public career in the temperance and abolitionist movements. Her continuing passions for other causes — improving working conditions for labor, for example — caused some conservatives to oppose women's political rights because they equated the suffragist cause with radicalism in general. Women could not easily overcome such views, and the long struggle for suffrage eventually drew millions of women into public life.
Meserve-Kunhardt Collection.

ity, argued that the black man held "his sufficient shield in his own hands. . . . Whatever he suffers will be largely now, and in future, wholly, his own fault." In essence, northern Republicans declared victory and scratched the "Negro question" from the agenda of national politics.

The Struggle in the South

While Northerners believed they had discharged their responsibilities with the Reconstruction Acts and the amendments to the Constitution, Southerners knew that the battle had just begun. Black suffrage and large-scale rebel disfranchisement that came with congressional reconstruction had destroyed traditional southern politics and established the foundation for the rise of the Republican Party. Gathering together outsiders and outcasts from traditional society, the Republicans in the South won elections, wrote new state constitutions, and formed new state governments.

Challenging the established class for political control was dangerous business. Equally dangerous were the confrontations that took place on farms and plantations from Virginia to Texas. In the countryside, blacks sought to give practical, everyday meaning to their newly won legal and political equality. But ex-masters and other whites had their own ideas about the social and economic arrangements that should replace slavery. Freedom, then, remained contested territory, and Southerners fought pitched battles with each other to determine the boundaries of their postemancipation world.

Freedmen, Yankees, and Yeomen

African Americans made up the majority of southern Republicans. Freedmen emerged from bondage illiterate and politically inexperienced, but they understood their own interests. They realized that without the ballot they were almost powerless, and they threw themselves into the suffrage campaign. Southern blacks gained voting rights in 1867, and within months virtually every eligible black man had registered to vote. While almost all voted Republican, blacks (like whites) did not have identical political priorities. Free-born, light-skinned southern blacks were often educated, property-holding artisans who tended to be economically conservative but socially radical. Concentrated in the South's towns and cities, they showed little enthusiasm for land reform, but they ached to tear down racial barriers that inhibited their everyday lives. Ex–field hands, in contrast, showed less concern about "whites only" signs in hotels and restaurants than they did about land of their own. Blacks united, however, in their desire for education and equal treatment before the laws.

Northern whites who decided to make the South their home after the war were a second element of the South's Republican Party. Conservative white Southerners called any northern migrant a "carpetbagger," a man so poor that he could pack all his earthly belongings in a single carpet-sided suitcase and swoop southward like a buzzard to "fatten on our misfortunes." Some Northerners who moved south were scavengers, but most were rest-

less, relatively well-educated young men, often former Union officers and Freedmen's Bureau agents who looked upon the South as they did the West—as a promising place to make a living. Only a few chose politics, but in the early years of Reconstruction carpetbaggers exercised leadership in the fledgling Republican Party far beyond their limited numbers. Illinois-born Henry C. Warmoth, for example, arrived in Louisiana with the army in 1864 and within months became the state's first Republican governor. Northerners in the southern Republican Party consistently supported programs that encouraged vigorous economic development along the lines of the northern free-labor model.

Black suffrage and large-scale rebel disfranchisement that came with congressional reconstruction had destroyed traditional southern politics and established the foundation for the rise of the Republican Party.

The Republican Party gained even more recruits among white Southerners. Some businessmen found Republican economic policies attractive and hoped that an infusion of northern capital, know-how, and bustle would cure the sick southern economy. But yeoman farmers in the Piedmont accounted for the vast majority of white Republicans in the South. Many were Unionists who emerged from the war with bitter memories of Confederate persecution. Some small farmers also nursed long-standing grievances against planter domination and welcomed the Republican Party because it promised to end favoritism toward plantation interests. Yeomen usually supported initiatives for public schools and for expanding economic opportunity within a reinvigorated southern economy. Approximately one out of four white Southerners voted Republican. The other three never considered joining the party of Lincoln and cursed those who did. They condemned southern-born white Republicans as traitors to their region and their race and called them "scalawags," a term for runty horses and low-down, good-for-nothing rascals.

The Republican Party in the South, then, was made up of freedmen, Yankees, and yeomen—an improbable coalition. The mix of races, regions, and classes inevitably meant friction as each group maneuvered to define the party. Despite the stress and strain, Reconstruction represents an extraordinary moment in American politics: Blacks and whites joined together to pursue political change. The Republican Party defended the political and civil equality of black Southerners and struggled to bring the South into the mainstream of American social and economic development. Formally, of course, only men participated in politics—casting ballots and holding offices—but women also played parts in the political struggle. Women joined in parades and rallies, attended stump speeches, and even campaigned. In 1868, black maids in Yazoo, Mississippi, shocked their white employers when they showed up for work boldly wearing buttons depicting the Republican candidate for president: Ulysses S. Grant.

Reconstruction politics was not for cowards. Any political act, even wearing a political button, took courage. Congress had introduced hundreds of thousands of ex-slaves into the southern electorate against the will of the white majority. Then, according to one Democrat, the Republican Party herded them to the polls like "senseless cattle." Most whites in the South condemned the entire political process as illegitimate and felt justified in doing whatever it took to stamp out Republicanism. Violence against blacks—the "white terror"—took brutal institutional form in 1866 with the formation of the Ku Klux Klan. The Klan went on a rampage of whipping, hanging, shooting, burning, and throat-cutting to defeat reconstruction and restore white supremacy. (See Historical Question, page 628.) Rapid demobilization of the Union army after the war left only twenty thousand troops to patrol the entire South, a vast territory. Without effective military protection, southern Republicans had to take care of themselves.

Democratic Equality and the General Welfare

The Reconstruction Acts required southern states to draw up new constitutions before they could be readmitted to Congress. Beginning in the fall of 1867, states held elections for delegates to constitutional conventions. About 40 percent of the white electorate stayed home, either because they had been disfranchised or because they were boycotting politics. Republicans won three-fourths of the seats. About 15 percent of the Republican delegates were Northerners who had moved south, 25 percent were African Americans, and 60 percent were white Southerners. As a British visitor observed, the elec-

tions reflected "the mighty revolution that had taken place in America." But Democrats described the conventions as zoos of "baboons, monkeys, mules . . . and other jackasses." In fact, the gatherings brought together serious, purposeful men who hammered out the legal framework for a new order.

The reconstruction constitutions introduced extensive changes into southern life. In general, changes fell into two categories: those that reduced aristocratic privilege and increased democratic equality and those that expanded the state's responsibility for the general welfare. In the first category, the constitutions adopted universal male suffrage, abolished property qualifications for holding office, and made more offices elective and fewer appointive. In the second category, they enacted prison reform; made the state responsible for caring for orphans, the insane, and the deaf and mute; and aided debtors by exempting their homes from seizure.

These forward-looking constitutions provided blueprints for a New South. But they stopped short of the specific reforms advocated by particular groups within southern Republicanism. Despite the wishes of virtually every former slave, no southern constitution confiscated and redistributed land. Despite the prediction of Unionists that unless all former Confederates were banned from politics they

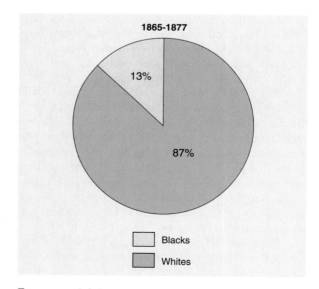

FIGURE 16.1
Southern Congressional Delegations
The statistics contradict the myth of black domination of Congressional representation.

THE STATE CONVENTION AT RICHMOND, VIRGINIA
*Between 1867 and 1869, every southern state except Tennessee held a convention to draft a
new constitution. For the first time in American history, black delegates joined whites in making laws. In Virginia, where blacks were more than 40 percent of the population, they made
up about 20 percent of the convention.*
Valentine Museum, Cook Collection.

would storm back and wreck reconstruction, no
constitution disfranchised ex-rebels wholesale. And
despite the desires of free-born blacks and others,
no constitution outlawed all forms of racial segregation.

But Democrats were blind to the limits of the
Republican program. In their eyes, they stared at
wild revolution. According to Democrats, Republican victories initiated "black and tan" (ex-slave and
mulatto) governments. But the claims of "Negro
domination" had almost no validity. Four out of five
Republican voters were black men, but more than
four out of five Republican officeholders were
white. Southerners sent fourteen black congressmen
and two black senators to Washington, but only 6
percent of Southerners in Congress during Reconstruction were black. With the exception of South
Carolina, where blacks briefly held a majority in one
house of the legislature, no state experienced
"Negro rule," despite black majorities in the populations of three states.

Democrats mocked black officeholders as ignorant field hands. Although many had only "agri-

cultural degrees" and "brick yard diplomas," most
were literate. One of Mississippi's two black U.S.
senators, free-born Hiram R. Revels, had attended
Knox College, and the other, ex-slave Blanche K.
Bruce, had learned to read while in bondage, run
away, and opened a school in Missouri. Francis Car-
dozo, South Carolina's secretary of state and secretary of the treasury, had studied at universities in
England and Scotland. But whatever their educational achievements, blacks were decidedly junior
partners in white-dominated Republican governments. Republicans sought to counter the racist attack by portraying themselves as "the poor man's
party" that promised to end the rule of the back-
ward-looking, arrogant planter aristocracy.

In almost every state, voters ratified the new
constitutions and swept Republicans into power.
After they ratified the Fourteenth Amendment, the
former Confederate states were readmitted to Congress. Southern Republicans then turned to the critical task of governing. They faced a staggering array
of problems. Wartime destruction still littered the
landscape. The war had destroyed one-third of all

What Did the Ku Klux Klan Really Want?

IN THE SUMMER OF 1866, six Confederate veterans in Pulaski, Tennessee, founded the Ku Klux Klan. Borrowing oaths and rituals from a college fraternity, the young men innocently sought fun and fellowship in a social club. But they quickly tired of playing pranks on one another and shifted to more serious matters. By the spring of 1868, when congressional Reconstruction went into effect, new groups or "dens" of the Ku Klux Klan had sprouted throughout the South.

According to former Confederate general and Georgia Democratic politician John B. Gordon, the Klan owed its popularity to the "instinct of self-preservation . . . the sense of insecurity and danger, particularly in those neighborhoods where the Negro population largely predominated." Everywhere whites looked, he said, they saw "great crime." Republican politicians organized ignorant freedmen and marched them to the polls, where they blighted honest government. Blacks drove overseers from plantations and claimed the land for themselves. Black robbers and rapists made white women cower behind barred doors. It was necessary, Gordon declared, "in order to protect our families from outrage and preserve our own lives, to have something that we could regard as a brotherhood—a combination of the best men of the country, to act purely in self-defense." According to Gordon and other conservative white Southerners, then, Klansmen were good men who stepped forward to do their duty, men who wanted nothing more than to guard their families and defend decent society from the assaults of degraded ex-slaves and a vindictive Republican Party.

Behind the Klan's high-minded and self-justifying rhetoric, however, lay another agenda. It was revealed in their actions, not their words. Klansmen embarked on a campaign to reverse history. Garbed in robes and hoods, Klansmen engaged in hit-and-run guerrilla warfare against free labor, civil equality, and political democracy. They aimed to terrorize their enemies—ex-slaves and white Republicans—into submission. As the South's chief terrorist organization between 1868 and 1871, the Klan whipped, burned, and shot in the name of white supremacy. Changes in four particular areas of southern life proved flash points for Klan violence: racial etiquette, education, labor, and politics.

The Klan punished those blacks and whites guilty of breaking the Old South's racial code. The Klan considered "impudence" a punishable offense. Asked to define "impudence" before a congressional investigating committee, one white opponent of the Klan responded: "Well, it is considered impudence for a negro not to be polite to a white man—not to pull off his hat and bow and scrape to a white man, as was done formerly." Klansmen whipped blacks for crimes that ranged from speaking disrespectfully to refusing to yield the sidewalk to raising a good crop to dressing well. Black women who "dress up and fix up like ladies" risked a midnight visit from the Klan. The Ku Klux Klan sought to restore racial subordination in every aspect of private and public life.

Klansmen also took aim at black education. White men, especially those with little schooling, found the sight of blacks in classrooms hard to stomach. Schools were easy targets, and scores of them went up in flames. Teachers, male and female, were flogged, or worse. Klansmen drove northern-born teacher Alonzo B. Corliss from North Carolina for "teaching niggers and making them like white men." In Cross Plains, Alabama, the Klan hanged an Irish-born teacher along with four black men. But not just ill-educated whites opposed black education. Planters wanted ex-slaves back in the fields, not at desks. Each student meant one less laborer. In 1869, an Alabama newspaper reported the burning of a black school and observed that it should be "a warning for them to stick hereafter to 'de shovel and de hoe,' and let their dirty-backed primers go."

Planters turned to the Klan as part of their effort to preserve plantation agriculture and restore labor discipline. An Alabama white admitted that in his area, the Klan was "intended principally for the negroes who failed to work." Masked bands

KU KLUX KLAN ROBE AND HOOD

The white robes that we associate with the Ku Klux Klan are a twentieth-century phenomenon. During Reconstruction, Klansmen donned robes of various designs and colors. It is unlikely that the man who wore this robe about 1866 — with its eye holes carefully trimmed with blue fabric — sewed it himself. Women did not participate in midnight raids, but mothers, wives, and daughters of Klansmen often shared their reactionary vision and did what they could to bring about the triumph of white supremacy.

Chicago Historical Society, Hope B. McCormick Center. Worn by Joseph Boyce Stewart, Lincoln County, Tenn., c.1866. Gift of W. G. Dithmer.

"punished Negroes whose landlords had complained of them." Sharecroppers who disputed their share at "settling up time" risked a visit from the night riders. Klansmen murdered a Georgia blacksmith who refused to do additional work for a white man until he was paid for a previous job. It was dangerous for freedmen to consider changing employers. "If we got out looking for some other place to go," an ex-slave from Texas remembered, "them KKK they would tend to Mister negro good and plenty." In Marengo County, Alabama, when the Klan heard that some local blacks were planning to leave, "the disguised men went to them and told them if they undertook it they would be killed on their way." Whites had decided that they would not be "deprived of their labor."

Above all, the Klan terrorized Republican leaders and voters. Klansmen became the military arm of the Democratic Party. They drove blacks from the polls on election day and terrorized black officeholders. Klansmen gave Andrew Flowers, a black politician in Chattanooga, a brutal beating and told him that they "did not intend any nigger to hold office in the United States." Jack Dupree, president of the Republican Club in Monroe County, Mississippi, a man known to "speak his mind," had his throat cut and was disemboweled while his wife was forced to watch.

Between 1868 and 1871, political violence reached astounding levels. Arkansas experienced nearly three hundred political killings in the three months before the fall elections in 1868, including Little Rock's U.S. congressman, J. M. Hinds. Louisiana was even bloodier. Between the local elections in the spring of 1868 and the presidential election in the fall, Louisiana experienced more than one thousand killings. Political violence often proved effective. In Georgia, Republican presidential candidate Ulysses S. Grant received no votes at all in 1868 in eleven counties, despite black majorities. The Klan murdered three scalawag members of the Georgia legislature and drove ten others from their homes. As one Georgia Republican commented after a Klan attack: "We don't call them democrats, we call them southern murderers."

It proved hard to arrest Klansmen and harder still to convict them. "If a white man kills a colored man in any of the counties of this State," observed a Florida sheriff, "you cannot convict him." By 1871, the death toll had reached thousands. Federal intervention—in the Ku Klux Klan Acts of 1870 and 1871—signaled an end to much of the Klan's power but not to counterrevolutionary violence in the South. Other groups continued the terror.

the South's livestock, and the $3 billion that was invested in slaves was gone. The South's share of the nation's wealth had fallen from 30 percent to only 12 percent. Manufacturing limped along at a fraction of prewar levels, agricultural production remained anemic, and the region's railroads had hardly advanced from the devastated condition in which Sherman had left them. Without the efforts of the Freedmen's Bureau, people would have starved. Moreover, reactionary violence and racial harassment dogged the steps of Southerners who sought reform. In this desperate context, Republicans struggled to breathe life into their new state governments.

Activity focused on three major areas. First, every state inaugurated a system of public education and began furiously building schools and training teachers. Before the Civil War, whites had deliberately kept slaves illiterate, and planter-dominated governments rarely spent tax money to educate the children of yeomen. By 1875, half of Mississippi's and South Carolina's eligible children (the majority of whom were black) attended school. Persistent underfunding meant too few schools, dilapidated facilities, and poorly trained teachers, but literacy rates rose sharply nevertheless. Although public schools were racially segregated, education remained for blacks a tangible, deeply satisfying benefit of freedom and Republican rule.

Second, states attacked racial discrimination and defended civil rights. Republicans especially resisted efforts by whites to establish separate facilities for blacks in public transportation. Texas replaced its law requiring segregation in its railroads with one that outlawed seating by race. Mississippi went further, levying fines of up to $1,000 and three years in jail for railroads, steamboats, hotels, and theaters that denied "full and equal rights" to all citizens. But passing color-blind laws was one thing; enforcing them was another. Fiercely determined that the South remain a white man's preserve, white Southerners sought to demonstrate the continued mastery of whites and the social inferiority of blacks. Segregation—the separation of blacks and whites in public places—developed at white insistence despite the law and became a feature of southern life long before the end of Reconstruction.

Third, Republican governments launched ambitious programs of economic development. They envisioned a South of diversified agriculture, roaring factories, and booming towns. Republican legislatures chartered scores of banks and industrial companies, appropriated funds to fix ruined levees

and to drain swamps, and initiated a vigorous program of internal improvements. The South went on a railroad-building binge, repairing old lines and adding some seven thousand miles of track during Reconstruction. The mania for railroads and state-sponsored economic development fell far short of solving the South's economic troubles, however. Republican spending to stimulate economic growth meant rising taxes and enormous debt that drained funds from schools and other programs.

The southern Republicans' record, then, was mixed. None of the initiatives in education, civil rights, or economic growth was an unqualified success. To their credit, the biracial Republican coalition had taken up an ambitious agenda to change the South. Success would have been difficult under the best of circumstances. As it was, money was scarce. In addition, Democrats kept up a constant drumbeat of harassment, while factionalism threatened the party from within. Moreover, corruption infected Republican governments in the South. Public morality reached new lows everywhere in the nation after the Civil War, and the chaos and disruption of the postwar South proved fertile soil for bribery, fraud, and influence peddling. Despite all of its problems and shortcomings, however, the Republican Party had made headway in its early efforts to purge the South of aristocratic privilege and racist oppression.

White Landlords, Black Sharecroppers

Reconstruction politics did not arise within a vacuum. Sharp dissatisfaction with conditions in the southern countryside politicized blacks and fueled political upheaval. On farms and plantations, freedmen confronted ex-masters who persisted in believing that blacks were unfit for free labor. A Tennessee man declared two years after the end of the war that blacks were "a trifling set of lazy devils who will never make a living without Masters." Blacks responded that if any class was lazy, it was the masters, "who lived in idleness all of their lives on stolen labor." Clashes occurred daily between ex-slaves who wished to take control of the conditions of their own labor and ex-masters who wanted to reinstitute old ways.

The system of agricultural labor that emerged in 1865 grew out of the labor program begun during the war by the federal military. When the war ended, supervision shifted to the Freedmen's Bureau, which renewed the army's campaign to restore production by binding black laborers and

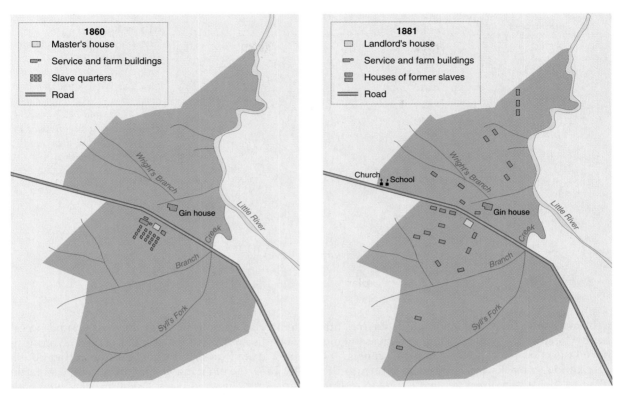

MAP 16.1

A Southern Plantation in 1861 and 1881

The maps of the Barrow plantation in Georgia illustrate some of the ways that ex-slaves expressed their freedom. Former slaves deserted the clustered living quarters behind the Big House, scattered over the plantation, built new family cabins, and farmed rented land. These ex-slaves also worked together to build a school and a church.

planters with wage contracts. Except for having to put down the whip and pay subsistence wages, planters were not required to offer many concessions to emancipation. Instead, they moved quickly to restore the antebellum world of work gangs, white overseers, field labor for black women and children, clustered cabins, minimal personal freedom, and even corporal punishment whenever they could get away with it.

Ex-slaves resisted every effort to roll back the clock. "The fact is, the colored people are very anxious to get land of their own to live upon independently," one black man remarked, "and they want money to buy stock [mules] to make crops." Disgusted planters confirmed that freedmen wanted to become "landholders" and not "hirelings." Blacks were equally determined to end planters' involvement in their personal lives. They wanted, for ex-

ample, to make their own decisions about whether women and children would labor in the fields. Indeed, within months after the war, black women (perhaps one-third of them) abandoned field labor and began working full time within their own households. Moreover, hundreds of thousands of black children enrolled in school.

The freedmen's dream of landownership never came true. Despite the ex-slaves' political agitation, Congress and southern legislatures refused to confiscate the planters' land. And without political intervention, landownership proved to be beyond the reach of all but a small fraction of blacks. Poverty-stricken freedmen were lucky to have two nickels to rub together, and few white people would offer them credit to purchase real estate. Even blacks who had money discovered that planters resisted selling them land. Whites who contemplated selling land

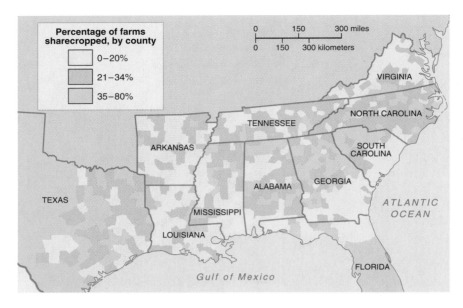

M A P 16.2
The Sharecropping System in the South, 1880
Fifteen years after the end of the Civil War, sharecropping dominated southern agriculture. White and black farmers found themselves enmeshed in a system that left them landless and impoverished.

to blacks knew they risked midnight raids from unhappy neighbors. Without land, ex-slaves would have little choice but to work on plantations.

Although blacks were forced to return to the planters' fields, freedmen resisted efforts to restore slavelike conditions. By working fewer days and shorter hours, by boycotting annual contracts, by striking, and by abandoning the most reactionary employers, they sought to force concessions. A tug-of-war between white landlords and black laborers took place on thousands of farms and plantations and out of it emerged sharecropping, a new system of southern agriculture.

Sharecropping was a compromise that offered both ex-masters and ex-slaves something but satisfied neither. Under the new system, planters divided their cotton plantations into small farms of twenty-five to thirty acres that freedmen rented, paying with a share of each year's crop, usually half. Sharecropping gave blacks more freedom than labor gangs and released them from the day-to-day supervision of whites. It meant that black families could now decide who would work, for how long, and how hard. Moreover, even half a crop seemed to promise a princely income after the subsistence of slavery and the puny wages of the Freedmen's Bureau's contract system. Still, most blacks remained dependent on the white landlord, who retained the power to expel them at the end of each season. For planters, sharecropping offered a way to resume agricultural production, but it did not allow them to reinstitute the unified plantation system or to administer what they considered necessary discipline. An experiment at first, sharecropping spread quickly throughout the cotton South. By 1870, the old gang system, direct white supervision, and clustered black living quarters were fading memories. As increasing numbers of white yeomen lost their land in the downward spiral of postwar southern agriculture, moreover, sharecropping ensnared small white farmers as well as black farmers.

Reconstruction Collapses

By 1870, Northerners looked forward to putting "the southern problem" behind them. They had written guarantees of civil and political rights for blacks into the Constitution and enacted a program of political reunification that had restored ex-Confederate states to the Union. Now, after a decade of engagement with the public issues of war and reconstruction, they wanted to turn to their own affairs. In Washington, matters that had taken a back-seat to the southern problem—economic development, foreign policy, scandal and corruption—clamored for attention. Increasingly, practical business-minded men came to the forefront of the Republican Party, replacing the band of reformers and idealists who had been prominent in the 1860s. Civil War hero Ulysses S. Grant succeeded Andrew Johnson as president in 1869 and quickly became an issue himself, proving that brilliance on the battlefield does not necessarily translate into competence in the White House.

Each year, events in the South received less of the North's attention. Reconstruction slipped further into the background, and Northerners signaled growing unwillingness to intervene in southern affairs. While northern resolve to defend black freedom withered, southern commitment to white supremacy intensified. Throughout the South, Democrats redoubled their attack on Republican rule. Without northern protection, southern Republicans were no match for the Democrats' economic coercion, political corruption, and violence. One by one, Republican state governments fell. The election of 1876 both confirmed and completed the collapse of reconstruction.

The Grant Regime: Cronies, Corruption, and Economic Collapse

When the Civil War ended, Ulysses S. Grant was easily the most popular man in the nation, at least north of the Mason-Dixon line. But the return of peace meant that the general risked slipping back into his former obscurity. Determined to avoid that fate, he settled in Washington and plunged into reconstruction politics, playing the political game on the dangerous middle ground between President Andrew Johnson and Congress. Lesser men might not have survived the crossfire, but Grant shrewdly maneuvered between the warring factions. At first he appeared to be Johnson's man, but during the impeachment crisis he broke with the president and linked arms with Congress.

While northern resolve to defend black freedom withered, southern commitment to white supremacy intensified.

Grant was the obvious choice for the Republican Party's presidential nomination in 1868. Radicals preferred someone with a deeper moral commitment to black equality, but Grant supported congressional reconstruction and that was enough for the Republican convention. The Democrats chose Horatio Seymour, former governor of New York. Their platform blasted congressional reconstruction as "a flagrant usurpation of power . . . unconstitutional, revolutionary, and void." Republi-

cans answered by "waving the bloody shirt," that is, they reminded the voters that the Democrats were "the party of rebellion," the party that stubbornly resisted a just peace. During the campaign, the Ku Klux Klan erupted in another reign of terror, murdering hundreds of southern Republicans. Terrorist tactics cut into Grant's tally, but he gained a narrow 300,000-vote margin in the popular vote and a substantial victory (214 votes to 80) in the electoral college.

Grant understood that most Northerners had grown weary of reconstruction. Conservative business-minded Northerners had become convinced that recurrent federal intrusion was itself a major cause of instability. Eager to invest in the South and especially to resume the profitable cotton trade, they sought order, not disruption. A growing number of northern Republican leaders began to question the wisdom of their party's alliance with the South's lower classes—its small farmers and sharecroppers. Grant's secretary of the interior, Jacob D. Cox of Ohio, proposed allying with the "thinking and influential native southerners . . . the intelligent, well-to-do, and controlling class."

The talents Grant had demonstrated on the battlefield—decisiveness, clarity, and resolution—deserted him in the White House. Unclear about his objectives, he grew tentative, unsure of himself, and bewildered. He gave the impression of a good man who was in over his head. Able advisers might have helped, but Grant surrounded himself with fumbling kinfolk and old cronies from his army days. He increasingly hobnobbed with the rich and powerful, even frequenting their expensive tailors. Grant was slow to realize that it was the desire for personal gain, not loyalty to him, that caused bankers and businessmen to cozy up to him. He also made a string of dubious appointments that led to a series of damaging scandals. Charges of corruption tainted his vice president, Schuyler Colfax, and brought down his secretary of war and secretary of the navy as well as his private secretary. Grant's dogged loyalty to liars and cheats only compounded the damage. While never personally implicated in any scandal, Grant was guilty of extreme gullibility. Before long, his administration was synonymous in many people's minds with greed, graft, and corruption.

Grant could not fairly be held responsible for the low moral tone that characterized the entire nation after the Civil War. New inventions, new technology, and new forms of business organization fed feverish growth throughout the economy. The head-

GRANT AND SCANDAL
This anti-Grant cartoon by the nation's most celebrated political cartoonist, Thomas Nast, shows the president falling headfirst into the barrel of fraud and corruption that tainted his administration. During Grant's eight years in the White House, many in his administration failed him. Sometimes duped, sometimes merely loyal, Grant stubbornly defended wrongdoers, even to the point of perjuring himself to keep an aide out of jail. Library of Congress.

long advance provided enormous opportunity for graft and corruption. Democrats stole at least as brazenly as Republicans. The Tweed Ring, the Democratic political machine in New York City, pocketed some $200 million of the citizens' money. The buying and selling of politicians at the state level dwarfed federal corruption. It was said that the Standard Oil Company could do anything it wanted with the Pennsylvania legislature except refine it. The spoils system, by which victorious parties rewarded loyal workers with public office, had become a fixture of public life before Grant moved into the White House. Still, Grant was aggravatingly naive and his administration filled with rot.

In 1872, disgusted anti-Grant Republicans bolted and launched a third party, the Liberal Republicans. The Liberals promised to create a government "which the best people of this country will be proud of." They condemned the Grant regime as a riot of vulgarity—crude graft, tasteless materialism, and blatant anti-intellectualism. To clean up the mess, they proposed ending the spoils system and replacing it with a nonpartisan civil service commission that would oversee competitive examinations for appointment to office. Moreover, they demanded that the government remove federal troops from the South and restore "home rule." Democrats especially liked the Liberal's southern policy, and the Democratic Party endorsed the Liberal presidential candidate, Horace Greeley, the longtime editor of the *New York Tribune*. Despite Grant's problems, however, the nation still felt enormous affection for the man who had saved the Union. In the 1872 election, voters gave him 56 percent of the popular vote, the most lopsided victory since Andrew Jackson swept into the White House forty-four years earlier.

Grant was not without accomplishments during his eight years as president. Ironically, he scored his greatest triumph on an issue he cared little about: the settlement of the U.S. claim against Great Britain for wartime damages caused by British-built Confederate ships. When Britain denied any wrongdoing, tempers flared. But in 1872, Hamilton Fish,

Grant's able secretary of state, skillfully orchestrated a peaceful settlement that paid the United States $15.5 million in damages.

Grant's great passion in foreign affairs—annexation of Santo Domingo in the Caribbean—ended in utter failure. Grant argued that the acquisition of this tropical land would permit the United States to expand its trade in the Caribbean and simultaneously provide a new home for the South's blacks, who were so desperately harassed by the Klan. Aggressive foreign policy had not originated with the Grant administration. Lincoln and Johnson's secretary of state, William H. Seward, had thwarted French efforts to set up a puppet empire under Maximilian in Mexico, and his purchase of Alaska ("Seward's Ice Box") from Russia in 1867 for only $7 million had fired Grant's imperial ambitions. But the Republican Party split over the president's scheme to acquire Santo Domingo, and in the end Grant could not marshal the votes needed to approve the treaty of annexation.

The Grant administration was caught up in a tangle of complicated economic problems, but by far Grant's most difficult was the depression that began in 1873. Railroads, which had fueled the postwar boom, led directly to the bust. Jay Cooke, head of a major Philadelphia bank, had poured enormous sums into railroads, became overextended with debt, and went under, initiating the panic of 1873. Like dominoes, other companies failed, and soon the nation sank into its most severe depression to that time. More than 18,000 businesses collapsed in two years, and more than one million workers lost their jobs. Urban dwellers who were lucky enough to avoid unemployment saw their wages shrivel by 25 percent while food costs declined only 5 percent. Government relief did not exist, and private charities were swamped. Desperate times arrived at the doorsteps of most working people. Industrial violence kept pace with economic hardship. The violence subsided as men and women returned to work, but only at the end of the decade did the depression lift. By then, southern Republican governments had fallen, and the experiment of reconstruction had ended.

Northern Resolve Withers

Although Northerners wanted desperately to shift their attention to the new issues, the old ones would not go away. When southern Republicans pleaded for federal protection from Klan violence, Congress enacted three laws in 1870 and 1871 that were intended to break the back of white terrorism. The severest of the three, the Ku Klux Klan Act, made interference with voting rights a felony and authorized the use of the army to enforce it. Intrepid federal marshals arrested thousands of suspected Klansmen. While the government came close to destroying the Klan, it did not end terrorism against blacks. Congress also passed the Civil Rights Act of 1875, which boldly outlawed racial discrimination in transportation, public accommodations, and juries. But federal authorities did little to enforce the law, and segregated facilities remained the rule throughout the South.

In reality, the retreat from reconstruction had begun in 1868 with Grant's election. Grant genuinely wanted to see blacks' civil and political rights protected, but he felt uneasy about an open-ended commitment that seemed to ignore constitutional limitations on federal power. Like his predecessor, he distributed pardons liberally and encouraged the passage of a general amnesty. In May 1872, Congress obliged and restored the right of officeholding to all but three hundred ex-rebels. Radicals did what they could to stiffen the North's resolve, but reform had lost its principal spokesmen. By 1874, Charles Sumner, Thaddeus Stevens, and Salmon Chase were all dead. Others, such as Benjamin Wade of Pennsylvania, had lost their seats in Congress. Still others had washed their hands of reconstruction, concluding that the quest for black equality was mistaken or hopelessly naive. Republicans who bolted to the Liberal Republican Party, for example, welcomed the South's "best people" back to power. Traditional white leaders, it seemed to them, offered the best hope for honesty, order, and prosperity.

The North's abandonment of reconstruction rested on more than weariness, greed, and disillusionment. Underlying everything was unyielding racial prejudice. Emancipation failed to uproot racism in either the South or the North. During the war, Northerners had learned to accept black freedom, but deep-seated prejudice prevented many from equating freedom with equality. Even the actions that they took on behalf of blacks often served partisan political advantage. Whether they expressed it quietly or boisterously, Northerners generally supported Indiana Senator Thomas A. Hendricks's declaration that "this is a white man's Government, made by the white man for the white man." Increasingly, when Radicals asked Northerners to remember reconstruction's victims, northern sympathy went out to white Southerners.

The U.S. Supreme Court also did its part to undermine reconstruction. From the first, Republicans had feared that the conservative Court would declare their southern policies unconstitutional. Indeed, at times the Court gave the impression of seeking to dismantle reconstruction. In the 1870s, a series of Court decisions significantly weakened the federal government's ability to protect black Southerners under the Fourteenth and Fifteenth Amendments. In the *Slaughterhouse* cases (1873), the Court distinguished between national and state citizenship and ruled that the Fourteenth Amendment protected only those rights that stemmed from the federal government. Since the Court decided that most rights derived from the states, it sharply curtailed the federal government's authority to protect black citizens. Even more devastating, the *United States v. Cruikshank* (1876) ruling said that the reconstruction amendments gave Congress power to legislate only against discrimination by states, not by individuals. The "suppression of ordinary crime," such as assault, remained a state responsibility. The Supreme Court did not declare reconstruction unconstitutional, but it gradually undermined its legal foundation.

The mood of the North found political expression in the election of 1874, when for the first time in eighteen years the Democrats gained control of the House of Representatives. Voters blamed the Grant administration for the economic hard times that had begun the previous year, but they also sent a message about reconstruction. As one Republican observed, the people had grown tired of the "negro question, with all its complications, and the reconstruction of the Southern States, with all its interminable embroilments." Voters turned to the Democrats, who had from the beginning attacked reconstruction as unconstitutional, unnatural, and unwise. After 1874, even the most stubborn Republicans knew that perpetuating reconstruction was political suicide.

Reconstruction had come apart in the North. Congress gradually abandoned it. President Grant grew increasingly unwilling to enforce it. The Supreme Court busily denied the constitutionality of significant parts of it. And the people sent unmistakable messages that they were tired of it. Rather than defend reconstruction from its southern enemies, Northerners backed away from the challenge. After the early 1870s, southern blacks faced the forces of reaction largely on their own.

White Supremacy Triumphs

Republican governments in the South attracted more bitterness and hatred than any other political regimes in American history. In the eyes of the majority of whites, each day of Republican rule produced fresh insults: Black militia patrolled town streets, black laborers negotiated contracts with former masters, black maids stood up to former mistresses, black voters cast ballots, and black legislators enacted laws. The northern retreat from reconstruction permitted southern Democrats to harness this white rage to politics. Taking the name "Redeemers," they promised to replace "bayonet

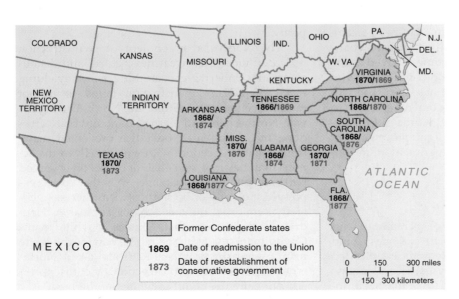

MAP 16.3
The Reconstruction of the South
Myth has it that Republican rule of the former Confederacy was not only harsh but long. In most states, however, conservative southern whites stormed back into power in only a matter of a couple of months or a very few years. By the election of 1876, Republican governments could be found in only three states. And they soon fell.

rule" (federal troops continued to be stationed in the South) with "home rule" (white southern control). They branded Republican governments a carnival of extravagance, waste, and fraud and promised that honest, thrifty Democrats would supplant the irresponsible tax-and-spend Republicans. Above all, they swore to save civilization from a descent into African "barbarism" and "negro rule." As one Redeemer put it, "We must render this either a white man's government, or convert the land into a Negro man's cemetery."

The Republican governments bore little resemblance to the Redeemer stereotypes. Nevertheless, numerous problems plagued their experiment in biracial democracy and made them vulnerable to attack. Republicans often promised more than they could deliver. Efforts to solve the massive economic problems of the devastated South often misfired. And while Democrats exaggerated in charging that "greed was unchecked and roguery unabashed," kickbacks, payoffs, and scams were common. But southern Republicans had no monopoly on corruption. During the Grant era, political dishonesty knew no particular party, region, or race.

By the early 1870s, however, Democrats understood that race was their most potent weapon. They adopted a two-pronged racial strategy to overthrow Republican governments. First, they sought to polarize the parties around color, and, second, they relentlessly intimidated black voters. They went about gathering all the South's white voters into the Democratic Party, leaving the Republicans to depend on blacks. The "straight-out" appeal to whites promised great advantage because whites made up a majority of the population in every southern state except Mississippi, South Carolina, and Louisiana.

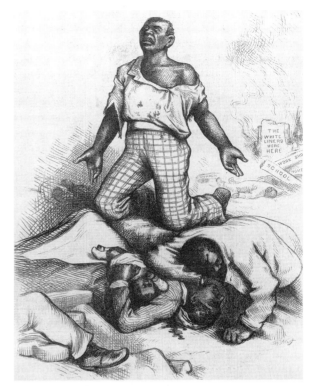

IS THIS A REPUBLICAN FORM OF GOVERNMENT?
This powerful 1876 drawing by Thomas Nast depicts the end of Reconstruction as the tragedy it was. As white supremacists in the South piled up more and more bodies, supporters of civil rights accused the Grant administration of failing to protect black Southerners and legitimately elected governments. They pointed specifically to the constitutional requirement that "[t]he United States shall guarantee to every State in this Union a Republican Form of Government, and shall protect each of them . . . against domestic violence" (Article IV, section 4).
Library of Congress.

Republican governments in the South attracted more bitterness and hatred than any other political regimes in American history.

Democrats employed several devices to dislodge whites from the Republican Party. First and foremost, they fanned the flames of racial prejudice. In South Carolina, a Democrat crowed that his party appealed to the "proud Caucasian race, whose sovereignty on earth God has proclaimed." Ostracism also proved effective. Local newspapers published the names of whites who kept company with blacks. So complete was the ostracism that one of its victims said, "No white man can live in the South in the future and act with any other than the Democratic party unless he is willing and prepared to live a life of social isolation."

In addition, Democrats exploited the small white farmer's severe economic plight by blaming it on Republican financial policy. Government spending soared during Reconstruction, and small farmers saw their tax burden skyrocket. Farms in Mississippi were taxed at four times the prewar level. When cotton prices fell by nearly 50 percent in the 1870s, yeomen farmers found cash in short supply. To pay their taxes, one man observed, "people are selling every egg and chicken they can get."

Those unable to pay lost their land. In 1871, Mississippi reported that one-seventh of the state's land —3,300,000 acres—had been forfeited for the nonpayment of taxes. The small farmer's economic distress had a racial dimension. Because few freedmen succeeded in acquiring land, they rarely paid taxes. In Georgia in 1874, blacks made up 46 percent of the population but paid only 2 percent of the taxes. From the perspective of the small white farmer, Republican rule meant not only that he was paying more taxes but that he was paying them to aid blacks. Democrats asked whether it was not time for hard-pressed yeomen to join the white man's party.

If racial pride, social isolation, and Republican financial policies proved insufficient to drive yeomen from the Republican Party, Democrats turned to terrorism. "Night riders" targeted scalawags as well as blacks for murder and assassination. By the early 1870s, then, only a fraction of southern whites any longer claimed allegiance to the party of Lincoln. White yeomen were willing for a time (as they would be again late in the century) to rise above racism and link arms with blacks to improve their common welfare, but the Republicans could not hold their allegiance. Racial polarization became a reality, and rich and poor whites united in opposition to reconstruction. Yeoman defection to the Redeemers proved a heavy blow to southern Republicanism.

The second prong of Democratic strategy—intimidation of black voters—proved equally devastating. Antiblack political violence escalated to unprecedented levels. In 1873 in Louisiana, a clash between black militiamen and gun-toting whites killed two white men and an estimated seventy black men. Half of the latter were slaughtered after they had surrendered. Although the federal government indicted more than one hundred white men, local juries failed to convict a single one.

Even before adopting the all-out white supremacist tactics of the 1870s, Democrats had already captured Virginia, Tennessee, and North Carolina. The new campaign brought fresh gains. The Redeemers regained Georgia in 1872, Texas in 1873, and Arkansas and Alabama in 1874. In 1875, Mississippi fell. The story in Mississippi was one of open, unrelenting, and often savage intimidation of black voters and their few remaining white allies. Planters warned the black sharecroppers who rented land from them: Vote Republican and find yourselves on the road. Whites used the flimsiest pretext to hunt down and shoot blacks who kept the Republican faith. In a "riot" in Vicksburg, Mississippi, thirty-five blacks and two whites lost their lives. As the state election approached in 1875, Republican Governor Adelbert Ames appealed to Washington for federal troops to control the violence, only to hear from the attorney general that the "whole public are tired of these annual autumnal outbreaks in the South." Abandoned, Mississippi Republicans succumbed to the Democratic onslaught in the fall elections. By 1876, only three Republican state governments—in Florida, Louisiana, and South Carolina—survived.

An Election and a Compromise

The centennial year of 1876 witnessed one of the most tumultuous elections in American history. Its chaos and confusion provided a fitting conclusion to the experiment known as reconstruction. The election took place in November, but not until March 2 of the following year, at 4 A.M., did the nation know who would be inaugurated president on March 4. For four months the country suffered through a constitutional and political crisis that jeopardized the peaceful transfer of power from one administration to the next. Sixteen years after Lincoln's election, Americans feared that a presidential contest would again precipitate civil war.

The Democrats had nominated New York's reform governor, Samuel J. Tilden, who immediately targeted the corruption of the Grant administration and the despotism of Republican reconstruction. The Republicans put forward a reformer of their own, Rutherford B. Hayes, governor of Ohio. Privately, Hayes considered "bayonet rule" a mistake, but he concluded that waving the bloody shirt, as threadbare as it was, remained the Republicans' best political strategy. "It leads people away from 'hard times,' which is our deadliest foe," Hayes said lamely.

On election day, Tilden tallied 4,284,000 votes to Hayes's 4,036,000. Yet in the all-important electoral college, Tilden fell one vote short of the majority required for victory. However, the electoral votes of three states remained in doubt and thus were uncounted. Both Democrats and Republicans claimed the nineteen votes of South Carolina, Louisiana, and Florida, the only remaining Republican strongholds in the South. To win, Tilden needed only one of the contested votes. Hayes had to have all of them to take the election. The two par-

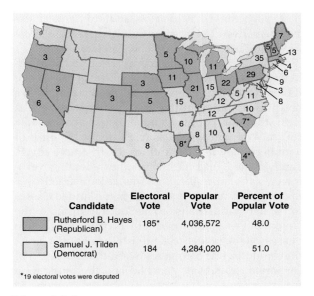

Candidate	Electoral Vote	Popular Vote	Percent of Popular Vote
Rutherford B. Hayes (Republican)	185*	4,036,572	48.0
Samuel J. Tilden (Democrat)	184	4,284,020	51.0

*19 electoral votes were disputed

MAP 16.4
The Election of 1876

ties traded charges of fraud and intimidation. To be sure, Republicans had stuffed some ballot boxes, but stepped-up violence by the Democrats had kept hundreds of thousands of southern Republicans from the polls.

Congress had to decide who had actually won the elections in the three southern states and thus who would be president. The Constitution provided little guidance. Moreover, Democrats controlled the House, and Republicans the Senate. To break the deadlock, Congress created a special electoral commission to arbitrate the disputed returns. An odd and cumbersome compromise, the commission was made up of five representatives (two Republicans, three Democrats), five senators (two Democrats, three Republicans), and five justices of the Supreme Court (two Republicans, two Democrats, and David Davis, considered to be an independent). But before the commission could meet, the Illinois legislature elected Justice Davis to the Senate. The other four justices filled his place with Justice Joseph Bradley, a fair-minded man but decidedly a Republican. The commissioners all voted the straight party line, giving every state to Hayes and putting him over the top in electoral votes.

Some outraged Democrats vowed to resist Hayes's victory. But the impasse was broken when negotiations behind the scenes between Hayes's lieutenants and some moderate southern Demo-

crats resulted in an informal understanding, known as the Compromise of 1877. In exchange for a Democratic promise not to block Hayes's inauguration and to deal fairly with the freedmen, Hayes vowed not to use the army to uphold the remaining Republican regimes. The South would also gain substantial federal subsidies for internal improvements. Less than two days later, the nation observed Hayes's peaceful inauguration.

Stubborn Tilden supporters bemoaned the "stolen election" and damned "His Fraudulency," Rutherford B. Hayes. Old-guard radicals such as William Lloyd Garrison denounced Hayes's bargain as a "policy of compromise, of credulity, of weakness, of subserviency, of surrender." But the nation as a whole celebrated. The Republic had weathered a grave crisis, and it had ended reconstruction. The last three Republican state governments fell quickly once Hayes abandoned them. The Compromise of 1877 confirmed the conservatism that had been growing in the North for years. New priorities meant that Northerners no longer wanted to intervene in the South, and, even without a deal, Hayes would probably have withdrawn the troops.

The nation's solution to this last sectional crisis marked a return to the antebellum tradition of sectional compromise. As in previous crises, whites had found a way to bridge their differences and retain the peace, and again blacks had paid the price. In 1877, Republicans followed a path of expediency and gained the presidency. Southern Democrats got home rule and a free hand in racial matters. When reconstruction ended, black Southerners were not completely subordinated to whites, but their prospects in the New South looked bleak.

Conclusion: "A Revolution but Half-Accomplished"

In 1865, when General Carl Schurz visited the South at President Andrew Johnson's behest, he discovered "a revolution but half-accomplished." Defeat had not prepared the South for an easy transition from slavery to free labor, from white racial despotism to equal justice, and from white political monopoly to biracial democracy. The old elite wanted to get "things back as near to slavery as possible," while ex-slaves and whites who had lacked power in the slave regime were eager to exploit the revolutionary implications of defeat and emancipation.

Congress pushed the revolution along. Although it refused to provide an economic underpinning to black freedom, it required defeated Confederates to accept legal equality and share political power. But conservative whites fought ferociously to recover their power and privilege. When they regained control of politics, they used the power of the state, along with private violence, to wipe out many of the gains of reconstruction. A visitor to the South in the late 1870s would have seen a landscape reminiscent of antebellum days. Blacks were back in the fields and kitchens, cotton had resumed its throne, and white Southerners again controlled the courthouses and state houses. So successful were the reactionaries that one observer concluded that the North had won the war but the South had won the peace.

But the Redeemer counterrevolution did not mean a return to slavery. Freedom meant something, and blacks knew it best. Abolition destroyed the old plantation of slavery days, and ex-slaves gained the freedom not to be whipped or sold, to send their children to school, to worship in their own churches, and to work independently on their own rented farms. The lives of impoverished sharecroppers overflowed with miseries and hardships, but even sharecropping provided more autonomy and economic welfare than bondage had. It was limited freedom, to be sure, but it was not slavery.

Emancipation set in motion the most profound upheaval in the nation's history, and nothing whites could do could entirely erase its revolutionary effects. War destroyed the richest and largest slave society in the New World. It cost masters $3 billion in lost property and destroyed the foundation of planter wealth. Slavery had defined the antebellum South, and abolition overturned the social and economic order that had dominated the region for nearly two centuries. The world of masters and slaves succumbed to that of landlords and sharecroppers. Even today, some Southerners divide history into "before the war" and "after the war."

The Civil War and emancipation mark a watershed not just in the South's history but in that of the entire nation. The scope of the revolution was not fully apparent in the 1870s, but already it was clear that the country had embarked on a new course. War had served as midwife for the birth of a modern nation-state, and for the first time sovereignty rested uncontested in the federal government. National unification was accompanied by a massive shift of power away from the landed classes to the new industrialists. The South returned to the Union, but as a junior partner. The victorious North possessed the power to establish the nation's direction, and it set its compass toward the expansion of corporate capitalism. War had laid the foundation for the power of big business and its captains in postwar America.

Still, the Civil War remained only a "half-accomplished" revolution. As such, Reconstruction represents a tragedy of enormous proportions. The nation did not fulfill the promises that it seemed to hold out to black Americans at war's end. The revolution raced forward, halted, and then slipped back, coming to rest far short of equality and justice. The failure had enduring consequences. Almost a century after reconstruction, the nation would embark on what one observer called a "second reconstruction," another effort to fulfill nineteenth-century promises. Many of the gains of the earlier reform effort had been negated, but the solid achievements of the Thirteenth, Fourteenth, and Fifteenth Amendments to the Constitution would provide a legal foundation for the renewed commitment. It is worth remembering, though, that it was only the failure of the first Reconstruction that made a modern civil rights movement necessary.

CHRONOLOGY

1863 **December.** Lincoln issues Proclamation of Amnesty and Reconstruction.

1864 **July.** Congress offers more stringent plan for reconstruction, Wade-Davis bill.

1865 **January.** General William T. Sherman sets aside land in South Carolina for black settlement.

March 4. Lincoln sworn in for second term as president of United States.

March. Congress establishes Freedmen's Bureau.

April 14. Lincoln shot, dies on April 15, is succeeded by Vice President Andrew Johnson.

Fall. Southern legislatures enact discriminatory black codes.

December. The Thirteenth Amendment abolishing slavery becomes part of U.S. Constitution.

1866 **April.** Congress approves Fourteenth Amendment making native-born blacks American citizens and guaranteeing all American citizens "equal protection under the laws." Amendment becomes part of Constitution in 1868.

April. Congress passes Civil Rights Act over President Johnson's veto.

May. Susan B. Anthony and Elizabeth Cady Stanton found Equal Rights Association to lobby for vote for women.

July. Congress extends Freedmen's Bureau over President Johnson's veto.

Summer. Ku Klux Klan founded in Tennessee.

November. Republicans triumph over Johnson in congressional elections.

1867 **March.** Congress passes Military Reconstruction Act imposing military rule on South and requiring states to guarantee vote to black men.

1868 **March–May.** Senate impeachment trial of President Johnson results in acquittal.

November. Ulysses S. Grant elected president of the United States.

1869 **February.** Congress approves Fifteenth Amendment prohibiting racial discrimination in voting rights. Amendment becomes part of Constitution in 1870.

1871 **April.** Congress enacts Ku Klux Klan Act in effort to end white terrorism in South.

1872 **November.** President Grant reelected.

1873 Economic depression sets in for remainder of decade.

1874 **November.** Elections return Democratic majority to House of Representatives.

1875 **February.** Civil Rights Act of 1875 outlaws racial discrimination, but federal authorities do little to enforce law.

1877 **March.** Special congressional committee awards disputed electoral votes to Republican Rutherford B. Hayes, making him president of United States; Hayes agrees to pull military out of South.

BIBLIOGRAPHY

GENERAL WORKS

W. E. B. Du Bois, *Black Reconstruction in America* (1935).

Eric Foner, *Reconstruction: America's Unfinished Revolution, 1863–1877* (1988).

John Hope Franklin, *Reconstruction after the Civil War* (1961).

James M. McPherson, *Ordeal by Fire: The Civil War and Reconstruction* (1982).

Rembert W. Patrick, *The Reconstruction of the Nation* (1967).

J. G. Randall and David Donald, *The Civil War and Reconstruction* (1967).

Kenneth M. Stampp, *The Era of Reconstruction, 1865–1877* (1965).

WARTIME RECONSTRUCTION

Richard H. Abbott, *The First Southern Strategy: The Republican Party and the South, 1855–1877* (1986).

Herman Belz, *Emancipation and Equal Rights: Politics and Constitutionalism in the Civil War Era* (1978).

Ira Berlin et al., eds., *Freedom: A Documentary History of Emancipation, 1861–1867* (1982–).

Louis S. Gerteis, *From Contraband to Freedman: Federal Policy toward Southern Blacks, 1861–1865* (1973).

Peyton McCrary, *Abraham Lincoln and Reconstruction: The Louisiana Experiment* (1978).

William S. McFeely, *Yankee Stepfather: General O. O. Howard and the Freedmen* (1968).

James M. McPherson, *The Struggle for Equality: Abolitionists and the Negro in the Civil War and Reconstruction* (1964).

Willie Lee Rose, *Rehearsal for Reconstruction: The Port Royal Experiment* (1964).

Brooks D. Simpson, *Let Us Have Peace: Ulysses S. Grant and the Politics of War and Reconstruction, 1861–1868* (1991).

Hans L. Trefousse, *The Radical Republicans: Lincoln's Vanguard for Racial Justice* (1969).

PRESIDENTIAL RECONSTRUCTION

W. R. Brock, *An American Crisis: Congress and Reconstruction, 1865–1867* (1963).

Albert Castel, *The Presidency of Andrew Johnson* (1979).

LaWanda F. Cox and John H. Cox, *Politics, Principles, and Prejudice, 1865–1866* (1963).

David H. Donald, *The Politics of Reconstruction, 1863–1867* (1965).

Edward L. Gambill, *Conservative Ordeal: Northern Democrats and Reconstruction, 1865–1868* (1981).

Martin E. Mantell, *Johnson, Grant, and the Politics of Reconstruction* (1973).

Eric L. McKitrick, *Andrew Johnson and Reconstruction* (1966).

Donald G. Nieman, *To Set the Law in Motion: The Freedmen's Bureau and the Legal Rights of Blacks, 1865–1868* (1979).

J. Michael Quill, *Prelude to the Radicals: The North and Reconstruction during 1865* (1980).

Patrick W. Riddleberger, *1866: The Critical Year Revisited* (1979).

Robert D. Sawrey, *Dubious Victory: The Reconstruction Debate in Ohio* (1992).

James E. Sefton, *Andrew Johnson and the Uses of Constitutional Power* (1980).

Hans L. Trefousse, *Impeachment of a President: Andrew Johnson, the Blacks and Reconstruction* (1975).

Hans L. Trefousse, *Andrew Johnson: A Biography* (1989).

CONGRESSIONAL RECONSTRUCTION

Eric Anderson and Alfred A. Moss Jr., eds., *The Facts of Reconstruction: Essays in Honor of John Hope Franklin* (1991).

Michael Les Benedict, *The Impeachment and Trial of Andrew Johnson* (1973).

Michael Les Benedict, *A Compromise of Principle: Congressional Republicans and Reconstruction* (1974).

Richard F. Bensel, *Yankee Leviathan: The Origins of Central State Authority in America, 1859–1877* (1990).

Fawn M. Brodie, *Thaddeus Stevens: Scourge of the South* (1959).

David H. Donald, *Charles Sumner and the Rights of Man* (1970).

William Gillette, *The Right to Vote: Politics and the Passage of the Fifteenth Amendment* (1965).

Victor B. Howard, *Religion and the Radical Republican Movement, 1860–1870* (1990).

Harold M. Hyman, *A More Perfect Union: The Impact of the Civil War and Reconstruction on the Constitution* (1973).

Stanley Kutler, *The Judicial Power and Reconstruction Politics* (1968).

Michael L. Lanza, *Agrarianism and Reconstruction Politics: The Southern Homestead Act* (1990).

William S. McFeely, *Grant* (1981).

James C. Mohr, *The Radical Republicans and Reform in New York during Reconstruction* (1973).

David Montgomery, *Beyond Equality: Labor and the Radical Republicans, 1862–1872* (1967).

William E. Nelson, *The Fourteenth Amendment: From Political Principle to Judicial Doctrine* (1988).

Patrick W. Riddleberger, *George Washington Julian: Radical Republican* (1966).

Joel H. Silbey, *A Respectable Minority: The Democratic Party in the Civil War Era, 1860–1868* (1977).

Mark W. Summers, *Railroads, Reconstruction, and the Gospel of Prosperity* (1984).

Margaret S. Thompson, *The "Spider Web": Congress and Lobbying in the Age of Grant* (1985).

Hans L. Trefousse, *The Radical Republicans* (1963).

THE STRUGGLE IN THE SOUTH

James D. Anderson, *The Education of Blacks in the South, 1860–1935* (1988).

Stephen V. Ash, *Middle Tennessee Society Transformed, 1860–1870: War and Peace in the Upper South* (1988).

Dwight B. Billings Jr., *Planters and the Making of a "New South"* (1979).

Randolph B. Campbell, *A Southern Community in Crisis: Harrison County, Texas, 1850–1880* (1983).

Dan T. Carter, *When the War Was Over: The Failure of Self-Reconstruction in the South, 1865–1867* (1985).

Barry A. Crouch, *The Freedmen's Bureau and Black Texans* (1992).

Richard N. Current, *Those Terrible Carpetbaggers: A Reinterpretation* (1988).

Joseph G. Dawson III, *Army Generals and Reconstruction: Louisiana, 1862–1877* (1982).

Edmund L. Drago, *Black Politicians and Reconstruction in Georgia* (1982).

Barbara J. Fields, *Slavery and Freedom on the Middle Ground: Maryland during the Nineteenth Century* (1985).

Michael W. Fitzgerald, *The Union League Movement in the Deep South: Politics and Agricultural Change during Reconstruction* (1989).

Eric Foner, *Nothing but Freedom: Emancipation and Its Legacy* (1983).

Steven Hahn, *The Roots of Southern Populism: Yeoman Farmers and the Transformation of the Georgia Upcountry, 1850–1890* (1983).

William C. Harris, *Day of the Carpetbagger: Republican Reconstruction in Mississippi* (1979).

Janet Sharp Hermann, *The Pursuit of a Dream* (1981).

Thomas Holt, *Black over White: Negro Political Leadership in South Carolina during Reconstruction* (1977).

Elizabeth Jacoway, *Yankee Missionaries in the South* (1979).

Jacqueline Jones, *Soldiers of Light and Love: Northern Teachers and Georgia Blacks, 1865–1873* (1980).

Peter Kolchin, *First Freedom: The Responses of Alabama's Blacks to Emancipation and Reconstruction* (1972).

Leon F. Litwack, *Been in the Storm So Long: The Aftermath of Slavery* (1979).

Richard Lowe, *Republicans and Reconstruction in Virginia, 1865–1870* (1991).

Jay R. Mandle, *Not Slave, Not Free: The African American Economic Experience since the Civil War* (1992).

Donald Nieman, *To Set the Law in Motion: The Freedmen's Bureau and the Legal Rights of Blacks, 1865–1868* (1979).

Michael Perman, *Reunion without Compromise: The South and Reconstruction, 1865–1868* (1973).

Michael Perman, *The Road to Redemption: Southern Politics, 1869–1879* (1984).

Lawrence N. Powell, *New Masters: Northern Planters during the Civil War and Reconstruction* (1984).

Howard Rabinowitz, ed., *Southern Black Leaders of the Reconstruction Era* (1982).

George C. Rable, *But There Was No Peace: The Role of Violence in the Politics of Reconstruction* (1984).

Roger L. Ransom and Richard Sutch, *One Kind of Freedom: The Economic Consequences of Emancipation* (1977).

William L. Richter, *Overreached on All Sides: The Freedmen's Bureau Administrators in Texas, 1865–1868* (1991).

C. Peter Ripley, *Slaves and Freedmen in Civil War Louisiana* (1976).

James L. Roark, *Masters without Slaves: Southern Planters in the Civil War and Reconstruction* (1977).

James E. Sefton, *The United States Army and Reconstruction, 1865–1877* (1967).

Crandall A. Shifflett, *Patronage and Poverty in the Tobacco South: Louisa County, Virginia, 1860–1900* (1982).

Joe G. Taylor, *Louisiana Reconstructed* (1974).

Allen Trelease, *White Terror: The Ku Klux Klan Conspiracy and Southern Reconstruction* (1967).

Ted Tunnell, *Crucible of Reconstruction: War, Radicalism, and Race in Louisiana, 1862–1877* (1974).

Clarence E. Walker, *A Rock in a Weary Land: The African Methodist Episcopal Church during the Civil War and Reconstruction* (1982).

Peter Wallenstein, *From Slave South to New South: Public Policy in Nineteenth-Century Georgia* (1987).

Michael Wayne, *The Reshaping of Plantation Society: The Natchez District, 1860–1880* (1983).

Jonathan M. Wiener, *Social Origins of the New South, 1860–1885* (1978).

Joel Williamson, *After Slavery: The Negro in South Carolina during Reconstruction* (1966).

Sarah Woolfolk Wiggins, *The Scalawag in Alabama Politics, 1865–1881* (1977).

Gavin Wright, *Old South, New South: Revolutions in the Southern Economy since the Civil War* (1986).

COLLAPSE OF RECONSTRUCTION

William Gillette, *Retreat from Reconstruction, 1869–1879* (1979).

Otto H. Olsen, ed., *Reconstruction and Redemption in the South* (1980).

Ian Polakoff, *The Politics of Inertia: The Election of 1876 and the End of Reconstruction* (1973).

Terry L. Seip, *The South Returns to Congress: Men, Economic Measures, and Intersectional Relationships, 1868–1879* (1983).

John G. Sproat, *"The Best Men"* (1968).

C. Vann Woodward, *Reunion and Reaction: The Compromise of 1877 and the End of Reconstruction* (1951).

KENTUCKY SUN QUILT

This carefully hand-stitched quilt, made from pieces of leftover wool clothing and blankets, shows how a woman named Nancy Miller Grider responded creatively to the challenges of her life in Russell County, Kansas, in the 1880s. Historically, women have produced quilts as a visual language, to tell something about themselves by using materials at hand. The circular pattern in Grider's quilt may represent the spokes of a wheel — a fitting symbol not only of her own migration west but of the mass migrations taking place after the Civil War when restless Americans on the move peopled the West and fed the growth of the big cities.

Collection of the Kentucky Quilt Project, Photograph courtesy of the Kentucky Quilt Project, Inc., Louisville, Ky.

AMERICANS ON THE MOVE: THE SETTLEMENT OF THE WEST AND THE RISE OF THE CITY

17

1860–1900

A MISSOURI HOMESTEADER REMEMBERED packing as the family pulled up stakes and headed west to Oklahoma:

> We were going to God's Country. Eighteen hundred and 90. . . . It was pretty hard to part with some of our things. We didn't have much but we had worked hard for everything we had. You had to work hard in that rocky country in Missouri. I was glad to be leaving it. We were going to God's Country. . . . We were going to a new land and get rich.

In the Dakotas an Oglala Sioux recalled moving with his family as a child:

> The snow was deep and it was very cold, and I remember sitting in another pony drag beside my father and mother, all wrapped up in fur. We were going away from where the soldiers were, and I do not know where we went, but it was west.

In the Midwest a young man turned his face to the city, leaving his hometown behind:

> He saw again in his mind's eye, as he tramped the road, a picture of the map on the wall of the railway station—the map with a picture of iron roads from all over the Middle West centering in a dark blotch in the corner. . . .
> "Chicago!" he said to himself.

And in Russia a young girl on her way to America bid good-bye to her village:

> I remember how the women crowded around mother . . . how, finally, the ringing of the signal bell set them all talking faster and louder than ever, in desperate efforts to give the last bits of advice, deliver the last messages, and, to their credit let it be said, to give the final, hearty, unfeigned good-bye kisses, hugs, and good wishes.

Americans in the nineteenth century were a people on the move, in search of jobs, land, and opportunity. In the last three decades of the century, their movement took many forms and went in many directions. The trek to the West continued apace as homesteaders, ranchers, miners, and settlers sought their fortunes. They in turn pushed Native Americans off the land and farther toward the sunset.

At the same time, the pull of the great industrial centers in the Northeast counterbalanced the westward migration. Farmers left the country to seek jobs in industrial centers like Chicago, New York, Pittsburgh, and Detroit. African Americans from the South began a migration to the northern cities, and Canadians crossed the border to work in the factories and mill towns of New England.

Fourteen million immigrants braved the Atlantic to come to America from Europe, creating the great migration that we think of as part of a worldwide westward movement. But the movement of peoples was by no means limited to one direction. Immigrants from Mexico and Latin America journeyed to "El Norte." Canadians headed south. Asians voyaged east across the Pacific to work on the "gold mountain" of California. It is not an exaggeration to say that the decades surrounding the turn of the twentieth century witnessed a migration unmatched in the history of the world.

Within the country, restless, footloose Americans joined the churning masses in motion. The typical urban American in the late nineteenth century moved, on the average, as much as or more than we commonly move today. An industrial worker might hold as many as thirty different jobs in perhaps a dozen cities during a lifetime.

By the end of the century, Americans on the move had peopled a continent and created the outlines of modern America. As industrial capitalism transformed the nation from a rural agrarian economy into an increasingly urban industrial society, it touched and transformed life not just in the burgeoning cities but also on the plains of the Dakotas, in the mines of Colorado, and on the farms of Texas and California. Iron rails and a national market economy inextricably linked the country and the city.

Land Fever

Americans by the hundreds of thousands packed up and moved, pinning their hopes and ambitions on the American West. In the three decades following 1870, this westward stream of migration swelled into a torrent, spilling across the remainder of the prairies, moving on to the Pacific coast, and even-

tually flooding back onto the Great Plains. During this brief span of time, more land was settled than in all the previous history of the country. Between 1876 and 1900, eight new states entered the Union—Colorado, Montana, North and South Dakota, Washington, Idaho, Wyoming, and Utah—leaving only three territories—Oklahoma, New Mexico, and Arizona—in the continental United States.

Two factors stimulated the rapid settlement of the trans-Mississippi West. The Homestead Act of 1862 promised 160 acres free to any citizen or prospective citizen, male or female, who settled on the land for five years. And railroads opened up new areas for settlement and actively recruited settlers. Those who took advantage of the government's offer of free land were called homesteaders, as distinguished from settlers, who purchased their land from private parties. Often they bought from speculators who took up land with an eye to profit, never intending to live on it. In the 1870s, the promise of land lured thousands west across the plains in covered wagons, a hard journey that took many months and cost many lives. With the completion of a transcontinental railroad system in the 1880s, settlers could choose from four competing rail lines and often made the trip in less than a week.

While the country was rich in land and resources, not all who wanted to own their own land were able to do so. Land prices soared to giddy heights as speculating drove prices up. At the same time, large landowners, often foreign investors, gobbled up huge ranches in California and the Southwest. The South, still reeling from the economic impact of the Civil War, saw the old plantation system give way to tenancy and peonage. A growing number of Americans found themselves dispossessed, forced to work for wages on land they would never own.

Moving West: Farmers, Homesteaders, and Speculators

Families who ventured west searching for "God's country" faced hardship, loneliness, and deprivation. To carve a farm from the raw prairie of Iowa, the plains of Nebraska, or the forests of the Pacific Northwest took more than fortitude and backbreaking toil. It took luck. Farming, as one historian acknowledged, was "a risky, uncertain, and often heartbreaking business." Blizzards, tornadoes, grasshoppers, hailstorms, drought, prairie fires, accidental death, and disease were only a few of the catastrophes that could befall even the best farmer.

RAILROAD LOCOMOTIVE
In the years following the Civil War, the locomotive replaced the covered wagon, enabling settlers to travel from Chicago or St. Louis to the West Coast in two days. By the 1890s, more than 72,000 miles of track stretched west of the Mississippi River. In this photograph, men and women hop aboard a locomotive to celebrate the completion of a section of track.
Library of Congress.

Debt was a constant nightmare. Homesteaders on "free" land needed as much as a thousand dollars for a house, a team of farm animals, a well, fencing, and seed. Poor sodbusters did without even these basics, living in dugouts carved in the land and using muscle instead of machinery.

Americans in the nineteenth century were a people on the move, in search of jobs, land, and opportunity.

"Father made a dugout and covered it with willows and grass," one Kansas girl recounted. When it rained, water flooded the dugout and "we carried the water out in buckets, then waded around in the mud until it dried." Rain wasn't the only problem. "Sometimes the bull snakes would get in the roof and now and then one would lose his hold and fall down on the bed, then off on the floor. Mother would grab the hoe . . . and after the fight was over Mr. Bull Snake was dragged outside."

For women on the frontier, simple daily necessities like obtaining water and fuel meant backbreaking labor. Women lugged bucketfuls of water from wells. Out on the plains, where water was scarce, women often had to trudge to the nearest creek or spring. "A yoke was made to place across the shoulders, so as to carry at each end a bucket of water," one daughter recollected, "and then water was brought a half mile from spring to house." Fifteen years of such unremitting hard labor, the daughter sadly observed, "brought her [mother] worn-out to the grave at the age of 58 years." Gathering fuel was another heavy chore. Without ready sources of coal or firewood, settlers on the prairies and plains turned to what substitutes they could scavenge. Anything burnable—twigs, tufts of grass, old corncobs, sunflower stalks—was used for fuel. But by far the most prevalent fuel used for cooking and heating were "chips", which were chunks of dried cattle and buffalo dung found in abundance on the plains and grasslands.

Food preparation provided another challenge to the farm wife. Cookstoves were virtually unknown in the territories. Settlers cooked in kettles suspended over the fireplace and boiled most of their food. Baking was accomplished using footed iron kettles set in the coals. Simplicity and monotony characterized the settlers' regular diet, which was heavy on corn, wheat, and potatoes. "Our living at first was very scanty," recalled one Kansas woman, "mostly corn coarsely ground and made into hominy." But things improved. The family raised a crop of wheat and ground it into flour. "We would invite the neighbors proudly telling them we

have 'flour doings.'" When the farm wife began to raise chickens, the family added "chicken fixings" to its diet, "and when we could have 'flour doings and chicken fixings' at the same meal we felt we were on the road to prosperity."

The costs and expenses of farming made farmers habitual debtors. The first years were critical. If the farm did not fare well, if the crop failed, the farmer faced a downward spiral into a mire of debt. Dependent on the weather, the bank, the railroad, and the market, the so-called independent farmer

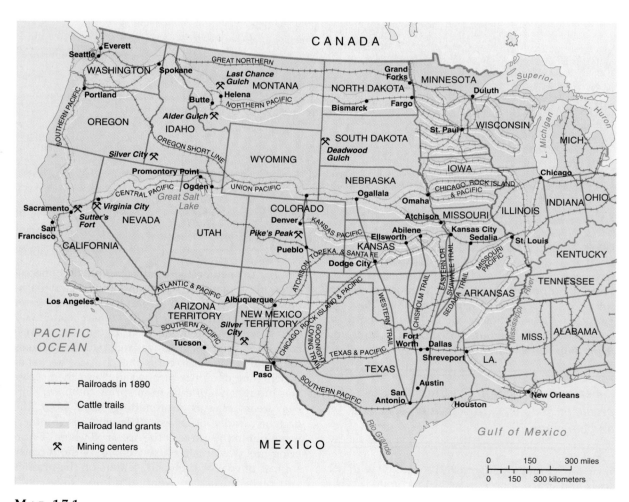

MAP 17.1

Federal Land Grants to Railroads and the Development of the West, 1850–1900
Generous federal land grants meant that railroads could sell the desirable land next to the track at a profit or hold it for speculation. Railroads received over 180 million acres, an area equal to the size of Texas. Note how the cattle trails connect with major railheads in Dodge City, Abilene, and Kansas City and to mines in Montana, Nevada, Colorado, and New Mexico.

OUR HOME
A mother and her children pose in front of their dugout near McCook, Nebraska, in the 1890s. With its real roof, glass windowpanes, and solid door, their dugout is more substantial than most.
Nebraska State Historical Society.

labored against heavy odds. No wonder some settlers didn't bother to farm at all. The West had more than its share of small-time speculators, who took up land in the hope of selling it for a profit.

Many homesteaders and settlers succeeded in building comfortable lives. But for others the opportunities of the West failed to materialize. Already by the 1870s, much of the best land had been taken, given to the railroads as land grants or to the states to finance education. Too often, the homesteaders found that only the least desirable tracts were left —poorer lands, far from markets, transportation, and society. Land speculators took the lion's share. "There is plenty of land for sale in California," one migrant complained in 1870, but "the majority of the available lands are held by speculators, at prices far beyond the reach of a poor man."

The railroads were by far the biggest single winners in the scramble for western land. To encourage railroad building in the decades after the Civil War, the federal government and the states gave public lands to the railroads. Together the land grants totaled approximately 180 million acres—an area almost one-tenth the size of the United States.

In California alone the railroads held some 20 million acres by 1870. Farmers who went west to homestead often ended up buying land from the railroads or from the speculators and land companies that quickly followed the railroads into the new territories. The value of Nebraska railroad land went from $8 an acre in 1870 to $25 an acre by 1890. Of the 2.5 million farms established on public lands between 1860 and 1900, homesteading accounted for only one in five; the vast majority of farmland sold for a profit.

As land for homesteading grew scarce on the prairie in the 1870s, farmers began to push farther westward, moving into western Kansas, Nebraska, and eastern Colorado—the land called the Great American Desert by settlers who had passed over it on their way to California and Oregon. The Homestead Act tempted settlers out onto the Great Plains, where 160 acres of plains land was too dry to support a farm. Although many agricultural experts warned that the semiarid land (where less than twenty inches of rain fell annually) should be reserved for grazing, their words of caution were drowned out by the extravagant claims of western promoters. Railroad companies pictured the plains as an agricultural paradise where settlers would "all become prosperous, and many will acquire fortunes in a short period." "Rain follows the plow" became the slogan of western boosters, who insisted that cultivation would alter the climate of the region and bring more rainfall.

It would have been more accurate to say that drought followed the plow. Periodic droughts at roughly twenty-year intervals were a fact of life on the Great Plains. Plowed up, the dry topsoil blew away in the wind. A period of relatively good rainfall in the early 1880s encouraged settlement, but a protracted drought in the late 1880s and early 1890s sent starving farmers reeling back from the plains. Hundreds of thousands retreated from western Kansas and Nebraska, some in wagons carrying the slogan "In God we trusted, in Kansas we busted." A popular ballad bitterly summed up the plight of the worst off, those too poor to leave:

How happy I am on my government claim,
Where I've nothing to lose and nothing to gain,
Nothing to eat and nothing to wear,
Nothing from nothing is honest and square.
But here I am stuck and here I must stay,
My money's all gone and I can't get away;
There's nothing will make a man hard and profane
Like starving to death on a government claim.

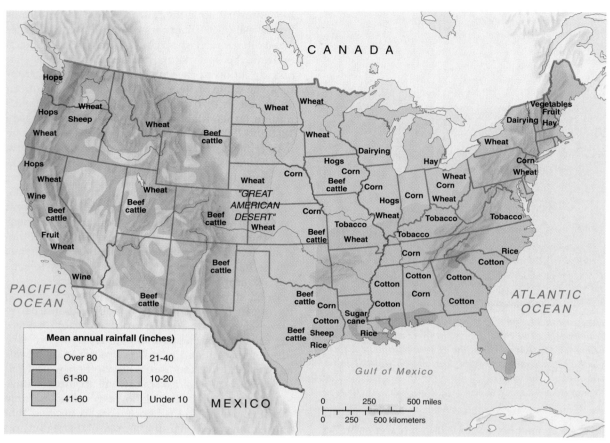

MAP 17.2
Rainfall and Agricultural Regions, around 1890
*Early travelers called the grasslands of the Great Plains "The Great American Desert" as they
hurried over this flat, semi-arid land on their way to California or Oregon. But by the 1870s
much of the best far western land was taken and land fever tempted farmers onto the plains in
western Kansas, Nebraska, and eastern Colorado. Many would go bust in the great droughts of
the late 1880s.*

The fever for fertile land set off a series of spectacular land runs in Oklahoma. When the government opened two million acres in former Indian territory to settlement in 1889, thousands rushed to grab a piece. Federal troops kept order as the homesteaders massed on the border. On April 22 at noon, pistol shots signaled the opening, and they were off. "Along the line as far as the eye could reach, with a shout and a yell the swift riders shot out, then followed the light buggies or wagons and last the lumbering prairie schooners and freighters' wagons," a reporter wrote. "Above all a great cloud of dust hover[ed] like smoke over a battlefield." It was a wild scramble, the reporter confessed, "a rough and tumble contest filled with excitement and real peril." By the end of the day, hundreds of homesteaders had staked claims, and Oklahoma boasted two tent cities with more than 10,000 residents.

In later years, other portions of Indian territory opened for settlement. In a frenzied land rush on the Cherokee strip in Oklahoma Territory in 1893, more than 100,000 homesteaders competed for 40,000 claims. Several settlers were killed in the stampede, and nervous men guarded their claims with rifles. Some simply moved onto Indian lands. Called "boomers" or "sooners," they had to be removed by force. As public lands grew smaller, the hunger for land grew even fiercer.

The Dispossessed: Tenants, Sharecroppers, and Migrants

Landownership, the symbol of the American dream in the nineteenth century, remained an elusive goal for many Americans—newly freed slaves, immigrants arriving from Europe and Asia, and Mexicans on the Texas border. In the post–Civil War period, as agriculture became a big business tied to national and global markets, an increasing number of dispossessed laborers worked land that they would never own.

In the southern United States, the farmer labored under particularly heavy burdens. The Civil War wiped out much of the region's capital, which had been invested in slaves, and crippled the plantation economy. The newly freed slaves rarely managed to obtain land of their own. Instead, they soon found themselves reduced to propertyless farm laborers. "The colored folks stayed with the old boss man and farmed and worked on the plantations," a black Alabama sharecropper observed bitterly. "They were still slaves, but they were free slaves."

Tenancy and sharecropping became a way of life for poor blacks and whites alike. The tenant rented land; the sharecropper worked someone else's land for a share of the proceeds. Even those who owned their own land faced enormous difficulties. In the states of the old Confederacy, both money and credit were in short supply. Southern farmers in desperation turned to the country merchant for credit. Before the war, tiny rural stores had dotted the South, serving the modest needs of small white farmers. After the war, thousands of small stores mushroomed across the landscape to provide food, clothing, and necessary supplies to the increased numbers of tenant and sharecropper farmers, both white and black. Some of the merchants were ex-masters who opened stores on their plantations. Under an arrangement called crop lien, local merchants supplied goods to the farmers on credit; in return, the farmers put up their next year's crop as collateral. The merchants charged exorbitant interest, up to 60 percent, on the goods they sold—from seed to a slab of bacon. At "settling up time," after the landlord took half the farmer's yield, the merchant consulted the debt ledger. Invariably, the farmer's expenses exceeded the income from his half of the cotton crop, and the cropper went home empty-handed, only to begin the cycle all over again.

There was no escape. Indebtedness bound the sharecropper to the landlord and to the merchant by prohibiting him from moving or buying from another store. Even small farmers who owned their own land suffered under the crop lien system. After seven years, farmers who did not "pay out" lost their land. Across the South the merchant became known as the "furnishing man." Black farmers called him simply "the man." The crop lien system over which he presided led generations of farmers, white and black, into a mire of debt and dependency. By the beginning of the twentieth century, a majority of white farmers had become landless share-

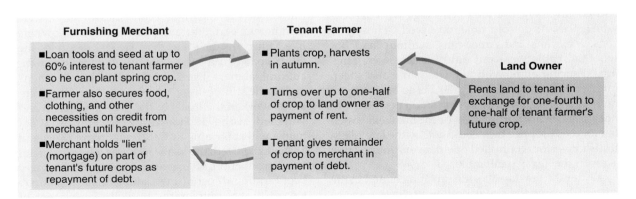

FIGURE 17.1
Tenancy and the Crop Lien System
The crop lien system was designed to deal with the shortage of money and credit in the post-Reconstruction South. The local furnishing merchant provided seed and supplies to farmers who pledged their crop as collateral. A complex skein of relationships developed between merchant, landowner, and tenant farmer.

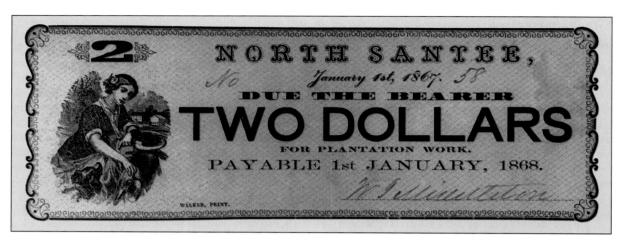

SHARECROPPER SCRIP

Both money and credit were in short supply in the South after the Civil War. To get around the problem, landowners issued scrip in lieu of cash to the landless sharecroppers who worked their fields. Redeemable only at the plantation store, the scrip locked the sharecroppers into an insidious system. The sharecroppers, forced to buy food and other goods at high prices from their creditors/employers, often fell into a cycle of debt and dependency. This note circulated in South Carolina in 1868.

The South Carolina Historical Society.

croppers, outnumbering even the freedpeople caught in the system.

In Texas, the coming of the railroads at the turn of the century undermined ranch culture and led to the rise of a segregated farm society in which a growing number of Mexican wageworkers labored on huge spreads owned by Anglos or by European syndicates. As early as the 1860s, the large ranchers had begun to enclose the open range with barbed-wire fences. As one old-timer observed, "Those persons, Mexicans and Americans, without land but who had cattle were put out of business by fencing." Fencing eliminated landless cattle and sheep ranchers, who had grazed their herds on the open range, and forced small-time landowners who could not afford to buy barbed wire or to sink wells to sell out for the best price they could get. By the late 1880s, British investors controlled one of every four or five acres in the Texas panhandle.

After the heyday of cattle ranching ended in the late 1880s came the rise of cotton production in the southeastern regions of Texas. Ranchers turned their pastures into sharecroppers' plots and hired displaced cowboys, most of them Mexican, as seasonal laborers for as little as seventy-five cents a day. Within the space of ten years, ranch life in southern Texas gave way to a growing army of agricultural wageworkers.

In California, a pattern of land monopoly and large-scale farming fostered tenancy and migratory labor. By the 1870s, less than one percent of the population owned half of the state's available agricultural land. A German, Henry Miller, in partnership with an Alsatian immigrant, Charles Lux, acquired thousands of acres in the rich San Joaquin valley. By 1900, the Miller-Lux empire constituted over a million acres. The rigid economics of large-scale commercial agriculture as practiced by rich owners like Miller and Lux and the seasonal nature of the crops spawned a ragged army of migratory agricultural laborers. Derisively labeled "blanket men" or "bindle stiffs," these homeless and landless transients worked the fields in the growing season and wintered in the flophouses of San Francisco. Bonanza wheat farming in California in the 1870s and 1880s exhausted the land and was replaced, with the introduction of irrigation, by fruit and sugar beet farming. Most of the California farm laborers were Chinese immigrants until the enactment of Chinese exclusion in 1882 forced big growers to tap other groups, including Mexicans, Filipinos, and Japanese, for farm labor.

The dispossessed—those with no land and no hope of owning their own land—became a growing part of the workforce in the United States by the end of the century.

The Changing Face of Rural America

In the late nineteenth century, America's population remained overwhelmingly rural. The 1870 census showed that nearly 80 percent of the nation's people lived in areas of less than eight thousand inhabitants. In 1900, the figure had dropped to 66 percent. But while the percentage of rural inhabitants fell, the number of farms grew—from 2 million in 1860 to more than 5.7 million in 1900. Rapid growth in the West accounted for the rise in the number of farms, but not all the nation's farmers lived in the West. The rural population spread evenly across the country, with rural inhabitants outnumbering city dwellers even in industrial states like Pennsylvania and New York as late as 1880. Like all aspects of American life, farm life changed rapidly in the last decades of the century. With the rise of industrialization and the growth of big cities, many farmers gave up their farms and moved to towns and cities. Those who stayed behind increasingly adopted new technologies, making farming less a way of life and more a business venture. In the states of the old

Confederacy, enthusiastic advocates of industrial development trumpeted the New South as the region scrambled to build blast furnaces and mills alongside its cotton fields. Nevertheless cotton remained king in the New South, and the region's emphasis on a cash-crop economy signaled a nationwide trend away from family farming and toward agribusiness.

The Colonial Economy of the New South

In the decades following the Civil War, the South struggled to regain its economic footing. The region's economy, devastated by war and altered forever by the abolition of slavery, foundered at the same time the North experienced an unprecedented industrial boom. No wonder some Southerners called for a New South modeled on the industrial North. Henry Grady, the ebullient young editor of the *Atlanta Constitution*, used his paper's substantial influence (it boasted the largest circulation of any weekly in the country) to extol the virtues of a new industrial South. Part bully, part booster, Grady exhorted the South to use its natural advantages—cheap labor and abundant natural resources—to go head to head in competition with northern industry.

Grady's message fell on receptive ears. Many Southerners, men and women, black and white, joined the national migration from farm to city, leaving the old plantations to molder and decay. Between 1870 and 1890, villages and towns in the South experienced unprecedented growth. With the end of military rule in 1877, southern Democrats, calling themselves "Redeemers," regained political power in the southern states. But whatever their plantation pedigrees, they readily cast their lot with the corporate North. The sons of the old planter class enthusiastically embraced northern promoters who promised prosperity and profits. Northern capital rushed south in the waning years of the 1870s as the country recovered from the hard times precipitated by the panic of 1873. The railroads came first, opening up the region for industrial development. Railroad mileage grew fourfold from 1865 to 1890. So too did the number of cotton spindles soar as textile mill owners abandoned New England en masse in search of the cheap labor, low taxes, and proximity to raw materials promised in the South. By 1900, the South had become the nation's leading producer of cloth, and more than 100,000 Southerners, many of them women and children, had traded agricultural labor for work in textile mills.

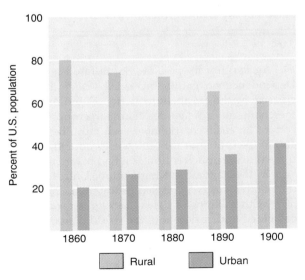

FIGURE 17.2
Changes in Rural and Urban Populations, 1860–1900
Between 1860–1900 not only did the number of urban dwellers increase, but the number of rural inhabitants fell. Mechanization made it possible to farm with fewer hands and fueled the exodus from farm to city throughout the second half of the nineteenth century.

In only one industry did the South truly dominate—tobacco. Soon after the Civil War, Julian Carr of North Carolina began to build Bull Durham tobacco with a massive advertising campaign that made the bull on the trademark an international symbol for smoking tobacco. Capitalizing on the invention of a machine for rolling cigarettes, the Duke family of Virginia challenged Bull Durham in the 1880s and boosted their fortunes, eventually dominating the industry with their American Tobacco Company. The new popularity of cigarettes, which replaced chewing tobacco among America's growing urban population, provided a booming market for Duke's "ready-made" cigarettes. James "Buck" Duke boosted sales by launching clever advertising campaigns that featured risqué pictures of "cigarette girls." Within four years, the company was selling 400,000 cigarettes a day.

The extractive industries, mining and lumber, also experienced a boom in the New South, but with devastating results. Coal from Appalachia could now be transported by rail to fuel the blast furnaces and factories of the nation. In the race to exploit the South's coal reserves, whole mountains were eaten up, often with catastrophic environmental and human costs. Fortunes were made, but few of them by Southerners. Investors in the North and abroad reaped the lion's share. The miners themselves violently protested their poor wages and dangerous working conditions in a series of strikes that gave one county in Kentucky the name Bloody Harlan. In the lumber industry, the demand for southern wood led to untrammeled growth. Northern lumber syndicates cut a wide swath through the virgin forests of the South, stripping them of timber and leaving the soil to erode. Warnings that such a course would lead to ecological disaster fell on deaf ears. Twenty years of milling led to what one contemporary forestry expert called "probably the most rapid and reckless destruction of forests known to history."

Of all its industries the New South was proudest of its iron and steel industry, which grew up in the area surrounding Birmingham, Alabama. Soon the smokestack replaced the white-pillared plantation as the symbol of the South. Would-be iron barons built twenty-five blast furnaces in Alabama alone. Pennsylvania iron magnate Andrew Carnegie toured the region in 1889 and observed, "The South is Pennsylvania's most formidable industrial enemy." But as long as control of southern industry remained in the hands of northern investors, Pennsylvania had nothing to fear. Whatever the South's natural advantages, northern bankers and investors had no intention of letting the South beat the North at its own game. Elaborate mechanisms rigged the price of southern steel, inflating it, as one northern insider confessed, "for the purpose of protecting the Pittsburgh mills and in turn the Pittsburgh steel users."

In practical terms the industrialized New South proved a chimera. While a handful of owners and managers prospered, the vast majority of Southerners, black and white, toiled for low wages in poor or dangerous conditions. Instead of thriving, the South found itself reduced virtually to the status of an economic colony of the North. Just as colonial economies the world over feature cheap labor, extractive industries, and exported raw materials, so too did the New South. Similarly, the region experienced low wages, absentee ownership, and little control over policy or pricing—key determinants of colonial status.

In practical terms the industrialized New South proved a chimera. Instead of thriving, the region found itself reduced virtually to the status of an economic colony of the North.

Agriculture in the New South fared no better. Dependence on cotton increased rather than decreased in the postbellum period. Landlords and merchants alike demanded that sharecroppers grow cotton, an easily marketable cash crop. Before the end of the century, the South was producing nearly three times as much cotton as it had before the Civil War in the heyday of King Cotton. Unfortunately, the South's vastly increased production, combined now with millions of bales from Egypt and India, coincided with a slowdown in world demand. Cotton prices plummeted. Even worse, relentless cotton cultivation exhausted the soil and eroded the countryside. It seemed that in agriculture, as in industry, Southerners had hitched their economic futures to a falling star. Although a few merchants and landowners managed to hold on and even profit, the majority of Southerners succumbed to the numbing poverty that settled over the rural South. Dissatisfaction with this state of affairs would fuel the Populist movement in the 1890s.

From the Family Farm toward Agribusiness

The promise of cheap land lured many settlers west at the same time the growing cities acted as a powerful magnet, particularly to young people, pulling them off the farm. By the 1890s, depopulation caused a growing chorus of alarm. Many feared that a way of life was dying. In the pages of popular periodicals, writers voiced the growing concern. "One by one, family by family, [the] inhabitants slip away in search of other homes," a New England writer lamented. "The young, the hopeful, the ambitious" left, while "the superannuated, the feeble, the dull" stayed. Although enough workers remained to carry on the common business of life, the writer noted sadly that "the world's real work is done elsewhere." Contrary to popular prejudice, however, it was not just the aged and dimwitted who chose to stay. Those who stayed behind increasingly adapted to changing conditions by adopting new technologies and moving toward commercial farming.

The loss of population was by no means limited to New England. More than half the rural townships of Ohio, Indiana, and Illinois lost population between 1880 and 1890, and the rate in Iowa was not far behind. Alarmed observers wondered who would be left to feed the growing city population if all the farmers left the fields. They needn't have

worried. The countryside in the late nineteenth century actually experienced surplus population. The birthrate in the country exceeded that in the city, while rural mortality rates ran significantly lower than urban rates. At the same time, scientific farming and mechanization enabled one farmer to do the work of several hands. New plows and reapers halved the time and labor cost of production. With fewer farmers producing more food, the drift from the countryside to the city was a healthy economic adjustment. The changes in rural America resulted as much from the push of a successful revolution in agriculture as from the failure of the farm to compete with the pull of urban economic opportunities.

To say that the farmer suffered from too much success, however, only obscures the economic realities as well as the social and cultural implications of the shift from the country to the city. In the 1870s and 1890s, crop failures and economic depression forced many farmers into foreclosure and off the land. For them the move from the farm represented a personal and economic defeat. That defeat came to be mirrored in the popular culture, where the farmer, who had once been the symbol of America, was increasingly ridiculed and caricatured. Derogatory terms like "hayseed" and "hick" entered the American vocabulary.

By the end of the century, a growing number of writers, influenced by the new trend toward literary realism, took a grim look at rural life. Hamlin Gar-

IOWA FARMHOUSE
This farmhouse in Clay County, Iowa, was built in the 1870s to replace the log cabin at the left where the homesteaders had lived when they first migrated from Kentucky. The rocking chair on the porch hints at the leisure the family could now occasionally enjoy. As some farmers prospered, they were able to construct white clapboard houses like this one, replicating the homes they had known back East.
Collection of Julia Booth.

land, a son of the Midwest who went east to school, revisited Iowa, Wisconsin, and North Dakota in the late 1880s. Garland's first collection of short stories, *Main Traveled Roads*, published in 1891, recounted his growing bitterness as he encountered "the ugliness, the endless drudgery, and the loneliness of the farmer's lot." Writers like Garland and Frederic Howe, who had themselves abandoned the farm for the city, acknowledged the farmer's diminished stature. "The farmer," wrote one novelist, "is as far out of it as if he lived in Alaska. Perhaps there was a time when a man could live in what the poet calls a daily communication with nature and not starve his mind and dwarf his soul, but this isn't the century."

However much the image of the farmer suffered in the popular culture of the time, in the late nineteenth century farming itself was thriving as an agricultural revolution transformed American farm life. The diversified family farm of the past began to give way to specialized, commercial farming. By the turn of the century, American agriculture had already entered the era of what would come to be called "agribusiness"—farming as a big business.

Industrialization and urbanization provided farmers with expanding markets for their produce, and railroads carried farmers' crops to markets thousands of miles away. At the same time, mechanization made it possible to farm vast tracts of land. Farming was on its way to becoming a business enterprise, not simply a way of life or a means of existence.

Business became the order of the day. Instead of extolling the virtues of the self-sufficient farmer, farm journals, agricultural societies, and educators pushed farmers to act more like businessmen, to specialize and to consolidate. Together they helped to create a striking new image of what constituted successful farming. "Farming for business, not for a living—this is the motif of the New Farmer," announced an agricultural writer at the turn of the century. The message was clear: The job of the up-to-date farmer was to produce money, not just crops.

East of the Mississippi, new farming techniques led to greater output and increased specialization. New Englanders gave up trying to compete with the Midwest in meat, grain, and wool and concentrated their energies instead on dairy farming, vegetables, and fruit. In the Midwest, Illinois and Iowa farmers turned the region into the nation's corn belt and feedlot. In the West, specialization led to huge bonanza wheat farms, some comprising over 100,000 acres, in California and the Red River valley

of North Dakota and Minnesota. In Washington, Oregon, and California, growers plunged headlong into the production of hops. In Oklahoma and the South, cotton remained king. Although general farming continued to prevail in large sections of the country, agricultural specialization marked the growing trend in late-nineteenth-century farming.

Farmers soon discovered that cash-crop farming had its hazards, subjecting the farmer to the twin risks of crop failure and soil depletion. Farmers who did not raise their own food had trouble surviving the periodic droughts and depressions that were common in the 1870s, 1880s, and 1890s. And in their determination to turn a profit, farmers used up the soil with as little regard for the depletion of its resources as the western miners, notorious for their rape of the land.

As farming moved onto the prairies and plains, mechanization took command. Steel plows, reapers, mowers, harrows, seed drills, combines, and threshers replaced human muscle on the farm. Horse-drawn implements gave way to steam-powered machinery. By 1880, a new harvester could reap and shock twenty acres of wheat in a day, and a single combine could do the work of twenty men. Farmers rushed to take advantage of the new technology, mortgaging their farms to pay for the expensive new machinery. Between 1860 and 1900, the value of farm machinery produced annually in the United States rose from $21 million to $101 million. Machines enabled farmers to vastly increase their acreage. Two men with one machine could cultivate 250 acres of wheat. Production soared. The agricultural revolution meant that by the second half of the nineteenth century, Americans raised more than four times the corn, five times the hay, and seven times the wheat and oats than they had before the Civil War.

The new farmer existed in a web of dependence, not only on weather and credit but increasingly on a world market.

The new farmer existed in a web of dependence, not only on weather and credit but increasingly on a world market. American foodstuffs fed people as far away as England and Germany. Farmers exported 217 million bushels of wheat by 1897 and 212 million bushels of corn. Like the cotton farmer in the South, northern grain and livestock

TECHNOLOGY IN AMERICA
The Combine

The mechanization of the farm helps explain how a declining farm population could greatly increase the output of farm products. The combine, pictured here, was so named because it combined the work of both a harvester and a thresher. Drawn by twenty-four horses, it reaped the grain, threshed it, and bagged it, all in one simultaneous operation. Benjamin Holt invented the combine in the early 1880s and founded what eventually became the Caterpillar Company.

The superiority of the new technology was not lost on contemporary observers. In the words of an early enthusiast, "If the total time required to build a combine is 300 man-days and the combine, doing the work of 1,000 men, is used 30 days per years for 10 years, the ratio of labor efficiency is 1,000 man-days saved for each day expended."

The effect of labor-saving machinery on the scale of agricultural operations can best be seen in the rise of huge wheat farms, like the one pictured here in Walla Walla, Washington. By the 1890s two men with the aid of machinery could farm well over 250 acres.
John Deere Museum.

farmers increasingly depended on foreign markets for their livelihood. A fall in commodity prices meant that a farmer's entire crop went to pay off debts. In periods of depression, great numbers of heavily mortgaged farmers lost their land to creditors.

The protective tariff, endorsed by every Republican president from Abraham Lincoln to William Howard Taft, further hurt the farmer. The tariff, designed to protect "infant industries," prevented foreign competition and effectively raised the price of manufactured goods. Almost everything the farmer purchased, from plows and reapers to kerosene and calico, cost more because of the tariff. Habitual debtors, farmers also suffered from the government's deflationary monetary policy. The gold standard caused a steady deflation, which forced debtors to repay loans with money worth much more than the money they had originally borrowed. Or put in terms of labor, a farmer who had borrowed a thousand dollars in 1868 had to grow twice as much wheat in 1888 than he would have had to grow twenty years earlier to pay back the loan. Farmers also resented the profits made by bankers and mort-

gage lenders and by the owners of grain elevators, who often made more money storing the farmers' grain than the farmers made when they sold it. "Every agent, pedlar, and Every profession of men is Fleecing the Farmer," a Texas cotton farmer complained in the 1890s. "By the time the World Gets their Liveing *out* of the *Farmer* as we have to Feed the World," he went on, his eloquence not blunted by his crude grammar and poor spelling, "we the Farmer has nothing Left but a Bear Hard Liveing."

Since the days of Thomas Jefferson, farming had been linked with the highest ideals of a democratic society. Now agrarianism itself had been transformed. The farmer was no longer the self-sufficient yeoman, but a businessman on the one hand or a dispossessed wage laborer on the other, both tied to a global market. And even as farm production soared, industrial production outstripped it. More and more farmers left the fields for the factories. Now that the future lay with the cities, was democracy itself at risk? This question would ignite a farmers' revolt in the 1880s and dominate political debate in the 1890s.

The American West: A Clash of Cultures

In the movies, the American West is portrayed in mythic terms as a picturesque landscape where strong-jawed heroes square off against villains. The good guys are always white, even their hats. Often the bad guys are red—Indians, the name Columbus mistakenly gave to Native Americans. In this masculine tableau the setting is so timeless that it is easy to forget that the action takes place at roughly the same time that waves of new immigrants sailed past the Statue of Liberty, engineers built the Brooklyn Bridge, and men like John D. Rockefeller consolidated their empires in emerging industrial America. The mythical West exists away from all of this, out of time.

Once the West is situated within its historical context, however, once it is seen as a particular place at a particular time, reality supersedes myth, and the West appears to be not so different from the rest of the country. The problems and issues facing the nation at the beginning of the twentieth century—the growing power of corporations, ethnic and racial animosity, the exploitation of labor and of natural resources—all played themselves out under western skies.

The Peoples of the Great Plains and the Far West

"West" has always been a relative term. Until the gold rush of 1849 focused attention on California, the West for settlers lay beyond the Appalachians and east of the Mississippi in the lands drained by the Ohio River, a part of the country that we now call the Old Northwest. But by the last three decades of the nineteenth century, the West increasingly referred to the land across the Mississippi, from the Great Plains to the Pacific Ocean.

The West of the late nineteenth century was a polyglot place, as much so as the big cities of the East. An illustrator on his way to the California goldfields deftly depicted the mix:

> The stranger, as he ascends the mountains towards the mining towns . . . notices the contrast in the scenes around him to anything he ever saw before. Indians are met in groups. . . . Strings of Chinamen pass, and greet you in broken English. . . . Next comes a Negro, with polite 'good morning, sar'; or Chileno, Mexican, or Kanaka.

The parade of peoples who came to the West included immigrants from England, Ireland, Wales, Germany, Greece, Scandinavia, Portugal, China, Japan, and Canada, not to mention New Englanders, Mormons, African Americans, Mexicans, Latinos, numerous Indians, and a sprinkling of European nobles. Prejudice and racial hostility erupted into violence on the frontier, just as they did in the cities. The Chinese suffered brutal treatment at the hands of employers and other laborers. Fearful of competition, workingmen rioted in the 1870s and fought to keep the Chinese out of the United States. Hispanic peoples, who had lived in Texas and the Southwest since Juan de Oñate led his pioneer settlers up the Rio Grande in 1598 and who had occupied the Pacific coast since San Diego was founded in 1769, overnight were reduced to a "minority" after the United States annexed Texas and took California in the Mexican War of the 1840s. African Americans who ventured out to the territories faced hostile settlers determined to keep the West "for whites only." And Native Americans, who once warred with one another, increasingly united to fight off white encroachment.

The sheer number of races that came together and mingled in the West produced a complex racism. One historian has noted, not entirely facetiously, that there were at least eight oppressed races in the West—Indians, Latinos, Chinese, Japanese, blacks, Mormons, strikers, and radicals.

The Mormons, followers of Joseph Smith, the founder and prophet of the Church of Jesus Christ of Latter-day Saints, fled west to avoid religious persecution. They believed that they had a divine right to the land, and their messianic militancy, as well as their favorable view of Indians and other pioneers' suspicions that they were abolitionists, contributed to making them outcasts. Although they were not the only religious sect of this period to practice plural marriage, the Mormons' polygamy became a convenient point of attack for those who hated and feared the group. After Smith was killed by an Illinois mob in 1844, Brigham Young led the flock, which numbered more than twenty thousand, over the Rockies to the valley of the Great Salt Lake in Utah. Often the pioneers pulled their carts by hand, dragging their children and belongings across the plains. The Utah land that they settled was a virtual desert, but the Mormons quickly set to work irrigating it. Lacking foreign or eastern capital to back them, they relied on cooperation and communalism. The church established and controlled water supplies, stores, insurance companies, and later factories and mining smelters. By 1882, the Mormons had built a thriving city of more than 150,000 souls with a grand tabernacle in Salt Lake City. Congress refused to grant Utah statehood until the church discontinued the practice of polygamy. Utah did not enter the Union until 1896.

One historian has noted, not entirely facetiously, that there were at least eight oppressed races in the West—Indians, Latinos, Chinese, Japanese, blacks, Mormons, strikers, and radicals.

Prospectors and cowboys have a special place in the lore of the West. The wide-open boomtowns of Nevada's Comstock Lode and the cattle towns on the Chisholm Trail—along with names like Virginia City, Tombstone, and Deadwood—conjure up visions familiar from American folklore. Yet by the 1870s, both mining and cattle had become big business. The colorful prospector, with his pan and his burro, gave way to huge underground operations and quartz mines in which rock was crushed to extract gold and base metals. Corporate control replaced individual prospecting, and New York replaced San Francisco as the center of speculation in mining stock.

The story of mining in the West is a tale of one rush after another in western lands rich with gold, silver, lead, zinc, and copper. Boomtown to ghost town in a matter of years was a pattern common in western mining, a pattern that left an ominous legacy of reckless exploitation. Labor as well as land was harshly treated. Miners in the West, like their counterparts in Kentucky, worked for low wages in dangerous conditions. In a scenario familiar in the East, desperate miners in Coeur d'Alene, Idaho, struck for union recognition in 1892, only to be put down by state troops.

COPPER MINE

This 1887 photograph of the Phelps-Dodge copper mining operation in Morenci, Arizona, indicates the development of western mining. In 1881, a westerner named William Church, who had bought out the original prospector, traveled to New York to persuade the giant Phelps-Dodge mining corporation to lend him $50,000 to develop a copper mine at Morenci. Phelps-Dodge agreed. Six years later Church sold out, leaving the corporation the sole owner of the mine. In a story told over and over again, mechanized mining replaced the prospector and his burro, and mining became a big business with western mines owned by large eastern conglomerates. Note the pollution attendant on copper mining evidenced by the slag heaps in the foreground.

Courtesy of the Arizona Historical Society, Tucson, #26,720.

Like mining, cattle ranching became a big business in the 1870s. On the range, the cowboy gave way to the cattle king. Cattle ranchers followed the railroads onto the plains, establishing in the years between 1865 and 1885 a cattle kingdom from Texas to Wyoming. Texas longhorns pushed the bison off the range, overgrazing the once abundant grasses. In three years the buffalo all but disappeared in Montana. Cattle ranching in the West, much of it financed by foreign capital, was characterized by speculation and absentee ownership. Wealthy Europeans and Americans occasionally tried their hand at ranching. The Marquis of Mores, complaining that he was "weary of civilization," came to ranch in the Dakotas. Not far away lived Theodore Roosevelt, a New Yorker who, in his typical fashion, sought to overcome his grief over the death of his wife by throwing himself headlong into the physical exertion of cowboy life.

By 1886, cattle overcrowded the range. Severe blizzards during the next two winters decimated the herds. "A whole generation of cowmen," wrote one chronicler, "went dead broke." As the heyday of the cattle kingdom came to an end, Roosevelt and the Marquis packed up and went home. Cattle ranching, like mining, became largely a corporate business with distant boards of directors in the East and wage-earning workers on the range.

The cowboy, that symbol of American independence, became, like the miner, a wage laborer. Though the cowboy was more colorful than his eastern counterparts in the factory, his life was no easier. "No class is harder worked or so poorly paid," observed Karl Marx's daughter on a trip to America. Many cowboys were African Americans and Mexicans (although western literature chose to ignore that fact and transformed the black cowboy Deadwood Dick into a white man). Like many other dissatisfied workers, cowboys organized labor unions in the 1880s and mounted strikes in both Texas and Wyoming.

The American West in the nineteenth century witnessed more than its share of bloodshed. Violence broke out between cattle ranchers and sheep ranchers, between ranchers and farmers, between strikers and bosses, between rival Indian groups, and between whites and those whom they judged "lesser breeds." At issue was who would control the vast resources of the emerging region. Each group claimed the public domain as its own, and each group was prepared to fight for it. In the ensuing struggle for preeminence, the biggest losers were those with the best claim to the land, the Americans who had been living on it since before Columbus or Coronado or de Soto arrived.

The Final Removal of the Indians

In the 1830s, President Andrew Jackson initiated the policy of Indian removal by pushing the Cherokee, Choctaw, Chickasaw, Creek, and Seminole tribes off their lands in the southern United States. Jackson's Indian removal forced thousands of men, women, and children to leave their homes in Georgia and Tennessee and walk hundreds of miles to lands across the Mississippi River. So many died of hunger, exhaustion, and disease along the way that the Cherokees called their path "the trail on which we cried." At the end of this trail of tears stood the Great Plains. Here, the government promised the Indians, they could remain "as long as grass shall grow."

But in the 1840s, the gold rush in California, the Mexican War, and Oregon land fever put an end to the promise. Settlers repeatedly trespassed onto Indian land and then were surprised when they encountered hostility. Indignantly, they demanded protection from the U.S. army. The result was thirty years of Indian wars that culminated in a final removal of the Indians.

The Indian wars on the plains lasted from 1861 until 1890. By the time they ended, only 250,000 Native Americans remained of the estimated 2.5 million who had lived on the continent when Columbus landed. To Americans filled with theories of racial superiority, the Indian constituted, in the words of a Colorado militia major, "an obstacle to civilization." Testifying before a congressional commission in 1864, the major concluded that they "should be exterminated." The federal government, acting through the army, adopted a different policy, succinctly summed up by General William T. Sherman: "Rather remove all to a safe place and then reduce them to a helpless condition." The government herded the Indians into ever dwindling reservations where the U.S. Bureau of Indian Affairs, a pitifully weak, badly managed agency, often acting through corrupt agents, supposedly ministered to their needs.

On the plains, the Sioux, Cheyenne, Arapaho, Nez Perce, Comanche, Kiowa, Ute, Apache, and Navajo nations put up a determined resistance. The Indian wars involved violence and atrocities on both sides. In 1864 at Sand Creek, Colonel John M. Chivington, leader of the local Colorado militia, slaughtered an entire village of Cheyenne. An up-

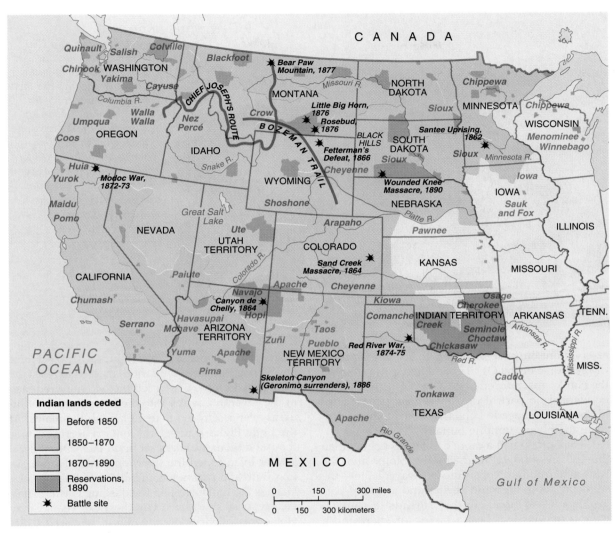

M AP 17.3
The Loss of Indian Lands, 1850–1890
By 1890, western Indians were isolated on small, scattered reservations. Native Americans strug-
gled to retain their land in major battles, from the Santee Uprising in Minnesota in 1862 to the
massacre at Wounded Knee, South Dakota, in 1890.

right Methodist elder, Chivington watched as his men mutilated their hapless victims and later justified the killing of Indian children with the terse remark "Nits make lice." The city of Denver treated Chivington and his men as heroes, but after a congressional inquiry he was forced to resign his commission to avoid court-martial.

Two years later, the Cheyenne united with the Sioux and retaliated on the Bozeman Trail. Captain William Fetterman, who had boasted that with eighty men he could ride through the Sioux nation, was killed, along with all eighty-one of his troops. The Sioux's impressive victories led to a treaty in 1868, under which the government promised to give the Indians lands stretching from the Missouri River to the Black Hills in western South Dakota in return for their promise to stop fighting. The great chief Red Cloud led many of his people onto the new

reservation. But several young chiefs, among them Crazy Horse of the Oglala band and Sitting Bull of the Hunkpapa, refused to go. Crazy Horse said that he wanted no part of the "piecemeal penning" of his people. Renegade bands of Sioux continued to roam the plains, hunting buffalo.

The buffalo had a more dangerous enemy than the Indian—the railroad. To the Sioux and the Kiowa the buffalo constituted a way of life—the source of food, fuel, and shelter and a central part of religion and ritual. To the railroads the buffalo were a nuisance, at best a target for sport and a source of cheap meat for the workers. Buffalo hunters hired by the railroads decimated the great herds; sport hunters fired at random from railroad cars just for the thrill of it. In the heyday of buffalo hunting in the 1880s, hunters sold as many as fifty thousand hides at a time to tanneries in the East. General Philip Sheridan applauded the hunters for "destroying the Indians' commissary." In thirty years, more than sixty million animals were slaughtered. The army took credit for subduing the Indians, but their defeat came about more as a result of the decimation of the buffalo herds.

In 1876, rumors of gold in the Black Hills effectively nullified the government's promise to Red Cloud. Miners began pouring into the area, and the Northern Pacific Railroad made plans to build tracks. Lieutenant Colonel George Armstrong Custer fed the gold fever by trumpeting news of the first strikes. Under the leadership of Crazy Horse and Sitting Bull, the Sioux tribes massed to resist the incursion. In June, Custer led the two hundred men of the Seventh Cavalry into the largest group of Indians ever assembled in one place on the plains. At the Little Bighorn River in Montana Territory, four thousand Sioux warriors set upon them. No federal soldier lived to tell the story, but Crazy Horse, Sitting Bull, and others recounted the killing of Long Hair, as the Indians called the dashing Custer. Their victory was short-lived. In the next year, Crazy Horse was killed and Sitting Bull surrendered. Chief Joseph of the Nez Percé resisted removal and fled toward Canada. Just forty miles from freedom, federal troops caught up with his band. With his people cold and starving, the chief surrendered. His speech stands as an eloquent statement of the plight of the Indians:

Tell Captain Howard I know his heart. What he told me before I have in my heart. I am tired of fighting. Our chiefs are killed. . . . It is cold and we have no blankets. The little children are freezing to death. My people, some of them, have run away to the hills, and have no blankets, no food; no one knows where they are—perhaps freezing to death. I want to have time to look for my children and see how many I can find. Maybe I shall find them among the dead. Hear me, my chiefs, I am tired; my heart is sick and sad. From where the sun now stands, I will fight no more forever.

The policy of rounding up Indians and herding them onto reservations gained momentum. After Custer's Last Stand, as the battle in 1876 came to be called, policy toward the Indians toughened. Even the most philanthropic Americans seemed convinced that the Indian way of life must go. Instead of remaining American Indians, they had to become Indian Americans. When Indians resisted, their children were taken off the reservations and sent to special schools to learn white ways—to play the piano, to farm, to act like white Americans.

In 1887, Congress passed the Dawes Act, breaking up the reservations and giving each Indian an allotment of land. The act effectively reduced Indian lands from 138 million acres to a scant 48 million, making it, in the words of one critic, "a bill to despoil the Indians of their lands and to make them vagabonds on the face of the earth." The surplus land was then opened to white settlement, setting off the great land rushes in Oklahoma. Well-meaning philanthropists viewed the Dawes Act as a way to foster individualism among the Indians and to extend to them the rights of citizenship. The result of this legislation, however, was the further destruction of Indian culture.

Faced with the extinction of their entire way of life and means of livelihood, the Indians turned to a compelling religious cult. The Paiute shaman Wovoka, drawing on a cult that had developed in the 1870s, combined elements of Christianity and traditional Indian religion to found the Ghost Dance religion in 1889. Wovoka claimed that he had received a vision in which the Great Spirit spoke through him to all Indians, urging them to unite and promising that whites would be destroyed in an apocalypse. The Indian warriors slain in battle would return to life, and buffalo once again would roam the land unimpeded. Followers of the Ghost Dance religion developed a ritual that involved five days of worship by dancing and meditation. Wearing white ghost shirts that were supposedly impervious to bullets, Indians danced until they dropped from exhaustion. This religion of despair with its message of hope spread like wildfire over the plains, alarming the whites, who feared that it would spark an uprising. "Indians are dancing in the snow and are wild and crazy," wrote the Bureau of Indian Affairs agent at the Pine Ridge reservation in South Dakota. Frantic, he pleaded for reinforcements. "We are at the mercy of these dancers. We need protection, and we need it now." President Benjamin Harrison dispatched several thousand federal troops to Sioux country to handle any outbreak.

In December 1889, when Sitting Bull sought permission to go to the Pine Ridge reservation to meet with Wovoka, the local Indian agent laid a trap for him, and Sitting Bull was shot. His people, fleeing the scene, were apprehended by the Seventh Cavalry, Custer's old regiment, near Wounded Knee Creek, South Dakota. As the Indians laid down their arms, a shot rang out and the army opened fire. In the ensuing melee, Indian warriors stormed the troops, killing more than thirty soldiers. But they were badly outgunned. Men, women, and children were mowed down in minutes by the army's brutally efficient Hotchkiss machine guns. More than two hundred Sioux lay dead or dying in the snow. Settler Jules Sandoz surveyed the scene the day after the massacre. "Here in ten minutes an entire community was as the buffalo that bleached on the plains," he wrote. "There was something loose in the world that hated joy and happiness as it hated brightness and color, reducing everything to drab agony and gray."

Although the massacre at Wounded Knee did not end the story of Native Americans, it ended a way of life. The Indian population would gradually recover; the 1990 census showed 1.9 million Native Americans. But their culture sustained a crushing blow. In the words of the visionary Black Elk, "The nation's hoop is broken and scattered. There is no center any longer, and the sacred tree is dead."

The West of the Imagination

Even as the Old West was dying, the myth of the West was being created. The dime novel, a precursor of today's paperback, capitalized on western heroes like Kit Carson, Wild Bill Hickok, Calamity Jane, and Deadwood Dick to entertain eastern readers seeking escapist fare. Published in the East and sometimes written by tenderfeet who had never ventured beyond the Hudson River, dime novels sold at a prodigious rate. The firm of Beadle and Adams pioneered the genre and published over a million copies a year.

The prince of the dime novel heroes was Buffalo Bill, featured in more than two hundred titles. A masterful showman, the real-life Buffalo Bill capitalized on his success and formed a touring Wild West company in 1883. Unlike the cowboy actors of the twentieth century, Buffalo Bill was the authentic article. Born William F. Cody, he had panned for gold, ridden for the Pony Express, scouted for the army, and earned his nickname hunting buffalo for the railroad. A ham actor and impresario, he turned

Did Whites Teach Indians to Scalp?

IN 1879, JUST THREE YEARS AFTER Custer and his troops were massacred at the Little Bighorn, Susette La Flesche, a member of the Omaha tribe, made a national tour to promote justice for Native Americans. Using her Indian name, Bright Eyes, La Flesche made a fascinating spokesperson for Indian rights. Her father, one of the best known of the Omaha chiefs, was of mixed blood, as was his wife. The La Flesche family embraced Christianity and advocated "progressive" Indian policy. Working closely with Presbyterian missionaries, they attacked the use of alcohol and urged Indians to take up farming. Susette grew up in the first frame house on the reservation in Nebraska. All the La Flesche children attended Presbyterian mission school at the Omaha agency. Later Susette and her sisters were sent to boarding school in New Jersey. Susette's sister Susan La Flesche Picotte became the first Indian woman to receive a medical degree, and her brother Francis became the first Indian anthropologist employed by the Smithsonian Institution. To Victorian society, the remarkable La Flesche family offered an inspiring example of the transition from "savagery" to civilization.

Susette La Flesche's East Coast tour was intended to publicize the plight of the Ponca Indians, who had lost their land in one of the many swindles perpetrated by the federal government. Boston audiences expecting an Indian "princess" dressed in deerskin encountered instead an educated young woman in a black velvet bonnet. But for all her modest demeanor, Susette did not hesitate in pointing out the routine barbarity of the U.S. army in its treatment of the Plains tribes. In Chicago, she was accosted by a reporter who chided her, pointing to the Indians' "barbarous . . . acts of atrocity upon captives and the bodies of the dead." La Flesche shot back, "Scalping, you mean, I suppose. Don't you know that the white man taught Indians that?" She insisted that "scalping was first practiced in New England on the Penobscot Indians." The General Court of the province of Massachusetts, she informed the reporter, "offered a bounty of forty pounds for every scalp of a male Indian brought in as evidence of his being killed, and for every scalp of a female or male Indian under twelve years, twenty pounds."

A hundred years later, La Flesche's charge that European colonists in New England had taught the Indians to scalp was well on its way to becoming accepted wisdom. Native American author Vine Deloria, in his widely read manifesto *Custer Died for Your Sins* (1969), echoed the belief that eighteenth-century European settlers with their bounty laws had introduced the practice of scalping among the eastern tribes.

Certainly scalping became synonymous with Indian barbarity. Europeans might draw and quarter, burn at the stake, and introduce the tortures of the iron maiden, but Indian mutilation of the dead remained the quintessential symbol of "savagery." Not surprisingly, La Flesche's effort to rehabilitate the popular image of the Indian in 1879 and Deloria's similar effort a century later began by calling into question the Indian origin of scalping. If whites had taught Indians to scalp, who, then, was the "savage"? As scholars became more sympathetic to the dispossession of American Indians and sought to rehabilitate the stereotype of the "fiendish savage," the charge that scalping was a white invention gained wide acceptance. But was it factual? Had the European settlers, with their bounties on scalps, introduced the practice?

Historian James Axtell set out to find the answer. But what sources would provide "proof"? Axtell drew on the records of early explorers and set-

SUSETTE LA FLESCHE

Susette La Flesche toured the country in 1879 using her Indian name, Bright Eyes, to publicize the plight of the Ponca Indians. It was La Flesche who alleged that whites had taught the Indians to scalp.

Nebraska State Historical Society.

tlers and on the work of ethnohistorians and archaeologists. All of the evidence seemed to point in the opposite direction from Susette La Flesche's confident assertion. Among the earliest visitors to American shores, Jacques Cartier in 1535 described "skins of five men's heads, stretched on hoops, like parchment." The practice was widespread, noted by Cartier in the North and by Hernando De Soto's men in Florida and the Southeast. As Axtell carefully demonstrated, "the list of Europeans who found scalping among the eastern Indians in the earliest stages of contact could be extended almost indefinitely."

Furthermore, although Europeans practiced many barbarities during the sixteenth and seventeenth centuries, nowhere was there evidence that they ever scalped their victims. The European languages did not even have a word to describe the practice. Archaeological evidence, too, pointed away from La Flesche's claim. Pre-Columbian skulls collected by early anthropologists showed distinct evidence of scalping.

What role, then, did scalping play in Indian culture? According to ethnohistorians and their Indian subjects, the practice, while widespread, varied markedly from tribe to tribe. Often the scalp served as more than physical proof of valor. The Iroquois believed that after death the soul hovered by the body. To take the scalp, they believed, was to take the spiritual life of the enemy. However, the practice of scalping took on a different character during the French and Indian War when both sides offered their Indian allies bounties for scalps, sometimes as

much as one hundred pounds (roughly two hundred dollars) for every scalp of an adult male. Soon the trading of scalps became part of the complex web that bound Indians and whites in colonial commerce. In Salem, Massachusetts, scalps that had been redeemed for bounties decorated the walls of the town courthouse until it was torn down in 1785.

By the nineteenth century, bounties had long been outlawed, and scalping existed among the Plains Indians in the context of tribal practice. Black Elk, an Oglala Sioux, recounted how he took his first scalp and proudly presented the trophy to his mother for her approval.

One final intriguing piece of the puzzle is the question of how Custer escaped scalping. Well known for his flowing locks, Custer, by all accounts, was not scalped after the battle, as were many of his men. Although no soldier lived to describe the battle scene, Indian accounts are unanimous in their assertion that Custer's body was not mutilated, except for one fingertip. Why did the Indians not take his scalp for a trophy? In large part the answer has changed as Custer's fortunes with historians and the public have waxed and waned. At the time of his death, when Custer was viewed as a brave martyr, writers conjectured that his Indian foes respected his bravery and refused to mutilate the man they called Pahuska, or Long Hair. As Custer's reputation sank to low ebb in the mid-twentieth century, writers became more skeptical. One author guessed that Custer, who was balding by 1879 and had cut his hair, was spared because from a warrior's point of view his scalp made a poor trophy.

BUFFALO BILL POSTER
Buffalo Bill Cody used colorful posters to publicize his Wild West show during the 1880s and 1890s. One of his most popular features was the reenactment of Custer's Last Stand, which he performed for Queen Victoria in London and at the World Columbian Exposition in Chicago.
Buffalo Bill Historical Center, Cody, Wyoming.

to melodrama in the 1870s and a decade later hit his stride with the Wild West Show. Part circus, part theater, the Wild West extravaganza featured exhibitions of riding, shooting, and roping and presented dramatic reenactments of great moments in western U.S. history. The star of the show was Annie Oakley, a crack shot who delighted the crowd by shooting a dime out of her husband's hand. A herd of buffalo, bucking broncos, and a sizable contingent of authentic cowboys and Indians trouped with the show. During the 1885 season, Sitting Bull toured with Buffalo Bill.

Cody performed in Europe for Queen Victoria, in Paris under the Eiffel Tower, in New York's Madison Square Garden, and on the road in hundreds of towns across the United States from 1883 until he went bankrupt in 1913. The centerpiece of his Wild West Show was the reenactment of Custer's Last

Stand, in which Indians in war paint and bonnets massacred the hapless Custer and his men. At the end, Buffalo Bill galloped in with a cloud of dust and dramatically mouthed the words "Too late!"

The Wild West that Buffalo Bill presented to the American people indiscriminately mixed the authentic with the romantic until reality itself was blurred in the popular mind. Cody had not arrived too late at the Little Bighorn. But some of the Indians in his troupe had been there and knew their parts firsthand. The rapid demise of the Wild West that Buffalo Bill enshrined in his show may perhaps best be comprehended if we juxtapose Cody with historian Frederick Jackson Turner. At the 1893 Columbian Exposition in Chicago, Turner addressed the American Historical Association on the significance of the frontier in American history. Turner noted that the frontier had vanished, that by 1890

American settlers had filled the map of the West so that no clear frontier line could be discerned. What Turner theorized—that the frontier which he claimed made America unique was now a part of the past —was perhaps nowhere better demonstrated than across the fairground in the spectacle of Buffalo Bill Cody's Wild West Show performing the "Battle of the Little Bighorn" to sellout crowds in the bleachers. After the show, fans sought out Indian "chiefs" and paid a dollar for the autograph of "the Indian who had killed Custer." The high drama of the struggle for the West in the years from 1876 to 1890 had become no more than a thrilling but harmless entertainment.

The images of the daring cowboy hero and the Indian (fiendish in victory but noble in defeat) that became so enshrined in the national imagination obscured the complex realities of the history of the American West.

The West of the imagination, the West of Buffalo Bill, of artists Frederic Remington and Albert Bierstadt, of novelists Owen Wister and Zane Grey, endured longer than its reality and was responsible for shrouding the region in myth. The images of the daring cowboy hero and the Indian (fiendish in victory but noble in defeat) that became so enshrined in the national imagination obscured the complex realities of the history of the American West, as much as the myth of moonlight and magnolias distorted the truth of the Old South.

The historical reality is every bit as dramatic as the fictions it sparked. But from the vantage point of the late twentieth century, it is no longer the simple morality tale of the triumph of good guys over bad guys, progress over primitivism, and civilization over the frontier that it once seemed. Whatever the moral ambiguities occasioned by the change, one thing was certain: By the 1890s, the American West had been transformed. More than seven-tenths of the farmland west of the Mississippi River was owned by investors who neither farmed nor ranched the land themselves. The shift from farming and ranching to agribusiness, not the disappearance of some magical frontier line, marked the end of an era in America. Far from being a mythic landscape out of place and time, the West was linked inextricably to the urban East by capital investment and iron rails that carried western goods to world markets.

The Rise of the City

"We cannot all live in cities, yet nearly all seem determined to do so," New York editor Horace Greeley complained. Greeley, who had urged young men to go West in the 1850s, lamented the growth of America's cities. Although much of the nation remained heavily rural, the last decades of the nineteenth century witnessed an urban explosion. Cities and towns grew more than twice as rapidly as the total population, far outstripping rural growth. Despite regional variations, the population of cities everywhere pushed upward, the greatest growth occurring in the industrial centers of New England, the Middle Atlantic states, and the Great Lakes states. Patterns of global migration contributed to the ascendancy of urban America. In the port cities, new immigrants from southern and eastern Europe lived in dense ghettos where the English language was rarely heard. The word *slum* entered the American vocabulary during these years and with it a growing concern over the gap between the rich and the poor, a gap only widened by the changing social geography of the cities. First horsecars, then trolleys and subways made it possible for those who could afford it to work downtown and flee after work to the "cool green rim" of the cities where residential tracts and suburbs catered to the middle class and well-to-do.

The Urban Explosion

The percentage of Americans living in towns and cities leaped from 20 percent in 1870 to 33 percent by 1900. In actual numbers, the urban population tripled, from nearly 10 million to over 30 million. The Census Bureau deemed any village of more than 8,000 inhabitants an urban place, lumping together Dubuque and Detroit, Kankakee and Cleveland. Growth in the urban population actually divided about evenly between large and small cities. But the emergence of the modern metropolis marked the most dramatic demographic development of the period. The number of cities with more than 100,000 inhabitants jumped from eighteen in 1870 to thirty-eight by 1900. Chicago grew at a meteoric rate, from 100,000 in 1860 to over a million in 1890, doubling its population each decade despite the ravages of the Great Fire of 1871, which destroyed three square miles and left 18,000 homeless. In the West, Los Angeles capitalized on its climate to explode from a sleepy village of 5,000 in 1870 to a metropolis of more than 100,000 by 1900. At the turn of the century, the United States could boast three cities with more than a million inhabitants—New York, Chicago, and Philadelphia.

Railroad growth stimulated urban development. In the West, the railroads moved in advance of settlement. Cities like Reno, Butte, and Cheyenne sprang up along the tracks long before the surrounding countryside was settled. The generous land grants given to promote railroad building made the railroads the largest private landholders in the country. Railroads encouraged settlement by selling the lands they had been granted in alternate sections along their right of way. Towns that the railroads bypassed failed to grow, while the transcontinental lines set off booms in Kansas City, Omaha, and Salt Lake City.

The astonishing growth of American cities that occurred from 1870 to 1900 came about not from the natural increase of the city population but from the internal and international movement of people.

Industrialization and urbanization went hand in hand. The continued growth of the urban population fueled a constantly expanding market. In a process that economists call the multiplier effect, the growing market in turn stimulated greater and greater production, creating more jobs in an expanding spiral. The emergence of a mass consumer market enabled cities to become centers for wholesaling and retailing, not just manufacturing and industry. Chicago, with its mail order houses like Montgomery Ward and Sears, Roebuck, along with its great department stores, Marshall Field and Carson Pirie Scott, led the country as an urban marketing center.

The astonishing growth of American cities that occurred from 1870 to 1900 came about not from the natural increase of the city population but from the internal and international movement of people.

From the Farm to the City: A Global Migration

The United States grew up in the country and moved to the city, or so it seemed by the late nineteenth century. Hundreds of thousands of farm boys and girls ran away to the city looking for jobs in the burgeoning industrial centers and hoping to make their fortunes. The lure of the bright lights and the promise of wages, coupled with the theaters, the dance halls, the great amusement resorts like Coney Island in New York, and the cultural and educational advantages offered by the city, served as a powerful magnet for many young women and men.

For at least one group of migrants, the move to the city promised something more. African Americans came north looking not just for economic opportunity. Demeaning laws that segregated blacks, called Jim Crow laws, became common throughout the South in the decades following Reconstruction. Further, the 1890s witnessed the systematic disfranchisement of black voters in state after state in the Old South. The South's efforts to segregate and subordinate African Americans gained federal endorsement when in 1896 the United States Supreme Court in the landmark case *Plessy v. Ferguson* upheld the legality of segregated facilities under the doctrine of "separate but equal." Intimidation and lynching, justified by white Southerners as necessary to "keep the Negro in his place," also became increasingly common throughout the South. These indignities combined with the lack of economic choices to move African Americans out of the South. "To die from the bite of frost is far more glorious than at the hands of a mob," proclaimed the *Defender*, Chicago's largest African American newspaper. As early as the 1890s, many blacks agreed. The African American migrants, nearly all of them rural, headed to the cities, settling in the great urban centers of the Northeast and the Midwest. There they found jobs, usually at the bottom of the occupational ladder as janitors, cooks, common laborers, or domestic servants. Racial discrimination and poverty limited blacks' options in the North, just as they had in the South. Yet the urban North continued to attract African Americans. By 1900, New York, Philadelphia, and Chicago contained the largest black communities in the nation. Although the greatest African American migration out of the South would occur during and after the end of World War I, 185,000 African Americans had already moved north by 1890. The great exodus was under way.

Rural migrants to the cities were by no means limited to American farmers and southern blacks. Worldwide in scope, the movement from rural areas to industrial centers attracted to the United States more than fourteen million Europeans in the waning decades of the nineteenth century. That migration came in two distinct waves that have been called

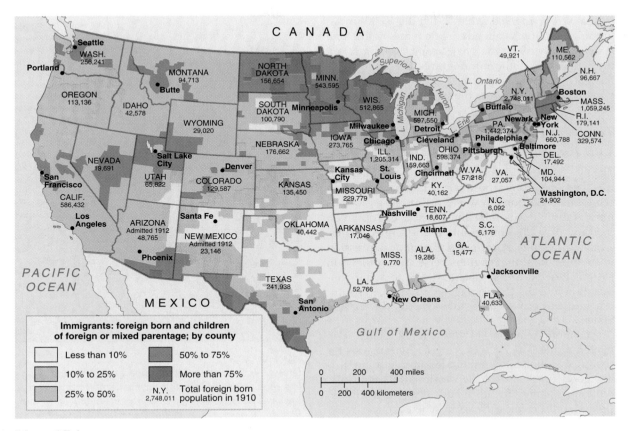

MAP 17.4
The Impact of Immigration to 1910
By 1910 the immigrant population was spread throughout the country, with the notable exception
of the southern states. In some areas — along the Canadian border and the Rio Grande and in the
nation's burgeoning cities — the foreign born and their children totaled more than 75 percent of
the population.

the old and the new immigration. Before 1880, the bulk of the new arrivals came from northern and western Europe, with the Germans, Irish, English, and Scandinavians making up approximately 85 percent of the newcomers.

After 1880, the pattern shifted, with more and more immigrant ships carrying passengers from southern and eastern Europe. Italians, Hungarians, eastern European Jews, Turks, Armenians, and Poles, Russians and other Slavic peoples accounted for more than 80 percent of all the immigrants by 1896. Alongside the tide of new European immigrants streamed Japanese coming east from Asia, French Canadians flowing south to work in New England's mill towns, and Mexicans and other Latin Americans heading north to settle in California and the Southwest.

In sheer numbers, the new immigration was unprecedented. In 1888 alone, more than half a million Europeans came to America, 75 percent landing in New York City. The Statue of Liberty, a gift from the people of France erected in 1886, stood sentinel in the harbor. An immigrant girl named Emma Lazarus penned the verse at Liberty's base:

Give me your tired, your poor,
Your huddled masses yearning to breathe free,
The wretched refuse of your teeming shore,
Send these, the homeless, tempest-tost to me,
I lift my lamp beside the golden door!

The tide of immigrants soon swamped the immigrant office at Castle Garden in New York harbor. An imposing new brick facility opened on Ellis Island in the harbor in 1900. Able to handle 5,000 immigrants a day, it was already inadequate by the time it opened. By 1907, the peak year of immigration, more than one million immigrants passed through the gates at Ellis Island, and on a record day inspectors processed more than 11,700.

The New Immigrants and the Call for Immigration Restriction

The new wave of immigration at the turn of the century resulted from a number of factors. Improved economic conditions in western Europe, as well as immigration to Australia and Canada, cut down on the flow of "old" immigrants to the United States. At the same time, a protracted economic depression in southern Italy, the religious persecution of Jews in eastern Europe, and a general desire to avoid conscription into the Russian army led many in southern and eastern Europe to move to the United States.

Economic factors in the United States also played a role. The need of America's industries for cheap, unskilled labor stimulated immigration during good times. In the depressions following the economic panics in 1873 and 1893, immigration slowed, only to pick up again when prosperity returned. Although the U.S. government did not offer direct inducements to immigrate, the steamship companies courted immigrants, who provided a highly profitable, self-loading cargo. Agents from the large lines traveled throughout Europe drumming up business. Colorful pamphlets and posters mingled fact with fantasy to advertise America as the land of promise.

Large economic and social forces affected immigration, but the decision to come to America remained an individual or a family choice. Immigrants were neither the passive "huddled masses" commemorated in Emma Lazarus's inscription on the Statue of Liberty nor bold adventurers determined at any cost to enter "the golden door." Increasingly, historians have rejected simplistic and monolithic views that treat immigrants collectively, instead acknowledging that each single individual or family decided to go or stay.

Nevertheless, immigration fever affected whole villages, as Mary Antin, writing of her Russian village in 1891, recounted:

"America" was in everybody's mouth. Businessmen talked of it over their accounts; the market women made up their quarrels that they might discuss it

IMMIGRANTS
Dressed in the clothing of the old country (cap and collarless shirt, apron and shawl), this immigrant couple carry their meager possessions, bedding in his bundle, food and utensils in her basket, and two umbrellas tied together. Note how the man gazes confidently, almost defiantly, into the camera, while the woman, looking miserable, averts her eyes. What do their postures tell about whose decision it was to come to America and about their hopes and apprehensions?
Wide World Photos, Inc.

from stall to stall; people who had relatives in the famous land went around reading their letters for the enlightenment of less fortunate folks; . . . children played at emigrating; old folks shook their sage heads over the evening fire, and prophesied no good for those who braved the terrors of the sea and the foreign goal beyond it;—all talked of it, but scarcely anybody knew one true fact about this magic land.

Would-be immigrants eager for information about America relied on letters, advertisements, and word of mouth—sources that were not always reliable or truthful. Promotional pamphlets exaggerated America's economic opportunities until Europeans dreamed of a land "where the streets were paved with gold." Glowing letters from immigrants to friends and relatives left behind boasted of life in America. Even photographs proved deceptive—

American workers dressed in their Sunday best looked more prosperous than they actually were to the eyes of relatives in the old country, where only the very wealthy wore white collars or silk dresses. As one Italian immigrant recalled, "Everything emanating from America reached [Italy] as a distortion. . . . News was colored, success magnified, comforts and advantages exaggerated beyond all proportions." No wonder immigrants left for America believing "that if they were ever fortunate enough to reach America, they would fall into a pile of manure and get up brushing the diamonds out of their hair."

In at least one respect, life in the new world differed markedly from that in the old. In their countries of origin, most of the newcomers had been rural peasants, farmers, and villagers. In America they became urbanites, both out of inclination and out of necessity. They were drawn by the availability of jobs in the nation's industrial centers at the same time poverty limited their ability to buy land in the West.

The concentration of immigrants in the nation's industrial cities was a characteristic of the age. By 1900, almost two-thirds of the country's immigrant population resided in cities. Although nowhere did the foreign-born population outnumber established inhabitants, the foreign-born and their American-born children did constitute a majority in many of the nation's largest cities. Fifty percent of Philadelphia's population was foreign-born or born of foreign parents, and the percentages were even higher in other cities: 66 percent in Boston, 75 percent in Chicago, and an amazing 80 percent in New York City.

Not all the newcomers came to stay. Perhaps eight million, mostly young men, worked for a year or a season and then returned to their homelands. American immigration officers referred to these young male immigrants as "birds of passage" because they followed a regular pattern of migration to and from the United States. By 1900, almost 75 percent of the new immigrants were single young men. Intent on making money as quickly as possible, they were willing to accept conditions that other workers regarded as intolerable. They showed little interest in labor unions and organized only when the dream of returning home faded, as it did for millions who ultimately remained in the United States.

Jews from eastern Europe most often came with their families and came to stay. In the 1880s, a wave of violent persecutions, or pogroms, in Russia and Poland led to the departure of more than a million Jews in the next two decades. They settled mostly in the port cities of the East. New York City's Lower East Side replicated the Jewish ghettos of eastern

STUDIO PORTRAIT OF IMMIGRANTS
Studio portraits of immigrant families, like this one of a Russian Jewish family taken at the turn of the century, showed everyone dressed in their finest clothes — the men in starched shirts and collars, the women in silk dresses or lacy shirtwaists. Mailed back to relatives in Europe, these pictures provided a tantalizing but not always entirely accurate picture of the promise of America.
Collection of Sharon Salinger.

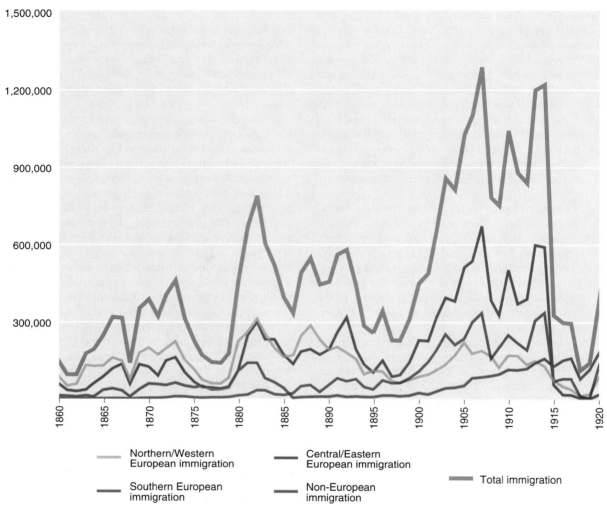

Figure 17.3
The Old and the New Immigration, 1860–1920
The immigration of the 1880s was dominated by southern and eastern Europeans. Before 1880, over 85 percent of immigrants had come from Western Europe — Germany, Ireland, England, and the Scandinavian countries. After 1880, 80 percent of the new arrivals came from Italy, Turkey, Hungary, Armenia, and Poland, Russia, and other Slavic countries.

Europe, teeming with street peddlers and pushcarts. Hester Street, at the heart of New York's Jewish section, rang with the calls of vendors hawking their wares, from pickles to feather beds.

The new immigration raised a chorus of criticism. The Italians, Russian Jews, and Slavs who formed the bulk of the new immigrants were compared unfavorably to the Germans, the Irish, the British, and the Scandinavians who had led the procession before the 1880s. To many older-stock Amer-

icans, the new immigrants from southern and eastern Europe seemed impossible to assimilate. "These people are not Americans," editorialized the popular journal *Public Opinion*, "they are the very scum and offal of Europe." The new immigrants were castigated for being uneducated, backward, and outlandish in appearance. Terence Powderly, head of the labor organization the Knights of Labor, complained that the newcomers "herded together like animals and lived like beasts."

Old-stock aristocrats such as Senator Henry Cabot Lodge of Massachusetts formed an unlikely alliance with organized labor to press for immigration restriction. A precedent for keeping out "undesirable" immigrants had been established in 1882, when labor agitation and racism in California led to passage of the Chinese Exclusion Act, which put a stop to the legal immigration of Chinese nationals. On the East Coast, Lodge and his followers championed a literacy test, a device designed to limit immigration from Italy and eastern Europe by requiring immigrants to demonstrate the ability to read and write in their native language. Since the vast majority of Italian and Slavic peasants had no schooling, it was assumed that few would be able to pass the test. In 1906, Congress approved a literacy test for immigrants, but President Grover Cleveland promptly vetoed it. "It is said," the president reminded Congress, "that the quality of recent immigration is undesirable. The time is quite within recent memory when the same thing was said of immigrants, who, with their descendants, are now numbered among our best citizens." Cleveland's veto forestalled immigration restriction but did not stop the forces seeking to close the gates. They would continue to press for restriction until they achieved their goal in the 1920s.

How Both Halves Lived

Much of what worried comfortable Americans about the new immigrants was the poverty and squalor of the immigrant ghettos in the big cities. In 1890, a young police reporter named Jacob Riis took his notebook and his camera into the tenements of New York's Lower East Side; the result was the best-selling book *How the Other Half Lives.* Riis invited his audience into a Cherry Street tenement:

> Be careful please! The hall is dark and you might stumble over the children pitching pennies back there. . . . Close? Yes! What would you have? All the fresh air that ever enters these stairs comes from the hall door and is forever slamming, and from the windows of dark bedrooms that in turn receive from the stairs their sole supply of the elements God meant to be free, but man deals out with such niggardly hand. . . .
>
> Here is a door. Listen! That short hacking cough, that tiny, helpless wail—what do they mean? They mean that the soiled bow of white you saw on the door downstairs will have another story to

tell—Oh! a sadly familiar story—before the day is at an end. The child is dying with measles. With half a chance it might have lived; but it had none. That dark bedroom killed it.

As Riis discovered, poverty, crowding, dirt, and disease constituted the daily reality of New York's poor. Riis's book, like his photographs, presented a world of black and white. He oversimplified the life of New York's working class by lumping together the day laborer, the unionized craftsman, the small-time artisan, the shop girl, and the pushcart peddler. There were many layers to the population Riis labeled "the other half" and distinctions furthered by ethnicity, religion, race, and gender. *How the Other Half Lives* must be read more as a call to action than as an accurate portrayal. Like many other middle-class Americans, Riis worried that the tenements would spawn not only disease and ignorance, but social unrest. In a chapter entitled "The Man with the Knife," Riis mused that a man driven by hunger to steal a loaf of bread for his family might also, driven by rage at injustice, rise in vengeance to strike at the comfortable middle class. Unlike the rest of his book, which sought to document the reality of immigrant life, the "man with the knife" was purely a figment of Riis's imagination. In reality, the underclass man with the knife more often turned it on his poor neighbors, for despite fears of social uprising, crime and violence rarely touched the well-off. Nevertheless, Riis's "man with the knife" was a potent symbol of the growing concern over the widening gap between the rich and the poor.

Jacob Riis's audience shivered at his revelations about the "other half." But middle-class Americans worried equally about the excesses of the wealthy. The chasm between the rich and the poor grew more visible in cities such as New York, where the mansions on Fifth Avenue stood only blocks from the tenements in Hell's Kitchen. Many middle-class Americans shared Jacob Riis's view that "the real danger to society comes not only from the tenements, but from the illspent wealth which reared them."

The excesses of newly minted millionaires in the decades following the Civil War were nowhere more visible than in the lifestyle of the Vanderbilts. "Commodore" Cornelius Vanderbilt, the uncouth ferryman who built the New York Central Railroad, died in 1877, leaving his son $90 million. William Vanderbilt doubled that sum and his two sons proceeded to spend it on French mansions and on "cottages" in Newport, Rhode Island, which, with their marble and gold leaf, rivaled the palaces of Europe.

MULBERRY STREET AND FIFTH AVENUE
These New York City streetscapes tell a tale of two cities. At the left is Mulberry Street, a crowded tenement district on the Lower East Side. Vendors hawk their wares, wash hangs out to dry, and children throng the street. Compare the teeming life of Mulberry Street with the fashionable crowd on Fifth Avenue. Here men and women promenade to see and be seen. Their dress is elaborate and formal — the women with sweeping skirts and large-brimmed hats, the men with canes and silk top hats. While Fifth Avenue seems as crowded as Mulberry Street, looks can be deceiving. The actual population density on the Lower East Side in 1894 rivaled that of Calcutta, India, with nearly ten thousand men, women, and children per acre.
Gift of John Worth Edmonds, Museum of the City of New York; Collection of the New York Historical Society.

Caroline (Mrs. William) Astor, who reigned as queen of established New York society, determined to act as gatekeeper and keep out the nouveau riche (newly rich). So Astor, whose husband had inherited old wealth and increased it by investments in slum property, spurned Alva Vanderbilt (Mrs. William K. Vanderbilt I), whose husband's railroad money was of more recent origin. In 1883, Alva Vanderbilt threw a costume party that promised to be so lavish and publicized that the Astor daughters forced their mother to relent and leave her calling card at the Vanderbilts, acknowledging them as social equals. The Vanderbilt ball became a legend in the annals of social excess. Dressed as a Venetian princess, Alva Vanderbilt greeted her 1,200 guests. But her sister-in-law capped the evening, appearing in cos-

tume as that miraculous new invention the electric light, resplendent in a white satin evening dress studded with diamonds. Many costumes cost as much as $1,500 apiece, three times the average yearly wage of a worker. The New York *World* speculated that the party as a whole had cost over a quarter of a million dollars. Alva got her money's worth. One guest observed that the ball had placed the Vanderbilts "at the top of the heap in what is recognized as good society in New York."

Such ostentatious displays of wealth became even more alarming when they were coupled with disdain for the general welfare of the people. When a reporter in 1882 asked William Vanderbilt whether he considered the public good in running his railroads, he shot back, "The public be damned." The fear that America had become a plutocracy—a society ruled by the rich—gained credence from the fact that the wealthiest one percent of the population owned more than half the real and personal property in the country (compare that with a century later, when the top one percent controlled less than a quarter).

Jacob Riis's audience shivered at his revelations about the "other half." But middle-class Americans worried equally about the excesses of the wealthy.

Although images of the Vanderbilt ball and the impoverished "other half" oversimplified the social reality of the city, the distortions highlighted a growing apprehension. In editorials, speeches, and conversations, well-to-do Americans uneasily evoked the image of the Paris Commune of 1871, when for seventy-three days the workers of Paris seized control of the city, burning and destroying monuments of the empire and attacking and murdering the clergy. The specter of revolution haunted America in the 1880s and 1890s. Uneasy politicians and judges were quick to call for repression whenever it looked as though angry workers might "threaten property." At the same time, urban growth fostered the very social fragmentation and division that fueled the flames of class antagonism.

The Social Geography of the City

In the 1870s, Cleveland, Ohio, was a small city, in both population and geographical area. Oil magnate John D. Rockefeller could, and often did, walk from his large brick townhouse on Euclid Avenue to his office downtown. On his way he passed the small homes of his clerks and other middle-class families. Behind these homes ran miles of alleys crowded with the dwellings of Cleveland's working class. Farther out, on the shores of Lake Erie, close to the factories and foundries, clustered the shanties of the city's poorest laborers.

Within two decades, the Cleveland that Rockefeller knew no longer existed. With the coming of mass transit, the walking city was transformed. In

CLEVELAND STREET SCENE
Horse-drawn carriages, pedestrians, and pushcarts vie with the new electric trolley line in Public Square, Cleveland, Ohio. The development of mass transit at the turn of the century, signaled here by the trolley lines, marked the end of the walking city and the development of a new urban and social geography.
Library of Congress.

its place emerged a central business district surrounded by concentric rings of residences graded by ethnicity and income. This pattern of development was repeated throughout the country as urban congestion and suburban sprawl forever altered the social geography of the city.

Mass transit drastically changed the American city. First the horsecar in the 1870s and then the electric streetcar in the 1880s made it possible to commute to work. City workers could enjoy single-family homes with lawns, gardens, and trees and still travel to work downtown for as little as five cents a day. By the early twentieth century, over half of Cleveland's residents rode the streetcars to work.

The central business district grew increasingly congested as banks, offices, department stores, wholesalers, theaters, restaurants, and clubs jostled one another for space on the city's main streets. Consumerism became a chief function of the central business district, and "going downtown to shop" constituted a typical outing. Some industries, like the garment trade and small manufacturers, competed with the commercial establishments for downtown space. Soaring real estate values in the central business district pushed many other manufacturers to the city's edge, along the railroad lines. Chicago's stockyards and the Homestead steel mills outside of Pittsburgh provide examples of this centrifugal movement.

The city's poor, unable to afford even the few cents for trolley fare, crowded into the inner city or lived "back of the yards" near the factories where they worked. There they lived in filthy, overcrowded, and overpriced dwellings: in dilapidated houses cut up into tenements, in shanties and cellars, and sometimes in alleyways and under bridges. The term *slum* came into common use by the mid-nineteenth century, coinciding with the increased social segregation of the poor in the least desirable areas of the city. This social segregation—rich and poor, ethnic and old-stock Americans—was one of the major social changes engendered by the rise of the industrial metropolis, and it occurred not only in Cleveland but in cities across the nation.

Race and ethnicity also affected the way in which cities evolved. Newcomers to the burgeoning cities, whether Jews and Italians "just off the boat" or African Americans up from the South, sought out their kin and countryfolk and struggled to maintain their culture in distinct neighborhoods that often formed around the synagogue or church. Blacks typically experienced the greatest residential segregation. Every large city had its ethnic neighborhoods, its Little Italy, Chinatown, Bohemia Flats, or Germantown, where one could walk for blocks without hearing a word of English. Jacob Riis observed, "A map of [New York] city, colored to designate nationalities, would show more stripes than on the skin of a zebra, and more colors than any rainbow."

City Life and City Images

In America, private enterprise built the cities. Boosters, builders, businessmen, planners, and politicians all had a hand in creating the modern city. With a few notable exceptions, such as Washington, D.C., there was no such thing as a comprehensive city plan. Cities simply mushroomed, formed by the dictates of private enterprise and the exigencies of local politics.

With the rise of the city came the need for public facilities, transportation, and services that would tax the imaginations of America's architects and engineers and provide the backdrop for the rough and tumble story of big-city politics and politicians.

Big-City Government

The physical growth of the cities required the expansion of public services and the creation of entirely new facilities: streets, subways, elevated trains, bridges, docks, parks, sewers, and public utilities. There was work to be done and money to be made. The professional politician—the colorful big-city boss—became a phenomenon of nineteenth-century urban growth. Although corrupt and often criminal, the boss saw to the building of the city and provided needed social services for the new residents. But not even the big-city boss could be said to rule the unruly city. The governing of America's cities resembled more a tug-of-war than boss rule.

The most notorious of all the city bosses was William Marcy Tweed of New York. At midcentury, Boss Tweed's Democratic Party machine held sway. A machine was really no more than a political party organized on the grassroots level. It existed to win elections and rewarded its followers with jobs on the city's payroll. New York's citywide Democratic organization, Tammany Hall, consisted of an army of party functionaries. At the bottom were the district captains. In return for votes, they provided services for their constituents, everything from a scuttle of coal in the winter to housing for an evicted family.

TAMMANY BANK

This cast-iron bank, a campaign novelty, is named after the New York City Democratic machine. It tells its political reform message graphically: When you put a penny into the politician's hand, he puts it in his pocket. Tammany Hall dominated city politics for more than a century, dispensing contracts and franchises worth millions of dollars. Some of those dollars invariably found their way into the pockets of Tammany politicians.
Collection of Janice L. and David J. Frent.

At the top were the powerful ward bosses who distributed lucrative franchises for subways and streetcars. They formed a shadow government, more powerful than the city's elected officials. Boss Tweed held the official title of alderman. But as a ward boss and chairman of the Tammany general committee, he wielded more power than the mayor. Through the use of bribery and graft he held the Democratic Party together and ran the city.

The cost of Tweed's rule was staggering. The construction of New York City's courthouse, budgeted at $250,000, ended up costing the taxpayers $14 million. The inflated sum represented bribery, kickbacks, and the greasing of many palms. The excesses of the Tweed ring soon led to a clamor for reform and cries of "Throw the rascals out." Cartoonist Thomas Nast pilloried Tweed in the pages of *Harper's Weekly.* His cartoons, easily understood even by those who couldn't read, did the boss more

harm than hundreds of outraged editorials. Tweed fled to Europe in 1871 to avoid prosecution, but eventually he was tried and convicted and died in jail.

The sheer extent and pervasiveness of corruption in Tweed's New York have led some historians to question whether the boss in fact "ruled" or whether he resorted to graft and bribery in a struggle to exercise a tenuous control over his followers. As Tweed himself complained, "This population is too hopelessly split up into races and factions to govern it under universal suffrage, except by the bribery of patronage and corruption."

New York was not the only city to be charged with bossism and corruption. The British visitor James Bryce concluded in 1888, "There is no denying that the government of cities is the one conspicuous failure of the United States." More than 80 percent of the nation's thirty largest cities experienced some form of boss rule in the decades around the turn of the century. Cincinnati's boss George B. Cox reigned undisputed over that city's Republican machine for a decade. Alexander R. Shepherd bossed Washington, D.C., and, to his credit (as well as his personal gain), helped to transform the city from a "swampy mudhole" into the beautiful capital envisioned by its architect, Pierre L'Enfant. Bossism did not stop at the Mississippi. Denver had its boss Robert Speer. Saloonkeeper Jim Pendergast dominated Kansas City politics. And "Blind Boss" Christopher Buckley ran San Francisco in the 1880s.

Infighting among powerful ward bosses was more typical in municipal government than domination by one big-city boss. "Czar" Martin Lomasney in Boston, "Big Tim" Sullivan in New York, and Chicago's "Bathhouse" John Coughlin and Michael "Hinky Dink" Kenna exemplified the breed. Their colorful nicknames signaled their distance from respectable society and hinted at unsavory connections with an underworld of crime and vice. The power they wielded belied the charge that any single boss enjoyed hegemony in the big cities.

Occasionally, a political strategist of more than ordinary skill emerged to become a bona fide boss. Less notorious but more powerful than Boss Tweed was Richard Croker of New York. Croker, who ruled Tammany Hall beginning in 1886, relied more on bureaucracy than boodle (bribery). He directed the distribution of lucrative construction contracts, he controlled franchises for street railways and public utilities, and he made sure these plums went to men who supported the party machine. Like Tweed, Croker held no elective office. As boss, he did not want to govern, he simply wanted to ensure that he and his supporters benefited from government. Unlike Tweed, who died in jail, Croker retired in 1901 to Wantage, his country estate in Ireland, a move that led one of his critics to quip, "New York's wastage is Croker's Wantage."

In the late nineteenth century, urban reformers and proponents of good government (derisively called "goo goos" by their rivals) challenged machine rule and sometimes succeeded in electing reform mayors. But the reformers rarely managed to stay in office for long. Their detractors called them "mornin' glories," observing that they "looked lovely in the mornin' and withered up in a short time." New York's William Strong is a fair example of the breed. A businessman, he won office in 1894 on the basis of his reputation for honesty and integrity. But Strong lacked the political skills needed to win reelection. However sporadic, the victories of urban reform signaled that the city boss was not without powerful rivals whom he had to counter or appease.

The bosses enjoyed continued success over the reformers for one main reason: the help the urban political machine handed out to the cities' immigrants and poor. In return for votes the machine provided legal aid, jobs, fuel, temporary shelter, and a host of small favors. In the words of Boston's Czar Lomasney, the immigrant poor needed "none of your law and justice, but help." The ability to combine philanthropy and politics was a hallmark of the urban boss. "What tells in holding your district is to go right down among the poor and help them in the different ways they need help," a Tammany ward boss observed. "It's philanthropy, but it's politics, too—mighty good politics." For the social services they received (and not because they were ignorant or undemocratic, as critics charged) the urban poor remained the bosses' staunchest allies.

Some reform mayors achieved success and longevity, however. In cities where they sponsored public services and championed the working class, reformers proved as unbeatable as any boss. Hazen S. Pingree of Detroit exemplified the successful reform mayor. A businessman who went into politics in the 1890s, Pingree, like most good-government candidates, promised to root out dishonesty and inefficiency. He did, but he also tangled with business interests when he tried to lower streetcar fares and utility rates. When the depression of 1893 struck, Pingree emerged as a champion of the working class and the poor. He hired the unemployed to build schools, parks, and public baths. And he fought for and got public ownership of electric utilities. By

providing needed services, he built a powerful political organization based on working-class support. Detroit's voters kept him in the mayor's office for four terms and then helped elect him governor twice.

Later reform mayors such as Toledo's Samuel "Golden Rule" Jones and Cleveland's Tom Johnson learned from Pingree. All three of these wealthy Yankee reform mayors won the support of ethnic voters by championing social services and avoiding so-called purity issues that might alienate working-class constituents. For example, while most good-government candidates harped on the Sunday closing of saloons and attacked vice and crime, Pingree demurred. "The most dangerous enemies to good government are not the saloons, the dives, the dens of iniquity and the criminals," he insisted. Detroit's problems could be "traced to the temptations which are offered to city officials when franchises are sought by wealthy corporations, or contracts are to be let for public works."

For all the color and flamboyance of the big-city boss, he was simply one of many actors in the drama of municipal government.

Not only the urban poor but the business class benefited from bossism and corruption, as Pingree shrewdly observed. The boss could juggle tax assessments for property owners and provide lucrative franchises. Through the skillful orchestration of rewards, an astute political operator like Croker exerted powerful leverage and lined up support for his party from a broad range of constituents, from the urban poor to wealthy industrialists. When journalist Lincoln Steffens wrote *The Shame of the Cities* in 1904, a series of articles exposing city corruption, he found that business leaders who fastidiously refused to mingle socially with the bosses nevertheless struck deals with them. "He is a self-righteous fraud, this big businessman," Steffens concluded. "I found him buying boodlers in St. Louis, defending grafters in Minneapolis, originating corruption in Pittsburgh, sharing with bosses in Philadelphia, deploring reform in Chicago, and beating good government with corruption funds in New York."

The complexity of big-city government, apparent in the levels of corruption Steffens uncovered, pointed to one conclusion: For all the color and flamboyance of the big-city boss, he was simply one of many actors in the drama of municipal government. The successful boss was not an autocratic ruler but a power broker. Businesspeople, old-stock aristocrats, new professionals, saloonkeepers, pushcart peddlers, and politicians all fought for their interests in the hurly-burly of city government. They didn't much like each other and they sometimes fought savagely. But they learned to live with one another. Compromise and accommodation—not boss rule—best characterized big-city government by the turn of the century.

Building Cities of Stone and Steel

"A town that crawled now stands erect," boasted an ironworker. "And we whose backs were bent above the [open] hearths know how it got its spine." Technology transformed the urban landscape in the late nineteenth and early twentieth centuries. Where once wooden buildings had stood rooted in the mire of unpaved streets, new cities of stone and steel sprang up. The skyscrapers and mighty bridges dominated the imagination and the urban landscape at the turn of the century. Less imposing, but no less significant, were the paved streets, the parks and public libraries, and the subways and sewers. In the late nineteenth century, Americans rushed to embrace new technology, making their cities the most modern in the world.

The Brooklyn Bridge opened in May 1883 and was quickly proclaimed "one of the wonders of the world." The world's longest suspension bridge soared over the East River in a single mile-long span connecting Brooklyn and Manhattan. Begun in 1869 during the days of Boss Tweed, the great bridge was the dream of John Roebling. Roebling never lived to see it completed. He died of an infection after he injured his foot while surveying the waterfront site. His son, Washington Roebling, carried on the great work.

The building of the Brooklyn Bridge called forth heroic effort. It took fourteen years and cost the lives of twenty men. To sink the foundation deep into the riverbed, laborers tunneled down through the mud and debris, working in reinforced wooden boxes called caissons, which were open at the bottom and pressurized to keep the water from flooding in. When the men emerged after a hard day's work, they often came up too quickly and suffered from the crippling effects of the bends. Washington Roebling himself fell victim to this disorder and ended up an invalid. He directed the completion of the bridge from his window in Brooklyn Heights through a telescope while his wife, Emily Warren Roebling, acted as site superintendent and general

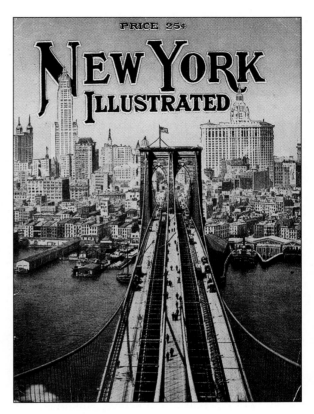

BROOKLYN BRIDGE
Completion of the Brooklyn Bridge in 1883 made possible the creation of Greater New York two years later by linking previously independent Brooklyn with Manhattan. Roebling's bridge has proven not only aesthetically pleasing, but remarkably functional for more than a century. The raised walkway allows pedestrians to enjoy their view above the traffic.
Picture Research Consultants & Archives.

engineer of the project. When the bridge was dedicated in 1883, Roebling turned to his wife and said, "I want the world to know that you, too, are one of the Builders of the Bridge."

Arching 130 feet above the East River, the bridge carried two roadways, one for vehicles and above it a pedestrian walkway. Together they pierced massive granite towers through two huge Gothic arches. John Roebling intended the bridge to stand as "a great work of art" as well as "a successful specimen of advanced Bridge engineering." Generations of artists and poets have testified to his success.

A decade after the Brooklyn Bridge opened, the growing city needed another bridge. This time engineers utilized the new technology of structural steel. The Williamsburg Bridge opened in 1903. More prosaic than its southern neighbor, it was longer by four feet and was completed in half the time. It became the model for future building as the age of steel supplanted the age of stone and iron.

Skyscrapers as well as bridges changed the cityscape. Competition for space in Manhattan pushed the city up into the air even before the use of steel. The invention of Elisha Otis's elevator (called a "safety hoister") in the 1850s led to the construction of cast-iron buildings with elevators that carried passengers as high as ten stories. In 1890, the Pulitzer Building climbed to 349 feet, the tallest office building in the world. But until the advent of structural steel, no building in Manhattan topped the spire of Wall Street's Trinity Church.

Chicago, not New York, gave birth to the modern skyscraper. Rising from the ashes of the Great Fire of 1871, Chicago offered a generation of skilled architects and engineers the chance to experiment with new technologies. Commercial architecture reached an art form at the hands of a skilled group of architects who together constituted the "Chicago school." Men of genius such as Louis Sullivan and John Wellborn Root gave Chicago some of the world's finest commercial buildings. Employing the dictum "form follows function," they built startlingly modern structures. The massive commercial buildings, in Root's words, "carried out the ideas of modern business life, simplicity, breadth, dignity." A fitting symbol of modern America, the skyscraper expressed and exalted the domination of corporate power.

Alongside the skyscrapers rose new residential apartments for the rich and middle class. The "French flat" gained popularity in the 1880s as city dwellers overcame their distaste for multifamily housing (which carried the stigma of the tenement) and gave in to "flat fever." Fashionable new apartments, built for affluent tenants, boasted such modern luxuries as electricity, telephones, central heating, elevators, and modern plumbing. The convenience of apartment living appealed particularly to women. "Housekeeping isn't fun," cried one New York woman. "Give us flats!" In 1883 alone, more than one thousand new apartments went up in Chicago.

The flush toilets, bathtubs, and lavatories of the new apartments would not have been possible without major improvements in city sewers and water mains. Under the direction of enlightened city engineers, municipalities enlarged and expanded their sewers and devised ingenious ways to bring

BANDSTAND AT CENTRAL PARK
Landscape architect Frederick Law Olmsted designed his great urban parks as places where city dwellers could retreat for solitude and silence. But New Yorkers had other ideas, using Olmsted's Central Park for entertainment and amusement as well. Here a crowd jostles shoulder to shoulder at a concert at the bandstand.
Lake County (Illinois) Museum, Curt Teich Postcard Archives.

clean water to the urban population. City engineer Ellis S. Chesborough tunneled two miles out into Lake Michigan to assure Chicagoans that the water they drank would not be tainted by sewage. Rudolph Herring earned the title Dean of Sanitary Engineering by planning the sewer systems for Philadelphia, New York City, Chicago, Los Angeles, Baltimore, Washington, D.C., Minneapolis, Montreal, Toronto, and Mexico City. By the 1890s, the residents of American cities demanded and received, at the twist of a faucet, water for their bathtubs, toilets, and even their lawn sprinklers. Those who could afford it enjoyed a standard of living that was the envy of European capitals.

Throughout the United States, municipal governments undertook public works on a scale unknown in European cities. They paved streets with asphalt, replaced gas lamps with electric lights, ran trolley tracks on the old horsecar lines, and dug underground to build subways and then tore down the unsightly elevated tracks that clogged the city streets. In San Francisco, Andrew Smith Hallidie mastered the city's hills, building a system of cable cars in 1873. Montgomery, Alabama, became the first city in the country to install a fully electrified streetcar system in 1886. Boston completed the nation's first subway system in 1897, and New York and Philadelphia soon followed.

To fight disease and dirt, cities enlisted an army of public health inspectors. European scientists may have discovered the microbe in the 1870s, but Americans led the fight against germs. Using the latest methods, they battled cholera, smallpox, and diphtheria. In 1874–1875 alone, New York vaccinated more than 126,000 people against smallpox. Municipal health departments, with the help of urban boosters, worked to make American cities among the healthiest in the world.

Cities became not only healthier, but also more beautiful. American cities created public parks that were unrivaled in their scope and execution. Much of the credit goes to one man—landscape architect Frederick Law Olmsted. Olmsted designed parks in Atlanta, Brooklyn, Buffalo, Boston, Rochester, Detroit, Chicago, Milwaukee, Bridgeport, Hartford, and Louisville. The indefatigable Olmsted also laid out the grounds for the U.S. Capitol, designed the campuses of Stanford University and Gallaudet College, and planned an entire city, Riverside, Illinois. The Boston park system, a seven-mile ring of green that Olmsted called the city's "emerald necklace," was his most ambitious and successful project. But he is best remembered for the creation of New York's Central Park. He and his partner Calvert Vaux directed the planting of more than five million trees, shrubs, and vines to transform the eight hundred acres between 59th Street and 110th Street into an oasis for urban dwellers. "We want a ground to which people may easily go after their day's work is done," he wrote, "where they may stroll for an hour, seeing, hearing, and feeling nothing of the bustle and jar of the streets."

Olmsted intended his parks for contemplation, but in the 1880s and 1890s, parks became playgrounds for the people. Lincoln Park in Chicago offered baseball diamonds, tennis courts, a zoo, bicycle and bridle paths, and a band shell. San Francisco's Golden Gate Park, built on a sandy waste, by 1900 stood as a magnificent recreational area complete with a Japanese tea garden and a herd of grazing buffalo.

American cities did not overlook the mind in their efforts at improvement. They created a comprehensive free public school system that educated everyone from the children of urban professionals to the sons and daughters of immigrants. The exploding urban population strained the system and led to crowded and inadequate facilities, but no one was

turned away. In 1899, more than 544,000 pupils attended school in New York's five boroughs. Schools in Boston, New York, Chicago, and Detroit as well as other cities and towns provided the only classrooms in the world where students could attend secondary school free of charge.

In addition to schools, the cities built libraries to educate their citizens. American cities in the late nineteenth century created the most extensive free public library system in the world. In 1895, the Boston Public Library opened its bronze doors under the inscription "Free to All." More than 700,000 volumes stood on the shelves, ready to be checked out. Designed in the style of a Renaissance palazzo, replete with a grand marble staircase and murals by John Singer Sargent, the library earned the description "a palace of the people." Across the United States, other cities participated in the public library movement. Cincinnati, Detroit, St. Louis, Chicago, and Cleveland sponsored libraries in the 1870s. And in New York, Philadelphia, and Buffalo, the city stepped in with support when private libraries faltered in the 1890s.

The enduring monuments of America's cities—the bridges, skyscrapers, apartments, parks, and libraries—stood as the undeniable achievements of the same system of municipal government that Lord Bryce dismissed as a "conspicuous failure."

Despite the Boston Public Library's legend "Free to All," the poor did not share equally in the advantages of city life. The parks, the libraries, and even the subways and sewers benefited some city dwellers more than others. Few library cards were held by Boston's laborers, who worked six days a week and found the library closed on Sunday. And in the 1890s there was nothing central about New York's Central Park. It was a four-mile walk from the tenements of Hester Street to the park's entrance at 59th Street and Fifth Avenue. Cities spent more money on plumbing improvements for affluent apartment dwellers than on public baths and lodging houses for the down and out. Even the uniform subway fare, which enabled Boston and New York riders to travel anywhere in the system for five cents, worked to the advantage of the middle-class commuter and not the downtown poor. Then, as now, the comfortable majority and not the indigent minority reaped a disproportionate share of the benefits in the nation's big cities.

Any story of the American city, it seems, must be a tale of two cities—or, more correctly, given the great diversity, a tale of many cities within each metropolis. At the turn of the century a central paradox emerged: The enduring monuments of America's cities—the bridges, skyscrapers, apartments, parks, and libraries—stood as the undeniable achievements of the same system of municipal government that Lord Bryce dismissed as a "conspicuous failure."

White City or City of Sin?

Americans have always been of two minds about the city. They boast of its skyscrapers and bridges, its culture and sophistication, and they pride themselves on its bigness and bustle. At the same time they fear it as the city of sin, the home of immigrant slums, the center of vice and crime. Americans in the late nineteenth century experienced the same ambivalence. Nowhere did the divided view of the American city take form more graphically than in Chicago in 1893.

In that year, Chicago hosted the Columbian Exposition, the grandest world's fair in the nation's history. The fairground, nicknamed the White City and built on the shores of Lake Michigan to honor the four hundredth anniversary of Columbus's discovery of America, offered a lesson in what Americans on the eve of the twentieth century imagined

a city might be. Only five miles down the shore of Lake Michigan from Chicago, the White City seemed light-years away. Its very name celebrated a harmony, a uniformity, and a cleanliness unknown in Chicago, with its stockyards, slums, and bustling terminals. "Formal," "academic," and "monumental" are words that best describe the city built for the Columbian Exposition. Frederick Law Olmsted and architect Daniel Burnham supervised the transformation of a wasteland on the shores of Lake Michigan into a pristine paradise of lagoons, fountains, wooded islands, gardens, and imposing white buildings. "Here," wrote the novelist Theodore Dreiser, "hungry men, raw from the shops and fields, idylls and romances in their minds, builded them an empire crying glory in the mud."

What did it mean, this harmony, this White City, juxtaposed against big-shouldered, brash Chicago? To Louis Sullivan, whose Transportation Building was judged the most innovative of the main buildings, the very harmony of the White City marked a triumph of uniformity over invention. Sullivan branded the fair a blight, a "virus." Its celebration of the neoclassical and Renaissance styles, he argued, set back modern architecture a generation.

But the average American delighted in the classical beauty of the White City. "Sell the cookstove and come," the novelist Hamlin Garland wrote to his parents on the farm. "You *must* see this fair." And come they did, in spite of the panic and depression that broke out only weeks after the fair opened in May 1893. More than 27 million people

FIRE AT THE WHITE CITY, CHICAGO
Spectators watch as the White City goes up in smoke in July 1894. After the World Columbian Exposition closed in 1893, the grounds became home to growing numbers of homeless unemployed thrown out of work following the panic of 1893. Unsure of what to do with the buildings, city officials may have been relieved by the fire, which broke out in a clash between federal troops and striking railway workers. Chicago Historical Society.

attended the Columbian Exposition. They marveled at the art and architecture, strolled the elaborate grounds, visited the exhibits—everything from an eleven-ton cheese to the gigantic Yerkes telescope—and were by turns educated and entertained. Half carnival, half culture, the great fair offered something for everyone. On the Midway Plaisance, a separate concession away from the White City proper, crowds thrilled to the massive wheel built by Mr. Ferris and watched agog as Little Egypt danced the hootchy kootchy.

William Dean Howells, an influential author and the unofficial dean of American letters, judged the fair an expression of America's utopian vision, "a glorious dream of universal brotherhood." For historian Henry Adams, one of the more astute observers of his era, the fair offered not so much a lesson as a riddle. "Chicago," Adams wrote, "asked in 1893 for the first time the question whether the American people knew where they were driving."

The White City's appeal seemed to lie in its distance from everyday life. But that distance could be disconcerting. Hamlin Garland treated his parents to a trip to the fair during the summer of 1893. His mother had grown old, worn down by the work and troubles of farm life. He fancied that the trip could somehow make it up to her. Eagerly he led his parents from one exhibit to another, from one grand vista to the next. The result was not what he anticipated.

> Stunned by the majesty of the vision, my mother sat in her chair, visioning it all yet comprehending little of its meaning. . . . These gorgeous scenes dazzled her, overwhelmed her. . . .
>
> At last, utterly overcome, she leaned her head against my arm, closed her eyes, and said, "Take me home. I can't stand any more of it."

In October the fair closed its doors in the midst of the worst depression the country had seen. The depression turned the decaying White City into a city of the poor and unemployed. During the winter of 1894, Chicago's homeless took over the grounds, vandalized the buildings, and frightened the respectable population. When Daniel Burnham was asked what should be done with the moldering remains of the White City, he responded, "It should be torched." And it was. In July 1894, in a clash between federal troops and striking railway workers, incendiaries set fire to the great buildings. In a matter of hours, nothing remained but a mass of rubble and twisted girders.

In the end, the White City remained what it had always been, a dreamscape. Buildings that looked like marble from a distance began to crumble even before fire destroyed the fairgrounds. Some had talked of preserving the vision, of building a permanent landmark for the city. But times were hard, and money was scarce. With the exception of the Arts Building, erected to house the Museum of Science and Industry, the White City remained a fantasy, never destined to endure. Perhaps it was not so strange, after all, that the legacy of the White City was felt most directly on Coney Island, where two new amusement parks, Luna and Dreamland, sought to combine, in a cheapened form, the beauty of the White City with the thrill of the Midway Plaisance.

Conclusion: The City and the Country

Those like Henry Adams who pondered the riddle of where the country was heading as the nineteenth century gave way to the twentieth would have been better advised to leave the White City and look to Chicago. There in the young metropolis, with its stockyards and skyscrapers, its terminals and rail yards, the answer could be found. Americans on the move had populated a continent and, along with a host of newcomers from around the world, filled the cities, doubling Chicago's population each decade. A vast spider web of railway tracks radiating out from Chicago linked burgeoning urban America with the orange groves of California, the cotton fields of Texas, and the cattle ranches of Montana, collapsing distance and difference. Increasingly, the city and the country were two parts of one whole, tied together by iron rails in an intricate web of dependence.

The story of Chicago was the story of America, where it had been and where it was heading. In the three decades between 1870 and 1900, the United States had filled out the map of the continent all the way to the Pacific Ocean. Iron rails crisscrossed the nation, carrying American goods and products to seaports for the world market. Settlers pushed into the trans-Mississippi West, forcing the Native Americans onto reservations and establishing eight new states and territories. A massive migration of peoples on the move, global in its scope, transformed the geography of the country, populating the West and leading to an urban explosion. No longer a set of isolated entities, the farms, the villages and towns, and the cities of the United States were by the twentieth century part of a vast network, linked to a global market by rails of steel.

CHRONOLOGY

1860–1900 2.5 million farms established on public lands.

1862 Homestead Act promises 160 acres of western land to anyone who settles on land for five years.

1870s Cattle ranching and mining become big business in the West.

1870 80 percent of the population lives in rural areas, according to U.S. census.

1871 William Marcy Tweed's rule in New York ends in ignominy.

Fire ravages Chicago and leads to new boom in architectural innovation as city rebuilds.

1873 Panic on Wall Street leads to nationwide economic depression.

1876 George Armstrong Custer and cavalry force of two hundred are killed by four thousand Indians near Little Bighorn River in Montana Territory.

Statehood granted to Colorado.

1880–1890 Rural areas of New England and Midwest suffer depopulation.

1880s Immigration patterns shift as more people arrive from southern and eastern Europe.

Heyday of buffalo hunting in the West leads to slaughter of 60 million animals.

1882 Chinese Exclusion Act prohibits immigration of Chinese nationals to U.S.

1883 Buffalo Bill Cody begins to tour with his Wild West company.

Brooklyn Bridge opens over New York City's East River.

1886 Statue of Liberty, a gift from France, dedicated in New York harbor.

1886–1887 Severe blizzards in Dakotas devastate cattle ranching.

1887 Congress passes Dawes Act, breaking up Indian lands.

1887–1890s Massive droughts defeat homesteaders on Great Plains.

1889 Rise of Ghost Dance religion among Native Americans in the West.

Sitting Bull killed by U.S. soldiers at Pine Ridge reservation.

Government opens two million acres of former Indian territory in Oklahoma to settlement.

Statehood granted to Montana, North Dakota, South Dakota, and Washington.

1890 Last remnant of Sioux surrender, and army troops kill 200 Indians at Wounded Knee, South Dakota. Only 250,000 Indians remain from an estimated 25 million living when Christopher Columbus landed.

Jacob Riis's *How the Other Half Lives* documents harsh poverty in New York City tenements.

Statehood granted to Idaho and Wyoming.

1890s First wave of African American migration from South to North begins.

1891 Author Hamlin Garland publishes *Main Traveled Roads,* his first collection of short stories about farm life in Midwest.

1893 Panic on Wall Street touches off major economic depression.

Columbian Exposition opens in Chicago.

Frenzied land rush takes place on Cherokee strip in Oklahoma Territory.

1895 Boston Public Library opens under the slogan "Free to All."

1896 Statehood granted to Utah.

1900 Ellis Island, in New York harbor, opens to process newly arrived immigrants.

Census finds that 66 percent of population live in rural areas, compared with 80 percent in 1870.

Three cities—New York, Chicago, and Philadelphia—top one million inhabitants.

BIBLIOGRAPHY

GENERAL WORKS

William Cronin, *Nature's Metropolis: Chicago and the Great West* (1991).

Allan Dawley, *Struggles for Justice: Social Responsibility and the Liberal State* (1991).

John Higham, *Strangers in the Land* (1955).

Nell Irvin Painter, *Standing at Armageddon: The United States, 1877–1919* (1987).

Jon C. Teaford, *Unheralded Triumph: City Government in America, 1870–1920* (1984).

Alan Trachtenberg, *Incorporation of America: Culture and Society, 1865–1893* (1982).

Richard White, *"It's Your Misfortune and None of My Own": A History of the American West* (1991).

Robert Wiebe, *The Search for Order, 1877–1920* (1967).

C. Vann Woodward, *The Origins of the New South, 1877–1913* (1951).

RURAL AMERICA

Jane Adams, *The Transformation of Rural Life, Southern Illinois, 1880–1990* (1994).

Edward L. Ayers, *The Promise of the New South: Life after Reconstruction* (1992).

Hal S. Barron, *Those Who Stayed Behind: Rural Society in Nineteenth-Century New England* (1984).

John B. Boles, *The South through Time* (1995).

Sucheng Chan, *This Bittersweet Soil: The Chinese in California Agriculture, 1860–1910* (1986).

Maisie Conrat and Richard Conrat, *The American Farm: A Photographic History* (1977).

Cletus E. Daniel, *Bitter Harvest: A History of Farmworkers, 1870–1941* (1981).

Everett Dick, *Sod-House Frontier* (1954).

Deborah Fink, *Agrarian Women, Wives and Mothers in Rural Nebraska, 1880–1940* (1992).

Gilbert C. Fite, *The Farmers' Frontier, 1865–1900* (1966).

Ian Frazier, *Great Plains* (1989).

John Brinckerhoff Jackson, *American Space: The Centennial Years, 1865–1876* (1972).

Julie Roy Jeffrey, *Frontier Women: The Trans-Mississippi West, 1840–1880* (1979).

Katherine Jellison, *Entitled to Power: Farm Women and Technology, 1913–1963* (1993).

Gerald McFarland, *A Scattered People: An American Family Moves West* (1985).

Sally McMurry, *Families and Farmhouses in Nineteenth-Century America: Vernacular Design and Social Change* (1988).

Carey McWilliams, *North from Mexico: The Spanish-Speaking People of the United States* (1948).

Carey McWilliams, *Factories in the Fields* (1971).

Eric H. Monkkonen, ed., *Walking to Work: Tramps in America, 1790–1935* (1984).

Sandra L. Myres, *Westering Women and the Frontier Experience, 1800–1915* (1982).

Nell Irvin Painter, *Exodusters: Black Migration to Kansas after Reconstruction* (1976).

Rodman W. Paul, *The Far West and the Great Plains in Transition, 1859–1900* (1988).

Paula Petrik, *No Step Backward: Women and Family on the Rocky Mountain Mining Frontier* (1987).

Glenda Gates Riley, *The Female Frontier: A Comparative View of the Prairie and the Plains* (1988).

Lillian Schlissel, Byrd Gibbens, and Elizabeth Hampsten, *Far from Home: Families of the Westward Journey* (1989).

Fred A. Shannon, *The Farmer's Last Frontier: Agriculture, 1860–1897* (1945).

Richard Slotkin, *Gunfighter Nation: The Myth of the Frontier in Twentieth-Century America* (1992).

Mary L. Smith, *Going to God's Country* (1941).

Joanna L. Stratton, *Pioneer Women: Voices from the Kansas Frontier* (1981).

Gregory R. Woirol, *In the Floating Army: F. C. Mills on Itinerant Life in California, 1914* (1988).

THE WEST

Rudolfo Acuna, *Occupied America: A History of Chicanos* (1981).

Stephen E. Ambrose, *Crazy Horse and Custer: The Parallel Lives of Two American Warriors* (1975).

Ralph K. Andrist, *Long Death: Last Days of the Plains Indians* (1964).

Lewis Atherton, *The Cattle Kings* (1961).

Gunther Barth, *Bitter Strength: A History of the Chinese in the United States, 1850–1870* (1964).

Monroe Lee Billington, *New Mexico's Buffalo Soldiers, 1866–1900* (1991).

Dee Brown, *Bury My Heart at Wounded Knee* (1970).

David Dary, *Cowboy Culture* (1981).

Sarah Deutsch, *No Separate Refuge* (1987).

Richard Drinnon, *Facing West: The Metaphysics of Indian-Hating and Empire-Building* (1980).

Robert R. Dykstra, *Cattle Towns* (1968).

C. Robert Haywood, *Victorian West: Class and Culture in Kansas Cattle Towns* (1991).

Robert V. Hine, *The American West: An Interpretive History* (2nd ed., 1984).

Richard Hogan, *Class and Community in Frontier Colorado* (1990).

Frederick E. Hoxie, *A Final Promise: The Campaign to Assimilate the Indians* (1984).

Howard R. Lamar, *The Far Southwest, 1846–1912* (1966).

Patricia Nelson Limerick, *The Legacy of Conquest: The Unbroken Past of the American West* (1987).

H. Elaine Lindgren, *Land in Her Own Name: Women as Homesteaders in North Dakota* (1991).

K. Tsiana Lowawaima, *They Called it Prairie Light: The Story of Chilocco Indian School* (1994).

Janet A. McDonnell, *The Dispossession of the American Indian, 1887–1934* (1991).

Devon A. Mihesuah, *Cultivating Rosebuds: The Education of Women at the Cherokee Female Seminary* (1993).

David Montejano, *Anglos and Mexicans in the Making of Texas, 1836–1986* (1989).

Donald J. Pisani, *From the Family Farm to Agribusiness: The Irrigation Crusade in California, 1850–1930* (1984).

Jules David Prown et al., *Discovered Lands, Invented Pasts* (1992).

Lillian Schlissel, Vicki Ruiz, and Janice Monk, eds., *Western Women, Their Land, Their Lives* (1988).

Richard Slatta, *Cowboys of the Americas* (1990).

Russell Thornton, *American Indian Holocaust and Survival: A Population History since 1492* (1987).

Robert A. Trennert Jr., *The Phoenix Indian School* (1988).

Kathleen Underwood, *Town Building on the Colorado Frontier* (1987).

Francis Utley, *The Last Days of the Sioux Nation* (1963).

Robert M. Utley, *The Indian Frontier of the American West, 1846–1890* (1984).

Robert M. Utley, *Cavalier in Buckskin: George Armstrong Custer and the Western Military Frontier* (1988).

Wilcomb Washburn, *The Indian in America* (1975).

Walter Webb, *The Great Plains* (1931).

Elliott West, *Growing Up with the Country: Childhood on the Far Western Frontier* (1989).

Donald Worster, *Rivers of Empire* (1985).

Donald Worster, *Under Western Skies* (1992).

THE CITY

Reid Badger, *The Great American Fair: The World's Columbian Exposition and American Culture* (1979).

Gunther Barth, *Instant Cities: Urbanization and the Rise of San Francisco and Denver* (1975).

Gunther Barth, *City People: The Rise of Modern City Culture in Nineteenth-Century America* (1980).

Josef J. Barton, *Peasants and Strangers: Italians, Rumanians, and Slovaks in an American City, 1890–1915* (1975).

Amy Bridges, *A City in the Republic: Antebellum New York and the Origins of Machine Politics* (1984).

David F. Burg, *Chicago's White City of 1893* (1976).

Edmund Chapman, *Cleveland: Village to Metropolis* (1964).

Charles W. Cheape, *Moving the Masses: Urban Public Transport in New York, Boston, and Philadelphia, 1880–1912* (1980).

Elizabeth Collins Cromley, *Alone Together: A History of New York's Early Apartments* (1990).

Mona Domosh, *Invented Cities, The Creation of Landscape in Nineteenth-Century New York and Boston* (1996).

Robert Fishman, *Bourgeois Utopias: The Rise and Fall of Suburbia* (1987).

James Gilbert, *Perfect Cities: Chicago's Utopias of 1893* (1991).

Thomas J. Gilfoyle, *City of Eros: New York City, Prostitution, and the Commercialization of Sex, 1790–1920* (1992).

Ray Ginger, *Altgeld's America* (1973).

Charles N. Glabb, ed., *The American City: A Documentary History* (1963).

Charles N. Glabb and A. Theodore Brown, *A History of Urban America* (1967).

David R. Goldfield and Blain A. Brownell, *Urban America: A History* (2nd ed., 1990).

Constance McLaughlin Green, *The Rise of Urban America* (1965).

William D. Griffin, *The Book of Irish Americans* (1990).

Peter B. Hales, *Constructing the Fair: Platinum Photographs by C. D. Arnold of the World's Columbian Exposition* (1993).

David C. Hammack, *Power and Society: Greater New York at the Turn of the Century* (1982).

Elizabeth Hawes, *New York, New York: How the Apartment House Transformed Life in the City, 1869–1930* (1993).

Leo Hershkowitz, *Tweed's New York: Another Look* (1977).

Melvin Holli, *Reform in Detroit: Hazen S. Pingree and Urban Politics* (1969).

Helen Lefkowitz Horowitz, *Culture and the City: Cultural Philanthropy in Chicago from the 1880s to 1917* (1976).

Kenneth T. Jackson, *Crabgrass Frontier: The Suburbanization of the United States* (1985).

Frederic C. Jaher, *The Urban Establishment: Upper Strata in Boston, New York, Charleston, Chicago, and Los Angeles* (1982).

Lawrence Karsen, *The Rise of the Urban South* (1985).

Ann Durkin Keating, *Building Chicago: Suburban Developers and the Creation of a Divided Metropolis* (1988).

Kenneth L. Kusmer, *A Ghetto Takes Shape: Black Cleveland, 1870–1930* (1976).

1860-1900

Donald A. Mackay, *The Building of Manhattan* (1987).

Seymour M. Mandelbaum, *Boss Tweed's New York* (1965).

Margaret Marsh, *Suburban Lives* (1990).

Carolyn Marvin, *When Old Technologies Were New: Thinking about Electric Communication in the Late Nineteenth Century* (1988).

Blake McKelvey, *The Urbanization of America, 1860–1915* (1963).

Ross Miller, *American Apocalypse: The Great Fire and the Myth of Chicago* (1990).

Zane L. Miller, *Boss Cox's Cincinnati* (1968).

Zane L. Miller and Patricia M. Melvin, *The Urbanization of Modern America: A Brief History* (2nd ed., 1987).

Raymond A. Mohl, *The New City: Urban America in the Industrial Age, 1860–1920* (1985).

Eric H. Monkkonen, *America Becomes Urban* (1988).

Humbert S. Nelli, *The Italians in Chicago, 1860–1920* (1970).

David E. Nye, *Electrifying America: Social Meanings of a New Technology, 1880–1940* (1990).

Maureen Ogle, *All the Modern Conveniences: American Household Plumbing, 1840–1890* (1996).

Gilbert Osofsky, *Harlem: The Making of a Ghetto, 1890–1930* (1966).

Kathy Peiss, *Cheap Amusements: Working Women and Leisure in Turn-of-the-Century New York* (1986).

Henry Petroski, *Engineers of Dreams* (1994).

Harold L. Platt, *The Electric City: Energy and Growth of the Chicago Area, 1880–1930* (1991).

Allan Pred, *Spatial Dynamics of U.S. Urban Growth, 1800–1914* (1971).

Samuel H. Preston and Michael R. Haines, *Fatal Years: Child Mortality in Late Nineteenth Century America* (1991).

William L. Riordan, *Plunkitt of Tammany Hall* (1905; reprint, 1963).

Moses Rischin, *The Promised City* (1962).

Roy Rosenzweig and Elizabeth Blackmar, *The Park and the People: A History of Central Park* (1992).

Luc Sante, *Low Life: Lures and Snares of Old New York* (1991).

David Schuyler, *The New Urban Landscape: The Redefinition of City Form in Nineteenth-Century America* (1986).

Richard Sennett, *Families against the City: Middle-Class Homes of Industrial Chicago, 1872–1890* (1970).

Joseph Siry, *Carson Pirie Scott: Louis Sullivan and the Chicago Department Store* (1988).

Carl Smith, *Urban Disorder and the Shape of Belief* (1995).

Allan H. Spear, *Black Chicago, 1860–1920* (1966).

Elizabeth Stevenson, *Park Maker: A Life of Frederick Law Olmsted* (1977).

John R. Stilgoe, *Borderland: Origins of the American Suburb, 1820–1939* (1988).

William R. Taylor, *In Pursuit of Gotham: Culture and Commerce in New York* (1992).

Jon C. Teaford, *City and Suburb: The Political Fragmentation of Metropolitan America, 1850–1970* (1979).

Stephan Thernstrom, *The Other Bostonians: Poverty and Progress in the American Metropolis* (1973).

Stephan Thernstrom and Richard Sennett, eds., *Nineteenth-Century Cities: Essays in the New Urban History* (1969).

John Emerson Todd, *Frederick Law Olmsted* (1982).

Alan Trachtenberg, *Brooklyn Bridge: Fact and Symbol* (1965).

David B. Tyack, *The One Best System: A History of American Urban Education* (1974).

Sam Bass Warner Jr., *Streetcar Suburbs* (1962).

Sam Bass Warner Jr., *The Urban Wilderness* (1972).

Gwendolyn Wright, *Moralism and the Model Home: Domestic Architecture and Cultural Conflict in Chicago, 1873–1913* (1980).

Oliver Zunz, *The Changing Face of Inequality* (1982).

IMMIGRANTS

Glenn C. Altschuler, *Race, Ethnicity, and Class in American Social Thought, 1865–1919* (1982).

Mary Antin, *From Plotzk to Boston* (1986).

John Bodnar, *Immigration and Industrialization: Ethnicity in an American Mill Town* (1977).

John Bodnar, *The Transplanted: A History of Immigration in Urban America* (1985).

Richard Ehrlich, ed., *Immigrants in Industrial America* (1977).

Steven Erie, *Rainbow's End: Irish-Americans and the Dilemmas of Urban Machine Politics, 1840–1985* (1988).

Donna Gabaccia, *From the Other Side, Women, Gender and Immigrant Life in the U.S., 1820–1990* (1995).

Oscar Handlin, *The Uprooted* (1951).

Thomas Kessner, *The Golden Door: Italian and Jewish Immigrant Mobility in New York City, 1880–1915* (1977).

Alan M. Kraut, *The Huddled Masses: The Immigrant in American Society, 1880–1921* (1982).

Robert Anthony Orsi, *The Madonna of 115th Street: Faith and Community in Italian Harlem, 1880–1950* (1985).

Gilbert Osofsky, *Harlem, the Making of a Ghetto: Negro New York, 1890–1930* (1971).

Thomas M. Pitkin, *Keepers of the Gate: A History of Ellis Island* (1975).

George Sanchez, *Becoming Mexican American: Ethnicity, Culture, and Identity in Chicano Los Angeles, 1900–1945* (1993).

CAMPAIGN LANTERN

Political parties gave out novelty items like this paper lantern from Republican Benjamin Harrison's 1888 presidential campaign. The log cabin, a staple political icon, celebrates the candidate's humble origins, while the reference to Tippecanoe highlights his relationship to President William Henry Harrison, his grandfather, the victor of the Battle of Tippecanoe in 1811. "Protection" in bold letters underscores the Republican Party's perennial support for a tariff designed to protect the country's industries from foreign competition.

Collection of Janice L. and David J. Frent.

BUSINESS AND POLITICS IN THE GILDED AGE 18

1877–1895

THROUGHOUT THE WINTER OF 1894–95, in the midst of the worst depression the country had yet seen, President Grover Cleveland walked the floor of the White House, sleepless over the prospect that the United States might go bankrupt. The Treasury's gold reserves had dipped so low that unless gold could be purchased abroad, the unthinkable might happen—the U.S. Treasury might not be able to meet its obligations.

Cleveland, like many honest and upright men of his era, believed that the only sound money was gold. Although other forms of currency circulated, notably paper money like banknotes and greenbacks, the government's support of the gold standard meant that all currency could be redeemed for gold. A major Wall Street panic in 1893 precipitated financial uncertainty, and in its wake banks and individuals rushed to cash in their banknotes and demand gold.

In late January 1895, with the Treasury's gold reserves sinking dangerously low, New York financiers August Belmont and John Pierpont Morgan suggested a plan whereby a private group of bankers would purchase gold abroad and supply it to the Treasury. Cleveland knew only too well that the scheme might give the financial community confidence, but it would bring a thunder of protest from people and politicians suspicious of the power the influential bankers wielded. Cleveland vacillated, hesitant to strike a deal.

Early in February 1895, J. P. Morgan traveled by private railway car to Washington to meet with the president. Cleveland, still brooding over his dilemma, refused to see Morgan. The great banker appeared unruffled by the snub. "I have come down to see the president," he told the crowd of reporters, "and I am going to stay here until I see him."

The next day, Cleveland summoned Morgan to the White House. When a phone call informed the president that only $9 million in gold remained in the New York branch of the Treasury, Morgan responded ominously that he knew of a $10 million debt outstanding. "What suggestion have you to make, Mr. Morgan?" Cleveland asked. To save the gold standard, the president had no choice but to turn to Morgan for help.

A storm of controversy erupted over the deal between Cleveland and Morgan. The press claimed that the president had lined his own pockets in the transaction and rumored that Morgan had made $8.9 million in profits. With the convenience of hindsight, it is difficult to see what all the fuss was about. The historical record has shown that Cleveland was an honest though stubborn man and that Morgan acted more from patriotism than for profit. (His share, far from the millions his critics claimed, amounted to $295,652.) Today, having survived as a nation for over half a century since President Franklin D. Roosevelt took the country off the gold standard, we find it hard to believe that a time existed when Americans expected to go to the bank and cash in dollar bills for real gold.

Yet the passions stirred by Cleveland's action in 1895 cannot be dismissed lightly. Undoubtedly, Morgan saved the gold reserves. But if President Cleveland managed to salvage the gold standard, his action did not save the country. The winter of 1894–95 was one of the hardest in American history. People faced unemployment, cold, and hunger. It never occurred to Cleveland that his great faith in gold prolonged the depression, favored creditors over debtors, and caused immense hardship for millions of Americans.

Perhaps the real meaning of the crisis of 1895 was what bothered the more thoughtful commentators of the time, who recognized that the issue was not gold but power. Cleveland's actions made it clear that J. P. Morgan, and not the president, had it in his power to save the Treasury. How had such enormous power accrued to businessmen? And what did it mean for the future of American democracy? Historian Henry Adams, the great-grandson of President John Adams and the grandson of President John Quincy Adams, voiced many Americans' fears about the growing power of the new business titans. Democracy itself, he feared, was threatened by what he called a "new caesarism"—a dictatorship of corporate power. The increasing emphasis on money and moneymaking stimulated by industrial development also worried the writer Mark Twain, who used the label "the Gilded Age" to highlight the crass materialism of the era.

In the years following the Confederate surrender at Appomattox, the country experienced a profound shift. President Rutherford B. Hayes observed, "We are in a period when the old questions are settled, and the new ones are not yet brought forward." Slavery and sectionalism, the twin forces fueling antebellum politics, yielded to new concerns as industry and the industrialists took center stage. After the end of the Civil War, industrial development in the United States speeded to a fever pitch. By the end of the century, the United States led the world in manufacturing, far surpassing Great Britain. America's manufacturing economy had its roots in the early nineteenth century, but in the years between 1865 and the 1890s the country was transformed, moving slowly but surely from a nation of farms to a nation of factories. Industrial progress, however, did not march forward smoothly at an even pace.

Economic growth was uneven, marred by cycles of boom and bust. Panics, sharp economic downturns usually precipitated by a stock market plunge and accompanied by bank failures and unemployment, occurred routinely and touched off two major depressions, one following the panic of 1873 and a more profound depression after the panic of 1893. Nor was industrial growth uniform across the country. Large areas of the United States, particularly in the South and the West, remained predominantly rural and agricultural. Industries developed more quickly in the Northeast and the areas touching the Great Lakes, where busy ports witnessed an influx of cheap labor and a correspondingly impressive outflow of American industrial goods.

The rise of industrialism in the United States and the interplay of business and politics strike the key themes in the Gilded Age, the period from the 1870s to the 1890s. Bound closer by a network of railroads and telegraphs, with the fate of small towns linked as never before to the fortunes of big cities, America in the late nineteenth century became united in fact as well as in name. Industrial development transformed the lives of all Americans, from factory workers to farmers. In the United States, the transition from a rural, agricultural economy to urban industrialism proved a deeply unsettling experience. The hopes and fears that industrialism inspired can be seen in the public's attitude toward the great business moguls of the day, men like Jay Gould, Andrew Carnegie, John D. Rockefeller, and J. P. Morgan. These larger-than-life figures dominated not only business but the popular imagination as the heroes and villains in the high drama of industrialization. At no other period in U.S. history would the industrial giants and the businesses they built (and sometimes wrecked) loom so large in American life.

Old Industries Transformed, New Industries Born

In the years following the Civil War, the scale and scope of American industry expanded dramatically. Old industries became modern big businesses, while discovery and invention stimulated new industries such as oil and electric power. A number of factors contributed to the prodigious growth of American industry. The country boasted an abundance of raw materials and energy sources—coal, iron, timber, oil, and water power. Human resources, too, seemed almost unlimited as record numbers of immigrants came to the United States and farmers migrated to industrial centers. American inventiveness also contributed to the growth of industry. The telephone, typewriter, electric light, sewing machine, refrigeration, and the automobile— all invented between the 1870s and 1890s—became integral parts of American life. Just as technological ingenuity created the machinery for industrial growth, a revolution in the management of industry enabled expanding businesses to organize their far-flung industrial networks.

The rise of the railroad played the key role in the transformation of the American economy in the post–Civil War period. The railroads created a national market that enabled businesses to expand from a local to a nationwide scale. Needing more and better rails to carry freight, the railroad radically changed the iron industry by speeding the transition from iron to steel. Railroads also made possible innovations in meatpacking and food processing. The railroad had what economists call a multiplier effect, speeding the pace of growth in many segments of the economy.

The Railroads, America's First Big Business

In the decades following the Civil War, the United States built the greatest railroad network in the world and in the process created America's first big business. The railroad in turn stimulated the development of many more businesses as the United States experienced an unprecedented industrial boom. Well before the Civil War, the railroad had replaced canals and turnpikes as a cheaper, more direct, and faster way to move goods and passengers. By 1857, the traveler who had once spent three weeks going from New York to Chicago could make the trip by rail in three days. And, more important for shippers, the railroads, unlike the canals, remained operable through the winter months. The steam locomotive ushered in a new era in American economic life as businesses grew in scale and scope. Given the central importance of the railroad to America's economic life, it is surprising to note that it was built with no central plan or vision. Instead it grew up piecemeal, built by speculators, promoters, boosters, merchants, manufacturers, capitalists, and outright crooks. Nevertheless, in less than twenty years, iron rails spanned the continent, and by the 1880s the enormous task of railroad building was virtually complete. To under-

stand how the railroads developed and came to dominate American life, there is no better study than the career of Jay Gould, a man who came to personify the Gilded Age.

The rise of the railroad played the key role in the transformation of the American economy in the post–Civil War period.

Jason "Jay" Gould bought his first railroad before he was twenty-five years old. It was only sixty-two miles long, in bad repair, and on the brink of failure. But within two years, he had sold it at a profit of $130,000. Thus began the career of the man who would pioneer the development of America's railway system and become the era's most notorious speculator. Gould, the sickly, frail son of a farmer, decided early to run away to the city to make his fortune. Like many Americans in the 1850s, he saw the railroad as the key to the future.

Gould, by his own account, knew little about railroads and cared less about their operation. Nevertheless, he became a master of corporate expansion, the architect of the vast railway systems that developed in the 1870s. The secretive Gould operated like a shark in the stock market, looking for vulnerable railroads, buying enough of their stock to take control, and threatening to undercut his competitors until they bought him out at a high profit. The railroads that fell into his hands, like the Erie, fared badly and often went bankrupt. But Gould's genius lay in cleverly buying and selling railroad stock, not in providing transportation.

Jay Gould's power and success underscored the haphazard development of the American railway system. To encourage railroad building, the federal and state governments provided the railroads with generous cash subsidies and grants of land. States and local communities clamored to offer inducements to railroad builders, knowing that towns and villages along the tracks would grow and flourish. Since the federal government held vast tracts of public land in the West, Congress did not hesitate to give it away to promote railroad building. The railroads not only received land for rights-of-way but were granted liberal sections on alternating sides of the track to do with as they pleased, most often to sell to the settlers who followed the railroads into the West. Over the years, the federal government alone granted the railroad builders a total of 175 million acres, an area larger than the state of Texas.

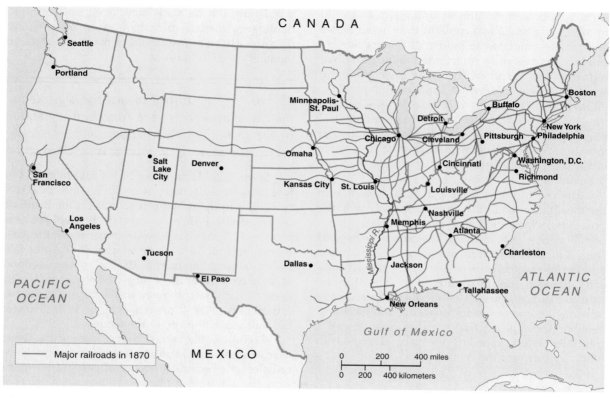

Major railroads in 1870

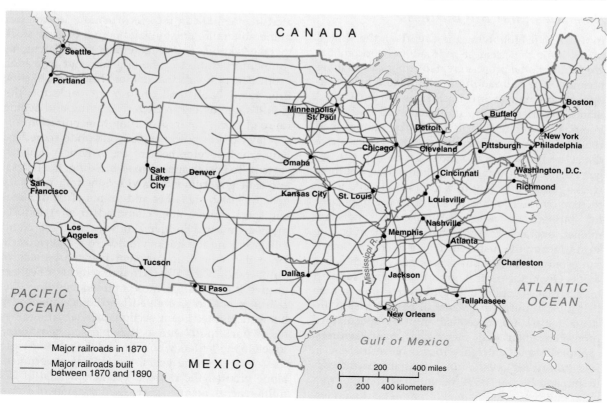

Major railroads in 1870

Major railroads built between 1870 and 1890

MAP 18.1
Railroad Expansion, 1870–1890
Railroad mileage nearly quadrupled between 1870 and 1890, with the greatest growth coming in the trans-Mississippi west. New transcontinental lines — the Great Northern, the Northern Pacific, the Southern Pacific, and the Atlantic and Pacific — were completed in the 1880s. Small feeder lines like the Oregon Short Line and the Atchison, Topeka & Santa Fe fed into the great transcontinental systems, knitting the nation together.

But the lion's share of capital for the railroads came from investors in the United States and abroad.

After a brief lull during the Civil War, a frenzy of railroad building took place. America's first transcontinental railroad system was completed in 1869 when the Union Pacific and Central Pacific tracks came together in Promontory Point, Utah, and a golden spike was driven to commemorate the occasion. Between 1870 and 1880, the amount of track laid in the country doubled, and it nearly doubled again in the following decade. By 1900, the country boasted over 193,000 miles of track, more than all of Europe and Russia combined. Despite the great leaps in growth, the railroads were in no sense well organized or integrated. Early rail lines, with the exception of the first transcontinental, did not connect with one another, and trains ran on tracks that had not yet been standardized to the same size and width. More than one thousand separate lines sprang up, often built more for financial speculation than for transportation. Speculators profited from "watered stock"—that is, stock issued in excess of the actual assets of the railroads. As long as investors remained optimistic about the future, a boom mentality prevailed. Buyers could be found for the overvalued stock, and speculators turned huge profits.

Lack of planning soon led to overbuilding. Already by the 1870s, the railroads competed fiercely with one another for business on the eastern seaboard. A manufacturer who needed to get goods to the market and who was fortunate enough to be in an area served by a number of competing railroads could get a substantially reduced shipping rate in return for promising the railroad steady business. Because this kind of competition caused the railroad owners to lose money, they tried to set up agreements or "pools" to divide up territory and set rates. But these informal combinations invariably failed because they had no legal standing and be-

cause men like Jay Gould could not resist undermining their competitors.

In the 1880s, Gould moved to put together a second transcontinental railroad to compete with the Union Pacific and Central Pacific. His decision meant that other railroads had no choice but to defend their interests by adopting his strategy of expansion and consolidation. By the 1890s, large railway systems, including the Southern Pacific, the Northern Pacific, and the Atchison, Topeka, and Santa Fe railroads, dominated American rail travel.

The unsung heroes of the railroad business were the managers, accountants, and financial officers—men like Daniel L. McCallum of the Erie and J. Edgar Thomson of the Pennsylvania. They developed new cost accounting methods and business structures that enabled the railroads to run at a profit and gave new meaning to the term "big business." In the 1850s, even the largest textile mill employed only 800 workers, most often working in one town or even one factory. The Pennsylvania Railroad in 1874, by contrast, employed more than 55,000 workers and managers and controlled more than six thousand miles of track spanning half the continent. Capitalized at over $400 million, the Pennsylvania could boast that it was the largest private enterprise in the world. The challenges to business posed by such size contributed to the creation of new systems of organization and operation that transformed American business as firms grew from small partnerships to huge corporations.

A similar revolution in communications accompanied and supported the growth of the railroads. In the 1840s, Samuel F. B. Morse developed a code to send messages across electrical wire. Morse's intricate series of dots and dashes, tapped out on a single key, enabled telegraphers to send messages virtually instantaneously over the wires, thus giving the country its first national communication system. The telegraph marched across the continent with the railroad, on rights-of-way furnished by the rail lines themselves. Telegraph wires formed the nervous system of the new industrial order. They provided the instantaneous communication the railroads needed to control their far-flung networks in order to avoid accidents and improve efficiency. Here again, Jay Gould had a hand. By 1878, through stock manipulation he had gained control of Western Union, the company that monopolized the telegraph industry.

Not all the early railroad builders were as unscrupulous as Jay Gould. James J. Hill built the Great Northern and built it well. Without benefit of

LET THEM HAVE IT ALL, AND BE DONE WITH IT!

RAILROAD TYCOONS

This political cartoon appeared in Puck, *a magazine with a partisan Democratic bent. Here the railroad barons, notably Jay Gould and William Vanderbilt, are caricatured carving up the country with long knives. The power wielded by these railroad tycoons worried many who feared that their machinations were detrimental to small business, farmers, and labor.*
Culver Pictures.

land grants or subsidies, Hill had to plan carefully and calculate which areas would best be served by the railroad in order to maximize returns to his investors. As a result, the Great Northern was one of the few major railroads able to weather the hard times of the 1890s. In contrast, speculators like Daniel Drew and James Fisk, Gould's partners at the Erie, could more accurately be described as wreckers than as builders. They ruined the Erie Railroad, gambling with its stock to line their own pockets. In the West, the Big Four railroad builders—Collis P. Huntington, Richard Crocker, Leland Stanford, and Mark Hopkins—became so powerful that critics charged that the Southern Pacific held California in the grip of an "octopus."

The public's alarm at the control wielded by the new railroads provided a barometer of attitudes toward big business itself. When Jay Gould died in 1892, the press described him as "the world's richest man," estimating his fortune at over $100 million. His competitor, "Commodore" Cornelius Vanderbilt, who built the New York Central Railroad, judged Gould "the smartest man in America." But to the American public, who found in Gould a symbol of all that most troubled them about the rise of big business, he was, as he himself admitted shortly before his death, "the most hated man in America." Why? Many no doubt remembered Gould's arrogant attempt to corner the gold market in 1869. Anti-Semitism also played a role since many mistakenly believed Gould to be Jewish. And a dislike of men who made their money by speculation rather than by producing goods further clouded Gould's reputation. Yet by the time Gould died, more than 150,000 miles of railroad track stretched across the continent and no one could claim to have had a greater hand in its building than Jay Gould.

Andrew Carnegie and Vertical Integration

Railroad building led directly to the development of a second major industry—steel. The first railroads ran on iron rails, which cracked and broke with alarming frequency. Steel, stronger and more flexible than iron, remained too expensive for use in rails until an Englishman named Henry Bessemer developed a way to make steel from pig iron. After the Civil War, with the discovery of rich iron ore deposits near the Great Lakes, the Bessemer process came into use in America. Andrew Carnegie was among the first to champion the new "King Steel," and he came to dominate the emerging steel industry.

If Jay Gould was the man Americans loved to hate, Andrew Carnegie was one of America's heroes. The hatred toward the one man and the popularity of the other testified to the country's divided reaction to industrialism. Carnegie, a Scots immigrant, landed in New York in 1848 at the age of twelve. He rose from a job cleaning bobbins in a textile factory at $1.20 a week to become one of the richest men in America. Before he died, he gave away more than $300 million of his fortune, most notably to public libraries. His generosity, combined with his own rise from poverty, gave him a positive image with the public. But he had another side—that of a shrewd businessman capable of making harsh demands on those who worked for him.

Carnegie's swift rise seemed to support the popular myth promoted by author Horatio Alger, who maintained that in America any boy could become a millionaire. Readers devoured novels with titles like *Ragged Dick, Mark the Matchboy,* and *Pluck and Luck* in which intrepid young men rose, if not from rags to riches, at least from rags to respectability. Carnegie, like Alger's fictional heroes, owed his success to both pluck and luck. When he was still a teenager, his skill as a telegraph operator caught the attention of Tom Scott, then superintendent of the Pennsylvania Railroad. Scott hired the young Carnegie, soon promoted him, and lent him the money for his first investments. Carnegie's

ANDREW CARNEGIE

Andrew Carnegie, shown here in 1861, made a small fortune as a young man. In 1868, he totaled his assets. "Thirty three and an income of $50,000 per annum," he recorded. "Beyond this never earn — make no effort to increase fortune, but spend the surplus each year for benovolent [sic] purposes." Carnegie didn't stick to his plan. In 1872, he founded Carnegie Steel and went on to become one of the richest men in America, giving away an estimated $300 million to charitable causes before his death in 1919.
Carnegie Library.

twelve years with the railroad furnished him with an unequaled education in business management, which he put to good use when he struck out on his own to reshape the iron and steel industries.

After making a small fortune in the stock market, he plunged into the steel business in 1872. "My preference was always manufacturing," he wrote at the age of twenty-seven. "I wished to make something tangible." By applying the lessons of cost accounting and efficiency that he had learned at the Pennsylvania Railroad, Carnegie turned steel into the nation's first manufacturing big business. In Braddock, on the outskirts of Pittsburgh, Pennsylvania, in 1872 he built the most up-to-date Bessemer steel plant in the world and began turning out steel at a furious rate. At that time, steelmakers were able to produce about seventy tons a week. Within two decades, Carnegie's blast furnaces poured out an incredible ten thousand tons a week. Using railroad accounting methods, he cut the cost of making rails in half, from $58 to $25 a ton. Carnegie's formula for success was simple: "Cut the prices, scoop the market, run the mills full; watch the costs and profits will take care of themselves." And they did. By 1900, Carnegie Steel earned $40 million in a single year.

To guarantee the lowest costs and the maximum output, Carnegie pioneered a system of business organization called vertical integration. All aspects of the business were under Carnegie's control. Vertical integration in steel meant, in the words of one observer, that "from the moment these crude stuffs were dug out of the earth until they flowed in a stream of liquid steel in the ladles, there was never a price, profit, or royalty paid to any outsider." Between 1875 and 1900, Carnegie sought to control every aspect of the steelmaking process, from the mining of iron ore to its transport on the Great Lakes to the production of crude steel and rails.

Always, Carnegie kept his eyes on the account books, looking for ways to cut costs and increase production. The great productivity that he encouraged came at a high price. He deliberately pitted his employees against one another, rewarding the winners with a small share in the company and firing the losers. His workers achieved the high productivity Carnegie demanded by enduring long hours, low wages, and dangerous working conditions. Steel workers toiled twelve hours a day in his Homestead plant, and when the shift changed every other week, they worked twenty-four hours at a stretch in the hazardous steel mills. Carnegie held an absolute majority of stock in his company and rarely paid dividends to his stockholders. Instead, he poured the profits back into new plants and new machinery. Even Carnegie's partners found his rule harsh.

Andrew Carnegie dominated the steel industry for three decades, building Carnegie Steel into an industrial giant, the largest steel producer in the world. Carnegie's steel built the first skyscraper in America, formed the skeleton of the Washington Monument, supported the elevated trains in Chicago and New York, and provided the superstructure for the Brooklyn Bridge. By the turn of the century, Andrew Carnegie had become the best-known manufacturer in the world and steel had replaced iron.

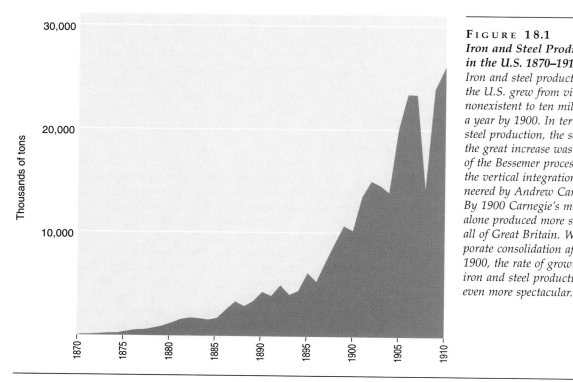

FIGURE 18.1
Iron and Steel Production in the U.S. 1870–1910
Iron and steel production in the U.S. grew from virtually nonexistent to ten million tons a year by 1900. In terms of steel production, the secret to the great increase was the use of the Bessemer process and the vertical integration pioneered by Andrew Carnegie. By 1900 Carnegie's mills alone produced more steel than all of Great Britain. With corporate consolidation after 1900, the rate of growth in iron and steel production was even more spectacular.

ADVERTISING IN THE GILDED AGE
*Trade cards were an important form of early advertising. Agents handed them out to retailers
and customers. In this early card advertising the H. J. Heinz Company, women bottle pickles
wearing aprons and caps and looking clean, happy, and attractive. How accurately do you think
the ad portrays the Heinz plant?*
Collection of Sally Fox.

The Emergence of Mass Marketing

By the 1880s, the railroads made possible a national mass market for consumer goods. Manufacturers integrated methods of mass production with those of mass distribution to achieve the first big consumer businesses in America. These enterprises came to dominate many of the nation's most vital industries. Successful organizational changes in the meatpacking and food processing industries enabled manufacturers to reap huge profits from products like hot dogs and ketchup.

What Carnegie did for steel, Gustavus Swift did for meatpacking. Until well after the Civil War, cattle were transported out of the West on the hoof to be slaughtered by local butchers. Swift, who first visited Chicago in 1875 to buy beef for a Boston company, realized that it would be more efficient to slaughter cattle in the Midwest and transport the meat to the East in refrigerated railway cars. He put together a vertically integrated meatpacking busi-

ness that controlled the entire process—from the purchase of cattle for slaughter to the mass distribution of meat to retailers and consumers. Swift pioneered the use of the refrigerated railroad car and warehouse, and, through high quality, low prices, and effective advertising, he won over consumers who at first worried about purchasing meat that had not been butchered locally. The success of Swift and Company led the older meatpackers, such as Philip Armour, to build similarly integrated businesses to compete with Swift, selling processed meat in the form of bologna and hot dogs.

Just as Swift combined mass production with mass distribution to revolutionize meatpacking, Henry John Heinz transformed the processed food industry. In 1880, Heinz was a local producer of pickles, sauces, and condiments. Operating outside of Pittsburgh, Heinz was still recovering from a bankruptcy brought on by the depression of the 1870s. In the 1880s, he adopted new, more efficient methods of canning and bottling and built a network of sales offices to advertise his fifty-seven varieties of condiments and sell them across the nation. To ensure a steady flow of vegetables and other food-stuffs into his factories, he created a large buying and storing organization to contract with local farmers. By 1888, Heinz had become one of Pittsburgh's wealthiest citizens, and ketchup had become an American staple. Using similar methods, other food processors, including Quaker Oats, Campbell Soup, and Borden Condensed Milk, coordinated mass production with mass distribution to produce low-priced, packaged consumer goods for the national market. Businesses in other industries, including tobacco, grain, matches, soap, and photography, integrated manufacturing and distribution to dominate their markets. Companies such as American Tobacco, Procter & Gamble, Quaker Oats, Pillsbury Flour, and Eastman Kodak are still a part of the American economy today.

Advertising played a vital role in helping new companies win a national audience. Just as the railroads made possible a national market, newspapers made possible advertising on a national scale. In its infancy, advertising bore little resemblance to the slick, sophisticated industry of today. Yesterday's ad agent neither wrote the copy nor selected the illustrative materials. All of that was done by the advertiser, the "client" in today's parlance. What the agent did was to buy and sell space in the newspapers. With more than eight thousand papers printed in the United States by 1876, few advertisers could afford the time away from their own businesses to learn the names and locations of the papers, let alone check the circulation figures and bargain for advertising space. The agent took on those tasks, accepting the advertiser's prepared copy and placing it in specified papers. The advertising agent was paid not by the advertiser directly but by the newspapers' publishers in the form of a commission, usually 15 to 25 percent of the cost of the space purchased. Given this anomalous position, an agent was hard put to say precisely whether he worked for the advertiser who hired him or the publisher who paid him. In practice most agents gave in to the temptation to increase their profits by getting from the advertisers all they could and paying the publishers as little as possible. The agents then pocketed the difference in addition to collecting their commissions.

Advertising in the Gilded Age suffered from its association with patent medicines, cure-alls for complaints ranging from dandruff to pneumonia. Products like Lydia E. Pinkham's Vegetable Com-

pound, a "sure cure for female complaints," pioneered early advertising and made Lydia Pinkham a household name. Reputable firms scorned advertising because of its dubious claims. Professional ethics crafted by organizations like the American Medical Association prohibited members from plying their trade in print. But by the turn of the century, advertising and attitudes toward it had begun to change. As companies sought a larger share of the emerging national market, they turned to advertising to stimulate sales by extolling the virtues of their products. Ivory soap ("99.44% pure", "It floats"), Quaker oats ("The easy food"), and Coca-Cola ("The ideal brain tonic") cashed in on the growing trend toward national advertising. For their part, advertising agents became more reputable and responsible, increasingly writing ads as well as placing them. By the twentieth century, advertising had become an important part of the product package.

Rockefeller, Standard Oil, and the Trust

Edwin Drake's discovery of oil in Pennsylvania in 1859 sent thousands rushing to the oil fields in search of "black gold." In the days before the automobile and gasoline, crude oil was refined into lubricating oil for machinery and kerosene for lamps, a major source of lighting for nineteenth-century Americans in the age before electricity. Observing the difference between the price of the crude oil gushing from wells at fifty cents a barrel (forty-two gallons) and the kerosene sold in the East at fifty cents a gallon, smart investors turned to oil refining. The amount of capital needed to buy or build an oil refinery in the 1860s and 1870s remained relatively low, less than $25,000, or roughly what it cost to lay one mile of railroad track. Since investment cost was low, the story of the new petroleum industry was one of riotous competition among many small refineries. Ultimately, one man came to dominate oil refining through the use of a new organizational strategy called the trust. That man, John D. Rockefeller, eventually succeeded in controlling nine-tenths of the oil refining business through his Standard Oil Company.

John D. Rockefeller grew up the son of a shrewd Yankee doctor who peddled quack cures for cancer. Under his father's rough tutelage, he learned early how to drive a hard bargain. "I cheat my boys every time I get a chance," Big Bill Rockefeller boasted. "I want to make 'em sharp." John D. started as a book-

JOHN D. ROCKEFELLER
Like Andrew Carnegie, John D. Rockefeller made his fortune at a young age. Shown here in 1884, the year he moved his Standard Oil offices from Cleveland to New York City, Rockefeller was already a millionaire many times over. Nevertheless, as a newcomer to the big city, he looks at once wary and diffident.
Courtesy Rockefeller Archive Center.

keeper in Cleveland and owned his own business by the time he turned twenty-one. One of the secrets of his success lay in his ability to obtain loans. He borrowed and borrowed to build up his profits, making other people's money work for him. A taciturn young man with a devouring passion for business, Rockefeller hired a substitute to fight for him during the Civil War, as did Gould, Carnegie, and J. P. Morgan. By the time the fighting ended, Rockefeller had become a moderately wealthy man. In 1865, he bought out his partner with borrowed money and took control of the largest oil refinery in Cleveland. Like a growing number of businessmen, Rockefeller abandoned partnership or single pro-

prietorship to embrace the corporation as a business structure best suited to maximizing profit and minimizing personal liability. In 1870, he incorporated his oil business, founding the Standard Oil Company, the precursor of today's Exxon Corporation.

As the largest refiner in Cleveland, Rockefeller demanded rebates, or secret refunds, from the railroads. These rebates enabled him to undercut his competitors. The railroads wanted his business so badly that they not only gave him the rebates on his shipping fares but also granted him a share of the rates paid by his competitors. This devil's bargain meant that not only did Rockefeller ship his oil at fully a dollar a barrel cheaper on the average than his competitors, but he also received fully a dollar a barrel "rake-off" on every barrel his competitors shipped. Using this kind of leverage, Rockefeller soon pressured competing refiners to sell out to him or face ruin. By 1871, Standard Oil had conquered the petroleum business in Cleveland, and Rockefeller set his sights on the national market.

Cleveland, Pittsburgh, Philadelphia, New York City, and the oil region in Pennsylvania competed for top place in the petroleum business. By combining railroad rebates with efficient production, Standard Oil strengthened its position. Major refiners began to sell out. In a series of secret mergers, or combinations, they received stock in Standard Oil and continued to run their refineries as before under their own names. Often stubborn independents who refused to sell to Rockefeller unwittingly sold to companies that were secretly controlled by Standard Oil. Not until 1879, when a legislative committee in New York investigated railroad practices in the state, did the American people learn the extent of Standard Oil's hidden empire.

John D. Rockefeller served as a lightning rod for the nation's fear of industrial consolidation. Americans vilified him because they feared the vast power of the Standard Oil trust.

Secrecy was necessary because at first such combinations were illegal. Laws forbade one corporation from controlling another. But Standard Oil developed an organizational structure called the trust, which had the advantage of being legal. Several trustees held stock in the various refineries "in trust" for Standard's stockholders. The trust was a form of horizontal integration, which differed

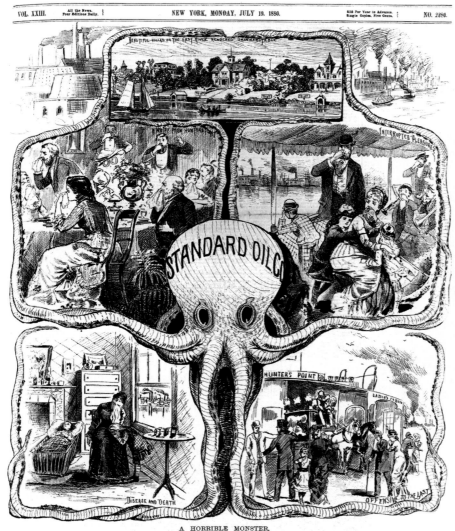

A HORRIBLE MONSTER,
WHOSE TENTACLES SPREAD POVERTY, DISEASE AND DEATH, AND WHICH IS THE PRIMAL CAUSE OF THE NUISANCES AT HUNTER'S POINT.

THE STANDARD OIL OCTOPUS

This 1880 cartoon from the New York Times *portrays the Standard Oil Company as an octopus, not for its monopolistic practices but for the dangerous pollution caused by its Hunter's Point, New York refinery. The environmental damage caused by burgeoning American industry rarely received the same attention the press and public focused on the trusts. Yet here is a graphic portrayal of the problems of pollution — houses rendered uninhabitable, boat passengers and diners forced to cover their faces to ward off noxious fumes, and a woman with an infant threatened by windborne "disease and death." Note the smokestacks spewing black clouds in the upper corners.*
Corbis-Bettmann.

markedly from Carnegie's vertical approach in steel. At first, Rockefeller did not attempt to control every aspect of the oil business from the crude oil at the well to the final product. Rather, he moved horizontally to control only the refining process by taking over virtually all the refineries. He used the trust to increase profits by controlling output, thus raising the price to the consumer. Because Standard Oil controlled so much of the market, it made a good target for people who argued that the trusts constituted a conspiracy against the public to extract private profit.

When the government threatened to outlaw the trust as a violation of free trade, Standard changed its tactics and in 1889 organized into a holding com-

pany. Holding companies operated in much the same way as trusts, but they were legal. Instead of competing companies entering into agreements to set prices and determine territories, the holding company simply combined competing companies under one central administration. New Jersey facilitated the development of the holding company by passing a law in 1889 that allowed corporations chartered in the state to hold stock in out-of-state ventures. Other businesses, such as Diamond Matches and the American Sugar Refining Company soon imitated Standard Oil's tactics, creating first trusts and later holding companies. By the 1890s, New Jersey had become the home of a number of holding companies, the largest of which was Standard Oil.

IDA TARBELL AND *MCCLURE'S*
Ida Tarbell's History of the Standard Oil Company *ran in McClure's magazine for three years. Her revelations of the ruthless practices Rockefeller used to seize control of the oil industry convinced many readers that it was time for economic and political reforms to curb the power of big business. Tarbell grew up in the oil region and knew firsthand how Standard Oil forced out its competitors.*
Culver Pictures; Corbis-Bettmann.

As Rockefeller's empire grew, central control became essential. Rockefeller moved to New York City in 1884. From his office at 26 Broadway he began to integrate Standard Oil vertically, even as he expanded horizontally. Through centralized control, Standard Oil ended the independence of the refinery operators and closed inefficient plants. Next Rockefeller moved to control sources of crude oil and took charge of the transportation and marketing of petroleum products. By the 1890s, Standard Oil controlled a vast, vertically integrated organization that was involved in every aspect of the petroleum business.

John D. Rockefeller enjoyed unequaled business success. Before he died in 1937, at the age of ninety-eight, he had become the country's first billionaire. For most of his adult life, he was unquestionably the richest man in America. But despite his modest habits, his pious Baptist faith, and his many charitable gifts, he never shared in the public affection that Carnegie enjoyed.

Journalist Ida M. Tarbell, whose *History of the Standard Oil Company* ran for three years (1902–1905) in serial form in *McClure's Magazine,* largely shaped the public's harsh view of Rockefeller. She had grown up in the Pennsylvania oil region, and her father had owned one of the small refineries gobbled up by Standard Oil. Her devastatingly thorough history chronicled the methods Rockefeller had used to gain control of the oil industry.

By the time she finished her story, Rockefeller slept with a loaded revolver by his bed to ward off would-be assassins. Standard Oil and the man who created it had become the symbol of heartless monopoly.

Rockefeller served as a lightning rod for the nation's fear of industrial consolidation. Americans vilified him because they feared the vast power of the Standard Oil trust. With its iron control of the market, its own secret codes and spy system, and its ruthless suppression of competition, the company Rockefeller created earned the title "the sovereign state of Standard Oil."

Electricity and the Telephone

Although Americans frequently disliked industrial giants like Rockefeller, they admired inventors. At the turn of the century, Thomas Alva Edison and Alexander Graham Bell became folk heroes. But no matter how dramatic the inventors or the inventions themselves were, the new electric and telephone industries they pioneered soon eclipsed their inventors and fell under the control of the bankers and the industrialists.

Alexander Graham Bell, a Scot with a passion to find a way to teach the deaf to speak, instead developed a way to transmit voice over wires—the telephone. The emperor of Brazil, dumbfounded by the telephone on display at the Philadelphia Centennial Exposition in 1876, cried out, "My God, it talks!" Bell's demonstration of the telephone immediately caught the attention of Western Union. But the telegraph company, momentarily distracted by a battle with Jay Gould, missed the opportunity to buy Bell's patent. Instead, American Bell, a company formed by the inventor in 1880, marketed the telephone under the skilled direction of a professional manager named Theodore N. Vail. Vail pioneered long lines, or long-distance telephone service, creating American Telephone and Telegraph (AT&T) to build the lines as a subsidiary of American Bell. In 1900, AT&T became the parent company of the system as a whole, controlling Western Electric, which manufactured and installed the equipment, and coordinating the Bell regional divisions. In practical terms, this complicated organizational structure meant that men and women could communicate not only locally in their towns and cities but across the country. And unlike a telegraph message, which had to be written out and taken to a telegraph station, sent over the wire, and then delivered by hand to

THE TELEPHONE IN THE HOME
The telephone achieved spectacular success, despite the daunting technical and marketing problems posed by a new technology that called for linking towns and cities by electrical wires to transmit voice. The number of phones soared from 310,000 in 1895 to over 1.5 million by 1900.
Corbis-Bettmann.

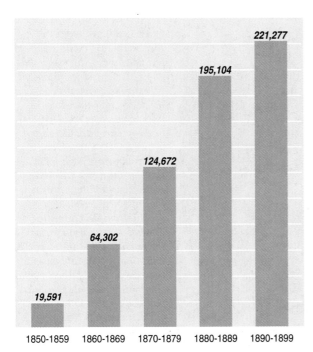

FIGURE 18.2
Patents Issued by Decade, 1850–1900
The second half of the nineteenth century was an age of invention, as witnessed by the striking increase each decade in the number of patents issued.

the recipient, the telephone connected both parties immediately and privately. Bell's invention proved a boon to business, contributing greatly to speed and efficiency.

Thomas Alva Edison embodied the old-fashioned virtues of Yankee ingenuity and rugged individualism that Americans most admired. A self-educated dynamo, he worked twenty hours a day in his laboratory in Menlo Park, New Jersey, vowing to turn out "a minor invention every ten days and a big thing every six months or so." He almost made good on his promise. At the height of his career, he averaged a patent every eleven days and invented such "big things" as the phonograph, the motion picture camera, and the electric lightbulb.

No industry that developed in the years following the Civil War faced a more difficult set of problems than electric light and power. Edison's development of a filament for the electric lightbulb in 1879 ushered in the age of electricity. But how was he to sell his wonderful invention? Before he could

begin marketing electric light and power, the inventor faced an enormous task. He had to develop an integrated system of conductors, power stations, generators, lamps, and electrical machines. And because electricity was so technically complex and so potentially dangerous, it demanded an entirely new system of marketing, one that relied on skilled engineers. At first the new industry depended on private generators. J. P. Morgan had electricity installed in his New York City mansion at 219 Madison Avenue in 1882, making it the first private home with electric lighting. An engineer visited the house daily to start the generator. When the lamp in Morgan's library short-circuited and set his desk on fire, the engineer promptly fixed the problem. Morgan, his faith in electricity restored, invested heavily in the Edison General Electric Company.

TABLE 18.1
NOTABLE AMERICAN INVENTIONS, **1850–1900**

Year	Invention
1851	Ice-making machine
1852	Elevator brake
1855	Gas burner
1857	Sewing machine
1860	Repeating rifle
1865	Web printing press
1865	Railroad sleeping car
1867	Typewriter
1867	Barbed wire
1868	Railroad refrigerator car
1869	Oleomargarine
1870	Stock ticker
1876	Telephone
1877	Phonograph
1879	Cash register
1882	Electric fan
1885	Adding machine
1886	Coca Cola
1888	Kodak camera
1889	Kinetoscope
1890	Electric chair
1891	Zipper
1895	Kellogg's Corn Flakes
1895	Safety razor
1896	Electric stove
1896	Ice cream cone
1899	Tape recorder
1900	Alkaline storage cells

AN UNRESTRAINED DEMON.

FEARS OF ELECTRICITY
Electricity was by no means a technology easy to sell, as this 1889 cartoon shows. Innocent pedestrians are electrocuted by the wires, a woman swoons, presumably as a result of the buzzing current, a horse and driver have collapsed, and a policeman runs for help. The skull in the wires attached to the electric lightbulb warns that this new technology is deadly. Ironically, inventor Thomas Alva Edison fueled the public's fears. In his battle with George Westinghouse over the virtues of direct versus alternating current, Edison repeatedly pointed to the dangers of electricity. Yet the gaslights it replaced posed risks of their own — gas leaks could cause explosions and fire.
The Granger Collection.

Edison worked steadily to build power stations and provide electric current. But his system had one major flaw—it relied on direct current, which could reach only two miles from a power station. Soon George Westinghouse, the inventor and manufacturer of the air brake for trains, experimented with alternating current, which could travel much greater distances. Westinghouse soon challenged Edison General Electric. Both companies created large, complex, vertically integrated enterprises to meet their unique marketing and distribution needs. They staffed sales offices with engineers trained to advise potential customers, safely install and operate equipment, and provide repair services. And they created research laboratories to find new uses for electricity. Despite Edison's protests, Westinghouse's superior alternating current became the accepted standard for electric power.

By 1900, electricity had become a part of American urban life. It powered trolley cars, subways, and factory machinery. It lighted homes, apartments, factories, and office buildings. Indeed, electricity became so prevalent in urban life that it became synonymous with the city, whose "bright lights" contrasted with a rural America, left largely in the dark. As late as the 1930s, only 10 percent of the nation's farms had electricity.

While Americans thrilled to the new electric cities, the day of the inventor quietly yielded to the heyday of the corporation. In 1892, J. P. Morgan consolidated the electric industry, selling Edison General Electric out from under its inventor and dropping Edison's name from the corporate title. The new General Electric Company, which was four times the size of Westinghouse, soon dominated the market.

TECHNOLOGY IN AMERICA
Vertical Transport: The Elevator

In 1890, for the first time a building in New York City exceeded the height of the steeple of Trinity Church in lower Manhattan. The Pulitzer Building gave New York its first skyscraper, a feat that would have been impossible without the development of vertical transport — the invention of the elevator.

The concept of the elevator was not new. As early as the Renaissance, Leonardo da Vinci had plans for one among his drawings, and by the mid-nineteenth century power elevators, often operated by steam, were used to convey materials in factories, mines, and warehouses. But not until Elisha Graves Otis perfected the "safety hoister" and patented it in the 1860s did the elevator become safe enough for people to use. Otis, a master mechanic in a bed factory, was an ambitious inventor who pioneered the safety elevator in a warehouse in Yonkers, New York. Otis devised an ingenious mechanism consisting of two metal pieces fastened to the elevator platform. If the rope or cable supporting the elevator broke, the metal pieces would spring out and stop the downward motion. In a dramatic demonstration at the Crystal Palace Exposition in New York in 1854, Otis cut the cable and proved the safety of his elevator.

Otis designed his first elevator to carry freight, but it was as a people mover that the elevator came into its own. The safety elevator transformed the value of urban real estate, making it possible to build into the air. As his son Charles later wrote, "I do not suppose that my father had the slightest conception at the time of what the outcome of this invention would be." Otis died in 1861 before his invention made him a fortune. His sons, who proved to be astute businessmen as well as skilled mechanics, founded the Otis Elevator Company and continued to pioneer vertical transportation, developing the escalator in 1900. In 1898, Otis Elevator, capitalized at $11 million, was formed through the merger of eight other elevator companies. The company went on to become one of the greatest industrial enterprises in America as well as one of the first multinational companies. Otis Elevator, currently a subsidiary of United Technologies, continues to be the world leader in elevator sales and service with a revenue of $2 billion a year.

Archive United Technologies Corporation, Hartford, Conn., 06101.

From Competition to Consolidation

Even as industrial giants like Rockefeller and Carnegie built their empires, their days were numbered. Business increasingly developed into the anonymous corporate world of the twentieth century as as the corporation became the dominant form of business organization and as corporate mergers restructured American industry, replacing the great business titans with faceless boards of directors.

Already by the end of the nineteenth century, the corporation had begun to eclipse the partnership and sole proprietorship as the major form of American business. Corporations had the advantage of limited liability, which protected investors from losing their own assets should the company fail. A corporation could outlive its owners and was not prey to the vagaries that plagued family businesses where one generation could ruin a business painstakingly built by its predecessors. Corporations had the added advantage of separating ownership and management, placing the actual day-to-day running of the company in the hands of professional managers. Since the corporation could raise money by issuing stocks and bonds, the owners in most

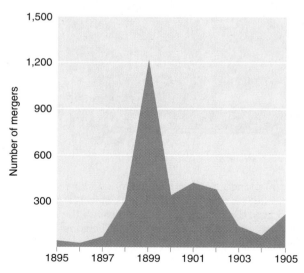

FIGURE 18.3
Merger Mania, 1890–1905
The depression of the 1890s fueled a "merger mania," as businesses consolidated and reorganized, often at the prompting of finance capitalists like J.P. Morgan. The number of mergers peaked in 1899 but continued into the first decade of the twentieth century.

cases were individual investors intent on making a profit and more than willing to leave management to elected boards of directors and operations to trained professionals. Also, because the law recognized the corporation as a "person" and granted it protection under the due process clause of the Fourteenth Amendment, it was difficult to regulate corporations through legislation. Last, corporations could buy out and control other corporate entities, and it was this power that came to dominate in the early twentieth century as businesses consolidated into ever larger corporate giants.

The merger mania that was apparent in the formation of Standard Oil and General Electric speeded up in the years between 1890 and 1903. When trusts came under fire, businesses consolidated into holding companies, as Standard Oil had done, to avoid prosecution. And as businesses foundered during the depression of the 1890s, many corporations went into bankruptcy courts where they were restructured, reorganized, and consolidated by court-appointed receivers. Banks and financiers played a key role in this consolidation, so much so that the era of the individual entrepreneur yielded to a new era of finance capitalism — investment sponsored by banks and bankers. The great banker J. P. Morgan took the lead in reshaping American business at the turn of the century, consolidating several major industries, including the railroads and steel. During these years, a new social philosophy based on the theories of Charles Darwin helped to justify consolidation and to inhibit state or federal regulation and control of business. The Supreme Court, a bastion of conservatism during this period, further proscribed attempts to control business by consistently declaring unconstitutional legislation designed to regulate railroad rates and to outlaw trusts and monopolies.

J. P. Morgan and Finance Capitalism

The great business leaders of the era loathed competition and sought whenever possible to substitute consolidation and central control. None had a greater passion for order, predictability, and profit than J. P. Morgan, the banker who became the architect of business consolidation. John Pierpont Morgan dominated the financial world of Wall Street. Aloof and silent, he looked down on the climbers and the speculators with a haughtiness that led his rivals to call him "Jupiter," after the Roman god. Physically, Morgan stood six feet tall, towering over Andrew Carnegie and Jay Gould, both of whom

J. P. MORGAN, PHOTOGRAPH BY EDWARD STEICHEN
Journalist Mark Sullivan wrote of financier J. P. Morgan,
"One thought of Morgan as of the bank buildings in
which he had his several thrones — structures impressing
the public (and designed to impress it), solid granite and
gold, marble and mahogany in every detail. He presented
no false facade to the public." Until the passage of the
Federal Reserve Act in 1913, Morgan functioned for all
intents and purposes as the bank of the United States. In
times of panic, two presidents would turn to him to inter-
vene in order to avert financial disaster.
Courtesy of George Eastman House, reprinted with permission of
Joanna T. Steichen.

were well under five feet five, the average height of
men at the time. Throughout his life, Morgan suffered from acne rosacea, which left him with a mis-
shapen strawberry of a nose. But it was his eyes that
people remembered—eyes so piercing that the
great photographer Edward Steichen observed that
"meeting his gaze was a little like confronting the
headlights of an express train." For three decades,
Morgan dominated American banking and finance,
exerting an influence so powerful that his critics
charged that he controlled a vast "money trust."

The son of a prominent banker, J. P. Morgan inherited along with his wealth the stern business
code of the old-fashioned merchant bankers, men
who valued character and reputation. From his own

age, Morgan absorbed some of the thrust and push
of enterprise. He moved investment banking into
the modern era, reaching out to reorganize business
and transform the stock market.

Morgan acted as a power broker in the reorganization of the railroads and the creation of industrial giants like General Electric and U.S. Steel.
When the railroads fell on hard times in the 1890s,
Morgan, with his passion for order and his access
to capital, took them in hand. He had already restructured the Baltimore and Ohio, the Reading,
and the Chesapeake and Ohio Railroads in the
1880s. After 1893, he added the Santa Fe, the Erie,
the Northern Pacific, and the Southern Railroads to
his list. In 1901, he crowned his achievement by
helping to create the Northern Securities Company,
a supersystem designed to bring peace between the
warring Great Northern and Northern Pacific Railroads. Other investment bankers managed similar
railroad reorganization, but none on the scale of
J. P. Morgan.

Morgan eliminated competition between the
railroads by creating a "community of interest"
among the managers, men he handpicked. Often,
Morgan partners sat on the boards of competing
firms, forming interlocking directorates. By the time
Morgan was finished, seven major groups controlled two-thirds of the nation's railroad mileage.

Banker control of the railroads rationalized, or
coordinated, the industry. But peace came at a high
price. Morgan heavily "watered" the stock of the
railroads, issuing new stock lavishly to keep old
investors happy and to guarantee huge profits.
Morgan's firm made millions of dollars from commissions and from blocks of stock acquired through
reorganization. The flagrant overcapitalization created by the watered stock hurt the railroads in the
long run, saddling them with enormous debts.
Equally harmful was the management style of the
Morgan directors who ran the railroads. They were
not railroad men. They looked at the railroads from
a banker's viewpoint, "as a group of men and a set
of books." Their conservatism discouraged the continued technological and organizational innovation
needed to run the railroads effectively.

In 1898, Morgan moved into the steel industry.
The story of his acquisition of Carnegie Steel is the
story of the passing of one age and the coming of a
new one. The era of the individual entrepreneur was
ending, and in its place came the rise of the huge
corporation. Carnegie represented the old order,
Morgan the new. As he began to challenge Carnegie's
control, Morgan supervised the mergers of several

**THE HOMESTEAD
STEEL MILL**
*The Homestead steel works
outside of Pittsburgh, Pennsylvania, was just one of the
mills J. P. Morgan purchased
from Andrew Carnegie in
1900 for $480 million. Mor-
gan's acquisition led to the
creation of the country's first
billion-dollar corporation, U.S.
Steel, known today as USX.*
Hagley Museum and Library.

smaller steel companies, which soon began to integrate vertically by moving from the manufacture of
finished goods into steel production. Carnegie, who
for decades had controlled the production of crude
steel, countered by creating a new plant for the manufacture of finished products such as tubing, nails,
wire, and hoops. A pugnacious Carnegie cabled his
partners in the summer of 1900: "Action essential:
crisis has arrived . . . have no fear as to the result;
victory certain."

*The era of the individual entrepreneur was
ending, and in its place came the rise of the
huge corporation. Carnegie represented the
old order, Morgan the new.*

The press trumpeted news of the impending
fight between the feisty little Scot and the haughty
Wall Street banker, but the "battle of the giants" in
the end proved little more than the wily maneuvering of two businessmen so adept that even today
it is difficult to say who won. The sixty-six-year-old
Carnegie, for all his belligerence, yearned to retire
to Skibo Castle, his home in Scotland, and may well
have invited Morgan's bid for power. Surely

Carnegie knew that Morgan was probably the only
individual who commanded the capital to buy him
out. When a go-between sought out Carnegie on the
golf course and asked him to name his price,
Carnegie scrawled a number in pencil on his score-
card. Hurrying to Morgan's office, the intermediary
handed him the scrap of paper. Morgan, who disdained haggling, glanced at it and said, "I accept
this price." Without blinking an eye, Morgan had
agreed to pay $480 million for Carnegie Steel.
Carnegie's personal share alone amounted to more
than $250 million. According to legend, when
Carnegie later teased Morgan, saying that he should
have asked $100 million more, Morgan had the last
word: "You would have got it if you had."

Morgan quickly moved to pull together Carnegie's chief competitors to form a huge new steel
corporation, United States Steel, known today as
USX. U.S. Steel, created in March 1901, became
America's first billion-dollar corporation. Capitalized (some said grossly overcapitalized) at $1.4 bil-
lion, U.S. Steel was the largest corporation in the
world. Yet for all its size, it did not hold a monopoly in the steel industry. Significant small competitors such as Bethlehem Steel remained independent,
creating a competitive system called an oligopoly,
in which several large combinations, not one alone,
controlled production. Other industries, such as

electricity and meatpacking, were also oligopolies. Businesses in the new oligopolies seldom competed by cutting prices, as older businesses had done. Instead, the smaller firms simply followed the lead of giants like U.S. Steel in setting prices and dividing the market so that each business held a comfortable share. Although oligopoly did not entirely eliminate competition, it did effectively blunt it.

When J. P. Morgan died in 1913, his estate totaled $68 million, not counting an estimated $50 million in art treasures. Andrew Carnegie, who gave away more than $300 million before his death six years later, is said to have quipped, "And to think he was not a rich man!" But Carnegie's gibe missed the mark. The quest for power, not wealth, characterized J. P. Morgan, and his power could best be measured not in the millions he owned, but in the billions he controlled. Morgan, even more than Carnegie or Rockefeller, left his stamp on twentieth-century America. When the country faced bankruptcy in 1895, it was Morgan to whom the president turned. And as the reorganizer of America's railroads and the creator of U.S. Steel, General Electric, and other large combinations, Morgan ushered in the era of oligopoly that has continued to characterize twentieth-century American business.

Social Darwinism and the Gospel of Wealth

John D. Rockefeller Jr., the son of the founder of Standard Oil, once told his Baptist Bible class that the Standard Oil Company, like the American Beauty rose, resulted from "pruning the early buds that grew up around it." The elimination of smaller, inefficient units was, he said, "merely the working out of a law of nature and a law of God."

The comparison of the business world to the natural world formed the backbone of a new theory of society based on the "law of evolution" formulated by British scientist Charles Darwin. In his monumental work *On the Origin of Species,* published in 1859, Darwin theorized that in the struggle for survival, the process of adaptation to environment triggered a natural selection process among species that led to evolutionary progress. In the late nineteenth century, Herbert Spencer in Britain and William Graham Sumner in the United States developed a theory called social Darwinism. Applying Darwin's teachings to human society, they concluded that progress came about as a result of relentless competition in which the strong survived and the weak died out.

In social terms, the doctrine of "survival of the fittest" had profound significance, as Sumner, a professor of political economy at Yale University, made clear in his 1883 book *What Social Classes Owe to Each Other.* "The drunkard in the gutter is just where he ought to be, according to the fitness and tendency of things," Sumner insisted. Any efforts by one class to aid another only tampered with the rigid laws of nature and slowed down evolution.

In an age when men like Rockefeller and Carnegie amassed hundreds of millions of dollars while the average worker earned $500 a year, social Darwinism justified economic inequality.

Social Darwinism's insistence that human interference hampered evolutionary progress acted as a strong curb to reform at the same time that it glorified great wealth. In an age when men like Rockefeller, Carnegie, Morgan, and Vanderbilt amassed hundreds of millions of dollars while the average worker earned $500 a year, social Darwinism justified economic inequality.

Andrew Carnegie, like most businessmen, never fully grasped social Darwinism, but he welcomed a philosophical system that placed money-making beyond good and evil and gave it scientific backing. In 1889 in his book *The Gospel of Wealth,* Carnegie offered his own American adaptation of social Darwinism. The millionaire, Carnegie insisted, acted as a "mere trustee and agent for his poorer brethren, bringing to their service his superior wisdom, experience, and ability to administer, doing for them better than they could or would do for themselves." Carnegie broke with rigid social Darwinists like Sumner, who rejected philanthropy as harmful to evolutionary progress. Instead, Carnegie preached the duty of the rich to "live unostentatious lives" and "administer surplus wealth for the good of the people." For Carnegie, whose vanity was nearly as big as his pocketbook, an element of self-promotion colored his charities; the public libraries he so generously endowed each contained a portrait of the donor. His Gospel of Wealth earned him much praise but converted few followers. J. P. Morgan, for example, though he gave to worthy causes, preferred to hoard private treasures in his marble library rather than to distribute his wealth as Carnegie counseled.

Social Darwinism and the Gospel of Wealth nicely suited an age in which the baffling changes accompanying industrialization seemed to cry out for some rational explanation. According to social Darwinism, the success of huge industries and great industrialists was a sign of their superiority and therefore inevitable. Social Darwinism claimed that to interfere with natural law would only slow evolutionary progress. This inflexible "law" assuaged the individual's conscience and made it possible to neglect the poor in the name of "race progress." When the poor were different—new immigrants, poor blacks—as they so often were, social Darwinism smacked of racism. This ugly aspect was never far from social Darwinist ideology, which judged Anglo-Saxons superior to all other groups. Carnegie's Gospel of Wealth, by stressing the responsibilities of the rich, replaced the pitiless social laws of Spencer with a doctrine that was more acceptable to American tastes. But either way, social Darwinism provided a comfortable system of belief that justified wealth and success.

Laissez-faire and the Courts

At first glance it seems ironic that William Graham Sumner, who so often sounded like an apologist for the rich, incurred the wrath of wealthy Yale alumni. But in 1890, they almost succeeded in getting him fired. The problem was that strict social Darwinists like Sumner insisted absolutely that the government ought not to meddle in the economy, subscribing to a doctrine called laissez-faire (literally, "let it alone"). In practice, Sumner opposed protective tariffs, which levied duties on imported goods to raise their prices so that they could not compete effectively with American products. Sumner rightly judged tariffs as government intervention in the market. His sharp attacks on the high tariffs angered Yale's alumni, who were not troubled by the discrepancy between theory and practice. While in theory laissez-faire constrained the government from playing an active role in business affairs, in practice businessmen fought for government favors— whether tariffs, land grants, or subsidies—that helped business. Only when it came to taxes or regulation were they quick to cry laissez-faire.

Business found a strong ally in the U.S. Supreme Court. During the 1880s and 1890s, the Court increasingly reinterpreted the Constitution to protect business from taxation, regulation, labor organization, and antitrust legislation. In a series of landmark decisions, the Court used the Fourteenth Amendment, originally intended to protect freed slaves from state laws violating their rights, to protect corporations. The Fourteenth Amendment declares that no state can "deprive any person of life, liberty, or property, without due process of law." By defining corporations as "persons" under the law, the Court determined that legislation designed to regulate corporations deprived them of "due process." Using this reasoning, the Court struck down state laws regulating railroad rates, declared income tax unconstitutional, and judged labor unions a "conspiracy in restraint of trade." In the face of the host of economic and social dislocations caused by industrialism, the Court insisted on elevating the rights of property over the rights of people. According to Justice Stephen J. Field, the Constitution "allows no impediments to the acquisition of property." Field, born to a wealthy family and educated at the best schools of his day, spoke with the bias of the privileged class to whom property rights were sacrosanct. Imbued with this ideology, the Court refused to impede corporate consolidation and did nothing to curb the excesses of corporate capitalism.

Party Politics in an Age of Enterprise

Writing of the late-nineteenth-century presidents, the novelist Thomas Wolfe observed, "Garfield, Arthur, Harrison, and Hayes, for me they were the lost Americans: Their gravely vacant and be-whiskered faces mixed, melted, swam together in the sea depths of a past intangible, immeasurable, and unknowable." Why do the great industrialists like Rockefeller, Morgan, and Carnegie jump vividly from the pages of the past while the presidents of that period remain so pallid? The answer rests in the relative weakness of the presidency and the federal government in the administrations between Abraham Lincoln (1861–1865) and Theodore Roosevelt (1901–1909). After the Civil War, power shifted from the government in Washington to leaders in business and industry. This waning of federal power in peacetime became a persistent pattern in American government interrupted only by the activism that accompanied the progressive movement in the first decade of the twentieth century and that emerged later in the Great Depression of the 1930s.

The presidents from Rutherford B. Hayes (1877–1881) to Grover Cleveland (1885–1889, 1893–1897) are indeed forgotten men, largely because so little was expected of them. Until the 1890s, few Americans seemed to think the president or the national government had any role in addressing the problems accompanying the industrial transformation of the nation. The dominant creed of laissez-faire, coupled with the dictates of social Darwinism, warned government to leave business alone: Intervention to soften even the most evil effects of industrialization would only slow evolutionary progress. This crippling view of the rights and responsibilities of the federal government in the economy and in society reduced it to something of a sideshow. The real action took place elsewhere—in party politics on the local and state levels and in the centers of business and industry.

Nevertheless, important changes transformed American political life in the decades following the Civil War, as industrialism replaced sectionalism as the driving force in national politics. The corruption and abuses associated with party politics produced civil service reform. By the 1880s, important economic issues such as the protective tariff, the currency, and federal regulation of the trusts and the railroads moved to the forefront. The presidents, for their part, were competent though not charismatic men who worked to bring the nation together after decades of sectional strife and to create one nation with a unified political life.

Politics and Culture

There is some irony when we observe that the voters of the day swarmed to the polls in record numbers to elect presidents who today seem so colorless. Voter turnout in the three decades following the Civil War averaged a hefty 80 percent, compared with a turnout of 49 percent in 1996. Why were voters then so eager to cast their ballots?

The answer lies in the role politics played in the culture of the late nineteenth century. Political parties used state, local, and federal jobs to reward voters for their support. Many voters owed their livelihood to party bosses. Political affiliation also provided a sense of group identity for many participants proud of their loyalty to the Democrats or the Republicans. Moreover, politics constituted one of the chief forms of entertainment for voters and nonvoters alike in an age before mass recreation and amusement. Political parties sponsored parades, rallies, speeches, picnics, torchlight processions, and Fourth of July fireworks, attracting millions of Americans. Outside the big cities, only religious revivals and traveling shows could compete.

Electoral politics, like tobacco, remained exclusively a male pursuit. Women did not vote until the 1890s and then in only four western states: Wyoming (1890), Colorado (1893), and Utah and Idaho (1896). Elsewhere, they continued to fight for suffrage by campaigning for state referenda across the nation. And, increasingly in the 1890s, politics became limited to white males only. Although black men gained the vote during Reconstruction, the withdrawal of federal troops from the South in 1877 led to a massive deterioration in black voters' power.

Until the 1890s, few Americans seemed to think the president or the national government had any role in addressing the problems accompanying the industrial transformation of the nation. . . . The real action took place elsewhere—in party politics on the local and state levels and in the centers of business and industry.

The Democratic Party, which traced its roots to Thomas Jefferson and Andrew Jackson, and the Republican Party of Abraham Lincoln remained the two dominant political forces after the Civil War. The parties vied vigorously for voter support, and most voters showed a strong party identification. Party loyalty in industrial America, however, had little to do with economic issues. Rather, it served to reinforce the cultural identity formed by allegiance to a region or to an ethnic or religious group.

After the end of Reconstruction, the old Confederate South voted Democratic in every election for the next seventy years. Labeling the Republican Party the agent of "Negro rule," Democrats urged white Southerners to "vote the way you shot." Opposing the "solid South" was the Republican Northeast, with nearly enough electoral votes to guarantee control of the presidency. To preserve Republican rule, the party had to carry key states such as Ohio, Indiana, and New York and had to prevent an alliance from developing between the agricultural South and the West. Republican politicians, like their Democratic rivals, encouraged sectional divisions by emotional appeals to the Civil War, a tactic known as "waving the bloody shirt," which had been used effectively in the election of 1868 and continued to rouse voters. Strong Unionist states in the Midwest responded by voting consistently Re-

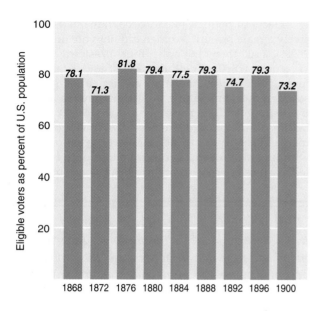

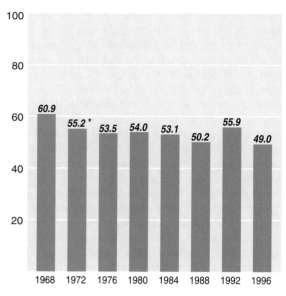

*Decrease because of expansion of eligibility with the enfranchisement of 18- to 21-year olds.

FIGURE 18.4
Voter Turnout 1868–1900 and 1968–1996
Despite the weakness of the presidency and the largely undistinguished men who filled the office, voters turned out in record numbers to vote in the late 19th century elections. Compare the robust rate of participation to the anemic turnout in the late 20th century elections. What factors do you think account for the change?

---

publican. "Iowa will go Democratic," one observer joked, "when Hell goes Methodist." Veterans of the Grand Army of the Republic formed an important base for the Republican Party, which rewarded their loyalty with generous pensions. By 1886, an astounding one-quarter of the federal budget went to pensions, not a penny of that to ex-Confederates.

Religion and ethnicity also played a significant role in politics. In the North, Protestants from the old-line denominations, particularly Presbyterians and Methodists, were drawn to the Republican Party, which championed a series of moral reforms such as temperance, the campaign against alcoholic beverages. The Democratic Party courted immigrants and attracted Catholic and Jewish voters by consistently opposing laws to close taverns and other businesses on Sunday and by charging that crusades against liquor only masked attacks on immigrant culture.

The power of the two major parties remained about equally divided throughout the 1870s and 1880s and into the 1890s. Although the Republicans captured the White House in four out of five elections, they rarely controlled the Congress. The Dem-

ocrats, noted more for their local appeal than for their national unity, for the most part dominated the U.S. House of Representatives.

During this period, senators were not directly elected by the voters but were selected by state legislatures. In an era noted for its tolerance of all but the most flagrant bribery and corruption, state legislatures frequently came under the influence of powerful business interests. In *Wealth against Commonwealth* (1894), his book on the Standard Oil Company, journalist Henry Demarest Lloyd wrote, "The Standard has done everything with the Pennsylvania legislature except to refine it." Senators were often closely identified with business interests, as in the case of Nelson Aldrich, the powerful Republican from Rhode Island. Aldrich, whose daughter married John D. Rockefeller Jr., did not object to being called "the senator from Standard Oil."

Corruption and Party Strife

The political corruption and party factionalism that were characteristic of the administration of Ulysses S. Grant (1869–1877) continued to trouble the nation in the 1880s. The spoils system—the awarding of jobs for political purposes—remained the driving force of party politics. The concept of ethics in government, precluding private individuals from getting rich from public office, remained an issue raised only by a small band of reformers during this period. Most respectable Americans viewed politics as a sordid business; corruption at the ballot box and in public office came to be taken for granted.

President Rutherford B. Hayes, whose disputed election in 1876 marked the end of Reconstruction in the South, proved to be a hardworking, well-informed executive who wanted peace, prosperity, and an end to party strife. Although he was ridiculed by the Democratic press as "Rutherfraud" and "His Fraudulency," Hayes was a figure of honesty and integrity who seemed well suited to his role as a national leader. But it was not an easy task. The Republican Party remained divided into factions led by strong party bosses who boasted that they could make or break a president.

The three Republican factions bore the colorful names Stalwarts, Half-Breeds, and Mugwumps. The Stalwarts, led by Senator Roscoe Conkling of New York, remained loyal to Grant and consequently carried with them the taint of corruption from the scandals of his administration. Opposing them were the Half-Breeds, led by Senator James G. Blaine of Maine, a group that was only slightly less corrupt in its pursuit of spoils. Standing against both factions was a small but prominent group of liberal Republican reformers, mostly from Massachusetts and New York, whose critics later dubbed them Mugwumps. The name came from an Indian chief of the Algonquian but was used derisively by those who insisted that the Mugwumps straddled the fence on issues of party loyalty, "with their mug on one side and wump on the other." Often Mugwumps were men of influence like former abolitionist and Union general Carl Schurz and E. L. Goodkin, editor of the *Nation*. They were eager to reform government and put it in the hands of competent, honest men like themselves. In their pursuit of reform, they largely evaded the complex and divisive economic issues of the day and called instead for the purification of the government through civil service reforms designed to set standards for officeholders and put an end to the spoils system.

President Hayes, despite his virtues, soon managed to alienate his party. A realist, he used federal patronage to build Republican strength by selecting for government jobs if not the best men, the best Republicans he could find. To the Stalwarts, who wanted more positions, his action constituted betrayal; to the Mugwumps, it smacked too much of the spoils system. Hayes soon found himself a man without a party and announced that he would not seek reelection in 1880.

The power of party bosses like Blaine and Conkling more than matched the limited power of the president. Fiery and dynamic leaders, they dominated national politics. The imperious Conkling combined in equal mixture vanity, brilliance, and petulance. Known for his biting insults and his close association with corporate interests, he had nothing but contempt for the Mugwumps. He ridiculed "snivel service" reform. "Parties," he lectured, "are not built up by deportment, or by ladies' magazines, or gush!" His archrival Blaine was a magnetic Irish American politician whose followers dubbed him the "Plumed Knight," and supported him so enthusiastically that they were called "Blainiacs." Blaine opposed the flagrant corruption of the Stalwarts but was himself tarnished by certain shady dealings in railroad bonds. They had come to light with the publication of a set of incriminating letters bearing the ominous but ignored warning "Burn this letter." More careless than criminal in his business dealings, Blaine, like so many in his era, drew no fine distinction between public service and private gain. The shadow of corruption would cost him the Republican nomination in 1880 and the presidency in 1884.

In 1880, the Republicans resisted Stalwart attempts to bring Grant back and passed over Blaine to nominate a dark horse candidate, Representative James A. Garfield from Ohio. To appease Conkling, they chose a Stalwart, Chester A. Arthur of New York, as vice presidential candidate. The Democrats made an attempt to break down sectionalism and establish a national party by selecting as their presidential standard-bearer the old Union general Winfield Scott Hancock. But as one observer noted, "It is a peculiarly constituted party which sends rebel brigadiers to Congress because of their rebellion, and which nominated a Union General as its candidate for president because of his loyalty." Although the popular vote was close, Garfield won 214 electoral votes to Hancock's 155.

Garfield, Guiteau, and Civil Service Reform

Government bureaucracy grew in the years following the Civil War until nearly 150,000 jobs existed on the federal payroll. The spoils system proved a poor way to select qualified individuals to serve as the clerks, civil engineers, and trained professionals needed in the new government posts. Politicians from the president down were tormented by a steady stream of office seekers. Critics soon called for civil service reform designed to mandate examinations and establish a merit system to screen applicants for government jobs. The cry for qualified employees was both an earnest attempt to be sure the "best men" served the government as well as a veiled attack on the increasing ethnic diversity in American politics. The struggle for civil service reform would come to a head with the assassination of President James Garfield.

"My God," President Garfield swore after only a few months in office, "what is there in this place that a man should ever want to get into it?" Garfield, like Hayes, faced the difficult task of remaining independent while pacifying the bosses and placating the reformers. To an indecisive man like Garfield, the presidency was a torment. He found the task of dispensing federal patronage grueling and distasteful. More than 140,000 federal jobs, not counting those in the military, needed filling. Thousands of office seekers swarmed to the nation's capital, each clamoring for a place. In an era before presidents received Secret Service protection, the White House door stood open to all comers. Garfield took a fatalistic view. "Assassination," he told a friend, "can no more be guarded against than death by lightning, and it is best not to worry about either."

On July 2, 1881, less than four months after taking office, Garfield was shot in the back at a Washington, D.C., railroad station while catching a train. His assassin, Charles Guiteau, though clearly insane, was a disappointed office seeker who claimed to be motivated by political partisanship. He told the police officer who arrested him, "I did it; I will go to jail for it; Arthur is president, and I am a Stalwart." Garfield lingered on through the hot summer while the nation held a long deathbed vigil. He died on September 19, 1881.

The press almost universally condemned the Stalwarts, if not for inspiring Guiteau, then for creating the political climate that produced him. Ironically, Guiteau's bullets led to the downfall of the very faction that he claimed to support. Stalwart leader Roscoe Conkling, who came under heavy attack for his partisanship in the wake of the assassination, had to give up his presidential ambitions and retire to a career in corporate law. Attacks on

the spoils system increased, as did a rising public demand for civil service reform. But though Garfield's death crystallized the desire for civil service reform, the debate was long and hard. Many of those who opposed reform recognized that civil service had built-in class and ethnic biases. They knew that when Mugwumps spoke of government run by the "best men," they meant men of their own class. Just as Irish Americans were beginning to carve out a place for themselves in local and state politics, civil service threatened to turn government back over to an educated Yankee elite. At a time when few men had more than a grammar school education, office seekers did not relish the prospect of written civil service examinations. One opponent argued, "George Washington could not have passed examination for a clerkship," noting that "in his will written by his own hand, he spells clothes, cloathes."

The legislation that established civil service reform—the Pendleton Act—passed in 1883, after more than a year of congressional debate and compromise. Both parties claimed credit for the act, which established a permanent Civil Service Commission of three members, appointed by the president. Some 14,000 jobs were placed under a merit system that required examinations for office and made it impossible to remove jobholders for political reasons. Half of the postal jobs and most of the customhouse jobs, the lion's share of the spoils system's bounty, passed to the control of the Civil Service Commission. The new law sought to prohibit federal jobholders from contributing to political campaigns, thus drying up a major source of the party bosses' revenue. Soon business interests replaced officeholders as the nation's chief political contributors. Ironically, civil service reform thus gave business an even greater influence in political life than it already had.

"Chet Arthur, president of the United States! Good God!" incredulous men exclaimed on hearing of Garfield's death. Surely little in his background made Chester A. Arthur seem like a man suited for the highest office in the country. Only four years earlier, he had been dismissed from his position in the customhouse in New York because of his close association with corrupt politicians. But as president, he quickly dispelled the nation's fears and acted independently, signing the Pendleton Act that his fellow Stalwarts had so long opposed. Arthur himself had little "faith in reform" but knew enough of politics not to stand in the path of public sentiment. Beyond civil service he did little, other than to refurbish the White House at his own expense and in keeping with his bachelor taste (he added a billiard room in the basement). As Carl Schurz observed, "whenever Arthur did a creditable thing, people would say, 'He is after all a better man than we thought he was.'" Arthur surprised his critics by turning out to be a competent president, but his was a lackluster administration. The Republicans quickly looked to Blaine to bear the party standard in 1884.

The Political Circus: The Campaign of 1884

With the downfall of Conkling and the Stalwarts, Blaine assumed leadership of the Republican Party and at long last captured the presidential nomination in 1884. But to many reformers, the Plumed Knight personified corruption. Led by Carl Schurz, who insisted that Blaine "wallowed in spoils like a rhinoceros in an African pool," the Mugwumps bolted the party and embraced the Democratic presidential candidate, the stolid Grover Cleveland, reform governor of New York. The burly, beer-drinking Cleveland distinguished himself from an entire generation of politicians by the simple motto "A public office is a public trust." First as mayor of Buffalo and later as governor of New York, he built a solid reputation for honesty, economy, and administrative efficiency. He soon alienated the Tammany Hall political machine; but with reform in the air, the enemies he made only added to his appeal. The Democrats, who had not won the presidency since 1856, rushed to nominate him. As was expected, Cleveland received the enthusiastic endorsement of the Mugwumps, who announced that "the paramount issue this year is moral rather than political."

They would soon regret their words. The 1884 contest degenerated into nasty mudslinging. One disgusted journalist styled it "the vilest campaign ever waged." Grover Cleveland, whatever his reform virtues, made an easy target. In July, his hometown paper, the Buffalo *Telegraph,* dropped the bombshell that the bachelor candidate had fathered an illegitimate child in an affair with a widow named Maria Halpin. The crestfallen Mugwumps tried to argue the difference between public and private morality. But robbed of their moral righteousness, they lost much of their enthusiasm. "Now I

fear it has resolved itself into a choice of two evils," one weary reformer confessed.

At public rallies, Blaine's partisans taunted Cleveland, chanting:

> Ma, ma, where's my pa?
> Going to the White House
> ha! ha! ha!

Cleveland supporters roared back:

> Blaine, Blaine, James G. Blaine
> Continental liar from the State of Maine
> Burn this letter!

The stoic Cleveland admitted responsibility for his illegitimate child. Silent but fuming, he waged his campaign in the traditional fashion by staying home. Blaine broke precedent by making a national tour. On a last-minute stop in New York, the exhausted candidate overlooked a remark by a local clergyman—and he may have lost the election as a result. The Reverend Samuel Burchard, while introducing Blaine, blasted the Democrats as the party of "Rum, Romanism, and Rebellion." An Associated Press correspondent hurriedly filed his story, crying, "If anything will elect Cleveland, these words will do it." By linking drinking and Catholicism, Burchard's unfortunate remark cast a slur on Irish Catholic voters, who had been counted on to desert the Democratic Party and support Blaine because of his Irish background.

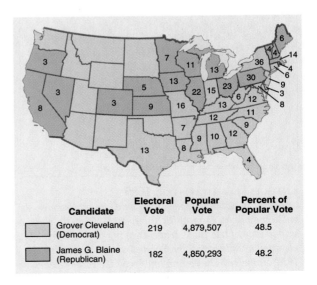

Candidate	Electoral Vote	Popular Vote	Percent of Popular Vote
Grover Cleveland (Democrat)	219	4,879,507	48.5
James G. Blaine (Republican)	182	4,850,293	48.2

MAP 18.2
The Election of 1884

With less than a week to go until the election, Blaine had no chance to recover from the negative publicity. He lost New York State by less than 1,200 votes and with it the election, although the vote was so close that the outcome remained uncertain for several days. In the final tally, the Democrats ended twenty-five years of Republican rule, defeating Blaine by a scant 30,000 votes nationwide, but winning 219 electoral votes to 182. Cleveland's followers had the last word:

Hurrah for Maria! Hurrah for the kid!
I voted for Cleveland,
And Damned glad I did!

ANTI-CLEVELAND POSTER, 1888
In this early example of negative campaign advertising, Republicans pillory Democratic President Grover Cleveland as an advocate of free trade, while dredging up the image of his illegitimate child, which had proved such a scandal in the 1884 campaign. The bottom lines echo the earlier campaign ditty "Ma Ma, Where's My Pa?" In this election the tariff became a potent issue, winning support from business and labor and helping to elect Republican Benjamin Harrison.
Collection of David J. and Janice L. Frent.

Economic Issues and Party Realignment

Four years later, in the election of 1888, fickle voters would turn Cleveland out, electing Republican Benjamin Harrison, the grandson of President William Henry Harrison. Then, in the only instance in America's history when a president who had been defeated at the polls was returned to office, the voters brought Cleveland back in the election of 1892. What factors account for such a surprising turnaround? The strengths and weaknesses of the men themselves partially determined the outcome. The stubborn Cleveland, newly married to Frances Folsom in 1886, resented demands on his time and refused to campaign in 1888. Although he won more votes than Harrison, he lost the electoral college. Once in office, Harrison proved to be a cold and distant leader. His critics called him "the human iceberg." But issues as well as personalities increasingly swayed the voters. The 1880s witnessed a remarkable political realignment as a new set of economic concerns replaced the Civil War rhetoric of carpetbaggers, rebels, and the bloody shirt. The tariff, federal regulation of the railroads and trusts, and the campaign for free silver restructured American politics.

The Tariff and the Politics of Protection

The concept of a protective tariff to raise the price of imported goods and stimulate American industry dated back to Alexander Hamilton in the founding days of the Republic. Congress enacted the first tariff following the War of 1812. The Republicans turned the tariff to political ends by enacting a measure in 1861 that rewarded their industrial supporters who wanted protection from foreign competition at the same time that it raised revenues for the Civil War. After the war, the Republicans continued to revise and enlarge the tariff at the prompting of northeastern industrialists. By the 1880s, the tariff posed a threat to prosperity—it generated too much money! Ironic as it may seem, the government found its enormous surplus revenue more embarrassing than today's huge deficits. The surplus sat in the Treasury's vaults, depriving the country of money that might otherwise have been invested to create jobs and products, while the government argued about how (or even whether) to spend it.

To many Americans, particularly southern and midwestern farmers who sold their crops in a world market yet had to buy high-priced protected goods, the answer was simple: Reduce the tariff. Advocates of free trade and moderates agitated for tariff reform. But those who benefited from the tariff—industrialists like Andrew Carnegie who insisted that America's "infant industries" needed protection and westerners producing protected raw materials such as wool, hides, and lumber—firmly opposed lowering the tariff. Many workers, too, believed that the tariff protected American wage levels by giving American products a competitive edge over goods imported from other countries.

The 1880s witnessed a remarkable political realignment as a new set of economic concerns replaced the Civil War rhetoric of carpetbaggers, rebels, and the bloody shirt. The tariff, federal regulation of the railroads and trusts, and the campaign for free silver restructured American politics.

The Republican Party seized on the tariff issue to forge a new national alliance. James G. Blaine shrewdly recognized its potent political uses. "Fold up the bloody shirt and lay it away," he advised a colleague in 1880. "It's of no use to us. You want to shift the main issue to protection." By encouraging an alliance among industrialists, labor, and western producers of raw materials, Blaine hoped to solidify the North and West against the solidly Democratic South.

Although his tactic failed in the election of 1884, it worked four years later. Cleveland, who straddled the tariff issue in the election of 1884, startled the nation in 1887 by calling for tariff reform. The Republicans countered by arguing that "tariff tinkering" would only unsettle prosperous industries, drive down wages, and shrink the farmers' home market. Benjamin Harrison, who supported the tariff, captured the White House in 1888. Cleveland won the popular vote by less than 1 percent, but Harrison carried all the northern and western states except Connecticut and New Jersey, winning 233 electoral votes to Cleveland's 168.

Back in office, the Republicans demonstrated their new commitment to economics over ideology by abandoning their support for freed slaves at the same time that they curried favor with the new industrialists. Senator Henry Cabot Lodge's Force Bill, a federal election law to restore the vote to African Americans in the South, died in the same Republican Congress that passed the highest tariff in the nation's history in 1890. The new tariff sponsored by representative William McKinley of Ohio stirred a hornet's nest of protest. The American people had elected Harrison to preserve protection, not to enact a higher tariff. The McKinley tariff set about solving the vexing problem of too much revenue by raising duties so high that foreign producers no longer wanted to sell their goods to Americans. Democrats condemned the McKinley tariff and labeled the Republican Congress that passed it the "Billion Dollar Congress" for its carnival of spending. The Fifty-first Congress earned its title by spending the nation's surplus on a series of "pork barrel" programs—legislation shamelessly designed to bring federal money to their constituents. In their haste to spend the federal surplus, members of Congress passed a series of giveaways, from veterans' pensions to public works. In the congressional election of 1890, angry voters swept the hapless Republicans, including tariff sponsor McKinley, out of office. Two years later, Harrison himself was defeated as Grover Cleveland, whose call for tariff revision had lost him the election in 1888, triumphantly returned to the White House vowing to lower the tariff. Such were the changes in the political winds whipped up by the tariff issue.

The Railroads, the Trusts, and the Federal Government

American voters may have divided on the tariff, but increasingly they agreed on the need for federal regulation of the railroads and federal legislation against the trusts. As early as the 1870s, angry farmers had organized to attack the railroads. The Patrons of Husbandry, or the Grange, founded in 1867 as a social and educational organization for farmers, soon became politicized. Grangers launched an independent political movement to do something about the high rates and unfair practices of the railroads. By electing Grangers to state office, farmers made it possible for several midwestern states to pass laws regulating the railroads. At first the Supreme Court upheld their right to do so. In *Munn v. Illinois* (1877), the Court ruled in favor of regulation. But in 1886, the Supreme Court reversed itself in the *Wabash* case (*Wabash, St. Louis, and Pacific Railway Co. v. Illinois*) and ruled that because railroads

VOL. XLI. No. 1044.   PUCK BUILDING, New York, March 10th, 1897.   PRICE TEN CENTS.

Puck

IN THE HANDS OF HIS PHILANTHROPIC FRIENDS.

**THE CORRUPTION OF GOVERNMENT
BY BIG BUSINESS**

In this Puck *cartoon, a gullible Uncle Sam is being led by
trusts and monopolies, satirically styled as "his philanthropic friends." Concern over the power of big business
led in 1890 to the passage of the Sherman Antitrust Act,
the first attempt to regulate business by making it illegal
to restrict competition.*

Picture Research Consultants & Archives.

crossed state boundaries, they fell outside state jurisdiction. With more than three-fourths of railroads
crossing state lines, the Supreme Court's decision
effectively quashed railroad regulation.

Anger over the Supreme Court decision finally
led to the passage of the first federal law to regulate the railroads, the Interstate Commerce Act,
passed in 1887 during Cleveland's first administration. The act established the nation's first federal
regulatory agency, the Interstate Commerce Commission (ICC). Belatedly, the federal government
used powers granted under the Constitution's interstate commerce clause to bring about railroad

regulation. In its early years, the ICC was never
strong enough or sure enough of what it should do
to pose a serious threat to the railroads. It proved
more important as a precedent than effective as a
watchdog.

Concern over the growing power of the trusts
led the federal government to pass the Sherman Antitrust Act in 1890. By then a consensus had emerged
favoring the regulation of business if it could be accomplished without hurting the economy. The Sherman Act allowed bigness but struck at the trusts.
Businesses could no longer enter into agreements to
restrict competition. The law outlawed pools and
trusts but did nothing to prohibit huge holding
companies like Standard Oil, since a holding company, no matter how big, was one entity and not an
agreement among separate businesses to set prices
or restrict trade.

The Sherman Act proved to be a weak sword
against the trusts. In the decade after its passage,
the government successfully struck down only six
trusts. However, the law was used four times
against labor by outlawing unions as a "conspiracy
in restraint of trade." In 1895, the Supreme Court
dealt the law a crippling blow in the *E. C. Knight*
case. The Court drastically narrowed the law by allowing the American Sugar Refining Company,
which controlled 98 percent of the production of
sugar, to continue its virtual monopoly on the
grounds that *manufacture* did not constitute *trade*.

Both the Interstate Commerce Commission and
the Sherman Antitrust Act testified to the nation's
concern about the abuses of big business and to a
growing willingness to use federal power to intervene on behalf of the public interest. Not until the
twentieth century would more active presidents
sharpen and use these weapons against the large
corporations.

The Fight for Free Silver

Although the trusts stirred up a good deal of public outrage, the most potent political issue to emerge
in the 1880s had to do with the currency. During the
Civil War, the Union printed greenbacks (paper
money), which provided funds for the war effort
and incidentally contributed to inflation since the
dollars were not backed with gold or silver. Debtors,
who could pay back their loans with the devalued
dollars, liked inflation; creditors of course opposed
it. Because many debtors were farmers in the West
and South and many creditors were investors and

bankers in the Northeast, the issue of inflation versus deflation in its many forms—greenbacks versus hard money and later gold versus silver—fostered a new sectionalism, this time with the West joining forces with the South to challenge the dominance of the Northeast.

In the 1870s, supporters of cheap money launched the Greenback Labor Party, arguing that the nation needed an expanding monetary system to keep up with population growth and commercial expansion. Greenbacks, their supporters insisted, were "the people's currency, elastic, cheap, and exportable, based on the entire wealth of the country." But in 1879, Congress supported creditors over debtors by voting to resume the gold standard, tying the nation's currency to its gold reserves. The Greenback Labor Party responded by running General James B. Weaver for president in 1880. Despite the broad appeal of inflation among southern and midwestern farmers, voters below the Mason-Dixon line could not bring themselves to cast their ballots for a former Union general, and the party fell apart.

In the 1880s, the currency problem refused to go away. After the nation returned to the gold standard in 1879, money became even tighter. By the 1890s, the call for easier money and credit resurfaced, this time in the demand not for greenbacks but for silver.

The silver issue stirred passions like no other issue of the day. On one side stood those who believed that gold constituted the only honest money. Many, but not all, were eastern creditors who did not wish to be paid in devalued dollars. On the opposite side stood the silver mining interests, whose stake in the battle was clear. The silver bonanza in the West in the 1860s and 1870s led to a flood of metal on the market, which drove down the price of silver. Mining states such as Nevada and Colorado wanted the government to buy silver and mint silver dollars to help jack up the price.

The appeal of silver extended well beyond the Rocky Mountain states. Allied with the silver interests for very different reasons were farmers from the West and South who had suffered economically during the 1870s and 1880s and who saw in silver an all-purpose solution to their problems. A grinding cycle of debt and deflation had left the farmers in desperate need of relief. "The farmer pays his debts with his labor," observed a Kansas newspaper editor in 1891. "His crops cost him as much labor now as in 1870, but he receives only from one-

fourth to one-half as much for them." The farmers hoped that increasing the money supply with silver dollars would give them some relief.

Advocates of silver pointed out that until 1873 the country had enjoyed a system of bimetallism, with both silver and gold minted into coins. In that year, Congress had demonetized (stopped buying and minting) silver, an act advocates of bimetallism denounced as the "crime of '73." They later branded it a conspiracy to limit the money in circulation and place the West and South at the mercy of eastern financiers. In 1878, Congress took steps to appease advocates of silver by passing the Bland-Allison Act over President Hayes's veto. The measure required the government to buy silver and issue silver certificates. The Bland-Allison Act helped mine owners, who now had a buyer for their ore, but it had little inflationary impact.

Pressures for inflation continued, but the silver advocates were unable to make any headway until 1890, when in return for their support of the McKinley tariff, Congress passed the Sherman Silver Purchase Act, increasing the amount of silver the government bought. Once again, the measure failed to produce the desired inflationary effect, and advocates began to call for "the free and unlimited coinage of silver," a plan whereby virtually all the silver that was mined would be minted into silver coins circulated at the rate of sixteen ounces of silver to one ounce of gold.

The silver issue crossed party lines, but the Democrats hoped to use it to achieve a union between western and southern voters. Unfortunately, Democratic President Grover Cleveland, a conservative in money matters, sat in the White House, where he supported the gold standard with his usual stubbornness. Overlooking the crying need for depression relief, he called a special session of Congress in August 1893 and bullied the legislature into repealing the Sherman Silver Purchase Act. Repeal did not produce recovery or save the gold reserves. But it did divide the country, making the Mississippi River for a time as potent a political boundary as the Mason-Dixon line. Angry farmers warned Cleveland not to travel west of the river if he valued his life.

As their economic plight worsened after the panic of 1893 touched off a deep economic depression, farmers increasingly talked of a conspiracy of eastern financial interests, or "gold bugs." A Nebraska newspaper adopted the rhetoric of class warfare, charging, "The conflict between the common people and the overbearing, despotic, insulting monied aristocracy, who have set themselves up as our dictators, is inevitable."

In the winter of 1894–95, Cleveland aggravated the already highly charged political climate by his deal with J. P. Morgan to save the country's gold reserves. The Morgan bond sale underscored the government's ties to the great money men. By the 1890s, the United States faced a crisis. Agrarian discontent, labor unrest, depression, unemployment—problems that were not only economic but also social and political—cried out for solutions. In the grim darkness of the winter of 1894–95, men and women talked of revolution, some of them in fear and some of them in anger.

Conclusion: Mark Twain and the Gilded Age

Mark Twain, humorist, author, and one of the shrewdist critics of his era, called the period following Reconstruction the "Gilded Age." He chose this title to ridicule the ugliness, crass materialism, and sham of a time when glitter on the outside masked what lay beneath.

The Gilded Age seemed to tarnish all who touched it. No one knew that better than Twain, who, even as he attacked it as an "era of incredible rottenness," fell prey to its enticements. Born Samuel Langhorne Clemens in a rough Mississippi river town, he first became a riverboat pilot. Taking the pen name Mark Twain, he gained fame as the chronicler of California's gold rush. Twain came east in 1866 to launch a career as an author and itinerant humorist. He played to packed houses, but his work was judged too vulgar for the genteel tastes of the time because he wrote about common people and used common language. *The Adventures of Huckleberry Finn*, his masterpiece of American realistic fiction, was banned in Boston when it appeared in 1884.

Huck Finn's creator eventually stormed the citadels of polite society, hobnobbing with the wealthy and living in increasingly expensive and elegant style. He built an ornate Victorian mansion in Hartford, Connecticut, and maintained a townhouse off Fifth Avenue in New York City. Succumbing without much struggle to the money fever of his age, Twain plunged into one scheme after an-

MARK TWAIN
Popular author Mark Twain (Samuel Langhorne Clemens) wrote acerbically about the excesses of the Gilded Age. No one knew the meretricious lure of the era better than Twain, who succumbed to a get-rich-quick scheme that left him virtually bankrupt.
Beinecke Rare Book and Manuscript Library, Yale University.

other in the hope of making millions. The Paige typesetting machine proved his downfall. This elaborate invention (it had more than eighteen thousand parts) promised to mechanize typesetting, replacing human labor with machine. The idea was a good one —Ottmar Mergenthaler soon patented the Linotype and made a fortune. But Paige's elaborate invention proved much too complicated and temperamental to be practical. By the 1890s, Twain faced bankruptcy. Only the help of Standard Oil millionaire Henry H. Rogers enabled him to begin his dogged climb out of debt. Twain's fall from fortune constituted a tale told over and over again in an age when the promise of wealth led as many to ruin as to riches.

A child of his age, Twain knew intimately the

allure of money and power and the giddy rise and fall of fortune. His indictment of his times was not the detached disdain of an observer, but the bitter recognition of a man deeply mired in the gaudy, meretricious lure of the era he named the "Gilded Age."

Mark Twain's label the "Gilded Age" has stood for more than a century as a fair representation of an era when political corruption strutted with the haughty arrogance of a Conkling and industrialists like William Vanderbilt cried, "The public be damned!" But if the age spawned greed, corruption, and vulgarity on a grand scale, it was not without its share of solid achievements. In these years, America made the leap into the industrial age. Factories and mills poured out American goods in unprecedented numbers. Where dusty roads and cattle trails once sprawled across the continent, steel rails now bound together a nation. Cities grew from the ground into the sky. In New York City, the Brooklyn Bridge spanned the East River with steel and stone, more strikingly beautiful than all the showy mansions on Fifth Avenue. In the offices and boardrooms of business, men like Rockefeller, Carnegie, and Morgan consolidated American industry. By the end of the century, the country had achieved industrial maturity. No other era in the nation's history witnessed such a transformation.

It remained to be seen whether the nation could curb the vast power of the industrialists and work to solve the social and economic problems accompanying industrialization.

CHRONOLOGY

1869 Completion of first transcontinental railroad.

1870 John D. Rockefeller incorporates Standard Oil Company in Cleveland.

1872 Andrew Carnegie builds largest Bessemer process steel plant near Pittsburgh.

1873 U.S. government decides to stop minting silver dollars.

Panic on Wall Street leads to major economic depression.

1874 Pennsylvania Railroad capitalized at $400 and employing 55,000; largest private enterprise in the world.

1876 Alexander Graham Bell demonstrates telephone at Philadelphia Centennial Exposition.

1877 Rutherford B. Hayes sworn in as president of United States after disputed election.

U.S. Supreme Court upholds right of states to regulate railroads in *Munn v. Illinois*.

1879 Congress votes to resume the gold standard.

Thomas Alva Edison perfects filament for incandescent lightbulb.

1880s Jay Gould becomes architect of a transcontinental railway system.

Gustavus Swift revolutionizes meatpacking with refrigerated railway cars to transport meat east.

H. J. Heinz pioneers mass production and distribution of his fifty-seven varieties of condiments.

1880 Greenback Labor Party runs General James B. Weaver for president.

Dark horse Republican candidate James A. Garfield elected president of United States.

1881 President Garfield assassinated by Charles Guiteau; Vice President Chester A. Arthur becomes president.

1882 Standard Oil develops the trust.

1883 Congress passes Pendleton Act establishing civil service reform.

1884 Grover Cleveland wins presidency, first Democrat to serve since before the Civil War.

Mark Twain's *Huckleberry Finn* published and subsequently banned in Boston.

1886 In *Wabash* case, U.S. Supreme Court reverses itself and disallows state regulation of railroads that cross state lines.

1887 Congress passes Interstate Commerce Act, first federal law to regulate railroads.

1888 Benjamin Harrison elected president of United States.

1889 Standard Oil reorganizes into holding company.

1890 Congress passes McKinley tariff and Sherman Siver Purchase Act.

Congress passes Sherman Antitrust Act.

1892 Grover Cleveland elected to second term as president.

J. P. Morgan consolidates electric industry, creating the General Electric Company.

1893 Panic devastates financial markets and touches off national depression.

1895 J. P. Morgan bails out U.S. Treasury and saves country's gold reserves.

1901 J. P. Morgan buys out Carnegie Steel and creates U.S. Steel, first billion-dollar corporation in United States.

BIBLIOGRAPHY

GENERAL WORKS

Sean Dennis Cashman, *America in the Gilded Age* (1984).

Alfred Chandler Jr., *The Visible Hand: The Managerial Revolution in American Business* (1977).

Alan Dawley, *Struggles for Justice: Social Responsibility and the Liberal State* (1991).

Vincent P. DeSantis, *The Shaping of Modern America, 1877–1920* (2nd ed., 1989).

Sidney Fine, *Laissez Faire and the General Welfare State: A Study of Conflict in American Thought, 1865–1914* (1956).

John A. Garraty, *The New Commonwealth, 1877–1890* (1968).

Ray Ginger, *The Age of Excess* (1963).

Samuel P. Hays, *The Response to Industrialism, 1885–1914* (1957).

Edward C. Kirkland, *Industry Comes of Age: Business, Labor, and Public Policy, 1860–1897* (1967).

Nell Irwin Painter, *Standing at Armageddon: The United States, 1877–1919* (1987).

Alan Trachtenberg, *The Incorporation of America: Culture and Society in the Gilded Age* (1982).

Robert Wiebe, *The Search for Order, 1877–1920* (1967).

BUSINESS

Robert Bannister, *Social Darwinism* (1979).

John Brooks, *Telephone: The First Hundred Years* (1976).

Travis Brown, *Historical First Patents* (1994).

W. Elliott Brownlee, *Dynamics of Ascent: A History of the American Economy* (rev. ed., 1979).

Robert V. Bruce, *Alexander Graham Bell and the Conquest of Solitude* (1973).

Stuart Bruchey, *Growth of the Modern American Economy* (1975).

Vincent P. Carosso, *The Morgans: Private International Bankers, 1854–1913* (1987).

John G. Cawelti, *Apostles of the Self-Made Man: Changing Concepts of Success in America* (1965).

Alfred D. Chandler Jr., *The Railroads, the Nation's First Big Business: Sources and Readings* (1965).

Alfred D. Chandler Jr., *Scale and Scope: The Dynamics of Industrial Capitalism* (1990).

Ron Chernow, *The House of Morgan* (1990).

Peter Collier and David Horowitz, *The Rockefellers: An American Dynasty* (1976).

Robert Fogel, *Railroads in American Economic Growth* (1964).

Edwin Gabler, *The American Telegrapher: A Social History, 1860–1900* (1988).

Louis Galambos, *The Public Image of Big Business in America, 1880–1940: A Quantitative Study in Social Change* (1974).

Robert W. Garnet, *The Telephone Enterprise* (1985).

Ellen Gruber Garvey, *The Adman in the Parlor, Magazines and the Gendering of American Culture* (1996).

Robert B. Gordon, *American Iron, 1607–1900* (1996).

Julius Grodinsky, *Jay Gould, 1867–1892* (1957).

David Freeman Hawke, *John D.: The Founding Father of the Rockefellers* (1980).

Robert L. Heilbroner, with Aaron Singer, *The Economic Transformation of America* (1977).

Morton J. Horowitz, *The Transformation of American Law, 1870–1960* (1992).

David H. Howard, *People, Pride, and Progress: 125 Years of the Grange in America* (1992).

Jonathan Hughes, *The Vital Few: The Entrepreneur and American Economic Progress* (1965; expanded ed., 1986).

John Ingham, *Making Iron and Steel: Independent Mills in Pittsburgh, 1820–1920* (1991).

Matthew Josephson, *The Robber Barons: The Great American Capitalists, 1861–1901* (1934).

Matthew Josephson, *Edison* (1959).

Justin Kaplan, *Mr. Clemens and Mark Twain* (1966).

John F. Kasson, *Civilizing the Machine* (1976).

Edward Chase Kirkland, *Dream and Thought in the Business Community, 1860–1900* (1956).

Maury Klein, *The Life and Legend of Jay Gould* (1987).

Maury Klein, *Union Pacific* (1987).

James T. Kloppenberg, *Uncertain Victory: Social Democracy and Progressivism in European and American Thought, 1870–1920* (1986).

Harold C. Livesay, *Andrew Carnegie and the Rise of Big Business* (1975).

Albro Martin, *Railroads Triumphant: The Growth, Rejection, and Rebirth of a Vital American Force* (1992).

Carolyn Marvin, *When Old Technologies Were New* (1988).

Andre Millard, *Edison and the Business of Innovation* (1990).

Ralph L. Nelson, *Merger Movements in American Industry, 1895–1956* (1959).

Allan Nevins, *Grover Cleveland: A Study in Courage* (1933).

Allan Nevins, *John D. Rockefeller: The Heroic Age of American Enterprise*, vol. 1 (1940); vol. 2 (1941).

James D. Norris, *Advertising and the Transformation of American Society, 1865–1920* (1990).

Douglass C. North, *Growth and Welfare in the American Past* (1966).

Richard O'Connor, *Gould's Millions* (1962).

Glenn Porter, *The Rise of Big Business, 1860–1910* (1973).

Andrew Sinclair, *Corsair: The Life of J. Pierpont Morgan* (1980).

William Graham Sumner, *What Social Classes Owe to Each Other* (1883; reprint, 1973).

George Rogers Taylor and Irene D. Neu, *The American Railroad Network, 1861–1890* (1956).

Peter Temin, *Iron and Steel in Nineteenth-Century America* (1964).

Joseph Frazier Wall, *Andrew Carnegie* (1970).

James A. Ward, *Railroads and the Character of America, 1820–1887* (1986).

John Hoyt Williams, *The Great and Shining Road: The Epic Story of the Transcontinental Railroad* (1988).

Oliver Zunz, *Making America Corporate, 1870–1920* (1990).

POLITICS

Paula Baker, *The Moral Frameworks of Public Life: Gender, Politics, and the State in Rural New York, 1870–1930* (1991).

Geoffrey Blodgett, *The Gentle Reformers* (1966).

Kenneth Davison, *The Presidency of Rutherford B. Hayes* (1972).

John M. Dobson, *Politics in the Gilded Age: A New Perspective on Reform* (1972).

Justus D. Doenecke, *The Presidencies of James A. Garfield and Chester A. Arthur* (1981).

Richard J. Ellis, *American Political Cultures* (1993).

Lewis L. Gould, *William McKinley: A Biography* (1988).

Ari Hoogenboom, *Outlawing the Spoils: The Civil Service Reform Movement, 1865–1883* (1961).

Ari Hoogenboom, *The Presidency of Rutherford B. Hayes* (1988).

Matthew Josephson, *The Politicos, 1865–1896* (1938).

Paul Kleppner, *The Cross of Culture: A Social Analysis of Midwestern Politics, 1850–1900* (1970).

Robert D. Marcus, *Grand Old Party: Political Structure in the Gilded Age* (1971).

Robert Green McCloskey, *American Conservatism in the Age of Enterprise, 1865–1910* (1951).

Gerald W. McFarland, *Mugwumps, Morals, and Politics, 1884–1920* (1975).

Michael E. McGerr, *The Decline of Popular Politics: The American North, 1865–1928* (1986).

H. Wayne Morgan, *From Hayes to McKinley: National Party Politics, 1877–1896* (1969).

D. Sven Nordin, *Rich Harvest: A History of the Grange, 1867–1900* (1974).

Arnold M. Paul, *Conservative Crisis and the Rule of Law: Attitudes of Bar and Bench, 1887 to 1895* (1969).

David J. Rothman, *Politics and Power: The United States Senate, 1869–1901* (1966).

Mary Ryan, *Women in Public: Between Banners and Ballots, 1825–1880* (1990).

Homer E. Socolofsky and Allan B. Spetter, *The Presidency of Benjamin Harrison* (1987).

John Sproat, *The Best Men: Liberal Reformers in the Gilded Age* (1968).

John Tomsich, *A Genteel Endeavor: American Culture and Politics in the Gilded Age* (1971).

Rexford Tugwell, *Grover Cleveland* (1968).

Irwin Unger, *The Greenback Era: A Social and Political History of American Finance* (1964).

Allen Weinstein, *Prelude to Populism: Origins of the Silver Issue, 1867–1878* (1970).

Richard E. Welch, *The Presidencies of Grover Cleveland* (1988).

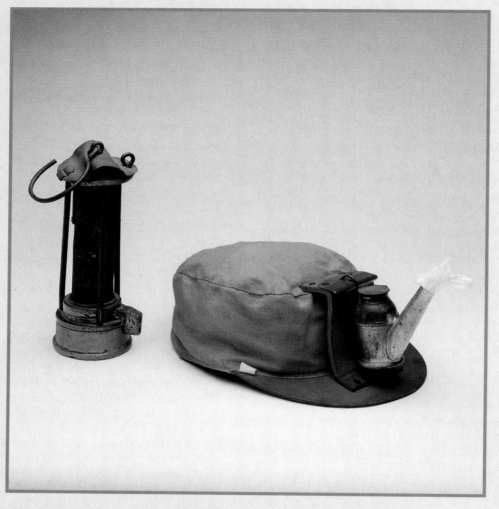

MINER'S SAFETY LAMP AND CANVAS CAP WITH OIL LAMP

This lamp and cap were used by coal miners in Pennsylvania in the mid to late nineteenth century. The oil-wick lamp, attached to the cap by a hook, was introduced by immigrant miners from Great Britain. The wick was soaked in oil stored inside the lamp and lit the miner's path with a smoky flame. Although these lamps were cheaper and burned longer than the candles they replaced, any open flame presented a serious danger: explosions and fires often resulted when flame came in contact with methane and other underground gases. Falling rock and cave-ins were also common occurrences, but the canvas hat offered little protection. Improvements in safety were implemented gradually. British inventors developed a lamp that enclosed the flame in steel netting to prevent reaction with gases. Because the flame grew higher when exposed to certain gases, the safety lamp (left) did double duty in lighting the miners' way and detecting dangerous gases. After World War I, cloth caps were replaced by hard hats with electric lights.

Pennsylvania Historical and Museum Commission, Bureau of Historic Sites and Museums, Anthracite Museum Complex.

AMERICA THROUGH THE EYES OF THE WORKERS

19

1870–1890

FOR TWO WEEKS DURING THE SUMMER OF 1877, President Rutherford B. Hayes faced an insurrection that was greater than any since the Civil War. Hayes met daily with his cabinet to plan military strategy and sat up late into the night receiving reports from his generals. He dispatched federal troops to nine states, ordered warships to protect the nation's capital, and threatened to declare martial law. Not since the Confederates fired on Fort Sumter had the nation witnessed such an alarm. Who posed this threat to the Republic? Not former rebels or foreign armies, but American workers engaged in the first nationwide labor strike in the country's history.

The summer of 1877 witnessed a spontaneous labor uprising known as the Great Railroad Strike. Economic depression following the panic of 1873 had thrown as many as three million people out of work. Those who were lucky enough to keep their jobs watched as pay cuts eroded their wages until they could no longer feed their families. When a Cincinnati cigar worker with a wife and three children was asked how he lived on $5 a week, he replied, "I don't live. I am literally starving. We get meat once a week, the rest of the week we have dry bread and black coffee."

The burden of the depression fell disproportionately on the backs of the country's working class. Corporations tried to economize by laying off workers and cutting wages so that the corporations could continue to pay dividends to their investors. When the Baltimore and Ohio (B&O) Railroad announced a 10 percent wage reduction in the same week that the company declared a 10 percent dividend to its stockholders, the brakemen in West Virginia, whose wages had already fallen from $70 to $30 a month, walked out on strike. One B&O worker described the hardship that had driven him to take such desperate action: "We eat our hard bread and tainted meat two days old on the sooty cars up the road, and when we come home, find our children gnawing bones and our wives complaining that they cannot even buy hominy and molasses for food."

The strike by brakemen in West Virginia touched off a nationwide uprising that spread rapidly, to Chicago and St. Louis, Kansas City and San Francisco. Within a few days, nearly 100,000 railroad workers went out on strike. The spark of rebellion soon fired other workers to action. An estimated 500,000 joined the striking train workers. Violence erupted as the strikers clashed with state militia. President Hayes, after hesitating briefly, called up federal troops. In three weeks it was over.

"The strikes have been put down by *force*," Hayes noted in his diary on August 5. "But now for the real remedy. Can't something be done by education of the strikers, by judicious control of the capitalists, by wise general policy to end or diminish the evil? The railroad strikers, as a rule, are good men, sober, intelligent, and industrious."

The uprising of the workers in 1877 underscored the tensions produced by rapid industrialization and pointed to many legitimate grievances on the part of labor. The explosion of industrial growth that occurred after the Civil War came about as a result of the labor of millions of men, women, and children who toiled in workshops and factories, in sweatshops and mines, on the railroads and on construction sites across America. Their stories provide a different perspective from that of the great industrialists and the politicians. Through their eyes it is possible to gauge how corporate capitalism transformed old work patterns and affected the social as well as the economic and political life of the United States.

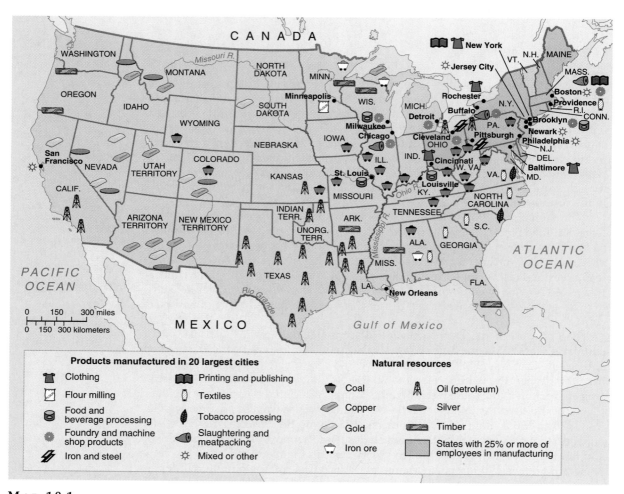

MAP 19.1

Industrialization, 1865–1900

Industrial development between 1865 and 1900 shows the clustering of industry in the Northeast and Great Lakes states. Only in these regions did industry employ 25 percent or more of the region's labor force. The West supplied raw materials — oil, minerals, and timber, while in the South and the Midwest agriculture and attendant industries such as tobacco processing and meatpacking dominated. Note, however, the movement of textile manufacturing from the Northeast to the South.

What were the lives of America's workers—white collar as well as blue collar—like? Who were they, and where did they come from? What did they do to earn their bread? Increasing business consolidation in the late nineteenth century had a significant impact on workers' lives. American society was profoundly reshaped by new corporate structures. As businesses consolidated and large corporations replaced partnerships and small proprietorships, work took on an increasingly impersonal quality. Traditional ideas about equal competition and the independence of employees broke down when the boss became a faceless corporation. Increasingly, workers tried to better their bargaining position by taking collective action. President Hayes's "sober, intelligent, and industrious" workers not only precipitated the uprising in 1877 but also stimulated the organization of nationwide labor unions to fight for the right to bargain collectively for better working conditions, shorter hours, and higher pay. Concern about the growing labor unrest led many comfortable, middle-class Americans to ask what could be done to curb the worst excesses of exploitation and inequity that accompanied corporate capitalism.

America's New Industrial Workers

America's industrial growth in the years following the Civil War brought about a massive redistribution of the country's population as agricultural workers moved to the city and became recruits in the industrial labor force. Burgeoning industrial centers such as Pittsburgh, Chicago, New York, and Detroit acted like giant magnets, attracting workers from the countryside.

The movement from the rural periphery to industrial centers was not just American in its scope. Farm boys and girls from western Pennsylvania who left for the mills of Pittsburgh were part of a global migration that included rural immigrants from Ireland, southern Italy, Russia, Japan, and China. As labor historian David Montgomery has pointed out, "the rural periphery of the nineteenth century industrial world became the primary source of supply for 'human machines.'"

The great diversity of American workers made it difficult for them to achieve solidarity. Differences in language, religion, ethnicity, and race raised powerful barriers that workers had to struggle to overcome if they wished to act collectively. Often forced to put their children in the mines and factories, to take in boarders, or to rely on women's paid work when one paycheck did not spell survival, the working class by the end of the century increasingly took action, whether through strikes, politics, or union organizing, to achieve a better life.

Workers from the Rural Periphery

By the 1870s, the world could be viewed as being divided into three interlocking geographic regions forming roughly concentric circles. At the center stood an industrial core bounded by Chicago and St. Louis in the West; Toronto, Glasgow, and Berlin in the North; Warsaw in the East; and Milan, Barcelona, Richmond, and Louisville in the South.

The ability to draw on cheap labor on a global scale helps explain why, in spite of the soaring demand for laborers after the Civil War, the wages of unskilled workers in the United States remained relatively stagnant.

Surrounding the industrial core and its urban outposts lay a vast agricultural domain encompassing Canada, much of Scandinavia, Russia and Poland, Hungary, Greece, Italy and Sicily, southern Spain, the defeated Confederate States and the Great Plains of America, central and northern Mexico, the hinterlands of Canton, China, and later the southern islands of Japan. (See Map 19.2, page 728.) Capitalist development in the late nineteenth century shattered traditional patterns of economic activity in this rural periphery. As old patterns broke down, the rural areas exported, along with other raw materials, new recruits for the industrial labor force.

Beyond this second circle lay an even larger "third world" including the Caribbean, Central and South America, the Middle East, Africa, India, and most of Asia. This area too became increasingly tied to the industrial core in the late nineteenth century, but its peoples largely stayed put. They worked on the plantations and railroads, in the mines and ports as part of a huge export network managed by foreign powers that staked out spheres of influence and colonies, often with gunboats and soldiers.

Beginning in the 1870s, railroad building and low steamship fares gave the world's peoples a newfound mobility that enabled industrialists to draw on a worldwide population for cheap labor.

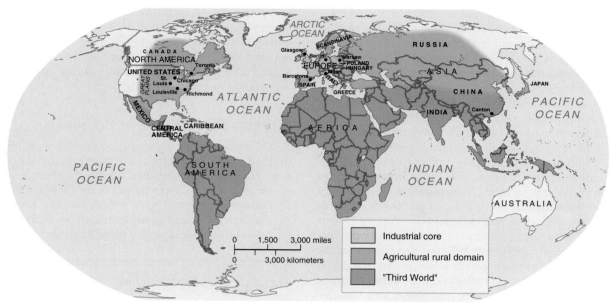

MAP 19.2
Economic Regions of the World
The global nature of the world economy at the turn of the century is indicated by three interlocking geographic regions. At the center was the industrial core —Western Europe and the northeastern United States; the agricultural rural periphery (rural domain) supplied immigrant laborers to the industries in the core. Beyond these regions lay a "Third World" tied economically to the industrial core by colonialism.

The Carnegie steel mills outside of Pittsburgh provide a good example. When Andrew Carnegie opened his first mill in 1872, Captain Billy Jones, his superintendent, hired workers for the blast furnaces from the Pennsylvania countryside. Jones's favorite workers were what he called "buckwheats"—young American boys just off the farm. By the 1890s, however, Carnegie's workforce was liberally sprinkled with other rural boys—Hungarians and Slavs who had migrated to the United States, willing to work for low wages.

The ability to draw on cheap labor on a global scale helps explain why, in spite of the soaring demand for laborers after the Civil War, the wages of unskilled workers in the United States remained relatively stagnant. Their pay fell dramatically during the depressions of 1873–1878 and 1893–1896 and did not regain 1872 levels before the end of the century.

Immigration, Ethnic Rivalry, and Racism

Ethnic diversity played a role in dividing skilled workers (those with a craft or specialized ability) from the unskilled (those who supplied muscle and brawn). As managers increasingly mechanized to replace skilled craftsworkers with lower-paid, unskilled labor, they played on ethnic prejudices to pit workers against each other. Carnegie's manager Henry Clay Frick hired Hungarians and Slavs as strikebreakers in the Pennsylvania coal fields in 1884, and when they went on strike six years later, he brought in Italians. With the bulk of the new, unskilled industrial laborers coming from southern and eastern Europe after 1880, the skilled workers, most of whom came from northern or western Europe, found it easy to criticize the newcomers. As one Irish worker complained, "There should be a law . . . to keep all the I-talians from comin' in and takin' the bread out of the mouths of honest people."

The Irish worker's resentment of the new Italian immigrants brings into focus the importance of the ideology and practice of racism in the experience of America's immigrant laborers. Throughout the nineteenth century, ethnic and even religious differences were perceived as *racial* characteristics. Members of the educated elite as well as workers spoke of the Polish "race" or the Jewish "race" in uncomplimentary terms. Each wave of newcomers was perceived as being somehow inferior to the

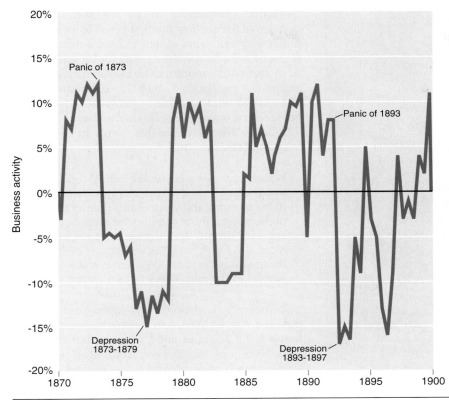

FIGURE 19.1
The U.S. Business Cycle,
1870–1890
The overall economy grew be-
tween 1865 and 1900, but the
growth was not steady. The
business cycle resembles a wild
roller coaster ride; deep troughs
represent major depressions —
one following the panic of
1873 and another following
the panic of 1893. The period
from 1882–1885 witnessed a
drop nearly as severe. During
these downward spirals tens of
thousands of Americans faced
unemployment and economic
hardship.

established residents. The Irish who judged the Italians so harshly had themselves been seen as a subhuman species just a generation before. But it is not surprising that immigrants, who brought their own religious and racial prejudices to this country, also absorbed the popular prejudices of American culture. Social Darwinism, with its strongly racist overtones, decreed that whites stood at the top of the evolutionary ladder. But who was "white"? The social construction of race is nowhere more apparent than in the testimony of an Irish dockworker, who boasted that he hired only "white men" to load cargo, a category that he insisted excluded "Poles and Italians."

Racism took its most blatant form in the treatment of African Americans and Asians. Like other migrants from the rural periphery, African American men in the South, former slaves and the children of slaves, found work as human machines. The labor gang system that was used in many industries reached its most extreme and brutal form in the South. There the convict lease system allowed private employers to contract prison labor, mostly African Americans jailed for such minor "crimes" as vagrancy. Shackled together by chains as they

worked under the watchful eyes of armed guards, these workers formed the bottom rung on labor's ladder. A Georgia man who escaped the brutal chain gang system remarked, "Call it slavery, peonage, or what not, the truth is we lived in a hell on earth."

The racism encountered by Asian immigrants in the western United States took a somewhat different form from that experienced by either European immigrants or black laborers. The Chinese and later the Japanese were vigorously attacked as the "tools of corporate interest" recruited by the bosses to undercut wages and threaten "white society." On the West Coast especially, Asian immigrants became the scapegoats of the changing economy. Politicians, newspaper publishers, preachers, labor leaders, and the general populace attacked Asians as "heathens," claiming that they jeopardized the whole fabric of economic opportunity and small enterprise. The labor movement itself played a key role in the struggle to exclude Asians from American life. Labor unions practiced exclusionary policies against both Chinese and Japanese workers and championed the 1882 Chinese Exclusion Act, which prohibited the immigration of Chinese nationals to the United States.

VOL. 13 NO. 330   FEBRUARY 11, 1888.   PRICE 10 CENTS.

Judge

SUPPLY AND DEMAND—SHALL IMMIGRATION BE RESTRICTED?
EMPLOYER—"As long as I am plentifully supplied with Immigrant Labor, I shall be deaf to the demands of the native workingmen."

THE COMPETITION OF CHEAP LABOR
Big business looks on approvingly as cheap immigrant labor outweighs American workers in this political cartoon published in the weekly Judge *in 1888. "As long as I am plentifully supplied with immigrant labor," says the portly manufacturer, "I shall be deaf to the demands of the native workingmen." Cartoons like this one underscored organized labor's concern with the number of foreign workers entering the country in the 1880s — nearly eight million, twice the number of the previous decade. Not only did the seemingly unlimited supply of immigrant laborers keep wages low, but the new recruits, who knew nothing of labor's struggles, often took work as strikebreakers.*
Judge, February 11, 1888.

The Family Economy: Women and Children

Many working-class families, whether native-born or immigrant, lived in poverty or near poverty. Family economic survival depended on the contributions of all, regardless of sex or age. In a wage economy, the paid and unpaid work of women and children became essential for family survival and economic advancement.

Rapid mechanization during the last two decades of the century made it possible for children under fourteen years of age to hold a much wider range of jobs. In the mines and textile mills, child labor had been common since midcentury. As other industries mechanized, they hired children, who often could tend machines as efficiently as adults, yet received wages considerably lower.

One worker recalled his youth in the textile mills of Massachusetts:

When I began as a boy in the mill, I worked fifteen hours a day. I used to go in at a quarter past four in the morning and work until a quarter to eight at night, having thirty minutes for breakfast and the same for dinner, drinking tea after ringing out at night. But I took breakfast and dinner in the mill as the time was too short to go home, so I was sixteen hour[s] in the mill. This I did for eleven years. . . .

Attempts to abolish child labor began before the Civil War. By 1863, seven states had passed laws limiting the hours of child workers, but often the laws were not strictly enforced. Most southern states refused to regulate child labor, and children continued to be widely employed in southern mills, some as young as six or seven years old. In the nation's mines, particularly in Appalachia, young boys were recruited to pick out the slate and waste from coal as it passed along chutes. Suspended on wooden boards over the moving coal, these breaker boys engaged in backbreaking, dangerous work. A boy who slipped into the coal had little chance of surviving without serious injury. When a child labor committee investigated conditions in Pennsylvania, it found that more than 10,000 children were illegally employed in the coal fields. Coal mining was not the only dangerous industry that employed children. At the turn of the century, over 98 percent of the 7,000 boys under sixteen years of age employed in America's glass factories worked in the intense heat of the furnace rooms where mortality figures ran high.

Child labor increased decade by decade, with the percentage of children under fifteen engaged in paid labor not dropping until after World War I. The 1900 census showed that 1,750,178 children age ten to fifteen were employed, an increase of more than one million since 1870. Children from ten to fifteen years old constituted over 18 percent of the labor force and 7 percent of all nonagricultural workers in 1900, compared with 1880, when ten-to-fifteen-year-olds constituted 16.8 percent of the total labor force and 6 percent of those employed in nonagricultural work.

Even children who didn't work for wages contributed to the family economy by scavenging firewood and coal for fuel. Gangs of children patrolled the railroad tracks, picking up the coal that fell from the coal cars that fueled the locomotives. Bands of street children roamed the towns and cities, sometimes stealing and breaking windows. Other children worked as street vendors, newsboys, and bootblacks. Although laws in many states mandated school attendance, enforcement proved difficult. Harried truant officers found it hard to collar children whose parents insisted it was their prerogative to put them to work rather than send them to school.

At the turn of the century, women entered the workforce in greater and greater numbers, although they were paid less than men. In the late nineteenth century, the number of women workers rose sharply, with their most common occupation changing slowly from domestic service to factory work and then to office work. The 1870 census listed 1.5 million women working in nonagricultural occupations. By 1900, more than 4.9 million women earned wages, and women constituted 18.8 percent of those employed in manufacturing.

Women's working patterns varied considerably according to race and ethnicity. White married women, even among the working class, rarely worked outside the home. In 1890, only 3 percent of white married women were employed. Nevertheless, many married women found ways to contribute money to the family economy. Families often took in boarders to supplement the family income. In many Italian families, homework, such as artificial flower making, allowed married women to contribute a wage to the family economy without leaving their homes and disrupting the cultural code that dictated that husbands guard the reputations of their wives. Black women, however, married and unmarried, worked for wages outside their homes at a much higher rate than white women. The 1890 census showed that 25 percent of African American married women worked outside the home, often in the houses of white families, where they did cooking and cleaning and child care.

Whatever activity wives and children performed, their contributions were often essential to the family's living. One statistician estimated that

"BREAKER BOYS"
Child labor in America's mines and mills was common at the turn of the century, despite state laws that attempted to restrict it. Here "breaker boys" in the 1890s take a rest from their twelve-hour day in the coal mines of Appalachia. Their unsmiling faces bear testimony to their hard and dangerous work. A committee investigating child labor found more than 10,000 children illegally employed in the Pennsylvania coal fields.
Brown Brothers.

in 1900, as many as 64 percent of working-class families relied on income other than the husbands' wages to make ends meet.

At Work

Throughout the nineteenth century, America's industrial workers toiled in a variety of settings. There were still skilled craftsmen and artisans who worked in small workshops or alone. But with the rise of corporate capitalism, large factories, mills, and mines increasingly dotted the landscape. Sweatshops and outwork, the contracting of piecework performed in the home, provided a different sort of work experience from that of the factory operative (machine tender) or the industrial worker who labored in the mines. Pick and shovel labor, whether on the railroads or in the building trades, constituted another kind of work. The best way to get a sense of the diversity of workers and workplaces is to look at several distinct types of industrial work: common labor, skilled work, factory work, sweatshop labor, and mining.

A Common Laborer

In her book *China Men,* Maxine Hong Kingston tells the story of Ah Goong, one of the *gam saan haak* (travelers to the gold mountain) who came to California in 1863 and went to work for the Central Pacific Railroad building the nation's first transcontinental railroad. Chinese work gangs laid the roadbed from San Francisco over the Sierra Nevada and across the Mojave Desert to Utah. For less than a dollar a day, Ah Goong hung in a basket on the cliffs above the American River, setting black powder in the crevices and firing the fuses to blast a path through the mountains. When the track came to a stop against a difficult stretch in the mountains, he tunneled through the granite with pick and shovel. The railroad experimented with the dangerous explosive nitroglycerine, and Ah Goong set the charges. To earn an extra dollar, he sometimes risked his life to go back into the tunnel to investigate when the highly volatile nitro had not exploded.

Working in the dark tunnel, Ah Goong toiled on eight-hour shifts seven days a week. When the railroad tried to increase the shift to ten hours, Ah Goong and ten thousand of his fellow workers went on strike in 1867. They demanded the same wages paid to the white, mostly Irish gangs, who earned

$40 a month compared with Ah Goong's $30. Construction superintendent Charles Crocker broke the strike, but in the end he raised the wages of the Chinese workers to $35 a month.

Common laborers built the railroads and subways, tunneled under the East River to anchor the Brooklyn Bridge, and helped to lay the foundation of industrial America.

Life was cheap on the Central Pacific. Men died on the cliffs when the ropes to the baskets broke or when the men failed to scramble out of the way before the blast. Men died in the tunnels when the nitroglycerine exploded without warning. The railroad received a subsidy for each mile of track laid, and Crocker worked the men throughout the win-

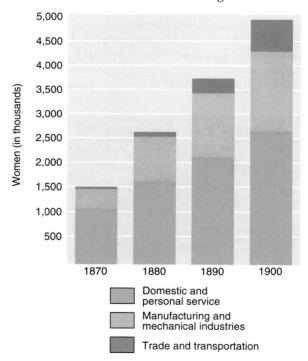

FIGURE 19.2
Women and Work, 1870–1900
In 1870 close to 1.5 million women worked in nonagricultural occupations. By 1900 that number had more than tripled to 4.9 million, with women constituting 18.8 percent of those employed in manufacturing. The total number of women workers rose sharply while the most common occupation changed from domestic work to industry and later to office work.

CHINESE RAILROAD WORKERS
*Chinese workers like this section gang pictured at Promontory Point, Utah, in 1869 made up
more than 80 percent of the workforce that built America's first transcontinental railroad. Charles
Crocker of the Central Pacific hired them, reasoning that the race that built the Great Wall could
build his road across the treacherous Sierra Nevada. Besides, the Chinese workers were a bargain:
Crocker paid them $10 dollars a month less than he paid his Irish section gangs.*
Denver Public Library, Western History Collection, photo by J. B. Silvis.

ters of 1866 and 1867, digging a tunnel through the Donner Summit, that infamous spot where, twenty years earlier, a party of settlers trapped in the snow had resorted to cannibalism to survive. More than forty-four feet of snow fell during the winter of 1867. In the freezing cold, the workers' fingers stuck to the iron rails and snow-blind men stumbled about with bandannas over their eyes. Blasting loosened walls of snow and buried workers alive. In the spring, when the snow melted, the crew uncovered the corpse of one worker, his tools still frozen in his hand.

Ah Goong was one of the lucky ones; he lived to see the Central Pacific reach Promontory Point, Utah, where it joined the Union Pacific to form the first transcontinental railroad in 1869. In the celebration that followed, orators basked in the accom-

plishment of the "greatest monument of human labor" and congratulated themselves that Californians had proved themselves "capable of any achievement." They made no mention of the Chinese although over 80 percent of the workers on the Central Pacific were Chinese. When the photographer took the famous picture of the driving of the golden spike to commemorate the meeting of the two railroads, the Chinese workers, whose prodigious labor had built the railroad, were nowhere in sight.

Common laborers like Ah Goong formed the backbone of the American labor force throughout the century. Although their pick and shovel work had changed little over the centuries, they nevertheless constituted an important part of such major modern industries as steel, railroads, and mining.

Common laborers built the railroads and subways, tunneled under the East River to anchor the Brooklyn Bridge, and helped to lay the foundation of industrial America.

A Skilled Ironworker

At the opposite end of the ladder from common laborers were skilled craftsmen like iron puddler James J. Davis. Davis, a Welsh immigrant boy, went into the iron mills in Sharon, Pennsylvania, at the age of eleven and won the title master puddler by sixteen. He later became a labor organizer and served in Congress and as secretary of labor in the 1920s.

Iron puddlers were an elite among skilled craftsmen. Using brains along with brawn, they took the melted pig iron in the heat of the furnace and, with long poles, formed the cooling metal into two-hundred-pound balls, relying on eye and intuition to make each ball uniform. Davis compared the task to baking bread: "I am like some frantic baker in the inferno kneading a batch of iron bread for the devil's breakfast. My spoon weighs twenty-five pounds, my porridge is pasty iron, and the heat of my kitchen is so great that if my body was not hardened to it, the ordeal would drop me in my tracks."

Possessing such a skill meant earning good wages, up to $7 a day, when there was work. But often no work could be found. Much industry and manufacturing in the nineteenth century remained seasonal; it was a rare worker who could count on year-round pay. In addition, the business cycle, those alternating periods of boom and bust regarded as inevitable by economists, produced two major depressions only twenty years apart, in 1873 and 1893, with accompanying unemployment and hardship. Davis, along with many other skilled workers, tramped the countryside looking for work in the 1890s.

Davis's experience demonstrated that even fiercely independent craftsmen like puddlers had no cushion against catastrophe. Once they could no longer work, whether because of unemployment, illness, or industrial accident, they faced impoverishment. In an era before unemployment insurance, workers' compensation, or old-age pensions, even the best worker could not guarantee security for his family. "The fear of ending in the poor-house is one of the terrors that dog a man through life," Davis confessed.

To protect their livelihood, highly skilled workers like iron puddlers jealously guarded their skill,

passing it from one generation to the next. Davis had to leave the mill at eighteen because his father was not yet ready to retire and turn his furnace over to his son. In the iron industry, puddlers ruled the furnace absolutely, controlling the pace of work, the organization of the job, and the rate of pay. Such worker control posed a challenge to employers, who, as the century wore on, tried as much as possible to limit the workers' autonomy by replacing men with machinery, breaking down skilled work into ever smaller parts, and replacing skilled workers with unskilled operatives who worked for less money at piece rates.

A Factory Operative

The textile mills provide a classic example of mechanized factory labor in the nineteenth century. Mary, a weaver at the mills in Fall River, Massachusetts, told her story to the *Independent* magazine in 1903. She had gone to work in the 1880s at the age of twelve and had begun weaving at fourteen. Mechanization of the looms had reduced the job of the weaver to watching for breaks in the thread. "At first the noise is fierce, and you have to breathe the cotton all the time, but you get used to it," Mary told her interviewer. "When the bobbin flies out and a girl gets hurt, you can't hear her shout—not if she just screams, you can't. She's got to wait, 'till you see her. . . . Lots of us is deaf," she confessed.

The majority of factory operatives were young, unmarried women like Mary. The gendered nature of the work kept pay low and limited chances for advancement.

Because their jobs as machine tenders were easily defined and measured, weavers increasingly received their pay by the piece rather than by the day or hour. Mary worked from six in the morning to six at night, six days a week, and took home about a dollar a day. To increase productivity, managers assigned workers to more looms. Mary complained, "You got so tired drivin' at eight looms, and when they gave us twelve looms I didn't see that we could make out to live at all. It makes you crazy watchin' 'em." The majority of factory operatives were young, unmarried women like Mary. The gendered nature of the work kept pay low and limited chances for advancement. Mary resented the gender division of labor in the mills that made female

TEXTILE MILL WORKER
This woman weaver is typical of factory operatives who worked in New England's textile mills. Young, unmarried women formed the majority of mill workers. The weaver's job was to watch the looms to be sure the threads did not break. The work was both nerve-racking and unhealthy — note the lint on the floor. What can't be seen is the tremendous racket made by the huge machines — so loud that many women lost their hearing.
Courtesy George Eastman House.

workers subject to sexual harassment from male supervisors. "Good lookin' girls get the best chance," Mary acknowledged. "Now there's French Charlie, he's one of the 'supers'—he will take only pretty girls; he takes mostly French girls, too, of course."

During the 1880s, the number of foreign-born mill workers almost doubled. At the Amoskeag mill in New Hampshire, foreign-born workers, many French Canadian, constituted over half the workforce. Ethnic rivalries between the old-stock English and Scots immigrants, like Mary and her family, and the newcomers made organizing difficult. "There's plenty waitin' at the gates for our jobs," Mary complained, using a common derogatory term to identify a rival group. "The Polaks learn weavin' quick, and they just as soon live on nothin' and work like that. But it won't do 'em much good for all they'll make out of it."

The seasonal nature of the work also drove wages down. "Like as not your mill will 'shut down' three months," and "some weeks you only get two or three days' work, when they're curtailin'," Mary recounted. After twenty years of working in the mill, Mary's family had not been able to scrape together enough money to buy a house. "We saved some, but something always comes."

With the growing move toward industry in the South, textile mills spread from New England into states like the Carolinas and Georgia. There, whole families went to work in the mills. But southern mill work remained largely for whites only; black men were hired only for the dirtiest, lowest-paid jobs. Because southern workers would work for less money, many of the textile mills in New England relocated in the twentieth century, often abandoning mills in New England to set up south of the Mason-Dixon line.

A Sweatshop Garment Maker

In the garment industry, the impact of mechanization transformed independent tailors into factory workers. The introduction of the foot-pedaled sewing machine in the 1850s and the use of mechanical cloth-cutting knives in the 1870s mechanized hand tailoring, but, paradoxically, mechanization at the same time revived primitive forms of homework. Particularly in the 1880s, specialization led manufacturers to distribute cut cloth in bundles to contractors, who bid against one another for the work and then hired other workers to help sew together the pieces. Working in sweatshops, small rooms hired for the season or even in the contractor's own tenement, women and children formed an important segment of garment workers.

Sadie Frowne, a sixteen-year-old Polish Jew, went to work in a Brooklyn sweatshop in the 1890s making underskirts. In a room twenty feet long and fourteen feet wide containing fourteen machines, Frowne sewed for eleven hours a day. "The machines go like mad all day, because the faster you work the more money you get," she recalled. She earned about $4.50 a week and, by rigid economy, tried to save $2. As a young, single woman with no family, a "woman adrift" in the common parlance of the time, she had to struggle to support herself. Like many other young women, she relied on her steady boyfriend to treat her to trips to Coney Island and other entertainment. Frowne enjoyed dancing and going out on the town and liked to buy stylish clothes. She justified her extravagance, observing, "A girl who does not dress well is stuck in a corner, even if she is pretty."

The typical woman wage earner in the late nineteenth century was young and single. The largest percentage worked in the needle trades, like Frowne, but factory work ranked a close second. In 1890, the average workingwoman had started to work at age fifteen and was now twenty-two, working twelve hours a day, six days a week, and earning less than $6 a week. These young workingwomen formed a unique subculture, seeking pleasure and autonomy in the "cheap amusements" of their day—dance halls, social clubs, and amusement parks. Their wage earning generally lasted eight to ten years at the most, until they married. Discrimination against women in the marketplace, where they earned less than men, served to reinforce their dependence and make them vulnerable economically and sexually.

An Underground Miner

Metal and coal mining, along with extractive industries such as lumbering, constituted the most hazardous work in the nation. To look closely at conditions in the mines, mills, and forests, in the words of one historian, is to enter a "chamber of horrors." Ross Moudy, a miner in Cripple Creek, Colorado, recounted the dangers he faced, first in a chlorination mill. For nine or ten hours a day, he worked for $1.50 to $2 a day, breathing sulfur dioxide or chlorine fumes and working in dust so thick that "one cannot see an object two feet away." On the advice of the company surgeon (who swore him

to secrecy lest the managers find out), he quit the chlorination mill and went to work in a Cripple Creek gold mine.

The mine, according to Moudy, was "safe," as mines went. The "dangers do not seem so great to a practiced miner, who is used to climbing hundreds of feet on . . . braces put about six feet apart . . . and then walking the same distance on a couple of poles sometimes not larger than fence rails, where a misstep would mean a long drop." When a group of stockholders came to tour the mine, Moudy recounted how one man, white as a ghost after a near fall, told the miner beside him "that instead of being paid $3.00 per day they ought to have all the gold they could take out."

Miners died in explosions, cave-ins, and fires. New technology eliminated some dangers but often added others. Machinery could maim and kill. Dust from machine-powered drills got into miners' lungs and led to serious respiratory illnesses. In the hard-rock mines of the West in the 1870s, accidents annually disabled one out of every thirty miners and killed one in eighty. Those who avoided accidents still breathed air so dangerous that respiratory diseases eventually disabled them.

After a year on the job, Moudy joined the union "because I saw it would help me to keep in work and for protection in case of accident or sickness." The union provided good sick benefits and hired nurses, "so if one is alone and sick he is sure to be taken care of." Moudy acknowledged that there were some "hotheads" in the union, the militant Western Federation of Miners. But he insisted that most union men "believe the change will come about gradually and not by revolution."

Moudy's biggest worry was the "mine gas" (carbon dioxide) that often filled the tunnels because of poor ventilation. "Many times," he confessed, "I have been carried out unconscious and not able to work for two or three days after." When asked how such conditions could exist, he replied, "The mining laws of Colorado are not enforced at all and it is on account of this that so many lives are lost." Moudy counted himself among the lucky ones. "Outside of getting a couple of toes smashed from falling rocks and a crack on the head from a bolt which fell about two hundred feet down the shaft . . . knocking me out for over a week, I got out of the district rather luckily." While still a young man, he quit mining and found work as assistant state chemist for Wyoming.

The conditions that Moudy described were no worse and probably a good deal better than those in other mines. An Appalachian anthracite coal miner, who had gone into the mine at twelve and worked for twenty-three years, confessed, "We get old quickly. Powder, smoke, after-damp, bad air— all combine to bring furrows to our faces and asthma to our lungs." In the 1890s, the miner earned $33 a month, barely enough to cover rent and groceries. Observing that the mine's mules were better fed than the miners, he concluded, "The luxuries of the rich we do not want; we do want butter for our bread and meat for our soup."

American workers lived close to the bone in the late nineteenth century. Although real wages (pay measured in terms of buying power) rose 15 percent between 1873 and 1893, workers did not share equally in the improvement. African American men and women, for example, continued to be paid at a much lower rate than white men, as did immigrant laborers and white women. And the protracted depressions following the panics of 1873 and 1893 undercut many of labor's gains. What most distin-

guished American wages by 1900 from those in industrialized Europe was not simply the higher average wage but rather the striking differential between workers.

Managers and White Collars

The late nineteenth century witnessed the growth of a new managerial class and a burgeoning army of new white-collar workers—those in sales, clerical, and service work. Business expansion and consolidation led to a managerial revolution, creating a need for a new class of managers and for a growing number of clerical and secretarial workers. As skilled workers saw their crafts erode, some moved into management positions as foremen or supervisors. At the same time, new white-collar jobs in department stores and offices attracted a growing number of women workers.

COAL MINERS
Coal miners come up out of the shaft in the "cage" in Scranton, Pennsylvania. As one observer commented, "Although the mines are always cold and wet, yet the labor of drilling and handling the coal is so great that the miner, stripped to his shirt, soon becomes wet with sweat while the dust from the coal is at times almost stifling. The work is thirst-provoking and each miner carries with him a bottle or can, often a quart or more of strong, black coffee for the purpose of washing the dust from his throat."
Picture Research Consultants & Archives.

The New Managerial Class

"The middle class is becoming a salaried class," the *Independent* magazine observed in 1903, "and is rapidly losing the economic and moral independence of former days." For better or for worse, the *Independent* articulated a trend that had begun decades earlier. As large business organizations consolidated and created national markets, they sought to control and rationalize business, replacing what economist Adam Smith had called "the invisible hand" of market forces with the "visible hand" of management. At the same time, corporate development separated management from ownership, and the job of directing the firm became the province of salaried managers and executives. The new managerial class drew its recruits primarily from the ranks of the white middle class; a group of workers who in the past might have started their own businesses now found employment working on salary for big business.

Bureaucracy was invented not by government, but by business. Business consolidation and expansion in the decades after the Civil War, led by the railroads, produced elaborate organizational hierarchies that were designed to bring order to operations and to maximize profits. A new rank of middle managers stood between the executives of a company and its workers. These salaried bureaucrats often regarded labor unions with hostility, seeing in unions a challenge to their right to manage.

The majority of these new middle managers were white men drawn from the 8 percent of the American population who held high school diplomas. In 1880, the middle managers at the Chicago, Burlington, and Quincy Railroad earned between $1,500 and $4,000 a year, while senior executives, generally recruited from the college-educated elite, took home $4,000 or more, and the company's general manager made $15,000 a year.

Not all managers came from the middle class. Some were skilled workers who were able to move into management at the very moment mechanization was eroding the independence of skilled craftsmen. Until late in the century, when engineering schools began to supply recruits, corporations drew on skilled workers trained on the job to provide expertise. As a result, many technical executives rose from the shop floor to positions of considerable responsibility.

The career of Captain William "Billy" Jones provides a glimpse of a skilled ironworker turned manager. Jones, the son of a Welsh immigrant, grew up in the heat of the blast furnaces, where he started working as an apprentice at the age of ten. During the Civil War, he served in the Union army and gained the rank of captain, a title he used for the rest of his life. When Andrew Carnegie opened his steelworks on the outskirts of Pittsburgh in 1872, he hired Jones as his plant superintendent. By all accounts, Jones was the best steel man in the industry. He loved his work and drove himself and his men. "Good wages and good workmen" was his motto. Carnegie constantly tried to force down wages, but Jones fought for his men. In 1881, he succeeded in shortening the shift from twelve to eight hours a day by convincing Carnegie that good labor policy could also mean good business because it would reduce absenteeism and accidents. Jones himself demanded and received a "hell of a big salary." Carnegie paid him $25,000—the same salary as the president of the United States—a stupendous sum in 1881 and one that testified to the value the tightfisted Carnegie placed on his superintendent. Captain Jones did not have long to enjoy his newfound wealth. He died in 1889 when a blast furnace exploded, adding his name to the estimated 35,000 killed each year in industrial accidents.

Office Work and Women "Typewriters"

The expansion and consolidation of business in the decades after the Civil War brought more and more workers into the office. As businesses became larger and more far-flung, the greater volume of correspondence and the need for more elaborate and exact records led to the hiring of more office workers. Mechanization soon transformed business as it had industry and manufacturing. The adding machine, the cash register, and the typewriter came into general use in the 1880s. Employers seeking literate workers soon turned to women, who not only worked for lower wages than men but tended to be better educated than the males available for clerical work. Men had too many other career choices. But for women, secretarial work constituted one of the few areas where they could put their literacy to use for wages. By 1900, they outnumbered men as stenographers and typists.

Sylvie Thygeson was typical of the young women who went to work as secretaries in the 1880s. Thygeson grew up in an Illinois prairie town in a middle-class family that valued education. Her father was a small-town lawyer, and her mother was

CLERICAL WORKER
A stenographer takes dictation in an 1890s office. Note that the apron, a symbol of feminine domesticity, has accompanied the woman into the workplace. In the 1880s, with the invention of the typewriter, many women were able to put their literacy skills to use for wages in the nation's offices.
Brown Brothers.

a woman who took pride in the fact that all eight of her children graduated from high school. When her father died in 1884, Thygeson went to work at the age of sixteen. After a brief stint as a country schoolteacher, she learned typing and stenography and found work as a secretary to help support her family. According to her account, she made "a fabulous sum of money." Nevertheless, she gave up her job after a few years when she met and married her husband.

Thygeson's story demonstrates the growing importance of clerical work for women workers, particularly those from the white middle class. Called "typewriters," these women workers were quite literally identified as indistinguishable from the machines they operated. But far from seeing their work as dehumanizing, young middle-class women like Sylvie Thygeson viewed it with pride and relished the economic independence it afforded them. By the 1890s, secretarial work was the overwhelming choice of white, native-born women, who constituted over 90 percent of the female clerical force. Not only was it considered more genteel than factory work or domestic labor, but office work meant more money for shorter hours. Boston's clerical workers made more than $6 a week in 1883, compared with less than $5 for women working in manufacturing. For Sylvie Thygeson and thousands of women like her, the office provided a welcome alternative to the limited options available to women workers.

The Department Store

The department store provides another good setting in which to examine the working life of the new white-collar class. With the rise of industrial capitalism, a new consumer culture came to dominate American life. Men and women increasingly sought security, comfort, material well-being, and pleasure. Indeed, the emphasis on acquisition and consumption gave the Gilded Age its name. Department stores became the symbol of this new consumer culture.

The department stores that emerged in the nineteenth century created a unique new urban environment. Shoppers learned the modern art of consumption in palaces designed to lend magic and glamour to even the most everyday things of life— such as men's trousers or bedsheets. Boasting ornate facades, large plate-glass display windows, marble and brass fixtures, and elegant skylights and galleries, department stores like Macy's in New York, Wanamaker's in Philadelphia, Filene's in

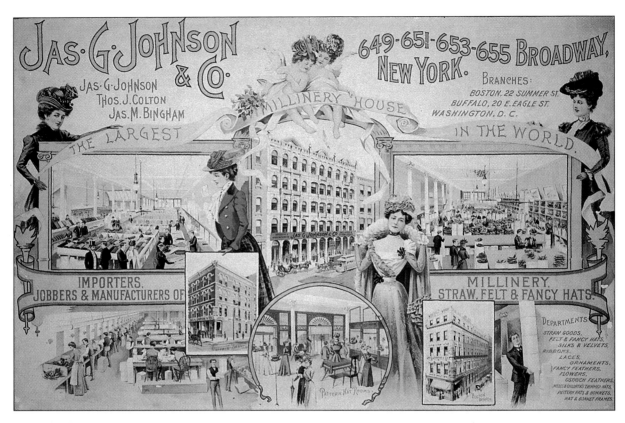

CONSUMER CULTURE

With the rise of consumer culture in urban America came huge new department and specialty stores. Johnson's Broadway store in New York advertised as "the largest millinery house in the world." In an era when no woman left her home without a hat, millinery stores sold the laces, flowers, ribbons, and feathers used to trim ladies' hats. The insatiable demand for fancy feathers led a group of prominent Boston women in 1896 to found the Massachusetts Audubon Society. Named for naturalist and painter John James Audubon, the group protested the indiscriminate slaughter of birds to provide feathers for the millinery trade.
Library of Congress.

Boston, and Marshall Field in Chicago stood as monuments to the material promise of the era and to the new culture of consumption.

With a vast array of personnel—stock boys, cashiers, salesclerks, elevator operators, bookkeepers, stenographers, telephone operators, buyers, and floorwalkers—the modern department store signaled the beginning of the shift in employment from production to services and heralded the rise of a new white-collar class. By the late 1890s, Macy's employed more than three thousand people, and Marshall Field more than doubled that figure within a few years.

Within these palaces of consumption, one could find cash girls, stock clerks, and wrappers who earned as little as $3 a week. At the top of the scale, buyers like Belle Cushman of the fancy goods department at Macy's earned $25 a week in 1871, an unusually high salary for a woman. But ordinarily, the gender segregation that kept women's wages low operated in the white-collar world of the department store just as it did in the office and the factory. Male supervisors, called floorwalkers, commanded salaries from $10 to $16 per week at a time when the typical Macy's saleswoman received $5 to $6. In all stores, saleswomen were subject to harsh and arbitrary discipline. Sitting was forbidden, and conversation with other clerks led to instant dismissal. The imperious Marshall Field fired any employee with ties to a labor union. Fines for tardiness or gum chewing pared down already meager wages. Yet white-collar workers counted themselves a cut above factory workers, even when their pay envelopes were thinner and did not justify the sense of superiority.

At Home and at Play

The growth of American industrial capitalism not only dramatically altered the workplace but indirectly transformed home and family life and gave rise to new forms of commercialized leisure. One of the major changes was the separation of work and home. In preindustrial society, trade and manufacturing generally took place in or close to the home. Industrialization redefined the very concepts of work and home. Increasingly, men went out to work for wages, while most white married women stayed home, either working in the home without pay—cleaning, cooking, and raising children—or supervising paid domestic servants who did the housework. The growing separation of workplace and home led to a new ideology, one that sentimentalized the home and women's role in it.

Domesticity and "Domestics"

The separation of the workplace and the home that marked the shift to industrial society in the early nineteenth century redefined the home as a "haven in the heartless world," presided over by a wife and mother who made the household her "separate sphere." The cultural ideology that dictated that woman's place was in the home has been called the "cult of domesticity," a phrase used to describe an ideal of womanhood that dominated the period from 1820 to the end of the nineteenth century.

The cult of domesticity purveyed an image of womanhood that was more appropriate for women of the middle and upper classes than for their working-class counterparts. With its insistence that the "true" woman confine her activities exclusively to the home, the cult soon fostered an invidious distinction between the "lady" and the working-woman. Since a lady, by definition, remained at home, women who worked for wages suffered a social stigma. In common slang, prostitutes were referred to as "working girls." Respectable working-class daughters who suffered by association struggled hard to transform the epithet into a term of dignity, but their task was complicated by the class

implications inherent in the nineteenth-century notion of true womanhood, which decreed that ladies remain in the home.

The cult of domesticity and the elaboration of the middle-class home in the nineteenth century led to a major change in patterns of hiring household help in the North (the South continued to rely on black female labor, first slave and later free). Domestic labor changed over the course of the nineteenth century from the "hired girl," who worked beside the housewife/employer, to the live-in servant, or "domestic." This transition reflected both economic and ideological change and was indirectly but distinctly tied to the maturing industrial capitalist economy, with its labor market, rising standard of living, system of unequal rewards, and created consumer "needs."

As the cult of domesticity and growing consumerism raised the expectations of the urban middle and upper classes, they relied more and more on paid domestic labor to perform menial household tasks. Domestics no longer "helped"; increasingly they carried the main burden of housework alone. In American cities by 1870, from 15 to 30 percent of all households included live-in domestic servants, more than 90 percent of whom were women.

The growth of American industrial capitalism not only dramatically altered the workplace but indirectly transformed home and family life and gave rise to new forms of commercialized leisure.

The life of the domestic was far from enviable. During the nineteenth century, native-born women took up other work and left domestic service to immigrants. By midcentury, the maid was so often Irish that "Bridget" became a generic term for female domestics. Investigators found that domestic servants not only worked longer hours than any other women workers but also spent the remainder of their time on call. "She is liable to be rung up at all hours," one study reported. "Her very meals are not secure from interruption, and even her sleep is not sacred."

Domestic servants by all accounts resented their lack of privacy and their limited opportunities for socializing. Furthermore, going into service carried a social stigma. As one young woman observed, "If a girl goes into the kitchen she is sneered at and called 'the Bridget,' but if she goes behind the counter she is escorted by gentlemen." No wonder domestic service was the occupation of last resort, a "hard and lonely life" in the words of one servant girl. With the opening of factory and office positions for women, only those with very limited skills chose service. "I would change my occupation if I knew enough to do anything else," confided one woman.

As workingwomen developed other options, the so-called servant problem became chronic, and white middle-class women lamented their inability to find "good help." For women of this class, domestics were a boon, freeing them from household drudgery and giving them more time to spend with their children or to pursue club work, reform, or woman suffrage. Thus, domestic service, while it supported the association of women with domesticity, created for those women who could afford it opportunities for activities that expanded women's horizons outside the home and worked to subvert accepted notions of "woman's place."

The House and the Home

As if to emphasize the new role of the home as a refuge and a haven in the decades after the Civil War, the typical middle-class dwelling itself became more embellished architecturally and its interiors more cluttered. Possession of such a home, indeed of any home at all, marked the gulf between the working poor and the middle class. Homeowners constituted only 36 percent of the housing population in 1900, compared with 64 percent today.

By 1890, the middle-class, urban home could boast such technological and sanitary improvements as central heating, hot and cold running water, and bathrooms. Electricity, which became available to city dwellers early in the twentieth century, expanded the hours of the day in a literal sense and also changed housework. As one architect noted, electricity "is used in operating telephones, call bells [for servants], for driving laundry, kitchen ventilating and pumping apparatus, and in some cases for refrigerating machinery."

Although few white women worked after marriage, the inequality of the incomes of their husbands created a yawning gulf between working-class wives and the wives of middle- and upper-class men. Wealthy and middle-class homemakers enjoyed sufficient income to purchase commodities women had previously produced at home and to avoid the drudgery of housework by hiring servants. This freedom enabled them to realize the cult of domesticity as a distinct and important social vocation.

The polarization between working-class austerity and the trappings associated with middle-class respectability becomes apparent in the comparison

SUNDAY DINNER
Sunday dinner at the home of the S.H. Fairfield family of Topeka, Kansas, is served by their African American domestic servant. Middle-class families as well as the wealthy relied on domestic help in the nineteenth century. Unlike white women, who rarely worked after marriage, more than 25 percent of African American married women worked for wages outside their homes, many as domestics. Often they had to leave their own homes and children and live in the homes of their white employers.
The Kansas State Historical Society, Topeka, Kansas.

of two households. Margaret Byington, a reformer who undertook a scientific survey of Homestead, the Carnegie mill town outside of Pittsburgh, recounted her visit to the family of a Slavic worker. The family lived in a two-room tenement, and she found the young mother doing the family laundry in a big washtub set on a chair in the middle of the room, struggling to keep her two babies from tumbling into the scalding water. Byington noted the sparse furnishings:

> On one side of the room was a huge puffy bed, with one feather tick to sleep on and another for covering; near the window stood a sewing machine; in the corner, an organ,—all these, besides the inevitable cook stove upon which in the place of honor was simmering the evening's soup. Upstairs in a second room, a boarder and the man of the house were asleep. Soon they would get up and turn their beds over to two more boarders, who were out at work.

Compare the Slavic family's household with the description of a middle-class home taken from *The Gilded Age,* the 1876 novel by Mark Twain and Charles Dudley Warner:

> Every room had its book-cases or book-shelves, and was more or less a library; upon every table was liable to be a litter of new books, fresh periodicals and daily newspapers. There were plants in the sunny windows and some choice engravings on the walls, with bits of color in oil or watercolors; the piano was sure to be open and strewn with music; and there were photographs and little souvenirs here and there of foreign travels.

In the eyes of Byington and many middle-class reformers, the Slavs' crowded tenement, with its boarders and its lack of privacy, could scarcely be dignified by the term "home." Yet for all the obvious differences between the households described, one can see in the workers' two feather ticks, sewing machine, and organ the same urge for sociability and impulse toward respectability that was apparent in the middle-class home.

Mill Towns and Company Towns

Mill towns like the one Byington studied became a feature of the industrial landscape in the nineteenth century. Many, like Homestead, grew up haphazardly. By 1892, eight thousand people lived in

Homestead, transforming a rural village into a bustling mill town that belied its pastoral name. As the Carnegie steelworks expanded, they encroached on the residential area, pushing the homes out of the flatlands along the Monongahela River. Workers moved into the hills and ravines. In an area called the Hollow, shanties hung precariously on the hillsides. These small, boxlike dwellings—many no larger than two rooms—housed the unskilled laborers from the mills.

Elsewhere, particularly in New England and the South, the company itself planned and built the town. The Amoskeag textile mill in Manchester, New Hampshire, was a self-contained world laid out according to a master plan conceived in the 1830s. Such planned communities rested on the notion of benevolent corporate paternalism. Viewing the workers as the "corporation's children," Amoskeag's owners sought to socialize their increasingly immigrant workforce to the patterns of industrial work and to instill loyalty to the company, curb labor unrest, and prevent unionization.

By the 1880s, Amoskeag employed tens of thousands of workers, housing many of them in corporation tenements. "The corporations," as workers called them, were three-to-five-story attached brick houses strung along the streets leading down from the center of the city to the mill yard. Workers paid the equivalent of $1 per room a month for company housing. To qualify, more than one family member had to work in the mill, a requirement that encouraged child labor. The substantial brick row houses with high ceilings and hardwood floors offered a striking comparison to the ramshackle shanties of Homestead. Only a third of Amoskeag's workers lived in company housing, however, making Manchester different from a classic company town. The majority of Amoskeag's workers rented houses in the city, and a significant number owned their own homes. The mill nevertheless exerted a powerful hold over the lives of its workers. "If you told the boss to go to hell, you might as well move out of the city," one mill worker acknowledged.

Perhaps the most famous company town in the United States was built by sleeping car king George M. Pullman nine miles south of Chicago on the shores of Lake Calumet. In the wake of the Great Railroad Strike of 1877, Pullman determined to remove his plant and workers from the "evil influences" of the city. In 1880, Pullman purchased 4,300 acres of bare prairie away from the "snares of the great city." On this isolated site he built his model town according to the principle on which he built the Pullman Palace cars that made his fortune—to be orderly, clean, and with the appearance of luxury. It was "to the employer's interest," he determined, "to see that his men are clean, contented, sober, educated, and happy." Pullman believed firmly that his practical philanthropy would guarantee larger profits by eliminating "loss of time and money consequent upon intemperance, labor strikes, and dissatisfaction," which, he insisted, "generally result from poverty and uncongenial home surroundings."

When the first family moved in on January 1, 1881, the model town of Pullman boasted parks, artificial lakes, fountains, playgrounds, an auditorium, a library, a hotel, shops and markets, a men's club, and 1,800 units of housing. Noticeably absent was a saloon. One worker lamented that he frequently walked by and "looked at but dared not enter Pullman's hotel with its private bar." The worker's intimidation underscored a major flaw in Pullman's plan. In his eagerness to inculcate what he referred to as the "habits of respectability," Pullman consulted his own wishes and tastes, never those of his workers.

With its clean, wide streets, its parks, and its model tenements, Pullman's town offered housing that was clearly superior to that in neighboring towns. But workers paid for the eye appeal. Pullman intended the town to support itself and expected a 6 percent return on his investment. As a result, Pullman's rents ran 10 to 20 percent higher than working-class accommodations in nearby communities. And a family could not own its own home in Pullman. George Pullman refused to "sell an acre under any circumstances." As long as he controlled the town absolutely, he held the powerful whip of eviction over his employees and could quickly get rid of troublemakers.

Although observers were at first dazzled by its beauty and order, it was not long before critics compared Pullman's model town to a "gilded cage" for workers. "The company owns everything," complained one critic, "and it exercises a surveillance over the movement and habits of the people." When labor organizers attempted to meet in Pullman, the company paid spies, or spotters, to report those who attended. The young economist Richard T. Ely went to the heart of what most concerned workers and critics alike when he concluded in 1884: "The idea of Pullman is un-American. . . . It is benevolent, well wishing feudalism, which desires the happiness of the people, but in such way as shall please the authorities."

The autocracy that many feared in Pullman was realized south of the Mason-Dixon line in the southern textile mill towns. "Practically speaking," a federal investigator observed, "the company owns everything and controls everything, and to a large extent controls everybody in the mill village." These largely nameless company towns, with their company-controlled stores, churches, schools, and houses, are a classic example of social control over workers. Paid in company currency, or scrip, workers had no choice but to patronize the company store, where high prices led to a mounting spiral of debt that reduced the workers to virtual captives of the company. At the turn of the century, 92 percent of southern textile workers' families lived in company towns.

The mill towns and company towns of America provide only the most dramatic examples of the ways in which industrialization and the rise of corporate capitalism changed the landscape of the United States and altered traditional patterns of work and home life. After the Civil War, communities where men and women of different classes knew and dealt with one another on a personal basis became more and more rare. In the face of increasing business consolidation and impersonality, traditional ideas about equal competition in the marketplace and the relative independence of employers and employees lost much of their hold.

Cheap Amusements

The poor and members of the working class took their leisure, when they had it, in the streets, the dance halls, the music houses, the ballparks, and the amusement arcades, which by the 1890s formed a familiar part of the landscape. For the most part the social divisions that marked American life existed in recreation. Poor and working-class people played largely apart from the retreats of the better-off. The tavern was the poor man's club. Saloons played a central role in workers' lives, often serving informally as political headquarters, employment agencies, or union halls. Not all the working class thronged to the saloons. Recreation varied according to ethnicity, religion, gender, and age. For many new immigrants, social life revolved around the family; weddings, baptisms, birthdays, and bar mitzvahs constituted the chief celebrations. Generally, older-stock American men spent more time away from home in neighborhood clubs, saloons, and fraternal orders than did their immigrant counterparts. German beer gardens, for example, were

TECHNOLOGY IN AMERICA
Moving Pictures at the Nickelodeon

The advent of projected motion pictures marked the culmination of the efforts of many inventors to present lifelike moving pictures on the screen. During the second half of the nineteenth century, a host of inventions, including the kinematoscope, the choreutoscope, the phasmatrope, and the zoopraxiscope, were designed to make pictures move. But it was Thomas Alva Edison's inventions in 1889 of the motion picture camera (kinetograph) and a peephole device to display the moving pictures (kinetoscope) that led to the commercial development of the cinema and the rise of the first moving picture theaters, the nickelodeons.

Edison launched the first exhibition of his motion pictures in a New York music hall in 1896. The result was an overnight sensation. Viewers marveled at the moving images — horses, dancers, waves on a beach. But the novelty soon wore off and audiences wanted a story. In 1903, *The Great Train Robbery*, an eleven-minute movie with a simple cops-and-robbers plot, proved such a hit that silent movies soon challenged the popularity of music halls, vaudeville houses, and penny arcades.

The years 1900 to 1907 were the heyday of the nickelodeons, the first motion picture theaters. The name came from combining *nickel*, the price of admission, with *melodeon*, the old reed organ sometimes played to accompany the silent films. Audiences flocked to these storefront theaters; by 1907, there were some five thousand nickelodeons across the United States. A viewer described the early shows: "A picture about 2 × 4 feet was projected from an Edison machine and a reel of film 300 to 400 feet in length was a complete show, lasting for four or five minutes. After each show the house was cleared and filled again."

It is not too much to say that modern cinema began with the nickelodeons, for their sudden growth stimulated the demand for movies, and the first studios quickly formed to feed the public's growing appetite for feature films. By the late 1920s, the film industry had taken root in Hollywood, California, and motion pictures had become one of the country's fastest-growing industries.

Corbis-Bettmann.

---

designed for the whole family. But more often, men and women took their leisure separately, except during the period of youth and courtship.

The growing anonymity of urban industrial society posed a challenge to traditional rituals of courtship. Adolescent working girls, immigrant and old stock, no longer met prospective husbands only

through their families. Fleeing crowded tenements, the young sought each other's company in dance halls and other commercialized retreats. Reformers worried that the commercial dance halls served as a breeding ground for drunkenness and prostitution. In 1884, millionaire heiress Grace Dodge, determined to help young working women find re-

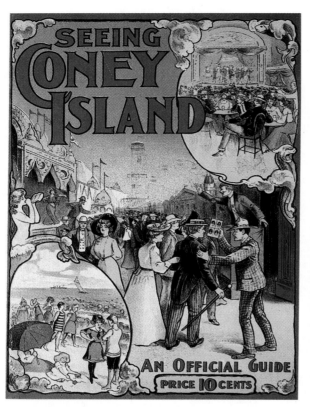

CONEY ISLAND
Coney Island became a pleasure resort in the 1870s, but at the turn of the century, with the development of elaborate amusement parks like Steeplechase, Luna, and Dreamland, Coney Island came into its own as the capital of commercialized leisure. This offical guide highlighted the beach, vaudeville hall, and the midway with its rides and its risqué harem dancers. In the foreground a barker gesticulates and a hawker urges a young man in a straw hat to buy souvenir photographs for his companion.
Brooklyn Historical Society.

Baseball became a national pastime in the 1870s —then, as now, one force in urban life that was capable of uniting a city across class lines. Cincinnati mounted the first professional team, the Red Stockings, in 1869. Teams proliferated in cities across the nation in the next decade. By 1888, as many as thirteen thousand fans regularly packed the Polo Grounds for weekend games of the New York Giants. Mark Twain hailed baseball as "the very symbol, the outward and visible expression, of the drive and push and rush and struggle of the raging, tearing, booming nineteenth century."

The increasing commercialization of entertainment in the last decades of the nineteenth century can best be seen at Coney Island. A two-mile stretch of beach that was close to Manhattan by trolley or steamship, Coney Island in the 1870s and 1880s attracted visitors to its beaches, its boardwalk, and its dance pavilions and penny arcades. In the 1890s, Coney Island was transformed into the site of some of the largest and most elaborate amusement parks in the country. Promoter George Tilyou built Steeplechase Park in 1897, advertising "10 hours of fun for 10 cents." With its mechanical thrills and funhouse laughs, the amusement park encouraged behavior that one schoolteacher aptly described as "everyone with the brakes off." By 1900, as many as half a million New Yorkers flocked to Coney Island on a weekend for fun. Other cities rushed to build their own playgrounds—Boston's Paragon Park and Revere Beach, Philadelphia's Willow Grove, Cleveland's Euclid Beach—but none rivaled Coney Island. The popularity of the amusement park signaled the rise of mass entertainment, making Coney Island the unofficial capital of a new mass culture.

spectability, set up a Working Girl's Club in New York City. Members contributed twenty-five cents a month to rent and furnish a comfortable club room where young women could relax and entertain. Designed as an alternative to commercial dance halls and amusement resorts, the Working Girl's Club sought to replicate patterns of middle-class courtship, where the young met under the watchful eye of older adults. By 1885, branches had sprung up in Brooklyn, Philadelphia, and Boston. But by far the majority of young workingwomen seemed to prefer the pleasure (and danger) of the dance halls.

The Labor Movement

Labor organization was not new in American society. Since colonial times, skilled workers had formed craft unions. And in the 1860s, William H. Sylvis, a Pennsylvania iron molder, briefly put together a National Labor Union to unite the skilled trades. With increased mechanization, craftsmen found their skills undermined as managers attempted to take control away from skilled workers through the use of machinery. Many of the old craft unions were broken up or badly weakened in the 1860s.

By the late nineteenth century, workers were losing control in the workplace. At the same time, the growing anonymity of corporate capitalism pitted the individual worker against huge corporations determined to cut costs. As labor became viewed less in human terms and more as a commodity, workers sought to act collectively to better their condition through politics and reform movements and also increasingly through labor unions.

Mechanization and the Erosion of Skilled Work

In 1883, a machinist described to a U.S. Senate committee the changes taking place in his shop:

> The trade has been subdivided and those subdivisions have been again subdivided, so that a man never learns the machinist's trade now. Ten years ago he learned, not the whole trade, but a fair portion of it. Also, there is more machinery used in the business, which again makes machinery. . . . It is merely laborers' work.

The machinist clearly recognized the way in which industrial capitalism was transforming the world of work. Jobs done by skilled craftsmen had increasingly been mechanized until the bulk of industrial workers were unskilled machine tenders or factory operatives by the end of the century. In the fierce competition to lower prices, industrialists like Andrew Carnegie invested heavily in new machinery that enabled them to replace skilled workers with unskilled workers. Wages fell accordingly, and workers found that they had less and less control over the workplace. The destruction of skill and the redefinition of labor as machine tending left the worker with a loss of independence and a growing sense of individual helplessness.

Along with the loss of independence came a threat to Americans' belief in individualism. The idea that a man could one day own his own business stood at the heart of the nineteenth-century ideology of the self-made man. Yet with the rise of large business combinations, the amount of capital that was required placed entrepreneurship out of reach for most Americans. The machinist testifying before the Senate committee expressed his growing disillusionment when asked whether his fellow workers ever hoped to become bosses or manufacturers:

> There is no chance. They have lost all desire to become bosses now . . . because the trade has become

demoralized. First they earn so small wages; and, next, it takes so much capital to become a boss now that they cannot think of it, because it takes all they can earn to live.

The ranks of wage laborers, those who worked by piece rates or by the hour, grew hand in hand with the rise of big business. In 1870, wage laborers represented more than half of those counted by the census as gainfully employed. The number of nonagricultural wage laborers increased after 1870 more than twice as rapidly as the country's population, and the number of male industrial wage laborers rose from 35.9 percent in 1870 to 48.3 percent in 1900. America, which prided itself on its small businesses and skilled craftsworkers, was rapidly becoming a nation of corporations and unskilled industrial laborers.

Alone, the worker might be helpless in the face of the anonymous corporation, but together, workers could challenge the bosses and reassert their power in the workplace.

For skilled workers, who prided themselves on their working-class identity, the loss of skilled positions meant a loss of control in the workplace. This erosion of individual power served as a spur to collective action. Alone, the worker might be helpless in the face of the anonymous corporation, but together, workers could challenge the bosses and reassert their power in the workplace.

The Great Railroad Strike of 1877

Labor flexed its muscle and showed its combined might with notable results during the summer of 1877 in the Great Railroad Strike. The strike, which began on the Baltimore and Ohio Railroad in West Virginia on July 16, quickly swept across the nation's rails until it involved 100,000 railroad workers on the B&O, the Pennsylvania Railroad, and the New York Central in cities from Baltimore to San Francisco. The strikers, whose wages had been repeatedly cut, aroused a good deal of public sympathy, even among the militia sent to put them down. In Reading, Pennsylvania, militiamen refused to fire on the strikers, saying, "We may be militiamen, but we are workmen first." Rail traffic ground to a halt, and for a brief period the nation lay paralyzed by the strike.

Violence erupted as the strike spread. In Pittsburgh, striking Pennsylvania Railroad workers were joined in the streets by steel rollers, mechanics, the unemployed, and women and children who were determined to "make a common fight against the corporations." Militiamen recruited from Philadelphia arrogantly boasted that they would clean up the "workingmen's town." Opening fire on the crowd, they killed twenty people. Angry workers retaliated, and the resulting conflagration destroyed 39 buildings, 104 engines, 46 passenger cars, and more than 1,200 freight cars and reduced an area of two miles along the track to smoldering rubble. Before the day ended, twenty more workers had been shot and the railroad had sustained property damage totaling $2 million.

Railroad officials stubbornly refused to arbitrate, hoping that federal and state authorities would step in to break the strike. Within the space of eight days, the governors of nine states, acting at the prompting of the railroad owners and managers, defined the strike as an "insurrection" and called for federal troops. President Rutherford B. Hayes (who, according to the New York *World*, owed his contested election in 1876 to the influence of Pennsylvania Railroad president Tom Scott) hesitated briefly, then called up the troops. By the time federal troops arrived, the violence had run its course. The army did not shoot a single striker in 1877. Its primary task consisted of acting as strikebreaker—opening rail traffic, protecting nonstriking "scab" train crews, and maintaining peace along the line.

Although the Great Strike was spontaneous and unorganized, it frightened the authorities and upper classes like nothing before in U.S. history. They quickly tried to blame the tiny radical Workingman's Party and predicted a bloody uprising. "Any hour the mob chooses it can destroy any city in the country—that is the simple truth," wrote future Secretary of State John Hay to his wealthy father-in-law. The *New York Times* editorialized about

MAP 19.3
The Great Railroad Strike of 1877
Starting in West Virginia and Pennsylvania, the Great Railway Strike of 1877 spread as far north as Buffalo, and as far west as San Francisco, bringing rail traffic to a standstill.

PITTSBURGH AFTER THE GREAT RAILROAD STRIKE
The Great Railroad Strike of 1877 left two miles of downtown Pittsburgh a mass of twisted rails and rubble. When the militia fired on the crowds, angry workers fought back. More than forty people were shot, and damage to property amounted to two million dollars. The middle class, which had initially sympathized with strikers, grew fearful of the violence and destruction. The shift in public opinion helped the railroad owners put down the strike.
Carnegie Library, Pittsburgh.

the "dangerous classes," and the *Independent* magazine offered the following advice on how to deal with "rioters":

> If the club of a policeman, knocking out the brains of the rioter, will answer, then well and good; but if it does not promptly meet the exigency, then bullets and bayonets, canister and grape . . . constitutes the one remedy and one duty of the hour.

Although many middle-class Americans had initially sympathized with the conditions that led the workers to strike, they blamed the strikers for the violence and property damage that occurred.

In the end, the strikers, whose united action had raised the specter of revolution, won few concrete gains. On most railroads, wage cuts remained in force, and hundreds of strikers were fired and their names circulated on a blacklist to prevent them from ever being rehired. But the workers were far from demoralized. They had learned the power of concerted action and would use it in the future. As labor leader Samuel Gompers acknowledged fifty years later, "The railroad strike of 1877 was the tocsin [alarm bell] that sounded a ringing message of hope to us all."

The Knights of Labor and the American Federation of Labor

The Great Strike served as a stimulus to labor organizing. The Knights of Labor, the first mass organization of America's working class, proved the chief beneficiary of labor's newfound consciousness. The Noble and Holy Order of the Knights of Labor had been founded in 1869 by Uriah Stephens, a Philadelphia garment cutter. A secret but peaceable society of workers, the Knights envisioned a "universal brotherhood" of all laborers, from the common laborer to the master craftsman. Although the Knights had played no active role in the 1877 strike, its membership swelled as a result of the growing interest in unionism. In 1878, the organization dropped the trappings of secrecy and launched an ambitious campaign to organize workers regardless of skill, sex, race, or nationality.

Under the direction of General Master Workman Terence V. Powderly, the Knights became the dominant force in labor during the 1880s. The union grew from 50,000 to a membership of over 700,000 by 1885. The Knights advocated a kind of workers' democracy that embraced a wide spectrum of reforms including free land, income tax, public ownership of the railroads, equal pay for work performed by women, and the abolition of child labor. The union sought to remove class distinctions and encouraged its local assemblies to welcome all comers, employees and employers alike. "I hate the word 'class' and would drive it from the English language if I could," Powderly stated. Only the "parasitic" members of society—gamblers, stockbrokers, lawyers, bankers, and liquor dealers—were denied membership.

In theory, the Knights of Labor opposed strikes. Powderly considered the strike "a relic of barbarism." He championed arbitration and preferred to use boycotts. But in practice, much of the organization's appeal came from the successful strike the Knights mounted in 1885 against three railroads controlled by Jay Gould. The Knights won a sweeping victory, including the revocation of a 15 percent pay cut. Despite the reservations of its leadership, the Knights of Labor was quickly becoming a militant labor organization that excited passionate support from working people with the slogan "An injury to one is the concern of all."

The Knights of Labor was not without rivals. Other trade unionists disliked the broad reform goals of the Knights and sought to focus on issues in the workplace. Samuel Gompers, a cigar maker born in London of Dutch Jewish ancestry, promoted what he called "pure and simple" unionism. Gompers founded the Organized Trades and Labor Unions in 1881 and reorganized it in 1886 into the American Federation of Labor (AFL), an organization to coordinate the activities of craft unions throughout the United States. His plan was simple: Organize skilled workers, those with the most bargaining power, and use strikes to gain immediate objectives such as higher pay and better working conditions. Gompers's "bread and butter" unionism at first drew few converts. The AFL had only 138,000 members in 1886, compared with 730,000 for the Knights of Labor. But events soon brought down the Knights and enabled Gompers to take control of the labor movement.

Haymarket and the Specter of Labor Radicalism

While the AFL and the Knights of Labor competed for members, more radical socialists and anarchists offered competing visions of labor's true path. The radicals, many of whom were immigrants steeped

SAMUEL GOMPERS
Samuel Gompers, pictured here in 1895, founded the American Federation of Labor in 1886 and served as its president continuously (except for 1895) until his death in 1924. Unlike the Knights of Labor, who supported the Populist Party in the 1890s, the AFL advocated "pure and simple unionism." Gompers, convinced that workers could gain little from politics, organized only skilled workers and focused on bread-and-butter issues.
The George Meany Memorial Archives.

in the tradition of European socialism, believed that reform was futile; they called for social revolution, in theory if not in practice. Anarchists also wanted revolutionary change but envisioned a smaller role for the state than the socialists did. Both groups, sensitive to criticism that they preferred revolution in theory to improvements here and now, rallied around the popular issue of the eight-hour day.

Ever since the 1840s, labor had sought to end the twelve-hour workday, which was standard in industry and manufacturing. To Ira Steward, who devoted his life to the struggle, the shorter workday meant not only greater leisure but also an opportunity for the workers to study politics and "escape from slavery and ignorance." By the mid-1880s, it seemed clear that labor shared too little in the new prosperity of the decade. Once again, pressure mounted for the eight-hour day. The radicals seized on the popular issue and launched major rallies in cities across the nation. Supporters of the movement set May 1, 1886, as the date for a nationwide general strike in support of the eight-hour day.

All factions of the nascent labor movement came together in Chicago on May Day, for what was billed as the largest demonstration in history in support of the eight-hour day. Chicago's Knights of Labor rallied to the cause even though Powderly and the union's leadership, worried by the increasing activism of the rank and file, refused to champion the movement for shorter hours. A group of radicals led by anarchist Albert Parsons, a *Mayflower* descendant, and August Spies, a German immigrant, spearheaded the eight-hour movement in Chicago. Combining passionate conviction with the fiery rhetoric of class warfare, they sent shivers of fear through the propertied classes with slogans like "Death to the foes of the human race."

Samuel Gompers was on hand, too, to rally the city's trade unionists, although he privately urged the AFL assemblies not to participate in a general strike. Gompers's skilled workers were labor's elite. Many still worked in small shops where negotiations between workers and employers took place in an environment tempered by personal relationships. In their Prince Albert coats and starched shirts, they stood in sharp contrast to the dispossessed strikers across town at Chicago's huge McCormick reaper works. There, strikers watched helplessly as the company brought in strikebreakers, or scabs, to take their jobs and marched them to work under the protection of the Chicago police and security guards supplied by the Pinkerton Detective Agency. Cyrus McCormick Jr., son of the inventor of the mechanical reaper, viewed labor organization as a threat to his power as well as to his profits; he was determined to smash the union.

On May Day, 45,000 workers paraded peacefully down Michigan Avenue in support of the eight-hour day, many singing the song that had become the movement's anthem:

> We mean to make things over;
>   we're tired of toil for naught
> But bare enough to live on: never
>   an hour for thought.
> We want to feel the sunshine; we
>   want to smell the flowers;
> We're sure that God has willed it,
>   and we mean to have eight hours.
> We're summoning our forces from
>   shipyard, shop, and mill:
> Eight hours for work, eight hours for rest,
>   eight hours for what we will!

Trouble came two days later, when strikers attacked scabs outside the McCormick works and police opened fire, killing or wounding six men. Angry radicals rushed out a circular urging workingmen to "arm yourselves and appear in full force" at a rally in Haymarket Square.

At Haymarket on the evening of May 4, the turnout was disappointing. No more than 2,000 to 3,000 gathered in the drizzle to hear Spies, Parsons, and the other anarchist speakers. Mayor Carter Harrison, known as a friend of labor, mingled conspicuously in the crowd, pronounced the meeting peaceable, and went home to bed. A short time later, police Captain John "Blackjack" Bonfield, a man who had made his reputation by cracking skulls, marched his men into the crowd (by now no more than 300 people) and demanded that they disperse.

Suddenly, someone threw a bomb into the police ranks, and the street echoed with the fiery blast. After a moment of stunned silence, the police drew their revolvers. "Fire and kill all you can," shouted a police lieutenant. Cries and curses mingled with the groans of the wounded as people took cover in doorways and behind walls and empty barrels, leaving the streets littered with bodies. When it was over, seven policemen and an unknown number of civilians lay fatally wounded. An additional sixty policemen and some thirty or forty civilians suffered injuries from the blast and the ensuing melee.

News of the "Haymarket riot" provoked a nationwide convulsion of fear, followed by blind rage directed not only at the bomb thrower, whose identity was never discovered, but also against anarchists, labor unions, strikers, immigrants, and the working class in general. The hysteria ran deepest in Chicago. The police rounded up Spies and the other Haymarket speakers and jailed hundreds of radicals. Although none of these men had thrown the bomb, seven of them, all German immigrants, were put on trial for conspiracy to commit murder. Parsons, who had managed to escape capture, turned himself in to stand trial with his fellows.

"Convict these men," cried State's Attorney Julius S. Grinnell, "make examples of them, hang them, and you save our institutions." The men were on trial for their ideas, not their actions. Although the state could not link any of the defendants with the bomb throwing, the jury nevertheless found all eight men guilty. Four were executed, one committed suicide, and three received prison sentences. On the gallows, August Spies spoke for the Haymarket martyrs: "The time will come when our silence will be more powerful than the voices you throttle today."

In 1893, Governor John Peter Altgeld, after a thorough investigation, pardoned the three remaining Haymarket anarchists. He denounced the trial as a shameless travesty of justice and concluded that Captain Bonfield was "the man really responsible for the death of the police officers." The governor's action brought on a storm of protest and cost him his political career. But through the entire process, Altgeld never wavered. "If I decide they are innocent, I will pardon them," he promised, "even if I never hold office another day." He did, and he didn't.

The bomb blast at Haymarket had lasting repercussions. For years, the memory of Haymarket and the dread of anarchy haunted the American consciousness and heightened the country's deep distrust of labor militancy. By the association of labor organization with terrorism and foreign radicals, the Haymarket bomb, in the eyes of one observer, proved "a godsend to all enemies of the labor movement." It effectively scotched the eight-hour movement and dealt a fatal blow to the Knights of Labor. On the same day as the Haymarket affair, Jay Gould, who had retaliated against the Knights of Labor in another strike, the Great Southwestern Railroad Strike of 1886, this time forced the union to come to terms. The Knights never recovered.

With the labor movement everywhere under attack, many workers severed their radical connections, and many skilled workers turned to the American Federation of Labor (AFL). Under the leadership of Samuel Gompers, the AFL soon became the dominant voice of American labor. Until his death in 1924, Gompers worked to shape skilled workers into a disciplined force able to exert bargaining leverage against employers.

Gompers developed a pragmatic philosophy concerning labor, a strategy forged in the aftermath of Haymarket. Disillusioned with broad reform goals, disappointed in politics as a route to change, and angry at radicals who jeopardized the future of labor, Gompers urged workers to focus on concrete gains. The AFL would push for changes here and now—higher wages, shorter hours—and use strikes and boycotts judiciously to win its demands. Gompers expected no help from the government, pointing out that the courts, the lawmakers, and the executive branch sided with property owners in every instance. Given the times, Gompers's narrow economic strategy made sense and enabled one segment of the workforce—the skilled—to organize effectively and achieve tangible gains. But the vast majority of unskilled workers remained largely untouched by the AFL's brand of "pure and simple" trade unionism.

Visions of a Better Life

Fear of social upheaval generated by the uprisings of workers in the 1870s and 1880s led to a search for social solutions. Liberal reformers, sympathetic to labor's plight but fearful of violence, sought schemes that would mitigate economic injustice without threatening bloodshed or class warfare. Two journalists, Henry George and Edward Bellamy, put forward visions of a better life that captured the imagination of their times. The utopian plans of George and Bellamy expressed both their fears about the present and their hopes for a better future.

Henry George and the Single Tax

The Great Railroad Strike of 1877 inspired San Francisco journalist Henry George to write a book that soon became a classic of American political economy. George knew poverty firsthand and harbored a deep sympathy for the underdog. In this spirit, he published *Progress and Poverty* in 1879, dedicating it "to those who, seeing the vice and misery that spring from the unequal distribution of wealth and privilege, feel the possibility of a higher social state and would strive for its attainment."

Liberal reformers, sympathetic to labor's plight but fearful of violence, sought schemes that would mitigate economic injustice without threatening bloodshed or class warfare.

In *Progress and Poverty*, George explored the paradox central to American life: Why, in a land so rich, was there such inequality? He had watched in frustration how the growth of monopoly went hand in hand with land speculation in California. In *Progress and Poverty*, he elaborated a theory that tied increasing inequality and growing monopoly to the scarcity of land caused by speculation (the practice of buying land and holding it till the price went up). Land speculators, he charged, contributed nothing to the economy yet made huge profits in "unearned increment."

As a cure for the nation's industrial problems, he championed a single tax on unimproved land. Once speculators could no longer turn large profits on the land they held, the way lay open to utopia, in George's view. Land would become available for farming. Industrial workers would leave the factories for the farms. Wages would naturally increase, and the life of industrial laborers would become more secure. Government, and with it the political corruption of the Gilded Age, would virtually disappear. George devoted an entire section of his book to a picture of the future that awaited the enactment of his simple law.

To underscore the urgent need for change, he ended his book with an apocalyptic vision of what would befall the United States if action were not taken: disease, pauperism, and an atmosphere of "brooding revolution." His single tax offered a way out, an alternative to class warfare. In George's view, venturesome capitalists and honest laboring people were not class enemies. The real villain was the grasping land speculator. The single tax, then, promised to bring America back from the brink of disaster and usher in a golden age.

George's message found many ready adherents who made the single tax a rallying cry for reform. George moved east after the publication of *Progress and Poverty* and became interested in politics. In 1886, in the aftermath of the Haymarket affair, he ran for mayor of New York City on the United Labor Party ticket. George appealed to labor, which saw him as one of its own. A printer, a unionist, and a member of the Knights of Labor, George believed that labor should take a more active role in politics, particularly on the municipal level. Tammany Hall attempted to buy him off, promising to run him for Congress on the Democratic ticket. "You cannot be elected," a Tammany pol told George, "but your running will raise hell." To which George responded, "I do not want the responsibility and the work of the Mayor of New York, but I do want to raise hell."

At first, George's opponents dismissed him as a "humbug" and a "busybody" with no real chance. But when 34,000 laborers signed a petition endorsing him, Democrats and Republicans began to take him seriously. Samuel Gompers himself became the chair of George's city organization and headed the speakers' bureau. Staunch Republican liberals, fearful of class war, threw their support to the Demo-

crats and tarred George as a "revolutionist" and "an apostle of anarchy and destruction." At the prompting of Tammany Hall, the Catholic archbishop of New York warned his flock not to "be deluded by men who advocate revolutionary doctrines." In what George accurately described as "one of the fiercest contests that ever took place in this or any other city," he lost the election by 20,000 votes, despite strong working-class support. The Democratic candidate beat George, who in turn nosed out his Republican rival, a political newcomer named Theodore Roosevelt.

Looking Backward from the Year 2000

While Henry George campaigned for mayor of New York and the country awaited the execution of the Haymarket anarchists, Edward Bellamy took up his pen to write one of the most influential novels in American history, a political work that ranks with Harriet Beecher Stowe's antislavery novel *Uncle Tom's Cabin* in terms of sales and influence. Bellamy, a Massachusetts newspaper writer forced by tuberculosis to give up his editorial career, had turned to writing novels. In 1888, he published *Looking Backward: 2000–1887*, a combination of utopian fantasy and genteel romance that spoke to the concerns of millions in the United States who were looking for a peaceful solution to the labor problem.

In *Looking Backward*, Edward Bellamy's hero, Julian West, falls asleep in Boston in 1887 and wakes in the year 2000 to find the world transformed. No labor strife, no class antagonism, no extremes of poverty and wealth exist in the twenty-first century. Instead, the people are organized into an efficient industrial army in which all men and women between the ages of twenty-one and forty-five work for the same guaranteed annual income. In Bellamy's highly centralized state, the disharmony, corruption, and party strife of the Gilded Age have vanished, replaced by benevolent bureaucracy.

Bellamy's utopia comes complete with visions of technological marvels that were unheard of in the 1880s—the radio and moving sidewalks. But although the material conditions of the people have improved, Bellamy makes it clear that the new world came about from a spiritual and not a material transformation. The Religion of Solidarity, or "nationalism," as it is called, transformed society. The Nationalist Party, Julian learns, grew almost overnight from a tiny band of evangelists to a force

From Rags to Riches: How Do Historians Measure Success?

THE RAGS TO RICHES FABLES of novelists like Horatio Alger fueled the dreams of countless young people at the turn of the century. Alger's formulaic novels feature fatherless young men who through the right combination of "pluck and luck" move ahead in the world. Yet despite the myth, few Americans rose from rags to riches. Even Alger's heroes, like his popular *Ragged Dick* (1866), more often traded rags for respectability.

Without exception, Alger's characters came from old stock and were not the new immigrants who poured through the "golden door" into the United States at the turn of the century. What were their chances of success? Literature written by the new immigrants themselves tells different stories. Abraham Cahan's *The Rise of David Levinsky* (1917) describes the experience of an eastern European Jewish immigrant who, as the title indicates, rises to gain material success. But the author laments that Levinsky's "rise" is paralleled by a spiritual loss. Mike Gold tells a darker story of immigrant life in *Jews without Money* (1930), an autobiographical tale of the implacable economic forces that devastated Gold's fictional family and turned its young protagonist to communism. Gold's characters inhabit a world of grinding poverty and ignorance, a landscape so bleak that one character comes to doubt the existence of a benevolent God, asking plaintively, "Did God make bedbugs?" Yet Gold's own success belied the grim economic determinism of his fiction. He made it out of the ghetto and into the world of literature and social activism.

Historians have been fascinated by the question of "making it" in America. Repeatedly they have attempted to measure economic and social mobility, from colonial times to the twentieth century. Looking at the lives of common folk, scholars have struggled to determine who made it and who didn't and why. Was America a land of boundless opportunity where the poor could rise? Or did the rich stay rich and the poor stay poor-to-middling, as pioneering studies of social mobility in the 1950s indicated?

By the 1960s, quantitative methods made possible by advances in computer technology promised to move history away from the "impressionistic," anecdotal evidence of fiction and memoirs and provide a statistical framework in which to measure success. But just what could historians measure with their new tools? Comparing Jewish and Italian immigrants in New York City at the turn of the century, one historian concluded that the Jews had done a better job of making it. By employing a table that categorized occupations, ranking them from professional, white-collar jobs to unskilled labor, the historian duly noted the movement from one category to another, concluding from his data that Jews moved more quickly into the white-collar class.

Studies of occupational mobility, however, contained major flaws. In a country where money has been and continues to be the common measure of success, historians' decision to use occupational categories and not income as the yardstick of mobility and success seemed to beg the question. Yet the choice was not surprising, given that census data, the staple of quantitative studies, provide information on occupation but not on income. Even occupational mobility proved difficult to measure accurately. For example, in the study cited, peddlers somewhat arbitrarily ranked at low white-collar status because they were self-employed. Yet the push-cart peddler and the Italian street vendor could hardly be said to have enjoyed white-collar status in the larger society in which they moved. Students must look carefully at what historians are measuring, recognizing that occupational mobility may not equate with social mobility or economic success.

The larger question remains: What is "making it" in America and how best can it be measured—in dollars and cents, in job satisfaction, occupational status, in comparison with the lives of one's parents or neighbors? And what of the immigrants them-

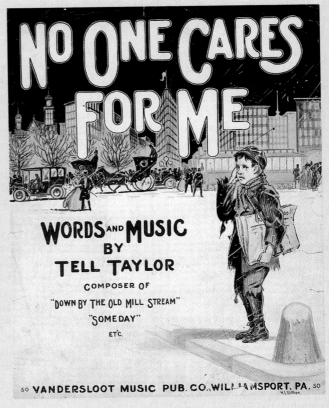

RAGS TO RICHES

Horatio Alger's novels like Ragged Dick *(1867), pictured here, invariably end with the young hero on the road to success. Contrast Alger's cheerful message with the bathos of the 1900 song "No One Cares for Me," in which the young newsboy in his rags replicates Alger's hero. But instead of getting ahead, his lot is portrayed as one of cruel neglect. Which portrait is more accurate? Historians for decades have wrestled with the question of social mobility and success.*

Picture Research Consultants & Archives; Culver Pictures.

selves? How did they define it? If becoming a bricklayer spelled success to the Italian immigrant and his family, do studies of occupational mobility based on statisticians' categories and job rankings distort his lived reality? In dealing with the issue of "making it" in America, historians have increasingly come to recognize that each immigrant group had its own unique definition of success. Not all immigrants sought upward mobility, whether economic or occupational. Cultural factors, such as the value Italians placed on loyalty to the family, also played a key role. Ultimately, questions of success and mobility cannot easily be quantified, and they demand attention to the larger cultural context that shaped individual economic and occupational choices.

that succeeded in eliminating the destructive energies of both capitalist greed and proletarian envy and hatred. All society had to do was recognize and cooperate in the inevitable evolutionary process from competition to cooperation.

Julian himself experiences a conversion and, by the book's end, overcomes the smug selfishness that was the hallmark of his class. Looking back at his old life, he compares society in the late nineteenth century to "a prodigious coach which the masses of humanity were harnessed to and dragged toilsomely along a very hilly and sandy road." The driver of the coach is hunger, and his whips cut deep into the backs of the struggling team below. On top of the coach, "well up out of the dust," perch the passengers, who occasionally call down encouragement to the toilers below, "exhorting them to patience, and holding out hopes of possible compensation in another world for the hardness of their lot." Such inhumanity, Julian patiently explains to his twenty-first-century audience, could be explained by the conviction that "there was no other way in which Society could get along, except that the many pulled at the rope and the few rode." Besides, the riders suffer from the hallucination that "they [are] not exactly like their brothers and sisters" but are made "of finer clay." "This seems unaccountable," Julian confesses, "but, as I once rode this very coach and shared that very hallucination, I ought to be believed."

In the parable of the stagecoach, Bellamy offered a scathing critique of social Darwinism and a call to action. The book caused a sensation. Within three years, over a million copies had been sold, and enthusiastic readers launched 165 Bellamy Clubs devoted to discussing nationalism and implementing the social goals expressed in *Looking Backward*. While neither George's single tax nor Bellamy's nationalist utopia produced the kind of massive social change envisioned by the two authors, the enthusiastic response to both books indicated that many Americans feared social cataclysm and were ready to take action.

Conclusion: The Workers' Own Struggle

The late nineteenth century witnessed many competing visions of a better life as Americans sought solutions to the problems attending urban industrialism and corporate capitalism. Henry George's single tax won supporters across the country and rallied New York's laborers to support him for mayor. Bellamy's nationalist utopia attracted followers drawn largely from the "sensible middle class." President Hayes called for "education" and a "wise judicious policy" to avoid labor upheavals like the Great Railroad Strike of 1877. American workers themselves had their own vision of what a better life might be—a life in which the independence eroded by industrialization could be countered by collective action, workers could regain some control of the workplace, and a shorter day and a higher wage promised escape from a brutal life of toil. Their vision and their willingness to fight for it made them active agents of social change, willing to risk their livelihood and sometimes their lives in the struggle.

Looking at the impact on his life occasioned by industrialization, a Massachusetts machinist declared in the 1890s:

> The workers of Massachusetts have always been law and order men. We loved our country and respected the laws. For the last five years the times have been growing worse every year, until we have been brought down so far that we have not much farther to go. What do the Mechanics of Massachusetts say to each other? I will tell you: "We must have a change. Any thing is better than this. We cannot be worse off, no matter what the change is."

Mounting anger and frustration would lead American workers and farmers to join forces in the 1890s and create a grassroots movement to fight for change under the banner of a new People's Party.

CHRONOLOGY

1869 Uriah Stephens founds Knights of Labor.

Cincinnati mounts first professional baseball team, the Red Stockings.

1870 Wage earners account for over half of those employed in 1870 census.

1872 Andrew Carnegie opens his steelworks outside Pittsburgh.

1877 Great Railroad Strike paralyzes nation's transportation system.

1878 Knights of Labor campaign to organize workers regardless of skill, sex, or race.

1879 Henry George publishes *Progress and Poverty*.

1880 George M. Pullman builds model town on 4,300 acres near Chicago.

1881 Samuel Gompers founds Organized Trades and Labor Unions.

1883 Andrew Carnegie acquires the Homestead Steel Mill outside Pittsburgh after labor strikes force owners to sell.

1884 Grace Dodge organizes first Working Girl's Club in New York City.

1886 Organized Trades and Labor Unions reorganized as the American Federation of Labor (AFL).

May 1. Massive rally in support of eight-hour workday takes place in Chicago.

Haymarket bombing in Chicago results in widening fear of anarchy and a blow to the labor movement.

Henry George campaigns for mayor of New York City on United Labor Party ticket and loses to Tammany Hall Democrat in close election.

1888 Edward Bellamy publishes *Looking Backward*.

1890 Average worker earns $500 per year.

1893 Governor John Peter Altgeld pardons three remaining Haymarket anarchists.

1897 Steeplechase amusement park opens on Coney Island.

BIBLIOGRAPHY

GENERAL WORKS

Alan Dawley, *Struggles for Justice: Social Responsibility and the Liberal State* (1991).

Melvyn Dubofsky, *Industrialism and the American Worker, 1865–1920* (1975).

Ray Ginger, *Altgeld's America* (1973).

Herbert C. Gutman, *Work, Culture, and Society in Industrializing America: Essays in American Working-Class and Social History* (1976).

David M. Katzman and William M. Tuttle Jr., *Plain Folk: The Life Stories of Undistinguished Americans* (1982).

David Montgomery, *The Fall of the House of Labor: The Workplace, the State, and American Labor Activism, 1865–1925* (1987).

Nell Irvin Painter, *Standing at Armageddon: The United States, 1877–1919* (1987).

Leon Stein and Philip Taft, eds., *Workers Speak* (1971).

WORKERS

Karen Anderson, *Changing Woman: A History of Racial Ethnic Women in America* (1996).

Eric Arnesen, *Waterfront Workers in New Orleans: Race, Class, and Politics, 1863–1923* (1991).

Cindy Sondik Aron, *Ladies and Gentlemen of the Civil Service: Middle-Class Workers in Victorian America* (1987).

Gunther Barth, *Bitter Strength: The History of the Chinese in the United States, 1850–1870* (1964).

Mary H. Blewett, *Men, Women, and Work: Class, Gender, and Protest in the New England Shoe Industry, 1780–1910* (1988).

John Bodnar, *Workers' World* (1982).

David Brody, *Steelworkers in America: The Nonunion Era* (1960).

David Brody, *Workers in Industrial America: Essays on the Twentieth-Century Struggle* (1980).

Milton Cantor and Bruce Laurie, eds., *Class, Sex, and the Woman Worker* (1977).

Ping Chiu, *Chinese Labor in California: An Economic Study* (1967).

Patricia A. Cooper, *Once a Cigar Maker: Men, Women, and Work Culture in American Cigar Factories* (1987).

Margery W. Davies, *Woman's Place Is at the Typewriter: Office Work and Office Workers, 1870–1930* (1982).

James J. Davis, *The Iron Puddler: My Life in the Rolling Mills and What Became of It* (1922).

Alan Derickson, *Workers' Health, Workers' Democracy: The Western Miners' Struggle, 1891–1925* (1988).

Sigmund Diamond, ed., *The Nation Transformed: The Creation of an Industrial Society* (1963).

Faye E. Dudden, *Serving Women: Household Service in Nineteenth-Century America* (1983).

Philip S. Foner, *Women and the American Labor Movement: From the First Trade Unions to the Present* (1979).

Michael H. Frisch and Daniel J. Walkowitz, eds., *Working-Class America: Essays on Labor, Community, and American Society* (1983).

John Debo Galloway, *The First Transcontinental Railroad* (1950).

Sherna Gluck, *From Parlor to Prison: Five American Suffragists Talk about Their Lives* (1976).

David M. Gordon, Richard Edwards, and Michael Reich, eds., *Segmented Work, Divided Workers: The Historical Transformation of Labor in the United States* (1982).

William H. Harris, *The Harder We Run: Black Workers since the Civil War* (1982).

Elizabeth Hasanovitz, *One of Them: Chapters from a Passionate Autobiography* (1918).

Jacqueline Jones, *The Dispossessed: America's Underclasses from the Civil War to the Present* (1992).

David M. Katzman, *Seven Days a Week: Women and Domestic Service in Industrializing America* (1978).

Susan E. Kennedy, *If All We Did Was to Weep at Home* (1979).

Alice Kessler-Harris, *Out to Work: The History of Wage-Earning Women in the United States* (1982).

Alexander Keyssar, *Out of Work* (1986).

Maxine Hong Kingston, *China Men* (1977).

S. J. Kleinberg, *The Shadow of the Mills: Workingclass Families in Pittsburgh, 1870–1907* (1989).

George Kraus, *High Road to Promontory: Building the Central Pacific across the High Sierra* (1969).

A. T. Lane, *Solidarity or Survival? American Labor and European Immigrants, 1830–1924* (1987).

Larry Lankton, *Cradle to Grave: Life, Work, and Death at Lake Superior Copper Mines* (1991).

Janet Lecompte, ed., *Emily [French]: The Diary of a Hard-Worked Woman* (1987).

Susan Levine, *Labor's True Women: Carpet Weavers, Industrialization, and Labor Reform in the Gilded Age* (1984).

Julie A. Matthaei, *An Economic History of Women in America: Women's Work, the Sexual Division of Labor, and the Development of Capitalism* (1982).

Cathy L. McHugh, *Mill Family: The Labor System in the Southern Cotton Textile Industry, 1880–1915* (1988).

Joanne J. Meyerowitz, *Women Adrift: Independent Wage Earners in Chicago, 1880–1930* (1988).

Gwendolyn Mink, *Old Labor and New Immigrants in American Political Development* (1986).

David Montgomery, *Workers' Control in America* (1979).

Victor G. Nee and Brett de Bary Nee, *Longtime Californ': A Documentary Study of an American Chinatown* (1972).

William L. O'Neill, ed., *Women at Work* (1972).

Cornelia Stratton Parker, *Working with the Working Women* (1922).

Samuel H. Preston and Michael R. Haines, *Fatal Years: Child Mortality in Late Nineteenth Century America* (1991).

Marilyn D. Rhinehart, *A Way of Work and a Way of Life* (1992).

Richard B. Rice, William A. Bullough, and Richard J. Orsi, *The Elusive Eden: A New History of California* (1988).

M. B. Schnapper, *Women at Work: The Autobiography of Mary Anderson as Told to Mary N. Winslow* (1951).

Dorothy Schweider, *Black Diamonds: Life and Work in Iowa's Coal Mining Communities, 1895–1925* (1983).

Carl Smith, *Urban Disorder and the Shape of Belief* (1995).

Daphne Spain, *Gendered Spaces* (1992).

Frank Hatch Streightoff, *The Standard of Living among the Industrial People of America* (1911).

Sharon Hartman Strom, *Beyond the Typewriter: Gender, Class, and Origins of Modern American Office Work, 1900–1930* (1992).

Ronald Takaki, *Strangers from a Different Shore: A History of Asian Americans* (1989).

Leslie Woodcock Tentler, *Wage-Earning Women: Industrial Work and Family Life in the United States, 1900–1930* (1979).

Carole Turbin, *Working Women of Collar City: Gender, Class, and Community in Troy, New York, 1864–1886* (1992).

Jules Tygiel, *Workingmen in San Francisco, 1880–1901* (1992).

Lynn Y. Weiner, *From Working Girl to Working Mother: The Female Labor Force in the United States, 1920–1980* (1985).

Robert E. Weir, *Beyond Labor's Veil: The Culture of the Knights of Labor* (1996).

Barbara Wertheimer, *We Were There: The Story of Working Women in America* (1977).

Richard White, *"It's Your Misfortune and None of My Own": A New History of the American West* (1991).

Mark Wyman, *Round-Trip to America: The Immigrants Return to Europe, 1880–1930* (1993).

Virginia Yans-McLaughlin, *Family and Community: Italian Immigrants in Buffalo, 1880–1930* (1977).

MILL TOWNS AND COMPANY TOWNS

William Adelman, *Touring Pullman: A Study in Company Paternalism* (1977).

Stanley Buder, *Pullman: An Experiment in Industrial Order and Community Planning, 1880–1930* (1967).

John S. Garner, *The Company Town: Architecture and Society in the Early Industrial Age* (1992).

Jacquelyn Dowd Hall, James Leloudis, Robert Korstad, Mary Murphy, Lu Ann Jones, and Christopher B. Daly, *Like a Family: The Making of a Southern Mill World* (1987).

Tamara K. Hareven, *Family Life and Industrial Time: The Relationship between the Family and Work in a New England Industrial Community* (1982).

Tamara K. Hareven and Randolph Langenbach, *Amoskeag: Life and Work in an American Factory-City* (1978).

LIFE AND LEISURE

Elaine Abelson, *When Ladies Go A'Thieving: Middle-Class Shoplifters in the Victorian Department Store* (1989).

Judith Adams, *The American Amusement Park Industry: A History of Technology and Thrills* (1991).

Gunther Barth, *City People: The Rise of Modern City Culture in Nineteenth-Century America* (1980).

Susan Porter Benson, *Counter Cultures: Saleswomen, Managers, and Customers in American Department Stores, 1890–1940* (1986).

George Chauncey, *Gay New York* (1994).

Warren Goldstein, *Playing for Keeps: A History of Early Baseball* (1989).

John F. Kasson, *Amusing the Million: Coney Island at the Turn of the Century* (1978).

William Leach, *Land of Desire: Merchants, Power, and the Rise of a New American Culture* (1993).

John Lucas and Ronald Smith, *The Saga of American Sport* (1978).

Karen Lystra, *Searching the Heart: Women, Men, and Romantic Love in Nineteenth Century America* (1989).

Steven Mintz, *A Prison of Expectations: The Family in Victorian Culture* (1983).

Steven Mintz and Susan Kellogg, *Domestic Revolutions: A Social History of American Family Life* (1988).

David Nasaw, *Going Out: The Rise and Fall of Public Amusements* (1993).

Kathy Peiss, *Cheap Amusements: Working Women and Leisure in Turn of the Century New York* (1986).

Steven Pope, *Patriotic Games: Sporting Traditions in the American Imagination, 1876–1926* (1996).

Steven A. Riess, *Touching Base: Professional Baseball and American Culture in the Progressive Era* (1980).

Roy Rosenzweig, *Eight Hours for What We Will: Workers and Leisure in an Industrial City, 1870–1920* (1983).

Sheila M. Rothman, *Woman's Proper Place: A History of Changing Ideals and Practices, 1870 to the Present* (1979).

Carol Smith-Rosenberg, *Disorderly Conduct: Visions of Gender in Victorian America* (1986).

LABOR STRIFE AND ORGANIZED LABOR

Paul Avrich, *The Haymarket Tragedy* (1984).

Robert V. Bruce, *1877: Year of Violence* (1959).

Henry David, *The History of the Haymarket Affair* (1963).

Melvyn Dubofsky, *When Workers Organize: New York City in the Progressive Era* (1968).

Leon Fink, *Workingman's Democracy: The Knights of Labor and American Politics* (1983).

Philip S. Foner, *The Great Labor Uprising of 1877* (1977).

William E. Forbath, *Law and the Shaping of the American Labor Movement* (1991).

Dee Garrison, *Mary Heaton Vorse: The Life of an American Insurgent* (1989).

Stuart B. Kaufman, *Samuel Gompers and the Origins of the American Federation of Labor* (1973).

John Laslett, *Labor and the Left: A Study of Socialist and Radical Influences in the American Labor Movement, 1881–1924* (1970).

Sidney Lens, *The Labor Wars: From the Molly Maguires to the Sitdowns* (1974).

Harold C. Livesay, *Samuel Gompers and Organized Labor in America* (1978).

Milton Meltzer, *Bread and Roses: The Struggle of American Labor, 1865–1915* (1967).

Henry Pelling, *American Labor* (1960).

Christopher L. Tomlins, *The State and the Unions: Labor Relations, Law, and the Organized Labor Movement in America, 1880–1960* (1985).

Robert E. Weir, *Beyond Labor's Veil: The Culture of the Knights of Labor* (1996).

Samuel Yellen, *American Labor Struggles* (1936).

Irwin Yellowitz, *Industrialization and the American Labor Movement, 1850–1900* (1977).

REFORMERS

Charles Albro Barker, *Henry George* (1955).

Edward Bellamy, *Looking Backward: 2000–1887* (1888).

Henry George, *Progress and Poverty* (1954).

Edward J. Rose, *Henry George* (1968).

John L. Thomas, *Alternative America: Henry George, Edward Bellamy, Henry Demarest Lloyd, and the Adversary Tradition* (1983).

FARMERS' ALLIANCE SONGBOOK

In the 1800s, the Farmers' Alliance recruited followers in the South and Midwest at the rate of twenty thousand a month, using lecturers, camp meetings, and even songs to educate and organize. This Farmers' Alliance songbook was offered for sale, by the copy and by the hundred — testimony to the growing movement. In the picture an Alliance farmer shakes the hand of a blacksmith, who bears a not coincidental resemblance to Abraham Lincoln. The handshake symbolizes the willingness of the alliance to make common cause with laborers of every stripe, a message reiterated in the four corners with images of school, farm, factory, and ship.

East Carolina Manuscript Collection, J. Y. Joyner Library, East Carolina University, Greenville, N. C. Photo by Dewan Frentger.

FIGHTING FOR CHANGE IN THE TURBULENT NINETIES

1890–1900

20

S T. LOUIS IN FEBRUARY 1892 played host to one of the most striking political gatherings of the century. Thousands of farmers, laborers, reformers, orators, and common people flocked to Missouri to attend a meeting that was, in the words of one observer, "different from any other political meeting ever witnessed in St. Louis." The cigar-smoking professional politicians who generally worked the convention circuit were nowhere to be found. In their place, a reporter noted, were "mostly gray-haired, sunburned and roughly clothed men" assembled under a banner that proclaimed, "We do not ask for sympathy or pity. We ask for justice."

Exposition Music Hall presented a colorful spectacle. "The banners of the different states rose above the delegates throughout the hall, fluttering like the flags over an army encamped," wrote one reporter. Ignatius Donnelly, the crowd's favorite orator, attacked the money kings of Wall Street. Mary Elizabeth Lease, a veteran campaigner from Kansas known for exhorting farmers to "raise less corn and more hell," lent her powerful voice to the cause. Terence V. Powderly, head of the Knights of Labor, called on workers to join hands with farmers against the "nonproducing classes." And Frances Willard of the Woman's Christian Temperance Union argued for temperance and woman suffrage. Between speeches the crowd sang songs like "Hurrah for the Toiler," "All Hail the Power of Laboring Men," and "Justice for the Farmer."

In the course of the next few days, delegates hammered out a series of demands that were breathtaking in their scope. They tackled the tough questions of the day—the regulation of business, the need for banking and currency reform, the rights of labor, and the role of the federal government in guaranteeing democracy. The convention, noted a reporter, ended its work amid a din of cheers. "As if by magic, everyone was upon his feet in an instant. Thundering cheers from 10,000 throats greeted these demands as the road to liberty. Hats, paper, handkerchiefs, etc., were thrown into the air; wraps, umbrellas and parasols waved; cheer after cheer thundered and reverberated through the vast hall reaching the outside of the building where thousands who had been waiting the outcome, joined in the applause till for blocks in every direction the exultation made the din indescribable."

What was all the shouting about? People were building a new political party, the People's, or Populist, Party. Dissatisfied with the Democrats and Republicans, a broad coalition of groups came together in St. Louis to fight for change. They determined to reconvene in Omaha in July to nominate candidates for the upcoming presidential election.

The 1890s witnessed one of the most turbulent decades in U.S. history. Unrest, agitation, agrarian revolt, labor strikes, and a severe financial panic and depression marked the decade. While the major parties continued to do business as usual, Americans flocked to organizations like the Knights of Labor, the Farmers' Alliance, and the Woman's Christian Temperance Union and worked together to create new political alliances. The St. Louis gathering marked just one milestone on the road to a new politics. The People's Party challenged laissez-faire by insisting that the federal government play a more active role to ensure greater economic equity in industrial America. This challenge to the status quo would culminate in 1896 in one of the most hotly contested presidential elections in the nation's history. At the close of this tumultuous decade, America entered the twentieth century after a war for expansion that healed the nation's wounds even as it raised new questions about the direction in which the United States was heading.

Militant Women

"Do everything," Frances Willard urged her followers in 1881. The new president of the Woman's Christian Temperance Union (WCTU) meant what she said. She soon led the organization into politics and reform. The path of the WCTU followed a trajectory that was common in the late nineteenth century. As women organized to deal with issues that touched their homes and families, they moved almost inevitably into politics, lending a new urgency to the cause of woman suffrage (the vote for women). Women's activism and reform were by no means limited to the white middle class, as Ida B. Wells's antilynching campaign forcefully demonstrated.

Frances Willard and the Woman's Christian Temperance Union

Frances Willard, the visionary leader of the WCTU, spoke for a group that was left almost entirely out of the electoral process—women. In 1881, only two territories, Utah and Wyoming, allowed women to vote. Elsewhere, woman suffrage was either nonexistent or severely limited. Michigan women voted in school elections, as did women in Minnesota and Kansas. But lack of the franchise did not mean that women were apolitical. The WCTU demonstrates

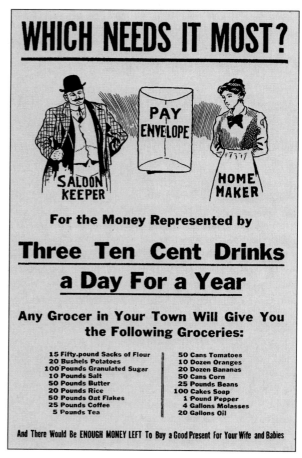

WCTU FLYER

This Woman's Christian Temperance Union flyer shows the wife pitted against the saloon keeper for her husband's pay. The economic consequences to the family of a drinker were a serious matter. At a time when the average worker made only $500 a year, the money spent on alcohol meant less to eat for the family. As the poster indicates, thirty cents a day for a year paid for a substantial amount of family staples. Beer and liquor lobbyists worked hard not only to counter the WCTU but to fight woman suffrage because they feared when women got the vote they would enact prohibition.
Culver Pictures.

the breadth of women's political activity in the late nineteenth century.

The WCTU was created in 1874 following a spectacular uprising in the Midwest known as the Woman's Crusade. During the winter of 1873–74, women, armed with Bibles and singing hymns, marched on taverns and saloons and refused to leave until the proprietors signed a pledge to quit selling liquor. The crusade spread like a prairie fire through small towns in Ohio, Indiana, Michigan, and Illinois and soon moved east into New York, New England, and Pennsylvania. Before it was over, more than 100,000 women marched in over 450 cities and towns. The crusade marked the first time since the days of the antislavery movement that middle-class, respectable churchwomen had taken to the streets.

The women's tactics were new, but temperance (the movement to ban the sale of alcoholic beverages and eliminate drunkenness) dated back to the 1820s. It had won significant victories in the 1850s when states, starting with Maine, passed laws to prohibit the sale of liquor (the laws became known as "Maine laws"). But by the late 1860s and 1870s, the liquor business was on the rise, with about one saloon for every fifty males over the age of fifteen. Willing to spend as much money as it took, the liquor interests mounted a powerful lobby to fight temperance.

Temperance was an especially explosive issue that divided communities, pitting middle class against working class, native-born against immigrant, Protestant against Catholic, and women against men. In 1869, a national Prohibition Party formed, but it attracted little support. In the North, most "drys," as the temperance advocates were called, stayed in the Republican Party, while the Democrats, with their strength in urban immigrant areas, won the support of the "wets." In practice, both major political parties avoided the divisive issue by leaving it up to counties and towns to decide whether to ban the sale of liquor.

After a decade of quiescence, the Woman's Crusade dramatically brought the issue of temperance back into the national spotlight. In 1874, women built on the success of the crusade to mount a new national organization, the Woman's Christian Temperance Union. Composed entirely of women, the new organization advocated total abstinence from alcohol. In its first five years, under the leadership of Annie Wittenmyer, the WCTU relied on education and moral suasion to achieve its goal. When Frances Willard became president in 1879, she radically changed the direction of the organization. Using "home protection" as her watchword, she capitalized on the cult of domesticity to move women into public life, arguing that they needed to attack the saloon to protect the home and family.

Women supported the temperance movement because they felt particularly vulnerable. The drunken, abusive husband epitomized the evils of a society in which women remained second-class citizens. Temperance provided women with a respectable outlet for their increasing resentment of women's inferior status and their growing recognition of women's capabilities. Seeing all women's interests as essentially the same, crossing class, ethnic, and racial lines, women reformers like the leaders of the Woman's Christian Temperance Union did not hesitate to use the singular *woman* to emphasize gender solidarity. Although largely white and middle class, the women of the WCTU resolved to speak for their entire sex.

As women organized to deal with issues that touched their homes and families, they moved almost inevitably into politics, lending new urgency to the cause of woman suffrage.

As the second president of the WCTU, Frances Willard greatly expanded the activities of the union. In its pursuit of temperance, the organization soon moved toward advocacy of woman suffrage (again the singular, "woman"), which Willard supported as early as 1875 and which the WCTU formally embraced in 1884 by calling for the "home protection ballot." A grassroots organization, the WCTU recruited members in every state and territory. By the 1890s, the WCTU network of local unions had penetrated all but the most isolated rural areas of the country. Strong and rich, with 150,000 dues-paying members, the WCTU was a force to be reckoned with.

Willard's "Do Everything" slogan accurately described the breathtaking sweep of the WCTU's concerns. Under her leadership, the WCTU moved closer to the view that alcoholism was a disease and not a sin and that poverty could be as much a cause as a result of drink. Accordingly, social action replaced prayer as women's answer to the threat of drunkenness. By 1896, twenty-five of the WCTU's departments dealt with nontemperance issues. The organization worked to establish women's reformatories and promoted the hiring of female police officers. The Chicago branch sponsored day nurseries, Sunday schools, an industrial training school, a mission for homeless women, a free medical dispensary, and a lodging house for men.

At the same time, the WCTU turned its attention to labor issues, joining with the Knights of Labor to press for better working conditions. One WCTU worker described the condition of factory operatives in a textile mill. "It is dreadful to see those girls stripped almost to the skin, wearing only a kind of loose wrapper, and running like racehorses from the beginning to the end of the day," she wrote in the *Union Signal,* the WCTU's monthly magazine. "The hard slavish work," she concluded, "is drawing the girls into the saloon."

Willard attempted to create a broad reform coalition in the 1890s, embracing the Knights of Labor, the People's Party, and the Prohibition Party. Until her death in 1898, Willard led, if not a women's rights movement, then the first organized mass movement of women united around a women's issue. As she herself observed, "All this work has tended more toward the liberation of women than it has toward the extinction of the saloon."

The WCTU under Willard's leadership secularized, politicized, and legitimized women's concerns. Frances Willard and the organization that she led championed a new kind of womanhood. Before 1873, most WCTU women had worked only in their churches. By 1900, women could claim a generation of experience in political action—speaking, lobbying, organizing, drafting legislation, and running private charitable institutions. Willard's death left a legacy of political activism.

The Suffrage Movement

Unlike the WCTU, the organized movement for woman suffrage was small and relatively weak in the late nineteenth century. But militant suffragists, like the temperance women, fought aggressively for change. The women's rights movement that had begun at Seneca Falls in 1848 had split over the issue of the Fourteenth Amendment, which had granted voting rights to African American men. Women's rights activists like Elizabeth Cady Stanton and Susan B. Anthony had wanted the Fourteenth Amendment to apply to women as well as to African Americans newly freed from slavery. "I will cut off this right arm of mine before I will ever work for or demand the ballot for the Negro and not the woman," Stanton had declared. But advocates of black suffrage such as Lucy Stone and Frederick Douglass urged women to wait, insisting that it was "the Negro's hour."

Stanton fought the Fourteenth Amendment because it did not include woman suffrage. Her strong stance led to a split among women's rights activists that produced two rival woman suffrage organizations. Stanton and Anthony formed the National Woman Suffrage Association (NWSA) in 1869,

launching the first independent women's rights movement in the United States. The more conservative American Woman Suffrage Association formed the same year. Unlike the NWSA, this group included men as well as women and welcomed many members who believed that women should vote in local but not national elections.

In 1890, the two groups united under the rubric of the National American Woman Suffrage Association (NAWSA). Twenty years had made a great change. Woman suffrage was not yet generally supported, but it was no longer considered a crackpot idea. Thanks to the WCTU's support of the "home protection ballot," suffrage had become accepted as a means to an end even when it was not embraced as woman's natural right. The NAWSA honored Elizabeth Cady Stanton by electing her its first president, but Susan B. Anthony, who took the helm in 1892, emerged as the leading figure in the new united organization.

In the 1890s, the NAWSA launched campaigns on the state level to gain the vote for women. The group won a victory in Colorado in 1893 and another in Idaho in 1896. In addition, two states joined the suffrage column when the territories of Wyoming and Utah entered the union in 1890 and 1896, respectively. But women suffered a bitter defeat in a California referendum in 1896.

Although it would take almost three decades for all women to gain the vote with the ratification of the Nineteenth Amendment in 1920, the unification of the two woman suffrage groups in 1890 signaled a new era in women's fight for the vote. And Frances Willard's place on the platform in 1892 at the founding of the People's Party in St. Louis symbolized women's growing role in politics and reform.

Ida B. Wells and the Antilynching Campaign

While most white women focused on reforms designed to counter the impact of urban industrialism in the North, black women followed a different path. The majority of African Americans were neither urban nor industrial. As late as 1890, more than 90 percent of the black population remained in the South, and those who migrated north found that discrimination blocked their employment in industry. As a result, African American women activists formed clubs and voluntary associations for self- and community improvement and organized around issues that affected life in the rural South. Foremost among their activities was the antilynch-

IDA B. WELLS

Ida B. Wells led the movement to end lynching, traveling the country to raise the nation's consciousness about this heinous and illegal practice. In 1895, Wells married Ferdinand L. Barnett, a black attorney, editor, and founder of the Chicago Conservator. *Shown here with Charles, the first of the couple's four children, Wells remained active in African American leadership, helping to found the National Association of Colored Women in 1896.*

Courtesy of University of Chicago, Department of Special Collections.

ing campaign mounted by Ida B. Wells. Wells mobilized black women throughout the country and stimulated the organization of the National Association of Colored Women.

In March of 1892, Ida B. Wells, editor of the African American newspaper *Free Speech,* learned of the murder of her friend Thomas Moss. Moss had been found in a field north of Memphis, his body riddled with bullets. Two other men, Calvin McDowell and Wil Stewart, had also been killed. The appalling crime, as Wells later recounted, "opened

my eyes to what lynching really was." For the three men had been killed not for some offense, real or imagined, against white womanhood—the common excuse for the murder or "lynching" of black men in the South. Instead their deaths could be traced to purely economic causes. The three men owned and operated the People's Grocery, a store that competed with a white-owned establishment just across the street. When the white owner instigated an attack on his black rivals, a shoot-out resulted that left three white men wounded. Despite the fact that they had acted in defense of their property, the three black grocers were arrested and jailed. In the dead of night, a lynch mob seized the men in their cells, dragged them to a waiting railroad car, carried them north of the city, and brutally shot them to death.

For Wells the crime underscored how lynching served "as an excuse to get rid of Negroes who were acquiring wealth and property and thus keep the race terrorized." Determined to do something, Wells began systematically to collect data on lynching. During 1892, she found, 241 people were lynched in twenty-six states. Of that number, 160 were identified as African Americans, and 152 of the 160 lynchings occurred in former slaveholding states. In the decade between 1882 and 1892, lynching in the South increased by an overwhelming 200 percent. The increase testified to the retreat of the federal government following Reconstruction and to Southerners' determination to maintain white supremacy through terrorism and intimidation.

At the time Wells began her antilynching campaign in 1892, she had already earned a reputation as a militant activist for African American rights. Born a slave in Holly Springs, Mississippi, in 1862, Wells grew up during Reconstruction. Her parents were active in the struggle for Negro rights and provided their daughter with strong role models. Their deaths from yellow fever left Wells an orphan at the age of sixteen. She took over as head of the family, leaving Rust College to support her five siblings. Wells found work in the Memphis city schools and became an active member in the local African Methodist Episcopal church. She also joined a local lyceum, or literary group. It was there that she began her career as a journalist, writing for the lyceum's newspaper. In 1889, she became the co-owner of the *Free Speech and Headlight,* later shortened to *Free Speech.*

Wells did not shrink from controversy. In 1884, after being forcibly removed from a seat in the ladies' car on the train, she had sued the Chesapeake, Ohio, and Southwestern Railroad and had won, only to see the decision overturned by the Tennessee Supreme Court. And in 1891, an editorial pressing for better school facilities for black children had cost her her teaching position in the Memphis schools. By the time she took up the antilynching cause, Wells had earned a reputation for her bold stand on race relations and for her work as a journalist whose syndicated columns appeared in African American papers across the country.

As the first salvo in her attack on lynching, Wells put to rest the "old threadbare lie that Negro men assault white women." As she pointed out, violations of black women by white men, which were much more frequent than black attacks on white women, went unnoticed and unpunished. Wells articulated lynching as a problem of race and gender, with the myth of black attacks on "white Southern womanhood" masking the reality that mob violence had more to do with economics and the shifting social structure of the South than with rape. She demonstrated in a sophisticated way how the southern patriarchal system, having lost its control over blacks with the end of slavery, used its control over women to circumscribe the liberty of black men.

Wells's strong stance immediately resulted in reprisal. While she was traveling in the North, her office was ransacked and her printing equipment destroyed. The warning that she would be killed on sight if she ever returned to Memphis only stiffened her resolve. As she wrote in her autobiography, *Crusade for Justice*, "Having lost my paper, had a price put on my life and been made an exile . . . , I felt that I owed it to myself and to my race to tell the whole truth now that I was where I could do so freely."

Antilynching became a lifelong commitment that took Wells twice to Britain, where she placed lynching on the international agenda. As a reporter, first for the *New York Age* and later for the *Chicago Inter-Ocean,* she used every opportunity to hammer home her message. After her marriage in 1895 to Ferdinand Barnett, she shifted the focus of her activities to Chicago, where she raised a family.

Wells's activities mobilized other black women, including Victoria Earle Matthews and Maritcha Lyons, who were already engaged in social reform and self-improvement. They hosted a testimonial dinner for Wells in New York in 1892 that led to the organization of a black women's club, the Women's Loyal Union. The club became a spearhead for the creation of the National Association of Colored Women (NACW) in 1896. The organization's first president, Mary Church Terrell of Washington, D.C., urged her followers to "promote the welfare of our race, along all the lines that tend to its development and advancement." Taking as their motto "Lifting As We Climb," the women of the NACW shouldered the double burden of self-improvement and social reform. They attacked myriad issues, including health care, housing, education, and the promotion of a positive image of the Negro race. (In their efforts, African American club women enjoyed little help from white women's clubs. The General Federation of Women's Clubs remained largely segregated at the insistence of its southern constituency.) The NACW played a critical role in Wells's antilynching campaign by lobbying for legislation that would make lynching a federal crime. Beginning in 1894 and continuing for decades after, antilynching bills were introduced in Congress only to be defeated by southern opposition.

Lynching did not end during Ida B. Wells's lifetime, nor did antilynching legislation gain passage in Congress; but Wells's forceful voice brought the issue to national prominence. At her funeral, black leader W. E. B. DuBois eulogized Wells as the woman who "began the awakening of the conscience of the nation."

The Farmers' Revolt

Hard times in the 1880s and 1890s created a groundswell of agrarian revolt. A bitter farmer wrote from Minnesota, "I settled on this Land in good Faith Built House and Barn Broken up Part of the Land. Spent years of hard Labor in grubing fencing and Improving." About to lose his land to foreclosure, he lamented, "Are they going to drive us out like tresspassers . . . and give us away to the Corporations?"

Farm prices fell, decade after decade. Wheat that sold for a dollar a bushel in 1870 dropped to eighty cents in 1885 and to sixty cents in the 1890s. The farmer actually got less, closer to thirty-five cents a bushel. Cotton plummeted from fifteen cents to five cents a pound. Corn started at forty-five cents and fell to thirty cents a bushel by the 1890s. In parts of Kansas, it sold for as little as ten cents a bushel, and angry farmers burned their crop for fuel rather than market it at that price. By 1894, almost half the farms in Kansas had fallen into the hands of the banks through foreclosure because poor farmers could not make enough money to pay their mortgages.

NEBRASKA FARM COUPLE
Many hardworking farmers like this Custer County, Nebraska, couple, photographed in 1888,
joined the Farmers'Alliance and later the Populist Party to give voice to their political, economic,
and social concerns about the direction in which America was heading.
Nebraska State Historical Society, Solomon D. Butcher Collection.

In the West, farmers rankled under a system in which railroads charged exorbitant freight rates while granting discounts to large shippers. Also, the railroads' policy of charging higher rates for a short haul than for a long haul meant that large grain elevator companies could ship their wheat from Chicago to New York and across the ocean to England for less money than it cost a Dakota farmer to send a crop to mills in nearby Minneapolis. In the South, the lack of currency and credit had driven farmers to the stopgap credit system of the crop lien, turning the entire region into a "vast pawn shop." The combined southern states actually had less money in circulation than did the state of Massachusetts.

During the depression of the 1890s, the human cost was staggering. "I Take my pen in hand to let you know that we are Starving to death," a Kansas farm woman wrote to the governor in 1894. Everywhere, the farmer seemed to be the victim of rules, such as the tariff, that worked to the advantage of big business. At the heart of the problem stood a banking system that was rooted in the gold standard and dominated by eastern commercial banks. In the face of their grievances, angry farmers across the United States raised a chorus of protest.

The Farmers' Alliance

Farm protest was not new. In the 1870s, farmers had supported the Grange and the Greenback Labor Party. But with the farmers' situation growing more desperate, the 1880s witnessed a spontaneous outbreak as farmers from Texas to Louisiana, from Kansas through the Dakotas organized into alliances. The first group of farmers gathered at a Lampasas County farm in Texas and banded together into the Farmers' Alliance to fight "land-sharks and horse thieves." In frontier farmhouses in Texas, in log cabins in backwoods Arkansas, in the rural parishes of Louisiana, separate groups formed similar alliances for self-help.

As the movement grew, the farmers consolidated into two regional alliances, the Northwestern Farmers' Alliance, which included the old Granger states of the Midwest, and the more radical Southern Farmers' Alliance, which began in Texas but soon spread into Georgia and united with groups in Louisiana and Arkansas. Determined to reach black farmers as well as whites, the Southern Alliance sponsored a separate National Colored Farmers' Alliance that recruited more than a quarter of a million members.

In the 1880s, traveling lecturers such as S. O. Daws and William Lamb in Texas spread the alliance message. Daws traveled far and wide, denouncing credit merchants, railroads, trusts, and the money power. Worn-out men and barefoot women reduced to extreme poverty by the crop lien system did not need to be convinced that something was wrong. The alliance lecturers articulated the indignation already felt by farmers. Overnight, scores of local alliances sprang up, each with its own lecturer, who in turn carried the word to every crossroads in the South. The Southern Alliance recruited at the amazing rate of 20,000 a month in the autumn of 1886. By 1887, the alliance had grown to more than 200,000 members, and by 1890 it counted more than three million members in the South alone.

At the same time, the Farmers' Alliance broadened its base by reaching out to workers during the Great Southwestern Strike against Jay Gould's Texas and Pacific Railroad in 1886. The Southern Farmers' Alliance issued a proclamation in support of the Knights of Labor, calling on farmers to boycott Gould's railroad, and rushed food and supplies to the strikers. William Lamb sponsored the boycott, observing simply that it was "a good time to help the Knights of Labor in order to secure their help in the near future." The alliance insisted that the farmer, too, was a worker and that the labor question was a crucial issue for both the farmer and the wage laborer. United as producers against those

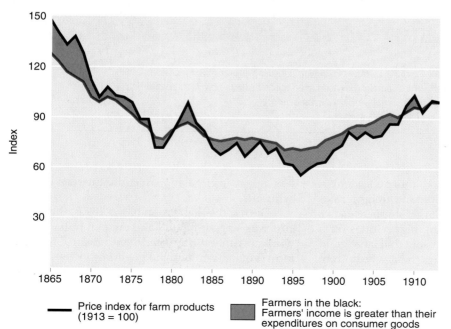

FIGURE 20.1
Consumer Prices and Farm Income, 1865 – 1913
In 1865 consumer prices and farm income were about equal. During the 1880s and 1890s, however, farmers suffered great hardships as prices for their crops declined steadily and the cost of consumer goods continued to rise.

Price index for farm products (1913 = 100)

Consumer Price Index (1913 = 100)

Farmers in the black: Farmers' income is greater than their expenditures on consumer goods

Farmers in the red: Farmers' income is less than their expenditures on consumer goods

ON THE WAY TO A POPULIST MEETING IN KANSAS
Populism was more than a political movement; it was a culture unto itself. For farmers in sparsely set-
tled regions, the movement assured them that they were not alone, that others shared their problems, and
that solutions could be found. When the Populists called a meeting, wagons came from miles around as
in this gathering in Dickinson County, Kansas. Men, women, and children were embraced by the Pop-
ulist movement, which recognized that a strong economic and political movement could be a social force.
Kansas State Historical Society, Topeka, Kansas.

who profited from their labor, the Farmers' Alliance and the Knights of Labor joined hands.

"The farmers seem like unto ripe fruit—you can gather them by a gentle shake of the bush," an alliance lecturer gloated in 1887. But ripe for what? Although its leadership insisted that the alliance was not political, it became increasingly politicized in the late 1880s. At the heart of the alliance movement was a series of farmers' cooperatives. By "bulking" their cotton, that is, selling it together, farmers could negotiate a better price. And by setting up trade stores and exchanges, they sought to escape the grasp of the merchant/creditor. Soon alliances in a dozen states competed to pioneer new purchasing cooperatives. Through the cooperatives, the Farmers' Alliance promised to change the way farmers lived. "We are going to get out of debt and be free and independent people once more," exulted one farmer. "We Georgia people are in earnest about this thing."

Cooperatives flowered throughout the South and West. In 1888, farmers scored a major victory when they defeated the jute-bagging trust in its scheme to double the price of the bags used to bale cotton. But the alliance failed in its attempt to re-

place the furnishing merchant in the South with cooperative stores. Opposition by merchants, bankers, wholesalers, and manufacturers made it impossible for the cooperatives to get credit. The Texas exchange survived only one season. Farmers soon realized that the alliance cooperatives stood little chance of working unless fundamental changes were made in the American money and credit system.

As the cooperative movement died, a new culture of politics was born. Cooperatives served as a recruitment vehicle through which huge numbers of farmers in the South and West became politicized. What had begun as an organization for self-help moved toward direct political action. Texas farmers drafted a set of demands in 1886 and pressured political candidates to endorse them. These demands became the basis of a platform proposed by the Southern Alliance in 1890 that called for railroad regulation and control, laws against land speculation, and currency and credit reform.

The alliance urged farmers to use the platform as a "yardstick," warning that candidates must "stand up and be measured." But it proved easier to get politicians to make promises than to get them to enact reform legislation. Confounded by the fail-

TABLE 20.1
THE 1892 POPULIST PARTY PLATFORM AND RESOLUTIONS

- Adoption of the sub-treasury plan
- Free and unlimited coinage of silver
- A graduated income tax
- Establishment of postal savings banks for safe deposit of earnings
- Government ownership and operation of railroads, telephone, telegraph, and postal system
- Return of land held by railroads and corporations (in excess of their "actual needs"); return of land owned by the foreign-born to native-born settlers
- Tariff reduction
- Payment of "fair and liberal" pensions to ex-Union soldiers and sailors
- Immigration restriction to prevent newcomers from undercutting and crowding out native-born wage-earners
- A shorter work day
- Prohibition of the use of Pinkerton agents to suppress strikers
- Electoral reforms including: direct popular election of senators, direct primaries, the initiative, the referendum, the secret ballot, and limiting the office of the president and vice president each to one term

ure of the Democrats and Republicans to break with commercial interests and support the farmer, the alliance moved, often reluctantly, in the direction of a third party.

At its start in 1877, alliance leader C. W. Macune had insisted, "The Alliance is a strictly white man's nonpolitical, secret business association." But by 1892, after more than a decade of organization, education, and politicization, the alliance was none of those things. Although some southern leaders, like Macune, made it clear that they would never threaten the unity of the white vote in the South by leaving the Democratic Party, advocates of a third party carried the day at the convention of laborers, farmers, and common folk in St. Louis. There, the Farmers' Alliance gave birth to the People's Party and launched the Populist movement.

The Populist Movement

"There is something at the back of all this turmoil more than the failure of crops or the scarcity of ready cash," a journalist observed in 1892. Populism was more than a set of demands and a list of economic grievances. At its heart were the emotion and the spirit of a religious revival. Wagon trains of ten thousand farmers gathered at camp meetings to listen to speeches by the angry prophets of the

movement. Populism, growing out of the Farmers' Alliance, was a mass movement with its own political language and its own slogan: "The alliance is the people and the people are together."

Henry Demarest Lloyd observed, "The People's Party . . . is the organized aspiration of the people for a fuller, nobler, richer, kindlier life for every man, woman, and child . . ."

The Populists mounted a critique of industrial society and a call for action. Convinced that the money and banking systems of the day worked to the advantage of the few and not the many, they demanded economic democracy. To solve the farmers' credit problem, C. W. Macune hit on the ingenious idea of the subtreasury, a plan that would allow farmers to store nonperishable crops in government storehouses until the market was advantageous. At the same time, they would receive commodity credit from the federal government that would enable them to buy needed supplies and seed. The subtreasury became an article of faith in the South, where it promised to eliminate the crop lien system once and for all. Although Macune's idea would be enacted piecemeal in Progressive and New Deal legislation after the turn of the century, at the time he proposed it in the 1890s it was dismissed by conservatives as far-fetched and communistic.

For the western farmer, whose enemy was not the merchant but the mortgage, Populism promised land reform. The Populists called for a plan that would reclaim excessive lands granted or sold to railroads and foreign investors. The Populists' boldest plan called for government ownership of the railroads and telegraphs to put an end to discriminatory rate practices. With the powerful railroads dominating politics and effectively nullifying the Interstate Commerce Act, which had passed in 1887 to regulate the railroads, Populists saw no solution short of government ownership. They did not shrink from advocating what their opponents called state socialism.

Money joined credit and land as the third major thrust of the Populist movement. Farmers in all sections rallied to the cry for cheaper currency, endorsing platform planks calling for free silver and greenbacks. To show their support for labor, Populists supported the eight-hour day and an end to contract labor. And to empower the common people, the platform called for the direct election of senators and electoral reforms including the secret ballot and the right to initiate legislation, to recall elected officials, and to submit issues to the people via referendum. More than just a response to hard times, Populism presented an alternative vision of what America could become. As Henry Demarest Lloyd, an enthusiastic supporter of Populism, observed, "The People's Party is more than the organized discontent of the people. It is the organized aspiration of the people for a fuller, nobler, richer, kindlier life for every man, woman, and child in the ranks of humanity." It represented, in Lloyd's words, "an uprising of principle."

The Labor Wars

While the farmers united to fight for change, industrial laborers fought their own battles in a series of bloody strikes so fiercely waged on both sides that one historian has called them the "labor wars." Coal miners struck to fight the use of convict labor in the mines of eastern Tennessee. Miners in Coeur d'Alene, Idaho, and Cripple Creek, Colorado, joined the militant Western Federation of Miners and battled the bosses. Railroad switchmen went on strike in Buffalo, New York, and a general strike

closed down the port of New Orleans. At issue was the right of labor to organize and speak through unions and to fight for better conditions and more control in the workplace.

The two major conflicts of the period, the Homestead lockout of 1892 and the Pullman strike of 1894, raised fundamental questions about the rights of laborers and the sanctity of private property.

Skilled workers had watched as management undermined their autonomy, replacing men with machines and systematically reducing skilled jobs to unskilled work. The proportion of craftsworkers had shrunk, and their control over the workplace diminished at the same time that a growing number of common laborers, many of them immigrants from southern and eastern Europe, came into the mills. Workers felt increasingly threatened. In the 1890s, they made a stand. The two major conflicts of the period, the Homestead lockout and strike of 1892 and the Pullman strike of 1894, raised fundamental questions about the rights of laborers and the sanctity of private property.

The Homestead Lockout and Strike

At first glance it seemed ironic that Carnegie steel's Homestead mill became the storm center of labor's fight for the right to unionize. Andrew Carnegie was unique among industrialists as a self-styled friend of labor. In 1886 he had written, "The right of the workingmen to combine and to form trades unions is no less sacred than the right of the manufacturer to enter into associations and conferences with his fellows, and it must sooner or later be conceded." Yet six years later at Homestead, Carnegie set out to crush a union in one of labor's legendary confrontations.

As much as he cherished his liberal beliefs, Carnegie cherished his profits more. Labor unions had worked well for him during the years when he was building his empire. Labor strife at Homestead during the 1870s had enabled Carnegie to buy the plant from his competitors at cost and take control of the steel industry. And during the 1880s, strong national craft unions ensured that competing mills could not undercut his labor costs. But by the 1890s, Carnegie held a dictatorial grasp on the steelmaking business, and the benefits of unionism were no longer so evident to the great steelmaker. Carnegie wanted complete control.

Standing in his way was the Amalgamated Association of Iron and Steel Workers, one of the largest and richest of the craft unions that made up the American Federation of Labor. In 1892, when the Amalgamated attempted to renew its contract at Carnegie's Homestead mill, its leaders were told that since "the vast majority of our employees are Non union, the Firm has decided that the minority must give place to the majority." While it was true that only eight hundred skilled workers belonged to the elite Amalgamated, the union had long enjoyed the support of the plant's three thousand nonunion workers. Slavs who did much of the unskilled work made common cause with the Welsh, Scots, and Irish who belonged to the union. Never before had the Amalgamated been denied a contract.

As the situation built toward a showdown, Carnegie sailed to Scotland. No doubt aware of his hypocrisy, he preferred not to be directly involved. He left Henry Clay Frick, the toughest antilabor man in the industry, in charge of the Homestead plant.

By summer a strike looked inevitable. Frick prepared for the showdown by erecting a fifteen-foot fence around the plant and topping it with barbed wire. With platforms for searchlights and holes for rifles, the fence gave the mill a distinctly military look. Workers aptly dubbed it "Fort Frick." To defend his fort, Frick hired three hundred mercenaries from the Pinkerton Detective Agency at the rate of five dollars per day, more than double the wage of the average Homestead worker.

The Pinkerton National Detective Agency, founded before the Civil War, came into its own in the 1880s as businessmen like Frick used Pinkerton agents as a private security force. Largely recruited from the ranks of the unemployed, the Pinkertons included some criminals and hoodlums as well as college boys on vacation. The "Pinks" earned the hatred of workers by protecting strikebreakers and acting as company spies.

On June 28, Frick locked the workers out of the mills. They immediately rallied to the support of the Amalgamated and declared a strike. Hugh O'Donnell, the young Irishman who led the union, vowed to prevent strikebreakers from entering the plant. On July 6 at four in the morning, a lookout spotted two barges moving up the Monongahela River in the fog. Frick was attempting to smuggle his Pinkertons into Homestead. Workers sounded the alarm, and within minutes a crowd of more than one thou-

sand, hastily armed with rifles, hoes, and fence posts, rushed to the riverbank to meet the enemy. When the Pinkertons attempted to come ashore, gunfire broke out, and more than a dozen Pinkertons and some thirty strikers fell, killed or wounded. The Pinkertons retreated back onto the barges.

In the twelve hours that followed, the strikers threw everything they had at the barges, but they could not blow them out of the water. Finally, the Pinkertons hoisted a white flag and arranged with O'Donnell to surrender. With eight strikers dead or dying and scores wounded, the crowd, now numbering perhaps ten thousand, was in no mood for conciliation. As the Pinkertons came up the hill, they were forced to run a gauntlet of screaming, cursing men, women, and children. One woman used her umbrella to poke out the eye of a hated "Pink." When a young guard dropped to his knees, weeping for mercy, he was clubbed unconscious. Only one Pinkerton had been killed in the siege on the barges, but in the grim rout that followed their surrender, three men died as a result of the beatings, and not one of the three hundred avoided injury.

The "battle of Fort Frick" ended in a dubious victory for the workers. They took control of the plant and elected a council to run the community. At first, public opinion favored their cause. Newspapers urged Frick to negotiate or submit to arbitration. The Populists, meeting in St. Louis, condemned the use of "hireling armies." A congressman castigated Carnegie for "skulking in his castle in Scotland."

But the action of the strikers struck at the heart of the capitalist system, pitting the workers' right to their jobs against the rights of private property. Four days after the confrontation, the Pennsylvania governor, who sympathized with the workers, nonetheless yielded to pressure and ordered eight thousand National Guard troops into Homestead to protect Carnegie's mills.

At first the strikers welcomed the guard, but they soon became disillusioned. The guard's ninety-five-day occupation not only protected Carnegie's property but also enabled Frick to reopen the mills using strikebreakers. "We have been deceived," workers bitterly complained. "We have stood idly by and let the town be occupied by soldiers who come here, not as our protectors, but as the protectors of non-union men. . . . If we undertake to resist the seizure of our jobs, we will be shot down like dogs."

Then, in a bizarre episode accompanying the Homestead lockout, Alexander Berkman, a Russian immigrant and anarchist, attempted to assassinate

THE BATTLE AT THE HOMESTEAD STEEL MILL
This contemporary lithograph portrays scenes from the battle between workers and strikebreakers in July 1892: workers attacking the barges, cannonading of the barges, surrender of the Pinkertons, captives being led to prison, and, finally, arrival of the militia and the soldiers in camp. The lithograph also shows (lower right) the revenge the strikers took on the hated "Pinks." Of the 316 Pinkertons, not one escaped injury as the angry crowd, armed with clubs, hoes, and brickbats, forced them to run a bloody gauntlet.
Carnegie Library, Pittsburgh.

Henry Clay Frick. Berkman's ally in his undertaking was the noted anarchist Emma Goldman, a Russian Jewish immigrant who had won a national reputation for her fiery speeches against capitalism and in favor of birth control. Together Berkman and Goldman planned the assassination of Frick in the belief that it would ignite a general uprising. But they badly miscalculated. Berkman bungled his attempt. Frick, shot twice, survived and showed considerable courage, allowing doctors to remove the bullets from his neck but refusing to leave his desk until the day's work was completed. "I do not think that I shall die," Frick remarked coolly, "but whether I do or not, the Company will pursue the same policy and it will win." Overnight, the man castigated for hiring Pinkertons won the nation's sympathy.

After the assassination attempt, in August, public opinion turned against the workers. Berkman was quickly tried and sentenced to prison. Although the Amalgamated and the AFL denounced his action, the incident served to couple anarchism and unionism, already associated in the public mind as a result of the Haymarket bombing in 1886. Hugh O'Donnell later wrote that "the bullet from Berkman's pistol, failing in its foul intent, went straight through the heart of the Homestead strike."

In the end, the workers' resistance was crushed. The strike collapsed after four and a half months. The Homestead mill reopened and the men returned to work, except for the union leaders, who were blacklisted in every steel and iron mill in the country. In the drama and melodrama of events surrounding Homestead, the ideological and political significance of what occurred often remained obscured: The workers at Homestead had been taught a lesson. They would never again, in the words of the National Guard commander, "believe the works are their's [sic] quite as much as Carnegie's."

"Our victory is now complete and most gratifying," Frick wired Carnegie. "Do not think we will ever have serious labor trouble again. . . . We had to teach our employees a lesson and we have taught them one that they will never forget." With the owners firmly in the saddle, the mills reopened. The company slashed wages, reinstated the twelve-hour day, and eliminated five hundred jobs. The workers lapsed into a demoralized and hopeless state. It would take another forty-five years before steelworkers successfully unionized. In the meantime, Carnegie's production tripled, even in the midst of a depression. "Ashamed to tell you profits these days," Carnegie wrote a friend in 1899. And no wonder; his profits had grown from $4 million in the year of the lockout to $40 million in 1900.

Eugene V. Debs and the Pullman Strike

A year after the Homestead lockout, a major panic and depression hit the nation. A stock market crash on Wall Street in the spring of 1893 led to bitter hard times. The ranks of the unemployed swelled to three million, almost half of the working population. Nowhere were workers more demoralized than in the model town of Pullman on the outskirts of Chicago. George M. Pullman, who made his millions by building Pullman Palace cars and leasing them to the railroads, prided himself on his enlightened approach to labor. But in 1893, Pullman's workers saw their pay sliced five times between May and December. Altogether, they sustained cuts of at least 28 percent.

At the same time, Pullman refused to lower the rents in his model town, insisting that "the renting of the dwellings and the employment of workmen at Pullman are in no way tied together." When workers went to the bank to cash their checks, the rent was taken out. One worker found that he had only forty-seven cents to live on for two weeks. When the bank teller asked him whether he wanted to apply it to his back rent, he retorted, "If Mr. Pullman needs that forty-seven cents worse than I do, let him have it." In the meantime, Pullman continued to pay his stockholders an 8 percent dividend, and the company accumulated a $25 million surplus.

At the heart of the labor problems at Pullman was not only economic inequity but the company's attempt to take control of the work process, substituting piecework for day wages and narrowing the difference between the skilled work performed by craftsworkers and the work of operatives. During the depression, Pullman's supervisors repeatedly imposed lower piece rates, forcing workers to make the same parts for less money and undermining the work of skilled craftsworkers. A woman complained of the "tyrannical and abusive treatment" meted out at Pullman. When workers protested, management instituted new forms of shop discipline, forbidding the workers to talk or assemble in a futile attempt to keep them from unionizing. Workers like painter Theodore Rhodie resented not only the drop in wages but also the loss of autonomy. Rhodie argued that it was his "right as an American citizen" to speak to whomever he chose.

The Pullman workers rebelled. During the spring of 1894, they flocked to the ranks of the American Railway Union (ARU), a new union led by Eugene Victor Debs. The ARU, unlike the skilled craft unions of the AFL, pledged to organize all railway workers from the elite engineers down to the lowliest engine wipers and section hands. Its belief in industrial democracy, however, was not matched by a commitment to racial equality; by a narrow margin, union members voted to exclude black workers.

Eugene V. Debs was a homegrown Hoosier labor leader with strong compassion for the unskilled workers at the bottom of labor's hierarchy. "It has been my life's desire," he wrote, "to unify railroad employees and to eliminate the aristocracy of labor, which unfortunately exists, and organize them so all will be on an equality." Workers who had long been excluded from the railroad's elite craft unions joined the new union at the rate of 200 to 400 a day in the fall of 1893. Within a year, the ARU had grown to 150,000.

George Pullman responded to his workers' grievances by firing three of the union's leaders the day after they led a delegation to protest wage cuts. Angry men and women walked off the job in disgust. What began as a spontaneous protest in May 1894 blossomed into a strike that involved more than 90 percent of Pullman's 3,300 workers. "We do not know what the outcome will be, and in fact we do not much care," one worker confessed. "We do know that we are working for less wages than will maintain ourselves and families in the necessaries of life, and on that proposition we refuse to work any longer." Pullman countered by shutting down the plant.

In June, the Pullman strikers appealed to the ARU to come to their aid. Debs sympathized with the strikers, but he hesitated to commit his fledgling union to a major strike in the midst of a depression. He pleaded with the workers to find another solution. When Pullman adamantly refused to arbitrate, the ARU, brushing aside Debs's call for caution, voted to boycott all Pullman cars. Beginning on June 29, switchmen refused to handle any train that carried Pullman cars.

The conflict escalated quickly. The General Managers Association (GMA), a combination of managers from twenty-four different railroads, acted in concert to quash the boycott. Determined to kill the ARU, they quickly retaliated by recruiting strikebreakers and firing all the switchmen who refused to handle Pullman cars. Their tactics set off a chain reaction. Disgusted with long hours, arbitrary treatment, and wage cuts, entire train crews walked off the job in a show of solidarity with the Pullman workers. In a matter of days the boycott/strike spread to more than fifteen railroads and affected twenty-seven states and territories. On day one, 18,000 workers walked out; on day three, the number grew to 40,000; and by the fourth day, more than 125,000 railroad workers were out on strike, despite the opposition of the conservative railroad unions in the AFL. By July 2, rail lines from New York to California lay paralyzed. Even the GMA was forced to concede that the railroads had been "fought to a standstill."

The strike remained surprisingly peaceful. Mobs stopped trains carrying Pullman cars and forced their crews to uncouple the cars and leave them on the sidings. But no major riots broke out, and no serious damage was done to railroad property. Debs, a whirlwind of activity, fired off telegrams to all parts of the country advising his followers to avoid violence, to use no force to stop trains, and to respect law and order. But the nation's newspapers, fed press releases by the GMA, distorted and misrepresented the strike. Across the country, papers ran headlines like "Wild Riot in Chicago," "Mob Is in Control," and "Law Is Trampled On." Editors rushed to denounce "Dictator Debs."

In Washington, Attorney General Richard B. Olney, a lawyer with strong ties to the railroads, determined to put down the strike. Acting in concert with the GMA, he sought to convince President Grover Cleveland that federal troops should intervene on the pretext of protecting the mails. When Cleveland balked, Olney advised the federal attorney in Chicago to obtain an injunction from a federal court requiring the workers to stop the boycott. Two Chicago judges quickly complied, issuing an order so sweeping that it prohibited Debs from even speaking in public. Through the use of the injunction, the court in effect made striking a crime punishable by a jail sentence for contempt of court, a civil process that did not require trial by jury. The injunction had the effect of outlawing the boycott and the strike. Even the conservative *Chicago Tribune* judged the injunction "a menace to liberty . . . a weapon ever ready for the capitalist." Furious, Debs risked jail by refusing to honor it.

Olney's strategy worked. With the strikers acting in violation of a federal injunction and with the mails in jeopardy (the GMA made sure that Pullman cars were put on every mail train), Cleveland called out the army. But he did so over the heated objections of the governor of Illinois, John Peter Altgeld. Altgeld, with his keen sense of fair play, had refused to use state militia to stop the strike. "At present some of our railroads are paralyzed," he had written the president calmly, "not by reason of obstruction, but because they cannot get men to operate their trains." When Cleveland called up federal troops, Altgeld protested that he had neither asked for nor desired the intervention of the army. He pointedly reminded Cleveland that "local self-government is a fundamental principle of our Constitution." Cleveland brushed aside Altgeld's objections, noting briefly that he thought it his duty to "restore obedience to law and to protect life and property."

On July 5, the army marched into Chicago, nearly two thousand strong, along with five thousand special federal deputy marshals, many reputedly recruited from the "dregs of the city." The GMA was jubilant. "It has now become a fight between the United States Government and the American Railway Union," a spokesman observed, "and we shall leave them to fight it out."

Violence immediately erupted. Crowds blocked railroad cars and set them on fire. In one day, more than $340,000 worth of property was destroyed, twenty-five workers were shot, and more than sixty were wounded. In the face of bullets and bayonets, the strikers held firm. "Troops cannot move trains," Debs reminded the striking ARU locals, a fact that was borne out as the railroads remained paralyzed despite military intervention. But if the army could not put down the strike, the injunction could and did. Debs was arrested and imprisoned for contempt of court. In a matter of days, the strike collapsed. With its leader in jail, its headquarters raided and ransacked, and its members demoralized, the ARU was defeated along with the strike. The Pullman factory reopened, hiring new workers to replace many of the strikers and leaving sixteen hundred workers without jobs and without the means to relocate. In August, Governor Altgeld toured Pullman, where he found widespread misery and starvation. The ARU and labor had suffered an overwhelming defeat.

In the aftermath of the strike, a special commission investigated the events at Pullman, taking testimony from 107 witnesses, from workers at the car company to George M. Pullman himself. Stubborn and self-righteous, Pullman spoke for the business orthodoxy of his era, steadfastly affirming the right of business to safeguard its interests through confederacies like the General Managers Association and, at the same time, denying labor's right to organize. In response to questioning, Pullman defended his actions. "If we were to receive these men as representatives of the union," he candidly confessed, "they could probably force us to pay any wages which they saw fit." Arguing that "no prudent employer would submit to arbitration," he insisted that there was a principle at stake: the company's "control of its own business."

In his Woodstock jail cell, Eugene Debs reviewed the events of the Pullman strike. With the army and the courts ready to come to the aid of property, labor had little recourse, Debs realized. Strikes seemed futile, and unions remained helpless; workers must take control of the state itself. Debs went into jail a trade unionist and came out six months later a socialist. After a brief flirtation with Populism, he would go on to form the Socialist Party in 1900 and run for president on its ticket five times, once from jail, where he again found himself in 1920 for opposing America's entry into World War I.

The Pullman strike revealed the evils of industrial paternalism, but it also demonstrated the power of organized management and the willingness of the government to come to the aid of the employers by wielding the court's power of injunction and by dispatching federal troops. When push came to shove at Pullman, as at Homestead, the federal government's police function of protecting property took precedence over labor's right to organize and to strike.

From Homestead to Coeur d'Alene, from Pullman to Cripple Creek, workers in the 1890s struggled to organize and to gain legitimacy for their right to bargain collectively and to have some say on the shop floor. Against them they found arrayed the might of the state, the power of the courts, and the influence of the press. In the end it was no contest. Although labor would make many gains in the coming decades, it would take the passage of the Wagner Act in 1935 before unions gained, once and for all, the right to bargain collectively. The labor wars of the 1890s rarely ended successfully for the strikers, but they dramatized the willingness of workers to fight for their rights and forced the nation to confront the issue of industrial strife.

Depression Politics

"A fearful crisis is upon us," wrote a labor publication in the winter of 1893. "Countless thousands of our fellow men are unemployed; men, women and children are suffering the pangs of hunger!" Railroad magnate Chauncey Depew concurred. "I have been through all the panics of the last thirty years," he wrote, "but I have never seen one in which the distress was so widespread and reached so many people."

The burden of feeding and sheltering the unemployed and their families fell to private charity, city government, and some of the stronger trade unions. The states and the federal government appropriated not a cent for aid.

The depression that began in the spring of 1893 and lasted for more than four years put nearly half of the labor force out of work. The country swarmed with people looking for jobs. They road the rails, slept in barns, begged for work, and, when they couldn't get work, begged for food. Dismissed as tramps or hoboes by the press, this army of the unemployed sought jobs, not handouts. Populist Governor Lorenzo Lewelling of Kansas, one of the few to sympathize with their plight, issued his "tramp circular" in December 1893. In it he lashed out at vagrancy laws that imprisoned "thousands of men, guilty of no crime but poverty," and promised that the poor would not be harassed in Kansas.

The burden of feeding and sheltering the unemployed and their families fell to private charity, city government, and some of the stronger trade unions. The states and the federal government appropriated not a cent for aid. Following the harsh dictates of social Darwinism and laissez-faire, the majority of Americans believed that it was inappropriate for the government to intervene. When Cincinnati set up a public works program for the unemployed, the business community complained that it "demoralized" the poor and attacked the program as "communistic" and a "waste of taxpayers' money."

The scope of the depression made it impossible for local agencies to supply relief, although they set up soup kitchens across the land to feed the hungry. Increasingly, voices called on the federal government to take action. The American Federation of Labor declared that the "right to work is the right

to life" and argued that "when the private employer cannot or will not give work, the municipality, state or nation must." Calls for government intervention mounted throughout the decade as poverty created its own politics.

Coxey's "Army"

Masses of unemployed Americans marched to Washington, D.C., in the spring of 1894 to call attention to their plight and to urge Congress to take action. From Seattle, from San Francisco, from Los Angeles, and from Denver, hundreds joined the trek to Washington. Jacob S. Coxey of Massilon, Ohio, led the most publicized contingent. Coxey, a wealthy manufacturer, had a plan to end unemployment. "What I am after," he told the press, "is to try to put this country in a condition so that no man who wants work shall be obliged to remain idle." He proposed to put the jobless to work building badly needed roads. Coxey had been an ardent

COXEY'S ARMY
Coxey's army called itself a "petition in boots." Here a group of Coxeyites in coats, ties, and bowler hats march behind the American flag as women and children join a curious crowd to greet the marchers as they pass. These well-dressed marchers hardly seem like a menacing army. But many feared Coxey and his followers, and the military rhetoric of the press only fueled their fears. Coxey dramatized the plight of hundreds of thousands of workers left unemployed in the wake of the panic of 1893.
Library of Congress.

Greenbacker (he named his son Legal Tender), and he planned to finance his program of public works by an issue of paper currency (greenbacks) and no-interest bonds. His plan won the support of the American Federation of Labor and the Populists.

Starting out from Ohio with one hundred men, Coxey's "army" swelled as it marched east through the spring snows of the Alleghenies. In Homestead, Coxey recruited several hundred from the ranks of those left unemployed in the wake of the lockout. Called by Coxey the "Commonweal of Christ," the army marched to the tune of "Marching through Georgia":

> We are marching to the Capitol,
>   three hundred thousand strong,
> With live petitions in our boots
>   to urge our cause along.
> And when we kick our congressmen,
>   they'll feel there's something wrong,
> As we go marching with Coxey.
>
> We are not tramps nor vagabonds,
>   that's shirking honest toil,
> But miners, clerks, skilled artisans,
>   and tillers of the soil
> Now forced to beg our brother worms
>   to give us leave to toil,
> While we are marching with Coxey.
>
> Hurrah! hurrah! for the unemployed's appeal
> Hurrah! hurrah! for the marching commonweal!
> Stop the trust and combine steal,
> For we are marching with Coxey.

On May 1, Coxey's army arrived in Washington. Given permission to parade but forbidden to speak from the Capitol, Coxey defiantly marched his men onto the Capitol grounds. Police set upon the band, cracking heads and arresting Coxey and his lieutenants. Coxey went to jail for twenty days and was fined five dollars for "walking on the grass."

Mass demonstrations of the unemployed served only to frighten comfortable Americans, who saw the specter of insurrection and rebellion everywhere in 1894. Those who had trembled for the safety of the Republic heaved a sigh of relief after Coxey's arrest, hoping that it would halt the march on Washington. But other armies of the unemployed, possibly as many as five thousand, were still on their way. Too poor to pay for railway tickets, they rode the rails as "freeloaders." The more daring contingents commandeered entire trains, stirring fears of revolution. Nervous midwestern

governors put trains at the marchers' disposal to speed them quickly out of the state. Journalists who covered the march did little to quiet the nation's fears. They delighted in military terminology, dubbing the marchers "armies" and describing themselves as "war correspondents." Their writing gave to the episode a tone of urgency and heightened the sense of a nation imperiled.

By August, the tattered armies dissolved. Although the "On to Washington" movement proved ineffective in forcing federal legislation, Coxey's army dramatized the plight of the unemployed and acted, in the words of one participant, as a "living, moving object lesson." Coxey's tattered "soldiers of misfortune" roused compassion among some they met along the way and stimulated discussion of what should be done. Although much of the eastern press heaped ridicule on Coxey and his motley crew of commonwealers, their uneasy laughter did not disguise the stark fact that something was seriously wrong. Like the Populist revolt, Coxey's army called into question the underlying values of the new industrial order and demonstrated how ordinary citizens turned to means outside the regular party system to influence politics in the 1890s.

The People's Party

"We meet in midst of a nation brought to the verge of moral, political, and material ruin," the Populists declared when they met in Omaha in July 1892 to nominate a national ticket. In the lengthy preamble to their platform, they cataloged their discontent:

> Corruption dominates the ballot-box, the legislatures, the Congress, and touches even the ermine of the bench. The people are demoralized. . . . The fruits of the toil of millions are boldly stolen to build up colossal fortunes for a few. . . . From the same prolific womb of governmental injustice we breed the two great classes—tramps and millionaires.

A sense of the world gone wrong, lurching toward catastrophe, fueled the Omaha convention. Ignatius Donnelly, author of the fiery preamble, spoke of a "vast conspiracy against mankind" and warned of "terrible social convulsions, the destruction of civilization." To answer this threat, he called on the Populists "to restore the government of the Republic to the hands of 'the plain people.'"

The Populists who arrived in Omaha on the Fourth of July to nominate a national slate for "the new party of the industrial millions" came by

CAMPAIGN RIBBONS

Political paraphernalia from the election of 1892 tells a good deal about each party's candidates and beliefs. The People's Party standard-bearer, General James B. Weaver, and his running mate are pictured under a banner promising "Homes for the Toilers, Equal Rights to All, Special Privileges to None." Populist issues are clearly spelled out — "Money, Land, and Transportation." The Populists' hope that these economic issues would replace sectional loyalties is evident in the symbolism of the blue Union and gray Confederate hands shaking. The beliefs of Democratic candidate Grover Cleveland are summed up in the phrase that became his motto, "Public Office Is a Public Trust." Republican Benjamin Harrison, who enjoyed the support of the business community, is aptly portrayed as sponsored by the Bankers and Brokers Republican Club.
Collection of Janice L. and David J. Frent.

wagon, by oxcart, and on foot. Few could afford train fare. The railroad chiefs had evidently read the St. Louis platform, with its call for government ownership of railroads. The Populists did not receive the reduced rates usually given to political delegates.

The Farmers' Alliance, remnants of the Grange, the Knights of Labor, and the WCTU were all on hand. Conspicuously absent was Leonidas L. Polk, the new party's first choice as its standard-bearer. He had died suddenly and the Populists scrambled to find a replacement. They nominated as their presidential candidate General James B. Weaver of Iowa,

a former Union general who had headed the Greenback Labor ticket in 1880. To balance the slate, they selected an ex-Confederate general as his running mate. The legacy of the Civil War cast its long shadow over Populist Party politics. Many southern Democrats, such as C. W. Macune, could not bring themselves to break with the Democratic "party of the fathers" and stayed away from the convention.

As befitted a party of principle, the longest ovation came not for the candidate but for the platform. When the chairman read the list of demands hammered out in St. Louis in February, the crowd went wild. To the eyes of a frightened eastern journalist, the enthusiasm evoked the spirit of the French Revolution. "Cheers and yells," he wrote, "rose like a tornado from four thousand throats and raged without cessation for thirty-four minutes, during which women shrieked and wept, men embraced and kissed their neighbors, locked arms . . . leaped upon tables and chairs in the ecstasy of their delirium."

The eastern press magnified the journalist's fears, rushing to denounce the Populists as "cranks, lunatics, and idiots." Righteous editors dismissed the Populists as "calamity howlers." Branding the Populist leaders with derogatory nicknames such as "Sockless" Jerry Simpson, Davis "Bloody Bridles" Waite, and James H. "Cyclone" Davis, the press denounced them as crackpots and dangerous radicals. The Populists shot back. "They say that I am a 'calamity howler,'" Lorenzo Lewelling of Kansas retorted. "If that is so I want to continue to howl until those conditions are improved." And Mary Elizabeth Lease, accused of being a communist, responded unperturbed, "You may call me an anarchist, a socialist or a communist, I care not, but I hold to the theory that if one man has not enough to eat three times a day and another man has $25 million, that last man has something that belongs to the first."

The Populists garnered more than a million votes in the election of 1892, a respectable showing for a new party. They won three governorships and ten seats in Congress, and they captured twenty-two electoral votes. On the local level, they won fifty state posts and put into office more than fifteen hundred county officials and state legislators. By working with the party out of power, usually the Democrats in the West and the Republicans in the South, they tipped the balance in the national election. This kind of fusion worked best in the West, where it took enough votes away from the incumbent Republican President Benjamin Harrison to allow Democrat Grover Cleveland to return to the White House. Viewing the election as a successful test of strength for a new party, Eugene Debs predicted, "The People's Party will come into power with a resistless rush as did the Republican party a little more than 30 years ago."

The fusion tactic worked in the West, but in the South the Populists made a disappointing showing. It was hard for southern Democrats to fuse with Republicans, especially to vote for a former Union general. Weaver proved an unpopular candidate south of the Mason-Dixon line. He had to cut short his

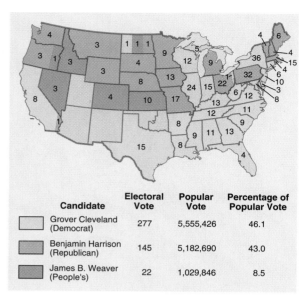

Candidate	Electoral Vote	Popular Vote	Percentage of Popular Vote
Grover Cleveland (Democrat)	277	5,555,426	46.1
Benjamin Harrison (Republican)	145	5,182,690	43.0
James B. Weaver (People's)	22	1,029,846	8.5

MAP 20.1
The Election of 1892

speaking tour in the South after Georgia crowds pelted him with rotten eggs until he looked like "a walking omelet." The People's Party fared better in the 1894 congressional elections, when, unencumbered by a Yankee general, the Populists added half a million voters to their column.

But more than their alliance with the Yankee North, it was the Populists' willingness to form common cause with black farmers that made them anathema in the South. Tom Watson of Georgia tackled the "Negro question" head on in 1892. Realizing that race prejudice obscured the common interests of black and white farmers, Watson campaigned as a Populist for Congress, promising "to wipe out the color line." He openly courted African Americans, appearing on platforms with black speakers. When angry Georgia whites threatened to lynch a black Populist preacher, Watson rallied two thousand gun-toting Populists to the man's defense. "We are determined," said the Populist sheriff of McDuffie County, "in this free country that the humblest white or black man that wants to talk our doctrine shall do it, and the man doesn't live who shall touch a hair of his head, without fighting every man in the people's party." The spectacle of white Georgians protecting a black man from lynching was symptomatic of the enormous changes Populism promised in the South.

McKinley, Bryan, and the Election of 1896

As the election of 1896 approached, depression intensified the need for currency reform. Once again, cries for free silver (the coinage of silver in addition to gold) stirred rebellion in the ranks of both the Democratic and Republican Parties. When the Republicans nominated Governor William McKinley of Ohio on a platform pledging the preservation of the gold standard, western advocates of free silver walked out of the convention. Open rebellion also split the Democratic Party as vast segments in the West and South repudiated President Grover Cleveland because of his support for the gold standard. In South Carolina, Benjamin Tillman won his race for Congress by promising, "Send me to Washington and I'll stick my pitchfork into [Cleveland's] old ribs!"

The spirit of revolt animated the Democratic convention in Chicago in the summer of 1896. "Pitchfork" Ben Tillman set the tone by attacking the party's president, denouncing the Cleveland administration as "undemocratic and tyrannical." But the man of the hour was William Jennings Bryan of Nebraska, the thirty-six-year-old "boy orator from the Platte," who whipped the convention to a frenzy with his passionate call for free silver. In his keynote address, Bryan masterfully cataloged the grievances of farmers and laborers, closing his dramatic speech with the ringing exhortation "Do not crucify mankind upon a cross of gold." Pandemonium broke loose. The delegates seized Bryan and hoisted him to their shoulders. In the demonstration that followed, delegates stampeded to support Bryan. Overnight, the young Nebraskan found himself propelled into the national spotlight, the youngest candidate ever to win a presidential nomination.

The juggernaut of free silver rolled out of Chicago and on to St. Louis, where the People's Party met a week after the Democrats adjourned. Smelling victory, many western Populists urged the party to endorse Bryan. In their haste, they were willing to jettison the Omaha platform and run on the issue of silver alone. "I care not for party names," declared Jerry Simpson, "it is the substance we are after, and we have it in William J. Bryan." A note of warning came from Populists like Tom Watson of Georgia. Watson denounced the Bryanites as opportunists and urged the Populists to steer clear of both major parties and stick to "the middle of the road." In the South, where Democrats had resorted to fraud and violence to steal elections from the Pop-

ulists in 1892 and 1894, support for a Democratic ticket proved especially hard for Populists to swallow. Another obstacle in the path of fusion was Arthur M. Sewall, Bryan's running mate. A Maine shipbuilder, railway director, and bank president, Sewall had been placed on the ticket to appease more conservative Democrats. But to the Populists, Sewall symbolized everything they opposed.

Populist delegates tried to remain true to their principles and their platform in St. Louis. They voted to support all the planks of the old Omaha platform, added to it a call for public works projects for the unemployed, and narrowly defeated a plank for woman suffrage. Only deceit and trickery enabled the fusionists to carry the day. In an unorthodox turn of events, the convention selected the vice presidential candidate first. By nominating Tom Watson to replace Sewall, the party undercut opposition to fusing with the Democrats. Bryan quickly wired the chairman of the convention, protesting that he would not drop Sewall as his running mate or run on a Populist ticket with Watson. Mysteriously, his message never reached the convention floor. Watson's nomination paved the way for the selection of Bryan by a lopsided vote. The Populists did not know it, but their cheers for Bryan in St. Louis signaled not a chorus of victory, but the death knell of the People's Party.

Few contests in the nation's history have been as fiercely fought and as full of emotion as the presidential election of 1896. On the one side stood Republican William McKinley, backed by the wealthy industrialist and party boss Marcus Alonzo Hanna. Hanna played on business fears of free silver to raise more than $4 million for the Republican war chest, double that of any previous campaign. J. P. Morgan and John D. Rockefeller reputedly contributed $174,000 each. McKinley, best known for the high protective tariff that he had sponsored while in Congress, styled himself the "advance agent of prosperity." Ironically, the advance agent had nearly gone bankrupt in the panic of 1893. Only the generous contributions of Hanna and his friends kept McKinley afloat and able to run in 1896. Following the time-honored tradition, McKinley waged a "front porch" campaign from his home in Canton, Ohio. But despite McKinley's low profile, the Republicans, with unlimited funds at their disposal, mounted an impressive campaign. The party relied on speakers, posters, buttons, and printed circulars —over 250 million of them. With so much literature and campaign paraphernalia, Theodore Roosevelt,

MECHANICAL REPUBLICAN CAMPAIGN CARD
In the fiercely contested election of 1896, Republicans, with a war chest of four million dollars, spent lavishly to get their message across. A colorful rotating campaign card promises "political object lessons." The candidates appear to receive even-handed treatment, but the message is clearly Republican. McKinley supports the gold standard with the positive slogans "Honest Payment of Honest Debts" and "Gold Is the Universal Standard of the World," while Bryan's free silver policy "Means Repudiation [of debts], Bankruptcy, and Dishonor." Idle workers outside a closed factory, an abandoned farm, and empty docks decorate the Bryan part of the card in contrast to the prosperity in the McKinley sections.
Collection of Janice L. and David J. Frent.

who harbored his own presidential ambitions, complained that Mark Hanna "advertised McKinley as if he were a patent medicine."

William Jennings Bryan had few assets beyond his silver tongue. The Democrats raised less than a tenth of what the Republicans spent, even with the support of silver barons such as the publisher William Randolph Hearst. Bryan struggled to make up in energy and eloquence what his party lacked in campaign funds. He set a new style for presidential campaigning, actively going to the voters. Crossing and recrossing the country in a whirlwind tour, he traveled more than eighteen thousand miles, visited twenty-seven states, and delivered more than six hundred speeches in three months. According to his own reckoning, he spoke to more than five million Americans. The poet Vachel Lindsay, growing up in Illinois during the race, likened Bryan's campaign to a cyclone:

> Prairie avenger, mountain lion,
> Bryan, Bryan, Bryan, Bryan,
> Gigantic troubadour, speaking like a siege gun,
> Smashing Plymouth Rock with his boulders from the West,
> And just a hundred miles behind, tornadoes piled across the sky,
> Blotting out the sun and moon,
> A sign on high.

While throngs in the West stirred to Bryan's "cross of gold" speech, editors in the East grew nearly hysterical in their condemnation of Bryan as a "dangerous revolutionary." Theodore Roosevelt, caught up in the fervor, compared the Democrats to French revolutionaries. In his typical bellicose fashion, he proposed "taking ten or a dozen of their leaders out, standing . . . them against a wall, and shooting them dead."

As election day approached, the silver states of the Rocky Mountains lined up for Bryan. The Northeast stood solidly for McKinley. Much of the South, with the exception of the border states, came back to the Democratic fold, leaving Tom Watson to lament that in the politics of fusion, "we play Jonah while they play the whale." The Midwest was in the balance. Bryan intensified his campaign in Illinois, Michigan, Ohio, and Indiana. But midwestern farmers could smell economic recovery and were less receptive to the blandishments of free silver than were voters farther west. In the cities, Democrats charged the Republicans with mass intimidation. "Men, vote as you please," the head of the Steinway Piano

Company reportedly announced on the eve of the election, "but if Bryan is elected tomorrow the whistle will not blow Wednesday morning."

Intimidation alone did not explain the failure of urban labor to rally to Bryan. In an effective campaign ploy, Republicans handed out wooden coins carrying Bryan's picture on one side and on the other side the inscription "In God We Trust . . . for the other 47 cents." Republicans repeatedly warned workers that if the Democrats won, the inflated silver dollar would be worth only fifty cents. However much farmers and laborers might insist that they were united as producers against the nonproducing plutocrats, it was equally true that inflation did not promise the boon to urban laborers that it did to western debtors.

On election day, four out of every five voters went to the polls in an unprecedented turnout. In the critical midwestern states, as many as 95 percent of the eligible voters cast their ballots. While some charged that the Republicans "voted the cemeteries" (stuffed the ballot boxes) for McKinley, fraud alone did not account for the high voter participation. To the voters in 1896, something momentous seemed to be at stake. Anxious crowds milled outside the newspaper offices and gathered on courthouse steps, waiting for news of the outcome. Bryan piled up a staggering total. He polled more than 6.5 million votes, double the number of any previous presidential candidate. McKinley bested him with 7.1 million. In the end the election outcome hinged on as few as one hundred to one thousand votes in several key states. Although McKinley won twenty-three states to Bryan's twenty-two, the electoral vote showed a lopsided 271–176. Despite his reputation in the East as a revolutionary firebrand, Bryan yielded with grace and cabled his congratulations to McKinley. Among the many telegrams that poured into McKinley's home in Canton came one from the jubilant Mark Hanna that said simply, "God's in his Heaven, All's right with the World!"

The biggest losers in 1896 turned out to be the Populists. On the national level, they polled less than 300,000 votes, over a million less than in 1894. In the clamor to support Bryan, Populists in the South drifted back into the Democratic Party. The People's Party was crushed, and with it died the agrarian revolt.

By the time William McKinley took the oath of office in March 1897, the political storms that had lashed the 1890s had died down. The decade had witnessed bold new political initiatives on the part of women, farmers, and laborers. For a time it looked as though they might forge a lasting alliance in the People's Party. In the end, although Populism proved unsuccessful, it set the political agenda for the United States in the next decades, highlighting issues such as banking and currency reform, electoral reforms such as the direct election of senators, and an enlarged role for the federal government in the nation's economic life. As the decade ended, the bugle call to arms drowned out the trumpet of reform as a "splendid little war" whipped up patriotic fervor, uniting the country and announcing the emergence of the United States as a major world power.

American Expansionism and the "White Man's Burden"

As the United States stood on the brink of the twentieth century, the European powers—Great Britain, France, Germany, Spain, and Belgium—as well as an increasingly powerful Japan competed for empires abroad, gobbling up what they liked to call the great "empty spaces" on the globe in Asia, Africa, Latin America, and the Pacific. Between 1870 and 1900, European nations gained control of more than 20 percent of the land and 10 percent of the earth's population. The United States, intent on con-

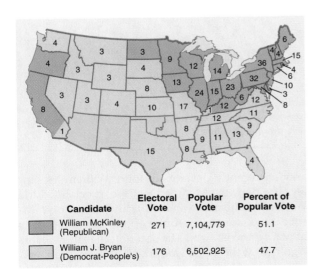

Candidate	Electoral Vote	Popular Vote	Percent of Popular Vote
William McKinley (Republican)	271	7,104,779	51.1
William J. Bryan (Democrat-People's)	176	6,502,925	47.7

MAP 20.2
The Election of 1896

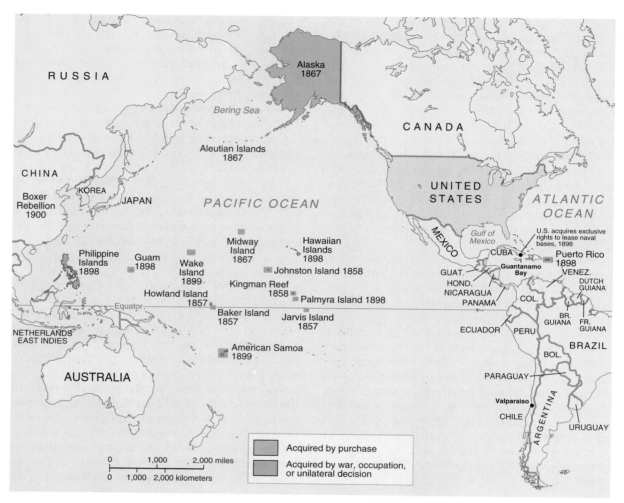

MAP 20.3
U. S. Territorial Expansion through 1900
The United States extended its interests abroad with a series of territorial acquisitions. Alaska was purchased in 1867; the Philippines and other Spanish island possessions, including Puerto Rico and Guam, were won in the Spanish-American War of 1898. Although Cuba was granted independence, the Platt amendment kept the new nation firmly under U.S. control. For good measure, President McKinley annexed Hawaii. In the wake of the Spanish-American War, the United States woke up to find it held an empire extending half way around the globe.

quering its own western frontier, had remained largely aloof from the scramble for colonies but not uninterested in the riches to be found abroad.

The Monroe Doctrine and the Open Door Policy

American foreign policy at the dawn of the twentieth century rested on two pillars, one that dated back to President James Monroe in the 1820s and another recently developed under William McKinley. The first, the Monroe Doctrine, proclaimed the Western Hemisphere an American "sphere of influence" and warned European powers to keep their hands off or risk war. The second pillar of U.S. foreign policy, the Open Door dealt with Asia, an area coveted by American merchants since the 1840s, the days of the clipper ships and the China trade. In the 1890s, China, weakened by years of warfare, looked as if it might be partitioned into spheres of influ-

THE OPEN DOOR

The trade advantage gained by the United States through the Open Door policy enunciated by Secretary of State John Hay in 1900 is portrayed graphically in this political cartoon. Uncle Sam stands prominently in the "open door" while representatives of the other Great Powers seek admittance to the "Flowery Kingdom" of China. Great Britain is symbolized by the stocky figure of John Bull; czarist Russia is portrayed by the bearded figure with the hat sporting the imperial double eagle. Other imperialist powers variously represented have yielded to Uncle Sam, who holds the golden key of "American Diplomacy" while the Chinese beam with pleasure. In fact, the Open Door policy promised only equal access for all powers to the China trade, not United States preeminence as the cartoon implies.

Culver Pictures.

ence by the imperial powers—England, Japan, Germany, France, and Russia. Concerned about American trade and, coincident to it, the integrity of China, Secretary of State John Hay in 1899–1900 hastily wrote a series of notes calling for an "open door" policy that would ensure trade access to all and maintain the semblance of Chinese sovereignty. The notes—sent to Britain, Germany, and Russia and later to France, Japan, and Italy—were greeted with polite evasions. Nevertheless, Hay boldly an-

nounced in 1900 that the Open Door was international policy.

American foreign policy reflected a curious paradox. Just as the United States wished to keep the Western Hemisphere (particularly Latin America and the Caribbean) closed to foreign influences, it wished to keep the Eastern Hemisphere (especially Asia) open for its own purposes. The twin pillars of U.S. foreign policy may not have been consistent, but they worked well to further America's economic interests. By insisting on its Open Door policy in Asia, the United States largely avoided the problems of maintaining a far-flung colonial empire while at the same time exerting its economic power.

Throughout much of the last half of the nineteenth century, the interests of the American public —and the American government—in foreign policy took a backseat to domestic developments. "Foreign relations," one historian has written, "were composed of incidents, not policies." One of these incidents occurred in 1889, when Germany threatened war with the United States. Eleven years after a treaty gave the United States the right to the harbor at the Pacific port of Pago Pago in the Samoan Islands, Germany, seeking dominance over the islands, sent warships to support its honor and its claims. But before any fighting broke out, a great typhoon destroyed the German and American ships. Acceding to the will of nature, the potential combatants divided the islands amicably between themselves.

American foreign policy reflected a curious paradox. Just as the United States wished to keep the Western Hemisphere closed to foreign influences, it wished to keep the Eastern Hemisphere open for its own purposes.

Elsewhere, America's foreign adventures appeared little more than a sidelight to business development. In Hawaii, American sugar interests fomented a rebellion in 1893, toppling the increasingly anti-American Queen Liliuokalani. They then proceeded to press President Cleveland to annex the islands, a move that would allow the planters to avoid the high duties on sugar recently imposed by the McKinley tariff. Cleveland balked. When he learned that the Hawaiian population opposed annexation, he withdrew the treaty from Senate consideration.

Closer to home, the United States actively worked to buttress the Monroe Doctrine, with its assertion of American hegemony (domination) in the Western Hemisphere. In the 1880s, Republican Secretary of State James G. Blaine promoted hemispheric peace and trade through Pan-American cooperation at the same time that he used American troops to intervene in Latin American border disputes. In 1891, war with Chile almost erupted after two American sailors were killed and several were injured in a barroom brawl in Valparaíso. President Benjamin Harrison threatened war but backed down after Chile apologized—he was wise to do so, for Chile had a better equipped navy than the United States. Late in the century, the United States began to strengthen its navy, but its army remained little more than a token force of 25,000, barely large enough to handle disturbances at home, let alone fight abroad.

Nevertheless, in 1895, Americans risked war with Great Britain to enforce the Monroe Doctrine. When a border dispute arose between Venezuela and British Guiana over lands where gold had been discovered, President Cleveland asserted the U.S. prerogative to step in and mediate, reducing Venezuela to the role of mere onlooker. Secretary of State Richard Olney boldly informed the British, "Today, the United States is practically sovereign on this continent," insisting that "its fiat is law." Unpersuaded, Britain refused to accept the United States as mediator. Conflict seemed imminent. "Let the fight come if it must," wrote Theodore Roosevelt. "I don't care whether our sea coast cities are bombarded or not; we would take Canada." Cleveland, less bellicose than Roosevelt, wished only to see America's presence in the hemisphere respected and its solution for peace accepted. He was relieved when the British, who also wished to avoid war, accepted the terms of U.S. mediation. The Venezuelan crisis signaled the willingness of the United States to play an active role beyond its borders, especially to preserve the Monroe Doctrine.

Markets and Missionaries

The depression of the 1890s provided a powerful impetus to American commercial expansion. As markets weakened at home, American businesses looked abroad for profits. Captain Alfred Thayer Mahan, leader of a growing group of American expansionists that included Henry Cabot Lodge, John Hay, and Theodore Roosevelt, prophesied as early as 1890, "Whether they will or not, Americans must now begin to look outward. The growing production of the country requires it." Although not all U.S. business leaders thought it advantageous to undertake adventures abroad, the logic of acquiring new markets to absorb the nation's growing capacity for production proved convincing to many. As the depression deepened, one diplomat warned that Americans "must turn [their] eyes abroad, or they will soon look inward upon discontent." Enthusiasts of expansion spoke glowingly of Asian markets: "Four hundred million Chinese without shoes!" American exports of cloth, kerosene, flour, and steel already constituted a small but significant percentage of the profits of American business. And where American interests led, businessmen expected American power and influence to follow to protect their investments. Companies like Standard Oil actively sought to use the government as their agent, often putting foreign service employees on the payroll. "Our ambassadors and ministers and consuls," wrote John D. Rockefeller appreciatively, "have aided to push our way into new markets to the utmost corners of the world." Whether by "our" he meant the United States or Standard Oil remained ambiguous; in practice, the distinction was of little importance in late-nineteenth-century foreign policy.

However compelling the economic arguments about markets and overproduction proved, material interest alone did not account for the new expansionism that seized the nation during the 1890s. As Mahan confessed, "Even when material interests are the original exciting cause, it is the sentiment to which they give rise, the moral tone which emotion takes that constitutes the greater force." Much of that moral tone was set by American missionaries intent on spreading the gospel of Christianity to the "heathen." No area on the globe constituted a greater challenge than China. In 1858, the Tientsin treaty admitted foreign missionaries — Roman Catholics from France, Protestants from Britain, Germany, and the United States — to spread the gospel to the hinterlands. Young women particularly were attracted to the independence and excitement promised by mission work. Missions accepted single women over twenty-six years of age. By 1890, women constituted more than 60 percent of the mission force. Young women from the rural Midwest who would not have ventured into Chicago alone set off for China. Foreign mission work promised adventure and autonomy few other callings for women could match.

Although they never lost their optimism, the missionaries' success proved limited and their converts few. By the turn of the century, an estimated 100,000 converts existed in a total population of 400 million Chinese. Nevertheless, as the missionaries pointed out, the number marked a significant increase over the 8,000 Christian converts counted in 1870.

Increased missionary activity and Western enterprise touched off a series of antiforeign uprisings in China that culminated in the Boxer Rebellion of 1900–1901. The Chinese particularly resented the interference of missionaries in village life and the preference and protection they afforded their Christian converts. Opposition to foreigners took the form of antiforeign secret societies, most notably the

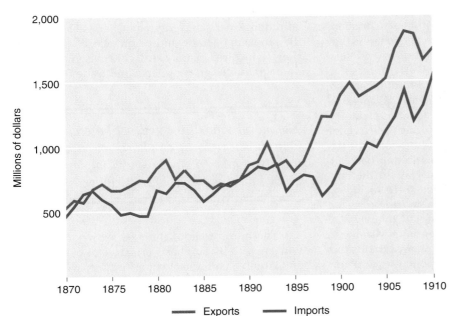

FIGURE 20.2
Expansion in U.S. Trade, 1870 – 1910

Between 1870 and 1910 American exports nearly tripled. Although imports rose, they were held in check by the high protective tariff championed by Republican presidents from Ulysses Grant to William Howard Taft. A decline in imports is particularly noticeable after passage of the prohibitive McKinley tariff in 1890.

WOMEN MISSIONARIES IN CHINA
Methodist women missionaries in the Szechuan province of China rely on traditional means of transportation, in this case "back chairs." The independence enjoyed by women missionaries, who made up more than 69 percent of the foreign mission force by 1890, stood in marked contrast to the restrictions placed on young women of their class at home.
Courtesy of the Yale Divinity School Library.

Boxers, whose Chinese name translated literally into "Righteous Harmonious Fist." No simple pugilists, the Boxers believed that through ritual they could induce a trance that would make them invincible to Western weapons. Under the slogan "Uphold the Ch'ing Dynasty, Exterminate the Foreigners," they began to terrorize Chinese Christians and later missionaries in the north of China. As they became bolder, they attacked railroads and telegraph lines, the twin symbols of Western imperialism. Their rampage eventually led to the massacre of some 2,000 Chinese converts and 250 missionaries and their families. The missionaries clamored for the American government to protect and avenge them. Fearing for their lives, they showed little toleration for the cautious diplomatic approach favored by Secretary of State John Hay. In the end, 2,500 U.S. troops joined an Allied force including British and German troops sent to save the besieged foreigners in Peking (now Beijing). The arrival of foreign troops chastened the imperial government, which adopted a tougher stance against the Boxers and a more accommodationist policy toward foreign missionaries.

In their fight against the Boxers, the missionaries saw no paradox in bringing Christianity to China at gunpoint. "It is worth any cost in money, worth any cost in bloodshed," argued one bishop, "if we can make millions of Chinese true and intelligent Christians." In truth, expansionists and missionaries worked hand in hand; trade and Christianity marched into China together. "Missionaries," admitted American clergyman Charles Denby, "are the pioneers of trade and commerce. . . . The missionary, inspired by holy zeal, goes everywhere, and by degrees foreign commerce and trade follow."

The moral tone of the age, set by social Darwinism with its emphasis on survival of the fittest and Anglo-Saxon racial superiority, proved ideally suited to imperialism.

The moral tone of the age, set by social Darwinism with its emphasis on survival of the fittest and Anglo-Saxon racial superiority, proved ideally suited to imperialism. Congregational minister Josiah Strong revealed the mix of racism and missionary zeal that fueled American adventurism abroad when he remarked, "It seems to me that God, with infinite wisdom and skill, is training the Anglo Saxon race for an hour sure to come in the world's future." British poet Rudyard Kipling put it better in verse.

> Take up the white man's burden
>   Send forth the best ye breed—
> Go bind your sons to exile
>   To serve your captive's need;
> To wait, in heavy harness,
>   On fluttered folk and wild—
> Your new-caught sullen people,
>   Half devil and half child.

The irony that is apparent in Kipling's poem evidently escaped those Americans who rushed to champion U.S. expansion. Jingoism, extreme nationalism tinged with belligerency, became the style. No one exemplified the new chauvinism more than Theodore Roosevelt, the rising young Republican from New York. Always more concerned with manliness than money, Roosevelt believed that nations and individuals needed the test of combat to maintain their virility. "This country needs a war," Roosevelt asserted in 1895. Power, not profits, motivated expansionists of Roosevelt's stripe. Intent on asserting the United States' place in the world of nations, they pressed for a more expansionist policy, judging imperialism "a fine expression of the American spirit."

Missionary zeal, patriotism, profit, and power all fueled American expansionism. The volatile mix reached the combustion point in 1898, propelling the United States into war and leading to the country's foray into colonialism.

The United States Becomes a World Power

As the leading industrial nation in the world, the United States was destined to play a significant role in world politics. Yet not until the end of the century did the country take its place on the world stage by confronting and easily defeating a European power. On the surface the Spanish-American War seemed a giant contradiction: A war begun as a humanitarian effort to free Cuba from Spain's colonial grasp ended with the United States itself becoming a colonial power. And in the jungles of

the Pacific, American troops fought a dirty guerrilla war with Filipino nationalists, who, like the Cubans, sought independence. Yet behind the contradiction stood the twin pillars of American foreign policy. The Monroe Doctrine's insistence on American control in the Western Hemisphere made Spain's presence in Cuba unacceptable, while the determination to keep an open door in Asia rendered the Philippines a convenient stepping-stone to China.

"A Splendid Little War"

Looking back on the Spanish-American War of 1898, Secretary of State John Hay judged it "a splendid little war; begun with the highest motives, carried on with magnificent intelligence and spirit, favored by that fortune which loves the brave." At the close of a decade marred by bitter depression, social unrest, and political upheaval, the war offered Americans a chance to wave the flag and march in unison. War fever proved as infectious as the tune of a John Philip Sousa march. Few argued the merits of the war until it was over and the time came to divide the spoils.

At the close of a decade marred by bitter depression, social unrest, and political upheaval, the Spanish-American War offered Americans a chance to wave the flag and march in unison.

The war began with moral outrage over the treatment of Cuban revolutionaries, who had launched a fight for independence against the Spanish colonial regime in 1895. In an attempt to isolate the guerrillas, Spanish General Valeriano Weyler y Nicolau herded Cubans into crowded and unsanitary concentration camps, where thousands died of hunger, disease, and exposure. Starvation soon spread to the cities. Tens of thousands of Cubans died, and countless others were left without food, clothing, or shelter. By 1898, fully a quarter of the island's population had perished in the revolution.

As the Cuban war dragged on, pressure for American intervention mounted. Public outrage at Spain was whipped to a frenzy by American newspapers. A fierce circulation war raged in New York City between William Randolph Hearst's *Evening*

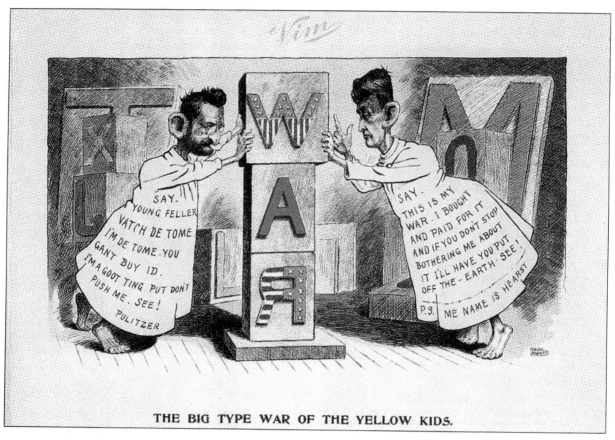

THE BIG TYPE WAR OF THE YELLOW KIDS.

YELLOW JOURNALISM
Newspaper publishers Joseph Pulitzer and William Randolph Hearst square off in "The Big Type War."
As the cartoon indicates, Hearst insisted he had the better right to cover the Spanish-American War be-
cause he "bought and paid for it." In their 1890s circulation war, Hearst and Pulitzer not only used big
type in sensational headlines, but employed color in new comic sections. Hearst's Sunday American
promised "eight pages of polychromatic effulgence that make the rainbow look like a lead pipe." Hearst
also stole the era's most famous cartoon character, the "Yellow Kid," from Pulitzer after a bidding war
for the cartoonist's talents. Soon all forms of sensational writing were labeled "yellow journalism."
Library of Congress.

Journal and Joseph Pulitzer's *World*. Their competition provoked what came to be called "yellow journalism," which pandered to the public's appetite for violence and sensationalism. The Cuban war provided Hearst with a wealth of sensational copy. His papers fed the nation a daily diet of "Butcher" Weyler and alleged Spanish atrocities. He sent artist Frederic Remington to document the horror, and when Remington wired home, "Everything is quiet. There is no trouble here. There will be no war," Hearst shot back, "You furnish the pictures and I'll furnish the war."

But other factors accounted for U.S. intervention. American interests, in the words of the U.S. minister to Spain, were more than "merely theoretical or sentimental." American business had more than $50 million invested in Cuban sugar, and American trade with Cuba, a brisk $100 million a year before the war, had dropped to near zero as a result of the revolution. Nevertheless, the business community balked, wary of a war with Spain. When industrialist Mark Hanna, Republican kingmaker and senator from Ohio, ever the barometer of business opinion, urged restraint, a hot-headed Theodore

Roosevelt exploded, "We will have this war for the freedom of Cuba, Senator Hanna, in spite of the timidity of commercial interests."

To expansionists like Roosevelt, more than Cuban independence was at stake. War with Spain opened up the prospect of expansion into Asia as well since Spain controlled not only Cuba but Puerto Rico, Guam, and the Philippine Islands. As assistant secretary of the navy, Roosevelt worked for preparedness whenever his boss's back was turned. While Secretary John D. Long was vacationing, Roosevelt audaciously ordered the U.S. fleet to Manila, in the Philippines. In the event of conflict with Spain, he put the navy in a position to capture the islands and gain an important stepping-stone to China.

President McKinley slowly and reluctantly moved toward intervention. In a show of American force, he dispatched the armored cruiser *Maine* to Cuba. On the night of February 15, 1898, a mysterious explosion destroyed the *Maine*, killing 266 crew members. Enraged Americans immediately blamed the Spanish government. Rallying to the cry "Remember the *Maine*," Congress declared war in April. In the surge of patriotism that followed, more than 235,000 men enlisted. War brought with it a unity of purpose and national harmony that ended a decade of internal strife. "In April, everywhere over this good fair land, flags were flying," wrote the Kansas editor William Allen White. "Little children on fences greeted the soldiers with flapping scarfs and handkerchiefs and flags; at the stations, crowds gathered to hurrah for the soldiers, and to throw hats into the air, and to unfurl flags."

They soon had something to cheer about. Five days after McKinley signed the war resolution, the U.S. navy under Admiral George Dewey destroyed the Spanish fleet in Manila Bay. Dewey's stunning

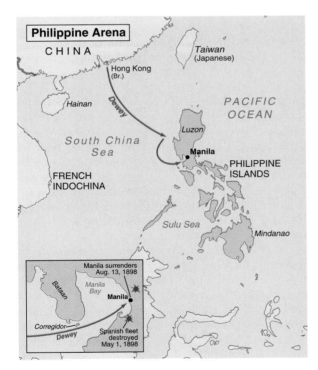

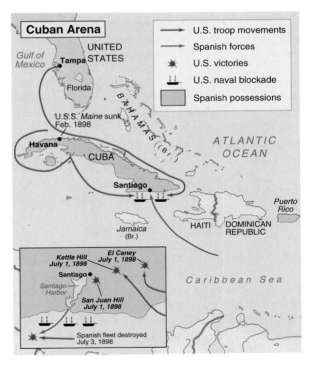

MAP 20.4
The Spanish-American War, 1898
The Spanish-American War was fought in two theaters, the Philippine Islands and Cuba. Admiral George Dewey captured Manila without the loss of a single American sailor five days after President William McKinley called for a declaration of war. The war lasted only a matter of months. U. S. troops landed in Cuba in mid-June and by mid-July they had taken Santiago and Havana and the Spanish fleet had been destroyed off Santiago.

The Spanish-American War: Eyewitness Accounts

*T*he Spanish-American War received more eyewitness news coverage than any previous war in American history. Hearst's papers had fanned the flames of war and, once it started in earnest, reporters fed a public hungry for news about the conflict. In addition to daily newspapers, weekly illustrated papers like Collier's, Leslie's, and Harper's covered the war, using dispatches wired from the front and illustrations by some of the leading artists of the day.

The press shared the country's enthusiasm for battle. Richard Harding Davis, a star foreign correspondent, observed on the eve of the troops' departure from Tampa, "It was a most happy-go-lucky expedition, run with real American optimism and readiness to take big chances, and with the spirit of a people who recklessly trust that it will come out all right in the end. . . . As one of the generals on board said, 'This is God Almighty's war, and we are only His agents.' "

*M*en's letters home spoke to more mundane aspects of army life.

DOCUMENT 1. Rough Rider Arthur Fortunatus Cosby, Letter to a friend, June 1898

Personally I expected anything and I have no complaints to make, but a lot of the "boys" don't like it. Our food on board ship is the same; coffee, hardtack, with canned beef (that must have been cooked it is so stringy and tasteless), canned tomatoes and beans. These are travel rations and we have now had ten days of them with 5 days more on the road. We get the coffee hot, but the other things are usually cold unless an enterprising fellow will make a mess of the whole thing which he calls a stew.

We have all gone expert in "rustling" food, begging it, buying it from the ship's cook who is supposed not to sell, smuggling it in from shore etc. . . .

All the boys have lost flesh at the most astonishing rate. . . . Then too although our passage has been remarkably quiet many of the boys have been sea-sick. This with the confinement and heat to which they are not accustomed, and poor food has weakened them. I am very much afraid that we shan't do much.

*W*hen the troops put ashore, General William Shafter attempted to hold the reporters on the ship until after the troops had landed. An irate Richard Harding Davis confronted the general, explaining that he was a "descriptive writer" and needed to be at the scene. Shafter retorted, "I do not care a damn what you are, I'll treat all of you alike." Davis managed to catch up to the troops and dispatch the following account of the landing.

DOCUMENT 2. Richard Harding Davis Reports on the Cuban Landing, June 1898

No one slept that night, for until two o'clock in the morning troops were still being disembarked in the surf, and two ships of war had their searchlights turned on the landingplace, and made Siboney as light as a ball-room. Back of the searchlights was an ocean white with moonlight, and on the shore red camp-fires, at which the half-drowned troops were drying their uniforms, and the Rough Riders, who had just marched in from Daiquiri, were cooking their coffee and bacon. . . .

It was one of the most weird and remarkable scenes of the war, probably of any war. An army was being landed on an enemy's coast at the dead of night, but with somewhat more of cheers and shrieks of laughter than rise from the bathers in the surf at Coney Island on a hot Sunday. . . . The men still to be landed from the "prison hulks," as they called the transports, were singing in chorus, the men already on shore were dancing naked around the camp-fires on the beach, or shouting with delight as they plunged into the first bath that had offered in seven days, and those in the launches as they were pitched headfirst at the soil of Cuba, signalized their arrival by howls of triumph.

Once on shore, Davis traveled with Theodore Roosevelt and General Leonard Wood, so close as to be almost a third commander. He was the first to spot Spanish troops and point them out to Wood. At one point, Davis picked up a rifle and fired a few shots at the enemy. No wonder his dispatches contain such a spontaneous account of the action, as in this description of the decisive charge up San Juan Hill, which took place on July 1, 1898.

Document 3. Richard Harding Davis at San Juan Hill

They had no glittering bayonets, they were not massed in regular array. There were a few men in advance, bunched together, and creeping up a steep, sunny hill, the tops of which roared and flashed with flame. The men held their guns pressed across their breasts and stepped heavily as they climbed. Behind these first few, spreading out like a fan, were single lines of men, slipping and scrambling in the smooth grass, moving forward with difficulty, as though they were wading waist high through water, moving slowly carefully, with strenuous effort. It was much more wonderful than any swinging charge could have been. They walked to greet death at every step, many of them, as they advanced, sinking suddenly or pitching forward and disappearing in the high grass, but the others waded on, stubbornly, forming a thin blue line that kept creeping higher and higher up the hill. It was inevitable as the rising tide. It was a miracle of self-sacrifice, a triumph of bull-dog courage, which one watched breathless with wonder.

[The journalist later recollected:]

I have seen many illustrations and pictures of this charge on the San Juan hills, but none of them seem to show it just as I remember it. In the picture-papers the men are running up a hill swiftly and gallantly, in regular formation, rank after rank, with flags flying, their eyes aflame, and their hair streaming, their bayonets fixed, in long, brilliant lines, and invincible overpowering weight of numbers.

Instead of which I think the thing which impressed one the most, when our men started from cover, was they were so few. It seemed as if someone had made an awful and terrible mistake. One's instinct was to call to them to come back.

Colonel Theodore Roosevelt himself kept diaries and later published his own account of the battle. He recalled that after his troops had taken nearby Kettle Hill, he called the Rough Riders to charge the line of Spanish trenches on San Juan Hill.

Document 4. TR Charges San Juan Hill

Thinking that the men would all come, I jumped over the wire fence in front of us and started at the double; but, as a matter of fact, the troopers were so excited, what with shooting and being shot, and shouting and cheering, that they did not hear, or did not heed me; and after running about a hundred yards I found I had only five men along with me.

[Going back to gather his forces, Roosevelt ordered them to charge.]

The men of the various regiments which were already on the hill came with a rush, and we started across the wide valley which lay between us and the Spanish intrenchments. . . . Long before we got near them the Spaniards ran, save a few here and there, who either surrendered or were shot down. When we reached the trenches we found them filled with dead bodies in the light blue and white uniform of the Spanish regular army. . . .

I was with Henry Bardshar [his aide-de-camp], running up at the double, and two Spaniards leaped from the trenches and fired at us, not ten yards away. As they turned to run I closed in and fired twice, missing the first and killing the second. My revolver was from the sunken battleship *Maine*.

There was very great confusion at this time, the different regiments being completely intermingled —white regulars, colored regulars [African American soldiers in the 21st Infantry], and Rough Riders. . . . We were still under heavy fire, and I got together a mixed lot of men and pushed on from the trenches and ranch-houses which we had just taken driving the Spaniards through a line of palm trees, and over the crest of a chain of hills. When we reached these crests we found ourselves overlooking Santiago.

Document 1. Frank Freidel, *The Splendid Little War* (Little, Brown, 1958), 75–76.
Document 2. Ibid., 95–97.
Document 3. Ibid., 162.
Document 4. Ibid., 167, 170.

THE BATTLE OF SAN JUAN HILL
*This idealized 1898 lithograph portrays a highly romantic version of the Battle of San Juan Hill,
far from the truth. The famous charge was much less glamorous than pictured here. Theodore
Roosevelt, whose Rough Riders had taken nearby Kettle Hill, called to his men to charge the next
line of Spanish trenches in the San Juan hills. But in the excitement of the battle, they didn't
hear him and Roosevelt found himself charging virtually alone. He had to go back and rally the
Rough Riders, who then charged the hill on foot. The illustration does get one thing right.
Theodore Roosevelt led the charge wearing his spectacles. Roosevelt was so myopic he feared he
might lose his glasses in battle and had Brooks Brothers, who custom-made his uniform, include
a dozen pockets for extra eyeglasses.*
Library of Congress.

victory caught the nation by surprise. Although
naval strategists like Roosevelt had been orches-
trating the move for some time, few Americans had
ever heard of the Philippines. Even McKinley confessed that he could not immediately locate the
archipelago on the map. He nevertheless dispatched
U.S. troops to secure the islands.

The war in Cuba ended almost as quickly as it
had begun. The first troops landed on June 22, and
after a handful of battles the Spanish surrendered
on July 17. (See Texts in Historical Context, page 792.)

The war lasted just long enough to elevate Theodore
Roosevelt to the status of bona fide war hero. Roosevelt, sensitive to charges that he and his friends
were no more than "armchair or parlor jingoes," resigned his post to lead a regiment. His Rough Riders, composed about equally of Ivy League polo
players and cowboys Roosevelt had met during his
sojourn in the Dakotas, made excellent copy for the
journalists and photographers hungry for stories
while the troops languished in Tampa awaiting
their orders. Roosevelt and his men staged daily

rodeos for the press, with the likes of New York blueblood William Tiffany busting broncs in competition with Dakota cowboy "Dead Shot" Jim Simpson. When the Rough Riders shipped out to Cuba, journalists fought for a berth with the colorful regiment. Roosevelt's charge up Kettle Hill and his role in the decisive battle of San Juan made front-page news. Overnight, Roosevelt became the most famous man in America. By the time he sailed home from Cuba, a coalition of independent Republicans was already busy making plans to nominate him for governor of New York. Tom Platt, nicknamed New York's "Easy Boss," voiced the only reservation. "If he becomes governor," Platt remarked, "sooner or later, with his personality, he will have to be President." Platt confessed that he was "afraid to start that thing going."

The Debate over American Imperialism

After a few brief campaigns in Cuba and Puerto Rico and Dewey's stunning naval victory in the Philippines, the American people woke up with an empire that stretched halfway around the globe. Cuba had been promised independence, but while it escaped Spanish colonialism, the United States stopped short of granting the island full autonomy. The Platt Amendment, tacked onto the peace treaty with Spain, gave the United States the right to intervene in Cuba whenever it pleased. The treaty ceded to the United States control of Puerto Rico and Guam, former Spanish colonies. McKinley added Hawaii for good measure, annexing the islands in July 1898. But what to do with the Philippines? After much prayer, the president resolved to keep this former Spanish colony. As Finley Peter Dunne, a popular humorist of the era, wryly observed through his mouthpieces, the barroom philosophers Hennessy and Mr. Dooley: "I know what I'd do if I was Mack," Hennessy insisted. "I'd hist a flag over th' Ph'lippeens, and I'd take in th' whole lot iv them." "An yet," his foil Mr. Dooley mused, "tis not more thin two months since ye larned whether they were islands or canned goods."

America would soon feel the weight of the "white man's burden" in the Philippines. Empire did not come cheap. When Spain balked, the United States agreed to pay an indemnity of $20 million for the islands. Nor was the cost measured in money alone. Filipino insurrectionaries under Emilio

Aguinaldo, who had greeted U.S. troops as liberators, bitterly fought the new masters. It would take seven years and four thousand American dead—almost ten times the number killed in Cuba—not to mention an estimated twenty thousand Filipino casualties, to defeat Aguinaldo and secure American control of the Philippines.

At home a vocal minority, composed largely of former Populists and Democrats, resisted the country's foray into empire, judging it unwise, immoral, and unconstitutional. William Jennings Bryan, who had enlisted in the army along with Roosevelt but contracted typhoid fever and never saw action, came to the conclusion that American expansionism served only to distract the nation from its real problems at home. What did imperialism offer the ordinary American? Bryan asked. His answer: "Heavier taxes, Asiatic emigration and an opportunity to furnish more sons for the army." Mark Twain, lending his bitter eloquence to the cause of anti-imperialism, lamented that the United States had become "yet another Civilized Power, with its banner of the Prince of Peace in one hand and its loot-basket and its butcher-knife in the other."

In the end the anti-imperialists would prove prophetic, and Hay's Open Door notes would demonstrate the principle that it was more effective for the United States to spread its influence abroad through economic power than by conquest. But in 1898, as the *Washington Post* trumpeted, "The taste of empire is in the mouth of the people," and Americans thrilled at the prospect of "an imperial policy, the Republic renascent, taking her place with the armed nations."

Conclusion: The End of a Tumultuous Decade

As the nineteenth century came to a close, the Spanish-American War symbolized America's entry onto the world stage as a significant player in global politics. A decade of domestic strife ended amid the blare of martial music and the waving of flags. During the 1890s, Americans, poised on the brink of the twentieth century, not only searched for order but fought for competing visions of who should manage the new industrial society. Women fought drunkenness and the conditions that fostered it and mounted a suffrage movement to secure their basic political rights. Ida B. Wells brought the brutality of lynching into the public spotlight. Laborers staged bloody strikes to determine once and for all who controlled the workplace, the workers who toiled there or the bosses who owned the machines and made the profits. The Homestead lockout and the Pullman strike demonstrated the power of property and the conservatism of the laissez-faire state. Like the striking workers, farmers in the 1890s demanded a greater voice and forged the People's Party to fight for a vision of economic democracy. Their willingness to increase the power of the federal government challenged the notion of laissez-faire and laid the foundation for a new liberal state capable of countering the power of large corporations. This shift away from laissez-faire and toward a more active role for the federal government marked the major political development of the period.

While none of the movements of the 1890s succeeded in that decade, they laid the groundwork for what was to come. Militant women, strikers, and farmers all fought for change and, in doing so, contributed to the forging of a new politics. In their struggles, the 1890s witnessed a decade of strife the likes of which the country would not see again for another seventy years.

CHRONOLOGY

1884   The Woman's Christian Temperance Union (WCTU), under leadership of Frances Willard, calls for "home protection ballot" (suffrage for women).

1887   Farmers' Alliance organized.

1890   National American Woman Suffrage Association (NAWSA) formed, elects Elizabeth Cady Stanton as president.

Wyoming enters Union with woman suffrage.

1892   Ida B. Wells begins her antilynching crusade.

People's Party (also known as Populist Party) founded in St. Louis.

Homestead lockout pits Carnegie steelworkers against hired Pinkertons.

Anarchist Alexander Berkman's attempt to assassinate Henry Clay Frick turns public opinion against Homestead workers.

People's Party wins more than one million votes for its presidential candidate, James B. Weaver.

Susan B. Anthony becomes president of NAWSA.

1893   Severe economic depression touched off by panic on Wall Street.

Referendum grants women right to vote in Colorado.

1894   Coxey's "army" marches from Ohio to Washington, D.C., to dramatize plight of unemployed.

Federal troops crush Pullman strike; union leader Eugene V. Debs jailed for violating court injunction.

1896   Democrats nominate William Jennings Bryan for president and adopt platform of free silver.

Republican William McKinley defeats Democrat William Jennings Bryan for presidency.

California voters defeat referendum granting women right to vote.

Women gain vote in Idaho. Utah enters Union with woman suffrage.

National Association of Colored Women formed, with Mary Church Terrell as president.

1898   Spanish-American War: United States intervenes in Cuba, defeating Spanish.

| 1898 | United States acquires Puerto Rico, Guam, and Philippines in wake of war with Spain and annexes Hawaii. Frances Willard, president of Woman's Christian Temperance Union, dies. | 1899–1900 | Secretary of State John Hay enunciates Open Door policy in China to guarantee U.S. trade access. |
| | | 1900–1901 | Boxer Rebellion in China leads to deaths of more than 250 missionaries and their families. |

BIBLIOGRAPHY

GENERAL

Alan Dawley, *Struggles for Justice: Social Responsibility and the Liberal State* (1991).

David Montgomery, *The Fall of the House of Labor: The Workplace, the State, and American Labor Activism, 1865–1925* (1987).

Nell Irvin Painter, *Standing at Armageddon: The United States, 1877–1919* (1987).

Alan Trachtenberg, *The Incorporation of America: Culture and Society in the Gilded Age* (1982).

Robert Wiebe, *The Search for Order, 1877–1920* (1967).

MILITANT WOMEN

Karen J. Blair, *The Clubwoman as Feminist: True Womanhood Redefined, 1868–1914* (1980).

Jack S. Blocker Jr., *"Give to the Winds Thy Fears": The Women's Temperance Crusade, 1873–74* (1985).

Ruth Bordin, *Women and Temperance: The Quest for Power and Liberty, 1873–1900* (1981).

Ruth Bordin, *Frances Willard: A Biography* (1986).

Ellen Carol DuBois, *Feminism and Suffrage: The Emergence of an Independent Women's Movement in America, 1848–1869* (1978).

Barbara Leslie Epstein, *The Politics of Domesticity: Women, Evangelism, and Temperance in Nineteenth Century America* (1981).

Sara M. Evans, *Born for Liberty: A History of Women in America* (1989).

Eleanor Flexner, *Century of Struggle: The Women's Rights Movement in the United States* (1973).

Glenda Elizabeth Gilmore, *Gender and Jim Crow: Women and the Politics of White Supremacy in North Carolina, 1896–1920* (1996).

Darlene Clark Hine, ed., *Black Women in America* (1993).

Beverly Washington Jones, *Quest for Equality: The Life and Writings of Mary Eliza Church Terrell* (1990).

Glenna Matthews, *The Rise of Public Woman: Woman's Power and Woman's Place in the United States, 1630–1970* (1992).

Glenda Riley, *Inventing the American Woman: A Perspective on Women's History, 1865 to the Present* (1986).

Jacqueline Jones Royster, *Southern Horrors and Other Writings: The Anti-Lynching Campaign of Ida B. Wells, 1892–1900* (1996).

Dorothy Salem, *To Better Our World: Black Women in Organized Reform, 1890–1920* (1990).

Anne Firor Scott, *Natural Allies: Women's Associations in American History* (1991).

Kathryn Kish Sklar, *Florence Kelley and the Nation's Work: The Rise of Women's Political Culture, 1830–1900* (1995).

Ian Tyrell, *Woman's World, Woman's Empire: The Woman's Christian Temperance Union in International Perspective, 1880–1930* (1991).

Charles Harris Wesley, *The History of the National Association of Colored Women's Clubs: A Legacy of Service* (1984).

THE FARMERS' REVOLT

Peter Argersinger, *Populism and Politics: William Alfred Peffer and the People's Party* (1974).

Edward L. Ayers, *The Promise of the New South: Life after Reconstruction* (1992).

Lawrence Goodwyn, *The Populist Moment: A Short History of the Agrarian Revolt in America* (1978).

Sheldon Hackney, *Populism and Progressivism in Alabama* (1969).

Steven Hahn, *The Roots of Southern Populism: Yeoman Farmers and the Transformation of the Georgia Upcountry, 1850–1890* (1983).

John D. Hicks, *The Populist Revolt: A History of the Farmers' Alliance and the People's Party* (1961).

Matthew Josephson, *The Politicos, 1865–1896* (1938).

Robert McMath, *Populist Vanguard* (1975).

Scott G. McNall, *The Road to Rebellion: Class Formation and Kansas Populism, 1865–1900* (1988).

Theodore R. Mitchell, *Political Education in the Southern Farmers' Alliance, 1887–1900* (1987).

Norman Pollack, *The Populist Response to Industrial America: Midwestern Populist Thought* (1962).

Norman Pollack, *The Just Polity: Populism, Law, and Human Welfare* (1987).

Norman Pollack, ed., *The Populist Mind* (1967).

Theodore Saloutos, *Farmer Movements in the South, 1865–1933* (1960).

Barton Shaw, *The Wool-Hat Boys: Georgia's Populist Party* (1984).

Lala Carr Steelman, *The North Carolina Farmers' Alliance* (1985).

George Brown Tindall, ed., *A Populist Reader: Selections from the Works of American Populist Leaders* (1966).

Urwin Unger, *The Greenback Era: A Social and Political History of American Finance, 1865–1879* (1964).

C. Vann Woodward, *Tom Watson: Agrarian Rebel* (1963).

THE LABOR WARS

Stanley Buder, *Pullman: An Experiment in Industrial Order and Community Planning* (1976).

Arthur G. Burgoyne, with afterword by David P. Demarest Jr., *The Homestead Strike of 1892* (1979).

Leon Fink, *Workingman's Democracy: The Knights of Labor and American Politics* (1983).

Philip S. Foner, *History of the Labor Movement in the United States*, vol. 2, *From the Founding of the American Federation of Labor to the Emergence of American Imperialism* (1955).

Edward C. Kirkland, ed., *Andrew Carnegie: The Gospel of Wealth and Other Essays* (1962).

Sidney Lens, *The Labor Wars: From the Molly Maguires to the Sitdowns* (1974).

Thomas G. Manning, ed., *The Chicago Strike of 1894: Industrial Labor in the Nineteenth Century* (1960).

Milton Meltzer, *Bread and Roses: The Struggle of American Labor, 1865–1915* (1967).

Nick Salvatore, *Eugene V. Debs: Citizen and Socialist* (1982).

William Serrin, *Homestead: The Glory and Tragedy of an American Steel Town* (1992).

Carl Smith, *Urban Disorder and the Shape of Belief: The Great Chicago Fire, the Haymarket Bomb, and the Model Town of Pullman* (1995).

Leon Stein, ed., *The Pullman Strike* (1969).

U.S. Strike Commission, *Report on the Chicago Strike of June–July 1894*, U.S. Congress, 53rd Cong., 3rd sess., Senate Executive Document no. 7 (1894).

Joseph Frazier Wall, *Andrew Carnegie* (1970).

Alice Wexler, *Emma Goldman: An Intimate Life* (1984).

Leon Wolff, *Lockout: The Story of the Homestead Strike of 1892* (1965).

Samuel Yellen, *American Labor Struggles* (1936).

DEPRESSION POLITICS

Robert A. Allen, *Reluctant Reformers: Racism and Social Reform Movements in the United States* (1974).

Robert W. Cherny, *A Righteous Cause: The Life of William Jennings Bryan* (1985).

Paolo Coletta, *William Jennings Bryan*, 3 vols. (1964–1969).

Robert F. Durden, *The Climax of Populism: The Election of 1896* (1969).

Paul W. Glad, *McKinley, Bryan, and the People* (1964).

Matthew Josephson, *The Politicos, 1865–1896* (1938).

Louis W. Koenig, *Bryan: A Political Biography of William Jennings Bryan* (1971).

Donald L. McMurry, *Coxey's Army: A Study of the Industrial Army Movement of 1894* (1968).

Samuel McSeveney, *The Politics of Depression* (1972).

Carol A. Schwantes, *Coxey's Army: An American Odyssey* (1985).

AMERICA ON THE WORLD STAGE

David Anderson, *Imperialism and Idealism: American Diplomacy in China, 1861–1898* (1985).

William Becker, *The Dynamics of Business-Government Relations* (1982).

Robert Beisner, *From the Old Diplomacy to the New, 1865–1900* (1975).

Charles Campbell, *The Transformation of American Foreign Relations, 1865–1900* (1976).

John Dobson, *America's Ascent: The United States Becomes a Great Power, 1880–1914* (1978).

Harold U. Faulkner, *Politics, Reform, and Expansionism, 1890–1900* (1959).

Philip S. Foner, *The Spanish-Cuban-American War and the Birth of American Imperialism*, 2 vols. (1972).

Frank Friedel, *The Splendid Little War* (1958).

Willard Gatewood Jr., *Black Americans and the White Man's Burden* (1975).

Kenneth Hagen, *American Gun-Boat Diplomacy* (1973).

Louis J. Halle, *The United States Acquires the Philippines: Consensus vs. Reality* (1985).

Jane Hunter, *The Gospel of Gentility: American Women Missionaries in Turn-of-the-Century China* (1984).

Walter LaFeber, *The New Empire: An Interpretation of American Expansion, 1860–1898* (1963).

Gerald F. Linderman, *The Mirror of War: American Society and the Spanish-American War* (1974).

H. Wayne Morgan, *America's Road to Empire: The War with Spain and Overseas Expansion* (1965).

Edmund Morris, *The Rise of Theodore Roosevelt* (1979).

Ivan Musicant, *The Banana Wars: A History of U.S. Military Intervention from the Spanish-American War to the Invasion of Panama* (1990).

Thomas Patterson, ed., *Imperialism and Anti-Imperialism* (1973).

Emily S. Rosenberg, *Spreading the American Dream: American Economic and Cultural Expansion, 1890–1945* (1982).

Mark Sullivan, *Our Times*, vol. 2, *America Finding Herself* (1927).

James C. Thompson Jr., Peter W. Stanley, and John Curtis Perry, *Sentimental Imperialists: The American Experience in East Asia* (1981).

Richard Turk, *The Ambiguous Relationship: Theodore Roosevelt and Alfred Thayer Mahan* (1987).

Albert K. Weinberg, *Manifest Destiny: A Study of Nationalist Expansion in American History* (1935).

William Appleman Williams, *The Tragedy of American Diplomacy,* rev. ed. (1962).

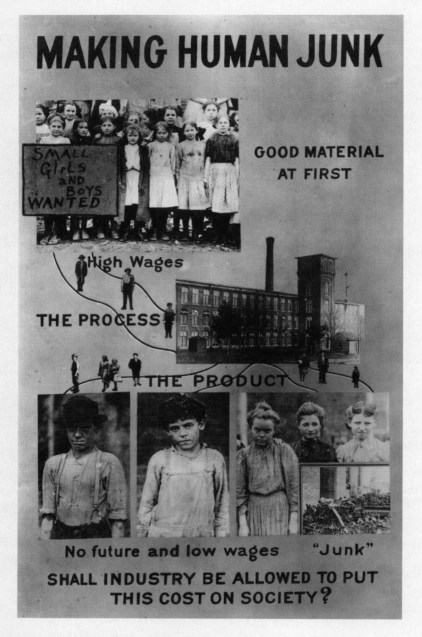

PROGRESSIVE POSTER CONDEMNING CHILD LABOR

This poster attacks child labor, borrowing the convention of the business flow chart to portray graphically how industries employing children are "making human junk." Progressives' concern for the plight of poor children won them the label "the child savers." Although activists worked hard to enact federal legislation prohibiting child labor in 1916, the Supreme Court declared the law unconstitutional two years later on the grounds that Congress had no right to regulate manufacturing within states.

Library of Congress.

PROGRESSIVE REFORM FROM THE GRASS ROOTS TO THE WHITE HOUSE

21

1890–1916

I N THE SUMMER OF 1889, a young woman leased the upper floor of a dilapidated mansion on Chicago's West Side in the heart of a burgeoning immigrant population of Italians, Russian Jews, and Greeks. Watching the preparations at number 335, the neighbors scratched their heads, wondering why the well-dressed woman, who surely could afford a better house in a better neighborhood, chose to live on South Halsted Street. For Jane Addams, the house built by Charles Hull precisely suited her needs. In September, she and her college friend Ellen Gates Starr moved in. "Probably no young matron ever placed her own things in her own house with more pleasure," she wrote. But Addams was no traditional matron. Her plan was to throw open the doors of Hull House to her immigrant neighbors in an attempt to bridge the gap between the rich and the poor.

For Jane Addams, personal action marked the first step in the search for solutions to the social problems fostered by urban industrialism. Her object was twofold: She wanted to help her neighbors and she wanted to offer an opportunity for educated women like herself to find meaningful work. As she later wrote in her autobiography, *Twenty Years at Hull-House* (1910), "I gradually became convinced that it would be a good thing to rent a house in a part of the city where many primitive and actual needs are found, in which young women who had been given over too exclusively to study might restore a balance of activity along traditional lines and learn of life from life itself." Addams's emphasis on the reciprocal relationship between the classes made Hull House different from other philanthropic enterprises. She wished to do things with, not just for, Chicago's poor.

By 1907, Hull House had expanded from one rented floor in the old brick mansion to some thirteen buildings that housed a remarkable variety of activities. The bathrooms in the basement had been converted into public baths; a coffee shop and restaurant sold take-out food to workingwomen too tired to cook after their long shifts; and a nursery and kindergarten provided care for neighborhood children. Clubs of every description and for every age met in the rooms. Hull House offered classes, lectures, art exhibits, musical instruction, and college extension courses. It boasted a gymnasium, a theater, a manual training workshop, a labor museum, and the first public playground in Chicago.

But Hull House was more than a group of buildings. From the first, it attracted a remarkable set of inhabitants. Some stayed for decades, as did Julia Lathrop before she went to Washington, D.C., in 1912 to head the Children's Bureau. Others, like Gerard Swope, who later became president of the General Electric Company, came for only a short while. Almost all had jobs, paid room and board, and devoted time to research and reform. The women and men who lived at Hull House were among the first to investigate the problems of the city with scientific precision. They surveyed housing conditions, investigated child labor and the sweatshop, documented the cocaine traffic in the neighborhood, studied the problems of juvenile delinquency, and conducted investigations into every aspect of urban life. Armed with statistics, they launched campaigns to improve housing, end child labor, fund playgrounds, mediate between labor and management, and lobby for protective legislation.

Although Addams had not intended to go into politics, Hull House soon became a political force. The evolution can best be dramatized in Addams's attempt to clean up Halsted Street. Piles of decaying garbage overflowed the street's wooden trash bins, breeding flies and disease. Investigation revealed that a contractor received a fat fee from the city to remove the garbage. The contract was a political plum awarded by the local ward boss, and the contractor felt under no obligation to provide adequate service. To end the graft, Addams herself applied for the contract. Instead, the mayor appointed her garbage inspector for the nineteenth ward. Out on the streets at six in the morning, Addams rode atop the garbage wagon as it made its rounds to be sure that the men did their work. Her diligence greatly annoyed the ward boss, who managed to have her removed after a year. What had begun as an attempt to clean up Halsted Street developed into a call for municipal reform as Addams squared off against the boss and his hirelings. In her attempt to oust the boss, she came to understand his role in city life. After backing several unsuccessful electoral campaigns to unseat him, Addams learned just how the machine worked among its poor constituency to provide jobs and favors. Judging the boss a symptom and not a cause of urban poverty, Addams moved on to press for state and national legislation designed to better the living conditions of the urban poor.

Addams had learned an important lesson. It was impossible to deal with urban problems without getting into politics. Her path led her not only to city hall but to the state capitol and on to Washington, D.C. A strong advocate of woman suffrage, she argued that city women needed the ballot, not the broom, to keep their neighborhoods clean.

JANE ADDAMS

Jane Addams was twenty-nine years old when she founded Hull House on Halsted Street in Chicago. Her desire to live among the poor, her insistence that settlement house work provide benefits for educated women like herself, as well as for the poor neighborhood residents, separated her from the charity workers who had come before her and marked the distance from philanthropy to progressive reform.

University of Illinois at Chicago, The University Library, Jane Addams Memorial Collection.

Under Jane Addams's leadership, Hull House became not only the premier social settlement in the United States but a "spearhead for reform," part of a broader movement that contemporaries called the progressive movement. The transition from personal action to political activism that Addams personified became one of the hallmarks of this reform period which lasted for almost three decades, from the 1890s to World War I.

What motivated comfortable, middle-class women and men to undertake the series of reforms that together constituted one of the major movements for social and political reform in U.S. history? There is no one answer because there is no single progressive profile. The "progressives," as they called themselves, were a diverse group with a variety of goals. A sense of Christian mission inspired some progressives. Others, frightened by the political tensions of the 1890s, feared social upheaval unless conditions were improved. Progressives shared a growing concern about the power of wealthy individuals and corporations and a strong dislike of the trusts. But often they feared the new immigrants as well and sought to control and Americanize them. Along with moral fervor, a belief in expertise and scientific principles informed progressivism and made the cult of efficiency part and parcel of the progressive movement. All of these elements—uplift and efficiency, social justice and social control—came together in the Progressive Era.

Grassroots Progressivism

Progressive reform began at the grassroots level and percolated upward into local, state, and eventually national politics as progressive reformers attacked the social problems fostered by industrialism. While reform flourished in many different settings across the country, the problems of urban America called forth the greatest efforts of the women and men who styled themselves progressives. A sense of moral outrage over conditions in the cities, coupled with a fear of growing class division, fueled progressive reform. In their zeal to "civilize the city," reformers founded settlement houses, professed a new Christian social gospel, and campaigned against vice and crime in the name of "social purity." Allying with the working class, they sought to better the lot of sweatshop garment workers and end child labor. (See Texts in Historical Context, page 804.) While their reform efforts often began on the local level, they just as often ended up being debated in state legislatures, in Congress, and in the Oval Office. From Hull House to the White House, progressivism became a major political force in the first decade of the twentieth century.

Civilizing the City

Progressive reform efforts were multifaceted, and reformers of many stripes participated in the campaign to civilize the city. Typically, progressives attacked the problems of the city on many fronts: The settlement house movement attempted to bridge the distance between the classes; the social gospel called for the churches to play a new role in social

reformation; and the social purity movement campaigned to clean up vice, particularly prostitution.

The settlement house movement, which originated in England, was imported to America in 1886 with the opening of the University Settlement House in New York City. In 1889, in the same month that Jane Addams moved into Hull House, a group of graduates from Smith College founded the College Settlement in Brooklyn. Americans modified the settlement significantly, abandoning the strong religious overtones of the English movement. Settlement house workers quickly recognized that it would be divisive and counterproductive to promote Protestantism among their largely Catholic and Jewish neighbors.

Another significant change from the English model was the substantial role that women, particularly college-educated women, played in American settlement houses. Women formed the backbone of the settlement house movement and helped it to grow in the decades between 1891 and 1911 from six settlements to more than four hundred. Eager to use their knowledge, educated women found themselves blocked by sex discrimination from medicine, law, and the clergy. Fewer than fifteen hundred women practiced law in 1900, and women constituted only 6 percent of the medical profession. College women like Jane Addams found settlements a way to put their talents to use in the service of society. In the process they created the new profession of social work. Florence Kelley, Julia Lathrop, Alice Hamilton, and Grace and Edith Abbott are only a few of the best known of these influential settlement house residents.

Progressive reform began at the grassroots level and percolated upward into local, state, and eventually national politics as progressive reformers attacked the social problems fostered by urban industrialism.

For their part, the churches confronted the social problems raised in the cities by enunciating a new "social gospel," one that saw its mission as being not simply to reform individuals but to reform society. On the simplest level, the social gospel offered a powerful corrective to the Gospel of Wealth, with its belief that riches somehow signaled divine favor. Washington Gladden, a prominent social gospel minister, challenged that view when he urged Congregationalists to turn down a gift from John D. Rockefeller, arguing that it was "tainted money." In place of the Gospel of Wealth, the clergy urged their congregations to put Christ's teachings to work in their daily lives. The Reverend William Stead made the point in the best-seller *If Christ Came to Chicago* (1894), and Charles L. Seldon's popular book *In His Steps* (1898) called on men and women to Christianize capitalism by asking the question "What would Jesus do?"

Women formed the backbone of the settlement house movement and helped it to grow in the decades between 1891 and 1911 from six settlements to more than four hundred. In the process they created the new profession of social work.

For Walter Rauschenbusch, a Baptist minister working in New York's Hell's Kitchen (a poor neighborhood in Manhattan), the social gospel grew out of the harrowing experience of the depression of the 1890s that left hundreds of thousands of people unemployed. "They wore down our threshold and they wore away our hearts," he later wrote. "One could hear human virtue cracking and crumbling all around." In *Christianity and the Social Crisis* (1907), Rauschenbusch called for the church to play a new role in promoting social justice.

Under the influence of the social gospel, churches began to provide social services. The Reverend George Rainsford of St. George's Episcopal Church in New York risked offending his most generous parishioner, J. P. Morgan, by inaugurating a gymnasium, a school for industrial training, and a boys' club to serve his immigrant neighborhood. Although the social gospel had its greatest effect among Protestant denominations, liberal Catholics like New York City's Father Edmund McGlynn also engaged in social action. McGlynn's strong support of the Irish working class, coupled with his attacks on capitalism, almost led to his excommunication. Like McGlynn, a radical fringe of social gospel ministers including Congregationalist George D. Herron called for Christian socialism—the nonviolent overthrow of capitalism and the creation of a cooperative society.

Ministers also played an active role in the social purity movement, the campaign to attack vice. The Reverend Charles Parkhurst shocked his New

York congregation in the 1890s by donning a disguise and touring the city's brothels, asking at each dive, "Show me something worse." As Parkhurst discovered, the brothel was a common feature of urban life. Progressives insisted that poverty bred prostitution and argued for higher wages. "Is it any wonder," asked the Chicago vice commission, "that a tempted girl who receives only six dollars per week working with her hands sells her body for twenty-five dollars per week when she learns there is a demand for it and men are willing to pay the price?"

To end the "social evil," as reformers euphemistically called prostitution, the social purity movement brought together doctors who were concerned about the spread of venereal disease, ministers like Parkhurst who wished to stamp out sin, and women reformers who were determined to fight the double standard that made it acceptable for men to engage in premarital and extramarital sex but punished women who strayed. Together, they attempted to shut down dance halls, saloons, and the dubious "employment agencies" that recruited women into prostitution. They waged campaigns to close "red-light districts" in cities across the country and lobbied for the Mann Act, passed in 1910, which made it illegal to transport women across state lines for immoral purposes. On the state level, they struck at venereal disease by securing legislation making it compulsory to have a blood test for syphilis before marriage.

Attacks on alcohol went hand in hand with the push for social purity. The temperance campaign launched by the Woman's Christian Temperance Union (WCTU) heated up in the early twentieth century. The Anti-Saloon League, formed in 1895 under the leadership of Protestant clergy, campaigned for an end to the sale of liquor. The clergy were joined by reformers who saw alcoholism as a threat to health, the family, and society. Reformers pointed to the links connecting drink with prostitution, wife and child abuse, unemployment, and industrial accidents. The powerful liquor lobby fought back, spending liberally in elections to defeat not only prohibition but woman suffrage and, in the process, fueling the charge that liquor corrupted the political process.

An element of nativism (dislike of foreigners) ran through the move for prohibition. Progressives failed to see the important role the tavern played in many ethnic communities. They sought to enforce Sunday closings of taverns and other forms of social control to deny the working class access to alcohol. By 1912, seven states had outlawed the liquor traffic.

Progressives' efforts to civilize the city, whether by launching social settlements or campaigning against prostitution and alcohol, demonstrated their willingness to take action, their belief that environment, not heredity alone, determined human potential, and their optimism that conditions could be corrected without radically altering America's economy or institutions. All of these attitudes characterized the progressive movement.

Progressives and the Working Class

Day-to-day contact with their neighbors made settlement house workers particularly sympathetic to labor unions. As Florence Kelley observed, "At Hull-House one got into the labor movement as a matter of course, without realizing how or when." When Mary Kenney O'Sullivan told Jane Addams that her bookbinders' union met in a dirty, noisy saloon, Addams invited the union to meet at Hull House. And during the Pullman strike in 1894, Hull House residents organized strike relief and lent their prestige and financial resources to the strike. "Hull-House has been so unionized," grumbled one Chicago businessman, "that it has lost its usefulness and become a detriment and harm to the community." But to the working class, the support of middle-class reformers marked a significant gain.

Attempts to forge a cross-class alliance became institutionalized in 1903 with the creation of the Women's Trade Union League (WTUL). The WTUL brought together middle-class "allies" and women workers. Its goal was to organize workingwomen into unions under the auspices of the American Federation of Labor (AFL). However, the AFL provided little more than lip service to the organization of women workers. From the leadership to the rank and file, the AFL men shared traditional notions of women's place. As one workingwoman confided, "The men think that the girls should not get as good work as the men and should not make half as much money as a man." When it came to women, the AFL's main concern seemed to be to protect men from female competition. Samuel Gompers, president of the AFL, endorsed the principle of equal pay for equal work, shrewdly observing that it would help male workers more than women, since many employers hired women precisely because they could be paid less. Given the AFL's attitude, it was not surprising that the money and leadership to organize women came largely from wealthy allies in the WTUL.

Two remarkable sisters provided the financial backing and leadership for the WTUL: Mary Dreier, who headed the New York branch, and Margaret Dreier Robins, president of the national league from

WOMEN STRIKERS
The "uprising of twenty thousand" pitted garment workers against their employers in a strike that lasted throughout the bitter winter of 1909–1910. The strikers, primarily young women from the Jewish and Italian immigrant communities, joined the International Ladies' Garment Workers Union and showed that women could be unionized and mount an effective strike.
Labor-Management Documentation Center, Cornell University.

What Do Early Documentary Texts Tell Us about the Men and Women Who Called Themselves Progressives?

IN THE 1880s, Jacob Riis took his camera into the tenements of New York City to document the living conditions of the poor. The result was the runaway best-seller *How the Other Half Lives* (1890). Riis, a Danish immigrant who covered the crime beat for the *New York Tribune,* had a keen eye for telling details and a colorful prose style. Through dozens of individual vignettes, piled one upon another, Riis built for his readers the concept of a slum.

Along with his descriptive text, he included his pictures. The first edition of *How the Other Half Lives* contained 39 images taken from Riis's photographs. The pictures are remarkable, both for the story they tell and for their place in the history of photography. The invention of flash powder made Riis's work possible by enabling him, literally, to shed light on his subjects. Lugging his bulky box camera and tripod into the dark alleys and dingy tenements of lower Manhattan, Riis pioneered photographic journalism. In Riis's day, photography was a dangerous business. He had to ignite magnesium flash powder in the close quarters of firetrap tenements.

Once he nearly blinded himself. Another time, when he was photographing the residents of a tenement on "Blind Man's Alley," he set the place on fire. He later claimed the tenement, nicknamed the "Dirty Spoon," was so filthy it wouldn't burn. He was able to douse the flames without his blind subjects ever realizing their danger.

Over a century after the book's publication, *How the Other Half Lives* is still a valuable tool for historians, as much for what it tells us about the progressive reformers who set out to document the evils of urban industrialism as for what it reveals about the conditions they brought to light.

Riis's ethnocentrism is immediately apparent. His pages are filled with racial and ethnic stereotypes—stealthy and secretive Chinese; colorful but murderous Italians; greedy, quarrelsome Jews; happy, fun-loving Negroes; dirty Arabs; orderly, thrifty Germans. The degree of his opprobrium rises in direct proportion to the distance his subjects are from Riis's native Denmark, a reminder that racism and prejudice were by no means native to American soil. Another troubling aspect of Riis's book is its voyeurism. Riis unabashedly invites his readers to go "slumming."

Riis's impressionistic view of the life of the urban poor was soon followed by more scientific studies. The gathering of information and the publicizing of urban conditions became staples of settlement house work. Jane Addams and Florence Kelley undertook a statistical survey of economic conditions in their Chicago neighborhood; they published the results in 1895 as *Hull-House Maps and Papers.* This passion for information was an important part of the progressive ethos. Sociology, a new field in the emerging "social sciences," was predicated on the need for accurate and precise infor-

1907 to 1922. The two sisters, daughters of a wealthy German-born merchant, grew up in Brooklyn, where they became interested in working girls' clubs and joined the fledgling WTUL. In 1906, Margaret married social activist Raymond Robins and moved to Chicago, where the couple lived among the working class in a cold-water flat not far from Hull House.

Although the alliance between the working-women, primarily immigrants and the daughters of immigrants, and their middle-class allies was not without tension, the WTUL helped workingwomen

achieve significant gains. The most notable success came in 1909 in the "uprising of twenty thousand."

In November 1909, hundreds of women employees of the Triangle Shirtwaist Company in New York City went on strike to protest low wages, dangerous and demeaning working conditions, and management's refusal to recognize their union, the International Ladies' Garment Workers Union (ILGWU). In support of the walkout, the ILGWU called for a general strike of all garment workers. An estimated twenty thousand workers, most of mation to stimulate reform. Soon sociologists attempted to supplant "storytellers" like Jacob Riis.

Their most ambitious project was the famous Pittsburgh survey undertaken under the auspices of the Russell Sage Foundation. Among the best-known volumes produced by the survey was Margaret Byington's study *Homestead: The Households of a Mill Town*, published in 1910. Byington lived in Homestead, Pennsylvania, for six months studying ninety families during the economic downturn of 1907–1908. Like Riis, she documented in text and photographs the lives of the workers in U.S. Steel's mills. And like Addams and Kelley, she provided a statistical analysis of her findings. Yet despite her rigorous claims to scientific method, the assumptions underlying Byington's study repeat the same ethnocentric patterns observed in Riis. Byington's treatment of Homestead's families is filtered through the nativist lens of her era. In dealing with family life, she can't hide her disapproval of the "Slavs," a catchall term for various nationalities of eastern and southern Europe. These poorest of the Homestead families supplemented their wages by taking in boarders. The practice appalled Byington, who subscribed to the middle-class notion that the home should remain inviolate. As a result, her study of Homestead's households defined family as she wished it to be, not as it was.

Historians seeking to uncover details about the daily lives of the urban poor turn to these documentary sources with the caveat that the cultural assumptions of the authors need to be looked at as closely as their photographs and text. The documentary evidence collected by early reformers reveals not only the everyday lives of the working poor but also a great deal about the men and women who called themselves "progressives"—their attitudes, their cultural beliefs, and their biases. Their greatest strength was their resolve for action, their determination to right the worst wrongs brought about by urban industrialism. They refused to believe the tenets of social Darwinism with its negation of human agency. Instead, they resolved to act. But often their actions aimed at the symptoms and not the causes of urban poverty. In Riis's case, he damned the tenement and not the economic system that produced it. Nor did Riis have a clear idea of the consequences of his battle against the tenement. He wanted to abolish substandard housing, but he never questioned what would happen to the people turned out on the street. In *How the Other Half Lives*, he noted with surprise that after he managed to get a building condemned, its pitiful inhabitants crept back in.

Riis, who had landed in New York in 1870 at the age of twenty-one and spent three years looking for work, knew firsthand the flophouses and the dirty alleys of New York. But he never lost faith in the promise of America. Riis never saw the slum as part of the burgeoning industrial economy just as he never subscribed to the growing criticism of capitalism.

Like Riis, most progressives rarely questioned the economic system or wished to tinker with it. Instead, they believed that publicity alone could solve problems. "The power of the fact is the mightiest lever of this or any day," Riis wrote with conviction. Too often, progressive reformers saw their role as simply to place the "facts" before the public. (For a Riis photo see page 810.)

These early documentary texts, then, profile not only the lives of the urban poor but present a progressive profile, pointing to the reformers' strengths and to their limitations.

them teenage girls and many of them Jewish and Italian immigrants, went out on strike and stayed out through the winter, picketing in the bitter cold. More than six hundred were arrested, and many were sent to jail for "streetwalking," a move by the authorities to try to break the spirit and impugn the morals of the striking women. By the time the strike ended in February 1910, the workers had won some important demands in many shops. But they lost their bid to gain recognition for their union, the ILGWU. The solidarity shown by the women workers proved to be the strike's greatest achievement. As Clara Lemlich, one of the strike's leaders, exclaimed, "They used to say that you couldn't even organize women. They wouldn't come to union meetings. They were 'temporary' workers. Well we showed them!"

The WTUL made enormous contributions to the success of the strike. The league provided volunteers for the picket lines, posted more than $29,000 in bail, protested police brutality, organized almost overnight a massive parade of ten thousand

TRIANGLE SHIRTWAIST FACTORY FIRE
A grim newspaper photo shows the broken bodies of garment workers who jumped to their death when fire broke out in the Triangle Shirtwaist Factory on Saturday, March 25, 1911. Nearly five hundred women and girls worked in the firetrap and many were unable to escape because the doors had been locked to prevent employees from taking breaks. Firefighters rushed to the scene, but their ladders reached only to the sixth floor, leaving those on the seventh, eighth, and ninth floors with little choice but to jump.
The New York Herald, March 26, 1911.

strikers, took part in the arbitration conference, arranged mass meetings, appealed for funds, and generated publicity for the strike. Mary Dreier herself marched on the picket line and was arrested. Under the leadership of the WTUL, women from every class of society, from J. P. Morgan's daughter Anne to socialists on the Lower East Side, joined the strikers in a dramatic demonstration of cross-class alliance.

But for all its success, the uprising of the twenty thousand failed fundamentally to change conditions for women workers, as the tragic Triangle fire dramatized in 1911. A little over a year after the shirtwaist makers' strike ended, fire alarms sounded at the Triangle factory. The ramshackle building, full of lint and combustible cloth, went up in flames in minutes. A WTUL member described the scene below on the street. "I was coming down Fifth Avenue on the Saturday afternoon, when a great, swirling, billowing cloud of smoke swept like a giant streamer out of Washington Square," she recounted. "Two young girls whom I knew to be working in the vicinity came rushing toward me, tears were running from their eyes and they were white and shaking as they caught me by the arm. 'Oh,' shrieked one of them, 'they are jumping. Jumping from ten stories up! They are going through the air like bundles of clothes, and the firemen can't stop them and the policemen can't stop them and nobody can help them at all.'"

The terrified Triangle workers had little choice but to jump. One door was blocked by flames, and the door to the fire escape had been locked to prevent the girls from sneaking out on breaks. The lucky ones made their way to the roof and escaped. Of 500 workers, 146 died and scores of others were injured. The owners of the Triangle firm were later tried for negligence, but they escaped conviction when authorities determined that the fire had been started by a careless smoker. The Triangle Shirtwaist Company reopened in another firetrap within a matter of weeks.

Outrage and a sense of futility overwhelmed Rose Schneiderman, a leading WTUL organizer, who made a bitter speech at the memorial service for the dead Triangle workers. "I would be a traitor to those poor burned bodies if I came here to talk good fellowship," she told her audience. "We have tried you good people of the public and we have found you wanting. . . . I know from my experience it is up to the working people to save themselves . . . by a strong working class movement."

The Triangle fire tested severely the bonds of the cross-class alliance. Along with Rose Schneiderman, WTUL leaders experienced a growing sense of futility. It seemed not enough to organize and to strike, particularly when the AFL paid so little attention to women workers. Increasingly, the WTUL turned its efforts to lobbying for protective legislation—laws that would limit hours and regulate working conditions.

The principle of protective legislation won a major victory in 1908 when the U.S. Supreme Court, in the landmark case *Muller v. Oregon*, reversed its previous rulings and upheld an Oregon law that limited the hours women could work to ten a day. A mass of sociological evidence put together by Florence Kelley of the National Consumers League and Josephine Goldmark of the WTUL and presented by Goldmark's brother-in-law, lawyer Louis Brandeis, demonstrated the ill effects of long hours on the health and safety of women. The "Brandeis brief" convinced the Court that long hours endangered women and therefore the entire race. The Court's ruling set a precedent, but one that separated the well-being of women from that of the rest of the workforce by arguing that women's reproductive role justified special treatment. Later generations of women fighting for equality would question the effectiveness of such a strategy and argue that it ultimately closed good jobs to women workers. But for the WTUL, protective legislation was greeted as a first stage in the attempt to ensure the safety not just of women but of all workers.

The National Consumers League, like the WTUL, fostered cross-class alliance. Formed in 1899 and led by Florence Kelley, the Consumers League urged middle-class women to boycott stores and exert pressure for decent wages and working conditions for women employees, primarily saleswomen. The league published a "white list" of stores that met its standards. But, like the WTUL, the Consumers League turned increasingly to protective legislation to achieve its goals in the first decade of the twentieth century. The tendency to seek legislative solutions to social problems was another hallmark of progressivism. Frustrated by the reluctance of the private sector to respond to the need for reform, progressives turned to the government at all levels. Critics would later charge that the progressives assumed too easily that government regulation could best solve social problems.

Reform also fueled the fight for woman suffrage. For women like Jane Addams and Florence Kelley, involvement in social reform led inevitably to support for woman suffrage. These new suffragists spoke less of natural rights than their predecessors Elizabeth Cady Stanton and Susan B. Anthony had done. Instead they emphasized the reforms that could be accomplished if women had the vote. When they talked of the need for the ballot, they often compared it to the broom. Jane Addams insisted that in an urban, industrial society a good housekeeper could not be sure the food she fed her family or the water and milk they drank were pure unless she became involved in politics and wielded the ballot instead of the broom to protect her family.

Progressivism: Theory and Practice

Progressive reformers developed a theoretical basis for their activist approach by countering social Darwinism with a dynamic new reform Darwinism and by championing the uniquely American philosophy of pragmatism. The progressives emphasized action and experimentation. No longer was the universe seen as a massive, slow-moving machine, but as a system amenable to tinkering by human intelligence. An unchecked admiration for speed and efficiency also characterized a significant component of progressive thought and led to enthusiasm for scientific management and a new cult of efficiency. These varied strands of progressive theory found practical application in state and local politics. Political progressivism originated at the local level and percolated upward to the state and national governments. The politicians who became premier progressives

PICTURING CHILD LABOR

Each of the photographs of children pictured here was designed consciously to carry a message. Jacob Riis intended his photograph of homeless newsboys sleeping in an alley to be emblematic of the plight of the city's poor children. The boy miner, photographed by the mining company he worked for, was intended to counter criticism of child labor. Entitled A Youthful Gold Digger, *the photograph carried the caption "Eight-year-old Bill Scott of [Clarksburg, West Virginia] is all set to go to work in the mines. He's fully outfitted for his day's labor — with pipe, headlight, pick axe, lunch can, high shoes, overall coat and bandanna." Ironically, the pictures evoke in a modern audience the opposite responses from those the photographers intended. The staged aestheticism of Riis's photo works against the grim reality Riis intended it to convey, while the mine's blatant promotion of child labor is shocking, and the plucky eight-year-old evokes our pity and horror.*
Homeless boys: The Jacob A. Riis Collection, #121, Museum of the City of New York; miner: Library of Congress.

were generally the followers, not the leaders, in a movement that was already well advanced at the grassroots level. Yet they left their stamp on the movement. Among the preeminent progressive politicians were Tom Johnson, the mayor of Cleveland, Ohio, and Robert La Follette, who as governor and later a senator, determined to make the state of Wisconsin a laboratory for progressivism.

Reform Darwinism and Pragmatism

The active, interventionist approach of the progressives directly challenged social Darwinism, with its insistence that the world operated on the principle of survival of the fittest and that human beings were powerless in the face of the law of natural selection. Without abandoning the evolutionary framework of Darwinism, a new group of sociologists argued that evolution could be advanced more rapidly if men and women used their intellects to alter the environment. Sociologist Lester Frank Ward put it clearly in his book *Dynamic Sociology* (1883), which emphasized an activist approach to the problems of urban industrialism. "I insist the time must soon come," he wrote, "when the control of blind natural forces in society must give way to human foresight." Dubbed "reform Darwinism," the new sociological theory condemned laissez-faire, insisting that the liberal state should play a more active role in solving social problems. Reform Darwinism provided a rationale for attacking social ills and became the ideological basis for progressive reform.

Although progressivism drew support from many people, much of its leadership came from the new urban middle class, a group composed of physicians, businesspeople, scientists, engineers, and social workers. These men and women put their skills and intellects to work to solve the problems caused by industrialization and to impose order on what many perceived as a dangerously chaotic society. This group of progressives championed the scientific method and promoted efficiency, seeking scientific solutions to social problems.

In their pursuit of reform, they were influenced by the work of two philosophers, William James and John Dewey. James and Dewey argued for a new test for truth, insisting that there were no eternal verities and that the real worth of any idea was in its consequences. They called their pluralistic, relativistic philosophy "pragmatism." Dewey put his theories to the test in the classroom of his laboratory school at the University of Chicago. A pioneer in American education, he emphasized process

rather than content and encouraged more child-centered schools where students learned by doing. By championing social experimentation, the American pragmatists provided an important impetus for progressive reform.

Scientific Management and the Cult of Efficiency

Increased emphasis on means as well as ends marked progressive reform. Efficiency and expertise became watchwords in the progressive vocabulary. The journalist and critic Walter Lippmann, in *Drift and Mastery* (1914), a classic statement of the progressive agenda, called for skilled technocrats who would use scientific techniques to control social change, substituting mastery for aimless drift. A fascination with "social engineering" was a characteristic of progressive reform. Ellen Richards, the first woman graduate and instructor at the Massachusetts Institute of Technology, urged college women and men to act as "social engineers." This emphasis on expertise inevitably fostered a kind of elitism. Whereas Populism had called for a greater voice for the masses, progressivism, for all its emphasis on social justice, insisted that experts be put in charge.

Although progressivism drew support from many people, much of its leadership came from the new urban middle class, a group composed of physicians, businesspeople, scientists, engineers, and social workers.

At its extreme, the application of expertise and social engineering took the form of scientific management, which alienated the working class while elevating productivity and efficiency above all other considerations. Frederick Winslow Taylor, who after a nervous breakdown left Harvard to become a machinist, pioneered "systematized shop management." Taylor was obsessed with making humans and machines produce more and faster. After he earned a master of engineering degree in 1885, he went back to work at Midvale Steel, restructuring the workplace, taking control away from individual workers, and placing it in the hands of managers. With his stopwatch he carefully timed workers and then attempted to break their work down into its simplest components, one repetitive action after another, on the theory that productivity would increase if tasks were reduced to their simplest parts. Employees at Midvale cursed him and called him a slave driver. When he died in 1915, with his stop-watch in his hand, workers bitterly pointed to the speedup—pushing workers to produce more in less time and for less pay—as his legacy. But Taylor's many advocates included progressives like Louis Brandeis who applauded the increased productivity and efficiency brought about under Taylor's system.

The progressive reformers who championed scientific management and social engineering as methods to solve social problems never faced the contradiction between the means they advocated and the ends they desired. The central paradox of progressivism was its insistence that social justice could be brought about by social engineering—that a just society could be achieved by applying scientific principles.

Progressivism in Action: Cleveland and Wisconsin

Progressivism burst forth at every level in 1901, but nowhere more forcefully than in Cleveland, Ohio, where the voters elected Thomas Lofton Johnson mayor. Johnson, a self-made millionaire by the age of forty, turned his back on business and entered politics after reading Henry George's *Progress and Poverty*. A Democrat and an advocate of free trade and Henry George's single tax, Johnson pledged during the campaign to reduce the streetcar fare to three cents. His election touched off a seven-year war between advocates of the lower fare and the entrenched interests who ran Cleveland's streetcars. Johnson believed that workingmen and -women paid a disproportionate share of their meager earnings for transportation. When the streetcar industry and its supporters argued that they couldn't meet costs with the lower fare, Johnson fought them. Arrayed against him were powerful adversaries, including Ohio Senator Marcus Alonzo Hanna, the Republican kingmaker who had managed William McKinley's successful campaign for president in 1896. When Johnson responded by building his own streetcar line, his foes tore up the tracks or blocked him with court injunctions and legal delays. At the prompting of his opponents, the state legislature sought to limit Johnson's mayoral power by revoking the charters of every city in the state, replacing home rule with central control from the state capital at Columbus.

During his tenure as mayor, Johnson fought for home rule, fair taxation, and municipal ownership

and championed greater democracy through the use of the initiative, referendum, and recall, devices that allowed the voters to have a direct say in legislative and judicial matters. Frustrated in his attempt to bring the streetcar industry to heel, he pushed for municipal ownership of street railways and public utilities, a tactic that progressives called "gas and water socialism." The city bought the streetcar system and instituted the three-cent fare. Under Johnson's administration, Cleveland became, in the words of journalist Lincoln Steffens, the "best governed city in America."

In Wisconsin, Robert M. La Follette, who as a young congressional representative had supported William McKinley, abandoned Republican conservatism and converted to the progressive cause early in the 1900s. An astute politician, La Follette capitalized on the grassroots movement for reform to launch his long political career, first as governor (1901–1905) and later as senator (1906–1925). A graduate of the University of Wisconsin, La Follette

THREE-CENT STREETCAR TOKEN
Tom Johnson, the reform mayor of Cleveland, Ohio, from 1901 to 1909, fought for a three-cent streetcar fare for more than seven years, winning the support of the working class at the same time he angered the business interests who ran the city's streetcars. To get his cheaper fare, Johnson finally called for municipal ownership of the transit system. Here Johnson uses a three-cent token in his re-election campaign in 1907.
The Western Reserve Historical Society, Cleveland, Ohio.

brought scientists and professors into his administration and used the university, only a few blocks from the state house in Madison, as a resource to help in drafting legislation. La Follette advocated railroad regulation, tax reform, and direct democracy. As governor, he lowered railroad rates, raised railroad taxes, improved education, championed conservation, established factory regulation and workers' compensation, instituted the first direct primary in the country, and inaugurated the first state income tax. Under his leadership, Wisconsin earned the title "laboratory of democracy."

A fiery orator, "Fighting Bob" La Follette united his supporters around issues that transcended old party loyalties. He successfully formed a coalition of farmers and laborers who reelected him many times. This emphasis on reforms rather than party identification became a characteristic of progressivism, which attracted followers from both major parties. Democrats like Tom Johnson and Republicans like Robert La Follette could lay equal claim to the label "progressive." When La Follette moved to the U.S. Senate in 1906, he joined a coalition of insurgent progressives, Democrats and Republicans alike, who crossed party lines to work together for reform.

Progressivism Finds a President: Theodore Roosevelt

On September 6, 1901, President William McKinley was shot and gravely wounded while attending the Pan American Exposition in Buffalo, New York. After lingering for a week, he died on September 14. When news of McKinley's assassination reached his friend and political mentor Marcus Alonzo Hanna, Hanna is said to have growled, "Now that damned cowboy is president." Hanna was speaking of Vice President Theodore Roosevelt, the colorful hero of San Juan Hill, who had indeed punched cattle in the Dakotas in the 1880s.

Roosevelt's status as a Spanish-American war hero had propelled him to the governorship of New York in 1898. A moderate reformer, he clashed with New York's Republican "Easy Boss," Tom Platt. To get rid of Roosevelt, the party bosses "kicked him upstairs" to the vice presidency in 1900, where he added luster to the ticket and helped reelect McKinley to a second term. As vice president, Platt and the party leaders reasoned, Roosevelt could do

little harm. But one bullet proved the error of their logic. Overnight, Roosevelt was president, and Mark Hanna was not alone in his concern that the world of conservative politics that McKinley personified had died with him. A skillful politician, Roosevelt would ride the wave of progressive reform, a wave that would swamp his successor, William Howard Taft.

An activist and a moralist, imbued with progressive spirit, Roosevelt would turn the White House into a "bully pulpit" and, in the process, shift the nation's center of power from Wall Street to Washington.

In the first days of his presidency, Roosevelt reassured the shocked nation that he intended "to continue absolutely unbroken" the policies of McKinley. But anyone who knew Roosevelt knew that that was impossible. McKinley had been Mark Hanna's man, taking his cue from the Ohio senator and the ruling clique of conservatives in Congress. Roosevelt was as different from McKinley as the twentieth century was from the nineteenth. An activist and a moralist, imbued with progressive spirit, he would turn the White House into a "bully pulpit" and, in the process, shift the nation's center of power from Wall Street to Washington.

The Square Deal

At the age of forty-two, Roosevelt was the youngest man ever to move into the White House. A patrician by birth and an activist by temperament, Roosevelt brought to the job enormous talent and energy. By the time he graduated from Harvard, he was already an accomplished naturalist, an enthusiastic historian, and a naval strategist. He could have picked from any of these promising careers. Instead, he chose politics, not a bad choice for a man who wanted power and relished competition.

Roosevelt was shrewd enough to realize that the path to power did not lie in the good-government leagues formed by his well-bred friends. Instead, he apprenticed himself to the local ward boss, who held court in a grimy, smoke-filled Republican club above a Manhattan saloon. Roosevelt's rise in politics was nothing less than meteoric. He went from the New York state assembly at the age of twenty-three to the presidency in twenty years, with time out to be a cowboy in the Dakotas, police commissioner of New York City, and colonel of the Rough Riders.

The "absolutely vital question" facing the country, Roosevelt wrote to a friend in 1901, was "whether or not the government has the power to control the trusts." The Sherman Antitrust Act of 1890 had been badly weakened by a conservative Supreme Court and by attorneys general more willing to use it against unions than against monopolies. To determine if the law had any teeth left, Roosevelt, in one of his first acts as president, ordered his attorney general to begin a secret antitrust investigation of the Northern Securities Company.

Roosevelt trained his sights on a good target. Northern Securities resulted from one of the most controversial mergers in American history. When Edward C. Harriman, who controlled the Union Pacific and the Southern Pacific Railroads, attempted to add the Northern Pacific to his holdings, James J. Hill of the Great Northern squared off against him. The result was a ruinous railroad war that precipitated a panic on Wall Street, bankrupting thousands of small investors. To bring peace, financier J. P. Morgan created the Northern Securities Company in 1901, linking under one management three competing railroads. This new behemoth monopolized railroad traffic in the Northwest. Small investors still smarting from their losses, farmers worried about freight rates, and the public in general saw in Northern Securities the symbol of corporate highhandedness.

In February 1902, Wall Street rocked with the news that the government had filed suit against Northern Securities. As one editor sarcastically observed, "Wall Street is paralyzed at the thought that a President of the United States would sink so low as to try to enforce the law." An indignant J. P. Morgan demanded to know why he had not been consulted. "If we have done anything wrong," he told the attorney general, "send your man to my man and they can fix it up." Roosevelt, amused, later noted that Morgan "could not help regarding me as a big rival operator." In a sense, that was just what Roosevelt intended. Roosevelt's thunderbolt put Wall Street on notice that the money men were dealing with a president who demanded to be treated as an equal and who was willing to use government as an instrument to control business. Perhaps sensing the new mood, the Supreme Court, in a significant turnaround, upheld the Sherman Act and called for the dissolution of Northern Securities in 1904.

"Hurrah for Teddy the Trustbuster," cheered the papers. Roosevelt went on to use the Sherman Act against forty-three trusts, including such giants as the American Tobacco Company, Swift and Company, Du Pont, and Standard Oil. But despite the reputation he earned, Roosevelt never believed in trust-busting alone. He was no foe of big business. Like Morgan, he recognized that combination was inevitable and not necessarily a bad thing. Always a moralist, he insisted on a "rule of reason." He would punish the "bad" trusts (those that broke the law) and leave the "good" ones alone. In practice, he preferred regulation to antitrust suits. In 1903, he pressured Congress to pass the Elkins Act, a law outlawing railroad rebates (money returned to a shipper to guarantee his business). And he created the new cabinet department of Commerce and Labor with a subsidiary Bureau of Corporations to act as a corporate watchdog.

Observing Roosevelt in action, journalist Joseph Pulitzer remarked, "He has subjugated Wall Street." Pulitzer exaggerated, but Roosevelt had masterfully asserted the moral and political authority of the executive, underscoring, in his words, the "duty of the President to act upon the theory that he is the steward of the people."

Roosevelt's handling of the anthracite coal strike in 1902 provided the country with another example of his willingness to use the power of the presidency, this time to mediate between labor and management. In May, more than fifty thousand coal miners in Pennsylvania went out on strike, demanding higher wages, shorter hours, and recognition of the United Mine Workers (UMW) union. "The miners don't suffer," scoffed George Baer, the operator's spokesman, "why they can't even speak English." Six eastern railroads owned over 70 percent of the anthracite mines. With the power of the railroads behind them, the mine owners refused to budge.

The strike dragged on through the summer and into the fall. Hoarding and profiteering drove the price of coal up from $2.50 to $6 a ton. Most homes were heated with coal, and, with winter approaching, near riots broke out in big cities. Labor's sympathizers called for national ownership of the coal mines. Business leaders urged Roosevelt to follow President Cleveland's example in 1894 and call out federal troops to break the strike. In the face of mounting tension, Roosevelt kept his balance and steered a middle course. In October, he issued a personal invitation to representatives from both sides to meet in Washington. His unprecedented intervention served notice that government counted itself an independent force in business and labor disputes. At the same time, it gave unionism a boost

THEODORE ROOSEVELT
At forty-two, Theodore Roosevelt was the youngest president to occupy the White House. He brought to the office energy, intellect, and activism in equal measure, moving the presidency into the twentieth century. Described aptly as a "steam engine in trousers," Roosevelt enjoyed the presidency and worked tirelessly to make the office a "bully pulpit" from which he advocated an astounding series of reforms, from conservation to simplified spelling.
Collection of the New-York Historical Society.

by granting the UMW a place at the table. At the meeting, Baer and the mine owners arrogantly refused to talk to the union representatives, managing to insult both the president and the attorney general. By comparison, John Mitchell of the UMW impressed Roosevelt as both honest and sincere. The meeting ended in impasse.

Beside himself at the "wooden-headed obstinacy and stupidity" of management, Roosevelt threatened to seize the mines and run them with federal troops. It was a powerful bluff, one that called into question not only the supremacy of private property but the rule of law. The specter of federal troops being used to operate the mines quickly brought management around. At the prompting of J. P. Morgan, the mine owners agreed to arbitration. In the end, the miners won a reduction in hours and a wage increase, and the owners succeeded in preventing formal recognition of the UMW.

Taken together, Roosevelt's actions in the Northern Securities case and the anthracite coal strike marked a dramatic departure from the tradition of William McKinley. Roosevelt's actions demonstrated conclusively that government intended to act independently to provide a countervailing force to the power of the big corporations. Pleased with his role in the anthracite strike, Roosevelt announced that all he had tried to do was give labor and capital a "square deal."

The phrase became his slogan in the 1904 election campaign. To win the presidency in his own right, Roosevelt had to wrest control of the Republican Party from Mark Hanna, the only man who stood between him and the nomination. By the time Hanna died of typhoid fever in 1904, Roosevelt was the undisputed leader of the party.

In the presidential election of 1904, Roosevelt easily defeated the Democrats, who abandoned William Jennings Bryan, their candidate in the previous two elections, to support Judge Alton B. Parker. Parker was a "safe" candidate who they hoped would win business votes away from Roosevelt. In the months before the election, the president prudently toned down his criticism of big business. Wealthy Republicans like J. P. Morgan, while they privately branded Roosevelt a class traitor, remained loyal to the party and gave it their money and their votes. In November 1904, Roosevelt swept into office with the largest popular majority any candidate had polled to that time.

Roosevelt and Regulation

"Tomorrow I shall come into my office in my own right," Roosevelt is said to have remarked on the eve of his election. "Then watch out for me!" The conservative Republicans who had helped to elect him intended to do just that. No longer under the illusion that Roosevelt would continue McKinley's role as a silent partner to business interests, they reassured themselves that Congress remained firmly in the grip of conservative, standpat Republicans. The old guard in the Senate was led by Nelson Aldrich of Rhode Island, who was called "the senator from Standard Oil" (an alliance cemented when his daughter married John D. Rockefeller Jr.). In an era when state legislatures still chose U.S. senators, many like Aldrich openly served special business interests. The old guard stood squarely in the path of Roosevelt and reform.

Roosevelt needed all the popularity and political savvy he could muster to guide the reform measures that he championed through the conservative Congress. His ability to compromise led more idealistic progressives like La Follette to judge him a "trimmer." Others, however, have been more impressed by his flexibility, concurring with the judgment that Roosevelt was a "skillful broker of the possible."

Roosevelt's pet project remained railroad regulation. The Elkins Act prohibiting rebates had not worked. No one could stop big shippers from wresting concessions from the railroads. The Interstate Commerce Commission (ICC), created in 1887 to regulate the railroads, had been stripped of its powers by the Supreme Court. In the face of a widespread call for railroad reform, Roosevelt determined that the only solution lay in giving the ICC real power to set rates and prevent discriminatory practices. A strengthened ICC, in Roosevelt's words, would enable "the corporation that wishes to do well from being driven into doing ill, in order to compete with its rival, which prefers to do ill." But for all Roosevelt's lectures on what was legally and morally right, business remained adamant in its opposition

to federal rate setting. The right to determine the price of goods or services was an age-old prerogative of private enterprise and one that business had no intention of yielding to government without a fight.

To ensure passage of the Hepburn Railway Act, a bill increasing the power of the ICC, Roosevelt worked skillfully behind the scenes. Once again, he showed his power to bluff. By threatening to call for tariff reform, a volatile issue that might split the party, he succeeded in getting a recalcitrant House of Representatives to pass the Hepburn Act. But the bill bogged down in the Senate, where the old guard, led by Aldrich, attempted to amend it to death. One amendment, intended to cripple the ICC's rate-making power, gave the railroads the right to appeal to the courts. To get the best bill possible, Roosevelt first worked with insurgent progressives and then, when they could not muster the needed votes, switched sides and succeeded in getting Aldrich and the Republican regulars to accept a compromise. In its final form, the Hepburn Act, passed in May 1906, gave the ICC power to set rates subject to court review. Progressives like La Follette judged the bill a defeat for reform. Die-hard conservatives branded it a "piece of populism." Both exaggerated. The bill was by no means perfect. It left the courts too much power, and it failed to provide adequate means for the ICC to determine rates realistically. But its passage marked a landmark in the evolution of federal control of private industry. For the first time, a government commission had the power to investigate private business records and to set rates. The Hepburn Act signaled a victory for President Roosevelt and stood as testimony to his stature as a political leader and a practical idealist.

Roosevelt as "Lame Duck"

Passage of the Hepburn Act in 1906 marked the high point of Roosevelt's presidency. In the years that followed, his power eroded, although he continued to be an active and resourceful president. In a serious political blunder, Roosevelt brought some of his problems on himself by announcing on the eve of his election in 1904 that he would not run again. By 1906, his term was starting to run out, and his influence on Congress and his party was waning. Ironically, he had become a "lame duck" at the very moment when he was enjoying his greatest public popularity and when he needed and wanted to press for more reform.

Roosevelt, always an apt reader of the public temper, witnessed a growing appetite for reform fed by the revelations of corporate and political wrong-doing that filled the papers and boosted the sales of popular periodicals. In October 1902, Lincoln Steffens's "Tweed Days in St. Louis" appeared in *McClure's Magazine*, the first part of a series entitled "The Shame of the Cities" (later published as a book). The next month, Ida Tarbell, a schoolteacher turned journalist, began her sharply critical series on Standard Oil in *McClure's*. S. S. McClure, the magazine's publisher, watched circulation skyrocket to more than 370,000. Soon other journalists such as Ray Stannard Baker and Robert Hunter tried their hand at the new brand of investigative reporting. Their hard-hitting exposés swelled magazine circulation and touched off a public clamor for reform.

Roosevelt, a man who brandished publicity like a weapon in reform and who assiduously cultivated the press, counted many of these new journalists, notably Jacob Riis and Lincoln Steffens, as his friends. But when David Graham Phillips attacked the Republican old guard in 1906 in a series of articles entitled "The Treason of the Senate," the character assassination of his fellow Republicans offended the president. Roosevelt cautioned restraint and warned journalists that they should not be like the allegorical character in *Pilgrim's Progress* who was so busy raking up muck that he took no notice of higher things. Roosevelt's criticism gave the American vocabulary a new word: *muckraker*. Journalists soon appropriated the term and turned it into a badge of honor.

Muckraking, as Roosevelt was keenly aware, had been of enormous help in securing progressive legislation. The passage of the Pure Food and Drug Act and the Meat Inspection Act were powerful examples of the role of the muckrakers. In 1905, the president had belatedly thrown his support behind legislation to outlaw misbranded and adulterated foods, drinks, and drugs. For years, Dr. Harvey Washington Wiley, chief chemist in the Department of Agriculture, had agitated for a federal law requiring accurate labeling of foods and drugs. "Let the Label Tell" became the slogan of reformers intent on stopping the trade in dangerous and adulterated products. Mark Sullivan's exposés of patent medicines in the *Ladies' Home Journal* and Samuel Hopkins Adams's "Great American Fraud" series in *Collier's* kept the issue before the public. "Gullible America," Adams announced in 1905, "will spend this year some 75 millions of dollars in the purchase of patent medicines . . . it will swallow huge quantities of al-cohol, an appalling amount of opiates and narcotics, a wide assortment of varied drugs . . . and far in excess of all other ingredients, undiluted fraud."

In the spring of 1906, the publicity generated by the muckrakers goaded Congress into action. With Roosevelt's backing and the support of the American Medical Association, the General Federation of Women's Clubs, and the National Consumers League, a pure food and drug bill passed the Senate and went to the House, where its opponents hoped to keep it locked up in committee. There it would have died, had not Upton Sinclair's novel *The Jungle*, with its sensational account of the filthy conditions in the meatpacking industry, sparked a massive public outcry that revived the pure food and drug debate. Public outrage led to the passage in 1906 of a tough Pure Food and Drug Act requiring medicine makers to list dangerous ingredients on their labels.

In the meantime, Roosevelt was so revolted by Sinclair's depiction of the meatpacking industry

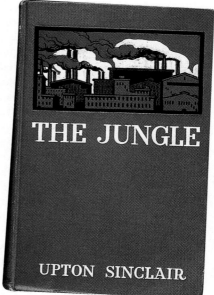

THE JUNGLE
Novelist Upton Sinclair, a lifelong socialist, wrote The Jungle *to expose the evils of capitalism. But readers were more horrified by the unsanitary conditions he described in the meatpacking industry, where Sinclair's hapless hero encountered rats, filth, and diseased animals processed into potted beef. It was rumored that after reading the book, President Theodore Roosevelt could no longer stomach sausage for breakfast. The president immediately ordered a thorough study of conditions in the meatpacking industry. The public outcry surrounding* The Jungle *contributed to the enactment of pure food and drug legislation and federal meat inspection. Sinclair ruefully remarked, "I aimed at the public's heart, but I hit them in the stomach."*
By permission of the Houghton Library, Harvard University.

that he launched his own investigation. Under public pressure, Congress hastily framed a meat inspection measure that passed the Senate. In the House, the bill languished until Roosevelt threatened to publish his "sickening report," which supported Sinclair's depiction of filthy conditions. In the glare of publicity, foreign markets moved to block exports of American meat. Knowing that they were beaten, the packers closed ranks to secure legislation "strong enough to still the public clamor, while not so drastic as to inconvenience them too greatly," in the words of one insider. The result was the passage in 1906 of a meat inspection provision that promised packers a government stamp of approval in return for meeting federal inspection standards.

As his term expired, Roosevelt moved to the left, allying with the more progressive elements of the Republican Party. In speech after speech he attacked the "malefactors of great wealth." Styling himself a "radical," he claimed credit for leading the "ultra conservative" party of McKinley to a position of "progressive conservatism and conservative radicalism." His rhetoric led John D. Rockefeller to predict early in 1907 that Roosevelt's attacks on big business would precipitate a depression.

When a sharp business panic developed in the fall of 1907, business interests quickly blamed the president. The panic of 1907 proved to be severe but short. Once again J. P. Morgan stepped in to avert disaster, switching funds from one bank to another to prop up weak institutions and keep them from failing. For his services, he claimed as a prize the Tennessee Coal and Iron Company, an independent steel business that had long been coveted by his U.S. Steel. Morgan dispatched his lieutenants to Washington, where they told Roosevelt that the sale of the company would aid the economy "but little benefit" U.S. Steel. Roosevelt, willing to take the word of a gentleman, tacitly agreed not to institute antitrust proceedings against U.S. Steel. As Roosevelt later learned, Morgan and his men had been less than candid. The acquisition of Tennessee Coal and Iron for a price under market value greatly strengthened U.S. Steel and undercut the economy of the Southeast. The episode would come back to haunt Roosevelt, as it gave rise to the charge that he acted as a tool of the Morgan interests.

The charge of collusion between business and government underscored the extent to which enlightened business leaders like Morgan and his partner George W. Perkins found federal regulation preferable to unbridled competition or harsher state measures. During the Progressive Era, advanced

business leaders participated in the creation of regulatory legislation and worked to develop a détente with government. Through a series of "gentlemen's agreements," like the one Morgan obtained in the Tennessee Coal and Iron merger, they sought the advice of the president and cooperated with government in the hope of avoiding antitrust prosecution. As much as Roosevelt attempted to make business subordinate to government, in practice Morgan still enjoyed equality with the chief executive and continued to operate on the principle of sending "my man to your man" that had so amused Roosevelt in 1902. Convinced that regulation was the best way to deal with big business, Roosevelt never acknowledged the extent to which his regulatory policies worked to further business interests and bring about business stability. As Roosevelt's actions in the panic of 1907 demonstrated, for all his harsh attacks on the "malefactors of great wealth," the president remained indebted to Morgan, who still functioned as the national bank and would continue to do so until the passage of the Federal Reserve Act six years later.

During the Progressive Era, advanced business leaders participated in the creation of regulatory legislation and worked to create a détente with government.

In at least one area, Roosevelt was well ahead of his time. Robert La Follette, who found much to criticize in Roosevelt's presidency, called his efforts in conservation of natural resources the progressive president's "greatest work." When Roosevelt took office, some 45 million acres of land remained as government reserves. He tripled that number to 150 million acres, buying land and creating national parks and wildlife preserves by executive order. To conserve natural resources, he fought not only the western cattle barons, lumber kings, and mining interests but powerful leaders in Congress, including Speaker of the House Joseph Cannon, who was determined to spend "not one cent for scenery." (See Map 21.1, page 819).

Roosevelt had no sooner entered the White House than he launched his conservation campaign, naming the able and enlightened Gifford Pinchot his chief forester. Together, the two worked zealously to put a stop to a century of exploitation. In one of their more effective ploys, they fought pri-

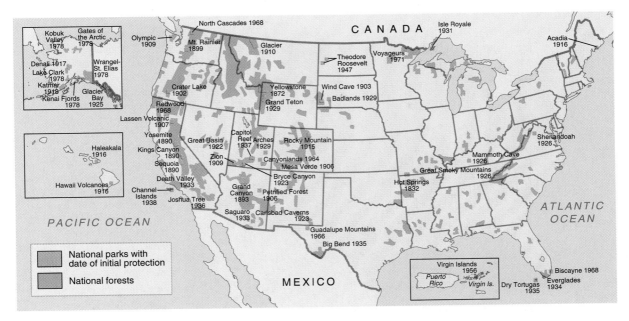

M A P 21.1

National Parks and Forests

The national park system in the West began with Yellowstone in 1872, followed in 1890 by Grand Canyon, Yosemite, King's Canyon, and Sequoia. During his presidency Theodore Roosevelt added six new parks — Crater Lake, Wind Cave, Petrified Forest, Lassen Volcano, Mesa Verde, and Zion.

vate utilities that were intent on gobbling up water-power sites and creating a monopoly of hydroelectric power. Pinchot withdrew 2,565 sites, often on the pretext that he planned to establish ranger stations on the lands. "Public rights come first and private interest second," Roosevelt insisted.

By 1907, Roosevelt had stepped on the toes of every major interest in the West. Timber, cattle, and mining kings, as well as eastern conservatives, were determined to stop him. Congress added a rider to an appropriations bill that barred the creation of any new reserves in six western states. The president could not veto the bill, but he worked feverishly in the ten days before it became law to establish twenty-one new reserves and save 16 million acres for posterity. Once again, he had outwitted his adversaries. "Opponents of the forest service turned handsprings in their wrath," he wrote gleefully, "but the threats . . . were really only a tribute to the efficiency of our action." Today, six national parks, sixteen national monuments, and fifty-one wildlife refuges stand as witness to Roosevelt's substantial accomplishments as a conservationist.

Roosevelt the Diplomat

Roosevelt took a keen interest in shaping foreign policy and hoped to see the United States take its place among world leaders. An active proponent of America's interest abroad, he was convinced that Congress was inept in foreign affairs, and he relied on executive power to effect a vigorous foreign policy, sometimes stretching those powers beyond legal limits in his pursuit of American interests.

A man who relished military discipline and viewed life as a constant conflict for supremacy, Roosevelt believed that the "civilized nations" should police the world and hold the "backward" countries in line. In his relations with the great European powers, he relied on military strength and diplomacy, a combination he aptly described with the aphorism "Speak softly but carry a big stick."

In the Caribbean, Roosevelt jealously guarded the Monroe Doctrine's American sphere of influence closed to rival European powers. In the Venezuelan dispute of 1902, he risked war with Germany to preserve the United States' prerogative in

ROOSEVELT AND MUIR
In this famous photograph, Theodore Roosevelt poses at Glacier Peak in Yosemite National Park in 1903 with John Muir, naturalist and founder of the Sierra Club. Roosevelt's years as a rancher in the Dakotas made him the first president to have experienced firsthand the American West. As president, he acted vigorously to protect the beauty and resources of the West for posterity, using executive power to set aside more than a hundred million acres in government reserves and to create six national parks.
Yosemite Museum/Leroy Radanovich.

the Western Hemisphere. Venezuela had borrowed money in Europe, and the country's dictator (whom Roosevelt dismissed as "a villainous little monkey") could not pay it back. When Germany threatened to intervene, Roosevelt issued an ultimatum to the kaiser, warning him to stay out of Latin American affairs or face war with the United States. The matter was eventually settled by arbitration.

Roosevelt's proprietary and paternalistic attitude toward the hemisphere became evident in the infamous case of the Panama Canal. A firm advocate of naval power and an astute naval strategist, Roosevelt had long been a strong supporter of an isthmian canal connecting the Caribbean and the Pacific. By enabling the navy to move quickly from the Atlantic to the Pacific, the canal would, in effect, double the nation's naval power. The United States began a joint venture with England to build a canal but in 1901 abandoned the partnership and moved forward alone. Two sites were possible, one in Nicaragua, which had the advantage of being at sea

level, and another in Panama, where the rough and hilly terrain demanded a system of locks. In the end, the choice was made not by logic but by politics. Private investors who held rights to build a Panamanian route lobbied Congress shamelessly until they won approval for the route.

A man who relished military discipline and viewed life as a constant conflict for supremacy, Roosevelt believed that the "civilized nations" should police the world and hold the "backward" countries in line.

The Panamanian isthmus was at this time part of Colombia, so in 1902, Roosevelt began negotiations to gain access to the land. He offered the Colombian government $10 million and an annual rent of $250,000. When the government in Bogotá

"THE NEWS REACHES BOGOTÁ"
*Like a modern Gulliver, President Theodore Roosevelt straddles the isthmus and begins digging
the Panama Canal. "I took Panama," Roosevelt boasted. This contemporary political cartoon evidently views Roosevelt's action in a favorable light, mocking the Colombian government with the
caption "The News Reaches Bogotá." Few raised objections at the time, but Roosevelt's successors would eventually apologize to Colombia and pay a $25 million indemnity; in 1978, the
United States signed a treaty to turn the canal over to the Panamanians.*
Theodore Roosevelt Collection, Harvard College Library.

refused to accept the offer, Roosevelt became incensed at what he called the "homicidal corrup-
tionists" in Colombia for trying to "blackmail" the
United States. The result was an uprising in Panama
in 1903 arranged by investors in New York and
staged with Roosevelt's implicit backing. The U.S.
government aided and protected the "revolution"
by placing the warship *Nashville* off the isthmus, and
the State Department recognized the new government of Panama within twenty-four hours after the
uprising. The new Panamanian government promptly accepted the $10 million, and the building of the
canal got under way. Roosevelt later boasted that he
"took Panama"; although most Americans applauded his action, the episode became a national disgrace.
President Woodrow Wilson would later insist on

paying the Colombian government $25 million,
much to Roosevelt's disgust and mortification.

In the wake of the Panama affair and the confrontation with Germany over Venezuela, Roosevelt
announced what became known as the Roosevelt
Corollary to the Monroe Doctrine. The United States
would not intervene in Latin America as long as nations conducted their affairs with "decency." But
Roosevelt warned that if any Latin American nation
proved guilty of "brutal wrongdoing," as in the case
of Venezuela's default on its debt to Germany, the
United States would insist on stepping in. The Roosevelt Corollary in effect made the United States the
policeman of the hemisphere and served notice to
the European powers to keep out. Critics called
Roosevelt's policy "gunboat diplomacy," and with

good reason. In the administrations of Roosevelt and his successor, William Howard Taft, U.S. marines were frequently dispatched to the Caribbean to take over customhouses or to show U.S. force. The legacy of gunboat diplomacy was a bitter anti-American sentiment that would last throughout the century.

In the Far East, Roosevelt inherited the Open Door policy initiated by Secretary of State John Hay in 1899, which was designed to ensure U.S. commercial entry into China. And as a result of victory in the Spanish-American War, the United States now enjoyed a foothold in the region with its pos-

session of the Philippines. As Britain, France, Russia, Japan, and Germany raced to secure Chinese trade and territory, Roosevelt was tempted to use force to enter the fray and gain economic or possibly territorial concessions. Sensibly, he held back. He realized that the American people would not support an aggressive Asian policy. In the end, he fell back on Hay's Open Door policy, which sought to maintain Chinese territorial integrity and guarantee the United States an equal share with the European powers in trade and investment.

In his relations with Europe, Roosevelt sought to establish the United States, fresh from its victory

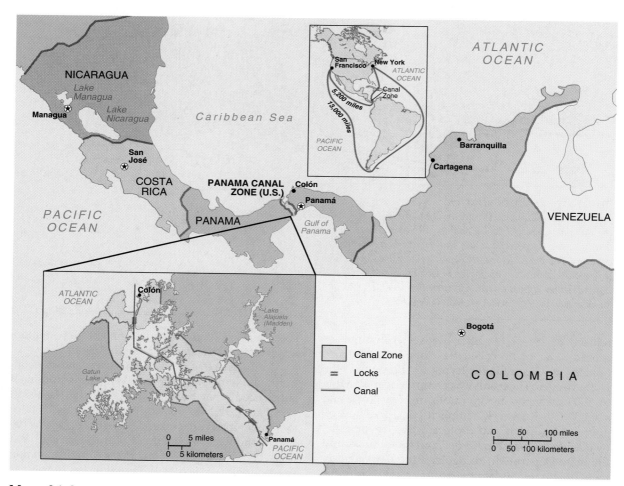

MAP 21.2

The Panama Canal, 1914

The Panama Canal, completed in 1914, bisected the isthmus in a series of massive locks and dams. As Theodore Roosevelt had planned, the canal greatly strengthened the navy by allowing ships to move from the Atlantic to the Pacific in a matter of days.

over Spain, as a rising force in world affairs. He proved himself a consummate diplomat when he succeeded in preserving peace after tensions flared between France and Germany in Morocco in 1905. Roosevelt set up a conference in Algeciras, Spain, where he worked to maintain a balance of power to help neutralize German ambitions. His skillful mediation of the dispute gained him a reputation as an astute player on the world stage and demonstrated the United States' new presence in world affairs.

In 1906, Roosevelt earned the Nobel Peace Prize for his role in negotiating an end to the Russo-Japanese War, which had broken out when the Japanese invaded Chinese Manchuria, threatening Russia's sphere of influence in the area. Again, Roosevelt sought to maintain a balance of power, in this case working to curb Japanese expansionism. Roosevelt admired the Japanese, judging them "the most dashing fighters in the world." But he did not wish Japan to become too strong in Asia. He offered to mediate and presided over the peace conference at Portsmouth, New Hampshire. At the peace conference, he was able to prevent Japan from dominating Manchuria, but he had no qualms about granting the Japanese control of Korea, a sovereign country.

Roosevelt fumed when the United States' good relations with Japan were jeopardized in 1906 by discriminatory legislation in California that called for segregated public schools for "Orientals." The Japanese government, sensitive to the racial slur, responded indignantly. Roosevelt castigated the "idiots" in California and managed to smooth over the incident by negotiating a "gentlemen's agreement" in 1907. He offered to reverse the segregation order in exchange for certain restrictions on Japanese immigration to the United States. This informal arrangement allowed the Japanese to save face, while at the same time placating nativist sentiment in California.

To counter Japan's growing bellicosity, Roosevelt dispatched the Great White Fleet, the navy's most up-to-date battleships, on a "goodwill" mission around the world. This show of American force constituted a classic example of his dictum "Speak softly but carry a big stick."

The Troubled Presidency of William Howard Taft

When Roosevelt retired from the presidency in 1909 at the age of fifty to go on safari and shoot big game in Africa, he turned the White House over to his handpicked successor, William Howard Taft. Any man would have found it difficult to follow in Roosevelt's footsteps, but Taft proved hopelessly ill suited to the task. A genial man with a talent for law, Taft had little experience in elective office, having served as governor of the Philippines and as Roosevelt's secretary of war. Taft had no talent or instinct for politics, no ability to compromise, and no nerve for controversy. His ambitious wife coveted the office and urged him to take it. He would have been better off listening to his mother, who warned, "Roosevelt is a good fighter and enjoys it, but the malice of politics would make you miserable."

Taft ran in 1908 with Roosevelt never far in the background. He soundly defeated the perennial Democratic candidate, the "Great Commoner," William Jennings Bryan, but his popular majority was only half of Roosevelt's record in 1904. On the eve of his inauguration, Taft showed little enthusiasm about his triumph and little zest for the future. In fact, the presidency for Taft proved an ordeal to be endured. As a symptom of his discomfort in office, his weight ballooned from an already hefty 297 pounds to over 350 pounds.

Taft proved a perfect tool in the hands of Republicans who yearned for a return to the days of McKinley. Whereas Roosevelt had moved in advance of his party, Taft was by nature cautious and was easily led. He saw his role as being to conserve the gains made by Roosevelt and not to press for additional reforms. With the country riding the crest of progressive reform, he was badly out of tune with his times.

Taft's greatest strength proved to be his greatest weakness. A lawyer by training and instinct, he believed that it was up to the courts, not the president, to arbitrate social issues. Roosevelt had carried presidential power to a new level, often castigating the judiciary and flouting the separation of powers. Taft the legalist found it difficult to condone such actions. Wary of the progressive insurgents in his own party and without Roosevelt to guide him, Taft relied increasingly on conservatives in the Republican Party. As a progressive senator lamented, "Taft is a ponderous and amiable man completely surrounded by men who know exactly what they want."

Taft's troubles began on the eve of his inaugural when he called a special session of Congress to deal with the tariff. Roosevelt had been too politically astute to tackle the troublesome tariff issue, even though he knew that rates needed to be lowered. Taft, with his stubborn courage, blundered into the fray. The House of Representatives passed a modest downward revision and, to make up for lost

WILLIAM HOWARD TAFT
William Howard Taft had little aptitude or stomach for politics. When Theodore Roosevelt tapped him as his successor in 1908, Taft had never held an elected office. A legalist by training and temperament, Taft moved congenially in the conservative circles of the Republican Party. His actions dismayed progressives and eventually led Roosevelt to challenge him for the presidency in 1912. The break with Roosevelt saddened and embittered Taft, who heartily disliked the presidency and was glad to leave it.
Library of Congress.

revenue, imposed a small inheritance tax. Led by Senator Aldrich, the conservative Senate struck down the tax and added more than eight hundred crippling amendments to the tariff. The Payne-Aldrich bill that emerged actually raised the tariff. Taft, as if paralyzed, neither fought for changes nor vetoed the measure.

Progressives and Democrats attacked the swollen tariff as a triumph for big business over consumers. Perhaps flummoxed by his conservative friends, Taft insisted that the tariff was "really a good bill" and that it represented a downward revision in tariff duties. On a tour of the Midwest in 1909, he was greeted with jeers when he claimed,

"I think the Payne bill is the best bill that the Republican party ever passed." In the eyes of a growing number of critics, his praise of the tariff made him either a fool or a liar.

Taft's legalism got him into hot water again in the controversy over conservation. Roosevelt, in his zeal to protect the wilderness, had not hesitated to bend the law. Taft refused to endorse his predecessor's methods. He undid Roosevelt's work to preserve water power sites when he learned that they had been improperly designated as ranger stations. Chief forester Gifford Pinchot, angry at what he perceived as a rollback of Roosevelt's conservation policies, publicly denounced Taft's secretary of the interior, Richard Ballinger, as a tool of western land-grabbers. Taft fired Pinchot, touching off a storm of controversy that hurt Taft and alienated Roosevelt.

Talk of substituting Roosevelt on the ticket in 1912 grew as Republican progressives became increasingly dissatisfied with Taft's policies. In June 1910, Roosevelt returned to New York, where he received a hero's welcome. Back at Sagamore Hill, his home in Oyster Bay, New York, the ex-president attracted a stream of visitors and reporters seeking his advice and opinions. Hurt, Taft kept his distance. By late summer, Roosevelt had taken sides with the progressive insurgents in his party. "Taft is utterly hopeless as a leader," Roosevelt confided to his son as he set out on a speaking tour of the West. Reading the mood of the country, Roosevelt began to sound more and more like a candidate.

With the Republican Party divided, the Democrats swept the congressional elections of 1910. Branding the Payne-Aldrich tariff "the mother of trusts," they captured a majority in the House of Representatives and won several key governorships. The revitalized Democratic Party could look to new leaders, among them the progressive governor of New Jersey, Woodrow Wilson.

With a Democratic majority in the House and progressive Republicans holding the balance of power in the Senate, Congress enacted a number of key reforms. Legislation to regulate mine and railroad safety, to create a Children's Bureau, and to establish an eight-hour day for federal workers passed. Two significant constitutional amendments —the Sixteenth Amendment, which provided for a modest graduated income tax, and the Seventeenth Amendment, which called for the direct election of senators (who had formerly been chosen by their state legislatures)—went to the states for ratification. While Congress rode the high tide of progressive reform, Taft sat on the sidelines.

In foreign policy as well as in the domestic arena, Taft had a difficult time following in Roosevelt's footsteps. In the Caribbean he pursued a policy of "dollar diplomacy," championing commercial goals rather than the strategic aims that Roosevelt had advocated. He provoked anti-American feeling by attempting to force commercial treaties on Nicaragua and Honduras and by dispatching the U.S. marines to Nicaragua and Santo Domingo in 1912.

In the Far East, Taft's foreign policy proved even more disastrous. He openly avowed his intent to promote in China "active intervention to secure for . . . our capitalists opportunity for profitable investment." Lacking Roosevelt's understanding of power politics, Taft naively believed that he could substitute "dollars for bullets." He never recognized that an aggressive commercial policy could not exist without military might. As a result, dollar diplomacy was doomed to failure. Even Taft was forced to recognize its limits when revolution broke out in Mexico in 1911. Under pressure to protect American investment, which amounted to more than $4 billion, he mobilized troops along the border. But in the end, he had to rely on diplomatic pressure to salvage American interests.

Always a legalist at heart, Taft hoped to encourage world peace through the use of a world court and arbitration. He unsuccessfully sponsored a series of arbitration treaties that Roosevelt, who prized national honor more than international law, vehemently opposed. By 1910, Roosevelt had become a vocal critic of Taft's foreign policy, which he dismissed as "maudlin folly."

The final breech between Taft and Roosevelt came in 1911, when Taft's attorney general filed an antitrust suit against U.S. Steel. In its brief against the steel giant, the government cited Roosevelt's agreement with the Morgan interests in the 1907 acquisition of Tennessee Coal and Iron by U.S. Steel. The incident greatly embarrassed Roosevelt by making it clear he had either been hoodwinked or had acted as a tool of Wall Street. Thoroughly enraged, Roosevelt lambasted Taft's "archaic" antitrust policy and began to hint that he might be persuaded to run for president again.

The Election of 1912

In February 1912, Roosevelt announced, "My hat is in the ring." Convinced that he was the only progressive who had a chance to win nomination and carry the election, he shoved aside Robert La Follette

and prepared to take on Taft. But for all his popularity, Roosevelt no longer controlled the party machinery. Taft, with uncharacteristic strength, refused to step aside. As he bitterly told a journalist, "Even a rat in a corner will fight." Roosevelt took advantage of newly passed primary election laws and ran in thirteen states, winning 278 delegates to Taft's 48. But at the Chicago convention, Taft's bosses refused to seat the Roosevelt delegates. Fights broke out on the convention floor as Taft won renomination on the first ballot. Crying robbery, Roosevelt's supporters marched out and bolted the party.

Seven weeks later, in the same Chicago auditorium, a hastily organized Progressive Party met to nominate Roosevelt. Few Republican officeholders joined the new party, but the advance guard of progressivism turned out in full force. Amid a thunder of applause, Jane Addams seconded Roosevelt's nomination. The convention resembled a religious revival with delegates singing "Onward Christian Soldiers" and "The Battle Hymn of the Republic." Full of reforming zeal, the delegates approved the most advanced platform since the Populists' in 1892. Planks called for woman suffrage, the direct election of senators, presidential primaries, electoral reforms, the recall of judges, conservation of natural resources, minimum wages for women, an end to child labor, workers' compensation, social security, and a federal income tax.

But for all the excitement and the cheering, the new Progressive Party was doomed, and the candidate knew it. The people may have supported the new party, but the politicians, even insurgents like La Follette, stayed within the Republican fold. The Progressive Party had only two assets: Roosevelt's personality and the money supplied by his many backers.

Roosevelt arrived in Chicago to accept the nomination and announced that he felt as "strong as a bull moose," giving the new party a nickname and a mascot. "I am under no illusion about it," he confessed to a friend. "It is a forlorn hope." But he had gone too far to turn back. He led the Bull Moose Party into the fray, exhorting his followers in ringing biblical tones, "We shall not falter, we stand at Armageddon and do battle for the Lord."

The Democrats, delighted at the split in the Republican ranks, smelled victory for the first time since 1892. Their convention turned into a bitter fight for the nomination. After forty-six ballots, William Jennings Bryan threw his support to Woodrow Wilson, and the party nominated the governor of New Jersey. Wilson's career in politics had proved even more astounding than Roosevelt's. After only eighteen months in office, the former professor and president of Princeton University found himself running for president of the United States.

Wilson ran on a platform hammered out by Democrats over the past fifteen years and designed to appeal to the constituent groups of the Democratic Party. To the farmers, the platform promised a lower tariff and cheaper agricultural loans; to labor unions, it promised to limit the use of injunctions and antitrust laws against labor; and to small business owners, it vowed to return to competition through the breakup of the trusts. As if that were not enough, Wilson's vice presidential candidate, Thomas R. Marshall, went on record avowing, "What America needs is a good five-cent cigar."

Voters in 1912 could choose from three candidates, each of whom claimed to be a progressive. That the term could stretch to cover all three underscored some major disagreements in progressive thinking about the relationship between business and government. Taft, for all his trust-busting, never succeeded in convincing the public of his progressivism and was generally conceded to be the candidate of the old guard. The real contest was between Roosevelt and Wilson and the two political philosophies summed up in their campaign slogans: "The New Nationalism" and "The New Freedom."

Roosevelt's New Nationalism enunciated his belief in federal planning and regulation. He accepted big business as inevitable but demanded that big government supervise it and act as a steward for labor and the consumer. Roosevelt called for an increase in the power of the federal government, a decrease in the power of the courts, and an active role for the president. He urged legislation creating a commission able to regulate manufacturing and trade along the lines of the ICC. As Herbert Croly pointed out in *The Promise of American Life* (1909), Roosevelt hoped to use the Hamiltonian means of greater centralization to further the Jeffersonian ends of greater democracy.

Voters in 1912 could choose from three candidates, each of whom claimed to be a progressive.

Woodrow Wilson, a Virginia-born Democrat schooled in the principle of limited government and states' rights, set a markedly different course with his New Freedom. He saw no benefit in bigness in

PASS PROSPERITY AROUND

BULL MOOSE POSTER
Accepting the nomination of the Progressive Party in 1912, Theodore Roosevelt exclaimed, "I feel as strong as a bull moose." Instantly the new party had a mascot and a nickname. The Bull Moose soon decorated party emblems, as in this poster where the animal is featured more prominently than Roosevelt or his vice presidential candidate, Hiram Johnson. The slogan "Pass Prosperity Around" may refer to the party's platform, which pledged to tax the great fortunes of the day by enacting the country's first graduated income tax.
Collection of Janice L. and David J. Frent.

business or government. Tutored in economics by *Muller v. Oregon* lawyer Louis Brandeis, who railed against the "curse of bigness," Wilson promised to use antitrust legislation to get rid of big corporations. He advocated strong antitrust laws that, he argued, would give small businesses and farmers better opportunities in the marketplace.

Throughout the campaign, Wilson and Roosevelt fought it out, each pointing to the weakness of his rival's program. Wilson labeled Roosevelt's New Nationalism a plan to "regulate monopoly," a thinly disguised partnership between government and business. Roosevelt castigated Wilson for being backward looking, for advocating a kind of "rural toryism." Each candidate's criticisms contained some truth. Roosevelt, in practice, did advocate détente between government and business. As Wilson never tired of pointing out, George Perkins, Morgan's ex-partner, was Roosevelt's campaign manager and chief financial backer. But it was equally true that Wilson's New Freedom was a rural program that affirmed the hopes and desires of the farmers and small business owners who formed the backbone of the Democratic Party.

In the end, only the energy and emotional enthusiasm of the Bull Moosers obscured the inevitable outcome of a race in which the Republican vote was split while the Democrats remained united. No candidate could claim a majority in the three-way race. Wilson captured a bare 42 percent of the popular vote, polling fewer votes than Bryan had received when he lost to Taft in 1908. Roosevelt and his Bull Moose Progressive Party won 27 percent of the vote, an unprecedented vote for a new party. The incumbent Taft ran third with 23 percent. But in the electoral college, Wilson won a decisive 435, with 88 going to Roosevelt and only 8 to Taft.

The election marked a triumph for the forces of reform. Clearly, Americans wanted a change from the policies of Taft. In the excitement for change, Eu-

gene V. Debs, the Socialist Party candidate, captured nearly a million votes. Wilson carried the traditional Democratic strongholds in the cities and the farmlands. But without the split in the Republican Party, the Democrats could not have won the White House. The real loser in 1912 was not Taft but the Bull Moose Party, which essentially collapsed after Roosevelt's defeat. It had always been, in the words of one observer, "a house divided against itself and already mortgaged."

Woodrow Wilson and Progressivism at High Tide

Born in Virginia and raised in Georgia, Woodrow Wilson was the first Southerner to be elected president since James K. Polk (in 1844) and only the second Democrat to occupy the White House since Reconstruction. Democrats who anticipated a wild celebration when Wilson took office soon had their hopes dashed. The son of a Presbyterian minister, Wilson was a teetotaler more given to Scripture than to celebration. He canceled the inaugural ball and called instead for a day of prayer.

This lean, ascetic man with an otherworldly gaze had come to politics by a strange route. A scholar and an academician, he had earned his doctorate at Johns Hopkins University and had taught at Bryn Mawr, Wesleyan, and Princeton, serving as president of the latter for eight years. In 1910, the New Jersey Democratic machine, looking for a respectable candidate, tapped him for governor. Once in office, he quickly cut his ties with the bosses and went over to the progressive camp. He was a man, his biographer conceded, whose "political convictions were never as fixed as his ambition."

As governor, Wilson put New Jersey in the vanguard of progressivism by signing laws to reform the election process, to provide workers' compensation, to end corrupt practices in state government, and to regulate railroads and public utilities. A year into his term, Wilson already had his eye on the presidency. Even though he loathed William Jennings Bryan, he courted him until he won Bryan's political blessing; afterward he rewarded the Great Commoner by naming him secretary of state. Always able to equivocate, Wilson was rarely able to compromise. At Princeton, he had split the university community in a bitter fight over the location of the graduate school. From an early age, Wilson believed that he was destined to lead and dreamed of

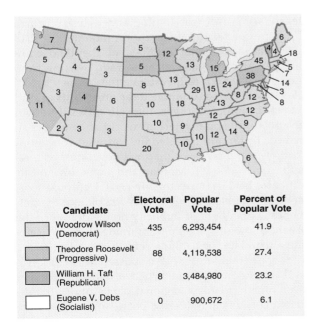

Candidate	Electoral Vote	Popular Vote	Percent of Popular Vote
Woodrow Wilson (Democrat)	435	6,293,454	41.9
Theodore Roosevelt (Progressive)	88	4,119,538	27.4
William H. Taft (Republican)	8	3,484,980	23.2
Eugene V. Debs (Socialist)	0	900,672	6.1

MAP 21.3
The Election of 1912

WOODROW WILSON
Woodrow Wilson's political career was meteoric, propelling him from the presidency of Princeton University to the presidency of the United States in three years. As governor of New Jersey from 1910 to 1912, Wilson turned his back on the Democratic machine that had backed him and made a reputation as a champion of progressive reform. Elected to the White House in 1912, he presided over the high tide of progressive reform.
Collection of Janice L. and David J. Frent.

moving the masses with great speeches. He brought to the White House a gift for oratory, a stern will, and a set of fixed beliefs. His tendency to turn differences of opinion into personal hatreds would impair his leadership and damage his presidency. Fortunately for Wilson, he came to power with a Democratic Congress ready to do his bidding.

Although he opposed big government in his campaign, Wilson viewed himself as the only leader who could speak for the country. He was prepared to work on the base built by Roosevelt to strengthen presidential power, exerting leadership and working through his party in Congress to accomplish the Democratic agenda. Before he was finished, Wilson would preside over progressivism at high tide and see enacted not only the platform of the Democratic Party but the humanitarian reforms championed by Roosevelt's Progressive Party as well.

Tariff and Banking Reform

In March 1913, Wilson, proud of his ability as an orator, became the first president since John Adams to go to Capitol Hill and speak directly to Congress, calling for tariff reform. "The object of the tariff," Wilson told his audience, "must be effective competition." Eager to topple the high tariff, the Democratic House of Representatives hastily passed the Underwood tariff, which lowered rates by 15 percent. To compensate for lost revenue, Congress added a provision for a moderate income tax made possible by the ratification of the Sixteenth Amendment a month earlier. In the Senate, lobbyists for industries quietly went to work to get the tariff raised, but Wilson rallied public opinion by attacking the "industrious and insidious lobby." Robert La Follette went further and demanded an investigation of the ties between business and the legislature. When senators for the first time had to disclose their finances, the public learned that more than a few were on the payrolls of big corporations. In the harsh glare of publicity, the Senate passed the Underwood tariff, which earned praise as "the most honest tariff since the Civil War."

Wilson turned his attention next to banking. The panic of 1907 had dramatically testified to the failure of the banking system. Once again, a president had had to turn to J. P. Morgan. But Morgan's legendary power was coming under close scrutiny. Pressure for federal intervention mounted in 1913 with the sensational findings of the Pujo committee. Arsène Pujo, a Democratic senator from Louisiana, set out to investigate the "money trust." Pujo's committee summoned the great lords of Wall Street, including Morgan himself, to testify about the powerful and mysterious world of New York finance. Testimony revealed an alarming concentration of banking power that had developed as a result of mergers. J. P. Morgan and Company and its affiliates held 341 directorships in 112 corporations, controlling assets of more than $22 billion. By casting the harsh light of publicity on the doings of the financial moguls, the Pujo committee helped to create a mandate for banking reform.

The Federal Reserve Act, passed in 1913 as a result of the outcry, established a national banking system composed of regional banks under the direction of a Federal Reserve Board appointed by the president. The bill was a compromise measure. Bankers initially fought for a central bank under banker control, while Bryan and the progressives insisted that government control the system and issue the currency. Influenced by his adviser Louis Brandeis, who sided with the progressives, Wilson backed public control of a central bank and stood firm against a howl of protest from the bankers. Progressives, who had wanted public control of regional banks as well, were disappointed. But southern agrarians did succeed in getting the regional reserve banks to issue short-term loans, the "corn tassel currency" that they had sought since the days of the Populists. To get his measure through the Senate, Wilson once again borrowed a tactic from Roosevelt and issued a public statement claiming that Wall Street was attempting to defeat his bill by creating fears of an impending panic.

Before he was finished, Wilson would preside over progressivism at high tide and see enacted not only the platform of the Democratic Party but the humanitarian reforms championed by Roosevelt's Progressive Party as well.

The Federal Reserve Act of 1913 was the most significant piece of domestic legislation in Wilson's presidency. It provided for twelve Federal Reserve banks, privately controlled but regulated and supervised by a Federal Reserve Board appointed by the president. It gave the United States its first efficient banking and currency system and, at the same time, provided for a larger degree of government control over banking than had ever existed before. The new system made currency more elastic and credit adequate for the needs of business and agriculture. It did not, however, attempt to take control of the boom and bust cycles in the U.S. economy that would produce another major depression in the 1930s.

Wilson and the Trusts

Flushed with success, Wilson tackled the trust issue. When Congress reconvened in January 1914, Wilson supported the Clayton bill to outlaw interlocking directorates (directors from one corporation sitting on the board of another) and unfair practices. By spelling out which practices were unfair, Wilson hoped to guide business activity back to healthy competition without resorting to regulation.

An anemic Clayton Antitrust Act finally passed in 1914. Its preamble declared, "The labor of human beings is not a commodity or article of commerce."

But the Clayton Act did not succeed in breaking the alliance of business and the judiciary. Despite the fact that AFL President Samuel Gompers hailed the Clayton Act as the "Magna Carta of labor," the conservative courts continued to issue injunctions and to use antitrust legislation against labor unions.

In the midst of the fight for the Clayton Act, Wilson, at the prompting of Louis Brandeis, changed his tactics. In a dramatic turnaround, he threw his support behind the creation of the Federal Trade Commission (FTC), precisely the kind of federal regulatory agency that Roosevelt had advocated under his New Nationalism and that Wilson had denounced. The FTC, created in 1913, had not only wide investigatory powers but the authority to prosecute corporations for "unfair trade practices" and to enforce its judgments by issuing "cease and desist" orders. Along with the Clayton Act, which outlawed "unfair competition"—practices such as price discrimination and interlocking directorates —Wilson's antitrust program worked to regulate rather than to break up big business.

With the enactment of antitrust laws, Wilson had exhausted the stock of ideas that made up the New Freedom. In the autumn of 1914, he alarmed progressives by declaring that the progressive movement had fulfilled its mission and that the country needed "a time of healing." During the next two years, Wilson consistently wooed bankers and businessmen. Having fought provisions in the Federal Reserve Act that would give bankers control, Wilson promptly named a banker, Paul Warburg, as the first chief of the Federal Reserve Board. Appointments to the new Federal Trade Commission also went to conservative businessmen. Disgruntled progressives charged that Wilson was attempting to nullify progressive legislation with his conservative appointments. But the progressive penchant for expertise helps explain Wilson's choices. Believing that experts in the field could best understand the complex issues at stake, Wilson appointed bankers to oversee the banks and businessmen to regulate business.

Wilson, Reluctant Progressive

Progressives watched in dismay as Wilson repeatedly obstructed or obstinately refused to encourage further progressive reforms. He failed to support labor's demand for an end to injunctions and for a promise to exempt unions from prosecution under antitrust laws as conspiracies "in restraint of trade." He twice threatened to veto legislation providing for farm credits on nonperishable crops. He refused to support child labor legislation or woman suffrage, and he vetoed legislation sponsored by labor to curb immigration. Wilson justified his actions in the rhetoric of the New Freedom by claiming that his administration would condone "special privileges to none." Virtually the only progressive measure that passed was the Seaman's Bill, a long overdue measure to improve the working conditions of sailors.

In the face of Wilson's obstinacy, reform might have ended in 1913 had not political motives forced the president to adopt the progressive agenda. In the congressional elections of 1914, the Republican Party, no longer split by Roosevelt's moribund Bull Moose faction, won substantial gains. Democratic strategists, with their eyes on the 1916 presidential race, recognized that Wilson needed to pick up support in the Midwest and the West by capturing votes from former Bull Moose progressives.

Wilson responded belatedly to this political pressure by championing reform in 1916. In a sharp about-face, he cultivated social reformers, farmers, and union labor. To please labor, he appointed Louis Brandeis to the Supreme Court. To woo farmers, he threw his support behind legislation to obtain rural credits. And he won support from advanced progressives such as Jane Addams by supporting workers' compensation and the Keating-Owen child labor law. When a railroad strike threatened in the months before the election, Wilson virtually ordered Congress to establish an eight-hour day at ten-hour pay on the railroads. He had moved a long way from his position in 1912 to embrace many of the social reforms championed by Theodore Roosevelt. As Wilson boasted, the Democrats had "opened their hearts to the demands of social justice" and had "come very near to carrying out the platform of the Progressive Party."

The Limits of Reform

Progressivism, no matter how much it challenged standpat conservatism, was never a radical movement. Its goal remained the preservation of the existing system, by government intervention if necessary, but without uprooting any of the traditional American political, economic, or social institutions. As Theodore Roosevelt, the bellwether of the movement, insisted, "The only true conservative is the man who resolutely sets his face toward the future." Roosevelt was such a man, and progressivism was such a movement. Its basic conservatism can be seen by comparing it to more radical movements of the era and by looking at the groups that were left out of progressive reform.

Radical Alternatives

It was inevitable, given the turbulence of the times, that the progressivism of Roosevelt and Wilson would be challenged by more radical voices. Some came from within the movement. Robert La Follette, always an implacable idealist, repeatedly called for stronger measures to curb corporate power and democratize the tax system. But the most cogent criticism of progressivism came from American socialists.

The year 1900 witnessed the birth of the Social Democratic Party in America, later called simply the Socialist Party. Like the progressives, the socialists were surprisingly middle class and native-born. They had broken with the older, more militant Socialist Labor Party precisely because of its dogmatic approach and immigrant constituency. (The party refused to allow the use of English at its meetings.) The new group of socialists, men such as Upton Sinclair, Walter Lippmann, and John Reed, were eager to appeal to a broad mass of Americans.

The socialists chose as their standard-bearer Eugene V. Debs, whose experience in the Pullman strike of 1894 convinced him that "there is no hope for the toiling masses of my countrymen, except by the pathways mapped out by Socialism." Debs's brand of socialism, which owed as much to the social gospel as to the theories of Karl Marx advocated cooperation to replace competition and urged men and women to liberate themselves from "the barbarism of private ownership and wage slavery." Described by his followers as "a poet, a saint, a sweetly strong man," Debs declared, "While there is a lower class I am of it, while there is a criminal class I am of it, while there is a soul in prison I am not free."

Roosevelt immediately labeled Debs a "mere inciter to murder and preacher of applied anarchy." Debs, for his part, pointed to the conservatism that underlay Roosevelt's fiery rhetoric. He urged workers not to be fooled by Roosevelt. In the 1912 election, Debs indicted both parties as Tweedledee and Tweedledum, each dedicated to the preservation of capitalism and the continuation of the wage system. The Socialist Party alone, he argued, was the "revolutionary party of the working class." Debs would

EUGENE DEBS CAMPAIGNING
*Socialist candidate Eugene Victor Debs ran for president five times, in 1900, 1904, 1908, 1912,
and 1920. Here he campaigns by cross-country train, the "Socialist Presidential Special." Debs,
in the back row holding a baby, argued in 1912 that Roosevelt and Wilson were as alike as
Tweedledee and Tweedledum and that only the Socialist Party spoke for the working class. He
polled almost a million votes.*
Indiana State University.

run for president five times, in every election (except 1916) from 1900 to 1920, when he ran from jail for opposing U.S. entry into World War I. But his biggest victory came in 1912, when he polled 6 percent of the popular vote, capturing almost a million votes.

Farther to the left of the socialists stood the Industrial Workers of the World (IWW), nicknamed the Wobblies. In 1905, Debs, along with Big Bill Haywood, created the IWW, "one big union" dedicated to organizing the most destitute segment of the workforce. The IWW preached syndicalism, the French doctrine that held that workers' unions or syndicates would lead the people to socialism. In practice, the IWW set out to organize the poorest and worst treated workers—western miners, migrant farmworkers, lumbermen, and immigrant textile workers. These unskilled workers were disdained by the craft unions of Samuel Gompers's AFL. Haywood, a craggy-faced miner with one eye

(he had lost the other in an industrial accident), was a charismatic leader and an authentic proletarian intellectual. While Debs insisted that change could come from ballots, not bullets, the IWW unhesitatingly advocated direct action, sabotage, and the general strike—tactics designed to trigger a workers' uprising. In the intolerant atmosphere of World War I, the IWW made a conspicuous target and was persecuted and prosecuted until it all but disappeared.

In contrast to political radicals like Debs and Haywood, who championed unionism and socialism, Margaret Sanger, a nurse and social activist, promoted birth control as a movement for radical change. Sanger coined the term *birth control* in 1915 and launched a movement with broad social implications. She and her followers saw birth control not only as a sexual and medical reform but also as a means to alter social and political power relationships and to alleviate human misery.

The movement for birth control during the Progressive Era was another example of a cross-class alliance, in which middle-class women like Sanger made common cause with the working class. The leading advocates of birth control from 1914 to 1920 came from the ranks of feminists and socialists. Radicals such as the anarchist Emma Goldman were the first to publicly advocate birth control. They saw it as a way to improve the plight of the workers and urged working-class women to quit producing recruits for the factory and the army.

In contrast to political radicals like Eugene Debs and Big Bill Haywood, who championed unionism and socialism, Margaret Sanger, a nurse and social activist, promoted birth control as a movement for radical change.

Sanger, the daughter of a radical Irish father and a mother who died at fifty after bearing eleven children, became the birth control movement's strongest advocate. As a nurse, she saw firsthand the desperation of poor women who sought to limit the size of their families. After watching one woman die from a botched abortion, Sanger vowed to do something.

Although birth control became a public issue only in the early twentieth century, the birthrate in the United States had been falling consistently throughout the nineteenth century, with the average number of children born to white women falling from 7 in 1800 to 3.6 by 1900. The desire for family limitation was widespread, and, in this sense, birth control was nothing new. But the open advocacy of contraception, the use of artificial means to prevent pregnancy, seemed to many people both new and shocking. Theodore Roosevelt fulminated against birth control as "race suicide" and castigated white middle-class couples for having small families, warning that the "white" population was declining while immigrants and "undesirables" continued to breed. Purity laws passed in the 1870s made it illegal to distribute information on birth control or contraceptive devices. Although there was a brisk underground trade in such items, limited access meant that many couples had to rely on methods such as withdrawal, abstinence, or abortion to reduce the size of their families.

Convinced that women needed to be able to control their pregnancies but unsure of the best methods for doing so, Sanger traveled to Europe in 1913 to learn more about contraceptive techniques. On her return in 1914, she promoted birth control in her newspaper, the *Woman Rebel*. When the post office declared the publication obscene and brought charges against Sanger, she responded defiantly by drafting a detailed pamphlet called "Family Limitation" and getting the IWW to distribute 100,000 copies. Facing arrest, she fled to Europe, where she worked with advanced sexual theorist Havelock Ellis. Sanger returned to the United States in 1916 something of a national celebrity. In her absence, birth control had become linked with free speech and had been taken up as a liberal cause. Under pressure from public opinion, the government dropped charges against her and Sanger undertook a nationwide tour to publicize the birth control cause.

Impatient with propaganda, Sanger turned to direct action in 1916, opening the first birth control clinic, in the Brownsville section of Brooklyn, New York. Located in the heart of a Jewish and Italian immigrant neighborhood, the clinic attracted 464 clients in the nine days it was open. On the tenth day, police shut down the clinic and put Sanger in jail. By then she had become a national figure, and the cause she championed had gained legitimacy if not legality. After World War I, the birth control movement would become much less radical as Sanger turned to doctors for support. But in its infancy, the movement that she led was part of a radical vision for reforming the world that made common cause with the socialists and the IWW in challenging the limits of progressive reform.

Progressivism for White Men Only

The day before President Woodrow Wilson's inauguration in March 1913, more than five thousand demonstrators marched in Washington to demand the vote for women. Inez Milholland, on a white horse, led the parade of women and men wearing the yellow suffragist emblem. A rowdy crowd on hand to celebrate the Democrats' triumph heckled the marchers, as did the police. "If my wife were where you are," a burly cop told one suffragist, "I'd break her head." But for all the marching, Wilson, who didn't believe that a "lady" should vote, pointedly ignored woman suffrage in his inaugural address the next day.

The march served as a reminder that the political gains of progressivism were not spread equally in the population. When the twentieth century

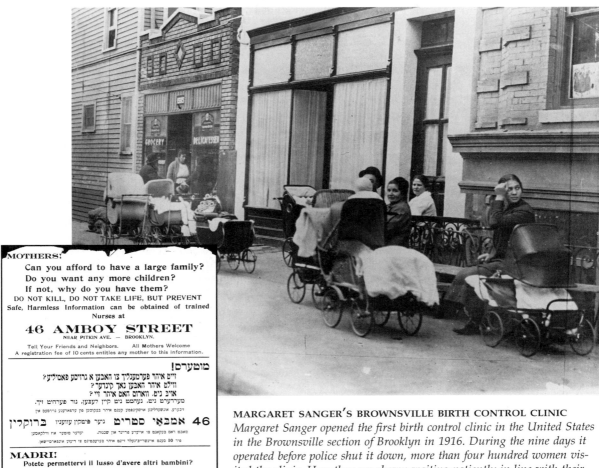

MOTHERS!
Can you afford to have a large family?
Do you want any more children?
If not, why do you have them?
DO NOT KILL, DO NOT TAKE LIFE, BUT PREVENT
Safe, Harmless Information can be obtained of trained
Nurses at

46 AMBOY STREET
NEAR PITKIN AVE. — BROOKLYN.

Tell Your Friends and Neighbors.   All Mothers Welcome
A registration fee of 10 cents entitles any mother to this information.

מוטערס!
זײט איהר פֿערמעגליך צו האבען א גרויסע פֿאמיליע?
ווילט איהר האבען נאך קינדער?
אויב ניט. וואָרום האט איהר זײ ?
זיכערע. אונשעדליכע אינפֿאָרמאציאָן קענט מען באקומען פֿון טרעאײנדע נוירסעס אין

46 אמבאי סטרים ניר פיטקין עוועניו **ברוקלין**

פֿיר 10 סענט אינשרייבען־געלד ווינט איהר בערעכטיגט צו דיעזע אינפֿאָרמאציאָן

MADRI!
Potete permettervi il lusso d'avere altri bambini?
Ne volete ancora?
Se non ne volete piu', perche' continuate a metterli
al mondo?
NON UCCIDETE MA PREVENITE!
Informazioni sicure ed innocue saranno fornite da infermiere autorizzate a
46 AMBOY STREET   Near Pitkin Ave. Brooklyn
a cominciare dal 12 Ottobre. Avvertite le vostre amiche e vicine.
Tutte le madri sono ben accette. La tassa d'iscrizione di 10 cents da diritto
a qualunque madre di ricevere consigli ed informazioni gratis.
Margaret H. Sanger

MARGARET SANGER'S BROWNSVILLE BIRTH CONTROL CLINIC
*Margaret Sanger opened the first birth control clinic in the United States
in the Brownsville section of Brooklyn in 1916. During the nine days it
operated before police shut it down, more than four hundred women visited the clinic. Here they are shown waiting patiently in line with their
baby carriages. Sanger published her flyers in English, Yiddish, and Italian, and her clinic attracted immigrant women, proving that Italian
Catholics and Russian Jews wanted birth control information as much as
their middle- and upper-class Protestant counterparts.*
Sophia Smith Collection.

dawned, women still could not vote in most states. Increasingly, however, woman suffrage had become an international movement. In Great Britain, Emmeline Pankhurst and her daughters Cristabel and Sylvia promoted a militant new suffragism. They seized the spotlight in a series of marches, mass meetings, and acts of civil disobedience, which sometimes escalated to include violence, riots, and arson. The activism of the British suffragists sparked new action in the United States, where progress toward full suffrage had moved slowly. After a victory in Washington state in 1910, suffragists experienced a stinging defeat in California in 1911. Kansas, Oregon, and Arizona joined the suf-

frage column in 1912, evidence that suffragists were perfecting their lobbying techniques. Yet some suffragists, attracted to the flamboyance of the British movement, urged more direct action. Alice Paul, a Quaker social worker who had visited England and participated in suffrage activism there, returned to the United States in 1910 at a time when suffrage was in the doldrums. Paul infused new life into the movement, planning the mass march on the eve of Wilson's inauguration and lobbying for a federal amendment to give women the vote. But Paul's dramatic tactics alienated many in the National American Woman Suffrage Association. In 1914, she broke with the group and continued her work

The Issue of Child Labor

*B*y the early years of the twentieth century, as many as four million children between the ages of ten and fifteen toiled long hours at low pay. They could be found in the depths of coal mines, in the searing heat of glass factories, in canneries and textile mills, in cotton fields —wherever employers coveted small size and nimble fingers. Progressive reformers, often called the "child savers," attempted to curb exploitation of children under the age of fourteen in sweatshops, mines, and mills across America. But they ran into solid opposition not only from employers, who had a vested interest in the cheap labor children performed, but also from parents, who counted on the meager wages of their children. For them the issue was at once economic and cultural. In rural America, no one had questioned a parent's right to put children to hard tasks in the fields and on the farm. Similarly, immigrants from rural Italy, Germany, or Russia could see no harm in putting children to work in factories or sweatshops in America's industrial cities and viewed it as the parents' prerogative to command their children's wages. Progressives found themselves up against stiff opposition.

Not just immigrants but old-stock Americans relied on child labor, particularly in the South, where entire families of poor whites left the land to work side by side in the textile mills. On May 22, 1914, a South Carolina mill owner testified before the House of Representatives Committee on Labor on why child labor was necessary in the South.

DOCUMENT 1. Testimony from Lewis W. Parker

It is not possible for a man who has been working on a farm who is an adult—after the age of 21 years, for instance—to become a skilled employee in a cotton mill. His fingers are knotted and gnarled; he is slow in action, whereas activity is required in working in the cotton mills. Therefore, as a matter of necessity, the adult of the family had to come to the cotton mill as an unskilled employee, and it was the children of the family who became the skilled employees in the cotton mills. For that reason it was the children who had to support the families for the time being. I have seen instances in which a child of 12 years of age, working in the cotton mills, is earning one and one-half times as much as his father of 40 or 50 years of age.

*P*rogressives countered these arguments with poignant testimony about the plight of young workers and the failure of the states to enforce the law. At the same 1914 committee hearings, reformer Florence Kelley described her experiences investigating child labor practices in Illinois.

DOCUMENT 2. Florence Kelley Testimony before the Congressional Committee on Labor, 1914

. . . I was at one time chief inspector of factories and workshops in the State of Illinois. I found great numbers of children working at night—working illegally. The superintendent of a glass-bottle company told me himself that this occurred once when he was rushed with work: A widow had come to him bringing two little boys, one still in kilts [baby skirts worn by small boys] and one in knee breeches. She told him that their father had just been killed on the railroad, and that they were penniless; and she wanted the older little boy to go to work in the glassworks, where he would get 40 cents a day. The superintendent was pressed for boys, and said, "I won't take the bigger fellow alone, but if you will take the baby back home and put him into knee pants, and then bring them both back in trousers, I will take them both." She did so, and those two little fellows, aged 9 and 7 years, began their work on the night shift.

Despite heavy odds against them, progressives achieved victory in 1916 when the National Child Labor Committee finally convinced Congress and President Woodrow Wilson to enact the Keating-Owen Bill forbidding the regular employment of children under sixteen.

The child savers' victory proved short-lived, however. Powerful business interests and a Supreme Court sympathetic to their views took advantage of the waning fervor for reform and in 1918 in Hammer v. Dagenhart struck down the child labor law on the grounds that Congress could not regulate manufacturing within states. This decision made it legal for the chief plaintiff in the case, Roland Dagenhart, to continue having his young sons work in a North Carolina cotton mill. It also protected the boys' "constitutional right" to continue to work at the mill, where they put in twelve-hour days and sometimes worked night shifts as well.

Ironically, one of the plaintiffs in the Dagenhart case had a very negative view of its outcome. In 1923, reporter Lowell Mellett tracked down Reuben Dagenhart, one of the boys in whose favor the Supreme Court had ruled six years earlier. In an article published in Labor in November 1923, Mellett recounted his meeting with Dagenhart.

Document 3. Lowell Mellett Interview with Reuben Dagenhart.

I found him at his home in Charlotte. He is about the size of the office boy—weighs 105 pounds, he told me. But he is a married man with a child. He is 20 years old.

"What benefit," I asked him, "did you get out of the suit which you won in the United States Supreme Court?"

"You mean the suit the Fidelity Manufacturing Company won? (It was the Fidelity Company for which the Dagenharts were working.) I don't see that I got any benefit. I guess I'd been alot better off if they hadn't won it. . . .

"Look at me! A hundred and five pounds, a grown man and no education. I may be mistaken, but I think the years I've put in in the cotton mills have stunted my growth. They kept me from getting any schooling. I had to stop school after the third

grade and now I need the education I didn't get."

"How was your growth stunted?"

"I don't know—the dust and the lint, maybe. But from 12 years old on, I was working 12 hours a day—from 6 in the morning till 7 at night, with time out for meals. And sometimes I worked nights besides. Lifting a hundred pounds and I only weighed 65 pounds myself."

He explained that he and his sister worked together, "on section," spinning. They each made about a dollar a day, though later he worked up to where he could make $2. His father made $15 a week and infant John, at the time the suit was brought, was making close to $1 a day.

"Just what did you and John get out of that suit, then?"

"Why, we got some automobile rides when them big lawyers from the North was down here. Oh, yes, and they brought both of us a coca-cola! That's all we got out of it."

"What did you tell the judge when you were in court?"

"Oh, John and me never was in court! Just Paw was there. John and me was just little kids in short pants. I guess we wouldn't have looked like much in court. We were working in the mill while the case was going on. But Paw went up to Washington."

Reuben hasn't been to school, but his mind has not been idle.

"It would have been a good thing for all the kids in this state if that law they passed had been kept. . . . I know one thing. I ain't going to let them put my kid sister in the mill. . . . She's only 15 and she's crippled and I bet I stop that!"

Despite the efforts of committed reformers, child labor persisted into the 1920s, immune from federal law and condoned by states reluctant to exercise their authority against the force of private money and growing public indifference.

Documents 1 and 2. House of Representatives Hearings before the Committee on Labor (1914), 93, 35-36.

Document 3. Labor (November 17, 1923).

WOMAN SUFFRAGE

The campaign for woman suffrage in its final phase in the 1910s argued that women needed the vote to fulfill their domestic duties. This 1916 poster echoed this sentiment, arguing that women as mothers needed the vote to protect their children. The more militant National Woman's Party, led by Alice Paul, insisted that women as women, not simply as housewives or mothers, deserved the vote.
Collection of Janice L. and David J. Frent.

through the Congressional Union for Woman Suffrage, which provided a base from which to press for a national strategy to achieve the vote. In 1916, she founded the militant National Woman's Party (NWP), which became the radical voice of the suffrage movement, advocating direct action and civil disobedience. Paul and her followers rejected the state-by-state strategy of the NAWSA and continued to press for a constitutional suffrage amendment, called by its supporters the Susan B. Anthony amendment, to provide woman suffrage.

The NAWSA, spurred by the actions of Paul and her followers, gained new direction when Carrie Chapman Catt became president in 1915. Catt revitalized the organization with a carefully crafted "winning plan" designed to achieve suffrage in six years. While Paul and her Woman's Party held a six-month vigil outside the White House with banners that read "Mr. Wilson, What Will You Do for Woman Suffrage?" Catt led a carefully disciplined and centrally directed effort that worked on several levels. In states where women already voted, Catt lobbied for a federal amendment. Where state referenda could be won, she launched campaigns to maintain the suffrage momentum. Catt's strategy was to "keep so much 'suffrage noise' going all over the country that neither the enemy [n]or friends [of suffrage] will discover where the real battle is." Catt's "winning plan" worked effectively, taking only four years instead of the six Catt had predicted.

World War I would provide the final impetus for woman suffrage. Paul and the NWP refused to work for the war and insisted that "democracy should begin at home." Arrested and jailed, they used hunger strikes to publicize their cause. For her part, Catt seized the mantle of patriotism, insisting that there was no conflict between fighting for suffrage and aiding the war effort. It would take several more years before the Nineteenth Amendment became part of the U.S. Constitution, but when it was ratified in August 1920, the victory belonged both to Catt and to Paul, for without the militancy of the Woman's Party, the NAWSA would not have seemed so moderate and respectable.

Women were not alone in being left out of progressive advances. African Americans fared even worse. The Progressive Era witnessed the systematic disfranchisement of black voters and the enactment of statutes, known as "Jim Crow" laws, to segregate public facilities. (The name "Jim Crow" derived from a character in a popular minstrel song.) It was one of the great ironies of progressivism that, as it was practiced south of the Mason-Dixon line, it preached disfranchisement of black voters as a "reform." During the bitter electoral fights that had pitted Populists against Democrats in the 1890s, the charge was often made that the party of white supremacy held its power only by the votes of the black belt. To guard against electoral fraud, where, it was alleged, African American votes were purchased by money or threats of coercion, southern progressives proposed to "reform" the electoral system by eliminating the black vote entirely. Southern states, beginning in 1890 with Mississippi, sought to curtail the African American vote through devices like the poll tax (a fee required to vote) and the literacy test. Not coincidentally, these measures also denied access to poor, illiterate whites likely to vote against the reigning Democrats and for the Populist Party. But the racist intention of southern voting legislation became clear when states resorted to such transparent ruses as the "grandfather clause," a legal device that allowed anyone to vote whose grandparent had cast a ballot, thus including virtually any southern white and excluding every black voter, whose grandparent had most likely been a slave.

It was one of the great ironies of progressivism that, as it was practiced south of the Mason-Dixon line, it preached the disfranchisement of black voters as a "reform."

The rise of the railroad precipitated segregation in the South where it had rarely existed, at least on paper, before. Blacks found themselves increasingly relegated to separate "Jim Crow" train coaches, even when they paid a first-class fare. Soon separate waiting rooms, separate bathrooms, and separate dining facilities sprang up across the South. In courtrooms in the state of Mississippi, blacks were even required to swear on a separate Bible.

In the face of this growing repression, Booker T. Washington, the preeminent black leader of the day, urged caution and restraint. A former slave, Washington founded the Tuskegee Institute in Alabama to teach vocational skills to African Americans. Washington emphasized education and economic progress for his race and urged African Americans to put aside issues of political and social equality. In an 1895 speech in Atlanta, which came to be known as the "Atlanta Compromise," he stated, "In all things that are purely social we can be as separate as the fingers, yet one as the hand in all things essential to mutual progress." Washington presided over an alliance of northern philanthropists and white leaders of the New South in which blacks agreed to segregation and disfranchisement in return for the promise of a share in economic growth. His accommodationist policy appealed to whites in all sections, who elevated Washington to the role of national spokesman for African Americans.

The year after Washington proclaimed the Atlanta Compromise, the Supreme Court upheld the legality of racial segregation, affirming in *Plessy v. Ferguson* the constitutionality of the doctrine of "separate but equal." Blacks could be segregated in separate facilities, from schools to rest rooms, as long as the facilities were "equal." In actuality, facilities rarely were equal. In the North, where the growing tide of new immigrants led to a clamor for restrictive legislation, support for African American rights found few advocates. Increasingly, the doctrine of "white supremacy" found support in all sections of the country.

When Theodore Roosevelt invited Booker T. Washington to dine at the White House in 1901, a storm of racist criticism erupted. One southern editor fumed that the White House "had been painted black." But Roosevelt's racist detractors missed the point. Roosevelt summoned Washington to talk politics and patronage, not African American rights. Busy tearing apart Mark Hanna's Republican machine and creating his own, Roosevelt wanted Washington's counsel in selecting black Republicans for party posts in the South. The president remained more interested in his own political fortunes than in those of African Americans. His attitude was obvious in the Brownsville incident in 1906, when he dishonorably discharged three companies of black soldiers because he believed that they were shielding the murderer of a white saloonkeeper who had been killed in a shoot-out in the Texas town.

When Woodrow Wilson came to power, he brought with him southern attitudes toward race and racial segregation. Despite the support of prominent African American intellectuals such as William Monroe Trotter and W. E. B. Du Bois, Wilson showed no compunction in allowing his postmaster general to segregate facilities, including drinking fountains and rest rooms, in the nation's capital. When critics attacked the policy, Wilson insisted that segregation was "in the interest of the Negro."

Faced with intolerance and open persecution, educated blacks in the North rebelled against the conservative leadership of Booker T. Washington. Harvard graduate W. E. B. Du Bois challenged Washington's political power. In *The Souls of Black Folk* (1903), he attacked the "Tuskegee Machine," comparing Washington to a political boss and charging that he used his influence to silence his critics and reward his followers. Du Bois founded the Niagara movement in 1905, calling for univer-

BOOKER T. WASHINGTON AND THEODORE ROOSEVELT DINE AT THE WHITE HOUSE
When Theodore Roosevelt invited Booker T. Washington to the White House in 1901, he stirred up a hornet's nest of controversy that continued into the election of 1904. Here in a Republican campaign piece, the meeting is portrayed positively, with TR and Washington pictured under a portrait of Abraham Lincoln, signaling the party's historic commitment to African Americans. Democrats portrayed the meeting in a very different light, their campaign buttons pictured Washington with darker skin and implied that Roosevelt favored "race mingling."
Collection of Janice L. and David J. Frent.

sal suffrage, civil rights, and leadership by a black intellectual elite. In 1909, the Niagara movement helped found the National Association for the Advancement of Colored People (NAACP), a coalition of blacks and whites that sought legal and political rights for African Americans. Like many progressive reform coalitions, the NAACP contained a diverse group—social workers, socialists, and black intellectuals. In the decades that followed, the NAACP came to represent the future for African Americans, while Booker T. Washington, who died in 1915, represented the past.

Conclusion: Progressivism in Perspective

The limitations of progressive reform should not obscure its very real achievements. The progressive movement brought significant gains as government moved away from laissez-faire and social Darwinism to embrace a more active role designed to bring about social justice and to achieve a better balance between business and government. Progressivism contained many paradoxes. A diverse coalition of individuals and interests, the progressive movement began at the grass roots but left as its legacy a stronger presidency and unprecedented federal involvement in the economy and social welfare. A movement that believed in social justice, progressivism often promoted social control. And while progressives called for greater democracy, they worshiped experts and efficiency. Many threads made up this complex reform movement. But whatever its inconsistencies, progressivism attempted to deal with the problems posed by urban industrialism and, by increasing the power of the presidency and expanding the power of the government, helped to launch the liberal state into the twentieth century. War on a global scale would provide progressivism with yet another challenge even before it had completed its ambitious agenda.

CHRONOLOGY

1889 Jane Addams opens Hull House in Chicago.

1895 Booker T. Washington enunciates "Atlanta Compromise," accepting segregation in return for economic opportunity.

Anti-Saloon League founded by Protestant clergy.

1896 U.S. Supreme Court upholds doctrine of "separate but equal" in *Plessy v. Ferguson*.

1900 Socialist Party founded with Eugene V. Debs as standard-bearer.

1901 Thomas Lofton Johnson elected mayor of Cleveland, Ohio.

Robert M. La Follette elected governor of Wisconsin.

Theodore Roosevelt succeeds to presidency following assassination of William McKinley.

Roosevelt intervenes in anthracite coal strike to bring labor and management to bargaining table.

Roosevelt initiates investigation of Northern Securities Company for antitrust violations.

1902 Dispute between United States and Germany over Venezuelan debt ends in arbitration.

Lincoln Steffens's muckraking series "The Shame of the Cities" begins to run in *McClure's Magazine*.

U.S. government files antitrust suit against Northern Securities Company.

1903 U.S.-backed uprising in Panama leads to Panamanian independence and to U.S. acquisition of rights to build canal.

In *The Souls of Black Folk*, W. E. B. Du Bois challenges Booker T. Washington.

Women's Trade Union League (WTUL) founded.

1904 Theodore Roosevelt wins presidential election in landslide.

1905 Industrial Workers of the World (IWW) founded by Big Bill Haywood.

1906 Pure Food and Drug Act and Meat Inspection legislation passed after publicity generated by Upton Sinclair's muckraking novel *The Jungle*.

Robert M. La Follette elected U.S. senator.

Congress passes Hepburn Act to regulate railroads and strengthen Interstate Commerce Commission.

Roosevelt receives Nobel Peace Prize for his role in mediating Russo-Japanese War.

1907 Social gospel minister Walter Rauschenbusch publishes *Christianity and the Social Crisis*.

Panic on Wall Street. J. P. Morgan's U.S. Steel acquires Tennessee Coal and Iron Company.

Roosevelt dispatches navy's Great White Fleet on world cruise to display U.S. naval power.

1908 U.S. Supreme Court upholds Oregon state law limiting women's working hours to ten a day (*Muller v. Oregon*).

William Howard Taft elected president to succeed Theodore Roosevelt.

1909 "Uprising of twenty thousand" occurs in New York City, a shirtwaist makers' strike backed by WTUL.

National Association for the Advancement of Colored People (NAACP) formed.

President Taft defends Payne-Aldrich tariff.

1911 Triangle fire in New York City kills 146 workers.

1912 President Taft sends marines into Nicaragua and Santo Domingo.

Theodore Roosevelt runs for president on Progressive Bull Moose Party ticket after losing Republican nomination to

incumbent President William Howard Taft.

Democrat Woodrow Wilson elected president, defeating Taft and Theodore Roosevelt.

1913 Federal Reserve Act reforms nation's banking system by providing twelve regional banks supervised by a Federal Reserve Board.

Woodrow Wilson signs legislation establishing Federal Trade Commission (FTC).

1914 Congress passes Clayton Antitrust Act.

Walter Lippmann publishes *Drift and Mastery*, a statement of the progressive philosophy.

1915 Carrie Chapman Catt takes over leadership of national woman suffrage movement.

1916 Alice Paul launches National Woman's Party.

Margaret Sanger opens first birth control clinic, in Brooklyn, New York.

BIBLIOGRAPHY

GENERAL WORKS

John Whiteclay Chambers II, *The Tyranny of Change: America in the Progressive Era, 1900–1917* (2nd ed., 1992).

Allen F. Davis, *Spearheads for Reform: The Social Settlements and the Progressive Movement, 1890–1914* (1967).

Alan Dawley, *Struggles for Justice: Social Responsibility and the Liberal State* (1991).

Vincent P. DeSantis, *The Shaping of Modern America, 1877–1920* (2nd ed., 1989).

Arthur Ekrich, *Progressivism in America* (1974).

Sara M. Evans, *Born for Liberty: A History of Women in America* (1989).

Harold U. Faulkner, *Politics, Reform, and Expansion, 1890–1900* (1959).

Samuel P. Hays, *The Response to Industrialism, 1885–1914* (1957).

Richard Hofstadter, *The Age of Reform* (1955).

Linda K. Kerber, Alice Kessler-Harris, and Katherine Kish Sklar, *U.S. History as Women's History* (1995).

Gabriel Kolko, *The Triumph of Conservatism* (1963).

Bruce Kuklick, *The Rise of American Philosophy* (1977).

Arthur Mann, ed., *The Progressive Era* (1975).

George Mowry, *The Era of Theodore Roosevelt* (1958).

William L. O'Neill, *The Progressive Years: America Comes of Age* (1975).

Nell Irvin Painter, *Standing at Armageddon: The United States, 1877–1919* (1987).

Alan Trachtenberg, *The Incorporation of America: Culture and Society in the Gilded Age* (1982).

James Weinstein, *The Corporate Ideal in the Liberal State, 1900–1918* (1969).

Robert H. Wiebe, *The Search for Order, 1877–1920* (1967).

GRASSROOTS PROGRESSIVISM

Jane Addams, *Twenty Years at Hull-House* (1910).

Joyce Antler, *Lucy Sprague Mitchell* (1987).

Karen J. Blair, *The Clubwoman as Feminist: True Womanhood Redefined, 1868–1914* (1980).

Steven Boyer, *Urban Masses and Moral Order in America, 1820–1920* (1978).

Kathleen Brady, *Ida Tarbell: Portrait of a Muckraker* (1984).

Robert Bremmer, *From the Depths: The Discovery of Poverty in the United States* (1956).

John D. Buenker, *Urban Liberalism and Progressive Reform* (1973).

Mina Carson, *Settlement Folk: Social Thought and the American Settlement Movement, 1885–1930* (1990).

Robert Cross, *The Church in the City* (1958).

Robert M. Crunden, *Ministers of Reform: The Progressive Achievement in American Civilization, 1889–1920* (1982).

Allen F. Davis, *American Heroine: The Life and Legend of Jane Addams* (1973).

Allen F. Davis and Mary Lynn McCree, *Eighty Years at Hull-House* (1969).

Nancy Schrom Dye, *As Equals and as Sisters: Feminism, Unionism, and the Women's Trade Union League of New York* (1980).

John H. Ehrenreich, *The Altruistic Imagination: A History of Social Work and Social Policy in the United States* (1985).

Ellen Fitzpatrick, *Endless Crusade: Women, Social Scientists, and Progressive Reform* (1990).

Philip S. Foner, *Women and the American Labor Movement.* vol. 1, *From Colonial Times to the Eve of World War I* (1979).

Lynn D. Gordon, *Gender and Higher Education in the Progressive Era* (1989).

Samuel Haber, *Efficiency and Uplift: Scientific Management in the Progressive Era, 1899–1920* (1964).

Alice Kessler Harris, *Out to Work: A History of Wage Earning Women in the United States* (1982).

Helen Lefkowitz Horowitz, *Culture and City: Cultural Philanthropy in Chicago from the 1880s to 1917* (1976).

Hull-House Maps and Papers (1895; reprint, 1970).

Michael B. Katz, *In the Shadow of the Poorhouse: A Social History of Welfare in America* (1986).

Seth Koven and Sonya Michel, eds., *Mothers of a New World: Maternalist Politics and the Origins of the Welfare State* (1993).

Christopher Lasch, *The Social Thought of Jane Addams* (1965).

William Leach, *True Love and Perfect Union: The Feminist Reform of Sex and Society* (1980).

James Lieby, *A History of Social Work in the United States* (1978).

Walter Lippmann, *Drift and Mastery* (1914).

Rivka Lissak, *Pluralism and Progressives: Hull House and the New Immigrants, 1890–1919* (1989).

Roy M. Lubove, *The Progressives and the Slums* (1962).

Henry F. May, *Protestant Churches and Industrial America* (1949).

Kathleen McCarth, ed., *Lady Bountiful Revisited: Women, Philanthropy, and Power* (1990).

David Montgomery, *Workers' Control in America* (1979).

Robyn Muncy, *Creating a Female Dominion in American Reform* (1991).

David Musto, *American Disease: Origins of Narcotic Control* (expanded ed., 1987).

Donald Nelson, *Frederick W. Taylor and the Rise of Scientific Management* (1980).

Charles Parkhurst, *Our Fight with Tammany* (1895).

Peggy Pascoe, *Relations of Rescue: The Search for Female Moral Authority in the American West* (1990).

Elizabeth Payne, *Reform, Labor, and Feminism: Margaret Dreier Robins and the Women's Trade Union League* (1988).

David Pivar, *The Purity Crusade: Sexual Morality and Social Control* (1973).

Jean B. Quandt, *The Social Thought of Progressive Intellectuals* (1970).

Ruth Rosen, *The Lost Sisterhood: Prostitutes in America* (1984).

Rosalind Rosenberg, *Beyond Separate Spheres: The Intellectual Roots of Modern Feminism* (1982).

John Rury, *The Cultural Moment: The New Politics, the New Woman, the New Psychology, the New Art, and the New Theatre in America* (1991).

Anne Firor Scott, *Natural Allies: Women's Associations in American History* (1991).

Peter R. Shergold, *Working Class Life: The "American Standard" in Comparative Perspective, 1899–1913* (1982).

Kathryn Kish Sklar, *Florence Kelley and the Nation's Work: The Rise of Women's Political Culture, 1830–1900* (1995).

Theda Skocpol, *Protecting Soldiers and Mothers* (1992).

Barbara Miller Solomon, *In the Company of Educated Women* (1985).

Sharon Hartman Strom, *Beyond the Typewriter: Gender, Class, and the Origins of Modern American Office Work, 1900–1930* (1992).

Meredith Tax, *The Rising of the Women* (1980).

Barbara Mayer Wertheimer, *We Were There: The Story of Working Women in America* (1977).

Harold S. Wilson, *McClure's Magazine and the Muckrakers* (1970).

R. Jackson Wilson, *Reform, Crisis, and Confusion, 1900–1929* (1970).

LOCAL AND STATE REFORM

Melvin Holli, *Reform in Detroit: Hazen S. Pingree and Urban Politics* (1969).

William A. Link, *The Paradox of Southern Progressivism, 1880–1930* (1992).

Carl Lorenz, *Tom L. Johnson, Mayor of Cleveland* (1911).

Richard L. McCormick, *From Realignment to Reform: Political Change in New York State* (1981).

George Mowry, *The California Progressives* (1951).

Spencer Olin Jr., *California's Prodigal Sons: Hiram Johnson and the Progressives, 1911–1917* (1968).

Judith Sealander, *Grand Plans: Business Progressivism and Social Change in Ohio's Miami Valley, 1890–1919* (1988).

David P. Thelen, *The New Citizenship: Origins of Progressivism in Wisconsin, 1885–1900* (1972).

David P. Thelen, *Robert M. La Follette and the Insurgent Spirit* (1985).

C. Vann Woodward, *The Origins of the New South* (1951).

James Wright, *The Progressive Yankees* (1987).

PROGRESSIVISM AND NATIONAL POLITICS

Donald E. Anderson, *William Howard Taft* (1973).

Judith Icke Anderson, *William Howard Taft: An Intimate History* (1981).

Howard K. Beale, *Theodore Roosevelt and the Rise of America to World Power* (1956).

John Morton Blum, *Woodrow Wilson and the Politics of Morality* (1956).

John Morton Blum, *The Republican Roosevelt* (2nd ed., 1977).

John D. Buenker, *Urban Liberalism and Progressive Reform* (1973).

Ron Chernow, *The House of Morgan* (1990).

Ron Chernow, *The Warburgs: The Twentieth Century Odyssey of a Remarkable Jewish Family* (1993).

Lewis L. Gould, *Reform and Regulation: American Politics from Roosevelt to Wilson* (2nd ed., 1986).

Lewis L. Gould, *The Presidency of Theodore Roosevelt* (1991).

Otis Graham Jr., *The Great Campaigns: Reform and War in America, 1900–1929* (1971).

William H. Harbaugh, *The Life and Times of Theodore Roosevelt* (rev. ed., 1982).

Samuel P. Hays, *Conservation and the Gospel of Efficiency* (1959).

James Kloppenberg, *Uncertain Victory: Social Democracy and Progressivism in European and American Thought, 1870–1920* (1986).

Arthur S. Link, *Woodrow Wilson*, 5 vols. (1947–1965).

Arthur S. Link, *Woodrow Wilson: Revolution, War, and Power* (1979).

Richard L. McCormick, *The Party Period and Public Policy* (1986).

James L. Penick Jr., *Progressive Politics and Conservation: The Ballinger-Pinchot Affair* (1968).

Emily S. Rosenberg, *Spreading the American Dream: American Economic and Cultural Expansion, 1890–1945* (1982).

Lincoln Steffens, *The Autobiography of Lincoln Steffens*, vols. 1 and 2 (1931).

Phillipa Strum, *Louis D. Brandeis* (1984).

David P. Thelen, *Robert M. La Follette and the Insurgent Spirit* (2nd ed., 1985).

Craig West, *Banking Reform and the Federal Reserve* (1977).

William Appleman Williams, *The Tragedy of American Diplomacy* (1959).

Clarence E. Wunderlin Jr., *Visions of a New Industrial Order: Social Science and Labor Theory in America's Progressive Era* (1992).

James Harvey Young, *Securing the Federal Food and Drug Act of 1906* (1989).

RADICAL ALTERNATIVES

Mary Jo Buhl, *Women and American Socialism, 1870–1920* (1981).

Ellen Chesler, *Woman of Valor: Margaret Sanger and the Birth Control Movement in America* (1993).

John Diggins, *The American Left in the Twentieth Century* (1973).

Melvyn Dubofsky, *"Big Bill" Haywood* (1987).

Melvyn Dubofsky, *We Shall Be All: A History of the Industrial Workers of the World* (2nd ed., 1988).

Leslie Fishbein, *Rebels in Bohemia: The Radicals of the Masses, 1911–1917* (1982).

David J. Goldberg, *A Tale of Three Cities: Labor Organization and Protest in Paterson, Passaic, and Lawrence, 1916–1921* (1988).

Linda Gordon, *Woman's Body, Woman's Right* (1977).

J. Morgan Kousser, *The Shaping of Southern Politics* (1974).

Neil R. McMillen, *Dark Journey: Black Mississippians in the Age of Jim Crow* (1989).

Bruno Ramirez, *When Workers Fight: The Politics of Industrial Relations in the Progressive Era, 1898–1916* (1978).

Salvatore Salerno, *Red November, Black November: Culture and Community in the Industrial Workers of the World* (1989).

Nick Salvatore, *Eugene V. Debs: Citizen and Socialist* (1982).

L. Glen Seretan, *Daniel DeLeon: The Odyssey of an American Marxist* (1979).

David Shannon, *The Socialist Party* (1955).

Elliott Shore, *Talkin' Socialism* (1988).

Ann Huber Tripp, *The IWW and the Paterson Silk Strike of 1913* (1987).

Alice Wexler, *Emma Goldman: An Intimate Life* (1984).

RACE RELATIONS AND WOMAN SUFFRAGE

Eleanor Flexner, *Century of Struggle: The Women's Rights Movement in the United States* (1959).

Kevin K. Gaines, *Uplifting the Race, Black Leadership, Politics, and Culture in the Twentieth Century* (1996).

Louis R. Harlan, *Separate and Unequal: Public School Campaigns and Racism in the Southern Seaboard States, 1900–1915* (1968).

Louis R. Harlan, *Booker T. Washington: The Making of a Black Leader, 1856–1901* (1972).

Louis R. Harlan, *Booker T. Washington: The Wizard of Tuskegee, 1901–1915* (1983).

Charles F. Kellogg, *NAACP: A History of the National Association for the Advancement of Colored People, 1909–1920* (1967).

Jack Temple Kirby, *Darkness at the Dawning: Race and Reform in the Progressive South* (1972).

Ann J. Lane, *The Brownsville Affair: National Crisis and Black Reaction* (1971).

Christine Lunardini, *From Equal Suffrage to Equal Rights: Alice Paul and the National Woman's Party, 1910–1928* (1986).

Mary E. Odem, *Delinquent Daughters, Protecting and Policing Adolescent Sexuality in the United States, 1885–1920* (1995).

Elliot M. Rudwick, *W. E. B. Du Bois* (1968).

Donald Spivey, *Schooling for the New Slavery: Black Industrial Education, 1868–1915* (1978).

Cheryl A. Wall, *Women of the Harlem Renaissance* (1995).

Booker T. Washington, *Up from Slavery* (1901).

John D. Weaver, *The Brownsville Raid* (1970).

Joel Williamson, *The Crucible of Race* (1984).

C. Vann Woodward, *The Strange Career of Jim Crow* (1955).

WAR

Which Bird?

As viewed by Life

LIFE MAGAZINE COVER
This 1914 magazine cover provides a vivid visual demonstration of the American press's very early tendency to support U.S. entry into World War I. The image makes no bones about the way a viewer should answer the question posed below it. The American eagle in the center, wings spread and screaming for action, dominates the picture and makes the dove holding an olive branch appear pathetically weak. Considering the stereotyped knife, gun, and bomb-wielding foreigners lurking in the background, the sailor has understandably turned toward the eagle for inspiration to intervene in the British lion's battle against the enemies of democracy.
Picture Research Archives and Consultants.

THE UNITED STATES AND THE "GREAT WAR" 22
1914–1920

I N AUGUST 1914, after more than forty years of peace, Europe exploded in war. The booming of the great guns could be heard in Paris and even in London when conditions were right. Washington, D.C., was three thousand miles from the tragedy, but President Woodrow Wilson felt it deeply nevertheless. When the news arrived that war had broken out, the American progressive president cried: "What a pathetic thing to have this come just as we were so full of hope!" Dazed by the suddenness of events and weighed down by the thought of the renewal of barbarism, he paced the corridors of the White House. Wilson also shouldered a crushing personal burden. His beloved wife, Ellen, lay dying. He received war reports while sitting at her bedside, holding her hand. When she died on August 6, 1914, Wilson was devastated. According to the White House physician, he was a "man with his heart torn out."

Although nearly numb with grief, Wilson formulated a national policy regarding the war in Europe. He never had any doubt that the only possible course was absolute neutrality. There were compelling reasons for not intervening. Even though his sympathies lay with Great Britain and France, Wilson concluded that blame for the war did not lie entirely with Germany. Moreover, he believed that the United States had no vital stake in the outcome of the war. It was a remote European contest, and nothing required that the United States give up its safety and security. Wilson agreed with the American ambassador in London, who declared, "Again and ever I thank heaven for the Atlantic Ocean." In addition, the United States was a nation of immigrants, millions of whom had only recently come from countries that were now at war. As Wilson told the German ambassador, "We definitely have to be neutral, since otherwise our mixed populations would wage war on each other."

There was another reason to stay out of the European struggle. On August 19, 1914, Wilson explained to the American people the international good that could come from strict neutrality. As a great neutral power, he said, the United States could offer "impartial mediation" and show the world the way to reconciliation and a healing peace. Because support for one side or the other would wreck this opportunity for service, Wilson told the American people that they must remain "impartial in thought as well as action." If they could curb their emotions and show the "true spirit of neutrality, which is the spirit of impartiality and fairness and friendliness to all concerned," then, Wilson declared, Americans could help him persuade the warring nations to lay down their arms in exchange for a just peace.

Like Wilson, the great majority of the American people were pro-peace and antiwar. They showed almost no sympathy for intervention. The nation wrapped itself in the concept of neutrality and tried to go about its business. If attention strayed outside the country, it fixed on the grand opening of the Panama Canal on August 15, 1914. By the beginning of 1915, newspaper coverage of the war had shrunk to a few columns. Few Americans felt the least worry over any prospect of involvement in the war in Europe. So secure and distant did Congress feel that in 1915 the House came within a few votes of slashing the Navy Department's moderate program for battleship construction.

But U.S. citizens learned that the Atlantic was no moat. Trade and travel webbed the modern world. After nearly three years of trying to steer a neutral course, Woodrow Wilson went before Congress on April 2, 1917, to ask for a declaration of war against Germany. He attempted to square America's entrance with his original progressive hopes for neutrality. America's military might would end the carnage of war, he said. And America's goodness and disinterestedness would ensure a just peace. The country's participation would make the First World War the war to end wars, the war "to make the world safe for democracy."

Called the "Great War," the First World War was great in its destructive power and in its transformative influence. It defined an era of revolutionary upheaval, cataclysmic conflict, and shifts in the balance of power that threatened the very foundations of the international order. The fighting that raged in Europe was the most savage the world had ever witnessed. War stretched across continents, and nations measured their casualties in the millions. When peace arrived in 1919, both the victors and the vanquished were decimated and exhausted.

America's experience was different, however. At home, war and prosperity went hand in hand. But America paid a price as citizens and the government cracked down on dissent and demanded conformity. "Over There," as Americans called the war theater in Europe, the nation lost 112,000 soldiers, but their performance on the battlefields affected the outcome of the war. In the peace negotiations that followed the armistice, Woodrow Wilson played a principal role, but the results did not confirm Wilson's impossible vision of himself as personal savior of the world. He had promised more than anyone could deliver, and the nation turned bitter and disillusioned.

In December 1919, Wilson's personal friend and chief foreign policy adviser, Colonel Edward House, summarized the nation's ordeal: "We came near doing a great thing in a great way, but Fate ordained otherwise and while something may still be done, it will be done in a small way and in a way full of humiliation for those who wished to see the United States lead in a new world movement."

Woodrow Wilson and the World

Shortly after winning election to the presidency in 1912, Woodrow Wilson confided to a friend: "It would be an irony of fate if my administration had to deal chiefly with foreign affairs." Indeed, Wilson had based his life and career on local attachments. He had never shown an interest in venturing far from where he was born and worked and had traveled abroad only on brief vacations. As president of Princeton University and then governor of New Jersey, his career kept him rooted in domestic concerns. During his campaign for the presidency, Wilson had argued passionately for domestic reform, referring only rarely to foreign affairs.

But Wilson could not avoid the world. The Wilsonian foreign policy that emerged in 1913–1914 reflected his conviction that the United States should be a moral example in international affairs. He championed the principles of liberal democracy. Those principles included respect for human rights and the rule of law, the right of self-determination to ensure that people could choose their own governments and leaders, and the reduction of tariffs that would impede trade and cause international conflict. Support for these principles meant opposing imperialism, large armed forces, and trade barriers. "We dare not turn from the principle that morality and not expediency is the thing that must guide us," Wilson announced loftily, "and that we will never condone iniquity because it is most convenient to do so."

A rising tide of militarism, nationalism, and violence severely tested Wilson's liberal principles. His first challenge arose in the Western Hemisphere, where according to the Monroe Doctrine the United States had special responsibilities and power. Reflecting that perspective, Wilson found the urge to intervene irresistible. When war broke out in Europe in 1914, however, Wilson claimed no such right to intervene. Instead, he offered his services as a peace broker. Fervently, Wilson sought acceptance of a "peace without victory," but the prevailing conviction among the warring nations that honor required defeat of the enemy ruled out compromise.

It was only a matter of time before the escalating fight caused incidents that wounded America's own interests and sense of honor and drew the nation into the tragic conflict.

Taming the Americas

When Wilson came to office, he sought to distinguish his foreign policy from that of his Republican predecessors. To Wilson, Theodore Roosevelt's "big stick" smacked of the blatant use of military force. William Howard Taft's "dollar diplomacy" appeared to be a crude flexing of economic muscle. Wilson sought a morally superior alternative. He underlined the new direction in foreign policy by appointing William Jennings Bryan to be Secretary of State. A pacifist on religious grounds, Bryan immediately turned his attention to making agreements with thirty nations for the peaceful settlement of disputes.

But Wilson and Bryan, like Roosevelt and Taft, also believed that the Monroe Doctrine bestowed on the United States special rights and responsibilities in the Western Hemisphere. The Wilson administration wanted to encourage justice and democracy and also to protect and expand American investments. Both principle and economic aspiration promoted American intervention as vigorous as that of the Roosevelt and Taft administrations. Wilson accepted the 1912 occupation of Nicaragua by U.S.

marines to thwart a radical revolution that threatened order and American property. In 1915, he sent marines into Haiti to quell lawlessness and to protect American interests. In 1916, Wilson followed a similar course in the Dominican Republic. So firm was his view of American dominance in the hemisphere that when the Central American court of justice issued a ruling against the American military presence as a violation of traditional rights of national sovereignty, Wilson simply ignored it.

> *The Wilson administration wanted to encourage justice and democracy in the Western Hemisphere and also to protect and expand American investments there.*

Wilson's most serious and controversial involvement in Latin America came in Mexico. Just weeks before Wilson was elected, Francisco Madero, who had become president of Mexico after the democratic revolution of 1911, was assassinated by henchmen of the reactionary General Victoriano Huerta. Most European nations promptly recognized Huerta, but Wilson balked, declaring that he would not support a "government of butchers." In April 1914, Huerta's refusal to apologize for briefly detaining American sailors in Tampico prompted

"PANCHO" VILLA AND GENERAL PERSHING
Here in 1914 Mexican revolutionary Francisco "Pancho" Villa and American general John J. Pershing (right) pose genially as allies in the struggle to overthrow the dictatorial ruler of Mexico, Victoriano Huerta. Soon afterward Villa and Pershing would be adversaries. After a raid by "Villistas" across the New Mexico border in 1915 to punish Americans for aiding Villa's revolutionary rivals, Pershing pursued Villa into Mexico.
Corbis-Bettmann.

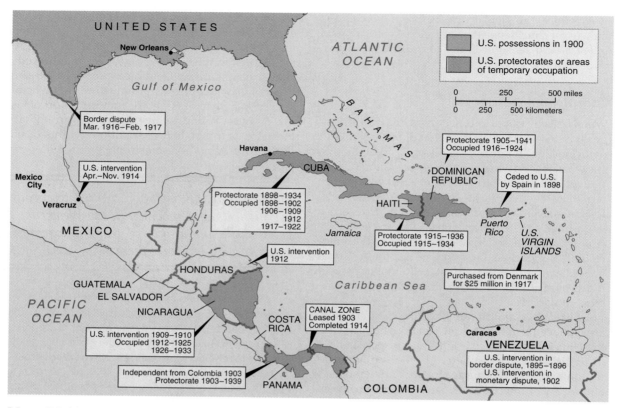

MAP 22.1

U.S. Involvement in the Caribbean and Latin America, 1895–1941

Victory against Spain in 1898 made Puerto Rico an American possession and Cuba a protectorate. America also gained control over the Panama Canal and was quick to protect expanding economic interests with military force to make sure that stable, if not necessarily democratic, governments prevailed.

Wilson to declare that it was time "to teach the South American republics to elect good men!" The president ordered eight hundred marines to seize the port of Veracruz and prevent the unloading of a large shipment of arms for Huerta, who was by then involved in a civil war of his own. In the fighting that followed, 19 Americans and 126 Mexicans died. Huerta, seeing the handwriting on the wall, fled to Spain, and the United States recognized a new government in Mexico.

Wilson was not able to escape from Mexico that easily, however. A rebellion erupted among desperately poor farmers who believed that the new government, aided by American business interests, had betrayed the revolution's promise to help the common people. Their leader, Francisco "Pancho" Villa, had instilled in his followers a brutal willingness to strike back at their oppressors. In January 1916, a

band of Villistas seized a trainload of gold from an American-owned mine deep within Mexico and killed the seventeen American engineers who were carrying it to Texas. Emboldened by that profitable act of revenge, another Villista band crossed the border on March 9 for a predawn raid on the town of Columbus, New Mexico, that cost several lives and left the town in flames. Wilson promptly dispatched twelve thousand troops led by General John J. Pershing, who years earlier had chased the Apache chief Geronimo through the same Mexican desert and who would soon command American forces in France. The American cavalry never managed to catch and punish Villa's raiders. In January 1917, Pershing finally led his weary troops back across the border, ending Woodrow Wilson's heavy-handed intervention into Mexican affairs. The cataclysmic revolution raged on in Mexico until 1920, however, and ended in the death of about two million people, one out of every eight Mexicans. Well before then, American attention had shifted to the situation in Europe.

The European Crisis

Early in the twentieth century, European leaders often proclaimed proudly that they had done away with war. But the many years of peace enjoyed by the great powers before 1914 masked profound tensions caused by imperial rivalries and nationalist desires. The consolidation of the German and Italian states into unified nations and the similar ambition of Russia to create some sort of "Pan-Slavic" union initiated new rivalries throughout Europe. As the conviction spread that colonial possessions were a mark of national greatness, competition expanded onto the world stage. In particular, Germany, under the leadership of Kaiser Wilhelm II, sought national greatness by creating an empire abroad and building industrial muscle at home. Its desire for colonies and economic might, together with its obsession with building a navy to overcome Britain's traditional domination of the sea, threatened Europe's balance of power and stimulated anxious competition among other nations.

Within this explosive atmosphere, a complex web of military and diplomatic alliances grew. By 1914, Germany, Austria-Hungary, and Italy (the Triple Alliance) stood opposed to Great Britain, France, and Russia (the Triple Entente). In their effort to avoid war, the nations of Europe had actually magnified the possibility of conflict by creating national borders that were in effect trip wires between two heavily armed power blocs. With rising dismay, those who had hoped for safety through a balance of power came to realize that the system gave a lone assassin the power to set off a catastrophe.

The fuse to the European powder keg was lit in southeastern Europe, in the Balkans. On June 28, 1914, a Bosnian Serb terrorist fatally shot Archduke Franz Ferdinand of Austria as he toured the city of Sarajevo, then part of the Austro-Hungarian Empire. The assassin sought to dramatize Serbia's persistent desire to extend its territory all the way to the Adriatic Sea. The nations of Europe mobilized their armies. Austria-Hungary, holding Serbia to account for the assassination, declared war on that nation on July 28. The alliance system locked into place, and in swift sequence the nations of Europe plunged into war. Russia, determined to protect its Slavic kin, announced that it would back the Serbs.

Germany felt compelled to support Austria-Hungary as a kindred Germanic state and declared war on Russia and on Russia's ally France. In response, Great Britain, upholding its treaty with France, declared war on Germany. Halfway around the globe, Japan saw an opportunity to rid itself of competition in China and went to war against Germany, making the conflict the First World War.

It became the most devastating and most hideous war the world had ever known. England's foreign secretary, Edward Grey, sighed his epitaph for the civilization he had known: "The lamps are going out all over Europe. We shall not see them lit again in our lifetime." But the foreign secretary and other national leaders who had been charged with tending the lamps faced the task of explaining why they had snuffed them out. With his usual grave dignity, Grey assured Parliament that Great Britain would rally to the cause of war when it "realizes what is at stake, what the real issues are." The next day on the other side of the barricades, the German imperial chancellor, Theobald von Bethmann Hollweg, insisted that Germany had grown strong "in the works of peace" and that "only in defense of a just cause shall our sword fly from its scabbard." But beyond vague assertions from each side that aggression must be halted and honor upheld, little was done to define "just cause."

Across the Atlantic, Woodrow Wilson perceived no just cause and labored to keep the United States neutral and its progressive mission intact.

The Ordeal of Neutrality

When the United States declared its neutrality, it also claimed neutral rights. The concept of neutrality was fuzzy in international law, but the United States had traditionally insisted on the broadest possible definition. In the American view, "free ships made free goods," that is, neutral nations had the right to trade freely with all nations at war, to send their ships safely through the open seas, and to demand the safe passage of their citizens on the merchant and passenger ships of all belligerents. More was involved in upholding neutral rights than principle. The year before Europe went to war, the American economy had started to slide into a recession that threatened to rival the depression of the 1890s. American trade with Europe offered hope of ending unemployment and hardship at home; a disruption of European trade would add greatly to the distress.

It was inevitable that the United States would run into trouble if it insisted on continuing to ship

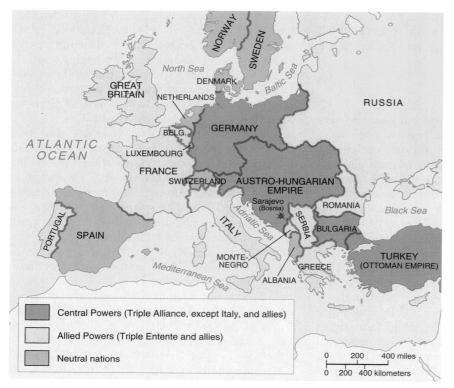

MAP 22.2
European Alliances after the Outbreak of World War I
With Germany and the Austro-Hungarian Empire wedged between their Entente rivals, and all parties fully armed, Europe was poised for war when the Archduke Franz Ferdinand of Austria was assassinated in Sarajevo in July 1914.

goods to Europe. Great Britain was the first to step on tender neutral rights. Britain's powerful fleet controlled the seas, and it quickly threw up a blockade around Germany. By denying Germany maritime imports, Britain hoped to bring its enemy to its knees. The United States vigorously protested British action, but Britain refused to give up its naval advantage. In the fall of 1914, the Wilson administration reluctantly accepted the British blockade, thus indicating the widespread sympathy for Britain within the State Department and beginning the fateful process of alienation from Germany. American anger about the violation of its neutral rights was undercut by the huge volume of war-related trade that sprang up between the United States and Britain. So great was the demand for American agricultural and industrial goods to break the German blockade that wartime orders succeeded in pulling the American economy out of its prewar slump.

The debate over the definition of neutrality also involved American loans to belligerents. In August 1914, Secretary of State William Jennings Bryan outlawed loans to nations at war on the grounds that for bankers to continue business as usual would be "inconsistent with the true spirit of neutrality." But

in 1915, when lack of funds threatened Britain's ability to continue its trade with the United States, Secretary of the Treasury William G. McAdoo warned Wilson: "To maintain our prosperity, we must finance it." Neutrality would henceforth be defined not by restrictions on the United States but in terms of the country's right to trade freely and to lend money. Although some continued to argue that vast loans to Britain would tie the United States to Britain and draw it into war, between 1914 and the spring of 1917 the United States advanced almost $2.5 billion in loans to the Allies and only $27 million to Germany. Trade showed an even greater imbalance. Driven by war-related goods, exports to Britain escalated some 300 percent, while British sea power reduced trade with Germany and its allies to the vanishing point.

Faced with the almost totally effective British blockade, Germany retaliated with a blockade of its own. But there was a difference. The British fleet was a surface fleet, and the German navy consisted primarily of deadly, torpedo-firing submarines. The German *Unterseebooten,* or U-boats, could not operate according to traditional rules. Surface ships could halt American freighters. Submarines could only sink them. Subs were effective only when they surprised their quarry. And once they sank a ship, the tiny, cramped U-boats could not possibly pick up the survivors. To much of the world, submarine warfare violated notions of how a "civilized" nation waged war. Nevertheless, in February 1915, the German high command declared the waters around Britain a war zone and warned that any ship in the area would be subject without notice to attack.

Woodrow Wilson responded harshly, branding the sinking of a merchant ship "a wanton act." He declared that the United States would regard the loss of an American ship or the loss of American lives on a belligerent ship as "a flagrant violation of neutral rights" and would hold Germany to "strict accountability." What "strict accountability" meant was still unclear when Wilson received the shocking news of the sinking of the British liner *Lusitania*

on May 7, 1915, off the coast of Ireland. The *Lusitania* was one of the great passenger ships of its day, the "Queen of the Atlantic." Journalist Mark Sullivan later recounted that for years afterward people could "remember the surroundings in which they read [the news of the sinking], the emotions they had, their actions the rest of the day." The sinking caused the loss of 1,198 lives, including 128 Americans.

American newspapers appeared with drawings of drowning women and children and cries for war. The majority of Americans, however, did not want to break relations with Germany. Some pointed out that the German embassy had warned prospective passengers that they would be entering a war zone where the ship would be subject to attack. Others observed that the *Lusitania* carried millions of rounds of ammunition as well as passengers.

SINKING OF THE LUSITANIA *Military prowess and civilian tragedy came together with shocking effect in the sinking of the British passenger liner* Lusitania, *on May 7, 1915. Captain Walter Schwieger, commander of the German submarine U-20, who spotted the ship off the coast of Ireland, skillfully sank the great liner with a single torpedo. After watching the chaos that ensued in which more than 1,200 people lost their lives, he remembered the scene as the most awful one he had ever witnessed. For Americans, the fate of the* Lusitania *was crucial in turning public sentiment against Germany. This poster by Fred Spear captured the outrage felt at the loss of many women and almost 100 children. Nearly two years before America entered the war, posters like this urged Americans to enlist as preparation for the day when they must surely save civilization from German barbarism.*
UPI/Bettmann Archive; Library of Congress.

Woodrow Wilson maintained his commitment to peace and neutrality, declaring on May 10 that "there is such a thing as a man being too proud to fight." Former president Theodore Roosevelt, a leading advocate of arming the nation against German aggression, never forgave Wilson for being such a "flub dub and mollycoddle," for not realizing he should be too proud *not* to fight. Yet Wilson's policy was not passive. He sent strongly worded notes to Germany condemning the sinking as an "illegal and inhuman act" and demanding payment for damages. Any further destruction of ships, Wilson warned, would be regarded as "deliberately unfriendly" and might lead the United States to break diplomatic relations with Germany.

Although the sinking of the *Lusitania* did not result in war, it turned Wilson against the peace movement within his administration. Secretary of State Bryan, the leading pacifist voice in the cabinet, argued that Germany had a right to protect itself from British importation of armaments. A ship carrying war materials, he said, "should not rely on passengers to protect her from attack—it would be like putting women and children in front of an army." He asked Wilson to warn American citizens using ships of belligerent countries that they traveled at their own risk. Instead, Wilson branded the sinking as a brutal attack on innocent people and reasserted the rights of American citizens to travel unharmed across the oceans. Bryan realized that Wilson had left Germany little choice but to cease submarine warfare and abandon its blockade of Britain or to risk war with the United States. In protest, Bryan resigned as secretary of state, and Robert Lansing, a veteran State Department officer and a strong advocate of the Allied cause, took his place.

Then the tension subsided. Germany, anxious not to provoke the United States into joining the Allied cause, apologized for the *Lusitania* deaths and offered an indemnity. After the sinking of the English steamer *Sussex* in 1916, at the cost of two more American lives, the German government quickly acted to head off war by promising that there would be no more submarine attacks without warning and without provisions for the safety of civilians. Observers hailed the pledge as a victory for Wilson's policy of careful negotiation between the poles of Bryan's pacifism and Roosevelt's bellicosity.

The lull stirred hope that a peaceful end to the war might be found. Colonel Edward House, Wilson's trusted adviser on foreign affairs, set off for London, Paris, and Berlin in January 1916. His hope was to get the belligerents to the conference table. How the bitterly hostile sides could reconcile their differences remained a mystery, but at least there would be a chance if they agreed to meet. On the basis of that slender thread of hope, Wilson appealed for a "peace without victory," speaking eloquently about the need to establish a new world order after the fighting ceased. He called for a peace settlement that would guarantee freedom of the seas, a reduction in military arms, free and open trade, and national self-determination. To provide the means for peaceful resolution of disputes in the future, he endorsed British Foreign Secretary Grey's suggestion to create a "league of nations" that would "insure peace and justice throughout the world."

Although the sinking of the Lusitania *did not result in war, it turned Wilson against the peace movement within his administration.*

Wilson's efforts for peace served him well in his bid for reelection in 1916. Still, controversies over neutrality, intervention in Mexico, and the government's role in regulating the economy made Wilson's chances uncertain. Unlike the situation in 1912, Wilson faced a united Republican challenge after Theodore Roosevelt declined to run for the Progressive Party. Wilson's opponent was the able associate justice of the Supreme Court Charles Evans Hughes, who had formerly been governor of New York. The Democratic Party ran Wilson under the slogan "He kept us out of war," but Wilson shied away from the claim, protesting that "they talk of me as though I were a god. Any little German lieutenant can push us into the war at any time by some calculated outrage." But Wilson said nothing when the Democrats also argued that the Republican candidate was more likely to lead the nation into war. Ultimately, Wilson's case for neutrality appealed to the majority in favor of peace. Wilson won, but the Democratic incumbent squeaked through by only 600,000 popular votes and only 23 electoral votes. The narrowness of his victory left in doubt whether Wilson spoke for the nation in foreign policy.

The United States Enters the War

In the end, the determination by the warring sides to achieve peace on their own terms scuttled any chance for a negotiated peace. The Germans refused to specify their war aims as a condition for mediation. The Allies made mediation difficult in any event by announcing aims that would have broken up the Austro-Hungarian Empire and required the Germans to pay damages for the war. In early January 1917, the German military high command forced the issue by persuading the kaiser that the country could no longer afford to allow neutral shipping to reach Great Britain while the enemy blockade threatened to starve Germany. Instead, Germany would resume unrestricted submarine warfare at the end of the month and sink without warning any ship found in the waters off Great Britain. The German military understood that it risked war with the United States but gambled that Germany would achieve a quick military victory before the United States could bring its armed might to bear.

Most of Wilson's advisers joined Theodore Roosevelt in demanding a declaration of war as soon as Germany announced its unrestricted submarine policy, but Wilson, still hoping for a peaceful way out, would only go so far as to sever diplomatic relations with Germany. Then on February 25, 1917, British authorities informed Wilson of a secret telegram sent by the German foreign secretary, Arthur Zimmermann, to the German minister in Mexico. It promised that in the event of war between Germany and the United States, Germany would see that Mexico regained the territories it lost in the Southwest in the Mexican-American War in exchange for a declaration of war against the United States. Wilson angrily responded to the Zimmermann telegram by asking Congress to approve a policy of "armed neutrality" that would equip merchant ships to fight back against any attackers. On a deeper plane, as the newspapers played up the Zimmermann note to sensational effect, the president moved to the conclusion that the war was, indeed, a defense of democracy against autocratic German aggression.

In mid-March, German submarines sank five American vessels in the sea lanes to Britain. After agonizing over the probable consequences, the president prevailed on Congress to issue a declaration of war on April 6. No longer too proud to fight, Wilson accused Germany of "warfare against mankind." But he insisted that the destruction of Germany was not the U.S. goal. Instead, the United States fought to make the world "safe for democracy" and to "vindicate the principles of peace and justice" in which a reconstructed Germany would find a democratic place.

Wilson did not overlook the tragic difference between those lofty aims and the brutal means chosen to achieve them. He spoke despairingly to a friend just before his appearance before Congress. "Once lead this people into war, and they'll forget there ever was such a thing as tolerance. To fight you must be brutal and ruthless, and the spirit of ruthless brutality will infect Congress, the courts, the policeman on the beat, the man in the street." Wilson then set out to lead the fight for American ideals.

The Crusade for Democracy

Wilson embraced the war as a mission to rescue a troubled world. His high-minded and idealistic goals for American participation rallied leading progressives to his side. Progressives hoped that war would improve the quality of American life as well as free Europe from its bondage to tyranny and militarism. The American Expeditionary Force (AEF) that eventually carried two million troops to Europe, by far the largest military venture the United States had ever undertaken on foreign soil, was trained to be morally straight and knowledgeable about the civilization they were to save. Progressive enthusiasm also powered the mobilization of industrial and agricultural production. Unfinished items on the progressive agenda achieved success. Moreover, labor shortages provided new opportunities in the booming wartime economy. African Americans and women found work where once they had been excluded, and women also gained new respect and recognition for their wartime endeavors.

The crusade strove for loyalty from a general public whose ancestry was rooted in all the belligerent nations. Wilson favored democratic persuasion, and to instill loyalty he supported indoctrination in the schools, set up a government agency to promote official propaganda, and sponsored parades, rallies, films, and other forms of patriotic expression. But with commitment to patriotism also went suppression of dissent. The government launched a harsh assault on civil liberties. In addition, mobs assaulted those whom they considered disloyal. Increasingly, attachment to the war stressed emotion rather than reason. In the end, as Wilson predicted, the progressive ideal of rational progress and free expression suffered grievous loss as the nation undertook its crusade for democracy.

The Call to Arms

When the United States entered the war in April 1917, the nation was woefully unprepared. It was clear, however, that the Allies could win only with massive and swift American involvement in Europe. War-weary Britain and France were virtually exhausted after almost three years of conflict. Hundreds of thousands of British and French soldiers had perished in the trenches. Morale in the French army was so bad that troops in the rear were firing on troops who deserted the front. Food supplies were dangerously short. Russia was in turmoil: A democratic revolution had forced Czar Nicholas II's abdication in March 1917, and eight months later the Bolshevik Revolution removed Russia from the war. To meet the demand for fighting men, food, and war materiel, the United States would have to mobilize not only an army but its economy as well.

On May 18, 1917, Wilson signed a sweeping Selective Service Act, which transformed a tiny volunteer armed force of 80,000 men, spread thinly around the United States and outposts from the Caribbean to China, into a vast army and navy. In 1917, about half of the standing military forces manned coastal artillery batteries. The rest were tactical units bearing light weaponry. There were no heavy field artillery, tanks, or modern planes. But in just two months, more than 9 million men had registered for the draft. Although almost 350,000 inductees either failed to report or claimed conscientious objector status, the draft boards eventually inducted 2.8 million men into the armed services. Another 2 million volunteered. Almost half of the 4.8 million American military eventually served in Europe.

But first, training camps had to transform raw recruits into fighting men. Progressive reformers viewed the camps as laboratories where medical examinations, along with recently developed sociological and psychological techniques, could take the measure of American youth. The shocking news that almost 30 percent of those drafted were rejected on physical grounds acted as a crucial stimulus to the public health and physical education movements. Intelligence tests given to recruits yielded even more disheartening results. According to the data (which later proved flawed), 47 percent of all whites and 89 percent of all blacks were below the mental age of thirteen. Some analysts used these results as proof that the lower classes had little interest in education. Others concluded that they proved genetic differences between the races. So

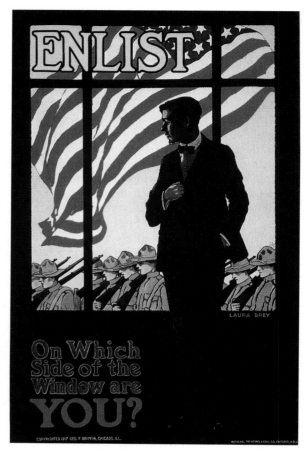

WORLD WAR I RECRUITING POSTER
Recruiting posters often appealed to young men's concerns about chivalry and manhood. One navy poster showed a uniform draped over a chair, with the words "It takes a man to fill it." In another, a provocative woman beckoned saying, "I want you . . . for the navy." In this poster, anxiety is the key. The fastidious appearance and somewhat languid pose of the worried civilian in his darkened interior contrasts with the bright, flag-filled outdoors of the marching troops. Of course, anyone with an ounce of spunk would go out and fall in line.
Library of Congress.

deep-seated was the cultural bias toward native-born middle-class white standards that it did not occur to the experts that farmers, factory workers, and recent immigrants might not be expected to notice that a net was missing from the picture of a tennis court or to know that mauve is a color.

Progressives in characteristically optimistic fashion accepted the dismal physical and mental data as an opportunity for improvement. Secretary of War Newton D. Baker, whose outlook had been shaped by reform crusades as mayor of Cleveland, created a Commission on Training Camp Activities staffed by YMCA workers and veterans of the settlement house and playground movements. They saw to it that military training merged with games, singing, and college extension courses. To further ensure a healthy environment, the Military Draft Act of 1917 prohibited prostitution and alcohol near training camps. Never before had there been such armed encampments, which Baker described in full progressive fervor as "national universities—training schools to which the flower of American youth is being sent." These "universities" taught recruits how to sing as well as to fight. They sought to provide the youthful crusaders with an "invisible armor" of education, comradeship, and moral fitness.

Wilson's selection of General John J. Pershing to command the new American Expeditionary Force recognized the need for hard professionalism in the lead, not the sort of romantic patriotism that had given amateurs like Theodore Roosevelt the chance to command combat troops in the Spanish-American War. Pershing had graduated from West Point in the 1880s and had seen combat in the Indian wars on the plains and against the Spanish in Cuba, where his command of black troops had earned him the nickname "Black Jack." Pershing's impeccable military bearing—erect, dignified, unflappable—enhanced his professional standing and gave promise that he would carry out his duties in the cool, efficient way required of modern war on a vast scale. Pershing's stoic fortitude had hardened to steel in 1915 when he learned that his wife and daughters had perished in San Francisco in a fire.

When Pershing and the wide-eyed troops of the AEF marched through Paris on the Fourth of July 1917, just a week after the first troopship landed, a grateful populace showered them with flowers. Even the impassive general was moved by the parade. "With wreaths about their necks and bouquets in their hats and rifles," Pershing recalled, "the column looked like a moving flower garden." At the statue of the hero who symbolized France's aid to the American Revolution, an officer stepped out and proclaimed in an inspired phrase that summed up the spirit of the occasion, "Lafayette, we are here!"

The Progressive Stake in the War

The idea of the war as an agent of social improvement fanned the old zeal and earnestness of the progressive movement. In particular, the war captivated progressives who were believers in strong government and who had been lukewarm about Wilson's cautious New Freedom. The Wilson administration realized that Washington would have to assert greater control to mobilize the nation's resources and to avoid chaos. To oversee the transformation of the economy, the administration established a multitude of new federal war agencies to deal with specific war needs.

The War Industries Board (WIB), created to direct and stimulate industrial production, was fortunate in the choice of Bernard Baruch to head it. Because he was at once a wealthy southern gentleman, a Jewish Wall Street stockbroker, and a reform Democrat, Baruch could speak to many constituencies. Shrewdly bullying and wheedling, he managed to weld scientists, industrialists, public administrators, and public relations experts into units that maximized production, limited waste, and delivered according to tight schedules. Efficient production of everything from boots to bullets made the American soldier the most fully equipped in the world, though it took time for the quality of his weaponry to catch up with that of the Europeans who had long fielded large armies.

Alongside Baruch's coordination of industry, Herbert Hoover, self-made millionaire engineer, headed the Food Administration. Sober and tireless, he led remarkably successful "Hooverizing" campaigns for conservation, with "wheatless" Mondays and "meatless" Tuesdays. By guaranteeing high prices for wheat, the Food Administration caused a dramatic increase in production. The American heartland not only supplied the needs of the American people and its armed forces but also became the breadbasket of America's allies, France and Britain. By planting fallow land, farmers provided feed to boost meat production from 640,000 tons to almost 3.5 million tons. The First Family, including Wilson's new wife, Edith Galt, joined countless others in answering the call to do their part. During the growing season, sightseers could gawk at the White House "victory garden" and the sheep munching the White House lawn in place of the gardeners, who had moved on to new work in the war effort.

Washington soon bristled with other hastily created agencies charged with managing the war effort. The Railroads' War Board directed railroad traffic, the Fuel Administration coordinated the coal industry and other fuel suppliers, the Shipping Board organized the merchant marine, and the National War Labor Policies Board resolved labor disputes. The administration gave progressives reason to believe that the new federal agencies would serve as mediating forces between business and government and encourage harmony in the public interest. Adding to the enthusiasm of industrial leaders was the fact that, while agencies often achieved greater production and efficiency, they also presided over the tripling of corporate profits, despite higher wartime taxes. Buoyed by these developments, influential voices like those of philosopher-educator John Dewey and journalist-critic Walter Lippmann argued for public support of the war as a means of progressive reform at home as well as abroad.

Reformers brought high expectations to the war and had cause to celebrate the way the less advantaged shared in some of the benefits. Full mobilization meant high prices for farmers and plentiful jobs in the new war industries.

The Wilson administration also devised shrewd and rousing strategies of raising the funds to pay for the war. No one could have guessed that the war would eventually cost the nation $33 billion (more than the federal government's total expenses from 1789 to 1917), but Secretary of the Treasury McAdoo, a witty and outgoing political operator

who also happened to be Wilson's son-in-law, deftly appealed to Americans to sacrifice through higher taxes. He also became the principal cheerleader for the purchase of war bonds, called Liberty Bonds. McAdoo's fund-raising, which included parades, posters, celebrity endorsements, and musical salutes, often left the line between patriotism and showmanship hard to discern, but it was wildly successful.

Reformers brought high expectations to the war and had cause to celebrate the way the less advantaged shared in some of the benefits. Full mobilization meant high prices for farmers and plentiful jobs in the new war industries. Reformers who had battled for workers' rights celebrated labor's gains. Increased industrial production required peaceful labor relations and the avoidance of strikes. The National War Labor Policies Board and other agencies, therefore, accepted the eight-hour day, a living minimum wage, and collective bargaining rights in industries that had long resisted them. Even merchant sailors, one of the most notoriously ill-treated groups throughout the nation's history, finally gained enough sympathy because of the submarine menace for Congress to legislate seamen's insurance and better working conditions. Wages rose sharply during the war, and the American Federation of Labor saw its membership soar from 2.7 million to over 5 million. Mobilization also aided the struggle to provide workers with insurance against injury on the job. After long resisting all efforts in this free en-

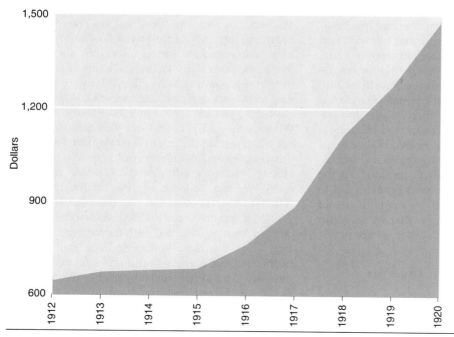

FIGURE 22.1
Industrial Wages, 1912–1920
With help from unions and Progressive reformers, wage workers gradually improved their economic condition. The entry of millions of young men into the armed forces caused labor shortages and led to a rapid surge in wages.

terprise area, Congress bowed to the patriotic cause of providing death and disability insurance for the armed forces.

The war also presented new opportunities for women. More than twenty thousand women served with the armed forces, a large number of them as nurses in France. In the private sector, long-standing barriers against hiring women fell when millions of workingmen became soldiers and few new immigrant workers succeeded in finding safe passage across the Atlantic. The growing presence of women in the war effort moved the government to create the Women's Bureau of the Department of Labor. This agency, along with the Women's Trade Union League (WTUL), helped open jobs to women, often against the opposition of the major trade organization, the American Federation of Labor (AFL). For the first time, women in sizable numbers found work with the railroads and in defense plants as welders and heavy machine operators. Some gained entry to labor unions, whose members usually earned far higher wages than nonunion workers. The future for women looked bright. "This is the women's age," exulted Margaret Dreier Robins, president of the Women's Trade Union League. "At last . . . women are coming into the labor and festival of life on equal terms with men."

In addition to gains in the workplace, women claimed victory in another arena. The struggle for woman suffrage dated back to the Seneca Falls convention of 1848, where women voiced their first formal demand for the ballot. But on the eve of the First World War, decades of grueling effort had produced only a few local victories. Using a state-by-state approach, suffragists had achieved success in Wyoming in 1890 and in several other western states in the following years, but elsewhere in the nation they met tremendous resistance and defeat. In New York, for example, suffragists waged a massive referendum campaign in 1915 for an amendment to the state constitution. In an attempt to canvass all of New York City's 661,000 registered voters, hundreds of women trudged up and down tenement stairs, visited shops and factories, and called at huge office buildings with their thousands of workers. Still, New York voters rejected woman suffrage resoundingly. Two years later in Ohio, suffragists succeeded in convincing the legislature to approve a bill that allowed women to vote in presidential elections, only to have opponents mount a petition drive that put the issue on the ballot, where a majority voted in favor of taking the vote away from women.

But riding a wave of wartime idealism and energized by increasingly militant tactics, the crusade for woman suffrage finally triumphed. Suffragists continued to struggle state by state, but they increasingly focused on the national level and on an amendment to the Constitution. Women's wartime service as nurses, factory workers, and patriotic vol-

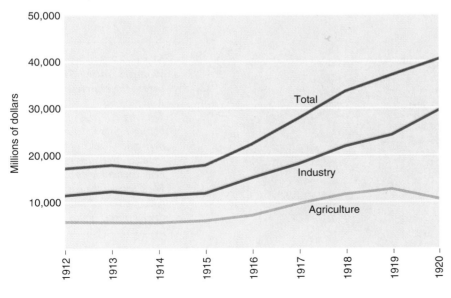

FIGURE 22.2
Manufacturing and Agricultural Income, 1912–1920
Following the postwar decline in demand for food and materiel, agriculture quickly fell into recession. Industry, spurred by new inventions and technologies, maintained a steady upward momentum.

Agriculture: cash receipts.
Industry: includes mining, electric power, manufacturing, construction, and communications.

unteers convinced many American men that women could shoulder public responsibilities. It would be wrong, Woodrow Wilson conceded, not to reward the "partnership of suffering and sacrifice" with a "partnership of privilege and right." Militant suffragists, such as Alice Paul, head of the new National Woman's Party, made it impossible for the nation to dodge the suffrage issue. Radical women picketed the White House. When they refused police orders to disperse, they were sent to jail, where they went on hunger strikes. In 1919, Congress passed the Nineteenth Amendment, granting woman suffrage, and by 1920 it had been ratified by the required two-thirds of the states and had become law. Looking back on the struggle, two suffrage leaders remarked: "How much of time and patience, how much work, energy and aspiration, how much faith, how much hope, how much despair went into it." To the women involved, "its success became a monumental thing."

Progressives found that the war provided a huge boost to another stalled campaign for a constitutional amendment. Before the war, progressives had campaigned widely against alcoholic beverages, and by 1917, nineteen states had gone dry. Liquor's opponents now claimed that America's success in the war rested on the national prohibition of liquor. Outlawing strong drink would make the cause of democracy powerful and pure, they claimed. Shutting down the distilleries would save millions of bushels of grain that could feed the United States and its allies. And taking aim at the nation's breweries, especially those with German names like Schlitz, Pabst, and Anheuser-Busch, would be a patriotic blow at Kaiser Wilhelm and the German cause. In December 1917, the Eighteenth Amendment, which banned the manufacture, transportation, and sale of alcohol, passed Congress. After ratification, the amendment went into effect on January 1, 1920.

The "Great Migration" of African Americans

In 1900, thirty-five years after emancipation, African Americans had made little progress toward achieving full citizenship. Nine of every ten African Americans were Southerners, and disfranchisement, segregation, and violence dominated their lives. The majority of black men still toiled in agriculture, either mired in the new servitude of tenancy or working for wages of sixty cents a day. Black women worked in the homes of whites as domestics for two dollars or less a week. Vicious racial violence descended on anyone whites considered "uppity." As the Vicksburg *Commercial Appeal* warned: "Don't monkey with white supremacy; it is loaded with determination, gun-powder, and dynamite." If blacks somehow managed to climb off the bottom, whites pushed them back down. "If we own a good farm or horse, or cow, or bird-dog, or yoke of oxen," a black Mississippian observed in 1913, "we are harassed until we are bound to sell, give away, or run away, before we can have any

Full voting with effective date

Partial voting rights for women (presidential vote in all; local, county vote in some)

No voting rights for women

MAP 22.3
Women's Voting Rights before the Nineteenth Amendment
The long campaign for women's voting rights reversed the pioneer epic — rolling eastward from its first successes in the new democratic openness of the West toward the entrenched male-dominated public life of the Northeast and South.

WOMAN SUFFRAGE

This cartoon sought to help the cause of woman suffrage by linking tradition with prejudice. Against the old-guard claim that the moral influence of women would decline if they became involved in the rough and tumble of politics, the woman racing toward the light escapes the spooky oppression of those who had claimed to be women's guardians.

Collection of Grunwald Center for the Graphic Arts, UCLA. Gift of Mr. and Mrs. Kenneth Chamberlain.

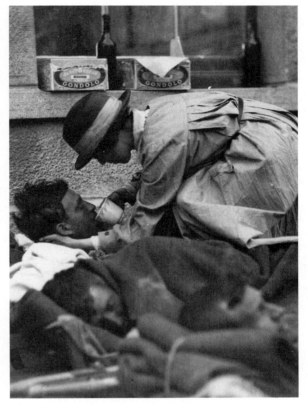

WORLD WAR I RED CROSS WORKER

An American Red Cross worker gives water to a badly wounded British soldier on a French railway platform in May 1918. More than twenty thousand women served with the armed forces, many of them as nurses in France.

National Archives.

peace in our lives." Southern blacks accommodated to what they could not change, but they looked for a way out.

The First World War provided African Americans with the opportunity to escape the South's cotton fields and kitchens. The labor shortage in northern industries during the war meant that blacks who were once welcome in the urban North only in personal service occupations now found work as unskilled and semiskilled industrial workers. Job opportunities were trumpeted by black newspapers like the militant Chicago *Defender* and by industrial recruiters who flooded the South looking for black workers. Young black men, who made up the bulk

of the migrants, found jobs in steel mills, shipyards, munitions plants, railroad yards, and mines. From 1915 to 1920, half a million blacks (approximately 10 percent of the South's black population) boarded trains bound for Philadelphia, Detroit, Cleveland, Chicago, St. Louis, and other industrial cities.

Blacks who joined the "great migration" were not just moving north. They were fleeing the South. In addition to jobs, they sought human dignity and personal freedom. The émigrés wrote letters that were read aloud in their home churches. One man announced proudly that he had recently been elevated to "first assistant to the head carpenter." "What's the news generally around Hattiesburg?"

What Did the War Mean to African Americans?

WHEN THE UNITED STATES ENTERED the First World War, some black leaders remembered the crucial role of African American soldiers in the Civil War. They rejoiced that military service would again offer blacks a chance to prove their worth. Robert Moton, president of the nation's foremost black college, Tuskegee Institute, recollected clearly when that thought had come to him. He was sitting in the midst of "dignified bankers [and] merchants" gathered in the Waldorf-Astoria hotel in New York City to promote the sale of Liberty Bonds. At that moment of patriotic inclusion, Moton "could not but feel that my people by their contribution, their loyalty, and their spirit . . . realized fully that they are heirs of America, and that as such they must be sharers of her struggles as well as partakers of her glory."

More surprising was the support for the war voiced by W. E. B. Du Bois. Known for his bold dissent against the white power structure, Du Bois shocked many readers with his editorial in the NAACP's journal the *Crisis*, urging blacks to "close ranks" and "forget our special grievances" until after a unified nation had won the war. The enemy of the moment, Du Bois insisted, was German "military despotism." Unchecked, that despotism "spells death to the aspirations of Negroes and all darker races for equality, freedom, and democracy."

Although critics bitterly assailed Du Bois for not demanding equal treatment for blacks who fought for their country, African Americans generally followed his advice and closed ranks. On the first day of registration for military service, July 5, 1917, more than 700,000 black men signed in at their draft boards. By war's end, 370,000 blacks had been inducted, some 31 percent of the total registered. The figure for whites was 26 percent.

During training, black recruits suffered the same prejudices that they had encountered in civilian life. Rigidly segregated, they were usually assigned to labor battalions. They faced crude abuse and miserable conditions. One base in Virginia that trained blacks as cargo handlers quartered troops in tents without floors or stoves and provided no changes of clothes, no blankets for the winter, or even facilities for bathing. Only several deaths from disease and exposure moved the authorities to make conditions barely tolerable.

When black soldiers began arriving in Europe, white commanders made a point of maintaining racial distinctions. A special report from the headquarters of the American commander, General John J. Pershing, advised the French that their failure to draw the color line threatened Franco-American relations. They should resist the urge, the report declared, to accept blacks as equals or to thank them for their efforts, for fear of "spoiling the Negroes."

Under such circumstances, German propagandists raised some painful questions. One leaflet distributed by the Germans to black troops reminded them that they lacked the rights that whites enjoyed and that they were segregated and were often lynched. "Why, then, fight the Germans," the leaflet asked, "only for the benefit of the Wall Street robbers and to protect the millions they have loaned to the British, French, and Italians?" Why, indeed?

Black soldiers hoped to prove a point. While they worked at first mainly as laborers and stevedores, before long they had their chance to fight. In February 1918, General Pershing received an urgent call from the French for help in the Meuse-Argonne sector. Reluctant to lose command over the white troops he valued the most, he sent black soldiers— the 369th, 370th, 371st, and 372nd Regiments of the 92nd Division—to the front, where they were integrated into units of the French army. In the 191 days spent in battle—longer than that spent by any other American outfit — the 369th Regiment won the most medals of any American combat unit, more than one hundred Croix de Guerre alone, and had no prisoners taken. In June 1918, the French high command paid its highest respect by asking the Americans to send all the black troops they could spare.

When the battle-scarred survivors of the 92nd Division returned home, they marched proudly past cheering crowds in Manhattan and Chicago. Black spokesmen proclaimed a new era for black Americans. In May 1919, Du Bois argued that it was time for African Americans to collect what was due them. "We return from fighting," Du Bois declared. "We return fighting. Make way for Democracy. We saved it in France, and by the Great Jehovah, we will save it in the U.S.A., or know the reason why."

Reasons soon presented themselves. Segregation remained entrenched, and its defenders con-

AFRICAN AMERICAN MACHINE GUN COMPANY
*This company from the 370th Regiment of the Illinois National Guard, shown early in their train-
ing, exemplifies the proud determination of black soldiers to prove their worth in battle. Once in
France, the 370th encountered resistance from American commanders reluctant to use combat-
ready black troops for anything but hard labor behind the lines. When desperation in the face of a
German offensive in the spring of 1918 gave them the chance to fight with French units, the
370th showed its mettle and received the Croix de Guerre. Adding to the irony of black soldiers
having to gain respect as Americans by serving with the French was the fact that the first black
soldier from Lincoln's state of Illinois to fall in battle was a private named Robert E. Lee.*
Picture Research Consultants and Archives.

tinued to hold power in Congress and in the White House. Postwar recession left blacks worse off economically than before their wartime glory and also made them scapegoats for white resentments. Whites launched race riots against blacks in two dozen cities. The willingness of blacks to stand their ground showed a more determined self-esteem, but it also meant more suffering from escalating violence. Nor did the armed services permanently offer new opportunities. Until the late 1940s, after the next world war, the American military remained segregated and almost devoid of black officers. Discrimination extended even beyond the ultimate sacrifice. When the organizers of a trip to France for parents of soldiers lost in the First World War announced that the boat would be segregated, black mothers felt honor-bound to decline the offer to visit the cemeteries where their sons lay.

It took decades for the nation to recognize the sacrifice and heroism of black soldiers in France. As one critic observed about the 92nd Regiment, "the example [they set] was so bright that most eyes closed against it." But in 1991, as the nation cheered American success in the Persian Gulf War, Americans began to see the light. A Defense Department investigating team, though insisting it had found no evidence of discrimination in the fact that none of the 127 Medals of Honor awarded during World War I had gone to blacks, declared that the time had come to correct an "administrative oversight." For leading a charge on September 28, 1918, up a German-held hill that cost him and 40 percent of his company their lives, Corporal Freddie Stowers would receive the Medal of Honor—until then the only one attained by an African American in the world wars. The slain soldier's elderly sister, who had survived seventy-three years to accept the award for her hero brother, could take solace that recognition came under the command of General Colin Powell, the first black chairman of the Joint Chiefs of Staff.

AFRICAN AMERICANS MIGRATE NORTH
This group of newcomers to a northern city in 1912 poses in its best dress on the threshold of a changed life. Several factors combined to prompt almost four and a half million African Americans to leave the South by midcentury. To the burden of racism was added the steady erosion of opportunities to make a living. In the 1920s many rural blacks lost work when a boll weevil invasion reduced the cotton crop drastically. Subsequently, mechanization and government programs to support crop prices by reducing acreage drove many more people off the land.
Schomburg Center for Research in Black Culture, New York Public Library.

he asked. "I should have been here 20 years ago. I just begin to feel like a man. It's a great deal of pleasure in knowing that you got some privileges. My children are going to the same school with the whites and I don't have to [h]umble to no one. I have registered—will vote the next election and there ain't any 'yes sir'—it's all yes and no and Sam and Bill." Whole churches, almost entire communities, sometimes transplanted themselves to northern cities. By 1930, for example, Chicago claimed nearly forty thousand black Mississippians, almost as many as Jackson, Meridian, and Greenville combined.

But blacks discovered that the North was not all milk and honey. As poor southern blacks poured into blighted northern slums looking for work and housing, they encountered a white backlash. To whites, fearful of losing jobs and status, the "great migration" looked more like a great invasion. They lashed out against the latest immigrants. In 1918, the nation witnessed ninety-six lynchings of blacks, some of them veterans still wearing their military uniforms. Race riots ripped two dozen northern cities. One of the worst occurred on a hot July night in 1917 in East St. Louis, Illinois. A mob of whites invaded a section of the city crowded with blacks who had been recruited to help break a strike. The

white attackers killed at least thirty-nine people and set a series of fires that left most of the black district in flames.

African Americans in the military also experienced racial violence. The most disastrous episode occurred in August 1917 when a group of armed black soldiers went to Houston, Texas, to avenge incidents of harassment by the police. In the clash that followed, thirteen whites, including several policemen, and one black soldier were killed. With vengeful swiftness that denied any appeal to the War Department, thirteen of the black soldiers were hanged and forty-one others sentenced to life imprisonment. Black leaders responded grimly that the incident demonstrated the tragic shortcomings of America's crusade for democracy.

Through it all, the hope for a better life kept the great black migration flowing northward. Although often disappointed with what they found, black émigrés rarely went back. As one man said in 1919: "When a man's home is sacred; when he can protect the virtue of his wife and daughter against the brutal lust of his alleged superiors; when he can sleep at night without the fear of being visited by the Ku Klux Klan . . . then I will be willing to return to Mississippi."

The Struggle over National Purpose

From the moment war broke out in Europe in 1914, Wilson's foreign policy had become a lightning rod for critics. Interventionists like Theodore Roosevelt hounded Wilson to abandon his announced policy of neutrality and to enter the war on the side of the British. Noninterventionists like William Jennings Bryan declared that Wilson's insistence on protecting American passengers on ships carrying war materials to England failed the neutrality test and could lead to war against Germany. When Wilson finally did commit the nation to war, most peace advocates rallied around the flag. The Carnegie Endowment for International Peace, for example, issued a resolution that "the most effectual means of promoting peace is to prosecute the war against the Imperial German Government" and adopted new stationery with the heading "Peace through Victory."

As prewar peace societies converted from pacifism to patriotism, a handful of new groups took up the cause of peace. As early as 1914, a group of professional women, led by settlement house leader Jane Addams and economics professor Emily Greene Balch, convened a group to resist what Addams described as "the pathetic belief in the regenerative results of war." The Women's Peace Party that emerged in 1915 and its foreign affiliates in the Women's International League for Peace and Freedom (WILPF) led the struggle to persuade governments to negotiate peace and spare dissenters from harsh punishment. It was discouraging, unpopular work. Participants were routinely labeled cowards and Communists, their efforts crushed by the steamroller of war enthusiasm. (See Texts in Historical Context, pages 870–872.)

Wilson's major strategy for fending off criticism of the war was to whip up patriotism with fervent flag-waving. To promote the cause and his leadership, in 1917 the president created the Committee on Public Information (CPI) under the direction of a progressive journalist, George Creel. Handsome and dynamic, Creel thumped for the war like an enthusiastic cheerleader at the big game. He sent "Four-Minute Men," a squad of 75,000 volunteers, around the country to give brief pep talks on the need to "make the world safe for democracy." His energetic team distributed millions of press releases that described successes on the battlefields and in the factories. But information and education slid easily into propaganda. The CPI created a stream of posters and cartoons that depicted brave American soldiers and sailors defending freedom and democracy against the evil Hun.

To help Creel's campaign, the film industry, then primarily a medium for working-class entertainment, sent movie stars to appear at fund-raising rallies. Hollywood cranked out reels of melodrama about battle-line and home-front heroes and gave audiences the chance to hiss at the German kaiser,

THE LIBERTY LOAN CHOIR
In promoting the war as a moral crusade, religion and patriotism often fused in the spirit of the popular hymn "Onward Christian Soldiers." On the steps of New York's City Hall in April 1918, the Liberty Loan Choir add their voices to the chorus of opera singers, movie stars, and political celebrities who were used throughout the war to rally the public to buy bonds to finance the war.
NA, US Army Signal Corps, AU, 1651, Paul Thompson.

PROPAGANDA POSTER

All the primal fears of rape, invasion, and violence at the hands of a monster wielding the weapon of "Kultur" are brought together in this 1916 scare poster. Germans so resented the dehumanizing portrait of themselves that in World War II, Nazi propagandists reproduced the poster with the warning that the poster had really been telling the American people to "destroy the German people."
Library of Congress.

otherwise known as "the Beast of Berlin" and "the Leper of Potsdam." For the more privileged, colleges and universities churned out war propaganda in the guise of scholarship and added courses designed to show the war as a culmination of the age-old struggle for civilization. Professor Samuel Harding of Indiana University declared that "if the teacher cannot conscientiously and wholeheartedly lend his influence to supporting the war with Germany, . . . he ought at least to keep silent." When Professor James McKeen Cattell of Columbia decided not to be quiet about his view that America should seek peace with

Germany short of victory, university president Nicholas Murray Butler arranged to get him fired. In a blunt summation of the campaign for patriotic conformity, Butler declared in his 1917 commencement address that "what had been folly is now treason." The university would not hesitate to purge "all who are not with whole heart and mind and strength committed to fight with us to make the world safe for democracy."

Encouraged thus by schools and government, a firestorm of anti-German passion swept the nation. Campaigns with the slogan "100% American" enlisted ordinary people eager to act as vigilantes sniffing out disloyalty and treason. German, the most widely taught foreign language in 1914, virtually disappeared from the high school and college curriculum. German-born Americans were ostracized, including Karl Muck, conductor of the Boston Symphony Orchestra, and the renowned violinist, Fritz Kreisler, who were driven from the concert stage. The rabid attempt to punish the enemy reached its extreme, however, with the lynching of Robert Prager in Collinsville, Illinois. In the atmosphere of mob rule, it was enough that Prager was German-born and had socialist leanings, even though he had not opposed American participation in the war. The defense lawyer for the drunken men who had beaten Prager and dragged him through the streets praised what he called a "patriotic murder." The local jury took only twenty-five minutes to acquit.

As hysteria increased, absurdity mingled with cruelty. In Montana, a school board barred a history text that had good things to say about medieval Germany. Menus across the nation changed German toast to French toast and sauerkraut to liberty cabbage. The fearful saw evidence of the enemy everywhere. One vigilant citizen claimed to see a periscope in the Great Lakes, and on the dunes of Cape Cod the fiancée of one of the war's leading critics was caught dancing and was held on suspicion of signaling to German submarines.

The Wilson administration took up the task of suppressing dissent with an eagerness that stood in ironic contrast to the army's commitment to defend democracy. The administration guided through Congress reckless legislation that went far beyond the legitimate goal of protecting the nation from espionage and sabotage. The Espionage Act (June 1917), the Trading with the Enemy Act (October 1917), and the Sedition Act (May 1918) gave the government sweeping powers to crush dissent. Among other things, the government could punish any opinion it considered "disloyal, profane, scurrilous, or abusive" of the American flag or uniform.

Two members of Wilson's cabinet, Attorney General Thomas Gregory and Postmaster General Albert Burleson, spearheaded the frenzy of repression. Both Texans, they had been active before the war in efforts to improve the lot of farmers, but after 1917 their antiforeign perspective and tendency to divide the world into friends and enemies moved them to crack down on dissent. Eventually, the government charged some fifteen hundred individuals with sedition. All but a dozen of them had merely spoken words the government found objectionable. Gregory also sponsored the American Protective League, made up of zealous private citizens, to carry out "slacker raids" against those thought to have avoided service or to have doubted official war aims. The league's net caught a carelessly accused mix of young men out of uniform and foreigners thought to be radical opponents of war. The vigilante spirit fomented several violent assaults against the Industrial Workers of the World (IWW), a radical union opposed to the war on grounds that it was capitalist exploitation of the workers who were forced to fight it.

Postmaster General Burleson, a zealot of such self-importance that Wilson dubbed him "the Cardinal," blocked mailing privileges for journals and books he personally considered disloyal. Burleson's suppression eventually hounded one of the leading literary journals, *Seven Arts,* out of business and intimidated another, the *Dial,* into removing Randolph Bourne, the most articulate voice against the war, from his editorial post. The Socialist Party, favored by Bourne and other rebellious young intellectuals, also came under attack for opposing the war. In a mortal blow, the party's leader, Eugene V. Debs, who had received almost a million votes for president in 1912, was convicted under the Espionage Act for speeches condemning the war as a capitalist plot and was sent to the Atlanta penitentiary.

Encouraged by schools and government, a firestorm of anti-German passion swept the nation.

At the center of the mounting hysteria, Wilson vacillated between backing repression, sometimes in strong language, and mildly protesting when his subordinates went to extremes. Though he had dreaded such a twist of fate, Wilson allowed his administration to evolve from the celebration of free expression characteristic of progressive reform to authoritarian insistence on loyalty to wartime goals.

ANTI-GERMAN SENTIMENT
Patriotic fervor during World War I condemned all things German — even in Cincinnati, long a center of German "Kultur." The photograph shows Dr. Ernst Kunwald, who had been driven from his post as conductor of the Cincinnati Symphony Orchestra in 1917, being escorted into custody as a prisoner of war.
War Department.

Even chief propagandist George Creel noted the sad disparity between the "great crusade" he promoted and some of the means being employed to force it on the nation.

Wilson hoped that national commitment to the war would subdue partisan politics. He could not legitimately repress his Republican rivals, however, and they found many opportunities to use the war as a weapon against the Democrats. The trick was to oppose Wilson's conduct of the war but not the war itself. For example, Republicans outshouted Wilson on the nation's need to mobilize for war but then complained that Wilson's War Industries Board was a tyrannical agency that crushed free enterprise. Republican attacks appealed to widely diverse business, labor, and patriotic groups. With each month of the war, Republicans gathered power against the coalition of Democrats and progressives that had narrowly reelected Wilson in 1916.

Wilson erred when he attempted to make the off-year congressional elections of 1918 a referendum on his leadership. His effort backfired, and he was roundly denounced for playing politics with the war. The Republicans gained a narrow majority in both houses of Congress. The end of Democratic control of Congress not only halted any possibility of further domestic reform but also meant that the United States would advance toward victory with authority divided between a Democratic presidency and a Republican Congress.

HELL

As the war dragged on, artistic visions of combat as a means to promote the war effort gave way to angry and despairing images of suffering. Georges Leroux was moved to paint this picture after seeing soldiers — alive and dead — illuminated by shell bursts at night in giant shell craters half full of water. He called the painting Hell *both because the landscape was horrifying, and because the scene resembled so closely traditional religious images of the inferno.*

L'Enfer (Hell), 1916 by Georges Paul Leroux (1877–1957), Imperial War Museum, London/Bridgeman Art.

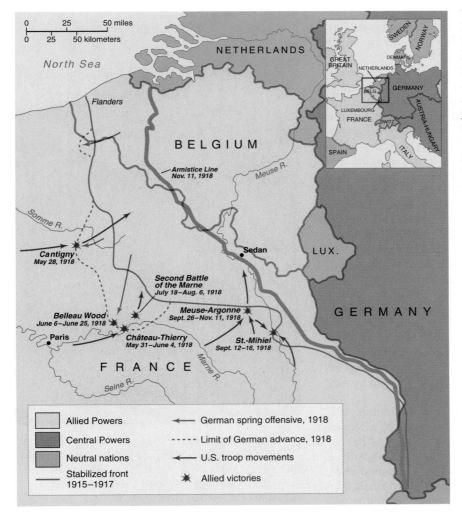

MAP 22.4
The American Expeditionary Force, 1917–1918
In the last year of the war, the American Expeditionary Force joined the French army on the western front to counterattack the final German offensive and pursue the retreating enemy until surrender.

Over There

As the struggle over leadership and aims unfolded at home, the American Expeditionary Force gathered strength in Europe. At the front, however, the AEF discovered a desperate situation. The three-year-old war had degenerated into a stalemate of armies dug defensively into mile upon mile of trenches snaking across France. Miserable, hollow-eyed soldiers huddled in the stinking mud, separated from the enemy only by a few hundred yards of "no-man's-land." When ordered "over the top," troops raced furiously toward the enemy's trenches, only to be entangled in vicious barbed wire and mowed down by machine guns and artillery. In 1915, Germany added poison chlorine gas to its lethal arsenal. Enormous casualties did not lead to decisive victories. At the Battle of the Somme in

1916, French and British forces lost 600,000 dead and wounded, while German losses reached 500,000. As a result, the French and British advanced their trenches a few muddy miles across devastated land.

General John J. Pershing, leader of the AEF, was appalled by what he saw. He was not about to commit his fresh new army of crusaders to the tactics of stalemate. The lessons that Civil War veterans had given him at West Point and his service in swift, mobile warfare on the plains and in Cuba left him permanently committed to what has been termed the "American way of war"—heavy frontal pressure through weight of numbers combined with swift surprise attacks on the flanks by infantry and cavalry. Pershing refused to allow his troops to merge with French and British units, despite the warning of the Allied commander in chief, General Ferdinand Foch, that a separate American command would leave the Allies dangerously uncoordinated. Pershing would, instead, save his soldiers for the moment when a series of lightning strikes might prove decisive.

In the best army fashion, then, American troops had hurried to France, only to wait. They saw almost no combat in 1917. But they were not exactly idle either. Young men who had never been far from home thought of going to France as a great adventure and carried with them all sorts of rumors about "Gay Paree." American officials did not object to some tourism, provided that it was high-minded and enlightened. Flustered officials quickly declined French Premier Georges Clemenceau's offer to supply American troops with licensed prostitutes. In only partly mock horror, Secretary of War Baker warned his deputy not to tell the president, "or he'll stop the war." Instead, the YMCA gave cultural tours, and servicemen used their unorganized moments to sightsee. Soldiers filled diaries and letters with serious attempts to explain what they had seen and done. Most often they expressed their awe at the antiquity of European society and the groomed landscapes they had seen before only in paintings. In contrast, their hosts, after three exhausting years of war, were most impressed by how the Yanks laughed and sang.

Sightseeing ended abruptly in March 1918 when the Germans launched a massive offensive aimed at French ports on the Atlantic. After six thousand cannons had let loose the heaviest barrage in history, a million German soldiers smashed a hole forty miles deep into the French and British lines west of the Somme River at a cost of a quarter of a million casualties on each side. Paris became gripped with the greatest terror of the war when shells fired eighty miles away by "Big Bertha" cannons began falling on the city. More than a thousand civilians died, and a mood of defeatism began to rise. Pershing, who had waited impatiently for months for a call to the front, visited Commander in Chief Foch to ask for the "great honor" of becoming "engaged in the greatest battle in history." Overcome, Foch agreed to Pershing's terms of a separate American command and in May assigned a combined army and marine force to the central sector.

Once committed, the Americans remained true to their way of war. At Cantigny and then at Château-Thierry, the fresh but green Americans checked the German advance with a series of dashing assaults. Then they headed toward the forest stronghold of Belleau Wood. The American force,

AVENUE OF THE ALLIES
Childe Hassam, the impressionist painter famous for his colorful portrayals of New York City, expressed his strong support of World War I through a series of paintings of flags draped along the "Avenue of the Allies" section of Fifth Avenue. This 1918 painting featuring French flags had great emotional impact on its viewers as American troops were fighting in France, helping to bring the war to a close. A French critic praised Hassam's uniquely American character: "No one had ever painted flags before; so now when one thinks of flags one thinks of Hassam's flag pictures. . . . He made the flags symbols of his heritage."
Musée National de la Cooperation Franco-Americaine © photo RMN-Jean.

with the Fifth and Sixth Marine Regiments in the lead, made their way against streams of refugees and retreating Allied soldiers who cried to them that the Germans had won: "*La guerre est finie!*—(The war is over)!" But when a French officer commanded the marines to turn and retreat with them, the Amer-

THE WORLD VICTORIOUS
This 1919 painting by Arthur Crisp was the center panel behind the speaker's platform on the
"Victory Way" parade route in New York City. The bold array of flags identifies the victorious
nations and projects a vision of postwar international unity of the sort the League of Nations
sought to establish.
Photography Collection, Miriam and Ira D. Wallach Division of Art, Prints and Photographs.
The New York Public Library.

ican commander replied sharply, "Retreat, hell. We just got here." After charging through a wheat field against withering machine gun fire, the marines plunged into a hand-to-hand forest battle of stalking and ambush. Victory came hard. On the single day of June 6, 1918, the marine spearhead lost 1,087 men, more than had been killed in the previous 143 years of Marine Corps history. In praise of the enemy's spirit, a German report noted that "the Americans' nerves are not yet worn out." Indeed, it was German morale that was on the verge of cracking.

In July 1918, the Allies launched a massive counteroffensive that would end the war. A quarter of a million American troops joined in the rout of German forces along the Marne River. In September, more than a million Americans joined the assault that threw the Germans back from positions along the Meuse River. American forces drove toward the town of Sedan, where the French had lost a war to Germany in 1870 and whose capture was thus of great symbolic importance. In early November, the Allies overran stubborn German resistance

around Sedan and sent the survivors trudging northward. Soon after, a revolt against the German government sent Kaiser Wilhelm fleeing to Holland. On November 11, 1918, a delegation from the newly established German republic met with the French high command in a railroad car in Compiègne to sign an armistice that brought the fighting to an end.

The adventure of the AEF was brief, bloody, and victorious—just the right combination to fix vivid memories of a successful crusade. When Germany resumed unrestricted U-boat warfare in 1917, it had gambled that it could defeat Britain and France before the Americans could raise and train an army and ship it to France. The German military had miscalculated. Of the 2 million American troops in Europe, 1.3 million saw at least some action. Some 112,000 soldiers of the AEF perished, their deaths divided equally between wounds and disease. Another 230,000 Americans suffered casualties but survived, many of them with permanent physical and psychological disabilities. Only the Civil War, lasting for a much longer period, had been

For and Against World War I

*W*orld War I became a battleground of loyalties as well as of guns. Through the Committee on Public Information (CPI), the Wilson administration developed the art of propaganda far beyond anything known before. The CPI promoted the war by organizing rallies and parades, blanketing the country with posters and cartoons, publishing a daily Official Bulletin, and mobilizing 75,000 volunteers to give speeches to hometown audiences. Only a few conscientious objectors, socialists, and disillusioned idealists were left to argue that war could not produce democracy but would instead destroy many lives and perhaps cherished values of progress and reform as well.

The Committee on Public Information recruited volunteers in local communities to carry the official version of the war directly to their neighbors. Called "Four-Minute Men" because their speeches were supposed to be only four minutes long, these enthusiasts spoke from carefully crafted scripts. The following example indicates how audiences were encouraged to buy war bonds by rousing their indignation against the Germans.

Document 1.
A "Four-Minute Man" Speech

While we are sitting here tonight enjoying a picture show, do you realize that thousands and thousands of Belgians, people just like ourselves, are *languishing in slavery* under Prussian masters? . . .

Prussian "Schrecklichkeit" (the deliberate policy of terrorism) leads to almost unbelievable besotten brutality. The German soldiers—their letters are reprinted—were often forced against their wills, they themselves weeping, to carry out unspeakable orders against defenseless old men, women, and children, so that *"respect"* might grow for German "efficiency." For instance, at Dinant the wives and children of 40 men were forced to witness the execution of their husbands and fathers.

Now, then, do you want to take the *slightest* chance of meeting Prussianism here in America?

If not, then you'll have to help in summoning all the resources of this country for the giant struggle. For resources will win the war.

Here's the way you can help save our resources. Instead of throwing money away on unnecessary things, buy Thrift Stamps, 25 cents, and War-Savings-Stamps, $4.12, worth $5 in five years, 4 percent compound interest. They're good as government money; like a mortgage on the U.S.A.

*T*o influence public opinion, the War Department enlisted journalists and professors to write a series of "war information pamphlets." In the following example, history professor John S. P. Tatlock of Stanford University describes the sort of invasion that could be expected if the German hordes were not checked.

Document 2. John S. P. Tatlock, "Why America Fights Germany," 1918

Now let us picture what a sudden invasion of the United States by these Germans would mean; sudden, because their settled way is always to attack suddenly. First they set themselves to capture New York City. While their fleet blockades the harbor and shells the city and the forts from far at sea, their troops land somewhere near and advance toward the city in order to cut its rail communications, starve it into surrender and then plunder it. One body of from 50,000 to 100,000 men lands, let us suppose, at Barnegat Bay, New Jersey, and advances without meeting resistance, for the brave but small American army is scattered elsewhere. They pass through Lakewood, a station on the Central Railroad of New Jersey. They first demand wine for the officers and beer for the men. Angered to find that an American town does not contain large quantities of either, they pillage and burn the post office and most of the hotels and stores. Then they demand $1,000,000 from the residents. One feeble old woman tries to conceal $20 which she has been hoarding in her desk drawer; she is taken out and hanged (to save a cartridge). Some of the teachers in two district schools meet a fate which makes them envy her. The Catholic priest and Methodist minister are thrown into a pig-sty, while the German soldiers look on and laugh. Some of the officers quarter themselves in a handsome house on the edge of the town, insult the ladies of the family, and destroy and defile the contents of the house. By this time some of the soldiers have managed to get drunk . . . and then hell breaks loose. Robbery, murder and outrage run riot. Fifty leading citizens are lined up against the First National Bank building, and shot. Most of the town and the beautiful pinewoods are burned, and then the troops move on to treat New Brunswick in the same way—if they get there.

This is not just a snappy story. It is not fancy. The general plan of campaign against America has been announced repeatedly by German military men. And every horrible detail is just what the German troops have done in Belgium and France.

True to her belief in reason, not force, the leader of the settlement house movement, Jane Addams, helped form the Women's Peace Party in 1915. Soon afterward Addams participated in the Hague Conference of Women in Holland and then, with a group of the delegates, visited the capitals of six warring nations to urge the leaders to those countries to seek peaceful resolution of the conflict. On July 9, 1915, Addams spoke to a New York City audience about the conclusions she had drawn from her tour of Europe.

Document 3. Jane Addams, Address at Carnegie Hall, New York City, July 9, 1915

The first thing which was striking is this, that the same causes and reasons for the war were heard everywhere. Each warring nation solemnly assured you it is fighting under the impulse of self-defense. . . .

In each of the warring nations there is this other point of similarity. Generally speaking, we heard everywhere that this war was an old man's war; that the young men who were dying, the young men who were doing the fighting, were not the men who wanted the war, and were not the men who believed in the war; that somewhere in church and state, somewhere in the high places of society, the elderly people, the middle-aged people, had established themselves and had convinced themselves that this was a righteous war. . . .

I quote a letter published in the *Cambridge Magazine* at Cambridge University and written by a young man who had gone to the front. . . .

" . . . Just when the younger generation was beginning to take its share in the affairs of the world, and was hoping to counteract the Victorian influences of the older generation, this war has come to silence us,—permanently or temporarily as the case may be. Meanwhile, the old men are having field days on their own. In our name, and for our sakes as they pathetically imagine, they are doing their very utmost, it would seem, to perpetuate, by their appeals to hate, intolerance and revenge, those very follies which have produced the present conflagration." . . .

It seemed to me . . . that the older men believed more in abstractions, shall I say; that when they talked of patriotism, when they used certain theological or nationalistic words, these meant more to them than they did to the young men; that the young men had come to take life much more from the point of view of experience . . . and when they went to the trenches and tested it out, they concluded that it did not pay, that it was not what they wanted to do with their lives.

Perhaps the most shocking impression left upon one's mind is this, that in the various countries the temper necessary for continuing the war is worked up and fed largely by the things which have occurred in the war itself. . . .

Let us say that there are two groups of boys in a boys' club, and I have much experience of that sort in boys' clubs to draw upon. If one says, "We did this because the other fellows did that," you will simply have to say, "I won't go into the rights and wrongs of this, but this thing must stop, because it leads nowhere and gets nowhere." . . .

. . . And what it needs, it seems to me, and to many of us, is a certain touch of human nature. . . . When you find that you can't talk to a woman on any subject, however remote from the war, without finding at once that she is in the deepest perplexity, —that while she is carrying herself bravely and going on with her accustomed activities because she thinks thereby that she is serving her country, her heart is being torn all the time,—it is borne in upon you that at last human nature must revolt. . . . Then men must see the horrible things which have happened; they will have to soberly count up the loss of life, and the debt they have settled upon themselves for years to come. . . .

Continued

Encouraged by civilian and military officials to make their crusade in Europe an enlightening experience, many soldiers recorded their impressions in diaries and letters. In the case of one anonymous soldier, the task became so absorbing that it eventually found its way into print as Wine, Women, and War: A Diary of Disillusionment *(1926). As time in combat dragged on, the diary changed its tone and looked critically at war aims and their probable outcome.*

DOCUMENT 4. Diary of an Anonymous American Soldier

25 August 1918: Base Hospital at Neuilly: Has the Lord ordained that from hideous mangling of flesh beautiful things should come? . . . Can't evade it—there is sublimity in war. Man made in mold of divinity, and more than a flavor of his origin still clinging to his soul. The cheer of these lads, their quiet grave resignation, too beautiful for marring touch of praise. . . .

One comes away from this eddy of human wreckage, a little sick at heart. But one presently forgets the bodies shattered, the faces marred, the freshness of lives become stale and useless, and remembers only that "God fulfills himself in many ways." The singular evangelism of blood. . . .

18 October 1918: Three hundredth day from Hoboken! Damned cold. Shivering, fingers numb as lead, and not even November yet. . . . Race between Kaiser and my pants still on. Vital interest in early termination of conflict! Each day another seam opens or another button drops from fatigue—and can't keep pants up by merely gritting teeth. Each morning, scan communiques first—then breeches. Strain beginning to tell.

After the war problems of readjustment, hitherto kept in background, going to make all sorts of trouble. League of Nations, not mere imaginative sentimental Utopia, but only practicable solution of world in chaos. . . . The real victors in this war will be determined 10 or 20 years afterwards, and they will be the nation who will be the best able to face the growing discontent of a disillusioned people, to ward off impending famine, and to save their people from the appalling consequences of the universal bankruptcy to which Europe is speeding every day with increasing pace.

Vast amount of nonsense about Germany. Silly idea of demanding huge indemnities, and in same breath refusing to allow access to raw material, i.e., ask tree to give fruit, but shut off sun and air. . . . Either slaughter entire Teutonic race, or take them back and try to make something of them. No middle ground. No sense hating Germans. Only proper object for hate, to anyone with brains God gave little snails, is an idea. And can't destroy ideas, or crush them, or punish them. Can only substitute good ideas for bad ones.

This life hard on illusions. Not many left. A hell of a way from best of all possible worlds, and man certainly a son-of-a-bitch when he puts his mind to it. But hope not to travel too far along road on which so many realists stub their silly toes, of believing there is no angel worth mentioning in poor, complex human heart. Heaven and hell both there.

Document 1. James R. Mock and Cedric Larson, *Words That Won the War* (Princeton, 1939), 123-124.

Document 2. John S. P. Tatlock, "Why America Fights Germany," War Information Series pamphlet no. 15, War Department, 1918.

Document 3. Jane Addams, "The Revolt against War" *Survey,* July 17, 1915.

Document 4. Anonymous, *Wine, Women, and War: A Diary of Disillusionment* (New York, 1926).

more costly in American lives. European nations suffered much greater losses, however: 2.2 million Germans, 1.9 million Russians, 1.4 million French, and 900,000 Britons died in the war. Where they had fought and died, the landscape was as blasted and barren as the moon. One grim jest made the telling point that the war would last one hundred years— four years of fighting and ninety-six more to roll up the barbed wire.

A Compromised Peace

Wilson decided to reaffirm his noble war aims by announcing his peace aims even before the end of hostilities was in sight. He hoped that America's allies would rally around his generous ideas. He soon discovered, however, that the worldwide popular appeal he enjoyed as the savior of Europe did not translate into ready acceptance of his plan for international democracy. The leaders of England, France, and Italy understood that Wilson's principles jeopardized their own postwar plans for the acquisition of enemy territory, new colonial empires, and reparations. In his effort to draw public opinion to his side, Wilson had to confront bitter political opposition at home as well as abroad. In the end, Wilson failed to convince the world's leaders to create a new world order based on democratic ideals, and he stood repudiated.

Wilson's Fourteen Points

On January 8, 1918, ten months before the armistice in Europe, President Woodrow Wilson delivered before Congress a speech that summarized U.S. war aims and provided his vision of a liberal peace. In his famous "Fourteen Points," Wilson provided a

THE BIG FOUR
Cynics who sought a glimpse behind the flags and victory parades suspected that the world war had been orchestrated by leading politicians, bankers, and industrialists for their own advantage. This cartoon was typical of the view that deals struck behind closed doors made a mockery of Wilson's profession that "open covenants of peace, openly arrived at" would "make the world safe for democracy."
Catherine LeRoy/AP, print courtesy Time Inc. Picture Collection.

blueprint for a new democratic world order. Echoes of his New Freedom and progressive thought reverberated as he eloquently spoke of a generous peace, a peace without vengeance, a peace that would transform the sordid, self-interested war into something permanently good and uplifting. Only if the war resulted in a peaceful and stable world could the American sacrifices be justified, he insisted.

Wilson's Fourteen Points provided a blueprint for a new democratic world order, affirmed basic liberal ideals, and supported the right of European peoples to self-determination.

Wilson's Fourteen Points dealt with broad principle as well as practical matters. The first five points affirmed basic liberal ideals: "open covenants of peace, openly arrived at," that is, an end to secret treaties; freedom of the seas in war and peace; removal of economic barriers to free trade; reduction of weapons of war; and recognition of the rights of colonized peoples. The next eight points supported the right to self-determination of European peoples dominated by Germany or its allies. Wilson's final point called for a "general association of nations"—a League of Nations—to provide "mutual guarantees of political independence and territorial integrity to great and small states alike." Wilson's insistence on a League of Nations reflected his lifelong dream of a "parliament of man." Only such an organization, he believed, could resolve and justify the war. Wilson concluded his speech by assuring Germany that the United States did not seek its destruction or humiliation. Instead, if it would renounce its militarism and imperialism, the United States would welcome Germany into the family of "peace-loving nations."

The Fourteen Points roused popular enthusiasm in the United States and every Allied country. Armed with such public support, Wilson felt confident that he could prevail against undemocratic forces at the peace table. During the final year of war, he pressured the Allies to accept the Fourteen Points as the basis of the settlement. Through a barrage of speeches and leaflets, Wilson conveyed his willingness, if necessary, to speak over the heads of government leaders directly to the people and so expand his presidential role as spokesman for American citizens to the grand role of champion of all the world's people. The Allies had won the war; Wilson would win the peace.

The Paris Peace Conference

Buoyed by his sense of mission, Wilson decided to attend the Paris peace conference in 1919 as head of the American delegation himself. The decision to leave the country at a time when his opponents were sharply contesting his leadership was risky in itself. But his stubborn refusal to include prominent Republicans in the delegation proved foolhardy. The ranking Republican on the Senate Foreign Relations Committee, the formidable Henry Cabot Lodge of Massachusetts, had never cared much for Wilson. Now he began to despise him. Ignoring his critics, Wilson set sail for Europe on the liner *George Washington*. He sought the great feat of converting skeptical, even cynical, Allies to his idealistic vision without having his own nation firmly behind him.

Still, the peace venture began well. As Wilson's motorcade made its way from the port of Le Havre to Paris, huge crowds cheered the American president. After four terrible years of war, men and women in Europe looked upon Wilson as a kind of savior, someone who would create a safer, more decent world.

When the peace conference convened at Louis XIV's magnificent palace at Versailles, however, Wilson encountered a very different reception. Representing the Allies were the decidedly unidealistic David Lloyd George of Britain, Georges Clemenceau of France, and Vittorio Orlando of Italy. To them, Wilson was a naive and impractical man who understood little about hard European realities. The Allies wanted to fasten blame for the war on Germany, totally disarm it, and make it pay so dearly for the destruction it had wrought that it would never be able to threaten its neighbors again. The French, in particular, upon whose soil most of the fighting was waged and who suffered an enormous loss of young manhood, demanded retribution in the form of territory and assurances that the German attack of 1914 would never be repeated.

Wilson was forced to measure success in inches, each small victory the product of tough negotiations and often unsavory compromise. He persuaded the Allies to agree that Germany would not be dismembered. Although France recovered Alsace-Lorraine, which Germany had won in the Franco-Prussian War of 1871, it did not gain additional German territory. Still, Germany's Rhineland was demilitarized and the mineral-rich Saar region was placed under international control, with France having the right to work the coal mines until an election after fifteen years would determine which nation the people of

the region would join. In return for French moderation of their territorial claims, Wilson agreed to support Article 231 of the peace treaty, assigning war guilt to Germany, and to endorse the concept of German repayment for damage to civilian property. Germany was outraged at being singled out as the instigator of the war and saddled with more than $33 billion in damages. Although the United States decided to waive its share of the reparations, the Germans felt betrayed by Wilson, who they believed had falsely promised that the peace terms would be based on his generous Fourteen Points.

Among the most pressing questions was where to draw national boundaries. Wilson proposed that dependent emerging nations, called mandates, would develop into democratic states under the guidance of the League of Nations, which would assign the mandates to small nations that had retained their virtue by not creating colonial empires. He gained considerable agreement on the principle of self-determination, though Italian ambitions to acquire coastal regions of the Balkans along the Adriatic Sea and French demands for Alsace-Lorraine had to be appeased. In applying democratic principles of self-determination, the conference redrew the map of Europe. Portions of the Austro-Hungarian Empire were ceded to Italy, Poland, and Romania, and the remainder reassembled into Austria, Hungary, Czechloslovakia, and Yugoslavia—independent republics with boundaries determined according to concentrations of ethnic groups. More arbitrarily, the Ottoman Empire was carved up into small mandates (including Palestine) under the control of France and Great Britain, partly to meet Allied concerns about stability in the Middle East and partly in accord with historical patterns of national sovereignty. Thus, with varying degrees of danger from ethnic and nationalist rivalries, each reconstructed nation faced the challenge of trying to make a new democratic government work.

Wilson hoped that Germany's colonies in Asia and Africa would be turned over to the League of Nations as mandates and either granted independence or ruled temporarily by smaller, nonimperialist nations. The Allies had other ideas. They had taken control of the colonies during the war, and they planned to keep them. A compromise left the colonies in the major powers' hands, but they agreed that the League of Nations would help administer them through the mandate system. Technically, the mandate system rejected imperialism. Yet it smacked of the old imperialist ways and drew

MAP 22.5
Europe after World War I
The post–World War I settlement redrew boundaries to create new nations based on ethnic groupings. This left bitter peoples within defeated Germany and Russia who resolved to recover territory that the new arrangements took from their homelands.

criticism from reformers and those who had suffered domination by the Western powers.

Adding to the taint was the refusal of the peace conference to endorse the proposal of Japan, an Allied nation during the war, for a clause proclaiming the principle of racial equality. Wilson's belief in the superiority of whites, as well as his apprehension about how Americans would respond to such a declaration, led him to oppose the clause. To soothe hurt feelings, Wilson agreed to grant Japan a mandate over the Shantung Peninsula in northern China, which had formerly been controlled by Germany. The gesture mollified Japan's moderate leaders, but the military faction getting ready to take over the country remained bitter about Western colonialism and racial prejudice.

Revolutionary changes that had taken place in Russia during the war intensified and confused certain key issues. In March 1917, after terrible defeats in the war, Czar Nicholas II was forced to abdicate, and reformers announced a new democratic era. To Wilson, who was just then leading his country into war, the Russian Revolution seemed to confirm his hopes that democracy would rise from the ashes of destruction. In reckless enthusiasm, Wilson declared that Russia had always been "democratic at

heart." With the autocracy gone, he continued, "the great, generous Russian people have been added in all their naive majesty and might to the forces that are fighting for freedom." A very different reality soon emerged, however. Appealing to a widespread desperation in Russia to leave the war, a group of Marxist radicals calling themselves Bolsheviks seized control of the nation in November 1917 and made their leader, Vladimir Ilyich Lenin, total ruler of the revolutionary state that came to be known as the Soviet Union. On December 15, 1917, Lenin concluded an armistice with Germany. To make matters worse for Wilsonian idealists, Lenin insisted that the war was being fought not for democracy but to extend the power of capitalist nations. Outraged by what he considered the Bolsheviks' betrayal of the Russian Revolution, Wilson reacted as he had to the Mexican revolution by refusing to recognize the new Russian government.

Respect for self-determination kept Wilson from agreeing with his British ally Winston Churchill that "the Bolshevik infant should be strangled in its cradle" by direct military action. The president did agree, nonetheless, to send fourteen thousand troops in September 1918 to join British and French forces in Siberia. Officially, the military mission was only to safeguard the movement of British war materiel and a contingent of Czech soldiers to the western front; but in addition, Allied troops assisted the so-called White Army, loyal to the deposed czar, in trying to overthrow Lenin and annul the Bolshevik Revolution. Wilson finally withdrew the expedition in April 1920 but continued to oppose Lenin's regime. Public opinion divided significantly in the face of these momentous events. A few observers were inspired by the Russian Revolution to believe that the war had created possibilities for suffering millions throughout the world to overthrow the tyrants who had oppressed them. Most Americans, however, saw the outcome as evidence that the cause of democracy had fallen short and left the world full of radical menace. The decision of subsequent American administrations to continue withholding recognition of the Soviet Union until 1933 indicated how deeply Americans disapproved of communism and everything that seemed tainted with its radical, alien mark.

Despite his many frustrations, however, Wilson gained what he most wanted at Versailles—acceptance of the League of Nations. He considered the league, an international organization designed to promote peace, as the cornerstone of international order, a forum for the nations of the world to solve their common problems. Wilson envisioned the league actively stopping aggression, pursuing disarmament, and protecting freedom of the seas and free trade. If necessary, it could invoke economic and even military sanctions against aggressor nations. Wilson realized the shortcomings of the treaty that the Allies were hammering out at Versailles, but he hoped that the league could remedy the imperfections born of compromise. Moreover, he knew that the postwar world was a precarious place, beset with national and ethnic rivalries, psychological wounds, and shattered economies and societies. The league, Wilson believed fervently, would provide peace its strongest ally.

To many Europeans and Americans whose hopes had been stirred by Wilson's lofty aims, the Versailles treaty came as a bitter disappointment. Wilson's admirers were shocked that the president dealt in compromise, like any other politician. But compromise and concession were inevitable. And without Wilson's presence, the treaty that was signed in the Hall of Mirrors at Versailles on June 28, 1919, would surely have been more vindictive. Wilson returned home in July 1919 convinced that the treaty he carried was the best obtainable.

The Fight for the Treaty

The tumultuous reception Wilson received when he arrived home persuaded him that the American people supported the treaty as well as American membership in the League of Nations. But the people would not vote on the treaty. The United States Senate would. Exhausted by six months of wrangling at Versailles, Wilson returned to Washington grimly determined to win the two-thirds vote needed for Senate approval.

On July 10, 1919, Wilson submitted the treaty to the Senate, warning that failure to ratify it would "break the heart of the world." But by then, news of the treaty's provisions had spread, and criticism was mounting. The most raucous voices raised against it were those of Americans still concerned about their countries of ethnic origin. German Americans complained that forcing Germany to pay heavy reparations and lose territory meant that the Fatherland was being blamed for a war that was really caused by many national rivalries. Italian Americans protested Wilson's refusal to cede more territory on the Adriatic coast to Italy. Irish Americans deplored Wilson's failure to follow his principle of self-determination by supporting the independence of Ireland from British rule. Even Wilson's liberal supporters worried that the president's concessions at Versailles had jeopardized the treaty's capacity to provide a generous plan for rebuilding Europe and guarantee the peace.

The treaty's most potent critics were found in the U.S. Senate. After the election of 1918 had given Republicans a slight edge over Democrats, forty-nine to forty-seven, a group of Republican "irreconcilables," which included such powerful senators as Hiram Johnson of California and William Borah of Idaho, condemned the treaty for entangling the United States in world affairs. They favored a return to the tradition of noninvolvement. A larger group of Republicans did not object to U.S. participation in world politics but feared that membership in the League of Nations would jeopardize the nation's independence in foreign affairs. No Republican, moreover, was eager to hand Wilson and the Democrats a foreign policy victory with the 1920 presidential election little more than a year away.

At the center of Republican opposition was Wilson's archenemy Senator Henry Cabot Lodge of Massachusetts. A spare man of sixty-nine whose piercing eyes and pointed beard gave him a slightly satanic look, Lodge found many reasons to loathe

WOODROW WILSON
An exhausted Wilson shows the flag in San Francisco during his 1919 cross-country tour to rouse support for the Versailles treaty. Reaction on the West Coast was mixed. Bitter labor unrest brought hecklers into the San Francisco crowds; before that, in Seattle, where a general strike had recently been crushed, the IWW lined the streets with protesters who stood in stony silence as the rattled president drove by. A week after this photograph was taken, a stroke felled Wilson and brought this mission to an end.
UPI/Bettmann Archive.

Wilson, personal pride prominent among them. Before Wilson had entered politics, Lodge, with his Ph.D. and historical publications, had become known as "the Scholar of the Senate." It rankled Lodge to be eclipsed by a rival of greater intellectual eminence who had also risen above him politically to become president. In the midst of one argument with the administration, Lodge exclaimed: "I never expected to hate anyone in politics with the hatred I feel toward Wilson." The enmity between the two men was especially acute over foreign policy. Lodge was no isolationist. Like his friend Theodore Roosevelt, who had died in January 1919, Lodge expected the United States' economic might and strong army and navy to propel the nation into a major role in world affairs. But Lodge insisted that mem-

bership in the League of Nations, which would require collective action to maintain the peace, threatened the nation's freedom of choice in foreign relations.

To undermine public support of the treaty, Lodge used his position as chairman of the Senate Foreign Relations Committee to air every sort of complaint. Out of the committee hearings came several "reservations," or amendments, that sought to limit the consequences of American membership in the league. For example, several reservations required approval of both the House and the Senate before the United States could participate in league-sponsored economic sanctions or military action. Eventually, it became clear that ratification of the treaty depended on acceptance of the Lodge reservations. Democratic senators, who overwhelmingly supported the treaty, urged Wilson to accept the reservations, arguing that they left the essentials of the treaty intact. Wilson, however, insisted that the reservations amounted to a "nullification" of the treaty. "*Lodge* reservations?" he thundered. "Never! I'll never consent to adopt any policy with which that impossible name is so prominently identified."

Whether American membership could have prevented another war in Europe in 1939 is debatable, but America's failure to join the League of Nations certainly left it a much weaker institution.

With the treaty about to be reported from the Foreign Relations Committee to the full Senate with reservations attached, Wilson decided to take his case directly to the people. On September 3, 1919, he set out by train on the most ambitious speaking tour ever undertaken by a president. Always uncomfortable with stump speaking and warned by his doctors that his health would not stand the strain, Wilson nevertheless became more eloquent, more forceful each week. But in Pueblo, Colorado, on September 25, just as his appeal seemed to be gaining momentum, Wilson collapsed and had to return to Washington. There he suffered a massive stroke that partially paralyzed him. From his bedroom, Wilson sent messages through his wife and cabinet instructing Democrats in the Senate to hold firm against any and all reservations. In the end, Wilson commanded enough loyalty to ensure a vote against the Lodge reservations. But his victory in that battle cost him the war. When the treaty came up for a vote in the Senate in March 1920, the combined opposition of the Republican irreconcilables and Republican reservationists left Wilson six votes short of the two-thirds majority needed for passage.

The nations of Europe went about organizing the league at Geneva, Switzerland, but the United States never became a member. Whether American membership could have prevented another war in Europe in 1939 is debatable, but America's failure to join certainly left the league a much weaker institution. Brought low by their feud, Woodrow Wilson and Henry Cabot Lodge both died in 1924, never seeing international order or security, never knowing the whirlwind that would eventually follow the failure to make the world safe for democracy.

Postwar Change

The defeat of Wilson's idealistic hopes for international democracy was the crowning blow to progressives at home who had hoped that the war could serve as a vehicle for reform. The reaction against idealism included an urge to demobilize swiftly. In the process, servicemen, defense workers, and farmers lost their connection to national purpose and much of their economic security. The combination of displaced veterans returning home, a stalled economy, and leftover wartime patriotism looking for a new cause was so volatile that it could hardly fail to explode. The American people moved toward the view that the main benefit of victory in the war had been to protect the nation against alien menace. It followed that postwar policy should strive to root out similar enemies at home, especially supporters of the Bolshevik Revolution in Russia. Then the country could move from wartime sacrifice to the normal pursuits of wealth and happiness.

Economic Hardship and Labor Upheaval

With news of the armistice came the need to convert the United States back to a peacetime economy. The impulse to end the wartime experiment in government-business cooperation, dismantle the federal agencies responsible for war production, and return to the hallowed traditions of free enterprise proved irresistible to economic and political leaders. Deconversion of the economy and demobilization of the armed forces came swiftly and was largely unplanned. The government simply abandoned its wartime controls on the economy and almost overnight canceled millions of dollars in orders for war materiel. In a matter of months, more than three million soldiers were mustered out of the military with only sixty dollars and a one-way ticket home. When war production ceased and veterans flooded the job market, unemployment rose sharply. At the same time consumers went on a postwar spending spree, and inflation soared. In 1919, prices rose an astonishing 75 percent over prewar levels, and in 1920, while inflation slowed, prices rose another 28 percent.

Labor had enjoyed a share of wartime prosperity, but most of the gains for workers evaporated in the postwar period. Business, freed from control and eager to restore the more favorable position it

After the Welcome Home— a JOB!
U.S. EMPLOYMENT SERVICE *Dep't of Labor*

RETURNING VETERANS AND WORK

After the triumphal parades passed by, attention turned to the question of what the heroes would do at home. The Department of Labor poster tries to convey a strong image of purposefulness and prosperity by framing a soldier in a victory arch in front of a booming industrial landscape. Under the circumstances, though, the soldier can best be regarded as a displaced person, teetering on a windowsill, dangerously high in the air. The U.S. Employment Service had little to offer veterans beyond posters such as this; and unions were unprepared to cope with the massive numbers of former soldiers who needed retraining. As workplace conditions deteriorated, the largest number of strikes in the nation's history broke out in 1919. The Chicago steel strikers in the photograph look very different from the returning soldier in the poster. Their fate was to lose the strike and return to harsh conditions. No record was kept of ex-servicemen, left to find their own way in the postwar world.

Library of Congress; UPI/Bettmann Archive.

held before the war, turned against the eight-hour day and declared war on labor unions. Rather than sit back and watch inflation eat up their paychecks and bosses destroy their unions, labor fought back. The year 1919 witnessed nearly 3,600 strikes involving four million workers.

In February 1919, a spectacular strike in the Northwest vividly demonstrated the depth of workers' discontent. In Seattle, large numbers of metalworkers and shipbuilders had been put out of work by demobilization. A coalition of two labor organizations—the radical Industrial Workers of the World (IWW) and the moderate American Federation of Labor (AFL)—called a general strike. The strike, the largest in American history, shut down the city for several days. Nationwide, elected officials and newspaper editorials echoed claims in the Seattle *Times* that the walkout was "a Bolshevik effort to start a revolution" engineered by "Seattle labor criminals." An effort to deport strike leaders failed because they were citizens, not aliens, but the suppression of the general strike by Seattle's anti-union mayor, Ole Hanson, and widespread alarm about radicalism cost the AFL much of the support it had gained through its wartime service and contributed to the destruction of the IWW soon afterward.

The ominous linkage of labor unrest and radical subversion reflected the Wilson administration's encounter with revolutionary socialism. Since the late nineteenth century, refugees from autocratic regimes in Europe had flocked to America, often bringing with them radical ideas about replacing private ownership of the means of production with a welfare state controlled by the working class. Socialists had played only a minor part in the progressive debate about how the United States should be reformed, but they had irked Wilson by challenging his New Freedom ideal of decentralized democracy. Under the pressures of socialist and Bolshevik denunciation of the war, Wilson's antagonism slid easily into the conviction that his radical critics were a subversive menace.

The outcome of a strike for higher pay by Boston policemen in the fall of 1919 also demonstrated rising postwar hostility toward labor militancy. Without police walking their beats, looters sacked the city. After two days of near anarchy, Boston's mayor fired the police force and began hiring new officers. The mayor had the approval of the Massachusetts governor, Calvin Coolidge, who gained national fame by calling out the National Guard to restore order. The public, frightened by news of radicalism abroad and yearning for peace and quiet at home, was grateful for Coolidge's reassurance that "there is no right to strike against the public safety by anybody, anywhere, any time."

Labor suffered an even more serious blow in the defeat of a widespread steel strike in 1919. Steelworkers had serious grievances, but for decades the steel industry had succeeded in beating back all their efforts to unionize. In 1919, however, the AFL, still led by its founding father, Samuel Gompers, caught wind of the steel industry's plan to renew the oppressive prewar system of seven-day weeks and twelve-hour days for weekly wages of about twenty dollars. Having loyally supported the government's war effort, the AFL expected federal support for its effort to unionize steelworkers. When Gompers began to recruit union members, however, he learned that he faced the steel barons alone. Elbert Gary, director of U.S. Steel, and Charles Schwab, his counterpart at Bethlehem Steel, announced that they would not negotiate a contract with the AFL. Gompers called for a strike, and 350,000 workers in fifteen states responded by walking out in September 1919.

Denying that the workers had legitimate complaints, the steel industry hired 30,000 strikebreakers (many of them African Americans) and turned public opinion against the strikers by portraying them as Bolsheviks bent on subverting the Republic. State and federal troops blocked an effective response by the union by keeping striking members from getting close to the steel mills and discouraging scabs from crossing their picket line. In January 1920, after 18 workers had been killed, the strike collapsed. The failure in the steel industry initiated a sharp decline in the fortunes of the labor movement, a trend that would last throughout the 1920s.

The steel strike offered dramatic testimony to the continuation of a nasty wartime development. To whip up popular enthusiasm for the defense of the American heritage, government and private propagandists had demonized the nation's enemies, transforming, for example, Germans into evil Huns. The steel barons took advantage of Americans' suspicion and hatred of foreigners by pinning the label Red, or Communist, on the strikers, many of whom were recent immigrants from the much hated Austro-Hungarian Empire. The leader of the steelworkers' union within the AFL, William Z. Foster, though born in the slums of Philadelphia, had once been a member of the IWW. As such, and for having uttered the conviction that the government represented capitalist oppression, he was lumped in with "dangerous" foreign radicals.

A new organization for veterans of the war, the American Legion, played an important role in the controversy over bolshevism, patriotism, and security. The organization provided a peacetime identity for veterans, with a name that harked back to the Roman ideal of a vigilant citizenry permanently ready to defend against the enemies of the state. Initially, the American Legion responded to the fact that, after the parades had ended for the two million American troops who returned from Europe, the veterans were left to make their way in an uncertain world. To assist them, the Legion persuaded Congress to award veterans' bonuses and create a Veterans' Bureau to provide medical care and other benefits. But the Legion's sense of patriotic service, expressed by its motto, "For God and Country," also included taking action against individuals and groups that showed disloyalty toward established institutions. In the struggle to maintain order and quell radical dissent, the Legion proved to be a potent weapon.

The Red Scare

In 1919–1920, fear of internal subversion swept the nation. The "Red scare" of that time far outstripped the hysteria, violence, and systematic denial of civil liberties during the war. This sad episode stemmed in part from the severe stresses and strains in American society, including the postwar recession, labor unrest, and the return of millions of veterans. But unsettling events abroad also added to Americans' anxieties. The victory of the Bolsheviks in Russia, itself disturbing, became even more menacing in March 1919 when the new Soviet leaders created the Third International to foment revolution in capitalist countries. The chance of a Communist revolution in the United States was zero, but a flurry of isolated terrorist acts in 1919 made it seem to edgy Americans that revolutionaries were at the door. Thirty-eight mail bombs were sent to prominent Americans, including Supreme Court Justice Oliver Wendell Holmes and financier J. P. Morgan Jr. The post office intercepted all but one of the bombs, but that one blew off the hand of the maid of a Georgia senator.

Fear and anger, mingled with bafflement over how to understand the motives of terrorists, led swiftly to a hunt for scapegoats. Middle-class Americans had long stigmatized immigrants as radicals. Business had stereotyped labor organizers as subversives. And most Americans identified socialists and others on the political left as dangerous to the

Republic. In 1919 and 1920, Attorney General Thomas Gregory and his successor, A. Mitchell Palmer, helped galvanize the nation's prejudices into an all-out assault on alleged conspirators. To protect the country from "Bolshevik tyranny," Mitchell decided that "there could be no nice distinctions drawn between the theoretical ideals of the radicals and their actual violations of our national laws." Targeting men and women who had broken no laws but who harbored what Mitchell considered dangerous thoughts, the Justice Department unleashed a witch-hunt against the supposed enemies of America.

> *The chance of a Communist revolution in the United States was zero, but a flurry of isolated terrorist acts in 1919 made it seem to edgy Americans that revolutionaries were at the door.*

In January 1920, Palmer ordered a series of raids that netted six thousand suspected subversives. He expected to discover plans for revolution and caches of weapons. Three pistols did not constitute a revolutionary armory, but Palmer nevertheless ordered five hundred of the suspects deported. Catching the spirit of the occasion, one Protestant minister suggested that the "Reds" should be sent away on ships of stone, with sails of lead, the wrath of God at their backs for a breeze and the port of hell for their destination. Government officials had already deported the country's most notorious radical, the Russian immigrant Emma Goldman. Before the war, Goldman's passionate support of labor strikes (including the Homestead lockout), women's rights, and birth control had made her a leading symbol of subversion and outspoken disrespect for mainstream opinion. During the war, she attacked conscription and earned a stay in prison. Her activities caught the eye of the fervent young director of the Radical Division of the Justice Department, J. Edgar Hoover, who targeted her for deportation. In December 1919, officials loaded Goldman and 250 other unwanted alien radicals on a ship for exile in the Soviet Union. When a jeering bystander yelled "Merry Christmas, Emma!," the unchastened rebel turned, thumbed her nose, and disappeared from the deck. A lawyer, commenting on her departure, noted, "With Prohibition coming in and Emma Goldman goin' out, 'twill be a dull country."

The effort to rid the country of alien radicals was matched by efforts to crush those entitled to remain. The climax was reached on Armistice Day, November 11, 1919, in Centralia, Washington. A rugged lumber town, Centralia contained one of only two IWW halls left in the state. Rumors circulated that the hall would be raided on the first anniversary of the end of the war. When members of the local American Legion post gathered in front of the hall, nervous IWW members fired into their ranks, killing three Legionnaires. Several union members were captured and later convicted of murder, but one, Wesley Everest, an ex-soldier, was tortured, castrated, and hung from a bridge, where his body was riddled with bullets. The coroner ruled the death a suicide, his report stating that Everest "jumped off [the bridge] with a rope around his neck and then shot himself full of holes." The incident roused other law enforcement officials to conduct raids to rid their cities and towns of "Reds."

Public institutions of all kinds joined the attack on civil liberties. Local libraries removed dissenting books. Schools and colleges fired unorthodox teachers. Police shut down radical newspapers. State legislatures refused to seat duly elected representatives who professed socialist ideas. In 1919, Congress removed its lone Socialist representative, Victor Berger, on the grounds that he was a threat to national safety. And that same year, the Supreme Court provided a formula for restricting the exercise of free speech. In upholding the conviction of Socialist Charles Schenck for publishing a pamphlet urging resistance to the draft during wartime (*Schenck v. United States*), Justice Oliver Wendell Holmes for the Court established a "clear and present danger" test. Such utterances as Schenck's during a time of national peril, Holmes wrote, could be considered the equivalent of shouting "Fire!" in a crowded theater. Congress had the right to protect the public against such an incitement to panic, the Court ruled. But the analogy was a false one. Schenck's pamphlet echoed faintly in the open air, not in a crowded theater, and had little power to provoke a public firmly opposed to its message.

In time, the relentless cries of Attorney General Palmer and other government leaders that the Communists were coming lost credibility. The lack of any

real radical menace became clear after newspaper headlines carried Palmer's warning that radicals were planning to celebrate the Bolshevik Revolution with a nationwide wave of violence on May 1, 1920. Palmer supplied all federal buildings with armed guards. Throughout the nation, officials responded by calling out state militia, fortifying public buildings and churches, mobilizing bomb squads, even putting machine gun nests at major city intersections. When May 1 came and went without a single disturbance, the public mood turned from fear to scorn, and Palmer, who had taken to calling himself the "Fighting Quaker," was jeered as the "Quaking Fighter."

Conclusion: Troubled Crusade

At home and abroad, the First World War was a traumatic experience for the American people. Woodrow Wilson sought to keep the nation out of war, but when war arrived in 1917, he promised that American intervention would further the noble cause of worldwide democracy. Serving under idealistic banners, American soldiers and sailors encountered unprecedented horrors—submarines, poison gas, machine guns—and more than 100,000 died. Rather than redeem their sacrifice, the peace that followed the armistice tarnished it. Few found consolation in the fact that the war thrust the nation into a position of international preeminence. At home, war brought prosperity, but rather than permanently improve working conditions, advance public health, and spread educational opportunity as progressives had hoped, the war threatened to undermine the achievements of the previous two decades. The immediate postwar years witnessed unemployment, inflation, racial conflict, labor unrest, and a ruthless crackdown on dissent.

In 1920, a bruised and disillusioned society stumbled into a new decade. The era coming to an end had called on Americans to crusade and sacrifice. Now whoever could promise them peace, prosperity, and a good time would have the best chance to win their hearts.

CHRONOLOGY

1914 In an attempt to impose democracy on Mexico, President Woodrow Wilson sends marines to occupy port of Veracruz.

August 6. All-out conflict when Germany declares war on Russia.

1915 German submarine sinks British liner *Lusitania*, with loss of almost 1,200 lives, including 128 Americans.

Settlement House reformer Jane Addams helps form Women's Peace Party to seek peaceful resolution of war.

1916 General Pershing leads military expedition into Mexico in pursuit of rebel leader "Pancho" Villa.

1917 British authorities inform Wilson of Zimmermann telegram.

April 6. Submarine attacks on American vessels convince Wilson to declare war on Germany.

Wilson creates Committee on Public Information, to promote U.S. war aims.

Selective Service Act authorizes military draft that brings 2.8 million men into armed services.

Espionage Act passed, limiting First Amendment rights.

Resentment against blacks migrating northward in search of work ignites violent race riot in East St. Louis, Illinois.

Armed action by black soldiers against racial discrimination in Houston results in execution of thirteen of the soldiers and life sentences for forty-one more.

Bolshevik Revolution ends Russian participation in the war.

1918– American forces deployed in Russia
1920 to protect Allied supplies and ports from Germany and then to support White Russian efforts to undo Bolshevik Revolution.

1918 **January 8.** President Wilson outlines his fourteen-point plan for peace.

May – June. American marines succeed in their first major combat with the Germans at Cantigny and Château-Thierry.

November 11. Armistice signed ending World War I.

1919 **January 18.** Paris peace conference begins, with President Wilson as head of U.S. delegation.

June 28. Versailles peace treaty signed.

Wilson undertakes speaking tour to rally support for ratification of Versailles treaty and League of Nations.

Postwar recession and ending of wartime support for labor unions lead to wave of strikes.

1919– Attorney General A. Mitchell Palmer
1920 leads effort, known as Red scare, to rid country of anarchists and aliens.

1920 **January 1.** Prohibition goes into effect, following ratification of Eighteenth Amendment.

Organized labor suffers its greatest defeat by ending the steel strike without a settlement.

Senate votes against ratification of Versailles peace treaty.

August 18. Nineteenth Amendment, granting women the vote, ratified by states.

BIBLIOGRAPHY

GENERAL WORKS

John Milton Cooper Jr., *Pivotal Decades: The United States, 1900–1920* (1990).

Robert H. Ferrell, *Woodrow Wilson and World War I, 1917–1921* (1985).

Ellis W. Hawley, *The Great War and the Search for a Modern Order: A History of the American People and Their Institutions, 1917–1933* (1979).

Derek Heater, *National Self-Determination: Woodrow Wilson and His Legacy* (1994).

David Kennedy, *Over Here: The First World War and American Society* (1980).

Nell Irwin Painter, *Standing at Armageddon: The United States, 1877–1919* (1987).

Robert D. Schulzinger, *American Diplomacy in the Twentieth Century* (1984).

David Steigerwald, *Wilsonian Idealism in America* (1994).

David Stevenson, *The First World War and International Politics* (1988).

J. M. Winter, *The Experience of World War I* (1989).

Neil A. Wynn, *From Progressivism to Prosperity: World War I and American Society* (1986).

EUROPEAN CONTEXT

Modris Ecksteins, *Rites of Spring: The Great War and the Birth of the Modern Age* (1990).

James Joll, *The Origins of the First World War* (1992).

Dwight Lee, *Europe's Crucial Years: The Diplomatic Background of World War I, 1902–1914* (1974).

George L. Mosse, *Fallen Soldiers: Reshaping the Memory of the World Wars* (1990).

Roland Stromberg, *Redemption by War: The Intellectuals and 1914* (1982).

Barbara W. Tuchman, *The Guns of August* (1962).

WOODROW WILSON AND THE WORLD

Kendrick A. Clement, *William Jennings Bryan, Missionary Isolationist* (1982).

Kendrick A. Clement, *Woodrow Wilson, World Statesman* (1987).

Patrick Devlin, *Too Proud to Fight: Woodrow Wilson's Neutrality* (1974).

John S. D. Eisenhower, *Intervention! The United States and the Mexican Revolution, 1913–1917* (1993).

Lloyd C. Gardner, *Safe for Democracy: The Anglo-American Response to Revolution, 1913–1923* (1987).

Burton I. Kaufman, *Efficiency and Expansion: Foreign Trade Organization in the Wilson Administration, 1913–1921* (1974).

Thomas Knock, *To End All Wars: Woodrow Wilson and the Quest for a New World Order* (1992).

Gordon N. Levin, *Woodrow Wilson and World Politics: America's Response to War and Revolution* (1970).

Arthur S. Link, *Wilson*, 5 vols. (1947–1965).

Manuel A. Machado Jr., *Centaur of the North: Francisco Villa, the Mexican Revolution, and Northern Mexico* (1988).

THE CRUSADE FOR DEMOCRACY

Daniel Beaver, *Newton D. Baker and the American War Effort, 1917–1919* (1966).

William T. Breen, *Uncle Sam at Home: Civilian Mobilization, Wartime Federalism, and the Council of National Defense, 1917–1919* (1984).

Jean Conner, *The National War Labor Board: Stability, Social Justice, and the Voluntary State in World War I* (1983).

Robert D. Cuff, *The War Industries Board: Business-Government Relations during World War I* (1973).

Carol S. Gruber, *Mars and Minerva* (1975).

John F. McClymer, *War and Welfare: Social Engineering in America, 1890–1925* (1980).

Ronald Schaffer, *America in the Great War: The Rise of the War Welfare State* (1991).

Stephen Vaughn, *Holding Fast the Inner Lines: Democracy, Nationalism, and the Committee for Public Information* (1980).

PACIFISM AND DISSENT

Charles Chatfield, *For Peace and Justice: Pacifism in America, 1914–1941* (1971).

Emma Goldman, *Living My Life* (1931).

Frederick C. Griffin, *Six Who Protested: Radical Opposition to the First World War* (1977).

C. Roland Marchand, *The American Peace Movement and Social Reform* (1973).

Marian J. Morton, *Emma Goldman and the American Left* (1992).

Paul L. Murphy, *World War I and the Origin of Civil Liberties in the United States* (1979).

Cass Sunstein, *Democracy and the Problem of Free Speech* (1993).

THE WAR IN MEMORY AND IMAGINATION

Peter Aichinger, *The American Soldier in Fiction, 1880–1963: A History of Attitudes towards Warfare and the Military Establishment* (1975).

Stanley Cooperman, *World War I and the American Novel* (1970).

Richard Cork, *The Bitter Truth: Avant-Garde Art and the Great War* (1994).

Paul Fussell, *The Great War and Modern Memory* (1975).

Jon Glover and Jon Silkin, eds., *The Penguin Book of First World War Prose* (1989).

Ernest Hemingway, *A Farewell to Arms* (1929).

Michael T. Isenberg, *War on Film* (1981).

Lyn Macdonald, *1914–1918: Voices and Images of the Great War* (1988).

BLACK AMERICA

Arthur E. Barbeau and Florette Henri, *The Unknown Soldiers: Black American Troops in World War I* (1974).

Carole Marks, *Farewell—We're Good and Gone: The Great Black Migration* (1989).

Bernard C. Nalty, *Strength for the Fight: A History of Black Americans in the Military* (1986).

Gerald Wilson Patton, *War and Race: The Black Officer in the American Military, 1915–1941* (1981).

Joe William Trotter Jr., ed., *The Great Migration in Historical Perspective* (1991).

GENDER AND SOCIETY

Nancy F. Cott, *The Grounding of American Feminism* (1987).

Sara Evans, *Born for Liberty: A History of Women in America* (1989).

Maurine Weiner Greenwald, *Women, War, and Work: The Impact of World War I on Women Workers in the United States* (1980).

Margaret Randolph Higonnet, Jane Jenson, Sonya Michel, and Margaret Collins Weitz, eds., *Behind the Lines: Gender and the Two World Wars* (1987).

Barbara J. Steinson, *American Women's Activism in World War I* (1982).

MILITARY ORGANIZATION AND EXPERIENCE

Michael C. Adams, *The Great Adventure: Male Desire and the Coming of World War I* (1990).

John Whiteclay Chambers II, *To Raise an Army: The Draft Comes to Modern America* (1987).

J. Garry Clifford, *The Citizen Soldiers* (1972).

Edward M. Coffman, *The War to End All Wars: The American Military Experience in World War I* (1968).

Kenneth J. Hagan, *This People's Navy: The Making of American Sea Power* (1990).

Lee Kennett, *The First Air War, 1914–1918* (1990).

Allan R. Millett and Peter Maslowski, *For the Common Defense: A Military History of the United States of America* (1984).

G. Kurt Piehler, *Remembering War the American Way* (1995).

Dominick A. Pisano, Thomas J. Dietz, Joanne M. Gernstein, and Karl S. Schneide, *Legend, Memory, and the Great War in the Air* (1992).

Daniel M. Smith, *The Great Departure: The United States and World War I* (1965).

Donald Smythe, *Pershing* (1986).

David F. Trask, *The AEF and Coalition War-Making, 1917–1918* (1993).

Russell F. Weigley, *The American Way of War: A History of United States Military Strategy and Policy* (1977).

Stanley Weintraub, *A Stillness Heard Round the World: The End of the Great War, November 1918* (1985).

PEACE AND POSTWAR CHANGE

David Brody, *Labor in Crisis: The Steel Strike of 1919* (1965).

Melvyn Dubofsky, *We Shall Be All: A History of the Industrial Workers of the World* (1969; reprint, 1988).

Melvyn Dubofsky, *The State and Labor in Modern America* (1994).

David S. Fogelsong, *America's Secret War against Bolshevism: U.S. Intervention in the Russian Civil War, 1917–1920* (1995).

John L. Gaddis, *Russia, the Soviet Union, and the United States* (1978).

John Maynard Keynes, *The Economic Consequences of the Peace* (1920).

Charles L. May Jr., *The End of Order: Versailles, 1919* (1980).

Robert K. Murray, *Red Scare: A Study in National Hysteria, 1919–1920* (1955).

William Pencak, *For God and Country* (1989).

Richard Polenberg, *Fighting Faiths: The Abrams Case, the Supreme Court, and Free Speech* (1987).

William G. Ross, *Forging New Freedoms: Nativism, Education, and the Constitution, 1917–1927* (1994).

Francis Russell, *A City in Terror: 1919, the Boston Police Strike* (1975).

Richard Severo and Lewis Milford, *The Wages of War: When America's Soldiers Came Home—from Valley Forge to Vietnam* (1989).

Ralph A. Stone, *The Irreconcilables: The Fight against the League of Nations* (1970).

William Tuttle Jr., *Race Riot: Chicago and the Red Summer of 1919* (1970).

Arthur Walworth, *Wilson and His Peacemakers: American Diplomacy at the Paris Peace Conference, 1919* (1986).

William C. Widenor, *Henry Cabot Lodge and the Search for an American Foreign Policy* (1980).

PANORAMIC HATBOX

Illustrated hatboxes, like the hats within them, were a favorite symbol of affluent style in the 1920s. This hatbox displays the extravagance of life on Fifth Avenue, the most fashionable milieu of all. Americans looked to New York wit and sophistication as a guide to how to transform the nation into an urban society.

Picture Research Consultants & Archives.

FROM "NORMALCY" TO THE GREAT DEPRESSION

23

1920–1932

O N A GRAY CHRISTMAS MORNING IN 1922, Federal Prisoner #9653 began his last day at the Atlanta penitentiary. The frail old man glanced at the crucifix on his cell wall before exchanging his jailhouse fatigues for the cheap new suit the guard had brought. Then he gathered his few belongings and prepared to leave. For Eugene Victor Debs, the leader and five-time presidential candidate of the Socialist Party, a long ordeal was over. President Warren G. Harding had granted him the pardon Woodrow Wilson had so bitterly refused. After three long years in prison for opposition to World War I, Debs was at last a free man.

As he neared the main prison gate, Debs remembered, he heard behind him "what seemed a rumbling of the earth as if shaken by some violent explosion." He turned back to face the stark walls and watched as a cry of farewell thundered from the other prisoners. Against every rule, the warden had allowed all 2,300 inmates out of their cells to witness this unprecedented departure. They responded with cheers for the man they had come to know as a sympathetic friend. Debs had an uncanny hold on their hopes and feelings. His cell mate, Sam Moore, recalled many years later the vivid impression that Debs made. "As miserable as I was I would defy fate with all its cruelty as long as Debs held my hand, and I was the most miserably happiest man on earth when I knew he was going home Christmas."

Debs's first stop was the White House, where his benefactor, President Harding, curious to meet America's most famous political prisoner, had invited him for a visit. The genial Harding bounded from behind his desk to shake Debs's hand, exclaiming, "Well, I have heard so damned much about you, Mr. Debs, that I am now very glad to meet you personally."

At the end of his journey, in Terre Haute, Indiana, a crowd estimated at 25,000 met Debs at the station. They lifted the old warrior into the same horse-drawn wagon that had carried him back from his imprisonment in 1895, when he had gone to jail for defying a federal injunction during the Pullman strike. When the parade arrived at the family home near the railroad tracks, Debs gave an impromptu speech from the porch, urging his cheering supporters to view his release as a step toward the ultimate victory of socialism and the working class.

It was a touching moment, but despite Debs's show of the old revolutionary fire, he faced a society very different from the one he envisioned. By pardoning America's leading antiwar martyr, the Harding administration shrewdly eased opposition to the "normalcy" it was putting in place to prevent the success of any new radical champions. The old radicals and reformers, bitterly disillusioned with the outcome of World War I, no longer thrilled to the Christian moralism or idealism that had fueled the crusades of the socialists and progressives. Although Debs's stature as a jailed martyr had won him 919,000 votes (the most ever for a Socialist candidate) when he ran for president from his cell in 1920, the Socialist Party itself was in drastic decline. By the time Debs left prison, Socialist membership had fallen to 120,000. The party had to sell its headquarters in Chicago and move into an attic to stave off bankruptcy.

The nation had turned a corner. The failure of the war to make the world safe for democracy and the tawdriness of the Versailles treaty had ended the craving for reform that had characterized the Progressive Era. The lack of strong leadership once Wilson fell ill left a vacuum at the center of American life that the energy released by the war and the subsequent development of America's economy rushed to fill. The nation enjoyed a spectacular burst of economic prosperity. The freewheeling economy mirrored a new sense of freedom in popular culture. The war seemed to accelerate the pace of American life, so much so that Secretary of Commerce Herbert Hoover declared that Americans had entered a "new era."

The 1920s were not without contradictions, however. The nation was enduring the final stages of the transition from a rural, agricultural nation to a modern, urban, machine-oriented one. Signs of tension and stress were clearly visible. Cities and industry grew enormously, yet nostalgia idealized the farm and the small town. The nation prospered, but the new wealth widened the gap between rich and poor. City life and diversity flourished, but they met renewed intolerance and demands for conformity. While millions admired the new, sophisticated style, millions of others condemned the vulgarity of postwar society. And in one of the most significant outpourings of creative talent in the nation's history, artists of all types indicted the United States for being artistically barren.

Competing myths and legends about the 1920s found expression in the labels attached to the age. Some labels express the era's high-spirited energy: "Roaring Twenties," "Jazz Age," "Flaming Youth," and "Age of the Flapper." Others echo the rising importance of money—"Dollar Decade," "Golden Twenties," "Prosperity Decade"—or reflect the sinister side of gangster profiteering—"Lawless Decade." Still other terms emphasize fragile dreams and loneliness: "the Lost Generation," "the Beautiful and the Damned." Ultimately, perhaps, it was an age best summed up by President Calvin Coolidge, who declared, "The business of America is business." During the 1920s, the values and ide-

ology of the business community reigned supreme, only to be toppled abruptly with the stock market crash and subsequent depression.

Normalcy

In a speech during his campaign for the presidency in 1920, Republican candidate Warren G. Harding told the people that "America's present need is not heroics, but healing; not nostrums [questionable remedies] but normalcy; not revolution but restoration; . . . not surgery but serenity." But what was "normalcy"? Harding explained: "By 'normalcy' I don't mean the old order but a regular steady order of things. I mean normal procedure, the natural way, without excess." So defined, "normalcy" (Harding's speechwriter had written the more familiar "normality"), captured the electorate and made its way into the dictionary. The urbane *New York Times* understood its appeal, observing, "Mr. Harding is not writing for the super-fine weighers of verbs and adjectives but for the men and women who see in his expressions their own ideas." In the 1920s, it was Harding and the Republican Party that spoke the people's language. From 1921 to 1933, power rested securely in business-minded and conservative Republican hands.

Postwar Politics and the Election of 1920

The economic chaos that accompanied the return to a peacetime economy after World War I spelled serious trouble for the Wilson administration. As inflation soared, people on fixed salaries—teachers, ministers, social service workers, store clerks, and others of the middle class who had formed the backbone of progressive support for Wilson—watched inflation shrink their purchasing power. Organized labor, having lost its great effort to strike for better conditions in 1919, faced grim prospects. By the winter of 1920–21, the national unemployment rate hit 20 percent, the highest ever suffered up to that time. For those still working, inflation and the fear of unemployment ruined any hope of enjoying a higher standard of living. Farmers fared worst, as their bankruptcy rate increased tenfold and real farm income fell far below wartime levels. For a decade that would become known for its economic miracles, the twenties began with a thud.

REPUBLICAN CAMPAIGN DECAL

Looking grimly dignified, these 1920 Republican candidates seek to persuade voters that they can put an end to radical and alien disruption and restore old-fashioned American values. Harding, the Washington insider from the traditional Republican stronghold of Ohio, stares out from beneath the slogan "Back to Normal"; his running mate, Calvin Coolidge, the Massachusetts governor who gained national fame by crushing the Boston police strike, appears as the exemplar of law and order.

Collection of Janice L. and David J. Frent.

President Woodrow Wilson, bedridden and partially paralyzed from the stroke he had suffered in 1919, squandered his party's chances by refusing to allow anyone within his administration to construct a program for the new postwar era. Instead, Wilson insisted that the 1920 election would be a "solemn referendum" on the League of Nations. The Democratic nominee for president, James M. Cox, three-time governor of Ohio, and for vice president, the New York aristocrat Franklin Delano Roosevelt, bearer of his uncle Teddy's famous name, dutifully campaigned on Wilson's international ideals.

The Republican Party chose a presidential candidate who embodied the change in national sentiment from global crusade to peaceful prosperity. Handsome and gregarious, with a pleasing, resonant voice, Senator Warren Gamaliel Harding of Ohio stood as an accurate representative of his age. A jovial joiner who belonged to a host of fraternal orders, Harding epitomized the essence of conventional small-town life.

Unlike the increasing number of young men from small towns who headed for the city to make their fortunes, Harding had stayed home in Marion, Ohio, to edit the town newspaper. At a Repub-

lican gathering, Harding attracted notice from a shrewd local lawyer, Harry Daugherty. Watching Harding make his way with casual charm through a throng of politicians, Daugherty thought immediately, "What a president he'd make!" Under Daugherty's guidance, Harding's rise in party politics was more a tribute to charm and amiability than to any political commitment. He vaguely opposed the prevailing progressive policies of economic regulation, agricultural subsidies, and graduated income taxes. Harding repeatedly demonstrated an ability to land on the winning side of an issue without having to grapple with conscience or complexity. On the two most heated domestic issues of the day—woman suffrage and prohibition—Harding showed little knowledge or conviction. He remarked that he saw no good reason for the reforms, but eventually he voted for them in a nod to public opinion.

The keys to Harding's success in 1920 lay in his image—it was generally agreed that he looked like a president—and in his appeal to harmony and good fellowship. Eager to put the poisonous atmosphere of the Red scare and the labor strife of 1919 behind them, the voters responded to Harding's call for normalcy by giving him the largest margin of victory any presidential candidate had ever received. The contrast between Harding's determinedly optimistic administration and the moribund one he replaced became immediately evident to the nation. In early March, as the Washington weather started to thaw, the Hardings arrived at the White House, threw open the barred gates, which had been closed since the declaration of war in 1917, and raised the window blinds. Bright flowers, birdhouses on the lawn, and, above all, a welcome to the public, who came by the thousands to see the Harding White House, lifted the national pall and signified a new era of easygoing good cheer.

The Republican Party chose a presidential candidate who embodied the change in national sentiment from global crusade to peaceful prosperity. Handsome and gregarious, with a pleasing, resonant voice, Harding stood as an accurate representative of his age.

Harding managed to choose some talented people for his cabinet, including Charles Evans Hughes, former associate justice of the Supreme Court, for secretary of state. Herbert Hoover, the self-made millionaire and former head of the wartime Food Administration, was tapped for secretary of commerce. The new president picked the leading champion of scientific agriculture, Henry C. Wallace, as secretary of agriculture. But wealth also counted. Conservative Republicans pressed Harding to name Andrew Mellon, one of the richest men in America (and a heavy contributor to the party), as secretary of the treasury. Harding also remembered his friends. "God, I can't be an ingrate," he is said to have remarked. Regardless of their experience, friends found themselves in high office. This curious combination of merit and cronyism would typify Harding's administration and set the stage for both a few "best minds" to argue over national needs and for lesser men to tarnish themselves and the Harding administration in scandal.

The "Noble Experiment" and Woman Suffrage

The shift from reform earnestness to normalcy showed in the public reaction to the last two great progressive achievements passed prior to Harding's

inauguration—prohibition and woman suffrage. In January 1920, the Eighteenth Amendment prohibiting the sale of alcohol took effect. Thus began what advocates of the measure referred to as "the noble experiment." While it succeeded in lowering the consumption of alcohol, at least in rural America, the ultimate result of prohibition was widespread disregard for the law. Federal enforcement of prohibition was lax, and any citizen who wanted a drink could find one. The "speakeasy," a place where men (and, increasingly, women) drank publicly, became a common feature of the urban landscape. Liquor dealers, called "bootleggers" because they hid bottles in their tall boots, provided the thirsty with their drink of choice. Liquor was smuggled in from Canada or concocted in makeshift stills, giving rise to the term "bathtub gin." Mort Mortimer, who operated in Washington, D.C., boasted a card that styled him as the "President's Bootlegger."

But, eventually, serious criminals took over most of the liquor trade. Al Capone became the era's most notorious gang lord by establishing a bootlegging empire in Chicago that reputedly grossed more than $60 million in a single year. Gangsters employed hundreds of gunmen, and gang wars raged in several American cities, most notably Chicago, where Al Capone held sway. The violence that marked the struggle for control of the lucrative market encouraged public cynicism about the

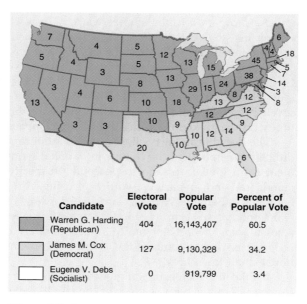

Candidate	Electoral Vote	Popular Vote	Percent of Popular Vote
Warren G. Harding (Republican)	404	16,143,407	60.5
James M. Cox (Democrat)	127	9,130,328	34.2
Eugene V. Debs (Socialist)	0	919,799	3.4

MAP 23.1
The Election of 1920

SATURDAY NIGHT
With a sly wink, the young dandy dips for movie money, while his date looks dubious about what will go on in the dark of that dry night. With this title, Harry Ruby, the popular songwriter, capitalizes on the expectation that resourceful Americans out for a good time will find ways around the prohibition amendment's attempt to enforce sober morality.
Picture Research Consultants & Archives.

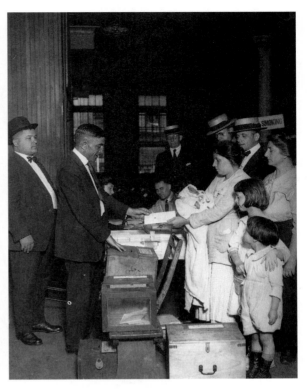

WOMEN VOTING IN NEW YORK CITY
Sharply attired New York City officials look wearily resigned or bemused as one of them hands ballots to two women voting for the first time in 1920. The contrast in appearance and demeanor of the two groups facing each other is strikingly reminiscent of photographs of apprehensive new immigrants applying for entry.
UPI/Bettmann Archive.

"noble experiment." Each year, the constituency supporting prohibition shrank, until in 1933 opponents succeeded in repealing the Eighteenth Amendment.

The Nineteenth Amendment, ratified in 1920, granted women the vote, ending nearly a century of struggle to achieve political rights for women. But how would women vote? Alice Paul, head of the militant National Woman's Party, wanted them to vote as a bloc and fight for an Equal Rights Amendment (ERA) that she put before Congress in 1923. The more moderate National American Woman Suffrage Association pursued a different course. The organization disbanded, forming the nonpartisan League of Women Voters (LWV) to educate the new electorate on the issues. Most activists in both groups, as well as many political observers

outside, looked to woman suffrage, the greatest single change ever made in voting eligibility, to reshape the political landscape. Female activists hoped to have decisive influence in enacting protective legislation for women and children that had long been high on their reform agenda.

As with prohibition, however, reality did not bear out utopian expectations. Ignorance of their right to vote and male domination, especially among immigrant groups and Southerners, kept many women away from the polls. Partly for that reason, in 1920 and 1924, for the first time in American history, less than a majority of eligible voters cast ballots in the presidential elections. Those women who did vote showed no unified commitment to the goals of suffrage leaders. Conservatives had wrested control of the Republican Party from

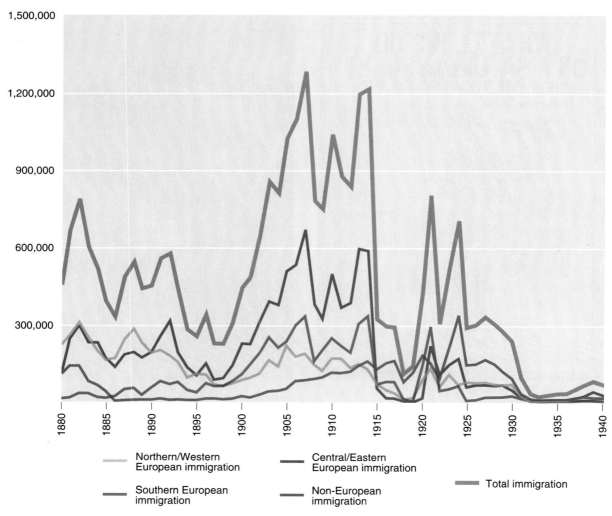

FIGURE 23.1
Immigration, 1880–1940
Reflecting harsh and unstable conditions in many foreign countries, emigration to the United
States increased sharply in the early twentieth century. After World War I, Americans reacted
to failed hopes and fear of outsiders by imposing stringent immigration quotas.

the progressives and were in charge of the White House and the congressional majority. In the Democratic Party, conservatives had also routed Wilsonian liberals, and antifeminist, segregationist Southerners took charge. Ruefully, Abe Martin, the cracker-barrel philosopher of the Indianapolis *News*, lamented in 1926: "Wouldn't the way things are goin' these days make a fine argymint in favor of woman's suffrage if we didn't already have it!"

But it took a while for politicians to realize that they need not fear any female voting bloc. Assuming that women would have considerable political leverage, the new Congress passed the Sheppard-Towner bill in 1921, providing federal funds for maternal and infant health care. As the weakness of the new voters' influence sank in, however, and doctors protested "socialist" interference, Congress reduced funds for the program and in 1928 eliminated it altogether. Those women who stuck with a progressive agenda had to join others seeking change outside the mainstream. Within a network of private agencies and reform associations, they continued to press the causes of birth control, protective legislation for the work place, legal equality for minorities, and the end of child labor. They looked toward the day when their efforts would be supported by those in power.

The United States Retreats from the World

Harding's desire for harmony equipped him well to preside over the country's retreat from international leadership. He began by shedding some responsibilities that stemmed from the world war. Only four months after his inauguration, he concluded peace treaties with Germany, Austria, and Hungary that removed the United States from supervision over their affairs. To lessen tensions closer to home, he handed over $25 million to Colombia as compensation for the loss of territory that nation had suffered when President Theodore Roosevelt "took Panama" to build the canal. Harding's most ambitious effort, however, was the Washington Disarmament Conference he convened in 1921 to establish a global balance of naval power. By gaining agreement on the proportional reduction of naval might among the major powers—Britain, France, Japan, Italy, and the United States—Harding hoped to provide a measure of security for the nation without the trouble of joining the League of Nations. A grateful citizenry breathed a sigh of relief that the threat of war seemed so easily removed at a conference noted for its international goodwill and optimism.

The campaign to limit immigration, however, was more ominous. Its barely veiled intent was to keep the nation's destiny in the hands of people of Anglo-Saxon stock. Though the Red scare had petered out before Harding's election, the specter of bomb-throwing radicals from revolutionary countries of eastern and southern Europe continued to haunt the American imagination.

The trial of Italian anarchists Nicola Sacco and Bartolomeo Vanzetti testified to a new wave of hysteria. Arrested in 1920 for robbery and murder in South Braintree, Massachusetts, the two were sentenced to death by a judge who openly referred to them as "anarchist bastards." Mounting public opinion called the verdict into question: It appeared to many that the men had been convicted because of their ideas and nationality. The governor of Massachusetts named a blue ribbon committee of establishment notables, including the presidents of Harvard and MIT, who found the trial judge guilty of a "grave breach of official decorum." Nevertheless, they closed ranks and refused to recommend a motion for retrial.

Supporters tried for six years to save Sacco and Vanzetti. Instead, on August 23, 1927, the two men were sent to the electric chair. More than fifty thousand protesters marching beside the coffins at the funeral seemed to bear out Vanzetti's defiant martyr's statement just before he died: "Never in our full life could we hope to do such work for tolerance, for justice, for man's understanding of man, as now we do by accident. . . . This agony is our triumph!" But

AGITATING FOR SACCO AND VANZETTI
This image appeared in the anarchist journal that Bartolomeo Vanzetti's friend and fellow immigrant Aldino Felicani created to raise support for pardoning Sacco and Vanzetti. By writing in English under an Italian masthead, Felicani sought to make the two accused men symbols of both immigrant and working-class suffering. In the cartoon's dramatic version of events, capitalism's executioner, leaning on the electric chair like a sinister barber, summons working-class victims to their doom. In fact, deportation and mob violence were the typical weapons used against alien radicals and others deemed dangerously un-American.
L'Agitazione, August 20, 1921.

many of the mourners saw things differently. One of them, the writer John Dos Passos, spoke for those who viewed the incident as proof that America was in the grip of a ruling class that would act viciously to suppress dissent and immigrant minorities. In *The Big Money* (1936), Dos Passos's panoramic novel about how the culture of wealth and privilege works, one of the mourners standing in the rain sums up the executions as a death blow to the idea of inclusive democracy. "All right," he declares with grim resignation, "all right, we are two nations."

By the time Harding took office, tensions about ethnic class differences had convinced public opinion that the time had come for drastic immigration restriction. Alongside the "100 percenters"— native-born Americans totally opposed to immigration on racist and patriotic grounds—stood union members, who feared immigrant competition for jobs, and traditionalists, who felt that the nation had completed its destined growth. In full accord, Harding made it one of his first acts to sign a quota law. The law limited the number of immigrants to no more than 357,000 per year and gave each European nation a quota, based on 3 percent of the number of people from that country listed in the U.S. census of 1910. The law effectively reversed the trend toward immigration from southern and eastern Europe, which by 1914 had amounted to 75 percent of the total. From an open welcome to millions of "huddled masses yearning to breathe free," the United States built high walls. In 1923, Congress cut the quota in half. The following year it specifically excluded Asians and increased the advantage for northern Europeans by shifting the census standard back from 1910 to 1890, before the great influx of southern and eastern Europeans.

Scandal

Having pulled back from international responsibilities and shut the door to undesirable immigrants, the Harding administration concentrated on prosperity at home. Harding sought to strengthen the power of American business but cast his policies in terms of benevolence and the general welfare. Profit making and public service, he declared, joined to form the core of the American way. He supported high tariffs, price supports for agriculture, and the complete dismantling of wartime government control over industry in favor of unregulated private direction. Passage of the Fordney-McCumber tariff in 1922 raised duties on imports to unprecedented heights. Ironically, by making it more difficult for

foreign countries to sell goods in the United States, the tariff prevented European nations from paying off their wartime debts to the U.S. treasury.

Eventually Harding's small-town congeniality and trusting ways became a liability. Wheeler-dealers, including many of his old friends from Ohio, descended on Washington, lured by visions of easy pickings. This "Ohio gang" held forth at what became known as the "little green house on K Street," a hideaway where whiskey and poker mixed with business, some of it illegal. The affable Harding resisted for as long as he could the recognition that some of his friends were involved in lawbreaking more serious than drinking bootlegged gin.

The scandals began when Charles Forbes, an army colonel Harding had met playing poker and offhandedly appointed director of the Veterans' Bureau, was caught defrauding the government. Forbes and a collaborator had found a number of ways to line their pockets, including selling off hospital equipment. Together they stole an estimated $200 million. Enraged by the betrayal of trust, Harding called Forbes into his office and, as the president told it, "shook him as a dog would a rat." Harding nevertheless allowed Forbes to flee to Europe and tried to write off the scandal. But the suicide of Forbes's henchman brought on a congressional hearing and with it a tide of trouble for Harding.

Before the investigations concluded, three of Harding's appointees would go to jail and others would come under indictment. Secretary of the Interior Albert Fall was convicted of accepting bribes of more than $400,000 from oil magnates Harry Sinclair and Edward L. Doheney. Fall had received the money at the taxpayers' expense by leasing Sinclair and Doheney oil reserves on public land in Teapot Dome, Wyoming, and Elk Hills, California. Doheney and Sinclair escaped conviction, but Fall went to jail, and "Teapot Dome" became a term synonymous with political corruption. Later, Attorney General Daugherty, the president's oldest crony, was indicted for selling political influence. Early inklings of these wrongdoings shattered Harding's confidence and, with it, his health.

Harding set off on a trip to Alaska in the summer of 1923 to escape his troubles. Baffled about how to deal with "my God-damned friends," the president found no rest and his health continued to decline. On August 2, 1923, a shocked nation learned of President Harding's sudden death at the age of fifty-eight from a stroke. Subsequent scandals revealed the extent of the rot in the Harding administration. Harding himself was not involved in any financial wrongdoing, but only his death saved him from further embarrassment. As president, he was a man in over his head and he knew it. When Nicholas Murray Butler, his friend and the president of Columbia University, found him up late one night doggedly answering routine mail and protested that the president should not waste time on such matters, Harding responded, "I suppose so, but I am not fit for this office and should never have been here."

The Business of America

By 1922, the American economy had pulled out of the nosedive that followed the war and began a long period of vigorous growth. Despite the conservatism of the Republican administrations of the 1920s and their claims that the best government was one that did the least, the federal government worked closely with business to sustain and extend the business prosperity of the decade. Henry Ford, the man who put America on wheels, broadcast a compelling vision of the new age, complete with new terms of production, promotion, and distribution. The key to abundance, he preached, was modern mass production. Ford liked to say that his business principles "are all summed up in the single word 'service.'" Others liked to frame the "New Era" in terms of advanced technology, business efficiency, and scientific management. Others simply said that the age was caught up in "money madness." According to the caustic Baltimore journalist H. L. Mencken, the businessman "is the only one who always seeks to make it appear, when he attains the object of his labor, i.e., the making of a great deal of money, that it was not the object of his labors." And for every product manufacturers produced, someone had to buy.

A Business Government

Vice-president Calvin Coolidge was vacationing at his family's farmhouse in Plymouth Notch, Vermont, when he was wakened during the night with the news of Harding's death. The family gathered in the parlor where, by the flickering light of an oil lamp, Coolidge's father, a justice of the peace, swore his son in as president. This rustic drama had a calming effect on the nation. Americans welcomed as Harding's successor a man seemingly steeped in the country ways of the Yankee past.

A spare, solemn man—one critic thought he must have been "weaned on a pickle"—Coolidge had won national publicity in 1919 when as governor of Massachusetts he had called out the National Guard to maintain order during the Boston police strike. In 1920, the Republican convention chose him as a man of decisiveness to stand behind the more pliable Harding. When he became president in 1923, the nation soon recognized differences between the Coolidge administration and its discredited predecessor—a more formal and proper White House, a close-mouthed presidential style, and absolute uprightness. But these differences obscured the basic similarities in their policies, particularly regarding business.

Despite the conservatism of the Republican administrations of the 1920s and their claims that the best government was one that did the least, the federal government worked closely with business to sustain and extend the business prosperity of the decade.

Coolidge, who once remarked, "The man who builds a factory builds a temple, the man who works there worships there," shared the era's infatuation with businessmen. As president, he proved an even stronger ally of business than Harding had been. He said baldly: "The business of America is business.... This is a business country, and it wants a business government." While Coolidge himself rarely stirred in the White House (he took a nap every afternoon), his administration made every effort to help businesses operate efficiently and profitably. Secretary of the Treasury Andrew Mellon, millionaire aluminum magnate, focused on getting tax cuts for corporations and the rich. Under his prodding, Congress cut taxes by about half. Secretary of Commerce Herbert Hoover devoted his efforts to building trade associations. He believed that cooperation, rather than cutthroat competition, among rival firms within a particular industry would reduce waste and increase stability.

The Supreme Court played its part in the pro-business thrust. After a period of validating a series of advanced social and economic legislation during the Progressive Era, the Court joined the nation in attempting to roll back the reform tide, launching a powerful attack on the rights of state and federal governments to regulate business. The Court op-

COOLIDGE POSING AS A FARMER

After the labor wars subsided, the idea of Coolidge as the enforcer of law and order gave way to the more placid image of "Silent Cal." Though he knew the ways of farming from his youth, the hay and pitchfork of this image are mere props for playing a political game Coolidge does not manage to disguise. His gleaming dress shoes and the official car with Secret Service men in the background show how the old rural imagery had become window dressing for the New Era of wealth and power.
Brown Brothers.

posed any federal regulation of hours, wages, and working conditions. In 1916, the Court had struck down the Child Labor Act, making it clear that its prohibition of federal labor regulation included the work done by children. Taking aim at state regulation in 1923, the Court declared unconstitutional the District of Columbia's minimum-wage law for women, asserting that the law interfered with the freedom of employer and employee to make labor contracts. In addition, the Court limited the rights of labor unions to organize, while confirming the rights of businesses to form trade associations.

The election of 1924 underscored the defeat of progressive principles. Coolidge easily won the Republican presidential nomination, while the Democrats nominated John W. Davis, a corporate lawyer whose conservative views differed little from Republican principles. In a last-gasp attempt to offer a reform alternative, the feisty Progressive Party made Senator Robert La Follette of Wisconsin its presidential nominee. Though ailing, La Follette remained fiercely loyal to progressive reform principles favoring strong labor unions, regulation of business, and civil liberties. In the showdown, for which Republicans coined the slogan "Coolidge or Chaos," the mostly silent president managed to capture more votes than both his opponents put

together, and the Republicans strengthened their majorities in both houses of Congress.

American business expressed its appreciation for the Coolidge administration's pro-business activity. "The American businessman is the most influential person in the nation," the United States Chamber of Commerce said proudly. "Never before, here or anywhere else, has a government been so completely fused with business." A close connection was not new, of course. During World War I, government and business had forged a partnership to produce war materiel to defeat the Germans. In the 1920s, the relationship no longer needed the stimulation of war. To many Americans, it seemed entirely natural.

Henry Ford and the Automobile

According to several surveys in the 1920s, the most admired man in America was Henry Ford. Ford and the automobiles he created stood at the center of the New Era. He began life in 1863 on a farm in Dearborn, Michigan, just outside Detroit. From the first, Ford hated the drudgery and animal messiness of farmwork and turned instead to tinkering with machines. In 1893, he built one of the first successful gasoline-driven carriages in the United States. In

1903, equipped with $28,000 from a few backers impressed by his mechanical skills, Ford left for Detroit to create the Ford Motor Company with twelve workers in a 250-by-50-foot plant.

Ford's timing and location could not have been better. The growing country had moved to its outer limits, leaving Americans, especially those west of the Mississippi, distant from neighbors and community services. With fewer than ten people to a square mile, the Midwest needed machinery to help its farmers make a living and to escape isolation on the vast tracts they called home. Ford's Detroit was well situated. The mining and manufacture of key materials for the automobile and the tractor—steel, oil, glass, and rubber—were concentrated in nearby cities in Pennsylvania, Ohio, Indiana, and Illinois. The waterways of the Great Lakes and the railroads stretching across the flat midwestern landscape made it easy to supply Detroit with what it needed. The automobile industry's demands for lead, nickel, plate glass, rubber, and especially steel proved so great that by 1929 an estimated one American in four found employment directly or indirectly in the industry. It was no wonder that one commentator quipped that "Give us our daily bread" was no longer addressed to the Almighty, but to Detroit. Henry Ford's reward was dominance over the market. The Fordson tractor and Model T automobile set the standards before World War I and stayed out front for many years after that. Despite the vast expansion of the automotive industry in the 1920s, the

Ford Motor Company remained the industry leader throughout the decade, peaking in 1925 when it outsold all its rivals combined.

When Ford began his rise, progressive critics were vilifying the industrial giants of the nineteenth century as "robber barons." While the industrialists lived in luxury, progressives charged, laboring people lived in rags. In contrast, Ford styled himself as a poor farm boy trying to get ahead and offered lacerating comments of his own about the modern-day robber barons who stood in his way. Expressing sympathy for the common folk he hoped to enlist as employees, Ford was able to claim his place as benefactor of a nation yearning to be free and mobile.

The key to Ford's success in the factory was mass production. By installing a continuous conveyor belt or assembly line in his plant in 1913, Ford was able to produce a car every ninety-three minutes, in contrast to the fourteen hours it had taken before. Mass production enabled Ford to drop the price of his cars from $845 to less than $300. Soon the working class joined the wealthy on the roads. The Model T—homely and available only in black, but rugged and cheap—became a prime symbol of the New Era. Aided by a new federal road-building program, cars, trucks, and buses surged past the railroads by the end of the 1920s as the primary haulers of passengers and freight.

At the start of the decade there were about 9 million vehicles on the road—one for every 11 citizens. With the Ford Motor Company leading the

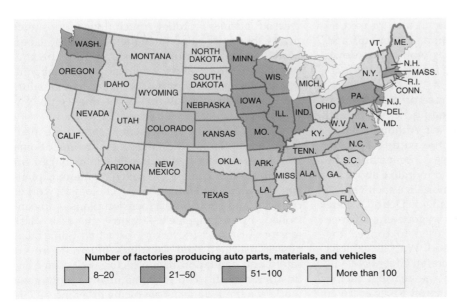

M A P 2 3 . 2
Auto Manufacturing
By the mid-1920s, the massive coal and steel industries of the Midwest had made the region the center of the new automobile industry. A major road-building program by the federal government carried the thousands of new cars produced each day to every corner of the country.

Number of factories producing auto parts, materials, and vehicles

8–20   21–50   51–100   More than 100

way, some ten thousand Model T engine blocks rolled off the assembly line every day by mid-decade, and the total number of buses, trucks, autos, and motorcycles on the road in 1929 rose to twenty-seven million—one for every 4.5 citizens.

The automobile changed the face of America. It blurred the distinction between country and city. At first rural folk greeted the horseless carriage as a "devil wagon" associated with rich city people who frightened the horses they so often needed to pull their cars out of the mud. But Ford's cheap, durable autos soon became, as Ford intended them to be, invaluable to rural dwellers. In 1920, about 30 percent of farmers owned a car; by 1930, the figure was 60 percent.

Hundreds of small towns and villages declined or died within the decade, largely because the automobile could connect people in rural communities with distant cities and thus bypass the small towns that had formerly provided services in simpler, duller ways. The one-room schoolhouse and the crossroads church began to vanish from the landscape. At the same time, some larger towns prospered by catering to the new auto trade. Country "guest cottages" were thrown up for auto tourists, and the word *motel* was coined to describe roadside accommodations. More prosperous towns paved and widened city streets, cutting down the trees on Main Street to make way for parking spaces —all in the name of the automobile age.

Americans took to the wheel in surprising numbers. That men drove came as no surprise, but even before women voted they demanded and got the right to drive. The automobile, in fact, proved an important asset in the long campaign for suffrage. And for young people, the car won hands down over the horse-drawn carriage for the privacy it accorded a courting couple.

Nobody entertained grander or more contradictory visions of the new America he had helped to create than Henry Ford himself. Although his automobile plants represented the cutting edge of modern technology and business organization, he also liked to look backward and moralize about the country's rural values. To memorialize such values, he created Greenfield Village outside Detroit, where he relocated buildings from a bygone era, such as his parents' farmhouse, and tried to convey the rural simplicity of his childhood. With its exhibits of homespun family life and crafts, Greenfield Village contrasted sharply with the roaring, racing Ford plant farther along the Detroit River at River Rouge. In the factory toiled the African American

and immigrant workers left out of Ford's village idyll. All would be well, Ford insisted, if Americans somehow remained loyal to the virtues of an agrarian past and yet were modern and scientific at the same time.

Specialization and Scientific Management

With reform in eclipse and the government promoting the unbridled interests of business, those interested in progress turned to technology and science. After the First World War, planners and efficiency experts shifted their talents to the private sector to help make industries and corporations more productive. Scientific management, which Frederick Winslow Taylor had pioneered at the end of the nineteenth century at Midvale Steel Company in Pennsylvania, reached its heyday during the 1920s, when industrial engineers fanned out across the nation searching for greater efficiencies in machines and labor. No one did more to advance Taylor's principles and the cult of productivity than Henry Ford. Ford's staggering success with the assembly line broadcast modern production techniques throughout American industry. Radios, refrigerators, washing machines, vacuum cleaners, and other mass-produced goods flooded the nation. Productivity—the efficiency of production—increased about 75 percent during the decade. Although the number of workers remained approximately the same, the workforce produced almost twice as many goods. Mass production resulted in vastly increased business profits, much lower consumer prices, but only slightly higher wages for labor. Moreover, as the moving assembly line became standard in almost every American factory, laborers lost whatever skills they had managed to retain during the industrial revolution of the nineteenth century and much of the fulfillment of work.

But scientific management meant more than time-and-motion studies and assembly lines. Some industries adopted new paternalistic management techniques that came to be called "welfare capitalism." Owners used industrial psychologists, worker councils, and contributory pension plans—all controlled by management—to try to ease class tensions by increasing labor satisfaction. Some businesses instituted paid vacations; others improved safety and sanitation inside factories. In some industries, carefully controlled company unions gave workers a limited means of voicing grievances. This "welfare capitalism" promoted by business in the

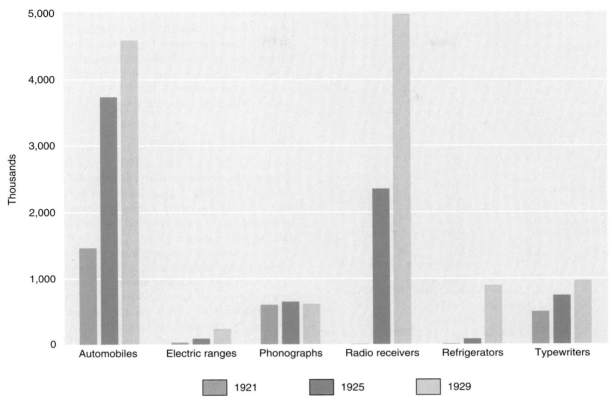

FIGURE 23.2
Production of Consumer Goods, 1920–1930
Transportation, communications, and entertainment changed the lives of consumers in the 1920s.
While labor-saving devices for the home were popular, vastly greater sales of automobiles, and radios
showed that consumerism was more powerful in moving people's attention beyond their homes.

economic boom of the 1920s would wither in the bust of the 1930s, but it had lasting effects, promoting new expectations among workers who came to see job security, high wages, and health benefits as achievable goals.

Scientific management in the 1920s also meant the culmination of the revolution in business organization that had been under way for decades. In an effort to become more streamlined and efficient, corporations established increasingly bureaucratic management structures. Businesses created specialized divisions—procurement, production, marketing, employee relations—each with its own team of managers who were increasingly professionally trained.

Belief in scientific management also helped advance the cause of higher education and the pro-

fessions: Corporations needed educated managers. By the end of the decade, enrollment in colleges and universities had more than tripled since the turn of the century. During the 1920s, graduate education expanded at an even faster rate. Funding agencies such as the Rockefeller Foundation, the John Simon Guggenheim Foundation, and the Social Science Research Council were established to support scientific research and channel it into useful applications. Private business kept pace by increasing the number of industrial research laboratories from around three hundred in 1920 to more than a thousand by the end of the decade.

These trends were not limited to business and research science. Welfare service also underwent professional change, especially in the growing new field of social work. Trained social workers often

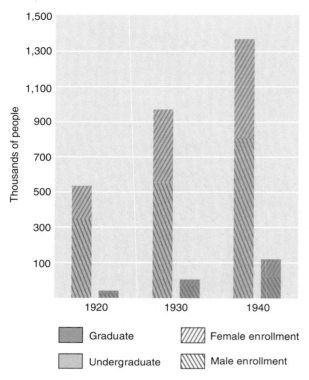

FIGURE 23.3
Higher Education Enrollments, 1920–1940
Both the prosperity of the twenties and the anxious striving for improvement of the thirties drew rising numbers of people to college. The steady ratios of men to women and undergraduate enrollment to graduate showed that the distribution of opportunity in higher education remained much the same in good times and bad.

discarded as amateur the social justice concerns of the settlement house founders in favor of a hard-headed casework method that increasingly focused on individual psychology as the main cause of problems. In the process, understanding of human behavior became more precise, but also more detached and fragmented. The aim was to adjust clients to the new, highly organized, tensely hurried business civilization all around them, not to nurture an independent sense of community and identity.

During the 1920s, as American economic dominance increased, scientific management cast a lengthening shadow over the thinking of industrial nations. In France, Germany, and Great Britain, Henry Ford's autobiography, *My Life and Work* (1922), inspired a wave of critical interest among intellectuals, artists, and manufacturers alike. Enthusiasts concentrated on the promise that efficiency in

the new industrial system would combine maximum economic benefit with functionally beautiful design. Even the Soviet Union turned to Ford and Taylor for guidance. Joseph Stalin predicted that the "essence" of his country's revolutionary future lay in "the combination of the Russian revolutionary sweep with American efficiency."

The New Consumers

Following the recession of 1921–1922, the nation's economy grew spectacularly during the rest of the decade. Per capita income increased by a third, the cost of living stayed the same, and unemployment remained low. Americans enjoyed the highest standard of living on the globe. Although the rewards of the economic boom were not evenly distributed, white, urban, middle-class, and upper-class Americans had more spending money and more leisure time to spend it. Mass production meant an explosion of affordable new products—especially those powered by electricity—and produced a consumer-goods revolution. In this new era of abundance, millions of Americans sought the American dream, the good life, through consumption.

No better guide exists to how the business boom and business values of the 1920s affected average American life than the sociological classic *Middletown* (1929). The authors, Robert Lynd, trained as a Protestant minister, and his wife, Helen, a professional sociologist, visited the small city of Muncie, Indiana, to compile data on secular and spiritual life. The almost entirely native-born, white population of Muncie (referred to as "Middletown" in the study) closely approximated the national ideal in the age of normalcy. At the end of five years of study, the Lynds determined that Muncie was, above all, "a culture in which everything hinges on money."

Mass production meant an explosion of affordable new products—especially those powered by electricity—and produced a consumer-goods revolution.

To the Lynds, Middletowners had been caught in what the fashionable term of the day called a "cultural lag." Technological and organizational change had become too complex for the average citizen to comprehend. Mystified and feeling increasingly powerless, many Middletowners had

INDIAN DETOUR TOUR GUIDES

Entrepreneurs in the 1920s found ways to draw restless, monied people to new and exotic places. The wealthy often went to Paris and the French Riviera. Others settled for less dazzling destinations. These four tour guides advertise an "Indian detour" — off the beaten track — for the Santa Fe Railroad in 1926. For several years, the Indian cultures of the Southwest had attracted writers and artists in search of peace and the mystical wisdom of Native American pueblo dwellers. The "detourists" were more interested in bargain prices for native crafts and jewelry. Resourcefully, Pueblo Indians and Hispanics mass-produced trinkets and even invented "traditional" dances to entertain the new consumers.

Hunter Publishing Company.

lost confidence in their ability to play an effective role in town meetings and civic organizations. Instead, they deferred to the supposed expertise of leaders in politics and economics and even in the domestic sphere of child raising. The new passivity had a spiritual cost as well, the Lynds lamented. Religion, once a "spontaneous and pervasive part of the life of the city," had been reduced to a social ritual.

The pied piper of these disturbing changes, according to the Lynds, was the rapidly expanding business of advertising, which "pounded away" to convert an independent community into a homogenized consumer aggregate. Indeed, a mature industrial society required radical adjustments by the American people. The values and habits that had built the economy of the 1920s seemed hopelessly inadequate to cope with new realities. The New Era required new truths. Independence and self-suffi-

ciency were out of place in a modern, integrated society where most people lived and worked in complex bureaucracies and organizations. America had solved the age-old problem of production—its factories could produce unimaginable quantities of goods. The question became: How could people be persuaded to buy?

Advertising attacked the old notions of thrift, frugality, and savings, replacing them with a buy-now, pay-later mentality that kept the goods moving, whether consumers had cash or not. Advertising, which became a massive business in the 1920s, touted products and titillated consumers. Newspapers, magazines, radios, and billboards told Americans what they had to have in order to be popular, secure, and successful. And installment buying—a little down, a payment each month—allowed them to buy expensive items before they had saved the

THE SHOPPERS
In this satirical painting, New York City scenic artist Martin Lewis shows two shoppers of the 1920s so attuned to fashion that they are wearing identical outfits and standing as if dancing the Charleston. Shown from the back to accent their anonymity, the pair look at store dummies who outdo them in style and grace, while a man nearby glances at the shoppers dully. The composition captures a certain awkward, comic yearning within the consumption boom of the 1920s for ways of purchasing elusive qualities of elegance and class.
Collection of John P. Axelrod.

cessful advertising agent, Bruce Barton, in 1925. The man nobody knew turned out to be Jesus Christ, who, according to Barton, had been mistakenly portrayed as spiritual and effeminate. The real Jesus, Barton argued, had been a salesman and businessman whose parables were "the most powerful advertisements of all time." Jesus, Barton explained, was a genius at management, a man who "picked up twelve men from the bottom ranks of business and forged them into an organization that conquered the world."

New Era Culture and Its Discontents

When Sigmund Freud visited the United States in 1908, his pioneering work in the psychology of the unconscious remained relatively unknown. But by the 1920s, Freud had become a household name. Most Americans, who didn't bother to read Freud, knew nothing of the complexity and pessimism of his works. They learned about Freud in the popular magazines, which simplified and distorted him. Still, people knew enough to realize that Freud offered a new way of looking at the world that was as radically different and important to the twentieth century as Charles Darwin's theory of evolution had been to the century before.

Freudian psychology, with its probing of the unconscious and its emphasis on the sexual origins of neurotic behavior, sought to break through the resistance of Victorian morality and to deal openly and honestly with sexuality. Freud's aim was to help people face problems and control their destructive impulses. Americans in the 1920s turned Freud on his head. If it is wrong to deny that we are sexual beings, they reasoned, then the key to health and happiness must lie in following impulse freely. Those who doubted this reasoning were simply "repressed." "I'm hipped on Freud," one of F. Scott Fitzgerald's fictional flappers announced, demonstrating her commitment to sexual freedom.

That new ethic excited a significant number of Americans to seek pleasure without guilt in a frenzy of activity that earned the decade the name "the Roaring Twenties." Others, held back by conscience or concern for appearances, enjoyed the spectacle through the miracles of modern technology and new means of mass communication.

money. Radios, vacuum cleaners, washing machines, and automobiles were bought by people who, according to the old values, could not afford them. But to keep the new economy humming, it appeared that people had to spend all they had, and more. As one newspaper announced, "The first responsibility of an American to his country is no longer that of a citizen, but of a consumer."

The extent to which the new values overwhelmed the old became apparent in the runaway best-seller *The Man Nobody Knows*, written by a suc-

TECHNOLOGY IN AMERICA
Frozen Foods

In this 1939 picture a grocer in Springfield, Massachusetts, stands beside a freezer that the Birdseye company had provided him, ready to be one of the first to introduce frozen foods to the nation. This sweeping advance in making food available in all seasons began accidentally during a government-sponsored survey of wildlife in Labrador in the early 1920s. Biologist Clarence Birdseye noted that fish rapidly frozen in that drastically cold climate retained freshness far better than did food frozen in slow-acting food lockers. Back at his seaport home in Gloucester, Massachusetts, Birdseye determined that quick freezing preserved food better because it produced smaller ice crystals that did not damage food cells or dry them out. With a patented process, Birdseye set up his own tiny General Foods Company in 1924 and began marketing locally caught frozen haddock. Five years later, when the large C. W. Post Company bought out the Birdseye name and patents, observers predicted that the Birdseye company would soon have sales of $1 billion per year. But it was not for another decade, when redesign had lowered the cost of freezers by 75 percent, that Birdseye moved beyond supplying steamships and hotels with special long-range storage needs and introduced frozen food to the general public. Typical of the rosy expectations that followed was a 1944 prediction in *Science Digest* that

"high frequency radio waves" would make feasts prepared "under the direction of world-famous chefs" ready for dinner tables. Beyond the imagination of the time was the actual exodus from the dining room altogether, led by the well-named TV-dinner.

BIRDSEYE is a registered trademark of Kraft General Foods, Inc. Reproduced with permission.

At the Movies

Americans seeking pleasure and escape increasingly went to the movies. Starting with the construction of the Regent Theatre in New York City in 1913, thousands of movie palaces, some of them larger and more ornate than European opera houses, sprang up in cities across the country. Uniformed ushers escorted patrons through cavernous foyers lined with mirrors that let plain people see themselves in classy surroundings. Admission was inexpensive for everyone, and the ideal of the good life for common folk and the privileged alike could be savored in the dark.

Little did Thomas Edison realize when he invented the kinetoscope in 1896 that his device for projecting moving images would form the technological base for one of the country's greatest industries. Soon, "nickelodeons," so named for the five cents admission, flourished throughout the country. These early peep shows treated people to little more than scenes of disconnected actions, usually some form of chase. But narrative sophistication came swiftly. *The Great Train Robbery*, made in 1903, became the first action film with a plot. Before World War I, audiences for the new motion pictures came mostly from the working class, while the more well-to-do retained their attachment to the live theater. But by 1910, the phenomenal success of the movies had produced ten thousand movie houses nationwide.

The center of the new industry moved in the 1920s from makeshift sound stages in New York City to Hollywood, California, where producers found open space to film any sort of epic and, more important for camera work, endless sunshine. Like

Ford's River Rouge plant, the Hollywood dream factory mass-produced enough pictures to satisfy Americans' growing appetite for vicarious experience. By 1929, as many people went to the movies in a single week as lived in the entire country.

In the 1920s, significant numbers of Americans sought pleasure without guilt in a frenzy of activities that earned the decade the name "the Roaring Twenties."

In Hollywood, a new breed of industrial entrepreneur, the movie mogul, soon hit upon the successful formula of combining images of opulence, sex, and adventure in thrillers, westerns, and Bible epics. Actors with exotic names like Pola Negri, Rudolph Valentino, and Vilma Banky drew audiences into films of romance in foreign lands where passion was allegedly freer. For settings closer to home, "America's Sweetheart," Mary Pickford, and her real-life husband, Douglas Fairbanks, offered more wholesome adventure. Comedy made the closest connection with audiences, however. Buster Keaton and Harold Lloyd were especially innovative in calling sympathetic attention to the pitfalls and absurdity ordinary people faced. Through slapstick and daring stunts they poked fun at the regimentation and stuffy social custom that made it hard for the average person to be secure and successful. Most versatile of all the comics was Charlie Chaplin, whose famous character the wistful tramp showed an endearing inability to cope with the rules and complexities of modern life.

Moralists who worried that the alluring images on the screen might subvert propriety soon pressed for government regulation. To head off censorship, in 1922 the Motion Picture Producers and Directors of America hired former Postmaster General Will Hays to monitor films for "decency and taste." Hays screened films and tried to balance the interests of public morality, creativity, and commerce without eliminating the raciness that made the movies so popular.

To match the grand surroundings of the theater palaces, Hollywood created the "movie star." Actors and actresses, with their furs, tuxedos, and perfect forms and faces, attended world premieres at the leading theaters, while searchlights broadcast the event beyond the horizon and humble ticket-paying admirers stood mesmerized by the circle of

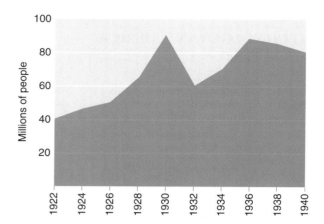

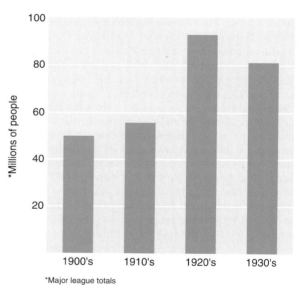

FIGURE 23.4
Movie and Baseball Attendance
America's favorite pastimes, movies and baseball, served as a fever chart for the economy. The percentage of national income spent by spectators of movies and major league baseball remained nearly constant during the interwar years; the rise and fall of weekly movie attendance and seasonal baseball attendance mirrored the rise and fall of prosperity.

light. Like a magnet, the movie industry drew its leading figures from all points of the compass. Many studio owners and producers came from eastern European immigrant communities, while directors were often refugees from the stage or European film studios. Actors came from all over. People of color were still largely excluded (except when they were used for comic relief or as villains). But among the white majority, anyone who looked

HEROES AND HEROINES

Within popular lore of the 1920s, two kinds of women looked up adoringly at two kinds of heroes. A wholesome image is seen on this 1927 cover of the Popular Monthly Homecraft Magazine. *Here the healthy outdoor girl type, smartly turned out in her raccoon coat and pennant, seems in flattering control of a naive college football hero. The pale, sensitive damsel Vilma Banky kneels imploringly before the hypnotic gaze of the movies' greatest heartthrob, Rudolph Valentino. The 1926 ad titillates with ambivalence. Is the pale heroine beseeching her kidnapper to release her? Or is she swooning with desire as the sheik begins to disrobe?*

Picture Research Consultant & Archives; Billy Rose Theatre Collection, The New York Public Library at Lincoln Center

good on screen and could invent an elegant or rugged-sounding name could hope to become a star. Hollywood turned out to be entertainment's best contribution to the melting pot ideal. In the 1920s, the movies' focus on fun and happiness, vicarious thrills and romance, held American audiences spellbound.

Sports and Hero Worship

Along with celluloid heroes, Americans found their heroes in sports. Baseball, professionalized since 1871, became the national pastime. Early in the cen-

tury, New York and Philadelphia built large stadiums, signaling the arrival of the sport into a new age of big money and influence. Still, by the 1920s, baseball remained essentially a game played by and for the working class, an outlet for raw energy and even a tinge of rebelliousness. Babe Ruth was the most cherished free spirit of the time. An orphan who never really grew up, Ruth mixed his record-setting home runs with rowdy escapades, satisfying the general view that sports offered a way to break out of the ordinariness of everyday life.

The public also fell in love with a young boxer from the grim mining districts of Colorado. As a teenager, Jack Dempsey had made his living hanging around saloons betting he could beat anyone in the house. When he took the heavyweight crown just after World War I from the giant champion Jess Willard in a spectacular slugfest, he was revered as America's equalizer, a stand-in for the average American who felt increasingly detached from natural impulses and hemmed in by complex bureaucracies and a machine-made culture.

The greatest football player of the decade, Red Grange of the University of Illinois, was a quiet, straitlaced son of the prairies whose steady attention to the business side of football proved crucial to the development of the professional game. The most celebrated college coach, Knute Rockne of Notre Dame, was beloved for his earnest advocacy of football as a parable of the good life of hard work and teamwork. Let the professors make learning as interesting as football, Rockne advised, and the problem of getting youth to learn would disappear.

The decade's hero worship reached its zenith in the celebration of a young pilot, Charles Lindbergh. On May 20, 1927, Lindbergh took off in his monoplane and became the first person to fly solo across the Atlantic. It took thirty-three hours, and as far as the lanky, painfully shy young man was concerned, the feat ended when he landed in Paris. But the American people would not let the adventure end. Lindbergh became the idol of the nation. His return home was a triumphant entry, unmatched in the nation's history.

Newspapers tagged Lindbergh the "Lone Eagle." One magazine declared: "Charles Lindbergh is the heir of all that we like to think is best in America. He is the stuff out of which have been made the pioneers that opened up the wilderness. His are the qualities which we, as a people, must nourish." Americans who celebrated Lindbergh lived in a world in which solitary, courageous achievement was rapidly becoming almost impossible. The United States was rapidly becoming a modern, urban, machine-oriented civilization, a world of bureaucracies and institutions, a place in which men and women did not act independently but found themselves cogs in large corporate or government organizations. It was painful for some to accept that success had become more a matter of cooperation, winning friends, and influencing people than courageous independent achievement.

But "Lucky Lindy," as he was known, referred to himself and his plane as "we," and he cautioned cheering crowds not to forget the wonderful engine that made it all possible. Man and machine (the most advanced piece of technology America's modern industrial economy had produced) were partners, not enemies, Lindbergh said. He sought to reassure Americans that possibilities for adventure remained in the modern, technological, and bureaucratic world. In the end, the celebration embraced both the heroic individual and the complex machine. It was a fitting response from a people who were enduring the final stages of the transition from a rural, agricultural nation to an urban, industrial one.

Women and Men of the Jazz Age

The first licensed radio station, KDKA in Pittsburgh, began broadcasting in 1920, and soon American airwaves buzzed with news, sermons, market information, police calls, soap operas, labor reports, sporting events, comedy shows, music, and advertisements. Americans in the most isolated outposts of the high plains laughed at the latest jokes from New York or Chicago. For the first time, citizens were able to listen to the voices of political candidates without leaving home. And, most important, radio allowed advertisers to reach prospective customers in the intimacy of their own living rooms. Door-to-door salesmen, traditionally rebuffed at the door, now came into the nation's parlors via the airwaves to pitch their products. Between 1922 and 1929, the number of radio stations increased from 30 to 606. In those seven short years, the number of homes with radios jumped from 60,000 to a staggering 10,250,000.

Jazz challenged its audience to be—or seem to be—young and carefree. For the first time, in the 1920s youth became a social class distinct in itself.

Along with advertising and consumer goods, radio added to the growth of popular music, especially jazz. Jazz, with its energetic style and its suggestion of youthful freedom and sexual openness, was the product of African American artists. But in the 1920s, although a radio broadcast might occasionally feature the headlong, ragged rhythms of the King Oliver Creole Jazz Band or the "walking bass" stride piano style of James P. Johnson, white audiences for the most part embraced a classically trained musician aptly named Paul Whiteman. Although Whiteman's "symphonic jazz," with its strict tempos and avoidance of improvisation, left most black jazz fans cold, Whiteman helped make jazz the national favorite with white audiences. George Gershwin composed his jazz-classical hybrid *Rhapsody in Blue* for Whiteman's orchestra, and it was Whiteman on the radio who spread Jazz Age dances like the shimmy, the black bottom, and, most popular of all, the Charleston.

Jazz, even white jazz, challenged its audience to be—or seem to be—young and carefree. For the first time, in the 1920s youth became a social class distinct in itself, much idolized and fretted over. As the traditional bonds of community and religion eroded, family constraints loosened and the young felt less pressure to imitate their elders. Instead, they developed their own culture. An increasing number of college students helped the "rah-rah" style of college life become a fad, promoted in movies, songs, and advertisements. The collegiate set was the vanguard of the decade's "flaming youth."

Most stunning were the changes in the behavior of young women. In the 1920s, the typical urban woman shed up to twelve yards of clothing, "parked" her corset in the cloakroom (if she wore one at all), bared her knees, smoked cigarettes, drank in speakeasies, and generally played havoc with traditionally conservative notions of female behavior. The daring "flapper," as she was called, became the symbol of youthful revolt. As her contemporary and chronicler F. Scott Fitzgerald described her in his novel *This Side of Paradise* (1920), she was "lovely and expensive and about nineteen."

For all their spirit, the youth of the 1920s managed to disappoint reformers by their lack of interest in politics as much as they angered traditionalists with their unconventional morality. For the most part, young people remained apathetic about social issues and eager to participate in the new consumer culture. Rarely did they pose a threat to the status quo. "Flaming youth" rapidly cooled in office jobs and suburbs, and high-spirited flappers eventually settled down to become wives and mothers and employees.

Yet, even at home women's lives reflected the changes of the new era. Thanks to the greater availability of birth control devices, married people could remain passionate and yet have fewer children to take care of. New home appliances also lightened the load. While men are judged by how successfully they delegate work, one advertisement declared, "the wise woman delegates to electricity all that electricity can do." Advertisers went too far, however, in claiming that electricity had made

HELD MAGAZINE COVER
Artist John Held drew and lived the extravagant life of the flaming youth of the Roaring Twenties. Raised in Mormon, Utah, Held followed his artistic and journalistic skills to New York City and there found endless subjects to amuse himself. His caricatures of the Jazz Age came to typify it and made him a fortune. Like the high-living sorts he satirized, Held married and divorced a couple of times, dividing his time among his New York penthouse, Palm Beach cabana, and estate in Connecticut. Then, following the curve, he went broke in the Great Crash of 1929. Held gave up cartooning for landscape painting and sculpture and settled down on a small farm. Shown here is Held's inimitable style on the cover of the 1920s leading humor magazine: sporty convertible, the flapper, and Held's signature caricature of the round-headed, almost puppetlike young man.
Culver Pictures.

housewives ladies of leisure. Most rural homes were beyond the reach of power lines; and urban middle class women who had appliances, still spent a lot of hours cooking, mending, and cleaning.

For women who worked outside the home, the changing economy of the 1920s offered fresh, but still limited, opportunity. Many factory jobs, such as those in the booming automobile industry, and most management positions remained male domains, but "pink-collar" jobs (in poorly paying service occupations) became readily available. Women continued to become teachers and nurses, but even more found work as secretaries, typists, and file clerks, keeping the modern corporation afloat while receiving few of its rewards. Women also worked as salesclerks, playing a crucial role in the new consumer society. By 1930, nearly eleven million women were employed, constituting 24 percent of the workforce, compared with 18 percent in 1900.

Black Assertion and the Harlem Renaissance

Cheers for the black soldiers who marched up Broadway after the First World War soon faded, and grim days of race riots and hardship followed. Still, a sense of optimism remained strong among African Americans. It was in New York City that the key elements of hope and talent came together to form an exceptionally dynamic moment in black history. In the years before the war, black people in New York had moved uptown from their cramped confinement in Hell's Kitchen to the spacious heights of Harlem. A highly cosmopolitan population soon filled the new area, including poor migrants from the South responding to the economic opportunities offered by the war and a more sophisticated wave of immigrants from the West Indies. On the crest of the new wave were black artists and writers who made Harlem a special place. There the "New Negro," as critic and historian Alain Locke put it in a book by that name, could rise from the ashes of a subjugated past and discover the race's true, creative identity.

That quest for autonomy would prove more aggressive than it had been before the war. The military service of black troops raised expectations of higher status in American society. Disillusioned with mainstream politics, African Americans looked for new leadership, and many poor urban blacks turned to a forceful Jamaican visionary named Marcus Garvey. Garvey urged African Americans to rediscover the heritage of Africa and to take pride in their own culture and achievements. In 1917, Garvey launched the Universal Negro Improvement Association (UNIA) to help African Americans gain economic and political independence entirely out-

side of white society. Through their own shipping company, the Black Star Line, Garvey's followers aimed to finance their Back to Africa movement. The dream of returning to a "promised land" in Africa linked anticolonialist fervor with pride in race. UNIA proposed a return to Africa for the Africans so that the true beauty and nobility of blacks could emerge from beneath the mask of servility forced upon them by white oppression in the United States.

Garvey excelled in stirring support for his vision. In parades, he cut a fine figure, riding in an open car in a feather-plumed uniform while his African Legion marched behind. His black nationalist message drew enthusiastic crowds in Harlem and brought delegates from many countries to the UNIA convention of 1920. But Garvey was a naive businessman and was unprepared for the rough opposition he encountered. Sharp operators sold bad ships to the Black Star Line, and the federal government, opposed to minority movements that challenged the status quo, jailed Garvey briefly on dubious mail fraud charges and then in 1927 deported him to Jamaica. But Garvey's black nationalist vision survived and continued to find spokesmen in the African American community. Moreover, other black people pondered the questions Garvey raised about black identity, racial pride, and the search for equality and security.

Black writers and artists who explored the African American experience unleashed an artistic explosion in the 1920s called the Harlem Renaissance. They embraced a cultural tradition far removed from the world of the white elite. The poet Langston Hughes summed up the central thrust of the movement when he shouted: "I am a Negro— and beautiful." Probing the black cultural tradition, African American intellectuals celebrated the rich achievement within harsh conditions.

In his music and writing, James Weldon Johnson focused on the migrants from the South, the gritty working people and churchgoers of Harlem. In 1903, he had written the "Negro national anthem," "Lift Every Voice," and in 1927, in "God's Trombones," he offered an interpretation of black folktales. Zora Neale Hurston came to Harlem from Florida, and as a scholarship student at Barnard College she studied anthropology and later collected black folktales. Her masterpiece, *Their Eyes Were Watching God* (1937), explores the indomitable spirit of poor, uneducated black people. Langston Hughes, Claude McKay, Countee Cullen, Nella Lar-

NOAH'S ARK

The Harlem Renaissance gained its principal visual expression at the hands of Kansas-born painter Aaron Douglas. When Douglas arrived in New York City in 1925, he quickly attracted the attention of W. E. B. DuBois, who placed great importance on the arts as a carrier of the African American soul. At Du Bois's urging, Douglas sought ways of integrating the African cultural heritage with American experience. This depiction of an African Noah commanding the loading of the ark displays a technique that became closely associated with African American art: strong silhouetted figures awash in misty color, indicating a connection between Christian faith and the vital, colorful origins of black Americans in a distant, mythologized African past.

Fisk University Art Galleries, Nashville, Tennessee.

sen, and other writers eloquently expressed both the plight of black Americans and their vital culture. Artist Aaron Douglas tried to capture slave and African folklore on canvas. His bold symbolic figures were a striking example of the Harlem Renaissance's clear assertion of self-esteem.

Whites who finally became aware of Harlem usually chose to go to the area at night and hardly noticed its serious side. For them Harlem was an exotic dark continent just up the street. They sought a modern version of the old-time minstrel show, and Harlem nightclubs sprang up to provide black performers for whites-only audiences. The most famous white outpost in Harlem, the Cotton Club, was a gangster-owned outlet for the bootleggers who made fortunes out of the prohibitionist society that club patrons were fleeing. As for the black performers, they had to enter by the delivery doors and make careful preparations not to need the restrooms, which were for whites only.

Garvey's Back to Africa movement and the Harlem Renaissance signified a new awareness among African Americans. The Great Migration that had carried a million blacks out of the South and their subsequent northern urban experiences altered black ideas and attitudes. Urban blacks, not just in Harlem, were showing a stronger racial consciousness and a willingness to act on it.

The Lost Generation

Observing the collection of American writers and artists who flocked to her salon in Paris during the 1920s, the writer Gertrude Stein remarked, "They are the lost generation." Out of step with American society, despising its business mentality, its consumer culture, and its small-town hypocrisy, a number of artists and critics renounced America altogether. Rather than try to reform it as the progressives had done before the war, they chose to leave it. The writer Harold Stearns announced the secession most conspicuously when he gathered a group of some thirty authors to publish a book of essays scornfully entitled *Civilization in the United States* (1922). Relentlessly, their essays condemned the way sexual prudery and greed blighted virtually every aspect of the America they knew. Then, amid much public fanfare, Stearns and other alienated critics set sail for France.

Young, and mostly college-educated men, these expatriates, as they were called, were profoundly embittered by World War I. The devastation wrought by the war had left them feeling betrayed and deceived by the older generation. The poet Ezra Pound asked what so many young men had died for. His answer:

For an old bitch gone in the teeth
For a botched civilization.

Fed up with Wilsonian rhetoric, skeptical of the possibility of progress, and appalled by the vulgarity and materialism of the New Era, the young exiles scattered throughout Germany, Spain, and France. Mostly, however, they favored Paris, where the cost of living was low and the culture receptive to their hopes and struggles. Far from the complications of home and steady work, they helped launch the most creative period in American art and literature in the twentieth century.

The novelist whose sparse, clean style best exemplified the expatriate writers' efforts to strip writing of its cant and make language into the exact mirror of things was Ernest Hemingway. Born in suburban Chicago, Hemingway had served in a volunteer ambulance corps during the war. In his novel *The Sun Also Rises* (1926), Hemingway's main character is impotent, the result of a war wound. Void of conventional beliefs, he and his friends set out on an aimless journey through France and Spain, discovering little in the world to sustain them. In Hemingway's view, paring words and images down to basics showed life as a struggle with brute forces. His own stern personal code of honor dismissed creeds, ideologies, and patriotism as pious attempts to cover up the fact that life is a losing battle with death. His ideal of macho courage, "grace under pressure," guided a lonely, doomed struggle with the inevitable.

Writers who remained in America were exiles in spirit who hoped that freedom from claims of duty and convention would help them in exploring the limits of creativity. One prominent critic boosted his reputation for good judgment by proclaiming that "the great problems of the world — social, political, economic, and theological — do not concern me in the slightest." Within that atmosphere novelist Sinclair Lewis in *Main Street* (1920) and *Babbitt* (1922) devastatingly satirized his native Midwest as a cultural wasteland. Humorists like James Thurber and Don Marquis created outlandish forms and characters to poke fun at taboos and inhibitions. And southern writers, led by William Faulkner, rallied against the South's reputation as a literary Sahara by exploring the dark undercurrents of that region's class and race heritage. But doubts about the new freedom surfaced as well. From the vantage of his own fame and wealth as chronicler of flaming youth, F. Scott Fitzgerald spoke with guilty brilliance in *This Side of Paradise* (1920) of a disillusioned generation "grown up to find all Gods dead, all wars fought, all faiths in man shaken."

Rural America and Resistance to Change

Rural America and urban America had eyed each other warily since the nineteenth century. But suspicion turned to outright hostility in the 1920s. Though the number of people in small towns and rural areas continued to increase, country people saw the center of gravity of American life shift from farm to city. The 1920 census established that for the first time more Americans lived in towns and cities than in the country. The rapid growth of cities and suburbs cost rural America its dominance over the nation's political and cultural life.

It also put economic distance between city and country. The prosperity of the 1920s was very much an urban phenomenon. Between 1918 and 1921, the value of farmland and farm incomes fell by 30 to 50 percent. Technological advances benefited large-scale farming, but the average farm family had to incur huge and risky debts to buy the new machinery it needed to compete. Most farmers held fast to the agrarian ideal of self-reliant individualism, but by the end of the decade, 40 percent of the nation's farmers had become landless tenants. Moreover, despite the flood of new technology, 90 percent of rural homes in 1930 were still without indoor plumbing, gas, or electricity.

In the eyes of many country folk, the cities stood for everything that rural areas stood against. Rural Americans saw themselves as Anglo-Saxon (conveniently forgetting that most blacks still lived in the rural South), while the cities filled with strangers from around the world. Rural America was the home of traditional Protestant values, and the cities were the home of Catholics, Jews, liberal Protestants, and atheists. Rural America championed old-fashioned Puritan moral standards of abstinence and self-denial, and the cities seemed to be places of unbounded hedonism and sexual vice. Rural youth were not children of the Jazz Age, running around with raccoon coats and hip flasks or with stockings rolled daringly at the knee.

Increasingly, the nation divided along the line drawn between the country and the city. At the end of the previous decade, rural Americans had helped enact prohibition and in the 1920s they defended it while urban dwellers lined up at speakeasies. The defense mechanisms of rural America began working overtime in the 1920s. Country people joined with other frightened Americans to push through immigration restrictions, cutting off the foreign flood that they feared was going to engulf them. Religious fundamentalism challenged modern values. And in 1928, the clash of cultures reached national politics, as city and country squared off in a presidential election.

The Rebirth of the Ku Klux Klan

Some of those who felt slighted or offended by the modern world channeled their desperation into a revived version of the Ku Klux Klan that first appeared in 1915. Although the new Klan rose once again in the South, where its predecessor had been created to curb the rights of blacks during Reconstruction, it swiftly moved beyond the region. Imperial Grand Wizard Hiram Wesley Evans, a Texas dentist who styled himself as "the most average man in America," employed modern sales techniques to organize a network of klaverns (local societies) across the country. The nation, Evans argued, stood in need of a thorough cleansing. He promised that Klansmen would stoutly defend family, morality, and traditional values against the threat offered by blacks, immigrants, and radicals. In 1926, Evans complained that "the sacredness of our Sabbath, of our homes, of chastity, and finally even of our right to teach our children in our own schools fundamental facts and truths were torn away from us." This potent argument of a lost birthright brought into the Klan at its peak some three to four million members, a substantial fraction of whom lived in towns and cities.

The Klan's brand of narrow-mindedness and intolerance offered a certain counterfeit dignity for those who felt passed over by a changing society. It played on the decade's love of fraternal societies with their secrecy, uniforms, and rituals. Like the Elks or the Odd Fellows, the Klan also promised the practical advantage of forging business contacts. At the same time, it appealed to the vengeful and brutal, enabling its cloaked and hooded members to intimidate and punish anonymously and with little fear of consequences. The brotherhood and camaraderie of the Klan served also as a pathetic substitute for the fading village community. Nostalgia and violence came together in the KKK.

Like the original Klan, the new Klan terrorized blacks, but it also took aim at other people. Any group that threatened traditional values, as the Klan defined them, ran the risk of vigilante action. Klansmen threatened, roughed up, and even murdered bootleggers, drunks, wife beaters, advocates of birth control, and teachers who contradicted the Bible. They sought to drive Catholics, Jews, and foreigners from their communities. Economic insecurity underlay Klansmen's sense of a world out of control. Long-term economic changes had marooned white farmers and small merchants between corporate giants on the one hand and the growing army of wage laborers on the other. Economic inequality grew during the 1920s, and prosperity remained a stranger in the American countryside. Their old world was unraveling, and Klansmen sought reactionary means to knit it back together. By the mid-1920s, the Klan had gained considerable political power, virtually controlling Indiana and influencing politics in Illinois, California, Oregon, Texas, Louisiana, Oklahoma, and Kansas.

THE LAW IS TOO SLOW
This stark depiction of a lynching by George Bellows in 1923 appeared just as the revived Ku Klux Klan was proclaiming itself the defender of traditional virtue in a sinful modern world. Bellows, an athlete as well as an artist, had gained fame as a realist and tough-minded radical before World War I and continued until his death in 1925 to spur social conscience even after doing so had gone out of fashion.
The Art Institute of Chicago. All rights reserved, © 1996.

By the late 1920s, the Klan had withered away, partly because immigration restrictions removed the threat of invading foreigners and partly out of public disgust. Grand Dragon David Stephenson of Indiana, for example, went to jail after a sensational trial that found him guilty of the kidnap and rape of a woman who subsequently committed suicide. Yet the social grievances and hard economic problems that had produced such alienation and attracted recruits to the Klan remained.

The Scopes Trial

The clash between the old-time religion and the new spirit of science reached a dramatic climax in the Scopes trial in 1925. The confrontation occurred after several southern and border states passed legislation in the early 1920s against the teaching of Charles Darwin's theory of evolution in the public schools. Fundamentalist Protestants insisted that the Bible's creation story be taught as the literal truth. In answer to a clamor from scientists and civil liberties organizations for a challenge to the law, John Scopes, a young schoolteacher in Dayton, Tennessee, offered to test his state's ban on teaching evolution. When Scopes was brought to trial in the summer of 1925, Clarence Darrow, a brilliant defense lawyer from Chicago, volunteered to defend him. Darrow, an avowed agnostic, took on the state's attorney William Jennings Bryan, the old war horse of the Democratic Party and symbol of rural America. Bryan, now aging and ill, styled himself as the defender of Christian opposition to the idea that humans had evolved from apes.

The Ku Klux Klan and the Scopes trial dramatized and inflamed divisions between city and country, intellectuals and the unlettered, the privileged and the outcasts, the scoffers and the faithful.

The Scopes trial quickly degenerated into a freakish media circus, despite the serious religious and philosophical issues underlying it. As the first trial to be covered live on the radio, it attracted an avid nationwide audience. The reporters from big-city papers who converged on Dayton were for the most part hostile to Bryan, none more so than the incomparably cynical H. L. Mencken. Mencken gleefully painted Bryan as a sort of Darwinian missing link ("a sweating anthropoid," a "gaping primate"). When, under relentless questioning by Darrow, Bryan declared on the witness stand that he did, indeed, believe the world was created in six days and that Jonah had lived in the belly of a whale, his humiliation in the eyes of most urban observers was complete. Although the Tennessee court upheld the law in defiance of modern intellectual consensus and punished Scopes with a $100 fine, Mencken had the last word in a merciless obituary for Bryan, who died just weeks after the trial ended. Portraying the "monkey trial" as a battle between the country and the city, Mencken flayed Bryan as a "charlatan, a mountebank, a zany without shame or dignity," motivated solely by "hatred of the city men who had laughed at him for so long."

As Mencken's acid prose indicated, Bryan's humiliation was not purely a victory of reason and science. It also served to reduce the esteem in which country people and their old values were held. The Ku Klux Klan and the Scopes trial dramatized and inflamed divisions between city and country, intellectuals and the unlettered, the privileged and the outcasts, the scoffers and the faithful.

Al Smith and the Election of 1928

The shock of Calvin Coolidge's announcement in the summer of 1927 that "I do not choose to run for President in 1928" caught the country off guard and evened the playing field for the Democrats. But in the election of 1928, issues splitting the nation—prohibition, religious bigotry, and the clash between rural and urban values—emerged with a vengeance.

Among Republicans, the logical choice as Coolidge's successor seemed to be Herbert Hoover. Hoover enjoyed a great reputation as the wonder-working dynamo of the Commerce Department during the Harding and Coolidge administrations. Some uneasiness surfaced during the primaries about Hoover's lack of a common touch and a feel for electoral politics, but the powerful insiders who ran the party believed that Hoover was best able to continue Coolidge's pro-business programs and secured him the nomination.

The Democrats nominated Governor Alfred E. Smith of New York. Smith epitomized big-city values. Born to Irish Catholic immigrant parents, Smith had grown up on the sidewalks of New York. The Democrats balanced the ticket with a southern conservative, Senator Joseph Robinson of Arkansas, and sought to woo farmers with the promise of lower tariffs and labor with calls for reforms including collective bargaining. The platform advocated an active government, and Smith, an outspoken "wet" (an opponent of prohibition), actively championed repeal of the Eighteenth Amendment.

Very quickly the contest boiled down to controversy over the urban and religious values Smith represented. As the first Catholic to run for president, Smith made an easy target. An editorial in the *Baptist and Commoner* declared that the election of Smith "would be granting the Pope the right to dictate to this government what it should do." There would be edicts from the White House saying "to hell with our public schools" and "Protestants are now living in adultery because they were not married by a priest." Are you willing, the editorial asked, to accept a president who would tell us "our offspring are bastards"? Smith's connections with the Tammany Hall political machine cost him additional support in the countryside. Radio broadcasts also damaged Smith among listeners who found his New York City accent alien and offputting.

Smith supporters attacked Hoover as a heartless tool of big-money interests, but with little effect. It is doubtful anyone could have beaten Hoover, who neatly combined the image of morality, efficiency, service, and prosperity. But in 1928, a Catholic had very little chance. Hoover won the election by a landslide. He received 58 percent of the vote, taking all but eight states, and gained 444 electoral votes to Smith's 87. The Republicans managed to retain support of blacks in the South at the same time they made a calculated appeal to southern whites in the fundamentalist Bible belt. Hoover wrenched five states loose from the formerly solid Democratic South. But Republican strength in the cities and among discontented farmers suffered an ominous erosion. The nation's largest cities voted Democratic in a striking reversal from 1924, indicating the rising strength of ethnic minorities, including Smith's fellow Catholics.

From the New Era to the Great Crash

At his inauguration in 1929, Herbert Hoover told the American people, "We in America today are nearer to the final triumph over poverty than ever before in the history of any land. The poorhouse is vanishing from among us." The nation had not yet reached that goal, he said, "but, given a chance to go forward with the policies of the last eight years,

we shall soon with the help of God be in sight of the day when poverty will be banished from this nation." Those words came back to haunt Hoover, for in eight short months the Roaring Twenties came to a crashing halt. The prosperity Hoover touted collapsed with the stock market crash, and the nation fell into the most serious economic depression of all time. Hoover and his reputation were among the first casualties, along with the reverence for business that had been the hallmark of Hoover's New Era.

Herbert Hoover: The Great Engineer

It is ironic, and a little unfair, that the Great Depression struck during Hoover's presidency. Coming into office in 1929, Hoover seemed to have the credentials to be a great president. He was undoubtedly a vast improvement over his immediate predecessors. Born in 1874 into a poor Iowa farm family and orphaned at twelve, Hoover was raised by hardworking Quaker relatives who had braved the pioneer trail to Oregon. In 1896, he graduated with Stanford University's first class with a degree in geology and forty dollars in his pocket. By the time he was thirty, he was one of the world's top mining engineers. By the time he was forty, he had become a millionaire with offices in London, New York, San Francisco, Petrograd (St. Petersburg), and Paris. Hoover and his wife and Stanford classmate, Lou Henry Hoover, lived lives of high adventure in mining camps around the world, surviving primitive conditions, labor wars, and even bombardment during China's Boxer Rebellion.

The prosperity Hoover touted collapsed with the 1929 stock market crash, and the nation fell into the most serious economic depression of all time.

In 1914, Hoover's renown as an organizational genius and tireless worker won him the directorship of the task force set up to feed the Belgians, who had been devastated by the German attack through their country at the beginning of World War I. Hoover's success in heading the greatest relief effort in history won him the title "the Great Humanitarian" and led Woodrow Wilson to choose him for head of the Food Administration when the United States entered the war. In the 1920s, he

VOTE FOR HERBERT HOOVER
and CHARLES CURTIS
for the Prosperity of your Country *and the Happiness and your home....*

HOOVER CAMPAIGN POSTER
Herbert Hoover's 1928 campaign poster neatly framed his major positions: middle-class prosperity in a house in the suburbs, complete with a car in every garage and, presumably, a chicken in every pot. To complete the display, smoking chimneys at a discreet distance remind voters that Hoover as secretary of commerce had promoted industry that made the suburban idyll possible.
Collection of Janice L. and David J. Frent.

served in the Harding and Coolidge cabinets as secretary of commerce, where he put into practice the things he believed in—material welfare, efficiency, voluntary cooperative enterprise, and individual initiative in the context of government-business partnership.

In 1922, Hoover had formulated his political philosophy in a slender book titled *American Individualism*. He extolled rugged individualism—"a quality of the individual alone"—and assumed that the United States offered opportunity to everyone. He measured a person's stature and achievement by wealth. As he summed it up, a man who had not made a million dollars by the time he was forty didn't amount to much. Hoover thought of himself as a progressive, but his reluctance to use the government to force change and equalize conditions distanced him from the reform spirit of prewar progressives. Government's task, Hoover felt, was simply to promote private initiative and enforce rules of fair play. While government could encourage cooperation among businesses, a vibrant economy and free society required that businesses participate voluntarily.

For all his strengths, hindsight reveals that Hoover had significant liabilities when he became

president. The only elective office he had ever held was treasurer of his class at Stanford. Having spent most of his adult life abroad, he had never voted in a presidential election. He had very little political know-how. He had no network of political contacts. He had a poor political touch. He was too stiff and too thin-skinned. And he also suffered the liability of being oversold. Before he took office, Hoover told a friend: "I have no dread of the ordinary work of the presidency. What I do fear is the . . . exaggerated idea . . . I am a sort of superman, that no problem is beyond my capacity." And he added prophetically, "If some unprecedented calamity should come upon the nation . . . I would be sacrificed to the unreasoning disappointment of a people who expected too much."

Hoover's greatest liability, however, was his stubborn integrity. He knew what he believed, and he would not be shaken. He had developed precise ideas that to him spelled out the proper workings of an economy and the correct relationship between citizen and government. Those ideas were popular and at least partially successful during the 1920s. But the world changed in the 1930s, and Hoover became a victim of his own beliefs. He doggedly stuck to his principles, even as the nation slipped deeper and deeper into depression. In the end, the man who had fed Europe became a symbol of hunger, the brilliant administrator a symbol of disaster. He carried the shame of the depression on his shoulders until he died in 1964. To some, his name remains linked with reactionary conservatism. In reality, the depression was inevitable by the time he entered the White House. What he did to combat it once it struck is another matter.

The Unstable Economy

In the spring of 1929, when Hoover moved into the White House, the United States basked in the sunshine of economic prosperity. Most Americans saw no more than a few wispy clouds on the horizon. In fact, thunderheads loomed.

Abroad, an unstable international economy spelled trouble. Massive expenditures during the First World War had nearly bankrupted the European powers. The United States, new to its role as the world's dominant economic power, failed to step in and help rebuild Europe's shattered economy. Instead, it demanded that European nations repay their war loans. Unable to pay, the European countries asked for and received new loans to pay off the old ones. In addition, the United States erected tariff barriers that kept other nations from selling their goods to Americans. As a consequence, foreign nations had less money to buy American goods, which were pouring out in record abundance. To keep trade with other nations alive, the United States extended more credit. Debt piled onto debt in an absurd pyramid. By the end of the decade, the United States accounted for 40 percent of the world's economic production and acquired most of the world's gold in return for its exports.

At home, too, prosperity rested on shaky foundations. Behind the glittering facade of affluence, poverty was rampant. Farmers continued to suffer from low prices for their crops and chronic indebtedness. The average income of families on the land amounted to only $240 per year, and 54 percent earned less than $1,000. Labor's wages rose slightly in the 1920s, but they failed to keep up with productivity and corporate profits. Nearly two-thirds of all American families lived on less than the $2,000 per year that was needed to "supply only basic necessities." The 1920s produced fabulous wealth, but most of it settled in the corporate sector. By the end of the decade, the top 1 percent of the population received 15 percent of the nation's income, an amount equal to that received by the bottom 42 percent of the population.

The imbalance of wealth produced a serious problem in consumption. Money rushing to the top prompted extravagant behavior—the acquisition of opulent houses, cars, and polo ponies. The rich, brilliantly portrayed in F. Scott Fitzgerald's *The Great Gatsby* (1925), gave the era much of its mythical glitter with their careless spending. But they could absorb only a tiny fraction of the nation's output. Ordinary folk, on whom the system ultimately depended, did their best, but they were too poor to buy all that American industry produced. At first, Americans thought that credit would handle the problem of consumer demand. Installment buying became a standard practice. At the end of the decade, four out of five automobiles and two out of three radios were bought on credit. Personal indebtedness swelled, but credit had its limits.

Signs of the economic slowdown began at middecade. Between 1921 and 1928, during the heyday of the New Era, some five thousand banks had failed. Two crucial industries began to totter. After 1925, the boom in the construction industry subsided, and the automobile industry also faltered. With nearly thirty million cars already on the road, demand had been met and producers began to cut back and lay off workers. The warning signs went largely unnoticed, however. Confidence in fundamental soundness and eagerness to profit from it created a blindness to underlying flaws in the economy.

The Great Crash of 1929

The most spectacular example of the credit binge of the 1920s occurred in the stock market—the nerve center and symbol of the boom. Even after the economy began weakening in the mid-1920s, a get-rich-quick mania hit Wall Street. There, buying stocks on margin—that is, putting up only part of the money at the time of purchase—became rampant. The lure of vast returns for very little investment lured tens of thousands of speculators into the market. And many got rich in paper profits. But those who bought on credit could finance their loans only if their stock increased in value. Thus, the stock market became dependent on continued expansion. Many naively believed that the market would continue to go up forever. There was some reason to think so. Between 1924 and 1929, the values of stocks listed on the New York Stock Exchange increased more than 400 percent. From that height it was hard to imagine what would happen were the market to fall and speculators forced to meet their margin loans with cash they never had.

When stock purchased on margin rose to about 20 percent of the total by the summer of 1929, Hoover summoned Richard Whitney, the head of the New York Stock Exchange, to urge him to tighten requirements. But Whitney, who later went to Sing Sing prison for stealing money from trust funds to cover his own bad investments, gave only empty promises of cooperation. Other representatives from prestigious banks and investment houses assured Hoover that all was well. Former President Coolidge stated tersely that at current prices, stocks were a bargain. The prudent Hoover, however, decided to sell some of his own stocks. In rejecting the optimistic advice of the boosters, Hoover took to a saying he kept repeating for the rest of his battle-scarred life: "The only trouble with capitalism is capitalists. They're too damned greedy."

Finally, in the fall of 1929, the market hesitated. Like rabbits sniffing danger, investors nervously began to sell their overvalued stock. The dip quickly became a rush, building to panic on October 24, the day that came to be known as Black Thursday. Brokers jammed the stock exchange and overflowed into the street. Stirred by the cries of "Sell! Sell!" just outside their windows, the giants of finance gathered in the offices of J. P. Morgan Jr., son of the nineteenth century Wall Street lion, to plot ways of restoring confidence. They injected $100 million of their assets to bolster the market and issued brave declarations of faith. But more panic selling came on Black Tuesday, October 29, the day the market suffered the greatest drop in history.

During the month of October alone, the listings on the New York Stock Exchange lost more than one-third of their value and continued steadily downward until 1932. During that slide, stocks worth $87 billion at the crest of the boom dropped to only $18 billion. In one of the few jaunty quips the panic produced, the weekly theatrical trade journal *Variety* headlined, "Wall Street Lays an Egg."

It was a very large egg out of which hatched the deepest, longest-lasting depression in the nation's history. It was once thought that the Great Crash *caused* the Great Depression. It did not. In 1929, the national and international economies were riddled with severe problems, but the collapse of Wall Street was significant nevertheless. The dramatic loss of 10 percent of Americans' total personal wealth and the fear of risking what was left acted

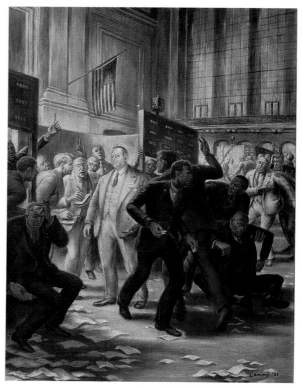

BLACK FRIDAY

Edward Laning, a mural painter who lost his personal fortune in the stock market crash, gained a measure of revenge in this melodramatic version of panic on the Stock Exchange floor. The painting shows Stock Exchange president Richard Whitney standing firm in the center as prices and brokers collapse around him. A few years later, however, Whitney went to prison for stealing from other people's accounts to cover his own losses. Laning, on the other hand, went on to fame for the murals he painted to adorn Ellis Island and the New York Public Library. Collection of John P. Axelrod.

as a great brake on economic activity. With the collapse of the stock market went the aggressive confidence in America's future as a land of perpetually expanding prosperity. That faith had been crucial to the New Era.

Hoover and the Limits of Individualism

Admirers of American capitalism at first shrugged off the Great Crash with the explanation that human nature and bad judgment accounted for recurring cycles of boom and bust. They insisted that holding resolutely to free market principles would bring things right again. "Prosperity," the boosters insisted, "is just around the corner"—close at hand, though out of sight. President Herbert Hoover stubbornly maintained that the American economic system was "fundamentally sound."

Hoover's first act in the aftermath of the crash was characteristic. He called a White House conference of business and labor leaders and urged them to join in a voluntary plan for recovery. The president asked businesses to forge ahead with their pre-crash investment plans, maintain production, and keep their workers on the job. He asked labor to accept the status quo and relinquish demands for improvements in wages, hours, or conditions. Within a few months, however, the bargain had fallen apart. As demand for their products declined, industrialists cut production, sliced wages, and laid off workers. Poorly paid or unemployed workers could not buy much, and decreased buying led to further cuts in production and further loss of jobs. And thus began the terrible spiral of economic decline.

Hoover did not just sit back and watch the depression cut its swath through American society. He worked long hours, wracked his brain for solutions, and, despite what people thought, felt the suffering of the American people. But he confronted the unprecedented problems of the depression within the constraints of the ideology he brought to the White House. He remained wedded to the notion of voluntary compliance and resisted plans that called for the federal government to intervene in the private sector. But he was not a do-nothing president. He did not agree with his secretary of the treasury, Andrew Mellon, who counseled that there was nothing the administration could do but let the depression run its course and eventually right itself. The people, Mellon said, would simply have to endure.

Hoover called on Congress to use its legitimate power to combat the depression. In 1930, he got Congress to authorize $420 million for public works projects to give the unemployed something useful to do and create greater purchasing power. Congress also agreed to cut taxes by $140 million to stimulate investment. To deal with the problems of rural America, Congress in 1930 passed the Agricultural Marketing Act. It created the Farm Board, which used its budget of $500 million to buy up agricultural surpluses and thus, it was hoped, raise prices. Although the Farm Board bought one-third of the nation's wheat supply, conditions worsened. Hoover also thought that American farmers would benefit from protective tariffs on agricultural goods. The Hawley-Smoot tariff of 1930 established the highest rates in history. None of Hoover's initiatives halted the downward slide of the economy, however. Each year of his administration, conditions grew more desperate. Some of his programs were well conceived but too puny to do much good. Others, such as the new tariff, ran contrary to what was needed. Dismayed foreign nations retaliated with increased tariffs of their own that further crippled American farmers' ability to sell abroad.

The nation's most pressing problem, however, was the relief of the unemployed. Each month, hundreds of thousands of additional workers lost their jobs. By 1932, one-quarter of the American workforce—more than 12 million men and women— were unemployed. There was no federal relief, and state services and private charities were swamped. Cries grew louder for the federal government to give hurting people relief. But Hoover absolutely refused. He believed that relief of suffering was a local responsibility. Federal aid, which he called a "dole," would destroy an individual's "moral fiber," he declared again and again. Hoover's fidelity to "rugged individualism" caused immeasurable suffering. In time, he fudged his principles a little. In 1931, he began to allow the Red Cross to distribute federal agricultural surpluses to the hungry. And in 1932, he allowed states to receive small federal loans, not gifts, to help them in their relief efforts. But Hoover's concessions were no more than Band-Aids on deep wounds.

By 1932, however, Hoover was forced to step up federal action. He reluctantly sponsored the Reconstruction Finance Corporation (RFC), a federal agency empowered to lend government funds to endangered banks, insurance companies, and railroads. The idea was that the RFC would lend money to these large enterprises so that they could keep going and continue to provide their employees with paychecks. It was a "trickle-down" theory: Pump money into the economy at the top, and in the long run the people at the bottom would benefit. Critics called the RFC a "millionaires' dole." Others charged that Hoover "tried to feed the sparrows by feeding the horses." In the most notorious instance, the RFC refused money to the city of Chicago to provide welfare for suffering victims of the crash but allocated $90 million to the Central Republic Bank in that city, headed by Charles Dawes, former head of the RFC.

None of Hoover's initiatives, including the RFC, turned the economy around. The great need

PRIVATE CAR

In the mid-1930s, LeConte Stewart, an artist who spent most of his life painting the landscapes of his native Utah, noticed a new sight. From his remote hillside above the Union Pacific railroad tracks, he witnessed a stream of tramps heading west. The sight of one young man jauntily braced in the doorway of a boxcar made Stewart think of the elegant private cars of millionaires that used to travel along those same tracks. Stewart entitled this painting Private Car *and achieved fame for his beautifully ironic depiction of a new wave of pioneers fleeing trouble.*
Private Car *by Le Conte Stewart. © The Church of Latter-Day Saints. Used by permission.*

was to increase consumer demand and in the process create jobs. Hoover's insistence on individual self-reliance severely limited the role that the federal government could play in fighting the depression and helped guarantee that the economy would continue to slump.

Life in the Great Depression

In 1930, the nation woke up to the realization that prosperity was not "just around the corner." The trouble was too deep, the engine too cold to restart. Suffering and trial on a massive scale began, and a mood of cold despair settled over the land. Americans were wracked with want and fear. It was not just a matter of hunkering down and waiting for

bad times to pass. Each year of the Hoover administration, times got harder. Hollow-eyed men and women were bewildered. They saw agricultural surpluses in the countryside and knew that their children were going to bed hungry. They saw factories standing idle and knew that they and millions of others were willing to work. The gap between Herbert Hoover and the American people widened as the depression deepened. By 1932, America's economic problems had become a dangerous social crisis.

The Human Toll

Statistics provide a scaffolding for understanding the human dimension of the Great Depression. When Herbert Hoover took office in 1929, the American economy stood at its peak. When he left in 1933, it had reached its twentieth-century low. More than nine thousand banks had shut their doors, and depositors had lost more than $2.5 billion. In 1929, national income was $88 billion. By 1933, it had declined to $40 billion. In 1929, unemployment was 3.1 percent, one and a half million workers. By 1933, unemployment stood at 25 percent, twelve and a half million workers. One by one, the nation's great steel mills and foundries, once the noisy centers of industrial might, had fallen quiet. U.S. Steel, the country's largest producer, operated at only 12 percent capacity in 1932. The reduction reflected in part the huge cutback of automobile and railroad manufacture, which also made the streets emptier and added to the stillness. After having produced an average of six hundred locomotives a year during the 1920s, the American Locomotive Company turned out only one in 1932. "Once I built a railroad," lamented one of the popular songs of the year, "now it's done. Brother, can you spare a dime?"

Jobless, homeless victims wandered in search of work, and the tramp, or hobo, became one of the most visible figures of the decade. Young men and women unable to land their first job, made up about half of the million-strong army of hoboes. Many hit the road so that their younger brothers and sisters at home could have more to eat and a bed to sleep in. Riding the rails or hitchhiking, the vagabonds tended to move southward and westward, toward the sun and warmth and opportunities, they hoped, for seasonal agricultural work.

In addition to provoking industrial workers and farmers into militant protest, hard times also revived the left in America.

Other unemployed men and women, less hopeful or sick, huddled in doorways—human "junk," as one writer put it. Scavengers haunted alleys behind restaurants and picked over garbage dumps in search of food. In describing what he called the "American Earthquake," the writer Edmund Wilson told of an elderly woman who always took off her glasses to avoid seeing the maggots crawling over the garbage she ate. Starvation claimed more than a few victims. Four New York City hospitals reported 95 deaths from hunger in 1931. But enervating, rampant malnutrition posed the greater threat. The Children's Bureau announced that one of five schoolchildren did not get enough to eat.

The worst hardships hit the jobless and their families, estimated by *Fortune* magazine to include 34 million persons. But those at work also felt the

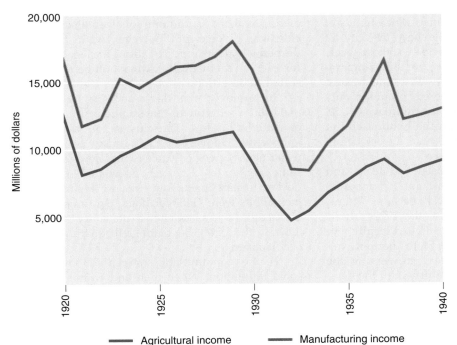

FIGURE 23.5
Manufacturing and Agricultural Income, 1920–1940

After economic collapse, recovery in the 1930s began under New Deal auspices. Sharp declines in 1937–1938, when federal spending was reduced, indicated that restoring manufacturing and agricultural income still needed New Deal stimuli.

pinch. The average weekly wage in 1932 was only $16.21. Some paychecks dwindled away to virtually nothing. In Chicago, the majority of workingwomen received less than 25 cents an hour. In the lumber industry, hourly rates fell to 10 cents, in general contracting to $7\frac{1}{2}$ cents, and in the sawmills to a nickel. Having a job, then, did not necessarily mean avoiding hunger or destitution.

Rural poverty was most acute. Landless tenant farmers and sharecroppers, mainly in the South, came to symbolize the ways poverty crushed the human spirit. In 1930, eight and a half million people, three million of them black, lived in tenant and sharecropping families—amounting to one-quarter of the total southern population. Often illiterate, usually without cash incomes, they crowded into two- and three-room cabins lacking screens or even doors, without plumbing, electricity, running water, or sanitary wells. They subsisted—just barely—on salt pork, cornmeal, molasses, beans, peas, and whatever they could hunt or fish. All the diseases of dietary and vitamin deficiencies wracked them. When the English economist John Maynard Keynes was asked whether anything like this degradation had existed before, he replied, "Yes, it was called the Dark Ages and it lasted four hundred years."

To meet this human catastrophe, the nation was equipped with the most limited welfare system in the Western world. There was no federal assistance, only a patchwork of voluntary institutions and pinchpenny state and local agencies. For a family of four without any income, the best the city of Philadelphia could do was provide $5.50 per week. That was not enough to live on, but still comparatively generous. New York City, where the greatest number of welfare cases gathered, provided only $2.39 per week. In Mississippi, the figure was $1.50. And Detroit, devastated when the bottom fell out of the auto industry, allotted 60 cents a week before the city ran out of money entirely.

The deepening crisis roused old fears and caused some Americans to cast about for scapegoats. Mexican Americans quickly became victims. During the prosperous years of the 1920s, cheap agricultural labor from Mexico flowed legally and unrestricted across the United States border, welcomed by the large farmers and growers. In the 1930s, however, public opinion turned on the newcomers, styling them as dangerous aliens who took jobs from Americans. Government officials, most prominently those in Los Angeles County, targeted all Mexican residents for deportation, without regard to citizenship status. With support from the Department of Labor, as many as half a million Mexicans and Mexican Americans were deported or fled to Mexico. Among them were children born in the United States, American citizens who had never lived outside the country.

The depression deeply affected the American family. Young people postponed marriage, and when they did marry, they produced so few children that demographers warned that, for the first time, the United States was on the verge of losing population. White women, who generally worked in low-paying service areas—cooks, salesclerks, and secretaries—did not lose their jobs as often as men who worked in industry. Even as hostility to women workers increased during the depression, economic necessity drove unmarried women as well as married women, who usually stayed in the home before the depression, into the marketplace. Married women's employment actually rose during the decade from about 12 percent to 15 percent. Overall, some 25 percent more women were employed for wages in 1940 than in 1930.

As more women became breadwinners and men sat at home unemployed, families experienced enormous stress. After a decade of exuberant consumption, smaller incomes led to significant belt tightening. Working women became increasingly decisive and self-reliant at the same time idle men fell prey to guilt and loss of self-esteem. Family violence escalated, as did rates of alcoholism and suicide. The divorce rate, however, went down; the desperately poor could not afford the legal expense. Instead, in dramatically rising numbers, men resorted to desertion.

Increasingly, the down-and-out huddled in makeshift shantytowns that sprang up on the edges of America's cities. The clusters of shacks were known as "Hoovervilles." So many people were using newspapers as blankets that newspapers became known as "Hoover blankets." An empty pocket turned inside out was a "Hoover flag." Jackrabbits were "Hoover hogs." In times of trouble, people have a tendency to personify their problems. In the 1930s, the blame fell squarely on Herbert Hoover.

As the economy sank, so too did Hoover's personal reputation. When men and women weren't cursing him, they were busy making him the butt of a thousand bitter jokes. One asserted that there was no question about Hoover being the world's greatest engineer: "In a little more than two years, he has drained, ditched, and damned the United States." Another told of Hoover's request to Andrew Mellon for a nickel to call up a friend. Mellon replied, "Here's a dime, call up all your friends."

Denial and Escape

In the midst of the mounting crisis, J. P. Morgan Jr., the living symbol of American capitalism, testified before a congressional committee where he defended the importance of preserving an economic elite. "If you destroy the leisure class," he declared, "you destroy civilization." When pressed to define the "leisure class," Morgan responded that it included all those who could afford a maid—about twenty-five or thirty million people, he reckoned, until informed that there were only about two million servants in the entire country. Morgan's ignorance was typical of many from his class who appeared before the committee. Under scrutiny, those who had presided over the economic collapse and now sought to lead the nation back to prosperity showed how little they had troubled to learn about the society that had made them rich. Morgan had learned enough, it turned out, to avoid paying income tax from 1929 to 1932. This revelation did little to win him support among the rising chorus of critics who, only a short time ago, had worshiped wealth and those who had it.

Although Herbert Hoover was no J. P. Morgan, he too was perceived as uncaring. His steadfast refusal to provide federal aid for the victims of the depression encouraged the image of the heartless millionaire in the White House. Hoover's personal habits did not help. Throughout the ordeal, the president sought to provide a personal example by keeping up appearances. Like his favorite comic strip hero, Daddy Warbucks in "Little Orphan Annie," he favored formal dress and manners. For dinner, with or without guests, he appeared in tuxedo, attended by a retinue of valets and waiters. No one was starving, he calmly assured the American people.

Not that his administration considered it the business of the federal government to find out. Walter Gifford, president of the American Telephone and Telegraph Company, appointed by Hoover to coordinate private relief efforts, acknowledged to a Senate subcommittee that he had made no attempt to get figures on how many people were out of work or on relief. Exasperated, Senator Robert La Follette asked if Gifford had any impulse to find out the facts of the situation. Gifford's response reflected the serene way the nation's business leadership distanced itself from the problems of failure and poverty. "Well," said Gifford genially, "I will not say that I did not make any estimate for my own interest and amusement."

While the wealthy practiced denial, other Americans sought refuge from reality at the movies. Throughout the depression, between sixty and seventy-five million people (nearly two-thirds of the nation) managed to scrounge up enough dimes to fill the movie palaces every week. People sought diversion and escape in the plush darkness. They momentarily forgot their troubles as the silver screen filled with wild comedies by the Marx Brothers or lavish musicals. Hollywood excelled at producing musical extravaganzas. Box office successes typically blended nostalgia for the lost Golden Twenties with the hope that renewed prosperity lay just around the corner. The leading musicals in 1933, *Forty-Second Street* and *Gold Diggers*, each offered a variation on the old rags-to-riches story of the chorus girl who makes the most of her big break. In *Gold Diggers*, as the sheriff arrives to foreclose on a bankrupt Broadway show, a wealthy banker suddenly realizes the value of entertainment and his love for a chorus girl. He breaks with his stuffy family to underwrite the show, and everyone dances off toward the dawn of a new day.

But as conditions in the country worsened, filmmakers also turned to grittier material. Films such as King Vidor's *Our Daily Bread* (1932) and John Ford's *The Grapes of Wrath* (1940) were razor-sharp social commentaries. Gangster films taught grim lessons about ill-gotten gains. Indeed, under the new production code of 1930, designed to protect public morals, all movies had to find some way to show that crime did not pay. In *Little Caesar* (1930), the main character is gunned down when he tries to get too much of what belongs to the big boys. *Public Enemy* (1931), a classic story of a hoodlum with a saintly mother, presents a cautionary tale about the doom that awaits those who succumb to easy money and reject virtue.

Despite Hollywood's efforts to keep Americans on the right side of the law, crime increased in the 1930s. Away from the movie palaces, out in the countryside, the plight of people who had lost their farms to bank foreclosures cut so deep that lawlessness gained a romantic popular appeal. In the wake of bank-robbing sprees across the Midwest and Southwest, a legend took shape that the thieves

Was Samuel Insull a Villain or a Victim?

HENRY FORD BECAME the most famous American of his time for his production-line success in putting America on wheels. But most of the rest of the technological marvels that transformed society during the 1920s — the bright lights on Main Street, the movie palaces, radios, phonographs, labor-saving appliances, and gadgets of all kinds — depended on the way Samuel Insull organized the mass production of electricity.

Born the son of a poor dairyman in England, Insull showed an aptitude for business from the time he left school at fourteen and hired on with an auction firm in London. His quickness with numbers attracted the attention of Thomas Edison's representative in England and led to Insull's coming to America in 1881 as the great inventor's private secretary. Impressed by his assistant's shrewd attention to detail—as "tireless as the tides" and "always thinking of the dollar angle"—Edison rewarded Insull in 1893 by making him president of the Chicago Edison Company.

Within fifteen years, Insull had gained control of the electric industry in Chicago. From there his rise to vast wealth and international prominence was swift. He served as president of 11 companies and board chairman or member of 150 more. His Edison Commonwealth empire, which included six thousand power plants in thirty-nine states, manufactured more than 10 percent of the nation's power and sold to twenty million customers. Honors showered down on Insull, and he responded by becoming a patron of culture. In 1929, Insull made his grandest gesture by building Chicago a new opera house that dazzled the eye with its gilt and murals. To a proud city, Insull seemed the perfect model of success, a strong moral contrast to the notorious criminal wealth flaunted by Al Capone and other Chicago gangsters.

Insull had no doubt that he deserved Chicago's adulation. When one of his opera singers gushed that he was like another Napoleon, Insull reminded her that Napoleon was only a soldier. Yet, like Napoleon, Insull overreached himself. Much of his empire had been bought on credit through the use of investors' money. To cover his tracks, Insull used his accounting genius to construct a network of holding companies. As the dominant shareholder—usually with about 25 percent of the total stock—Insull could run the companies' boards of directors and thus decide how to use their entire assets. The higher Insull's pyramid of holding companies rose, the wider the gap between Insull's actual cash assets and the paper value of his empire. By the end of the 1920s, Insull's inner circle, including his brother and his son, held assets with a market value of about $2.5 billion, for which they had invested only $100 million, most of it other people's money.

The stock market crash in October 1929 brought down Insull's paper empire. Besieged by debt and unable to borrow more money, Insull resorted to the tactic of declaring bankruptcy for his holding companies. As more and more investors learned that they had lost everything in the bankruptcy maneuvers and the nation lurched into the depression, the conviction grew that Insull personified those whose fake prosperity had brought on the Great Crash. They laughed bitterly at cowboy comedian Will Rogers's definition of a holding company as "a thing where you hand an accomplice the goods while the policeman searches you." The Union League Club, a Chicago watering hole for conservative investors, expressed its contempt for Insull by papering its dining room with Insull's worthless stock certificates. But the bottom was not reached until October 1932, when a grand jury indicted Insull and his brother on charges of embezzlement, larceny, and use of the mails to defraud. *Who's Who* rendered its own verdict by dropping the former first citizen of Chicago from its roster.

Insull read about the indictment in Paris, where he had fled after signing over all his bankrupt assets. Yet even with a trail of ruined lives behind him and ample time to reflect on his career, Insull still could not understand why he had lost favor. "Why am I not more popular in the United States?" he asked. "What have I done that every banker and business magnate has not done in the course of busi-

SAMUEL INSULL

This May 1934 Time *magazine cover shows Samuel Insull hiding his face as he enters the courtroom to face criminal charges. The quotation underneath reminds readers that Insull had a key role both in building up and in tearing down the country. Journalists and moralists were eager to use Insull, America's most famous fugitive from justice, as the main symbol in a morality tale of how ruthlessly greedy tycoons had brought on the Great Depression.*

ness?" When extradition orders for income tax evasion arrived, Insull fled to Italy and then eastward through Athens until he was finally cornered in a dank jail cell in Istanbul, where he was being held as a vagrant.

The captive's return to depression-wracked America in the spring of 1934 had the usual melodramatic touches of courtroom drama and disgrace. Insull appeared on the cover of *Time* magazine in the typical fugitive pose, hat pulled down over his face as he was hustled up the courthouse steps, while all around the country pundits declaimed that he had betrayed the public trust.

In the end, however, the incredible complexity of the financial empire that led to Insull's ruin also saved him. With checks, bonds, and stock certificates moving swiftly from one Insull subsidiary to another, who could tell what belonged to whom at any particular moment? No sleuth could match Insull's ingenuity in devising what one headline called the "Insull Daze-Maze." Even the U.S. Senate Banking and Currency Committee, which was investigating the stock market collapse, was stymied. One expert witness, Owen D. Young, a distinguished banker, confessed to "a feeling of complete helplessness when I began to examine the complicated structure of the Insull group. . . . It was impossible to get an accounting system that would not have misled even the officers themselves."

While the state attorney thrashed about for incriminating evidence, Insull pleaded his case directly to the jurors. Abandoning his pose as a Napoleonic commander of industry, Insull presented himself as just another seeker of the American dream, who like other Americans, from office boys to tycoons, had been caught in a terrible historical accident. For hours, he told the jury of his struggle to overcome meager origins and his bewilderment now, as just a poor old man, over how disaster had befallen the era of prosperity. In his summation to the jury, Insull's lawyer drove the point home. "You have had a description here of an age in American history which we hope will never be repeated. I say that we are trying that age." The jury agreed and found the age guilty, but Insull innocent.

Free but unwilling to remain in America as a nobody, Insull returned to anonymity in Paris, where he died in 1938. According to the police report, Insull collapsed and died of a heart attack in the Paris subway with only about 85 cents of loose change on him. But that was not quite right. Insull had ample resources stashed away and always carried a considerable amount of cash. Someone else from humble origins and similarly committed to the advancement of self-interest must have found the body first. Then Samuel Insull, the artful dodger of American finance, had his own pocket picked, and the police never noticed.

stole to get back what the banks had taken from the poor. Woody Guthrie, the populist folk singer from Oklahoma, captured the public's inclination to see criminals as modern Robin Hoods in his widely admired tribute to a murderous bank robber with a choirboy face, "The Ballad of Pretty Boy Floyd":

Yes, as through this world I ramble,
I see lots of funny men,
Some will rob you with a six-gun,
Some will rob you with a pen.
But as through your life you'll travel,
Wherever you may roam,
You won't never see an outlaw drive
A family from their home.

The Rise of Working-Class Militancy

Although the nation's working people bore the brunt of the economic collapse, the labor movement, including the dominant American Federation of Labor (AFL), was slow to respond. Organized labor had been hobbled during the 1920s by the willingness of the courts to issue injunctions curtailing the right of unions to organize and strike. Early in the depression, William Green, head of the AFL, sounded like Hoover's twin when he argued that a dole would turn the worker into "a ward of the state." But by 1931, the normally benign Green had turned ferocious. "I warn the people who are exploiting the workers," he shouted at the AFL's annual convention, "that they can drive them only so far before they will turn on them and destroy them. They are taking no account of the history of nations in which governments have been overturned. Revolutions grow out of the depths of hunger." Green's lieutenant, Edward F. McGrady, told a Senate subcommittee that, if the government did not act to create work for the unemployed, "as far as I am personally concerned, I would do nothing to close the doors of revolt if it starts."

Like the labor leaders, the American people were slow to anger. At first, they were too numb to raise protests about the depression. More likely, they turned the blame inward, wondering what they had done to lose their jobs, feeling ashamed when they could not find new ones. As the shock wore off and they realized that millions were in the same circumstances, people began to get angry. On the morning of March 7, 1932, several thousand unemployed autoworkers massed at the gates of the

Ford Company's River Rouge factory in Dearborn, Michigan, to demand work. Henry Ford sent out his private security forces, who told the demonstrators to disperse. The workers refused and began hurling rocks. The Ford army responded with tear gas and freezing water but quickly escalated to gunfire. When they stopped, four demonstrators were dead and dozens more wounded. An outraged public—forty thousand strong—turned out for the unemployed men's funerals. People from coast to coast denounced Ford's callous and brutal resort to violence.

Farmers, who desperately needed relief, mounted the broadest protest. Their spokesmen in Washington asked the government to guarantee farm prices that would at least equal the cost of production, but Congress would not budge. On May 7, 1932, some three thousand farmers, led by the flamboyant Milo Reno, created the National Farmers' Holiday Association. Invoking the Boston Tea Party, they promised vigilante action to keep farm produce from reaching the markets until prices improved. Although the rebellion was short-lived, Reno and his followers barricaded roads around Sioux City, Iowa, turned back farmers heading for market, and dumped thousands of gallons of milk in the ditches.

Farm militants had more success with their "penny sales." With so many farms falling under the auctioneer's hammer, farm dissidents packed auctions with members pledged to pay only a few cents to buy the foreclosed property and return it to the bankrupt owners. Under this kind of pressure, some states suspended debts or reduced mortgages. Where evictions continued, farmers stepped up their protests. In early 1933, some Iowa farmers hauled Judge Charles Bradley out of his courtroom in midtrial. Taking him to a remote place, they beat him, smeared him with grease, and finally released him when he lost consciousness with a noose around his neck. That same year in California, where landowners cut their already substandard wages, more than fifty thousand farmworkers, most of them Mexicans, went on strike. In 1933, John Simpson, president of the National Farmers Union, observed that "the biggest and finest crop of revolutions you ever saw is sprouting all over the country right now."

In addition to provoking industrial workers and farmers into militant protest, hard times also revived the left in America. When the crash struck, Eugene Debs was dead and so, for all purposes, was the Socialist Party. But the Great Depression—the massive failure of Western capitalism—provided a hothouse environment that brought socialism back to life and the American Communist Party to its greatest size and influence in American history. Eventually, some 100,000 disillusioned Americans —workers, intellectuals, college students—joined the Communist Party and sought radical change in the United States. Party leader William Z. Foster sketched the future in his book *Toward a Soviet America* (1932).

Although the American Communist Party declared that it was homegrown, purely American, and beholden to no one, it clearly followed the party line laid down by the Soviet Union. By the late 1930s, Moscow's demands for conformity had driven most Americans out of the party, but in the early years of the depression, members engaged in protest on a broad front. In 1931, the party entered the labor wars. In Harlan County, Kentucky, Communists fearlessly faced the mine owners' thugs and increased membership in the National Miners Union from one hundred to twenty-five thousand. Newspapers and newsreels graphically portrayed the violence unleashed against the strikers. Eventually, the miners lost, but the Communist Party emerged from the coal fields stronger than before.

Jobless, homeless victims wandered in search of work, and the tramp, or hobo, became one of the most visible figures of the decade.

Almost alone among American organizations, the Communist Party attacked racism and spoke out on behalf of African Americans. When nine young black men in Scottsboro, Alabama, were arrested on trumped-up rape charges, the party rushed to their defense. The Communists managed to save the defendants from the electric chair and thereby gained wide publicity as crusaders against racism. The party also gained publicity by organizing black sharecroppers in Alabama who faced expulsion by white landlords. Efforts on behalf of African Americans attracted new recruits to the party. From only about fifty black members in 1930, the Party counted ten thousand by the end of the decade.

It was not only Communists who believed that capitalism meant poverty and unemployment. Protest by workers and farmers who never had a radical thought in their lives dwarfed the effort of

the left. Breadlines, soup kitchens, foreclosures, unemployment, and cold despair drove patriotic men and women to question American capitalism. "I am as conservative as any man could be," a Wisconsin farmer explained, "but any economic system that has in its power to set me and my wife in the streets, at my age—what can I see but red?"

Conclusion: The Era of Boom and Bust

The decade of the 1920s has persistently defied generalization. To many observers, it looked like the New Business Epoch and the New Era. Living standards rose, economic opportunity increased, and the flow of consumer goods appeared endless. Others focused on the thrill of cultural liberation and called the decade the Great Spree, the Roaring Twenties, and the Jazz Age. But the dominant images of the decade had little meaning for many Americans. They experienced neither the glitter nor the jazz and lacked the power to offer labels of their own. Instead of plunging into speculation on Wall Street or shimmying at the Cotton Club, the nation's farmers and industrial laborers struggled to make ends meet.

Almost overnight, the 1920s ended. In just a little over ten years following the triumph of World War I, the United States veered dizzily from its steepest rise in power and wealth to a free fall into its deepest depression. Smug urbanites were humbled, but men and women already living on the margins suffered more. The 1930s found new symbols: glut without buyers; empty apartments and homes alongside rude cardboard shantytowns; mountains of oranges rotting in the California sun while guards with shotguns chased away the hungry. As government stubbornly refused to alleviate the suffering and some of the rich seemed immune, sullen apathy increasingly turned to angry revolt.

On a night in June 1931, on the outskirts of Gary, Indiana, a man driving a large car slammed on the brakes when a brick crashed through the windshield. "What's the big idea?" he shouted out. Out of the darkness came the reply: "All rich guys ought to be strung up." "Who are you?" the driver asked. "We're the fellows that'll do the stringing." Later that night a hotel clerk tried to explain: "Their patience is at an end. . . . Another four years of Hoover and . . . ."

CHRONOLOGY

1920 Eighteenth Amendment, prohibiting the sale of liquor, goes into effect.

Nineteenth Amendment, granting women the vote, ratified.

Station KDKA in Pittsburgh begins first regular commercial radio broadcasts.

Marcus Garvey hosts Universal Negro Improvement Association conference in Harlem.

Republican Warren G. Harding elected president.

1921 Sheppard-Towner Act, providing infant health care, passes in Congress.

1922 Fordney-McCumber Act sets protective tariffs at record heights.

Principles of new business-minded era expressed in publication of Henry Ford's *My Life and Work* and Herbert Hoover's *American Individualism*.

About thirty artists and intellectuals renounce American society in *Civilization in the United States*.

1922, 1924 New laws imposing quotas according to nationality end historical tradition of open immigration.

1923 Equal Rights Amendment introduced in Congress.

August. Harding dies in office and is succeeded by Calvin Coolidge.

1924 Calvin Coolidge elected president.

1925 John Scopes convicted for violating Tennessee statute forbidding teaching of evolution.

Alain Locke expresses cultural aspirations of Harlem Renaissance in *The New Negro*.

1926 Ernest Hemingway's novel of expatriate Paris, *The Sun Also Rises*, published.

1927 Charles Lindbergh becomes America's most famous hero by flying alone across Atlantic.

Italian anarchist immigrants Sacco and Vanzetti executed.

1928 Herbert Hoover defeats Alfred E. Smith.

1929 Robert and Helen Lynd publish their study of an average American small city, *Middletown*.

October 24. Stock market collapses on Black Thursday.

1931 Nine black men arrested in Scottsboro case.

1932 Several thousand demonstrators at Ford plant protest unemployment; security forces fire on crowd, killing four.

Farmers' Holiday movement blocks roads and pours milk on ground to protest falling prices.

BIBLIOGRAPHY

GENERAL WORKS

Frederick Lewis Allen, *Only Yesterday: An Informal History of the Nineteen-Twenties* (1930).

Dorothy Brown, *Setting a Course: American Women in the 1920s* (1987).

Norman Cantor, *Twentieth Century Culture: Modernism to Deconstruction* (1988).

Paul A. Carter, *Another Part of the Twenties* (1977).

Stanley Coben, *Rebellion against Victorianism: The Impetus for Cultural Change in 1920s America* (1991).

Lynn Dumeril, *The Modern Temper: American Culture and Society in the 1920s* (1995).

Ellis W. Hawley, *The Great War and the Search for a Modern Order: A History of the American People and Their Institutions, 1917–1933* (1979).

William E. Leuchtenburg, *The Perils of Prosperity, 1914–1932* (1958).

Robert S. Lynd and Helen M. Lynd, *Middletown: A Study in Modern American Culture* (1929).

Michael Parrish, *Anxious Decades: America in Prosperity and Depression, 1920–1941* (1992).

Geoffrey Perrett, *America in the Twenties: A History* (1982).

MAINSTREAM POLITICS

David Burner, *Herbert Hoover: A Public Life* (1979).

Warren I. Cohen, *Empire without Tears: America's Foreign Relations, 1921–1933* (1987).

Frank Costigliola, *Awkward Dominion: American Political, Economic, and Cultural Relations with Europe, 1919–1933* (1984).

Paula Elder, *Governor Alfred E. Smith: The Politician as Reformer* (1983).

Lewis Ethan Ellis, *Republican Foreign Policy, 1921–1933* (1968).

Christine A. Lunardini, *From Equal Suffrage to Equal Rights: Alice Paul and the National Woman's Party, 1912–1928* (1986).

Donald R. McCoy, *Calvin Coolidge* (1967).

Michael E. McGerr, *The Decline of Popular Politics: The American North, 1865–1928* (1986).

Robert K. Murray, *The Harding Era: Warren G. Harding and His Administration* (1969).

Francis Fox Piven and Richard A. Cloward, *Why Americans Don't Vote* (1988).

William Appleman Williams, *The Tragedy of American Diplomacy* (1959).

Joan Hoff Wilson, *Herbert Hoover: Forgotten Progressive* (1975).

THE NEW ERA OF SCIENCE AND CONSUMPTION

Susan Porter Benson, *Counter Cultures* (1986).

James J. Flink, *The Automobile Age* (1988).

Louis Galambos and Joseph Pratt, *The Rise of Corporate Commonwealth: U.S. Business and Public Policy in the Twentieth Century* (1988).

Kenneth T. Jackson, *Crabgrass Frontier: The Suburbanization of the United States* (1985).

Robert E. Kohler, *Partners in Science: Foundations and Natural Scientists, 1900–1945* (1991).

T. J. Jackson Lears, *Fables of Abundance: A Cultural History of Advertising in America* (1994).

Roland Marchand, *Advertising the American Dream: Making Way for Modernity, 1920–1940* (1985).

David F. Noble, *America by Design: Science, Technology, and the Rise of Corporate Capitalism* (1977).

Ronald C. Tobey, *The American Ideology of National Science, 1919–1930* (1971).

Reynold M. Wik, *Henry Ford and Grass-Roots America* (1972).

LABOR

American Social History Project, *Who Built America? Working People and the Nation's Economy, Politics, Culture, and Society*, vol. 2, *From the Gilded Age to the Present* (1992).

Irving Bernstein, *The Lean Years: A History of the American Worker, 1920–1933* (1960).

Colin Gordon, *New Deals: Business, Labor, and Politics in America, 1920–1935* (1994).

Sanford M. Jacoby, *Employing Bureaucracy: Managers, Unions, and the Transformation of Work in American Industry, 1900–1945* (1985).

John A. Salmond, *Gastonia 1929: The Story of the Loray Mill Strike* (1995).

Winifred Wandersee, *Women's Work and Family Values, 1920–1940* (1981).

Robert H. Zeiger, *Republicans and Labor, 1919–1929* (1969).

RURAL AND SMALL-TOWN LIFE

Michael L. Berger, *The Devil Wagon in God's Country: The Automobile and Social Change in Rural America, 1893–1929* (1979).

James N. Gregory, *American Exodus: The Dust Bowl Migration and Okie Culture in California* (1989).

Jack Temple Kirby, *Rural Worlds Lost: The American South, 1920–1960* (1987).

Donald Worster, *Dust Bowl: The Southern Plains in the 1930s* (1979).

POPULAR CULTURE

Ann Douglas, *Mongrel Manhattan in the 1920s* (1994).

Ronald Edsforth, *Popular Culture and Political Change in Modern America* (1991).

Lewis Erenberg, *Steppin' Out: New York City Nightlife and the Transformation of American Culture, 1890–1930* (1981).

Paula S. Fass, *The Damned and the Beautiful: American Youth in the 1920s* (1977).

Larry May, *Screening out the Past: The Birth of Mass Culture and the Motion Picture Industry* (1980).

Kathy H. Ogren, *The Jazz Revolution: Twenties America and the Meaning of Jazz* (1989).

Kathy Peiss, *Cheap Amusements* (1986).

Arnold Shaw, *The Jazz Age: Popular Music in the 1920s* (1987).

Robert Sklar, *Movie-Made America* (1975).

Robert Smith, *Babe Ruth's America* (1974).

Susan Smulyan, *Selling Radio: The Commercialization of American Broadcasting, 1920–1934* (1994).

Ted Vincent, *Mudville's Revenge: The Rise and Fall of American Sport* (1981).

EDUCATION AND ART

Charles C. Alexander, *Here the Country Lies: Nationalism and the Arts in Twentieth-Century America* (1980).

Malcolm Cowley, *Exile's Return* (1934).

Malcolm Cowley, *The Dream of the Golden Mountains: Remembering the 1930s* (1980).

Helen Lefkowitz Horowitz, *Campus Life: Undergraduate Cultures from the End of the Eighteenth Century to the Present* (1987).

Lary May, *Outside In: Minorities and the Transformation of American Education* (1989).

Maren Stange, *Symbols of Ideal Life: Social Documentary Photography in America, 1890–1950* (1989).

William Stott, *Documentary Expression and Thirties America* (1973).

Elizabeth Hutton Turner, *American Artists in Paris, 1919–1929* (1988).

RESISTANCE TO CHANGE

David H. Bennett, *The Party of Fear: From Nativist Movements to the New Right in American History* (1988).

Kathleen M. Blee, *Women of the Klan: Racism and Gender in the 1920s* (1991).

Lyle W. Dorsett, *Billy Sunday and the Redemption of Urban America* (1991).

Ray Ginger, *Six Days or Forever? Tennessee v. John Thomas Scopes* (1958).

Nancy MacLean, *Behind the Mask of Chivalry: The Making of the Second Ku Klux Klan* (1994).

George M. Marsden, *Fundamentalism and American Culture* (1980).

Daniel Joseph Singal, *The War Within: From Victorian to Modernist Thought in the South, 1919–1945* (1982).

REFORM AND DISSENT

Daniel Aaron, *Writers on the Left* (1960).

Milton Cantor, *The Divided Left: American Radicalism, 1900–1975* (1978).

Clarke Chambers, *Seedtime of Reform, 1918–1933* (1956).

Nancy F. Cott, *The Grounding of Modern Feminism* (1977).

John P. Diggins, *The Rise and Fall of the American Left* (1992).

Donald J. Lisio, *The President and Protest: Hoover, MacArthur, and the Bonus Riot* (1994).

Nick Salvatore, *Eugene V. Debs: Citizen and Socialist* (1982).

David Thelen, *Robert M. La Follette and the Insurgent Spirit* (1976).

William Young and David E. Kaiser, *Postmortem: New Evidence in the Case of Sacco and Vanzetti* (1985).

RACE AND MINORITIES

Rodolfo Acuna, *Occupied America: A History of Chicanos* (1980).

Francisco E. Balderrama and Raymond Rodriguez, *Decade of Betrayal: Mexican Repatriation in the 1930s* (1995).

William B. Barlow, *"Looking Up at Down": The Emergence of Blues Culture* (1989).

Dan T. Carter, *Scottsboro: A Tragedy of the Modern South* (1969).

John Higham, *Strangers in the Land: Patterns of American Nativism, 1860–1925* (1955).

James de Jongh, *Vicious Modernism: Black Harlem and the Literary Imagination* (1990).

David Levering Lewis, *When Harlem Was in Vogue* (1989).

Manning Marable, *W. E. B. Du Bois: Black Radical Democrat* (1986).

Donald L. Parman, *Indians and the American West in the Twentieth Century* (1994).

Judith Stein, *The World of Marcus Garvey* (1986).

Ronald Takaki, *A Different Mirror: A History of Multicultural America* (1993).

Cheryl A. Wall, *Women of the Harlem Renaissance* (1995).

Raymond Wolters, *Negroes and the Great Depression* (1970).

THE CRASH AND RESPONSE

William J. Barber, *From New Era to New Deal: Herbert Hoover, the Economists, and American Economic Policy, 1921–1933* (1985).

Andrew Bergman, *We're in the Money: Depression America and Its Films* (1971).

Peter Fearon, *War, Prosperity, and Depression* (1987).

John Kenneth Galbraith, *The Great Crash: 1929* (1961).

Charles Hearn, *The American Dream in the Great Depression* (1973).

Charles Kindleberger, *The World in Depression* (1973).

Robert McElvaine, *The Great Depression: America 1929–1941* (1984).

David P. Peeler, *Hope among Us Yet: Social Criticism and Social Solace in the Depression Years* (1987).

Studs Terkel, *Hard Times: An Oral History of the Great Depression* (1979; reprint, 1986).

Tom Terrill and Jerrold Hirsch, *Such As Us* (1978).

T. H. Watkins, *The Great Depression: America in the 1930s* (1993).

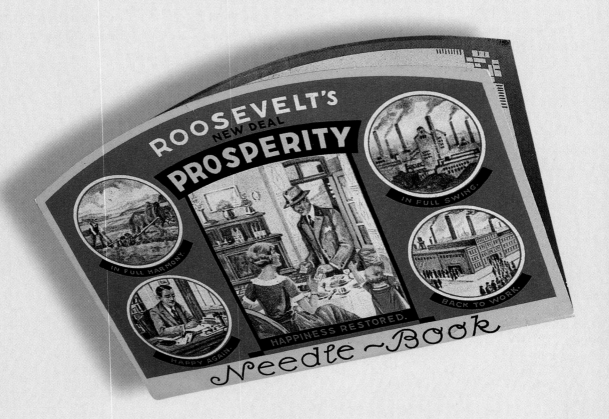

SOUVENIR SEWING NEEDLE BOOK

Borrowing the current popular tune "Happy Days Are Here Again" as the theme song for Roosevelt's 1932 campaign was an inspired act of wishful thinking in those dark days. By 1936, conditions had improved enough that this souvenir needle book could celebrate "Happiness Restored" a bit more realistically. The major places where economic recovery was to be created — farm, factory, and office — are shown operating in full swing on the cover of this little container that held sewing needles. But in accord with the New Deal emphasis on security at home, the figure of domestic happiness looms largest in the center under the arch of prosperity.
Collection of Janice L. and David J. Frent.

THE NEW DEAL ERA
1932–1939

24

Iℕ JULY 1932, A RAGGED, DUSTY CONTINGENT of some fifteen thousand World War I veterans marched into Washington, D.C. Calling themselves the Bonus Expeditionary Army, the men came to lobby Congress. Eight years earlier, Congress had voted to award veterans a bonus for their military service; the bonus was supposed to be paid in 1945. The Bonus Army had come to convince Congress that they needed the bonus now. Many of these unusual lobbyists came to Washington in boxcars, shipped free by sympathetic railway workers, sometimes under the label "Livestock." Unable to afford hotels, they camped in unfinished federal buildings just three blocks from the Capitol, and as their numbers swelled they spilled onto the mud flats along the Anacostia River.

The Bonus Army angered President Hoover. The Republican Party had recently nominated him for a second term as president, and he was eager to demonstrate his capacity for leadership and decisive action. The veterans were trespassing on official government property, Hoover said. They were an embarrassing eyesore that undercut his efforts to restore public confidence that prosperity was just around the corner. While the bonus marchers were setting up camp, Hoover prompted Congress to vote down immediate payment of the bonus because its $2.4 billion cost was too expensive.

Hoover also encouraged the press to spread a cloud of misinformation about the veterans. Hoover and other critics claimed that the bonus marchers were not veterans at all, although a careful Veterans Administration study showed that 94 percent had served in the armed forces. The *New York Times* called the marchers ingrates who should be satisfied with their regular service pensions. In fact, only career soldiers qualified for military pensions, not enlisted men like the bonus marchers. The most telling falsehood was that the marchers were led by Communists ("insurrectionists," Hoover said) who posed a revolutionary threat to the government. Everyone who came to know the Bonus Army discovered that almost all of its members believed in traditional values, although the depression had stripped them of jobs, homes, and hope. They came to Washington to regain their respectability, not to overthrow the government.

Isolated in the White House behind heavy drapes and tight security, Hoover became increasingly defensive and out of touch. A visiting reporter found him greatly changed. "He didn't look like the Hoover I had been seeing," the reporter recalled. "His hair was rumpled. He was almost crouching behind his desk." Hoover's military advisers, especially Army Chief of Staff Douglas MacArthur, argued that a show of force would quickly get rid of the Bonus Army and impress the nation with the government's authority. Feeling besieged, Hoover ordered the military to disperse the defenseless veterans and their families.

Late in the afternoon of July 28, commuters leaving their offices on Capitol Hill were surprised to see a thousand soldiers clogging Pennsylvania Avenue—cavalry with sabers drawn, infantry with bayonets ready, backed up by tanks. Hoover watched from the window of the Oval Office as the soldiers, under General MacArthur's command, headed for the Bonus Army's camp. They lobbed tear gas into the buildings occupied by the bonus marchers, forcing them to flee. In the gathering twilight, the troops paused as MacArthur surveyed the scene. Hoover had ordered MacArthur not to send his troops into the main camp on the Anacostia flats. MacArthur defied Hoover's order and commanded his troops to charge. The soldiers routed the Bonus Army, set the camp on fire, and sent the men and their families fleeing. Several marchers suffered bayonet wounds and one infant died of gas poisoning.

MacArthur was immensely pleased with the success of the attack. "Had [President Hoover] let it go on another week, I believe that the institutions of our government would have been severely threatened," he said. Privately, Hoover was bitter about MacArthur's insubordination, but he issued a public statement endorsing the dispersal of the bonus marchers, calling them "not veterans" but "Communists and persons with criminal records."

The beleaguered veterans fled into oblivion. As they traveled west, the police in each state hustled them to the next border. The remnants of the Bonus Army who made it across the Mississippi River were herded onto a special train that rumbled off to an unknown destination on the plains. There they scattered among the thousands of dispossessed Americans roaming the countryside in search of work and hope.

On the day after the Bonus Army was driven from Washington, Franklin D. Roosevelt, Hoover's Democratic rival in the 1932 presidential campaign, sat in bed surrounded by newspapers. Disabled by polio, he usually started his day immersed in the news of the world. As he read about the attack on the bonus marchers, he was overcome by "a feeling of horror," his wife, Eleanor, later recalled. Roosevelt summoned his campaign aide Rexford Tugwell to speak with him about the attack. Roosevelt wondered why Hoover hadn't just offered coffee and doughnuts to the protesters, rather than unleashing the army on them. The Bonus Army seemed to be desperate family men, he said, not dangerous subversives threatening the nation's capital. Were it up to him, Roosevelt declared, he would

have used the men for reforestation projects or found land where they could farm and regain their independence.

Roosevelt's instinctive response to news of MacArthur's attack on the Bonus Army echoed the slogan Roosevelt had announced when he accepted the Democratic nomination: "I pledge you, I pledge myself, to a new deal for the American people." Roosevelt's "new deal" did not include support for payments of the veterans' bonus; like Hoover, he thought the bonus was too expensive. But, unlike Hoover, Roosevelt declared repeatedly that if people desperately needed help, the government should try to help them.

Almost a year later—after Roosevelt had been elected president—a second group of about 3,000 veterans gathered in Washington to lobby again for payment of the bonus. Roosevelt arranged for the men to be fed and housed in military barracks at government expense while they petitioned Congress. Shortly after the men assembled, Eleanor Roosevelt strode into their camp to express her personal concern and to lead the men in singing favorite wartime songs. The occasion was so stirring that these bonus marchers elected Franklin Roosevelt an honorary member. He received a delegation at the White House and genially recalled how they had *all served together* in the war and reassured them that the government was prepared to rescue victims of the depression, although he could not support the bonus. In the end, 2,600 of the 3,000 marchers seized the chance to enroll in the government's Civilian Conservation Corps, designed to put people to work conserving the nation's natural resources, rather than accepting government transportation home.

The Second Bonus Army came to Washington as angry protesters and left with government-sponsored jobs, while Roosevelt's opposition to the bonus bill stayed in place. Roosevelt's deft response to the veterans stood in stark contrast to Hoover's refusal to meet with the first bonus marchers for fear that it would lend legitimacy to an invading mob. As the Second Bonus Army prepared to break camp, a reporter overheard remarks that brought into focus part of the meaning of Roosevelt's reform program that he called the New Deal. One rain-soaked veteran asked, "What is this bird Roosevelt up to?" Another shrugged and replied, "All I know is he's a hooman bein'."

The veteran caught the point that the New Deal would approach the downtrodden and the desperate with the simple proposition that they were peo-

WASHINGTON BONUS MARCH
This watercolor is one of a series executed by twenty-four-year-old Lewis Rubenstein in 1932
after traveling as an observer with the bonus marchers. Here he depicts the march in its early
stages as a hopeful, somewhat theatrical adventure. The figure on the runningboard of the car,
megaphone in hand, seems almost like a cheerleader encouraging the team as it advances on its
goal — in this case the steps of the United States Capitol.
Janet Marqusee Fine Arts Ltd.

---

ple in need of a helping hand to get back on their feet. The New Deal would prove to be remarkably free of concern about ideology. With a zest for experimentation, the Roosevelt administration set about to find work for the unemployed, to end chronic hard times in the countryside, and to stabilize business and financial practices so that the economy would be protected against future crashes. In the process, it created a coalition of supporters that gave the Democrats national power for twenty years.

How the American people were to be made productive and secure was the question. It was related most urgently to the millions of farmers and workers whose livelihood had been destroyed by the depression. But the issue involved Americans at all levels, since the depression left no one unscathed. At the center of these inclusive, progressive aims was the new president, Franklin Roosevelt, whose characteristics as a "hooman bein'" guided both the substance and the symbolism of the vast New Deal experiment. Roosevelt left the presidency and the nation fundamentally changed. The power of the president grew, the federal government assumed responsibility for the well-being of the nation, and citizens established a new relationship with Washington.

Franklin D. Roosevelt: A Patrician in Government

The man elected president in 1932 was very different from the people who elected him. To the manner born, he was every inch an aristocrat. Yet he managed to establish an extraordinary relationship with the American people, especially the poor and dispossessed. The explanation of his success lay partly in the circumstances in which he held office. In his twelve-year reign, he experienced two of the nation's greatest crises—the Great Depression and World War II. But simply presiding over economic catastrophe and war was no guarantee of popularity or greatness. The personality, the outreach, the actions, the times—all combined to make Franklin Roosevelt the dominant figure of his age. No other American politician in the twentieth century has had an impact as great as that of FDR.

The Growth of a Politician

Franklin Delano Roosevelt grew up in comfort and security on a beautiful Hudson River estate in New York. Born in 1882, the only child of a family with substantial inherited wealth, Roosevelt grew up in a safe and secure environment that steeped him in the values of Christian service. He absorbed early a belief, which never left him, that the privileged had a duty to look after the poor and weak. His education at Groton Academy and Harvard University prepared him to take his place within the leadership of his elite social class.

After a brief career as a reform member of the New York state legislature from 1910 to 1912, Roosevelt campaigned ardently for Woodrow Wilson, who appointed him assistant secretary of the navy in 1913. Roosevelt's bold and innovative efforts to modernize the navy during World War I and his attractive, crowd-pleasing ways moved the Democratic Party to nominate him for the vice presidency in the doomed campaign against Warren Harding in 1920. Roosevelt emerged from that campaign with a glowing reputation; a golden career in politics seemed to be ahead. He carried the name of a former president, was married to an earnest, public-spirited woman from his social class, and had strong state and national political connections.

Fate, however, had a grim detour in store for Roosevelt. In the summer of 1921, after a vigorous day of swimming in the icy water of the Bay of Fundy near his summer home on Campobello Island just over the Maine border in Canada and then fighting a ferocious brush fire, Roosevelt suffered a chill and collapsed. Within a few hours, he was paralyzed from the waist down, a victim of the polio virus. Though he battled the affliction with cheerful fortitude, Roosevelt would never again walk unassisted. With the help of his devoted wife, Eleanor, and his tireless aide Louis Howe, Roosevelt regained his intense desire for an active political career.

Roosevelt became a student of public life and gathered an encyclopedic knowledge of local conditions and political activities. Going places and getting to know people in their own setting had always been Roosevelt's personal and political style. After the polio attack, he reversed the tactic by finding ways to draw people to him. Maps, letters, phone calls, receptions, dinner parties, cruises, and the Warm Springs, Georgia, polio sanitarium that he founded all served that purpose. Roosevelt's uncomplaining adjustment to his disability convinced an uncle that he was "twice-born," that his ordeal had forced him to move beyond his shallow and spoiled youth to become a strong and compassionate person. Those closest to Roosevelt—Eleanor Roosevelt and Louis Howe among them—insisted that the illness did not transform him but merely shifted his focus. Tempered by constant suffering and no longer able to distract himself in physical activity, he concentrated on the art and practice of politics, including the persuasive uses of verbal and visual symbols.

Governor Roosevelt

Roosevelt's chance to return to political office came sooner than he expected. When New York Governor Al Smith prepared for his run at the presidency in 1928, he convinced Roosevelt to run for his vacated position and to help Smith capture the state's electoral votes. The tactic did not save Smith, who was defeated by Herbert Hoover, but Roosevelt managed a narrow upset victory. As the newly elected governor, he rejoiced at the opportunity to build New York's prosperity through a balanced program of conservation and scientific farming in the countryside combined with improved social services and working conditions in the cities.

The 1929 stock market crash forced him to confront a grim, unexpected reality. Unlike President Hoover, Governor Roosevelt was only momentarily at a loss. Because he believed that government's prime role was to respond to social need rather than to defend general principle, he was eager to act. He operated in the American tradition of the great patrician innovators, especially Thomas Jefferson, whose trust in the basic framework of American society was such that they felt free to try almost any approach that promised to answer particular needs. Unlike Hoover's fealty to a dogma of self-reliance, Roosevelt resisted ideology that would curb his ability to try out any new ideas that appealed to him. As the depression worsened, he urged experimentation to find more democratic and humane ways of dealing with the crisis.

Roosevelt accepted the progressive view that the genius of American government was the opportunity to use states as laboratories for national policy.

Roosevelt accepted the progressive view that the genius of American government was the opportunity to use states as laboratories for national policy. In that experimental spirit, he concluded that the severe economic crisis might require government to set aside conventional theories and customs in favor of whatever expedients would work to alleviate hardship and protect democracy. When a noted economist visited the State House in Albany to explain that a high level of human distress was inevitable while the laws of supply and demand permitted the free market system to recover its balance, Roosevelt cut him off and scolded, "People aren't cattle, you know."

Rather than rugged individualism or control by experts and economic law, Roosevelt preferred Abraham Lincoln's view that the government's duty was to step in when citizens were no longer able to help themselves. In an address to the New York legislature in August, 1931, Roosevelt declared:

> The duty of the State toward the citizen is the duty of the servant to its master. . . . One of these duties of the State is that of caring for those of its citizens who find themselves the victims of such adverse circumstances as make them unable to obtain even the necessities for mere existence without the aid of others. . . . To these unfortunate citizens aid must be extended by governments, not as a matter of charity but as a matter of social duty. . . . [No one should go] unfed, unclothed, or unsheltered.

On that basis of compelling necessity, Roosevelt set aside his budget-balancing orthodoxy and supported the largest state relief program in the nation's history. Yet he resisted even the appearance of radical change by naming the initiative the Temporary Emergency Relief Act (TERA). By labeling his innovations "temporary" and "emergency," Roosevelt sought to root new initiatives firmly within the established traditions of democracy and capitalism. He wanted to shore up the existing social and economic order, not subvert it. At the head of TERA, Roosevelt placed a social worker named Harry Hopkins, who was admired as an advocate of child welfare. Hopkins had grown up poor in Iowa, the son of a harness-maker. Nurtured in social gospel fervor at Iowa's Grinnell College, he set out for New York City, where he became a resident of the Christadora settlement house in the impoverished Lower East Side. Sallow and thin, with a hollow face, usually sucking on a cigarette, Hopkins resembled some of the neediest of those he sought to help. His empathy with the poor and their feelings of despair combined with his zestful energy to invigorate his leadership of New York's relief program.

The other mainstay of Roosevelt's relief effort was Frances Perkins, whom he named state labor commissioner. A veteran of hard-fought battles to reform industrial working conditions, Perkins was a tough-minded yet courtly woman with a com-

mitment to social service that had been ingrained during her student days at Mount Holyoke College. While serving in Al Smith's state administration, she had become acquainted with Eleanor Roosevelt and had helped in her personal struggle to escape the confines of her upper-class origins and to overcome her psychological wounds at having been considered an awkward and homely child. Perkins's plainspoken and witty remarks also helped Eleanor Roosevelt direct her husband's attention to the plight of industrial workers.

To coordinate New York's relief efforts, Roosevelt established in 1930 the Commission on Stabilization of Industry. The commission coordinated relief efforts in local communities and worked with industry to reduce unemployment. In a nation accustomed to letting the market take its course, it was the first state agency ever created to deal with problems of people who were out of work. Roosevelt sponsored another first in government cooperation by convening a conference of state governors at Salt Lake City in June 1930 to discuss the problems of the depression. There Roosevelt argued that the nation should follow the example of World War I by mobilizing national resources and enacting short-term emergency measures to win the war against economic collapse and hopelessness.

Roosevelt's highly visible efforts to do something constructive gained him the gratitude of constituents and the attention of national politicians. In 1930, New Yorkers reelected him governor by a margin of 750,000 votes and assured his position as the Democratic Party's leading candidate in the 1932 presidential election.

The Presidential Campaign of 1932

Roosevelt announced his candidacy for the presidency in January 1932, just a week before his fiftieth birthday. On the surface, he seemed to have everything going for him. Roosevelt's name, his earlier service in Washington, and his stature as a vice presidential candidate had made him a national figure. His smashing reelection and leading role among governors in combating the depression gave him stature as the most active champion of recovery. His record contrasted with Hoover's dismal image as a last-ditch defender of the old order. And Roosevelt was blessed with radiant personal charm, including a vibrant radio voice.

To supply him with fresh ideas, Roosevelt assembled a group of experts on national issues. Raymond Moley, a professor of government at Co-

ROOSEVELT CALLS FOR ACTION

*Franklin Roosevelt charged toward the presidential nomi-
nation in 1932, stressing the need for government action
against the depression. To dramatize his point, he broke
with custom by flying to the convention in Chicago. Once
at the podium to accept the call to launch a "New Deal,"
Roosevelt spoke with animated force to establish a contrast
with the stolid lecturing style of his opponent, Herbert
Hoover. As this and all other authorized pictures demonstrate, Roosevelt insisted that his activist image never be
undermined by any indication that without leg braces and
assistance, he could not walk.*

Franklin D. Roosevelt Library.

lumbia University, headed a team of advisers that
a journalist dubbed the "Brain Trust." The Brain
Trust's other leading figures were another Columbia professor, Rexford Tugwell, and a lawyer and
economist, Adolf Berle. Roosevelt's Brain Trust
equipped him with an arsenal of information and
the latest reform ideas. From his advisers, Roosevelt
heard passionate arguments in favor of government
planning to introduce stability and fair play into the
marketplace and a welfare state to aid the helpless
and end poverty.

Despite support from the Brain Trust and his
own personal and political strengths, Roosevelt still
had to overcome the old split in the Democratic
Party between rural strongholds in the South and
working-class enclaves in the cities, many of them
filled with recent immigrants. Moreover, he had to
devise a plan to attack the nation's woes that did
not alienate the Democratic Party faithful, who did
not agree among themselves. Roosevelt identified
himself with what he called "the forgotten man at
the bottom of the pyramid" and declared that helping that forgotten man called for "bold, persistent
experimentation." He tried to steer clear of divisive
issues and factional disputes within the party and
instead concentrated on building a victorious coalition by adding the West to his eastern and southern
base. He hoped to capture the party's nomination
with his support of direct cash subsidies to farmers
and with his commitment to the West's interest in
conservation of natural resources and water development.

Roosevelt needed all his impressive political
skills to overcome his rivals within the Democratic
Party. From the right, Al Smith, the party's 1928
presidential candidate, resented being overshadowed by Roosevelt and attacked him as a fomenter
of class conflict. On the left, progressives chided
Roosevelt for his unwillingness to offer bold plans
for redistributing wealth and regulating the economy,
steps considered class warfare by Smith's faction of
the party. Roosevelt's western strategy faltered
when the rival candidacy of John "Cactus Jack" Garner of Texas, Speaker of the House of Representatives, attracted so many supporters that Roosevelt
finally had to offer him the vice presidential nomination. At the end of the scramble for votes, Roosevelt
won the nomination at the head of a peculiar new
coalition. It lumped together his friends within the
Democratic Party's eastern establishment, big-city
machine bosses, old Wilsonian reformers, entrenched
southerners—many of them deeply conservative

and racist—along with angry farmers, labor unions, and urban ethnic communities. To galvanize that unwieldy coalition, Roosevelt realized that he needed to establish a personal, symbolic presence above the fray of political battle.

Roosevelt dramatized his candidacy by breaking with the precedent that the nominee should stay at home during the party's convention and await word of the party's choice. Instead, he flew to the Democratic convention in Chicago to deliver his acceptance speech in person. Roosevelt came before the delegates to restate his main case for innovation and experimentation. The flight, he declared, signified his intention to be bold and active. "Let it also be symbolic that in so doing I broke traditions. Let it be from now on the task of our Party to break foolish traditions and leave it to the Republican leadership, far more skilled in that art, to break promises." Roosevelt proposed to lead the party in the direction "of liberal thought, of planned action, of enlightened international outlook, and of the greatest good to the greatest number of our citizens." In conclusion, Roosevelt expressed his twin allegiance to the New Freedom of Woodrow Wilson and the Square Deal of Theodore Roosevelt by forging the label for his own program: the New Deal. As the delegates' applause died away, the band struck up "Happy Days Are Here Again," a bouncy new popular tune that became the anthem of Roosevelt's New Deal optimism.

During the presidential campaign, Roosevelt continued to make bold declarations of optimism and of the need for fresh initiatives in government, followed by careful hedging on specifics. In Topeka, Kansas, he promised wholesale reorganization of the Department of Agriculture to establish closer relationships between farmers and the government. In Seattle, he attacked high tariffs. In Portland, Oregon, he called for full disclosure of the financial activities of utility companies, where payoffs and corruption were rampant. In Detroit, where the slump in the automobile industry had created massive unemployment, Roosevelt declared his intention to eliminate the causes of poverty. The most thoroughgoing appeal to change came at the Commonwealth Club in San Francisco, where Roosevelt argued that the closing of the frontier meant that the days of boundless natural resources were over and that prosperity required careful public management of the nation's limited natural endowment.

President Hoover, the nominee of the Republican Party, attacked Roosevelt's proposed New Deal

as un-American collectivism of the sort that Russian Communists used to subdue the masses. Exhausted and angry, Hoover declared that his opponent was a "chameleon on plaid" who threatened to undermine the foundation of American society by advocating handouts and bureaucratic controls instead of relying on the tried-and-true efforts of hardworking, self-disciplined individuals. During the campaign, Hoover's motorcade took him past somber, silent crowds. When he spoke, many in the audience sat on their hands. Hoover sensed the nation's desperation, but he had little idea what to do about it. "Perhaps what this country needs," he said just weeks before the voters went to the polls, "is a great poem. . . . We need something to raise our eyes beyond the immediate horizon . . . something simple enough for a child to put his hand on his chest and spout in school on Fridays."

The electorate, however, did not hunger for poetry. Many voters heard Hoover's appeals for individual effort and sacrifice as coldhearted, pompous rhetoric that ignored their suffering. While Roosevelt exuberantly thumped the tub for a New Deal for the "forgotten man," Hoover became the scapegoat for all ills. One Democratic slogan proclaimed, "A Vote for Roosevelt Is a Vote against Hoover." The

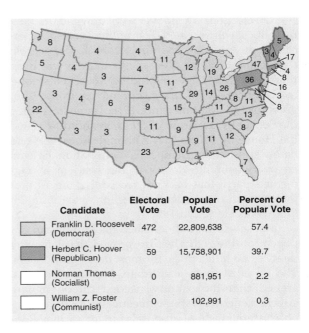

Candidate	Electoral Vote	Popular Vote	Percent of Popular Vote
Franklin D. Roosevelt (Democrat)	472	22,809,638	57.4
Herbert C. Hoover (Republican)	59	15,758,901	39.7
Norman Thomas (Socialist)	0	881,951	2.2
William Z. Foster (Communist)	0	102,991	0.3

MAP 24.1
The Election of 1932

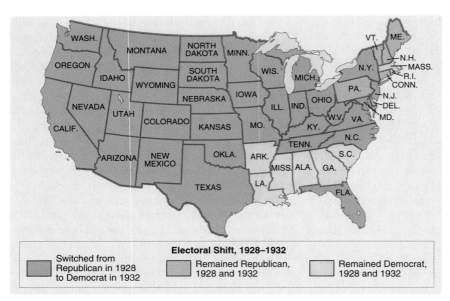

M A P   24.2
Electoral Shift, 1928–1932
Democratic victory in 1932
signaled the rise of a New
Deal coalition within which
women and minorities, many
of them new voters, made the
Democrats the majority party
for the first time in the twentieth century.

Electoral Shift, 1928–1932

☐ Switched from Republican in 1928 to Democrat in 1932   ☐ Remained Republican, 1928 and 1932   ☐ Remained Democrat, 1928 and 1932

president's name became a label for poverty. New York City's Park Department officially designated as "Hoover Valley" a gully where derelicts huddled in Central Park. When home-run king Babe Ruth was criticized for requesting a salary higher than President Hoover's, the Babe shot back with indisputable accuracy, "So what? I had a better year."

On election day, Hoover went down to utter defeat. Roosevelt received 22.8 million votes, 57 percent of the total, to 15.8 million votes for Hoover. In the electoral college, Roosevelt's margin was even more lopsided, 472 to 59. Riding Roosevelt's political coattails, Democrats swept into control of Congress for the first time since 1916. Democrats ruled the Senate by a margin of 59 to 36 and dominated the House by 313 to 117. Although Roosevelt had barely secured the Democrats' nomination, he won an overwhelming victory at the head of a fragmented party that had not received a majority of the votes in a presidential election since Franklin Pierce was elected in 1852.

Roosevelt not only crushed his Republican opponent on the right; he also proved that left-wing politics had little appeal for most depression voters. The Socialist Party candidate, Norman Thomas, argued that the country needed thoroughgoing government ownership of the means of production, not the tepid welfare proposals put forward by Roosevelt. But the Socialist Party polled only 881,951 votes, leaving the party with no significant electoral future. The Communists did even worse. They gained

only 102,991 votes. Tiny, remote Crosby, Minnesota, an outpost of Finnish immigrant miners devastated by the industrial collapse, was the only place to give the Communists a majority. Even the Farm Laborites, with a Populist heritage nourished by a half-century of rural grievances, managed only to elect five members of Congress and a single senator.

The landslide for Roosevelt and the Democrats in 1932 was the greatest change in voter choice in the nation's history. A new coalition came together to repudiate Republican leadership and policy and place their faith in a man who promised change.

The electoral switch from a landslide for Hoover and the Republicans in the 1928 election to a landslide for Roosevelt and the Democrats in 1932 was the greatest change in voter choice in the nation's history. It began what political analysts have termed the "Roosevelt Revolution"—a fundamental realignment of voter allegiance that swept the New Deal into power. A new coalition of farmers, industrial laborers, white-collar workers, African Americans, immigrants, women, intellectuals, and others —came together to repudiate Republican leadership and policy and place their faith in a man who promised change.

The New Deal in Action: The Hundred Days

At noon on March 4, 1933, Americans anxiously gathered around their radios to listen to Franklin Delano Roosevelt deliver his first inaugural address. A frightened people heard a serene and confident new president declare that the "only thing we have to fear is fear itself." The United States was "a stricken nation in the midst of a stricken world," Roosevelt said, but the "people . . . have not failed." Rather than dealing with the depression by "talking about it," he promised "direct, vigorous action." He would even be willing to "ask the Congress for the one remaining instrument to meet the crisis — broad Executive power to wage a war against the emergency, as great as the power that would be given to me if we were in fact invaded by a foreign foe."

Roosevelt's confident optimism and his determination to do *something* offered Americans hope and the sense that at last someone in Washington was listening. Roosevelt had been too vague and contradictory in the campaign for the people to have a clear road map of his administration, but they knew to expect strong presidential leadership and bold action. The first months of his administration, called "the Hundred Days," were a blur of action. For the hurry-up new order, the most immediate task was to offer relief to the destitute, including the 25 percent of the workforce that was unemployed. Their plight pointed toward a second need: the recovery of business and farming so that jobs would be available to all workers. And that goal led in turn to the third challenge: how to reform the system to guard against any future economic collapse.

The New Dealers

Reformers looking for a chance to translate their ideas into action hurried to Washington in the spring of 1933, drawn by the combination of public desperation and the chance to serve under a president interested in active reform. "As for those first New Deal days," Gardiner C. Means, an economic adviser, recalled, "much of the excitement came from improvisation. Nothing was fully set in the minds of the people there. They were open to fresh ideas. Always." Means reveled in the "yeastiness of experimentation" and an atmosphere that was "highly personal and highly charged."

The New Deal was the only moment in American history when a president receptive to reforms took office in bad times rather than good. Roosevelt's reform heroes — Andrew Jackson, Theodore Roosevelt, and Woodrow Wilson — had the good fortune to serve during economic booms. Roosevelt confronted the more daunting task of reversing an economic depression without violating the nation's allegiance to democracy and capitalism. Rather than responding to bad times by blaming the victims, as Herbert Hoover had done, Roosevelt let it be known that he sympathized with the victims and that he was eager for new ideas to break the depression's merciless stranglehold.

In recognition of his sprawling party base, Roosevelt selected his cabinet and staff to represent important constituencies. He also chose advisers who would be loyal to him and who would be unlikely to become rivals for power. Vice President Garner was a source of pride to the Southwest and a shrewd negotiator with Congress. For secretary of state, Roosevelt chose an old Wilsonian southerner, Cordell Hull, a former senator from Tennessee and a longtime advocate of Wilsonian free trade. For secretary of the treasury, Roosevelt called upon Will Woodin, a former industrialist and lifelong Republican who was nonetheless eager to carry out Roosevelt's experimental approach. In these appointments, Roosevelt made clear his intention to establish a friendly, cooperative relationship with businessmen and bankers yet to proceed openly to test ways of rescuing the economic system.

For the heads of the Labor and Agriculture Departments, whose constituencies were more fully the forgotten and the hard-pressed, Roosevelt turned to reformers. Frances Perkins became the first female secretary of labor, much to the outrage of traditional labor leaders. Henry A. Wallace of Iowa, a voice for scientific experiment and government regulation of markets, was tapped to be secretary of agriculture. For secretary of the interior, Roosevelt also looked west when he selected the irascible progressive Republican lawyer from Chicago Harold A. Ickes. Roosevelt followed the principle of diversity in other, less central appointments and ended up with a cabinet and set of advisers that represented virtually all sections, both major parties, the three major religions, and both sexes. Roosevelt — happily responding to his new nickname, "the Chief" — took the responsibility to knit these disparate advisers into some semblance of cohesion.

Through it all, Roosevelt radiated good cheer and relished his task as the impresario of a great rescue operation and the restorer of public confidence. Lights burned late in the White House most nights. Roosevelt wore out his assistants, picking their brains, prodding them to find fresh solutions. To communicate with the public, he began his practice of frequent news conferences, which brought him face to face with the press thirty times during the Hundred Days and at least once a week thereafter. His wide grin and infectious optimism made him the personal symbol of recovery, the emblem of hope for millions.

Banking and Finance Reform

The new administration first targeted the disaster engulfing America's banking system. By March 4, 1933, when Roosevelt was inaugurated, the nation's governors had suspended almost all banking operations within their states. That was a desperate action, but since 1930, more than five thousand banks with $3.4 billion in assets had gone under. On March 5, 1933, Roosevelt made good his inaugural pledge for "action now" by announcing a four-day "bank holiday" that converted emergency state action into federal policy. Three days later, Roosevelt sent Congress the Emergency Banking Act, and four hours later a compliant Congress passed the administration's plan for rescue. Under the provisions of the

bill, the secretary of the treasury could decide which banks were stable enough to reopen and could authorize the Reconstruction Finance Corporation (RFC) to supply funds for immediate circulation. A few months later, Congress rounded out these regulatory changes by creating the Federal Deposit Insurance Corporation (FDIC) to insure bank customers against the loss of their deposits if their bank should fail.

The New Deal's more radical supporters were disappointed that Roosevelt had not nationalized the banks and made them a firm cornerstone for national planning. Instead, the private banking system was propped up with federal funds, banks were subjected to federal regulation and oversight, and individual deposits were secured with the full faith and credit of the United States government. Within a few days, most of the nation's major banks had reopened.

On March 12, Roosevelt broadcast his first "fireside chat" to the nation, explaining why the banking legislation was needed and how it gave good reason for confidence. That radio talk, suggesting a cozy gathering of the nation at the family hearth to discuss what was left in the sugar bowl, was a masterstroke. Roosevelt, speaking in cheerful, simple, fatherly terms, came through as a friendly savior echoing his inaugural address with his reassurance against fear. In the minds of a majority of Americans, the New Deal had established its competence

TABLE 24.1

MAJOR LEGISLATION OF THE NEW DEAL'S FIRST HUNDRED DAYS

Name of Act	Date Passed	Basic Provisions
Emergency Banking Act	March 9, 1933	Provided for reopening stable banks and authorizing RFC supply funds
Civilian Conservation Corps Act	March 31, 1933	Provided jobs for unemployed youth
Agricultural Adjustment Act	May 12, 1933	Provided funds to pay farmers for not growing surplus crops
Federal Emergency Relief Act	May 12, 1933	Provided relief funds for the destitute
Tennessee Valley Authority Act	May 18, 1933	Set up authority for development of electric power and conservation
National Industrial Recovery Act	June 16, 1933	Specified cooperation among business, government, and labor in setting fair prices and working conditions
Glass-Steagall Banking Act	June 16, 1933	Created Federal Deposit Insurance Corporation (FDIC) to insure bank deposits

and humaneness, and a glimmer of the nation's old optimism returned. The banking panic ended, and the money that anxious Americans had stuffed in mattresses and buried in backyards began to flow back into the banks.

To provide a firm financial basis for economic recovery, the New Deal turned to the stock market, whose scandals so vividly symbolized the 1920s. While governor of New York, Roosevelt had frequently denounced shady dealings on Wall Street, and now as president he was eager to enact provisions that would end dubious practices such as the pyramiding of holding companies that created Samuel Insull's false fortune or profitable stock trading on the basis of insider information. At his insistence, Congress passed the Securities Act of 1933 and the Federal Securities and Exchange Act of 1934, which created the Securities and Exchange Commission (SEC). The new agency licensed investment dealers, monitored all stock transactions, restricted margin buying, and required corporate officers to make full disclosures of their stock offerings and be responsible for any claims they made about their companies.

Roosevelt named an abrasive and successful Wall Street trader, Joseph P. Kennedy, chairman of

the SEC. Critics opposed the choice of someone whose reputation had been clouded by shrewd stock manipulation, but Roosevelt replied wickedly, "Set a thief to catch a thief." Kennedy proved to be tough enough to face down threats by brokers, some of them with things to hide, to boycott the exchange or even move it out of the country. Soon the SEC won praise for its effectiveness, and Wall Street regained respect within business circles. In the end, the most spectacular casualty was not a brash upstart like Joe Kennedy but the impeccably well-bred stock exchange president, Richard Whitney, who went to jail for stealing from others' accounts to cover his own bad investments.

In addition to his efforts to save the financial structure at home, Roosevelt attempted to repair a sputtering international economy. He inherited a conference President Hoover had convened in London to find a way to stabilize the world's depressed monetary system and revive international trade. Hope for cooperation soon faded, however. When the conference deadlocked on the gold standard and trade policies, Roosevelt brought the conference to an abrupt end with a sharp rebuke of what he called "old-fashioned fetishes of so-called international bankers." Instead, he decided, the United States

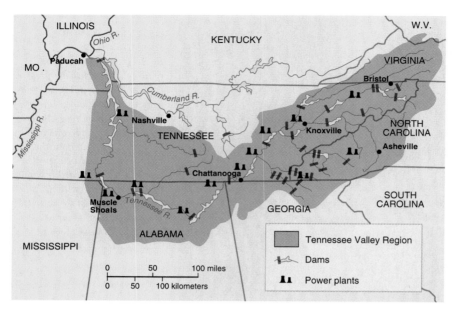

MAP 24.3
The Tennessee Valley Authority
The New Deal created the Tennessee Valley Authority to modernize a vast impoverished region with hydroelectric power dams and, at the same time, to reclaim eroded lands and preserve old folkways.

would take care of its own problems first and return to the international bargaining table when other nations learned to be more cooperative and balance their books. Though Roosevelt's decision to pull out of the conference left the rest of the world in a precarious state, it enabled his New Deal administration to concentrate on domestic problems.

Relief and Conservation Programs

Having rescued the banks, Roosevelt took on the plight of those with no means of support—the unemployed, the landless, the disabled, and those who were too old or too young to work. The Federal Emergency Relief Administration (FERA) Act made good on the president's promise that he would not abandon Americans to hunger and homelessness. The new initiative provided cash subsidies to bankrupt local relief agencies. Soon, the FERA supported from four to five million households each month and funded thousands of work projects for the unemployed. In Alabama, Dera Johnson, whose husband, a coal miner, had become too sick to work, got a teaching job with FERA. "That class was a lifesaver to my family," she remembered. "I taught it for a year, and his rest had improved Johnson so much that he went back to work." To publicize the terrible suffering that provoked this unprecedented federal initiative, FERA's director, Harry Hopkins, sent reporters out into the field to describe conditions. With support from an aroused public, FERA took the lead in providing vaccinations and immu-

nizations for millions of unprotected poor people, helped build desperately needed flood protection systems, and supported literacy classes for the most ill prepared citizens.

Having rescued the banks, Roosevelt took on the plight of those with no means of support—the unemployed, the landless, the disabled, and those who were too old or too young to work.

Agreeing with Hoover about the dangers of a federal "dole," the Roosevelt administration intended its efforts as temporary emergency measures to relieve suffering and jump-start the economy, without threatening individual self-reliance. Whenever possible, the administration favored aid in the form of a job that saved the recipient's dignity while accomplishing something useful. The New Deal's second major relief program, the Civil Works Administration (CWA), under Hopkin's direction, put more than four million Americans to work building schools and parks. But New Dealers perceived work relief as an emergency measure also, and within a year the Roosevelt administration began whittling back the CWA.

More enduring was Roosevelt's favorite work relief program, the Civilian Conservation Corps (CCC), which offered unemployed young men, mostly from the cities, a chance to perform useful outdoor work. The CCC reflected Roosevelt's long-standing enthusiasm for the outdoors and conservation. By the time the vigorous program ended in 1942, it had enrolled three million young people. From a big family, Blackie Gold had "to go out and beg for coal, buy bread that's two, three days old." In 1937, when he was seventeen, he joined the CCC at thirty dollars a month. "I really enjoyed it," he remembered. "I had three wonderful square meals a day." The CCC achieved significant results. Trees planted on the plains checked the disastrous dust storms that ravaged the Southwest in the early years of the decade. The CCC reversed the long-standing depletion of forest preserves by planting more than two billion new trees, fighting forest fires, and erecting more than five million dams to check soil erosion. It strung 83,000 miles of telephone wires, constructed 122,000 miles of minor roads and trails, and located 23,000 new water sources in the nation's wilderness. In the end, the CCC created magnificent outdoor recreation areas and made them accessible to millions of people.

The most spectacular accomplishment of the New Deal's conservation efforts was the Tennessee Valley Authority (TVA). The project fulfilled the long-frustrated aim of progressives to use government lands in Muscle Shoals, Alabama, along the Tennessee River for planned regional development, rather than selling them off to private developers. In April 1933, Roosevelt presented legislation to Congress designed to transform the Tennessee valley, one of the nation's most depressed areas and largely untouched by modern technology, into a model of cooperative development. The act creating the TVA set up a regional organization empowered to build hydroelectric power dams along the Tennessee River and to use the electricity generated to bring power and light to rural communities. To help guide the new prosperity, the TVA planned to build model towns for power station workers and provide new homes for farmers who would benefit from electricity and flood control. At the same time, the New Deal expressed its commitment to the con-

CIVILIAN CONSERVATION CORPS WORKERS
No New Deal program was more popular among its participants and the general public than the Civilian Conservation Corps. It offered healthy outdoor work for young men that got them out of the cities and eased their unemployment blues. To the public it showed that the New Deal would act against the depression in a way that would repair neglect of America's natural resources.
Forest Service Photo Collection.

servation of social custom, as well as natural resources, by including programs within the TVA to encourage local crafts and other folkways.

The most spectacular accomplishment of the New Deal's conservation efforts was the Tennessee Valley Authority (TVA).

"It is time to extend planning to a wider field, in this instance comprehending in one great project many States directly concerned with the basin of one of our greatest rivers," Roosevelt declared when he signed the TVA bill. Crossing the state lines of Kentucky, Virginia, North Carolina, Tennessee, Georgia, Alabama, and Mississippi, the TVA set out to demonstrate that a partnership between the federal government and local residents could overcome traditional limitations of state boundaries and free enterprise to make efficient use of abundant resources and break an ancient cycle of poverty. The TVA became the most ambitious example of New Deal enthusiasm for planning. But hampered by bitter resistance from competing private power companies, the TVA never fully realized its utopian ends. It did, however, succeed in bringing electric power, flood protection, soil reclamation, and, therefore, sharply improved prosperity to the area it served.

Agricultural Initiatives

New Dealers formulated other plans to meet the crisis in agriculture that stretched far beyond the Tennessee valley. Farmers typically responded to low prices for their crops by increasing production, causing a self-defeating cycle of crop surpluses and still lower prices. At the same time, unemployment robbed consumers of the money to buy even low-priced farm products. Congress first considered the McNary-Haugen bill, which proposed dumping crop surpluses overseas at below market prices, with a subsidy from the government to make up the difference. That way, domestic supplies would not exceed demand and farmers would enjoy a good return. When the bill failed to pass, a farm economist named M. L. Wilson devised a new approach. His voluntary domestic allotment plan called for the federal government to pay farmers to leave some of their land idle, thus reducing crop surpluses and thereby boosting prices. Left for another day was the problem of feeding the hungry who could not afford the higher prices the plan was designed to set.

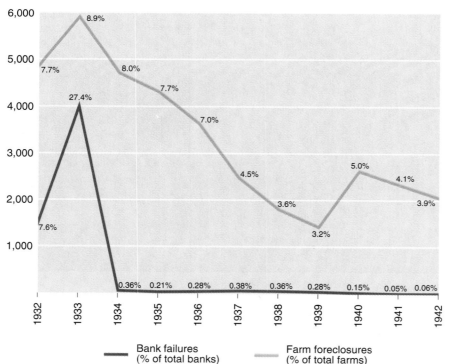

FIGURE 24.1
Bank Failures and Farm Foreclosures, 1932–1942
New Deal legislation to stabilize the economy had its most immediate and striking effect in preventing banks, along with their depositors, from going under and farmers from losing their land.

SKETCH FOR A WPA MURAL
This sketch for a mural commissioned for Lenoir City, Tennessee, is typical of the Federal Arts Program's goal to memorialize significant moments of achievement in every region of the country. For rural folk, the sight of Rural Electrification Authority workers extending power lines was one of the more exciting symbols of the New Deal. When the REA came into existence in 1935, less than 10 percent of the nation outside the cities had electricity. By 1941, REA programs had increased that number to 40 percent; ten years later the figure had risen to 90 percent, and the gulf of silence and darkness between town and country was successfully bridged.
Public Buildings Service, General Services Administration.

The Agricultural Adjustment Act (AAA), which incorporated the domestic allotment plan and the Agricultural Adjustment Administration to apply it, sailed easily through Congress in May 1933. On the heels of the landmark AAA legislation, the Farm Credit Act eased another old farm grievance by providing credit to forestall foreclosures on mortgaged farm property and prevent debt-ridden farmers from being evicted from their land.

Once in place, these reforms dampened the urge for farm revolts and nudged prices upward. An Iowa farmer remembered, "People could now see daylight and hope. It was a whole transformation of attitude." Results, however, were mixed. New Dealers relied on grass-roots democracy to administer the programs fairly. In the corn, hog, and wheat region of the Midwest, farmers came together on a democratic basis, and a reasonably equitable distribution of benefits followed. In the South, however, local control meant that sharecroppers and tenant farmers on cotton plantations were denied a decent share of the benefits, while large growers reaped huge subsidies for putting land out of production—and tenant farmers out of work. Nonetheless, the AAA guided agriculture toward greater overall prosperity. With almost all major crops limited, surpluses declined and gross farm income rose from $6.4 billion in 1932 to $8.5 billion in 1934.

Moreover, loans sponsored by the Farm Credit Administration (FCA) arrested farmers' steep slide into bankruptcy. The trickle of 7,800 federal loans in 1932 rose to a flood of 287,881 in less than a year after the FCA was enacted in 1933—a record 3,174 loans winning approval in a single day. By the end of the decade, the federal government had financed 40 percent of farm mortgage debt, and the shadow of foreclosure had receded from most farmers' doorsteps.

With both the TVA and AAA in place, the administration turned to fulfilling the old progressive dream that electricity and all its modern benefits be extended to rural America. When Roosevelt became president, about 90 percent of the country outside the cities and towns was without electricity. Power magnates like Samuel Insull saw little profit in sending expensive transmission lines into sparsely settled territory. Thus, the further cities moved into the electric age, the more rural America seemed backward, rather than the backbone of the country, as Jefferson had intended.

In May 1935, the New Deal finally overcame the resistance of the private power industry and created the Rural Electrification Administration (REA). Encouraged by the successes of the AAA and TVA in communal cooperation, the REA gave low-cost loans to farm cooperatives so that they could bring power into their communities. By 1941, the REA succeeded in raising to 40 percent the number of farms with electricity. One man recalled the lights coming on in his Arkansas farmhouse in 1940. "The lights just barely glowed," he said. But his mother was smiling, and "tears started to run down her cheeks." Others remembered their first radios and hearing Roosevelt's voice. By 1950, nine out of every ten American farms were electrified. With the possible exception of the automobile, nothing did as much to brighten the quality of rural life and close the gap between country and city.

Industrial Recovery

Industry was as devastated as any sector of the nation's economy. But the New Deal's National Recovery Administration (NRA), established in June 1933 under the National Industrial Recovery Act (NIRA), was a far less successful experiment than the agricultural programs. The NRA's objective was to coordinate management, labor, and the federal government through a network of industrial codes that governed industrial working conditions, prices, and trade practices. In exchange for the easing of antitrust regulations, business leaders agreed to allow the bill to guarantee labor's right to collective bargaining. The NRA hoped to set nationwide terms for how much each industry should produce, what it should charge consumers, and, subject to collective bargaining agreements, what pay and benefits workers should receive.

Under the energetic leadership of General Hugh Johnson, a veteran of the War Industries Board during World War I, the NRA captured public attention through speeches and gala parades with floats, movie stars, West Point cadets, and even a Miss NRA displayed in a shell-shaped float like Venus emerging from the sea. By the end of 1933, most industries were represented within the 541 NRA codes, and the Blue Eagle symbol displayed in store windows let the public know.

The stage seemed set for a major transformation of American industry, but opinions differed widely on the direction it would take. The New Dealers emphasized the possibilities for rational management and fair competition. They hoped that

NRA QUILT
The blue eagle of the National Recovery Administration, fiercely clutching a machine gear and lightning bolts, symbolized the government's determination to bring American industry around to a coordinated plan for recovery. The attempt to balance the interests of producers, workers, and consumers proved too much for the blue eagle however. Yet, as this backcountry quilt indicates, the blue eagle was sometimes able to carry the spirit of cooperation far from the centers of industrial turmoil.
Franklin D. Roosevelt Library.

coordination would produce a collective social conscience that would inhibit industry from cheating customers or destroying the environment and would make sure that workers were treated fairly. Critics, however, saw bureaucratic oppression. Because the NRA skirted antimonopoly laws and left industry subject to federal management, they claimed that the economy would become rigidly controlled from the top. The NRA scheme of linking business with government seemed to its critics an American version of Mussolini's corporate fascism in Italy, a means for controlling individuals by directing their economic lives.

In reality, neither prediction was accurate. The outcome was more an extension of conventional business practice than a radical change to either the right or the left. Johnson's sloppy management gave business leaders the opportunity to gain control of the code-writing mechanism, and they made sure the codes would first serve the interests of corporate profits rather than worker benefit or the general welfare. By the mid-1930s, prospects for a rationally coordinated business system had faded, and even New Dealers began to hope for some way to make a graceful escape from the NRA as it had developed.

The Hundred Days that initiated the First New Deal produced a blizzard of new agencies and programs.

The Hundred Days that initiated what became known as the First New Deal produced a blizzard of new agencies and programs. The central idea uniting the legislative onslaught was planning and coordination, in both industry and agriculture. The effort succeeded in reversing the economic decline and restoring the nation's confidence, but it did not produce full recovery. The magnitude and scope of the depression and the speed of the New Deal attack ensured that the Roosevelt administration would have as many failures as successes. Inevitably, resistance mounted.

Challenges to the New Deal

A majority of Americans supported the New Deal's initiatives and programs. After the early rush of excitement, however, discontent began to grow. Business expressed open hostility to the philosophy and practice of the First New Deal. Conservatives insisted that New Deal changes had been too radical, undermined economic stability, and threatened American democratic values. But the continuation of severe distress across much of the nation caused others to fault the administration for not having programs radical enough to meet the people's needs. Increasingly, opponents mounted political challenges to Roosevelt's initiatives.

Resistance to Business Reform

Backlash within the business community and among others opposed to government interference in the economy went beyond material self-interest.

Since the New Deal sought economic recovery, New Dealers expected business leaders to come around eventually and welcome cooperative economic planning. In that respect the administration was sorely disappointed. In the Tennessee valley, private power companies battled the TVA as "creeping socialism" and unfair competition. The NRA took even greater abuse. The alliance of the New Deal with urban labor and constant feuding between business representatives and NRA officials about how to devise codes of competition caused strain from the outset. Moreover, although business conditions improved steadily and the business failure rate declined to levels below those of the boom years of the 1920s, business leaders never reconciled themselves to the administration's planning concept. To one Republican senator, the creator of the NRA was "Frankenstein" Roosevelt and the Blue Eagle symbol was really "the Soviet duck" in disguise. The relentlessly anti-NRA Hearst newspapers chimed in with a poem that characterized the Roosevelt administration as

The Red New Deal with a Soviet seal
Endorsed by a Moscow hand;
The strange result of an alien cult
In a liberty-loving land.

Ironically, the business community kept up its criticism even though its situation improved more steadily during the depression than did that of most other social groups, including farmers and workers. The managerial elite remained mostly intact—despite some spectacular jailings, flights from prosecution, and suicides. So did the hierarchical corporate structure that had been developed during the boom years at the turn of the century. The greatest wounds had been to business leaders' confidence and pride. A desire by business leaders to ward off threats of government regulation, higher taxes, and union organization moved them to create public relations offices and—more ominously—a system of company spies and police forces to seek out disloyal workers. The rage of businessmen toward the New Deal fastened on Franklin Roosevelt as the source of their loss of public admiration and government favor. In the typical commuter line club car—otherwise known as the "assassination special"—rumors flew about that "traitor to his class," about "that man in the White House." Hostility among the well-to-do became so pervasive that when high society's leading party giver, Elsa Maxwell, planned a "Pet Hates" ball, she asked guests not to come dressed as the president or his wife to prevent everyone from wearing the same costume.

The most extreme example of anti–New Deal agitation was the American Liberty League, founded in 1934 as the NRA came under bitter attack. Prominent members of the league had once been leaders in the Democratic Party, but now they decried the New Deal as a betrayer of basic constitutional guarantees of freedom and individualism. These critics included the party's 1928 presidential candidate, Al Smith, his campaign chairman, John Jacob Raskob, and Jowett Shouse, a former chairman of the Democratic National Committee. The league furiously attacked almost every feature of the New Deal. The AAA was a "trend toward Fascist control of agriculture," relief programs marked "the end of democracy," and the NRA had plunged the nation into a "quicksand of visionary experimentation." Although the league's membership never exceeded 125,000 zealots, its well-financed publicity campaign inflamed the rift between Roosevelt and the business class. By 1935, the two major business organizations—the National Association of Manufacturers and the Chamber of Commerce—had become openly anti-New Deal.

Conservatives insisted that New Deal changes had been too radical, undermined economic stability, and threatened American democratic values.

Planners and labor leaders who favored more worker control attacked the New Deal from the other direction. In their view, the NRA had stifled enterprise by permitting monopolistic practices. They pointed out that industrial trade associations twisted codes to suit their aims, thwarted competition, and engaged in price gouging. Labor leaders especially resented the willingness of the NRA to allow companies to form their own unions, blocking the organization of genuine grass-roots unions that permitted workers to bargain on terms they chose for themselves.

In the midst of the cross fire of criticisms, the Supreme Court in May 1935 declared that the NRA unconstitutionally conferred legislative power on an administrative agency and overstepped the limits of federal power to regulate interstate commerce. The agency lingered briefly, but its codes evaporated, and business leaders rejected most proposals for cooperation with government. The failure of the NRA demonstrated both historic American resistance to economic planning and the refusal of the business community to yield its autonomy unless it was forced to do so.

Reaction against the New Deal Farm Program

The AAA survived its battering by champions of the old order. Contentment among the majority of farmers was at a higher level than among the businessmen affected by the NRA. Even though farmers were reluctant to abandon their traditional practice of trying to increase production as a matter of pride and survival, the allotment checks for keeping land fallow and the higher prices for their produce created loyalty among those with enough acreage to participate.

Protest stirred, however, among those with smaller farms who were not fortunate enough to qualify for allotments. The Southern Farm Tenants Union, formed by tenant farmers themselves, argued passionately that the AAA was a device for enriching large farmers at the expense of the most vulnerable. By taking out of production the land on which tenants had lived, owners could simultaneously qualify for government subsidies and be relieved of the need to provide for those who had been dependent on them. Already at the bottom of the economic ladder, tenant farmers and sharecroppers faced a grave situation. One black sharecropper explained to an interviewer why only seventy-five dollars a year from the plantation cotton subsidies made its way down to her: "De landlord think he ought to have *all* the acre p'duction checks, cause it his land." Bypassing the intention of New Deal programs to benefit owners and tenants alike was simple enough in her part of Arkansas because "de landlord is landlord, de politicians is landlord, de judge is landlord, de shurf is landlord, ever'body is landlord, en we ain' got nothin'!" Stories like this convinced critics that the New Deal was fostering just the sort of inequality and misery—among both whites and blacks—that it had set out to eliminate.

The AAA's most potent critics, however, were not the dispossessed but agricultural processors and distributors. They were unhappy that the AAA reduced the volume of production—the source of their profits—while they were required to pay for the very program that disadvantaged them. In 1936, the Supreme Court agreed to their contention that they were the victims of an illegal attempt to regu-

BLACK SHARECROPPERS
*A painful, unintended conse-
quence of the New Deal plan
to maintain farm prices by reducing acreage in production
was the eviction of tenant
farmers when the land they
worked was unused. Champions of the tenant farmers, most
notably the Southern Farm
Tenants Union, protested that
federal crop subsidies should be
shared between owners and
those who usually worked the
land. Often, however, sharecroppers like these were simply
cast adrift, and lobbies for farm
owners thwarted any governmental challenge. The sad state
of tenant farmers continued
until World War II provided
opportunities for displaced tenants to escape to the cities.*
UPI/Bettmann Archives.

late agriculture and to tax one group (processors
and distributors) to enrich another (farmers). The
AAA rebounded from the Supreme Court ruling by
redesigning its allotment provisions with legislation
that focused more on conservation measures the
Court found acceptable.

By establishing the principle of keeping prices
up by keeping production down, the New Deal
went far toward making American agriculture profitable. Success came, however, by favoring large-
scale, capital-intensive agribusiness over the needs
of small farmers. Those with large holdings could
benefit most from crop subsidies; those with little
land or on marginal land were the first to be displaced by plans to put surplus acreage out of production.

Politics on the Fringes

The New Deal also faced challenges from outside
the bounds of organized politics or labor unions.
These critics included a small but growing minority
drawn to radical movements. The depression had
given radicals many opportunities to use their talents
for organizing discontent. Socialists and Communists
accused the New Deal of mounting a feeble resistance

to business elites or, worse, rescuing capitalism
from its self-inflicted crisis. Many intellectuals and
artists moved left during the 1930s to embrace
Marxist critiques of capitalism and ruling-class exploitation. They voiced powerful arguments for
radical change. Socialist author Upton Sinclair ran
for governor of California in 1934 on the EPIC (End
Poverty in California) ticket. He lost a close race
when a harsh smear campaign charging Sinclair
with being a dangerous Communist caused Roosevelt to withdraw support for the EPIC plan to put
the unemployed to work in idle factories.

With that one exception, the left was never able
to mount a serious electoral challenge to the New
Deal. And for all the doctrinaire talk of violent overthrow of the government by the proletariat or some
other aggrieved group, there was no real chance of
that happening after Roosevelt's election. The United
States was a highly organized modern nation where
legal means of exerting force were mostly in the
hands of the authorities, and constitutional provisions for realizing individual and democratic values
were already in place, although they were not always
honored.

The poor and alienated largely shied away from
radical change. Instead, as the Bonus Army demon-

strations showed, they clung desperately to the belief that their status as loyal Americans entitled them to respect, material security, and the opportunity to improve their lot. With varying degrees of militancy, most Americans sought inclusion, not revolution, fundamental entitlements, not radical novelties. Accordingly, homespun populist agitators preaching old-style religion and harping on birthrights drew the biggest crowds looking for an alternative to the status quo.

The most formidable coalition of down-and-outers challenging the New Deal was led by a Catholic priest in Detroit named Charles Coughlin. Father Coughlin expressed his outrage at the depression in a series of radio broadcasts that gained him an unequaled nationwide audience of forty million by 1930. The "Radio Priest" found villains in all the conventional places. He began by denouncing Communists as traditional foes of the church but soon shifted to bankers and other "predatory capitalists," who, he increasingly insisted, were dominated by Jews. To his formula he added a touch of Midwest populism by calling for an expanded money supply backed by silver so that the poor could be rescued from the "cross of gold" that William Jennings Bryan had so famously associated with business domination of the economy.

In 1932, Father Coughlin, like most other urban, working-class Catholics, pinned his hopes on the Democratic Party and Roosevelt's election. But his pronouncements in favor of confiscating wealth for redistribution to the deserving poor and his growing insistence on his own importance set him at odds with the New Deal. After first welcoming Roosevelt as the nation's political savior, Coughlin soon turned against the administration for its failure to "drive the moneychangers from the temple." In 1935, Coughlin founded the National Union for Social Justice to promote legislation that would advance his cause. As the presidential election of 1936 neared, Coughlin converted his organization into the Union Party and called on other dissidents to join him in mounting an election challenge to Roosevelt.

One of those who answered Father Coughlin's call was a man of very different temperament and background. Dr. Francis Townsend was a sixty-six-year-old public health officer in Long Beach, California, when the New Deal began. Townsend's anger that his elderly patients existed in misery in the golden land roused him to action. As a remedy, he proposed the Old Age Revolving Pension in late 1933, which would pay all persons over age sixty

$200 a month on the condition that they spend the entire amount within thirty days and thereby stimulate the economy. Buoyed by 90 percent of all Long Beach voters who endorsed his petition to the federal government, Townsend organized pension clubs that soon sprouted across the country among older people looking for security. By the time Father Coughlin announced his National Union for Social Justice, there were between 2 and 3.5 million paying members of the Townsend movement looking for a political home. Townsend found the Coughlin organization attractive as another populist insurgency outside the status quo.

The most important of the rebellious populists came from another region ripe for protest. Huey Pierce Long, son of a backcountry farmer, had used his immense talents to become governor of Louisiana in 1928, the same year Roosevelt was elected governor of New York. Long, calling himself "the Kingfish" after a sly character in a radio comedy show, electrified the plain people of his state with brash rhetoric and country humor. With their support, he swept out of power a reactionary political machine that had kept Louisiana one of the poorest and most backward states. By delivering on his promises to build roads, schools, and hospitals and provide jobs, Long stood out as a beacon of hope among the desperate during the early depression years. The dark side, however, was that Long achieved his revolution in Louisiana by ruthlessly gathering power into his own hands.

Elected to the Senate in 1932, Long, like Coughlin, at first tried to tie his fortunes to the New Deal. But he too became disaffected when he could not bend Roosevelt to his will and simply use him to further his own ambition to become president. Long's national popularity rested on his Share Our Wealth plan for "making every man a king." Vaguely, the plan advocated steeply progressive income taxes to reduce large fortunes and to redistribute wealth through guaranteeing every family a "homestead" worth $5,000 and an annual income of $2,500. Like Townsend and Coughlin, Long scorned conventional economics, but his calculations sounded good to many poor people. A Chicago shoe salesman wrote Long: "I voted for President Roosevelt but it seems Wall St. has got him punch drunk. What we need is men with guts to go farther to the left as you advocate." Roosevelt called Long "one of the two most dangerous men in America"—the other was Douglas MacArthur, the general who had so offended him with his strong-arm tactics against the Bonus Army.

The populist threat mounted by Coughlin, Townsend, and Long stirred the New Deal administration to solidify its winning coalition. An early test came in the 1934 elections, normally a time when a seated president loses support as disillusion sets in among those who expected too much. Roosevelt approached the elections cautiously, wishing to keep himself within the reform center and at a safe distance from radical and crank causes on the right and left. In August, Roosevelt embarked on a national tour to express support for loyal Democratic candidates before large, friendly crowds who convinced him that the electorate would endorse his active efforts to jolt the country out of depression.

Roosevelt's keen appraisal of the situation was confirmed by the unusually high percentage of voters who turned out to give New Dealers a landslide victory. Democrats increased their numbers in the House of Representatives from 310 to 319 out of a total of 422; and in the Senate, the party gained 10 new seats to take a commanding two-thirds majority, the greatest margin ever achieved in that body.

The New Deal also escaped the threat of Huey Long's challenge in a way that some observers of his provocative career predicted. Long's ambitions reached the heights of bravado in 1935 when he published *My First Days in the White House*, which explained what he would do as president. But in September 1935 it all ended. While visiting the Louisiana State House to make sure his absolute power still prevailed, Long was fatally shot by one of the many Louisianans he had antagonized. With the disappearance of Long's brilliant personality, the followers he had whipped up scattered like dust in a whirlwind. Some of Long's admirers carried their alienation into the campaigns of Coughlin and Townsend. Most turned toward the New Deal. In the election to fill the Kingfish's seat, the candidate who pledged loyalty to the Roosevelt administration swept the field by a wide margin.

The Second New Deal and the Rise of the Welfare State

Following the congressional elections of 1934, newspaper editor William Allen White observed, "He has been all but crowned by the people." Roosevelt and the Democrats had triumphed, but New Dealers found the outlook troubling. While the First New Deal had made sweeping improvements in American life, halted the economic decline, and restored

hope, the nation was not restored to economic health. A glance at almost any economic index— employment, production, income—revealed how anemic the economy remained. The Hundred Days had spent itself, and major programs were faltering (AAA) or invalidated by the Supreme Court (NRA). Angry criticism was sprouting on the right and the left. "The air has been filled of late with the noise of things breaking up," reported the Washington *Star* in March 1935. Roosevelt decided that it was time for a departure.

> *Out of the welter of legislative and executive action that made up the Second New Deal emerged the first elements of an American welfare state.*

In 1935, New Dealers surged ahead with a flurry of new policies that has been called the Second Hundred Days or the Second New Deal. The Second New Deal moved away from central economic planning, represented by the NRA and AAA, toward provision for the special needs of various social groups. By providing security for the downtrodden, Roosevelt sought to blunt the appeal of radicals on the left and the right. The keystone of the emerging coalition was labor. Workers had felt overlooked in the 1920s, and Roosevelt reached out with both legislation and his genuine concern and sympathy. Remarkably, the aristocratic president captured the hearts of working people across the country. In the opinion of a North Carolina mill worker, "Mr. Roosevelt is the only man we ever had in the White House who would understand that my boss is a sonofabitch." Out of the welter of legislative and executive action that made up the Second New Deal emerged the first elements of an American welfare state. An understanding that individual sufferers were more often victims of economic forces beyond their control, rather than failures who had only themselves to blame, moved reformers to look to the government as the legitimate, even sole, power able to improve the nation's economic health and guard its citizens' well-being.

Relief for the Unemployed

Roosevelt directed attention to the millions of Americans still out of work. Conditions had improved, but 20 percent of the nation's labor force

Huey Long:
Demagogue or Champion
of the Dispossessed?

FROM THE TIME HE HAD BEEN A SMALL CHILD, Huey P. Long was what one exasperated neighbor called a "pesterance." Defiant at school, artful at avoiding any disagreeable chores, ruthlessly driven to be the center of attention, Long had gotten ahead through the shrewdness of his extraordinary intelligence and brash willingness to flout conventional rules. Though he spent only brief periods at the University of Oklahoma and Tulane University, he cajoled a judge to convene a special bar examination, which he passed easily at the age of twenty-one. Declaring that he came out of that examination "running for office," Long rose swiftly from election as state railroad commissioner in 1918 to governor ten years later. Along the way, he dazzled the public with rhetorical gifts never before approached in the state and argued successfully before the Supreme Court with a skill that archconservative Chief Justice William Howard Taft—not a man to be taken in by a small-town southern lawyer—judged to be as keen as any he had ever encountered.

Circumstances and temperament dictated the political stance Long took all his life. The populist tradition of Winn Parish, where he grew up, instilled a basic loyalty to poor, rural folk. The small population of blacks in the parish and a history of blacks and whites forming a common front against rich sawmill and plantation owners meant that there never had been much race baiting in Winn. The rest of the state was very different, however. There, blacks and whites divided evenly, and the state's leaders made white supremacy the cornerstone of their rule. Out of step with majority opinion on race, Long could only hope to advance his fortunes by appealing to class division—rich against poor, rural against urban, the humble against the elite.

Long decided to focus his reform program on a more equitable distribution of income and opportunity. At St. Martinsville, deep in swampy Cajun country, he asked, "Where are the schools that you have waited for your children to have, that have never come? Where are the roads and the highways that you sent your money to build . . . ? Where are the institutions to care for the sick and disabled?" When Long assumed the governorship, Louisiana had only 331 miles of paved roads outside the cities. It was also the most illiterate state in the country. In 1893, when Long was born, 45 percent of those above the age of ten could not read; by 1920, the rate of illiteracy was still 22 percent, including 38 percent of all blacks.

Long articulated the grievances and hopes of the poor people of Louisiana; he also behaved utterly ruthlessly. After overcoming an impeachment effort in 1929, Long moved to consolidate his power. "I used to try to get things done by saying 'please,'" he said. "That didn't work and now I'm a dynamiter. I dynamite 'em out of my path." By 1930, Long completely dominated the state. Journalists around the country routinely referred to him as "the dictator of Louisiana." He made no effort to hide his power. Once, an angry opponent thrust a volume in his face and shouted, "Maybe you've heard of this book. It's the constitution of the state of Louisiana." Long shrugged and said, "I'm the constitution here now." He bullied and bribed the state legislature into a rubber-stamp body that passed a series of laws giving him the power to count ballots and thus determine the outcome of elections. He intimidated the courts and made them heel to his demands. Every state employee knew that his or her job depended on loyalty to the Kingfish.

His grasp on Louisiana firm, Long made his leap into the national limelight by winning election to the United States Senate in 1932. With none of the freshman senator's expected deference to senior members, his arms flailing, Long introduced a sweeping "soak-the-rich" tax bill that would outlaw annual personal incomes of more than $1 million and inheritances of more than $5 million. Swift rejection by the Senate, as Long expected, triggered his long-range strategy of becoming president by mobilizing the vast numbers of low-income Americans into a Share Our Wealth protest movement. Long's plan was to mount a presidential campaign in 1936 that would take enough votes from Roosevelt to tip the election to the Republican candidate. After four years of Republican failure to alleviate the depression with conservative policies, Long would sweep into the presidency in 1940, the savior of a suffering people.

HUEY LONG

Huey Long's ability to adapt his captivating stump speech style to the radio made him the one rival politician who gave Roosevelt serious concern in the mid-1930s. Here Long is shown in 1932 campaigning in Arkansas in support of Hattie Carraway's bid for election to the United States Senate. Carraway, stigmatized as both a women and a populist reformer, seemed a sure loser until Long crossed the border from Louisiana on her behalf. In a mere two weeks of speaking and pressing the flesh, Long brushed aside criticism that he was an interloper and boosted Carraway to victory as part of his crusade to share the wealth.

UPI/Bettmann Archive.

The electoral showdown never came, however. On September 8, 1935, a young physician named Carl Austin Weiss, enraged by the dishonor Long had visited on his family by removing his father from the Louisiana bench and suggesting black ancestry, fatally shot Long in a corridor of the Louisiana State House and was immediately gunned down by Long's bodyguards. The long lines of worn and ragged people passing by Long's coffin in the capitol and the smaller, better-dressed mourners at Weiss's funeral testified to the split in Louisiana along class lines. Some people at Weiss's funeral even proposed erecting a monument to Long's assassin.

Long always answered charges that he was a dictator, rather than a man of the people, by insisting that the polite ways of conventional democratic rules could never cure the nation's deepest ills. Only forceful means, he insisted, could finally break the hold of the privileged and extend opportunity to everyone. He could point to real achievements in Louisiana. As promised, he taxed the oil companies and utilities that had run Louisiana for decades and funneled the revenue into programs to benefit those who had been continuously left out. While he built monuments to his own vanity, like the thirty-four-story state capitol with his profile in bronze on the elevator doors, Long addressed some of the state's real social needs. At one time, Louisiana's road-building program was the biggest in the nation, and by 1935 the state had ten times more paved roads than when Long became governor. He made Louisiana State University a major university. He greatly expanded the state's pitiful public health facilities. For children, he provided free schoolbooks and new schools. For adults, he started night schools that attacked illiteracy.

Critics responded that Long was a homegrown fascist. They called him "the Messiah of the Rednecks," disdainful both of Long and those who turned to him. They compared him to Mussolini or Hitler and expressed relief that his life, and thus the damage he and the rabble who supported him could do, was cut short. The bitter controversy over Long related to vital American political issues. Roosevelt had recognized that the New Deal must reach out to the "forgotten man." Long reached farther to connect with dispossessed outsiders who could never be forgotten because they had never even been noticed. He offered Americans the only chance they ever had, for better or worse, to vote for a candidate with a broad national following who offered sweeping change comparable to parties on the radical right and left in other countries.

After Long's death, the hopes of the underclass to share the wealth lapsed into silent neglect. Mostly, they voted for Roosevelt, when they voted at all, but remained largely alienated from the prevailing system. They did achieve connection in memory, however. In 1974, a Louisiana newspaper asked citizens to name the greatest governor in the history of the state. Much to the paper's editorial dismay, the overwhelming choice was Huey Long.

had no jobs, which, Roosevelt said, was a devastating blow to "their self-respect, their self-confidence and courage and determination." As a remedy, he endorsed Harry Hopkins's innovative proposal to set up an independent agency that would employ people who lacked jobs and let them work for the public benefit. Roosevelt created the Works Progress Administration (WPA) by executive order in May 1935. The WPA imposed few limits as to the sort of work to be done. Instead, general guidelines specified that the projects be useful, be undertaken in places where unemployment was high, and produce results that would bring revenues back to the Treasury as soon as possible. The program was respectful of local initiative: State and municipal agencies had the responsibility to propose what needed to be done. By the time the WPA received its "honorable discharge" in 1943, it had generated jobs costing $10 billion that provided an average of a year's worth of work for each of the thirteen million unemployed put on the payroll.

Construction amounted to about three-fourths of the total WPA projects and left the mark of the New Deal broadly distributed over the countryside. By 1943, the WPA had built 572,000 miles of country roads, 40,000 buildings, 67,000 miles of city streets, 78,000 bridges, 8,000 parks, and 350 airports, along with a variety of smaller projects.

In a striking departure from the usual pick and shovel relief program, the WPA also allowed unemployed artists, musicians, and writers to make use of their talents for public benefit. When asked if artists should be included, Roosevelt replied, "Why not? They are human beings. They have to live. I guess the only thing they can do is paint and surely there must be some public place where paintings are wanted." Indeed, scores of artists painted murals on post office walls. At its peak, the WPA employed some six thousand artists, musicians, actors, journalists, Ph.D.'s, poets, and novelists. The roster included many unknowns but also towering figures such as novelist John Steinbeck and poet

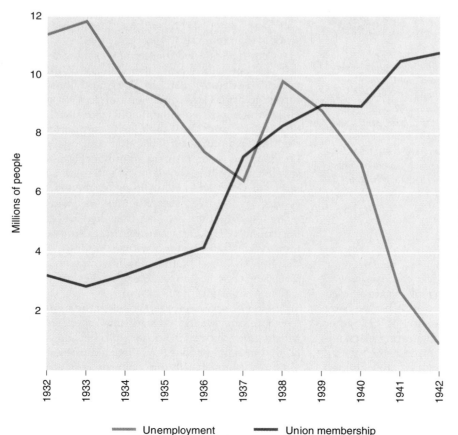

FIGURE 24.2
Unemployment and Union Membership, 1932–1942
The intersecting lines of this graph suggest a close relationship between prosperity, unemployment, and union membership. With New Deal support and economic recovery, unions gained strength until the number of unemployed dropped far below union membership in 1942. Only when the economy dipped during the recession of 1937–1938 did the trend reverse and unemployed workers again outnumber union members.

MACBETH OPENS IN HARLEM
The New Deal Federal Theater Project, which began in 1935, had the good fortune of attracting as one of its directors a twenty-year-old genius named Orson Welles. Acting on news that Welles and an African American theater group had prepared a version of Macbeth *set in Haiti, an opening night crowd in 1938 mobbed the Lafayette theater in Harlem. As one reviewer put it, the play was "a classic stunt" that ensured the director's reputation and indicated new directions for the American theater.*
Library of Congress.

Conrad Aiken. WPA Theater brought sixty million people into its performances. In the first fifteen months of the WPA Music Project, fifty million Americans heard concerts. The artist Robert Gwathmey recalled that the government imposed no restrictions: "You were a painter: Do your work. You were a sculptor: Do your work. You were a printmaker: Do your work. An artist could do anything he damn pleased." The entire cost of the WPA Arts Project was only $23 million, but the paintings, sculptures, and prints created continue to grace America's courthouses, public buildings, and museums.

Empowering Labor

Many workers desired more far-reaching change than that supported by the First New Deal or the old craft unions. In 1934, a series of local uprisings, mostly by unskilled workers who had no unions to join, set in motion a labor revolution. Striking workers in Toledo, Minneapolis, and San Francisco asserted their right to picket their employers. The pickets encountered ferocious opposition by police and the National Guard, who were deployed by state authorities sympathetic to employers to safeguard private property and to subdue strikers. Bloody battles erupted in the streets and on the docks. The uneasy stalemate that emerged roused militant labor leaders to seek new ways to break the dominance that industrial management had achieved over workers during the 1920s.

After the violence of 1934 subsided, the main focus of labor leaders settled on a bill to create federal supervision of labor disputes. The sponsor of the National Labor Relations Act (NLRA), Senator Robert Wagner of New York, was a veteran of progressive efforts to secure decent working conditions. Wagner's sympathy for working people reflected his own impoverished childhood after coming to the United States from Germany. The NLRA—justly termed a Magna Carta for labor—guaranteed workers the right to organize freely. It created a National Labor Relations Board to oversee elections for union representation. If the majority of workers voted for a union, the union became the sole bargaining agent for the entire workplace, and employers were required to negotiate with the duly elected union leaders. At first, Roosevelt was reluctant to see his NRA ideal of cooperative decision making replaced by adversarial collective bargaining. But he signed the Wagner Act into law in July 1935 as the best way available to protect the rights of workers and unions and attach them to the New Deal. At last, organized labor had a federal guarantee for collective bargaining and some legal protection against employers' power to fire labor organizers, suppress strikes, and stifle unions.

While the Wagner Act moved through Congress, unskilled workers who had been largely unrepresented within organized labor began to press for inclusion. Under the aggressive leadership of John L. Lewis, head of the United Mine Workers (UMW), and Sidney Hillman, head of the Amalgamated Clothing Workers, a coalition of unskilled workers gathered in 1935 to form the Committee for Industrial Organization (CIO; later the Congress of Industrial Organizations). The CIO struggled with the leadership of the American Federation of Labor (AFL) over who would take advantage of the New Deal's encouragement for union organization. After Lewis ended an argument on the main platform at the 1935 AFL convention in Atlantic City by dropping "Big Bill" Hutcheson of the Carpenters Union with a right cross to the jaw, the CIO went its own way. The following year, Lewis and Hillman broke with organized labor's apolitical tradition by forming the Non-Partisan League to support Roosevelt's reelection.

By mobilizing unskilled workers, who had always been scattered, the CIO greatly reduced the lordly power of industrialists and began to win significant concessions on wages and working conditions. Starting with a successful effort to organize rubber workers, the CIO began an embattled decade of triumph and disappointment. The CIO overcame fierce opposition to unionize the major steel and automobile companies. But fear and the habit of deference to authority were too great in textile manufacturing areas of the South to force unionization on that industry, despite the exploitation and misery that plagued its workers.

The achievements that flowed from the new militancy of labor and a sympathetic government were formidable. When Roosevelt took office in 1933, AFL membership stood at three million, down by half since the end of World War I. Cowed by business dominance, workers had shied away from the old unions. Work stoppages by demoralized union members actually decreased during the first years of the depression. Defeated workers tended to blame themselves for their plight. But after the Wagner Act took hold after 1935, unions expanded almost five-fold to fourteen million members by the time of Roosevelt's death in 1945. Thirty percent of the workforce was then unionized, the highest union representation ever reached.

Not only were more workers unionized, but different workers were unionized. Much of the union membership at the start of the 1930s, especially its leadership, was native-born, northern European in ancestry, and employed in the skilled trades. During the New Deal era, large numbers of unskilled assembly line workers, many of them African Americans or recently arrived immigrants, flocked to the unions.

CIO leaders admired the exceptional courage and organizing skill of Communists and other radicals, and they permitted committed leftists to help them take on the entrenched centers of resistance to unionism, the automobile and steel industries. The campaign by the United Auto Workers (UAW) to unionize workers at General Motors (GM) climaxed in January 1937 in a "sit-down" strike in the main assembly plant in Flint, Michigan. Workers simply sat down at their workstations, refusing either to work or to leave the premises. They were not completely inactive, however. When a police detachment charged the barricaded plant, strikers responded by throwing ball bearings at the fleeing lawmen in what the strikers jeeringly called the "battle of bulls run." The strikers reduced the plant's production of

15,000 cars a week to a mere 150. In desperation, General Motors gained court injunctions against the sit-down. But neither Roosevelt nor Michigan Governor Frank Murphy would act. Although they did not approve of the strikers' illegal occupation of the plant, they were unwilling to end the strike by force. Stymied, General Motors came to terms with the UAW. The agreement made the UAW the sole bargaining agent for all GM workers, prohibited the company from interfering with union activity, and arranged for contract negotiations to begin on February 15. Having beaten the automobile industry's leading producer, the UAW successfully organized throughout the auto industry, increasing its membership almost fourfold by the summer of 1937. In 1941, Henry Ford, who in 1937 had hired thugs to beat labor organizers, finally gave in and the UAW completed its campaign to unionize the entire automotive industry.

The CIO hoped to ride success in automobile plants to success in steel mills. But the steel industry managed to check the CIO short of full victory. A coalition of smaller steel firms, aided by the reaction of the courts and public opinion against the sit-down strike's infringement of property rights, impeded CIO efforts. In May 1937, a crowd of strikers gathered in a field outside Chicago to get ready for a march on Republic Steel, where they planned to set up a picket line. Without warning, police who had been sent there to keep order charged the crowd, firing their sidearms and wielding clubs, killing ten and injuring scores. The steelworkers halted their organizing campaign. They would finally succeed in 1941 when the war in Europe and the military buildup at home created a demand for steel and steelworkers.

In the same spirit of partnership, southern textile mills also received enough support from police and local officials to thwart an organizing drive. A steep recession in 1937 and 1938 threw thousands of textile workers out of work and further stalled the union campaign. The southern textile industry remained locked in uncertain battle until mobilization for war after 1940 revived the economy, gave laborers greater bargaining power, and brought unions into all major industries.

Despite setbacks, labor made enormous gains because of the Wagner Act. As Roosevelt hoped, labor remembered its benefactor and settled securely within Roosevelt's Democratic coalition. That attachment revealed itself most powerfully in the 1936 election.

Social Security and Tax Reform

Standing alongside the Wagner Act and the WPA as a major New Deal accomplishment in 1935 was the Social Security Act. Putting unemployed persons on relief was the most immediate priority of the New Deal, but taking care of hard-hit elderly people was a closely related goal. The population over the age of sixty-five doubled between 1870 and 1930 at the same time that work for the elderly declined. The tradition of self-reliance, boosted by the free enterprise spirit of the 1920s, inhibited government action to help poor, jobless older Americans. When the depression struck, only a third of the men and about 8 percent of the women over sixty-five had jobs. Of the tiny minority who worked, only 15 percent had pension plans. Insolvent corporations and banks often could not come up with funds during the depression to pay the meager pensions they had promised. Just eighteen states provided elderly assistance, which usually amounted to about a dollar a day for impoverished individuals.

These desperate circumstances lured millions to Dr. Townsend's pension scheme. Townsend's challenge, in turn, helped move Congress toward adopting a federal pension plan. Roosevelt became the first president to advocate protection for the elderly, describing it as "our plain duty to provide for that security upon which [the general] welfare depends." With the aggressive agitation of Townsend, Fr. Coughlin, and Huey Long rumbling ominously in the background, Roosevelt appointed Frances Perkins to chair a committee that readied the Social Security Act for his signature in August 1935.

The struggle for Social Security brought out class differences in their starkest form. Coming together in support of the measure was a coalition of advocate groups for the elderly and the poor, traditional progressives, leftists, social workers, labor unions, and educators. Arrayed against them were economic conservatives, including the Liberty League, the National Association of Manufacturers, the Chamber of Commerce, the American Medical Association, the conservative wing of the Republican Party, and assorted other defenders of wealth and privilege. Enact the Social Security system, these conservatives warned, and the government will gain a whip hand over private property, initiative will be destroyed, and proud individuals will be reduced to spineless loafers.

Obvious need and the large New Deal majority in Congress carried the day against the very well financed opposition. The strong objections to federal involvement in matters traditionally left to individual and local charity meant that Social Security had to strike a balance between federal, state, and personal responsibility. The Social Security program, therefore, required that pensions for the elderly be funded by tax contributions from workers and their employers. It also created unemployment insurance, paid for by employers' contributions. In a bow to traditional local responsibility for public assistance, Social Security also issued grants for the states to use to support dependent mothers and children, public health services, and the blind. A Supreme Court decision in 1937 upheld the right of Congress to require all citizens to pay for Social Security through their federal taxes and allowed the Social Security Act to be expanded to include benefits for dependent survivors of deceased recipients. Social Security raised the elderly out of the lowest economic status and established the principle that older Americans should be protected in their declining years from the crushing effects of poverty. As with the WPA and the Wagner Act, it helped secure the loyalty of the ordinary worker to the New Deal. At first, Social Security covered less than half of all workers, but over the years more and more workers were brought into the system.

The opposition to Social Security struck New Dealers as evidence that the rich and well-born had learned little from the depression. They apparently were still willing to clothe their opposition to federal insurance as a defense of a kind of individual opportunity that simply did not exist for most Americans. Roosevelt had long felt contempt for the moneyed elite, and he looked for a way to redistribute wealth that would, in a single stroke, weaken conservative opposition, advance the cause of social equity, and defuse populist challenges on the fringe. In June 1935, as the Social Security Act was being debated, Roosevelt delivered a message to Congress outlining comprehensive tax reform. He urged a graduated tax on corporations, a similar tax on holding company dividends used to shelter corporate income, an inheritance tax, and an increase in maximum personal income taxes from 63 to 79 percent. These measures aimed to pay for federal recovery and relief programs and balance the federal budget with a progressive tax that required those with the most money to pay the highest taxes.

Roosevelt promoted his plan by declaring that large fortunes put "great and undesirable concentration of control in [the hands of] relatively few individuals over the employment and welfare of many, many others." He insisted that a more progressive tax structure would increase opportunity for the common people at the bottom of the economic ladder, "restrain the growth of unwholesome and sterile accumulations [of wealth], and . . . lay the burdens of Government where they can best be carried." Against charges that higher taxes on the rich would dampen their initiative, Roosevelt contended that the new measures would instead stimulate competition. If the idle rich were stripped of their unfair advantages of monopolies and inherited fortunes, there would be more opportunities for innovative enterprises and for the small businesses that employed so many Americans.

Roosevelt's tax package was more timid than Huey Long's "soak-the-rich" plan, and Congress was more timid still. But Congress endorsed Roosevelt's basic taxation principle by enacting a slightly progressive tax on undistributed corporate profits. From there, with the Revenue Act of 1937, Roosevelt moved to close loopholes that he considered outrageous. Threatening to name names of the wealthy who were not paying their fair share of taxes, Roosevelt persuaded Congress to eliminate a number of tax shelters, including such relics from the New Era as deductions for company yachts and country estates.

Broadening the New Deal Coalition

The largest groups that had been persistently excluded from economic and political benefits were women and African Americans. Their stories were strikingly parallel. Both received wages substantially lower than white men and owned only a tiny sliver of the nation's property. Though constitutionally entitled to vote since Reconstruction, most African Americans had been disfranchised by intimidation and legal subterfuge. Women, too, had the right to vote, which they won by 1920, but they were only starting to exercise their electoral power in numbers comparable to those of men. With relatively few voters in either group, women and African Americans had little influence within the political establishment and were largely unrepresented when the New Deal came into being. Although women and minorities had strong claims on the New Deal's commitments to assist those most in need, they had little political leverage to translate those commitments into action.

Eleanor Roosevelt was determined to use her position as First Lady to increase the political par-

ELEANOR ROOSEVELT MEETING WOMEN REPORTERS
Even though the editorial opinion of newspaper owners was about 80 percent opposed to the
president and his wife, both Franklin and Eleanor Roosevelt had close rapport with the working
press. Making the point that women had something important to contribute to public affairs and
that the First Lady could be more than simply a White House hostess, Eleanor Roosevelt wrote a
daily column, "My Day," and held regular news conferences to which only women reporters
were admitted. She used the occasions to reinvigorate the commitment women had begun in the
Progressive Era to education, equal rights, decent working conditions, and child welfare.
Stock Montage.

ticipation and influence of women and minorities.
Her long-standing involvement in women's causes
helped draw women into the New Deal and to
mobilize them as a distinctive force for reform. In
1933, President Roosevelt allowed the Democratic
National Committee to create a Women's Division
to define women's issues and to screen candidates
for administration positions. Molly Dewson, a former leader in the suffrage movement and the National Consumers League, became head of the
Women's Division. Dewson created a talent pool of
eighty thousand women from which the New Deal
hired an unprecedented number for government
positions.

Most remarkable was the entry of women into
executive positions that had always been considered

for men only. Frances Perkins became the first woman
cabinet officer; Ruth Bryan Owen the first woman
to hold an ambassadorial post as envoy to Denmark; Florence Allen the first woman judge on a
district court of appeals; Nellie Tayloe Ross the first
director of the Mint; and Marion Glass Banister the
first assistant secretary of the treasury. Alongside
these breakthroughs, women social workers and educators helped the New Deal to bring women into
its programs of relief and welfare. Under the broad
WPA umbrella, Ellen Woodward headed Women's
and Professional Projects, Hallie Flanagan directed
the Federal Theater Project, and Hilda Smith organized Workers' Education. Women also played key
roles in the Division of Labor Standards, in the Children's Bureau, and in the administration of relief to

the unemployed and destitute, both locally and in Washington.

These activities did not, however, result in equality between the sexes, either economically or politically. Attitudes that women should earn less and be subordinate in the public realm, if they chose to leave the home at all, were too pervasive. Indeed, the efforts women made within the New Deal were limited to improving particular social conditions; any service to the cause of equal opportunity and women's status was merely a by-product. In New Deal agencies, women devoted their energies to children, the infirm, the unemployed, and others who lacked the ability to take care of themselves. Nonetheless, the experience of women in community organization and the design of welfare legislation established a foundation of skill and influence that buttressed future efforts to attain equal rights.

Eleanor Roosevelt also helped link the causes of gender and racial discrimination through her identification with the underdog and her abhorrence of racism. One of her strongest allies among African American women was Mary McLeod Bethune, the founder of the Daytona Normal and Industrial Institute for Negro Women in Florida and a cofounder of the National Council on Negro Women in 1935. Her accomplishments brought Bethune to the attention of Eleanor Roosevelt and resulted in her appointment as the highest-ranking black official within the federal government, heading the office of minority affairs within the National Youth Administration. Like Molly Dewson and the women's network she created, Bethune used her New Deal post and the National Council to guide a core group of black professionals and civil rights activists to posts within the New Deal. This group, nicknamed the "Black Cabinet," was the first sizable African American presence within the federal government. Its members used their influence to inform the president of hardship and discrimination. Because of Eleanor Roosevelt, the Black Cabinet, and New Dealers, African Americans participated in some New Deal relief programs. By mid-decade, about one-quarter of all blacks received some sort of federal assistance.

The conditions with which the Black Cabinet grappled were bleak in the extreme. At the outset of the New Deal, about half of urban blacks were out of work, twice the unemployment rate among whites. The rural black majority had slim prospects of making a living or even retaining their place on the land, whether as owners or tenants. The racial atmosphere at mid-decade was ominous. During

MARY MCLEOD BETHUNE
At the urging of Eleanor Roosevelt, Mary McLeod Bethune, a southern educational and civil rights leader, became director of the National Youth Administration's Division of Negro Affairs. The first black woman to head a federal agency, Bethune used her federal position to promote social change. Here Bethune takes her mission to the streets to protest the Peoples Drug Store chain's discriminatory hiring practices within the nation's capital.
Moorland Spingarn Research Center, Howard University.

the depression, lynching increased after years of decline. In Alabama, the "Scottsboro Boys" faced the death penalty for a rape they did not commit, and black radical Angelo Herndon toiled as a prisoner on a Georgia chain gang for trying to organize black workers. In 1935, a riot in Harlem, where the artistic Renaissance had once flourished, dramatized blacks' despair.

The New Deal response, despite sympathy for the plight of minorities, was cautious. Roosevelt believed that in order to enact ambitious New Deal reforms, he was obliged to appease conservative, segregationist, southern Democratic members of Congress. Reflecting these political pressures, landmark New Deal achievements—the NRA, WPA, and AAA—failed in large measure to serve African Americans. Because the NRA refused to require manufacturers to eliminate racial discrimination, the agency's initials were derided as "Negro Run Around" or "Negroes Ruined Again." Work gained through the WPA was also prejudicial. Only eleven of more than ten thousand WPA supervisors in the South were black. The AAA harmed blacks by rewarding white landowners for evicting their black tenants to get crop reduction bonuses for themselves.

Stymied administratively and legislatively, New Dealers turned to coalition building as a long-range way of overcoming entrenched opposition to improving the lot of blacks. Off the record, Roosevelt spoke of a time when politics would be realigned into opposing conservative and progressive parties, with the Republicans and southern Democrats making up the former and the New Deal coalition the latter. Blacks played a key role in Roosevelt's conception. At the time of Roosevelt's first presidential campaign, black journalist Robert Vann had called on African Americans to "turn Lincoln's picture to the wall. That debt has been paid in full." In 1934, the first significant electoral evidence surfaced that black voters were shifting from the Republican to the Democratic Party. Those who could cast ballots voted their hopes and helped elect New Deal Democrats in numerous congressional and gubernatorial races.

The new leverage of black voters lent weight to the efforts of Eleanor Roosevelt and the Black Cabinet for greater racial equity. During Roosevelt's first two terms, the numbers of blacks in federal service tripled, and white officials showed unprecedented willingness to hear what black leaders had to say. The frequent interviews Mary McLeod Bethune and Walter White, head of the National Association for the Advancement of Colored People (NAACP), held with the president, along with Eleanor Roosevelt's many visits to black institutions, led to an identification of black reform aims with the New Deal. The symbolic climax occurred in 1939 when the great black contralto Marian Anderson was refused permission by the Daughters of the American Revolution (DAR) to sing in the organization's Constitution Hall in Washington. Eleanor Roosevelt promptly resigned her membership in the DAR, and Interior Secretary Harold Ickes, himself a former president of an NAACP chapter in Chicago, arranged to have Anderson per-

form on the steps of the Lincoln Memorial. Anderson sang from the steps of the monument to an integrated throng of 75,000 in an electrifying demonstration of the tie between black aspirations and the spirit of the New Deal.

Concrete accomplishments were another matter, however. In 1940, the end of Roosevelt's second term, blacks still suffered severe handicaps. Most of the thirteen million black workers toiled at low-paying menial jobs. Infant mortality was half again as great as for whites, and life expectancy twelve years shorter. Segregation in the South was unmoved by the New Deal. Nor was the equal part of "separate but equal" much advanced. Black schools had less money and worse facilities than those of whites, and only 1 percent of black students earned college degrees. In southern states, where most blacks lived, there were no black police officers or judges and hardly any lawyers. Lynching of blacks went unpunished. By mid-decade, little had happened to refute the grim witticism that, for African Americans, America was "the land of the tree and the home of the grave."

Hispanic Americans and Asian Americans had even fewer voters than women and blacks and consequently less political clout. Without significant numbers and organizational strength, neither could lobby effectively with the New Deal coalition builders in Washington. Mexican Americans, already at the economic margins of American life, suffered greatly from the depression's effect on agriculture. Engaged throughout the West as farm laborers, they saw their wages in California's fields plummet to not much more than a dime an hour. Part of the explanation was new competition from other victims of the depression. When persistent drought raised huge dust storms and turned large areas of the plains into a "dust bowl," hundreds of thousands of ruined farmers—called "Okies" and "Arkies" because most of them came from Oklahoma and Arkansas—moved westward and competed with Mexican Americans for scarce agricultural work. In addition, local administration of many New Deal programs meant that the treatment of minorities rested in the hands of established leadership. In the West, when Hispanics and Indians were permitted to join government work projects, they often received lower pay than white Americans received. Relief programs also reflected local prejudice, with minorities receiving less aid.

Asian Americans fared no better than Mexican Americans. Asian immigrants to the United States were still excluded from citizenship, and in many

HISPANIC-AMERICAN ALLIANCE BANNER
Between 1910 and 1940, when refugees from the Mexican revolution poured across the American border, the Hispanic-American Alliance and other such organizations sought to protect Mexican American rights against nativist fears and hostility. In the years between the world wars, many alliance banners such as this one flew in opposition to the deportation of Mexican aliens, an attempt in 1926 to bar Mexican Americans from city jobs in Los Angeles, and the disproportionately high use of the death penalty against Mexicans convicted of crimes. Throughout these and other trials, the alliance steadfastly emphasized the desire of Mexican Americans to receive permanent status in the United States.
The Oakland Museum.

states they were not permitted to own land. But by 1930, more than half of the Japanese American population had been born in the United States. Still, no Japanese American was immune from discrimination, which the depression only reinforced. Even college-educated Japanese Americans worked at family shops, hotels, and fruit stands. As one frustrated young man said: "I am a fruitstand worker. I would much rather it were doctor or lawyer . . . but my aspirations of developing into such [were] frustrated

long ago by circumstances [and] I am only what I am, a professional carrot washer." Chinese Americans tended to remain in Chinatown sections of cities, where they labored in laundries and restaurants. The nation had always been a hard place for Asian Americans, and the depression offered no relief.

Native Americans, however, experienced a major change in their circumstances, especially in their relationship with the federal government. Ever since the Dawes Act of 1887, the government had tried to solve the "Indian problem" by encouraging assimilation, that is, an end to a separate Indian identity. Because of the remarkable commitment of John Collier, commissioner of Indian affairs, Congress adopted the Indian Reorganization Act of 1934, which ended the government's assault on the tribal structure that had undergirded Indian culture. The act restored to Native Americans the right to own land communally, a right they had lost in 1887. The change brought little immediate benefit, however. Indians remained the poorest of Americans. But it did provide a foundation for economic and cultural resurgence a generation later.

Throughout Roosevelt's first term, socialists and Communists had denounced the slow pace of change and charged the New Deal with failing to serve the interests of "the people"—the workers and farmers who produced the nation's wealth but kept only a meager portion of it. But in 1935, as the Second Hundred Days reached flood tide, the left made a surprising switch. The Soviet Union, which was worried about the threat of fascism in Europe, instructed Communists throughout the world to cease their attacks on moderates and to join hands in a "Popular Front" against fascism. Thus, even though one radical critic declared that Roosevelt reform was "about as exciting as near beer," most of those on the left joined the New Deal coalition.

In the summer of 1935, therefore, Roosevelt announced a new direction for the New Deal. He gave up trying to build a total coalition of all interests and instead focused on the growing antibusiness feeling among the public. The WPA had reached out to the unemployed, the Wagner Act to labor, and the Social Security Act to all working people; and his administration grew more sensitive to women and blacks. All bulwarks against radical challengers to the New Deal, these overtures established foundations for federal welfare policies for the next six decades. But Roosevelt's opponents never made peace with the New Deal's welfare state. It was clear that most of big business would remain stubbornly opposed to most New Deal programs. Roosevelt saw the situation as a struggle between a Hamiltonian faction of wealth and privilege and the heirs of Jeffersonians like himself who favored shared wealth and equal opportunity. The people would express their views in the presidential election of 1936.

The New Deal's Final Phase: From Victory to Deadlock

Neither the First nor the Second New Deal cured the depression. Economic recovery remained agonizingly slow. The tardy return to prosperity left the future of reform very much in doubt at the end of Roosevelt's first term in 1936. The Second New Deal's move to the left, however, had blunted the

attack from that direction. Long was dead, and Townsend's and Coughlin's power was waning. Most radicals felt compelled to support the New Deal's welfare and labor reforms, even though the reforms stopped well short of revolutionary change. But forces on the right, especially conservative Republicans and southern Democrats, grew more unified and more powerful. Roosevelt's frustration led him into an ill-advised attack on the Supreme Court in an effort to defend and extend his programs. But even without judicial obstacles, reform was running out of steam. With one last flurry of legislation, the New Deal ended.

The Election of 1936

Roosevelt believed that the presidential election of 1936 would be a test of his leadership and New Deal policy. Republicans welcomed a national referendum and had reason to be hopeful. Public opinion

JOHN COLLIER MEETS WITH NAVAJO REPRESENTATIVES
Commissioner of Indian Affairs John Collier receives a Navajo delegation protesting restrictions set down by the Indian Reorganization Act of 1934. The Navajos display a blanket made from the wool of their own sheep to protest a limit set on the number of sheep they could raise. Collier had crafted the Act to revive Native American society by granting tribes an independent land base and many self-governing powers. However, his attempt to make the reservations economically viable through land conservation measures, including restrictions on grass-devouring sheep, roused resistance on the part of Indians who chose traditional ways of using resources. The tension between federal benevolence and Indian views of their own way of life has remained a painful issue.
Wide World Photos, Inc.

G.O.P. CONVENTION, CLEVELAND
This illustration of the 1936 Republican convention for an article in the progressive journal
Common Sense *displays artist Thomas Hart Benton's gift for energetic satire. Benton's aged
and grotesque conventiongoers underscore the article's contention that the Republican old guard
is preparing "to join the Tyrannosaurus, the Pterodactyl and the Three-toed Horse." Unexpected
circumstances prevented Benton's illustration from being used, however, and the GOP survived
the article's prediction that "the Republican elephant [would become] as extinct as the dinosaurs,"
though the term "dinosaur" remained an epithet to be hurled at conservatives.*

Thomas Hart Benton, American, 1889-1973. G.O.P. Convention, Cleveland, 1936. Black crayon, pen and black ink, and black wash, over graphics, 37.4 x 53.4 cm. © The Cleveland Museum of Art, 1996. Leonard C. Hanna, Jr., 1995. 70.

polls showed that Roosevelt's popularity had dipped. Between 8.5 million and 12.5 million workers were still unemployed, depending on which source one believed, and most farmers remained poor. The business community raged at any attempts to raise its taxes for fresh initiatives to cure the problems. A telephone poll by the magazine *Literary Digest,* which had always been very accurate, predicted that the Republican candidate would win handily. Republican Party leaders believed that the American people were poised to vote against power-mad politicians and bureaucrats in Washington who were undermining the traditional values that had made the country strong.

In their nostalgic appeal to the good old days, the Republicans turned to the Kansas heartland to select Governor Alfred Landon as their nominee for president. Henry Ford, in what he intended to be a compliment, dubbed Landon the "Kansas Coolidge." But Landon was a far cry from Coolidge. As governor, he had supported New Deal measures for conservation and farm relief. An independent oil producer, he endorsed Interior Secretary Ickes's efforts to better regulate the oil industry. He promised labor and independent unions a fair deal. He sought to keep blacks in their original party by speaking out strongly against racial prejudice. But Landon was not a Republican Roosevelt either. In traditional Republican language, he proposed to replace wasteful government spending with a balanced budget and businesslike efficiency and to ease the perils of illness and old age with old-fashioned neighborliness instead of Social Security.

Roosevelt put his faith in the growing coalition of New Deal supporters. He believed that they shared his conviction that the New Deal was the nation's liberator from a long period of privilege and wealth for a few and "economic slavery" for the rest. At the end of the campaign, Roosevelt struck a defiant pose before a thunderous crowd at Madison Square Garden. Assailing his "old enemies —monopoly, speculation, reckless banking, class antagonism"—he proclaimed, "Never before in all our history have these forces been so united against one candidate as they stand today. They are unanimous in their hate for me—and I welcome their hatred." When the crowd's roar subsided, Roosevelt concluded:

> I should like to have it said of my first Administration that in it the forces of selfishness and of lust for power met their match. I should like to have it said of my second Administration that in it these forces met their master.

Roosevelt did not let such intensity rob him of his light touch. Toward Alf Landon he took a relaxed, amused attitude, characterizing his opponent as a misguided throwback who fronted for sinister interests. He pointed out that while Landon and his supporters denounced the New Deal, Kansas drew 70 percent of its relief funds from New Deal programs. He cast doubt on Landon's status as a foe of big government by disclosing that, as governor, Landon had requested a federal grant of $35 million for a state-owned natural gas pipeline. Republican hypocrisy was accurately reflected, Roosevelt said, in the Kansas state flower that Landon had adopted as his symbol: The sunflower is yellow, has a black heart, is good only for parrot food, and dies before November.

Roosevelt triumphed in spectacular fashion. He received eleven million *more* votes than Landon. His 60.8 percent majority was the widest ever in a pres-

idential race and won him every state except the Republican strongholds of Maine and Vermont. Third parties on the right as well as the left—the Union of Social Justice Party, the Socialists, the Communists—attracted few supporters. Congressional results were equally lopsided, with Democrats outnumbering Republicans by more than three to one

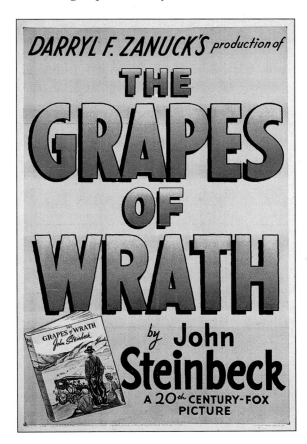

THE GRAPES OF WRATH
Movies had their greatest popularity in the depression when they offered momentary escape from the hard times outside. Through most of the 1930s, musicals like Top Hat, *with elegant dancers Fred Astaire and Ginger Rogers, set the pace, with comedies and costume dramas not far behind. By the end of the decade, however, years of labor strife, farm distress, and reform agitation had also created an audience for social problem films. The Grapes of Wrath, adapted in 1940 from John Steinbeck's novel of the flight of impoverished farmers from the midwestern Dust Bowl to California, made one of the most successful cinematic appeals to Americans' sympathy for the underdog and belief in social justice.*
The Oakland Museum.

in both houses. And in the states, Democrats won twenty-six of thirty-three gubernatorial races, including Landon's Kansas.

Roosevelt's triumph emerged from the New Deal's distinctive political coalition. Many Americans who had been alienated from politics during the 1920s rallied around Roosevelt's standard. Only about 45 percent of eligible voters actually voted in national elections during the 1920s; in 1936, in contrast, 57 percent of eligible voters turned out. New voters—women, blacks, young people, and especially laborers and ethnic minorities—boosted Roosevelt's margin of victory. Northern blacks gave Roosevelt 76 percent of their votes and provided the margins needed to swing the key states of Illinois, Michigan, and New Jersey away from the Republicans. In the nineteen northern cities where more than half the population was composed of first- and second-generation immigrants, the Democratic vote increased by 205 percent, Republican votes by only 29 percent. Roosevelt also managed to retain the support of every traditionally Democratic southern state, delaying Hoover's dream of bringing the South into the Republican Party.

Emphasizing his mandate from the voters, Roosevelt made it plain that he would try to ensure a decent standard of living for all citizens. In response to news that sixty million people had an income of less than $1,000 per year, he declared in his inaugural address: "In this nation I see tens of millions of its citizens—a substantial part of its whole population—who at this very moment are denied the greater part of what the very lowest standards of today call the necessities of life. . . . I see one third of a nation ill-housed, ill-clad, ill-nourished." With the voters' support, Roosevelt committed himself to do all that he could to help these disadvantaged citizens.

Court Packing

In the afterglow of his electoral triumph, Roosevelt went on a cruise to ponder how to remove the remaining obstacles to New Deal reforms. He returned intent on targeting the Supreme Court. Ladened with conservatives left over from the discredited Republican era, the Court had invalidated eleven New Deal measures as unwarranted interference with free enterprise; in more than 140 years before 1932, the Court had nullified only sixty laws. In Roosevelt's view, the Court's recent decisions had cast doubt "upon the ability of the Congress ever at any time to protect the Nation against catastrophe

by squarely meeting modern social and economic maladjustment." At that moment, Social Security, the Wagner Act, the Securities and Exchange Commission, and other New Deal innovations were moving toward an ominous rendezvous with the Court. Roosevelt concluded that he must do something to make sure the Court's "horse and buggy" notions did not nullify the popular will and demolish the New Deal.

A nationwide opinion poll showed that more than two-thirds of Americans believed that the Supreme Court should be free from political interference. Nevertheless, in 1937 Roosevelt moved toward a showdown with the Court and "judicial tyranny." He sent a bill to Congress proposing that one new justice be added to the Court for each existing judge who had already served for ten years and was over the age of seventy. It would give the president the power to overwhelm the elderly, conservative Republican justices by naming up to six New Dealers to the bench.

A nationwide opinion poll showed that more than two-thirds of Americans believed that the Supreme Court should be free from politician interference.

But the president had not reckoned with Americans' deeply rooted deference to the independent authority of the Supreme Court. Even Roosevelt's supporters were disturbed by the "court-packing" scheme. The implication that individuals over seventy had diminished mental capacity affronted many members of Congress who were past that age. Roosevelt's proposal also aroused the ire of the oldest Supreme Court justice, Louis Brandeis, the astute mentor of several able New Dealers and the Court's most liberal justice. Roosevelt deviously insisted that the bill was intended to improve the efficiency of an "overworked" Court, although it was plain to everyone that the real purpose was to make room for supporters of New Deal initiatives.

A storm of public protest, egged on by conservatives delighted that they had finally found a popular cause to use against the New Deal, sank the Court bill. Business spokesmen waxed indignant because Roosevelt's plan blatantly violated constitutional ideals and cleared the way, as the journalist Walter Lippmann claimed, "to establish the political framework for, and to destroy the safeguards against, a dictator."

Although the Court reform plan failed, it apparently sent a message to the Supreme Court justices. After the furor abated, Chief Justice Charles Evans Hughes and fellow moderate Owen Roberts reversed their views on certain New Deal cases. Their votes kept the Court from invalidating the Wagner Act and Social Security, inspiring a wit to point out that "a switch in time saves nine." Soon afterward, the most resistant of the elderly justices —the "four horsemen of reaction," as New Dealer and future Supreme Court Justice Felix Frankfurter called them—began to retire. After appointing no one to the Supreme Court during his first term, Roosevelt went on to name eight justices—more than any other president. His choice of liberals to fill the vacancies on the Court ultimately ensured safe passage of New Deal laws through the shoals of judicial review. But Roosevelt's error in proposing his court-packing scheme also did powerful damage to his administration. He had handed conservatives a popular issue to use against the New Deal.

Reaction and Recession

The court-packing fiasco stirred Republicans and southern Democrats to rally around their common conservatism and to jointly obstruct additional reform. Other factors also began to work against the extension of the New Deal. The progress made in reviving the economy and alleviating hardship tended to reduce the enthusiasm of many people for new efforts. Arguments over how to proceed and how far to go weakened the consensus among reformers and, as the Court fight showed, sparked antagonisms between Congress and the White House. The rise of belligerent regimes in Germany, Italy, Japan, and elsewhere in the 1930s also slowed reform; some Americans began to demand that the nation concentrate on defending what it had rather than striving for change. In a surprisingly short time, these impediments mounted and Roosevelt's 1936 landslide began to seem like a mirage.

No action by New Deal opponents was more damaging than the administration's self-inflicted wounds. Soon after his second term began, Roosevelt accepted the view that the steady, though incomplete, economic recovery since 1933 had largely eliminated the depression crisis. He was persuaded that additional deficit spending designed to pump up the economy was no longer necessary. He also worried that inflation would reduce the value of savings and new investments the New Deal had so earnestly tried to build up. Accordingly, Roosevelt moved cautiously toward a balanced budget by cutting funds for relief projects. At his urging, the Federal Reserve raised interest rates to discourage borrowing on easy terms for unwise speculation. *Time* magazine soothingly reported that in recent weeks, with the "Depression lapsing into memory, the portents of Boom drummed excitingly throughout the land."

Roosevelt's fiscal retrenchment soon backfired. Rather than preventing inflation, the reduction in deficit spending cooled down the economy too much. Roosevelt's anxiety about inflation had failed to take into full consideration how far the economy had to go before it would reach inflationary levels. Even at the high-water mark of recovery in the summer of 1937, unemployment remained at about 14 percent of the workforce, some seven million people in all. In the next few months, national income and production slipped backward so steeply that almost two-thirds of the economic gains since 1933 were lost by June 1938. The stock market followed suit with a sharper decline between August 1937 and May 1938 than in the Great Crash. Farm prices dropped 20 percent, and unemployment rose by more than two million.

This economic downturn hurt the New Deal politically. Conservatives argued that the recession proved that New Deal measures were fundamentally wrong and had produced only an illusion of progress. They maintained that the New Deal's progressive tax policy helped cause the recession by funneling money away from productive investment. Herbert Hoover had been right after all, they claimed. The way to weather the recession was to spend less, save more, and wait for the laws of the free enterprise system to restore prosperity.

Many New Dealers believed instead that the recession showed there was no going back to the orthodoxies of free enterprise. They insisted that the crash and the Great Depression had demonstrated the shortcomings of an unregulated economy. They demanded that the administration revive federal spending and redouble efforts to stimulate the economy. In 1938, Congress heeded Roosevelt's plea to enact a massive new program of spending to revitalize the economy.

The New Deal's methods received support from new economic ideas advanced by the brilliant British economist John Maynard Keynes. Keynes played a prominent role in shaping British economic policy, and he capped his career in 1936 with the publication of the most influential work on economics in the twentieth century, *The General Theory of Employment, Interest, and Money*. Keynes made a sophisticated, theoretical argument in favor of practices that New Deal relief agencies had developed in an ad hoc, commonsense way. A nation's economy, Keynes declared, could not automatically reach its full potential in the complex, interdependent modern world. The depression had painfully illustrated that economic activity could become stalled at a level far short of a society's true potential. When that happened, only government intervention could pump enough money into the system to revive production, boost consumption, and restore prosperity. In bad times, Keynes contended, government should provide paid jobs for unemployed workers in order to spread purchasing power throughout the economy. In good times, government should restrict the supply of money to prevent the economy from producing more goods and services than consumers can absorb.

Roosevelt never had the inclination or the time to follow his economic advisers into the thicket of Keynesian theory. But the recession scare of 1938 taught him the Keynesian lesson that economic growth had to be carefully nurtured. To clear the way for renewed government intervention in the economy, Roosevelt reemphasized the greed and irresponsibility of "economic royalists." In April 1938, as the economy reeled and conservatives gloated over the defeat of the Court bill, Roosevelt sent a message to Congress asking for "a thorough study of the concentration of economic power in American industry." The result was a congressional study that led to the establishment of the Temporary National Economic Committee (TNEC) in June 1938.

Debates within TNEC over economic reform revived the old argument that had divided progressives since the beginning of the century. As TNEC uncovered plentiful evidence of ruthless and corrupt business practices, some New Dealers argued in the spirit of Theodore Roosevelt for increased government planning to make the economy more rational and efficient. Another group echoed Wilsonian Democrats and urged the government to break up monopolies that restricted competition, reduced efficiency, and hindered the growth of new enterprises so vital for economic recovery. But an antimonopoly campaign lacked political support. Efforts to revive central planning also sputtered.

The Keynesian message, however, had great impact on New Deal policy. The notion of an active federal government freed from rigid economics and willing to engage in large-scale spending to alleviate distress appealed to the Roosevelt administration. Harry Hopkins's economics had always consisted largely of a desire to "feed the hungry, and Goddamn fast."

The Last of the New Deal Reforms

From the moment he entered office, Roosevelt had tinkered with the small and antiquated office of the presidency. He believed that the powers of the presidency were inadequate, especially during emergencies such as the depression. He also wanted more power over the federal bureaucracy. Arguing the need for "efficiency," Roosevelt submitted an ambitious plan of executive reorganization to Congress in 1937. The bill failed, but in September 1939, Congress passed the Administrative Reorganization Act, which gave Roosevelt part of what he desired and strengthened the office of the president. With a Democratic majority in Congress, a now friendly Supreme Court, the Keynesian fruits of the TNEC, and the revival of deficit spending, the newly empowered White House seemed to be in a strong position to move ahead with a third New Deal.

Resistance was also on the rise, however. Conservatives argued that the New Deal had pressed its centralization too far and was bent on creating what later came to be known as "the imperial presidency." Even the New Deal's friends became weary with one emergency program after another, especially while economic recession still shadowed New Deal achievements. By the midpoint of Roosevelt's second term, restive members of Congress balked at new initiatives. Clearly, the New Deal was winding down, but enough energy remained for one last burst of reform.

Desperate need among poor people in rural America still claimed federal attention. In 1937, the Agriculture Department created the Farm Security Administration (FSA) to provide housing and loans that would help tenant farmers become owners and give them the best possible chance to prosper. But the FSA was starved for funds and ran up against the major farm organizations, which were intent on serving the interests of the large farms. With only minor successes to show, the FSA petered out.

The New Deal completed its efforts to raise the farm sector to a secure plateau of prosperity with

NEW DEAL HOUSING GOALS

The eradication of slum housing (above) such as this in Atlanta in 1936 came to be a prime test of overcoming the depression. In his inaugural address for his second term, Roosevelt focused on the need to rescue the one-third of the nation still "ill-housed, ill clad, and ill-nourished." The most famous attempt to point the way was the greenbelt town program run by the Resettlement Administration of the Department of Agriculture to relocate people forced off the farms. The picture of Greendale, Wisconsin, (below) taken in 1939, offers an idea of the uniform utopia the Roosevelt administration favored but was prevented from continuing by the shifting of resources to fight World War II.
Library of Congress.

TECHNOLOGY IN AMERICA
Mechanized Cotton Picking

Here in 1935 two of the most important farm machines of the time, the Farmall tractor and the Rust cotton picker, cut through a sea of cotton, showing how mechanization could eliminate the backbreaking work of harvesting cotton by hand. Within ten years tractors would displace horses as the main means of doing heavy farm work, but success for mechanical cotton pickers was longer in coming. For a century and a half after the invention of the cotton gin in 1793 made cotton farming feasible, inventors tried to create a device that would make picking cotton as efficient as ginning it. The first patent for a crude mechanical picker was granted in 1850 and nearly 2,000 more followed before John Rust in 1931 demonstrated a machine that could pick more bales of cotton in a day than the average farmer in the deep South grew in a year.

Ironically, though Southerners had at last realized their dream of mechanizing cotton picking, the machine was so efficient that it was ill-suited to most southern cotton farms, whose yearly crop was relatively modest. Nor could most cotton growers afford the new machinery. In the midst of the Great Depression, when Rust demonstrated his invention in 1931, cotton prices had plunged from 35 cents a bale in 1919 to only 6 cents a bale.

In the next two decades, large farms using the new mechanical cotton picker became dominant and

that change shifted most cotton growing to the West, where vast agricultural holdings were the rule. Displaced by the decline of King Cotton in the South, field hands like the woman shown above migrated in thousands to the North in search of jobs.

Cotton picking machine: Mississippi State University Libraries; Cotton picker: Courtesy of the Harvard University Art Museums. Gift of Bernarda B. Shahn, Estate of Ben Shahn.

the Agricultural Adjustment Act (AAA) of February 1938. Secretary of Agriculture Henry Wallace centered the new act around the ancient Chinese tradition of an "ever normal granary." The plan combined production quotas on five staple crops—cotton, tobacco, wheat, corn, and rice—with storage loans through its Commodity Credit Corporation to moderate price swings by making sure that supply was at an "ever normal" level, sufficient to satisfy the market and prevent hunger. A grateful Iowa farmer remembered, "Henry Wallace and his ever-normal granary was the man who saved the farmer. The farmer would have passed clear out of the picture." The measure benefited well-endowed farmers but added an element of charity by providing surplus food for the poor through the act's Federal Surplus Commodities Corporation. Begun on a modest scale, the food stamp plan introduced a basic welfare role for agriculture in aiding the third of the nation that Roosevelt identified as ill fed. The AAA of 1938 brought stability to American agriculture for the next several years.

Advocates for the urban underclass also had modest luck gaining attention after decades of neglect. New York Senator Robert Wagner used a massive statistical study of suffering to convince Congress to pass the National Housing Act in September 1937. By 1941, some 160,000 residences had been made available at rates affordable for those below the poverty line. The project did not come close to meeting the need for affordable housing; but for the first time, the federal government took an active role in trying to replace the squalor of American cities with housing that met standards of decency and answered Roosevelt's inaugural pledge to aid the ill housed.

The last major piece of New Deal labor legislation, the Fair Labor Standards Act of June 1938, reiterated the original New Deal pledge to provide workers with a decent standard of living. After unprecedented haggling and compromise that revealed the waning strength of the New Deal, Congress finally agreed to intervene in the long sacrosanct free enterprise realm of contracts between employers and workers. The act set minimum-wage and maximum-hours standards and curbed the use of child labor. The minimum-wage level was modest —twenty-five cents an hour for a maximum of forty-four hours a week. And the act exempted merchant seamen, fishermen, domestic help, and farm laborers from these wage and hours standards in order to attract enough conservative votes to pass

the act. Nevertheless, the passage of minimum-wage and maximum-hours standards was an important step toward realization of the New Deal promise to work actively to eliminate poverty.

The final New Deal reform effort failed to make much headway against the hidebound system of racial segregation. Although Roosevelt was willing to denounce lynching as murder, he would not jeopardize his vital base of political support in the South by designating antilynching bills as "must" legislation. In 1934 and 1935, Congress voted down attempts to make lynching a federal crime, and in 1938 the last antilynching bill of the decade died in a Senate filibuster. Laws to eliminate the poll tax—used to deny blacks the opportunity to vote—encountered the same overwhelming resistance. African Americans received some meager benefit from employment opportunities in northern relief projects and federal agencies, but the New Deal refused even to confront the injustice of racial segregation.

The last major piece of New Deal labor legislation, the Fair Labor Standards Act of June 1938, set minimum-wage and maximum-hours standards and curbed the use of child labor.

By the end of 1938, the New Deal had run out of fresh ideas and into stiff opposition. As legislative initiative waned and programs played themselves out, the conservative tide rose. In the congressional elections of 1938, Republicans picked up seven seats in the Senate and eighty in the House, making them a power for the first time since 1932. New Dealers could claim unprecedented and resounding achievement since 1933 when Roosevelt entered the White House, but ten million unemployed five years later, about two-thirds as many as in 1932 under Hoover, were powerful reminders that the depression had not been whipped. In his annual message to Congress in January 1939, however, Roosevelt called a halt to the great reform movement of the Second New Deal. He spoke of preserving the reforms already achieved, not of extending them. The major theme of his address, in fact, was not domestic affairs at all. It was the enormity of the totalitarian threat overseas to international peace and American happiness.

Conclusion: A New Departure

"This election," Herbert Hoover announced in 1932, "is not a mere shift from the ins to the outs. It means deciding the direction our nation will take over a century to come." Franklin Roosevelt's election, he warned, would result in "a radical departure from the foundations of 150 years which have made this the greatest nation in the world." Hoover was right that Roosevelt's election would mean a significant departure, but like many conservatives, he misjudged his successor's radicalism.

Franklin Delano Roosevelt took the helm of a nation near collapse, starvation, and revolution. He confronted the unprecedented crisis head on, confident that vigorous government action could overcome the depression and its devastating human consequences. Roosevelt's constant improvisation, alleviation of suffering, and warmhearted sympathy restored hope and faith. The people agreed with the president that society should help those in need and that the federal government was an appropriate vehicle to deliver aid. In the process of fighting the blight of the depression, the Roosevelt administration vastly expanded the size and power of the federal government and changed the way the American people looked upon Washington. It won major successes such as Social Security, labor's right to organize, and measures to ensure that people could hold on to their savings, homes, and farms. The federal government assumed new responsibilities for the nation's economy and the people's welfare.

To Hoover and many of his contemporaries, Roosevelt appeared to be a dangerous radical who threatened the foundations of democracy and capitalism. But as Frances Perkins said, Franklin Roosevelt took capitalism as much for granted as he did his family. Rather than attack capitalism, he boldly sought to save it. The daring innovation and persistent experimentation took place within ideological boundaries that precluded radical and revolutionary transformation. Like his cousin Teddy, Franklin Roosevelt understood that things would have to change in order to remain the same. He left America greatly changed, but America also remained profoundly the same.

CHRONOLOGY

1932	The Bonus Army marches on Washington.
1933	Franklin D. Roosevelt assumes presidency.
	Roosevelt closes nation's banks for four-day "holiday" to allow time to stabilize the banking system.
	March–June. New Deal established through passage of reform legislation of the Hundred Days.
	The Civil Works Administration (CWA) begun under Harry Hopkins to provide relief for unemployed.
1934	Securities and Exchange Commission formed to license and regulate stock exchanges.

	Upton Sinclair loses bid to become governor of California and enact his EPIC work relief program.
	Wealthy conservatives of American Liberty League oppose New Deal.
	"Radio Priest" Father Charles Coughlin begins National Union for Social Justice.
	Dr. Francis Townsend devises Old Age Revolving Pension scheme to provide money to the impoverished elderly.
	Congress adopts Indian Reorganization Act.
1935	Louisiana Senator Huey Long assassinated.

As part of Second New Deal, legislation creates Works Progress Administration (WPA).

The Committee for Industrial Organization (CIO) founded to provide union representation for unskilled workers.

Congress passes Wagner Act to guarantee workers the right to organize unions and bargain collectively.

1936   John Maynard Keynes publishes *The General Theory of Employment, Interest, and Money*, providing theoretical justification for government deficit financing.

Franklin Roosevelt reelected by landslide over Republican Alfred Landon.

1937   CIO stages successful sit-down strike at the General Motors plant in Flint, Michigan.

Roosevelt's "court-packing" legislation defeated in Senate.

1937–1938   Economic recession slows recovery from depression.

1938   Second Agricultural Adjustment Act and Fair Labor Standards Act bring New Deal legislation to an end.

Congress fails to pass administration's antilynching bill.

1939   Administrative Reorganization Act enlarges scope and power of presidency.

African American contralto Marian Anderson gives concert at Lincoln Memorial.

BIBLIOGRAPHY

GENERAL WORKS

Anthony Badger, *The New Deal: The Depression Years, 1933–1940* (1989).

Alan Brinkley, *The End of Reform: New Deal Liberalism in Recession and War* (1995).

Paul Conkin, *The New Deal* (1967).

Kenneth S. Davis, *FDR*, 3 vols. (1972; reprint, 1985, 1986).

Steve Fraser and Gary Gerstle, eds., *The Rise and Fall of the New Deal Order* (1988).

William E. Leuchtenburg, *Franklin D. Roosevelt and the New Deal, 1932–1940* (1963).

William E. Leuchtenburg, *The FDR Years: On Roosevelt and His Legacy* (1995).

Katie Loucheim, ed., *The Making of the New Deal: The Insiders Speak* (1983).

Richard H. Pells, *Radical Visions and American Dreams: Culture and Social Thought in the Depression Years* (1973).

David Plotke, *Building a Democratic Political Order: Reshaping American Liberalism in the 1930s and 1940s* (1996).

Arthur M. Schlesinger Jr., *The Coming of the New Deal* (1959).

Arthur M. Schlesinger Jr., *The Politics of Upheaval* (1960).

Harvard Sitkoff, ed., *Fifty Years Later: The New Deal Evaluated* (1985).

THE ROOSEVELT LEADERSHIP

Philip Abbott, *The Exemplary Presidency: Franklin D. Roosevelt and the American Political Tradition* (1990).

John M. Allswang, *The New Deal and American Politics* (1978).

Kristi Andersen, *The Creation of a Democratic Majority, 1928–1936* (1979).

James MacGregor Burns, *Roosevelt: The Lion and the Fox* (1956).

Blanche Wiessen Cook, *Eleanor Roosevelt* (1992).

Joseph Lash, *Eleanor and Franklin* (1971).

Richard Polenberg, *Reorganizing Roosevelt's Government, 1936–1939* (1966).

Albert U. Romasco, *The Politics of Recovery: Roosevelt's New Deal* (1983).

Eleanor Roosevelt, *Autobiography* (1961).

Eliot A. Rosen, *Hoover, Roosevelt, and the Brains Trust: From Depression to New Deal* (1977).

Sean J. Savage, *Roosevelt: The Party Leader, 1932–1945* (1991).

Richard W. Steele, *Propaganda in an Open Society: The Roosevelt Administration and the Media, 1933–1941* (1985).

Geoffrey C. Ward, *A First-Class Temperament: The Emergence of Franklin Roosevelt* (1989).

Susan Ware, *Beyond Suffrage: Women in the New Deal* (1981).

Susan Ware, *Partner and I: Molly Dewson, Feminism, and New Deal Politics* (1987).

ECONOMICS AND PLANNING

William J. Barber, *From New Era to New Deal: Herbert Hoover, the Economists, and American Economic Policy, 1921–1933* (1985).

Donald R. Brand, *Corporatism and the Rule of Law: A Study of the National Recovery Administration* (1988).

Mark Gelfand, *A Nation of Cities: The Federal Government and Urban America, 1933–1945* (1975).

Otis L. Graham Jr., *Toward a Planned Society: From Roosevelt to Nixon* (1976).

Erwin C. Hargrove, *Prisoners of Myth: The Leadership of the Tennessee Valley Authority, 1933–1990* (1990).

Ellis Hawley, *The New Deal and the Problem of Monopoly: A Study in Economic Ambivalence* (1966).

Susan Estabrook Kennedy, *The Banking Crisis of 1933* (1973).

Mark Leff, *The Limits of Symbolic Reform: The New Deal and Taxation, 1933–1939* (1984).

Dean May, *From New Deal to New Economics* (1981).

Michael Parrish, *Securities Regulation and the New Deal* (1970).

Theodore Rosenof, *Patterns of Political Economy in America: The Failure to Develop a Democratic Left Synthesis, 1933–1950* (1983).

REFORM AND WELFARE

W. Andrew Achenbaum, *Shades of Gray: Old Age, American Values, and Federal Policies since 1920* (1983).

Edward D. Berkowitz, *America's Welfare State: From Roosevelt to Reagan* (1991).

William R. Brock, *Welfare, Democracy, and the New Deal* (1987).

John A. Clausen, *Looking Back at the Children of the Great Depression* (1993).

Phoebe Cutler, *The Public Landscape of the New Deal* (1986).

Linda Gordon, *Pitied but Not Entitled: Single Mothers and the History of Welfare* (1994).

William Graebner, *A History of Retirement: The Meaning and Function of an American Institution, 1885–1978* (1980).

Joseph Hutmacher, *Senator Robert Wagner and the Rise of American Liberalism* (1968).

Paul A. Kurzman, *Harry Hopkins and the New Deal* (1974).

Roy Lubove, *The Struggle for Social Security, 1900–1935* (1968).

Paul E. Mertz, *New Deal Policy and Southern Rural Poverty* (1978).

James T. Patterson, *America's Struggle against Poverty, 1900–1980* (1981).

John Salmond, *The Civilian Conservation Corps, 1933–1942* (1967).

Bonnie Fox Schwartz, *The Civil Works Administration, 1933–1934* (1984).

CHALLENGES TO THE NEW DEAL

Alan Brinkley, *Voices of Protest: Huey Long, Father Coughlin, and the Great Depression* (1983).

Otis L. Graham Jr., *An Encore for Reform: The Old Progressives and the New Deal* (1967).

William Ivy Hair, *The Kingfish and His Realm* (1991).

Harvey Klehr, *The Heyday of American Communism* (1984).

R. Alan Lawson, *The Failure of Independent Liberalism, 1930–1941* (1971).

Donald J. Lisio, *The President and Protest: Hoover, Conspiracy, and the Bonus Riot* (1974).

Huey Long, *Every Man a King: The Autobiography of Huey P. Long* (1933).

Huey Long, *My First Days in the White House* (1935).

James T. Patterson, *Congressional Conservatism and the New Deal* (1967).

Leo P. Ribuffo, *The Old Christian Right: The Protestant Far Right from the Great Depression to the Cold War* (1983).

Frank A. Warren, *Liberals and Communism: The "Red Decade" Revisited* (1966; reprint, 1993).

Clyde P. Weed, *The Nemesis of Reform: The Republican Party During the New Deal* (1994).

T. Harry Williams, *Huey Long* (1969).

George Wolfskill, *The Revolt of the Conservatives: A History of the American Liberty League, 1934–1940* (1962).

RURAL AMERICA, SOUTH AND WEST

David E. Conrad, *The Forgotten Farmers: The Story of the Share-Croppers in the New Deal* (1965).

Cletus E. Daniel, *Bitter Harvest: A History of California Farmworkers, 1870–1941* (1981).

David E. Hamilton, *From New Day to New Deal: American Farm Policy from Hoover to Roosevelt, 1928–1933* (1991).

Jack Temple Kirby, *Rural Worlds Lost: The American South, 1920–1960* (1987).

Richard Lowitt, *The New Deal and the West* (1984).

LABOR

John Barnard, *Walter Reuther and the Rise of the Auto Workers* (1983).

Irving Bernstein, *A Caring Society: The New Deal, the Worker, and the Great Depression* (1985).

Bert Cochran, *Labor and Communism* (1977).

Lizbeth Cohen, *Making a New Deal: Industrial Workers in Chicago, 1919–1939* (1990).

Sidney Fine, *Sitdown: The General Motors Strike of 1936–1937* (1969).

Steve Fraser, *Labor Will Rule: Sidney Hillman and the Rise of American Labor* (1991).

Gary Gerstle, *Working-Class Americanism: The Politics of Labor in a Textile City, 1914–1960* (1989).

Colin Gordon, *New Deals: Business, Labor, and Politics in America, 1920–1935* (1994).

James A. Hodges, *New Deal Labor Policy and the Southern Cotton Textile Industry, 1933–1941* (1986).

August Meier and Elliot Rudwick, *Black Detroit and the Rise of the UAW* (1979).

David Milton, *The Politics of United States Labor: From the Great Depression to the New Deal* (1980).

Judith Sealander, *As Minority Becomes Majority: Federal Reaction to the Phenomenon of Women in the Work Force, 1920–1963* (1983).

Robert H. Zieger, *John L. Lewis: Labor Leader* (1988).

RACE AND MINORITIES

Francisco E. Balderrama and Raymond Rodriguez, *Decade of Betrayal: Mexican Repatriation in the 1930s* (1995).

Christine Bolt, *American Indian Policy and American Reform* (1987).

Dan T. Carter, *Scottsboro* (1969).

Robin D. G. Kelley, *Hammer and Hoe: Alabama Communists during the Great Depression* (1990).

John B. Kirby, *Black Americans in the Roosevelt Era: Liberalism and Race* (1980).

Clifford Lytle, *American Indians, American Justice* (1983).

Doug McAdam, *Political Process and the Development of Black Insurgency, 1920–1970* (1982).

Harvard Sitkoff, *A New Deal for Blacks: The Emergence of Civil Rights as a National Issue: The Depression Decade* (1978).

Patricia Sullivan, *Days of Hope: Race and Democracy in the New Deal Era* (1996).

Graham D. Taylor, *The New Deal and American Indian Tribalism: The Administration of the Indian Reorganization Act, 1935–1945* (1980).

Nancy J. Weiss, *Farewell to the Party of Lincoln* (1983).

Robert L. Zangrando, *The NAACP Crusade against Lynching* (1980).

PUBLIC CULTURE

Kenneth J. Bindas, *All of This Music Belongs to the Nation: The WPA's Federal Music Project and American Society* (1996).

Jerre Mangione, *The Dream and the Deal* (1972).

Karal Ann Marling, *Wall-to-Wall America: A Cultural History of Post-Office Murals in the Great Depression* (1982).

Jane De Hart Mathews, *The Federal Theatre, 1935–1939: Plays, Relief, and Politics* (1967).

Richard McKinzie, *The New Deal for Artists* (1973).

Francis V. O'Connor, ed., *Art for the Millions: Essays from the 1930s by Artists and Administrators of the WPA Federal Art Project* (1973).

Geoffrey O'Gara, *A Long Road Home: In the Footsteps of the WPA Writers* (1989).

GOD BLESS AMERICA

MEMENTO OF WAR

To mark the seriousness of going to war, servicemen and their families often mounted photos in special settings, such as this painted-on-glass frame. Symbols of God and country sum up patriotic devotion to a just cause. And in the midst of these ritualized sentiments, as if looking back through a window draped in his honor, an unknown sailor seems about to tell us something more.

Private Collection.

THE UNITED STATES AND THE SECOND WORLD WAR

25

1939–1945

EXCITED AND UNCERTAIN ABOUT WHAT TO EXPECT, a noisy crowd of eight thousand jostled into the America First rally in Des Moines, Iowa, on the evening of September 1, 1941. They came to hear Charles Lindbergh, the first person to fly solo across the Atlantic, the nation's most famous hero. Lindbergh was speaking against President Franklin Roosevelt's order that would allow American warships to "shoot on sight" any German vessel that interfered with American shipping to Great Britain. A firestorm was the last thing Lindbergh wanted to ignite. A shy, private man, he resisted every effort by the media to make him a celebrity. Only a compelling sense of duty convinced him that he must suffer the spotlight again to take a stand against American involvement in another war.

Lindbergh's speech was sponsored by the America First Committee (AFC), organized in the fall of 1940 to keep the United States out of the war that had erupted in Europe the year before. The AFC's youthful organizers attracted a considerable following among those of draft age, including two future presidents, Gerald Ford and John Kennedy. But America Firsters, especially Lindbergh, had suffered harsh denunciation. Secretary of the Interior Harold Ickes labeled Lindbergh "America's No. 1 Nazi fellow traveler." "No one," Ickes pointed out in July 1941, "has ever heard Lindbergh utter a word of horror at, or even aversion to, the bloody career that the Nazis are following, nor a word of pity for the innocent men, women, and children who have been deliberately murdered by the Nazis." A year earlier, Roosevelt had gone even further. "I am absolutely convinced," he told Secretary of the Treasury Henry Morgenthau, "that Lindbergh is a Nazi."

Yet the man who had flown the Atlantic alone still had such a strong hold on the American imagination that the crowd in Des Moines settled down immediately when he stepped onto the stage, straight and tall, still at thirty-nine the godlike young aviator. In his clear, earnest voice Lindbergh declared that war would needlessly take the lives of the nation's best young men and bleed precious resources. He promised the "utmost frankness" in laying bare the forces behind the interventionist "subterfuge." Bluntly, he declared that "the three most important groups who have been pressing this country toward war are the British, the Jewish, and the Roosevelt administration." Lindbergh received a standing ovation when he identified the war "agitators." But elsewhere, accusations mounted that Lindbergh was anti-Semitic, if not pro-Nazi, and even close associates backed away. In the few months left before the United States entered the war, the "Lone Eagle" was alone again.

When the United States went to war in December 1941, the America First Committee shut its doors, and true to their insistence that they were patriots committed to the defense of their country, its members hurried to defend the flag. Lindbergh, however, had his way blocked by the implacable hostility of the Roosevelt administration. Denied a renewal of his commission in the air force, Lindbergh finally found work on the sidelines testing fighters and bombers for the Ford Motor Company. In 1944, Lindbergh seized the chance to continue flight testing in the Pacific war zone. His superb flying skills persuaded the fighter squadron on remote Biak Island to let him fly fifty combat missions. "Lucky Lindy" proved he had some luck left; in one firefight he barely escaped being shot down, and in another he finally destroyed an enemy plane just a few yards short of a head-on collision.

Even when the war ended in victory, however, Lindbergh believed that his dire predictions about the conflict had been correct. Although he had fought courageously, he steadfastly refused to draw sharp distinctions between the Allied and Axis sides, between "our" good and "their" evil. The brutality of war, he argued, "is not a thing confined to any nation or to any people. What the German has done to the Jew in Europe, we are doing to the Jap in the Pacific. . . . It is not the Germans alone, or the Japs, but the men of all nations to whom this war has brought shame and degradation."

In 1940–1941, millions of other Americans shared Lindbergh's concern that the nation would be drawn into war, but few resisted as hard or as long as he did. Haltingly at first, then boldly, the American people rallied behind Roosevelt and accepted his interpretation of the Nazi menace. When the nation entered the war, Americans threw themselves unreservedly into the struggle. They believed that they were engaged in a necessary war to preserve democracy, a righteous war to save civilization. Much more than during World War I, Americans said it was a "good war."

There was no specific moment when foreign affairs replaced domestic reform as Roosevelt's chief priority. Throughout the 1930s, as Roosevelt battled the depression, foreign problems gradually grew more insistent. The growth of fascism, the power of Germany and Japan, the Ethiopian War, the Spanish Civil War, and the war in China drew Roosevelt and the nation into a more active foreign policy.

After September 1939, when fighting erupted in Europe, an American president once again had to negotiate the treacherous waters of neutrality. Like Woodrow Wilson, Roosevelt promised to keep the nation out of the European conflict, but as he became convinced that a fascist victory would be catastrophic, he sought to educate the American people into a more aggressive defense of the Allied cause. Debate ended on December 7, 1941, when the Japanese attacked the American naval base at Pearl Harbor, Hawaii. The United States entered World War II, the most devastating and transforming conflict in history.

The American experience in World War II was unique. No bombs fell at home, no civilian starved, and no government toppled. Yet the nation engaged in a total war that influenced every American and almost every aspect of American life. The war put Americans to work again and ended the depression. It ended the New Deal's drive for reform and the nation's isolationism. American soldiers and sailors who had never been beyond their hometowns fought on distant continents and seas and came home changed. As one rifleman said of his experience abroad: "I went there a skinny, gaunt mama's boy, full of wonderment. I came back much more circumspect in my judgment of people. And of governments." Nearly four years of war also changed individuals and society at home. Women did "men's" work, minorities stepped out of their "places," and, as one woman remembered, people came out of the war "with more money than they'd had in years." But hundreds of thousands of families also lost fathers, husbands, and sons, wounds that would never heal. A victorious nation, grieving yet optimistic, emerged from World War II the most powerful industrial and military power in the world.

Peacetime Dilemmas

With the Japanese invasion of Manchuria in 1931, the arms buildup and talk of the glories of war in fascist Italy, and the swearing in of Adolf Hitler as chancellor of Germany in 1933, the world grew steadily more dangerous. The forces of aggression in Europe and in the Far East mocked the peace structure so hopefully put into place during the Versailles Peace Conference following World War I. The United States had rejected Woodrow Wilson's plea to join the League of Nations and commit to the principle of collective international security. The rising tide of violent nationalism throughout the world in the 1930s roused old fears of foreign entanglements and caused Americans to pull back behind their ocean shields. That recoil from international conflict paralleled the decision of New Dealers to concentrate on domestic policies first and not allow international complications to hinder the country's economic recovery from the depression. With few exceptions, American policy took on a peculiar polarity: In the face of crises, the nation's leaders took bold action at home but shrank from being involved abroad.

FDR and Reluctant Isolation

Nowhere was the contrast between domestic boldness and international caution more evident than in the change in Franklin Delano Roosevelt's public position on foreign policy. Roosevelt grew up within activist international circles. The Delano family had long been involved with China, and the family home in Hyde Park, New York, was filled with books, mementos, and talk about Asia. Moreover, his famous cousin Theodore had played a premier role in bringing the United States onto the world stage and had capped his achievements by winning the Nobel Peace Prize for negotiating an end to the Russo-Japanese War in 1905. In that heady atmosphere, when the twentieth century was young and the United States was beginning to flex its economic muscle, Franklin Roosevelt came to believe strongly that naval dominance determines the balance of power. When he joined the Wilson administration as assistant secretary of the navy in 1913, Roosevelt zestfully welcomed international action. He had urged American preparedness when World War I broke out in Europe and welcomed U.S. entry into the fray as an uplifting adventure.

True to Wilson's vision that the United States should take the lead in making the world "safe for democracy," Roosevelt went against the isolationist tide in the 1920s by arguing for American membership in the League of Nations. When he reentered politics in 1928 to run for governor of New York, he charged that the Republicans had undermined chances for a prosperous peace by setting high tariffs while also insisting that the exhausted Europeans pay off their loans and reparations.

The depression forced Roosevelt to retreat from his internationalism. Hard times made it easy for isolationists to persuade other Americans that ex-

pending effort and money on foreign ventures was a risky diversion from domestic recovery. During his 1932 run for the presidency against Herbert Hoover, Roosevelt was unnerved by charges that he was an international adventurer. He pulled back from his endorsement of the League of Nations and reversed his position on forgiving European war debts. With regret, Roosevelt concluded that the New Deal coalition he sought required him to curb his internationalism.

Once in office, Roosevelt wanted to join domestic economic recovery with a foreign policy that encouraged free trade and disarmament. He had always believed that peace, prosperity, and free trade were linked. "Foreign markets must be regained if America's producers are to rebuild a full and enduring domestic prosperity for our people," Roosevelt declared in 1935. "There is no other way if we would avoid painful economic dislocations, social readjustments, and unemployment." The concept of an interdependent and open world led to the most successful initiative of his first year in office — the recognition of the Soviet Union, which had been shunned as a revolutionary menace since the Bolshevik Revolution of 1917. After a careful survey of American public opinion convinced him that the nation supported bringing the USSR into the world community, Roosevelt pressed forward with negotiations that resulted in formal recognition on November 17, 1933.

The recoil from international conflict paralleled the decision of New Dealers to concentrate on domestic policies first and not allow international complications to hinder the country's economic recovery from the depression.

Despite this bold initiative, he also believed that until the American economy regained its balance, unhindered experimentation at home called for a safe distance from the world's troubles. He hoped that the United States would recover quickly and then be in a position to give active support to disarmament and removal of barriers to free trade. Instead, the depression dragged on and a series of crises abroad provoked wars and rivalries, rather than the spirit of cooperation that disarmament and free trade required.

Thus Roosevelt was hemmed in by circumstances. Because the New Deal needed support from isolationists in Congress, Roosevelt could not offer to help the League of Nations curb aggression. Nor could he agree to abide by decisions of the World Court, which was established by the League of Nations to settle international disputes. American endorsement of international cooperation could go no further than to express watery praise for the concept of collective security.

Almost as soon as Roosevelt entered office, the ability of the League of Nations to maintain peace declined when Japan withdrew from the league and rejected limitations on its naval strength imposed after World War I. In the fall of 1933, the new Nazi chancellor of Germany, Adolf Hitler, further dimmed the league's prospects by recalling Germany's representatives to the league and joining Japan in condemning the organization as an obstacle to Germany's national aspirations. Shocked by the ominous turn of events, Roosevelt reassured Americans that support of the league's objectives would not involve the United States in war. Under no circumstances, he declared, would the nation "use its armed forces for the settlement of any dispute anywhere."

Unable to launch foreign policy initiatives, Roosevelt turned to building U.S. defenses. In 1934, to counter the threatened Japanese naval buildup, Roosevelt authorized the largest expansion of the U.S. navy since 1916. At the same time, he instructed the State Department to play down Japan's expansion in China. Most citizens, absorbed in their domestic woes, paid little attention to foreign problems and were thankful for the oceans they thought could shelter them from involvement.

The Good Neighbor Policy

In his inaugural address in 1933, Franklin Roosevelt dedicated the United States to "the policy of the good neighbor" in foreign affairs. A few weeks later, he specifically applied the phrase to the nation's Latin American policy. Although the Hoover administration had moved away from the Roosevelt Corollary under which the nation had arrogantly claimed the right to intervene in the internal affairs of Latin American nations, the United States and other nations in the Western Hemisphere were hardly cordial neighbors when Roosevelt took office.

Roosevelt and Secretary of State Cordell Hull were committed to establishing a genuine Pan-American accord. By offering a "helping hand" and

enjoying "the cooperation of others," Roosevelt declared, the United States could "have more order in this hemisphere and less dislike." In the Western Hemisphere, unlike elsewhere, isolationist Americans were willing to allow significant international cooperation. In December 1933, Hull traveled to Montevideo, Uruguay, to participate in the Inter-American Conference. The intense anti-American feeling he encountered abated when he signed the joint declaration that asserted that no nation has the right to intervene in the internal or external affairs of another.

The United States' commitment to nonintervention was quickly put to the test. When Mexico nationalized American oil holdings and when revolution boiled over in Nicaragua, Guatemala, and Cuba, Roosevelt refrained from his cousin Theodore's easy resort to sending in the marines to defend the interests of American corporations. In 1934, moreover, Roosevelt withdrew American marines from Haiti, where they had been since 1916. But nonintervention was a double-edged sword. While it honored the principle of national self-determination, it did not necessarily promote freedom. American business, emboldened by Roosevelt's policy, entered into lucrative arrangements with dictators like Anastasio Somoza in Nicaragua and Fulgencio Batista in Cuba that enabled those tyrants to become wealthy and powerful by exploiting and terrorizing the rest of the population.

Adoption of the "good neighbor policy," therefore, did not mean that Roosevelt had abandoned Woodrow Wilson's aim of achieving economic preeminence in the region. Roosevelt did not so much retreat from empire in Latin America as reject military force as a means of retaining it. With Roosevelt's blessing, Hull engineered passage of the Reciprocal Trade Agreements Act of 1934. The act gave the president power to reduce the nation's high tariffs on a nation-by-nation basis. By 1940, Hull's initiative persuaded twenty-two nations to sign reciprocal treaties and has broadened since to cover most of America's foreign trade. Trade reciprocity had significant results. Between 1929 and 1932, American exports to Latin America had fallen from $2 billion to $500 million. From 1933 to 1940, American exports doubled. Trade reciprocity, however, did not prevent a widening of the gap between American economic power and that of the rest of the Western Hemisphere. Still, Roosevelt's new departure in Latin America planted the seeds of friendship and solidarity, an achievement that grew in importance as events in Europe and Asia eroded the hope for peace.

The Price of Noninvolvement

Increasingly in the 1930s, international order broke down. Countries beset by economic hardship, ethnic rivalries, and historic grievances turned to aggressive nationalism as the way to end their troubles. Italian strongman Benito Mussolini set the pattern. Through harsh militarist means, Mussolini constructed an authoritarian state that created a semblance of order and efficiency. Even those who lamented the loss of democracy were likely to accept the myth that, in Italy, "at least the trains ran on time." But Mussolini's philosophy of aggression eroded European resolve to settle disputes peacefully. "War is to the man what maternity is to the woman," Mussolini proclaimed with a theatrical strut, eyes bulging and jaw thrust out. "I do not believe in perpetual peace; not only do I not believe in it, but I find it depressing and a negation of all the fundamental virtues of man."

In Germany, Hitler was feverishly rearming his nation in open defiance of the Versailles treaty. British, French, and Italian leaders had the power to compel German compliance, but they contented themselves with verbal protest. In 1935, Britain concluded a treaty with the Nazis that conceded Germany equality in submarines and the right to build a surface fleet one-third the size of the British navy. Still, Hitler ranted against the Jews as the enemies of the Aryan master race and threatened action to avenge humiliating defeat in World War I. His statements about restoring territories with German inhabitants to the "Fatherland" became harder to ignore.

Political and economic tensions in the Far East also gave rise to a militant movement in Japan that resembled European fascism in the way it subordinated the economy to a ruling caste and sought national advantage through conquest. After absorbing Manchuria in 1932, Japan's military rulers began a campaign to take the five northern provinces of China. What they believed would be a mere skirmish became a long and vicious war when Chinese Nationalist leader Chiang Kai-shek rallied his troops and courageously resisted the Japanese invasion.

At first, alarm in the United States over escalating hostility abroad played into the hands of the isolationists. Disillusionment over the failure of World War I to make the world safe for democracy convinced many Americans that the opponents of the war had been right all along. America's participation seemed useless and even foolish. And after 1933, it also seemed malicious. In that year, the Senate established a committee to conduct an investigation into the U.S. entry into the war. Chaired by Republican Gerald Nye of North Dakota, who became one of Lindbergh's most prominent allies in the fight against going to war again, the committee concluded that the greed of American munitions makers, bankers, and financiers was responsible for dragging the country into war. Although it had little evidence, the Nye committee nevertheless convinced thousands of Americans that such a tragic mistake must never happen again.

The Nye committee's report and the rapidly deteriorating international situation prodded Congress into action. Between 1935 and 1937, legislators passed a series of neutrality acts designed to prevent the recurrence of the circumstances that they now believed had dragged the country into World War I. One act forbade loans to nations at war. Another gave the president the power to warn Americans about traveling on ships of belligerent nations. A third prohibited arms sales to nations at war.

But by 1937, trade in nonmilitary goods had also become an issue. Some Americans argued that any trade, not just in munitions, could draw the nation into war and argued for a total embargo of all American products to warring countries. Most members of Congress, however, recognized that a total trade ban would devastate the shaky American economy. And yet, trade with nations at war might lead to American involvement. Was there a way out? Congress believed that it found a way with the Neutrality Act of 1937. Legislators decided to allow nonmilitary goods to continue to flow to nations at war *if* the foreign nations paid cash (thus avoiding American loans) and shipped the goods in their own vessels (thus avoiding the use of American ships in war zones). The so-called cash-and-carry policy seemed to promise that the United States could have both peace and prosperity.

Constrained by law and public opinion, the Roosevelt administration could do no more in the face of international aggression than express moral disapproval. Emboldened by democracy's presumed lack of military toughness and resolve to stand firm against pressure, Germany, Italy, and Japan went from one triumphant strike to the next. In March 1936, Nazi troops marched unopposed into the Rhineland on Germany's western border in blatant violation of the Treaty of Versailles, which had placed the area under French authority. One month later, Italian armies completed their conquest of Ethiopia, a cloud of bombers and poison gas preparing the way for their grand entry into the capital at Addis Ababa. Aggression in the Far East reached its climax in December 1937 when Japanese troops captured Nanking and celebrated their triumph with a murderous rampage that cost the lives of 200,000 Chinese civilians. Yet the rest of the world continued to stand aside, the League of Nations unable to mount sanctions and U.S. action limited to moral outrage and feeble warnings.

These brutal events occurred alongside a tragic drama in Spain that demonstrated the threat of fascist power to democracy. In 1936, Spain erupted in a civil war between the Loyalists, a coalition representing the existing republican government, and the Falangists, rebel fascists led by General Francisco Franco. In what became widely described as a rehearsal for the next world war, Germany and Italy sent troops and arms to Franco, and the Soviet Union, on a much smaller scale, came to the aid of the Loyalists. The American government and public opinion favored the Loyalists as the democratically elected government, but the United States, and European democracies as well, offered no assistance to either side. This neutrality meant that Loyalist forces were at a disadvantage against fascist forces amply supplied by allies that welcomed war. Rather than sit helplessly on the sidelines, however, more than three thousand Americans enlisted in the Lincoln Brigade and joined several thousand volunteers from other countries to fight with the Loyalists. Nevertheless, in 1939, the Loyalists went down to defeat. The Spanish Civil War dramatized the tragic consequences of neutrality legislation while offering a glimpse of what a war against fascism was apt to be like.

Increasingly convinced that the United States needed to play a stronger role in stopping fascist aggression in Europe and Asia, Roosevelt sought to break the hold of isolationists on American foreign policy. On October 5, 1937, in a speech in Chicago, the heartland of isolationist sentiment, the president attempted to persuade Americans to allow the government to take a more assertive international stance. He harked back to his internationalist sense of the link between intervention and peace. "America hates war," he said. "America hopes for peace. Therefore, America actively engages in the search for peace." Thinking particularly of the horrors of Japanese aggression in China, Roosevelt declared that aggressors must be "quarantined" by the international community. Otherwise, the "contagion" of war would spread to every shore.

The speech advocated no specific action, but just the hint of a desire for the United States to cross its ocean moat was enough to ignite a storm of protest. Peace groups unloosed a letter-writing campaign to newspapers and politicians. The *Chicago Tribune* charged that the president wanted to replace "Americanism" with "internationalism." Most ominously, leaders in Congress remained silent. Roosevelt, who already had his hands full with fighting the depression, pulled back. "It's a terrible thing," he remarked to an aide, "to look over your shoulder when you are trying to lead and find no one there."

The public's reaction was a sharp reminder that the American people had made Roosevelt president to wage war against domestic ills. To enlist support for the vigorous action he urged at home, Roosevelt had to be cautious in dealing with the rest of the world. Most Americans still preferred the isolationist policies of the previous decade, partly to protect the fragile American economy from foreign competition and disruption and partly because disillusionment over America's failed crusade in World War I still lingered.

The Onset of War

Events had not spiraled far enough into disaster by the start of Roosevelt's second term to convince the public that noninvolvement would have to give way to an active role in foreign affairs, backed up by expanded armed forces. To be sure, the saber-rattling rhetoric and actual aggression of fascist dictators had alerted some observers to the danger. But troubles in China, Ethiopia, and Spain seemed too remote and minor to bring most Americans around to the president's view that it was time to take a stand. While Americans strongly condemned ruthless aggression abroad, they even more strongly opposed any measure to halt aggression that might conceivably lead to war. By 1939, however, world events and Roosevelt's efforts to educate Americans to the dangers of isolationism were bringing about a profound change of attitude. When war finally came to America, the nation united to defeat the Axis powers.

Nazi Aggression and War in Europe

Under the spell of neutrality, Americans watched helplessly as Adolf Hitler continued his campaign to dominate Europe. In the name of Germany's "destiny" to unite all German peoples, Hitler in 1938 bullied his native land of Austria into accepting incor-

THE HARVEST
Cartoonist Daniel Robert Fitzpatrick of the St. Louis Post-Dispatch *captures the rising impression of the Nazis as ghoulish scavengers stripping dead victims of their valuables. This cartoon appeared in 1938, soon after Germany incorporated Austria and seized the Sudetenland from Czechoslovakia. Fitzpatrick is obviously skeptical of British Prime Minister Neville Chamberlain's claim that appeasing Hitler's appetite for other people's possessions had achieved "peace in our time."*
Daniel Robert Fitzpatrick/*St. Louis Post-Dispatch*/John F. Kennedy Library.

poration—"Anschluss"—into the Nazi Third Reich. He then turned his attention to the German-speaking Sudetenland, granted to Czechoslovakia by the Versailles settlement. Although the Czechs were prepared to fight rather than surrender territory, the British and French wanted peace and sought to strike a deal with Hitler. British Prime Minister Neville Chamberlain went to confer with the German ruler in Munich. Chamberlain offered terms of "appeasement," as he called it, that would turn over the Sudetenland to Germany in exchange for leaving the rest of Czechoslovakia alone. On September 29, 1938, Hitler accepted the offer, solemnly promising that he would make no more territorial claims in Europe. Chamberlain returned home convinced that he had obtained "peace in our time." In March 1939, Hitler marched the German army into weakened Czechoslovakia and took over the entire country without a shot being fired.

Hardly pausing for breath, Hitler in April demanded that Poland return the German territory that it had been awarded after World War I. At this point, Britain and France finally recognized that the policy of appeasement was a failure. They assured Poland that they would go to its aid if Hitler attacked. Intent on avoiding a two-front war, Hitler offered Joseph Stalin concessions to prevent the Soviet Union from joining Germany's adversaries in the West. Despite deep enmity between Nazi Germany and the Communist Soviet Union, the two powers shocked the world by signing a Nazi-Soviet treaty of nonaggression in August 1939. The agreement not only provided that Germany and the Soviet Union would not attack one another but stipulated that in the event of territorial rearrangement in Eastern Europe, the Soviet Union would profit.

Hitler mobilized his armies and prepared to seize Poland. He fretted, "I am afraid some pig-dog will make a proposal for mediation as at Munich." To prevent any such interruption, he exhorted his generals to be as ruthless as possible. "Close your hearts to pity! Act brutally! . . . In starting and waging a war it is not Right that matters, but Victory." At dawn on September 1, 1939, fully in accord with Hitler's wishes and spirit, the German army crossed the Polish border, mechanized to a swift and crushing degree never before conceived. France and Britain kept their word by declaring war. The greatest conflict in history had begun.

From Neutrality to the Arsenal of Democracy

When war erupted, Roosevelt issued an official proclamation of American neutrality. But unlike Woodrow Wilson, he did not ask Americans to be impartial in thought as well as deed. "This nation will remain a neutral nation," he explained, "but I cannot ask that every American remain neutral in thought as well. Even a neutral has a right to take account of facts. Even a neutral cannot be asked to close his mind or his conscience." Roosevelt and the vast majority of Americans were decidedly not neutral. They favored Britain, France, and the Allied cause, but almost no one advocated going to war on their behalf. An antifascist neutral, the nation debated what it should do short of war to aid the Allies.

Roosevelt's immediate objective was to persuade Congress to repeal the arms embargo mandated by the neutrality legislation. He believed that France and Britain could defeat Germany only if they had access to weapons. The president's request

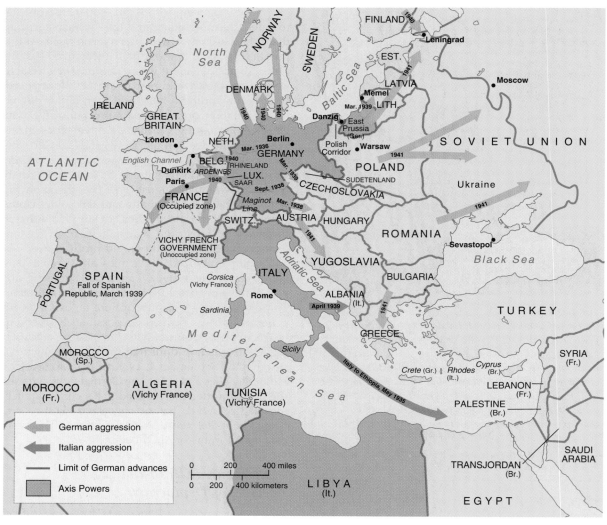

MAP 25.1
Axis Aggression to 1941
In a series of surprise military strikes, Hitler reclaimed German territories occupied by France after World War I, annexed Austria, and then launched World War II to extend German power over the "inferior" peoples across Germany's borders.

provoked frenzied debate across the nation. Charles Lindbergh said that the war was a European matter and that the United States should stay out of it. Senator William Borah of Idaho declared that Roosevelt's proposal was equivalent to taking sides and would drag the United States into war. But Congress finally consented to modify neutrality legislation so that selected belligerents could purchase armaments in the United States on a cash-and-carry basis. The narrow victory gained over vigorous isolationist

protest gave the Allies what Roosevelt hoped would be crucial assistance without involving the United States directly in the dangers of carrying war goods to Europe through the German submarine blockade.

After Hitler's armies overran Poland, they paused, but fighting resumed in the spring of 1940 with a series of Nazi hammer blows. In a lightning-fast attack called a "blitzkrieg," German dive-bombers and tanks smashed through Denmark, Norway, Belgium, and Holland and into northern

France. The French held out behind the Maginot Line, a massive concrete fortification that stretched from the Swiss border to the Ardennes forest on the edge of Belgium. But in early summer, Mussolini brought Italy into the war when his armies invaded France from the south, while Hitler's blitzkrieg flanked the Maginot Line in the north. British forces that had defended the north were cut off from their French allies by the swift German advance and retreated to the port of Dunkirk. By an extraordinary evacuation effort between May 26 and June 4, on every form of seagoing vessel available, 215,000 British troops, along with 120,000 French troops, were ferried safely back to Britain before the onrushing Germans could capture them. Less than three weeks later, reeling from a German sweep southward, the French surrendered the largest army in the world and signed an armistice that placed three-fifths of the country under German control. In the words of a British military expert, the French sword had turned out to be a broomstick.

The fall of France and the real possibility of British defeat shocked and frightened Americans. They watched breathlessly as Britain faced Germany alone. The British turned the appeaser Neville Chamberlain out of office and welcomed as prime minister the defiant Winston Churchill. With mounting fury, Churchill had watched from the sidelines as Chamberlain had kowtowed to Hitler. When the Germans attacked Britain itself, Churchill was ready with a vengeance to take over the last-ditch defense of the nation. Churchill's oratorical genius shone through the intensive bombing campaign the Germans inflicted on English cities in the summer and fall of 1940 in an attempt to break the nation's spirit. By the time the Royal Air Force won the Battle of Britain in November, ridding the skies of German bombers, Churchill (who even looked like an English bulldog) had become the symbol of indomitable British resistance.

Roosevelt strove for a comparable role as leader and symbol. His task was complicated, however, by

THE COUNTY OF LONDON ORCHESTRA
Gallant British resistance to the bombing of their cities captured American sympathy and helped to build support for U.S. entry into the war. Here in the Chelsea section of London in 1942, both the County of London Orchestra and an audience of mostly children demonstrate how to carry on in the ruins with poise and a stiff upper lip.
Hulton Deutsch Collection.

neutrality and distance from the conflict. In the spring of 1940, the president prevailed on Kansas journalist William Allen White to form the Committee to Defend America by Aiding the Allies. The committee mounted a nationwide campaign to combat isolationism and generate public support for Roosevelt's policy of providing all aid to the Allies short of war. Inevitably, isolationists (or noninterventionists, as they called themselves) organized in response. The America First Committee consisted of an odd assortment of pro-Nazi spokesmen, anti-British Irish Americans, and Italian Americans, socialists, Communists, pacifists, idealists, and thousands of patriotic Americans who genuinely thought the United States' safety depended on remaining in the Western Hemisphere and staying out of Europe's troubles.

In the midst of this hugely important debate about American foreign policy, the presidential election of 1940 unfolded. Having decided to run for an unprecedented third term rather than step aside in the midst of crisis, Roosevelt looked forward to a campaign pitting the reformist, internationalist thrust of the New Deal against Republican isolationism and business conservatism. Instead, progressive Republicans gained the nomination for Wendell Willkie, a former Democrat who supported most of the New Deal domestic program and generally agreed with Roosevelt's foreign policy. But realizing that he trailed Roosevelt badly, Willkie changed course and attacked Roosevelt as a warmonger, forcing the president to declare, "Your boys are not going to be sent into any foreign wars. . . . Your President says this country is not going to war." Although the margin of his victory was smaller than in 1936, Roosevelt won easily, 27.3 million votes to 22.3 million votes, and 449 electoral votes to 82.

The president interpreted his victory as a mandate to continue to support Britain in every way short of war. Indeed, Roosevelt's campaign to convince Americans that the United States could stay out of war with Germany only if Great Britain succeeded had won thousands of converts. But in the fall of 1940, Great Britain was in desperate straits. The British had exhausted their treasury and no longer could pay cash for weapons as required by the cash-and-carry policy. Rather than see American aid end, Roosevelt came up with a plan that he announced to the American people in a fireside chat.

On December 16, 1940, the president explained that only the British stood between the United States and Nazi aggression. To prevail, Britain needed war materiel. "We must be the great arsenal of democracy," he declared. As for how the British would pay,

he offered the homely example of a man who lent his neighbor a garden hose when his house caught on fire. "I don't say to him . . . 'you have to pay me $15 for it.' I don't want $15—I want my garden hose back after the fire is over."

The public response was overwhelmingly favorable, and the administration introduced the Lend-Lease Act to Congress in January 1941. In March, following sharp debate, Congress approved the measure, which allowed the British to obtain armaments from the United States and return them or their equivalent after the war was over. Lend-Lease was a transparent charade. As one observer noted, "Lending war materiel is a little like lending chewing gum. You don't want it back." With Lend-Lease, the United States dropped its pretense of neutrality. It engaged in full-fledged economic warfare against Germany. And since Britain could not sustain its shipping in the face of losses to German submarines, the United States would need inevitably to build and protect a vast merchant fleet. It was only a matter of time before an armed attack occurred of the sort that had precipitated World War I.

The predictable series of events began on June 11, 1941, when a German U-boat (submarine) sank the American freighter *Robin Moor* off the coast of Africa. Several months later, an American destroyer, the *Greer*, helped a British plane track a German submarine and then engaged it in a firefight. Roosevelt seized upon the incident as cause for issuing a "shoot on sight" policy for American escort vessels, and in September 1941 an "undeclared war" was under way. A month earlier, Roosevelt and Churchill had met on shipboard off the coast of Newfoundland to devise what became known as the Atlantic Charter. Although the United States was not officially at war, the joint statement of "certain common principles" looked forward to the destruction of the Nazis and the creation of a peaceful postwar world order.

As danger in the Atlantic mounted, Hitler took a terrible gamble by launching a massive invasion of the Soviet Union on June 22, 1941. Until that violent rupture of the Nazi-Soviet pact, Americans generally thought no better of the Communists than they did of the Nazis. But now things were different. Churchill bluntly welcomed his old archenemy Joseph Stalin to the cause, stating that he would not hesitate to deal with the devil if Hitler invaded hell. Roosevelt hailed the diversion of German forces away from the hard-pressed British and quickly persuaded Congress to extend Lend-Lease to the Russians.

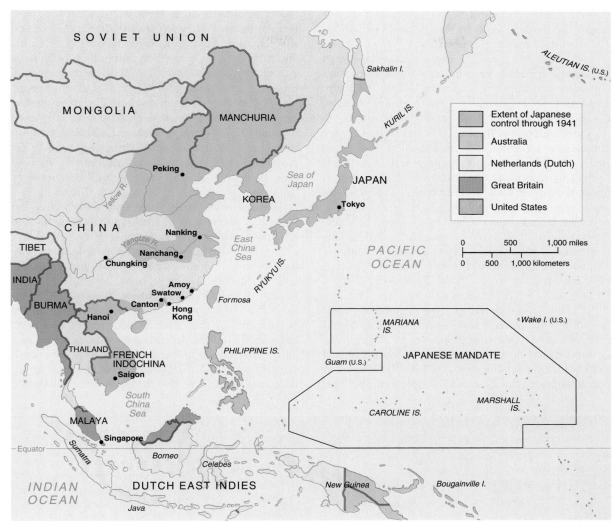

MAP 25.2
Japanese Aggression through 1941
Beginning with the invasion of Manchuria in 1931, Japan sought to force its imperialist control
over most of East Asia. Japanese aggression was driven by the need for raw materials for the
country's expanding industries and by the military government's devotion to martial honor.

War Comes to America

Despite the United States' primary concern with
Europe, the expansion of the Japanese empire made
the danger of war most immediate in Asia. The rising tide of Japanese imperialism clashed with U.S.
aspirations and commitments, especially in China.
America's China policy had been set in 1899 when
Secretary of State John Hay issued the Open Door
notes demanding that the United States have equal

access to the rich markets of China and that China
maintain its territorial integrity. But the island-
bound Japanese also wanted raw material and markets and their weak neighbor China was the natural
place to turn. The military invasion of Manchuria
in 1931 proved to be the opening salvo of continuing Japanese aggression in China. Each act of territorial conquest received a stern rebuke from the
Roosevelt administration, but toothless proclamations caused the Japanese little concern. They dis-

missed American opinion and marched forward under the banner "Asia for the Asians," which really meant China for the Japanese.

In 1940, the crisis in Asia escalated. Japan signed the Tripartite Pact, a defensive alliance with Germany and Italy. It also obtained from the Vichy government, the German puppet regime in France, the right to build airfields and station troops in northern Indochina. In 1941, U.S. naval intelligence cracked the Japanese code and learned that Tokyo had set its sights on the resource-rich Dutch East Indies. In response, the Roosevelt administration announced a complete trade embargo, which denied Japan access to essential oil and scrap iron. Roosevelt understood that he had given Japan a choice. Japan would either have to knuckle under, halt its aggression, and restore relations and trade with the United States, or it would have to find new sources of vital supplies, most likely by seizing British, French, and Dutch possessions in the Far East.

Despite apprehensions, the American public generally supported Roosevelt's increasingly bold responses to Japanese imperialism. In part, public opinion rested on ill-informed prejudices that had grown strong over the decades. Like the Roosevelt administration, the American people believed that Japan would shy away from war against the superior Americans. They felt secure, therefore, in using the economic boycott to force Japan out of China and reinstate the Open Door. Rather illogically, most Americans looked upon the Japanese as comically inferior, yet diabolically clever. "Made in Japan" was a term of derision for shoddy merchandise turned out by small, near-sighted people who lived in paper houses and substituted obedience to authority for creative thought. Throughout the 1930s, American newspapers and newsreels showed Japanese troops, sinister yet ludicrous in their baggy uniforms, swarming into wrecked Chinese cities.

Japanese nationalists were increasingly offended by American pressure against Japan's economic and territorial ambitions. In October 1941, a military clique took control from a more moderate group that believed Japan should avoid war with the United States. The new head of state, General Hideki Tojo, persuaded other leaders, including Emperor Hirohito, who originally called the idea "harebrained," that swift destruction of American bases in the Pacific would force a quick peace and leave Japan free to follow its destiny. Despite knowledge from decoded Japanese messages that an attack was imminent, the Roosevelt administration

PEARL HARBOR, DECEMBER 7, 1941
A rescue fireboat is hopelessly dwarfed by the enormous catastrophe of the battleship West Virginia *aflame and sinking at its mooring in Pearl Harbor. With the dramatic force of a vast seascape painting, this photograph was widely reproduced as a graphic indication of how great a crime the Japanese had committed.*
U.S. Army.

disastrously underestimated the reach of Japanese military power. Consequently, American forces were unprepared for the blow that struck the Pearl Harbor naval base in Hawaii on December 7, 1941. At dawn, a swarm of Japanese carrier-borne fighters, bombers, and torpedo planes found most of the American fleet at anchor and American planes neatly crowded together at Hickam Field. In two hours, the raiders sank or damaged all eight battleships of the fleet and disabled ten other ships. Three hundred and forty airplanes were wrecked and more than 3,500 Americans were killed or wounded.

Though the raid scored a stunning tactical success, in the larger sense it was a colossal blunder. Overnight, disagreement in the United States about foreign policy ended. Americans united in their commitment to war. Pearl Harbor also created a powerful rage for getting even. In his message to Congress declaring war, Roosevelt said:

> Yesterday, December 7, 1941—a date which will live in infamy—the United States of America was suddenly and deliberately attacked by naval and air forces of the Empire of Japan. . . . Always will we remember the character of the onslaught against us. No matter how long it may take us to overcome this premeditated invasion, the American people in their righteous might will win through to absolute victory.

Congress endorsed the message unanimously, except for Quaker pacifist Jeannette Rankin, who had also voted against U.S. entry into World War I. Although Hitler and Mussolini had not known about the Japanese attack in advance, Germany and Italy declared war against the United States on December 11.

Fighting Back: 1941–1943

Never had the United States faced such a desperate military situation or so staggering a task as it did in 1941. Hitler and his armies had conquered most of Europe, and the Japanese military machine was slicing through the Pacific with amazing speed. From the beginning, American concern had centered on the fascist menace in Europe. American policy held it necessary to save Britain and the Soviet Union from defeat so that the United States would not have to face Hitler alone. To that end, Roosevelt and his military commanders decided on a strategy that would concentrate on Germany first and then bring the nation's full armed might to bear on the Japanese. But before turning to Hitler, the United States and its allies would have to stop the Japanese advance through the Pacific. By 1943, the Allies had checked their enemies and were pushing them back. But the Allies could claim victory in neither Europe nor Asia. The "good war" would also be a long one.

Turning the Tide in the Pacific

Following Pearl Harbor, Japan's leading military genius, Admiral Isoroku Yamamoto, ordered an all-out offensive in the Pacific on the belief that, if his forces did not win quickly, Japan would lose the war to America's far greater manpower and resources. With lightning speed, the Japanese attacked American airfields in Manila in the Philippines and captured the American outposts of Guam and Wake Island. Singapore, the great British naval base in Malaya, surrendered in February 1942. Most of Burma had fallen by March. All that stood in the way of Japan's total domination of the southwestern Pacific were the Philippine Islands.

Though the raid on Pearl Harbor scored a stunning tactical success, in the larger sense it was a colossal blunder. Overnight, disagreement in the United States about foreign policy ended. Americans united in their commitment to war.

Under intense attack, General Douglas MacArthur, who commanded the Philippine defenses, retreated to fortifications on the Bataan Peninsula across the harbor from Manila. In March, MacArthur escaped to Australian command headquarters, leaving General Jonathan Wainwright to hold out as long as possible. When Wainwright surrendered the Corregidor fortress in May, Japanese soldiers marched the starved and ill survivors sixty-five miles to a concentration camp. Hundreds of Americans and as many as ten thousand Filipinos died en route. Of those who survived the Bataan Death March, sixteen thousand died within weeks of disease and mistreatment in the brutal prison camp. By summer 1942, the Japanese war machine had also conquered the oil-rich Dutch East Indies and was poised to strike at Australia and New Zealand.

The dark events that followed Pearl Harbor struck hard at American confidence. Jukeboxes may have been blaring "Goodbye, Mama, I'm Off to Yokohama," but the nation had learned that the soldiers of the Rising Sun were tough and fearless. They were highly trained sharpshooters carrying better weapons and more ammunition than American infantrymen, and they were prepared to fight to the death for honor and the emperor. On sea, the Japanese had larger, faster, heavier armored ships with bigger guns and more accurate torpedoes. And the four different kinds of airplanes that descended on Pearl Harbor outperformed anything the Americans could send up against them.

The string of unbroken Japanese victories caused Americans at home to worry about their own safety. A false report that Japanese fighter planes had been spotted near Los Angeles set off an antiaircraft barrage and inspired the commander of West Coast defenses to announce that "death and destruction [from enemy planes] are likely to come at any moment." Antiaircraft guns sprouted up and down the Pacific coast. In Hawaii, still shaken from the attack on Pearl Harbor, one vigilant citizen advised the authorities that he had spotted a dog on the beach "barking in Morse code to Japanese subs offshore." Americans needed some sort of success to take the edge off panic.

By April 1942, the United States was ready to strike back. The new offensive began with a demonstration to the Japanese that they were not safe anywhere, even in the imperial capital. A squadron of sixteen B-25 bombers under the command of Lieutenant Colonel James H. Doolittle launched a bombing raid on Tokyo from the deck of the carrier *Hornet*. The raid did little material damage but created an authentic hero to cheer Americans at home.

Much more substantive was a mighty two-pronged offensive that the Americans hoped would stop and then reverse the Japanese advance. The plan called for forces under the command of General MacArthur to move north from Australia and recapture the Philippines, while forces under Admiral Chester W. Nimitz sailed west from Hawaii and retook the Japanese-held islands in the mid-Pacific. Both offensives scored immediate victories. On May 7, 1942, in the Coral Sea just north of Australia, planes from the *Lexington* and *Yorktown* stopped the Japanese fleet that was sailing around the coast of New Guinea.

The Battle of the Coral Sea was a prelude to an even more significant encounter. Learning that the Japanese were sending an invasion force against Midway Island, an outpost guarding the Hawaiian

Islands, Admiral Nimitz moved his carriers and cruisers into the Central Pacific. In a wild melee that raged from June 3 to June 6, American planes sank four Japanese carriers, a heavy cruiser, and two destroyers, while losing only one carrier and a destroyer. The Battle of the Coral Sea and the Battle of Midway marked the high tide of Japanese power in the Pacific. The Americans had stopped the Japanese advance. They began the long, bloody march to Tokyo.

For Admiral Yamamoto, the end came in April 1943 when he was on his way to one of his remaining air force units on the island of Bougainville in the Solomon Islands. Having intercepted a message describing Yamamoto's plan, Nimitz went after his nemesis. Swift P-38 fighters rushed out of ambush to send Yamamoto's plane down in flames. Deprived of its naval genius, the Japanese navy was even more vulnerable to American power.

The Campaign in Europe

Once the Japanese offensive in the Pacific was halted, American attention focused on defeating Germany. In the dark months after Pearl Harbor, the war news from Europe was as depressing as that from the Pacific. While imperial Japanese forces were spreading through Asia, Hitler's army smashed deep into the Soviet Union and prepared for an invasion of Britain. American efforts to come to the rescue had first to contend with the German attempt, as in World War I, to starve Britain into submission by destroying its seaborne lifeline. Advances in technology meant that the U-boats were far more effective than in World War I, and at first German submarines sank American ships faster than they could be built. The toll eventually reached 4,786 merchant ships, nearly double the number in World War I. Submarines also exacted a high military cost. Before the war ended, almost 200 warships became victims of torpedoes. The human toll reached 40,000 Allied seamen and almost as many Germans who perished in their 781 stricken U-boats.

The Germans profited from the fact that the Allies had done little to prepare for another battle on the Atlantic. The British had not laid down mines to defend coastal waters nor armed merchant vessels. Because Americans did not institute blackouts until the spring of 1942, shorelines brilliantly illuminated merchant targets. Using only 6 U-boats, the Germans sank 82 ships off the American East Coast and more than 200 additional ships in the waters around Bermuda and the Caribbean islands. Bathers at Virginia Beach in the bright sunshine of June 15, 1942, watched aghast as a U-boat on the surface sank two merchant vessels. Soon afterward the beach was awash with oily debris and bodies.

Until 1943, the war in the Atlantic remained in doubt and the British Isles hung by a precarious thread over the cruel sea. But with the use of newly invented effective radar detectors and production of sufficient destroyer escorts for merchant vessels, the United States gained the ability to move massive amounts of supplies to England and to the Soviet ports of Murmansk and Archangel. The battle of the Atlantic had been won.

While imperial Japanese forces were spreading through Asia, Hitler's army smashed deep into the Soviet Union and prepared for an invasion of Britain.

The big question was how to return to the European continent, which was dominated by the formidable German war machine. In the west, a buildup of Nazi military might threatened an invasion of Great Britain across the English Channel, and in the east two hundred Nazi armies devoured vast Soviet territory and millions of soldiers and citizens. Soviet Premier Joseph Stalin begged the Allies to open a second, western front against the Nazis to divert German divisions away from his bloody doorstep before they delivered a final, crushing blow. The issue was where the Allies should open a second front against Hitler. Stalin strongly urged an immediate and massive invasion of France across the English Channel, but Churchill favored something smaller, perhaps a Mediterranean target such as Europe's "soft underbelly," the Balkans. Roosevelt worried about a plan that would merely "peck on the periphery," but ultimately he backed an invasion of North Africa first. Since the United States' rapidly expanding military force was clearly the vital element in any western front, Roosevelt's wishes prevailed.

In October 1942, at El-Alamein in Egypt, the British halted General Erwin Rommel's Nazi soldiers who were driving on Egypt and the Suez Canal. In November, the Americans made their long-awaited landing in French Morocco under the leadership of the supreme commander of American forces in Europe, General Dwight D. Eisenhower. General George Patton, the ablest U.S. tank commander, joined with the British in pursuit of the Axis armies. In May

1943, Allied armies closed the jaws of a gigantic vice on the last German and Italian troops in North Africa. The North African campaign cost the Axis dearly—some 350,000 dead and captured—and reopened the Mediterranean to Allied shipping. But in Stalin's view, North Africa was a miserable excuse for a second front, for it diverted only 15 German divisions from the Soviet Union, not the 40 Stalin wanted.

As the North African campaign unfolded, Roosevelt arrived at the Moroccan city of Casablanca in January 1943 to confer with his fellow Allied leaders. Joining him were Winston Churchill and General Charles de Gaulle, the leader of the Free French government in exile. Stalin, preoccupied with the desperate defense of Stalingrad at the easternmost penetration of the German advance, was an absent but watchful partner. Pledged to rid the world of the Axis menace, the Allied leaders announced that they would insist on "unconditional surrender." Of equal importance was their decision to postpone the cross-channel invasion of France. The decision meant that the Soviet Union would continue to absorb the brunt of the Nazi attack. Before the war ended, Soviet casualties would reach approximately 20 million, far more than those of any other nation. Instead of invading France, Roosevelt decided to strike Italy, while troop strength was building up in England for the crucial return to France. The plan was for Allied troops to invade Sicily first and then drive quickly up the boot of Italy, knocking the Axis's junior partner out of the war.

On July 10, 1943, a combined American and British amphibious operation, the largest in history, landed 160,000 troops in Sicily. The badly equipped Italian defenders, many of whom had lost their will to fight in the disastrous North African campaign, quickly withdrew to the mainland. The Allied capture of Sicily marked the end for Mussolini. The Fascist Grand Council expelled him from power. In September, the Allies invaded the Italian mainland. Five days later, the Italian government surrendered unconditionally. But the Germans rushed additional divisions into the country and seized Rome. The military campaign in Italy became a war of liberation against German occupation.

Success came hard against the Germans, who waited in sophisticated fortifications atop the mountainous Italian terrain. Not until June 1944, after a long and bloody campaign, did massive firepower finally breach the German lines and enable Allied forces to liberate Rome. From then to the end of the war, the Allies struggled against German

AN ITALIAN TOWN SURRENDERS
In 1943 the Roosevelt administration authorized a special unit of "combat artists" to present an "in-
tegrated picture of war in all its phases." Edward Reep, a trained infantryman as well as an artist,
achieved rare authenticity from his own combat experience. Contorted body postures and tilted build-
ings express the frenzied moment when Italian partisans celebrated the liberation of their town and
terrified German soldiers ran to Reep's invading unit to escape revenge.
Courtesy U.S. Army Center of Military History.

mountain defenses in northern Italy. The Italian campaign was the costliest of the war to the American infantry. Eventually it diverted 25 German divisions that might otherwise have been thrown against the Russians or a second front in France. Still, it was not the all-out second front that an increasingly embittered Stalin demanded.

The War at Home

The experience of Americans during World War II was unlike that of other peoples around the world. For millions of French, German, Russian, Chinese, and Japanese, the war meant air raids, invasion, and occupation, devastation and terror, cities and countryside turned into battlefields. In the United States,

no physical destruction occurred, no territorial lines were redrawn, no governments fell, no one starved, and no civilians lost their lives in the fighting. Still, World War II changed the nation. Inevitably, a war as vast and as long as World War II disrupted the traditional social patterns it sought to defend. Total war meant that millions of troops went to unheard of places to face unimagined dangers. Total war also meant the mobilization of the entire home front to serve the nation's armed forces abroad.

Conversion of the economy to war purposes drew millions away from their roots to seize opportunities they never had before in places where they never expected to live. Women welding in the shipyards in California, men building tanks in the factories of Detroit, and children everywhere stripping scarce tinfoil from empty cigarette packs—all felt the impact of the war and were changed by it.

From Reform to Recovery

There is partial truth in the observation that Adolf Hitler was more responsible for ending the depression in the United States than was Franklin Roosevelt. The nation's military buildup of 1940–1941 did more to revive industry and reduce unemployment than had any New Deal program. But preparedness spending confirmed the Roosevelt administration's deficit-spending approach. It simply showed that Roosevelt's insistence on trying to balance the budget while defeating the depression was naive. In 1939, the federal budget was $9 billion. By 1945, it had grown to $100 billion. When Keynesian economics were allowed to work, the nation pulled out of the economic doldrums. But it did not do so overnight. In 1940, some 14.6 percent of the nation's workforce was unemployed. In 1941, when defense industries were starting to hum, unemployment still stood at nearly 10 percent. But after Pearl Harbor, war work at home and military service abroad virtually ended unemployment.

By 1941, there was no longer much talk about reform. The New Deal had run out of ideas and had been hampered by effective conservative opposition years before. Now the last thoughts of reform gave way to war. As Roosevelt said later, he had given up being "Dr. New Deal" in order to become "Dr. Win the War." The nation had entered World War I in the context of progressivism and its idealist expectations. But the U.S. entry into World War II came in the context of the depression and was less romantic than practical. The feeling was that there was a job to be done. Industry had to be converted to wartime production and an army and navy had to be raised. Preparedness campaigns before the war had put some men in uniform, but not enough. And the Lend-Lease program had begun to transform American industry, but industry remained far from a wartime footing.

The Roosevelt administration oversaw a miracle of production. The president brought to Washington businessmen from private industry to carry out the swiftest and fullest possible mobilization of the nation's productive capacity. These "dollar-a-year men" (so called because they served without pay) headed the rapidly multiplying war production agencies. The federal government invested billions in factories, military bases, power plants, and transportation facilities. The huge sums flowing into California shipyards and aircraft factories transformed the sleepy western state into one of the nation's most dynamic. Despite confusion and chaos, the country's economic achievement was staggering. The United States produced 275,000 airplanes during the war and by 1945 was launching a new ship every twenty-four hours. The United States not only produced what it needed to fight the Axis but also supplied the British, French, and Russians with a large part of what they required. By 1942, American production equaled that of Germany, Italy, and Japan combined. By 1944, it doubled Axis production.

Almost as impressive was the nation's mobilization of its armed forces. Draft boards registered 31 million men, of whom 10 million were inducted into service. In addition, more than 5 million men and women volunteered. When the war ended, 10,400,000 had served in the army, 3,900,000 in the navy, 600,000 in the marines, and 240,000 in the coast guard.

There is partial truth in the observation that Adolf Hitler was more responsible for ending the depression in the United States than was Franklin Roosevelt.

The war boom favored large businesses and farms. In agriculture, family farms declined and tenant farmers virtually disappeared. The change was dramatically demonstrated by the migration of black farmworkers to urban centers, both North and South. By 1950, the census showed that only 115,000 African Americans remained on the land out of a total of 1,406,000 who had lived on farms when the war started. In general, however, agriculture prospered. To feed both Americans and Allies, American farmers increased production in 1942 by 25 percent and continued to increase it at that rate for the rest of the war. In business, large firms did better than small ones, but by 1943, business profits in general had soared well beyond those of 1929.

The war also restored prosperity to American workers. Rather than too little work for too many workers, as in the depression, the war years witnessed a booming economy and labor shortages. With more than 15 million adults in the military, new workers—the old, the young, and especially women—were brought into the labor force. The cost of living increased 30 percent from 1941 to 1945, while weekly earnings of workers employed in manufacturing increased 70 percent. But civilians

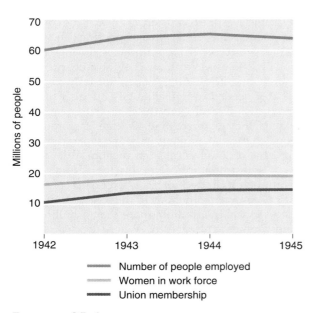

FIGURE 25.1
World War II and the Economy, 1942–1945
The end of the Depression followed by war mobilization sent employment and union membership to high levels that continued into peacetime. Women lost many jobs in heavy industry after the war, but their increased numbers in the total work force were sustained by the strong economy that followed.

on the home front also felt the pinch of war. Government management of the economy meant a system of wage and price controls that hurt some and aided others. Production for war meant that some items—automobiles, washing machines, refrigerators—were no longer being produced. The government also instituted a system of rationing of many basic items. Coffee was rationed because of the decline in ocean shipping, canned goods because of insufficient tin, and shoes because of the needs of soldiers and sailors. The government also rationed gasoline, which was plentiful, in order to save rubber tires, which were not. Americans were cautioned with the slogan "Hitler Smiles When You Waste Miles." Ration books were a tremendous bother, but they did not symbolize real privation.

Although the profits of war were not evenly distributed and rationing was a daily aggravation, Americans on the home front rallied around the war effort in unprecedented unity. Economic gains were broadly enough distributed so that the harsh rhetoric that characterized relations between rich and poor during the 1930s largely disappeared.

Moreover, after Pearl Harbor, Americans were convinced that they were engaged in a necessary war against evil regimes. With few dissenters, vigilantes rarely attacked other Americans in the name of patriotism. Wanting to avoid hysteria and hatred, Roosevelt opposed the creation of a high-powered propaganda campaign such as Wilson's during World War I. The government did not forgo control of news and opinion, however. It exercised censorship, especially of bad news from the war zone. But with one great and tragic exception, the nation survived the war without a wholesale violation of citizens' civil rights.

Political Crosscurrents

With the nation enjoying full employment and the need for New Deal programs waning, the Roosevelt administration had difficulty holding its governing coalition together. Resentment over price controls and shortages of rationed goods, white indignation over blacks leaving their subordinate place on southern farms, and dismay that the war was not going as well as it should provoked discontent with the Democratic administration. Moreover, in the congressional elections of 1942, Democrats were denied considerable support from soldiers and defense workers who were unable to cast their usual Democratic votes because the war had taken them away from the hometowns where they were registered. As a consequence, voter turnout was low in 1942, and Republicans gained forty-four seats in the House and nine in the Senate.

Republican opponents saw the war years as an opportunity to roll back New Deal reforms in favor of traditional American free enterprise values. The conservative coalition of Republicans and southern Democrats succeeded in abolishing several New Deal agencies in 1942 and 1943, including the Work Projects Administration and the Civilian Conservation Corps. But the Democratic administration did not sit idly by while Republicans dismantled their work of the 1930s. By persuading states to ease residency requirements and Congress to guarantee absentee ballots for servicemen, they arranged to bring scattered members of the New Deal coalition back into the fold.

Roosevelt also made strategic changes in preparation for the presidential election of 1944. Although exhausted and ill, he announced that he would run for an unprecedented fourth term. "All that is within me," he declared, "cries out to go back to my home on the Hudson River. . . . But as a good soldier . . . I will accept and serve." Convinced that many Americans had soured on liberal reform, Roosevelt replaced Vice President Henry Wallace, an outspoken progressive, with a more politically viable running mate, Senator Harry S. Truman of Missouri. A reliable party man from a border state, Truman seemed safe to urban Democratic leaders and to southerners nervous about challenges to segregation.

The Republicans, confident of riding the strong conservative upsurge to the White House, nominated the governor of New York, Thomas E. Dewey. Dewey was handicapped in the campaign by his general agreement with much of the New Deal and with Roosevelt's handling of the war. Dewey's chief advantage was Roosevelt's failing health, but the Republicans

OWI PROPAGANDA POSTER
The Office of War Information mobilized art and propaganda in many ways to connect the home front with the battlefield. Though little fat actually went from the frying pan into the firing line, this poster is a visually startling example of attempts to remind people that even the simplest acts could contribute to the war effort.
Library of Congress.

underestimated the unwillingness of the American people to change presidents at the height of a foreign war. Roosevelt's victory was his narrowest (53.5 percent of the popular vote), but it assured him of four more years in the White House, if he lived.

Women, Family, and the War

World War II meant astonishing changes in women's lives. Public attitudes about working-women changed overnight. During the depression, workingwomen were often accused of taking a husband's or father's job, but with the war, government and industry actively recruited women. Old ideas were not dead, of course. Women found themselves caught between the idealized role of the girl left behind to keep the home fires burning and the need to take up in the workplace where the warriors had left off. However uncomfortable their ambivalent situation, millions of women entered the workforce during the war, increasing by more than half the number of workingwomen. Three-fourths of the women entering were married and nearly four million had children. Women who were already working for wages often quit jobs as domestic servants and waitresses for war work at better pay.

The ambivalence for women between their place at home and in the factory showed in the fact that the average age for marriage went down to just over twenty and the birthrate rose, while at the same time women increased their presence in industry, especially in war production. By 1944, some 18 million women had jobs, 50 percent more than in 1939. The symbol for women performing what was traditionally men's work was "Rosie the Riveter," who according to a popular song was busy "making history working for victory." *Chicago Tribune* columnist Mike Royko remembered: "My sister became Rosie the Riveter. She put a bandanna on her head every day and went down to this organ company that had been converted to war work. There was my sister in slacks. It became more than work. There was a sense of mission about it. Her husband was Over There." The nation celebrated these women who loaded shells, packed parachutes, and built tanks, ships, and airplanes, and the women were rightfully proud of their accomplishments.

Women were often amazed at the salaries they earned. A mountain woman remembered her first job after the depression at a munitions plant in Viola, Kentucky. "We made the fabulous sum of thirty-two dollars a week," she said. "To us it was just an absolute miracle. Before that, we made nothing." A black woman from Clarksville, Tennessee, went to Los Angeles to work as a maid but ended up working in the aircraft industry at $40 a week. "When I left Tennessee," she remembered, "I was only makin' two-fifty a week, so that was quite a jump." Yet women's weekly wages averaged about $31, men made $54, a discrepancy reflecting women's more menial jobs and lower seniority.

World War II meant astonishing changes in women's lives. Public attitudes about working women changed overnight. By 1944, some 18 million women had jobs, 50 percent more than in 1939.

Alongside women in the civilian workforce stood 350,000 women who joined the Nurse's Corps and the newly created military units the army WACs, navy Waves, coast guard Spars, and the Women's Marine Corps. Women also served as pilots in the WASPs (Women Air Service Pilots). While barred from combat duty, women worked at nearly every noncombat assignment. Women in the military never achieved a secure place within the staunchly male system, but the Nurse's Corps, drawing on a respected tradition of service in America's wars, gained officer rank and attracted many recruits.

Despite the war's dynamic social changes, most women remained in the home and worked only part-time or not at all. The yearning in the midst of war for the peacetime joys of security and family, felt mutually by isolated women and fighting men, reinforced traditional attitudes. Those attitudes became more practical, too. With men no longer unemployed and wages up, family survival depended less on women earning money outside the home. The increase in consumer wealth also nurtured hopes for a comfortable home and the ability to raise children in vastly better circumstances than during the depression. While most women enjoyed the economic and social freedom that came with work outside the home, a substantial number saw work as necessary and temporary, something to set aside when the men came home.

Not all trends pointed in the direction of middle-class stability, however. The absence of millions of able-bodied young men left many families without a father in the house or traveling from one military base to the next. Drastic housing shortages near military installations and in cities where war work

boomed forced many families into poor living conditions. When one woman, who was fourteen years old in 1941, was asked about her wartime experience, she replied: "What I feel most about the war, it disrupted my family. That really chokes me up, makes me feel very sad that I lost that. On December 6, 1941, I was playing with paper dolls. . . . After Pearl Harbor, I never played dolls again."

The war took a toll on families. The number of marriages and the birthrate rose, but so too did illegitimacy and divorce. Teenagers encountered an unstable mix of opportunity and danger as they increasingly entered the workforce. The absence of older men also meant that young people had less guidance than usual. Juvenile delinquency, especially among girls, increased dramatically. Other children, however, pitched in and gained the satisfaction of

FEMALE DEFENSE WORKER
The war effort brought persons and activities together in unlikely ways, leading to unexpected outcomes. In this photo, for example, the Army magazine, Yank, *sought to boost morale by presenting a defense worker as pin-up girl. No one could know that the young propeller technician, nineteen year-old Norma Jean Baker Dougherty, would later remake herself as the most glamorous of movie stars, Marilyn Monroe.*
David Conover Images © Norma Jean Enterprises, a division of 733548 Ontario Limited.

being part of the war effort. Boy scouts, for example, sponsored scrap drives collecting iron, steel, brass, bronze, tin, and wastepaper. Wartime disruption redoubled the yearning for a stable, secure life when the war ended and the veterans came home.

Prejudice and the War

Fighting against Nazism and its ideology of Aryan racial supremacy under the banner of democracy forced Americans to examine prejudice in their own society. No one needed to instruct Asian Americans, Mexican Americans, African Americans, or Native Americans about the chasm between assertions of freedom and equality and the realities of prejudice and discrimination. War forced minority Americans to consider what they owed their country. On his way to the European front, a young Mexican American soldier reflected on his dilemma. "Why fight for America when you have not been treated as an American?" he asked. He answered that America was where he had been born, his home. "All we wanted," he decided, "was a chance to prove how loyal and American we were."

African American leader W. E. B. Du Bois defined World War II as a War for Racial Equality and a struggle for "democracy not only for white folks but for yellow, brown, and black."

Minorities rallied to the war effort as Americans, but winning the war meant more than just defeating Hitler and Tojo. African American leader W. E. B. Du Bois defined World War II as a "war for racial equality" and a struggle for "democracy not only for white folks but for yellow, brown, and black." More than 13,000 Chinese Americans and more than 25,000 Native Americans fought in the armed forces. Mexican Americans feared that the war would mean deportation; instead, more than 200,000 laborers were imported from Mexico to cultivate American crops in the federal government's *"bracero"* program. Some 500,000 Mexican Americans served in the U.S. armed forces, but even while they were fighting for democracy abroad, they suffered racial violence at home. In 1943, "zoot suit" riots exploded in Los Angeles when hundreds of white servicemen

DOUBLE V BUTTON
The Double V became African Americans' special version of the official "V for victory" symbol. Thousands of these buttons were worn as a reminder that both the Axis powers and racial discrimination should surrender unconditionally. Private Collection.

claiming they were punishing draft-dodgers, chased and beat young Chicano men who dressed in distinctive broad-shouldered, peg-legged suits. Racial prejudice, sometimes severe, remained in place to mock the nation's democratic war aims. Japanese Americans especially found their fellow Americans less accepting, not more. European Jews, who knew from experience that racism could become genocide, searched desperately for a haven from the horrors of the Holocaust but found small comfort in the United States.

African Americans and the Double V

As they had done in World War I, African Americans regarded the war as a chance to prove their patriotism and advance their condition. Such aspirations squared perfectly with official proclamations of the war as a fight for democracy. In a letter to the Southern Negro Youth Congress, Roosevelt declared that blacks were in the war "not only to defend America but . . . to establish a universal freedom under which a new basis of security and prosperity can be established for all—regardless of station, race, or creed." His opponent for the presidency in 1940,

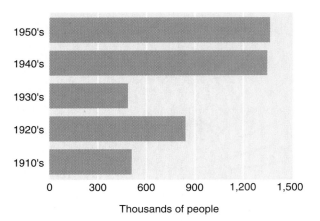

FIGURE 25.2
Black Migration from the South, 1910–1960
Spurred by desire for better economic and social condi-
tions, African Americans after 1910 headed north in un-
precedented numbers. The flow grew to a flood in the
1940s and 1950s, driven by the availability of defense
work in the North and the decline of the sharecropping
system in the South.

Wendell Willkie, pressed the issue even more insistently. The United States, Willkie stated, could not justly eliminate "the forces of imperialism abroad and maintain any form of imperialism at home." Encouraged by signs of sympathetic concern, the Pittsburgh *Courier*, a leading black newspaper, rejoiced that, though "war may be hell for some," it appeared ready to "open up the portals of heaven for us."

When the American defense industry moved into high gear in 1940–1941, however, African Americans learned that old discriminatory patterns pervaded the arsenal of democracy. Black organizations sent a barrage of petitions to Congress and the White House demanding that the federal government require companies receiving defense contracts to integrate their workforces. In the summer of 1941, black labor leader A. Philip Randolph, who had opposed World War I as a white man's cause, finally got Roosevelt's attention. As head of the Brotherhood of Sleeping Car Porters, a union made up overwhelmingly of blacks, he promised that 100,000 marchers would descend on Washington if the president did not eliminate discrimination in defense industries.

Alarmed at the prospect of such an embarrassment and persuaded by Eleanor Roosevelt's argument for justice, the president overcame his nervousness about offending old southern and union allies. He issued Executive Order 8802 directing defense contractors to hire blacks and whites on an equal basis and establishing a Committee on Fair Employment Practices to investigate violations of the order. Randolph called the march off, and civil rights champions hailed the historic significance of the first direct presidential intervention on behalf of black civil rights.

Actual progress developed slowly, however. Five and a half million blacks abandoned the rural South in the 1940s and flooded into industrial cities, making African Americans a predominantly urban population for the first time. Early black migrants discovered that industry policies barred them from many prospective jobs, skilled and unskilled. The rapidly expanding aircraft industry provided the most striking example of exclusion. Aircraft manufacture nationwide included only 240 black employees at the start of the war. Douglas Aircraft, a major supplier, had only 10 black workers. Much of organized labor, particularly the older AFL craft unions, defended exclusionary practices. Eighteen major unions, including such vital participants in the defense industry as the machinists, iron shipbuilders, and railway workers, had explicit bans against black membership.

In time, however, severe labor shortages and government pressure opened up defense plants to African American workers. Black unemployment dropped by about 80 percent during the war, and the percentage of blacks in the defense industry doubled to a level almost equal to the percentage of blacks in the general population. Earnings and union membership went up impressively. The end result, however, was not enough to wipe out centuries of discrimination. By the end of the war, the average income of black families was only half that of white families.

While migration into industrial cities improved African Americans' economic fortunes, it also led to racial friction. Racial antagonism boiled over in the hot summer of 1943. That year, there were 242 racial outbreaks in forty-seven different cities, far surpassing the total of 26 riots in the grim Red scare year of 1919. Worst of all were the two days of mayhem in Detroit. The city was coping with more than half a million newcomers, more than 50,000 of them black, who had come mostly to seek jobs at auto factories converted to war production and at the vast new Willow Run aircraft plant. Conflict between whites and blacks at a city park ignited a race war that saw whites smash their way with clubs through black neighborhoods and blacks retaliate by destroying and looting white-owned businesses in their neighborhoods. In the end, scores of persons suffered injury and thirty-four died, including twenty-five African Americans.

But race relations on the home front were not uniformly dismal. The National Association for the Advancement of Colored People (NAACP) launched the "Double V" campaign—victory at home and abroad—and attacked racism on a broad front. In 1942, civil rights activists who wanted to move more swiftly than the NAACP founded a new organization, the Congress of Racial Equality (CORE), that attacked segregation vigorously. CORE took direct action by organizing sit-ins against Jim Crow restaurants and theaters. By war's end, both the NAACP and CORE could point to large memberships and significant triumphs.

The military was no more free of discrimination than was the home front. Secretary of War Henry Stimson, who presided firmly over the war effort, opposed any change in the segregation of blacks and whites into separate units and declared that the military effort should not serve as a "sociological laboratory." In 1942, Stimson fumed in his diary about what he deemed the absurdly presumptuous claims of black reformers: "What these foolish leaders of the colored race are seeking is at bottom social equality." Top military brass echoed Stimson's sentiments and worked to keep African Americans in segregated units that were restricted to menial tasks. "Experiments to meet the wishes and demands of the champions of every race and creed for the solution of their problems," the army adjutant general's office warned, "are a danger to efficiency, discipline and morale, and would result in ultimate defeat."

Denied desegregated armed forces, blacks joined anyway, and by the end of the war nearly one million African American men and women had served. Segregated practices loosened as the war progressed. Blacks were trained as pilots for the first time, served on warships with white sailors, and saw extensive combat duty in the ground war in Europe and the Pacific. Yet military facilities remained segregated, and the Red Cross even segregated by race the blood it supplied to treat battlefield casualties.

In 1944, the Swedish sociologist Gunnar Myrdal in his classic report on race in America, *The American Dilemma*, concluded that "not since Reconstruction, has there been more reason to anticipate fundamental changes in American race relations." Indeed, World War II marked a watershed in the history of black Americans. Their wartime move upward inspired hope and shaped the tactics that blacks would use thereafter in the quest for rights and opportunity. But much of that battle lay ahead. Perhaps nothing more poignantly captured the reality of wartime race relations than the moment when Lloyd Brown, a black soldier caught in the dusty heat of a Kansas summer day, gazed past the restaurant owner denying him entry and saw a row of German prisoners of war enjoying their lunch at the counter.

The Plight of Japanese Americans

World War II did not witness a repetition of the madness, hysteria, and viciousness that had characterized the home front during World War I. Few questioned the war, and there was little to provoke repression. Americans were worried about espionage, however. Walls were plastered with slogans such as "Loose lips sink ships" and "Enemy agents are always near; if you don't talk, they won't hear." But the government engaged in no high-powered propaganda campaign to whip Americans into a frenzy against its enemies and mounted no wholesale attack on civil liberties.

There was one major exception—the drastic violation of the rights of Japanese Americans. Americans of Japanese ancestry were the only minority group to lose ground during the war. From the time of their first entry into the country in significant numbers in the 1890s, mainly to settle on the West Coast, the Japanese had encountered hostility as economic competitors and intruders in a "white man's country." Although they were law-abiding and successful in small businesses and farming, white prejudice prevailed. In 1907, the Japanese government was forced to accept a humiliating "gentleman's agreement" that reduced the numbers of new Japanese immigrants in exchange for the right of Asians to attend public schools in California.

In 1924, the federal government went even further by declaring that Japanese immigrants were "aliens ineligible to citizenship." In rejecting an appeal that the law violated the right of all citizens to equal protection, the Supreme Court declared that the Fourteenth Amendment conferring that right applied only to whites and ex-slaves. As intended, the ruling halted the influx of Japanese and left unnaturalized Japanese immigrants (called "Issei") permanently in limbo as residents who could never become citizens. The absurdity of the situation was heightened by the fact that the Issei's children ("Nisei") were automatically citizens by virtue of having been born in the United States.

Japanese Internment

*A*ngrily determined that the bombing of Pearl Harbor would not be followed by more sneak attacks, military and political leaders on the West Coast targeted persons of Japanese descent—alien and citizen alike—as potential saboteurs. Early in 1942, General John DeWitt, commander of the Western Defense Command, persuaded President Franklin Roosevelt to issue an executive order authorizing the removal of the Japanese. Subsequently, some 110,000 Japanese Americans were confined to relocation camps in remote areas, surrounded by barbed wire and armed guards. DeWitt's recommendation expressed concern for military security within racist conceptions long used to curb Asian immigration.

DOCUMENT 1. Final Recommendations of the Commanding General, Western Defense Command and Fourth Army, Submitted to the Secretary of War

February 14, 1942

Memorandum for the Secretary of War.

Subject: Evacuation of Japanese and Other Subversive Persons from the Pacific Coast.

1. In presenting a recommendation for the evacuation of Japanese and other subversive persons from the Pacific Coast, the following facts have been considered:

    a. Mission of the Western Defense Command and Fourth Army.

       (1) Defense of the Pacific Coast of the Western Defense Command, as extended, against attacks by sea, land, or air;

       (2) Local protection of establishment and communications vital to the National Defense for which adequate defense cannot be provided by local civilian authorities.

    b. Brief Estimate of the Situation.

       (1) . . . The following are possible and probable enemy activities: . . .

          (a) Naval attack on shipping on coastal waters;

          (b) Naval attack on coastal cities and vital installations;

          (c) Air raids on vital installations, particularly within two hundred miles of the coast;

          (d) Sabotage of vital installations throughout the Western Defense Command.

Hostile Naval and air raids will be assisted by enemy agents signaling from the coastline and the vicinity thereof; and by supplying and otherwise assisting enemy vessels and by sabotage.

In the war in which we are now engaged racial affinities are severed by migration. The Japanese race is an enemy race and while many second and third generation Japanese born on United States soil, possessed of United States citizenship, have become "Americanized," the racial strains are undiluted. To conclude otherwise is to expect that children born of white parents on Japanese soil sever all racial affinity and become loyal Japanese subjects, ready to fight and, if necessary, to die for Japan in a war against the nation of their parents. . . .

It, therefore, follows that along the vital Pacific Coast over 112,000 potential enemies, of Japanese extraction, are at large today. There are indications that these are organized and ready for concerted action at a favorable opportunity. The very fact that no sabotage has taken place to date is a disturbing and confirming indication that such action will be taken. . . .

*I*mprisoned in bleak surroundings far from home, Japanese internees were prey to despair and bitterness. Looking back after forty years, Kazue Yamane recalled her confinement as a disturbing and baffling experience.

DOCUMENT 2. An Oral History of Life in the Japanese American Detention Camps

In April 1942, my husband and I and our two children left for camp, and my mother-in-law and father-in-law came about a month later. I wasn't afraid, but I kept asking in my mind, how could they? This is impossible. Even today I still think it was a nightmarish thing. I cannot reconcile myself to the fact that I had to go, that I was interned, that I was segregated, that I was taken away, even though it goes back forty years. . . .

I was separated from my husband; he went to the Santa Fe, New Mexico, camp. All our letters were censored; all our letters were cut in parts and all that. So we were not too sure what messages was getting through and not getting through, but I do know that I informed him many times of his mother's condition. He should have been allowed to come back to see her, because I thought she wouldn't live too long, but they never did allow him to come back, even for her funeral. They did not allow that. I learned that a lot of the messages didn't get to him; they were crossed out. I now have those letters with me.

In 1944 I was left with his parents and our kids. But I had no time to think of what was going to happen because my child was always sick and I had been quite sick. . . .

My son knew what was going on, and he too had many times asked me why . . . you know, why? why? Of course, I had no explanation why this was happening to us. . . .

Forcibly removed from the tension between his life as a student at the University of California at Berkeley and his unassimilated family, Charles Kikuchi sought in his prison camp diary to make sense of the internment and to judge where it would lead.

Document 3. The Kikuchi Diary

December 7, 1941, Berkeley, California
Pearl Harbor. We are at war! Jesus Christ, the Japs bombed Hawaii and the entire fleet has been sunk. I just can't believe it. I don't know what in the hell is going to happen to us, but we will all be called into the Army right away.

. . . The next five years will determine the future of the Nisei. They are now at the crossroads. Will they be able to take it or will they go under? If we are ever going to prove our Americanism, this is the time. The Anti-Jap feeling is bound to rise to hysterical heights, and it is most likely that the Nisei will be included as Japs. I wanted to go to San Francisco tonight, but Pierre says I am crazy. He says it's best we stick on campus. In any event, we can't remain on the fence, and a positive approach must be taken if we are to have a place in fulfilling the Promise of America. I think the U.S. is in danger of going Fascist too, or maybe Socialist. . . .

I don't know what to think or do. Everybody is in a daze.

April 30,1942, Berkeley
Today is the day that we are going to get kicked out of Berkeley. It certainly is degrading. . . .

I'm supposed to see my family at Tanforan as Jack told me to give the same family number. I wonder how it is going to be living with them as I haven't done this for years and years? I should have gone over to San Francisco and evacuated with them, but I had a last final to take. I understand that we are going to live in the horse stalls. I hope that the Army has the courtesy to remove the manure first. . . .

July 14, 1942
Marie, Ann, Mitch, Jimmy, Jack, and myself got into a long discussion about how much democracy meant to us as individuals. Mitch says that he would even go in the army and die for it, in spite of the fact that he knew he would be kept down. Marie said that although democracy was not perfect, it was the only system that offered any hope for a future, if we could fulfill its destinies. Jack was a little more skeptical. He even suggested that we [could] be in such grave danger that we would then realize that we were losing something. Where this point was he could not say. I said that this was what happened in France and they lost all. Jimmy suggested that the colored races of the world had reason to feel despair and mistrust the white man because of the past experiences. . . .

In reviewing the four months here, the chief value I got out of this forced evacuation was the strengthening of the family bonds. I never knew my family before this and this was the first chance that I have had to really get acquainted. . . .

Document 1. *Final Recommendations,* report by General John Lesesne Dewitt to the United States Secretary of War, February 14, 1942.

Document 2. John Tateishi, *And Justice for All.* Copyright ©1984 by John Tateishi. Reprinted by permission of Random House, Inc.

Document 3. John Modell, ed., *The Kikuchi Diary: Chronicle from an American Concentration Camp,* 43, 51, 183, 252. Copyright 1973 by the Board of Trustees of the University of Illinois. Used with the permission of the University of Illinois Press.

Hostility did not end with the cessation of immigration, however. In the 1930s, the *Los Angeles Times* led a fresh anti-Japanese campaign, arguing that Japanese Americans were still a threat because they would multiply endlessly and then, closed off within their sinister enclaves, conspire to outcompete "real" Americans. The argument made no demographic or economic sense. In 1940, there were only 127,000 Japanese Americans. They were concentrated in agriculture in California, and their role in the economy was to provide cheap food, exactly what white workers, managers, and homemakers should have hailed. What little tolerance there was evaporated in the storm of hatred that followed the attack on Pearl Harbor.

The idea that the Japanese were unassimilable, aliens who were forever loyal to the land of their ancestors, provided an excuse to regard them as a subversive threat. Even though a military survey concluded that Japanese Americans posed no danger, General John DeWitt, army commander for the West Coast, and California law officials decided to take them into custody. "A Jap's a Jap," DeWitt explained. "It makes no difference whether he's an American or not." On February 19, 1942, Roosevelt gave that racist premise the force of law in an executive order that authorized the roundup of all Americans of Japanese descent. Allowed little time to secure or sell their property, the victims lost most of their assets, their jobs, and their homes. Most were American citizens; no one was charged with a crime; and not a single case of subversion or sabotage was ever uncovered. Still, Japanese Americans were sent to "relocation centers"—makeshift prison camps—in remote areas of the Southwest and Great Plains—penned in by barbed wire and armed guards for more than three years. Remarkably, thousands of young Japanese American men went directly from these desert prisons to Europe, where they fought in the U.S. military against the Axis enemy. Only in 1988 did Congress award modest reparations to Japanese Americans for their wartime losses.

MAP 25.3
Western Relocation Authority Centers
Responding to prejudice and fear of sabotage, in 1942 President Roosevelt authorized the roundup and relocation of all Americans of Japanese descent. Taken from their homes in the cities and fertile farms of the far West, Japanese Americans were confined in desolate areas scattered as far east as the Mississippi River.

Gays in the Military

War posed challenges for homosexual Americans in some ways comparable to those faced by other marginalized groups. The view that gays were a threat to good order and were apt to crack under stress had long dominated military thinking. In World War I, that prejudice began to harden into a system of exclusion. The introduction of psychological testing prompted authorities to use traits associated with gays as a way of eliminating men they considered undesirable. Their efforts stalled, however, when a hunt for gay sailors at the naval training station in Newport, Rhode Island, created a sensation. Stung by revelations of entrapment tactics and the denial of rights of self-defense for the accused, the navy in 1921 established strict rules of fair courtroom procedure for trying homosexual acts as criminal conduct. That same year, the army, wanting to head off trouble at the outset, tightened its psychological screening process by issuing a set of standards that barred recruitment of sexual "perverts" and "psychopaths."

Despite their broad powers, authorities showed little inclination to act against gays in the period between the world wars when the military shrank into a small volunteer force. A few men did serve time in prison for sodomy, but psychological screening was seldom used, since officers were ill equipped to understand it. Essentially, those in charge ignored the issue of gays whenever they could conveniently do so.

FBI SEARCHING JAPANESE AMERICAN HOME
When President Roosevelt informed military commanders that they might "from time to time"
remove persons deemed dangerous, he had reason to suspect that virtually all Japanese Americans
would be affected. An army "expert" on Asian culture had already advised the War Department
that, "as you cannot . . . penetrate the Oriental thinking . . . the easiest course is to remove them
all from the West Coast and place them . . . under guard." Intent on getting to the bottom of one
Japanese American family's allegiance, an FBI agent in 1942 scrutinizes a picture album, while
family members whose home has been invaded look on helplessly.
Los Angeles Daily News Morgue, Department of Special Collections, University Research Library, UCLA.

World War II aroused a new sense of crisis. Once the Selective Service Act of 1940 began bringing vast numbers of recruits into the armed forces, Secretary of War Henry Stimson reminded all commanding generals that they were expected to prosecute cases of sodomy. To screen effectively for persons who might commit such acts, the authorities turned to psychological experts in the latest theories of character disorders. Though many psychologists believed that homosexuality was a maladjustment that could be corrected, military authorities seized the experts' definition of homosexuality as a form of "disturbed sex development" and used it as grounds to purge gays from the ranks.

Stigmatized, gay Americans, like other disadvantaged minorities, found the war to be a special sort of transforming experience. Ironically, the very crisis that renewed prejudice also worked against

enforcing it thoroughly. The need to build a huge fighting force made those in charge less able, or willing, to discriminate closely against potential recruits. During the course of the war, only four to five thousand men out of eighteen million examined for induction were excluded as homosexuals. And because screening procedures had been set up with only men in mind, lesbians volunteering for the newly formed women's branches of service had an even lower proportion of their numbers screened out.

Gays in the military thus served in about as many ways as other inductees, and studies made at the end of the war showed their records to be much the same. Like black and Japanese American service people, gays sought to demonstrate their worth under fire. "I was superpatriotic," explained a combat veteran. "And being a homosexual, I had that constant compelling need to prove how virile I was."

The brute experience of war put issues of sexual inclination into a blunt new perspective. In the midst of life or death realities, as one gay survivor of the Iwo Jima campaign put it, "who in the hell is going to worry about this shit?"

When peace came, gay veterans, both those who made it through the war undetected and those expelled without any veterans' benefits, tended to cluster in large cities where their sense of mutual interests and loyalty shaped their communities. Toughened by the military ordeal and angry that they had been part of a successful war against oppression while remaining oppressed themselves, veterans led the way in promoting the gay liberation movement. In 1950, a group of gay veterans formed the Mattachine Society to combat discrimination, and five years later lesbians in San Francisco followed their example by founding the Daughters of Bilitis. These efforts provided the impetus for gay activism to join in the broad front of civil rights insurgency that eventually arose in the 1960s.

Refugees from the Holocaust

As American resolve against totalitarian oppression stiffened, refugees from fascism and Nazism posed an increasingly difficult challenge to the national conscience. Throughout the 1930s, Spanish Loyalists fleeing Franco, opponents of Mussolini, and, most numerous, the targets of Hitler's maniacal racism clamored for asylum. As Hitler expanded his campaign to "purify" Germany and to clear conquered land for the Aryan master race, Jews, gypsies, religious dissenters, homosexuals, avant-garde artists, and other "degenerates" came under increasing pressure to flee or risk extermination. Within the United States, there arose a desperate contest between those who would rescue the victims of persecution and those who would bar the gate.

Roosevelt sympathized with the pleas for help, but only to an extent that did not jeopardize his foreign policy or his hold on the electorate. After the German army took over Austria in March 1938, crowds of Jews besieged the American embassy in Vienna, seeking immigration visas. Roosevelt tried to raise the annual quota, which allowed only 1,400 Austrians into the country, but Congress, trying to keep out of war and mindful of polls showing that 82 percent of Americans were against admitting Jewish exiles, refused the request. Roosevelt then sought to persuade countries in Latin America and Africa to accept refugees. None would agree. In a

last attempt before war broke out, friends of the refugees introduced legislation in Congress in 1939 that would grant asylum to 20,000 German refugee children, most of them Jewish. Anti-Semitism, as well as isolationism, was undoubtedly a factor in the defeat of the bill, for the following year refugee English children who were not predominantly Jewish gained entry without delay.

After fending off efforts to accept more refugees before the war, Congress maintained harsh terms of exclusion even after January 1942, when Hitler devised a comprehensive plan for the "final solution": Jews and other undesirables would be sent to concentration camps in remote areas. There, old people, children, and others deemed too weak to work would be gassed and cremated immediately; the able-bodied would be put to work until lack of food and harsh conditions killed them. The Nazis made the extermination of the Jews of Europe a top secret, but news leaked out. The World Jewish Congress then took the lead for a terrified, grieving Jewish community in seeking help from the Allies. But skeptical U.S. State Department officials stood firmly in the way. When the American consul in Geneva conveyed news of Hitler's concentration camps, he added a recommendation that the report be set aside because of "the fantastic nature of the allegation, and the impossibility of our being of any assistance if such action were taken."

After fending off efforts to accept more refugees before the war, Congress maintained harsh terms of exclusion even after January 1942, when Hitler devised a comprehensive plan for the "final solution."

The State Department's resistance to evidence reflected the way victims of Nazi persecution had long been cut off from adequate help. Most nations had repeatedly refused to admit many refugees from Nazi Germany, partly out of prejudice against Jews, partly to avoid additional new burdens during the economic hard times of the 1930s. In all, up to the start of war, only 152,000 Jews managed to gain entry into the United States. From there the numbers dropped steadily to a mere 2,400 in 1944. Those trapped in Europe could only wait for rescue by Allied armies, while their champions abroad vainly pleaded with the Allies to bomb the Nazi death camps and the railroad tracks leading to them to hamper the killing operation. (See Historical Question, page 1006).

When Russian troops arrived at Auschwitz in Poland in February 1945, they found only a handful of emaciated prisoners, some of them too weak to survive their liberation. Skeletal corpses, some half burned, lay around them; nearby were ponds and pits filled with the ashes of those who had perished. The Russians discovered sheds filled with loot stripped from the dead—clothing, gold fillings, false teeth, even cloth made from human hair. Two months later, the American Third Army came to Nordhausen, where they found 700 survivors and 3,000 bodies. At last, the truth about Nazi atrocities breached the wall of denial. But by then, Nazi extermination had reached its final toll of 9 million victims.

Military Victory: 1943–1945

By early 1943, the defensive phase of the war was over. Having halted the German and Japanese offenses in Europe and in Asia, the Allies faced the daunting task of driving the Axis back, retaking vast conquered areas, and finally defeating Germany and Japan on their home territory. The Allied alliance of the United States, Britain, and the Soviet Union suffered enormous stress over the matter of the "second front" in Europe to relieve the Soviet Union from the brunt of battle against Hitler. By June 1944, when a true second front was launched, the Soviet Union had already broken German power. In the Pacific, the United States, fighting with Australia and New Zealand, defeated the Japanese and ended World War II.

From Normandy to Berlin

In November 1943, as the Italian campaign ground on at its cold, muddy pace, Churchill, Roosevelt, and Stalin held meetings in Teheran, the capital of Iran, and Cairo to plan the final assault on Hitler. Stalin finally succeeded in getting Roosevelt and Churchill to commit to a definite time for the great invasion of Europe—May 1944. The Allies had been gathering an enormous army and navy in Great Britain for nearly two years in anticipation of a return to France. General Dwight D. Eisenhower, with his great tact and organizing skills, became Supreme Commander of the Allied Forces—American, British, and Free French—while General Sir Bernard Montgomery, the hero of victory in North Africa, took charge of the landing itself.

Led by the master tactician General Erwin Rommel, the German forces strengthened the Atlantic wall by fortifying the cliffs and mining the beaches of northwestern France. Yet, as Rommel realized more clearly than Hitler, the huge deployment of German forces in the East trying to contain the massive Soviet offensive that began in the spring of 1943 left Rommel without adequate forces to stop the 3 million Allied soldiers waiting in England. Even more of a handicap was Rommel's inability to control the air. Hitler and his air marshall, Hermann Göring, thought of air power as support for assault troops and so concentrated on short-range fighters and dive bombers to cover ground offensives. The concept had served well in the blitzkriegs, but now the Luftwaffe had only 300 fighter planes to face 12,000 Allied aircraft of all types poised for massive bombardment.

The Germans expected the invasion to come in the Pas de Calais area, where the England Channel is narrowest. False radio signals, invented armies, and fake air sorties encouraged German suspicions, but the actual invasion took place miles to the south on the beaches of Normandy. First came raging air and naval attacks, then the landing of paratroopers behind the German lines, and then at 7:30 in the morning on June 6, 1944, referred to as "D Day," seaborne soldiers hit the beaches. For a perilous moment, rough seas and fortified machine guns stopped the assault in a chaos of overturned tanks, drowning men, and frantic attempts by those who made it ashore to find cover against the withering fire from the cliffs above. But paratroopers coming up behind the German line and rangers scaling the cliffs to knock out enemy gun emplacements finally secured the beachhead. As General Omar N. Bradley observed, the Allies prevailed only by "guts, valor, and extreme bravery."

Within a week, Allied forces had broken out of the Normandy pocket and had begun to drive toward the Rhine River. As the German army was being hammered badly on both its western and eastern fronts, some German military officers began to doubt the wisdom of the war. Hoping to replace the Nazis with a new government that would negotiate a peace, they made an unsuccessful bomb attempt against Hitler in July 1944. Suspicion mistakenly fell upon Rommel, who retired to his home and committed

Why Did the Allies Refuse to Bomb the Death Camps?

ONLY A FEW DAYS AFTER the German Blitzkrieg swept through Poland in September 1939, Adolf Hitler traveled to the front to exult over victory. He summoned military commanders to one of the cars of his special train and instructed them to begin, as swiftly as possible, making room for Germans by "housecleaning" the territory of its clergy, aristocracy, intelligentsia, and Jews. Soon afterward, Nazi soldiers began shooting clusters of men, women, and children standing in burial pits the victims had dug themselves. Seeking faster and more efficient means to annihilate millions of people that would also relieve reluctant army forces from the bloody horror of shooting them, Nazi engineers then designed airtight vans that roamed the countryside suffocating the condemned with carbon monoxide gas.

With the implementation of Hitler's "final solution," killing became quicker and more efficient. Though the Nazis endeavored to keep the final solution a secret, news of what was happening to Jews, gypsies, political prisoners, and others sent away in cattle cars for "resettlement" had surfaced by the summer of 1942. In July, a shaken German businessman with mines in Poland near Auschwitz, the main death camp, informed a Jewish associate in Switzerland of the plan he had discovered to exterminate 3.5 to 4 million Jews. The World Jewish Congress then led the horrified Jewish community in a campaign to get the Allies to take action.

Once the war started and the Nazis sealed the borders of their territories, opportunities for rescue narrowed considerably. With hope waning for the hundreds of thousands of European Jews not yet sent to their deaths, pleas mounted for the Allies to bomb the death camps and the railroad tracks leading to them in order to hamper the killing operation and block further shipments of victims. Insistence rose to frenzy in April 1944, after escapees from Auschwitz brought word to the outside world of the unimaginable horror of murder and starvation. The nightmare deepened on April 19, when Jews in the ghetto of Warsaw began an armed rebellion against slow death by attrition at the hands of the Nazis. For twenty-eight days, the Jewish defenders held and then suffered total annihilation.

The rising volume of proposals to bomb the railroads and camps got no farther than the desks of Assistant Secretary of War John J. McCloy in Washington and British Foreign Secretary Anthony Eden in London. Both men were seasoned members of foreign service elites, which Jews had never penetrated. Intent on achieving military victory as soon as possible without distraction, they routinely turned aside bombing requests by insisting that the air forces could not spare resources from their strictly military missions. There was an element of moral indifference, as well. Eden's Foreign Office was especially distant and patronizing, as if fending off the usual special-interest group looking for petty favors. An eloquent plea from Chaim Weizmann, one of the most imposing Jewish leaders, elicited a routine rejection letter that ended with tragic understatement: "I understand that this decision will be a disappointment to you, but be sure that the matter was considered exhaustively."

The value of bombing the death camps was not considered exhaustively, however. Tactically, there was no reason to hesitate. The German air force could offer little resistance after 1943, when the Allies gained full control of the air. The Allies had many extra planes that could have been assigned to bomb the death camps without any hindrance to the military advance into Germany. Worries expressed about loss of life were similarly hollow. Refusing to commit heavy bombers to the mission because they would kill *some* innocent people in the camps overlooked the fact that if nothing were done *all* the innocents would die. Testimony from Auschwitz survivors shows that inmates appreciated the distinction and strongly hoped the increasing number of Allied planes they saw overhead meant that their hell would soon be bombed into oblivion.

Cautious calculation of the public interest and doubt about what could be verified also prevented action. The Office of War Information (OWI) avoided the subject of death camps out of fear that charging the Germans with crimes against humanity would incite them to greater resistance that would prolong the war and cause more American casualties. Deprived of information to dispel widespread skepticism that death camps could really exist,

THE DEAD AT BUCHENWALD
In this stark moment, all distance between official Washington and the Holocaust is breached. Soldiers and civilians pause somberly in the background as Senator Alben Barkley of Kentucky, stooped in sadness, tries to comprehend the incomprehensible.
Pentagon, U.S. Army Signal Corps.

newspapers and journals relegated news of the Holocaust to the back pages. Better to wait until the victorious armed forces could prove or refute such charges than to risk giving fake propaganda the same prominence that had so discredited journalists in World War I.

In the midst of blackout and denial, the will to disbelieve grew so strong that, when verification of the true horror did finally filter through, it tended to induce numbness. Even Supreme Court Justice Felix Frankfurter, a Jew himself and a veteran of agonizing fights against bigotry and persecution, found the truth incomprehensible. After a member of the Polish underground gave him a detailed account of the mass murder in Poland, Frankfurter denied the information as beyond the realm of possibility. "I did not say this young man is lying," he explained. "I said I cannot believe him. There is a difference." McCloy clung to the same rationalization that the nightmare could not be real. At least once, though, the will to disbelieve wavered. Leon Kubowitzki of the World Jewish Congress, after repeatedly being rebuffed by false arguments masquerading as "technical reasons" for not intervening, remembered a tense meeting with the assistant

secretary in December 1944. McCloy took Kubowitzki aside and said anxiously, "We are alone. Tell me the truth. Do you really believe that all those horrible things happened?"

By then it was too late. The Nazis had shut down the killing operations in Poland in November and were about to flee to Germany. When Russian troops arrived at Auschwitz in February 1945, they found only a handful of emaciated prisoners, some of them too weak to survive their liberation.

We have since learned that, aside from the Nazis' hasty attempt just before they fled to hide what they had been doing by wrecking the gas chambers and crematoria, the only destruction of killing apparatus was carried out by the victims themselves. In the fall of 1944, when the debate over bombing the death camps reached its peak, four women prisoners smuggled dynamite from the munitions plant at Auschwitz to men assigned to take ashes from the furnaces. Realizing that their deed was suicidal, the ash men managed to blow up one of the four furnaces and kill several SS guards. Immediately, the women were hanged and the men shot, their heroic act unknown to those who dared not send bombers instead.

MAP 25.4
The European Theater of World War II, 1942–1945
Russian reversal of the German offensive by breaking the sieges of Stalingrad and Leningrad,
combined with Allied landings in North Africa and Normandy, placed Germany in a closing vise
of armies from all sides.

suicide to spare his family and himself the pain of Nazi retaliation. Hitler, who now doubted the loyalty of his officer corps, retreated more and more into directing the war on the basis of his own intuition.

On August 25, the Allies liberated Paris from four years of Nazi occupation. A month later, they succeeded in pushing the Germans out of most of France. In another month, they made their first foray into Germany to capture the city of Aachen. As the giant pincers of the Allied and Soviet armies closed on German headquarters in Berlin, Hitler took a mad gamble. In December 1944, he ordered

D DAY LANDING
*Amid a dense thicket of landing craft, men and equipment lucky enough to have made it through
rough seas and enemy fire struggle onto the beach at Normandy on June 6, 1944, to open a second front in Europe. An intrepid photographer caught this brief moment of safe passage just before the troops advanced into withering enemy fire from the high cliffs beyond the beach.*
UPI/Bettmann Archive.

a counterattack through Belgium to recapture the
port of Antwerp and deny the Allies their major
supply port. Massive German forces drove fifty-five
miles into Allied lines in what was known as the
Battle of the Bulge before being stopped at Bastogne.
German losses of 82,000 men and hundreds of
tanks were disastrous. By committing so many of
his reserves to the Bulge, Hitler left the part of his
army facing the Russians close to collapse.

In February 1945, with the end in sight,
Churchill, Roosevelt, and Stalin met secretly at the
Russian Black Sea resort town of Yalta to discuss the
structure of the postwar world. Discussions centered
on three major topics: rearranging the political map
of Europe; creating a new international organization;
and achieving victory over Japan. Roosevelt arrived
showing the ashen pallor and shaking hands of a
man who was seriously ill. Although his stamina
and mental alertness flickered, he still managed to
secure a major share of what he sought. The Soviets

agreed to a declaration of self-determination for the
countries their armies occupied in Eastern Europe.
Chiang Kai-shek would receive Allied support as
leader of China in the war against Japan. The Soviet Union would gain control over the Kuril and
southern Sakhalin Islands near Japan and have a
say in the governance of Korea and Manchuria in
exchange for entering the war against Japan after
the defeat of Germany.

The "Big Three" also agreed on the creation
of a new international organization, the United
Nations, the details of which had been decided the
year before at a conference at Dumbarton Oaks estate
outside Washington, D.C. All nations would have a
place in the United Nations General Assembly, but
the Security Council would wield decisive power.
The Security Council would be composed of temporary members and of permanent representatives
from China, France, Great Britain, the Soviet Union,
and the United States, each of which would retain

the veto. Delegates from fifty nations, inspired by the conviction that they must not fail a second time to secure the peace after a world war, met in San Francisco in April 1945 to approve the charter of the United Nations. The response of the United States was startlingly different than it had been to the League of Nations in 1919. Internationalism triumphed over isolationism when Republican Senator Arthur Vandenberg of Michigan declared that it was his mission to "end the miserable notion that the Republican Party will return to its foxhole when the last shot in this war has been fired and will blindly let the world rot in its own anarchy." The Senate ratified the charter in July by a vote of eighty-nine to two.

Following the Yalta agreement, the Allies began the final assault on Hitler. While American forces pounded Germany from the west, the Soviets, having swept through Poland, arrived at the outskirts of Berlin in April 1945. Hitler, who had descended into his underground bunker on January 16, committed suicide on April 30. His body was burned amidst the din of Russian cannons and the remains hurriedly buried under what is now the median strip of a superhighway. A provisional German government surrendered on May 7, 1945, ending the Nazi nightmare in Europe.

Franklin Roosevelt did not live to witness the end of the Nazi horror. On April 12, while resting in Warm Springs, Georgia, the president suffered a fatal stroke. Americans grieved publicly for the man who had led them through more than twelve years of depression and world war. And they worried aloud about his successor, Vice President Harry S. Truman. The world stood at a fateful moment in its history, and Truman was largely unknown and

TECHNOLOGY IN AMERICA
Penicillin

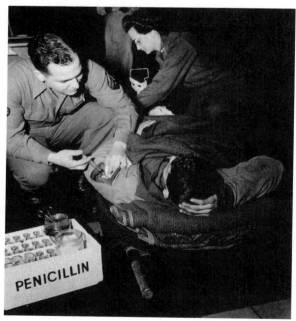

National Archives.

The antibacterial drug, penicillin, shown being injected into a soldier, did more than any other medical advance to save lives on the battlefield during World War II. This success was the culmination of an intense period of discovery and debate that came to fruition just in time to meet the desperate wartime need for drugs to fight infection. In 1928, the English biochemist, Alexander Fleming, accidentally discovered that mold left on laboratory culture plates could kill bacteria. Subsequent tests on mice using the organic form of arsenic extracted from the mold, which Fleming called penicillin, proved highly effective against a wide variety of bacterial infections. These experiments succeeded in 1940, just as the Battle of Britain against the German bombing blitz was reaching its climax. After the lifesaving use of penicillin on wounded airmen and later on soldiers in North Africa, a team of British researchers rushed to the United States in 1941 to urge mass production of the drug. The campaign came to a dramatic conclusion when the Pearl Harbor bombing ended a conference on battlefield medicine being held in Honolulu the day before the British team was to present its case for penicillin. American authorities moved cautiously to make use of the new wonder drug. By April 1943 fewer than 500 men had received penicillin, but word of its astonishingly successful results convinced U.S. authorities early in 1944 to urge all medical personnel to use penicillin "without hesitation." In the final tally of the war's damage, death rates in battle were half those of World War I, and largely because of penicillin, mortality rates for disease were 27 times lower.

YALTA CONFERENCE
In February 1945, President Roosevelt and British Prime Minister Winston Churchill met with Russian leader Joseph Stalin at the Black Sea resort of Yalta to plan the postwar reconstruction of Europe. Roosevelt, near the end of his life, and Churchill, soon to suffer reelection defeat, look weary next to the resolute "Man of Steel." Controversy would later arise over whether a stronger stand by the American and British leaders could have prevented the Soviet Union from imposing communist rule on Eastern Europe.
U.S. Army.

untested. He had been vice president less than three months, and Roosevelt had consistently left him out of discussions of the conduct of the war. Truman's colleagues in Congress generally agreed that he would preside over the end of the war as little more than a caretaker, another Harding perhaps. Truman seemed to agree. When a reporter called him "Mr. President," he replied uneasily, "I wish you didn't have to call me that." He said to other reporters, "Boys, if newspapermen pray, pray for me now." He soon showed himself to be tough-minded and a quick learner, with a knowledge of history deeper than that of almost any other president. He could be blunt and earthy, calling more than one opponent a "son of a bitch." But he had a clear sense of who he was, and it soon became clear that he did not hesitate to make hard decisions.

The Defeat of Japan

American victories at sea in early 1942 halted the Japanese advance in the Pacific. By mid-1942, the Americans had taken the offensive. Japan had intended to use its navy to shield a vast economic empire in China and Southeast Asia. Instead, it had to fend off a revived and aroused foe in the Pacific while also trying to quell renewed resistance on the Asian mainland. In China, the Japanese armies had scored many victories but were unable to finish off Chiang Kai-shek. Japanese forces had advanced westward almost to India, but in 1943 British and American forces, along with Indian and Chinese troops, were preparing for a counterthrust through Burma and into China. The most decisive action, however, came in the Pacific, where the Allies

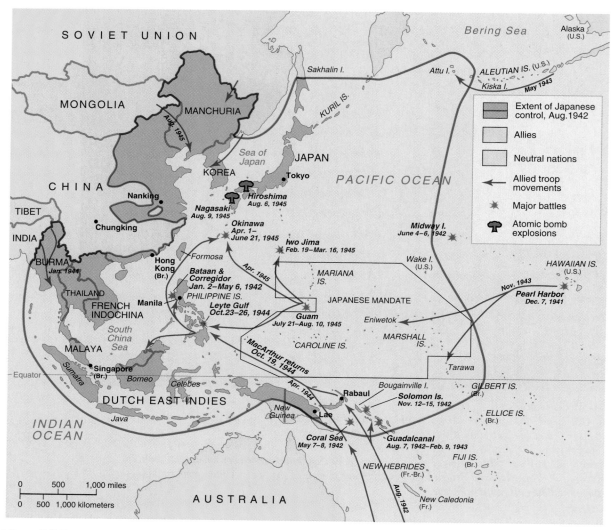

M A P 25.5
The Pacific Theater of World War II, 1941–1945
To drive the Japanese from their far-flung empire, the Allies launched two combined naval and military offensives — one to recapture the Philippines and then attack Japanese forces in China, the other to hop from island to island in the central Pacific toward the Japanese mainland.

moved slowly and painfully, island by island, toward the Japanese homeland.

Victory at sea led to Allied success on land. In August 1942, the First Marine Division landed on Guadalcanal Island, where the Japanese were constructing an airfield. For the next six months, a savage battle raged for control of the strategic area. Both sides suffered terrible losses, but gradually the American navy won control of the seas, and the marines and army beat back the Japanese on land.

Japanese forces withdrew during the night of February 7, 1943. Guadalcanal was a significant victory, but it signaled just how costly the long march to Japan would be.

In mid-1943, American, Australian, and New Zealand forces under the naval and military commanders, Admiral Chester Nimitz and General Douglas MacArthur, launched new offensives that penetrated the outer perimeter of Japanese defenses. Bloody campaigns in New Guinea and the Solomon

GUADALCANAL: *GHOST TRAIL*
This painting, Ghost Trail *by combat artist Kerr Eby, captures the eerie, murky quality of jungle warfare first experienced fully in the campaign to capture the Pacific island of Guadalcanal. The troops blend into a dense maze of black and green that compounds the difficulties of detecting the hidden enemy.*
Navy Art Collection/Gift of Abbott Laboratories.

Islands gradually secured the South Pacific. In the central Pacific, amphibious forces, borne by the greatest fleet in history, took the Gilbert and Marshall Islands, which served eventually as forward positions for launching the decisive air and ground assaults on the Japanese home islands.

As the Allied offensive pressed on, resistance grew fiercer and more resourceful. Japanese soldiers were instructed to stand firm to the death to defend their homeland. The landing on Tarawa made plain the tenacity of the Japanese soldiers. Stymied by a tide that grounded their landing craft far from shore, the invading marines had to wade a half mile, waist-deep, through brutal enemy fire. Survivors of that barrage then faced concrete emplacements manned by well-armed troops who had no intention of retreating. Within three days, the marines had suffered 1,000 dead and another 2,000 wounded—all to take a barren coral island not three square miles. Only 17 of the 3,000 Japanese defenders were left alive to surrender. The island to island warfare took on an awful sameness of rooting the enemy

out of bunkers and caves with explosives and flamethrowers.

In October 1944, the Allies invaded the Philippines. In the battle for Leyte Gulf, the greatest naval battle in history, the Japanese lost practically their entire fleet—three battleships, four carriers, nine cruisers, and eight destroyers. Even before MacArthur had retaken the Philippines, Allied forces captured Iwo Jima, 750 miles from Japan, and Okinawa, only 370 miles from Tokyo. To defend Okinawa, the Japanese called on thousands of suicide pilots, known as "kamikaze" ("divine wind"). Their mission was to crash bomb-laden planes into Allied ships and thus, it was hoped, make the landing forces turn back. The kamikaze made life harrowing for the fleet but did not deter it. Rather, the suicide gesture destroyed the last vestige of the Japanese air force. By June 1945, the Japanese were virtually defenseless on sea and air. Thousands of B-29 Superfortresses bombed Japanese cities virtually unopposed, and the navy set up a total blockade of the Japanese homeland. The United States prepared to invade.

JAPANESE KAMIKAZE
In this painting by Sentaro Iwata, Japanese suicide pilots prepare to fly to the defense of Okinawa. The pilots, some wearing swords, look heavenward before going aloft as kamikaze, "divine wind," to deliberately crash their bomb-laden planes into enemy warships. In the fight for Okinawa, kamikaze caused over 4,000 U.S. casualties.
Painting by Sentaro Iwata, National Archives.

Atomic Warfare

Just as the island campaigns drew to an end, American scientists were completing work on a secret weapon. The race to develop an atomic bomb had been a long one. In 1942, warned by refugee scientists that the Nazis were working to convert nuclear energy into a superbomb, the Roosevelt administration had authorized the top-secret Manhattan Project —the largest organized scientific effort that had ever been undertaken—to develop the bomb before the Germans did. In thirty-seven locations across the country, coordinated by leading theorists at Los Alamos, New Mexico, 100,000 persons worked at top speed to win the race.

Germany surrendered before it produced a bomb and before the United States was ready to test its own. But just before dawn on July 16, 1945, a test explosion lit up the sky in an isolated corner of the Alamogordo Air Base near Los Alamos. Project

scientists had wagered in a betting pool that the blast, if the test device worked at all, would be equivalent to a few hundred tons of TNT. No one guessed the actual force of 20,000 tons. Nor was anyone prepared for a flash of multicolored light more brilliant than ever seen before—visible even to a blind woman miles away—or the vast fireball and mushroom-shaped cloud of dust and debris that rose eight miles into the upper atmosphere.

The small circle of scientists and officials who knew about the top-secret project had debated for months how atomic weapons should be used. Some scientists, troubled by the power they had unleashed, proposed a public demonstration of the bomb's doomsday force to persuade Japan to surrender. It seemed a prudent time for such a warning shot. With Japan's armed forces incapable of offensive action and Japan totally blockaded, test proponents argued that the United States could afford to wait until the point of the demonstration sank in. The

HIROSHIMA BOMBING
This rare shot taken by a news photographer in Hiroshima immediately after the atomic bomb ex-
ploded on August 6, 1945 suggests the shock and incomprehension that survivors would describe
as their first reaction. Three days later another atomic bomb devastated Nagasaki.
U.N. photo.

Japanese government had already sent emissaries to see if a negotiated peace could be reached. The sticking point was that the Japanese wanted to retain their emperor, while the American government remained committed to unconditional surrender.

In the end, all reluctance to unleash the atomic monster on populated targets yielded to other urgent considerations. When President Harry Truman heard about the bomb test, he was involved in hard bargaining with the Soviets in Potsdam, Germany, about how to reorganize the postwar world. Truman showed his distrust of the Russians by keeping the news of the test secret. Then he adjusted his strategy to make use of the new weapon. Clearly, the bomb made it unnecessary to call on the Russian promise to hasten victory by declaring war on Japan. Rather, a surprise use of the new superweapon might have the advantage of ending the conflict before the Soviet Union could gain a foothold in Korea and Manchuria by attacking the Japanese armies

still there. Perhaps, also, the bomb's devastation would convince the Soviets that they could not safely challenge American leadership after the war.

A more basic motive was to save American lives. As Truman pondered his options, American troops and supplies were massing on the island of Saipan for Operation Downfall—the invasion of the Japanese home islands in the fall. Experience with Japanese who fought to the death filled American military and civilian leaders with dread. In the battle for Okinawa alone, which ended the island-hopping campaign just before the atomic bomb test, 7,000 American fighting men lost their lives. By resisting to the end, 70,000 Japanese soldiers and 80,000 Okinawans also died in the two-month-long battle. Intelligence reports indicated that an invasion of the Japanese homeland would be a bloodbath on a much vaster scale. More than 2 million Japanese army troops were available for a last-ditch defense of their homeland. Behind them were 28 million men, women, and boys of the civilian militia, armed with sharpened bamboo stakes and any other weapons they could muster.

Truman, who had been a commander of combat troops on the ground in World War I, was keenly sympathetic to the ordeal facing an invading army. He saw no reason not to use a weapon of war, even a terribly destructive one, if it would save American lives. But first he issued an ultimatum that Japan must surrender unconditionally or face utter destruction. When the Japanese failed to respond by the deadline, Truman turned to his advisory committee's recommendation that, to shock the Japanese into surrender, the bomb be dropped without warning on cities that had not already been heavily damaged. On August 6, a single B-29, the *Enola Gay*, droned over Hiroshima and released one of the three operational atomic bombs the Americans possessed. As the plane banked sharply away, crew members could see behind them the mushroom cloud that signified the obliteration of the city and the death of 78,000 inhabitants. Russia then declared war on Japan on August 8, and the next day a second atomic bomb obliterated Nagasaki, with more than 100,000 deaths.

According to one estimate, the death toll during World War II reached 35 million, evenly divided between military and civilian losses.

In the midst of ruin, a peace faction took control of the Japanese government from diehard military leaders, and with assurance that the emperor could retain his throne under Allied control, Japan surrendered on August 14. Whether allowing the Japanese to retain their emperor before using atomic bombs would have been enough to induce surrender can never be known. Emperor Hirohito's power to shift the Japanese spirit from war to peace became clear, however, when he informed his people in a radio broadcast—the first words that the public had ever heard the emperor utter—of his divine will that they cease fighting. Loyally, his subjects lay down their arms and stood quietly by as the giant battleship *Missouri* sailed into Tokyo harbor for the formal signing of surrender on September 2, 1945.

Conclusion: Victory and Uncertainty

For Americans, the attack on Pearl Harbor was just the first shock of a war whose scope and violence was unprecedented. World War I had meant ghastly destruction for parts of Europe, but never before had armies been flung across such vast stretches of the globe. And on the seas there were more battles, with more ships lost, than in all other modern wars combined. An accurate tally of the dead is impossible. According to one estimate, the death toll reached 35 million, evenly divided between military and civilian losses. Some countries suffered much more than others. Approximately 400,000 Americans lost their lives in military service; the Soviet Union lost more in the single battle of Stalingrad. Eventually, the Soviets suffered nearly 20 million civilian and military deaths. Despite its relatively light losses, the United States experienced far-reaching changes, none of which was more decisive than its rise to global power.

When World War II ended, the United States was unquestionably the most powerful nation on earth. Determined not to repeat the failure to secure a stable peace after World War I, the Roosevelt administration had begun to plan a postwar world even before the United States entered the conflict. But Roosevelt's hope for a peaceful and democratic postwar world was shadowed by wartime events and postwar developments. The Holocaust exposed humankind's capacity for unimaginable evil and raised indelible misgivings about postwar prospects. The annihilation of Hiroshima and Nagasaki by atomic bombs cast additional doubts about modern technology. Moreover, the United States and Western Europe soon found themselves at odds with dictatorial Communist countries led by the Soviet Union and soon to be joined by China. Efforts by Britain and France to maintain their colonial empires also violated democratic principles and met mounting resistance from national forces seeking liberation.

Nevertheless, most Americans emerged from World War II convinced that good had triumphed over evil. What purposes victory would ultimately serve, however, quickly became debatable, as the confidence bred of winning the "good war" gave way to the anxious uncertainties of the "cold war."

CHRONOLOGY

1933 Adolf Hitler becomes chancellor of Germany.

United States recognizes Soviet Union.

1935– 1937 Congress seeks to shield America from world conflicts with neutrality acts.

1936 Nazi Germany occupies the Rhineland.

Mussolini's fascist Italian regime conquers Ethiopia.

Civil war breaks out in Spain.

1937 Japanese troops capture Nanking.

Roosevelt delivers speech urging "quarantine" against aggressor nations.

1938 Hitler annexes Austria.

British Prime Minister Chamberlain meets with Hitler in Munich and agrees to German seizure of Sudetenland in Czechoslovakia.

1939 German troops occupy remainder of Czechoslovakia without resistance.

Nazi Germany and Soviet Union sign nonaggression pact.

September 1. Germany's attack on Poland begins World War II.

United States and Great Britain conclude cash-and-carry agreement.

1940 **May–June.** British troops evacuated at Dunkirk.

June. French sign armistice with Germany that puts most of France under direct German control.

Isolationists, including Charles Lindbergh, create America First Committee.

Roosevelt wins reelection against Wendell Willkie.

1941 Lend-Lease Act enables Britain to obtain war materials in United States on credit.

June. Germany invades Soviet Union.

August. Atlantic Charter devised by Roosevelt and Allies to guarantee human and international freedoms after war.

December 7. Japanese launch surprise attack on Pearl Harbor. United States declares war on Japan.

1942 Japan captures the Philippines.

Civil rights activists found Congress of Racial Equality (CORE).

U.S. navy scores its first major victories in Battle of Coral Sea and at Midway.

Roosevelt authorizes top-secret Manhattan Project.

November. U.S. forces invade North Africa.

Roosevelt authorizes internment of Japanese Americans.

1943 Allied leaders agree that war will end only with unconditional surrender of Axis forces.

"Zoot suit" riots explode in Los Angeles.

U.S. forces invade Sicily.

1944 **June 6.** Combined Allied army stages successful D Day landing at Normandy.

Roosevelt wins reelection against Thomas E. Dewey.

1945 The Allies meet to plan reconstruction of Europe after defeat of Germany.

April 12. Franklin Roosevelt dies and Harry Truman becomes president.

Delegates from fifty nations, meeting in San Francisco, approve charter of the United Nations.

May 7. Germany surrenders.

August 6. United States drops atomic bomb on Hiroshima.

August 8. United States drops atomic bomb on Nagasaki.

August 14. Japan surrenders and brings World War II to an end.

BIBLIOGRAPHY

GENERAL WORKS

Michael Adams, *The Best War Ever* (1994).

John Morton Blum, *V Was for Victory: Politics and American Culture during World War II* (1977).

Kenneth S. Davis, *FDR: Into the Storm, 1937–1940* (1993).

I. C. B. Dear and M. R. D. Foot, eds., *The Oxford Companion to World War II* (1995).

Paul Fussell, *Wartime* (1989).

Akira Iriye, *The Origins of the Second World War in Asia and the Pacific* (1987).

Richard Ketchum, *The Borrowed Years, 1938–1941: America on the Way to War* (1989).

Eric Larrabee, *Commander in Chief: Franklin Delano Roosevelt, His Lieutenants, and Their War* (1987).

Richard Polenberg, *War and Society: The United States, 1941–1945* (1972).

Michael S. Sherry, *In the Shadow of War: The United States since the 1930s* (1995).

Studs Terkel, *"The Good War": An Oral History of World War II* (1984).

Gerhard Weinberg, *World at Arms: A Global History of World War II* (1994).

FOREIGN POLICY

Robert Dallek, *Franklin D. Roosevelt and American Foreign Policy, 1932–1945* (1979).

Erwin F. Gellman, *Good Neighbor Diplomacy: United States Policies in Latin America, 1933–1945* (1979).

Waldo Heinrichs, *Threshold of War: Franklin D. Roosevelt and American Entry into World War II* (1988).

Robert Hilderbrand, *Dumbarton Oaks: The Origins of the United Nations and the Search for Postwar Security* (1990).

Akira Iriye, *The Globalizing of America, 1913–1945* (1995).

Walter LaFeber, *Inevitable Revolutions* (1983).

Frederick W. Marks, *Wind over Sand: The Diplomacy of Franklin Roosevelt* (1988).

Arnold Offner, *The Origins of the Second World War* (1975).

Robert Rosenstone, *Crusade of the Left: The Lincoln Battalion in the Spanish Civil War* (1969).

David F. Schmitz, *The United States and Fascist Italy, 1922–1944* (1988).

Gaddis Smith, *American Diplomacy during the Second World War, 1941–1945* (1985).

Jonathan Utley, *Going to War with Japan, 1937–1942* (1985).

PACIFISM AND ANTI-INTERVENTIONISM

Wayne S. Cole, *Roosevelt and the Isolationists, 1932–1945* (1983).

Robert A. Divine, *The Illusion of Neutrality* (1982).

Charles A. Lindbergh, *The Wartime Journals* (1970).

Charles A. Lindbergh, *Autobiography of Values* (1978).

Joyce Milton, *Loss of Eden: A Biography of Charles and Anne Morrow Lindbergh* (1994).

Geoffrey S. Smith, *To Save a Nation: American "Extremism," the New Deal, and the Coming of World War II* (1992).

John E. Wiltz, *In Search of Peace: The Senate Munitions Inquiry, 1934–1936* (1963).

MOBILIZATION AND THE HOME FRONT

Karen Anderson, *Wartime Women: Sex Roles, Family Relations, and the Status of Women during World War II* (1981).

D'Ann Campbell, *Women at War with America: Private Lives in a Patriotic Era* (1984).

Lewis A. Erenberg and Susan E. Hirsch, eds., *The War in American Culture: Society and Consciousness during World War II* (1996).

Mark Jonathan Harris, Franklin D. Mitchell, and Steve J. Schechter, *The Home Front: America during World War II* (1985).

Susan Hartmann, *The Homefront and Beyond: American Women in the 1940s* (1982).

Clayton R. Koppes and Gregory D. Black, *Hollywood Goes to War: How Politics, Profits, and Propaganda Shaped World War II Movies* (1987).

Nelson Lichtenstein, *Labor's War at Home: The CIO in World War II* (1983).

Gerald D. Nash, *The American West Transformed: The Impact of the Second World War* (1985).

William L. O'Neill, *A Democracy at War: America's Fight at Home and Abroad in World War II* (1993).

Geoffrey Perrett, *Days of Sadness, Years of Triumph: The American People, 1939–1945* (1985).

William Tuttle, *Daddy's Gone to War: The Second World War in the Lives of America's Children* (1993).

MILITARY ORGANIZATION AND CAMPAIGNS

Gar Alperovitz, *The Decision to Use the Atomic Bomb and the Architecture of an American Myth* (1995).

Stephen E. Ambrose, *D-Day, June 6, 1944* (1994).

Allan Berube, *Coming Out under Fire: The History of Gay Men and Women in World War Two* (1990).

Paul S. Boyer, *By the Bomb's Early Light: American Thought and Culture at the Dawn of the Atomic Age* (1985).

A. Russell Buchanan, *The United States and World War II,* 2 vols. (1964).

John Costello, *Virtue under Fire: How World War II Changed Our Social and Sexual Attitudes* (1986).

Albert E. Cowdrey, *Fighting for Life: American Military Medicine in World War II* (1994).

Gavan Daws, *Prisoners of the Japanese: POWs of World War II* (1992).

John Dower, *War without Mercy: Race and Power in the Pacific War* (1986).

Akira Iriye, *Power and Culture: The Japanese-American War, 1941–1945* (1982).

D. Clayton James, *A Time for Giants: The Politics of the American High Command in World War II* (1987).

Dan Kurzman, *Day of the Bomb: Countdown to Hiroshima* (1986).

William Manchester, *Goodbye, Darkness: A Memoir of the Pacific War* (1980).

Martin V. Melosi, *The Shadow of Pearl Harbor: Political Controversy over the Surprise Attack, 1941–1946* (1977).

Geoffrey Perrett, *Winged Victory: The Army Air Forces in World War II* (1993).

Gordon Prange, *At Dawn We Slept* (1981).

Richard Rhodes, *The Making of the Atomic Bomb* (1986).

Ronald Schaffer, *Wings of Judgment: American Bombing in World War II* (1988).

Michael Schaller, *Douglas MacArthur: The Far Eastern General* (1989).

Michael S. Sherry, *The Rise of American Air Power: The Creation of Armageddon* (1987).

E. B. Sledge, *With the Old Breed at Peleliu and Okinawa* (1990).

Ronald H. Spector, *Eagle against the Sun: The American War with Japan* (1985).

RACE AND MINORITIES

Alison R. Bernstein, *American Indians and World War II: Toward a New Era in Indian Affairs* (1991).

A. Russell Buchanan, *Black Americans in World War II* (1977).

Dominic Capeci, *The Harlem Race Riot of 1943* (1977).

Dominic Capeci, *Race Relations in Wartime Detroit* (1984).

Lyn Crost, *Honor by Fire: Japanese Americans at War in Europe and the Pacific* (1994).

Roger Daniels, *Concentration Camps: North American Japanese in the United States and Canada during World War II* (1971; reprint, 1989).

Peter H. Irons, *Justice at War: The Story of the Japanese Internment Cases* (1983).

Mauricio Mazon, *The Zoot-Suit Riots: The Psychology of Symbolic Annihilation* (1984).

Bernard C. Nalty, *Strength for the Fight: A History of Black Americans in the Military* (1989).

Lou Potter, with William Miles and Nina Rosenblum, *Liberators: Fighting on Two Fronts in World War II* (1992).

Page Smith, *Democracy on Trial: The Japanese American Evacuation and Relocation in World War II* (1995).

Ronald Takaki, *Strangers from a Different Shore: A History of Asian Americans* (1989).

Neil Wynn, *The Afro-American and the Second World War* (1976).

DEPICTING THE WAR

M. Joyce Baker, *Images of Women on Film: The War Years* (1981).

Thomas Doherty, *Projections of War: Hollywood, American Culture, and World War II* (1993).

Paul Fussell, *Wartime* (1989).

Library of America, *Reporting World War II*, 2 vols. (1995).

William Manchester, *Goodbye Darkness: A Memoir of the Pacific War* (1980).

Karal Ann Marling and John Wetenhall, *Iwo Jima: Monuments, Memories, and the American Hero* (1991).

Peter Maslowski, *Armed with Cameras: The American Military Photographers of World War II* (1993).

Mordecai Richler, *Writers on World War II* (1991).

George H. Roeder Jr., *The Censored War: American Visual Experience during World War II* (1993).

Vernon Scannell, *Not without Glory: Poets of the Second World War* (1976).

Holly Cowan Shulman, *The Voice of America: Propaganda and Democracy, 1941–1945* (1991).

E. B. Sledge, *With the Old Breed at Peleliu and Okinawa* (1990).

Frederick S. Voss, *Reporting the War: The Journalistic Coverage of World War II* (1994).

AMERICA AND THE HOLOCAUST

Robert Abzug, *Inside the Vicious Heart: Americans and the Liberation of Nazi Concentration Camps* (1987).

Richard Breitman and Alan Kraut, *American Refugee Policy and European Jewry* (1987).

Lucy Dawidowicz, *The War against the Jews, 1933–1945* (1986).

Leonard Dinnerstein, *America and the Survivors of the Holocaust* (1982).

Lawrence L. Langer, *Admitting the Holocaust: Collected Essays* (1995).

Deborah E. Lipstadt, *Beyond Belief: The American Press and the Coming of the Holocaust, 1933–1945* (1986).

Michael Marrus, *The Holocaust in History* (1987).

Verne W. Newton, ed., *FDR and the Holocaust* (1995).

COLD WAR COMIC BOOK

Americans barely had time to celebrate the Allied victory in World War II when they perceived another threat, that posed by the Soviet Union. Fear of communism dominated much of postwar American life and politics, even invading the realm of popular culture. Four million copies of this comic book, published by a religious organization in 1947, painted a terrifying picture of what would happen to Americans when the Soviets took over the country. Such takeover stories appeared in movies, cartoons, and magazines as well as in other comic books.

Collection of Charles Christensen.

COLD WAR POLITICS IN THE TRUMAN YEARS

26

1945–1953

O N NOVEMBER 5, 1946, President Harry S. Truman, his wife, and his daughter boarded the train back to Washington from Truman's hometown, Independence, Missouri, where they had gone to vote. During the congressional campaigns, Republicans had blasted Truman as incapable of dealing with economic problems and with the threat of communism at home and abroad. The president's standing with the public had sunk to a mere 32 percent approval rate. Many Democratic candidates avoided mentioning his name, hoping to stir voters with recordings of the late Franklin Roosevelt's voice. Playing poker with reporters on the train as the returns came in, Truman appeared unconcerned. But the results were devastating: The Republicans had captured both the House and the Senate by substantial majorities.

When Truman stepped off the train in the capital at the lowest point of his presidency, only one member of his administration showed up to greet him, Undersecretary of State Dean Acheson. Acheson's gesture signaled a developing relationship of central importance to the two men as well as to postwar history. The fifty-three-year-old Acheson shared most of Truman's political principles, but their backgrounds could not have been more dissimilar. Acheson had enjoyed a typical upper-class education: prep school, Yale University, where classmates voted him "wittiest" and the "spiciest" dresser, and Harvard Law School. After clerking at the Supreme Court, Acheson earned a comfortable living as a lawyer specializing in work for international corporations. In contrast, Truman, the son of a Missouri farmer, had not attended college and had failed in a business venture before entering local politics in the 1920s.

Despite his wealth and privilege, Acheson supported most of the New Deal and staunchly defended organized labor. He spoke out against isolationism in the late 1930s, and in 1941 he accepted President Roosevelt's offer of a job at the State Department. Shortly after Truman became president, Acheson wrote his son that he observed shortcomings in Truman's "judgment and wisdom that the limitations of his experience produce," but he also found the fledgling president "straightforward, decisive, simple, entirely honest," a man who "will learn fast and will inspire confidence." In June 1947, Acheson left the State Department, but Truman lured him back eighteen months later, this time as secretary of state during the president's second term. Acheson appreciated the president's willingness to make tough decisions and respected the man whose "ego never came between him and his job." Truman cherished Acheson's abiding loyalty. Relying on him as secretary of state until they both left office in January 1953, Truman called Acheson "my good right hand."

Truman needed all the help he could get. The "accidental" president lacked the charisma, experience, and political skills with which Roosevelt had transformed both foreign and domestic policies, won four presidential elections, and forged a Democratic Party coalition that dominated national politics. Initially criticized and abandoned by many Roosevelt loyalists, Truman faced a resurgent Republican Party as well as revolts from within his own party.

Part of Truman's challenge lay in domestic problems left over from the New Deal. Without the war to fuel the economy, how could the nation achieve economic growth that would ensure a decent livelihood for its citizens and avoid another depression? Truman failed to achieve his goal of extending the New Deal with ambitious reforms in health care, education, housing, and civil rights, but his administration did consolidate and modestly expand the welfare state. Riding a postwar economic boom, Americans enjoyed an unparalleled standard of living. Still, at the end of the 1940s, about one-third of the population remained mired in poverty.

A watershed in foreign policy that required increasing expenditures for defense and foreign aid helped to stimulate prosperity during the Truman years. The nation's central goals—protecting the United States from foreign aggression, encouraging other countries to follow its political and economic system, and fostering U.S. economic interests abroad—were not new. What changed in the postwar period were the international context and the means used to pursue these goals.

World War II had left in its wake ruin, instability, and power vacuums in large parts of the globe. Restoring order would have been a challenge under any circumstances, but growing hostility between the two most powerful nations—the United States and the Soviet Union—made it infinitely more difficult. As early as 1946, Dean Acheson became convinced that the Soviet Union posed the major threat to U.S. security. With other officials, he helped to shape a containment policy, with the goal of thwarting Soviet power and influence wherever they threatened to spread. By 1947, a new term had been coined to describe the intense hostility and rivalry between the superpowers—the "cold war."

The containment policy worked enormously well in Western Europe, but foreign policy reverses elsewhere combined with partisan politics at home to produce a wave of hysteria about Communists within the United States. This anti-Communist frenzy produced a large-scale purge of individuals from public service and private employment. Free-

DEAN ACHESON
No individual had more to do with transforming America's role in the world after World War II than Dean Acheson, President Truman's closest foreign policy adviser. Acheson, seen here in 1945, criticized those who saw the cold war in black and white terms and communism as an evil that the United States could expel from the earth. Rather, he advocated that American leaders learn "to limit objectives, to get ourselves away from the search for the absolute, to find out what is within our powers." Library of Congress.

dom to express unpopular ideas or to criticize U.S. policies and institutions became a major casualty of the cold war.

Although Acheson kept his job, as the preeminent foreign policy official and defender of a former colleague accused of being a Soviet spy, he too reaped abuse from Republicans for being "soft on communism." At the height of the anti-Communist hysteria, Acheson received so much hate mail that guards were posted at his house. Yet he kept a sense of humor. When cab drivers asked him, "Aren't you Dean Acheson?" he would reply, "Yes. Do I have to get out?"

From the Grand Alliance to Containment

No sooner had Americans finished celebrating the victory over Japan in August 1945 than they began to besiege the government with demands to bring the troops home. Baby shoes and photos of children arrived at the White House and Congress with notes pleading for the return of fathers and husbands to civilian life. Throughout the world, servicemen themselves staged demonstrations demanding to be sent home, and they booed the secretary of war in Manila. Under pressure, Truman approved a more rapid demobilization than most of his advisers thought prudent, but no one expected the postwar world to require a large military establishment. Most Americans expected that the Allies, led by the United States and working within the United Nations, would cooperate to manage international peace and order.

These expectations vanished quickly. When the wartime alliance forged by the United States, Great Britain, and the Soviet Union crumbled, the United States began to develop the military and diplomatic means to contain the spread of Soviet power. By 1949, the nation had reestablished the military draft, embarked on a nuclear arms race, entered into its first peacetime alliance, and committed itself to a multibillion-dollar foreign aid program.

Conflicts in the Wartime Coalition

"The guys who came out of World War Two were idealistic," reported Harold Russell, a young paratrooper whose hands had been blown off in a training accident. The veterans believed they were "coming home to build a new world. . . . We felt the day had come when the wars were all over." Public opinion polls revealed that most Americans shared the veterans' confidence in the prospects for peace.

Political leaders were less optimistic. Winston Churchill had always distrusted the Soviets; in a moment of frustration during the war, he had remarked that the only thing worse than fighting with allies was fighting without them. Indeed, once the Allies had overcome the Axis powers and no longer fought a common enemy, the prewar mistrust and antagonism between the Soviet Union and the West resurfaced as they sought to implement very different plans for the postwar world.

The Soviets' deep suspicions of the United States had scarcely diminished during the war, especially when the Western allies resisted Stalin's repeated pleas for a speedy opening of a second front in Western Europe. Soviet leaders knew that their nation had made supreme wartime sacrifices, losing more than twenty million of its citizens and vast portions of its agricultural and industrial capacity. Soviet leader Joseph Stalin wanted to require Germany to pay for the rebuilding of the Soviet economy, to eliminate any future threats to Soviet security from neighboring countries, and to expand Soviet influence in the world. Above all, Stalin wanted governments friendly to the Soviet Union on its borders in Eastern Europe, especially in Poland, which had been the path of German aggression against the Soviet Union twice within twenty-five years.

When the wartime alliance forged by the United States, Great Britain, and the Soviet Union crumbled, the United States began to develop the military and diplomatic means to contain the spread of Soviet power.

In contrast, only in the United States had war and prosperity marched hand in hand. Its land was untouched by enemy fire, and its 405,000 dead amounted to 2 percent of the Soviet loss. With its vastly expanded productive capacity and its monopoly on atomic weapons, the United States emerged from the war as the most powerful nation on the planet, replacing Britain as the dominant power in the Western world. America's sheer possession of that power, its economic interests, its leaders' understanding of how the recent war might have been avoided, and supreme confidence in American institutions all induced Truman and his associates to grasp the unprecedented role of world leadership.

With the specter of the depression still haunting the nation, U.S. officials believed that the economy's health depended in large measure on what went on in the rest of the world. To avoid a return to the hard times of the 1930s, the United States needed access to raw materials, markets for its goods, and security for American investments abroad. These needs could most readily be met in countries with economic and political systems much like its own, not in countries whose governments might institute economic controls that would interfere with the free flow of products and dollars. As Truman put it in 1947, "The American system can survive in America only if it becomes a world system."

Truman's definition of American goals reflected many citizens' feelings of national superiority. Boasting of the best economic and political system in the world, American leaders encouraged other nations to copy the United States. Convinced of the superiority of their institutions and values, Americans viewed their foreign policy not as a self-interested campaign to meet economic needs, but as an idealistic crusade to bring freedom, democracy, and capitalism to the rest of the world.

Recent history also shaped American approaches to foreign policy. Americans believed that World War II might have been avoided had Britain, France, and the United States resisted rather than appeased Hitler's initial aggression. As early as September 1945, Secretary of the Navy James V. Forrestal doubted that the United States should attempt to "buy [the Soviets'] understanding and sympathy. We tried that once with Hitler." This "Munich analogy" (referring to the 1938 conference at which Britain and France agreed to Hitler's plan to annex part of Czechoslovakia) would be evoked time and again when new challenges to the international status quo arose.

Moving toward a Cold War

The man with the ultimate responsibility for U.S. policy came to the White House with little international experience but with strong anti-Communist sentiments. When Germany attacked the Soviet Union in 1941, then Senator Truman expressed publicly the wish that the two countries would bleed each other dry. Yet as president, he hoped to maintain Soviet-American cooperation, remarking in 1945 that the Russians "have always been our friends and I can't see any reason why they shouldn't always be." For that friendship to continue, Truman demanded that the Soviet Union agree with U.S. plans for the postwar world and restrain its expansionist impulses. Proud of his ability to make quick decisions and never look back, Truman was determined to be firm about Soviet expansionism, and he knew well that America's nuclear monopoly gave him the upper hand.

Soviet and American interests clashed first in Eastern Europe. Stalin interpreted the Allies' wartime agreements as giving him a free hand in the countries that the Red Army had defeated or liberated, just as the United States was unilaterally reconstructing governments in Italy and Japan. In Poland and Bulgaria, countries bordering the Soviet Union, Stalin used harsh methods to install Communist governments that followed Moscow's party line. Elsewhere, the Soviets displayed more restraint, tolerating non-Communist governments in Hungary and Czechoslovakia before Soviet-Western hostility became intense.

To Stalin, U.S. policy seemed hypocritical in demanding elections in Eastern Europe while supporting dictatorships friendly to U.S. interests in Cuba, Nicaragua, and other Latin American countries. The United States clung to its own sphere of influence while adamantly denying one to the Soviets. But the tough words of the Western allies were no match for the Soviet armies occupying Eastern Europe: The United States and Britain sharply protested Soviet actions but would not use military force against the puppet governments installed by Stalin.

In contrast to his insistence on controlling Eastern Europe, Stalin backed down when the Western allies opposed his actions in Iran, the Soviet Union's neighbor to the southwest. Hoping to take advantage of declining British power and to gain access to Iranian oil, Stalin delayed removing troops that had been dispatched there during the war until confronted by strong Western and Iranian demands in the spring of 1946. Once the Soviets had withdrawn, the door opened for the United States to supplant British influence in Iran and to gain important oil concessions.

The Soviet Union had much more at stake in central Europe, where in 1946 the future of Germany became a central point of contention among the Allies. Having suffered two invasions by Germany in twenty-five years, the Soviet Union resolved to keep that country weak and to exact heavy reparations that it could use to rebuild the Soviet economy. American policymakers agreed on stripping Germany of its military capacity, but they also wanted a rapid industrial revival there. An economically strong Germany would foster the economic recovery of Europe and thus America's own long-term prosperity.

Unable to resolve their different plans for Germany, the Allies divided it. The Soviet Union seized industrial equipment and installed a puppet Communist government in the eastern part of the country, occupied by the Red Army. In December 1946, Britain, France, and the United States unified their occupation zones into a single body, beginning a

MAP 26.1
The Division of Europe after World War II
The "Iron Curtain," a term coined by Winston Churchill to refer to the Soviet grip on Eastern
and Central Europe, divided Europe for nearly fifty years. Communist governments controlled
every country along the Soviet Union's western border, except Finland, which remained neutral.

process that led to creation of the Federal Republic
of Germany (West Germany) in 1949.

Soviet and Western leaders faced off with hostile words in 1946. In February, Stalin called his former allies a more serious threat than Nazi Germany,
a pronouncement that Supreme Court Justice
William O. Douglas termed "the declaration of
World War III." One month later, Truman traveled
with Winston Churchill to Westminster College in
Fulton, Missouri, where the former prime minister
denounced Soviet suppression of the popular will
in Eastern and central Europe. "From Stettin in the
Baltic to Trieste in the Adriatic, an iron curtain has
descended across the continent," Churchill said.
Although Truman did not officially endorse

Churchill's words, his presence implied agreement
with the call for the development of joint British-
American strength to combat Soviet aggression. To
Stalin, Churchill's "iron curtain speech" sounded a
"call to war against the USSR."

As Soviet-Western conflict sharpened, in February 1946 career diplomat George F. Kennan sent
a memo to the State Department that furnished a
comprehensive rationale for the Truman administration's toughening stance. Kennan had spent
years working in U.S. embassies in Eastern Europe
and Moscow. Appalled at what he viewed as the
"cynicism, shamelessness, [and] contempt for humanity" displayed by Soviet officials and convinced
that optimistic assumptions about Soviet-American

cooperation were "pipe dreams," Kennan urged a hard line. He explained that "the traditional and instinctive Russian sense of insecurity" combined with Soviet leaders' need to maintain their authority at home prompted Stalin to exaggerate dangers from the capitalist world abroad. These circumstances, Kennan argued, made it impossible to negotiate with the Soviets, a conclusion shared by Secretary of State James F. Byrnes, Undersecretary Dean Acheson, Navy Secretary Forrestal, and other key Truman advisers.

Although Kennan downplayed the role of Communist ideology in Soviet foreign policy, he predicted that the Soviet Union would try to "fill every nook and cranny available to it in the basin of world power." Yet he found Soviet leaders cautious and flexible, having "no compunction about retreating in the face of superior force." Therefore, the United States should respond with "unalterable counterforce" wherever the Soviets tried to expand their influence, an approach that came to be called "containment." Forcing Russia to "face frustration indefinitely," Kennan predicted, would eventually end in "either the breakup or the gradual mellowing of Soviet power."

Kennan's message received a larger audience when he published his views under the pseudonym "X" in *Foreign Affairs* magazine in July 1947. His analysis did not so much change U.S. policy as provide a rationale for resisting Soviet actions. Kennan later expressed dismay when others used his ideas to justify what he felt was an indiscriminate American response wherever communism seemed likely to succeed. But his analysis marked a critical moment in the development of the cold war, providing a powerful argument and an intellectual framework for using U.S. power to check the spread of Soviet influence.

Although the American people displayed no enthusiasm for taking on substantial new burdens in the world, popular sentiment seemed to echo Kennan's hard-line approach to the Soviet Union. A majority of respondents to a March 1946 poll viewed Soviet actions as attempts to become the ruling power in the world and favored a strong American response. Truman's political opponents at home, the Republicans, were no more eager than their fellow citizens to send dollars or soldiers abroad. In fact, the Republican Party contained a strong isolationist element led by Ohio Senator Robert Taft. However, that did not stop Republicans from seeking political gains by charging the Truman administration with being "soft on communism."

Administration officials promoting a more conciliatory policy toward the Soviets found themselves out of work. Secretary of Commerce Henry A. Wallace, Truman's predecessor as vice president, persistently urged Truman to be more sensitive to Soviets' fears and concerns about their nation's security. In a major speech in September 1946, Wallace insisted that " 'getting tough' never brought anything real and lasting—whether for schoolyard bullies or businessmen or world powers." He urged Americans to realize "that we have no more business in the political affairs of Eastern Europe than Russia has in the political affairs of Latin America, Western Europe, and the United States." Because Wallace's words challenged the hardening direction of U.S. policy toward the Soviet Union, State Department officials were furious. When Wallace refused to be muzzled on foreign policy topics, Truman fired him in September 1946.

Containment and the Truman Doctrine

In 1947, the United States moved from tough words to action, implementing the doctrine of containment that would guide foreign policy for the next four decades. It was not an easy transition; despite public approval of a verbal hard line, Americans had had enough of international challenges. They were eager to make up for the deprivations of the depression and the war and wanted to keep their soldiers and tax dollars at home. In addition to selling containment to the public, Truman had to persuade a Congress controlled by the Republicans after the 1946 elections.

Crises in two Mediterranean countries triggered the implementation of containment. In February 1947, Britain informed the United States that its crippled economy could no longer sustain military assistance to Greece and Turkey. Turkey was trying to resist Soviet pressures, and the monarchist government in Greece, propped up by British aid, faced a challenge from internal leftists. Truman promptly decided to ask Congress for authority to send military and economic missions along with $400 million in aid to the two countries.

To pave the way for approval of the aid, Truman and his aides first met privately with congressional leaders. Dismayed at their lack of enthusiasm, Acheson painted the issue in catastrophic terms, predicting that if Greece and Turkey fell, communism would soon consume three-fourths of the planet and threaten the United States itself. After a stunned silence, Michigan Senator Arthur Vandenberg, the Republican foreign policy leader and a recent convert from isolationism, said that to get congressional approval, Truman would have to "scare hell out of the country."

Truman did just that. Speaking before Congress, he echoed Acheson's grim predictions and summoned the United States to a global commitment. He presented what would later be called the "domino theory," warning that if Greece fell to the rebels, "confusion and disorder might well spread throughout the entire Middle East . . . and would have a profound effect upon . . . Europe." Failure to step in "may endanger the peace of the world— and . . . shall surely endanger the welfare of the nation."

The assumption that American security depended on rescuing any anti-Communist government from internal rebels or outside pressure became the cornerstone of U.S. foreign policy from 1947 until the end of the 1980s.

"I told my wife to dust off my uniform," one veteran studying under the GI bill at the University of Oklahoma said in response to Truman's words. The president's crisis rhetoric along with its staggering global implications evoked dismay from Kennan himself. According to what came to be called the "Truman Doctrine," it was not just Soviet military power that must be resisted. The United States must "support free peoples who are resisting attempted subjugation by armed minorities or by outside pressures." In agreeing to aid for Greece and Turkey, Congress did not formally accept the Truman Doctrine. Yet the assumption that American security depended on rescuing any anti-Communist government from internal rebels or outside pressure became the cornerstone of U.S. foreign policy from 1947 until the end of the 1980s.

The Marshall Plan

In May 1947, in a steamy gym at Delta State Teachers College in Cleveland, Mississippi, Dean Acheson rolled up his sleeves and began to prepare the public for the next application of containment. His speech concerned Western Europe, where the war had left "factories destroyed, fields impoverished and without fertilizer or machinery, . . . transporta-

tion systems wrecked, populations scattered and on the borderline of starvation, and long-established business and trading connections disrupted."

Most Americans knew about the desperate conditions, and millions had already opened their hearts and pocketbooks, sending CARE packages and money to provide food, shelter, and clothing to people overseas. A California couple adopted a French village that the Germans had left in ruin; and a Nebraska farmer who had been able to pay off his debt during the war sent the dollar equivalent of a thousand bushels of corn. In all, Americans sent two billion dollars to alleviate suffering abroad during the first six years after the war.

Yet private generosity was not enough. Europe needed even larger-scale aid that, Acheson asserted, the United States should provide "as a matter of national self-interest." European economic recovery, U.S. policymakers believed, would halt the growth of socialist and Communist parties in France and Italy and confine Soviet influence to Eastern Europe. And because the United States could not prosper without world markets, it needed an economically strong Europe for trade.

Retired General George C. Marshall, the new secretary of state, formally unveiled the administration's plan for European recovery in a speech at Harvard University in June 1947. He invited all the European nations and the Soviet Union to cooperate in preparing a request for aid. As administration officials expected, the Soviet Union refused to meet the American terms of free trade and financial disclosure and ordered its Eastern European satellites likewise to reject the offer. Sixteen nations outside the Soviet orbit then drew up a proposal outlining their economic plans and requesting contributions from the United States. In March 1948, Congress approved the Marshall Plan, officially known as the European Recovery Program, and over the next five years the United States allocated $13 billion to restore the economies of Western Europe.

A program of economic rather than military assistance, the Marshall Plan was one of the outstanding achievements of postwar foreign policy. It helped the nations of Western Europe rebuild their war-ravaged economies and move toward a united European economy. It was also good business for the United States. The European recipients spent most of the dollars to buy American products loaded by American workers onto American ships. The economic recovery of Europe expanded the realm of raw materials, markets, and investment opportunities available to American capitalists.

U.S. AID TO EUROPE
In addition to the $13 billion of Marshall Plan aid that the U.S. government provided to Europe, private citizens also pitched in to help rebuild countries devastated by World War II. Residents of Jersey City, New Jersey, donated this snowplow being unloaded in Rome and destined for the small village of Capracotta in the Italian mountains.
Corbis–Bettmann.

Moreover, the Truman administration could point to another victory for containment, since every Western European government remained non-Communist.

While Congress debated the Marshall Plan, in February 1948 the Soviets tightened their grip on Central Europe by staging a brutal coup against the elected government of Czechoslovakia and installing a Communist regime. Truman stepped up his cold war rhetoric, condemning Stalin's "ruthless course of action" in destroying "the independence and democratic character of a whole series of nations in Eastern and Central Europe."

The president matched words with actions when the Soviets threatened Western access to Berlin in the spring of 1948. The former capital of Germany lay within the Soviet occupation zone, but all four Allies—the United States, Britain, France, and the Soviet Union— jointly occupied Berlin, dividing it into separate administrative units. When the Western Allies moved forward with plans to organize West Germany as a separate nation, the Soviets retaliated by blocking access by road and rail from West Germany to the Western-held sections of Berlin. Thus the two million inhabitants of the Western sectors were cut off from food, fuel, and other essentials.

"We stay in Berlin, period," Truman responded to this effort to force the West out. Yet he also wanted to avoid an armed confrontation with So-

viet troops. So for fifteen months, U.S. and British pilots—landing a plane every eight minutes—airlifted 2.3 million tons of goods, enough to sustain the West Berliners. Stalin hesitated to shoot down these cargo planes, and in 1949 he lifted the Berlin blockade. The city was formally divided into East Berlin, under Soviet control, and West Berlin, which became part of West Germany. To U.S. officials, the Berlin airlift confirmed the wisdom of containment: When challenged, the Russians would back down, as Kennan had predicted.

The policy of containment reflected the dashed hopes that the major powers would cooperate through the United Nations. Instead, the new international organization served more as a propaganda body for its member nations. It provided a mechanism for nations to discuss disputes, and perhaps its moral authority and ability to claim world attention exercised restraints on nations. But it could not act without unanimity on the Security Council, where the Soviet-American split prevented any effective action.

Creating a National Security State

The new policy of containment demanded a military capacity to back it up. During the Truman years, the United States fashioned a five-pronged defense strategy: (1) development of atomic weapons, (2) strengthening of traditional military power,

THE BERLIN AIRLIFT
These German children standing on the rubble of war wave to planes carrying food and other ne-cessities to Berlin during the Soviet blockade in 1948. Truman and his advisers were "prepared to use any means that may be necessary to stay in Berlin." To reduce the risk of war, the president decided on an airlift rather than attempting to send ground convoys through Soviet lines.
Corbis–Bettmann.

(3) military alliances with other nations, (4) programs of military and economic aid to friendly nations, and (5) an extensive espionage network and secret means to subvert Communist expansion.

When Truman's press secretary called reporters to his office and released a statement on September 23, 1949, they rushed so fast for the telephones that they destroyed a stuffed deer's head in the process. Sending them scrambling was Truman's announcement that the Soviets had detonated an atomic bomb. Even though U.S. policymakers had known that the Soviet Union was working on an A-bomb, its success came years ahead of most predictions and shocked the American public.

Losing its nuclear monopoly pushed the United States to build an even deadlier weapon. In January 1950, Truman approved development of the hydrogen bomb, a weapon based on a thermonuclear explosion equivalent to five hundred atomic bombs. At its first test explosion in March 1954, the hydrogen bomb—known as the "super bomb"—produced a force one thousand times greater than the atomic bomb used on Hiroshima. But America's

thermonuclear advantage was brief; in November 1955, the Soviet Union exploded its own super bomb.

From the 1950s through the 1980s, the United States conducted a nuclear defense strategy based on the concept of "deterrence": The Americans would strive to maintain a more powerful nuclear force than the Russians, thereby deterring the Soviets from attacking the United States. Because the Soviets pursued a similar policy, the superpowers became locked in an ever escalating race for nuclear dominance. Albert Einstein, whose mathematical discoveries had laid the foundations for nuclear weapons, commented grimly on the enormous destructive force now possessed by the superpowers. The war that came after World War III, he said, would be fought with stones.

Along with vastly increasing its nuclear arsenal, the United States beefed up its conventional military power to deter Soviet threats that might not warrant nuclear retaliation, such as the Berlin blockade. To curtail squabbling among the military branches and streamline defense strategy planning, Congress passed the National Security Act in 1947.

That law brought the military branches together under a single secretary of defense and created the National Security Council (NSC) to advise the president on defense policy.

As the Berlin crisis simmered in 1948, Congress stepped up appropriations for the air force and enacted a peacetime draft. Urged on by General Dwight D. Eisenhower and other military leaders, Congress also granted permanent status to the women's military branches, thereby allowing women to volunteer. With around 1.5 million men and women in uniform in 1950, the military strength of the United States stood at more than four times its prewar level, and in 1947, defense expenditures claimed one-third of the federal budget.

Collective security, the third arm of postwar military strategy and the sharpest break from America's past, also developed during the Berlin showdown of 1948. That June, the administration won Senate support for the general principle of regional alliances for collective security. One year later, the United States joined Canada and Western European nations in its first peacetime military alliance, the North Atlantic Treaty Organization (NATO), which was created to counter the Soviet threat to Western Europe. For the first time in its history the United States pledged to go to war should one of its allies be attacked.

The fourth part of postwar defense strategy operated foreign aid programs to strengthen friendly countries. Military and economic assistance to Greece and Turkey in 1947 was one example of this strategy. Another was the $13 billion Marshall Plan that helped Western European nations to revive their war-crippled economies. In addition, in 1949, Congress approved $1 billion of military aid to its NATO allies and began economic assistance to nations in other parts of the world.

Finally, the United States began to develop its espionage capacities and the means to subvert communism through secret activities, operations that would form a larger part of foreign policy after the Truman years. The National Security Act of 1947 created the Central Intelligence Agency (CIA) to gather information considered necessary to the national defense. Truman and his advisers assured legislators who were uneasy about a peacetime spying agency that the CIA's powers would be limited. Nonetheless, the legislation authorized the new agency to perform any "functions and duties related to intelligence affecting the national security" that the NSC might authorize. Eventually, CIA agents conducted secret operations that toppled legitimate foreign governments and violated the rights of U.S. citizens. In many respects, the CIA was unaccountable to Congress or the public.

By 1950, the United States had abandoned age-old tenets of foreign policy. In place of the isolationism and neutrality that had followed World War I, the country embarked on economic and military efforts to control events far beyond its borders. The new policy of containment worked reasonably well in Europe. Short of war, the United States could not stop the descent of the iron curtain, but it acted aggressively and successfully to promote economic recovery and a military shield for the rest of Europe, thereby diminishing the threat of any further extension of Communist power.

Superpower Rivalry around the Globe

Although Europe occupied the center of the Truman administration's attention, it was not the only place where the United States sought to implement containment. The defeat of Japan, Italy, and Germany and the declining power of Britain and France left immense power vacuums in parts of the world that these countries had controlled or colonized. Assuming that the Soviet Union would try to fill those vacuums, U.S. policymakers sought to promote stability in Asia and win friends among the nations casting off colonial domination throughout the world. These nations collectively came to be referred to as the "third world," a term denoting countries outside the Western and Soviet orbits (especially in Africa, the Middle East, and Asia) that had not developed industrial economies.

Assuming that the Soviet Union would try to fill power vacuums around the world, U.S. policymakers sought to promote stability in Asia and win friends among the nations casting off colonial domination.

The United States soon encountered enormous difficulties in attempting to extend containment beyond Western Europe. Political and economic conditions in the Middle East and Asia proved volatile and complex, and Truman failed to achieve the bipartisan consensus in Congress that had ensured approval of his European initiatives. The United States remained the most powerful nation in the world, but it could not manage events everywhere to suit its interests.

The Rise of National Liberation Movements

In Africa, the Middle East, and Asia, World War II furthered a tide of national liberation movements against war-weakened imperial powers. Between 1945 and 1960, forty countries containing more than one-quarter of the world's people won their independence. As these nations ousted their former colonial rulers, both the United States and the Soviet Union sought to foster governments that were friendly to their own interests and institutions.

Like Woodrow Wilson during World War I, Roosevelt and Truman promoted the ideal of national self-determination. The United States granted independence to its own dominion the Philippines on July 4, 1946. American officials applauded the British withdrawal from India, Burma, and Ceylon and the Dutch retreat from Indonesia in 1949, and they encouraged France to relinquish its empire in Indochina.

As the cold war intensified, however, the ideal of self-determination gave way to American leaders' worries about the nature of the new governments that had been established in the ruins of European and Japanese imperialism. Policymakers wanted to preserve opportunities for American trade, and U.S. corporations coveted the vast oil reserves in the Middle East. Access to that oil was also critical to the European nations.

Moreover, the United States viewed its own revolution as the best model for independence movements and expected newly emerging nations to create institutions in the American democratic and capitalist image. But many independence movements were more impressed with the Russian Revolution and the rapid economic growth it had spawned. Although they tended to have few or no direct ties with the Soviet Union, many newly independent nations adopted socialist or Communist ideas. American leaders insisted on viewing these movements as a threatening extension of Soviet power. And they increasingly demanded that new nations take sides in the cold war, forgetting the importance of neutrality in their own diplomatic tradition. The bipolar lens of United States–Soviet Union conflict colored the American and Soviet views of the entire world.

In 1949, the Truman administration initiated the Point IV program of technical aid to the third world. The program aimed to hold communism at bay by fostering economic development and political stability, but the dollars spent were few compared with those spent on European aid. For the most part, Africa and Latin America remained on the periphery of Truman's attention and did not become entangled in the global rivalry between the superpowers until the 1950s and 1960s. The Middle East and Asia were the third world hot spots of the Truman years.

Nationalist Turmoil in the Middle East

In 1943, when the U.S. government was doing little to save European Jews from the Nazi terror, then-Senator Harry Truman spoke passionately at a rally called to focus attention on the Holocaust. Urging the United States to do everything "humanly possible to provide a haven and a place of safety" for Hitler's victims, Truman maintained, "This is not a Jewish problem, it is an American problem—and we must . . . face it squarely and honorably."

As president, Truman grasped the opportunity to make good on his words when he confronted the establishment of a Jewish homeland in Palestine. Jews had been settling in Palestine since the nineteenth century, and Nazi persecution during World War II swelled the tide of Jewish migration. In 1917, Britain had promised the Jews a homeland in territory that Britain did not then control but that became a British protectorate with the defeat of the Turks in World War I.

After World War II, hundreds of thousands of European Jews sought refuge in Palestine. American immigration policy continued to allow relatively few Jewish refugees to settle in the United States, and Truman urged Britain to lift the limits it had set on Jewish immigrants to Palestine. Fighting between Palestinian Arabs and Jews raged into brutal terrorism on both sides, and the British were reluctant to do anything that might increase tensions or alienate Arabs in other parts of the Middle East who controlled oil resources.

Truman's support for a Jewish state in Palestine distressed nearly all of his foreign policy experts, who saw American-Arab friendship as a critical factor in blocking Soviet influence in the Middle East and securing U.S. interests in Arabian petroleum. The president was more sympathetic to the enormous pressure marshaled by Jewish organizations and to the resolutions from thirty-three state legis-

latures supporting a Jewish state in Palestine. His
position reflected a moral commitment to the Holocaust survivors as well as his interest in keeping the
American Jewish vote within the Democratic fold.

When Jews in Palestine declared the independent state of Israel in May 1948, Truman waited just
eleven minutes after the declaration became official
to recognize the new country. Arab forces immediately attacked Israel, and Truman pledged assistance, making the defense of Israel the cornerstone
of U.S. Middle Eastern policy. In acting on his moral
and political instincts, Truman uncharacteristically
defied his foreign policy advisers. A national homeland was scant compensation for the horrors inflicted upon European Jews during World War II,
yet its establishment drove thousands of Palestinians from their homes and left the Middle East in
turmoil for decades to come.

Communism Triumphs in China

On the other side of the globe, a civil war raged in
China, where the Communists, led by Mao Zedong
(Mao Tse-tung), fought the official Nationalist government under Chiang Kai-shek. Eight years of war
against the Japanese had taken a terrible toll, but
the Communists gained increasing support among
the peasants for their courageous stand against

the Japanese and their land reforms. In contrast,
Chiang's corrupt government and incompetent
management of the war against Japan alienated
much of the population.

The United States took a keen interest in China,
dating back to the Open Door policy of the turn of
the century. Although the Chinese Communists remained independent of Moscow and received very
little Soviet aid, many U.S. officials feared the expansion of Soviet power should the Communists
prevail in the civil war. Moreover, the Truman administration was under extreme pressure not to
"lose" China to the Communists from the so-called
China bloc, a lobby that included Republican members of Congress, religious groups with missionary
ties to China, and Henry R. Luce, the son of missionaries and the publisher of the influential *Time*
and *Life* magazines.

To Truman and his advisers, however, Europe
remained the hub of U.S. interests. They believed
that diversion of American resources from Europe
to China would be not only unwise, but also futile,
given the incompetence of Chiang's government.
After a failed effort at negotiations in 1946, the United
States provided some token aid to Chiang to mol-
lify the China bloc and to signal its interest, but the
Truman administration for the most part simply
awaited the inevitable downfall of the Nationalists.

In December 1949, Mao established the People's Republic of China (PRC); the Nationalists fled to the island of Taiwan two months later. Some administration officials urged accommodation with Communist China, but the outbreak of war in Korea in June 1950 foreclosed that option. The United States refused to recognize the existence of the PRC, blocked its admission to the United Nations, and continued to provide aid to Chiang's government in Taiwan.

"We picked a bad horse," Truman remarked, explaining the Communist victory as the result of the corrupt Nationalist government. The State Department viewed Mao's victory as "the product of internal Chinese forces, forces which this country tried to influence but could not." Nothing less than a massive U.S. military commitment could have stopped the Chinese Communists. But some Americans blamed Truman and his advisers. Republicans

CHIANG KAI-SHEK AND MAO ZEDONG
The leaders of the opposing sides in the Chinese civil war — the communist Mao Zedong (on the right) and the Nationalist Chiang Kai-shek — met in Chungking in 1945 to discuss forming a coalition government after driving out the Japanese. These negotiations failed. After four years of conflict, in 1949 the Communists established the People's Republic of China under Mao, while Chiang and his supporters fled to the island of Taiwan.
Jack Wilkes, *Life* Magazine © Time Inc.

cried that Truman had "lost" China, and one critic assailed "the pro-Communists in the State Department who . . . aided in the Communist conquest of China."

Truman's political wounds over the "loss" of China were partially self-inflicted. He had warned repeatedly of the threat of Communist expansion, and he had implied that the United States could contain that threat. China tested the boundaries of U.S. power and found it to be limited, a situation that was difficult for Americans to accept. It was easier to believe the Republicans when they blamed subversives in the U.S. government for the Communist victory in China. China became a political albatross for the Democrats, who resolved never again to be in a position that would allow their opponents to accuse them of being soft on communism.

The Reverse Course in Japan

As it became clear that China could not fulfill American hopes for a stable ally in Asia, the administration reconsidered its plans for postwar Japan. Initially, it had aimed to prevent Japan from threatening peace again by reforming its political and economic institutions. The U.S. military occupation headed by General Douglas MacArthur purged Japanese militarists from official positions, pushed Japan to adopt a democratic constitution, and made plans to break up huge concentrations of economic power.

As the situation in China worsened, Truman's advisers began to reassess the occupation strategy, and by 1948 they had reversed their original plans for the economic decentralization of Japan. Now the United States promoted the swift economic recovery of its former enemy, just as it had done in Germany. The new goals were to rapidly reindustrialize and to secure Japanese access to markets and natural resources in Asia. The United States also moved to silence leftist groups and return to power many officials who had promoted wartime Japanese aggression. After a sluggish start, the Japanese economy flourished. Within three decades, Japan would challenge the industrial supremacy of the United States.

American soldiers remained on military bases in Japan, but the official occupation ended when the two nations signed a peace treaty and a mutual security pact in September 1951. As had been the case with Germany, Japan sat squarely within the American orbit, ready to serve as an economic hub for Asia.

Truman and the Fair Deal at Home

Referring to the Civil War general who coined the phrase "War is hell," Truman said in December 1945, "Sherman was wrong. I'm telling you I find peace is hell." Challenged by thorny problems abroad, Truman also had to deal with shortages, strikes, inflation, and other problems attending the reconversion of the economy to peacetime production. At the same time, he tried to expand New Deal reform, most notably into the areas of civil rights, housing, education, and health care.

> *Referring to the Civil War general who coined the phrase "War is hell," Truman said in December 1945, "Sherman was wrong. I'm telling you I find peace is hell."*

Yet obstacles abounded to Truman's domestic agenda, which came to be known as the Fair Deal. Four years of war had left most Americans weary of government intervention in the economy, eager to hold on to their wartime gains but not disposed to engage in more social and economic experiments. Business leaders' role in the wartime production miracle had greatly elevated their influence, which they now directed against Truman's reform proposals. Not only did Truman battle Republicans in Congress, but even when the Democrats controlled Congress, he failed to win most of his legislative goals. For the most part, Truman had to settle for consolidation of reforms that were already in place.

Truman's Program and Postwar Politics

Despite the deprivations and inconveniences caused by World War II, most Americans had enjoyed a wartime standard of living that was higher than ever before. Economic experts and ordinary citizens alike worried about whether that standard could be sustained in peacetime and whether an economy no longer stimulated by massive government purchasing could provide jobs for millions of returning soldiers.

Truman wasted no time in unveiling his plan for converting the economy from military to peacetime production. Within days of the Japanese surrender, he went to Congress with a twenty-one-point program. Truman wanted to retain controls over the economy to ease the reconversion process and sought new authority to promote full employment. He proposed measures to assist minorities, low-income workers, farmers, and small businesses and called for long-range programs that would ensure decent housing, adequate medical care, and a good

TABLE 26.1
WORK STOPPAGES IN THE UNITED STATES, **1936–1947**

Year	Number	Average Length of Stoppage (days)	Workers Involved (in thousands)
1936	2,172	23.3	789
1937	4,740	20.3	1,860
1938	2,772	23.6	688
1939	2,613	23.4	1,170
1940	2,508	20.9	577
1941	4,288	18.3	2,360
1942	2,968	11.7	840
1943	3,752	5.0	1,980
1944	4,956	5.6	2,120
1945	4,750	9.9	3,470
1946	4,985	24.2	4,600
1947	3,693	25.6	2,170

Source: U.S. Department of Labor, *Handbook of Labor Statistics,* 1974.

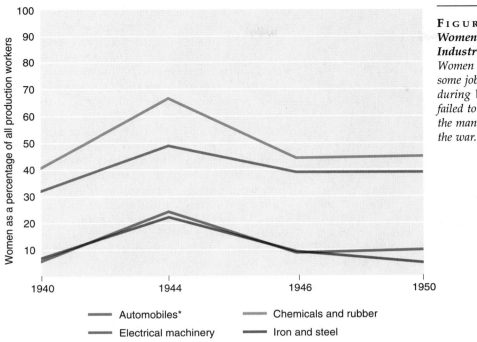

FIGURE 26.1
Women Workers in Selected Industries, 1940–1950
Women demolished the idea that some jobs were "men's work" during World War II, but they failed to maintain their gains in the manufacturing sector after the war.

Automobiles*   Chemicals and rubber
Electrical machinery   Iron and steel

*During World War II, this industry did not produce cars, but rather military transportation such as jeeps, tanks, aircraft, etc.

education for every citizen. "Not even President Roosevelt ever asked for as much at one sitting," exploded Republican leader Joseph W. Martin Jr.

Congress enacted Truman's proposal for full-employment legislation in a watered-down form. The Employment Act of 1946 declared it the "responsibility of the Federal Government . . . to promote maximum employment, production, and purchasing power," thereby formalizing what had been implicit in Roosevelt's actions to counter the depression—government's responsibility for maintaining a healthy economy. The law created a Council of Economic Advisers to assist the president in economic planning, but it authorized no new powers to translate the government's new obligation into effective action.

Inflation rather than unemployment turned out to be the most severe problem in the early postwar years. Unable to buy civilian goods during the war, in 1945 alone consumers had saved nearly $30 billion that they now itched to spend. But shortages of meat, automobiles, appliances, housing, and a host of other items persisted. Some six million people wanted new cars in 1946, but auto manufacturers managed to produce fewer than three million.

Housing was so scarce that returning veterans lived in basements, garages, and even automobiles.

Until industry could convert fully to civilian production, making more goods available, consumer demand could only drive up prices. Struggling with the problems of reconversion, Truman complained that the wartime unity had been replaced by greed. "The Congress [is] balking, labor has gone crazy, and management isn't far from insane in selfishness," he wrote his mother in October 1945.

Labor wanted to keep price controls but sought wage increases at the same time. Corporations, however, demanded that the government abandon price controls, and they found allies in Republicans and conservative Democrats. Truman took an inconsistent course until he scuttled the Office of Price Administration after the Republicans gained control of Congress in the 1946 elections. The consumer price index—an official measurement of the rate of inflation—shot up by 18 percent in 1946, but the shift to peacetime production occurred swiftly enough to save the United States from crippling inflation. However, it did not save the administration from taking the blame, during the 1946 elections, for rising prices.

What Happened to Rosie the Riveter?

ALTHOUGH STUDIES HAVE BEEN DONE of the post-war lives of World War II soldiers, we know much less about another group of "veterans," the women who helped fight the war on the domestic front. Statistics show that women's employment fell by more than two million between 1945 and 1947. But gross statistics don't reveal which women left the labor force and why, and they obscure the experiences of women who continued to work but in different jobs.

We do know what public officials and business and labor leaders expected of women who had taken up "men's" work during the war. With the shadow of the depression still hovering, Americans doubted that the economy could accommodate the six million new women workers along with millions of returning veterans once wartime production had ceased. A nearly universal response to anxieties about unemployment pushed a big part of the responsibility on women: In place of their wartime duty to produce the goods needed for victory came their postwar obligation to withdraw from the labor force.

The message that they should quit their jobs "for the sake of their homes as well as the labor situation" overwhelmed women. The company newspaper at Kaiser shipyards in the Pacific Northwest proclaimed in May 1945, "The Kitchen—Women's Big Post-War Goal." Putting words into the mouths of Kaiser's female employees, the article asserted, "Brothers, the tin hat and welder's torch will be yours! . . . The thing we want to do is take off these unfeminine garments and button ourselves into something starched and pretty." A General Electric ad predicted that women would welcome a return to "their old housekeeping routine" because GE intended to transform housework with new appliances. Some experts connected married women's employment to their obligations to help their husbands readjust to civilian life. A psychiatrist warned that women's economic independence might "raise problems in the future," urging women to realize

that "reunion means relinquishing it [their independence]—to some extent at any rate."

Other evidence suggests that many women did not have to be told to give up their wartime jobs. Skyrocketing marriage and birthrates reveal the attraction of home and family life to people compelled to postpone marriage and childbearing during the depression and the war. Thanks to the accumulation of wartime savings, veterans' benefits, and favorable opportunities for men in the postwar economy, many families found it possible to rely on a single earner.

The double burdens of married women who took wartime jobs suggest another reason for women's voluntary withdrawal from the workforce. The wartime scarcity of goods had made housekeeping much more difficult, especially for women who typically worked forty-eight hours a week with one day off. Shopping became a problem because stores often sold out of goods early in the day, and few shops kept evening or Sunday hours. Washing machines, refrigerators, vacuum cleaners, and other appliances that might have lightened women's burdens were not produced at all during the war. Child care centers accommodated only about 10 percent of the children of employed mothers. Employed women with families to care for were simply worn out.

Yet surveys reported that 75 percent of women in wartime jobs wanted—and usually needed—to keep them. As two women employed at a Ford plant in Memphis put it, "Women didn't stop eating when the war stopped." Those who needed and wanted to remain in the workforce experienced the most wrenching changes. The vast majority were able to find jobs; in fact, women's workforce participation began growing again in 1947 and reached the wartime peak by 1950. But women lost the traditionally male, higher-paying jobs in durable goods industries (such as iron and steel and automobile and machinery production) and were pushed back into the lower-paying light manufacturing and service industries that had customarily welcomed them.

Statistics tell part of the story of this displacement. Women virtually disappeared from ship-building, and their share of jobs in the auto industry fell from 25 percent in 1944 to 10 percent in 1950. In the burgeoning Los Angeles aircraft industry, the proportion of women plunged from a wartime peak of 40 percent to 12 percent in 1948, rising to just 25 percent in the 1950s. Even in light manufacturing,

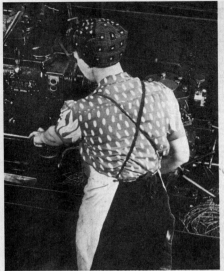

Sisters under the apron—Yesterday's war worker becomes today's housewife.

What's Become of Rosie the Riveter?

WOMEN'S POSTWAR FUTURE
This photograph headed an article in the New York Times Magazine *in June 1946. The article, written by the head of the Women's Bureau of the Department of Labor, discussed the needs of women workers, stressed their right to work and to equal pay, but also assumed that they would all but vanish from heavy manufacturing.*
Ellen Kaiper.

such as the electrical goods industry, where women had claimed one-third of the prewar jobs, women maintained their numbers but were bumped down to lower-paying work. During the war, women had narrowed the wage gap between men and women, but in 1950, women earned only 53 percent of what men did.

How women reacted to their displacement can be pieced together from what they were willing to say to reporters and oral history interviewers and what they wrote to government agencies and labor unions. "Women do not expect or want to hold jobs at the expense of returning soldiers," proclaimed a resolution passed by the Women's Trade Union League, expressing women's overwhelming support for veterans' claims to jobs based on seniority awarded for the years of their wartime service. According to Tina Hill, a black worker at North American Aircraft in Los Angeles, being laid off "didn't bother me much. I was just glad that the war was over . . . [and] my husband had a job." Nonetheless, after doing domestic work, when North American called her back, she recalled, "was I a happy soul!"

When management violated women's seniority rights by hiring nonveterans, some women protested bitterly. According to an automobile worker, "We have women laid off with seniority . . . and every day they hire in new men off the street. They hire men, they say, to do the heavy work. . . . During the war they didn't care what kind of work we did." When Ford laid off women with as many as twenty-seven years' seniority, 150 women picketed with signs that read, "The Hand That Rocks the Cradle Can Build Tractors, Too." A worker infuriated by her union's failure to protect women's seniority rights told a reporter, "We are making the bullets now, and we will give the [union executive] board members a blast that will blow them out of their shoes."

Protest from a minority of women workers could not save the jobs that "Rosies" had held during the war. Despite women's exemplary performance, most employers still saw women and men as different species fit for different roles and deserving of disparate rewards. Most labor unions paid lip service to representing all their members, but even the most progressive unions gave low priority to protecting women's seniority rights. In the absence of a feminist movement that could have given visibility and credibility to their claims for equal treatment, most Rosie the Riveters resigned themselves to the *status quo ante bellum.*

Labor Becomes More Militant

Labor relations constituted another thorn in Truman's side. Organized labor survived the war stronger than ever, its 14.5 million members making up 35 percent of the civilian workforce. Yet union members feared erosion of wartime gains. With wage controls in place throughout the war, the rising incomes enjoyed by working-class families had depended largely on the availability of new jobs and the chance to work longer hours. The end of overtime meant a 30 percent cut in take-home pay for most workers.

Women who had flocked into wartime jobs also saw their earnings decline. Many women were ready to return to their homes, but as many as 68 to 85 percent, according to some polls, wanted to keep their jobs. Most "Rosie the Riveters" (a nickname based on a wartime image of women factory workers popularized in a Norman Rockwell painting) who remained in the workforce did so only by accepting lower-paying jobs in light industry or the service sector. Displaced from her shipyard work, Marie Schreiber found work as a cashier. "You were back to women's wages, you know . . . practically in half," she recalled. Men replaced tens of thousands of women in iron, steel, and other heavy industries that paid relatively good wages. From a wartime high of 36 percent, in 1947 women held just 27 percent of all jobs.

Most unions paid scant attention to the problems of women workers as they struggled to defend labor's interests in the postwar economy. Using the power to strike, which unions had patriotically given up during the war, seemed the only way to avoid the hard times of the 1930s. As it had after World War I, labor militancy erupted soon after the surrender of Japan. From September 1945 to the end of 1946, five million workers stopped production in virtually every major industry. The nation lost more than twenty million worker-days in February 1946 alone, and more strikes took place in 1946 than at any other time in U.S. history.

Workers saw corporate owners and executives profiting at their expense. Shortly before his union took a strike vote, a twenty-four-year-old Pittsburgh steelworker and former marine read about a lavish party given by a company executive. He and his fellow carpoolers figured out that the party would cost more than their total earnings for a year's work in the steel mills. The veteran remembered, "That sort of stuff made us realize, hell, we *had* to bite the bullet . . . the bosses sure didn't give a damn for us."

Union members had reason to believe that Truman didn't give a damn for them either. Strikes interfered with rapid reconversion, and demands for higher wages threatened to thrust the economy into a spiral of inflation. Truman and his associates strong-armed both management and labor, but both sides frequently thumbed their noses at government recommendations. While the president vented his displeasure with labor and management alike, his efforts to curb strikes provoked angry attacks from labor leaders. When Truman tried to end the General Motors strike in December 1946, CIO President Philip Murray charged him with trying "to weaken and ultimately destroy labor union organization."

Although most Americans approved of unions in principle, they were fed up with labor stoppages, blamed unions for rising prices, and wanted more government restrictions on organized labor. Truman shared the public exasperation and resorted to drastic measures when strikes affected critical industries. In May 1946, after coal miners rejected government recommendations for a settlement, and their strike threatened the steel, auto, and railroad industries as well, Truman placed the mines under federal control.

Then, when the railroad workers walked out two days later, Truman decided to seek authority to draft into the armed services workers who struck in essential industries. Cautioned by his advisers who questioned the constitutionality of such a measure, Truman shot back, "We'll draft them and think about the law later." The plan to draft strikers infuriated labor and its liberal allies, and even conservative Republicans found his remedy too drastic. Settlement of the railroad strike just as Truman presented his proposal to Congress did little to quell the outrage against him.

Although strikes subsided by the end of 1946, antilabor sentiment lingered, and Truman faced the labor issue again in 1947. In general, labor's postwar militancy won wage increases of around 20 percent for unionized workers. But the loss of overtime combined with rising prices left labor's purchasing power only slightly higher than it had been in 1942, while real income in other sectors of the economy had risen.

Reconversion and the Economic Boom

By 1947, the nation had survived the strains of reconversion and avoided the nearly universally expected postwar depression. Wartime profits enabled businesses to invest in new plants and equipment.

Consumers used their billions of dollars in wartime savings to buy the houses, cars, and appliances that had been denied them during the depression and the war. Defense spending and the $38 billion in grants and loans that enabled war-torn countries to purchase American goods also stimulated the economy. A soaring birthrate, 25 percent higher in 1949 than in 1940, further sustained consumer demand.

The nation's gratitude to its returning warriors also boosted the economy. Under the Servicemen's Readjustment Act (the GI Bill), passed in 1944, sixteen million veterans could claim unemployment compensation while they looked for jobs; low-interest loans to purchase homes, farms, and small businesses; and funds for job training and educa-

tion. By 1948, some 1.3 million veterans had bought houses with government loans, and more than 7 million had received funds for tuition, books, and living expenses related to job training and education. Men who had dodged bullets at Normandy and Iwo Jima now poured into crowded college classrooms.

As a form of affirmative action program for veterans, the GI Bill inadvertently disadvantaged women, who filled just a tiny portion of military slots during the war. For example, women's enrollments grew after the war, but their share of college degrees dropped below the prewar level. Nor could the vast majority of women claim the preference in hiring that veterans enjoyed from private and public employers alike. As wives and daughters of veterans, women did benefit indirectly from the GI subsidies, which helped almost one of every four Americans.

Americans in the late 1940s went on a spending spree. Between 1946 and 1950, a population of about 150 million purchased more than 20 million automobiles and refrigerators, 5.5 million electric stoves, and 11.6 million television sets. The number of owner-occupied houses increased from 15.2 million in 1940 to 23.5 million in 1950; by the end of the decade, most families owned their own homes.

Yet economic prosperity was not universal. The real gains had been made during the war, and family income actually declined slightly between 1944 and 1950. Wages and salaries increased by 23 percent from 1945 to 1950, but prices went up by 36.2 percent. A recession in 1949 threw 7 percent of the labor force out of work; it abated only when the Korean War sparked economic recovery. Moreover, the one-third of all Americans who lived in poverty failed to receive any significant benefits from the return to peacetime production.

Black Protest and the Politics of Civil Rights

"I spent four years in the army to free a bunch of Frenchmen and Dutchmen," an African American corporal declared, "and I'm hanged if I'm going to let the Alabama version of the Germans kick me around when I get home." Black soldiers and civilians alike resolved that the return to peace would not be a return to the racial injustices of prewar America. Their political clout had grown with the migration of two million African Americans to northern and western cities, where they could vote

VETERANS GO TO COLLEGE
So many World War II veterans wanted to use their GI benefits for higher education that colleges were overwhelmed, and many had to turn away students. These veterans, sprinting out of the building where they have just registered, express their joy at having been admitted to Indiana University in 1947.
Indiana University Photographic Services.

and their ballots could make a difference. Even in the South, the proportion of blacks who cast ballots inched up from 2 percent to 12 percent in the 1940s. Pursuing civil rights through the courts and Congress, the National Association for the Advancement of Colored People (NAACP) counted half a million members.

"I spent four years in the army to free a bunch of Frenchmen and Dutchmen," an African American corporal declared, "and I'm hanged if I'm going to let the Alabama version of the Germans kick me around when I get home."

In the postwar period, individual blacks broke through the color barrier, achieving several "firsts" for their race. Jackie Robinson integrated major league baseball when he took over second base for the Brooklyn Dodgers in 1947. Overcoming abuse from both fans and players, Robinson performed brilliantly and ended the season with the rookie of the year award. Two other African Americans toppled racial barriers in 1950: Ralph J. Bunche, who received the Nobel Peace Prize for his contributions to the United Nations, and Gwendolyn Brooks, who won the Pulitzer Prize for poetry.

However, in most respects, African Americans found that little had changed after the war, especially in the South, where a wave of violence erupted when they tried to assert their rights. White men with guns turned back Medgar Evers (who would become a key civil rights leader in the 1960s) and four other veterans who were trying to vote in Mississippi. Angry crowds flogged another Mississippi veteran who attempted to register. A mob lynched Isaac Nixon for voting in Georgia, and an all-white jury acquitted those accused of his murder. Governors, U.S. senators, and other southern politicians routinely intimidated potential voters with threats of economic retaliation and violence.

"My very stomach turned over when I learned that Negro soldiers just back from overseas were being dumped out of army trucks in Mississippi and beaten," wrote Truman. Shaken by the violence against blacks and pressured by civil rights leaders and their liberal allies, he believed that his responsibility as chief executive compelled action against blatant injustice. Truman grasped the importance of black and liberal votes to Democratic Party fortunes in northern states, but he knew equally well how much the party relied on a solid bloc of white southern votes. Wrestling with these counterforces, Truman acted more boldly on civil rights than had any previous president.

In 1946, Truman created a Committee on Civil Rights. Not surprisingly, this committee of distinguished Americans found glaring and widespread racial discrimination, and it recommended measures to protect voting rights and eliminate segregation. In February 1948, Truman sent a special message to Congress calling for enactment of the committee's recommendations. The first president to address the NAACP, Truman announced to that group that all Americans should have equal rights to housing, education, employment, and the ballot.

JACKIE ROBINSON
John Roosevelt Robinson slides into home in a game against the Philadelphia Phillies in 1952. Before he became, in 1947, the first African American to play major-league baseball, Robinson had excelled at track as well as baseball at UCLA and had been an Army officer in World War II. Even his brilliant play for the Brooklyn Dodgers did not save him from fans' and players' racial taunts or exclusion from restaurants and hotels that catered to his white teammates. Having paved the way for other black players, Robinson played until 1956.
The Michael Barson Collection/Past Perfect.

To the dismay of civil rights leaders, the president did not always match his words with equally forceful deeds. He failed to follow up on his messages by having specific bills introduced into Congress. In the throes of the 1948 election campaign, and under threat of civil disobedience action proposed by A. Philip Randolph (who had pressured Roosevelt by threatening an African American march on Washington in 1941), the president did issue an executive order to desegregate the armed services. But he allowed the order to go unimplemented until the need for military personnel during the Korean War forced the military's hand.

Though Truman continued to call for civil rights legislation, a combination of southern Democrats and Republicans killed every bill that was in-

SEGREGATION
Signs like this were a normal feature of life in the South from the late nineteenth century until the 1960s. State and local laws mandated segregation in every aspect of life, literally from the cradle to the grave. African Americans could not use white hospitals, cemeteries, schools, libraries, swimming pools, playgrounds, restrooms, or drinking fountains. They were relegated to balconies in movie theaters and kept apart from whites in all public meetings.
Martin Magner/Courtesy, Center for Creative Photography, The University of Arizona.

troduced. Nor was he able to rally much popular support for his program. Among those polled in a national survey in 1949, nearly half opposed federal action against job discrimination, while just 34 percent believed that the government should "go all the way" to ensure equal opportunity.

Nonetheless, Truman's Justice Department aligned the administration with the NAACP by filing *amicus curiae* ("friend of the court") briefs supporting legal challenges to segregation and discrimination. In 1948, the Supreme Court struck a blow at housing discrimination in *Shelley v. Kramer.* Two years later, it ruled that a state university could not segregate black students (*McLaurin v. Oklahoma State Regents*) and that an inferior school established to keep African Americans out of the University of Texas Law School violated their right to equal protection (*Sweatt v. Painter*).

Although the gap loomed large between what Truman said about civil rights and what his administration accomplished, the desegregation of the military and the support of civil rights cases in the Supreme Court kindled far-reaching changes. Breaking sharply with the past, Truman used the prestige and visibility of his office to educate the public and set a moral agenda, thereby encouraging the struggles of African Americans that would bring more substantial progress in years to come.

The "Do-Nothing Congress" and the 1948 Election

Truman's difficulties with economic reconversion and strikes gave the Republicans an edge in the 1946 congressional elections. Portraying Truman as a little man in a big job that was way over his head, they accused his administration of "confusion, corruption, and communism" and jeered, "To Err Is Truman." Capturing Congress for the first time in fourteen years, the Republicans looked eagerly to the 1948 presidential campaign.

Although many Republicans campaigned against New Deal "regimentation," "bureaucracy," and "radicalism," their dominance of the 80th Congress, elected in 1946, failed to dismantle the reforms of the 1930s. Congress made slight assaults on reform programs with budget cuts and, overriding Truman's veto, favored higher income groups with tax cuts. Its most serious attack on the New Deal was the Taft-Hartley Act, passed in 1947.

Called a "slave labor" law and "Tuff-Heartless" by unions, Taft-Hartley imposed restrictions that

TRUMAN'S WHISTLE-STOP CAMPAIGN
Harry Truman rallies a crowd from his campaign train at a stop in Bridgeport, Pennsylvania, in October 1948. His campaign theme song, "I'm just wild about Harry," was borrowed, with the words slightly changed, from a musical written in 1921. This was the last election in which the pollsters predicted the wrong winner. They stopped taking polls in mid-October, after which many voters apparently changed their minds. One commentator praised the American citizenry, who "couldn't be ticketed by the polls, knew its own mind and had picked the rather unlikely but courageous figure of Truman to carry on its banner."
Photo: Truman Library; sheet music: Collection of Janice L. and David J. Frent.

limited the right to strike and made organizing workers more difficult. For example, it allowed states to pass "right to work" laws banning union shops, workplaces in which all workers were required to join a union once a majority had voted for it. The law also compelled union leaders to swear that they were not Communists and to report annually on their union's financial situation. From its role as supporter of unions, established in the Wagner Act of 1935, the federal government now

moved to a more neutral position between labor and management and between unions and individual workers. The New Deal principle of government protection for collective bargaining nonetheless remained intact.

Truman's impassioned attack on Taft-Hartley did not prevent Congress from overriding his veto, but it provided ammunition for his 1948 campaign. Planning to run as a strong liberal, he vetoed a number of bills that, he charged, favored the privileged.

Truman also took the offensive. Knowing that the Republican-controlled Congress would refuse his demands for liberal programs, he issued them anyway, constructing a case against what he called the "do-nothing Congress." Democratic Party leaders, unpersuaded that Truman could win, scurried around for an alternative candidate, but in the end they could not deny the president renomination.

Thomas E. Dewey, the Republican nominee who had lost to Roosevelt in 1944, was sure that his time had come, and so was nearly everyone else. In the 1948 elections, Truman faced not only a resurgent Republican Party, but also two revolts from within his own party. On the left, Henry Wallace, Roosevelt's vice president in the early 1940s and Truman's secretary of commerce, pushed out of the cabinet for his foreign policy views, led a new Progressive Party. On the right, South Carolina Governor J. Strom Thurmond headed the States' Rights Party—the Dixiecrats—formed by southern Democrats in opposition to the Democratic Party's growing support for civil rights.

Virtually alone in believing he could win, Truman crisscrossed the country by train, answering supporters' cries of "Give 'em hell, Harry," lambasting the 80th Congress, and warning voters against the return of "gluttons of privilege" to Washington. So bleak were Truman's prospects that the overconfident Dewey ran a low-key campaign and rarely went on the attack against Truman. Pollsters stopped polling, and on election night the *Chicago Tribune* printed its day-after-election issue with the banner headline "Dewey Defeats Truman."

But Truman surprised everyone, taking 303 electoral votes to Dewey's 189. The president's spirited campaign revitalized key segments of the Democratic coalition, including urban workers, farmers, and blacks. Not only did Truman hold on to his office, but his party also regained control of Congress. Even though Thurmond and Wallace collected more than a million votes each, mostly from Democrats, Truman finished more than two million votes ahead of Dewey. In addition to reflecting popular support for his foreign policy, Truman's win attested to his skills as a campaigner and to the enduring popularity of New Deal reform.

The Fair Deal Flounders

Truman viewed his victory as a mandate to enact the policies of his Fair Deal. But he found little support in Congress, where southern Democrats often joined the Republicans on domestic issues. Congress made modest improvements in Social Security and raised the minimum wage, but its only significant reform initiative was in housing. Sponsored by Ohio Republican Senator Robert Taft and passed in spite of strong opposition from the real estate industry, the Housing Act of 1949 furnished 350,000 units of government-constructed housing over the next fifteen years. Although it fell far short of actual need, and many projects were too cheaply built and poorly designed to provide a favorable environment for their inhabitants, the Housing Act represented a landmark commitment by the federal government to address the housing needs of the poor.

To the rest of the Fair Deal, Congress responded as it had to civil rights measures—with a resounding no. Congress rejected Truman's proposals for a federal health care program with national health insurance; for federal aid to education; and for a new agriculture program that would benefit small farmers, limit subsidies to giant commercial farmers, and keep prices low for consumers. Truman's proposals in civil rights, health, and education failed in the short run, but they laid foundations for enactment of similar programs in the 1960s.

Truman's efforts to revise immigration policy met a similar fate. In accord with the president's goals, the McCarran-Walter Act of 1952 ended

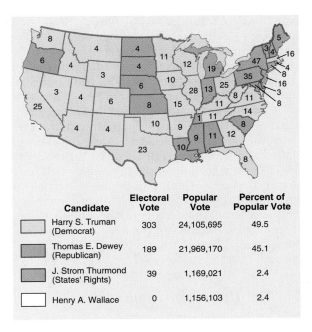

Candidate	Electoral Vote	Popular Vote	Percent of Popular Vote
Harry S. Truman (Democrat)	303	24,105,695	49.5
Thomas E. Dewey (Republican)	189	21,969,170	45.1
J. Strom Thurmond (States' Rights)	39	1,169,021	2.4
Henry A. Wallace	0	1,156,103	2.4

MAP 26.2
The Election of 1948

the outright ban on immigration and citizenship for Japanese and other Asians. But it authorized the government to bar suspected Communists and homosexuals. Most distressing to Truman, it maintained the quota system established in the 1920s, discriminating "deliberately and intentionally, against many of the peoples of the world," as Truman declared in his veto message. Overriding Truman's veto, Congress left the quota system intact for another fifteen years.

Although Truman blamed Republicans, conservative Democrats, and interest groups for defeating his Fair Deal, the reasons were much more complex, and some lay at his own doorstep. Truman devoted much more energy to foreign policy than to his domestic proposals. And he tended to throw many proposals at Congress without assigning priorities. Moreover, by late 1950 the Korean War embroiled Truman in controversy, diverted his attention from domestic affairs, and depleted his power as a legislative leader.

The Domestic Chill: A Second Red Scare

Truman's domestic program also suffered from a wave of anti-Communist hysteria that weakened leftist and liberal forces. "Red-baiting," the attempt to discredit individuals by accusing them of being Communists ("Reds") or sympathizers, was not new. Neither was official retaliation against leftist critics of government policies. Both had flourished during the Red scare at the end of World War I.

A second Red scare convulsed the United States after World War II. Born of partisan political maneuvering, collapse of the Soviet-American alliance, setbacks in U.S. foreign policy, and disclosures of Soviet espionage in the United States, Canada, and Britain, the postwar anti-Communist crusade swept through nearly every segment of American society. The new "witch-hunt" brought personal distress to thousands of citizens and created a climate of fear, stifling expression that did not conform to mainstream beliefs.

The Politics of Anticommunism

Republicans attacked New Deal programs by equating them with communism, and they jumped at the opportunities presented by the cold war to discredit

Democrats with the taint of communism. To Americans perplexed by the nation's inability to control events in Eastern Europe, China, and Korea, accusations of internal subversion offered simple explanations. As Wisconsin Republican Senator Joseph R. McCarthy, the leading anti-Communist, charged, "The Communists within our borders have been more responsible for the success of Communism abroad than Soviet Russia."

A second Red scare convulsed the United States after World War II. . . . The new "witch-hunt" brought personal distress to thousands of citizens and created a climate of fear, stifling expression that did not conform to mainstream beliefs.

Revelations of Soviet espionage and accusations made by former Communists furnished just enough credibility to such charges. In 1946, for example, the Canadian government discovered that several Canadian and British officials had passed military secrets to Russian agents. In the United States, a number of ex-Communists, including Whittaker Chambers and Elizabeth Bentley, testified that they and others had provided secret documents to the Soviets. In 1950, Klaus Fuchs, a British physicist attached to the atomic bomb project, confessed that he was a spy. He implicated several Americans, including a New York couple named Ethel and Julius Rosenberg. They pleaded innocent but were convicted of conspiracy to commit espionage; they were executed in the electric chair in 1953.

Most of the disloyalty charges against Americans involved allegations that they had connections to Communists long before the cold war had made the Soviet Union an enemy. At the peak of hysteria about internal subversives in the late 1940s, the U.S. Communist Party had only about twenty thousand members, some of them FBI agents. The party parroted the Soviet line on every issue and shrouded many activities in secrecy, but most members were open about their affiliation and acted within the law.

In addition to the twenty thousand party members, many more Americans had once been party members, had belonged to groups with Communist members, or had supported radical causes, but Red-hunters cared little for such distinctions. For more

THE RED SCARE
This map, entitled The Bear Grows and Grows, *appeared in the Sunday magazine section of the New York* News *in November 1947. What impact might such an image have on newspaper readers?*
The Michael Barson Collection/Past Perfect.

than ten years following World War II, the House Un-American Activities Committee (HUAC), the Senate Internal Security Subcommittee (SISS), and a host of other official bodies ordered citizens to testify about their past and present political associations.

Once witnesses admitted membership in a group that was deemed subversive, inquisitors asked them to name other members. If they tried to save their associates from a similar ordeal by refusing to identify them, they could be held in contempt of Congress. Consequently, many witnesses refused to answer any questions at all, claiming the Fifth Amendment protection from self-incrimination. Anti-Communists then charged that silence was tantamount to confession, and these "unfriendly witnesses" suffered the loss of jobs as well as public ostracism.

Nixon and McCarthy on the Attack

Richard Nixon was one of the Republicans who leaped at the chance to attack the Democrats for permitting subversives to operate in the United States. A member of HUAC during his first term in Congress in 1947–1948, Nixon took up the pursuit of Alger Hiss, a former New Dealer who had served in the wartime State Department. According to ex-Communist Whittaker Chambers, in the 1930s Hiss had belonged to a secret Communist cell that passed government documents to the Soviet Union.

Hiss denied the charges, but in 1950 a jury convicted him of lying to HUAC about his connections with Chambers, and Hiss spent four years in prison. The Hiss case became a hot spot of anti-Communist contention. Prominent Democrats such as Dean

SENATOR JOSEPH R. McCARTHY
In March 1950, McCarthy reads letters responding to his claim to have a list of 205 Communists in the State Department. Although McCarthy made his reputation from anticommunism, he seized that issue more from the need to have a campaign platform in 1950 than from genuine concern grounded in real evidence. McCarthy loved politics from his high school days in Appleton, Wisconsin, and easily distorted the truth to promote his political ambitions. He died from alcoholism at the age of forty-eight, three years after the Senate condemned his conduct.
Corbis-Bettmann.

Acheson and Adlai Stevenson defended Hiss, while Republicans vilified him as a prime example of "twenty years of treason" under the Democrats. Nixon's pursuit of Alger Hiss won him national fame.

But Joseph McCarthy exceeded Nixon in his zeal to purge the United States of nonconformists. So great was his influence that "McCarthyism" became a term synonymous with the anti-Communist crusade, even though the hysteria ranged far beyond the senator's activities. McCarthy jumped into the national spotlight in 1950, when he claimed to have a list of 205 "known Communists" working in the State Department. He attacked individuals reck-

lessly, and even though many of his charges were absurd—such as his allegation that retired General George C. Marshall belonged to a Communist conspiracy—the press covered McCarthy avidly, and his photograph was featured on the covers of *Time* and *Newsweek*.

Although their party led it, not all Republicans joined McCarthyism. In 1950, Senator Margaret Chase Smith and six other Republicans issued a "declaration of conscience" condemning Republican efforts to gain power through "fear, ignorance, bigotry, and smear." Nor was McCarthyism confined to Republicans. Mississippi Democrat John E. Rankin led the effort to make HUAC a permanent committee, and he relentlessly hounded the witnesses who were called to testify. Other Democrats matched his Red-baiting, particularly southern politicians who labeled any efforts for racial justice Communist-inspired.

The Official Purge

Under increasing pressure from the Republicans and with public opinion strongly against the employment of Communists in government jobs, in March 1947 Truman issued Executive Order 9835 requiring investigation of every federal employee. Those found guilty of Communist affiliation or even of "sympathetic association" with Communists—often interpreted as membership in groups with radical leanings—lost their jobs without a hearing. Esther Brunauer, a State Department official, and her husband, Stephen, a noted chemist employed by the navy, lost their jobs in the anti-Communist hysteria. Attacked as subversives by McCarthy in 1950, the Brunauers quickly got caught up in Truman's loyalty-security program—"a nightmare from which there [was] no awakening," in Esther Brunauer's words.

Stephen Brunauer had belonged briefly to a Communist youth organization in the 1920s, and the Brunauers had associated with individuals or organizations that were allegedly sympathetic to communism. But there was no evidence of disloyalty or subversion, and the Brunauers' superiors affirmed the couple's loyalty in 1948. After McCarthy's charges, however, the government began new investigations. In 1951, the navy suspended Stephen Brunauer on security grounds. Rather than contesting the suspension, he resigned. Esther Brunauer endured two more hearings, in which she was accused of "close and habitual association" with her husband, before being ousted from the

State Department in 1952. She then found some editorial work, and her husband took a job with a cement association, their careers and reputations irreparably damaged.

The Brunauers and others accused of association with subversives had no opportunity to confront their informers, and they bore the burden of proving that they were not disloyal. In effect, Truman's loyalty program violated the principles of American justice by allowing anonymous informers to make charges and then demanding that the accused clear themselves. The program extended into the mid-1950s, as more than two thousand civil service employees lost their jobs and another ten thousand resigned from 1947 through 1956. Years later, Truman privately admitted that the loyalty program had been a mistake. "It was terrible," he said.

The Truman administration also went directly after the Communist Party. Just before the 1948 elections, the Justice Department began prosecuting eleven Communist Party leaders under the Smith Act, passed in 1940, which made it a crime to "advocate the overthrow and destruction of the Government of the United States by force and violence." A jury found the leaders guilty, convicting them

not for their actions but for their beliefs. They were sentenced to five years in prison. Although civil libertarians argued that the verdicts violated First Amendment rights to freedom of speech, press, and association, the Supreme Court ruled in 1951 (*Dennis v. United States*) that the severity of the Communist threat overrode the guarantees of the Constitution. Other prosecutions under the Smith Act followed, resulting in more than one hundred convictions through 1956.

Despite his own anti-Communist actions, Truman denounced the extremism of men like Nixon and McCarthy. He vetoed the McCarran Internal Security Act in 1950, rebuking Congress for putting the government in the "thought control business." The legislation denied passports and government or defense industry jobs to Communist sympathizers and authorized the government to build concentration camps to confine "subversives" in times of national emergency. Testifying to the strength of anti-Communist sentiment, Congress easily overrode the veto.

Although Republicans castigated Truman for being soft on communism, Truman himself contributed to McCarthyism. He had whipped up support for containment with words that intensified

RED SCARE VICTIMS
Esther Brunauer speaks with her husband, Stephen, at the conclusion of her testimony in March 1950 before the Senate subcommittee investigating Senator Joseph McCarthy's charges that the State Department harbored Communist employees. As was true for thousands of government employees, McCarthyism terminated the Brunauers' professional careers.
Wide World.

fears of communism. The president and other Democrats engaged in Red-baiting against Henry Wallace in the presidential campaign of 1948. Moreover, the Truman administration's efforts to disarm the more rabid witch-hunters with the federal employee loyalty-security program actually fanned the flames.

The Pervasive Repression

The internal cold war spread beyond the nation's capital. State and local governments undertook their own investigations, demanded loyalty oaths from everyone from teachers to professional wrestlers, prosecuted Communist sympathizers, fired individuals suspected of disloyalty, banned books from public libraries, denied business licenses to alleged subversives, and more. Private organizations and businesses also purged dissidents and helped to create a climate of conformity.

McCarthyism drew sexual as well as political "deviants" into its web of victims. A 1950 Senate report claimed that homosexuals' "moral turpitude" and their susceptibility to blackmail made them unfit for government jobs. Purged from the civil service and drummed out of the military, gay men and women also suffered surveillance and harassment at the hands of the FBI, the post office, and local police forces.

Educational institutions grilled hundreds of teachers about their past and present political associations. When individuals refused to name associates, they often lost their jobs. Rutgers, Harvard, Michigan, Fisk, and a host of less prominent universities dismissed professors, and public school teachers lost their jobs in New York, Philadelphia, Los Angeles, and elsewhere. University of Chicago President Robert M. Hutchins decried the damage to freedom of inquiry: "The entire teaching profession of the U.S. is now intimidated." Teachers had every reason to fear the repercussions of expressing nonconformist political ideas.

Hollywood came under HUAC's scrutiny in 1947. Ronald Reagan, president of the Screen Actors Guild, and others in the movie industry cooperated with the committee, but ten writers and directors—who became known as the Hollywood Ten—refused to testify. After serving short prison terms, they found themselves barred from work in Hollywood, as did scores of others suspected of Communist associations. The entire entertainment industry blacklisted leftists, including the Weavers, Pete

Seeger's folksinging group whose "Goodnight Irene" had topped the record charts in 1950.

Labor unions, like other liberal organizations, were both victims and agents in the anti-Communist crusade. Although few workers were Communists, the party and its sympathizers had helped to reinvigorate the labor movement in the 1930s and continued to wield influence in several CIO unions. When employers used charges of communism to discredit unions, the CIO adopted a defensive strategy and expelled eleven unions whose leaders refused to take the anti-Communist line. Unions survived and continued to grow, but the labor movement wasted energy in internecine battles and lost many progressive activists who had placed the CIO on the cutting edge of reform in the 1930s.

Because the Communist Party championed racial justice, civil rights activists and organizations became the prey of McCarthyism. Again, one did not have to be a Communist Party member to be a target; it was enough simply to hold views that were shared by the party. As a chairperson of a government loyalty review board put it, "Of course the fact that a person believes in racial equality doesn't *prove* that he's a Communist, but it certainly makes you look twice, doesn't it?"

McCarthyism caused untold economic and psychological harm to individuals who were innocent of breaking any law. Thousands of people found themselves humiliated and discredited, hounded from their jobs, some put behind prison bars. The anti-Communist crusade violated fundamental constitutional rights of freedom of speech and association, stifled expression of dissenting ideas, and removed unpopular causes from public contemplation.

The Cold War Becomes Hot: Korea

The anti-Communist hysteria intensified after the cold war erupted into a shooting war in June 1950, when troops from Communist North Korea invaded South Korea. For the first time, Americans went into battle to implement containment. The United States in concert with the United Nations ultimately held the line in Korea but at great cost in lives, dollars, and domestic unity. Popular discontent with the Korean War helped sweep General Dwight D. Eisenhower into the White House. Confirming the global reach of the Truman Doctrine, U.S. involvement in Korea also marked the militarization of American foreign policy. Defense spending shot up sharply and remained high even after hostilities ended.

Korea and American Credibility

The war in Korea grew out of the artificial division of that country after World War II. Having expelled the Japanese, who had controlled Korea since the Russo-Japanese War of 1904, the United States and the Soviet Union divided Korea at the thirty-eighth parallel into two occupation zones. As various political factions vied for power, the Soviets supported the Korean Communist Party in the North. In the South, the United States backed the Korean Democratic Party, led by landowners, businessmen, and even former Japanese collaborators, and attempted to diminish the strength of the Communists and other forces on the left.

With Moscow and Washington unable to agree on a unification plan, in July 1948 the United Nations sponsored elections in South Korea. The American-favored candidate, a Korean nationalist named Syngman Rhee, who had spent most of his life in exile in the United States, was elected president, and the United States withdrew all but five hundred of its troops in July 1949. In the fall of 1948, the Soviets established a People's Republic of North Korea, and they too withdrew their occupation forces.

U.S. State and Defense Department officials did not consider Korea to be of vital strategic interest, and many officials doubted that Rhee's conservative government could sustain popular support. The Rhee government reacted with severe repression to economic problems and opposition from the left. What counted for the Truman administration, however, was Rhee's anticommunism, and Truman decided to supply a small amount of economic and military aid to the Rhee government.

Skirmishes between North and South Korean troops had occurred since 1948, with both sides crossing the thirty-eighth parallel. In June 1950, however, ninety thousand North Koreans swept into South Korea. Truman's advisers immediately assumed that the Soviet Union, China, or both had instigated the attack. Revelations by former Soviet

KOREA
During the winter of 1950–51, American soldiers in Korea faced bitter cold and bitter defeat as Chinese and North Korean troops pushed them back below the thirty-eighth parallel. Under the leadership of General Matthew Ridgway, American troops began to turn the tide again. When this photograph was taken, U.S. forces were close to regaining the thirty-eighth parallel in March 1951.
Corbis-Bettmann.

officials thirty years later indicated only that the Kremlin had acquiesced in North Korean plans.

Looking back on his presidency, Truman regarded his decision to defend South Korea as his most important one. As was his custom, he wasted no time in making it. On June 30, six days after learning of the attack, Truman decided to commit ground troops. In addition, the U.S. representative to the UN persuaded the Security Council to sponsor a collective effort to repel the attack. With the Soviet representative boycotting the meeting (in protest over the council's refusal to seat a representative from the People's Republic of China) and thus unable to exercise veto power, the Security Council authorized Truman to appoint a commander for the UN force. He named General Douglas MacArthur, hero of the American victory in the Pacific and head of the Allied postwar occupation in Japan.

> *Looking back on his presidency, Truman regarded his decision to defend South Korea as his most important one. As was his custom, he wasted no time in making it.*

Sixteen nations, including many of the NATO allies, sent troops to Korea, but the United States contributed most of the personnel and weapons. The United States deployed almost 1.8 million troops in Korea and essentially dictated military strategy. Yet Congress never declared war. Truman himself refused to call it a war. At first he said that it was simply the United States, as a member of the United Nations, "going to the relief of the Korean Republic to suppress a bandit raid." When pressed by a reporter, he agreed that it was a "police action under the United Nations," and "police action" became the official label for the war.

Truman acted within his legal powers in asking the United Nations to repel the aggression and in responding to the Security Council's call for troops. And Congress authorized the calling up of soldiers and the expenditures of funds to pursue the war. Yet some felt that fighting a war without an official declaration by Congress violated the spirit of the Constitution. Moreover, the president exposed himself to attacks by political opponents, who called it "Truman's war" when the military situation worsened.

The first American soldiers to reach Korea were woefully unprepared and ill equipped; some units rushed to the front without training. The North Koreans took the capital of Seoul and drove deeply into the south between June and September, forcing UN troops to retreat south to Pusan. Then in September, MacArthur launched a bold counteroffensive, staging an amphibious landing at Inchon, 180 miles behind the North Korean lines. Overcoming tough resistance, these units joined up with forces that had broken out of the Pusan area and liberated Seoul. By mid-October, UN forces had pushed the North Koreans back to the thirty-eighth parallel. The brilliant strategy enhanced not only MacArthur's heroic stature but also his already overwhelming confidence in his own genius. Now Truman had to decide whether to authorize an invasion of North Korea and seek to unify Korea under UN supervision.

From Containment to Rollback to Containment

"Troops could not be expected . . . to march up to a surveyor's line and stop," remarked Dean Acheson, reflecting sentiment in Congress, the public, and the administration to transform the military objective from containment to elimination of the enemy and unification of North and South Korea. Only George Kennan and a few others in the State Department had doubts about expanding the war. Truman received UN approval and on September 27, 1950, ordered MacArthur to move beyond the thirty-eighth parallel if necessary to destroy North Korean forces. Concerned about possible intervention by China and the Soviet Union, Truman directed the general not to send UN troops close to the Chinese border. In October, he met with MacArthur on Wake Island and received his assurance that neither China nor the Soviets would intervene and that the unification of Korea could be accomplished by the end of the year. However, expansion of the war to North Korea sent UN troops on a march to disaster.

By November, MacArthur's assurances about Chinese neutrality proved to be worthless. As UN forces moved to within 40 miles of the Korean-Chinese border, more than 150,000 Chinese troops crossed the Yalu River to join the war. By December 1950, they had forced UN armies back below the thirty-eighth parallel and recaptured Seoul. It took three months of grueling battle for UN forces to work their way back to the thirty-eighth parallel. At that point, Truman decided to seek a negotiated settlement.

As the goal of the war reverted to containment, MacArthur vented his fury. All along, he had considered Asia more important to U.S. security than

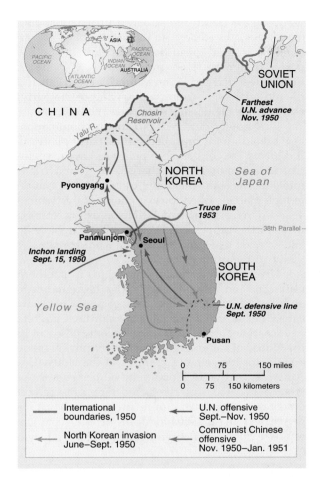

MAP 26.3

The Korean War, 1950–1953

After each side had plunged deep into its enemy's territory, the Korean War ended in 1953 with the dividing line between North and South Korea nearly the same as it had been before the war.

Europe. To him, a holding action against communism represented defeat. "There is no substitute for victory," he asserted. MacArthur was prepared to carry the war to China, to bring in Chinese Nationalist troops, and even to use nuclear weapons. Truman and his advisers, however, resolved to avoid a wider war in Asia. In the words of General Omar Bradley, chairman of the Joint Chiefs of Staff, the war that MacArthur wanted to wage was "the wrong war, at the wrong place, at the wrong time, with the wrong enemy."

Despite administration efforts to restrain him, MacArthur took his case public, in effect challenging the president's authority to make foreign policy and violating the principle of civilian control over the military. Fed up with MacArthur's insubordination, Truman relieved him of his command in April 1951. "Quite an explosion . . . letters of abuse by the dozens," Truman recorded in his diary. The general came home to a hero's welcome, and when he spoke to Congress, one legislator remarked that there was not "a dry eye on the Republican side nor a dry seat on the Democratic." Millions saw MacArthur's speech on television, and more than seven million people turned out for his triumphant parade in New York City. Three out of four Americans sided with MacArthur rather than with Truman. Republicans castigated the administration unmercifully.

Americans' adulation of MacArthur reflected their frustrations with containment. The general's view of the war coincided with the entire military history of the United States. In previous wars (except for the dimly remembered War of 1812), the United States marshaled its total resources to win all-out victory. Why should Americans die simply to preserve the status quo rather than to wipe out the enemy once and for all? To side with MacArthur enabled Americans to hold on to their belief that the United States was all-powerful and to pin the Korean stalemate on the government's ineptitude or willingness to shelter subversives within its ranks.

Truman's success in "scaring the hell" out of the American people came back to haunt him. If communism was so threatening, so evil, why not stamp it out as MacArthur wanted? When Congress investigated MacArthur's firing, all of the top military leaders supported the president, yet he never recovered from the political blows resulting from MacArthur's dismissal. Nor was Truman able to end the war. Cease-fire negotiations began in July 1951 as both sides held their ground roughly along the thirty-eighth parallel. Peace talks dragged on for two more years, while twelve thousand more U.S. soldiers met their deaths.

Korea, Communism, and the 1952 Election

Popular discontent with "Truman's war" gave the Republicans a decided edge in the election battles of 1952. Their presidential candidate, General Dwight D. Eisenhower, enjoyed immense stature as the architect of victory in Europe. Reared in modest circumstances in Abilene, Kansas, Eisenhower had attended West Point and had risen steadily through the army ranks, serving under MacArthur for a time in the 1930s. As supreme commander in Europe, he won widespread praise for his remarkable ability to forge the Allied armies into an effective coalition.

Reporters liked Eisenhower and portrayed him in the national media not only as a brilliant commander and vigorous leader but also as a sincere, decent, friendly individual. He quickly became a national hero, "Ike" to the general public as well as his friends. He spent his postwar years first in Washington as army chief of staff and then in New York City as president of Columbia University. In 1950, Truman appointed Eisenhower the first supreme commander of NATO forces.

As befitted a career soldier, Eisenhower had always refrained from public statements about political issues. His party preference was unknown, and both Republicans and Democrats had courted him for the presidency in 1948. Although he believed that civilian control over the military worked best when professional soldiers declined from office seeking, the political situation gave him compelling reasons to run for the presidency in 1952.

Eisenhower agreed with the broad scope of Democratic foreign policy—which he had helped to create and implement—while he deplored the Democrats' efforts to solve domestic problems with new federal programs and large expenditures. At the same time, he equally disliked the foreign policy

views of the leading Republican presidential contender, Senator Robert A. Taft, who attacked containment, sought to cut defense spending, and opposed assigning U.S. troops to NATO bases. Eisenhower decided to run as much to stop Taft and the old guard (the conservative wing of the party) as to get the Democrats out of the White House.

Eisenhower defeated Taft for the nomination, but the old guard prevailed on the party platform. It damned the containment policy as "negative, futile, and immoral" and charged the Truman administration with shielding "traitors to the Nation in high places." Eisenhower's choice of thirty-nine-year-old Senator Richard M. Nixon as his running mate further appeased the Republican right wing and ensured that anticommunism would be a major theme of the campaign.

Nixon came from modest origins in southern California and had to work his way through college and law school. After navy service and a brief law career, he helped the Republicans capture Congress in 1946, defeating a liberal incumbent for a seat in the House of Representatives. Nixon quickly made a name for himself as a member of the House Un-American Activities Committee and a pursuer of Alger Hiss. Accusing the Democrats of being soft on communism, Nixon found an issue to boost his own career. In his 1950 bid for the Senate, he ran an effective smear campaign against Helen Gahagan

THE 1952 REPUBLICAN TICKET
At the Republican convention in 1952, presidential nominee Dwight D. Eisenhower stands with his wife, Mamie (right), and his running mate, Richard Nixon, and Nixon's wife, Patricia (left), at the start of their campaign. The campaign button featured a theme common to candidates of the party currently out of power.
Corbis-Bettmann; Collection of Janice L. and David J. Frent

TABLE 26.2 THE ELECTION OF 1952			
Candidate	Electoral Vote	Popular Vote	Percent of Popular Vote
Dwight Eisenhower (Republican)	442	33,936,252	55.1
Adlai Stevenson (Democrat)	89	27,314,992	44.4

Douglas, charging her with being "pink [Communist] right down to her underwear."

Having decided not to run for another term, Truman persuaded Adlai E. Stevenson, governor of Illinois, to seek the Democratic nomination, which he easily won. Truman's unpopularity proved to be an unbearable burden for Stevenson, even though he was witty and eloquent and a popular governor, acceptable to both liberals and southern Democrats. Although Stevenson tried to distance himself from the president, he could not escape the domestic fallout from the Korean War.

The Republican campaign faltered just once, when the last item of its "Korea, Communism, and Corruption" campaign came back to haunt the party. A newspaper reported that Nixon had accepted $18,000 from supporters in California. Although such gifts were common in politics at that time, Democrats jumped on Nixon, hoping to divert attention from the scandals that involved several figures in the Truman administration and the Democratic Party. As newspapers printed editorials calling for Nixon to withdraw from the ticket, most of Eisenhower's advisers urged him to dump his running mate.

Nixon saved himself by exploiting the new medium of television. To a national audience, he made an emotional appeal, disclosing his financial affairs and documenting his modest standard of living. Referring to the family pet, Checkers, Nixon admitted that the cocker spaniel could be considered an illegal gift from supporters, but he vowed that he would not break his daughters' hearts by returning it. The overwhelming popular response to the "Checkers speech" turned the tide for Nixon. Eisenhower summoned his running mate and welcomed him with the words "You're my boy!" Despite these words, both men bore resentments about the incident, and their relationship was never easy or warm.

With the issue of corruption neutralized, the Republicans harped on communism at home and failure to end the Korean War. Eisenhower's most dramatic campaign statement came less than two weeks before the election. "I shall go to Korea," Eisenhower announced, and voters registered their confidence in his ability to end the war. Cutting sharply into traditional Democratic territory, Eisenhower won several southern states and 55 percent of the popular vote. His coattails carried a narrow Republican majority to Congress.

An Armistice and the War's Costs

Eisenhower made good on his pledge, flying to Korea a few weeks after the election. In July 1953, the two sides reached an armistice that left Korea divided as it had been three years earlier. The war took the lives of 54,000 and wounded more than 100,000 Americans. Total UN casualties included 118,515 killed, 264,591 wounded, and 92,987 captured, most of whom did not return alive.

THE CHECKERS SPEECH
Republican vice presidential nominee Richard M. Nixon poses with his wife, Patricia, just before going on radio and TV to respond to charges of having received illegal campaign funds during the 1952 campaign. In an emotional speech that he finished in tears, Nixon saved his place on the ticket and probably his political career. Pat Nixon did not like the speech, asking her husband, "Why do we have to tell people how little we have and how much we owe?"
Corbis-Bettmann.

Korean and civilian casualties were heavier still. More than 1.6 million North Koreans and Chinese were killed or wounded, and 3 million South Koreans died of war-related causes. The nature of the war and the unpopularity of the Rhee government made it difficult for soldiers to distinguish between friends and enemies, since civilian populations sometimes harbored North Korean agents. Consequently, as one journalist reported, the situation "forced upon our men in the field, acts and attitudes of the utmost savagery . . . the blotting out of villages where the enemy *might* be hiding, the shooting and shelling of refugees who *may* be North Koreans."

Viewing Korea as a test of its credibility, the Truman administration judged the war a success. It had shown the world that it would help nations that were resisting communism even if they were not vital to U.S. security and were run by undemocratic, repressive governments. Not only was communism checked at the thirty-eighth parallel in Korea, but both Truman and Eisenhower managed to contain what amounted to a world war, in which twenty nations were involved on both sides, within a single country. Moreover, despite both presidents' threats to use nuclear bombs, they limited the Korean War to a conflict fought with conventional weapons.

In April 1950, two months before the Korean War began, the National Security Council had given Truman a top-secret document on the nation's military strength. NSC 68, as the report was called, painted the world in gravely threatening terms. The survival of the nation and the world, it said, required a massive military buildup. Truman read the report but took no action on recommendations that would perhaps triple the current defense budget.

Nearly all of the military buildup called for in NSC 68 came about in the context of the Korean War, which vastly increased U.S. capacity to act as a global power. Using the Korean crisis to expand the American presence elsewhere, Truman got Congress to approve the rearming of West Germany and the commitment of troops to NATO. Military spending shot up from $14 billion in 1950 to $50 billion in 1953, and it remained in the $34–40 billion range throughout the 1950s. By 1953, defense spending claimed 60 percent of the federal budget, and the size of the armed forces had tripled.

To General Matthew Ridgway, who succeeded MacArthur as commander of the UN forces, Korea taught the lesson that U.S. forces should never again fight a land war in Asia. Eisenhower concurred. Nevertheless, the Korean War induced the Truman administration to expand its influence in Asia by increasing aid to the French, who were fighting to hang on to their colonial empire in Indochina. As marines retreated from a battle against Chinese soldiers in 1950, they—prophetically—sang, "We're Harry's police force on call, / So put back your pack on, / The next step is Saigon, / Cheer up, me lads, bless 'em all."

Conclusion: Meeting the Challenges of the Postwar World

More than any development in the postwar world, the cold war defined American politics and society during the Truman administration and for years to come. Truman's decision to oppose communism throughout the world marked the most momentous foreign policy initiative in the nation's history. It transformed the federal government, shifting its attention from domestic to external affairs, greatly expanding its budget, and substantially increasing the power of the president. The nuclear arms race attending the cold war put the people of the world at risk, diverted resources that could have been used to improve living standards, and skewed the economy toward dependence on military projects. While Americans continued to debate who was responsible for the cold war and whether it could have been avoided, none could question its impact on American society or the world.

The boost to industry from cold war spending and the reconstruction of Western Europe and Japan contributed to an economic boom that provided nearly full employment during most of the Truman years and turned out an array of consumer goods that lifted the standard of living for a majority of Americans. Preoccupied with foreign policy, Truman failed to mobilize support for his ambition to assist the disadvantaged with new initiatives in education, health, agriculture, and civil rights, but he successfully defended most of the New Deal reforms. Thus, in sharp contrast to foreign policy, the domestic policies of the postwar years reflected continuity with the past.

The anti-Communist hysteria that grew out of the cold war also contributed to the domestic status quo by silencing the left, stifling debate, and narrowing the range of acceptable ideas. Partisan politics and the Truman administration's constant rhetoric about the Communist menace fueled McCarthyism, but the obsession with subversion also fed on popular frustrations over the new policy of containment and the failure of this policy to produce clear-cut victories. Convulsing the nation in bitter disunity, McCarthyism reflected a loss of confidence in American power. It would be a major challenge of the next administration to restore that unity and confidence.

CHRONOLOGY

1945 Harry Truman becomes president of United States upon death of Franklin D. Roosevelt.

Japan and Germany surrender to Allies, ending World War II.

1946 Severe labor unrest erupts throughout United States.

Truman creates Committee on Civil Rights.

United States grants independence to Philippines.

Congress passes Employment Act signifying government's responsibility for healthy economy.

Congressional elections result in Republican control of 80th Congress.

1947 George F. Kennan's article on policy of containment appears in *Foreign Affairs* magazine.

National Security Act of 1947 unifies military services under secretary of defense and creates National Security Council (NSC) and Central Intelligence Agency (CIA).

Truman asks Congress to appropriate aid to Greece and Turkey to counter communism and announces Truman Doctrine.

1948 Congress approves Marshall Plan, providing massive aid to help European countries recover from World War II.

Congress enacts law to make women permanent part of armed services.

Truman issues executive order to desegregate armed services.

United States recognizes state of Israel.

Truman defeats Republican Thomas E. Dewey to win full term as president.

1948–1949 Soviets block access to West Berlin, setting off Berlin crisis and fifteen-month Western airlift of supplies to city.

1949 Communists under Mao Zedong win Chinese civil war and take over mainland China; Nationalists retreat to Taiwan.

NATO (North Atlantic Treaty Organization) organizes to counter Soviet threat to Western Europe.

Truman administration initiates Point IV technical aid program to third world nations.

Soviet Union explodes atomic bomb.

1950 Senator Joseph McCarthy begins campaign against alleged Communists in United States, giving his name to period of anti-Communist hysteria.

Truman approves development of hydrogen bomb.

United States sends troops to South Korea to repel North Korean assault.

1951 Truman relieves General MacArthur of command in Korea for insubordination.

United States ends postwar occupation of Japan; the two nations sign peace treaty and mutual security pact.

1952 Republican Dwight D. Eisenhower elected president of United States.

1953 Armistice signed in Korean War.

BIBLIOGRAPHY

GENERAL WORKS

John Patrick Diggins, *The Proud Decades: America in War and Peace, 1941–1950* (1988).

Robert J. Donovan, *Conflict and Crisis: The Presidency of Harry S. Truman, 1945–1948* (1977).

Robert J. Donovan, *Tumultuous Years: The Presidency of Harry S. Truman, 1949–1953* (1982).

Alonzo L. Hamby, *Man of the People: A Life of Harry S. Truman* (1995).

Michael J. Lacy, ed., *The Truman Presidency* (1989).

Melvyn Leffler, *A Preponderance of Power: National Security, the Truman Administration, and the Cold War* (1992).

Donald R. McCoy, *The Presidency of Harry S. Truman* (1984).

David McCullough, *Truman* (1992).

William L. O'Neill, *American High: The Years of Confidence, 1945–1950* (1986).

James T. Patterson, *Grand Expectations: The United States, 1945–1974* (1996).

William E. Pemberton, *Harry S. Truman: Fair Dealer and Cold Warrior* (1989).

Michael S. Sherry, *In the Shadow of War* (1995).

Harry S. Truman, *Year of Decisions* (1955).

Harry S. Truman, *Years of Trial and Hope* (1956).

DOMESTIC POLITICS AND POLICIES

William C. Berman, *The Politics of Civil Rights in the Truman Administration* (1970).

Bert Cochran, *Harry Truman and the Crisis Presidency* (1973).

Richard M. Dalfiume, *Desegregation of the U.S. Armed Forces: Fighting on Two Fronts* (1969).

Richard O. Davies, *Housing Reform during the Truman Administration* (1966).

Andrew J. Dunar, *The Truman Scandals and the Politics of Morality* (1984).

Robert H. Ferrell, *Harry S. Truman and the Modern American Presidency* (1983).

Susan M. Hartman, *Truman and the 80th Congress* (1971).

R. Alton Lee, *Truman and Taft-Hartley* (1966).

Nelson Lichtenstein, *The Most Dangerous Man in Detroit: Walter Reuther and the Fate of American Labor* (1996).

Norman D. Markowitz, *The Rise and Fall of the People's Century: Henry A. Wallace and American Liberalism, 1941–1948* (1973).

Allen J. Matusow, *Farm Policies and Politics in the Truman Years* (1967).

Donald R. McCoy and Richard T. Ruetten, *Quest and Response: Minority Rights and the Truman Administration* (1973).

Keith W. Olson, *The G.I. Bill, the Veterans, and the Colleges* (1974).

Monte M. Poen, *Harry S. Truman versus the Medical Lobby: The Genesis of Medicare* (1979).

David W. Reinhard, *The Republican Right since 1945* (1983).

Allen Yarnell, *Democrats and Progressives: The 1948 Presidential Election as a Test of Postwar Liberalism* (1974).

Robert Zieger, *The CIO, 1935–1955* (1995).

ORIGINS OF THE COLD WAR

Gar Alperovitz, *Atomic Diplomacy* (1985).

Lynn E. Davis, *The Cold War Begins: Soviet-American Conflict over Eastern Europe* (1974).

John L. Gaddis, *The United States and the Origins of the Cold War* (1972).

James L. Gormly, *The Collapse of the Grand Alliance, 1945–1948* (1987).

Fraser J. Harbut, *The Iron Curtain: Churchill, America, and the Origins of the Cold War* (1986).

Joyce Kolko and Gabriel Kolko, *The Limits of Power: The World and United States Foreign Policy* (1972).

Bruce R. Kuniholm, *The Origins of the Cold War in the Near East* (1980).

Deborah W. Larson, *Origins of Containment: A Psychological Explanation* (1985).

Ernest R. May, ed., *American Cold War Strategy: Interpreting NSC 68* (1993).

Wilson D. Miscamble, *George F. Kennan and the Making of Foreign Policy, 1947–1950* (1992).

Thomas G. Patterson, *Soviet-American Confrontation: Postwar Reconstruction and the Origins of the Cold War* (1973).

Thomas G. Patterson, *On Every Front: The Making of the Cold War* (1979).

Robert A. Pollard, *Economic Security and the Origins of the Cold War* (1985).

Michael Schaller, *The American Occupation of Japan: The Origins of the Cold War in Asia* (1985).

Hugh Thomas, *Armed Truce: The Beginnings of the Cold War, 1945–1946* (1987).

Randall B. Woods and Howard Jones, *Dawning of the Cold War: The United States' Quest for Order* (1994).

Daniel Yergin, *Shattered Peace: The Origins of the Cold War and the National Security State* (1977).

FOREIGN POLICY

Dean Acheson, *Present at the Creation* (1969).

William S. Borden, *The Pacific Alliance: United States Foreign Economic Policy and Japanese Trade Recovery, 1947–1955* (1984).

Gordon H. Chang, *Friends and Enemies: The United States, China, and the Soviet Union, 1948–1972* (1990).

Michael J. Cohen, *Truman and Israel* (1990).

Peter L. Hahn, *The United States, Great Britain, and Egypt: Strategy and Diplomacy in the Early Cold War* (1991).

Gary R. Hess, *The United States' Emergence as a Southeast Asian Power, 1940–1950* (1987).

Walter L. Hixon, *George F. Kennan: Cold War Iconoclast* (1989).

Michael J. Hogan, *The Marshall Plan: America, Britain, and the Reconstruction of Western Europe, 1947–1952* (1987).

Walter Isaacson and Evan Thomas, *The Wise Men: Six Friends and the World They Made: Acheson, Bohlen, Harriman, Kennan, Lovett, McCloy* (1986).

Lawrence S. Kaplan, *The United States and NATO: The Formative Years* (1984).

Stuart W. Leslie, *The Cold War and American Science* (1993).

Thomas J. McCormick, *America's Half-Century: United States Foreign Policy in the Cold War* (1989).

David S. McLellan, *Dean Acheson: The State Department Years* (1976).

Richard Rhodes, *Dark Sun: The Making of the Hydrogen Bomb* (1995).

John Snetsinger, *Truman, the Jewish Vote, and the Creation of Israel* (1974).

Nancy B. Tucker, *Patterns in the Dust: Chinese-American Relations and the Recognition Controversy, 1949–1950* (1983).

Imanuel Wexler, *The Marshall Plan Revisited* (1983).

Evan M. Wilson, *Decision on Palestine: How the U.S. Came to Recognize Israel* (1979).

Lawrence S. Wittner, *American Intervention in Greece, 1943–1949* (1982).

MCCARTHYISM

Michael R. Belknap, *Cold War Political Justice: The Smith Act, the Communist Party, and American Civil Liberties* (1977).

David Caute, *The Great Fear: The Anti-Communist Purge under Truman and Eisenhower* (1978).

Larry Ceplair and Steven Englund, *The Inquisition in Hollywood: Politics in the Film Community* (1980).

Sigmund Diamond, *Compromised Campus: The Collaboration of Universities with the Intelligence Community, 1945–1955* (1992).

Richard M. Freeland, *The Truman Doctrine and the Origins of McCarthyism: Foreign Policy, Domestic Politics, and International Security, 1946–1948* (1972).

Richard M. Fried, *Men against McCarthy* (1976).

Richard M. Fried, *Nightmare in Red: The McCarthy Era in Perspective* (1990).

Robert Griffith, *The Politics of Fear: Joseph R. McCarthy and the Senate* (1970).

Stanley I. Kutler, *The American Inquisition* (1982).

Harvey Levinstein, *Communism, Anticommunism, and the CIO* (1981).

David Oshinsky, *A Conspiracy So Immense: The World of Joe McCarthy* (1983).

Richard Gid Powers, *Not Without Honor: The History of American Anticommunism* (1995).

Ronald Radosh and Joyce Milton, *The Rosenberg File: A Search for the Truth* (1983).

Thomas C. Reeves, *The Life and Times of Joe McCarthy* (1983).

Ellen W. Schrecker, *No Ivory Tower: McCarthyism and the Universities* (1986).

Ellen W. Schrecker, *The Age of McCarthyism* (1994).

Peter L. Steinberg, *The Great "Red" Menace: United States Persecution of American Communists, 1947–1952* (1984).

Athan Theoharis, *Seeds of Repression: Harry S. Truman and the Origins of McCarthyism* (1971).

Allen Weinstein, *Perjury: The Hiss-Chambers Case* (1979).

KOREA

Bruce Cumings, *The Origins of the Korean War* (1981).

Rosemary Foot, *The Wrong War: American Policy and the Dimensions of the Korean Conflict, 1950–1953* (1984).

Gregory Henderson, *Korea: The Politics of the Vortex* (1968).

Burton I. Kaufman, *The Korean War: Challenges in Crisis, Credibility, and Command* (1986).

James I. Matray, *The Reluctant Crusade: American Foreign Policy in Korea* (1985).

Glenn D. Paige, *The Korean Decision: June 24–30, 1950* (1968).

David Rees, *Korea: The Limited War* (1964).

William Stueck, *The Road to Confrontation: American Policy toward China and Korea, 1947–1950* (1981).

William Stueck, *The Korean War: An International History* (1995).

John Toland, *In Mortal Combat: Korea, 1950–1953* (1992).

Richard Whelan, *Drawing the Line: The Korean War, 1950–1953* (1990).

1954 CADILLAC

The automobile reflected both corporate and family prosperity in the 1950s. This car was a product of General Motors, the biggest and richest corporation in the world and the first to sell a billion dollars' worth of products. Costing about $5,000, the Cadillac was GM's top product, one of the first purchases the McDonald brothers made when they struck it rich with their hamburger stand in California. Even the cheaper models that average Americans could afford featured the gas-guzzling size and space-age-inspired style of this Cadillac.
Ron Kimball.

THE POLITICS AND CULTURE OF ABUNDANCE

27

1952–1960

TRAILED BY REPORTERS AND PHOTOGRAPHERS, Vice President Richard M. Nixon led Soviet Premier Nikita Khrushchev through the American National Exhibition in Moscow in July 1959. The display of American consumer goods followed an exhibit of Soviet products in New York, part of a cultural exchange between the two superpowers that reflected a slight thaw in the cold war. Both Khrushchev and Nixon seized on the propaganda potential of their encounter, and as they made their way through the display their verbal sparring turned into a slugfest of words and gestures that reporters dubbed "the kitchen debate."

Showing off a new color television set, Nixon conceded that the Soviet Union "may be ahead of us . . . in the thrust of your rockets for . . . outer space," but he bragged that the United States outstripped the Soviets in consumer goods. "Any steelworker could buy this house," Nixon boasted, as they walked through a model of a six-room ranch-style house. Costing about $14,000, such houses were within reach of working-class families, he insisted. Khrushchev responded that in the Soviet Union, "you are entitled to housing," whereas in the United States, "if you don't have a dollar," you are reduced to sleeping on the pavement.

While the two leaders inspected appliances in the model kitchen, Nixon declared, "These are designed to make things easier for our women." Khrushchev responded that his country did not have "the capitalist attitude toward women"; the Soviet Union appreciated women's contributions to the economy, not their domesticity.

Mocking American consumers' fondness for gadgetry, Khrushchev asked, "Don't you have a machine that puts food into the mouth and pushes it down?" The Soviet premier found many of the items on display "interesting but they are not needed in life. . . . They are merely gadgets." When Nixon insisted, "Isn't it far better to be talking about washing machines than machines of war?" Khrushchev agreed. Yet he affirmed the persistence of severe cold war tensions when he later blustered, "We too are giants. You want to threaten—we will answer threats with threats."

The Eisenhower administration had in fact begun with statements deeply threatening to the Soviet Union. Republican campaigners vowed to roll back communism and liberate "enslaved" peoples under Soviet rule. In practice, however, Eisenhower settled for a containment policy that differed from Truman's only in particulars. Eisenhower shifted the means of containment to a greater reliance on nuclear weapons and on combating communism secretly through the CIA. Yet, as

Nixon's visit to Moscow demonstrated, Eisenhower took advantage of changes in the government of the Soviet Union to reduce tensions in Soviet-American relations.

Continuity with the Truman administration also characterized Eisenhower's domestic policies. Eisenhower did slow the pace of domestic reform. He proposed no major initiatives to deal with growing problems in such areas as health care and housing, and he failed to support the rising aspirations of black Americans. The Eisenhower administration favored the business community with tax cuts and preferred state and private control rather than federal management of important resources and functions. Yet all the important reform programs of the New Deal and the Fair Deal remained in place. A majority of Americans enjoyed prosperity under the immensely popular president and seemed content with his "moderate Republicanism."

The American display in Moscow testified to the unheard-of material gains savored by many Americans in the postwar era. Weapons production spurred business prosperity and contributed especially to the burgeoning populations and economies of the West and Southwest. Rising incomes enabled millions of Americans to purchase homes, television sets, and a host of other new products. Suburban development transformed patterns of living, economic enterprise, and politics. To many, it seemed that the spectacular economic growth would enable the nation to transcend problems of poverty and race without cost to the "haves."

The 1950s also witnessed tremendous enthusiasm for marriage and family life, both in the media and in practice. The "baby boom" that had begun in the 1940s accelerated. In his "kitchen debate" comments about the American housewife, Nixon reflected the popular celebration of traditional gender roles. Yet in this respect the United States moved closer to the Soviet model, as more and more married women took jobs outside their homes.

African Americans struck a much stronger blow against the status quo. The Supreme Court ruled segregation in the public schools unconstitutional. More significantly, African American protest took a dramatic new direction when blacks in large numbers turned to direct action against the system of segregation and disenfranchisement. By the end of the decade, African Americans had developed the institutions, leadership, strategies, and will to mount a civil rights movement of unprecedented size and power.

Eisenhower and the Politics of the "Middle Way"

Eisenhower pronounced moderation the guiding principle of his domestic agenda and leadership style. His first State of the Union message pledged a "middle way between untrammeled freedom of the individual and the demands for the welfare of the whole Nation." His administration would "avoid government by bureaucracy as carefully as it avoids neglect of the helpless." Claiming that Democrats appealed to divisive class interests, Eisenhower presented himself as a leader who stood above partisan politics and selfish interest groups and would govern by compromise and consensus.

Eisenhower presided over an era of remarkable domestic stability and prosperity that enabled most Americans to ignore the existence of substantial poverty, urban decay, and a growing crisis in race relations.

Those qualities, along with Eisenhower's heroic military reputation, made him one of the most popular and beloved presidents. But he failed to translate his personal prominence into a mandate for Republican rule, and he did not use his popularity to seek new solutions to social and economic problems. Eisenhower presided over an era of remarkable domestic stability and prosperity that enabled most Americans to ignore the existence of substantial poverty, urban decay, and a growing crisis in race relations. Although liberals called the 1950s "years of flabbiness and self-satisfaction and gross materialism," a majority of citizens found the decade one of opportunity and fulfillment. They expressed their complacency in their affection and votes for Ike.

Moderate Republicanism and the "Hidden Hand"

For most of his two terms (1953–1961), Eisenhower presided over a divided government. His coattails carried a meager Republican majority into Congress in the 1952 elections, but in 1954 the Democrats regained control and maintained it for the rest of the decade. The "moderate Republicanism" of the Eisenhower years was shaped not just by Eisenhower's convictions but also by a Democratic majority in Congress that maintained the course charted by the New Deal and the Fair Deal.

Eisenhower claimed to be above interest-group politics, yet he turned for advice almost exclusively to leaders of the business community. He selected John Foster Dulles as secretary of state because of Dulles's extensive experience in foreign affairs, devotion to hard work, and willingness to take presidential orders; but like many foreign-policy makers under Truman, Dulles came to public service from a career in corporate law. Because most of Eisenhower's cabinet appointees were wealthy businessmen, when he appointed Martin Durkin, president of the AFL plumbers union, as secretary of labor, a liberal journal quipped that Eisenhower had "picked a cabinet of eight millionaires and one plumber." The "plumber" lasted less than a year and was replaced by a retail executive. Eisenhower became the second president to appoint a woman to his cabinet, choosing former WAC commander and Texas newspaper publisher Oveta Culp Hobby to head the newly created Department of Health, Education, and Welfare in 1953.

Eisenhower also garnered advice informally from a group of wealthy businessmen, whom he called his "gang." They went along on his vacations and discussed politics and economics while the president played golf or bridge. Eisenhower relied heavily on his advisers, but he remained firmly in charge, leading one scholar to characterize his administration as the "hidden-hand" presidency.

While Eisenhower's choice of businessmen as official and informal associates reflected his personal preferences, it was also compatible with his goal of unifying the Republican Party. This required winning over the conservative old guard Republicans, who wanted to repeal most of the New Deal and who attacked the containment policy, especially its focus on Europe. Eisenhower chose Richard Nixon for his running mate in 1952 in part because Nixon had close ties to the Republican right wing. Keeping Nixon on the ticket in 1956 underscored the president's commitment to party unity and his continuing attempts to swing the old guard toward moderate Republicanism.

The President and McCarthy

Eisenhower's desire to placate conservative Republicans influenced his approach to the anti-Communist fervor that had plagued the Truman adminis-

tration. Eisenhower shared Senator Joseph McCarthy's goal of eliminating communism from American life. He refused to commute the sentences of Ethel and Julius Rosenberg, who were convicted of treason and sentenced to death for passing atomic secrets to the Soviets during the war. Eisenhower resisted worldwide pressure to grant clemency to these parents of young children, and they were electrocuted in June 1953.

Although Eisenhower deplored McCarthy's method, he made little effort to silence him. Privately, Eisenhower explained that he would not demean the presidency by getting "into a pissing contest with that skunk," insisting that presidential attention would only give the senator greater publicity. Recognizing McCarthy's popularity, Eisenhower feared that to denounce him would alienate

THE PERSISTENCE OF MCCARTHYISM
This political cartoon, created in 1954, took a jab at both President Eisenhower and the U.S. Senate for allowing Senator Joseph McCarthy to destroy careers and reputations with his indiscriminate charges of communism.
Herblock © 1954/*The Washington Post.*

old guard Republicans who held powerful positions in Congress. Moreover, Republicans benefited from McCarthy's attacks on the Democrats. Republican Senator John Bricker of Ohio called McCarthy an "SOB" but continued, "Sometimes it's useful to have SOBs around to do the dirty work."

The changeover to a Republican administration failed to stop McCarthy's allegations that the government was rife with Communists; thousands of federal employees charged with disloyalty lost their jobs while Eisenhower was president. Drunk with power, the senator attacked several of Eisenhower's appointees and got the State Department to remove from overseas libraries books by such "subversive" authors as Mark Twain and John Dewey.

Eisenhower correctly predicted that McCarthy would ultimately destroy himself. With the conclusion of the Korean War, popular frustrations over containment abated, and the anti-Communist hysteria subsided. Because Eisenhower came across to most Americans as a staunch anti-Communist, when right-wing Republicans continued to cry Red after he was in charge of the government, they sounded like crackpots.

McCarthy tightened his own noose in 1954 when he went after alleged Communists in the army. As he hurled reckless charges during weeks of televised committee hearings, public opinion turned against McCarthy, who came across as a cruel, disruptive bully. "Have you left no sense of decency?" demanded the army's lawyer, Joseph Welch. The Senate, too, had had enough and in December 1954 voted to condemn him. After the vote, Eisenhower remarked that McCarthyism had become "McCarthywasism." But the president's inaction had allowed the senator to spread his poison longer than he might otherwise have done. Like Truman, Eisenhower lent the prestige and power of his office to the postwar Red scare and suppression of dissent.

The New Deal Confirmed

During the 1952 presidential campaign, Eisenhower warned that "four years more of Democratic, uninterrupted, government . . . will put us so far on the road to socialism that there will be no return to a free enterprise." Yet he knew that many of the social policies of the past two decades had fostered economic stability, and he understood their great popularity with voters. He wrote in his diary in 1954, "The Republican party must be known as a progressive organization or it is sunk."

Convinced that government was best left up to the states and economic decisions to private business, Eisenhower determined to limit the scope and size of the federal government. Nonetheless, in some cases, he was willing to expand the welfare state and to involve the federal government in new projects. His "middle way" applied the brakes, but it did not reverse the growing federal responsibility for economic development and for the welfare of Americans who were unable to survive in the free market.

In 1954, Eisenhower signed legislation that expanded improvements in Social Security by providing higher benefits and extending coverage to some ten million workers and self-employed individuals. Whereas Truman had failed to win congressional approval for a new Department of Health, Education, and Welfare, Eisenhower succeeded. Moreover, the Housing Act of 1954 continued the federal government's role in financing public housing, although the amount of construction fell far short of meeting the need.

Eisenhower supported massive federal public works projects, including the St. Lawrence Seaway, which connected the Great Lakes with the Atlantic Ocean. But his greatest initiative was the Interstate Highway Act of 1956, involving the federal government in road-building activities that previously had been conducted by states and localities. Promoted as an essential arm of the nation's cold war defense strategy and as a spur to economic growth, the law authorized construction of a national system of highways, with the federal government paying most of the costs through increased fuel and vehicle taxes.

Millions of Americans would benefit from the ease of travel and the improved transportation of goods on the interstate highway system, but the most direct and substantial gains went to the trucking, construction, and automobile industries, which had lobbied hard for the law. Greater than any previous public works project, the Interstate Highway Act created a larger federal government with subsidies for business interests, not for the poor. Unforeseen at the time, the monumental highway construction project eventually exacted severe costs in the form of air pollution, wasteful energy consumption, declining mass transportation, and the decay of central cities.

In other areas, Eisenhower restrained the federal government in favor of state governments and private enterprise. He achieved large tax cuts, for example, that favored business and the wealthy.

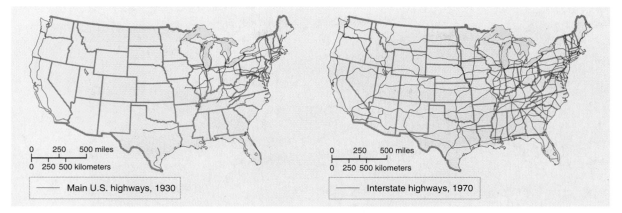

M A P   **27.1**

The Interstate Highway System, 1930 and 1970
Built with federal funds authorized in the Interstate Highway Act of 1956, superhighways soon
criss-crossed the nation. Trucking, construction, and gasoline were among the industries that
prospered, but railroads suffered from the subsidized competition.

Moreover, whereas Democrats sought to keep nuclear power in government hands, Eisenhower signed legislation authorizing the private manufacture and sale of nuclear power and directed the Atomic Energy Commission (AEC) to provide materials and services to private utilities at cost. Ground was broken at Shippingport, Pennsylvania, for the first commercial atomic power plant in the fall of 1954.

The president made only slight concessions to liberals who called for a larger federal role in the areas of health, education, and civil rights. Stubbornly resisting proposals that resembled Truman's national health insurance program, Eisenhower responded in very measured ways to the increasing difficulty Americans faced in securing adequate health care. For instance, the spread of polio, or infantile paralysis, the disease that had stricken Franklin D. Roosevelt in the 1920s, neared epidemic proportions in the 1950s. Terrified parents kept children away from swimming pools to protect them from the crippling disease. When Dr. Jonas Salk developed a vaccine, Eisenhower obtained funds from Congress for its distribution, even though conservatives preferred that states assume that responsibility.

The 1956 Election and the Second Term

Although Eisenhower retained his immense popularity, his health became a serious political issue in September 1955, when he suffered a heart attack that kept him away from the White House until the end of the year. After the heart attack, Eisenhower deliberated at length whether to run for a second term. When he announced his decision in February 1956, he knew that his health made the choice of running mate even more critical than it had been in 1952.

Eisenhower worried about placing Vice President Nixon a heartbeat away from the presidency. He admired Nixon's loyalty and dedication but doubted his maturity and ability to run the government. Eisenhower failed to lure Nixon off the ticket with an offer of a cabinet post but could not bring himself to dispose of Nixon forthrightly. He left the vice presidential choice up to the Republican national convention, where conservatives led a successful drive for Nixon's renomination.

Adlai Stevenson, chosen again by the Democrats, was hard-pressed to explain why voters should abandon Eisenhower in times of peace and prosperity. Stevenson's indirect references to Eisenhower's health helped little. He warned of the radioactive fallout from nuclear testing and called for a test ban, but most voters supported development of nuclear weapons and felt comfortable with Eisenhower's finger on the nuclear trigger. The president's experience in international affairs seemed even more important when crises erupted in Eastern Europe and the Middle East just before the election.

Losing only seven states, Eisenhower trounced Stevenson with 35.6 million to 26 million votes, doubling his 1952 margin. But even Ike's popularity could not break the Democrats' control of Congress.

POVERTY IN AN ERA OF ABUNDANCE
This photo of coal miner Orville Sturgill's family in front of their one-room shack on a country
road near Mayking, Kentucky, in 1959 represents the hidden side of the affluent 1950s. The in-
come from a very small truck mine that Sturgill worked with another man combined with the
produce from a garden patch behind the house was not enough to lift this family out of poverty.
Wide World.

Two years later, the Democrats all but wiped out the Republican Party, gaining a 64–34 majority in the Senate and a 282–135 advantage in the House. Though Eisenhower captured voters' hearts, a majority of them remained wedded to the programs and policies of the Democrats.

In part because of the Democratic resurgence, Eisenhower's leadership faced more serious challenges in his second term. Illness struck again, in the form of a stroke in November 1957. The economy plunged into a recession in late 1957, and unemployment rose to 7 percent. Eisenhower fought with Congress over the budget and vetoed a number of Democrat-sponsored bills providing for expanded public works projects, a high level of price supports for farmers, and housing and urban development. The president and Congress did reach agreement in two important areas: enacting the first civil rights legislation in a century and establishing a new role for the government in education.

In the end, Eisenhower's middle way altered very little the relationship between the federal government and the individual that had been established under Roosevelt and Truman. The first Republican administration after the New Deal left the size and functions of the federal government intact, as it tipped federal policy somewhat more in favor of corporate interests. Unparalleled prosperity graced the Eisenhower years, and inflation was confined to an annual average of 1.5 percent. The nation experienced two recessions in the 1950s, but the economy recovered without putting to a test the president's aversion to substantial federal intervention.

Nevertheless, the prosperity of the 1950s blinded most Americans to the poverty endured by a substantial minority of the population. In 1960, some forty million people—more than 20 percent of the population—lived below the income levels that had been established by the government as the minimum necessary to provide a decent livelihood.

Another thirty-nine million who were above the poverty line survived only on stringent budgets, denied most of the consumer goods that symbolized the decade of affluence. Rural poverty was particularly pronounced, with farm families earning less than 50 percent of the income of the nonfarming population. The policies of the middle way sustained the postwar economic boom, but they failed to bring that prosperity, or even comfort, to a sizable minority of the nation.

Liberation Rhetoric and the Practice of Containment

Like Truman, Eisenhower saw communism as a threat not only to the nation's physical security but also to U.S. economic interests. As he wrote in 1951, the nation's foreign policy should seek "for the United States to obtain certain raw materials to sustain its economy, and, when possible, to preserve profitable foreign markets for our surpluses." What distinguished Eisenhower's foreign policy from Truman's was its rhetoric, its means, and—after Stalin's death in 1953—its overtures toward accommodation with the Soviet Union.

Republican rhetoric—voiced most prominently by Secretary of State John Foster Dulles—deplored containment as "negative, futile, and immoral" because it accepted the existing Soviet sphere of influence and control. Yet, despite promises to roll back Soviet power, the Eisenhower administration carried out a policy of containment. It directed anticommunism at the margins of Communist power in Asia, the Middle East, and Latin America, not at its core in Europe. Eisenhower assigned nuclear weapons and secret operations larger roles in defense strategy. He avoided involvement in new wars and took steps to ease tensions between the superpowers.

The "New Look" in Foreign Policy

Eisenhower's concern about federal spending governed defense strategy. To meet his goals of balancing the budget and cutting taxes, he had to reduce military expenditures. Moreover, he feared the domestic effects of massive defense spending. To Eisenhower, the internal economic strength and stability of the nation were as critical to its security as military power. A state based on warfare could de-

stroy the very society it was intended to protect. As he declared in 1953, "Every gun that is made, every warship launched, every rocket fired signifies, in the final sense, a theft from those who hunger and are not fed, those who are cold and not clothed."

Eisenhower's strategy concentrated U.S. military strength in nuclear weapons. After the Korean War, he and most other Americans rejected the possibility of large-scale involvement in conventional wars. The nation's allies could defend themselves with U.S. aid. Eisenhower pointed out that while "it cost $3,515 to maintain an American soldier each year, for a Pakistani the price was $485, for a Greek, $424." Instead of spending huge amounts for a large standing army, the United States would arm its allies and step up its nuclear capabilities. This was Eisenhower's "New Look" in foreign policy: Give friendly nations American weapons and back them up with an ominous nuclear arsenal.

Air power and nuclear weapons provided, in Dulles's words, "maximum deterrent at bearable cost," or, as Defense Secretary Charles Wilson put it, a "bigger bang for the buck." The New Look would enable the United States to deter Soviet expansion with the U.S. capacity for "massive retaliation." According to Dulles, America's willingness to "go to the brink" of war with its intimidating nuclear superiority would cause the Soviets to back down from any efforts to extend the territory under their control.

> What distinguished Eisenhower's foreign policy from Truman's was its rhetoric, its means, and—after Stalin's death in 1953— its overtures toward accommodation with the Soviet Union.

The armed services, Democratic leaders, and some Republicans wanted to strengthen conventional military forces and maintain greater nonnuclear flexibility. Over their objections, Eisenhower stuck to his nuclear guns. He held the annual defense budget between $35 and $40 billion while maintaining U.S. nuclear superiority. The means for delivering weapons to their targets became more efficient, and bombs shrank in size even as they mushroomed in destructive force. By 1955, one U.S. bomber carried more force than all the explosives ever detonated in the entire history of humankind.

Although the Soviets quickly developed nuclear weapons, the United States retained its supe-

THE NUCLEAR ARMS RACE
This magazine-cover rendering of Soviet leader Nikita Khrushchev and President Dwight D. Eisenhower balanced on the head of a nuclear missile suggests the precarious world created by the nuclear arms race. The table on which the two men sit refers to the arms limitation negotiations under way when the magazine was published in 1959.

riority and deterrence capability. Nuclear bombs and missiles could not stop a Soviet attack, but they could inflict almost unimaginable destruction on the Soviet Union. Therefore, American bombers armed with nuclear weapons stayed airborne around the clock, ready to fly across the iron curtain and annihilate the enemy should it attack the United States. The certainty of that massive retaliation was meant to deter the Soviets from launching an attack on the United States. Because the Soviet Union could respond similarly to an American first strike, this delicately balanced nuclear standoff became known as "mutually assured destruction," or MAD. Winston Churchill called it a mutual balance of terror.

The balance of terror prevented the Eisenhower administration from fulfilling its promises to roll back the iron curtain and liberate peoples under Communist rule. The United States lacked the massive conventional forces necessary to pry the Soviets' grip from Eastern Europe. But the use of nuclear weapons would have destroyed the very people Eisenhower wanted to liberate. Thus, when an opportunity for liberation emerged, the administration's promises proved to be empty rhetoric.

In 1956, several Eastern European nations responded to Soviet leader Nikita Khrushchev's signals that the harsh policies of Stalin would be relaxed. Demonstrations in Poland won that nation a measure of independence from Soviet influence. In Hungary, students and workers massed in demonstrations against the Soviet puppet government and the Red Army. When Soviet tanks arrived to crush the revolt, the Hungarian Freedom Fighters sent a radio message that they were counting on American help: "SOS! They just brought us a rumor that the American troops will be here within one or two hours. . . . We are well and fighting." But no help came, and the Soviets suppressed the insurrection by killing thirty thousand Hungarians and executing the rebels' leader, Imre Nagy.

Eisenhower would not risk U.S. soldiers and a possible nuclear war to roll back the iron curtain. Talk of liberation had its partisan political uses, but it amounted to little more than grandstanding, since rollback lay outside the limits of American power.

From Korea to Vietnam

Accepting the status quo in Europe, the Eisenhower administration sought to contain communism in other parts of the world, just as the Truman administration had. Like Truman, Eisenhower assumed that the People's Republic of China (PRC) took its orders from Moscow. He continued the policy of nonrecognition—maintaining the fiction that the government of Chiang Kai-shek on Taiwan represented all the Chinese people—even though most nations had recognized the legitimacy of Mao Zedong's Communist government on the mainland. Twice the United States threatened to use nuclear bombs when the PRC made moves against the Nationalist-held islands Quemoy and Matsu, which lie close to mainland China. Continuing support of Nationalist China, Eisenhower and his advisers believed, provided a vital symbol of the nation's commitment to containment in Asia.

The major challenge to that commitment came in Southeast Asia, in Indochina, where a nationalist coalition called the Viet Minh, led by Ho Chi Minh, had declared the independence of Vietnam from France in 1945 after helping to defeat Japan. When France fought to maintain its colony, Ho fought back, plunging the area into war. U.S. officials found no direct connections between the Viet Minh and Soviet leaders. Nonetheless, because Ho declared himself a Communist, the Truman administration quietly began to provide aid to the French.

In 1950, after the Communist victory in China, the outbreak of the Korean War, and the Soviet recognition of the Viet Minh, the United States stepped up its support of the French. The United States recognized the puppet government of Bao Dai set up by the French in the south of Vietnam and began to supply it with economic aid and technical assistance. Soon the United States was paying 40 percent of the cost of the war against Ho Chi Minh.

Eisenhower fully agreed with Truman's Vietnam policy, viewing it as another domino about to topple from Communist aggression, much as Truman had regarded Greece and Turkey. "You have a row of dominoes set up," Eisenhower said, and "you knock over the first one, and what will happen to the last one is the certainty that it will go over very quickly." The president pointed to the "value of [Southeast Asia] in its production of materials that the world needs" and to "the possibility that many human beings [will] pass under a dictatorship that is inimical to the free world." He warned that the fall of Southeast Asia to communism could well be followed by the fall of Japan, Taiwan, and the Philippines. By 1954, the United States was contributing 75 percent of the cost of the war.

But the soldier-president also had a realistic view of American capabilities and interests. When in 1954 the French stood at the brink of defeat at Dien Bien Phu and demanded troops and airplanes from the United States, Eisenhower firmly said no. He was willing to pay for French combat but would not commit U.S. troops to another ground war in Asia. The British also turned down French appeals, and congressional leaders would not grant the president discretionary authority to dispatch U.S. forces without participation by allies. Dien Bien Phu fell in May 1954 and with it the French colony of Vietnam.

Two months later in Geneva, France signed a truce. The Geneva accords drew a temporary line across the seventeenth parallel of Vietnam and prohibited either the Viet Minh in the North or the government in the South from joining a military alliance or permitting foreign bases on their soil. Within two years, elections were to be held for the Vietnamese people to choose a unified government. The United States promised to support free elections, but it did not sign the accords.

The French defeat in Vietnam did not cause Eisenhower to abandon containment in Asia. Instead, he searched for allies. In September 1954, the United States organized the Southeast Asia Treaty Organization (SEATO), with Britain, France, Australia, New Zealand, Thailand, Pakistan, and the Philippines as members. A separate protocol to the SEATO pact committed the members to the defense of Cambodia, Laos, and South Vietnam. This was Eisenhower's attempt to prop up the dominoes of Southeast Asia after the French defeat.

The ink was barely dry on the SEATO alliance when the United States began to send weapons and military advisers to South Vietnam. Knowing that the election mandated by the Geneva accords would result in a victory for Ho Chi Minh, the United States supported South Vietnamese Prime Minister Ngo Dinh Diem in his refusal to hold the election, in effect violating the Geneva agreement. Diem did hold a referendum in the South: His government won 98 percent of the vote, including 605,000 votes from the city of Saigon, which had 405,000 registered voters. This fraudulent election marked but the first sign of the corruption and repression that characterized Diem's rule.

Seeking to make South Vietnam a bulwark against communism, the United States repeated most of the mistakes that had doomed the French. Between 1955 and 1961, the United States poured $1 billion into South Vietnam, 80 percent of which went to the South Vietnamese army (ARVN). However, Diem staffed the army with men known for their loyalty to him rather than for their military competence. Despite U.S. dollars, the ARVN proved to be grossly unprepared for the guerrilla warfare that the Vietminh began to mount in the late 1950s.

In 1959, Ho Chi Minh's government in Hanoi began sending military assistance to Vietminh rebels in the South, who stepped up their guerrilla attacks on the Diem government. The insurgents gained control over villages not only through sheer military power but also through support from peasants who were outraged by the Diem government's jailing of critics, failure to give peasants control over the land they worked, and relocation of peasants far from their homes. Unable to reverse the growing opposition to Diem in the South and unwilling to abandon his commitment to containment, Eisenhower would pass the deteriorating situation in Southeast Asia on to his successor, John F. Kennedy, in 1961.

Interventions in Latin America and the Middle East

While attempting to buttress friendly governments in Asia, the Eisenhower administration also worked to topple unfriendly ones in Latin America and elsewhere. Much more than Truman, Eisenhower relied on secret, behind-the-scenes efforts. His administration's covert activities against what it considered hostile governments justified the fears expressed in 1948 when Congress debated creation of the Central Intelligence Agency (CIA). Increasingly, the administration conducted foreign policy behind the back of Congress.

Taking extreme care not to leave a paper trail, Eisenhower authorized the CIA, headed by Allen Dulles, the brother of the secretary of state, to eliminate a threat to U.S. interests in oil-rich Iran. In

1951, Iran's left-leaning prime minister, Mohammed Mossadegh, nationalized oil fields and refineries, thereby upsetting the British monopoly of Iran's major national resource and setting a precedent that threatened Western oil interests throughout the Middle East. Mossadegh also challenged the power of the shah, Mohammad Reza Pahlavi, Iran's hereditary leader, who had favored foreign oil interests and the Iranian wealthy classes. Moreover, Mossadegh's acceptance of support from the Iranian Communist Party led U.S. officials to assume that he would draw closer to the Soviet Union.

With Eisenhower's approval, the CIA sent agents to Iran with funds to bribe Iranian army officers and to pay Iranians to demonstrate against Mossadegh's government. In August 1953, army officers took Mossadegh prisoner, and the shah's power was reestablished. Iran renegotiated oil concessions, giving U.S. companies a 40 percent share. Although the intervention worked in the short run, Americans in the 1970s and 1980s would harvest the full fury of Iranian opposition to the shah's repressive government that the United States had helped to reinstall.

FIDEL CASTRO TRIUMPHS IN CUBA
Castro came from a privileged family and attended law school at the University of Havana, but he spent his youth working for the overthrow of Cuban dictator Fulgencio Batista. After leading an assault on Batista's soldiers in 1953, he spent two years in prison and then slowly built up an army of guerrilla fighters. He is shown here during his triumphal entrance into Havana in January 1959.
Corbis-Bettmann.

Heady with the success in Iran, the Eisenhower administration soon turned to clandestine activities in Central America, where it perceived a Communist threat in Guatemala. As in Iran, the Guatemalan government was not Communist or Soviet-controlled, but it accepted support from the native Communist Party and threatened established economic interests. In both Guatemala and Iran, U.S. intervention thwarted the popular will, set up repressive dictatorships, and helped American corporations.

In 1951, Guatemalan voters elected Jacobo Arbenz as president. Arbenz sought to alleviate poverty through land reforms that nationalized the holdings of foreign companies, including the United Fruit Company, which was owned by U.S. investors. Eisenhower decided that Arbenz had to go and authorized the CIA to stage a coup in 1954.

The CIA organized a small army under its handpicked leader, Castillo Armas, supplied him with planes and bombs, and authorized CIA pilots to bomb Guatemalan targets. Unable to get support from the United Nations, Arbenz resigned, and a military dictatorship under Armas took over. The United Fruit Company got its land back, and Eisenhower achieved his primary objective: to prevent communism from gaining a foothold in Central America. He considered the Guatemalan coup among his proudest accomplishments.

"We're going to take care of Castro just like we took care of Arbenz," promised a CIA agent when Cubans' desire for political and economic autonomy erupted in 1959. An uprising led by Fidel Castro drove out dictator Fulgencio Batista, who had long been supported by the United States. American companies controlled a large portion of Cuba's critical resources, especially sugar and tobacco, and decisions made in Washington directly influenced the lives and livelihoods of the Cuban people. As a former ambassador to Cuba put it, "The American Ambassador was the second most important man in Cuba; sometimes even more important than the [Cuban] President."

CIA Director Allen Dulles warned Eisenhower that "Communists and other extreme radicals appear to have penetrated the Castro movement." When the United States denied Castro's requests for loans, he turned for help to the Soviet Union. After American companies refused Castro's offer to purchase them at their assessed value—which the Batista government had kept ridiculously low so that Americans could avoid heavy taxes—Castro began to nationalize their property. Eisenhower broke off diplomatic relations with Cuba and cast about for an alternative to Castro, authorizing the CIA to train Cuban exiles for an invasion of Cuba. Time ran out on the Eisenhower administration, and he bequeathed the Cuban situation, along with Vietnam, to the next administration.

Although Eisenhower expanded presidential power and conducted military operations that were kept secret from Congress and the public, he showed restraint when the risks of intervention seemed too high. He judged the risks of helping the French at Dien Bien Phu to be too great, and he reached similar conclusions when conflict erupted in the Middle East.

The Republican administration turned from Truman's all-out support for Israel and attempted to foster friendships with Arab nations. But these overtures to Arab states collapsed when the American insistence on complete loyalty to the United States conflicted with smaller nations' preference for nonalignment, which would allow them to seek aid from both the West and the Soviet Union and its allies. In 1955, Secretary of State John Foster Dulles began negotiating with Egypt about American support for building the Aswan Dam to control the Nile River. But in 1956, Egypt's leader, Gamal Abdel Nasser, declared his intention to obtain arms from Communist Czechoslovakia and negotiated a military alliance with other Arab nations. He also withdrew Egypt's recognition of the Nationalist Chinese government and recognized the People's Republic of China.

Unwilling to tolerate such independence, Dulles called off the deal for the Aswan Dam. On July 26, 1956, Nasser responded boldly by seizing the Suez Canal, then owned by Britain and France. Taking the canal advanced Nasser's prestige and power because it coincided with nationalist aspirations in the Arab world. Moreover, the revenue from the canal could provide capital for constructing the dam.

Britain and France immediately protested the canal seizure, but Eisenhower held back, announcing that the United States would not participate in military efforts to settle the Suez crisis. He recognized that the Egyptians, after all, had claimed their own territory, and he believed that Nasser "embodies the emotional demands of the people . . . for independence and for 'slapping the white Man down.'" To intervene against him, Eisenhower concluded, "might well array the world from Dakar to the Philippine Islands against us."

Ever since the establishment of Israel in 1948, Egyptian and Israeli forces had engaged in skirmishes along their common border. When Egypt seized the Suez Canal, Israel—with the knowledge of France and Britain—attacked Egypt. The two European nations then joined the military effort against Egypt. Shocked and angered by the Anglo-French intervention, Eisenhower declared an oil embargo on Britain and France while calling on the United Nations to arrange a truce. Without U.S. support, the French and British soon pulled back, and Israel was forced to retreat from territory it had captured in the Sinai Desert region of Egypt.

Although Eisenhower refused to intervene in the Suez crisis, he made clear that the United States would actively combat communism in the Middle East. In March 1957, Congress agreed to his request for a joint resolution approving economic and military aid to any Middle Eastern nation "requesting assistance against armed aggression from any country controlled by international communism." The president invoked this "Eisenhower Doctrine" to send aid to Jordan in 1957 and troops to Lebanon in 1958 to counter anti-Western pressures on those governments.

The Nuclear Arms Race

Although Eisenhower allowed his secretary of state to speak publicly of an "irreconcilable conflict" between the United States and the Soviet Union and to label the Soviet Union a nation of unmitigated evil, the president was determined to reduce superpower tensions. A number of events made accommodation with the Soviet Union a promising prospect. After Stalin's death in 1953, a more moderate leadership under Nikita Khrushchev emerged. For the first time, the Soviet Union withdrew troops from territory it had taken during World War II: After agreeing to a peace treaty with Austria that guaranteed Austrian neutrality, Soviet troops left that country. Like Eisenhower, Soviet Premier Khrushchev worried about the domestic costs of the cold war and wanted to reduce defense spending and check the arms race.

New developments in military technology and mounting evidence that radioactive fallout from nuclear testing produced horrible birth defects gave greater urgency to finding a way out of the nuclear arms race. By the mid-1950s, both superpowers had started to develop intercontinental ballistic missiles (ICBMs) armed with nuclear warheads. These new missiles, once launched, could not be recalled (as planes carrying conventional bombs could) and would strike their targets within minutes, thus rendering them much more vulnerable to human miscalculation. The nuclear button had become a hair trigger.

Eisenhower and Khrushchev met in Geneva in 1955 at the first summit conference since the end of World War II. Though the summit produced no significant agreements, it nevertheless symbolized a lessening of tensions—as Eisenhower put it, "a new spirit of conciliation and cooperation." Thereafter, the two nations exchanged offers and counteroffers for limiting nuclear arms. In 1959, Khrushchev visited the United States, and Nixon went to the Soviet Union. By 1960, the two sides were within reach of a ban on nuclear testing, and Khrushchev and Eisenhower agreed to meet again in Paris in May.

To avoid jeopardizing the summit, Eisenhower canceled espionage flights over the Soviet Union, but his order came one day too late. On May 1, as the last U-2 spy plane flew over the Soviet Union, Soviet gunners shot it down. Assuming that the pilot, Francis Gary Powers, had not survived, the State Department denied that U.S. planes had been deliberately violating Soviet air space. When the Soviets produced not only Powers but also the photos taken on his flight, they caught the United States in a lie. Eisenhower assumed responsibility but refused to apologize. He met with Khrushchev briefly in Paris, but the U-2 incident dashed all prospects for a nuclear arms agreement and aborted Eisenhower's planned visit to Moscow. Both nations had suspended nuclear testing in the atmosphere in 1958 and continued to do so, but they could not agree on a permanent test ban.

Intercontinental ballistic missiles, once launched, could not be recalled and would strike their targets within minutes, thus rendering them much more vulnerable to human miscalculation. The nuclear button had become a hair trigger.

Eisenhower's "more bang for the buck" defense budget increased enormously the U.S. nuclear capacity. Between 1958 and 1960 alone, the stockpile of nuclear weapons grew from six thousand to eighteen thousand. Moreover, by the time Eisenhower left office in 1961, the United States had installed seventy-two ICBMs in the United States and Britain, was prepared to deploy additional missiles in Italy and Turkey, and had several hundred more under

CHILDREN IN THE AGE OF NUCLEAR ANXIETY
As schools routinely held drills to prepare for possible Soviet attacks, children directly experienced the anxiety and insecurity of the 1950s nuclear arms race. The Soviet launching of Sputnik *in 1957 intensified American fears and led to an even greater focus on civilian defense.*
Archive Photos.

contract. The first Polaris submarine carrying nuclear missiles was launched in November 1960.

The spectacular growth in nuclear defense capability, however, did not spare Eisenhower from charges that he had allowed the United States to fall behind the Soviet Union. Insisting that the United States needed a "flexible response" to Communist aggression, leading Democrats and military experts attacked the administration's emphasis on nuclear weapons to the neglect of conventional forces. Moreover, critics charged, the Eisenhower administration had not adequately pursued development of new delivery systems, thus contributing to a "missile gap" between the United States and the Soviet Union.

In August 1957, the Soviets test-fired the first intercontinental ballistic missile; two months later, they launched *Sputnik,* the first artificial satellite to circle the planet. To Senate majority leader Lyndon Johnson, these developments amounted to a scientific Pearl Harbor. *Sputnik* spread a sense of national humiliation as journalists, politicians, and others reported that the United States lagged behind not only in missile development and space exploration but also in science, education, economic growth, and national resolve. When the United States tried to launch a response to *Sputnik,* its satellite exploded. Newspapers expressed the humiliation by calling it

a "Stayputnik" or a "Flopnik." The United States finally launched its first satellite in January 1958.

Eisenhower correctly insisted that the United States possessed nuclear superiority, but in 1957 he was unable to disclose his strongest evidence, information about the Soviet arsenal obtained from the top-secret U-2 surveillance. He took steps to diminish public panic, supporting the formation of the National Aeronautics and Space Administration (NASA) in July 1958 and approving a gigantic increase in the budget for space research and development. Eisenhower also signed the National Defense Education Act in 1958, providing loans and scholarships for students in math, foreign languages, and science.

In the 1960 election campaign, the Democrats exploited the "missile gap" issue, which after the election was exposed as a partisan myth. Yet nuclear superiority did not guarantee security, and the United States was no safer when Eisenhower left office than when he became president. Though it lagged behind the United States in virtually every aspect of military technology, the Soviet Union nonetheless possessed sufficient nuclear weapons to devastate the United States. American schoolchildren regularly dove under their desks during drills in preparation for a nuclear attack, and the Civil Defense Administration recommended that families construct home bomb shelters. In 1959, *Life* magazine featured newlyweds who spent their fourteen-day honeymoon in their 8-by-11-foot shelter. Most American families did not build shelters, but they realized how precarious nuclear weapons had made their lives.

Just before he left office, Eisenhower emphasized another menace of the nuclear age: the growing influence of "the military-industrial complex" in American government and life. To keep the defense budget within reasonable limits, Eisenhower had struggled against unrelenting pressures from defense contractors who, in tandem with the military services, sought more dollars for newer, more powerful weapons systems. In his farewell address, he warned that the "conjunction of an immense military establishment and a large arms industry . . . exercised a total influence . . . in every city, every state house, every office of the federal government." The cold war had created a warfare state.

Winners and Losers in an Economy of Abundance

Military spending helped to stimulate domestic prosperity. Economic productivity increased enormously in the 1950s, a multitude of new products came on the market, consumption became the order

of the day, and millions of Americans moved to the suburbs. Prosperity also provided the means for more young people to stay in school, and higher education became the norm for middle-class families. Although every section of the nation enjoyed the new prosperity, the West and Southwest especially boomed in production, commerce, and population.

As the economy surged, the nature of work itself changed: Farm labor continued to decline, white-collar employment overtook manufacturing jobs, and women constituted a growing share of the workforce. These economic shifts disadvantaged some segments of the population, but most Americans enjoyed a higher standard of living. In the 1950s, the United States became what economist John Kenneth Galbraith termed "the affluent society."

The Transformation of Agriculture

On October 2, 1944, on a plantation near Clarksdale, Mississippi, International Harvester demonstrated its first mechanical cotton picker. The machinery could replace fifty people and reduce the cost of picking a bale of cotton from forty dollars to five dollars. The mechanical cotton picker soon swept the South, transforming the sharecropping system that had been in place since Reconstruction and displacing hundreds of thousands of African Americans, who swelled an exodus to southern cities, the North, and the West.

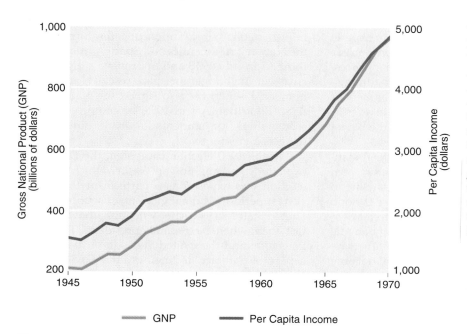

FIGURE 27.1
The Postwar Economic Boom: GNP and Per Capita Income, 1945–1970
American dominance of the worldwide market, innovative technologies that led to new industries such as computers and plastics, population growth, and increases in worker productivity all contributed to the enormous economic growth of the United States after World War II.

The cotton picker was just one element in a spectacular rise in agricultural production. Between 1940 and 1960, the output of American farms mushroomed, while the number of farmworkers declined by nearly one-third. In 1940, it took forty-four hours of work to yield one hundred bushels of wheat; by 1960, the same job took just eighteen hours. Farmers achieved nearly miraculous agricultural productivity through greater crop specialization, more intensive use of fertilizers, and, above all, mechanization. Tractors, mechanical corn and cotton pickers, and other forms of machinery increasingly replaced human labor and animal power.

Economic productivity increased enormously in the 1950s, a multitude of new products came on the market, consumption became the order of the day, and millions of Americans moved to the suburbs.

The decline of the family farm and the growth of large commercial farming, which came to be called "agribusiness," were both causes and consequences of mechanization. Larger farmers benefited handsomely from federal price support programs, and they more easily took advantage of technological improvements, while smaller producers lacked capital to invest in the machinery that was required to compete. Consequently, although the average farm size more than doubled between 1940 and 1964, the farm population declined from thirty million to thirteen million, and the number of farms decreased by more than 40 percent.

Many small farmers who hung on managed a bare subsistence standard of living and constituted a core of rural poverty that escaped the attention of those who celebrated the affluence of the 1950s. Southern sharecroppers were other victims of the transformation of agriculture, forced off the land when owners replaced them with machinery. Often they moved to cities, where a lack of jobs for which they could qualify and racial discrimination engendered growing urban poverty.

A Mississippi woman whose family had worked on a plantation since slavery confronted a difficult dilemma. She recalled that when her family got the news that "it was going to be machines now that harvest the crops, and there wasn't much we could do anymore," most of her relatives went to Chicago. Worrying that "it might be worse up

MECHANIZING AGRICULTURE
This farm equipment ad reflects the growing application of technology to agriculture. Ever more elaborate machinery created a long-term trend in which family farms were overtaken by agribusiness. Giant farms employed the latest technology and thus reduced the need for human labor. Between 1945 and 1960, the nation's population living on farms shrank from 17.5 to 8.7 percent.
John Deere Company.

there," she faced an agonizing choice: "I'm afraid to leave and I'm afraid to stay, and whichever I do, I think it might be real bad for my boys and girls."

New Jobs and New Workers

Tremendous gains in productivity were not confined to agriculture. Between 1945 and 1960, the gross national product (the value of all goods and services produced during the year) leaped by 250 percent, and per capita income rose by 35 percent. Although about one-fifth of the population continued to live below the poverty line, economists could claim that some 60 percent of the population en-

TECHNOLOGY IN AMERICA
Air Conditioning

Air conditioning developed primarily in response to the needs of industry. In 1902, Willis Haviland Carrier, an American engineer who formulated basic theories of air conditioning, designed the first system to control temperature and humidity and installed it in a Brooklyn printing plant. In 1915 he founded the Carrier Corporation to manufacture air-conditioning equipment. Because fibers are sensitive to moisture, the textile industry provided an early and important market for air conditioning. The process also helped to popularize movie theaters by making them a cool as well as entertaining retreat during hot summer months; and in the 1930s room air conditioners began to appear. This 1950 Carrier ad promoted the clean air in homes and offices that would come with purchase of a room air conditioner. Less than a million homes had room air conditioners in 1950, but nearly eight million did in 1960, and more than half of all homes had some form of air conditioning by 1975. Air conditioning was a mixed blessing: It improved air quality inside businesses, homes, and cars, but contributed to outdoor air pollution. Perhaps its greatest impact on the nation was to make possible the population explosion in the Sun Belt. One historian of the South, referring disparagingly to the impact of air conditioning on that region, proclaimed that "G.E. has proved a more devastating invader than even General Sherman."

Courtesy Carrier Corporation.

EXCUSE MY DUST

Carrier   AIR CONDITIONING • REFRIGERATION

---

joyed middle-class incomes. By the late 1950s, when the nation's population stood at 175 million, there were seventy-four million cars on the road. Four of every five families owned television sets and washing machines, and nearly all had refrigerators.

A number of forces spurred this unparalleled abundance. Even with Eisenhower's conservative fiscal policies, government spending reached $80 billion annually and stimulated not only the creation of jobs but also research and development. A population explosion—from 140 million in 1945 to 176 million in 1960—expanded demand for products, and the rapidly growing youthful segment of the population stimulated industries ranging from baby goods to records. Consumer borrowing also fueled the boom, as more and more people purchased houses, cars, and appliances on installment plans.

American prosperity reflected the nation's dominance in the international economy. With U.S.

aid, the economies of Western Europe and Japan began to recover from the devastation of World War II, but American producers still found abundant markets for their products abroad and faced relatively little competition from foreign imports in the domestic economy. By the end of the 1950s, however, Western Europe and Japan became more competitive in world markets. Japanese-made products such as cameras, televisions, and automobiles began to compete with American manufactures. The first Volkswagen appeared in the United States in 1949. In 1958, Americans purchased nearly 400,000 imported automobiles.

As in agriculture, technological innovation increased industrial production. In the automobile industry, for example, new technology cut the number of labor-hours needed to manufacture a car by one-half between 1945 and 1960. Technology also transformed such industries as electronics, chemicals, and air transportation and promoted the growth of newer industries, such as television and computers. The first electronic computers were developed in the mid-1940s, and by the 1950s corporations had begun to use computers for processing data.

Labor unions enjoyed their greatest success during the 1950s as production workers saw their real earnings increase by 40 percent. The merger of the AFL and CIO in 1955 lessened jurisdictional conflicts and enabled labor to speak with one voice. The Eisenhower White House was generally unresponsive to organized labor, but unions helped to elect liberals to Congress and exercised considerable political clout.

Although labor lost much of its militancy in the postwar era, unions achieved gains for their members that went beyond wage increases. Fringe benefits—including pensions, health care, insurance, and paid vacations—became a staple of union contracts in most industries, though workers in steel, automobiles, and other heavy industries did much better than those employed in food processing, garment making, and other areas of light manufacturing. In addition, the United Auto Workers (UAW) pioneered in achieving a modified form of guaranteed income for its workers. Under this plan, laid-off workers could receive payments from a company fund to supplement their government unemployment benefits.

Unlike other industrial nations, where government provided most workers' benefits, the United States developed a mixed system in which company programs won by labor through collective bargaining played a much larger role. This system resulted in wide disparities among workers and put people who were not represented by unions at a severe disadvantage. Those nonunion workers began to constitute an increasing share of the workforce.

The absolute number of union members continued to increase, but union membership as a percentage of the labor force peaked at 27.1 percent in 1957. Automation and other forces chipped away at jobs in heavy industry, where most union workers were concentrated. Competing against the trucking industry and private automobiles, the railroads saw a 40 percent decline in jobs between 1947 and 1961; technological advances reduced the number of workers in the steel, copper, and aluminum industries by 17 percent. Moreover, the most rapidly growing economies of the South and Southwest were traditionally inhospitable to unions.

Above all, the economy as a whole was shifting from a production to a service orientation. The typical worker replaced a blue collar with a white one, which did not always mean a fatter paycheck. By 1960, blue-collar workers constituted just 40 percent of the workforce. Instead of manufacturing products, the typical worker now engaged in the distribution of goods, provision of services, record keeping, education, or government work. Although union organizing made headway in some of these fields, notably among retail clerks, communication workers, and public employees, most white-collar employees resisted unionization.

The growing clerical and service occupations swelled the demand for female workers, and women moved into the workforce during the 1950s at a rate four times that of men. By 1960, 35 percent of all women over age sixteen worked outside the home—twice as many as in 1940—and women held more than one-third of all jobs. Moreover, the largest increases in employment occurred for married women and women with children. Joining the women who had always entered the labor market simply to earn a living, increasing numbers of women sought a second family paycheck to allow their families to take advantage of the new commercial abundance. As one woman remarked, "My Joe can't put five kids through college, and then Sue needed braces . . . and the washer had to be replaced, and Ann was ashamed to bring friends home because the living room furniture was such a mess, so I went to work."

When women took jobs, they entered a sharply segregated workplace. The vast majority earned their paychecks as clerical and service workers, factory operatives in light manufacturing, domestic workers, teachers, and nurses. Union organizers neglected most of these areas, and because they were female occupations, wages were relatively low. In 1960, the average female worker, employed full-time all year, earned just 60 percent of the average wage for a male worker. At the bottom of the employment ladder, black women earned, on average, 42 percent of what white men earned.

Burgeoning Suburbs and Declining Cities

Nothing symbolized the prosperity of the 1950s more than the upsurge in suburban living. Suburbs were not new in the United States, but they entered a period of unparalleled growth in that decade. Of the thirteen million new homes built in the 1950s, eleven million appeared in the suburbs. While cities

AN AFRICAN AMERICAN SUBURB
The pioneer of mass-produced suburban housing, William J. Levitt, reflected the racism that kept
blacks out of suburbia when he said, "We can solve a housing problem, or we can try and solve a
racial problem but we cannot combine the two." These African Americans developed their own
suburb, a planned community for middle-class blacks in Richmond, California, which welcomed
the first families in 1950.
Courtesy Richmond Public Library.

failed to grow, the number of people living just out-side cities increased by 45 percent, as more than one million Americans moved to suburban areas every year. By 1960, one in every four Americans lived in the suburbs.

A new feature of the suburban boom of the 1950s was its accessibility to families with modest incomes. William J. Levitt pioneered in constructing affordable housing with his 17,000-home develop-ment, called Levittown, on Long Island. Modifying the assembly line process developed for automo-biles by Henry Ford, Levitt planned nearly identi-cal houses so that each construction worker could move from house to house and perform the same single operation in each, such as caulking windows, hanging doors or cabinets, or installing bathtubs. Individuals could purchase these mass-produced houses for just under $8,000 in 1949. Developments similar to Levittown, as well as more luxurious ones, quickly went up around metropolitan areas throughout the country.

While private industry built the suburbs, the government made home ownership possible by guaranteeing long-term, low-interest mortgages through the Federal Housing Administration and the Veterans Administration. A veteran could move into Levittown with payments of just $58 per month for twenty-five years. Highway construction also in-directly subsidized suburban development. Cities constructed urban expressways linking suburbs to downtown areas, and the federal interstate system authorized 5,000 of its initial 41,000 miles to run through urban areas. Without the automobile and the freeway, the suburban explosion would not have been possible.

Suburban culture came in for its share of dis-approval in the 1950s. Architecture critic Lewis Mumford blasted the suburbs as "a multitude of uniform, unidentifiable houses, lined up inflexibly, at uniform distances, on uniform roads, in a tree-less communal wasteland, inhabited by people of the same class, the same income, the same age group." Suburban populations did tend to be homogeneous in terms of class, race, and age, but they sometimes brought together people of various ethnic ancestries. Moreover, within a few years, the initial sameness of the tract houses gave way to personal embellishments by individual home owners, and the barren land was softened by trees and shrubs. Regardless of what critics said, the new suburbanites enjoyed the convenience and spaciousness of their new homes and the social activities of their new neighborhoods.

Although suburbs fulfilled many of the dreams of their inhabitants, they contributed substantially to a more polarized society. The suburbs isolated women, many of whom spent their entire days with children and other mothers. Racial polarization was even more severe. Each family who purchased a house in Levittown signed a contract that "no dwelling shall be used or occupied by members of other than the Caucasian race." Although the Supreme Court declared such covenants unenforceable in 1948, and a few black families moved into Levittown in the 1950s, suburban America remained almost exclusively white.

Meanwhile, as white residents joined the suburban migration, blacks moved to cities in search of economic opportunity. As the white population declined by 13 percent in Chicago, the black population rose by 65 percent and constituted more than one-fifth of the total. In the 1950s, Washington, D.C., became the first major city with a black majority. In all cities of at least fifty thousand people, the number of black residents grew by 50 percent during the 1950s.

MOVING INTO THE SUBURBS

In the Los Angeles suburb of Lakewood, families gobbled up houses as fast as they could be built. Between 1946 and 1960, an average of 400 people moved into the Los Angeles area every day, and the population of Lakewood jumped from 2,000 to 100,000. What can you tell about the composition of the families moving into Lakewood?

J.B. Eyerman, Life Magazine © 1953 Time Inc.

TABLE 27.1

THE GROWING SUN BELT CITIES, 1920–1980

	1920	1940	1960	1980
Los Angeles	879	2,916	6,039	7,478
Houston	168	529	1,418	2,905
Dallas	185	527	1,084	2,430
Atlanta	249	559	1,017	2,030
San Diego	74	289	1,033	1,862
Miami	30	268	935	1,626
Phoenix	29	186	664	1,509
New Orleans	398	552	907	1,256
San Antonio	191	338	716	1,072
Tucson	20	37	266	531

(Population in thousands)

These newcomers came to cities that were already beginning to decline. Cities lost not only population to the suburbs, but also commerce and industry. New manufacturing and wholesaling facilities began to ring central cities, and shoppers gradually gave up downtown department stores in favor of suburban malls. Thus, many of the new jobs lay beyond the reach of new residents of the inner cities. Fewer people came downtown, and when they did, they preferred to drive their own automobiles along the new expressways, contributing to a decline in public transportation.

Urban governments faced falling tax revenues just as the poverty of their newer residents required greater services. With the move of manufacturing, retailing, entertainment, and transportation centers to the suburbs, downtown areas lost their diversity, becoming primarily office centers. When the workday ended, workers went home to the suburbs, leaving the downtown commercial areas dark and devoid of life.

The Democratization of Higher Education

The affluent postwar years spectacularly transformed higher education. Between 1940 and 1960, college and university enrollments leaped from 1.5 million to 3.6 million, vastly outstripping population growth. Whereas about 15 percent of college-age youths attended college in 1940, more than 40 percent did so by the mid-1960s. Higher education was no longer the domain of the privileged.

The general prosperity of the postwar years enabled many families to keep their children out of work and in school longer. Government policies, especially the GI Bill, also played a role in the democratization of higher education. Moreover, in waging the cold war, the federal government poured millions of dollars for defense-related research into universities and subsidized the education of more than 2 million World War II and Korean War veterans. In response to *Sputnik*, the National Defense Education Act of 1958 allocated $887 million for science, math, and foreign language education and $295 million in student loan funds.

Total tax dollars spent for higher education more than doubled from 1950 to 1960, as state and local governments also invested heavily. Municipalities began to build two-year junior or community colleges, and state governments vastly expanded the number of four-year colleges and universities. In 1960, California established a three-tier statewide system that made higher education accessible to all its inhabitants and that provided a model for other states to copy and adapt.

Initially, the democratization of higher education increased the gap in status between men and women. In absolute numbers, more women attended college than before, but their situation declined relative to that of men. In 1940, women constituted 40 percent of college graduating classes, but as veterans flocked to college campuses, women's proportion declined to just one-fourth in 1950. Even by 1960, women accounted for just 33 percent of college degrees, still below their 1940 share.

The large veteran enrollments did, however, bring a new group of women to college campuses and introduced a new feature of collegiate life: the married student. Colleges that had previously forbidden students to marry relaxed the rule to accommodate the mature, war-tempered population. The veterans' example made the combination of marriage and higher education an accepted pattern.

That pattern also encouraged women to drop out of college to marry. About half of the male students who started college received degrees, but only 37 percent of the women did so. Just as veterans' wives had taken jobs to make ends meet, female students often needed to find employment to enable their husbands to stay in school. These women talked of getting their Ph.T.'s, by "putting hubby through." Reflecting gender-role norms of the 1950s, most college women responding to a survey agreed that "it is natural for a woman to be satisfied with her husband's success and not crave personal achievement."

The GI Bill also made college possible for thousands of African Americans, the majority of whom attended black colleges. College enrollments of blacks surged from 37,000 in 1941 to 90,000 in 1961. Yet African Americans constituted only about 5 percent of all college students, less than half the percentage of African Americans in the general population. Unlike their white counterparts, black men and women attended college in nearly equal numbers.

Some observers of student life in the 1950s termed college students a "silent generation," complaining of their apparent passivity, caution, and conformity. Students seemed all too eager to suspend independent, critical thinking in favor of pleasing their professors and getting good grades to launch them on successful careers. In comparison to the "flaming youth" of the 1920s, *Time* mag-

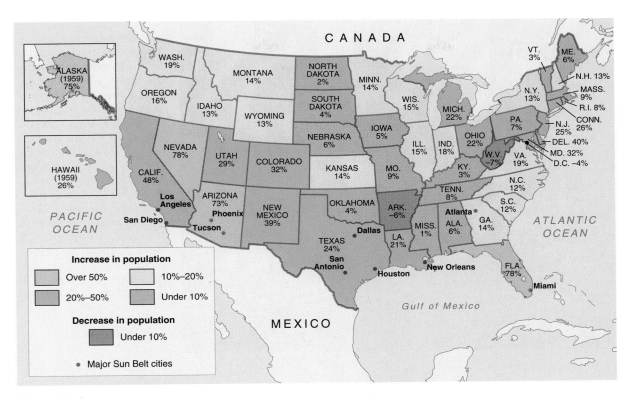

M AP 27.2
The Rise of the Sun Belt, 1940–1980
The growth of defense industries, a nonunionized labor force, and the spread of air conditioning all helped spur economic development and population growth, which made the Sun Belt the fastest growing region of the nation between 1940 and 1980.

azine called the 1950s generation "a still, small flame." Those who remembered favorably the activist student generation of the 1930s found students in the 1950s apolitical or safely conservative.

Regional Variations in the Economy of Abundance

The nation seemed to be tipped westward, quipped architect Frank Lloyd Wright: Everything not bolted down was sliding toward California. No region experienced the postwar economic and population boom more intensely than the West and Southwest. California's population more than doubled after World War II, reaching 19 million in 1960; California overtook New York as the most populous state in 1962. Low population density and a beautiful natural environment that promised a healthful and attractive lifestyle drew new residents to the West and

Southwest, but no magnet proved stronger than the promise of economic opportunity.

As railroads had spurred western growth in the nineteenth century, the automobile and airplane helped generate the post-World War II surge, providing efficient transportation for both people and products. The aerospace industry boomed in Los Angeles, Tucson, and Dallas-Fort Worth, and military bases helped underwrite prosperity in such cities as San Diego, San Antonio, and Seattle-Tacoma and throughout the so-called Sun Belt, which stretched from Florida to California.

Although defense dollars benefited regions such as New England, with its electronics and research and development operations, the West captured the lion's share of cold war spending for research and production of bombers, missiles, other weapons, and satellites. In California alone, the federal government spent more than $100 billion for

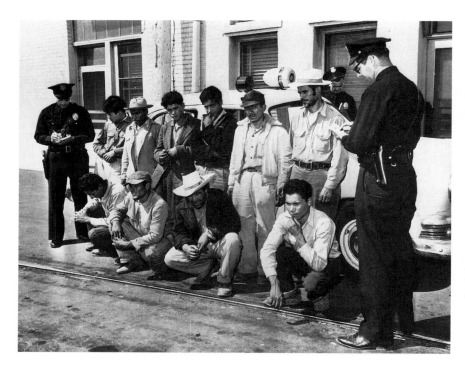

ROUNDING UP UNDOCUMENTED MIGRANTS *Not all Mexican Americans who wanted to work in the United States were accommodated by the* bracero *program. In 1953, Los Angeles police arrested these men who did not have the legal documents and were hiding in a freight train. Americans used the crude term* wetback *to refer to illegal immigrants because many of them swam across the Rio Grande, on the border between the United States and Mexico.*
Corbis-Bettmann.

defense between 1945 and 1965. By 1960, California captured one-quarter of all defense dollars. Nearly one of every three California workers held a defense-related job.

The high-technology basis of postwar economic development drew well-educated and highly skilled workers to the West. But the economic promise also attracted the poor. "We see opportunity all around us here, whether we can grab hold of it or not. We smell freedom here, and maybe soon we can taste it," commented a black mother, one of the millions of Americans who flocked to California. Between 1945 and 1960, more than one-third of the African Americans who left the South moved to the West.

The Mexican American, or Chicano, population also grew, especially in California and Texas. To supply California's vast agribusiness industry, the government continued the *bracero* program begun during World War II. Until the program ended in 1964, more than 100,000 Mexicans entered the United States each year to labor in the fields, and many of them stayed, legally or illegally. But while the government encouraged the use of Mexican labor, it responded to white Americans' opposition to permanent Mexican immigration. In 1954, the government launched a series of raids called "Operation Wetback." Designed to ferret out and deport

illegal immigrants, the operation made U.S. citizens of Mexican descent feel unwelcome and threatened them with incidents of mistaken identity.

Native Americans increased their numbers but also suffered under new government policies. In 1953 with a policy called "termination," the Eisenhower administration sought to end the special status of American Indians, eliminate their reservations, and do away with tribal sovereignty. Termination and relocation of Indians to cities fit well with Eisenhower's preference for a limited federal government, but it proved devastating for Native Americans and was abandoned in the 1960s. Yet 170,000 Indians moved off their reservations, and, like most of the blacks who moved out of the rural South, they most typically exchanged rural poverty for urban poverty.

Free of the discrimination that denied economic opportunity to minority groups, white Americans reaped the fullest fruits of prosperity in the West. In April 1950, California developers advertised the opening of Lakewood, a new housing development in Los Angeles County that was larger even than Levittown. On the first day of sales, thirty thousand people lined up to purchase tract houses for eight to ten thousand dollars. Many of the new home owners were veterans, blue-collar and lower-level white-collar workers whose defense-based jobs at

McDonnell Douglas, Hughes, Rockwell, and other aerospace corporations or at the Long Beach naval station and shipyard enabled them to fulfill the American dream of the 1950s. They could purchase the products of abundance at a huge regional shopping mall, Lakewood Center. And as California's master plan for higher education went into effect, their children had access to several community colleges, four campuses of California State University, and two campuses of the University of California system—all within easy reach of Lakewood.

Society and Culture in an Era of Abundance

Economic growth underlay the cultural counterparts of Eisenhower's politics of consensus and moderation. With prosperity, more people married and the birthrate soared. Interest in religion quickened at the same time that Americans sought satisfaction in material possessions. Television entered the homes of most Americans, helping to promote a "consumer culture."

The dominant values, which favored family life and traditional gender roles, consumption, conformity, and "belongingness," drew their share of crit-

ics. Undercurrents of rebellion, especially among young people, defied some of the dominant norms. But these challenges to mainstream trends did not disrupt the complacency of the 1950s.

The Great Domestic Revival

The entrance of married women into the workforce in unprecedented numbers coexisted with the dominant ideology that celebrated traditional family life and conventional gender roles. Even though greater numbers of women left the home for work, including more than one-third of mothers with school-age children, the family ideal defined by popular culture and public figures persisted: a male breadwinner, a woman who devoted her life to wifehood and motherhood, and three or four children living a safe, comfortable life in a new suburban home. Americans were eager to realize a traditional norm that had been disrupted by economic depression in the 1930s and war in the 1940s.

Writer and feminist Betty Friedan gave a name to the idealization of women's domestic roles in her book *The Feminine Mystique*, published in 1963. Friedan claimed that advertisers, social scientists, educators, women's magazines, and public officials all encouraged women to seek their ultimate fulfillment in serving others through marriage and

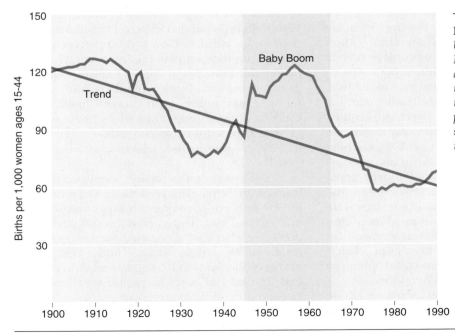

FIGURE 27.2
U.S. Birthrate, 1900–1990
Notice the long-term trend of decline in birthrate over the twentieth century. What helps to account for the unusual plunge in the 1930s and the steep but temporary ascent in the 1950s?

childrearing. The ideal woman, according to the feminine mystique, kept a spotless house, cooked creative meals, raised her children to be good citizens, served her husband's career, and provided him emotional and sexual satisfaction. In 1956, *Life* magazine had declared, "Of all the accomplishments of the American woman, the one she brings off with the most spectacular success is having babies."

The feminine mystique of the 1950s assumed that biological differences fitted men and women for entirely different roles in life. Women who sought independence or success in the masculine world were "neurotic," insisted one popular book. Another writer instructed women to realize that "just being a woman is her central task and her greatest honor. . . . Women must boldly announce that no job is more exacting, more necessary, or more rewarding than that of housewife and mother."

The entrance of married women into the workforce in unprecedented numbers coexisted with the dominant ideology that celebrated traditional family life and conventional gender roles.

Although the glorification of domesticity clashed with the increasing participation in the labor force of married women, the lives of many Americans did in fact embody the family ideal. Postwar prosperity enabled more people to rush to the altar and to have more children. Both women and men married at younger ages than in the past. In 1960, some 68 percent of all adults were married, the largest percentage in the twentieth century. After declining for a century, especially during the depression, the birthrate soared after 1945, reaching a peak in 1957 with 4.3 million births and producing the "baby boom" generation. The baby boom occurred, however, at the very time when more and more couples used contraception. Americans were planning their families, but they wanted more children than had their parents. Whereas women who came of age in the 1930s had an average of 2.4 children, women in the more prosperous and optimistic 1950s produced an average of 3.2 children.

The millions of mothers who turned for advice to Dr. Benjamin Spock found the norms for childrearing more demanding than ever before. Magnifying the importance of maternal attention in the

child's daily development, Spock's best-selling *Common Sense Book of Baby and Child Care* (1946) advocated a permissive approach in place of the more traditional emphasis on strictness and rigid schedules. Such an approach required that mothers devote their full time to childrearing, observe the child closely, and fine-tune their behavior to the needs of the child. Experts in the 1950s also urged fathers to cultivate family "togetherness" and spend more time with their children.

Although women had more children and faced more demanding standards for motherhood, they also enjoyed more child-free years. By spacing children closer together, the typical woman bore her last child by the time she was thirty-two. Having completed childbearing earlier, women looked forward to longer periods of decreasing domestic responsibilities. To the question of what women would do with those years, the feminine mystique offered no answer. One wife and mother, who wanted "more out of life," tried "large doses of everything from alcohol to religion, from a frenzy of sports activities to PTA. . . . Each served its purposes at the time, but . . . none had any real future."

The Rise of Religion

Along with a renewed emphasis on family life, the 1950s witnessed a surge of interest in religion. By 1960, about 63 percent of Americans belonged to churches and synagogues, up from 50 percent in 1940. Polls reported that 95 percent of all Americans professed a belief in God and 90 percent prayed. Evangelism took on new life, most notably in the nationwide crusades of Baptist minister Billy Graham, whose passionate and powerful oratory moved mass audiences to accept Christ. Roman Catholic Monsignor Fulton J. Sheen drew millions of Americans to his books and radio and TV shows; in 1954 he was named television's "man of the year."

President-elect Eisenhower expressed the enthusiasm of the religious revival when he proclaimed in 1952 that "our government makes no sense unless it is founded on a deeply felt religious faith—and I don't care what it is!" Congress linked religion more closely to the state by adding "under God" to the pledge of allegiance in 1954 and by requiring in 1955 that "In God We Trust" be printed on all currency. Eisenhower's indifference about exactly what religious faith should be practiced reflected a unifying trend among religions in the postwar era. Although religious conflict did not disappear, greater toler-

EVANGELIST BILLY GRAHAM
Crowds as large as this one in Times Square in New York City were usually New Year's Eve revelers, but in 1957 these people came to hear the Reverend Billy Graham, a young Baptist minister from North Carolina. He electrified mass audiences across the country, entreating them to find salvation in Jesus Christ and to uphold Christian moral standards. So large were his audiences that Graham extended this 1957 New York crusade from eight to sixteen weeks.
Billy Graham Center.

ance and cooperation was evident in ecumenical movements such as the World Council of Churches, which was organized in 1948. Eisenhower's pastor attributed the renewed interest in religion to economic progress, which "provided the leisure, the energy, and the means for a level of human and spiritual values never before reached." Others suggested that Americans sought reassurance and peace of mind from the anxieties of the cold war and the threat of nuclear annihilation. Perhaps the freedom to practice religion seemed all the more precious in contrast to the "godless communism" of the nation's enemy.

Social critics were skeptical about the depth of the religious revival, attributing the growth in church membership to a desire for conformity and a social outlet. One commentator, for example, noted that 53 percent of Americans could not name any book of the New Testament. The popularity of the Reverend Norman Vincent Peale, whose best-selling book *The Power of Positive Thinking* emphasized how to be successful and happy, suggested to critics the superficiality of Americans' attachment to religion.

Television Transforms Culture and Politics

Just as private family life and religion offered a respite from the anxieties of the cold war, so too did the new medium of television. In 1950, fewer than 10 percent of American homes boasted a television set, but by mid-decade, TV had entered a majority of households, and by 1960, an impressive 87 percent of all households owned a set. On the average, Americans spent more than five hours each day in front of the screen.

Television kept people at home more but did not necessarily enhance family relationships. Although parents and children gathered together, their attention focused on the TV screen and their conversation was limited. The new medium altered eating habits when, in 1954, the appearance of the frozen dinner, a complete meal in an easily portable tray, enabled families to spend the dinner hour in front of the TV set. Noticing that the heaviest water consumption took place on the hour and the half hour, civil engineers in Toledo, Ohio, recognized that television regulated even trips to the bathroom.

Variety shows and live drama became staples of early television. *Playhouse 90, Kraft Television Theatre,* and other programs aired plays by major dramatists performed by some of the most talented actors, including Humphrey Bogart, Henry Fonda, Laurence Olivier, and Joanne Woodward. Looking back on these ambitious productions, critics called the 1950s the "Golden Age of Television." *Ozzie and Harriet, Father Knows Best, The Honeymooners,* and other situation comedies were especially popular, but by the end of the 1950s, mystery, crime, and western series claimed a large share of the audience.

Situation comedies projected the family ideal and the feminine mystique into millions of homes. On TV, women with families did not work outside the home and ostensibly deferred to their husbands, though they often got the upper hand through subtle manipulation. In the most popular television show of the early 1950s, *I Love Lucy,* the husband-and-wife team of Lucille Ball and Desi Arnaz played the fictional couple Lucy and Ricky Ricardo. In step with the trends, they moved from an apartment to a house in suburbia. Ricky refused to allow his wife to work outside the home, and many of the plots revolved around Lucy's zany attempts to thwart his objections.

The show also reflected the childbearing mania of the 1950s. When Lucille Ball became pregnant, she wanted to continue working on the show and got the producers to write the pregnancy into the script. Although CBS would not allow the word "pregnant" to be spoken on the air, Americans followed the progress of Lucy's pregnancy, and forty-four million people watched the fictionalized birth, more than tuned in to Eisenhower's inauguration the next day. If Lucy Ricardo embodied the feminine mystique, Lucille Ball, who combined a career with motherhood, refused to let motherhood rule her life.

TV news, limited to just fifteen minutes a day on each network, did not become the public's main source of news until the 1960s. Yet television began to affect politics in the 1950s. Edward R. Murrow's documentaries on McCarthyism and the televised Army-McCarthy hearings helped to bring about the senator's downfall. Richard Nixon's televised "Checkers speech" enabled him to hang on to his place on the Republican ticket in 1952. The 1952 election campaign used TV advertising spots for the first time. Adlai Stevenson refused to participate in "selling the presidency like cereal," but Eisenhower succumbed to the new media and filmed forty ads.

THE MADE-FOR-TV FAMILY
This scene is from the popular television sitcom Father Knows Best, *which ran from 1954 to 1963 and which, along with other shows such as* Ozzie and Harriet *and* Leave It to Beaver, *idealized white family life. In these shows, no one got divorced or gravely ill, no one took drugs or seriously misbehaved, fathers held white-collar jobs, mothers did not work outside the home, and husbands and wives slept in twin beds.*
Culver Pictures/Rob Huntley, Lightstream/Picture Research Consultants, Inc.

But he was not happy about it, regretting that "an old soldier should come to this."

Television made political figures much more familiar to Americans and encouraged voters to place more emphasis on attractiveness and style than on experience and political wisdom. By 1960, television played a major role in candidates' chances for success. Reflecting on his narrow victory in 1960, President-elect John F. Kennedy remarked, "We wouldn't have had a prayer without that gadget."

Politics in turn affected television. Throughout the 1950s, networks boycotted writers and actors who were considered to be too closely linked with

Communist or radical causes. Murrow had to use his own funds to advertise his documentaries on McCarthyism because CBS refused to do so. That network and its sponsors found too controversial a script that portrayed neighborhood efforts to drive out an African American family. They persuaded the writer to make the unwelcome newcomer an ex-convict instead.

In little more than a decade, television came to dominate Americans' leisure time, influence their consumption patterns, and shape their perceptions of the nation's leadership and government.

Unlike government-financed television in Europe, private enterprise paid for American TV through advertising, and advertisers did not hesitate to interfere with shows that might jeopardize the sale of their products. On the *Camel News Caravan,* for example, the sponsor, producer of Camel cigarettes, insisted that any film clips showing "No Smoking" signs be cut. The American Gas Association, which sponsored *Judgment at Nuremberg,* censored the words "gas ovens" so as not to associate

the Nazi horrors with its product. Television became the major vehicle for selling the products of an affluent society; Procter and Gamble, for example, spent more than 90 percent of its advertising budget on TV.

In 1961, Newton Minow, chairman of the Federal Communications Commission, called television a "vast wasteland." Acknowledging some of TV's great achievements, particularly documentaries and drama, Minow depicted television programming as "a procession of game shows, violence . . . formula comedies about totally unbelievable families, blood and thunder, mayhem, violence, sadism, murder . . . and cartoons." Viewers disagreed—or at least they kept tuning in. In little more than a decade, television came to dominate Americans' leisure time, influence their consumption patterns, and shape their perceptions of the nation's leadership and government.

Countercurrents

Signals of unrest and dissent underlay the complacency of the 1950s. Some intellectuals took exception to the politics of consensus promoted by Eisenhower and to the materialism and conformity celebrated in popular culture. In *The Lonely Crowd*

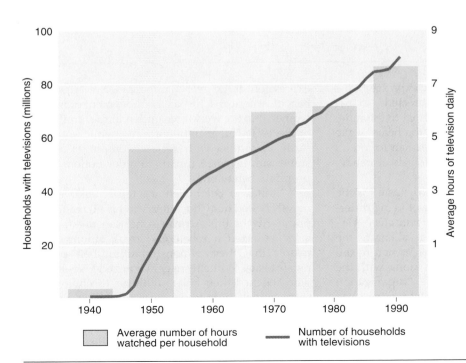

FIGURE 27.3
A Nation of Television Watchers
By the mid-1950s, television occupied a majority of U.S. homes. Set ownership and the number of hours Americans spent watching would continue to grow dramatically.

Average number of hours watched per household   Number of households with televisions

ELVIS PRESLEY
Young people seeking escape from white middle-class conformity thrilled to Elvis Presley's pulsating music, long sideburns and ducktail haircut, colorful clothing, and sensual movements. His gyrating hips illustrated in these 1956 photographs led to the appellation "Elvis the Pelvis," while adult reviewers complained about his "grunt and groin antics" and "unnecessary bump and grind routine."
Corbis-Bettmann.

(1950), sociologist David Riesman expressed dismay at a shift from the "inner-directed" to the "other-directed" individual. In contrast to the independent thinking that had been at the heart of the American character in the past, Riesman found an eagerness to adapt to external standards of behavior and belief.

Other critics shared Riesman's distaste for the importance of "belonging" and fear of being different. In his popular book *The Organization Man* (1956), William H. Whyte Jr. saw the villain as the modern corporation, whose employees had to tailor their behavior and ideas to get along with the group. According to Whyte, these "organization men" sacrificed the risk taking, individualism, and independence of the traditional American businessman, and they also displayed dull conformity in their suburban lives after work.

Less direct but more substantial challenges to the standards upheld in mainstream culture found

expression in the everyday behavior of large numbers of Americans. Just as the movement of married women into the workforce undercut the family ideal of the 1950s, other undercurrents, while not necessarily in conflict with society's emphasis on consumerism, revealed threats to older notions of appropriate behavior.

"Roll over Beethoven and tell Tchaikovsky the news!" belted out Chuck Berry in his hit record. The popularity of this African American rock-and-roll artist reflected a rebellious streak among young people that they demonstrated in their popular music tastes. White teenagers lionized Elvis Presley, who shocked their elders with his throbbing, sensuous music, tight pants, and hip-rolling gestures, considered by some TV producers so lewd that they would film him only from the waist up. Presley blended a country and western style with black rhythm and blues. In fact, rock and roll developed from the creativity of African American musicians such as Chuck Berry, Fats Domino, and Little Richard Penniman and Latino performers such as Ritchie Valens. Arthur Crudup, a black bluesman whose music Elvis exploited, noted, "I was makin' everybody rich and I was poor."

"Before there was Elvis . . . I started going crazy for 'race music,'" recalled a white man of his teenage years. "It had a beat. I loved it. . . . That got me into trouble with my parents and the schools." This man illustrated African Americans' contributions to rock and roll as well as the rebellion symbolized by white youths' attraction to black music. While some whites had been drawn to jazz for decades, white teenagers' infatuation with black music in the 1950s marked a turning point in cultural integration.

Just as rock and roll's sexual suggestiveness violated norms of middle-class respectability, the sexual behavior of many Americans departed from the family ideal of the 1950s. Two books published by Alfred Kinsey and a group of researchers at Indiana University, *Sexual Behavior in the Human Male* (1948) and *Sexual Behavior in the Human Female* (1953), uncovered a surprising range of sexual conduct. In a survey of eighteen thousand individuals, Kinsey found that 85 percent of the men and 50 percent of the women had had sex before marriage. Half of the husbands and one-fourth of the wives had engaged in extramarital sex. Although the vast majority considered themselves heterosexual, one-third of the men and one-seventh of the women reported homosexual experience. The books became best-sellers but also drew a firestorm of outrage. Evangelist Billy Graham protested "the damage this book will do to the already deteriorating morals of America," and the Rockefeller Foundation stopped funding Kinsey's work. Critics were most incensed by Kinsey's refusal to make moral judgments about his findings.

Just as rock and roll's sexual suggestiveness violated norms of middle-class respectability, the sexual behavior of many Americans departed from the family ideal of the 1950s.

Playboy magazine, which began publication in 1953 and quickly gained a circulation of one million, offered another challenge to reigning standards of domesticity and respectability. With its photographs of naked young women, *Playboy* pro-moted sexual freedom, at least for men. In contrast to most of the popular culture, the magazine idealized bachelorhood and pitied men who were "trapped" in marriages. Its publisher, Hugh Hefner, disparaged "foolish notions . . . about 'togetherness,' home, family, and all that jazz."

The most extreme rebellion against conventionality came from the self-proclaimed Beat generation, a small group of literary figures based in New York City's Greenwich Village and in San Francisco. Rejecting nearly everything in mainstream culture —patriotism, consumerism, technology, conventional family life, and discipline—they favored spontaneity and absolute personal freedom, which included drug consumption and freewheeling sex.

JACKSON POLLOCK
The leading artist in the post-World War II revolution in painting, Jackson Pollock here illustrates his technique of pouring and splattering paint onto the canvas. He worked with the canvas on the floor because, he said, "I feel nearer, more a part of the painting. . . . I can walk around it, work from the four sides and be literally 'in' the painting."
Jackson Pollock, 1950 photograph by Hans Namuth © 1991 Hans Namuth Estate. Courtesy, Center for Creative Photography, Tucson.

In his landmark poem *Howl* (1956), Allen Ginsberg inveighed against "Robot apartments! invisible suburbs! skeleton treasuries! blind capitals! demonic industries! . . . monstrous bombs!" and denounced the social forces that "frightened me out of my natural ecstasy!" Another leading member of the Beat generation, Jack Kerouac, wrote the best-selling novel *On the Road* (1957), but the Beats' shocking lifestyles affronted most "square" Americans. The Beats' rebelliousness would provide models for a much larger movement of youthful dissidents in the 1960s.

Developments in the visual arts also showed the 1950s to be more than a decade of bland conventionality. An artistic revolution that flowered in New York City redirected approaches to painting throughout the Western art world. Known as "action painting," "abstract expressionism," or the "New York school," this movement rejected the idea that painting should represent recognizable forms. Jackson Pollock and other abstract expressionists poured, dripped, and threw paint on canvases or substituted sticks and other implements for brushes. The work of the New York school emphasized energy and spontaneity, and it so captivated the art world that New York replaced Paris as its center.

Emergence of a Civil Rights Movement

African Americans challenged the status quo of the 1950s most dramatically as they sought to break the chains that had replaced the bonds of slavery. Every southern state mandated rigid segregation in public settings ranging from hospitals and schools to drinking fountains and rest rooms. Southern voting laws and practices disfranchised the vast majority of African Americans; employment discrimination kept them at the bottom of the economic ladder.

Although black protest was as old as American racism, in the 1950s that protest developed into a grassroots movement that attracted national attention and the support of white liberals. Pressed by civil rights groups and in the face of popular resistance and the will of elected officials, the Supreme Court initiated the most significant institutional reforms. But the most important changes of all occurred among blacks themselves. Ordinary African Americans in substantial numbers actively sought their own liberation, building a movement that would transform race relations in the United States.

A Sympathetic Court and a Reluctant President

A number of developments lay behind the rise of black protest in the 1950s. Between 1940 and 1960, more than three million African Americans moved out of the South into areas where they could vote and exert pressure on white politicians. White leaders also worried that the U.S.'s dismal record in race relations put the country at a disadvantage in cold war competition, as Soviet propaganda routinely exposed the gap between American ideals and practice.

Although black protest was as old as American racism, in the 1950s that protest developed into a grassroots movement that attracted national attention and the support of white liberals.

In the South, African Americans controlled resources that were essential to a mass movement. The very system of segregation encouraged the development of black institutions and kept black talents within the black community. In particular, black churches and colleges developed leadership skills within the African American community and provided a mass base and organizational network. Moreover, as African Americans moved into urban areas, their institutions grew in numbers and financial resources, and they shared in some economic benefits of the general postwar prosperity.

Growing even faster was the National Association for the Advancement of Colored People (NAACP), whose emphasis on litigation had begun to pay off in the late 1940s. Its crowning achievement came with the Supreme Court decision in *Brown v. Board of Education* in 1954. The *Brown* case resulted not just from the legal brilliance and financial resources of the NAACP, but also from the determination of black Americans to fight for their rights. One of the five suits consolidated into the *Brown* case began in 1951, when teenagers at Moton High School in Farmville, Virginia, initiated a strike to protest the inadequate schools set up for blacks.

NAACP lawyers, led by Thurgood Marshall, who would later be appointed to the Supreme Court, urged the Court to overturn the fifty-eight-year-old precedent established in *Plessy v. Ferguson,* which had enshrined "separate but equal" as the law of the land. A unanimous court, headed by Chief Justice Earl Warren, declared, "Separate edu-

SCHOOL INTEGRATION
In 1964, the popular artist Norman Rockwell painted The Problem We All Live With, *based on the experience of Ruby Bridges during the 1962 integration of the New Orleans public schools. He hoped through this painting to get people to realize what America was doing to its children. How effective is this painting in stirring emotions? What about the structure of the scene and the characteristics of the people indicate Rockwell's intentions?*
Norman Rockwell Family Trust and Curtis Archives.

cational facilities are inherently unequal" and thus violated the Fourteenth Amendment. In 1955, after waiting a year to deal with implementation, the Court called for desegregation "with all deliberate speed" but established no deadline.

As chief executive, President Eisenhower bore the ultimate responsibility for enforcement of *Brown*, but he refused to use his enormous popularity to win acceptance of the decision from Americans. Officially, Eisenhower announced his intention to obey the decision. But before the Supreme Court ruling, he had privately expressed to Chief Justice Warren his sympathy for white southerners. All they wanted, Eisenhower said, was that "their sweet little girls" not have to "sit in schools alongside some big black bucks." Asked if he had any advice to give the South in responding to *Brown*, he replied, "Not in the slightest." The president's failure to endorse the decision or to urge the South to comply reflected his own racial prejudice, insensitivity to the aspirations of blacks, preference for a limited fed-

eral role in the nation's affairs, and leadership style that favored consensus and gradual progress.

In some cases, Eisenhower used his executive powers against segregation, ordering the integration of public facilities in the District of Columbia and at army and navy bases, for example. More often, he remained aloof. In 1955, when whites lynched a fourteen-year-old black boy named Emmett Till for whistling at a white woman in Mississippi, Eisenhower rejected advice that he speak out against the atrocity. Nor would he act in March 1956, when the University of Alabama violated a federal court order to admit its first black student.

Eisenhower's inaction fueled southern officials' determined resistance to school desegregation and contributed to the gravest constitutional crisis since the Civil War. The crisis came in Little Rock, Arkansas, in September 1957. Local officials dutifully prepared for the integration of Central High School, but on the first day of school, Governor Orval Faubus sent National Guard troops to block

The Brown *Decision*

*T*he Brown *decision along with a second Supreme Court ruling in 1955 about implementing desegregation outraged many southern whites. In 1956, more than one hundred members of Congress signed a manifesto pledging resistance to the decision.*

*I*n 1954, Chief Justice Earl Warren delivered the unanimous opinion of the Supreme Court in Brown v. Board of Education of Topeka, declaring racial segregation in public education unconstitutional and explaining why.*

DOCUMENT 1. *Brown v.*
Board of Education of Topeka

In these days, it is doubtful that any child may reasonably be expected to succeed in life if he is denied the opportunity of an education. Such an opportunity, if the state has undertaken to provide it, is a right that must be made available to all on equal terms. . . .

We come then to the question presented: Does segregation of children in public schools solely on the basis of race, even though the physical facilities and other "tangible" factors may be equal, deprive the children of the minority group of equal educational opportunities? We believe that it does. . . .

In *McLaurin* [a 1950 case], the Court, in requiring that a Negro admitted to a white graduate school be treated like all other students, again resorted to intangible considerations: ". . . his ability to study, to engage in discussions and exchange views with other students, and, in general, to learn his profession." Such considerations apply with added force to children in grade and high schools. To separate them from others of similar age and qualifications solely because of their race generates a feeling of inferiority as to their status in the community that may affect their hearts and minds in a way unlikely ever to be undone.

We conclude that in the field of public education the doctrine of "separate but equal" has no place. Separate educational facilities are inherently unequal. . . .

DOCUMENT 2. Southern Manifesto
on Integration

We regard the decision of the Supreme Court in the school cases as a clear abuse of judicial power. It climaxes a trend in the Federal judiciary undertaking to legislate . . . and to encroach upon the reserved rights of the states and the people.

The original Constitution does not mention education. Neither does the Fourteenth Amendment nor any amendment. . . . The Supreme Court of the United States, with no legal basis for such action, undertook to exercise their naked judicial power and substituted their personal political and social ideas for the established law of the land.

This unwarranted exercise of power by the court, contrary to the Constitution, is creating chaos and confusion in the states principally affected. It is destroying the amicable relations between the white and negro races that have been created through ninety years of patient effort by the good people of both races. It has planted hatred and suspicion where there has been heretofore friendship and understanding. . . .

We pledge ourselves to use all lawful means to bring about a reversal of this decision which is contrary to the Constitution and to prevent the use of force in its implementation.

*I*n the face of white hostility, black children carried the burden of implementing the Brown *decision. The following accounts by black students reflect varied experiences, but even those who entered white schools fairly easily found obstacles to their full participation in school activities. Nonetheless, they cherished the new opportunities, favoring integration for reasons different from those given by the Supreme Court.*

Document 3. A High School Girl in the Deep South

The first day a news reporter rode the bus with us. All around us were state troopers. In front of them were federal marshals. When we got to town there were lines of people and cars all along the road. A man without a badge or anything got on the bus and started beating up the newspaper reporter. . . . He was crying and bleeding. When we got to the school the students were all around looking through the windows. The mayor said we couldn't come there because the school was already filled to capacity [and] if six of us came in it would be a fire hazard. He told us to turn around and go back. We turned around and the students started yelling and clapping. When we went back [after obtaining a court order] there were no students there at all. There were only two teachers left so they had to bring a couple of teachers from other places. [The white students did not return, so the six black students finished the year by themselves.] The shocking thing was during the graduation ceremonies. All six of the students got together to make a speech. After we finished, I looked around and saw three teachers crying. The principal had tears in his eyes and he got up to make a little speech about us. He said at first he didn't think he would enjoy being around us. You could see in his face that he was really touched. We said something like we really enjoyed school together and that we were glad they stuck it out and all that kind of stuff.

Document 4. A High School Boy in Oak Ridge, Tennessee

I like it a whole lot better than the colored school. You have a chance to learn more and you have more sports. I play forward or guard on the basketball team, only I don't get to participate in all games. Some teams don't mind my playing. Some teams object not because of the fellows on the team, but because of the people in their community. Mostly it's the fans or the board of education that decides against me. . . . The same situation occurs in baseball. I'm catcher, but the first game I didn't get to participate in. A farm club of the major league wrote the coach that they were interested in seeing me play so maybe I'll get to play the next time.

Document 5. A High School Girl in the Deep South

I chose to go because I felt that I could get a better education here. I knew that the [black] school that I was then attending wasn't giving me exactly what I should have had. As far as the Science Department was concerned, it just didn't have the chemicals we needed and I just decided to change. When I went over the students there weren't very friendly and when I graduated they still weren't. They didn't want us there and they made that plain, but we went there anyway and we stuck it out. The lessons there were harder, lots harder, but I studied and I managed to pass all my subjects.

Document 6. A High School Girl in Louisville, Kentucky

I'm accepted now as an individual rather than as a person belonging to the Negro race. People say to me, "I'm glad I met you because if I met someone else I might not have liked them." I don't think it's fair, this individual acceptance. I feel like I was some ambassador from some foreign country.

I couldn't go out for any extracurricular activities. Cheerleading, band, drum majorettes, the people who are members of these organizations, they go to camps in the summer which are segregated. Well, what can you do? It just leaves me out. It's not the school, it's the community.

Document 1. *Brown,* 347 U.S. 483 (1954).

Document 2. "Southern Manifesto on Integration" (1956).

Document 3. *In Their Own Words: A Student Appraisal of What Happened after School Desegregation* (Washington, D.C.: Department of Health, Education, and Welfare, Office of Education, 1966), 17–18.

Document 4. Dorothy Sterling, *Tender Warriors* (New York: Hill and Wang, 1958), 83.

Document 5. *In Their Own Words: A Student Appraisal of What Happened after School Desegregation* (Washington, D.C.: Department of Health, Education, and Welfare, Office of Education, 1966), 44.

Document 6. Dorothy Sterling, *Tender Warriors* (New York: Hill and Wang, 1958), 83.

MONTGOMERY CIVIL RIGHTS LEADERS
During the Montgomery, Alabama, bus boycott of 1955–1956, local white officials harassed African Americans with arrests and lawsuits. Here Rosa Parks, catalyst of the boycott and one of ninety-two defendants, ascends the steps of the Montgomery County courthouse in March 1956. She is accompanied by E.D. Nixon, a forceful civil rights leader and her longtime friend and associate in the Montgomery NAACP.
Wide World.

the enrollment of nine black students, claiming that it would cause public disorder.

Reluctant to intervene, Eisenhower waited nearly three weeks, until Faubus agreed to allow the black students to enter. But Faubus also withdrew the National Guard, leaving the nine students to face an angry mob of whites. As television cameras transmitted the ugly scene across the nation, the president was forced into action. He sent in one thousand regular army troops and took federal control of the Arkansas National Guard. In this first federal military intervention in the South since Reconstruction, Eisenhower took pains to point out that he acted not to achieve integration, but to enforce the law. Escorted by paratroopers, the black students stayed in school, and Eisenhower withdrew the army in November.

Other southern cities closed public schools to avoid integration and used tax dollars to support private, white-only schools. During the first three years after the *Brown* decision, 750 school districts, primarily in border states, began desegregation, but only 49 new efforts came between 1957 and 1960. When Eisenhower left office in 1961—nearly seven years after the Supreme Court had outlawed segregation—only 6.4 percent of southern black students attended integrated schools. (See Texts in Historical Context, page 1090.)

Eisenhower did support the first federal civil rights legislation since Reconstruction, the Civil Rights Acts of 1957 and 1960. Both laws focused on voting rights, and the 1957 legislation established the U.S. Commission on Civil Rights and a Civil Rights Division in the Justice Department. But the legislation lacked strong enforcement provisions and represented only marginal progress toward the enfranchisement of blacks. Baseball star Jackie Robinson spoke for many African Americans when he wired Eisenhower, "We disagree that half a loaf is better than none. Have waited this long for bill with meaning—can wait a little longer."

The Eisenhower years represented a retreat in presidential leadership on civil rights. Forceful and decisive in foreign affairs, the president saw no moral imperative in civil rights and moved in that arena only with the greatest reluctance. Eisenhower appointed the first black professional to the White House staff, but E. Frederick Morrow confided to his diary, "I feel ridiculous . . . trying to defend the administration's record on civil rights." Morrow later remembered Eisenhower as "a great, gentle, and noble man . . . but neither intellectually nor emotionally disposed to combat segregation in general."

Montgomery and Mass Protest

From individual acts of defiance and slave revolts through the legal and lobbying efforts of the NAACP, black protest enjoyed a long tradition in

**MARTIN LUTHER KING
IN MONTGOMERY**
*During the Montgomery bus
boycott, Martin Luther King
Jr. preaches at the First Baptist Church, the congregation
of Ralph D. Abernathy, the
man who would become King's
close associate in the crusades
to come. The crucial role that
black churches played in the
black freedom struggle was not
lost on white racists, who
bombed First Baptist and three
other black churches in Montgomery during the boycott.*
Dan Weiner, courtesy Sandra Weiner.

American society. What set the civil rights movement of the 1950s and 1960s apart from earlier
protests were the great numbers of people involved,
blacks' willingness to confront white institutions directly, and the use of nonviolence and passive resistance to bring about change. The Congress of
Racial Equality (CORE) and other groups had experimented with these innovations in the 1940s, but
the first sustained protest to claim national attention occurred in Montgomery, Alabama, in 1955 and
1956.

On December 1, 1955, Montgomery police arrested a black woman, Rosa Parks, for violating a
local segregation ordinance by refusing to give up
her seat on a city bus to a white man. Parks had
long been active in the local NAACP, and this was
not the first time that she had rebelled against segregation. Montgomery blacks who had been considering a challenge to segregation prepared to
move. Three groups helped to orchestrate the challenge: a women's organization, the NAACP chapter, and community ministers. In 1946, black professional women had founded the Women's
Political Council (WPC) to work on voter registration, desegregation of public facilities, and employment of blacks in municipal services. Its leader was
Jo Ann Robinson, an English professor at Alabama
State College in Montgomery, who had been humiliated by a bus driver when she inadvertently sat
in the white section. The WPC had already dis-

cussed plans for a boycott of the city bus system.
After Parks's arrest, the group consulted with E. D.
Nixon, head of the Montgomery NAACP and the
local Brotherhood of Sleeping Car Porters. Nixon
too had been looking for an opportunity to mount
a boycott, and he sought support from ministers.

In the early morning hours after Parks's arrest,
WPC members and Alabama State students and faculty blanketed the black community with leaflets
urging support of a bus boycott. On December 5,
leaders of local organizations founded the Montgomery Improvement Association (MIA) to organize and maintain the boycott. The MIA ran an alternative transportation system, marshaled more
than 90 percent of the black community to sustain
the year-long boycott, and mounted a legal challenge that persuaded the Supreme Court to strike
down the bus segregation ordinance in November
1956.

Elected to head the MIA was Martin Luther
King Jr., a newcomer to Montgomery. Born in 1929,
King was the son of a minister who had risen from
sharecropper origins and married the daughter of a
prominent pastor of Ebenezer Baptist Church in Atlanta. The younger King attended Morehouse College and preached his first sermon at Ebenezer at
the age of eighteen. He went on to Crozer Theological Seminary in Pennsylvania and then to
Boston University, where he earned his doctorate in
theology. In 1954, he answered the call to be pastor

at the Dexter Avenue Baptist Church in Montgomery.

Only twenty-six years old, King rose to the challenge of the boycott. As a minister, he held a prominent place in the institution that became the focal point of black protest, providing the movement with a mass base, talented leadership, a financial foundation, and meeting places. Day after day, Montgomery blacks gathered at their churches to plan strategy and receive instructions and inspiration. A captivating speaker, King summoned their courage and inspired commitment by linking racial justice to the redeeming power of Christian love. He asked his people to abandon "that patience that makes us patient with anything less than freedom and justice." He promised, "If you will protest courageously and yet with dignity and Christian love . . . historians will have to pause and say, 'There lived a great people—a black people—who injected a new meaning and dignity into the veins of civilization.' This is our challenge and our overwhelming responsibility."

Montgomery blacks summoned up their courage and determination in abundance. They walked miles when the carpool was unavailable, contributed their meager financial resources, and stood up with dignity and discipline to legal, economic, and physical intimidation. King himself endured arrest and the firebombing of his house. Montgomery blacks demonstrated that even without the ballot, African Americans could struggle successfully against their oppression.

In January 1957, black churchmen from across the South met to coordinate local protests against segregation and to secure the ballot for blacks. They founded the Southern Christian Leadership Conference (SCLC) and chose King to head it. Although ministers dominated the SCLC, its success owed much to Ella Baker, a seasoned NAACP activist who came from New York to set up the SCLC office and handle its organizational affairs.

King's face on the cover of *Time* magazine in February 1957 marked his rapid rise to national and international fame. He crisscrossed the nation and the world, speaking to large audiences, raising funds, and meeting with other activists. In June 1958, Eisenhower extended his first invitation to black leaders, and King and three others met with the president. Meanwhile, in the late 1950s, the SCLC, NAACP, and CORE developed centers in several southern cities, paving the way for a mass movement that would revolutionize the racial system of the South.

Conclusion: Assessing the "Ike Age"

By most measures, the Eisenhower years represented a time of tranquility, stability, and prosperity. The 1950s saw tremendous economic growth, a rising standard of living for most Americans, and low inflation rates. Cold war spending drove up the federal budget, which now played a permanent and significant role in the economy as a whole. One of every ten American jobs depended directly on defense spending. The Eisenhower administration restrained spending for domestic purposes and tipped the balance between the federal government and private enterprise in favor of big business, but it maintained the basic foundations of the welfare state.

The president's insistence on moderation, consensus, and a limited role for the federal government seemed to fit the mood of the 1950s well, but it also meant an accumulation of problems for the future. Although economic productivity reached a level sufficient to meet the material needs of all Americans, twenty percent of the U.S. population lived in poverty. Eisenhower refused to use his enormous popularity to rally the nation behind efforts to promote racial justice, and he launched no major programs to deal with urban slums or the growing inadequacies in health care and public education.

In large matters, Eisenhower's foreign policy demonstrated restraint and a recognition of the limits of U.S. power. He promoted development of more destructive atomic weapons, which held Americans under the threat of nuclear obliteration, but he kept the defense budget from skyrocketing, and the superpowers avoided war. Even though the United States and the Soviet Union made no substantive progress in solving cold war issues, Eisenhower began negotiations and helped to lessen tensions between the superpowers.

Eisenhower took from Truman the assumption that the United States must fight communism everywhere, reinforced it in his public utterances, and passed it on to the next administration. The president realized that the "protection of our own interests and our own system demands [understanding of] the spirit of nationalism, coupled with a deep hunger for some betterment in physical conditions and living standards." Yet when movements for such conditions in Iran, Guatemala, and Vietnam seemed to him too radical, too friendly to communism, or too inimical to American economic interests, he did not hesitate to oppose them, often deploying American power in operations kept hidden from congressional and public scrutiny.

Thus, although Eisenhower presided over eight years of peace, his foreign policy inspired anti-Americanism, established dangerous precedents for the expansion of executive power, and forged commitments that future generations would deem unwise. As Eisenhower's successors took on the struggle against communism and grappled with the domestic problems that he had avoided, the tranquility and consensus of the 1950s would give way to the turbulence and conflict of the 1960s.

CHRONOLOGY

1952 Dwight D. Eisenhower elected president of United States.

I Love Lucy becomes number one television show.

1953 The government begins policy of termination of special status of American Indians and relocates thousands off reservations.

CIA engineers coup against government of Prime Minister Mohammed Mossadegh in Iran.

Julius and Ethel Rosenberg executed for passing atomic secrets to Soviet Union.

Playboy magazine begins publication.

1954 CIA stages coup against government of Jacobo Arbenz in Guatemala.

Eisenhower administration continues many New Deal and Fair Deal initiatives, including expansion of Social Security.

Eisenhower administration begins aid program to government of South Vietnam.

Government launches "Operation Wetback," series of raids designed to seek out and deport illegal immigrants.

Ground broken in Pennsylvania for first commercial nuclear power plant.

U.S. Supreme Court declares segregation in public schools unconstitutional in *Brown v. Board of Education.*

United States organizes Southeast Asia Treaty Organization (SEATO) in wake of French defeat in Vietnam.

1955 Eisenhower and Khrushchev meet in Geneva for first superpower summit since end of World War II.

1955– Montgomery, Alabama, bus boycott
1956 by African Americans focuses national attention on civil rights.

1956 Interstate Highway Act involves federal government in road-building activities previously done by state and local governments.

President Eisenhower reelected by landslide to second term.

Allen Ginsberg publishes poem *Howl,* expressing rebelliousness of Beat generation.

1957 Southern Christian Leadership Conference (SCLC) organizes and elects Martin Luther King Jr. its president.

Soviets launch *Sputnik,* first satellite to orbit earth.

Labor union membership peaks at 27.1 percent of labor force.

1958 United States and Soviet Union suspend nuclear testing in atmosphere.

1958– U.S. nuclear weapons stockpile triples
1960 in size.

1960 Soviets shoot down U.S. U-2 spy plane, causing rift in U.S.-Soviet relations.

Women represent one-third of labor force; 35 percent of women work outside the home.

One-quarter of Americans live in suburbs.

BIBLIOGRAPHY

GENERAL WORKS

John Patrick Diggins, *The Proud Decades: America in War and Peace, 1941–1960* (1988).

Alan Ehrenhalt, *The Lost City: Discovering the Forgotten Virtues of Community in the Chicago of the 1950s* (1995).

David Halberstam, *The Fifties* (1993).

Douglas T. Miller and Marion Nowak, *The Fifties: The Way We Really Were* (1977).

J. Ronald Oakley, *God's Country: America in the Fifties* (1986).

William L. O'Neill, *American High: The Years of Confidence, 1945–1960* (1986).

DOMESTIC POLITICS AND POLICIES

Charles C. Alexander, *Holding the Line: The Eisenhower Era, 1952–1961* (1975).

Craig Allen, *Eisenhower and the Mass Media: Peace, Prosperity, and Prime-Time TV* (1993).

Stephen E. Ambrose, *Eisenhower*, vol. 2, *The President* (1984).

Jeff Broadwater, *Eisenhower and the Anti-Communist Crusade* (1992).

Robert F. Burk, *Dwight D. Eisenhower: Hero and Politician* (1986).

Fred I. Greenstein, *The Hidden Hand Presidency: Eisenhower as Leader* (1982).

R. Alton Lee, *Dwight D. Eisenhower: Soldier and Statesman* (1981).

Chester J. Pach Jr. and Elmo Richardson, *The Presidency of Dwight D. Eisenhower* (rev. ed., 1991).

Herbert S. Parmet, *Eisenhower and the American Crusades* (1972).

Gary W. Reichard, *The Reaffirmation of Republicanism* (1975).

Mark H. Rose, *Interstate: Express Highway Politics, 1941–1956* (1979).

FOREIGN POLICY

Stephen E. Ambrose, *Ike's Spies: Eisenhower and the Espionage Establishment* (1981).

Michael R. Beschloss, *Mayday: Eisenhower, Khrushchev, and the U-2 Affair* (1986).

Blanche Weisen Cook, *The Declassified Eisenhower: A Divided Legacy of Peace and Political Warfare* (1981).

Robert A. Divine, *Eisenhower and the Cold War* (1981).

Robert A. Divine, *The Sputnik Challenge* (1993).

Steven Z. Freiberger, *Dawn over Suez: The Rise of American Power in the Middle East, 1953–1957* (1992).

George C. Herring, *America's Longest War: The United States and Vietnam, 1950–1975* (2nd rev. ed., 1986).

Richard H. Immerman, *The CIA in Guatemala* (1982).

Richard H. Immerman, *John Foster Dulles and the Diplomacy of the Cold War* (1990).

Stanley Karnow, *Vietnam: A History* (rev. ed., 1991).

Walter LaFeber, *Inevitable Revolutions: The United States in Central America* (1983).

Donald Neff, *Warriors at Suez: Eisenhower Takes America into the Middle East* (1981).

Stephen G. Rabe, *Eisenhower and Latin America: The Foreign Policy of Anticommunism* (1988).

Andrew J. Rotter, *The Path to Vietnam: Origins of the American Commitment to Southeast Asia* (1987).

Robert W. Stookey, *America and the Arab States* (1975).

WOMEN, GENDER ROLES, AND THE FAMILY

Wini Breines, *Young, White, and Miserable: Growing Up Female in the Fifties* (1992).

Stephanie Coontz, *The Way We Never Were: American Families and the Nostalgia Trip* (1992).

Barbara Ehrenreich, *The Hearts of Men: American Dreams and the Flight from Commitment* (1983).

Peter Filene, *Him/Her/Self: Sex Roles in Modern America* (2nd ed., 1986).

Betty Friedan, *The Feminine Mystique* (1963).

Eugenia Kaledin, *Mothers and More: American Women in the 1950s* (1984).

Elaine Tyler May, *Homeward Bound: American Families in the Cold War Era* (1988).

Joanne Meyerowitz, ed., *Not June Cleaver: Women and Gender in Postwar America, 1945–1960* (1994).

Steven Mintz and Susan Kellogg, *Domestic Revolutions: A Social History of American Family Life* (1988).

Arlene Skolnick, *Embattled Paradise: The American Family in an Age of Uncertainty* (1991).

Rickie Solinger, *Wake Up Little Susie: Single Pregnancy and Race before* Roe v. Wade (1992).

ECONOMIC, SOCIAL, AND CULTURAL TRENDS

Erik Barnouw, *Tube of Plenty: The Evolution of American Television* (rev. ed., 1982).

William Boddy, *Fifties Television: The Industry and Its Critics* (1994).

Paul Boyer, *By the Dawn's Early Light: American Thought and Culture at the Dawn of the Atomic Age* (1985).

Richard O. Davies, *The Age of Asphalt: The Automobile, the Freeway, and the Condition of Metropolitan America* (1975).

Scott Donaldson, *The Suburban Myth* (1969).

Simon Frith, *Sound Effects: Youth, Leisure, and the Politics of Rock and Roll* (1981).

Herbert Gans, *The Levittowners: Ways of Life and Politics in a New Suburban Community* (2nd ed., 1982).

Serge Guilbaut, *How New York Stole the Idea of Modern Art: Abstract Expressionism, Freedom, and the Cold War* (1983).

Peter Guralnick, *Last Train to Memphis: The Rise of Elvis Presley* (1994).

Kenneth T. Jackson, *Crabgrass Frontier: The Suburbanization of the United States* (1985).

Barbara Kelly, *Expanding the American Dream: Building and Rebuilding Levittown* (1993).

Michael P. Malone and Richard W. Etulain, *The American West: A Twentieth Century History* (1989).

David Mark, *Democratic Vistas: Television in American Culture* (1984).

Karal Ann Marling, *As Seen on TV: The Visual Culture of Everyday Life in the 1950s* (1994).

Larry May, ed., *Recasting America: Culture and Politics in the Age of the Cold War* (1989).

Gerald D. Nash, *The American West in the Twentieth Century* (1973).

Lynn Spigel, *Make Room for TV: Television and the Family Ideal in Postwar America* (1992).

Jon C. Teaford, *The Twentieth-Century American City* (1993).

Cecelia Tichi, *Electronic Hearth: Creating an American Television Culture* (1991).

Stephen J. Whitfield, *The Culture of the Cold War* (1991).

Robert Wuthnow, *The Restructuring of American Religion: Society and Faith since World War II* (1988).

CIVIL RIGHTS

Taylor Branch, *Parting the Waters: America in the King Years, 1954–63* (1988).

Robert Fredrick Burk, *The Eisenhower Administration and Black Civil Rights* (1984).

Adam Fairclough, *To Redeem the Soul of America: The Southern Christian Leadership Conference and Martin Luther King, Jr.* (1987).

David J. Garrow, *Bearing the Cross: Martin Luther King, Jr., and the Southern Christian Leadership Conference* (1986).

David J. Garrow, ed., *The Montgomery Boycott and the Women Who Started It: The Memoir of Jo Ann Gibson Robinson* (1987).

Richard Kluger, *Simple Justice: The History of* Brown v. Board of Education *and Black America's Struggle for Equality* (1976).

Doug McAdam, *Political Process and the Development of Black Insurgency, 1930–1970* (1982).

Aldon D. Morris, *The Origins of the Civil Rights Movement: Black Communities Organizing for Change* (1984).

E. Frederick Morrow, *Black Man in the White House* (1963).

Mark V. Tushnet, *Making Civil Rights Law: Thurgood Marshall and the Supreme Court, 1936–1961* (1995).

"COUNTRY JOE" MCDONALD'S GUITAR

Music was an omnipresent element of protest movements in the 1960s. Civil rights demonstrators sang, "We Shall Overcome," anti-war rallies featured folk singers, and hippies turned on to acid rock. The guitar was the central musical instrument for each kind of music: traditional African American, folk, and rock. This wood acoustic guitar belonged to "Country Joe" McDonald who started his band, Country Joe and the Fish, at a draft protest in Oakland in 1965. The band was one of many that originated in the San Francisco Bay area, but its popularity soon spread across the country.

The Oakland Museum of California.

A DECADE OF REBELLION AND REFORM

28

1960–1968

I N THE SUMMER OF 1960, twenty-year-old white college student Tom Hayden went to Los Angeles to cover the Democratic National Convention for the University of Michigan *Daily*. He heard presidential candidate John F. Kennedy declare, "We stand on the edge of a New Frontier . . . of unfulfilled hopes and threats." The speech, Hayden reported, "stirred me deeply," but his encounter with Martin Luther King Jr. inspired him even more. By the time the Democrats met in Chicago eight years later, both Kennedy and King had been murdered. Hayden and thousands of other protesters were there in open rebellion against much of what the Democrats and the government stood for. Hayden's personal political journey through the 1960s—the fading of his initial hopes into anger and frustration—mirrored a more general shift among Americans from optimism and consensus to disillusionment and divisiveness.

In contrast to Kennedy's vague call for Americans to attack unsolved problems with idealistic service, King was specific. "Ultimately, you have to take a stand with your life," he told Hayden in 1960. In 1961, Hayden went south to work with black activists. There he joined a civil rights movement that shook the national conscience, raised hopes for the possibility of change, and provided a model of protest that inspired other marginalized groups.

The prosperity of the 1960s contributed to the nation's buoyant confidence and belief that the federal government should advance social welfare. Voters elected two Democratic presidents, John F. Kennedy and Lyndon B. Johnson, who favored an activist government and wanted to replace the complacency of the 1950s with a vigorous attack on social and economic problems. Nonetheless, grassroots movements representing people far from the centers of power built the strongest engine driving domestic reform and pushed official leaders beyond their original intentions.

Although foreign policy was Kennedy's supreme concern, as grassroots pressures mounted he began to push for innovative domestic programs in 1963. After Kennedy's assassination in November 1963, Johnson took up domestic reform with a passion, launching a multitude of programs aimed at promoting general economic growth and improving the conditions of racial minorities and the impoverished. These, along with education, health care, urban development, and environmental reforms, came to be known as the Great Society and constituted the most far-reaching innovations in U.S. domestic policy since the New Deal.

The Supreme Court also contributed substantially to this domestic revolution. Beginning in the 1950s, with pathbreaking decisions relating to civil rights, criminal justice, political representation, and the treatment of dissenters, the Court forcefully promoted the realization of equality in the United States. Many of its decisions were hotly contested, but most withstood challenge and contributed notably to the egalitarian thrust of public policy in the 1960s.

Underlying the transformation in domestic policy was the black freedom struggle, which took on new form and urgency in 1960 when African Americans in massive numbers began to apply the tactics of civil disobedience in demonstrations throughout the South. White repression and violence made the costs of progress high for the protesters, who endured brutality, saw their homes and churches burned, and sometimes lost their lives, but by the end of the decade, law had caught up with the American ideal of equality.

Yet it did not catch up fast enough. Legal guarantees of civil rights left untouched the deplorable economic conditions resulting from three centuries of poverty and oppression. By 1966, a minority of African American activists had discarded the original tenets of integration and nonviolence and demanded black power. Simultaneously, urban riots erupted in black neighborhoods throughout the nation. The second half of the decade saw a splintering among those who supported civil rights and a sharp decline in white support for its goals. Yet the black freedom struggle stimulated a multitude of new social movements. Other racial and ethnic minorities, students, and women benefited from the visibility of African American protest as well as from the civil rights movement's ideas, tactics, and policy precedents.

Tom Hayden went from civil rights activism to student organizing to protest against the U.S. role in the war in Vietnam. Hayden and other student radicals who formed what came to be called the New Left, scorned Kennedy's New Frontier and Johnson's Great Society for failing to strike at the roots of America's unjust political and economic system. Conservatives cried that the Great Society went too far and expressed outrage at the wholesale challenge to American values and institutions mounted by blacks, students, and others. Even before the decade's end, the optimism and idealism with which it had begun had given way to disillusionment and polarization.

Kennedy and the New Frontier

In his New Frontier speech that stirred Tom Hayden at the Democratic nominating convention in 1960, John F. Kennedy promised to confront "unsolved problems of peace and war, unconquered pockets of ignorance and prejudice, unanswered questions of poverty and surplus." Once in office, Kennedy instituted an aggressive foreign policy. Believing that most domestic problems could be solved by promoting economic growth, he asked Congress for a broad range of reform legislation, but he failed to back up his requests with effective leadership. Not until his final months did massive grassroots pressures spur Kennedy to launch a substantial assault on the problems of racism and poverty. Before these efforts reached fruition, an assassin ended his life.

The Election of 1960

John F. Kennedy grew up in privilege, the son of a wealthy Irish Catholic businessman who served in Franklin D. Roosevelt's administration and nourished his son's political career. With the aid of a distinguished World War II navy record, John Kennedy won election to the House of Representatives in 1946 and to the Senate in 1952. The Massachusetts senator set his sights on the White House for 1960, using his family's fortunes to build a superb political machine directed by his brother Robert. A major challenge was to woo Democratic liberals who were put off by Kennedy's undistinguished record in Congress and his failure to take a strong stand against McCarthyism.

Kennedy's opponents included Adlai E. Stevenson, Senate Majority Leader Lyndon B. Johnson of Texas, and Hubert H. Humphrey, the liberal senator from Minnesota. With his overwhelming financial advantage, his handsome appearance, and his dynamic style, Kennedy triumphed in a series of state primaries. A critical victory over Humphrey in West Virginia eliminated the question of his Catholicism, an issue that had doomed Al Smith's candidacy in 1928. Kennedy's impressive margin in that heavily Protestant state demonstrated that religious intolerance no longer raised an insuperable barrier between a Catholic and the presidency.

At the Democratic convention, after winning the nomination on the first ballot, Kennedy stunned nearly everyone by choosing Lyndon Johnson as his running mate. Although ticket balancing was a time-honored tradition, liberals detested the choice of a man whom they viewed as a typical southern conservative. The party platform, however, embodied liberal priorities, including the strongest civil rights plank the Democrats had ever endorsed. It also called for increased defense spending to bolster the nation's position in the cold war.

On the Republican side, Vice President Richard M. Nixon deflected challenges from liberal New York Governor Nelson Rockefeller and from Arizona Senator Barry Goldwater on the right. Support for Goldwater, who urged his party to "quit copying the New Deal," indicated that Eisenhower had not won over Republican conservatives to moderation. But the convention nominated Nixon on the first ballot.

While Nixon based his campaign on his experience as vice president, Kennedy took the initiative on issues. Kennedy called for a stronger defense system and a more vigorous approach to the cold war, and he promised to expand the welfare state and increase the rate of economic growth to "get this country moving again." Nixon, stuck with defending the policies of the Eisenhower administration, seemed less dynamic, though the two candidates actually differed little on defense and foreign policy questions.

Unmoved by any sense of moral urgency and concerned about the votes of southern whites, both candidates stepped gingerly around the issue of race. Yet Kennedy's advisers pushed him to seize an opportunity for attracting black support when Martin Luther King Jr. was arrested at a demonstration in Atlanta on October 19, 1960. Kennedy called King's wife to offer his sympathy, Robert Kennedy made a phone call to the judge, and the campaign circulated two million flyers about the incident in African American churches the Sunday before the election.

In the excruciatingly close election, Kennedy depended on black voters. Nixon won 52 percent of the white vote, but the black preference for Kennedy enabled him to outpoll Nixon by about 120,000 votes. African Americans provided essential margins in Illinois, Michigan, South Carolina, and other states vital to Kennedy's 303–219 majority in the electoral college. Of course, Kennedy needed more than black votes. Lyndon Johnson took credit for capturing most of the South for the Democratic ticket, but a third Eisenhower recession, which

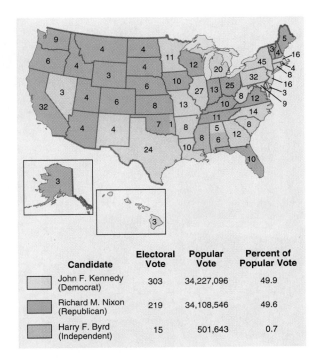

Candidate	Electoral Vote	Popular Vote	Percent of Popular Vote
John F. Kennedy (Democrat)	303	34,227,096	49.9
Richard M. Nixon (Republican)	219	34,108,546	49.6
Harry F. Byrd (Independent)	15	501,643	0.7

M A P 2 8 . 1
The Election of 1960

pushed unemployment above 6 percent in 1960, also contributed to the incumbent party's defeat. Kennedy's religion won him extra votes from Catholics in the North but caused him losses elsewhere.

Kennedy benefited from the first televised debates between presidential candidates. He came across as cool, experienced, handsome, and in command of the issues. Nixon appeared nervous, sweaty, and pale. Radio listeners declared the debate a draw, but television viewers came away more impressed with Kennedy. Television also helped to increase interest in the campaign: At 64 percent, voter turnout for this election was the highest in the twentieth century.

The Style and Promise of the New Frontier

The Kennedy administration projected an aura of dynamism, idealism, and glamour, reflecting the president's personal style as well as the tone of the government. He charmed the press corps with his grace, vigor, and self-mocking wit and was the first president to hold press conferences for a live TV au-

THE KENNEDY FAMILY
John F. Kennedy's youthful good looks, glamorous background, and attractive family added to his appeal and continue to fascinate many Americans decades after his death. Here he relaxes with his wife, Jacqueline, and their children, Caroline and John, at their vacation home in Hyannisport on Cape Cod. This photograph was taken in July 1963, a few months before Kennedy's assassination.
John F. Kennedy Library.

dience. The nation warmed to images of a young president competing in touch football, sailing with his chic and cultured wife, Jacqueline, and playing in the executive office with his toddler daughter and infant son. The Kennedys transformed the White House into a national showcase of culture and the arts, inviting prominent writers, artists, and musicians to visit and perform.

Kennedy surrounded himself with diverse advisers, including men from the Republican Party and Wall Street as well as liberal Democrats. Wanting to control foreign policy himself, Kennedy chose for secretary of state Dean Rusk, who was known for his loyalty in Truman's State Department. Most controversial was the appointment of Robert Kennedy as attorney general. Questioned about his brother's youth and lack of experience, Kennedy fell back on his wit, responding that he saw nothing wrong with "giving Robert some legal experience before he goes out to practice law."

The appointment of Robert S. McNamara as secretary of defense most reflected the style of the administration. Known for his keen analytic ability

and decisiveness, the hard-driving McNamara had risen to the top of the Ford Motor Company. A number of Kennedy's appointments to lower-level posts and the White House staff shared McNamara's youth, brilliance, and eagerness to apply technology and engineering to problem solving. Many were intellectuals from Ivy League schools, including fifteen Rhodes scholars; they exuded confidence, enjoyed competition, and welcomed crisis and risk. However, they were not especially well schooled in practical politics. When Lyndon Johnson told Speaker of the House Sam Rayburn how impressed he was with the brilliance of the Kennedy men, the older Texan replied, "I'd feel a whole lot better . . . if just one of them had run for sheriff once."

Kennedy's inaugural address called on all Americans to serve the common good. As the youngest elected president took the reins of government from the oldest president up to that time, Kennedy noted that he was the first president born in the twentieth century and that a "new generation" was assuming leadership. He asked Americans to cast off the complacency and self-indulgence of the 1950s, to "ask not what your country can do for you—ask what you can do for your country."

To what ends would this service be put? The brief, eloquent inaugural address described the cold war in a tone of crisis, emphasizing the United States' "role of defending freedom in its hour of maximum danger." Kennedy insisted, "If a free society cannot help the many who are poor, it cannot save the few who are rich"; yet his address gave domestic problems short shrift and delineated no specific programs. Nonetheless, the idealism of his speech touched many, especially the young, inspiring them to strive for the common good and to replace self-interest with service to a larger cause.

The Substance of the New Frontier at Home

Commenting on Kennedy's actions on civil rights, Martin Luther King Jr. described the president as "committed but . . . feeling his way," a characterization that King could easily have applied to Kennedy's domestic achievements in general. After campaigning on a party platform that promised to expand the welfare state, particularly in the areas of health care and education, Kennedy failed to achieve any major legislation. Nor did he assume leadership on behalf of racial justice until near the end of his life, when pressures from civil rights activists gave him no choice.

A number of factors account for the large gap between what Kennedy said he stood for and his achievements. Even though his party controlled Congress, a combination of southern Democrats and Republicans constituted a force that was large enough to block reform. Having been elected by a slim margin, Kennedy saw no reason to go out on a limb for social justice. He displayed much more zeal for foreign policy and consigned domestic reform to a back burner.

Kennedy did win support for several items that congressional Democrats had been pushing in the 1950s. New legislation included a two-billion-dollar slum clearance and urban renewal program; the Area Redevelopment Act of 1961, which aided depressed areas through incentives for companies to locate in them; and the Manpower Development and Training Act of 1962, which provided training for the unemployed. But two key items on the Democratic agenda, federal aid to education and health care for the elderly, got nowhere. Referring to a book Kennedy had written, *Profiles in Courage*, liberals

jokingly expressed their dissatisfaction with his leadership by asking that he show "less profile and more courage."

Two initiatives of the Kennedy administration —a presidential commission on women and equal pay legislation—received relatively little attention but had important ramifications. Although Kennedy had no particular interest in women's rights, he heeded the advice of Esther Peterson, head of the Women's Bureau in the Department of Labor. In 1961, she persuaded Kennedy that he could strengthen his support among women by appointing a President's Commission on the Status of Women.

Chaired by Eleanor Roosevelt and composed of leaders from the government and private organizations, the commission reported its findings in October 1963, eight months after Betty Friedan had attacked sex discrimination in her best-selling book *The Feminine Mystique*. The commission report, *American Women*, identified widespread discrimination against women, insisted that such discrimination harmed the country as well as individuals, and made recommendations for action. Spawning counterparts at the state level, the president's commission helped to create networks of women aware of sex discrimination and eager for action, providing an impetus for the launching of a grassroots women's movement a few years later.

Having been elected by a slim margin, Kennedy saw no reason to go out on a limb for social justice. He displayed much more zeal for foreign policy and consigned domestic reform to a back burner.

The president's commission addressed the age-old custom of paying women less than men for doing the same work. Although Kennedy's domestic agenda did not list sex discrimination among even the minor issues, he allowed Peterson to spearhead a drive for equal pay legislation, a goal that women's organizations and labor unions had been pushing for two decades. After Kennedy signed the Equal Pay Act in June 1963, wage disparities based solely on gender became illegal. Within a few years, women began to win wage increases and back pay worth millions of dollars.

The phrase "a rising tide lifts all boats" expressed Kennedy's belief that economic growth could solve most problems, that increased production provided the best means to eradicate poverty. In addition to meeting domestic needs, greater productivity would make the nation more competitive with the Soviet Union, whose rate of economic growth exceeded that of the United States throughout the 1950s. Consequently, Kennedy sought to increase the government's role in restraining inflation, eliminating recessions, and promoting economic growth.

Restraining inflation depended on cooperation from organized labor and corporations. When U.S. Steel and other big companies announced price increases in excess of rising labor costs in 1962, the president marshaled all of his resources to bring them back into line. He publicly criticized the steel executives, had the Justice Department begin investigations of price-fixing, and canceled government orders from the offending companies. "I'm beginning to sound like Harry Truman," he remarked, referring to Truman's lambasting of business. His vigorous action, unparalleled on other domestic fronts, ultimately forced the steel industry to retreat.

Although Kennedy called big businessmen "sons of bitches" in a widely reported comment during the steel controversy, he was also prepared to treat business kindly to further his goal of economic growth. Through new tax guidelines and legislation granting credits for new investment, corporations won a 10 percent tax cut in 1962.

Kennedy's biggest innovation in "getting the country moving again" came with his call for an enormous tax cut in 1963. Key economic advisers persuaded him that infusing money into the economy by reducing taxes would increase demand, boost production, and decrease unemployment. This use of fiscal policy to stimulate the economy even when there was no recession gained the name "the new economics." Kennedy, however, failed to sell his tax bill to Congress even after modifying it to make it more advantageous to the rich. Legislators worried that the tax cut would result in a budget deficit. Organized labor opposed the bill because the largest share of the reduction would go to the wealthy.

Kennedy did not live to see approval of his bill. Passed in February 1964, the law provided $10 billion in tax cuts over 1964 and 1965, and it received major credit for the greatest economic boom since World War II. Unemployment dropped to 4.1 percent, and the gross national product shot up by 7 to 9 percent annually between 1964 and 1966.

Questioning the wisdom of the tax cut, critics disputed its economic impact, pointing out that the surge was already under way before the law went into effect. Conservatives warned that cutting taxes would spark inflation. John Kenneth Galbraith and other liberals maintained that economic growth alone would not eliminate poverty, arguing instead for increased spending on schools, hospitals, urban renewal, and other public programs and facilities directed at the needs of ordinary citizens.

Some of these needs had gained the Senate's attention in 1960, when a subcommittee reported "a growing and intense problem," the poverty of eight million older Americans, whose "declining years are without dignity. . . . They are sick . . . they are without money." That same year Kennedy came face to face with the rural poor of Appalachia when he asked for their votes in his 1960 campaign in West Virginia. In 1962, he read *The Other America*, Michael Harrington's devastating account of the hopelessness and wretched conditions in the lives of more than one in every five Americans. And by 1963, Kennedy's key economic advisers recognized that economic growth in itself would not eradicate poverty.

The summer of 1963 marked a turning point in Kennedy's attitude toward domestic reform. In addition to asking aides to plan an attack on poverty, he issued a dramatic call for passage of a comprehensive civil rights bill. Whether he could have achieved these breakthroughs in domestic policy was left unanswered by his assassination on November 22, 1963.

Assassination of a President

The murder of the president in Dallas, Texas, seared the consciousness of Americans as had no other event since the end of World War II. Within minutes of the shooting, radio and television broadcast the unfolding horror to the nation. Millions watched the return of *Air Force One* to Washington bearing the president's coffin, his widow in her bloodstained suit, and the new president, Lyndon Baines Johnson, who had taken the oath of office aboard the jet.

From Friday afternoon until the burial on Monday, Americans shared in the tragedy through television, which abandoned regular programming. They saw newsreels of President Kennedy in life, experts assessing his career, somber-faced world leaders arriving to pay their respects, and thousands of tearful Americans filing past his coffin in

JOHN F. KENNEDY'S FUNERAL
For the few days following November 22, 1963, normal life stopped in the United States. Schools
and businesses were closed, while tens of thousands of Americans traveled to Washington, D.C.,
to file past Kennedy's coffin in the rotunda of the Capitol. The relatively new medium of television
unified the nation, as it allowed millions of viewers to experience every moment of that long, terrible
weekend, culminating in the funeral procession, shown here. The president's widow, Jacqueline
Kennedy, is escorted in the procession by the president's brothers Robert (left) and Edward.
© Henri Dauman NYC.

the Capitol. Even many of Kennedy's opponents and critics expressed their shock and personal grief.

Stunned Americans struggled to determine what had happened and why. As Kennedy had ridden with his wife and Texas Governor John B. Connally in a motorcade in an open car, three shots were fired, killing Kennedy and injuring Connally. The police quickly arrested Lee Harvey Oswald, a loner with an irregular past, and concluded that he had fired the shots from a nearby building. Two days later, as a television audience watched Oswald being transferred from one jail to another, a local nightclub operator and gambler, Jack Ruby, killed him.

Suspicions arose that Ruby had killed Oswald to cover up a conspiracy. Some people believed there had been a plot among ultraconservative Texans who hated Kennedy. Others, pointing to Oswald's Russian wife, his three-year residence in the Soviet Union, and his activities on behalf of Cuba's Castro, suspected a Communist plot. To get at the truth and calm public fears, President Johnson ap-

pointed a commission headed by Chief Justice Earl Warren, which concluded in September 1964 that both Oswald and Ruby had acted alone. Several experts pointed to errors and omissions in the report, and later investigations both supported and contested the lone-killer explanation. As with Lincoln's assassination, the controversy persisted for decades. The weight of opinion favored the original Warren report but never became conclusive enough to satisfy skeptics.

Debate also continued over how to assess Kennedy's domestic record. It had been unremarkable in his first two years, but his initiatives on taxes, civil rights, and poverty in 1963 suggested an important turning point. Whether Kennedy could have persuaded Congress to translate his proposals into legislation cannot be known. In the words of journalist James Reston, "What was killed was not only the president but the promise. . . . He never reached his meridian: We saw him only as a rising sun."

Johnson and the Great Society

Within six months after becoming president, Lyndon Johnson had a theme for his administration. In May 1964, he announced the goal of a "Great Society, [which] rests on abundance and liberty for all. It demands an end to poverty and racial injustice, to which we are totally committed." In pursuing that Great Society, Johnson not only signed a host of measures that had lain beyond Kennedy's grasp —the tax cut, a civil rights law, federal aid to education, and medical care for the aged and poor. He also got Congress to approve two more civil rights acts, an antipoverty program, a massive housing program, and legislation to protect consumers, control pollution, and preserve the environment.

In pursuing the Great Society, Johnson got Congress to approve three civil rights acts, an antipoverty program, a massive housing program, and legislation to protect consumers, control air and water pollution, and preserve the environment.

The legislation of the 1960s constituted a remarkable record of reform yet fell short of achieving the Great Society. A backlash arose to thwart African Americans' aspirations before equality became a reality for all. The number of Americans living in poverty was cut in half, but inadequately funded and hastily designed programs achieved only partial success. Above all, the Great Society fell victim to an escalating war in Vietnam, which depleted federal revenues, diverted the president's attention from domestic affairs, and damaged the credibility of his leadership.

Fulfilling the Kennedy Promise

Johnson assumed the presidency with a wealth of political experience. A self-made man from the poor Texas hill country, he won election to the House of Representatives in 1937 and to the Senate in 1948. Although his Texas base required caution on civil rights and attention to the needs of the oil industry and other business interests, Johnson's growing ambitions for national leadership led him to take more liberal stands. By 1955, he had secured the top post of Senate majority leader, which he used brilliantly

to forge a Democratic consensus on the Civil Rights Acts of 1957 and 1960 and other liberal programs.

Johnson's coarse wit, excessive vanity, intense ambition, and Texas accent put off many who were accustomed to the sophisticated Kennedy style. His extreme need to dominate reached the point of humiliating aides and friends. Lacking Kennedy's eloquent and dynamic speaking style, Johnson excelled at behind-the-scenes planning, maneuvering, and persuading. Legislators found themselves enticed, cajoled, or threatened into support of his objectives. The famous "Johnson treatment" became legendary. In his ability to achieve his overriding goal of consensus—and in the means to which he was willing to resort—he had few peers in American history.

Johnson masterfully led the nation through the trauma of Kennedy's murder, stressing above all continuity and consensus. Mobilizing emotions aroused by the assassination, he asked Congress to act so that "John Fitzgerald Kennedy did not live or die in vain." He quickly applied his political skills to the slain president's tax proposal. By trimming the federal budget and promising government frugality, he won over fiscal conservatives and signed the tax cut in February 1964.

Still more revolutionary was the Civil Rights Act of 1964. Although Johnson gave responsibility for managing the bill to Robert Kennedy, who stayed on as attorney general until the fall of 1964, the president also worked mightily to line up enough Republicans and southern Democrats to ensure passage. "No memorial oration or eulogy could more eloquently honor President Kennedy's memory," he asserted. Referring to the "Johnson treatment" applied to Senate Republican leader Everett Dirksen, an aide reported that the president "never left him alone for thirty minutes." Enacted in July 1964, this act was the strongest civil rights measure since Reconstruction.

Antipoverty legislation followed fast on the heels of the Civil Rights Act. Still in an embryonic stage when Kennedy died, the poverty program captured Johnson's immediate attention. While Kennedy's body still lay in state, Johnson instructed an aide, "Give it the highest priority. Push ahead full tilt." In his first State of the Union message, Johnson called for "an unconditional war on poverty." Just two months later, the administration sent a draft bill to Congress, and in August Johnson signed the Economic Opportunity Act of 1964.

The new measure authorized ten programs to be administered by an Office of Economic Opportunity, allocating $800 million dollars for the first

THE "JOHNSON TREATMENT"

Abe Fortas was a distinguished lawyer who had argued one of the major criminal rights cases, Gideon v. Wainwright *(1963), before the Supreme Court and who was a close friend and adviser to President Lyndon Johnson. When Johnson asked him to serve on the Supreme Court, he was reluctant to leave his lucrative law practice, and Johnson had to use his famous persuasive powers to secure his assent. This photograph of the president and Fortas taken in July 1965 illustrates how Johnson used his body as well as his voice to bend people to his will.*
Yoichi R. Okamoto/LBJ Library Collection.

year (around 1 percent of the federal budget). Many provisions were targeted at youth, from Head Start, a preschool program for poor children, to the Upward Bound program and work-study grants for college students. There were also job training programs for youth (the Job Corps) and adult heads of families; loans to businesses willing to hire the long-term unemployed; aid to small farmers and rural businesses; and the VISTA program, which funded modest subsidies for volunteers to work on behalf of the disadvantaged. A legal services program that provided lawyers for the poor resulted in lawsuits that expanded and enforced impoverished Americans' rights to welfare programs.

The most novel and controversial part of the law, the Community Action Program (CAP), required "maximum feasible participation" of poor people themselves in coordinating poverty programs. Unlike other aspects of the poverty program, which sought to equip the poor to succeed in the existing system, this provision offered potential challenges to the system itself and a redistribution of power. In cities that took maximum feasible participation seriously, poor people began to organize community action programs to take control of their neighborhoods and to reform the welfare agencies, school boards, police departments, housing authorities, and other agencies on which they relied for services. Within months, mayors complained to the White House that activists were using federal funds to attack local governments and to "foster class struggle."

The last thing Johnson wanted was conflict, and he expressed his irritation at the "kooks and sociologists" involved in administering CAPs who caused him problems with Democratic mayors. Under his direction, federal poverty officials became less insistent on genuine representation for the poor, and local leaders found means to obtain federal funds without empowering people likely to challenge their control. Although the CAP failed to live up to its promise, for the first time in many cities those who were routinely excluded from the governmental process gained a voice, an incentive to act on their own behalf, and the opportunity to develop leadership skills.

A young black antipoverty worker in Mississippi reported that his Head Start project could offer poor people "doctors for their kids and good food," as well as employ "poor people who never had seen a check in their lives" to work as aides at the centers. "They're learning how to spell right and speak right," reported a mother with children in Head Start, but even more important to her, they were "learning about . . . us the colored people and what we've gone through . . . and what we've done for the country."

The 1964 Landslide

With the tax cut, civil rights, and antipoverty measures behind him, Johnson prepared to claim the presidency in his own right. He faced only one significant problem as the Democrats gathered for their

TABLE 28.1
REFORMS OF THE GREAT SOCIETY, 1964–1968

1964

24th Amendment	Abolished poll tax as prerequisite for voting.
Tax Reduction Act	Provided $10 billion in tax cuts over 1964–1965.
Civil Rights Act	Banned discrimination in public accommodations, public education, and employment.
Economic Opportunity Act	Created programs for the disadvantaged, including Head Start, VISTA, Job Corps, and CAP.
Wilderness Preservation Act	Set aside 9.1 million acres of national forest for protection.

1965

Elementary and Secondary Education Act	Provided $1.3 billion in aid to elementary and secondary schools.
Medical Care Act	Provided health insurance (Medicare) for all citizens age 65 and over. Extended federal health benefits to welfare recipients. (Medicaid)
Voting Rights Act	Banned literacy tests and other voting tests and authorized the federal government to act directly to enable African Americans to register and vote.
Executive Order 11246	Banned discrimination on the basis of race, religion, and national origin by employers awarded government contracts and required them to "take affirmative action to ensure equal opportunity."
Department of Housing and Urban Development (HUD)	New government department created to provide programs to address housing and community issues.
National Arts and Humanities Act	Created National Endowment for the Humanities (NEH) and National Endowment for the Arts (NEA) to support the work of artists, musicians, writers, and scholars.
Water Quality Act	Required states to set and enforce water quality standards.
Immigration and Nationality Act	Abolished fifty-year old quotas based on national origins, increasing the number of non-Western and Northern European immigrants.
Air Quality Act	Imposed air pollution standards for motor vehicles.
Higher Education Act	Expanded federal assistance to colleges and universities.

1966

National Traffic and Motor Vehicle Safety Act	Established federal safety standards.
Highway Safety Act	Required federally approved safety programs at the state level.
Department of Transportation	New government department created to administer transportation programs and policies.
Model Cities Act	Authorized more than $1 billion to ameliorate nation's slums.

1967

Executive Order 11246	Order extended to allow discrimination ban and requirement of affirmative action to cover women.

1968

Civil Rights Act of 1968	Banned discrimination in housing and in jury service.
National Housing Act	Subsidized the private construction of 1.7 million units of low-income housing.

MISSISSIPPI FREEDOM DEMOCRATIC PARTY RALLY
*These activists are singing at a rally outside the Democratic National Convention hall in 1964,
supporting the Mississippi Freedom Democratic Party (MFDP) in its challenge to the all-white
delegation sent by the regular Mississippi Democratic Party. In the foreground are Fannie Lou
Hamer, one of the MFDP delegates; Eleanor Holmes Norton, a civil rights lawyer; and Ella
Baker, who helped organize the Southern Christian Leadership Conference (SCLC) and later
managed MFDP headquarters in Washington, D.C.*
Matt Herron.

national convention in the summer of 1964. In Mississippi, blacks and their supporters had organized a delegation to challenge the all-white state contingent chosen by party regulars. Determined that consensus would reign over his convention, Johnson instructed Minnesota Senator Hubert H. Humphrey to arrange a settlement that would avoid a fight on the convention floor. The resulting "compromise" allotting them just two at-large seats while leaving the forty-four-member all-white delegation intact outraged black Mississippians, but Humphrey received his reward when Johnson chose him for his running mate.

The Democrats' refusal to guarantee racial justice within the party did not cost their ticket much support from civil rights advocates. They had nowhere else to go. At a bitterly divided Republican national convention, Arizona Senator Barry M. Goldwater won the nomination, defeating the liberal and moderate wing that had dominated the party since the 1940s.

Republican Phyllis Schlafly wrote a book to promote Goldwater's candidacy, calling it *A Choice Not an Echo* and aptly capturing right-wing Republicans' frustration with what they considered the "me-tooism" of their party. Goldwater told the convention that "extremism in defense of liberty is no vice" and embarked on a campaign that indeed put him near the extreme right of U.S. politics. He attacked the entire framework of the welfare state and called for the government to leave the economy to "free enterprise." Criticizing the Democrats' failure to use every means available to crush communism in Vietnam, he suggested that he would use nuclear weapons if necessary.

Goldwater proved an easy mark for Johnson. Having safely steered the nation through the assassination trauma and established his capacity for national leadership, Johnson projected stability and security. With the economy booming, only a minority of voters proved willing to risk a change as dramatic as Goldwater promised. Although Goldwater captured five states in the Deep South, Johnson accomplished a record-breaking landslide of 61 percent of the popular vote. On his coattails came resounding Democratic majorities in the House (295–140) and Senate (68–32).

Completing the Great Society Agenda

"I want to see a whole bunch of coonskins on the wall," Johnson told his aides, using a hunting analogy to stress his determination to make the most of his mandate. He wanted to surpass even the domestic achievements of his mentor, Franklin Roosevelt. In the sheer amount and breadth of new legislation, Johnson succeeded extraordinarily, and public opinion polls gave impressively high marks to both the president and Congress. Reporters called the legislation of the 89th Congress (1965–1966) "unprecedented" and "a political miracle"; organized labor lauded that Congress as "the most productive congressional session ever held."

The Economic Opportunity Act of 1964 had been just the opening shot in the War on Poverty. Congress increased the program's funding in 1965 to $2 billion and initiated two new assaults on poverty. The Appalachian Regional Development Act and the Public Works and Economic Development Act attacked poverty in depressed regions that the general economic boom had bypassed. Rather than combatting poverty directly, these programs—like the tax cut of 1964—sought to help the poor indirectly by stimulating economic growth and providing jobs through road building and other public works projects.

A second approach, one that was new to the 1960s, promised to equip the poor with the training and skills necessary to find jobs. The 1964 antipoverty legislation included the Head Start and Job Corps programs for just this purpose. But the largest assault on poverty through education was the Elementary and Secondary Education Act of 1965.

Ever since establishing the land-grant college system in the nineteenth century, the federal government had promoted education, but only in the form of funds for a specific purpose, such as science education in the National Defense Education Act of 1957. Legislators who opposed federal involvement in what had always been the preserve of state and local governments had stalled Truman's proposal for general aid to public education for two decades. Other conflicts concerned whether aid to parochial schools violated the constitutional separation of church and state.

To sidestep the religious issue, Johnson proposed aid for "the educational needs of educationally deprived children" rather than to schools per se. Thus private and parochial schools could receive aid for equipment and supplies to be used for poor children, and public school districts would be granted funds on the basis of the number of poor children in their schools. When Congress passed the Elementary and Secondary Education Act in April 1965, Johnson flew to the little school in Texas where he had begun his education to sign the bill with his first teacher at his side.

With the Higher Education Act of 1965, Congress also vastly expanded federal assistance to colleges and universities, providing not only funds for buildings and programs but also scholarships and low-interest loans for students. In 1966, Congress renewed its commitment to education, appropriating nearly $4 billion for higher education for the next three years and $6.1 billion for a two-year extension of the elementary and secondary education program.

The administration broke a second congressional deadlock in the area of health care. Trimming down the plan for universal care that Truman had first proposed, Johnson focused his proposal on the elderly, who constituted a large portion of the nation's poor. Congress responded with the Medicare program, which provided the elderly with universal compulsory hospital insurance financed largely through Social Security taxes and a voluntary insurance program for doctors' bills and other costs funded by the government and individual contributions. Congress took the initiative in authorizing the Medicaid program, a system of federal grants to supplement state programs paying for medical care for poor people below the age of sixty-five. Demonstrating again his flair for the dramatic, Johnson flew to Independence, Missouri, to sign the Medicare-Medicaid bill under the gaze of former

President Truman, who had first called for a national commitment to adequate health care.

The whirlwind of legislation from the 89th Congress included additional efforts to assist the impoverished. A food stamp program, begun as a demonstration project in 1961, replaced the distribution of surplus commodities, giving poor people greater choice in obtaining food. Rent supplements allowed some poor families to acquire another basic necessity without resort to public housing. Congress attacked the environment of poverty with the Model Cities Act, authorizing more than $1 billion to improve conditions in the nation's slums.

In response to the growing force of the civil rights movement, Johnson persuaded Congress to pass the Voting Rights Act of 1965. The Immigration and Nationality Act of 1965 eliminated a different form of discrimination. The new law continued to restrict the numbers of immigrants and for the first time placed limits on immigration from the Western Hemisphere. But it also did away with the fifty-year-old quotas based on national origins, thereby ending discrimination against immigrants from areas outside northern and western Europe.

The benefits of the Great Society reached well beyond the poverty-stricken. Pressures from a growing consumer movement led by liberal activist Ralph Nader and others produced legislation to make automobiles safer and to raise standards for the food, drug, and cosmetics industries. In 1965, Johnson became the first president to send Congress a special message on the environment, and Congress responded with measures to control water and air pollution and to preserve the natural beauty of the American landscape. Another law, the National Arts and Humanities Act of 1965, created programs to support artists, musicians, writers, and scholars and to bring their work to public audiences.

The flood of reform legislation dwindled to a trickle after 1966, when midterm elections reduced the overwhelming majorities that the Democrats previously enjoyed. Even though a sizable majority of the poor were whites, who benefited proportionately from the war on poverty, the public tended to associate antipoverty programs with African Americans. White support for black aspirations withered, and a wave of urban riots between 1964 and 1968 caused many voters and legislators to contend that the poor needed "law and order," not more government assistance. The appearance of buttons reading "I fight poverty—I work" indicated a growing backlash against the disadvantaged.

The Vietnam War dealt the largest blow to domestic reform, for at the same time that Johnson pursued his Great Society at home he rapidly escalated the U.S. presence in Vietnam. Growing opposition to the war diverted the president's attention from domestic affairs and put his entire leadership in jeopardy. Even more damaging was the war's cost, which rose to more than $2 billion a month by 1966 and increased the federal deficit. Moreover, rising military expenditures began to exert inflationary pressures on the economy.

The Vietnam War dealt the largest blow to domestic reform, for at the same time that Johnson pursued his Great Society at home he rapidly escalated the U.S. presence in Vietnam.

In August 1967, Johnson called for a temporary tax increase to control the deficit and check inflation. While Congress hesitated, the president reduced spending, cutting especially deeply into social welfare programs. Congress finally enacted an income tax surcharge, but not until July 1968. By then, consumer prices were increasing at what was considered a high annual rate of 5 percent, and inflation continued despite the tax increase.

The declining years of the Johnson administration were not completely lacking in significant reforms. The president pried one more civil rights law out of Congress in 1968, and he also secured a new housing program. Construction of public housing over the previous two decades had lagged behind need, and millions of people continued to live in substandard dwellings. Moreover, public housing often took the form of massive high-rise buildings that afforded a poor environment for children. In addition, projects tended to be located in areas that offered minimal employment opportunities and inadequate public transportation and services.

Johnson proposed both an enormous increase in construction of low-income housing and a new way of providing it. The National Housing Act of 1968 authorized construction of 1.7 million units in the next three years but left construction and ownership in private hands. Poor people could purchase houses with low-interest loans guaranteed by the government, and developers could obtain low-interest loans to construct housing for the needy.

Assessing the War on Poverty

Measured by statistics, the reduction in poverty in the 1960s was significant. The number of impoverished Americans fell from forty million in 1959 to twenty-five million in 1968, reducing the poor from 22 percent of the population to around 13 percent. Certain groups fared much better than others. Large numbers of the aged and members of male-headed families rose out of poverty, while the economic circumstances of female-headed families actually worsened. Moreover, although African American family income grew from 54 percent of white family income to 61 percent, whites escaped poverty at a faster rate than blacks, and blacks constituted one-third of the poor population at the end of the decade.

Intangible changes flowed from the War on Poverty in the form of shifting attitudes. In the 1960s, a substantial part of the population expressed a concern about poverty, located its causes in economic and social circumstances rather than in individuals' shortcomings, and assumed a national responsibility for alleviating it. Especially through the Community Action Programs, poor people themselves gained more control of their circumstances and a sense of their right to a fairer share of America's bounty.

The rising tide of the economy played a large role in the reduction in poverty. Yet government programs that transferred funds and services to the poor also contributed. Whereas the distribution of surplus food benefited about fifty thousand participants at the cost of $1 million in 1961, by the 1970s, twelve million people received more than $2 billion in food stamps. Within ten years after their inauguration, Medicare and Medicaid provided $32 billion worth of health care for the elderly and the poor. In addition, the War on Poverty helped to make the needy aware of their eligibility for aid programs and to remove restrictions that discouraged them from applying for aid. Between 1960 and 1970, the number of recipients of Aid to Families with Dependent Children (AFDC), a program launched by the New Deal, grew from three million to ten million.

The heart of the antipoverty program, the Office of Economic Opportunity (OEO), remained underfunded throughout its life. Poverty experts projected expenditures of $6.5 billion for OEO by 1968, but they never rose above $2 billion. Moreover, despite the large increases in direct subsidies for

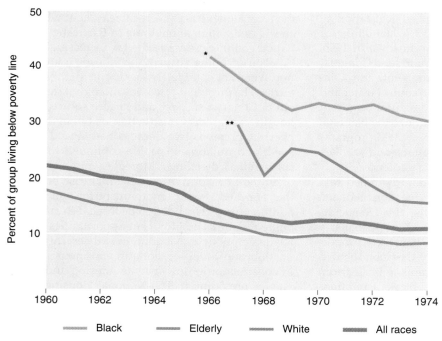

FIGURE 28.1
Poverty in the U.S., 1960–1974
The short-term effects of economic growth and the Great Society's attack on poverty are seen here. Which groups experienced the sharpest decline in poverty and what might account for the differences?

*Statistics on blacks for years 1960–1965 not available.
**Statistics on the elderly for years 1960–1966 not available.

AFDC, food stamps, housing, and medical care, no significant redistribution of income resulted. The poorest 20 percent of the population received 5.1 percent of total national income in 1964 and 5.4 percent in 1974.

Conservatives charged that the Great Society programs discouraged initiative among the poor by giving them "handouts." Critics on the left claimed that the emphasis on training and education placed the responsibility for poverty on the poor themselves rather than on the economic system. Most job training programs prepared graduates for low-level occupations and could not guarantee that jobs would be available on the completion of training. Surveys in 1966 and 1967, for example, found 28 percent of Job Corps graduates unemployed six months after completing their training.

Who reaped the greatest benefits from the Great Society programs? Critics pointed out that most of the funds for Appalachia and other depressed areas went to highway building and thus to the construction industry. Real estate developers, investors, and moderate-income families reaped the lion's share of benefits from the mortgage subsidies under the National Housing Act of 1968. Noting that in slum clearance programs, commercial development and high-income housing often displaced poor families, blacks called urban renewal "Negro removal." Physicians' fees and hospital costs soared after enactment of Medicare and Medicaid. Other beneficiaries of the Great Society programs were middle-class professionals who staffed the growing bureaucracy that was needed to run them.

Some critics of the War on Poverty suggested that the solution to poverty lay in a major redistribution of income, through raising taxes and using those funds in the public sector to create jobs, overhaul social welfare systems, and rebuild slums. The Johnson administration programs did invest more heavily in the public sector, but they had little effect on the existing distribution of resources. Determined above all to promote consensus and avoid conflict, Johnson would not take from the advantaged to provide for the poor. Funds for the poverty programs had to come from increasing revenues generated by economic growth, not from new taxes on the rich or middle class. Economic prosperity allowed spending for the poor to rise and significantly improved the lives of millions, but that spending never approached the amounts that would have been required to declare a victory in the war on poverty.

The Second Reconstruction

Unlike many of the Great Society reforms, which failed to live up to their promise and evoked widespread criticism, the civil rights movement effected a revolution in the legal status of African Americans and won widespread acceptance. The first Reconstruction in the aftermath of the Civil War had ended slavery and written racial equality into the Constitution; the second Reconstruction a century later made the guarantee of equal status under the law a reality. That accomplishment depended heavily on the courage, resourcefulness, and determination of black people themselves. In the words of Sheyann Webb, one of the thousands of marchers in the Selma, Alabama, campaign for voting rights, "We were just people, ordinary people, and we did it."

Unlike many of the Great Society reforms, which failed to live up to their promise and evoked widespread criticism, the civil rights movement effected a revolution in the legal status of African Americans and won widespread acceptance.

Begun as an effort to end legal segregation and discrimination in the South, the civil rights movement in the mid-1960s expanded its purpose in two ways. It extended its concern to racial injustice throughout the country, and it attacked the deplorable economic conditions of African Americans that equal rights left untouched. The movement to extend legal equality to blacks initially won broad support from white Americans. But when the movement began to seek equality through systematic change in the economic system, white support declined, and a strong backlash developed. By the end of the 1960s, the revolution in the legal status of blacks was complete, but the black freedom struggle had lost much of its momentum, and African Americans remained at the bottom of the economic ladder.

The Flowering of the Black Freedom Struggle

The Montgomery bus boycott in the mid-1950s had given national visibility to the plight of southern blacks, produced a national leader in Martin Luther

LUNCH COUNTER SIT-IN
John Salter Jr., a professor at Tougaloo College, and students Joan Trumpauer and Anne Moody take part in 1963 in a sit-in at the Woolworth lunch counter in Jackson, Mississippi. Shortly before this photograph was taken, whites had thrown two students to the floor, and police had arrested one student. Salter was spattered with mustard and ketchup. Moody would write a popular book in 1968 about her experiences in the black freedom struggle, Coming of Age in Mississippi.
State Historical Society of Wisconsin.

King Jr., and demonstrated the effectiveness of mass mobilization. Nevertheless, although it took enormous energy and determination, the boycott remained in a way a passive action—Montgomery blacks avoided riding the buses. In the 1960s, the form of protest underwent a major change, mobilizing blacks into direct and personal confrontation with the people and institutions that segregated them or discriminated against them: lunch counters, department stores, public parks and libraries, buses and depots, municipal service providers, and voting registrars.

Direct action as a mass movement began in February 1960, when four African American freshmen at North Carolina A&T College in Greensboro sat at the whites-only Woolworth's lunch counter and asked for service. Within days, hundreds of young

people joined their demonstration. By the end of February, blacks had launched sit-ins in thirty-one cities in eight southern states. These local movements received encouragement from the NAACP, the Congress of Racial Equality (CORE), and the Southern Christian Leadership Conference (SCLC). At the SCLC, executive secretary Ella Baker picked up the phone and challenged her contacts at various colleges: "What are you going to do? It's time to move."

In April, Baker got student activists together at Raleigh, North Carolina. With her support they decided to remain independent from the older generation and its established civil rights organizations. They founded the Student Nonviolent Coordinating Committee (SNCC, pronounced "snick"), creating a decentralized, nonhierarchical structure that encouraged the development of leadership and decision making at the grassroots level.

Although SNCC rejected the organizational patterns of the older groups, it embraced the strategy of civil disobedience and the nonviolent principles of Martin Luther King Jr. and others in the SCLC and CORE. Directly confronting the agents of oppression, students would stand up for their rights, but they would not practice self-defense against their enemies. At SNCC's founding conference, minister James Lawson defined a strategy for blacks that he believed could change the hearts of their oppressors: "We affirm . . . nonviolence as a foundation of our purpose, the presupposition of our faith, and the manner of our action." Love was at the heart of nonviolence, he pointed out: "It matches the capacity of evil to inflict suffering with an even more enduring capacity to absorb evil, all the while persisting in love." With its appeal to human conscience, "nonviolence nurtures the atmosphere in which reconciliation and justice become actual possibilities."

When students returned to the field, their optimism and commitment to nonviolence met severe testing. Although some local leaders managed to negotiate quiet accommodations to student demands, in most cases authorities and local citizens reacted with violence. Hostile whites poured food over demonstrators, burned them with cigarettes, called them "nigger," and pelted them with rocks. Local police went after protesters with clubs, fire hoses, and tear gas; they arrested more than 3,600 civil rights demonstrators in the year following the Greensboro sit-in. Spurning complicity with an unjust system, demonstrators frequently refused to pay fines, choosing jail instead.

Another wave of protest arose in 1961, when CORE organized Freedom Rides to integrate interstate transportation. On May 4, six whites and seven blacks boarded two buses in Washington, D.C., for a thirteen-day ride to New Orleans. The riders crossed the color line without harm in bus stations in Virginia and North Carolina, but in Alabama, white hoodlums bombed a bus and beat the riders with baseball bats. When the brutality turned some Freedom Riders back, SNCC members rushed in to take their places.

A mob of more than a thousand people attacked the Freedom Riders when they arrived in Montgomery. Angry whites knocked unconscious a federal government observer who tried to help the protesters. After failing to get the activists to call off the rides, Attorney General Robert Kennedy dispatched

federal marshals to restore order. Alabama and Mississippi authorities agreed to protect the buses, but when they reached Jackson, Mississippi, the Freedom Riders were promptly arrested. Refusing to post bail, several hundred spent parts of the summer in Mississippi jails.

Encouraged in part by Kennedy administration officials who viewed voting rights as less controversial than civil disobedience (and more likely to benefit the Democratic Party), SNCC and other groups began a Voter Education Project in the summer of 1961. Yet as activists sought to register black voters in the Deep South, they met no less violence than had the Freedom Riders. Whites beat Robert Moses, an African American and the first SNCC activist in Mississippi, and police arrested him as he worked to get blacks registered to vote. When a Mississippi legislator killed Herbert Lee, one of the first blacks to attempt to register, no charges were brought against the murderer.

When African Americans mobilized, whites bombed their churches, threw tenant farmers out of their homes, and beat and jailed the activists. Plantation worker Fannie Lou Hamer, for example, lost her job and home when she attempted to register to vote in Mississippi in 1962. Undeterred, she continued her efforts, and one year later police arrested and battered her so savagely that she would not show her face to her family for a month. In June 1963, a white man gunned down Mississippi NAACP leader Medgar Evers in front of his house in Jackson.

Television brought home to the entire world the brutality of southern resistance to racial equality in May 1963, when Martin Luther King Jr. and the SCLC launched a campaign in Birmingham, Alabama, to integrate public facilities and open jobs to blacks. As blacks massed in demonstrations, the city's police chief, Eugene "Bull" Connor, responded with police dogs, electric cattle prods, and high-pressure hoses. Hundreds of demonstrators, including school-age children, went to jail, and firebombs exploded at King's motel and his brother's house. Four months later, a bomb killed four black children attending Sunday school in a Birmingham church.

The largest demonstration took place in Washington, D.C., in August 1963. Civil rights leaders revived the march on Washington strategy used by A. Philip Randolph in 1941 to get President Roosevelt to ban discrimination in defense jobs. Sponsored by the major civil rights organizations and coordinated by Bayard Rustin, a pacifist, socialist, and civil

BIRMINGHAM DEMONSTRATORS
In April 1963, Martin Luther King Jr. and the Southern Christian Leadership Conference (SCLC) initiated a campaign to integrate Birmingham, Alabama, known as the most segregated city in the nation. City officials filled the jails with demonstrators, including King himself, and nine hundred children, like these young people being attacked with powerful hoses. One police officer remarked to a colleague, "Ten or fifteen years from now, we will look back on all this and we will say, 'How stupid can you be?'" Photographs like this one evoked outrage around the country.
Charles Moore/Black Star.

rights activist, the march drew 250,000 blacks and whites to the nation's capital. Gathered below the Lincoln Memorial, they heard from many singers and speakers, but it was King who put his indelible stamp on the day.

Moved by the intense emotions of the crowd, King departed from his formal speech, using all the passion and skills that made him the greatest orator of his day. His words came from the Bible, from Negro spirituals, and from the nation's patriotic anthems. "I have a dream," he repeated again and again, spelling out a future when "the sons of former slaves and the sons of former slave owners will be able to sit down together at the table of brotherhood." With the crowd roaring in support, he looked toward the day "when all of God's children . . . will be able to join hands and sing . . . 'Free at last, free at last; thank God Almighty, we are free at last.'"

Media and public response to the March on Washington was overwhelmingly positive, but the buoyant euphoria of that day quickly faded as activists returned to continued resistance throughout the South. The movement next launched the Mississippi Freedom Summer Project in 1964. Organized primarily by SNCC, the project mobilized more than one thousand northern college students, who paid their own expenses to conduct voter ed-

ucation classes and help blacks register to vote in Mississippi. Resistance was fierce. By the end of the summer, only twelve hundred new voters had been placed on the rolls, several people had been killed, eighty had been beaten, more than a thousand had been arrested, and thirty-five black churches had been burned.

Still the movement persisted. In January 1965, the SCLC and SNCC launched a voting drive in Selma, Alabama, where for two months local authorities met demonstrators with clubs, whips, cattle prods, and arrests. In March, Alabama troopers used such brutal force to turn back a fifty-mile march from Selma to the state capitol in Montgomery that the incident earned the name "Bloody Sunday." Hundreds of representatives from religious groups and other organizations then poured into Selma to support the demonstrators. Finally, President Johnson called up the Alabama National Guard, and the march proceeded under the guard's protection to the capitol. Before the Selma campaign was over, whites had shot or beaten to death three demonstrators.

John Lewis, chairman of SNCC and a leader of the march on Bloody Sunday, was beaten and hospitalized but managed to make the final march. Looking back on that demonstration, he recalled it as one of the most meaningful events in his life: "In

THE MARCH ON WASHINGTON
More than a quarter of a million Americans, including fifty thousand whites, gathered on the
Mall in the nation's capital on August 28, 1963, to pressure the government to support the civil
rights of African Americans. After Martin Luther King Jr. gave his "I have a dream" speech,
Malcom X said to march organizer Bayard Rustin, "You know this dream of King's is going to
be a nightmare before it's over."
James P. Blair/National Geographic Society Image Collection.

October of that year the Voting Rights bill was passed and we all felt we'd had a part of it." The black freedom struggle brought untold changes in the dignity and self-confidence of southern blacks, but for Lewis and other activists the nation's capital was the site of the first major fruits of their struggle.

The Response in Washington

Civil rights leaders would have to wear sneakers, Lyndon Johnson said, if they were going to keep up with him. But he misrepresented cause and effect in the history of civil rights. Indeed, although both Kennedy and Johnson went further than any previous president, and although Johnson's civil rights leadership far surpassed Kennedy's, both presidents acted more in response to events created by the black freedom struggle than on their own initiative.

During his first two years in office, Kennedy used the Civil Rights Act of 1957 to file voting rights suits in southern counties, and he appointed black justices to federal courts, including NAACP lawyer Thurgood Marshall to the U.S. circuit court of appeals. Yet he also appointed several segregationist justices, who would hamper civil rights enforcement in the South. Moreover, Kennedy hesitated when it came to executive action and legislation. During the campaign, Kennedy had promised to end discrimination in housing with "a stroke of the presidential pen." Not until late in 1962, after activists had sent thousands of pens to the White House, did Kennedy issue an executive order to ban discrimination in federally insured housing.

The president moved most forcefully when events in the South gave him little choice. He sent federal marshals to Montgomery to protect the Freedom Riders. In 1962, he dispatched federal troops to enable James H. Meredith, a black air force veteran, to enroll in the all-white University of Mississippi. And he called up the Alabama National

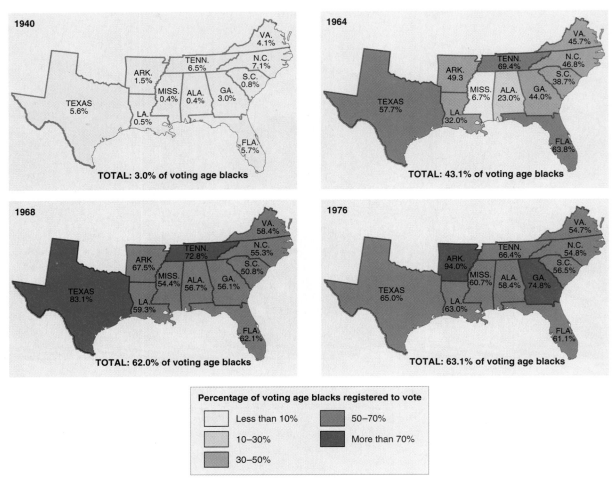

MAP 28.2
The Rise of the African American Vote, 1940–1976
Voting rates of Southern blacks increased gradually in the 1940s and 1950s, but shot up dramatically in the Deep South after the Voting Rights Act of 1965 provided for federal agents to enforce African Americans' right to vote.

Guard during the Birmingham demonstrations in May 1963. But to activists who wanted more federal protection, Kennedy replied that law enforcement was a local matter. Well aware of the political costs of deploying federal force against fellow Democrats who headed state and local governments, the president and attorney general made it clear that when they intervened it was to enforce the law, not to support the demonstrators.

Seeking to contain civil rights activism, the Kennedys frequently proposed cooling-off periods and even tried to get black leaders to call off the March on Washington, though the president did invite them to the White House after the march. In response to one of these appeals, CORE leader James Farmer pointed out that blacks had been "cooling" for a hundred years. "If we got any cooler we'd be in a deep freeze," he said.

In June 1963, the president finally made good on his campaign promise to seek legislation. In a nationally televised speech, he called civil rights "a moral issue . . . as old as the scriptures and . . . as clear as the American Constitution" and specifically supported voting rights and equal access to public schools and accommodations. Pointing to the discrimination and humiliations experienced by blacks, Kennedy asked white Americans, "Who among us would then be content with the counsels of patience and delay?"

Johnson took up Kennedy's commitment with zeal, and a number of factors assisted his efforts. Television captured the dignity and courage of African Americans and the brutal repression of southern officials. Many whites were appalled at the violence against peaceful black demonstrators, who were often on their knees in prayer. The growing public support for civil rights, the "Johnson treatment," and the president's ability to turn the measure into a memorial to the martyred Kennedy produced the Civil Rights Act of 1964.

Passed in July 1964, the Civil Rights Act guaranteed access for all Americans to public accommodations, public education, employment, and voting, thus sounding the death knell for the South's system of segregation and discrimination. Title VII of the measure, which banned discrimination in employment, also attacked racial inequality outside the South. The ability of a massive civil rights movement to sway a majority of the white population secured passage of the law. At the same time, it spotlighted Johnson's political capabilities and enabled him to cast off his sectional identity and become a genuinely national leader. Many southern whites called the first southerner in the White House since Woodrow Wilson a traitor to his race and region.

Title VII of the Civil Rights Act also prohibited sex discrimination in employment, although this provision came not from the administration but from a conservative southern representative, Howard W. Smith, an opponent of civil rights. Its adoption resulted from the efforts of Representative Martha Griffiths, a Democrat from Michigan and a women's rights advocate, intense lobbying by a tiny band of feminists, and support from southerners who hoped that including the sex provision would defeat the entire bill. Because Title VII applied not just to wages but to every aspect of employment, including hiring and promotion, it represented a giant step toward equal employment opportunity for women as well as racial minorities.

Within months after passage of the Civil Rights Act of 1964, Johnson ordered his aides to draft a new law, one that would remove "every remaining obstacle to the right and the opportunity to vote." A week after the violent Bloody Sunday in Selma, Johnson went to Congress to plead for its passage. In his televised speech, he insisted, "Should we defeat every enemy, should we double our wealth and conquer the stars" without achieving racial equality, "we will have failed as a people and as a nation." Invoking the freedom song of the movement, he concluded, "We shall overcome." The Voting Rights Act, which empowered the federal government to act directly and immediately to enable African Americans to register and vote, was signed by Johnson in August 1965. A major transformation began in southern politics. (See Historical Question, page 1120.)

THE SELMA MARCH
In 1963, the Student Nonviolent Coordinating Committee (SNCC) began a campaign for voting rights in Selma, Alabama, where white officials had registered only 335 of the 15,000 African Americans old enough to vote. As often happened, after younger activists had gotten things started, Martin Luther King Jr. came to Selma in January 1965 and made the city his primary focus. Here King leads the third — and successful — effort, begun March 21, 1965, to walk the fifty-four miles from Selma to Montgomery, the state capital. On the right is Ralph Abernathy, King's close associate.
Bob Adelman/Magnum Photos, Inc.

What Difference Did Black Voting Rights Make?

BORN TO POOR BLACK SHARECROPPERS in the Mississippi Delta, Unita Blackwell hearkened in church one Sunday in 1964 when a SNCC worker talked about voter registration. The very next day she went to the courthouse where, predictably, officials refused her application. Undeterred, she succeeded on the third try, threw herself into activism as a SNCC organizer, and saw her share of jail cells. In fact, she and her husband planned their protest activities so that only one would risk arrest and the other would remain free to care for their child. A founder of the Mississippi Freedom Democratic Party, which was established to challenge the all-white state organization, Blackwell saw the challenge compromised away at the 1964 Democratic national convention. But four years later, she participated in the national convention with Mississippi's reconfigured biracial delegation. Subsequently, she served as vice chair of the state Democratic Party and on the Democratic National Committee. When her small town of Mayersville incorporated in 1976, Blackwell won election as its first mayor and the first black female mayor in Mississippi.

Blackwell's career is but one measure of the transformations generated by African Americans' struggle for the most basic right of citizenship. Their determination to register to vote and the resulting resistance and violence of southern whites created a crisis that the federal government could not ignore. Its response, the Voting Rights Act of 1965 and subsequent extensions, suspended the literacy tests that had been used to disqualify blacks but not whites, and brought electoral operations in most southern states under federal supervision. The law required the Justice Department to approve in advance any changes in state procedures that might disadvantage black voters, and it empowered the attorney general to send federal agents to observe registration and election processes and even to register voters in areas of continued white resistance.

"Legislation is not self-implementing," noted NAACP leader Roy Wilkins. "There is work to be done." As was the case with its passage, implementation of the Voting Rights Act depended on the efforts of African Americans themselves. More than two hundred voter registration drives between 1966 and 1968 paid off in dramatic increases in the numbers of blacks registered. Throughout the South, the proportion of African Americans on voter rolls jumped from 43 percent in 1964 to 62 percent in 1968. In Mississippi, the percentage leaped from just 6.7 in 1964 to 68 percent in 1968.

African Americans also gained political offices in unprecedented numbers. Fewer than two dozen blacks held elective office in the South in 1964. In 1970, they claimed almost five hundred elected government posts, and two years later the number reached nearly twelve hundred. Just seven years after whites bludgeoned civil rights activists during the Selma voting drive, black candidates won half of the ten seats on Selma's city council. With the victories of Barbara Jordan from Houston, Texas, and Andrew Young from Atlanta, Georgia, in 1972, the former Confederacy sent its first African Americans to the House of Representatives since Reconstruction. Black electoral success was not limited to the South. Across the nation, African Americans held fifteen hundred elected positions in 1970, and by 1990 that number exceeded seven thousand. The total of black representatives in Congress inched up from ten in 1970 to twenty-five in 1990 and then soared to thirty-eight in the 1992 elections.

The greatest progress came at the local level. The number of black mayors grew sixfold to more than 300 in the 1990s; the number of black city council members vaulted from 552 in 1970 to nearly 3,000 in 1989. Electoral success translated into tangible benefits. When black officials took office, their constituents saw improvements in public facilities, police protection, roads, trash collection, and other basic services. Referring to Unita Blackwell's accomplishments as mayor, a Mayersville resident noted, "She brought in the water tower. Mostly it was pumps then. . . . Sewage, too. There wasn't nothing but those little old outdoor houses." Another constituent pointed to "old folks' houses. And paved streets. I grew up here when they wasn't paved." Black local officials also awarded more gov-

ernment jobs to African Americans and contracts to minority businesses. Elected mayor of Atlanta in 1973, Maynard Jackson appointed a black police chief and increased blacks' share of city jobs from 42 percent to 51 percent.

Most black officials had far less power than Jackson, but even when they were outnumbered by whites, their mere presence on local governing bodies paid dividends. They could at least introduce issues of concern to blacks that whites had ignored, and they gained access to information about behind-the-scenes government. An African American serving on a city council in Florida pointed out that "no matter what happened," his white colleagues "knew I was listening to everything that went on." Activist Fannie Lou Hamer noted the psychological benefits of electoral progress. When blacks had no political voice, she recalled, "some white folks would drive past your house in a pickup truck with guns hanging up on the back and give you hate stares. . . . Those same people now call me Mrs. Hamer."

Yet political power did not readily guarantee African Americans economic equality or even ma-

terial security. Their minority status in the population and residential dispersion, combined with many whites' disinclination to vote for blacks, meant that even by the 1990s, African Americans occupied fewer than 2 percent of all elected positions in the nation. As African Americans looked to increase their political force and shape policy to meet their needs, they recognized that they would have to revive grassroots activism and seek coalitions with nonblacks. In addition they considered a number of electoral strategies to solidify black and minority strength in a majoritarian system: reducing the number of at-large elections, which dilute minorities' power, and increasing the number of single-member district systems; monitoring electoral redistricting to ensure as many black-majority districts as possible; and proportionate or cumulative voting.

Despite the limited reach of black enfranchisement, most experts nonetheless view the voting rights revolution as the most successful of all civil rights initiatives. As Unita Blackwell put it, "We didn't have nothing, and we changed the whole world with nothing. We changed a whole outlook."

Johnson had also pronounced the need "to move beyond opportunity to achievement," to achieve "not just equality as a right and theory, but equality as fact and as result." To this end, he used his authority as president to issue Executive Order 11246 in September 1965. Not only did that order ban discrimination by employers holding government contracts (affecting about one-third of the labor force), but it also required them to take affirmative action to ensure equal opportunity.

Extended to cover women in 1967, the affirmative action program provoked more controversy than any of the civil rights measures. Calling it "reverse discrimination," many people thought—incorrectly—that affirmative action required absolute quotas for hiring minorities and women or that it required hiring or promoting unqualified candidates. In fact, the order sought to overcome the effects of centuries of discrimination by requiring employers not just to stop discriminating but to act forcefully to bring the composition of their labor force into line with the available pool of qualified candidates. Despite its controversial nature, affirmative action withstood attacks until the 1990s and came to be seen as a good employment practice by most large businesses.

Johnson's final effort to reconcile the actuality of race relations with the nation's vision of itself was the Civil Rights Act of 1968. That measure banned racial discrimination in housing—the most controversial provision—and in jury selection, and it empowered the federal government to intervene to protect civil rights workers from violence.

Like Kennedy, Johnson tried, unsuccessfully, to keep the movement from getting ahead of him. Johnson sided with Democratic mayors, such as Richard J. Daley in Chicago, when Martin Luther King Jr. and others began to attack discrimination in housing, education, and employment outside the South. Moreover, under Johnson the FBI continued the wiretapping and electronic surveillance of King that had begun under Kennedy and expanded its activities to "expose, disrupt, misdirect, discredit, or otherwise neutralize" the activities of militant black protest organizations.

The three civil rights measures of the 1960s formed the most important legal gains for African Americans since Reconstruction and constituted Johnson's most far-reaching contributions to domestic reform. Yet the progress failed to match the rising aspirations of African Americans or to satisfy the needs of blacks that antidiscrimination measures in themselves could not address. As the cry

for racial equality moved outside the South and intensified in militancy, the president most committed to promoting civil rights became the object of bitter criticism from a large segment of the black freedom movement.

Black Nationalism and the End of the Civil Rights Coalition

By 1966, the black freedom struggle had undergone dramatic changes. Initially focused on the South, the movement sought integration and legal equality, and activists assumed that blacks and whites could work together through nonviolent direct action to change the hearts and behavior of white oppressors. By 1966, movement leaders' attention encompassed racial oppression throughout the nation; their goals had broadened to eliminate the poverty and miserable living conditions that defined the lives of millions of African Americans; and many activists had given up both on white allies and the tactics of nonviolence.

In part the new emphases resulted from the very success of civil rights legislation, as one layer of oppression receded only to reveal others more subtle but just as pervasive. Civil rights leaders knew that equal access to public facilities and institutions did little to improve the material conditions of blacks throughout the country. What did it matter that African Americans had the freedom to patronize a restaurant if they could not afford the price of a meal?

King himself realized that racism reached beyond the South, even though northern whites liked to think otherwise. In 1965, he moved his campaign north, and the SCLC mounted a drive for better jobs, schools, and housing in Chicago. King also pressed the government for more adequate funding of the antipoverty program and initiated plans for a Poor People's March to the nation's capital in 1968. Yet even as his goals changed, King clung to the principle of nonviolence and attempted to work with white supporters and government officials. For this he came increasingly under criticism from activists in CORE and SNCC.

African Americans suffering the daily terror associated with civil rights activism in southern communities deplored the federal government's failure to protect them from violence. Their disillusionment with white allies increased even as hundreds of white students came to organize in Mississippi in 1964. Black organizers felt that white students too often tried to run things, and they doubted the commitment of students who would return to lives of ease and security at the end of the summer. The Democratic Party's rejection of the black-based Mississippi Freedom Democratic Party at the 1964 convention intensified skepticism about playing by the rules. Expressing the black delegates' bitter disillusionment over the sellout by white liberals, Fannie Lou Hamer declared, "We didn't come all this way for no two votes."

In the North, a powerful voice rose to challenge the dominant ethos of the civil rights movement. Malcolm Little had grown up in poverty, first in Nebraska and then in Michigan. His father, a supporter of Marcus Garvey's pan-Africanism, was harassed

MALCOLM X

Malcolm X addresses a Black Muslim rally in New York City on July 1963. The name of the newspaper he displays refers to the organization's leader, Elijah Muhammad, who had headed the Nation of Islam since 1934. In 1964, Malcolm broke with the leader. He did not abandon black nationalism and continued to urge radical change, but he no longer equated whites with the devil. "The white man is not inherently evil," he said, "but America's racist society influences him to act evilly."
Wide World.

by the Ku Klux Klan and died after whites pushed him under a streetcar. Convicted of attempted burglary at the age of twenty-one, Malcolm Little went to prison, where he educated himself and converted to the Nation of Islam, whose adherents were called Black Muslims. The Nation drew on a long African American tradition of nationalism and separatism.

Released from jail in 1952, Malcolm Little changed his name to Malcolm X, to symbolize the African identity stripped from his ancestors, and went to work for the Nation of Islam. He attracted a large following, especially in urban ghettos, to his doctrine of separation from the "corrupt [white] society," black pride and autonomy, and self-defense against white violence. In 1964, Malcolm broke from the Black Muslims, began to cultivate a wider constituency, and expressed an openness to working with whites. At a Harlem rally in February 1965, three members of the Nation of Islam shot and killed him. Yet his ideas outlived his death and began to resonate in CORE and SNCC.

Black rage and impatience with legal changes erupted into a wave of riots that ignited cities in the North, Midwest, and West every summer from 1964 to 1968. Usually sparked by an incident between white police and local blacks, the most intense of these riots involved thousands of people who battled with the police, burned buildings, and looted stores. The Watts district of Los Angeles in 1965, Newark and Detroit in 1967, and the nation's capital in 1968 saw the most destruction and violence, but hundreds of other eruptions occurred across the country. In Detroit, rioters swept through fourteen square miles of the black ghetto; the result was 43 deaths, 7,000 arrests, 1,300 destroyed buildings, and 2,700 shops looted. Surveying the carnage, Detroit's mayor remarked, "It looks like Berlin in 1945."

Rioters exhibited pride and exhilaration in their new defiance and sense of power, however fleeting. They generally remained in African American neighborhoods and tried to avoid damaging black-owned and public buildings, saving their rage for white businesses and local police. "Our nation is moving toward two societies, one black, one white —separate and unequal," warned an investigating commission appointed by President Johnson in 1967. But Johnson ignored the commission's recommendations for a more vigorous campaign against racism and poverty, and little was done to ameliorate the basic conditions from which the riots sprang.

Revealing the intensity of black discontent, the rebellions suggested to some activists the potential for a more militant assault on racism. At a rally in Greenwood, Mississippi, in June 1966, SNCC chairman Stokely Carmichael gave that new approach a name. Using slang that belied his university education, Carmichael asserted, "This is the twenty-seventh time I have been arrested—I ain't going to jail no more." Then he shouted, "We want black power!" again and again as the audience cheered and called back the words. "Black power" quickly became the rallying cry in SNCC and CORE. Though embraced by only a minority of African Americans, the black power movement claimed the lion's share of national attention in the late 1960s.

Activists issued no single systematic definition of black power, but the words and deeds of Carmichael and other leading exponents delineated its major elements. Black power meant separation from whites. Carmichael called integration "a subterfuge for the maintenance of white supremacy." Working with white liberals perpetuated "a paternalistic, colonial relationship."

The black power movement rejected assimilation into the dominant society because that implied the superiority of white institutions and values. The phrase "Black is beautiful" emphasized the authenticity and worth of African American culture and racial pride. African Americans were encouraged to develop independent businesses and control their own schools and other community institutions. They were also encouraged to form their own all-black political organizations, such as the Black Panther Party, founded in Oakland, California, in 1966 to combat police brutality.

To black power advocates, nonviolence only brought more beatings and killings. Malcolm X had said, "If someone puts a hand on you, send him to the cemetery." Carmichael agreed: "Black people should and must fight back." The press paid an inordinate amount of attention to black radicals, and the black power movement sparked a severe white backlash. Some black power advocates, including Carmichael, H. Rap Brown, and Eldridge Cleaver, carried guns and openly called for black insurrection. Although the urban riots erupted spontaneously, triggered by specific incidents, horrified whites blamed them on black power militants. By 1966, a full 85 percent of the white population thought that blacks were pressing for too much too quickly; two years earlier, only 34 percent had thought so.

King agreed with black power advocates about the need for "a radical reconstruction of society" but clung to nonviolence and integration as the means

to this end. In March 1968, the thirty-nine-year-old leader took his movement to Memphis to support a strike of municipal garbage workers, most of whom were black. There, on April 4, King was shot and killed while standing on the balcony of his motel. James Earl Ray, an escaped white convict, was arrested and confessed to the murder but later denied that he had killed King and insisted that he was a scapegoat for a wider conspiracy.

Black power advocates receded from national visibility by the end of the decade. Never able to command substantial support in the African American community, which revered King and his philosophy, black militants were harassed by the FBI, jailed, and sometimes killed by the police, whom they also sometimes killed. Black nationalism's emphasis on black pride and black culture and its critique of American institutions, however, resonated broadly and helped to shape the protest of other groups.

Demands for Power to the People

Beyond its impact on the lives and status of African Americans, the black freedom struggle encouraged a multitude of movements that fueled social change in the 1960s. With its incontrovertible moral claims, the civil rights movement helped to make protest respectable, and its ability to capture national attention and move the federal government suggested possibilities for other groups with grievances. College students, opponents of the war in Vietnam, women, Native Americans, Mexican Americans, and other minority groups all drew in some measure on the black freedom struggle for inspiration, models of protest, and critiques of American institutions. These groups became more militant, engaging in direct action protests, expressing their own cultural nationalism, and challenging existing institutions and values.

Native American Protest

Protest was not new to the group with the oldest grievances, but Native American activism took on new militancy and goals in the 1960s. The cry "red power" reflected the influence of black radicalism on Native Americans who rejected the goal of assimilation into the mainstream. As one Indian put

THE AMERICAN INDIAN MOVEMENT
Dennis Banks (right), a Chippewa who had served in the U.S. air force, was a founder and leader of the American Indian Movement (AIM). Russell Means, a Sioux born on the Pine Ridge reservation, joined AIM in 1969. This photo was taken in 1973 when Banks and Means led an occupation of Wounded Knee, a part of the Pine Ridge reservation where the army had massacred the Sioux in 1890. The two-month stand by two hundred occupiers, during which the Indians and federal agents exchanged gunfire that killed two Indians, produced no substantive reforms but called attention to the plight of Native Americans. Wide World.

it, the civil rights struggle led by King "was within the System, and the System had nothing to do with Indians." Rather, American Indians sought tribal sovereignty and just treatment as independent nations.

College students, opponents of the war in Vietnam, women, Native Americans, Mexican Americans, and other minority groups all drew in some measure on the black freedom struggle for inspiration.

In 1963, Northwest Indians mounted "fish-ins" to enforce fishing rights that were guaranteed by century-old treaties. Elsewhere, Native Americans demonstrated and occupied territory and public buildings, claiming rights to natural resources and lands that they had owned collectively before European settlement. A new, more militant generation participated in these demonstrations through the National Indian Youth Council, founded in 1961. In the most dramatic action, Indians seized Alcatraz Island in San Francisco Bay and used it as a cultural and educational center from 1969 until the federal government ran them out in 1971.

"The American Indian Movement hit our [Lakota Sioux] reservation like a tornado," recalled Mary Crow Dog. Two Chippewa, Russell Banks and George Mitchell, founded the American Indian Movement (AIM) in 1968 in Minneapolis initially to deal with problems in cities, where about 300,000 Indians lived. AIM focused on Native Americans encouraged or forced by the relocation and termination programs of the 1950s to migrate to urban areas only to find unemployment, poverty, and alienation from their traditions. In addition to protecting Indians from police harassment and securing antipoverty program funds for Indian-controlled organizations, AIM chapters established "survival schools" where children were educated in the history and values of their own culture.

The appeal of AIM spread beyond urban areas, electrifying Native Americans like Mary Crow Dog. When AIM members first visited her reservation in South Dakota, it "loosened a sort of earthquake inside me," she later wrote. The AIM people "had a new look about them, not that hangdog reservation look I was used to." The militant tactics of AIM and other radical groups rarely achieved their goals, but—in addition to stirring Native American self-respect—they helped sensitize Americans to Indian grievances and fostered more moderate aims.

CHICANO POWER
This mural in Los Angeles with symbols used by Chicano activists illustrates Mexican American pride.
Craig Aurness/Woodfin Camp.

Native American protest won more responsiveness from the Bureau of Indian Affairs, legislation to meet educational and health needs of Indians, and government decisions recognizing Indian rights to ancestral lands. Taos Indians, for example, regained sacred lands in New Mexico, and the government paid the Sioux more than $100 million for lands that were taken when gold was discovered there in the nineteenth century. Native Americans recovered a measure of identity and pride, a greater respect for and protection of their culture, and, in the words of President Johnson's special message to Congress in 1968, a recognition of "the right of the First Americans to remain Indians while exercising their rights as Americans."

Hispanic American Struggles for Justice

The fastest-growing minority group in the 1960s was Hispanic Americans, people of Mexican, Puerto Rican, Caribbean, and other Spanish-speaking origins. Hispanics of Puerto Rican and Caribbean descent tended to live in urban areas on the East Coast. But the largest group, comprising more than half of the Hispanic population of the United States, was some six million Mexican Americans, who were concentrated in California, Texas, Arizona, New Mexico, and Colorado. In addition, thousands of immigrants illegally crossed the unguarded two-thousand-mile border between Mexico and the United States in search of economic betterment.

Throughout the twentieth century, Mexican Americans had formed local and national organizations to push for political power and economic rights. But, as was true among African Americans and Native Americans in the 1960s, young Hispanics increasingly rejected the traditional politics practiced by their elders in favor of militant strategies of direct action. One symbol of this generational challenge was the adoption of the name "Chicano" by young Mexican American activists.

The first organizing among Chicanos that gained national attention occurred in California, where migrant workers endured wretched living and working conditions as they followed the harvests of fruits and vegetables around the state. In 1963, Cesar Chavez organized the United Farm Workers Association (UFW) to improve conditions for Chicanos through union representation. UFW marches and strikes gained widespread support, and a national boycott of California grapes helped the UFW to win union recognition and a wage increase in 1970.

Chicanos mobilized elsewhere to end employment and educational discrimination, win their share of antipoverty funds, and combat police brutality. Starting in East Los Angeles in 1968 and spreading through the Southwest, a series of strikes, called "Blow Outs," among thousands of high school students protested the racism experienced by Mexican Americans in the public schools. In Denver, Rodolfo "Corky" Gonzales organized the Crusade for Justice, setting up "freedom schools," where Chicano children learned Spanish and studied Mexican American history and culture and marched down the halls chanting, "Chicano power." The separatist and nationalist strains of Chicano protest were evident in La Raza Unida (the United Race), a third party founded by José Angel Gutierrez in Texas and based on cultural pride and brotherhood.

Mexican Americans gradually won greater representation in government and more effective enforcement of antidiscrimination legislation. With blacks and Native Americans, they continued to be overrepresented among the poor but gained a sense of their potential power and respect for their culture through such programs as bilingual education in the schools and Chicano studies programs.

Student Rebellion and the New Left

Connections between civil rights and other protest movements appeared direct and immediate, as white activists returned from civil rights projects in the South to organize student protests, the antiwar movement, and the new feminist movement. Their confrontation with extreme racism and their disillusionment with the federal government radicalized and sensitized them more deeply to injustice. They also developed greater self-confidence and learned new tactics.

Tom Hayden's first meeting with SNCC activists in the fall of 1960 "was a key turning point, the moment my political identity began to take shape." He became involved with Students for a

Democratic Society (SDS), a small group of whites formed in 1960 from the remains of an older socialist-oriented student organization. In 1961, Hayden went south, where he was beaten and jailed while working with SNCC in Georgia. In 1962, he played a key role in defining the purpose and structure of SDS, which soon became the organizational focus of white student protest in the 1960s.

Idealistic students criticized the complacency of their elders, the remoteness of decision makers from the will of the people, and the powerlessness and alienation that people experienced in a society run by large, impersonal bureaucratic institutions.

The Port Huron Statement, named for the site in Michigan where about sixty student leaders and a few older activists met, articulated SDS's principles. "We are people of this generation, bred in at least modest comfort, housed now in universities, looking uncomfortably at the world we inherit," the statement began. The idealistic students criticized the complacency of their elders, the remoteness of decision makers from the will of the people, and the powerlessness and alienation that people experienced in a society run by large, impersonal bureaucratic institutions.

SDS aimed to mobilize a new social movement, called the New Left, with civil rights, peace, and universal economic security as its major targets. Both the means and ends of change were to be a "participatory democracy" in which each individual would "share in those social decisions determining the quality and direction of his life." SDS remained small until 1965, but other forms of student activism soon followed in its wake.

The first large-scale white student protest arose in the Free Speech movement at the University of California at Berkeley in the fall of 1964, when university officials banned student organizations from a campus site where they had set up tables to recruit support for civil rights and other causes. Led by Mario Savio and other whites who had worked for civil rights in the South, the students claimed the right to freedom of expression and political action. They occupied the administration building and confronted police in their attempts to disobey the ban. More than seven hundred students were arrested before they got the California Board of Regents to overturn the new restrictions.

Hundreds of student rebellions followed. Opposition to the Vietnam War activated the largest number of students, who marched, rallied, and occupied buildings in protest against universities' activities linked to the war. But they did not stop there. Attacking the impersonality of universities and their unresponsiveness to students' needs, protesters issued a broad range of demands, including curricular reforms, more financial aid for minority and poor students, independence from paternalistic rules over their lives outside the classroom, the freedom to hear controversial speakers on campus, and a larger voice in campus decision making.

Student protest spread from large universities and elite institutions to small colleges and religious schools. It ranged far beyond SDS, which exercised virtually no control over its local chapters. According to surveys taken in 1967 and 1968, more than 140,000 students (about 2 percent of the college population) were affiliated with SDS, and nearly 13 percent identified themselves as radicals. In addition to its contributions to the antiwar movement, student insurgency also brought about changes ranging from new black, Chicano, and women's studies programs to coed dormitories.

Student rebels came from the "baby boom" generation that swelled enrollments in higher education in the 1960s and gave young people a sense of power and generational solidarity. Most white students came from middle- and upper-class families. Materially secure and free of the immediate need to provide for themselves, they enjoyed the luxury of attacking the very system that made their rebellion possible. Such conduct bewildered and angered older Americans, who were equally shocked by a growing revolt against nearly every conventional standard of behavior.

The Counterculture

By 1967, national media had begun to take notice of another revolution that was under way. Growing up alongside the New Left and student movements and often overlapping them, the counterculture drew on the ideas and behavior of the Beats of the 1950s. Although many young people were both cultural and political rebels, the cultural revolution focused on personal rather than political and institutional change.

Cultural radicals, or "hippies," as they were called, scorned mainstream norms that valued the work ethic, material possessions, rationality, order, and sexual control. The phrase "Do your own thing" expressed their belief in spontaneity, living for the moment, and distrust of all authority. Hippies stood out with their long hair and unusual, wildly colorful and often ragged clothing, including tie-dyed and Indian fabrics, jeans, beads, and sandals, when they wore shoes at all. The Haight-Ashbury district of San Francisco harbored the most widely known hippy community, but thousands of cultural radicals established communes in cities or on farms, where they renounced the concept of private property and shared everything, often including sex partners. Seeking heightened perceptions and freedom from all inhibitions, they replaced the alcohol, nicotine, and tranquilizers of their elders with illegal drugs such as marijuana and experimental drugs like the new hallucinogenic drug LSD (lysergic acid diethylamide), unaware of its harmful effects.

Rock music played a central role in both the counterculture and the political left. English groups such as the Beatles and the Rolling Stones and homegrown products including Bob Dylan, Janis Joplin, the Jefferson Airplane, and Jerry Garcia's Grateful Dead took American youth by storm. Rock music shared with rock and roll the sensual, pulsating beat that had thrilled young people in the 1950s. Lyrics encouraged drugs—"I'd love to turn you on"—and spontaneous sex—"Why don't we do it in the road."

But the 1960s music often carried insurgent political and social messages. "Eve of Destruction," a top hit of 1965, despaired of the violence around the world and the threat of nuclear annihilation—"There'll be no one to save with the world in a grave"—and reminded young men, "You're old enough to kill but not for votin'." Other popular songs derided authority, touted the mind-expanding thrills of marijuana and LSD, celebrated sexual freedom, and called for peace, love, and revolution.

Although cultural rebels remained a small minority, many elements of the counterculture—from rock music to jeans and long hair—filtered into the mainstream. Sexual relations outside marriage and tolerant attitudes about sexual morality increased to such an extent that experts proclaimed a "sexual revolution." Self-fulfillment became a dominant concern of many Americans, and questioning of government and other authority became much more widespread. Even though the counterculture was just one of several forces promoting changes in American society, it continued to influence American society after the hippies faded away in the early 1970s.

WOODSTOCK

The Woodstock Music Festival, held on a farm near Bethel, New York, in August 1969, featured the greatest rock and folk musicians of the era and epitomized the values and hopes of the counterculture. Despite terrible conditions created by bad weather and the failure of festival organizers to plan for so many people, the youthful crowd of 400,000 created a loving, peaceful community for three days filled with music, sex, and drugs.

Image Works.

Beginnings of a Feminist Movement

Both the civil rights struggle and the New Left served as inspiration and models for a new women's movement. The ban against sex discrimination in the Civil Rights Act of 1964 and President Johnson's executive order extending affirmative action to women reflected feminists' efforts to "piggyback" onto civil rights measures. The new laws raised women's expectations, and feminists grew impatient when the government moved slowly against sex discrimination in employment. Deciding that they needed a "civil rights organization for women," Betty Friedan and others founded the National Organization for Women (NOW) in 1966.

A more radical wing of the new feminism grew out of young women's activism in civil rights and the New Left. In SNCC and SDS, women absorbed the values of self-determination and individual worth but faced significant barriers to the full use of their talents, quickly grasping a contradiction between the ideal of equality and the actual status of women. Two white women, Mary King and Casey Hayden, first raised the issue in SNCC in 1964, and in 1965 they began circulating their ideas to women who were active in SDS and other New Left groups.

King and Hayden pointed out that, like blacks, women "seem[ed] to be caught up in a common-law caste system . . . forcing them to work around or outside hierarchical structures of power which may exclude them." Women, they contended, were also exploited and subordinated in personal relations. The 1965 memo struck a responsive chord among white activist women, but the chief response from male radicals was indifference or ridicule. Consequently, feminists moved to form an independent women's liberation movement.

FEMINISTS PICKET THE MISS AMERICA PAGEANT
These picketers were among the feminists who demonstrated at the Miss America pageant at Atlantic City, New Jersey, in 1968. They protested society's conditioning of women "to compete for male approval, enslaved by ludicrous 'beauty' standards." They set up a "freedom trash can" and invited women to throw away their "bras, girdles, curlers, false eyelashes, wigs, and Cosmopolitan." And they decorated a live sheep with ribbons and crowned it Miss America. Wide World.

By the end of the 1960s, radical women had established women's liberation groups in Chicago, New York, Boston, New Orleans, and elsewhere across the nation. They translated black pride into pride of womanhood, and they implemented the "participatory democracy" of SDS in all their activities. Staging marches, sit-ins, and other demonstrations, they began to gain public attention, especially when in 1968, one hundred demonstrators picketed the Miss America beauty pageant, throwing girdles, bras, and hair curlers into a "freedom trash can" in protest against being forced "to compete for male approval, enslaved by ludicrous 'beauty' standards." Activism by radicals and more moderate feminists surged into a mass movement that dramatically changed public policy and popular attitudes in the 1970s.

The Judicial Revolution

For more than a decade, beginning with the *Brown* school desegregation decision in 1954, the Supreme Court under Chief Justice Earl Warren (presiding from 1953 to 1969) spearheaded another form of change. During the 1960s, Eisenhower referred to the appointment of Warren as "the biggest damn-fool mistake I ever made." Eisenhower was especially upset with Court decisions on the rights of Communists and criminals. Other critics charged the Warren Court with usurping power from the states, the president, and Congress. Liberal supporters praised the Court for infusing new life into the Bill of Rights and serving as the nation's conscience.

In articulating the rights of disadvantaged groups, Supreme Court decisions in the 1950s and 1960s departed from judicial tradition and often got out ahead of legislators' sentiment and public opinion. Upsetting customary practices in race relations, personal liberty and privacy, criminal justice, political representation, and religion, the Warren Court's rulings protected the constitutional rights of marginal and powerless Americans—minorities, the poor and uneducated, and political dissenters.

Civil Rights and Voting Rights

Following the pathbreaking *Brown* decision, the Warren Court ruled against all-white public facilities in a number of cities and states and struck down educational plans devised by southern states to avoid integrating their schools. Moreover, by upholding the constitutional rights of African Americans to freedom of assembly and freedom of speech, the Court enabled the black freedom struggle to continue sit-ins, mass marches, and other civil disobedience tactics that were so critical to its success.

Upsetting customary practices in race relations, personal liberty and privacy, criminal justice, political representation, and religion, the Warren Court's rulings protected the constitutional rights of marginal and powerless Americans.

Chief Justice Earl Warren considered *Baker v. Carr* (1963) the most important decision of his sixteen-year tenure. This case grew out of a complaint that Tennessee electoral districts were so inequitably drawn that sparsely populated rural districts had far more representatives in the state legislature than did densely populated metropolitan areas. Other states had also failed to redraw voting districts to reflect growing urban populations, thereby exaggerating the influence of rural interests. Congressional districts were less badly apportioned, but in some states they too diluted the power of urban and suburban voters in favor of rural constituents.

Grounding its decisions on the Fourteenth Amendment guarantee of "equal protection of the laws" in *Baker* and companion cases, the Court established the principle of "one person, one vote" for

both houses of state legislatures and for the House of Representatives. Requiring most states to redraw electoral districts, the "one person, one vote" rulings helped to revitalize state legislatures and make them more responsive to metropolitan interests and problems. The decisions struck at entrenched power bases, and many politicians denounced them as unwarranted judicial intervention in political matters.

Criminal Justice

The egalitarian thrust of the Warren Court also touched the criminal justice system. Between 1957 and 1967, the Court overturned a series of convictions on the grounds that the accused individuals had been deprived of "life, liberty, or property, without due process of law" and thus had been denied their rights under the Fourteenth Amendment. Furthermore, the Court interpreted that amendment to prevent the states as well as the federal government from violations of the Bill of Rights. These rulings dramatically reformed law enforcement practices and the treatment of individuals accused of crime. As one plaintiff, Clarence Gideon, remarked, "I didn't start out to do anything for anybody but myself, but this decision has done a helluva lot of good."

In the case he initiated, *Gideon v. Wainright* (1963), the Court ruled that states must provide lawyers to poor people accused of serious crime who cannot afford to pay lawyers themselves. In *Escobedo v. Illinois* (1964), the justices extended the right to counsel to the period when suspects are being questioned by police officers. Two years later, in *Miranda v. Arizona*, the Court issued general guidelines requiring officers to inform suspects that they may remain silent, that anything they say can be used against them, and that they are entitled to a lawyer.

The Court established additional guidelines that law enforcement officials must follow in obtaining evidence. In a series of cases, it overturned convictions resulting from evidence obtained by unlawful arrest, by wiretapping and other kinds of electronic surveillance, and by entering property without a search warrant. These decisions pressured police officials to pay careful attention to suspects' rights, since evidence that was obtained illegally could not be used in court.

Critics accused the Supreme Court of letting criminals go free (Escobedo, in fact, ran afoul of the law soon after his release) and obstructing law enforcement. Liberals, however, argued that these rulings promoted equal treatment in the criminal justice system: The wealthy always had access to legal counsel, and practiced criminals were well aware of their right to remain silent. The beneficiaries of the decisions were the poor, the ignorant, and the weak as well as the general population whose right to privacy was strengthened by the Court's stricter guidelines for admissible evidence.

Dissent and Religious Issues

The Warren Court also strengthened protections for individuals suspected of being Communists or subversives. For example, it set limits on the states and federal government in investigating and prosecuting suspected subversives and prevented state bar associations from denying membership to those suspected of having Communist associations. Like the criminal justice cases, these rulings guaranteed the rights of people on the margins of American society and reaped their share of criticism.

The Warren Court's decisions on prayer and Bible reading in the public schools provoked even greater outrage. In *Abington School District v. Schempp* (1963), the Court overturned a Pennsylvania law requiring Bible reading and recitation of the Lord's Prayer at the beginning of the schoolday. Such a law, it ruled, violated the First Amendment principle of separation of church and state. Later decisions ruled out prayer in public schools even if students were not required to participate. An outraged Alabama legislator fumed, "They put Negroes in the schools and now they've driven God out." The Court's supporters, however, declared that the religion cases protected the rights of non-Christians and atheists.

Two or three justices, who believed that the Court was overstepping its authority, often issued sharp dissents in decisions on voting rights, criminal rights, and other cases. Outside the Court, opponents worked to pass laws or constitutional amendments that would upset despised decisions, legal experts pleaded for the Court to exercise judicial restraint, and billboards demanded, "Impeach Earl Warren." Nonetheless, the Court's major decisions withstood Warren's retirement in 1969 and the test of time.

The innovations of the Supreme Court in the 1950s and 1960s constituted a watershed in domestic policymaking. In expanding the Constitution's promise of equality and protection of individual rights, the Court shifted power from the states to the judicial branch of the federal government. The Warren Court recast the Constitution from a document concerned primarily with restricting injustices by government to one requiring the government to act to prevent injustice and discrimination.

Conclusion: Achievements and Limitations of 1960s Liberalism

Surveying the record of the Johnson administration, Senate majority leader Mike Mansfield concluded that the president "has outstripped Roosevelt. . . . He has done more than FDR ever did, or ever thought of doing." Yet opposition to his leadership grew so strong by 1968 that Johnson abandoned hopes for reelection. As his liberal vision lay in ruins, he asked, "How was it possible that all these people could be so ungrateful to me after I have given them so much?"

The egomania reflected in that question was but one of several factors that contributed to Johnson's demise and the waning of Democratic liberalism. Inadequately planned and funded, many of the antipoverty programs ended up benefiting particular industries and the nonpoor as much as or more than they helped the impoverished. Because Johnson refused to ask for sacrifices from prosperous Americans, the Great Society never approached the redistribution of wealth and resources that would have been necessary for the elimination of poverty.

Black aspirations exceeded white Americans' commitment to genuine equality. It was easy for nonsoutherners to be sympathetic (and self-righteous) when a civil rights movement focused on crude and blatant forms of racism in the South. But when the movement attacked the subtler forms of racism that existed throughout the nation and sought equality in fact as well as in rights, the black freedom struggle confronted a powerful backlash.

Most surprising was the opposition to liberalism from the left. Radicalized by the black freedom struggle, a small but vocal minority of whites and blacks emphasized the shortcomings of the Great Society and questioned whether real reform could be achieved within the framework of traditional American institutions and values. Young radicals engaged in direct confrontations with the government and the universities that, together with racial conflict, escalated into political discord and social disorder not seen since the union wars of the 1930s.

The war in Vietnam polarized American society as much as did the question of race or the behavior of young people. Johnson's conduct of the war undermined faith in his leadership, as his darker side—his arrogance, vindictiveness, secrecy, and carelessness with the truth—manifested itself apace with the growing opposition to the war. The war starved the Great Society, devouring revenues that might have been used for social reform. Vietnam not only cut short the promise of reform; it also eclipsed the substantial progress that had actually been achieved.

CHRONOLOGY

1960 African American college students in Greensboro, North Carolina, stage sit-in at whites-only lunch counter.

John F. Kennedy elected president of United States.

Student Nonviolent Coordinating Committee (SNCC) established to mobilize young people for direct action for civil rights.

Students for a Democratic Society (SDS) founded.

1961 Congress of Racial Equality (CORE) sponsors Freedom Rides to desegregate interstate transportation in South.

President Kennedy establishes President's Commission on the Status of Women.

1963 *Baker v. Carr* mandates electoral redistricting to enforce "one-person, one-vote" principle.

Betty Friedan's best-selling book *The Feminine Mystique* published.

Equal Pay Act makes wage disparities based solely on gender illegal.

Mississippi NAACP leader Medgar Evers assassinated in Jackson.

Bayard Rustin organizes March on Washington, largest civil rights demonstration in U.S. history.

President's Commission on the Status of Women issues report detailing widespread discrimination against women.

President Kennedy assassinated in Dallas, Texas; Vice President Lyndon B. Johnson becomes president.

Cesar Chavez founds United Farm Workers Association (UFW).

1964 Congress enacts Civil Rights Act of 1964, the strongest such measure since Reconstruction.

Economic Opportunity Act passed.

Free Speech movement, first large-scale white student protest of 1960s, organized at University of California at Berkeley.

Malcolm X breaks from Nation of Islam and attracts wide following with his message of black pride and autonomy.

President Johnson elected to a full term in landslide over Republican Senator Barry Goldwater.

Tax cut bill proposed by Kennedy administration passed.

1965 Malcolm X assassinated in New York City.

Selma-to-Montgomery march for voting rights takes place; Johnson orders federal protection for marchers after they are attacked.

Congress passes Voting Rights Act.

1965– 89th Congress passes most of Johnson's
1966 Great Society domestic programs, including antipoverty measures, public works acts, aid to education, and Medicare-Medicaid.

1966 Black Panther Party founded, advocating African American economic and political autonomy.

In *Miranda v. Arizona,* Supreme Court requires police to inform suspects of their rights.

National Organization for Women (NOW) founded.

1968 The American Indian Movement (AIM) founded.

BIBLIOGRAPHY

GENERAL WORKS

John Morton Blum, *Years of Discord: American Politics and Society, 1961–1974* (1991).

David Farber, *The Age of Great Dreams: America in the 1960s* (1994).

Hugh Davis Graham, *The Civil Rights Era: Origins and Development of National Policy, 1960–1972* (1990).

Jim F. Heath, *Decade of Disillusionment: The Kennedy-Johnson Years* (1975).

Allen J. Matusow, *The Unraveling of America: A History of Liberalism in the 1960s* (1984).

Douglas T. Miller, *On Our Own: Americans in the Sixties* (1996).

Edward P. Morgan, *The Sixties Experience: Hard Lessons about Modern America* (1991).

William L. O'Neill, *Coming Apart: An Informal History of America in the 1960s* (1971).

Barbara L. Tischler, ed., *Sights on the Sixties* (1992).

Irwin Unger, *The Best of Intentions: The Triumph and Failure of the Great Society* (1996).

THE BLACK FREEDOM STRUGGLE

Peter J. Albert and Ronald Hoffman, eds., *We Shall Overcome: Martin Luther King, Jr., and the Black Freedom Struggle* (1990).

Jervis Anderson, *Bayard Rustin: Troubles I've Seen* (1997).

Taylor Branch, *Parting the Waters: America in the King Years, 1954–63* (1988).

Carl M. Brauer, *John F. Kennedy and the Second Reconstruction* (1977).

James W. Button, *Black Violence: Political Impact of the 1960s Riots* (1978).

Clayborne Carson, *In Struggle: SNCC and the Black Awakening of the 1960s* (1981).

David J. Garrow, *Protest at Selma: Martin Luther King, Jr., and the Voting Rights Act of 1965* (1978).

David J. Garrow, *Bearing the Cross: Martin Luther King, Jr., and the Southern Christian Leadership Conference* (1986).

Peter L. Goldman, *The Death and Life of Malcolm X* (1979).

Ralph G. Gomes and Linda Faye Williams, eds., *From Exclusion to Inclusion: The Long Struggle for African American Political Power* (1992).

James C. Harvey, *Black Civil Rights during the Johnson Administration* (1973).

Steven F. Lawson, *Black Ballots: Voting Rights in the South, 1944–1969* (1976).

Steven F. Lawson, *Running for Freedom: Civil Rights and Black Politics in America since 1941* (1991).

Doug McAdam, *Freedom Summer* (1989).

August Meier and Elliott M. Rudwick, *CORE: A Study in the Civil Rights Movement, 1942–1968* (1973).

Stephen B. Oates, *Let the Trumpet Sound: The Life of Martin Luther King, Jr.* (1982).

Charles Payne, *I've Got the Light of Freedom: The Organizing Tradition and the Mississippi Freedom Stuggle* (1995).

Kenneth O'Reilly, *"Racial Matters": The FBI's Secret File on Black America, 1960–1972* (1989).

Frank R. Parker, *Black Votes Count: Political Empowerment in Mississippi after 1965* (1990).

Bruce Perry, *Malcolm: The Life of a Man Who Changed Black America* (1991).

James R. Ralph Jr., *Northern Protest: Martin Luther King, Jr., Chicago, and the Civil Rights Movement* (1993).

William L. Van Deburg, *New Day in Babylon: The Black Power Movement and American Culture, 1965–1975* (1993).

POLITICS AND POLICIES OF THE NEW FRONTIER AND GREAT SOCIETY

Henry J. Aaron, *Politics and the Professors: The Great Society in Perspective* (1978).

Vaughn Davis Bornet, *The Presidency of Lyndon B. Johnson* (1983).

David Burner, *John F. Kennedy and a New Generation* (1988).

Robert Caro, *The Years of Lyndon Johnson,* vols. 1 and 2 (1982, 1990).

Paul K. Conkin, *Big Daddy from the Pedernales: Lyndon Baines Johnson* (1986).

Robert A. Divine, ed., *Exploring the Johnson Years* (1981).

Robert Alan Goldberg, *Barry Goldwater* (1995).

Eric Goldman, *The Tragedy of Lyndon Johnson* (1969).

Doris Kearns, *Lyndon Johnson and the American Dream* (1976).

Sar Levitan and Robert Taggart, *The Promise of Greatness* (1976).

Robert Mann, *The Walls of Jericho: Lyndon Johnson, Hubert Humphrey, Richard Russell, and the Struggle for Civil Rights* (1996).

Gerald Posner, *Case Closed: Lee Harvey Oswald and the Assassination of JFK* (1993).

Jill Quadagno, *The Color of Welfare: How Racism Undermined the War on Poverty* (1994).

Richard Reeves, *President Kennedy: Profile of Power* (1993).

Mark Stern, *Calculating Visions: Kennedy, Johnson, and Civil Rights* (1992).

James L. Sundquist, *Politics and Policy: The Eisenhower, Kennedy, and Johnson Years* (1968).

PROTEST MOVEMENTS

Terry H. Anderson, *The Movement and the Sixties* (1995).

Stewart Burns, *Social Movements of the 1960s: Searching for Democracy* (1990).

David Chalmers, *And the Crooked Places Made Straight: The Struggle for Social Change in the 1960s* (1991).

Martha F. Davis, *Brutal Need: Lawyers and the Welfare Rights Movement, 1960–1973* (1993).

Vine Deloria Jr., *Behind the Trail of Broken Treaties* (1974).

Alice Echols, *Daring to Be Bad: Radical Feminism in America, 1967–1975* (1989).

Sara Evans, *Personal Liberation: The Roots of Women's Liberation in the Civil Rights Movement and the New Left* (1978).

Jo Freeman, *The Politics of Liberation* (1975).

Ignacio M. Garcia, *United We Win: The Rise and Fall of La Raza Unida Party* (1989).

Todd Gitlin, *The Sixties: Years of Hope, Days of Rage* (1987).

Juan Gómez-Quiñones, *Chicano Politics: Reality and Promise, 1940–1990* (1990).

Richard Griswold del Castillo and Richard A. Garcia, *Cesar Chavez: A Triumph of Spirit* (1995).

Cynthia Harrison, *On Account of Sex: The Politics of Women's Issues, 1945–1968* (1988).

Laurence M. Hauptman, *The Iroquois Struggle for Survival: World War II to Red Power* (1986).

Maurice Isserman, *If I Had a Hammer . . . : The Death of the Old Left and the Birth of the New Left* (1987).

George Katsiaficas, *The Imagination of the New Left: A Global Analysis of 1968* (1987).

Cyril Levitt, *Children of Privilege: Student Revolt in the Sixties* (1984).

Peter B. Levy, *The New Left and Labor in the 1960s* (1994).

Peter Matthiessen, *In the Spirit of Crazy Horse* (1983).

James Miller, *"Democracy Is in the Streets": From Port Huron to the Siege of Chicago* (1987).

Joan Moore and Harry Pachon, *Hispanics in the United States* (1985).

Donald L. Parman, *Indians and the American West in the Twentieth Century* (1994).

Manuel P. Servin, *An Awakened Minority: The Mexican Americans* (2nd ed., 1974).

William Wei, *The Asian American Movement* (1993).

THE SUPREME COURT

Archibald Cox, *The Warren Court: Constitutional Decision as an Instrument of Reform* (1968).

Richard Y. Funston, *Constitutional Counterrevolution? The Warren Court and the Burger Court: Judicial Policy Making in Modern America* (1977).

Philip B. Kurland, *Politics and the Warren Court* (1970).

Paul L. Murphy, *The Constitution in Crisis Times, 1918–1969* (1972).

Bernard Schwartz, *Super Chief: Earl Warren and His Supreme Court, a Judicial Biography* (1983).

Melvin I. Urofsky, *The Continuity of Change: The Supreme Court and Individual Liberties, 1953–1986* (1991).

FATIGUE HAT WITH PROTEST BUTTONS

The button on this fatigue hat of a veteran who had served two tours of duty evinces veterans' response to the many Americans who just wanted to forget the war that the United States had failed to win. Because their war was so different from other American wars, Vietnam veterans often came home to hostility or indifference. The POW-MIA pin referred to prisoners of war and those missing in action.

Nancy Gewitz/Antique Textile Resource/Picture Resource Consultants, Inc.

VIETNAM AND THE LIMITS OF POWER

29

1961–1975

As Charles Anderson's plane prepared to land, the pilot announced, "Gentlemen, we'll be touching down in Da Nang, Vietnam, in about ten minutes. . . . Fasten your seat belts, please. On behalf of the entire crew and staff, I'd like to say we've enjoyed having you with us . . . and we hope to see all of you again next year on your way home. Goodbye and good luck." As did most soldiers after 1966, Charles Anderson went to war on a commercial jetliner, complete with stewardesses (as they were called then) in miniskirts.

Military personnel traveling to battle as if they were businessmen or tourists was not the only thing that made the Vietnam War so different from America's previous wars. Marine infantry officer Philip Caputo landed at Da Nang in March 1965 confident that the enemy "would be quickly beaten and that we were doing something altogether noble and good." But in just a few months, "what had begun as an adventurous expedition had turned into an exhausting, indecisive war of attrition in which we fought for no other cause than our own survival."

Another soldier discovered even more quickly that "something was wrong." Wondering why the bus taking him from the air base to the compound had wire mesh over the windows, he was told, "It's the gooks man. . . . The gooks will throw grenades through the windows." Looking out, he saw "shriveled, little old men squatting beside the road. . . . They looked up at me with real contempt on their faces. Here we are at one of the largest military installations in the world and we have to cover the windows to protect ourselves from little old men."

Soldiers in Vietnam initially used the racist word *gook* to refer to the enemy—the North Vietnamese or their supporters in the South—but it quickly became a term used for any Vietnamese. "From one day to the next, you could see for yourself changes coming over guys on our side—decent fellows, who wouldn't dream of calling an Oriental a 'gook' back home," reported one American. The problem was that in this civil war, "they couldn't tell who was their friend and who wasn't. Day after day, out on patrol we'd come to . . . a shabby village, and the elders would welcome us and the children come running with smiles on their faces, waiting for the candy we'd give them. But . . . just as we were leaving the village behind, the enemy would open up on us, and there was bitterness among us that the villagers hadn't given us warning."

Americans' horrifying and bewildering experiences in Vietnam grew out of cold war commitments made in the 1940s and 1950s by presidents Harry S. Truman and Dwight D. Eisenhower. John F. Kennedy wholeheartedly took on those commitments, promising more innovative, flexible, and vigorous efforts to thwart communism. In the most memorable words of his inaugural address he declared, "Let every nation know, whether it wishes us well or ill, that we shall pay any price, bear any burden, meet any hardship, support any friend, oppose any foe to assure the survival and the success of liberty."

Kennedy asked the American people to pay a steep price. It included enormous increases in spending to bolster U.S. nuclear superiority and arm the country for both conventional and guerrilla warfare. Moreover, when the Soviet Union attempted to install nuclear missiles in Cuba in 1962, Kennedy asked Americans to risk nuclear war to stand up to the Soviets.

The conflict in Vietnam became the foremost test of what the United States would or could do to "assure the survival and the success of liberty." Kennedy sent increasing amounts of American arms and personnel to help sustain the South Vietnamese government, and Johnson dramatically escalated that commitment. By 1965, the civil war in Vietnam had become America's war.

The Americanization of the war increased the number of U.S. military personnel in Vietnam to 540,000 at peak strength in 1968 and to more than three million total throughout the war's duration. Yet not only did this massive intervention fail to defeat the North Vietnamese and their allies in South Vietnam, but it added a new burden to the costs of fighting the cold war—intense discord among the people at home. Believing that the war was immoral or futile, hundreds of thousands of Americans protested it.

The Vietnam War cost President Johnson another term in office and contributed to the political demise of his Republican successor, Richard M. Nixon. Nixon gradually withdrew ground troops, but neither efforts to strengthen the South Vietnamese nor ferocious bombing campaigns daunted the enemy. The peace treaty signed in 1973 did little more than provide a short interval between American withdrawal and victory for the North Vietnamese.

Lieutenant David Donovan, sent to Vietnam as a counterinsurgency expert, gave a bitter twist to Kennedy's rousing inaugural words. In Vietnam, according to Donovan, the United States found "a price too high, a burden too heavy, a friend too incompetent, a foe too intractable for us to continue to hold high the cause of liberty." Those who agreed with Donovan lauded the American goal in Vietnam and damned only the nation's unwillingness

to pursue it effectively. Others believed that preserving a non-Communist South Vietnam was neither in the best interests of the United States nor within its capacity to achieve.

But none could deny the war's enormous costs. "The promises of the Great Society have been shot down on the battlefield of Vietnam," said Martin Luther King Jr. In addition to derailing domestic reform, the Vietnam War inflicted a heavy cost in American lives and dollars, kindled internal conflict and disorder, and led to the violation of the rights of antiwar protesters. With the exception of the African American freedom struggle, no post-World War II event affected Americans so intensely.

New Frontiers in Foreign Policy

John F. Kennedy moved quickly to fulfill his campaign promises of a tougher, more aggressive, more flexible foreign policy. He embraced the goal of containment and believed that the United States could pursue it much more effectively than his predecessors had done. With his like-minded secretary of defense, Robert S. McNamara, Kennedy expanded the nation's nuclear arsenal, increased its ability to fight conventional battles, and developed its capability for combating guerrilla warfare. To ensure U.S. superiority over the Soviet Union in every area, Kennedy accelerated the nation's space exploration program and increased American attention to the third world, with new programs to promote economic development, political stability, and friendly governments.

Believing that Eisenhower's caution and passivity had encouraged Soviet and Chinese expansion, and mindful of charges that he was too young and inexperienced, Kennedy resolved to present a tough posture. To demonstrate his unflinching determination to halt communism, he took the United States to the brink of nuclear war during the 1962 Cuban missile crisis. Less dramatically, but no less tenaciously, Kennedy stepped up American contributions of arms, aid, and personnel to save the government of South Vietnam from Communist insurgents. During his last months in office, Kennedy moved to decrease Soviet-American tensions, but he did not waver from his commitment to South Vietnam.

Meeting the "Hour of Maximum Danger"

Kennedy and other Democrats criticized the Eisenhower administration for placing too much reliance on nuclear weapons, thereby denying the nation a "flexible response" to Communist expansion. Moreover, Kennedy charged, Eisenhower's desire to limit defense spending had allowed the United States to fall behind even in nuclear capability, thereby creating a "missile gap" with the Soviet Union. In January 1961, Kennedy warned that the nation faced a grave peril: "Each day the crises multiply. . . . Each day we draw nearer the hour of maximum danger."

Although Kennedy exaggerated the actual threat to national security, several developments in 1961 heightened the sense of crisis and provided rationalization for a military buildup. In a speech made shortly before Kennedy's inauguration, So-

viet Premier Nikita Khrushchev had encouraged "wars of national liberation," thereby aligning the Soviet Union with independence (usually anti-Western) movements in the third world. Khrushchev wanted to bolster Soviet leadership of the Communist world, which was then being challenged by the People's Republic of China; and he needed to shore up his political position at home by projecting forcefulness abroad. U.S. officials, however, interpreted Khrushchev's words as signaling new efforts to upset the status quo of containment.

The status quo had already shifted in 1959, when Fidel Castro's revolution moved Cuba—only ninety miles from the United States—into the Soviet orbit. Under Eisenhower, the CIA had been planning an invasion by anti-Castro exiles. Kennedy ordered the invasion to proceed even though his military advisers gave it only a "fair" chance of success. To do otherwise, the president

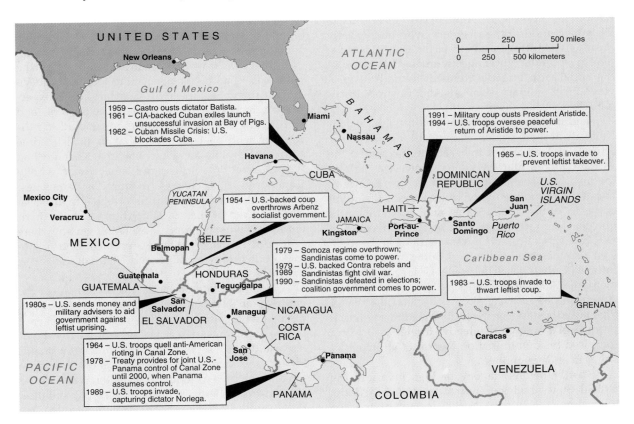

MAP 29.1
U.S. Involvement in Latin America and the Caribbean, 1954–1996
During the Cold War, the U.S. frequently intervened in Central American and Caribbean countries to suppress Communist or leftist movements.

felt, would create an appearance of weakness. Kennedy believed that to deal effectively with the Soviets, the United States had to do more than simply possess superior power. The nation also had to demonstrate the will to exercise that power and to project an image of strength.

To demonstrate his unflinching determination to halt communism, Kennedy took the United States to the brink of nuclear war during the 1962 Cuban missile crisis.

Kennedy's efforts to hide the American role in the Cuban invasion resulted in an operation that was poorly planned, inadequately manned, and without sufficient air and naval support. On April 17, 1961, about 1,300 anti-Castro exiles, who had been trained and armed by the CIA, landed at the Bay of Pigs on the south shore of Cuba. Contrary to the anticipation of the planners, who had gravely miscalculated the sentiments of the Cuban population, no popular uprising materialized to support the anti-Castro brigade. Kennedy would not provide direct military support, and Castro's forces quickly defeated the invaders.

The Bay of Pigs disaster was humiliating for Kennedy and the United States. Although Kennedy refused direct military intervention, no one in the world doubted that the United States was behind the invasion. The attempted armed interference in the affairs of another nation compromised the moral authority of the United States, and its failure raised questions about the wisdom and effectiveness of U.S. foreign policy and military strategy. The invasion also increased Cubans' support for Castro, reinforced Cuba's ties to the Soviet Union, and evoked memories of Yankee imperialism among Latin American nations. The sorry debacle at the Bay of Pigs posed a stark contrast to Kennedy's inaugural promise of a new, more effective foreign policy and increased his determination to project an image of strength and toughness.

Shortly before the Bay of Pigs invasion, the United States had suffered a psychological blow when Soviet astronaut Yuri Gagarin orbited the earth, the first human to do so. In the late 1950s, the Eisenhower administration had stepped up American research on space exploration in response to *Sputnik*, the Soviet satellite that had orbited the earth. But the United States still lagged behind in "manned" spaceflight competition, having sent only monkeys into space on suborbital missiles. The first American entered the new frontier in space on May 5, 1961, when Alan B. Shepard Jr. made a three-hundred-mile flight.

That same month, Kennedy called for a huge new commitment to the space race, which he clearly viewed as one element of U.S.-Soviet competition. "If we are to win the battle that is now going on around the world between freedom and tyranny," he told Congress, the United States must "take a clearly leading role in space achievement." His goal: an American on the moon within six to eight years. Congress authorized the Apollo program and substantially boosted appropriations for space exploration. In 1962, John H. Glenn orbited the earth, less than a year behind the Soviets. And in 1969, the United States surpassed the Soviet Union in the space race when two Americans, Neil A. Armstrong and Edwin E. ("Buzz") Aldrin Jr., became the first humans to set foot on the moon.

In the early months of his presidency, Kennedy sought a meeting with Khrushchev. "I have to show him that we can be as tough as he is," Kennedy said. "I'll have to sit down with him and let him see who he's dealing with." Their meeting took place in Vienna, Austria, in June 1961. Contrary to his expectations, Kennedy met a strident, belligerent, and threatening Khrushchev, and the president left the meeting with his confidence shaken. British Prime Minister Harold Macmillan noted that Kennedy had "for the first time in his life . . . met a man wholly impervious to his charm." To journalist James Reston, the shocked president reported, "He just beat [the] hell out of me. . . . If he thinks I'm inexperienced and have no guts . . . we won't get anywhere with him. . . . Now we have a problem in trying to make our power credible, and Vietnam looks like the place."

The immediate problem was Berlin, one of the earliest points of conflict in the cold war. Khrushchev demanded an agreement recognizing the existence of two Germanys; otherwise, he warned, the Soviets would sign a separate treaty with East Germany. Should this happen, the Soviet Union would no longer recognize American occupation rights in and access to West Berlin, which lay some one hundred miles within East Germany. Kennedy held his ground. Returning home, he ordered more troops to Europe and a large increase in military forces. West Berlin, he declared, was "the great testing place of Western courage and will."

A major embarrassment for the Communists was the massive exodus of East Germans into West

HUMANS REACH THE MOON
In July 1969, less than a decade after President John F. Kennedy announced the goal of "landing a man on the moon and returning him safely to the earth," the space capsule Apollo 11 *carried astronauts Edwin E. Aldrin Jr. and Neil A. Armstrong to the moon. As millions of people watched on television, Armstrong became the first human to step on the moon's surface, saying, "That's one small step for a man, one giant leap for mankind." Armstrong and Aldrin collected rock samples and conducted scientific experiments. Other missions to the moon followed. In this 1971 photograph of the* Apollo 15 *mission, astronaut James B. Irwin salutes near the lunar module and lunar roving vehicle.*
NASA/Johnson Space Center.

Berlin. To stop the flow of escapees from behind the iron curtain, on August 13, 1961, East Germany stunned the world by erecting a wall between East and West Berlin. To Kennedy, the wall was "a hell of a lot better than a war," and the United States did not interfere, although at one point in the crisis, armed American tanks faced off with Soviet tanks less than a football field away. With the Berlin Wall stemming the tide of East German migration, Khrushchev backed off from his threats. But not until 1972 did the superpowers settle the issue of the two Germanys with recognition of East and West Germany as separate nations and a guarantee of Western access to West Berlin.

Kennedy used the Berlin crisis to diversify and fortify the nation's military establishment. In the summer of 1961, he got Congress to add $3.2 billion to the defense budget. By increasing draft calls and mobilizing the reserves and National Guard, he expanded the size of the military by 300,000. This buildup in conventional forces met Kennedy's demand for "a wider choice than humiliation or all-out nuclear action" by providing a "flexible re-

sponse" strategy. When the Soviet Union terminated its three-year moratorium on nuclear testing, the United States followed suit, and Kennedy pushed the development of new nuclear weapons and delivery systems.

New Approaches to the Third World

Kennedy administration officials believed that they had found new ways to deal with the wave of nationalism, reform, and revolutionary movements that had convulsed the world since the end of World War II. Much more than his predecessors had, the president publicly supported third world democratic and nationalist aspirations. He proposed that foreign aid be based on the recipient country's willingness to undertake democratic reform. By helping to fulfill hopes for independence and democracy, he asserted, the United States could win the hearts and minds of people in the developing nations.

To that end, Kennedy created the Alliance for Progress, promising $20 billion in aid for Latin America over the next decade. Like the Marshall

PEACE CORPS VOLUNTEERS IN BOLIVIA
The majority of Peace Corps volunteers worked on educational projects in developing countries. Others helped to increase food production, build public works, and curb diseases, as did these volunteers vaccinating a young Bolivian girl. President John F. Kennedy saw the Peace Corps volunteers, with their dedication to freedom, "overcoming the efforts of Mr. Khrushchev's missionaries who are dedicated to undermining that freedom." In the course of their missions, however, some volunteers came to question the single-minded focus of U.S. policy on anticommunism.
David S. Boyer©National Geographic Society.

The Peace Corps exemplified the idealism and sacrifice that Kennedy had called for in his inaugural address. One volunteer spoke of easing his conscience "that I and my peers were born between clean sheets when others were issued into the dust with a birthright of hunger." Peace Corps volunteers studied a country's language and culture before going to work directly with its people. Some seven thousand of them by the end of Kennedy's presidency and more than sixty thousand by the mid-1970s fanned out around the globe, serving two-year stints in villages in Latin America, Africa, and Asia, where they opened schools, provided basic health care, assisted with agriculture and nutrition projects, and helped develop small economic enterprises.

Nonetheless, Kennedy's foreign aid initiatives fell far short of their objectives. Though almost universally welcomed, Peace Corps projects numbered too few to make a dent in the poverty and suffering in third world countries struggling to develop their economies. By 1969, the United States had provided only half of the $20 billion promised to the Alliance for Progress. Much of the aid was military, and ruling elites in the receiving countries skimmed off a large part while failing to initiate meaningful social and economic reforms. In addition, a soaring birthrate in Latin America counteracted most of the gains made in economic productivity, and these nations increasingly bore burdens of foreign indebtedness.

Kennedy did not neglect more direct, military means to bring political stability to the third world. Although his speeches aligned the United States with popular movements seeking independence and better living conditions, he drew the line at uprisings that appeared to have Communist connections or goals. Thus his actions frequently contradicted his words. Even when increasing hostility between the Soviet Union and Communist China presented an opportunity for improving U.S. relations with China, Kennedy continued to adhere to the basic tenet of the cold war: that communism was a monolithic force and had to be contained, no matter what form it took. To that end, he promoted counterinsurgency forces to put down revolutions or insurrections that smacked of communism.

The showcase of the administration's counterinsurgency strategy was an elite corps from the army, air force, navy, and coast guard that was trained to wage unconventional warfare. Called "special forces," the corps had been established under the Eisenhower administration to aid groups

Plan, the Alliance for Progress was a cold war measure designed to thwart communism and hold nations within the American sphere by fostering economic development. Kennedy also brought foreign assistance programs together in a new Agency for International Development (AID) and reversed the emphasis from military to economic aid. With an idea borrowed from Senator Hubert H. Humphrey, Kennedy launched his most dramatic third world initiative. He established the Peace Corps in 1961, under the direction of his brother-in-law R. Sargent Shriver.

that were sympathetic to the United States in their fight against Communist-leaning national liberation movements. Kennedy rapidly expanded the special forces and authorized their new name and official headgear, the green beret, which he called "a mark of distinction in the fight for freedom." He sought to recruit the best officers and enlisted men for the Green Berets and to make them a highly disciplined, daring force, equipped with the latest technology and trained for guerrilla warfare.

The Arms Race and the Nuclear Brink

The final piece of the Kennedy-McNamara defense strategy involved U.S. nuclear strength. Kennedy realized quickly that the "missile gap" he had warned about during the 1960 campaign was a myth, but that knowledge did not lessen his determination to make the United States even stronger. Because the Soviets had the ability to expand their own nuclear arsenal, Kennedy and McNamara reasoned that the United States should push ahead to enlarge its superiority. The drive for nuclear dominance continued into the Johnson administration. By then, the United States had increased the number of nuclear weapons based in Europe from 2,500 to 7,200, and it had multiplied fivefold its supply of intercontinental ballistic missiles (ICBMs).

To the Soviets, the American nuclear buildup suggested that the United States wanted not just superiority, but the capacity to launch a first strike, wiping out the Soviet missile sites before the Soviets could respond. The Kremlin therefore stepped up its own ICBM program, and the most intense arms race ever ensued. McNamara would later conclude that the U.S. superiority was "in fact more than we require[d]." Despite the enormous American buildup, the Soviets were closer to parity with the United States when McNamara resigned in 1967 than they had been in 1961.

In October 1962, the superpowers came perilously close to using those weapons of terror, when Cuba once again took center stage. During the summer of 1962, Khrushchev made his biggest gamble of all: He decided to install nuclear missiles in Cuba. When American U-2 spy planes spotted defensive, surface-to-air missiles in Cuba, Kennedy warned the Soviets not to attempt to install offensive, ground-to-ground missiles.

The Soviet ambassador to the United States conveyed assurances from Khrushchev that they had no such intentions. But on October 16, 1962, the CIA showed Kennedy new surveillance pho-tographs that exposed Khrushchev's lie. Launching sites in Cuba were being constructed for missiles that had ranges of one thousand and twenty-two hundred miles. The ensuing thirteen-day Cuban missile crisis brought the world closer to nuclear annihilation than ever before or since.

Working with a small group of top advisers meeting secretly and daily during the crisis, Kennedy developed the American position. Though determined to keep offensive missiles out of Cuba, he rejected suggestions for nuclear or conventional strikes against the sites or an invasion of the island. On October 22, the president told a television audience that he had placed the military on full alert and was imposing a "strict quarantine on all offensive military equipment" headed from the Soviet Union to Cuba. The U.S. navy would stop, search, and, if necessary, turn back any Soviet vessel suspected of carrying offensive missiles to Cuba. (Only later did the United States find out that offensive missiles were already in Cuba.) Kennedy warned Khrushchev that any attack launched from Cuba would trigger a full nuclear attack against the Soviet Union.

The president called the missiles an "unjustified change in the status quo which cannot be accepted . . . if our courage and our commitments are ever to be trusted again either by friend or foe." Kennedy's aides later conceded that the missiles would not in reality have shifted the balance of power. As McNamara put it, "It makes no great difference whether you're killed by a missile fired from the Soviet Union or from Cuba." But to Kennedy, projecting the appearance of toughness was paramount. According to his speechwriter, Theodore Sorensen, although the missiles did not "alter the strategic balance in fact . . . that balance would have been substantially altered in appearance; and in matters of national will and world leadership . . . such appearances contribute to reality."

Although Kennedy was willing to risk nuclear war for appearances, he also exercised considerable caution. To avoid a confrontation, which neither side wanted, he refused advice from the military to bomb the missile sites and instead called for the quarantine to allow time for negotiations. On October 24, Russian ships carrying nuclear warheads suddenly stopped or turned back. Secretary of State Dean Rusk then remarked, "We are eyeball to eyeball, and I think the other fellow just blinked." Kennedy matched Khrushchev's restraint. When one ship crossed the blockade line, he ordered the navy to follow it rather than to attempt to stop it.

THE CUBAN MISSILE CRISIS
In October 1962, President John F. Kennedy dispatched more than one hundred U.S. ships to quarantine Cuba and prevent the importation of Soviet offensive nuclear missiles. After Soviet leader Nikita Khrushchev agreed to remove the missiles already in Cuba, the U.S. navy continued to monitor the movement of Soviet ships. Here the U.S.S. Barry *steams alongside a Soviet freighter, outbound from Cuba and carrying military equipment.*
Corbis-Bettmann.

"We don't want to push him [Khrushchev] to a precipitous action," he said. But a small number of Americans believed that Kennedy helped create a crisis, playing "chicken, with mankind on the bumpers."

While Americans experienced the most fearful days of the cold war, Kennedy and Khrushchev exchanged offers and counteroffers. Finally, the Soviets removed the missiles and pledged not to introduce new offensive weapons into Cuba. In exchange, the United States promised not to invade the island. Secretly, the United States also agreed to remove its own missiles based in Turkey and aimed

at the Soviet Union, a decision that Kennedy had made months before but had not implemented.

Although the United States' no-invasion promise was face-saving for Khrushchev, in miscalculating the resolution of Kennedy he lost badly. As a result, the Soviets suffered in their contest with China for the allegiance of third world countries, and Khrushchev himself was so weakened that he was deposed two years later. Kennedy emerged triumphant. The image of a new, inexperienced president fumbling the Bay of Pigs invasion and being bullied by Khrushchev in Vienna gave way to that of a brilliant leader combining firmness with restraint and bearing the United States through its "hour of maximum danger."

Having proved his toughness, Kennedy could afford to be conciliatory. After the Cuban missile crisis, the president acted to reduce the danger of future confrontations. He and Khrushchev agreed to install a special telephone "hot line" to speed top-level communication in moments of crisis. In a major speech at American University in June 1963, Kennedy called for a reexamination of the assumptions of the cold war. Appealing for a greater understanding of the Soviet Union, he asked Americans "not to see only a distorted and desperate view of the other side, not to see conflict as inevitable." Acknowledging that the superpowers could not quickly resolve all their differences, Kennedy pointed to what they had in common: "We all inhabit this small planet. We all breathe the same air. We all cherish our children's future and we are all mortal."

Responding in part to pressures from scientists and other Americans alarmed by the dangers of nuclear testing and the threat of nuclear war, Kennedy called for an end to "a vicious cycle" in which "new weapons beget counterweapons." The United States would stop testing nuclear weapons aboveground and begin negotiations with the Soviet Union for a permanent ban on nuclear testing, he announced. In August 1963, the United States, the Soviet Union, and Great Britain signed a limited test-ban treaty, a goal that had eluded Eisenhower. Because France and China refused to sign, the agreement failed to stop the proliferation of nuclear weapons, and it did not apply to underground testing. The limited test ban did, however, reduce the threat of radioactive fallout from nuclear testing, and it raised hopes for accommodation between the superpowers on other issues.

Venturing into a Quagmire in Vietnam

Whether the new approach to the cold war that Kennedy outlined at American University could have been realized was left forever unanswered by his assassination. It was clear, however, that the new approach did not mean abandoning efforts to save the South Vietnamese government from its Communist foes and their supporters. Kennedy had criticized the idea of "a Pax Americana enforced on the world by American weapons of war," but he continued to increase the flow of those weapons into South Vietnam.

The foreign policy setbacks during Kennedy's first six months in office suggested the need to make a strong stand somewhere. As he remarked to an associate, "There are just so many concessions that one can make to the Communists in one year and survive politically." Kennedy also remembered the political blows to the Democratic Party when in 1949 "China was lost. . . .We don't want that." Moreover, the pro-United States government in Laos, which bordered Vietnam, also confronted insurrection, and Kennedy subscribed to the falling domino theory enunciated by Eisenhower.

Kennedy's strong anticommunism, his interpretation of "the lessons of history," and his commitment to a tough, activist foreign policy prepared him to take a stand in Vietnam. The new counterinsurgency program provided the means. Kennedy's key military adviser, General Maxwell Taylor, thought that Vietnam would be a good testing ground for the Green Berets. Author of the "flexible response" strategy, Taylor believed that holding firm in Vietnam would show the Soviets that wars of national liberation were not "cheap, safe, and disavowable [but] costly, dangerous, and doomed to failure."

Kennedy's strong anticommunism, his interpretation of "the lessons of history," and his commitment to a tough, activist foreign policy prepared him to take a stand in Vietnam.

Two major problems, however, undercut Taylor's analysis. First, the South Vietnamese insurgents—called Vietcong, short for Viet Nam Cong-san ("Vietnamese Communists"), by the Americans—were a genuine indigenous force, whose initiative came from within, not from the Soviet Union or China. Even Ho Chi Minh's Communist government in North Vietnam did not begin to supply the rebels in the South with weapons or soldiers until 1959, after local insurgents had initiated guerrilla activities against the South Vietnamese government on their own. Because the government in South Vietnam had failed to hold the elections promised in the Geneva accords and, in fact, was doing everything possible to exterminate its opponents, the rebels saw no choice but to take up arms.

The second problem lay in the South Vietnamese government and army (the Armed Forces of the Republic of Vietnam, or ARVN), which proved to be ineffective vehicles for the American goal of suppressing wars of liberation. The government in Saigon consistently avoided economic reforms that could have gained popular support. In fact, its corruption and repression of opponents of all stripes alienated growing portions of the South Vietnamese population, not just the Communists. Ngo Dinh Diem, South Vietnamese premier from 1954 to 1963, chose military leaders for their personal loyalty, and they, in turn, made decisions to protect their own positions rather than to defeat the enemy.

The growing intervention by North Vietnam made matters worse. In 1960, the Hanoi government established the National Liberation Front (NLF), composed of South Vietnamese rebels but directed by the North. Although the NLF recruited most of its forces from among the South Vietnamese and fought largely with American weapons captured from ARVN, Hanoi constructed a network of infiltration routes (called the "Ho Chi Minh Trail") in neighboring Laos through which it sent people and supplies to help liberate the South. Violence escalated between 1960 and 1963, and the Saigon government seemed close to collapse.

When Kennedy took office, more than $1 billion of aid and about seven hundred military advisers from the United States had failed to stabilize the South Vietnamese government. Some Kennedy aides urged applying any force necessary to save South Vietnam from communism. Opposing views came from two advisers who believed that the Saigon government was unsalvageable. W. Averell Harriman, former diplomat and foreign policy adviser under Roosevelt and Truman, thought that the United States should not "stake its prestige in Vietnam," and Undersecretary of State Chester Bowles warned that the country was "headed full blast up a dead end street."

Kennedy resisted pressure for an all-out effort, but beginning in the spring of 1961, he gradually escalated the American commitment. He remained skeptical about the prospects for victory and suspicious of the continuing pressure for additional forces. "It's like taking a drink," he said. "The effect wears off, and you have to take another." Yet he would not bring himself to abandon the commitment. Between 1961 and 1962, Kennedy doubled the amount of military aid and increased to nine thousand the number of American military advisers, whose activities expanded from training and advice to occasional participation in the fighting. Although

the United States extracted new promises of reform from Diem with every increase of aid, the South Vietnamese government never made good on them.

Kennedy and most of his advisers assumed that the latest military technology and sheer vastness of U.S. power would eventually stem the Communist tide in South Vietnam. Yet that power and technology was ill suited to a guerrilla-type war, and it hurt the very people it meant to save. Military personnel had trouble distinguishing the Vietcong and their supporters from the general population. Thousands of peasants were uprooted from their land and villages (which in Vietnamese culture are sacred) and resettled in new "strategic hamlets," where they were supposed to be out of the reach of the Communists. Those left in the countryside suffered bombing and strafing by South Vietnamese forces, which used bombs containing the highly flammable substance napalm. In January 1962, United States planes began to spray leaf and plant killers such as Agent Orange in efforts to wipe out the Vietcong's jungle hideouts and devastate their food supply.

A new threat to the South Vietnamese government developed in 1963, as Buddhist monks protested the repressive and unrepresentative nature of Diem's Catholic-dominated government. ARVN troops shot at Buddhist demonstrators, triggering more protests and extreme actions by individual monks, who committed suicide by dousing themselves with gasoline and setting themselves on fire. Diem resisted U.S. demands that he stop persecuting the Buddhists, and in August 1963, U.S. officials signaled ARVN officers that Diem's overthrow would not be unwelcome.

South Vietnamese military leaders effected a coup on November 2, 1963, brutally executing Diem and his brother Ngo Dinh Nhu, who headed the secret police. The killings shocked Kennedy, but in the three weeks he had left to live, he gave no indication of any change in policy. In a speech scheduled to be given in Dallas on the very day he was assassinated, Kennedy would have called Americans to their responsibilities as "the watchmen on the walls of world freedom." Referring specifically to Southeast Asia, his undelivered speech warned, "We dare not weary of the task."

Though never going as far or as fast as his military advisers advocated, Kennedy radically raised the U.S. stakes in Vietnam. At his death, sixteen thousand Americans served in Vietnam, and one hundred of them had died there. He bequeathed to

Lyndon Johnson a vastly expanded commitment to a South Vietnamese government that was no more in control than it had been before the infusion of American power.

Lyndon Johnson's War against Communism

Following the basic outlines of Kennedy's foreign policy, Johnson retained his predecessor's key foreign policy and military officials. Secretary of Defense McNamara continued the massive buildup of nuclear weapons and conventional and counterinsurgency forces that had begun in the early 1960s. At the same time, Johnson built on the less hostile climate between the United States and the Soviet Union that had followed the Cuban missile crisis. In 1968, he signed a nuclear nonproliferation agreement with the Soviet Union, Britain, and fifty-eight nonnuclear nations, and he initiated plans for Soviet-American negotiations to control the arms race.

Johnson's adherence to the basic assumptions of the cold war was manifested in his approach to Latin America and Southeast Asia, two major trouble spots that had consumed Kennedy's attention. In 1965, when the South Vietnamese government approached collapse, Johnson took the fateful steps of ordering U.S. troops into combat and initiating sustained bombing of the North. Yet even this enormous intervention did not break the enemy's capability. That same year, closer to home, Johnson sent U.S. marines to the Dominican Republic to crush a leftist rebellion.

Toward an All-Out Commitment in Vietnam

During the first year of his presidency, Lyndon Johnson stuck to the course laid out by Kennedy in Vietnam, deciding "to do more of the same and do it more efficiently." He expanded secret raids on North Vietnam, boosted military and economic aid to the South Vietnamese, and increased the number of American advisers to twenty-three thousand by the end of 1964. Johnson appointed General William Westmoreland, a World War II and Korean War veteran, to command the U.S. military effort. Westmoreland confronted a South Vietnam in which the Vietcong controlled more than 50 percent of the population and more than 40 percent of its land.

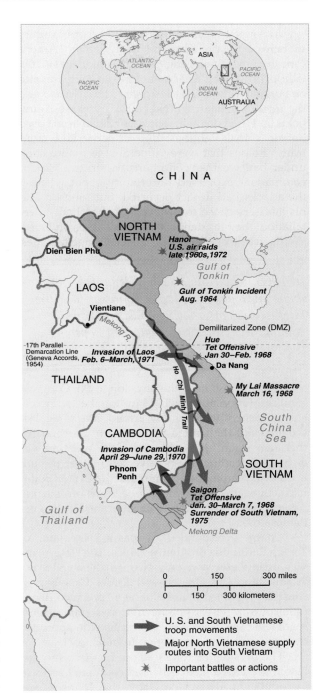

M A P 29.2
The Vietnam War, 1964–1975
The United States sent more than two million soldiers to Vietnam and spent more than $150 billion on the longest war in American history; but it was unable to prevent the unification of Vietnam under a Communist government.

In August 1964, Johnson seized an opportunity to increase the pressure on North Vietnam. American ships routinely engaged in espionage in the Gulf of Tonkin off the coast of North Vietnam, and on August 4, two U.S. destroyers, the *Maddox* and the *Turner Joy*, reported that North Vietnamese gunboats had fired on them. The reports had been based not on actual sightings, but on sonar and radar transmissions that were vulnerable to malfunction under bad weather conditions. Later, the *Maddox* commander expressed uncertainty about whether the attacks had in fact occurred, but Johnson and his advisers chose to believe that they had. In retaliation, the president ordered air strikes on North Vietnamese torpedo bases and oil storage facilities.

In 1965, when the South Vietnamese government approached collapse, Johnson took the fateful steps of ordering U.S. troops into combat and initiating sustained bombing of the North.

Johnson also used the occasion to ask Congress for a resolution authorizing him to take "all necessary measures to repel any armed attacks against the forces of the United States and to prevent further aggression." His portrayal of the situation was at best misleading, for he revealed neither the uncertainty about the attacks nor that the United States had engaged in provocative actions in staging covert raids and operating close to the North Vietnamese coast.

Congress responded by passing the Gulf of Tonkin Resolution on August 7, 1964. The House vote was unanimous, and only two senators voted no, Wayne Morse of Oregon and Ernest Gruening of Alaska, who called the resolution a "predated declaration of war." Public opinion mirrored congressional sentiment. The percent of Americans who approved U.S. policy in Vietnam shot up from 52 to 71.

The president's tough stance just two months before the 1964 elections helped counter charges of his opponent, Barry Goldwater, that Johnson was "soft on communism." Yet Johnson also presented himself as the peace candidate when Goldwater proposed massive bombing of North Vietnam and even entertained the possible use of atomic weapons. Johnson countered that bombing would expand the war and send American forces into battle. "We are not going to send American boys nine or ten thousand miles away from home to do what

Asian boys ought to be doing for themselves," Johnson insisted. Again and again, he claimed, "We seek no wider war."

Within months, however, Johnson did widen the war. He rejected peace feelers from North Vietnam, which insisted on American withdrawal and establishment of a coalition government in South Vietnam as steps toward the ultimate unification of the country. McNamara and most advisers urged Johnson to begin a bombing campaign against the North. Bombing North Vietnam, they said, would boost South Vietnamese morale, reduce Hanoi's ability to infiltrate personnel and equipment into the South, and thereby break the will of what Johnson called a "raggedy-ass little fourth-rate country" to continue the war.

In February 1965, Johnson initiated Operation Rolling Thunder, a strategy of gradually intensified bombing of North Vietnam. The administration did not reveal that strategy to the public but instead justified the initial strikes as a reprisal for recent Vietcong attacks on U.S. military quarters. Less than a month later, two battalions of marines landed near Da Nang, South Vietnam, the first U.S. combat troops to serve in Vietnam. In July, Johnson shifted the previously defensive mission of U.S. troops to that of offensive operations and authorized the dispatch of fifty thousand more soldiers.

Johnson took pains to obscure the significance of those two decisions, ordering aides to "minimize any appearance of sudden changes of policy." He told reporters, "I know of no far-reaching strategy that is being suggested or promulgated." Yet those decisions, whose import was kept from Congress and the public, marked a critical turning point in the war. Now it was genuinely America's war.

Preventing Another Castro in Latin America

Closer to home, Johnson faced perpetual problems, despite the efforts of the Alliance for Progress, in Latin America. Thirteen times during the 1960s, military coups replaced Latin American governments, and local insurgencies grew apace. The administration's response to such turmoil varied from case to case but centered on the determination to prevent any more Castro-type revolutions.

In 1964, riots erupted in the Panama Canal Zone, which the United States had seized early in the century and made a U.S. territory. Instigated by Panamanian nationalists who viewed the United States as a colonial power and wanted sovereignty

U.S. TROOPS IN THE DOMINICAN REPUBLIC
These United States paratroopers were among the twenty thousand troops sent to the Dominican Republic in April and May 1965. The American invasion helped restore peace, but it also kept the popularly elected government of Juan Bosch from regaining office. Dominicans expressed their outrage in anti-American slogans that greeted troops throughout the capital, Santo Domingo. Bosch himself said, "This was a democratic revolution smashed by the leading democracy in the world."
Corbis-Bettmann.

over all Panamanian territory, the riots resulted in the death of four U.S. soldiers and more than twenty Panamanians. Johnson authorized U.S. troops to quell the rioting, but he also initiated negotiations with Panamanian leaders. These talks dragged on until 1978 when they produced treaties providing for Panama to assume full authority over operation of the canal and for neutrality of the Canal Zone territory by the year 2000.

In 1965, Johnson's Latin American policy generated a new surge of anti-Americanism and cries of "Yankee imperialism." Voters in the Dominican

Republic had ousted the decades-old dictatorship of Rafael Trujillo and elected a constitutional government headed by Juan Bosch in 1961. After a military coup in 1963 overthrew Bosch, his supporters rallied in an uprising against the military government in April 1965. When the revolt was just four days old, Johnson ordered marines to the island and eventually sent more than twenty thousand soldiers to take control.

The president defended the intervention as necessary because the Boschist rebels included Communists who were likely to take over the Dominican Republic, a view that was never substantiated. Along with the marines, Johnson also sent a special ambassador, who arranged a truce between the opposing sides and installed an interim government. When Dominican elections in 1966 established a constitutional government under a moderate rightist, it appeared that Johnson's policy had worked.

Yet as the first outright show of Yankee force in Latin America in forty years, the Dominican intervention damaged the Johnson administration's credibility both at home and abroad. It quickly became clear that Communists had played no significant role in the revolt, and U.S. intervention kept the reform-oriented Boschists from returning to power. Moreover, the president had acted without the consent of the Dominicans or the Organization of American States (OAS), to which the United States had pledged to respect national sovereignty in Latin America. Once the troops landed in the Dominican Republic, Johnson did ask for approval and joint occupation from the OAS members, but several nations, including Mexico, Chile, Peru, and Venezuela, refused to support the United States.

Fear of being compared unfavorably with Kennedy obsessed Johnson throughout his presidency. The Texan's lowly origins and lack of an Ivy League education left a sense of insecurity that appeared in his efforts to show that he was just as smart and tough as Kennedy. Johnson also believed that demonstrating strength in the Caribbean would help convince the enemy in Vietnam of the depth of American resolve. In turn, the apparent success in the Dominican Republic no doubt encouraged the president to press on in Vietnam.

The Americanized War

From Operation Rolling Thunder in 1965 to early 1968, the United States employed a strategy of gradually escalating attacks against the North Vietnamese and their Vietcong allies, with the goal of

HELICOPTERS IN VIETNAM
This helicopter has just delivered soldiers on a mission near the Ho Chi Minh Trail in April 1968.
Because the enemy in Vietnam was widely dispersed, the helicopter became a key implement of war
and an example of American reliance on technology. The United States used helicopters to evacuate
wounded, or drop napalm and defoliants. The helicopter's mobility enabled efficient placement of
troops, and as gunships, they combined built-in weapons with the fire of soldiers on board.
Philip Jones Griffith/Magnum Photos, Inc.

breaking the will of the North Vietnamese while avoiding massive intervention by the Chinese. Johnson crudely explained the strategy to reporters as one of "seduction," from which the United States might ease off, rather than one of "rape," which might provoke China to respond as it had done in Korea. Intensely concerned with the bombing of the North, Johnson liked to boast, "They can't even bomb an outhouse without my approval."

Bombing intensified in both the North and the South, and over the course of the war U.S. pilots eventually dropped 3.2 million tons of explosives, more than the United States had launched in all of World War II. By 1967, the war was costing more than $2 billion a month, and nearly 500,000 Americans were fighting in Vietnam. By 1968, American GIs were dying at the rate of more than 1,000 a month.

The intensive bombing claimed monthly death tolls of more than 2,000 North Vietnamese civilians and military personnel but failed to dampen the North's commitment. The Hanoi government dispersed and concealed industrial and military facilities, taught its citizens how to protect themselves from bombing, and relied on human labor to rebuild transportation routes. Both the Soviet Union and China helped North Vietnam replace what the bombing destroyed, supplying an estimated $2 billion worth of materials between 1965 and 1968.

In South Vietnam, General Westmoreland conducted a strategy of attrition designed to search out and kill the Vietcong and North Vietnamese regular army. Military officials calculated the progress of the war not in territory gained or strategic positions seized, as they had in previous wars. Instead, they computed "body counts" and "kill ratios," the number of enemies killed in relation to the cost in American and ARVN lives. Under these circumstances, GIs did not always take care to distinguish between the enemy and noncombatants. Lieutenant Philip Caputo reported that the operating rule was "If it's dead and Vietnamese, it's VC [Vietcong]."

To carry out the strategy of attrition, Westmoreland could count on the best-equipped army in history. In addition to massive firepower and highly maneuverable helicopters that could move troops and artillery at a rapid pace, American forces used sophisticated computers and enemy-detecting systems as well as herbicides to destroy millions of acres of forests where the enemy hid. The United States relied even more heavily on airpower in the South, raining down more than twice the tonnage of bombs dropped on North Vietnam.

In contrast to World War II, when the average soldier was twenty-six years old, teenagers fought the Vietnam War. Until a constitutional amendment reduced the voting age from twenty-one to eighteen in 1971, most U.S. soldiers, whose average age was nineteen, could not even vote for the officials who sent them to Vietnam. As Americanization of the war progressed, the ratio of draftees to enlisted men increased, and the war's dependence on the draft added to its unique character.

Mike Clodfelter, sent to Vietnam in 1965, noticed that working-class youth did most of the fighting. "From my own small hometown [Plainville, Kansas] all but two of a dozen high school buddies would eventually serve in Vietnam and all were of working-class families," he observed. "I know of not a single middle-class son of the town's businessmen, lawyers, doctors, or ranchers from my high school graduating class who experienced the Armageddon of our generation."

Unlike World War II, which distributed the fighting among young men of various economic levels, the Vietnam War was the war of the poor and working class, who constituted about 80 percent of the troops.

Unlike World War II, which distributed the fighting among young men of various economic levels, the Vietnam War was the war of the poor and working class, who constituted about 80 percent of the troops. More privileged youth enjoyed greater ability to avoid the draft, usually through college deferments. Others evaded service in Vietnam by using family connections to get into the National Guard. Whereas 21 percent of high school graduates served in Vietnam, only 12 percent of college graduates did so, and these were half as likely to see combat as were soldiers with less education. In

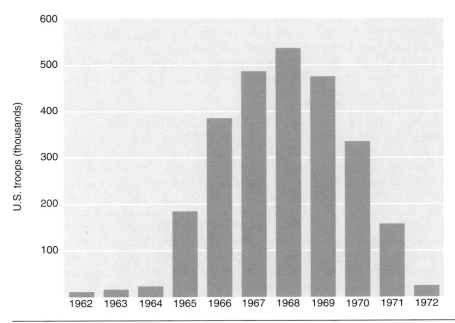

FIGURE 29.1
U.S. Troops in Vietnam, 1962–1972
The steepest increases in the American military presence in Vietnam came in 1965 and 1966. Although troop levels declined in 1971 and 1972, the U.S. continued massive bombing attacks.

Why Couldn't the United States Bomb Its Way to Victory in Vietnam?

WORLD WAR II DEMONSTRATED the critical importance of airpower in modern war. According to the official U.S. study of strategic bombing during World War II, "No nation can long survive the free exploitation of air weapons over its homeland." In the Vietnam War, U.S. planes delivered even more explosives than they had in World War II. Why, then, did strategic bombing not bring victory in Vietnam?

"Our airpower did not fail us; it was the decision makers," asserted Admiral U. S. Grant Sharp, World War II veteran and commander in chief of the Pacific Command during the Vietnam War. Military officials welcomed President Johnson's order to begin bombing North Vietnam in February 1965 as a means to destroy the North's capacity and will to support the Communist insurgents in South Vietnam. But they chafed at Johnson's strategy of gradual escalation and the restrictions he imposed on Operation Rolling Thunder, the three-and-a-half-year bombing campaign. Military officials believed that the United States should have begun Operation Rolling Thunder with all-out massive bombing and continued until the devastation brought North Vietnam to its knees. Instead, they charged, civilian decision makers compelled the military to fight with one hand tied behind its back. Their arguments echoed General Douglas MacArthur's criticism of Truman's policy during the Korean War—though they did not repeat MacArthur's insubordination.

Unlike military officials, who could single-mindedly focus on defeating the enemy, the president balanced political considerations against military objectives and found compelling reasons to limit the application of airpower. Recalling the Korean War, Johnson noted that "China is there on the [North Vietnamese] border with 700 million men," and he studiously avoided action that might provoke intervention by the Chinese, who now possessed nuclear weapons. Johnson's strategy also aimed to keep the Soviet Union out of the war, to avoid inflaming antiwar sentiment at home, and to avert international criticism of the United States.

Consequently, the president would not permit bombing of areas where high civilian casualties might result and areas near the Chinese border. He banned strikes on airfields and missile sites that were under construction and thus likely to contain Chinese or Soviet advisers, and he refused to mine North Vietnam's harbors, through which Soviet ships imported goods to North Vietnam. But Johnson did escalate the pressure, increasing the intensity of the bombing fourfold by 1968. In all, Operation Rolling Thunder rained 643,000 tons of bombs on North Vietnam between 1965 and 1968.

Military leaders agreed with Johnson's desire to spare civilians. The Joint Chiefs of Staff never proposed, for example, strikes against a system of dikes and dams that could have disrupted food production and flooded Hanoi under twenty feet of water. Rather, they focused on destroying North Vietnam's industry and transportation system. Even after the Tet Offensive in early 1968, military advisers did not suggest direct attacks on civilians. Noncombatant casualties in North Vietnam contrasted sharply with those in World War II, when Anglo-American bombing of Dresden, Germany, alone took more than 35,000 civilian lives and the firebombing of Japan caused 330,000 civilian deaths. Operation Rolling Thunder's three and a half years of bombing claimed an estimated 52,000 civilian lives.

The relatively low level of economic development in North Vietnam and the North Vietnamese government's ability to mobilize its citizens counteracted the military superiority of the United States. Sheer man-, woman-, and child-power compensated for the demolition of transportation sources, industry sites, and electric power plants. When bombs struck a rail line, civilians rushed with bicycles to unload a train's cargo, carry it beyond the break, and load it onto a second train. Three hundred thousand full-time workers and 200,000 farmers labored in their spare time to keep the Ho Chi Minh Trail usable in spite of heavy bombing. When bridges were destroyed, the North Vietnamese resorted to ferries and pontoons made from bamboo, and they rebuilt bridges slightly underwater to make them harder to detect from the air. They dispersed oil storage facilities and production centers throughout the countryside, and when bombs knocked out electric power plants, the Vietnamese turned to more than two thousand portable generators and used oil lamps and candles in their homes.

North Vietnam's needs were relatively small, and officials found ample means to meet them. In 1967, North Vietnam had only about 55,000 soldiers in South Vietnam, and because they waged a guerrilla war with only sporadic fighting, the insurgents in the South did not require huge amounts of supplies. What U.S. bombs destroyed, the North Vietnamese replaced with Chinese and Soviet imports. In 1967 alone, China provided 600,000 tons of rice, and it supplied small arms and ammunition, vehicles, and other goods throughout the war. Competing with China for influence in North Vietnam and favor in the third world, the Soviets contributed tanks, fighter planes, surface-to-air missiles, and other sophisticated weapons. Foreign aid substantially curtailed the effect of Operation Rolling Thunder, and the Soviet-installed modern defense systems made the bombing more difficult and dangerous for U.S. pilots.

In July 1969, Seventh Air Force commander General William W. Momyer commented on Operation Rolling Thunder to the retiring air force chief of staff, "We had the force, skill, and intelligence, but our civilian betters wouldn't turn us loose." Johnson refused to turn the military loose because in addition to the goal he shared with the military —breaking Hanoi's ability to support insurgency in the South—he also wanted to keep China and the Soviet Union—and nuclear weapons—out of the war and to contain domestic and international criticism of U.S. policy. Whether a more devastating air war would have provoked Chinese or Soviet intervention, of course, can never be known.

Nor can we know whether all-out bombing of the North could have guaranteed an independent non-Communist government in the South. We do know that Johnson's military advisers imposed their own restraints, never recommending the wholesale attacks on civilians that took place in World War II. Short of decimating the civilian population, it is questionable whether more intense bombing could have completely halted North Vietnamese support for the Vietcong, given the nature of the North Vietnamese economy, the determination and ingenuity of its people, and the plentiful assistance from China and the Soviet Union. Whether the strategic bombing that worked so well in a world war against major industrial powers could be effective in a third world guerrilla war remained in doubt after the Vietnam War.

the early years of the war, African Americans constituted 31 percent of all combat troops, often having enlisted in the military because their opportunities were so meager in the civilian economy. Death rates among black soldiers were twice as great as the proportion of black to white soldiers in Vietnam until 1966, when the military adjusted assignments of personnel to produce a more racially balanced distribution of sacrifice.

American troops faced extremely difficult conditions. This was a war whose purpose was unclear, a war without established battle lines. "There were no Normandies or Gettysburgs for us," wrote infantry officer Philip Caputo. For most combat troops, the war meant "weeks of expectant waiting and, at random intervals, of conducting vicious manhunts through jungles and swamps where snipers harassed us constantly and booby traps cut us down one by one."

Soldiers fought in thick jungles and swamps filled with leeches and in oppressive heat, rain, and humidity that rotted their feet and legs. Search-and-destroy missions sent platoons out into the darkness where ambushes, traps, and snipers could spring up at any moment. A harmless-looking civilian might be a deadly enemy. In the war of attrition, the U.S. military inflicted great losses on the enemy, estimated at more than 200,000 by the end of 1967. Yet the United States could claim no more than a stalemate.

After a series of coups and short-lived regimes, in 1965 the South Vietnamese government settled into a period of stability, if only in terms of personnel. Air Marshal Nguyen Cao Ky became prime minister, and General Nguyen Van Thieu took over as commmander in chief of the military. In 1967, in elections boycotted by the Buddhists, the South Vietnamese selected a constitutional assembly. It produced a document that was modeled after the U.S. and French constitutions, but with numerous provisions designed to enable the current leaders to remain in power. In subsequent elections, Thieu won the presidency, with Ky as his vice president. However, the Thieu-Ky ticket could muster only 35 percent of the vote, while an opponent who called for negotiations with the Vietcong won 17 percent.

The Thieu-Ky government was no more able than Diem had been to rally popular support for the war. Graft and corruption continued to flourish, and the massive American presence often made things worse. In the intensified fighting and inability to distinguish friend from foe, thousands of South Vietnamese civilians were killed and wounded, and

FIGHTING THE CLIMATE AND GEOGRAPHY
Steamy tropical conditions and an inhospitable terrain were among the nonhuman enemies U.S. troops faced in Vietnam. Soldiers like these men making their way through rice paddies in 1968 were soaked for weeks on end. Veteran Philip Caputo wrote about "being pounded numb by ceaseless rain" during the monsoon; "at night we squatted in muddy holes, picked off the leeches that sucked on our veins."
C. Simon Pietri/Sygma.

South Vietnamese farms and villages were bombed and burned. By 1968, five million people, nearly 30 percent of the population, had become refugees; many were forced into camps or urban centers. Massive infusions of American dollars and goods produced rampant inflation, more opportunities for graft, the demise of local industries, and an increased dependence on foreign aid.

Americanization of the war also strained relations between the United States and its key allies. Australia, New Zealand, the Philippines, South Korea, and Thailand supported the U.S. effort by sending small military contingents to Vietnam. But no help came from the United States' most important allies. In fact, French President Charles de Gaulle openly criticized U.S. policy in Vietnam, while Canadian, British, and West German leaders more quietly sought an end to the war. Some of the allies had moral or practical reservations about U.S. intervention, and all wanted the United States to concentrate its attention and resources in areas that they deemed more critical to the West.

Johnson's Americanization of the war resulted from decisions that were carefully considered and cautiously reached, and they flowed logically from the commitments made by three presidents before him. All the same, 1965 marked a critical turning point because Americanization of the war shifted the rationale for involvement from the need to contain communism in Southeast Asia to the need to prove to the world the will and ability of the United States to make good on its commitments. As George F. Kennan, a chief architect of the containment policy, insisted in 1966, American withdrawal from Vietnam would result in damage to U.S. interests that would be "greater than any that might have been involved by our failure to engage ourselves in the first place."

A Nation Polarized

By 1968, President Johnson was fighting a war on two fronts. Unable to secure a non-Communist government in South Vietnam, yet unwilling to withdraw and admit American defeat, the United States entered into a period of internal conflict and violence unparalleled since the Civil War. Domestic opposition to the war grew rapidly after 1965, and radical groups became more vocal and visible, challenging not just the war but the most basic values and institutions of American society.

In response to his critics, President Johnson presented optimistic appraisals of the war and engaged the CIA and FBI in illegal operations to destroy the antiwar movement. In 1968, however, Johnson realized that he must find a way out of Vietnam. Torn between his domestic critics and the military's clamor for more and more troops, in March 1968 the president announced restrictions on the bombing, a new effort at negotiations, and his decision not to pursue reelection.

Those announcements did not quell the domestic unrest. Throughout 1968, demonstrations, violence, and assassinations convulsed the nation.

Vietnam took center stage in the election, and voters chose by a narrow margin the Republican candidate, former Vice President Richard Nixon, who promised to "bring Americans together again" and to achieve "peace with honor."

The Widening War at Home

Before 1965, American actions in Vietnam evoked little criticism in the United States. Small groups of pacifists and radicals had objected to the sending of American advisers and arms since the early 1960s. There were also a few military and civilian officials whose experiences in Vietnam gave them second thoughts. Accepting the basic assumption that the United States must preserve a non-Communist South Vietnam, such critics argued that success depended on transforming the South Vietnamese government and army into institutions that could win popular support.

> *Domestic opposition to the war grew rapidly after 1965, and radical groups became more vocal and visible, challenging not just the war but the most basic values and institutions of American society.*

Johnson's decision to launch Operation Rolling Thunder in the spring of 1965 sparked a mass movement against the war. In April 1965, Students for a Democratic Society (SDS) launched the first major protest and surprised everyone by recruiting 20,000 people for a rally in Washington, D.C. Thereafter, SDS chapters multiplied rapidly across the country, springing up on more than three hundred college campuses and enrolling more than 100,000 members. Although the vast majority of students did not join SDS, thousands of young people joined campus protests against Reserve Officers Training Corps (ROTC) programs, recruiters from the CIA, companies that manufactured war materials, and university departments that conducted research for the Defense Department. A new draft policy in 1967, which ended deferments for postgraduate education, gave students a greater stake in seeing the war end. In the spring of 1968, as many as one million college and high school students participated in a nationwide strike.

Though a critical element, students constituted just one part of the antiwar movement, which entered society's mainstream. The *New York Times*

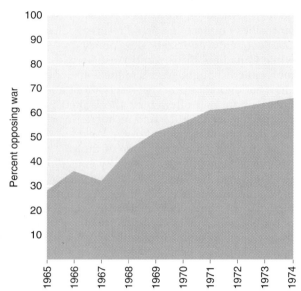

FIGURE 29.2
Public Opinion about the Vietnam War, 1965–1974
This chart reflects the percent of people answering yes to a Gallup poll question, "In view of the developments since we entered the fighting in Vietnam, do you think the United States made a mistake in sending troops to fight in Vietnam?"

AFRICAN AMERICAN ANTIWAR PROTEST
The first expression of African American opposition to the war in Vietnam occurred in Mississippi in July 1965 when a group of civil rights workers called for draft resistance. Blacks should not fight for freedom in Vietnam "until all the Negro People are free in Mississippi," they said, nor should they "risk our lives and kill other Colored People in Santo Domingo and Viet Nam." This protester on the West Coast in April 1967 expresses similar sentiments.
Robert LeBeck/Black Star.

began to question the administration's policy in 1965, and by 1968 media critics included the *Wall Street Journal, Life* magazine, and popular TV journalist Walter Cronkite. The organization Clergy and Laymen Concerned about Viet Nam, founded in 1965, attracted primarily Protestants but also Catholics and Jews who opposed the war. Businesspeople, scientists, and physicians formed their own groups to pressure Johnson to stop the bombing and start negotiations. Although most of organized labor supported the president, some unions and their leaders joined the peace movement. In-

creasing numbers of prominent Democratic senators, including J. William Fulbright, George McGovern, and majority leader Mike Mansfield, urged Johnson to substitute negotiation for force. Popular dissatisfaction brought out some 200,000 people who protested in New York City in April 1967.

Opposition to the war took diverse forms: letter-writing campaigns to officials; teach-ins on college campuses; mass marches in Washington, D.C., and cities throughout the nation; student strikes; withholding of federal taxes; and draft card burnings. Protests also included shouting down officials attempting to defend the war in public forums, civil disobedience against military centers and manufacturers of war materials, efforts to stop trains carrying troops, and burnings of ROTC facilities.

Prominent writers Arthur Miller and Robert Lowell turned down invitations to the White House. Singer Eartha Kitt attended a White House luncheon hosted by Lady Bird Johnson, the president's wife, and used the occasion to condemn the war. Father Philip Berrigan and three other Catholics poured pig blood on draft records. Army doctor

Howard Levy refused to train special forces, announcing that training "murderers of women and children" violated the Hippocratic Oath that all doctors must uphold. Although the peace movement never claimed a majority of the population, it brought the war to the center of media attention and severely limited the administration's options. Above all, it revealed that the twenty-year-old consensus about cold war foreign policy had been broken.

Substantial numbers of young men refused to fight in the war. The World Boxing Association stripped Muhammad Ali, heavyweight champion of the world, of his title when he refused to serve in what he called a "white man's war." More than 170,000 young men who opposed the war on moral grounds became conscientious objectors and performed nonmilitary duties at home or in Vietnam. Whether for moral or other reasons, others avoided military service in different ways. About 60,000 young men fled the country to escape the draft, more than 200,000 were accused of failing to register for the draft or other draft offenses, and 25,000 were indicted.

Opponents of the war held far from unanimous views. Some condemned the war on moral grounds, challenging the right of the United States to interfere in the affairs of another country. To them, U.S. intervention had only propped up a corrupt, repressive government, magnified the suffering of the North and South Vietnamese people, and damaged the moral authority of the United States throughout the world. Their goal was total withdrawal from the war and major reorientation of U.S. foreign policy.

The largest segment of antiwar sentiment reflected practical considerations. As draft calls increased, young men and their families wondered whether American interests in Southeast Asia were worth their lives. Liberals recoiled at the mounting costs of the war in American lives, dollars, and the sacrifice of domestic reform. As American intervention escalated with no tangible results, many concluded that the war could not be won or, if it could, that the cost would be too great to bear. Not demanding withdrawal, they wanted Johnson to stop bombing North Vietnam and seek a negotiated settlement.

The antiwar movement outraged millions of Americans who supported the war. The domestic conflict sometimes cut through families; the older generation that had fought against Hitler could not understand a younger generation that failed to stand one hundred percent behind the government. Most repellent to many Americans were antiwar

THE ACCIDENTS OF WAR
As this Vietnamese boy walked to church in Saigon in 1968, he was struck by a rocket and later died. A U.S. helicopter, aiming at Vietcong three hundred yards away, overshot its mark. In a war without a defined front and with the enemy hiding potentially anywhere, such mistakes were not uncommon. Images like this one, showing the human devastation of war, appeared regularly on American TV and helped to stir antiwar sentiment.
Philip Jones Griffith/Magnum Photos, Inc.

PRO-WAR DEMONSTRATORS
Supporters as well as opponents of the war in Vietnam took to the streets, as these New Yorkers did in support of the U.S. invasion of Cambodia in May 1970. Construction workers — called "hard hats" — and other union members marched with American flags and posters supporting President Nixon's policies and blasting New York Mayor John Lindsay for his antiwar position. Following the demonstration, supportive union leaders presented Nixon with an honorary hard hat.
Paul Fusco/Magnum Photos, Inc.

leaders like Tom Hayden, who went to North Vietnam and praised its people, and thousands of peace advocates who expressed support for the enemy. "How can Americans take sides against their own young men sent to Vietnam to fight and perhaps die?" asked supporters of government policy, who demonstrated with banners declaring, "Support our boys in Vietnam." A firefighter whose son had died in Vietnam expressed his hatred for the peace advocates: "They don't really love this country. Some of them almost seem glad to have a chance to criticize us. . . . To hell with them! Let them get out, leave, if they don't like it here. My son didn't die so they can look filthy and talk filthy and insult everything we believe in."

This man reflected the views of many working-class people. While they expressed doubts about the war as often as middle-class Americans, working-class people were conscious of the class dimensions of both the war and the public opposition to it. The

firefighter maintained, "It's people like us who give up our sons for the country. The businesspeople, they run the country and make money from it. The college types . . . go to Washington and tell the government what to do. . . . But their sons don't end up in the swamps over there, in Vietnam." His wife added her view that antiwar protesters' "hearts are with other people, not their own American people, the ordinary kind of person in this country."

In his domestic economic policies, Johnson tried to contain opposition to the war by avoiding actions that would focus attention on its burdens. Therefore, he escalated the war without asking Americans to pay higher taxes. In 1967, however, the growing costs of the war and resulting budget deficits began to stimulate a rise in the cost of living. The president refused to ask for price and wage controls, which had been employed in other wars to control inflation, but at the end of 1967 he did ask for a tax increase. In June 1968, Congress agreed to a 10 percent surcharge on federal income taxes only after Johnson pledged to trim the budget deficit by reducing domestic spending. Johnson's Great Society programs suffered, but the surcharge failed to reverse the inflationary surge.

The rising cost of living and diversion of funds from reform programs broadened antiwar sentiment, to which Johnson reacted harshly. He agonized over casualty reports and was personally hurt by protesters who chanted outside the White House, "Hey, hey, LBJ, how many kids have you killed today?" The president also recognized public opinion as a critical weapon in the war effort. He told a reporter in 1967 that the enemy was not the major problem; rather, it was opposition at home, which was "leading the enemy to believe that we might quit." In addition to undertaking a public relations campaign that cast the war's progress in a deceptively optimistic light, Johnson sought to discredit opponents by labeling them "nervous Nellies," Communists, or unwitting dupes of the enemy.

The administration also employed direct means to silence its critics. On Johnson's orders, the CIA spied on peace advocates, compiling secret files on more than seven thousand citizens. Law enforcement officials indicted not just draft resisters but also those like Dr. Benjamin Spock, the famous baby care expert, who counseled them. Without the president's specific authorization, the FBI launched COINTELPRO (for "counterintelligence programs"), infiltrating the peace movement and disrupting its work. FBI agents schemed to discredit antiwar leaders' reputations by, for example, sending anonymous letters to the press suggesting that a peace activist was a homosexual. However, even the resort to illegal measures failed to subdue the opposition.

The Tet Offensive and the Decision to Deescalate

Although the majority of Americans remained detached from the peace movement and many opposed it vigorously, by late 1967 public impatience and frustration had intensified. Television brought the carnage of the Vietnam War into American homes day after day, making it the first "living room war." The public also watched leading members of Congress question administration officials about the war. Major newspapers around the country editorialized for a change in policy, and in October 1967, public opinion polls found that a mere 28 percent of Americans approved of Johnson's conduct of the war.

Among those dissatisfied with the president's leadership, the "hawks" charged that the United States was fighting with one hand tied behind its back and wanted to apply more power against North Vietnam. The "doves" wanted deescalation or withdrawal. Most Americans were torn between their weariness of the war and their worry about abandoning the American commitment. As one woman said to a pollster, "I want to get out but I don't want to give up."

By the spring of 1967, grave doubts about the war had penetrated the administration itself. The most important defector was Secretary of Defense McNamara, a principal architect of U.S. involvement who now doubted that the war was winnable. Ho Chi Minh, he believed, "won't quit no matter how much bombing we do." McNamara also feared for the image of the United States, "the world's greatest superpower killing or seriously injuring 1,000 noncombatants a week, while trying to pound a tiny, backward nation into submission on an issue whose merits are hotly disputed." Although Johnson shared some of his adviser's concerns, he rejected McNamara's suggestions for deescalation. McNamara did not disclose his views to the public until thirty years later, but in early 1968 he left the administration to head the World Bank.

The critical turning point for Johnson came with the Tet Offensive, which began on January 30, 1968. Just a few weeks after General Westmoreland had reported to Washington that "the enemy has been driven away from the population centers [and] has been compelled to disperse and evade contact," the North Vietnamese and Vietcong attacked key cities and towns and every major American base in South Vietnam. The enemy even invaded the grounds of the U.S. embassy in Saigon, killing two American MPs and holding the compound for six hours. Meanwhile, marines hustled the U.S. ambassador, in pajamas, from his residence to safety.

The Tet Offensive, named for its occurrence during the Vietnamese lunar new year celebration, Tet, was the biggest surprise of the war—and not simply because it violated a truce that both sides had generally observed during the holiday. More important, Tet displayed the enemy's vitality and refusal to let the presence of half a million American soldiers deter it from launching its most daring offensive. Militarily, the Vietcong and North Vietnamese suffered a defeat, losing more than 30,000 men, ten times the casualty rate of ARVN and U.S.

forces. The ARVN fought unusually well, and within a few weeks the enemy had been routed.

Psychologically, however, the Tet Offensive was a devastating blow. It highlighted the credibility gap between official statements and the actual progress of the war, in part because the press emphasized the magnitude of the attacks rather than how quickly they had been repelled. The Tet Offensive created one million more South Vietnamese refugees along with widespread destruction, especially in the ancient city of Hue, whose archaeological treasures were left in rubble after three weeks of intense fighting. Referring to a village that he had helped to defend, a U.S. army official said, "We had to destroy the town to save it." This statement epitomized for more and more Americans the contradiction between means and ends in Vietnam and the brutality and senselessness of the war.

In the aftermath of the Tet Offensive, Johnson reversed the direction the war had taken since the spring of 1965. When Westmoreland requested 200,000 additional troops in Vietnam by the end of the year, the president conferred with his civilian advisers in the Department of Defense, now headed by Clark Clifford, a Washington lawyer and former aide to Harry Truman. He also sought advice from an unofficial group of foreign policy experts who had played key roles in designing cold war policies under successive presidents since World War II. Dubbed the "Wise Men," they met with Johnson in March. Dean Acheson, one of Truman's secretaries of state, summarized their conclusion: "We can no longer do the job we set out to do in the time we have left and we must begin to take steps to disengage."

On March 31, 1968, Lyndon Johnson addressed the nation on television. He announced that the United States would henceforth cut back its bombing of North Vietnam to a small area north of the South Vietnamese border and that he was prepared to begin peace talks with North Vietnam. Then he stunned his audience by concluding, "I shall not seek, and I will not accept, the nomination of my party for another term as your president."

Johnson's decision marked the end of the gradual escalation that had begun in 1965. It signaled the beginning of a shift from "Americanization" to "Vietnamization" of the war, but it was a shift in strategy rather than policy. The United States did not abandon the goal of a non-Communist South Vietnam; it simply hoped to reach that goal by relying more heavily on the South Vietnamese. In that sense, Johnson's announcement represented a return to the pre-1965 policy.

Johnson's explanation for withdrawing from the presidential campaign stressed his need to devote full attention to ending the war and reducing the bitter discord at home. He also hoped that the dramatic step would convince North Vietnam of his sincere desire for a negotiated settlement. Concerns about his health and the possibility of losing the election also motivated his decision. Before Johnson announced his withdrawal, Senator Eugene McCarthy of Minnesota had already begun a race for the Democratic nomination on an antiwar platform and had nearly defeated the president in the New Hampshire primary. Shortly thereafter, Senator Robert F. Kennedy, the late president's brother, began his own campaign.

North Vietnam quickly seized on Johnson's overture, and on May 10, 1968, the two sides began negotiations in Paris. But the United States would not agree to recognition of the NLF, a coalition government, and an American withdrawal. The North Vietnamese would agree to nothing less. Although the talks continued, so did the fighting. The American presence neared its peak at 540,000 in mid-1968, but the cost in American lives was nearly as high after peace talks began as before.

1968: Year of Upheaval

Violence escalated at home. Two months after the murder of Martin Luther King Jr. and the riots that erupted in its wake, another assassination stunned the nation. Senator Robert F. Kennedy had just celebrated his triumph in the California Democratic primary when he was shot in the head by a Palestinian Arab refugee, Sirhan Sirhan, who was outraged by Kennedy's recent statement of support for Israel. Heroic efforts to save Kennedy failed, and he died twenty-six hours later on June 6. For millions of Americans, his death seemed to foreclose the possibility of peace in Vietnam and the renewal of attention to the needs of society's least privileged members.

The spring of 1968 also saw campus violence escalate, as students in France, Britain, Germany, and elsewhere took to the streets and barricades. Of some two hundred campus protests in the United States in the first half of the year, the bloodiest occurred at Columbia University. There, students took over five buildings, demanding that the university stop uprooting African Americans as it sought to expand into the neighboring community and do more to meet the needs of black students. The students also wanted the university to stop sponsoring research for the Department of Defense and grant amnesty to past and current student demonstrators. When negotiations failed, university officials called in the New York City police, who cleared the buildings, sent more than one hundred demonstrators to the hospital, and arrested more than seven hundred students. An ensuing student strike brought the academic year to a premature end.

In August, protesters battled the police in Chicago, where the Democratic Party convened to nominate its presidential ticket. Several thousand demonstrators came to Chicago, some to show their support for Eugene McCarthy's peace candidacy, others mobilized by the Youth International Party (Yippies), a splinter group of SDS. Its leaders, Abbie Hoffman and Jerry Rubin, urged students to demonstrate their hatred of the establishment by creating chaos and disorder in the backyard of the Democratic convention and provoking the police to violence.

Chicago's mayor and leading Democrat, Richard J. Daley, had already made clear his intention to brook no civil disorder when he ordered police to "shoot to kill" arsonists and "shoot to maim" looters during the riots following King's assassination. Now he forbade demonstrators to hold rallies or marches, insisted that the parks be cleared after 11 P.M., and mobilized thousands of police to carry out his will. When police ordered demonstrators in Lincoln Park to disperse on August 25, only to be met with taunts and jeers, they attacked the protesters with tear gas and clubs.

Street battles between police and protesters continued for three days, culminating in what an

PROTEST IN THE STREETS
The worst violence surrounding the 1968 Democratic National Convention in Chicago came on August 28 when protesters attempted to march to the convention site. Near the Hilton Hotel, where most of the delegates stayed, some three thousand protesters came up against a line of police. The police attacked the demonstrators, as well as reporters, hotel guests, and bystanders, with nightsticks and mace, driving a crowd through the plateglass window of the Hilton's cocktail lounge. What other police confrontation in Chicago does the name of the bar in the background recall?
Corbis-Bettmann.

official commission later termed a "police riot" on the night of August 28. Taunted by cries of "Gestapo pigs" and pelted with rocks and bottles, the police attacked with mace and nightsticks, clubbing not only those who had come in hopes of provoking violence, but also reporters, peaceful demonstrators, convention delegates and workers, and bystanders.

The bloodshed in the streets had little effect on the outcome of the convention. Peace Democrats lost their battle for a platform plank offering some concessions to North Vietnam that might break the deadlock in the peace talks. They also lost the presidential nomination, as Vice President Hubert H. Humphrey trounced Eugene McCarthy by nearly three to one. McCarthy's refusal to share the podium with Humphrey on the final night of the convention provided a stark illustration of the bitter split within the party.

In contrast, the Republican convention, which had occurred three weeks earlier, provided little drama. Referring to the lack of excitement and Miami's heat and humidity, one columnist wrote that the convention had been "planned in advance by six bores and a sadist." Former Vice President Richard Nixon won on the first ballot. For his running mate, Nixon chose Maryland Governor Spiro T. Agnew, hoping to gather southern support while not alienating northern and western voters.

For the first time in nearly fifty years, a strong third party entered the electoral scene. Former Alabama Governor George C. Wallace, who had gained national attention for his all-out efforts to maintain "segregation forever" in Alabama schools, ran on the ticket of the American Independent Party. Although his support was strongest in the Deep South, Wallace appealed to Americans throughout the country who were alarmed and disgusted by the changes that were sweeping their society and frustrated by the nation's inability to work its will in Vietnam.

Wallace supporters included considerable numbers of lower-class and working-class whites, who believed that civil rights initiatives and antipoverty programs benefited the undeserving at their expense. And he appealed to citizens outraged by the assault on traditional values that had reverberated through the 1960s. Privileged students attacking their universities, antiwar protesters resorting to civil disobedience and sometimes violence, young people experimenting with drugs and flouting sexual mores—all seemed to threaten the very foundations of American society. Wallace promised to restore law and order, respect for authority, disci-

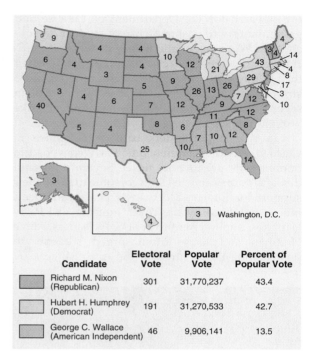

Candidate	Electoral Vote	Popular Vote	Percent of Popular Vote
Richard M. Nixon (Republican)	301	31,770,237	43.4
Hubert H. Humphrey (Democrat)	191	31,270,533	42.7
George C. Wallace (American Independent)	46	9,906,141	13.5

MAP 29.3
The Election of 1968

pline, and patriotism. Striking a chord with those Americans who could not accept the limitations of U.S. power in the world, he called for stronger measures against America's enemies, both at home and in Vietnam.

Voters could discern very little difference between the two major party candidates on the central issue of Vietnam. Nixon had the advantage because he could criticize the incumbent party for "four years in Vietnam with no end in sight." He promised "to bring an honorable end" to the war but gave no indication of how he would do it. Attacking the Great Society for "pouring billions of dollars into programs that have failed" and appealing to "the forgotten Americans, the non-shouters, the non-demonstrators," Nixon more guardedly played on the resentments that fueled the Wallace campaign.

Humphrey had strong reservations about U.S. policy in Vietnam, yet as vice president he wanted to avoid a break with Johnson. In late September, Humphrey distanced himself marginally from official policy by expressing willingness to "stop the bombing of the North as an acceptable risk for peace." At the end of October, Johnson gave

Humphrey's campaign a further boost when he announced a halt to the bombing of North Vietnam. By election eve, Nixon and Humphrey were in a neck-and-neck race.

With nearly ten million votes (13 percent of the total), the American Independent Party produced the strongest third-party finish since 1924. Nixon squeaked by Humphrey with a popular vote of 31.8 million to Humphrey's 31.3 million, prevailing more strongly in electoral college votes, with 301 to Humphrey's 191 and Wallace's 46. The Democrats lost a few seats in Congress but maintained control of both the House and the Senate.

The 1968 elections revealed deep cracks in the coalition that had, with the exception of the Eisenhower years, kept the Democrats in power for thirty years. Opposition to the Democrats' policies on race moved most of the South behind Nixon or Wallace, as that region decidedly broke a century of Democratic Party ascendency. Although union leaders rallied strongly behind Humphrey, significant numbers of the rank and file and unorganized blue-collar workers demonstrated their displeasure with recent tumultuous changes and frustration over the Vietnam War by voting for Wallace or Nixon. Voters aimed grievances concerning civil rights policies, Great Society reforms, inflation, antiwar protesters, campus rebels, changing sexual mores, drug use, urban riots, and America's impotence in Vietnam at the Democratic Party. These resentments continued to simmer, later to be mobilized into a resurging right in American politics.

Nixon's Failed Search for Peace with Honor

"I'm not going to end up like LBJ, holed up in the White House afraid to show my face on the street," the new president asserted. "I'm going to stop that war. Fast." Yet, having promised "peace with honor," Nixon was no more willing than Johnson had been to allow South Vietnam to fall to the Communists and no more able to find a way to prevent it. Like Johnson, he faced two obstacles: A majority of Americans did not want to see the war drag on, and North Vietnam and the National Liberation Front would settle for nothing less than an independent, united nation.

To quiet domestic opposition to the war, in 1969 Nixon began a gradual withdrawal of U.S. ground troops combined with attempts to strengthen the South Vietnamese military. He pursued peace through negotiations while expanding military operations into neighboring Cambodia and Laos and engaging in sporadic but ferocious bombing of North Vietnam, thereby intensifying opposition to the war. The Nixon administration further polarized the nation and outdid its predecessor in deceiving Congress and the public and in harassing dissenters.

Having promised "peace with honor," Nixon was no more willing than Johnson had been to allow South Vietnam to fall to the Communists and no more able to find a way to prevent it.

Unable to marshal support at home or to defeat the enemy abroad, in January 1973 the administration concluded a truce that ended the direct involvement of the United States. Far from achieving peace with honor, the United States accepted conditions that led to total victory for the North Vietnamese in April 1975. By then, public disclosure of the illegal means Nixon had applied to silence his critics and defeat the political opposition at home had driven the president from office.

Vietnamization and Negotiations

"No secretary of state is really important," Nixon remarked in 1967. "The president makes foreign policy." Both his secretary of state and his secretary of defense found themselves overshadowed in the making of foreign policy and often left in the dark on important initiatives. Nixon's most important adviser was Henry A. Kissinger, a German-born refugee from Hitler's Holocaust and a Harvard professor of international relations. During the 1968 campaign, Kissinger had manuevered himself into the favor of both Humphrey and Nixon by offering advice to each. In the new administration he became the president's assistant for national security.

Nixon and Kissinger embraced the goal of the three preceding administrations: a non-Communist South Vietnam. By 1969, however, that goal had become almost incidental to the larger objective of maintaining American credibility. According to Kissinger, regardless of the wisdom of the initial intervention, "the commitment of five hundred thousand Americans has settled the importance of Vietnam. For what is involved now is confidence in American promises."

From 1969 to 1972, Nixon and Kissinger pursued a four-pronged approach. First, they aimed to strengthen the South Vietnamese military and government. Second, they negotiated with both North Vietnam and the Soviet Union. Third, they agreed to apply sufficient force to make Hanoi amenable to American terms at the bargaining table. Fourth, to disarm the antiwar movement at home, Nixon gradually withdrew U.S. soldiers from combat. Serving in their place would be South Vietnamese soldiers and American technology and bombs.

U.S. military officials carried out an ambitious program to strengthen South Vietnam. ARVN forces grew to more than one million, supplied with the latest American equipment and supported with improved training, increased pay scales, and added benefits. The South Vietnamese air force became the fourth largest in the world. U.S. advisers and funds also assisted "pacification" efforts in the countryside, which involved land reform, holding village elections, and building schools, hospitals, and transportation facilities. Despite these improvements, whether South Vietnam could stand on its own remained doubtful.

The other side of Vietnamization was the withdrawal of U.S. forces. The number of GIs peaked at 543,000 in June 1969 and thereafter decreased to 334,600 in 1970 and 140,000 by the end of 1971. Casualties likewise declined, the average monthly death rate of American soldiers falling from nearly 800 in 1969 to 352 in 1970. Decreasing draft calls and casualties helped undercut the strength of the antiwar movement, yet more than 20,000 Americans perished in Vietnam during the last four years of the war.

Morale fell among the Americans left in Vietnam. Having been exposed to the antiwar movement at home, many of these soldiers had less faith in the purpose or value of the war than their predecessors had. In addition to mounting racial tensions among soldiers, more incidents of "fragging" (attacks on officers by enlisted men) occurred than in any previous wars. A government study in 1971 reported that half of the U.S. army personnel sought escape from boredom and horror by smoking marijuana, and one-fourth used heroin, opium, and other drugs.

While reducing the U.S. presence in Vietnam, Nixon and Kissinger also endeavored to capitalize on Soviet interest in expanded trade and arms reductions by linking U.S. desires in Vietnam with Soviet concerns elsewhere. However, their breakthroughs in summit diplomacy with the Soviet

Union and China (discussed in chapter 30) failed to change the course of the war. The Communist leaders in Vietnam zealously pursued their goal of unification and national independence, and little that either the Soviet Union or China could or would do deterred them from the objective to which they had dedicated twenty or more years of their lives.

Nor did intensification of force against the enemy achieve its objective. While maintaining the general halt in the bombing of North Vietnam, Nixon approved several ferocious assaults throughout Vietnam and ordered secret attacks on enemy strongholds in neighboring Cambodia and Laos. Kissinger believed that a "fourth-rate power like North Vietnam" had to have a "breaking point," but the hundreds of thousands of tons of bombs delivered by U.S. pilots failed to find it. Fierce application of American power bought time, but little else. (See Historical Question, page 1152.)

The bombing inflamed passions at home, and the antiwar movement plagued the Nixon administration through 1971. Some protesters devised new and extravagant methods. A small group called Women against Daddy Warbucks invaded a draft board in New York City in July 1969, removed draft files, and stripped typewriters of the 1 and the A keys, which were used to type the code 1-A, designating those who were eligible for the draft. Other protests were legal and peaceful and involved massive numbers of people. On October 15, 1969, two million citizens across the nation took part in marches, rallies, and readings of the names of dead soldiers. One month later, tens of thousands of people marched from Arlington National Cemetery to Capitol Hill, wearing black armbands, each bearing a card with the name of a dead American or a destroyed village. Passing the White House, each marcher called out a victim's name. More than half a million people gathered the next day at the Washington Monument.

Vietnam Becomes Nixon's War

In the spring of 1969, Nixon began a fierce air war in Cambodia. Pilots were commanded to destroy their orders after every mission, and Nixon kept the bombing hidden from Congress and the public for more than a year. Designed to knock out North Vietnamese sanctuaries in Cambodia, from which the enemy launched attacks on South Vietnam, the campaign, dropping more than 100,000 tons of bombs, resulted only in sending the North Vietnamese to other hiding places. To support a new, pro-Western

Cambodian government that came to power in 1970 through a military coup and "to show the enemy that we were still serious about our commitment in Vietnam," in April 1970 Nixon ordered a joint U.S.-ARVN invasion of Cambodia.

With that order, the president made Vietnam "Nixon's war" and provoked immediate outrage at home. Aware that he was "going to get unshirted hell" for the attack, Nixon made a belligerent speech announcing his move, which he called an "incursion" because the Cambodian government acquiesced in it. He concluded by emphasizing the importance of American credibility: "If when the chips are down, the world's most powerful nation acts like a pitiful helpless giant, the forces of totalitarianism and anarchy will threaten free nations . . . throughout the world."

"This will make the students puke," a cabinet member said when he read Nixon's speech. They did more. A protest in Washington drew upward of 100,000 people, and students demonstrated and boycotted classes on hundreds of campuses. At Kent State University in Ohio, where protesters had burned an ROTC building, the governor called out National Guard troops. At a peaceful rally on May 4, 1970, nervous troops fired at students, killing four, two of whom were bystanders, crippling another for life, and wounding ten others. "They're starting to treat their own children like they treat us," commented a black woman in Harlem. In a confrontation at Jackson State College in Mississippi on May 14, police shot into a dormitory, killing two black students. In August, a national Chicano antiwar rally held in Los Angeles erupted in violence when police used clubs and tear gas against the protesters.

Furious at the secret bombing and invasion of Cambodia, legislators attempted to rein in the president. The Senate voted to terminate the Gulf of Tonkin Resolution, which had been passed in 1964 and gave the president virtually a blank check in Vietnam, and to cut off all funds for the Cambodian operation by the end of June. The House of Representatives refused to go along, but Congress was clearly becoming an obstacle to the Nixon administration's plans. By the end of June, Nixon pulled out all U.S. soldiers from Cambodia. But he also authorized an intensified assault on his domestic opponents, one that ultimately drove him from the White House.

The Cambodian invasion inflicted heavy blows on the North Vietnamese but failed to break their will. Instead, it set in motion a terrible tragedy for the Cambodian people. The North Vietnamese moved farther into Cambodia and increased their support of the Khmer Rouge, Communist insurgents attempting to overthrow the U.S.-supported government of Lon Nol. Cambodians endured heavy bombing until Congress forced its end in 1973. A brutal civil war lasted until 1975, when the Khmer Rouge triumphed and quickly imposed a savage genocidal rule over the Cambodian population. The Khmer Rouge slaughter and the murderous effects of the war took millions of lives, giving the name "killing fields" to the land of this historically peaceful people.

After the spring of 1971, there were fewer massive antiwar demonstrations, but vehement protest continued in other forms. Public attention focused on the horrors of U.S. intervention in Vietnam at the court-martial of Lieutenant William Calley, which began in November 1970 and resulted in his conviction. During the trial, Americans learned that Calley's company had massacred more than two hundred civilians in the hamlet of My Lai in March 1968. Among those murdered were children and women, some of whom were raped first. The military had covered up the atrocity for more than a year.

In 1971, Vietnam veterans themselves became a visible part of the peace movement, the first men in United States history to oppose a war in which they had fought. Veterans held a public investigation of U.S. "war crimes" in Vietnam, rallied in front of the U.S. Capitol and cast away their war medals, and occupied the Statue of Liberty. In May 1971, veterans numbered among 40,000 protesters who engaged in civil disobedience in an effort to shut down Washington. Officials made more than 12,000 arrests, which courts later ruled violations of protesters' rights.

Administration policy suffered a greater blow in June 1971 with publication of the *Pentagon Papers*, a secret, critical government study of U.S. policy in Vietnam. While working as an aide to Henry Kissinger, Daniel Ellsberg, who had previously served as a civilian adviser in Vietnam, came across the documents. Convinced that the war was futile and frustrated in his attempts to persuade officials of his view, Ellsberg copied the papers and gave them to the *New York Times*.

The Nixon administration quickly obtained a court injunction against further publication of the papers, only to have the injunction overturned by the Supreme Court as a violation of freedom of the press. Ellsberg then became another victim of Nixon's obsession with punishing his enemies. Instructed by the president to do anything necessary to discredit Ellsberg, a group of men hired by Nixon

aides broke into the office of Ellsberg's psychiatrist, stole confidential records, and leaked them to the press. Although these actions escaped public notice until 1973, the *Pentagon Papers* episode spurred disillusionment with the war by casting doubts on the government's credibility. Seventy-one percent of respondents to public opinion polls in 1971 thought that it had been a mistake to send American troops to Vietnam; 58 percent considered the war to be immoral.

The Peace Accords and the Fall of Saigon

In 1972, Nixon and Kissinger continued to pursue a combined strategy of military force and negotiations. In March, responding to the heaviest offensive by the North Vietnamese since the Tet Offensive of 1968, the United States resumed sustained bombing of the North, mined Haiphong and other harbors for the first time, and announced a naval blockade. Nixon boasted, "The bastards have never been bombed like they're going to be bombed this time."

The escalation of the war probably heightened North Vietnam's interest in a settlement, and by October, secret negotiations between Kissinger and North Vietnamese envoy Le Duc Tho brought the two sides close to agreement. But when the talks sputtered to a new deadlock in December 1972, Nixon turned once again to intimidation. Over the Christmas holiday, he ordered the most devastating bombing of North Vietnam yet: In twelve days, U.S. planes dropped more bombs than they had in all of 1969–1971. On January 27, 1973, representatives of the United States, North Vietnam, the South Vietnamese government, and the Vietcong (now called the People's Revolutionary Government) signed a formal accord in Paris.

The agreement required removal of all U.S. troops and military advisers within sixty days but allowed North Vietnamese forces to remain in place. Both sides agreed to return prisoners of war, including hundreds of Americans, some of whom had been held since the mid-1960s. The Thieu government continued in power, but the People's Revolutionary Government won a role in determining the political future of South Vietnam. The peace treaty allowed the United States a face-saving withdrawal but fell far short of the goal for which the United States had intervened in the first place, since it was doubtful that South Vietnam would remain non-Communist for long.

EVACUATING SOUTH VIETNAM
As Communist troops rolled south toward Saigon in the spring of 1975, desperate South Viet-
namese attempted to flee along with the departing Americans. Here an American official punches
a man trying to get on an already overloaded plane leaving Nha Trang on April 1. Thousands of
Vietnamese who wanted to be evacuated were left behind. But not South Vietnamese President
Nguyen Van Thieu, who escaped with fifteen tons of baggage on a U.S. plane to Taiwan.
Corbis-Bettmann.

Though the Paris agreement had established a cease-fire, fighting resumed immediately among the Vietnamese, and the United States continued to bomb Cambodia. Nixon found his efforts to support the South Vietnamese government, and indeed his ability to govern at all, increasingly eroded by a series of revelations of administration wrongdoing that came to be known as the Watergate scandals (discussed in chapter 30). In June 1973, Congress enacted legislation that ended all military operations in Laos and Cambodia. The House upheld Nixon's veto, but public opposition compelled the president to stop the bombing.

In 1975, North Vietnam launched a new offensive in South Vietnam, calculating that it would take two more years to achieve victory. It took just five months. As South Vietnam neared collapse, Congress approved funds to evacuate Americans and to serve "humanitarian" purposes but refused to authorize any more military aid. On May 1, 1975, Vietcong troops occupied Saigon and renamed it Ho Chi Minh City in honor of the Communist leader, who had died before seeing his goal of Vietnamese unification and independence achieved.

Confusion, humiliation, and tragedy marked the hasty evacuation of Americans and their South Vietnamese allies. The United States got its own citizens out, as well as 150,000 Vietnamese. But there were not enough aircraft and ships and not enough time to evacuate all those who wanted to leave. U.S. marines beat back some of the desperate Vietnamese who tried to escape through the U.S. embassy. Some South Vietnamese troops, frightened and angry at being left behind, even fired on departing Americans.

The Legacy of Defeat

It took Nixon four years to end the war; twenty thousand additional Americans lost their lives, the conflict expanded into Laos and Cambodia, and Southeast Asia endured massive bombing campaigns. During that time, the Vietnam War became a genuinely bipartisan war. And it was not only the president's war. Although increasing numbers of legislators criticized the war, Congress never denied the funds to fight it. "This chamber reeks of blood," George McGovern had declared on the Senate floor in 1970, castigating his colleagues for "our pitiful willingness to let the Executive carry the burden that the Constitution places on us." Congress moved slowly to assert itself, not repealing the Gulf of Tonkin Resolution until the end of 1970.

Only after the U.S. military withdrawal from Vietnam in 1973 did the legislative branch stiffen its constitutional authority over the making of war. In November 1973, Congress enacted the War Powers Act over Nixon's veto. The law required the president to report to Congress within forty-eight hours when he deployed military forces in places where hostilities existed or were likely to occur. If Congress failed to endorse his action within sixty days, the troops would have to be withdrawn.

Because both Democrats and Republicans bore responsibility for America's involvement in Vietnam, the defeat did not become a subject of partisan debate. In fact, most Americans wanted simply to forget the war. Moreover, the dire predictions of three presidents did not materialize. The failure to preserve a non-Communist South Vietnam did not open the floodgates to Communist expansion, the original premise of U.S. intervention. Although

Vietnam, Laos, and Cambodia all fell within the Communist camp in the spring of 1975, Thailand, Burma, Malaysia, and the rest of Southeast Asia did not. When China and Vietnam soon reverted to their historical relationship of hostility, the myth of a monolithic Communist power overrunning Asia evaporated.

Three features of the war denied Vietnam veterans the traditional homecoming: its lack of strong support at home, its character as a guerrilla war, and its ultimate failure.

The Americans most directly affected by the nation's first military defeat were the veterans and those who had lost loved ones to the war. The nation had always honored soldiers' sacrifices for a noble and victorious cause. However, three features of the war denied Vietnam veterans the traditional homecoming: its lack of strong support at home, its character as a guerrilla war, and its ultimate failure. As one veteran remarked, "The left hated us for killing, and the right hated us for not killing enough."

Because the Vietnam War was in large part a civil war without easily identifiable enemies, combat was especially brutal. As antiwar opposition grew, more and more GIs could find no purpose in the war beyond staying alive, no redeeming quality beyond comradeship and loyalty to their fellow soldiers. For combat soldiers, the terrors of conventional warfare were multiplied, and so were the opportunities and motivations to commit atrocities. The massacre of civilians by U.S. troops in My Lai was the most publicized war crime, but 9 percent of a sample of veterans in a government study reported that they had committed abusive violence against civilians or prisoners of war, and 30 percent had witnessed such acts.

To demonstrate the immorality of the war, peace advocates stressed the atrocities, to which the media also gave substantial coverage in the later stages of the war. This emphasis on the war's cruelties contributed to an image of the Vietnam War veteran as dehumanized and violent and thus deserving of public hostility or indifference. Veterans themselves who had committed or witnessed atrocities carried a severe burden of guilt.

Veterans expressed two kinds of reactions to the defeat. Many regarded the commitment as an honorable one and castigated the government for

---

TABLE 29.1

VIETNAM WAR CASUALTIES

United States

Killed in action	47,382
Wounded	153,303
Died, non-combat	1,811
Missing, captured	10,753

South Vietnam

Killed in action	110,357
Military wounded	499,026
Civilians killed	415,000
Civilians wounded	913,000

Communist regulars and guerrillas

Killed in action	666,000

Source: U.S. Department of Defense.

betraying them and their dead comrades by not letting them win the war. Others, sometimes expressing shame or guilt, blamed the government for sacrificing its youth in an immoral or useless war. The soldiers themselves best expressed the sense of the war's futility in the slang term they used in referring to a comrade's death: He was "wasted."

No parades or other heroes' welcomes greeted the returning soldiers. Some were treated to first-class seats by sympathetic airline attendants, but the common advice was to get out of uniform as quickly as possible. Returning veterans sometimes faced harassment from antiwar activists who did not distinguish the war from the warriors. A veteran who had stepped on a mine in Vietnam reported that being spit on "hurt as much as the wounds I sustained." Another veteran remembered the "feelings of rejection and scorn that a bunch of depressed and confused young men experienced when they re-

turned home from doing what their country told them to do."

Most military personnel came home to public indifference. Government benefits were less generous to Vietnam War veterans than they had been to World War II and Korean War soldiers. Many felt unwelcome even by veterans of earlier wars, who could not relate to soldiers who had failed to win their war. The 11,500 women who had served in Vietnam felt even more isolated and ignored by the government, the public, and veterans' groups.

Two-thirds of Vietnam veterans said that they would serve again, and most veterans readjusted well to civilian life under difficult conditions. Yet a substantial minority endured the aftereffects of war for decades. The Veterans Administration (VA) estimated that nearly one-sixth of the three million veterans suffered from posttraumatic stress disorder, with its symptoms of fear, recurring nightmares, feelings of guilt and shame, violence, drug

THE VIETNAM VETERANS MEMORIAL
These Vietnam veterans honor their dead comrades at the memorial in the nation's capital. Many veterans found a healing moment in standing before the wall. As one explained at the memorial's dedication in 1982, they came "to find the names of those we lost in the war, as if by tracing the letters cut into the granite we could find what was left of ourselves."
Peter Marbottom/Magnum Photos, Inc.

and alcohol abuse, and suicidal tendencies. More than fifteen years after the war's end, veterans remained on long waiting lists for treatment.

Symptoms of another kind of war casualty began to appear among veterans in the late 1970s. In greater proportions than the general population, those who had served in Vietnam bore deformed children and fell ill themselves with cancer, severe skin disorders, and other ailments. Veterans claimed a link between these illnesses and Agent Orange, an herbicide that contained the deadly poison dioxin. The military had sprayed twenty million gallons of Agent Orange and similar herbicides over five million acres in Vietnam.

For a decade the Veterans Administration insisted that no direct link could be proved, and it rejected virtually all veterans' applications for benefits based on claims that Agent Orange had caused their diseases. In response to a suit filed by 15,000 veterans, manufacturers of the chemical refused to admit fault but settled the suit by agreeing to pay $180 million in claims. Scientists continued to disagree about the chemical's effects on veterans, but in 1989 the VA began to use less severe standards in evaluating veterans' claims. In 1991, Congress enacted legislation extending benefits to veterans with diseases linked to Agent Orange and mandating further research.

Reversal of the government's position on Agent Orange coincided with a shift in the climate surrounding Vietnam War veterans. "It wasn't until the early 1980s," one veteran observed, "that it became 'all right' to be a combat veteran." Before then, he had never seen crowds cheer Vietnam War veterans who marched in Fourth of July parades. The Vietnam War began to enter the realm of popular culture with novels, TV shows, and hit movies depicting a broad range of military experience—from soldiers reduced to brutality to men and women serving with courage and integrity.

The incorporation of the Vietnam War into the collective experience was symbolized most dramatically in the Vietnam Veterans Memorial, designed by Maya Lin and unveiled in Washington, D.C., in November 1982. The black, V-shaped wall inscribed with the names of 58,000 men and women lost to the war became the second most visited site in the capital. It evoked emotional responses from visitors, many of whom adorned it with flowers, flags, messages, and mementos. In an article describing its dedication, a Vietnam combat veteran spoke to and for his former comrades: "Welcome home. The war is over."

Conclusion: The Limits of American Power

The Vietnam War was America's longest war. The United States spent $150 billion and sent more than 3 million of its young men and women to Southeast Asia. Fifty-eight thousand never returned, and 300,000 suffered wounds. The war shattered consensus at home and contributed to the most severe internal disorder in a century. It created opportunities for the aggrandizement of presidential power at the expense of congressional authority and public accountability and led to the downfall of two presidents.

The Vietnam War was a logical extension of the United States' post–World War II commitment to contain communism everywhere on the planet. Truman had begun that commitment when the United States had enjoyed an extraordinary margin of power, largely because World War II had so ravaged the other major nations. As other nations recovered, the United States lost its artificial and temporary advantage. Defeat in Vietnam did not make the United States the "pitiful helpless giant" predicted by Nixon, but it did suggest the relative decline of U.S. power and the impossibility of containment on a global scale.

One of the constraints on U.S. power was the tenacity of revolutionary movements that were determined to achieve national independence and autonomy. Failing to learn from the French experience in Vietnam, U.S. officials badly underestimated the sacrifices that the North Vietnamese and Vietcong were willing to make for the goal of national liberation. Policymakers overestimated the effectiveness of American technological superiority, and they failed to realize how easily the United States could be perceived as a colonial intruder, no more welcome than the French had been.

A second constraint on Eisenhower, Kennedy, Johnson, and Nixon in their decisions about Vietnam was their resolve to avoid a major confrontation with the Soviet Union or China. Johnson, who conducted the largest escalation of the war, especially needed to be cautious to avoid provoking direct intervention by the Communist superpowers. After China exploded its first atomic bomb in 1964, the potential heightened for the Vietnam conflict to escalate into worldwide disaster.

Third, in Vietnam the United States faced the problem of containment by means of an extremely weak ally. The South Vietnamese government never won the support of a majority of its population, and the intense devastation and suffering the war brought to the civilian population only made things worse. Short of taking over the South Vietnamese government and military, the United States could do little to strengthen South Vietnam's ability to resist communism.

Finally, domestic opposition to the war constrained the options of Johnson and Nixon. Although the antiwar movement never claimed a majority of the population, by 1968 it counted significant portions of mainstream America and the voices of prominent religious, media, business, and political

leaders. Moreover, as the war dragged on, with increasing American casualties and no signs of victory and with growing evidence of the damage being inflicted on the Vietnamese, more and more Americans simply became weary of the war.

By 1968, distinguished experts who had fashioned and implemented the containment policy recognized that erosion of support for the war made its continuation untenable. Yet the United States fought on for five more years before Nixon and Kissinger bowed to the resolution of the enemy and the limitations of U.S. power.

CHRONOLOGY

1961 CIA-backed Cuban exiles launch unsuccessful invasion of Cuba at Bay of Pigs.

Berlin Wall erected, dividing East and West Berlin.

Kennedy administration increases military aid and military advisors in South Vietnam.

Kennedy administration creates the Alliance for Progress and the Peace Corps.

1962 Cuban missile crisis.

1963 Limited nuclear test-ban treaty signed by United States and Soviet Union.

South Vietnamese military overthrows President Ngo Dinh Diem.

1964 U.S. troops quell anti-American rioting in Panama Canal Zone.

President Johnson uses Gulf of Tonkin incident to get congressional resolution of support for escalating the war.

1965 First major protest demonstration in Washington, D.C., against the Vietnam War attracts 20,000 people.

Johnson administration initiates Operation Rolling Thunder, intensified bombing of North Vietnam.

Johnson orders increase in the number of U.S. troops in Vietnam, which rises to 543,000 by 1969.

U.S. troops invade Dominican Republic to prevent leftist government from taking power.

1968 Hundreds of thousands of Americans demonstrate against war.

Vietnamese Communists' Tet Offensive leads Johnson administration to reverse its policy in Vietnam and seek negotiated settlement.

In wake of Tet Offensive, President Johnson decides not to seek second term.

Richard Nixon elected president.

1969 Nixon orders secret bombing of Cambodia.

1970 Nixon orders joint U.S.–South Vietnamese invasion of Cambodia.

1971 *New York Times* publishes *Pentagon Papers,* a secret, critical government study of U.S. policy in Vietnam.

1973 The Paris accords between United States, North and South Vietnam, and Vietcong bring formal end to U.S. role in Vietnam.

Congress enacts War Powers Act, limiting president's ability to send Amercans to war without congressional consent.

1975 North Vietnam launches final offensive and takes over all of South Vietnam, ending war in Vietnam.

BIBLIOGRAPHY

GENERAL WORKS

David Halberstam, *The Best and the Brightest* (1972).

George C. Herring, *America's Longest War: The United States and Vietnam, 1950–1975* (1986).

Walter A. McDougall, *The Heavens and the Earth: A Political History of the Space Age* (1985).

Kim McQuaid, *The Anxious Years: America in the Vietnam and Watergate Era* (1989).

James S. Olson and Randy Roberts, *Where the Domino Fell: America and Vietnam, 1945–1990* (1996).

Irwin Unger and Debi Unger, *Turning Point: 1968* (1988).

Marilyn B. Young, *The Vietnam Wars, 1945–1990* (1991).

FOREIGN POLICY IN THE 1960S

Graham T. Allison, *Essence of Decision: Explaining the Cuban Crisis* (1971).

Trumbull Higgins, *The Perfect Failure: Kennedy, Eisenhower, and the CIA at the Bay of Pigs* (1987).

Walter Isaacson, *Kissinger: A Biography* (1992).

Jerome Levinson and Juan de Onis, *The Alliance That Lost Its Way* (1970).

Abraham Lowenthal, *The Dominican Intervention* (1972).

Charles Murray and Catherine Bly Cox, *Apollo: The Race to the Moon* (1989).

James A. Nathan, ed., *The Cuban Missile Crisis Revisited* (1992).

Thomas G. Paterson, *Contesting Castro: The United States and the Triumph of the Cuban Revolution* (1994).

Thomas G. Paterson, ed., *Kennedy's Quest for Victory: American Foreign Policy, 1961–1963* (1989).

Gerald T. Rice, *The Bold Experiment: JFK's Peace Corps* (1986).

Robert D. Schulzinger, *Henry Kissinger: Doctor of Diplomacy* (1989).

D. Michael Shafe, *Deadly Paradigms: The Failure of U.S. Counterinsurgency Policy* (1988).

Deborah Shapley, *Promise and Power: The Life and Times of Robert McNamara* (1993).

Robert Smith Thompson, *The Missiles of October: The Declassified Story of John F. Kennedy and the Cuban Missile Crisis* (1992).

THE WAR IN VIETNAM

David L. Anderson, *Shadow on the White House: Presidents and the Vietnam War* (1993).

Loren Baritz, *Backfire: A History of How American Culture Led Us into Vietnam and Made Us Fight the Way We Did* (1985).

Larry Berman, *Lyndon Johnson's War: The Road to Stalemate in Vietnam* (1989).

Robert Buzzanco, *Masters of War: Military Dissent and Politics in the Vietnam Era* (1996).

Mark Clodfelter, *The Limits of Air Power: The American Bombing of North Vietnam* (1989).

Bernard Fall, *The Two Vietnams: A Political and Military Analysis* (1967).

Frances FitzGerald, *Fire in the Lake: The Vietnamese and the Americans in Vietnam* (1972).

Lloyd C. Gardner, *Lyndon Johnson and the Wars for Vietnam* (1995).

James William Gibson, *The Perfect War: Technowar in Vietnam* (1986).

Allan E. Goodman, *The Lost Peace: America's Search for a Negotiated Settlement of the Vietnam War* (1978).

Ellen J. Hammer, *A Death in November: America in Vietnam, 1973* (1987).

Arnold Isaacs, *Without Honor: Defeat in Vietnam and Cambodia* (1983).

Stanley Karnow, *Vietnam: A History* (1983; rev. ed., 1991).

Gabriel Kolko, *Anatomy of a War: Vietnam, the United States, and the Modern Historical Experience* (1985).

Guenter Lewy, *America in Vietnam* (1978).

Robert S. McNamara, *In Retrospect: The Tragedy and Lessons of Vietnam* (1995).

Harold G. Moore, *We Were Soldiers Once—and Young: Ia Drang, the Battle That Changed the War in Vietnam* (1992).

John M. Newman, *JFK and Vietnam: Deception, Intrigue, and the Struggle for Power* (1992).

David Rudenstine, *The Day the Presses Stopped: A History of the Pentagon Papers Case* (1996).

Ronald H. Spector, *After Tet: The Bloodiest Year in Vietnam* (1993).

Roger Warner, *Shooting at the Moon: The Story of America's Clandestine War in Laos* (1997).

THOSE WHO FOUGHT

Christian G. Appy, *Working-Class War: American Combat Soldiers and Vietnam* (1993).

Lawrence M. Baskir and William A. Strauss, *Chance and Circumstance: The Draft, the War, and the Vietnam Generation* (1978).

Philip Caputo, *A Rumor of War* (1977).

David Donovan, *Once a Warrior King: Memories of an Officer in Vietnam* (1985).

Bernard Edelman, ed., *Dear America: Letters Home from Vietnam* (1985).

Peter Goldman, *Charlie Company: What Vietnam Did to Us* (1983).

Bob Greene, *Homecoming: When the Soldiers Returned from Vietnam* (1989).

Ron Kovic, *Born on the Fourth of July* (1976).

Myra MacPherson, *Long Time Passing: Vietnam and the Haunted Generation* (1984).

Kathryn Marshall, *In the Combat Zone: Vivid Personal Recollections of the Vietnam War from the Women Who Served There* (1987).

Harry Maurer, *Strange Ground: Americans in Vietnam, 1945–1975, an Oral History* (1989).

Al Santoli, *Everything We Had: An Oral History of the Vietnam War* (1981).

Neil Sheehan, *A Bright Shining Lie: John Paul Vann and America in Vietnam* (1988).

John Wheeler, *Touched with Fire: The Future of the Vietnam Generation* (1984).

THE ANTIWAR MOVEMENT

Charles DeBenedetti, with Charles Chatfield, *An American Ordeal: The Antiwar Movement of the Vietnam Era* (1990).

Adam Garfinkle, *Telltale Hearts: The Origins and Impact of the Vietnam Antiwar Movement* (1995).

Todd Gitlin, *The Whole World Is Watching* (1980).

Thomas Powers, *Vietnam: The War at Home* (1973).

Melvin Small, *Johnson, Nixon, and the Doves* (1988).

Melvin Small and William D. Hoover, eds., *Give Peace a Chance: Exploring the Vietnam Antiwar Movement* (1992).

Amy Swerdlow, *Women Strike for Peace: Traditional Motherhood and Radical Politics in the 1960s* (1993).

Michael Useem, *Conscription, Protest, and Social Conflict: The Life and Death of a Draft Resistance Movement* (1983).

Nancy Zaroulis and Gerald Sullivan, *Who Spoke Up? American Protest against the War in Vietnam* (1984).

DOMESTIC POLITICS

Dan T. Carter, *The Politics of Race: George Wallace, the Origins of the New Conservatism, and the Transformation of American Politics* (1995).

David Halberstam, *The Unfinished Odyssey of Robert Kennedy* (1969).

Stephan Lesher, *George Wallace: American Populist* (1994).

Jonathan Schell, *The Time of Illusion* (1976).

Theodore H. White, *The Making of the President, 1968* (1970).

Jules Witcover, *85 Days: The Last Campaign of Robert Kennedy* (1969).

EARTH DAY HOT AIR BALLOON

This hot air balloon, floated by students at Cerritos Junior College in Los Angeles, exemplified the theater and ritual attending the nationwide celebration of the first Earth Day in April 1970. The popularity of the event, observed on some 1,500 college campuses and at thousands of other sites, reflected a rising environmental movement that along with feminism carried social activism into the 1970s. Environmentalism's emphasis on a finite environment and the need for self-restraint went against the American grain. Yet it paralleled a dominant aspect of the decade, as Americans confronted limitations on government's ability to solve economic and social problems at home and to shape events abroad.

Julian Wasser/Time Magazine.

THE DECLINE OF TRUST AND CONFIDENCE

30

1968–1980

ON THE EVENING OF JULY 25, 1974, Representative Barbara Jordan gazed solemnly into the television cameras. Not since the 1954 McCarthy hearings on charges of alleged Communists in the army had the activities of a congressional committee so riveted Americans to their TV screens. In a deep, commanding voice, Jordan said, "I am not going to sit here and be an idle spectator to the diminution, the subversion, the destruction of the Constitution." Thus began Jordan's argument for the impeachment of Richard M. Nixon, president of the United States.

That an African American woman from the South could influence the fate of the presidency indicated the significance of the civil rights struggles of the preceding decade. Born in 1936, Jordan grew up in an all-black neighborhood in Houston, Texas, living with her grandparents, parents, and two sisters in a two-bedroom house. Her father's income as a warehouse clerk and part-time minister provided a modest standard of living but few extras. Instilled with discipline and ambition by her parents, Jordan attended a segregated high school and then went to the all-black Texas Southern University. Riding at the back of the bus, drinking out of water fountains marked "colored," and attending segregated, underfunded schools were routine for Jordan and her friends in the 1950s.

In high school and college, Jordan discovered and honed her skills as an orator and debater. When she decided to attend law school at Boston University, her entire family scrimped to pay her expenses. After earning her degree in 1960, she returned home and set up a law practice. Local Democrats recognized her remarkable speaking skills, sent her out campaigning, and supported her candidacy for the Texas House of Representatives in 1962 and 1964. Running in countywide at-large elections, she lost both times to white candidates.

But the U.S. Supreme Court's "one person, one vote" decisions in the 1960s forced Texas to reapportion its legislative districts and opened political doors for Jordan. In 1966, she won election to the Texas Senate from her district, now heavily populated by African Americans, Chicanos, and white labor unionists, and became one of the first two African Americans to serve as Texas senators since 1882. In 1972, voters sent her to the U.S. House of Representatives, where she was appointed to the House Judiciary Committee.

Jordan's argument for impeachment reflected lifelong habits of painstaking research and careful deliberation, as she measured the illegal activities of President

Nixon against historical and legal standards. If Nixon's offenses did not add up to impeachment, Jordan concluded, "then perhaps that eighteenth-century Constitution should be abandoned to a twentieth-century paper shredder." The next day, billboards sprang up in Houston reading, "Thank you, Barbara Jordan, for explaining the Constitution to us."

Before the House could act on impeachment, Nixon resigned the presidency in disgrace. His successor, Gerald R. Ford, occupied the Oval Office for little more than two years, losing his bid for a full term when Jimmy Carter led the Democrats back into the White House in the 1976 election. After a single term, Carter, too, was voted out of office.

This rapid turnover in the presidency reflected in part a widespread loss of trust and confidence in government in the 1970s, expressed cynically by some Americans whose bumper stickers exhorted, "Don't vote . . . It only encourages them." Public opinion polls reported a drop from 56 percent to 29 percent in citizens' belief that government would "do what is right most of the time." Those who thought that "the people running the country don't really care what happens to you" shot up from 26 percent to 60 percent. And voter turnout continued to decline, reaching only 52.3 percent in 1980.

Nixon's moral failings and Ford's and Carter's weak leadership contributed to the demise of all three. Yet Ford and Carter also confronted problems that might well have defeated more talented politicians. Changes in the institutions of politics and government made effective leadership more difficult just when new domestic and foreign challenges demanded great vision and heroic efforts at persuasion and consensus building.

Barbara Jordan came to a Congress determined to reassert its authority in reaction to the expansion of presidential power under Johnson and Nixon. Yet at the same time, the House and Senate instituted reforms that dispersed power more broadly throughout Congress and undercut the traditionally strong position of congressional party leaders. Moreover, political parties lost influence as primary elections replaced party conventions as the vehicle for nominating candidates. Elected officials depended less on party support and relied more on campaign funds from special interest groups. They used these contributions to appeal directly to voters, largely through television. Consequently, while the legislature set limitations on presidential power, the decline of party influence undermined the ability of Congress itself to provide coherent leadership.

BARBARA JORDAN

After gaining national attention for her role in the Nixon impeachment hearings, Barbara Jordan served in the House of Representatives until she retired in 1978. The representative from Texas supported women's rights as well as civil rights; here she addresses the government-sponsored National Women's Conference in Dallas, Texas, in 1977.

Owen Franken/Sygma.

This fragmented leadership confronted critical challenges during the 1970s, including shifting relations between the superpowers and new shock waves in the Middle East that threatened Western access to oil. Economic problems further shook national confidence as the United States suffered simultaneous galloping inflation and rising unemployment and as a sluggish economy and declining productivity replaced the rapid economic growth of the 1960s.

An increasingly vocal minority of Americans joined right-wing political groups in the 1970s, yet the reforming impulse of the 1960s did not come to a complete halt. Even though the black freedom struggle had been devastated by government harassment, assassination of its leaders, internal conflicts, and white backlash, civil rights advocates retained some influence in Washington, and a few

African Americans, such as Barbara Jordan, slowly edged into the margins of the power structure. Key elements of Lyndon Johnson's Great Society actually expanded in the early 1970s, and a reconstituted Supreme Court under Chief Justice Warren Burger maintained most of the Warren Court's protections of individual rights. Two social movements that had begun late in the 1960s—environmentalism and feminism—achieved their greatest strength during the decade.

Yet a more prevalent pessimism overshadowed these signs of faith that the government could still tackle social problems and promote the general welfare. By the end of the 1970s, a majority of Americans saw their standard of living slipping and the global position of their nation in decline. The heady optimism of the post–World War II era, badly shaken by defeat in Vietnam, shattered with the economic crises and foreign policy setbacks of the 1970s. Limitations rather than possibilities characterized both the popular mood and the state of the nation.

Politics and the Persistence of Reform

Richard Nixon took his victory in 1968 and the strong showing made by George Wallace as evidence that most Americans were fed up with social protest and government efforts to expand individual rights and opportunities. As president, Nixon continued to appeal to those frustrations, and the pace of reform slackened considerably during his administration. Yet in defeating Ronald Reagan on the right and Nelson Rockefeller on the left, Nixon had won the Republican nomination as a centrist. Like Eisenhower, he did not try to turn the clock back a decade, nor did his presidency bring reform efforts to a screeching halt.

Congress remained in the hands of a Democratic majority, and the government faced pressures from popular movements that survived the 1960s. Supporters of the black freedom struggle retained some clout in Congress and the courts, which compelled the Nixon administration to accept civil rights advances that were at odds with the president's antireform rhetoric. Two newer movements prompted Congress and the president to enact reforms in women's rights and environmental protection.

Nixon's "Southern Strategy" and Race Relations

Nixon's 1968 campaign had exploited southern antipathy to black protest and new civil rights policies to woo white southerners away from the Democratic Party. This "southern strategy" delivered the electoral votes of the Upper South to Nixon, yet George Wallace ran strongly in the South and made inroads into traditional white voting blocs in northern and western cities. The prospect of another Wallace campaign in 1972 encouraged Republicans to write off the black vote and appeal to whites who thought racial progress had gone far enough.

Nixon himself believed that "the laws have caught up with our consciences" and that legal solutions had done about as much as they could to improve the status of African Americans. His key adviser, Daniel Patrick Moynihan, a Democrat who had worked in the Johnson White House, claimed that the issue of race had been "taken over by hysterics, paranoids, and boodlers" and called for a period of "benign neglect" in which "Negro progress continues and racial rhetoric fades." Although blacks made some advances during the Nixon administration, the president's public rhetoric and policies sought to slow the momentum of racial change and reap the political benefits of the white backlash.

Richard Nixon took his victory in 1968 as evidence that most Americans were fed up with social protest and government efforts to expand individual rights and opportunities.

In 1968, fourteen years after the *Brown* decision, school desegregation had barely touched the South: Two-thirds of African American children did not have a single white schoolmate. Nixon wanted a freedom-of-choice approach that forbade discrimination but did not use federal power to compel integration. Nonetheless, when the Supreme Court overruled efforts by the Justice Department to delay court-ordered desegregation, in 1969 the administration agreed to enforce the law. By the time Nixon left office, fewer than one in ten black children attended totally segregated schools in the South.

In fact, school segregation was more extreme in northern and western cities, where segregated residential patterns left half of all African American

SCHOOL BUSING
Controversy over busing as a means to integrate public schools erupted in Boston when the school year started in autumn 1974. Opposition was especially high in white ethnic neighborhoods like South Boston, whose residents resented liberal judges from the suburbs assigning them the burden of integration. Clashes between blacks and whites in South Boston prompted authorities to dispatch police to protect black students.
Ira Wyman.

children attending virtually all-black schools. By 1971, busing students from white to black neighborhoods to achieve desegregation had become one of the most inflammatory civil rights issues. That year, in *Swann v. Charlotte-Mecklenburg Board of Education,* the Supreme Court ruled unanimously that busing in Charlotte, North Carolina, and the surrounding county was an appropriate remedy to overcome segregation previously sanctioned by the city. Subsequently, federal courts approved busing plans in cities outside the South that had not offi-

cially maintained segregated schools but that had residential patterns resulting in de facto segregation.

Although children had been riding buses to school for decades, especially in rural areas, busing for racial integration provoked outrage. When busing began at the formerly all-white South Boston High School in 1974, virtually all of the white students boycotted classes while angry opponents of busing threw rocks at black students. The whites most likely to be bused came from working-class families, who remained in cities that more affluent whites had fled and who already felt their status eroding while the government attended to the needs of minorities and the poor. Moreover, white children rode buses to predominantly black schools where overcrowding and deficient facilities often meant inferior education. African Americans themselves were divided over the desirability of busing children across district lines.

Nixon attacked "forced integration" but failed to persuade Congress to end court-ordered busing. But with four new justices appointed by Nixon, the Supreme Court moved in the president's direction in 1974. In a five-to-four decision concerning the Detroit public schools (*Milliken v. Bradley*), the Court imposed strict limits on the use of busing to achieve racial balance.

Despite Nixon's conservative rhetoric and practice, his administration did take some initiatives against discrimination. Secretary of Labor George Shultz implemented the so-called Philadelphia plan, later extended to other cities, which required contractors and unions to increase the number of minority members employed on construction projects funded by the federal government. The Nixon administration also gave a modest boost to African American entrepreneurs by increasing the number of government contracts and loans awarded to minority businesses.

Congress took the initiative in other areas. Overcoming administration opposition, in 1970 Congress extended for five more years the Voting Rights Act of 1965, one of the most important instruments for the empowerment of African Americans. Pressured by feminists and civil rights activists, in March 1972 Congress strengthened the Civil Rights Act of 1964. It enlarged the jurisdiction of the Equal Employment Opportunity Commission, the act's enforcement agency, and granted it authority to initiate lawsuits against employers who were suspected of discrimination.

The Supreme Court after Earl Warren

To Nixon, the Warren Court had been "unprecedentedly politically active . . . too often using their interpretation of the law to remake American society according to their own social, political, and ideological precepts." Through his judicial appointments, Nixon planned both to reverse the Court's directions and to implement his "southern strategy." When Chief Justice Earl Warren resigned in June 1969, Nixon replaced him with Warren E. Burger, a federal appeals court judge, who was seen as a more conservative strict constructionist. Burger easily won Senate confirmation, but Nixon's next nominations provoked bitter fights.

Unions and civil rights groups mounted strong campaigns against Nixon's next two nominees, southern federal judges known for their conservative positions, especially on civil rights. The Senate defied Nixon on both nominations, forcing him to settle on a candidate acceptable to the Senate, federal judge Harry A. Blackmun from Minnesota, who over the years turned out to be a moderate in his rulings. Two more vacancies enabled Nixon to appoint Lewis F. Powell and William H. Rehnquist, both of whom Nixon hoped would be more sympathetic to his political agenda.

Even with Nixon's more conservative justices, the Supreme Court in the 1970s maintained considerable continuity with the 1960s Court, carrying on social reform through judicial rulings. Several decisions of the Burger Court, for example, expanded the rights of welfare recipients. The Court narrowed somewhat the protections that the Warren Court had extended to accused criminals, but it also nullified all state death penalty laws in 1972, primarily on the grounds that the death penalty was arbitrarily applied. Four years later, the Court upheld the rights of states to impose capital punishment if they established specific procedural safeguards.

Although the Court restricted busing to achieve school integration, overall its decisions favored victims of discrimination based on race and sex. A unanimous court, for example, established the rule of "disparate impact," deciding in *Griggs v. Duke Power Company* (1971) that under the Civil Rights Act of 1964 a company's employment practices, even when established in good faith, could be found illegal if the result was to discriminate against women and minorities.

The issue of affirmative action, however, sharply divided the Court. In *Regents of the Univer-*

sity of California v. Bakke (1978), the Court ruled in favor of a white man who had been denied admission to a University of California medical school even though his test scores were higher than those of some minority applicants who were admitted. Yet the Court sanctioned affirmative action programs to attack the results of past discrimination as long as strict quotas or racial classifications were not involved. The Court also took giant steps in protecting women's rights and minimizing sex discrimination.

The New Feminism

On August 26, 1970, fifty years after women won the right to vote, tens of thousands of women took to the streets. In nationwide protests, called Women Strike for Peace and Equality, they carried signs reading "Sisterhood Is Powerful," "Don't Cook Dinner—Starve a Rat Today," and "Don't Iron While the Strike Is Hot." Some of the banners proclaimed, "The Women of Vietnam Are Our Sisters," and others demanded racial justice. But this time, women placed their own liberation at the forefront.

Conceived by Betty Friedan and organized largely by chapters of the National Organization for Women (NOW), the strike reflected the diverse strands that constituted the new feminism of the 1970s: radical women in jeans and conservatively dressed former suffragists, peace activists and politicians, teenagers and older women, and a sprinkling of women of color. The strike centered on NOW's three main demands: equality for women in employment and education; child care centers throughout the nation; and women's control over reproduction, including the right to abortion.

Feminism came into its own in the 1970s, spawning hundreds of new organizations, radical changes in how women perceived themselves and their interests, and policy changes that amounted to a revolution in women's status under the law. Women's liberation, the radical wing of feminism, erupted from women's experiences in the civil rights and antiwar movements of the 1960s. Representing feminism's mainstream was NOW, founded in 1966, an outgrowth of the publication of Friedan's *The Feminine Mystique,* the work of the President's Commission on the Status of Women, and federal attention to sex discrimination in the Equal Pay Act of 1963 and the Civil Rights Act of 1964.

Although NOW elected a black president, Aileen Hernandez, in 1970, white middle-class

TECHNOLOGY IN AMERICA

The Pill

Two reform-minded women and three male scientists played prominent roles in the development of the birth control pill. Margaret Sanger had fought for women's control over reproduction since the 1910s. In the 1950s her main priority was the development of an oral contraceptive and she persuaded wealthy heiress Katharine Dexter McCormick, the second woman to graduate from MIT, to bankroll research on the pill with a portion of her enormous fortune. McCormick supported the work of biologists Gregory Goodwin Pincus and M.C. Chang, who then brought physician John Rock into their research on hormones. They began testing the pill in 1956, and the Food and Drug Administration approved it in 1960.

"Modern woman is at last free as man is free," declared Clare Boothe Luce, playwright and former congresswoman. Separating contraception from the act of intercourse for the first time, the pill afforded greater spontaneity in sexual relations. It also was more reliable than other forms of birth control since it was nearly one hundred percent effective in preventing pregnancy. Within three years more than two million women were "on the pill" and their numbers continued to increase as doses were adjusted to reduce side effects and risk of stroke, cancer, and other ailments. In the 1990s, nearly twenty million women relied on the pill, the most widespread form of contraception aside from sterilization.

Wyeth-Ayerst Laboratories.

---

women in the political mainstream provided most of the national leadership and much of the constituency for the new feminism. They were justifiably criticized for their frequent indifference to the concerns of women who were unlike themselves. Yet support for feminism was exceedingly multifaceted. Although most black women, for example, remained cool to NOW and other mainstream groups, polls showed that their support for feminist goals exceeded that of white women.

Like other women of color, most African American women worked through their own groups such as the older National Council of Negro Women and the National Black Feminist Organization, founded in 1973. Similarly, women from forty-three Indian nations established the Native American Women's Association in 1970, Mexican American women held the first national Chicana conference in 1971, and Asian American women formed their own local movements. Blue-collar women organized the National Coalition of Labor Union Women in 1974, clerical workers founded Nine-to-Five, and women

over forty founded the Older Women's League. Lesbians established collectives in communities throughout the country as well as their own caucuses in organizations such as NOW. Women formed a host of other groups that focused on single issues such as health, abortion rights, education, and violence against women.

Feminist activism produced the most sweeping changes in laws and policies concerning women since the Nineteenth Amendment in 1920 guaranteed women's right to vote.

The range of feminist activism ran the gamut from lobbying Congress to direct action. In 1970, nine San Francisco women upset a meeting of CBS stockholders, protesting against "derogatory images of women in programming and commercials." (Later that year, CBS executives circulated a memo calling for "a new image of a woman as a doer, as

an educated, serious-minded individual person.")
Women began to speak out publicly about personal
experiences, such as rape and abortion, that had always been shrouded in secrecy. Tens of thousands
marched throughout the country to demand an
Equal Rights Amendment to the Constitution, and
a handful of women illegally occupied state capital
buildings and went on hunger strikes. In 1972, journalist Gloria Steinem and other women founded
Ms., a feminist magazine that sold 300,000 copies in
a week and became the popular voice of feminism.
Throughout the nation, women joined conscious-
ness-raising groups where they discovered that
what they had considered "personal" problems reflected a well-entrenched system of discrimination
against and devaluation of women.

Common threads underlay the great diversity
of organizations, issues, and activities. Above all,
feminism represented the belief that women were
barred from, unequally treated in, or poorly served
by the entire male-dominated public arena, whether
the political system, the medical establishment, the
law enforcement bureaucracy, the educational system, or organized religion. Feminists challenged traditional norms that identified women primarily as
wives and mothers, and they sought equality in
both the private and public spheres.

The women's movement was an effect rather
than a cause of women's rising employment, but
feminism lifted female aspirations and helped lower
barriers to jobs historically monopolized by men.
Women made some inroads into skilled crafts and
management positions. During the 1970s, their share
of law degrees shot up from 5.4 percent to nearly 30
percent, and their proportion of medical degrees
from 8.4 percent to 23 percent. In political officeholding at all levels of government, women started
from a near-zero base, and their gains came at an excruciatingly slow pace. Yet by the late 1980s, women
served as mayors in ten large cities and held 15 percent of municipal offices and state legislative seats.

Feminist activism produced the most sweeping
changes in laws and policies concerning women
since the Nineteenth Amendment in 1920 guaranteed women's right to vote. In 1972, Congress
passed Title IX of the Education Amendments Act,
banning sex discrimination in education. Covering
athletics as well as admissions, hiring, and student
services, the law evoked outrage from the male
sports establishment, which did not want to share
its subsidies. Nonetheless, women's participation in
high school and college athletics grew enormously
over the next two decades. Congress outlawed sex

discrimination in granting credit in 1974 and in 1978
prohibited discrimination against pregnant women.
It opened the military academies to women and
gave an official stamp to the women's movement
by appropriating funds for the first National
Women's Conference. This conference, attended by
a cross section of American women, met in Houston, Texas, in 1977 and established a national policy agenda for women.

Changes in other areas came largely at the state
and local levels and often resulted from the efforts
of radical feminists. They spoke out about rape,
forced law enforcement agencies to treat rape victims more humanely, and won new state laws that
banned cross-examination of rape victims about

MS. MAGAZINE
*In 1972, Gloria Steinem and other journalists and writers
published the premier issue of the first mass-circulation
magazine to be controlled for and by women.* Ms.: The
New Magazine for Women *ignored the recipes and
fashion tips of typical women's magazines. It featured literature by women writers and articles on a broad range of
feminist issues. What concerns are suggested by the cover
of this premier issue?*
Courtesy, Lang Communications.

past sexual history and eliminated the traditional requirement that victims produce either a witness or proof of resistance. Domestic violence was another issue made visible by feminists. Throughout the country, groups of women set up shelters to provide safety for battered women and their children. Nearly every state passed laws affording greater protection for victims of domestic violence and more effective prosecution of offenders. A number of states used revenues from marriage license fee increases for domestic violence programs.

Women's demand for reproductive freedom focused on the right to abortion. Feminists pressured state legislatures to reform or repeal restrictions on abortion, and many testified publicly about their own illegal abortions. They also filed lawsuits, and in 1973 the Supreme Court issued the landmark *Roe v. Wade* decision. Upholding the individual rights of both women and physicians, the Court ruled that the Constitution protects the right to abortion and that states could not prohibit abortions in the early

stages of pregnancy. However, later decisions allowed state governments to refuse to pay for abortions under Medicaid and other government-financed health programs.

The Court also struck down laws that treated men and women differently, for example, in granting Social Security and welfare benefits, workers' compensation, and access to military programs; in establishing the age of adulthood; in forming juries; and in determining alimony. Although the Court refused to adopt the same strict standard for laws differentiating on the basis of sex as it did for those involving race, these and other rulings overturned centuries of law based on women's dependency as daughters, wives, and mothers.

Public opinion polls registered majorities in favor of most feminist goals, yet by the mid-1970s, feminism faced a strong countermovement. The movement was led by Phyllis Schlafly, who had built her political career in the right-wing politics of fervent anticommunism, demands for a stronger defense establishment, and opposition to big government and social welfare programs. In the 1970s, Schlafly and other conservatives broadened their program to include a defense of conventional sex roles and the traditional family. For example, an organization called the Moral Majority, led by fundamentalist minister Jerry Falwell, combined long-standing conservative positions with opposition to nearly every goal of the women's movement.

Antifeminism achieved its greatest victory in blocking ratification of the Equal Rights Amendment (ERA). Stating simply that "equality of rights under law shall not be denied or abridged by the United States or by any State on account of sex," the ERA would outlaw any differential treatment of men and women under all state and federal laws. Initially proposed by a small band of feminists in 1923, the ERA rode through Congress in 1972 on the wave of the new feminism. Most states rushed to ratify the amendment, but by 1973, Schlafly and others had begun to organize massive resistance. When the time limit on ratification ran out in 1982, after Congress had extended it in 1978, only thirty-five states had ratified the amendment, three short of the necessary three-fourths majority.

A handful of male votes in a few state legislatures made the difference, yet conservative women played prominent roles in defeating the amendment. Arguing that the ERA would deprive women of important privileges, including their right to stay home and be supported by their husbands and their exemption from military service, and that it would

TABLE 30.1
WOMEN ENTER THE PROFESSIONS, 1975 AND 1988

Occupation	Percent of women of total employed	
	1975	1988
Airplane pilot, navigator	—	3.1
Architect	4.3	14.6
Bus driver	37.7	48.5
Carpenter	0.6	1.5
Child care worker	93.8	97.3
Computer programmer	25.6	32.2
Computer systems analyst	14.8	29.5
Data entry keyer	92.8	88.2
Dentist	1.8	9.3
Economist	13.1	35.5
Elementary school teacher	85.4	84.8
College, university teacher	31.1	38.5
Lawyer, judge	7.1	19.5
Mail carrier	8.7	22.0
Physician	13.0	20.0
Police officer	2.7	13.4
Registered nurse	97.0	94.6
Secretary	99.1	99.1
Telephone installer, repairer	4.8	12.1
Telephone operator	93.3	89.8

Source: U.S. Bureau of Labor Statistics.

PHYLLIS SCHLAFLY

As one of the few nonsouthern states that rejected ratification of the proposed Equal Rights Amendment, Illinois was the scene of feverish activity by supporters and opponents. Here STOP ERA *leader Phyllis Schlafly rallies her followers in the rotunda of the Illinois capitol in Springfield in June 1978.* STOP ERA *women handed legislators apple pies bearing the words "For the sake of the family please vote no."*
Corbis-Bettmann.

BETTY FRIEDAN AND GLORIA STEINEM

Two prominent feminists, Betty Friedan (foreground) and Gloria Steinem (to her right), sign telegrams in July 1977 entreating President Jimmy Carter to help get three more states to ratify the proposed Equal Rights Amendment. The appeal to Carter urged him to translate his commitment to human rights abroad into vigorous support of human rights at home.
Corbis-Bettmann.

MAP 30.1
The Fight for the Equal Rights Amendment
Many states that failed to ratify the Equal Rights Amendment had previously refused to ratify the women suffrage amendment (or ratified it decades later, as did North Carolina in 1971). Why do you think so many nonratifying states were in the South?

destroy the traditional family, grassroots antifeminists wrote letters, lobbied, and demonstrated. These women had invested a lot in their traditional roles, which they saw as God-given, and feared a breakdown of gender differences. The antifeminists defeated the major goal of the women's movement, even though public opinion polls showed that a majority of both men and women favored the ERA.

Opposition to a second major goal of the women's movement, the right to abortion, was more complex. Many Americans believed that human life begins with conception, and they equated abortion with murder. The Catholic Church and other religious organizations provided institutional support for their protest. Right-wing politicians and their supporters, who identified abortion with the emancipation of women and the destruction of conventional sex roles and the family, constituted another segment of the right-to-life movement. As did opponents of the ERA, the right-to-life movement mobilized thousands of women who believed that abortion devalued motherhood and saw feminism as a threat to their traditional roles.

Although the right-to-life movement failed to achieve a constitutional amendment banning abortion, it helped defeat pro-choice politicians and achieved restrictions on abortion at the state and federal levels. In 1977, Congress began to deny the use of Medicaid and other federal funds for abortions. States also enacted laws that made it more difficult for women, especially poor women, to obtain abortions.

Defense of abortion rights was just one of the challenges feminists faced as the 1970s ended. For all the highly publicized inroads women made into male-dominated occupations, the vast majority of women still worked in traditionally female jobs. Pay scales in such occupations as clerical work, nursing, and teaching reflected the historic devaluation of women's worth and seemingly lay beyond the reach of antidiscrimination legislation.

Women continued to bear primary responsibility for the care of their homes and families even while they increasingly worked outside the home. Most husbands of women in the labor force expanded their share of domestic duties only marginally, while women worked a "double day"—one at the workplace and one at home. As the number of female-headed families grew from 10 percent to 20 percent of all families between 1970 and 1990, the situation of employed mothers became even more critical. Congress's only significant effort to ease the problems of employed mothers—the passage of a comprehensive child care bill—fell to President Nixon's veto in 1971. At the end of the 1970s, feminists needed stamina not only to preserve the gains of the past decade, but also to address the problems that were untouched by the legal revolution of the 1970s.

A Movement to Save the Environment

Mass demonstrations in the 1960s and early 1970s were not confined to the civil rights, antiwar, and feminist movements. In April 1970, millions of Americans observed the first Earth Day to register their concern over the ravaging effects of industrial development on the environment. In Wisconsin, students distributed flyers encouraging recycling, and a group of Detroit women picketed a steel plant that discharged industrial waste into a river. Girl scouts cleaned garbage from the Potomac River, Berkeley citizens attended an environmental teach-in, and African Americans in St. Louis dramatized the effects of poisons in lead paint. Some students in Michigan shattered a Ford to protest automobile emissions, and people planted trees all over the country.

Inheriting their concern for the natural world from the decades-old conservation movement, the new environmentalists had a far broader agenda. Even more important than preserving portions of the natural world for aesthetic and recreational purposes was protecting human beings from the devastating side effects of industrial development and economic growth—polluted air and water and the spread of deadly chemicals. This pollution threatened wildlife, plants, and a delicate ecological balance and had the potential to imperil human life itself.

Biologist Rachel Carson had drawn the first national attention to environmental concerns in 1962 with her best-seller *Silent Spring,* which stressed the harmful effects of toxic chemicals, particularly the pesticide DDT. Older conservation organizations like the Sierra Club and the Wilderness Society expanded the scope of their concerns, and they were

joined by a host of new organizations. The Environmental Defense Fund, for example, specialized in litigation. In 1971, environmentalists founded Greenpeace, an organization that protested nuclear testing around the world and campaigned to save whales, other ocean animals, and tropical rain forests. Even more militant was Earth First!, created in 1980 and committed to direct action and sabotage of projects injurious to the environment.

President Nixon asserted that the nation must begin "reclaiming the purity of its air, its waters, our living environment" and urged legislation to "end the plunder of America's natural heritage." Yet he obstructed several objectives of the environmental movement and forced Congress to override his veto to continue the anti–water pollution measures begun in the 1960s. Nixon gave priority to economic growth and increasing the nation's energy supply over environmental considerations. Against objections from environmentalists, he pushed Congress to authorize construction of a 789-mile-long pipeline to carry oil across Alaska.

Inheriting their concern for the natural world from the decades-old conservation movement, the new environmentalists had a far broader agenda: protecting human beings from the devastating side effects of industrial development and economic growth.

In other respects, the Nixon administration proved a friend—or at least not an enemy—of the environmental movement. In 1970, he established the Environmental Protection Agency (EPA). Charged with enforcing clean air and water policies and regulating pesticides, the EPA soon became the largest federal regulatory agency. Nixon also signed the Occupational Safety and Health Act (OSHA), which safeguarded workers against workplace accidents and disease. For example, it set limits on worker exposure to cotton dust, which caused devastating brown lung disease among textile workers, and imposed restrictions on the use of cancer-causing asbestos.

The strongest measure supported by the Nixon administration was the Clean Air Act of 1970. It established national standards for air quality, imposed restrictions on factory and automobile emissions, and included penalties of jail sentences as well as

EARTH DAY

*Because of its association with nature and the earth, green was the color of the
environmental movement, and environmentalists called themselves "greens." These
activists leave no doubt about their affiliation at an Earth Day celebration in New York City
in April 1970. The button, a takeoff on the antiwar slogan "Give Peace a Chance," reflects the continuing impact of the antiwar movement.*
Dennis Stock/Magnum Photos, Inc.; button: private collection.

fines. Twenty years after enactment, no major city
met the new health standards, and more than half
the population lived in areas that defied the law's
promise that "air . . . shall have no adverse effects
on any American's health." But even with lenient
enforcement, the Clean Air Act cut the amount of
air pollutants by one-third, despite population and
economic growth. Denver residents could see the
mountains more clearly after pollution was cut in
half, and even Los Angeles experienced less smog
after the controls.

The environmental movement made further
progress during the Carter administration (1977–
1981). With the president's sponsorship, Congress
passed legislation to improve clean air and water
programs; to preserve vast areas of Alaska; to control strip mining, which left ugly scars along moun-

tainsides; and to provide $1.6 billion for cleanup of
hazardous wastes left by the chemical industry.

Nuclear energy posed an even greater threat.
When Carter took office in 1977, nuclear power
plants produced about 11 percent of the country's
electricity. A growing antinuclear movement
warned of the hazards of radiation leakage, the potential for accidents, and the problem of disposing
of nuclear wastes. The perils of nuclear energy came
into dramatic focus in March 1979, when an accident occurred at the Three Mile Island nuclear facility in Pennsylvania. Technicians worked for days
to prevent a meltdown of the reactor core, while
thousands of people who lived in the vicinity of the
plant fled their homes and the threat of fatal radiation. A combination of economic factors (mainly the
staggering costs of building nuclear plants) and

popular opposition stalled further development of the nuclear power industry, but antinuclear activism remained on the environmental movement's agenda. The environmental movement persisted into the 1980s as it sought to preserve the advances of the past two decades against attempts to relax or repeal environmental laws.

Domestic and Foreign Initiatives of the Nixon Era

Not all of the reforms of the 1970s originated outside the White House. Much of Richard Nixon's public rhetoric appealed to Americans unhappy with the expanding federal programs of the 1960s and frustrated by the nation's seeming inability to deter its great enemy, communism. Yet in practice, the Nixon administration not only moved the United States toward cooperation with China and the Soviet Union but also pursued a domestic agenda that bore marks of the very government activism that Nixon decried in his speeches.

The Nixon administration not only moved the United States toward cooperation with China and the Soviet Union but also pursued a domestic agenda that bore marks of the very government activism that Nixon decried in his speeches.

Nixon's domestic policies grew out of political expediency, a Congress controlled by the Democrats, a body of advisers representing a broad spectrum of political positions, the president's desire for history's approving gaze, and serious economic problems. Thus his administration sustained many of the reforms of the 1960s and advanced the government's role in some areas. While transferring some power from the federal government to the states through a revenue-sharing program, the Nixon administration also enlarged the federal government's role in the economy with expanded aid to the poor, new environmental regulations, deficit spending, devaluation of the dollar, and price and wage controls—all heretical deviations from traditional Republican economics.

Nixon's foreign policy also deviated from Republican orthodoxy, most markedly in its moves toward accommodation with the Soviet Union and China. Yet at the same time, in Vietnam, the Middle East, and Latin America, the administration pursued policies straight out of the cold war book of unrelenting opposition to communism.

Extending the Welfare State

Richard Nixon's second inaugural address in 1973 encapsulated his objections to much of Lyndon Johnson's Great Society: "In trusting too much to government, we have asked more of it than it can deliver. . . . Government must learn to take less from people so people can do more for themselves." The Great Society's efforts to solve every social problem, Nixon argued, both overextended federal power and proved ineffective in practice. Nixon's words also played to "middle America," which resented government's apparent disregard for its interests while favoring individuals who lacked the discipline and willingness to help themselves: "America was built not by government, but by people—not by welfare, but by work."

Congress successfully resisted many of Nixon's attacks on programs that had been initiated with the War on Poverty, refusing, for example, to eliminate the Office of Economic Opportunity. Skirmishes between the president and Congress resulted in some changes in antipoverty programs but left intact key programs such as Head Start, Legal Services, and job training. At the same time, Nixon blocked congressional efforts at reform. Although he supported day care programs for welfare recipients, the president vetoed the child care bill passed by Congress in 1971. He objected not only to the program's $2 billion cost but also to "communal approaches to child rearing," which he believed had "family-weakening implications."

Nixon also reached beyond his veto powers to undermine congressional initiatives. Concerned about the budget deficit and angry at Congress for appropriating more funds than he wanted for social welfare, environmental protection, and other programs, in 1972 Nixon simply refused to spend nearly $9 billion of appropriations. Federal courts later found this "impoundment" of appropriations to be a violation of presidential powers.

More significant than the Nixon administration's battle against federal programs was its extension of government assistance to the disadvantaged. Budgets for social services during Nixon's presidency exceeded defense spending for the first time since World War II. Social Security benefits went up and for the first time were legally required to rise with the cost of living. Subsidies for low-income housing, which totaled less than $1 million in 1969, reached nearly $3 billion in 1973. A new program, the Basic Opportunity Grant program, provided $1 billion in so-called Pell grants (named for Democratic Congressman Clayborne Pell, who sponsored the law) for low-income students to attend college.

Much of the expansion of the welfare state during the Nixon years was simply maintenance of existing programs or acquiescence to congressional initiatives. However, the Nixon administration itself proposed a major reform, a Family Assistance Plan (FAP) that would provide a guaranteed minimum income for all families. With this bold proposal, Nixon hoped to eliminate problems in the welfare system, reduce the welfare bureaucracy, aid the working poor, and secure his place in history. Unlike existing policy, established in the 1930s and administered through the Aid to Families with Dependent Children (AFDC) program, Nixon's proposal established a national standard for benefits and provided income supplements to the working poor. As Nixon expected when he presented the FAP in August 1969, conservatives immediately objected to the cost and to increasing the number of welfare recipients. White southerners especially feared its impact on the ability to hire poor blacks at low wages: "There's not going to be anybody left to roll these wheelbarrows and press these shirts. They're all going to be on welfare," commented one southern representative.

Liberals and grassroots movements representing the poor attacked the low level of the income guarantee—even after the administration increased it from $1,600 to $2,400 a year. Groups such as the National Welfare Rights Organization decried a work requirement that would force mothers of young children into substandard jobs. Organized labor, too, deplored a work requirement that would compel recipients to work at jobs below the minimum wage and, in effect, "subsidize the employers of cheap labor."

The FAP foundered over the dilemma inherent in an economy that failed to provide sufficient jobs at adequate wages: how to provide satisfactory support for those who cannot earn a decent livelihood while at the same time containing welfare expenditures and retaining incentives to work. Conservatives believed that Nixon's FAP would weigh too heavily on taxpayers, reduce work incentives, and encourage a reliance on welfare; liberals argued that its level of support was woefully inadequate.

WELFARE
Beginning in the 1960s, Congress repeatedly attempted to reform welfare (the program's official name was Aid to Families with Dependent Children, or AFDC), usually with requirements to encourage or force welfare recipients to take jobs. This mother of three children who was separated from her husband was trying to become self-supporting by attending college, but officials in Schenectady, New York, removed her from the welfare rolls when she refused to take a job.
Wide World.

Although Congress refused to pass the FAP and establish a guaranteed annual income for poor families, it did so for the aged, blind, and disabled by enacting Supplementary Security Income in 1972. Moreover, in response to growing public attention to undernourishment and indications that the Democrats were going to capitalize on the issue of hunger, Nixon proposed a huge expansion of the food stamp program. The new guidelines mandated a nutritionally adequate diet for everyone, including the working poor, and the number of recipients of food stamps grew from 2.5 to 15 million between 1969 and 1974. By 1975, the value of food stamps available to a family of four had risen to almost $2,000 a year.

The New Federalism

Nixon called his domestic agenda the New Federalism, expressing traditional Republican distaste for federal control and preference for state and local autonomy and responsibility. To this end, he made revenue sharing, the transfer of federal funds to state and local governments, a cornerstone of his domestic program, even though he thought it didn't have much political "sex appeal." Revenue sharing gave states and localities considerable discretion in spending decisions and strengthened their financial foundations. State and local governments, many of which faced budget crises, provided a powerful lobby, and Congress enacted the measure in October 1972. The law transferred more than $5 billion of federal funds annually to state and local governments. Not designated for specific programs, these funds supplemented existing federal transfers for education, urban development, and the like.

When it came to transferring funds for and authority over existing programs, Congress balked. That approach would have constituted a more substantial attack on the national bureaucracy while increasing decision making at lower levels of government. In later years, the administration moved in this direction by consolidating several funding programs into broad block grants, as with the Comprehensive Employment and Training Act (CETA), which was designed to provide jobs and training for the poor. Although still targeted for a specific purpose such as community development or job training, block grants allowed local governments greater discretion in their use. Both general revenue sharing and block grants continued after the Nixon administration, but represented only a small step in the decentralization of government power.

Indeed, the expansion of federal controls in other areas overshadowed the New Federalism's revenue sharing. Despite Nixon's aversion to a growing federal bureaucracy, certain problems eluded solution on the state level or posed economic or political threats that were too great to risk inaction. Thus, in addition to approving new environmental controls, Nixon expanded the government's role in dealing with energy shortages, inflation, and unemployment.

In the 1970s, Americans confronted two costs of the post–World War II economic boom that had amply enriched their standard of living: environmental damage and an insatiable demand for energy that left the nation increasingly dependent on foreign sources of oil. The nation's own abundant oil deposits along with access to huge, cheap supplies of Middle Eastern oil had encouraged entrepreneurs to build large cars, suburban housing developments, and glass-enclosed skyscrapers and houses with no concern for fuel efficiency. The traditional American assumption that energy resources were boundless and the resulting wasteful practices meant that by the 1970s, the United States, with just 6 percent of the world's population, consumed one-third of its fuel resources.

In the fall of 1973, the United States faced its first energy crisis. Furious at the Nixon administration's support of Israel during the Yom Kippur War, Arab nations cut off oil shipments to the United States, and nations that did not join the embargo raised prices nearly tenfold. As supplies of oil fell in the winter of 1973–74, long lines formed at gas stations, where prices had nearly doubled. Shortages of heating oil meant that many homes were cold and some schools had to close. A traveling salesman complained, "I can't get gas to go on the road," while a laid-off airline pilot said, "We've never had a crunch like this before."

In response to the energy crisis, Nixon relaxed deadlines on environmental regulations, pressed for the Alaska pipeline bill, and pushed ahead on the production of nuclear energy. He signed legislation authorizing temporary emergency powers to allocate petroleum and establishing a national 55-mile-per-hour speed limit to save gasoline. But Nixon opposed rationing gasoline and vetoed a bill that, in an effort to prevent oil companies from unduly profiting from the crisis, set ceilings on domestic crude oil prices. By the spring of 1974, the energy crisis had eased, thanks largely to voluntary conservation, a relatively mild winter, and cessation of the Arab oil embargo. But the United States had yet to come to grips with its seemingly unquenchable demand for fuel and its dependence on foreign oil.

Soaring energy prices contributed to the second serious economic problem: a rising cost of living. From the Johnson administration, Nixon inherited an economy under strong inflationary pressures. In 1969, the inflation rate rose to 7 percent, an enormous increase to Americans used to inflation rates of about 2 percent. By 1970, unemployment had joined inflation as a serious problem. This unprecedented combination of a stagnant economy and inflation soon received the name "stagflation."

Domestic troubles were compounded by the decline of American dominance in the international economic system. Having fully recovered from World War II with U.S. aid, the economies of Japan and Western Europe grew faster than the economy of the United States. Cars, electronic equipment, and other foreign products competed favorably with American goods throughout the world. In 1971, for the first time in decades, the United States imported more than it exported, which meant that more dollars were flowing out of the country than were coming in. As the United States spent billions of dollars abroad for defense purposes, the amount of dollars in foreign hands exceeded U.S. gold reserves. The nation could no longer back up its dollars with gold.

Political considerations helped to shape the president's response to these economic problems, a response that deviated considerably from conventional Republican doctrine. With an eye to the 1972 election and believing that Eisenhower's recession had ensured his defeat by Kennedy in 1960, Nixon announced a "New Economic Policy" in August 1971. He abandoned the convertibility of dollars into gold, devalued the dollar to make American goods cheaper in foreign markets and thus increase exports, and imposed a 10 percent surcharge on most imports. Nixon also froze wages and prices, thus enabling the government to stimulate the economy without fueling more inflation.

In the short run, these policies worked. Exports surged ahead of imports, inflation subsided, unemployment fell below 5 percent, and Nixon was resoundingly reelected in 1972. Yet the New Economic Policy treated only the superficial wounds of the economy. The lifting of price and wage controls in 1973, the Arab oil embargo, and rising food prices (the result of a drought in the Midwest and huge Soviet purchases of American grain) sent the consumer price index soaring again. In 1974, inflation reached 11 percent, while unemployment edged back up. Nixon's bold intervention in the economy proved only a temporary respite, and his successor inherited the most severe economic crisis since the depression of the 1930s.

New Opportunities and Dangers in a Multipolar World

The challenges and opportunities of foreign policy captured Nixon's greatest enthusiasm, and his highest hopes to make his mark on history lay in the international arena. He possessed a broad understanding of international relations and the ability to analyze how changing world patterns would affect national interests. The discord between the Soviet Union and China and the growing power of Europe and Japan, Nixon believed, indicated that the "rigid and bipolar world of the 1940s and 1950s" was giving way to "the fluidity of a new era of multilateral diplomacy." With his chief foreign policy adviser, Henry Kissinger, Nixon prepared to grasp a "historic opportunity to turn the transformations of the last twenty-five years into new avenues for peace."

New approaches to China and the Soviet Union formed the keystone of Nixon's foreign policy, and his most important innovation was to deflate ideology as the driving force. As Kissinger put it in 1969, "We will judge other countries, including Communist countries, . . . on the basis of their actions and not on the basis of their domestic ideology." Nixon repeated that premise in 1972: "What is important is not a nation's internal political philosophy. What is important is its policy toward the rest of the world and toward us."

Nixon and Kissinger moved to exploit the deterioration in Soviet-Chinese relations that had begun in the early 1960s and escalated into military clashes along their common border in 1969. If these two nations balanced and checked each other's power, the threat of either of them to the United States would lessen. As Nixon later recalled, "The hostility between China and the Soviet Union served our purposes best if we maintained closer relations with each side than they did with each other."

U.S. overtures through intermediaries, followed by Kissinger's secret visit to China in July 1971, set the stage for Nixon's most dramatic act as president. With his arrival carefully orchestrated to take advantage of prime-time television, in Febru-

NIXON IN CHINA
"This was the week that changed the world," proclaimed President Richard M. Nixon in February 1972, emphasizing the dramatic turnaround in relations with America's former enemy the People's Republic of China. The Great Wall of China forms the setting for this photograph of Nixon and his wife, Pat.
Nixon Presidential Materials Project.

ary 1972 Nixon became the nation's first president to set foot on Chinese soil—an astonishing act by a man who had climbed the political ladder as an all-out anti-Communist. Indeed, it was Nixon's irreproachable anti-Communist credentials that enabled him to conduct this shift in U.S.-Chinese relations with no significant objections at home. As he remarked to the Chinese leader, Mao Zedong, "Those on the right can do what those on the left only talk about."

Neither side expected concrete, immediate results from Nixon's historic but largely symbolic visit. Plans proceeded for cultural and scientific exchanges, and American producers began to find markets in China. The United States did not abandon the Nationalist Chinese government on Taiwan, but Nixon acknowledged that Taiwan was a part of China, its fate to be settled by the Chinese themselves. By ending the isolation of China, Nixon's visit brought U.S. policy more into conformity with the actual world and paved the way for normal diplomatic relations by the end of the decade.

As Nixon and Kissinger hoped, the warming of U.S.-Chinese relations increased Soviet responsiveness to the Nixon-Kissinger strategy of détente, the term given to efforts to ease conflicts with the Soviet Union. In pursuing détente, Nixon and Kissinger did not abandon the principle of containment but instead concentrated on issues of common concern to the two superpowers. Containment would be achieved not only by military threat, but also by ensuring that Russia and China had stakes in a stable international order and would therefore refrain from precipitating crises. The goal, as Nixon defined it in 1972, was "a stronger, healthy United States, Europe, Soviet Union, China, Japan, each balancing the other."

Arms control, trade, and stability in Europe were three areas of common interest. In November 1969, the United States and the Soviet Union resumed the Strategic Arms Limitation Talks (SALT), and in 1971 they moved to defuse potential crises by improving the hot line between Moscow and Washington. Conflict over Berlin eased through an agreement in August 1971, when the Soviet Union guaranteed access routes to West Berlin and in turn won permission to open a consulate there.

Nixon turned the spotlight on détente in May 1972, when—three months after his trip to China—he made another historic visit. Meeting with Soviet leaders in Moscow, Nixon came away with several agreements regarding trade and cooperation in science and space. Most significantly, Soviet and U.S. leaders signed arms limitation treaties that had grown out of SALT. Both sides gave up the pursuit of a defense against nuclear weapons, agreeing to restrict antiballistic missile systems (ABMs) to two each. Curbing offensive weapons proved more difficult, but the superpowers reached an interim five-year agreement limiting the number of strategic missile launchers each could build.

The SALT agreement left the Soviets ahead in absolute numbers of missiles, but U.S. weapons were more accurate, and the United States retained the lead in bombers, which were not covered by the treaty. The agreement deterred neither side from weapons research and development, so both the Soviet Union and the United States pursued qualitative improvements in strategic arms. Kissinger him-

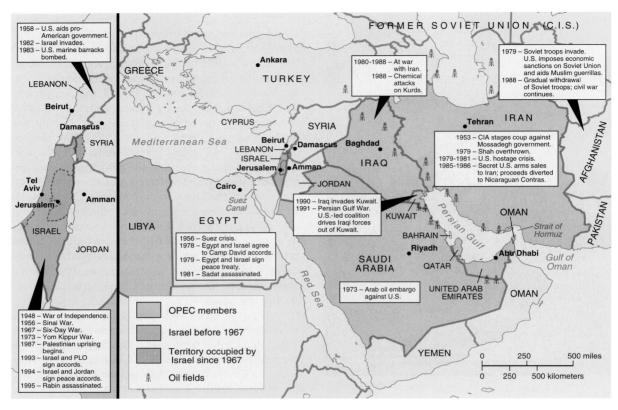

1958 – U.S. aids pro-American government.
1982 – Israel invades.
1983 – U.S. marine barracks bombed.

1980-1988 – At war with Iran.
1988 – Chemical attacks on Kurds.

1979 – Soviet troops invade. U.S. imposes economic sanctions on Soviet Union and aids Muslim guerrillas.
1988 – Gradual withdrawal of Soviet troops; civil war continues.

1953 – CIA stages coup against Mossadegh government.
1979 – Shah overthrown.
1979-1981 – U.S. hostage crisis.
1985-1986 – Secret U.S. arms sales to Iran; proceeds diverted to Nicaraguan Contras.

1990 – Iraq invades Kuwait.
1991 – Persian Gulf War. U.S.-led coalition drives Iraqi forces out of Kuwait.

1956 – Suez crisis.
1978 – Egypt and Israel agree to Camp David accords.
1979 – Egypt and Israel sign peace treaty.
1981 – Sadat assassinated.

1973 – Arab oil embargo against U.S.

1948 – War of Independence.
1956 – Sinai War.
1967 – Six-Day War.
1973 – Yom Kippur War.
1987 – Palestinian uprising begins.
1993 – Israel and PLO sign accords.
1994 – Israel and Jordan sign peace accords.
1995 – Rabin assassinated.

OPEC members

Israel before 1967

Territory occupied by Israel since 1967

Oil fields

MAP 30.2
The Middle East, 1948–1996
U.S. determination to preserve access to the rich oil reserves of the Middle East and its commit-ment to the security of Israel were the fundamental — and sometimes conflicting — principles of U.S. foreign policy in that region.

self suggested the limited nature of détente: "The way to use this freeze is for us to catch up."

In his second inaugural address, Nixon said, "The time has passed when America will make every other nation's conflict our own . . . or presume to tell the people of other nations how to manage their own affairs." Yet even while Nixon and Kissinger dealt with China and the Soviet Union on the basis of practical politics rather than ideology, in Vietnam and elsewhere they continued to equate the ideology of Marxism with a threat to U.S. interests and actively resisted social revolutions that might lead to communism.

In Chile, the Nixon administration found that threat in Salvador Allende, a self-proclaimed Marxist. Since 1964, the CIA and U.S. corporations concerned about nationalization of their Chilean properties had provided funds to Allende's opponents.

When Allende won the 1970 presidential election, Nixon announced that the United States "accepted that decision." Yet the CIA had taken covert action, including plans for a military coup, to overthrow Allende. Thereafter the United States continued to exert political and economic pressure to destabilize the Allende government. "I don't see why we have to let a country go Marxist just because its people are irresponsible," Kissinger remarked privately. In 1973, the Chilean military engineered a coup, killed Allende, and established a dictatorship under General Augusto Pinochet.

The Nixon administration moved closer to repressive governments in other parts of the world. It eased pressures on ruling white minorities in southern Africa, believing that the "whites are here to stay. . . . There is no hope for the blacks to gain the political rights they seek through violence, which will lead only to chaos and increased opportunities for Communists." In the Middle East, the United States found in Iran a stable anti-Communist ally—one with enormous petroleum reserves. In 1972, the Nixon administration began secretly to provide massive amounts of arms to the shah of Iran, cementing a relationship that would ignite a new crisis for the United States when the shah was overthrown in 1979.

Like its predecessors and successors, the Nixon administration pursued a delicate balance between honoring its commitments to Israel's security and seeking the goodwill of Arab nations that were strategically and economically important to the United States. Conflict between Israel and the Arab nations had escalated into all-out war (the Six Day War) in 1967, in which Israel won a stunning victory over Egyptian, Syrian, and Jordanian forces. The Six Day War ended with Israel occupying the Sinai Peninsula and Gaza Strip (Egyptian territory), the Golan Heights of Syria, and the West Bank of Jordan, which included the Arab sector of Jerusalem—territory that amounted to twice the original size of Israel.

After Israel's decisive victory in the Six Day War, Palestinian refugees stepped up guerrilla attacks against the Israelis, and the Soviet Union expanded military aid to Arab countries. American diplomats' efforts to reduce tensions in the Middle East had little success in the late 1960s and early 1970s. The Arab countries refused to recognize Israel's right to exist; Israel would not withdraw from the territories occupied during the Six Day War; and no solution could be found for the Palestinian refugees who had been displaced by the creation of Israel in the late 1940s.

In October 1973, on Yom Kippur, the holiest day in the Jewish calendar, Egypt and Syria surprised Israel by launching a full-scale attack. After the Nixon administration sided with the Israelis, the Arab nations imposed an oil embargo. Although the Soviets threatened to intervene, the United States held its ground, and Israel repulsed the attack. Shortly after the war, the United States adopted the role of mediator as Kissinger embarked on "shuttle diplomacy," moving back and forth across the Middle East. Although unable to resolve the underlying conflicts, he achieved some limited disengagements between Israeli forces and their enemies. As a result, the Arab nations lifted the oil embargo, and Soviet influence in the area declined as U.S. credibility among Arabs increased.

Constitutional Crisis and Restoration

In the 1972 presidential election, Richard Nixon turned his narrow victory of 1968 into a massive landslide. At year's end, he and Henry Kissinger graced the cover of *Time* as the magazine's Men of the Year, and the president's approval ratings in the polls neared 70 percent. Less than two years later, Nixon abandoned the presidency in disgrace. He was not turned out of office by voters dissatisfied with his domestic or foreign policies. Rather, Nixon's abuse of presidential power and his efforts to cover up crimes that had been committed by subordinates betrayed the public trust and forced the first presidential resignation in history.

Nixon's handpicked successor, Gerald Ford, brought to the White House a reputation for decency and openness that helped to restore confidence in the presidency. Ford maintained the basic policy directions set by the Nixon administration, but he faced economic problems even more severe. In 1976, Ford lost the presidency to Democrat Jimmy Carter in an election that failed to stir much excitement for either candidate.

The Landslide Election of 1972

Nixon's most spectacular foreign policy initiatives, détente with the Soviet Union and the opening of relations with China, heightened his prospects for reelection in 1972. Although the war in Vietnam continued, antiwar protests diminished with the decrease in American casualties and the continuing withdrawal of U.S. ground forces. Nixon's New Economic Policy had temporarily checked both inflation and unemployment, and his attacks on busing and antiwar protesters had solidified his support on the right. At their convention in Miami Beach in August 1972, the Republicans resoundingly renominated Nixon and his vice president, Spiro Agnew.

A large field of contenders vied for the Democratic nomination, including Hubert Humphrey, back for a third effort, and New York Representative Shirley Chisholm, the first African American politician to make a serious bid for the presidency. Senator George S. McGovern of South Dakota chalked up primary victories in key states, while on the right, Governor George Wallace of Alabama won a series of southern primaries as well as those in Michigan and Maryland. Wallace's campaign was cut short, however, when a deranged man shot him, leaving him paralyzed below the waist.

McGovern's primary victories established him as the clear leader by the time the Democrats convened in Miami Beach in July, and the composition of the convention delegates made his position even stronger. After the bitter 1968 convention, the party had initiated major reforms requiring delegations to represent the relative proportions of minorities, women, and youth in their states. These newcomers displaced many regular Democrats—officeholders, labor leaders, and representatives of urban political machines and traditional ethnic groups. Some party regulars such as Representative Edith Green thought that "the Democratic Party was taken over by kooks" and stayed home. Referring to the significant numbers of young people and women, a labor leader remarked that there was "too much hair, and not enough cigars at this convention."

Nixon's abuse of presidential power and his efforts to cover up crimes that had been committed by subordinates betrayed the public trust and forced the first presidential resignation in history.

McGovern won the nomination easily, and his supporters pushed through platform planks calling for an immediate end to the Vietnam War, support for busing, and other controversial issues. Women constituted 40 percent of the delegates, and feminists organized at the convention for the first time. McGovern's handpicked running mate, Senator Thomas F. Eagleton of Missouri, won nomination easily, but women rallied 13 percent of the vice presidential vote behind Texas politician Frances Farenthold and wrote fifteen women's rights planks into the platform.

The Democratic campaign floundered almost immediately when the press reported that Eagleton had undergone psychiatric treatment for nervous exhaustion and depression during the 1960s. Refusing to bow to prejudice concerning mental illness, McGovern declared, "I am one thousand percent behind Tom Eagleton." But he soon changed his mind and replaced Eagleton with R. Sargent Shriver, former head of the Peace Corps and Johnson's antipoverty program. The incident hurt McGovern by casting doubt on his judgment, decisiveness, and sincerity.

Moreover, the Democratic nominee failed to capture the middle ground of his party. Many Democrats objected to his call for immediate withdrawal from Vietnam, his pledge to cut $30 billion from the Pentagon's budget, and his waffling on welfare reform. Republicans portrayed McGovern as an extremist on the left. Capitalizing on many of his early statements, they construed them as demands for legalizing marijuana and liberalizing abortion laws. Labor leader George Meany called McGovern "the candidate of amnesty, acid, and appeasement." Traditional Democrats defected from the party in massive numbers.

Nixon received 60.7 percent of the popular vote and carried every state except Massachusetts in a landslide victory second only to that of Johnson in 1964. Although the Democrats maintained control of the House, the Senate, and thirty-one governorships, Nixon won a majority of votes among southerners, Catholics, urbanites, and blue-collar workers, all traditionally strong supporters of the Democratic Party. But the president had little time to savor his triumph or consolidate his support, as a series of revelations began to emerge about crimes and misdemeanors that had been committed to ensure the victory.

Watergate

During the early morning hours of June 17, 1972, five men working for Nixon's reelection campaign crept into Democratic Party headquarters housed in the Watergate apartment and office complex near the Potomac River, just a mile from the White House. Wearing surgical gloves, they carried Mace, lock-picking equipment, cameras, and telephone-bugging devices to repair a bugging device installed in an earlier break-in. Their arrest on the scene and the subsequent efforts of Nixon and his aides to cover up their connections to administration officials set in motion the most serious constitutional crisis since the Civil War. The crisis took its name, "Watergate," from the scene of the burglary.

As the events of Watergate unfolded over the next two years, Americans learned that Nixon and his associates had engaged in a host of other abuses. These included accepting illegal campaign contributions, using "dirty tricks" to sabotage Democratic candidates, and unlawfully attempting to silence critics of the Vietnam War.

Nixon was by no means the first president to lie to the public or to misuse presidential power. On the eve of World War II, Franklin Roosevelt misled

WATERGATE SHOOTOUT
This political cartoon by Edward Sorel portrays a besieged President Richard Nixon and his associates who were involved in Watergate and other scandals. Some, such as Vice President Spiro Agnew, in the center of the floor, and Attorney General John Mitchell, to his right, are already down. What could be the artist's intention in putting a picture of Eisenhower on the wall?
Collection of Byron Dobell.

the public about U.S. naval operations in the Atlantic Ocean that violated congressional intentions to keep the nation out of war. Every president after Roosevelt had enlarged the powers of the presidency, justifying his actions as necessary to protect national security in the cold war. This expansion of executive powers, often called the growth of the "imperial presidency," weakened some of the traditional checks and balances on the executive branch and opened the door to abuses.

Some of Nixon's activities followed patterns set by his predecessor. Lyndon Johnson deceived Congress about the Gulf of Tonkin attacks, for example, and allowed CIA and FBI interference in the affairs of civil rights and antiwar activists. Moreover, Nixon and Johnson shared certain personality traits —the self-righteousness of self-made men, a sense of insecurity, exhilaration over presidential power, suspiciousness, and a tendency to see opposition as a conspiracy against them. All of these traits encouraged both men to employ the vast powers of the executive against their enemies.

Johnson, however, enjoyed more self-confidence as well as an openness to advice. He abandoned the opportunity for reelection rather than intensifying his efforts to silence the opposition. Nixon, introverted and socially ill at ease, had few intimate friends. His relationships with most of his

closest aides rested on political calculations rather than on trust and loyalty. These aides tried above all to protect themselves, and few would confront him with the truth and the opportunity to save his presidency. Unable to distinguish his real enemies from those who simply disagreed with him, Nixon saw opposition to his policies not only as a personal attack but also as an attack on the presidency and the country.

Watergate began when White House adviser Charles Colson established a secret unit nicknamed the "plumbers" to stop the kind of "leaks" that had led to publication of the *Pentagon Papers* in 1971. Former CIA agent E. Howard Hunt and former FBI employee G. Gordon Liddy led the plumbers, some of whom soon turned to projects to disrupt the Democratic presidential nomination process and discredit potential candidates. They went to work for the Committee to Re-elect the President (CRP, called "CREEP" by its critics), a group that was independent of the Republican Party and directed by Nixon's former attorney general John Mitchell. The CRP funneled money, including illegal campaign contributions, into the campaign, and in 1972 CRP officials authorized the Watergate break-in to bug the Democratic Party's phones and find out whether the Democrats had any information that they could use against the Republicans.

When police arrested the five men found in the Watergate—four Cuban Americans and James Mc-Cord, a former CIA agent and current security director for CRP—they discovered papers linking them to Hunt and Liddy. The Nixon administration immediately denied any connection with the break-in. A grand jury indicted Hunt, Liddy, and the five alleged burglars, but Democratic charges of a cover-up during the 1972 elections fell on deaf ears in the media and among the public.

Brought to trial in early 1973 in the federal district court of John J. Sirica, all seven men either pleaded guilty or were convicted of theft and illegal electronic surveillance. McCord then broke ranks with the cover-up. In March 1973, he told Judge Sirica that perjury had been committed at the trial and suggested that administration officials had been involved in the break-in. A grand jury began to investigate these charges, and the Senate soon began its own inquiry. As press reports began to implicate Mitchell, John W. Dean, counsel to the president, and presidential aides John Ehrlichman and H. R. Haldeman, Nixon decided that it was time to act.

In a television address at the end of April 1973, Nixon accepted official responsibility for Watergate but denied any personal knowledge of the break-in or of a cover-up. He also cleaned house, announcing the resignations of Dean, Ehrlichman, Haldeman, and Attorney General Richard Kleindienst. In May, he authorized the appointment of an independent special prosecutor, Archibald Cox, to conduct an investigation.

Meanwhile, sensational revelations exploded in the Senate investigating committee, headed by Sam J. Ervin of North Carolina. TV audiences watched as John Dean described White House projects to harass "enemies" through income tax audits and other illegal means and asserted that the president had long known of efforts to cover up the Watergate burglary. White House aide Alexander Butterfield struck the most damaging blow when he disclosed that the Oval Office in the White House had a voice-activated taping system that automatically recorded conversations.

Both Cox and the Ervin committee immediately asked for tapes on which Nixon discussed Watergate with his aides. When Nixon refused to give them up, citing executive privilege and separation of powers, Cox and Ervin took their case to Judge Sirica's federal district court. Sirica ruled that the tapes should be turned over to him for review so that he could decide whether they should be released to the special prosecutor.

In the midst of the battle for the tapes, Nixon had to deal with more disclosures that expanded the scandal to include the suggestion of personal gain through public office. The General Services Administration reported that Nixon had spent $10 million of federal funds on his personal homes. Later, the IRS disclosed that Nixon owed a half million dollars in back taxes and in 1970 and 1971 had paid federal income taxes of less than $1,000, an amount usually paid by individuals earning $10,000.

In August 1973, the Justice Department announced that Vice President Agnew was under investigation for taking bribes when he was governor of Maryland. Maintaining his innocence and claiming he was a victim of politics, Agnew struck a deal, pleading no contest to a lesser charge of income tax evasion in exchange for a suspended sentence and his resignation. Although Nixon's choice of House minority leader Gerald Ford of Michigan to succeed Agnew won widespread approval, the vice president's resignation further tarnished the administration and led some to think that the president, too, might be replaceable.

Nixon continued to hold on to the tapes. On October 19, 1973, he ordered special prosecutor Cox to cease his efforts to get them. When Cox refused, Nixon ordered Attorney General Elliot Richardson to fire Cox. Richardson balked and resigned instead, as did William D. Ruckelshaus, second in line at the Justice Department. Finally, the solicitor general, Robert Bork, agreed to carry out the president's order. The press called the series of dismissals and resignations the "Saturday night massacre." Nixon's defiance outraged the public, who fired off 250,000 telegrams condemning his action. Stunned by the reaction, Nixon appointed a new special prosecutor, Leon Jaworski, but failed to quell editorials in major newspapers demanding that he resign and serious talk about impeachment in Congress. The president's support in public opinion polls plummeted to 27 percent.

In February 1974, the House of Representatives voted to begin an impeachment investigation. In April, Nixon began to release transcripts of the tapes that he himself had edited. As the public read passages sprinkled with "expletive deleted," House Republican leader John Rhodes abandoned his support of the president, calling the transcripts a "deplorable, shabby, disgusting, and immoral performance by all." The transcripts included Nixon's orders to Mitchell and Dean in March 1973: "I don't give a shit what happens. I want you all to stonewall it, let them plead the Fifth Amendment, cover up or anything else, if it'll save it—save the plan."

In July 1974, the House Judiciary Committee began its nationally televised debate over specific charges for impeachment: (1) obstruction of justice, (2) abuse of power, (3) contempt of Congress, (4) unconstitutional waging of war by the secret bombing of Cambodia, and (5) tax evasion and the selling of political favors. The committee approved the first three charges, with two to six Republicans joining the Democrats on each vote. The last two counts failed to get a majority, but the committee had enough to take its three charges to the House, where a vote of impeachment seemed certain.

On July 24, a unanimous Supreme Court ordered Nixon to comply with Judge Sirica's request for the tapes. When the president released transcripts of three previously unheard tapes on August 5, he sealed his fate. Conversations between Nixon and Haldeman just six days after the break-in revealed that Nixon had tried to manipulate the CIA to hinder the FBI investigation of the burglary. This was the "smoking gun," evidence sufficient to persuade even his staunchest supporters. An angry Senator Barry Goldwater told a Nixon aide, "The president has only twelve votes in the Senate. He has lied to me . . . [and] to my colleagues for the last time."

On August 8, 1974, Nixon announced his resignation to a television audience. Acknowledging that he had made some incorrect judgments, he insisted that he had always tried to do what was best for the nation. The next morning, Nixon ended a rambling, emotional farewell to his staff with some advice: "Always give your best, never get discouraged, never get petty; always remember, others may hate you, but those who hate you don't win unless you hate them, and then you destroy yourself." Had he but practiced that advice, he might have saved his presidency.

The Ford Interregnum

As Nixon's jet sped him back to private life in California, Gerald Ford took the presidential oath of office. "Our Constitution works," he declared. "Our great Republic is a government of laws and not of men." The new leader of that Republic had represented Michigan in the House of Representatives since 1948. He was elected minority leader in 1965,

NIXON RESIGNS
President Richard M. Nixon, just before his resignation took effect on August 9, 1974, waves good-bye to his staff from a helicopter on the White House lawn.
Nixon Presidential Materials Project.

having built a reputation as a conservative, solid party loyalist who treated opponents with openness and cordiality. Neither a brilliant thinker nor an eloquent speaker, Ford was known for his integrity, humility, and dedication to the responsibilities of public office. "I'm a Ford, not a Lincoln," he acknowledged. Most of official Washington and the American public looked favorably on his succession.

Upon taking office, Ford announced, "Our long nightmare is over," but he shocked many Americans one month later when he ended the particular nightmare of the former president. On September 8, 1974, Ford granted Nixon a pardon "for all offenses against the United States which he . . . has committed or may have committed or taken part in" during his presidency. In its universality and its promulgation even before any charges were filed, the pardon was the most extravagant one ever issued, and it saved Nixon from nearly certain indictment and trial. It also provoked a tremendous outcry from Congress and the public. A majority of Americans opposed the pardon, and many suspected that Nixon had made a deal with Ford when he appointed him vice president. (See Historical Question, page 1198.) Capitalizing on the revulsion

Was Ford Right in Pardoning Nixon?

I N NOVEMBER 1973, during Gerald R. Ford's confirmation hearings for the vice presidency, a senator asked Ford whether he believed that a new president could stop criminal proceedings against the president he replaced. Ford replied, "I do not think the public would stand for it." Yet less than a year later, Ford did exactly that when he gave a blanket pardon to Richard M. Nixon just one month after Nixon had resigned the presidency to escape impeachment.

After returning from church on Sunday morning, September 8, 1974, President Ford called reporters to the White House, where he read a statement and signed a proclamation granting Nixon a "full, free, and absolute pardon" for all crimes that he "committed or may have committed or taken part in" while president. When Ford called congressional leaders just before announcing the pardon, Democratic leader Tip O'Neill had said, "You're crazy." And so thought a large segment of the public. White House switchboards lit up immediately, with opinion running strongly against the pardon. Ford's approval rating in public opinion polls plunged by twenty percentage points.

There were immediate charges that Ford had made a deal to pardon Nixon. Certainly, some of Nixon's aides—and no doubt Nixon himself— gave thought to a pardon even before he resigned. J. Fred Buzhardt, one of Nixon's lawyers, drafted a pardon in Ford's name while Nixon was still president. When Nixon's chief of staff, Alexander Haig, met with Ford to brief him on the release of tapes that would probably lead to Nixon's resignation, Haig outlined various strategies, one of which was that Nixon could be pardoned even be-

fore any indictment had taken place. When Ford reported the conversation to his own advisers, they insisted that he call Haig and tell him that nothing he had discussed with Haig should figure in Nixon's decision about whether to resign. Scholars have found no evidence of a deal, and Ford steadfastly denied any such thing. Nonetheless, Haig impressed on Ford the notion that a president had the power to issue a pardon even without an indictment.

If there was no deal, why did Ford pardon Nixon? First of all, the question of a possible pardon hovered over the White House throughout Ford's first weeks in office. Some of Nixon's aides whom Ford had kept on—including Haig, Henry Kissinger, and special counsel Leonard Garment— lobbied the new president to pardon their former boss. In addition, staff members at Nixon's home in San Clemente sent reports emphasizing the former president's serious health problems. The press hammered administration officials about a possible pardon, and reporters opened Ford's first televised press conference by asking whether Nixon should have immunity from prosecution. Ford later remarked, "I thought they had wasted my time," distracting him and the nation from important issues concerning the economy and foreign policy.

In the pardon proclamation and the statement accompanying it, Ford gave a number of reasons for his decision. He said that the "serious allegations and accusations hang[ing] like a sword" over the former president threatened his health. He insisted that "Nixon and his loved ones have suffered enough, and will continue to suffer no matter what I do." Drawing on private opinions that he had sought from special prosecutor Leon Jaworski (along with the understanding that Jaworski would not oppose a pardon), the president suggested that pretrial publicity and lengthy delays would prevent Nixon from getting a fair trial and "equal justice." Ford questioned whether having "already paid the unprecedented penalty of relinquishing the highest office in the United States," Nixon should be exposed "to further punishment and degradation."

Although moved by compassion for Nixon, Ford insisted that "it is not the ultimate fate of

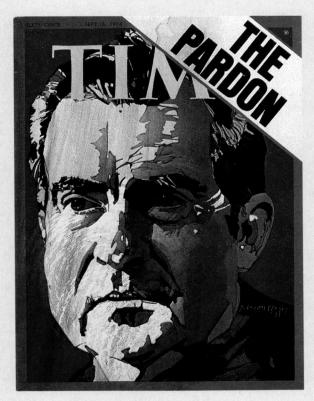

GERALD FORD'S MOMENTOUS DECISION
On September 8, 1974, President Gerald Ford granted for-mer president Richard Nixon a "full, free, and absolute pardon" for whatever crimes he may have committed in the Watergate affair. The pardon enabled Nixon to build a post-Watergate career as elder statesman, while it clouded the remainder of Ford's presidency and contributed to his defeat at the polls in 1976.

©1974 Time Inc. Reprinted by permission.

Richard Nixon that most concerns me." Most of all, he said, the pardon was necessary to get rid of Wa-tergate, the "ugly passions" that it aroused and the "polarization" that it engendered. During the de-bate over the proposed Constitution, Alexander Hamilton had envisioned the pardon provision being used at "critical moments, when a well-timed offer of pardon . . . may restore the tranquility of the commonwealth." Ford did not refer to the Founders, but he declared it his duty "to shut and seal this book" to ensure "domestic tranquility."

In the long run, the pardon probably furthered Ford's goal of getting the political establishment to put Watergate behind it and focus on what Ford considered the real issues confronting the nation. In the short run, however, it reopened the wounds, be-cause many people believed that the pardon vio-lated the principle that all Americans are equal under the law. Upon learning that Ford was going to issue the pardon, his press secretary, Jerald F. ter-Horst, submitted his resignation. It was "ethically wrong," he said, to "put just one man above the law," especially when all of Nixon's aides "were left to run the gauntlet of our judicial system."

TerHorst lamented that "Ford could throw away the new national mood of trust . . . without getting in return a signed confession." Adding fuel to the firestorm of protest was Nixon's response to the pardon. He failed to acknowledge guilt or ex-press contrition for the abuses of power and ob-struction of justice that were charged against him in the articles of impeachment and supported by the tapes. In Nixon's statement, which had been nego-tiated by Ford and Nixon's aides before the pardon was issued, he expressed only "regret" that he had made "mistakes and misjudgments" and acknowl-edged merely that he was "wrong in not acting more decisively and more forthrightly in dealing with Watergate."

Although we cannot measure the degree to which the pardon turned voters against the presi-dent and the Republican Party, Ford did pay a po-litical price for it. Two months after the pardon, Re-publicans lost an exceedingly high number of seats in the congressional elections, and the pardon un-doubtedly played a role in Ford's painfully close de-feat for reelection in 1976. For Nixon, the pardon meant a new political life. His ability over the next two decades to rebuild his image into that of an elder statesman rested in large part on having gained a pardon without having to admit that he had broken the law, violated his oath of office, and betrayed his constituents' trust.

over Watergate, Democrats made impressive gains in the congressional elections in November.

To defend the pardon, Ford testified before Congress, the only president since Lincoln to do so. Although the president has absolute authority to issue pardons, Congress did prevent Ford from turning presidential papers and tapes over to Nixon. In addition to escaping criminal prosecution, the former president also avoided testifying in trials of other Watergate defendants because he was ill with phlebitis and had to undergo surgery. Thirty Nixon associates ultimately were convicted or pleaded guilty, though none served very long sentences; the longest was the nineteen-month imprisonment of former Attorney General John Mitchell.

The grilling of President Ford about the pardon reflected Congress's determination to reassert its authority. Legislators also subjected Ford's choice for vice president, former New York governor Nelson Rockefeller, to long, hard questioning before permitting him to take office in December. To prevent future abuses in election campaigns, Congress enacted the Federal Election Campaign Act of 1974, which established public financing of presidential campaigns.

Having set limits on presidential power in foreign policy by enacting the War Powers Act over Nixon's veto, Congress now moved to check abuses by intelligence agencies both at home and abroad. Special committees in the House and Senate undertook investigations that implicated the FBI and the CIA in a host of illegal activities stretching back to the 1950s. Both agencies had operated programs to harass and discredit political dissenters, and the CIA had even intercepted mail from the Senate Intelligence Committee's chair, Frank Church, to his mother-in-law. The CIA not only had harassed administration critics at home, but also had taken part in plans to assassinate Fidel Castro and other foreign leaders. In response to these revelations, Ford established new controls on covert operations and brought George Bush, head of the U.S. Liaison Office in China, home to head the CIA. Congress established permanent committees to oversee the intelligence agencies.

These measures did little to diminish the public cynicism and lack of trust in government that had been developing since the Johnson years. The Democrats had had their own share of scandals. Wilbur Mills, chair of the House Ways and Means Committee and erstwhile presidential candidate, turned up one night drunk and in the company of a stripper known as "the Argentine Firecracker." In

1976, an employee of Wayne Hays, another prominent Democratic representative, reported that she was on the congressional payroll purely for sexual services: "I can't type, I can't file, I can't even answer the phone." And a cloud continued to hover over Massachusetts Senator Edward M. Kennedy, who in 1969 was driving a car involved in an accident in which a young woman drowned. The accident took place after a party on Chappaquiddick Island, off Martha's Vineyard; Kennedy never managed to give satisfactory explanations of how the accident happened or why he delayed in reporting it.

Public confidence in the federal government's ability to solve critical economic problems also slumped. Both joblessness and inflation intensified in 1974 and 1975 as the president and Congress quarreled over appropriate remedies. Lacking Nixon's flexibility and boldness, Ford reverted to traditional Republican policy, proposing to fight inflation by tightening the money supply and by cutting spending and increasing taxes to balance the federal budget. This set him on a collision course with the heavily Democratic Congress, which pursued a tax cut and increased spending to stimulate the economy and create jobs.

Dubbed by Democratic opponents "the most veto-prone Republican president in the twentieth century," Ford curtailed some federal programs over the objections of Congress. Yet Congress prevailed with a tax cut, increased Social Security benefits, a higher minimum wage, and a $4 billion public works program. Unemployment and inflation abated somewhat, but underlying weaknesses in the U.S. economy remained: a low rate of growth, higher than normal unemployment, a deficit in foreign trade, and high energy prices tied to dependence on oil from abroad.

Keeping Nixon's key foreign policy adviser, Henry Kissinger, as secretary of state, Ford pursued foreign policy goals set by his predecessor. Just two weeks after South Vietnam's collapse in April 1975, the Ford administration seized upon an incident to reassert U.S. power when Cambodian patrol boats captured an American cargo ship, the *Mayagüez*, which was sailing along the Cambodian coast. Ford quickly ordered U.S. forces to bomb Cambodian boats and authorized a plan to rescue the crew of the *Mayagüez*. The president and the U.S. military were unaware that Cambodia had already released the crew, and the attack was carried out, costing forty-one American lives. Although it was unnecessary, the attack produced a burst of approval and pride at home. Senator Barry Goldwater exulted, "It was wonderful. It shows we've still got balls in this country."

Ford and Kissinger, however, failed to sustain widespread support of détente. The secrecy and failure to consult with Congress during the Nixon-Kissinger initiatives had alienated some legislators, and members of both parties worried that Soviet strength was overtaking that of the United States. Some Democrats charged that détente ignored Soviet violations of human rights. In response, Congress derailed trade agreements with the Soviet Union, refusing economic favors unless the Soviets stopped their harsh treatment of internal dissidents and gave Jews who wanted to leave the country permission to emigrate.

Although negotiations continued, the superpowers achieved no further agreements to limit strategic arms during Ford's presidency. The administration's most notable international agreement took place in 1975 in Helsinki, Finland, where Ford, Soviet leader Leonid Brezhnev, and European leaders formally recognized the existing post-World War II boundaries in Europe. In signing the Helsinki accords, the United States accepted the Soviets' domination over their satellite countries in Eastern Europe—a condition to which it had objected so bitterly thirty years earlier as the cold war began.

The Election of 1976

Opposition to détente fueled the biggest challenge to Ford's nomination for a full term in 1976, a challenge that came from the Republican right. The president's leading opponent in the Republican primaries, former California Governor Ronald Reagan, deplored the "collapse of the American will and the retreat of American power," charging that Nixon and Ford had allowed the United States to become "number two in a world where it is dangerous—if not fatal—to be second best." Taking a position to the right of Ford on domestic issues as well, Reagan came close to snatching the nomination from Ford. But in an attempt to unify the party, Ford bowed to conservative Republicans on key platform planks that criticized his own foreign policy and selected conservative Senator Robert Dole of Kansas as his running mate.

Smelling victory, Democratic contenders came out in abundance. Former Georgia Governor James Earl (Jimmy) Carter Jr. began early, traveling across the country campaigning for congressional candidates in 1974 and for himself by early 1975. A graduate of the U.S. Naval Academy, Carter spent seven

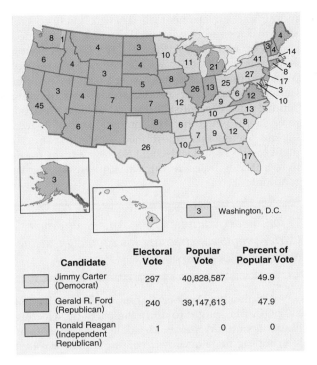

Candidate	Electoral Vote	Popular Vote	Percent of Popular Vote
Jimmy Carter (Democrat)	297	40,828,587	49.9
Gerald R. Ford (Republican)	240	39,147,613	47.9
Ronald Reagan (Independent Republican)	1	0	0

M A P   3 0 . 3
The Election of 1976

years in the navy before his father's death called him back to Plains, Georgia, in 1953 to take over the family peanut farming business. In 1962, he won election to the Georgia state senate, where he served for four years. After a failed bid for the governorship in 1966, he won election in 1970 and served a successful four-year term. As soon as he left office in early 1975, he threw himself into the presidential campaign.

Well financed by businessmen, Carter at first ran a lonely yet sophisticated and grueling campaign that took him into every state's contest for convention delegates and gained extensive media coverage. Highly intelligent and well prepared on the issues, the soft-spoken Carter stressed his small-town roots, deep religious commitment, unpretentiousness, and distance from the popularly suspect national government. Although not a riveting speaker, after the revelations of corruption in the Nixon administration, the candidate who carried his own bags, lived modestly, and went home almost every week to teach a Bible class at his Baptist church had considerable appeal.

"I will never tell a lie to the American people," Carter promised, stressing his campaign theme of morality in government. Pledging vaguely to "restore to our country what has been lost," he avoided stands on controversial issues. The Georgian won endorsements from black religious leaders, but black politicians remained wary, especially after Carter approved of neighborhoods maintaining "ethnic purity" against "intrusion of alien groups," remarks for which he was compelled to apologize. Liberal Democrats questioned Carter's commitment to the New Deal-Great Society reform tradition, but they failed to rally around an alternative candidate.

> *"I will never tell a lie to the American people,"*
> *Carter promised, stressing his campaign theme*
> *of morality in government.*

Winning the Democratic nomination on the first ballot, Carter sought to unify the party by selecting liberal Senator Walter F. Mondale of Minnesota as his running mate and by accepting a platform that affirmed broad goals compatible with traditional Democratic principles. His nomination nonetheless represented a decided rightward turn in the party, reflected in Carter's campaign promises to eliminate the budget deficit and reduce federal controls and regulations on business.

Carter benefited from the Watergate backlash, the economic problems that plagued the Ford administration, the damage that the Reagan challenge had done to Ford, and his own ability to attract sufficient votes from the traditional Democratic coalition of blacks, southerners, organized labor, and ethnic groups. Yet his victory over Ford was narrow. Democrats retained substantial margins in the House and Senate, but Carter received just 50.1 percent of the popular vote to Ford's 48 percent.

The "Outsider" Presidency of Jimmy Carter

In his campaign autobiography, *Why Not the Best?*, Jimmy Carter (the name he used even when signing state documents) held out the ideal of a government that was "competent," as well as "honest, decent, open, fair, and compassionate." Carter was extremely well informed and hardworking, a kind and decent individual who was uninterested in personal or political aggrandizement. Yet while Carter

refrained from abusing the power of his position, he seemed unable to wield his legitimate authority effectively and failed to win a second term.

Carter's undoing stemmed from his style of leadership and from a configuration of domestic and foreign crises that culminated during his last year in office. Prone to attempt too many initiatives at once, Carter worked poorly with Congress, even though it remained under Democratic control. He faced at more intense levels the energy shortages and stagflation that had confounded his predecessors. Carter also reaped the blame for deteriorating Soviet-American relations and for the rise of an intensely anti-American government in Iran, which held fifty-two Americans hostage through his last year in office.

The disastrous final year of Carter's presidency overshadowed some significant accomplishments of his administration, most notably in environmental and energy policies. In foreign affairs, Carter obtained ratification of treaties ending U.S. control over the Panama Canal—the most blatant symbol of Yankee imperialism—and, following up on Nixon's initiatives, he established normal diplomatic relations with China. His most brilliant achievement was securing a peace treaty between Israel and Egypt.

Retreat from Liberalism

Jimmy Carter promised "to help the poor and aged, to improve education, and to provide jobs" but at the same time "not to waste money." He wanted a humane government that would help those in need, but one that also was efficiently managed and prudent in its spending. When these two aims conflicted, especially when inflation threatened economic stability, Carter's commitment to reform assumed second place. Liberal Democrats accused him of deserting the Democratic reform tradition that stretched back to Franklin Roosevelt.

Symbolizing his desire to be known as a "man of the people," Carter substituted a business suit for the traditional formal dress at his inauguration and with his wife, Rosalynn, led the inaugural parade on foot rather than riding in a car. Carter stressed his status as an "outsider" to the deals, bargaining, and inefficiency that characterized national politics. Believing that congressional action was unduly shaped by powerful special interests and legislators' concerns for the next election, Carter saw his job as countering those special interests by acting as the trustee of all the people.

PRESIDENT CARTER'S INAUGURAL DAY
*After his inauguration in January 1977, Jimmy Carter eschewed the customary presidential limousine and instead walked with his family down Pennsylvania Avenue from the Capitol to the White
House. He wanted to emphasize his opposition to some of the trappings of office that separated the
government from the people. Ordering cabinet heads to drive their own cars, he said, "Government
officials can't be sensitive to your problems if we are living like royalty here."*
Jimmy Carter Presidential Library.

Although Carter's outsider status helped him
into office, it left him without strong ties either to
party insiders or to prominent legislators. He lacked
experience in the horse trading and compromise
that got things done in Washington and opposed
them in principle. His desire to propose comprehensive solutions to national problems went against
the congressional tendency to take a piecemeal, incremental approach. Legislators complained of inadequate consultation with the White House during policy formulation, and they grew exasperated
when Carter flooded them with a large number of
unprioritized proposals.

Even a president within the mainstream of the
Democratic Party and an expert in the art of congressional persuasion might not have done much
better than Carter. Congress was flexing its muscles
in response to Watergate and the aggrandizement
of presidential power under Johnson and Nixon. In
addition to reasserting its authority vis-à-vis the executive branch, in the 1970s Congress reduced the
power of its own committee chairs and instituted
reforms that weakened party control over legislators and decentralized the decision-making process.

*Carter worked poorly with Congress and
faced energy shortages and stagflation. He
also reaped the blame for deteriorating Soviet-
American relations and for the rise of an
intensely anti-American government in Iran.*

For his White House staff, Carter relied heavily on associates from Georgia—who, like him,
lacked experience in national politics—but his cab-

AN ACTIVE FIRST LADY
Rosalynn Carter was the most active First Lady in public affairs since Eleanor Roosevelt. Various members of Congress and diplomats criticized President Jimmy Carter for sending her on an official mission to Latin America to emphasize his administration's commitment to human rights and democracy there. Though critics said Latin American leaders wouldn't take her seriously, the seven-country visit in June 1977 proved successful. Here she meets with President Carlos Andrés Pérez of Venezuela.
Walter Bennett/Sygma.

inet appointments included several men from the Kennedy and Johnson administrations. Continuing their relationship as business and political partners, the president discussed nearly everything with his wife, who played a larger role in affairs of state than any First Lady since Eleanor Roosevelt. Carter involved other women in policymaking (including three at cabinet-level rank), far surpassing his predecessors in appointing women as well as members of minority groups to federal judgeships and high government positions. He also undertook a reorganization of the executive branch and won congressional approval for the creation of two new departments, the Department of Education and the Department of Energy.

Carter began his presidency confident that he could solve the unusually formidable set of prob-

lems that had eluded the efforts of the Nixon and Ford administrations—unemployment, inflation, a slow rate of economic growth, and energy shortages. Though some critics complained that his program didn't do enough, Carter signed bills pumping $14 billion into the economy through public works and public service jobs programs and cutting taxes by $34 billion over a three-year period. Unemployment, which had hovered near 8 percent in late 1976, fell below 6 percent in 1978.

However, rising inflation quickly overshadowed the creation of new jobs. Carter refused the mandatory controls on prices and wages that Nixon had implemented briefly in 1971. Instead, while the Federal Reserve system tightened the money supply by increasing interest rates, Carter tried to curtail federal spending. These policies not only failed to halt inflation, which surpassed 13 percent in 1980, but also contributed to rising unemployment, reversing the progress that had been made in Carter's first two years.

The Carter administration achieved little progress on issues traditionally central to the Democratic Party. The president's commitment to holding down the federal budget frustrated Democratic legislators pushing for comprehensive welfare reform and a national health insurance program. To ensure solvency in the Social Security system, Carter and Congress agreed on measures to increase employer and employee contributions. Although these measures shored up the Social Security fund, they also increased the tax burden of lower- and middle-income Americans.

Carter, however, won approval for several proposals that favored business. As Social Security taxes went up, a sharp cut in the maximum rate on capital gains reduced the tax burden on the wealthy. When the Chrysler Corporation approached bankruptcy in 1979, Congress responded with $1.5 billion worth of loan guarantees to ensure the survival of the tenth largest corporation in the country. The government also reduced federal controls in several industries. Congress approved Carter's proposals to deregulate airlines in 1978 and the banking, trucking, and railroad industries in 1980. Airline deregulation at first stimulated lower fares and the rise of new companies, but the 1980s saw reduced service to smaller communities, increasing concerns about safety, and the dominance of a few large conglomerates because of the demise of financially insecure airlines and a series of mergers.

Response to the Energy Crisis

Designating the energy issue "the moral equivalent of war," Carter fought for a comprehensive energy program. But his goal to limit consumption and to reduce U.S. dependence on foreign oil fell victim to his uneasy relationship with Congress and to competing demands among energy producers and consumers. In 1978, Congress passed the National Energy Act of 1978, a compromise measure that included penalties on gas-guzzling automobiles and other incentives to conserve energy. The legislation also provided measures to promote alternative fuel sources and changes in natural gas policies to increase supplies and achieve more equitable distribution.

In 1979, before even this limited program could have an effect, declines in oil production abroad, linked in part to a revolution in Iran, created the most severe energy shortage yet. Hundreds of cars lined up at gas stations in some areas, and motorists' tempers rose even higher when prices at the pumps began to reflect enormous price hikes by the Organization of Petroleum Exporting Countries (OPEC). Carter appealed to the public for support

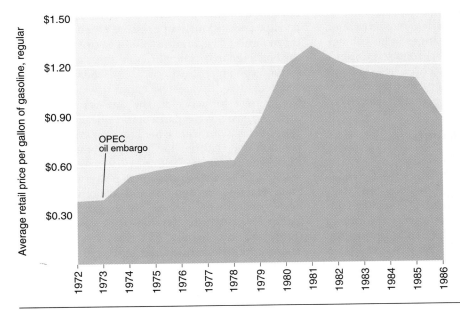

FIGURE 30.1
The Price of Gasoline, 1972–1986

The sharp increase in gasoline prices in 1973 and the even sharper one beginning in 1978 reflected price increases by the Organization of Petroleum Exporting Countries (OPEC) and contributed to inflation in the United States.

of new energy measures, and Congress eventually authorized programs to stimulate alternative fuel sources at the same time that it reduced controls on oil and gas and imposed a windfall profits tax on producers to redistribute some of the profits that would accrue with deregulation. Still falling short of Carter's initial proposal, the energy measures represented the nation's first comprehensive efforts to limit consumption and decrease its dependency on foreign oil.

In July 1979, Carter told a national TV audience that the country faced a "crisis of confidence." Along with losing their faith in progress, too many Americans had sacrificed their pride in "hard work, strong families, close knit communities and our faith in God" to the "worship of self-indulgence and consumption."

In July 1979, Carter told a national TV audience that the nation's problems went far beyond the energy crisis. The country, he said, faced a "crisis of confidence." Along with losing their faith in progress, too many Americans had sacrificed their pride in "hard work, strong families, close-knit communities and our faith in God" to the "worship of self-indulgence and consumption." To many listeners, Carter's speech seemed to blame the American people for his own failure to lead the way to solutions for national problems. Perceptions of flawed leadership multiplied when, two days later, Carter announced sweeping changes in his cabinet. By the end of the month, pollsters reported Carter's approval rating at just 25 percent. Developments abroad would undermine even further the nation's confidence in Carter's ability to govern effectively.

Idealism and Human Rights in Carter's Foreign Policy

Moral principles, Jimmy Carter promised, would guide his approach to America's relationships with the rest of the world. His predecessors' obsession with protecting and expanding U.S. power by any means, Carter believed, had violated the nation's principles of freedom and human dignity. "We've seen a loss of morality . . . and we're ashamed of what our government is as we deal with other nations around the world," he said. The cynical support of dictators, the

secret diplomacy, the interference in the internal affairs of other countries, the excessive reliance on military solutions—Carter promised to reverse them all.

Human rights formed the cornerstone of Carter's approach. Led by the president, U.S. officials took every opportunity to focus attention on governments that denied their citizens basic political and civil rights or freedom of religion and expression. The administration also used economic sanctions, denying aid or trading privileges to nations that oppressed their citizens. It applied economic pressure against a number of countries, including Argentina, Chile, El Salvador, and the white minority governments of Rhodesia and South Africa, which blatantly violated the rights of their black majorities.

Yet the administration implemented the human rights policy with glaring inconsistencies. In 1979, the United States established formal diplomatic relations with the People's Republic of China, concluding the process that Nixon and Kissinger had begun. In this case, improved relations with China took priority over attempts to secure democratic rights for the Chinese people. Moreover, in dealing with staunch, anti-Communist U.S. allies, Carter sacrificed human rights to strategic and security considerations. The administration invoked no sanctions against Iran, South Korea, and the Philippines, even though official oppression was obvious in those countries.

Cold war considerations dominated concern for human rights in the administration's approach to Nicaragua, which had been ruled since 1936 by the corrupt and viciously oppressive regime of the Somoza family. The administration complained about the Nicaraguan dictatorship's excesses and invoked some economic sanctions, but when civil war erupted there, its greatest concern was to contain Communist influence in the anti-Somoza movement. Officials were particularly uneasy about the Sandinistas, who were a leading element in the opposition and had ties to Cuba. Nonetheless, when the Somoza regime fell in 1979 and Sandinista leader Daniel Ortega assumed power, the United States extended recognition and economic aid to the new government. Critics on the right attacked Carter for pressuring Anastásio Somoza on human rights and thus helping to undermine his regime. These critics demanded the more typical test for U.S. support during the cold war years: whether a country was anti-Communist and friendly to U.S. interests, not how it treated its citizens.

THE CAMP DAVID ACCORDS
President Jimmy Carter oversees the meeting of Egyptian President Anwar Sadat, left, and Israeli Prime Minister Menachem Begin at Camp David, Maryland, in September 1978. Carter's passionate commitment to promoting peace helped produce the first easing of hostility between Arabs and Israelis in thirty years.
Corbis-Bettmann.

The president took on even greater political burdens in applying moral principles to relations with Panama. Carter sped up the negotiations over control of the Panama Canal that had been under way since the Johnson administration. In 1977, the United States and Panama reached agreement on the terms of two treaties, one providing for joint control of the canal until the end of the century and the second defining U.S. rights after Panama assumed control.

The treaties evoked intense opposition. Although Carter and his supporters viewed them as recompense for the blatant use of U.S. power in obtaining the canal in 1903, others insisted on maintaining control of this vital waterway. "We bought it, we paid for it, it's ours, and we're going to keep it," claimed Ronald Reagan in his 1976 campaign for the Republican nomination. Behind the opposition lay anxieties about the decline of U.S. power. After the Carter administration undertook a massive campaign to rally popular and congressional support, the Senate ratified the treaties by the narrowest margins. Opponents continued to use the Panamanian accords as a political weapon: Several pro-treaty senators lost reelection bids, and Carter

saw the issue as an important factor in his own defeat in 1980.

In applying his moral authority toward peace in the Middle East, Carter achieved his most brilliant victory, one that was not tarnished by acrimony at home. He took advantage of the courage and foresight of Egyptian President Anwar Sadat, the first Arab leader to risk his political future by talking directly with Israeli officials. When initial discussions between Sadat and Israeli Prime Minister Menachem Begin faltered, Carter invited the two leaders to the presidential retreat at Camp David, Maryland, in September 1978. Carter studied all the issues down to the smallest details and then spent thirteen days at Camp David mediating between Begin and Sadat, carrying proposals and counterproposals from one cabin to the other. His enormous investment paid off in the form of a tentative agreement known popularly as the Camp David accords.

When subsequent negotiations for an official treaty bogged down, Carter flew to Jerusalem and Cairo and applied his tenacious diplomacy once more, obtaining a treaty that Begin and Sadat signed on the White House lawn in March 1979. Under the terms of the treaty, Egypt recognized Israel, and Israel agreed to gradual withdrawal from the Sinai Peninsula, territory that it had seized in the 1967 war. The issues of Palestinian self-determination in other Israeli-occupied territories (the West Bank and Gaza) and the plight of Palestinian refugees remained unresolved. Nonetheless, the first real steps toward peace in the Middle East had been taken, and Jimmy Carter had earned much of the credit.

Foreign Policy in Disarray

The last two years of the Carter administration saw both a shift in policies and severe setbacks to Carter's original goals. Relations between the United States and the Soviet Union deteriorated, and the administration began a sizable military buildup. Although external events in 1979, particularly the Soviet invasion of Afghanistan and the Iranian revolution, stimulated the turn toward militarism, it also reflected currents that had existed within the administration from the beginning.

For counsel on foreign policy issues, Carter leaned most heavily on his secretary of state, Cyrus Vance, and his national security adviser, Zbigniew Brzezinski. Even though the two had recommended each other for their respective posts, once in office they discovered acute differences in their approaches to policy. Polish-born Brzezinski, an international relations professor at Columbia University, held traditional cold war views, emphasizing the Soviet and Communist threat and urging the maximization of U.S. power. Vance, a New York lawyer who had served in the Kennedy and Johnson administrations, had come to see the limitations of American power and the need to work with the Soviet Union to reduce the threat of nuclear war.

Preferring to pursue national security through nonmilitary means, Carter initially approached the Soviet Union with an air of accommodation and reassurance. Although the president never ceased to speak out about Soviet suppression of Jews and dissidents, he set Vance to work on a new strategic arms limitation agreement to replace SALT I, which was due to expire in 1977. He also cast a cautious eye on new weapons systems and canceled production of the neutron bomb, a high-radiation weapon designed to be used on the battlefield. Carter also halted production of the new B-1 bomber, thereby infuriating a large number of its supporters in Congress.

Two years of negotiations with the Soviet Union produced a SALT II treaty in 1979, but by then

Carter had accepted Brzezinski's warnings about the need to counter a Soviet military buildup. The president authorized development of new intermediate-range missiles to be deployed in Western Europe as well as an enormous new missile system (known as MX) to be built in the United States. However, this new emphasis on military strength did not defuse criticism of SALT II and arms control, opposition that had grown with Carter's cancellation of the B-1.

With Senate ratification of SALT II becoming increasingly unlikely, Carter withdrew the treaty in December 1979. He acted shortly after the Soviet Union invaded its neighbor Afghanistan, whose recently installed pro-Soviet government was threatened by Muslim opposition. Carter asserted that the invasion "could pose the greatest threat to peace since the Second World War." In response, he imposed economic sanctions on the Soviet Union, canceled U.S. participation in the 1980 Olympic Games in Moscow, and persuaded Congress to approve legislation requiring all nineteen-year-old men to register for the draft.

The president claimed that Soviet actions posed a threat to oil supplies from the Middle East and announced his own "Carter Doctrine," stating that the United States would intervene with any means necessary should an outside force try to gain control of the Persian Gulf. The human rights policy fell by the wayside as the United States stepped up aid to Pakistan, Afghanistan's neighbor, controlled by a military regime that had overthrown and executed the popularly elected head of state. Finally, Carter called for hefty increases in defense spending over the next five years.

On November 4, 1979, a crowd broke into the U.S. embassy in Teheran and held more than sixty Americans captive there, demanding that the United States return the shah for trial.

Events in Iran fueled this reversion to a hardline, militaristic approach. All the U.S. arms and support had not enabled the shah to suppress growing opposition to his regime. Iranian dissidents still resented the CIA's role in the overthrow of the Mossadegh government in 1953, and they deplored the Westernization of their country that accompanied the shah's rule as well as his savage attempts to silence opposition. On New Year's Eve 1977, Carter toasted the shah's "great leadership" at a banquet in Teheran. But in little more than a year, a revolution forced the shah to abandon his throne and country. By March 1979, the Iranian government was in the hands of the Ayatollah Ruholla Khomeini and other Shiite Islamic fundamentalists who were intensely hostile to the United States, which they blamed for supporting the shah's brutalities and undermining the religious foundations of their country.

When Carter permitted the shah to enter the United States for medical treatment, anti-American demonstrations escalated in Teheran. On November 4, 1979, a crowd broke into the U.S. embassy and held more than sixty Americans captive there, demanding that the United States return the shah for trial. When Khomeini supported the captors and refused to negotiate, Carter froze Iranian assets in U.S. banks and placed an embargo on Iranian oil. The only Iranian concessions were to free thirteen blacks and women and later a seriously ill hostage. For the next year, the hostage crisis received an inordinate amount of television coverage and vast amounts of the administration's time and energies.

Every attempt to negotiate was frustrated, and in April 1980, Carter resorted to force to rescue the hostages. But the small military operation ran into

AMERICAN HOSTAGES IN IRAN
Iranian militants display one of the hostages they took when they occupied the American embassy in Teheran on November 4, 1979. Until the hostages were released in January 1981, Americans regularly watched TV images of the American captives being paraded before angry Iranian crowds. The bound, blindfolded hostages served as humiliating symbols of the limitations of American power.
Ph. Ledru/Sygma.

difficulties landing in the Iranian desert and had to abort the mission. Eight Americans died when a U.S. plane and helicopter collided during the evacuation. Secretary of State Vance, who had opposed a rescue attempt and had been kept out of the plans, resigned in protest. Failure of the rescue mission further embarrassed the president, and the hostage crisis burdened Carter's campaign for reelection. Continuing efforts to reach an agreement with Iran finally produced release of the hostages on the day Carter left office.

Conclusion: The Loss of American Ascendency

Public confidence and trust in government declined in the 1970s, partially in response to Watergate and other revelations of deception and corruption among public officials. Presidents Ford and Carter restored morality to the White House, but both were deficient in political skills. The 1970s saw continuation of key domestic reforms of the 1960s as well as new legislation in response to movements for women's rights and environmental protection. Yet the government seemed unable to deal with the gravest economic problems since the Great Depression—a low rate of economic growth, inflation combined with unemployment, and an increasing trade deficit.

Nor could Americans take much comfort in their country's relationships with the rest of the world. They applauded Carter's success in inching the Middle East slightly in the direction of stability, but the Israeli-Egyptian accord failed to resolve the larger Middle East problems that affected Americans directly by disrupting energy supplies. And even though the Panama Canal treaties moved the United States toward more equitable relations with Latin American countries, they provoked strong opposition.

Normalization of relations with the People's Republic of China won widespread support, but critics of strategic arms limitation and Soviet-American détente gained the upper hand. This opposition, combined with the Soviet invasion of Afghanistan, nullified the thaw in Soviet-American relations that Nixon and Kissinger had begun. By 1980, the hostile tone of the United States toward the Soviet Union and the growing emphasis on military expansion resembled the early years of the cold war.

Officials in both parties who supported a more militaristic approach to foreign policy found support in a public perplexed by the nation's apparent inability to influence global events. Four years after the fall of South Vietnam, another humiliation rocked the nation when Iran erupted into a burst of anti-Americanism and the United States proved unable to rescue its citizens who were held hostage there.

Americans' feeling of impotence in the face of the hostage crisis did reflect a decline in U.S. power, but it was a relative descent from an artificially high base. The global political and economic ascendancy of the United States existed only as long as it took for other countries to recover from the ravages of World War II. The growing power of the Soviet Union and China set limits on the ability of the United States to intervene throughout the world without risking superpower confrontation. And the rise of nationalism in the third world posed further constraints on American power.

The recovery of Europe and Japan challenged U.S. economic supremacy and contributed to the domestic problems that plagued each administration in the 1970s, particularly the loss of foreign and domestic markets; the decline in electronics, steel, automobile, and other major industries; and the accompanying rising unemployment and sluggish economy. Whether and how the United States could regain its economic and political power provided the script for the 1980 elections.

CHRONOLOGY

1968 Richard Nixon elected thirty-seventh president of the United States.

1969 Warren E. Burger appointed chief justice of United States by Nixon.

1970 Earth Day demonstrations held to support environmental goals.

Congress passes Occupational Safety and Health Act.

Environmental Protection Agency established by Nixon.

Native American Women's Association founded.

Women Strike for Peace and Equality demonstrations take place nationwide.

1971 First national Mexican American women's conference held.

In *Swann,* Supreme Court upholds legality of busing to achieve integration.

Nixon announces abandonment of gold standard in his New Economic Policy.

Nixon vetoes comprehensive child care bill.

1972 Congress passes federal revenue-sharing laws.

Congress passes Title IX of Education Amendments Act, banning sex discrimination in education.

Ms. magazine founded by Gloria Steinem and other feminists.

Nixon becomes first U.S. president to visit China.

Nixon visits Moscow to sign arms limitation treaties with Soviets.

Nixon campaign aides apprehended breaking into Democratic Party headquarters in Watergate apartment complex in Washington, D.C.

Richard Nixon reelected president in landslide.

1973 Arab oil embargo in retaliation for U.S. support of Israel creates energy crisis in United States.

National Black Feminist Organization founded.

Senate Watergate hearings reveal widespread abuses of power in Nixon administration.

In *Roe v. Wade,* Supreme Court rules that abortion is constitutionally protected.

1974 Nixon resigns as president in face of certain impeachment by House of Representatives over his role in Watergate affair; Gerald Ford becomes thirty-eighth president of United States.

Ford pardons Nixon of any crimes he may have committed while president.

Supreme Court imposes some limitations on use of busing to achieve racial integration in schools.

1976 Jimmy Carter, former Democratic governor of Georgia, elected thirty-ninth president of United States, defeating Ford.

1978 Carter helps negotiate peace agreement between Israel and Egypt (Camp David accords).

Congress passes National Energy Act.

In *Bakke,* Supreme Court rules against racial quotas and "reverse" discrimination.

Congress passes law banning discrimination against pregnant women.

1979 **November 4.** Beginning of hostage crisis in Iran.

1980 Attempt to free U.S. hostages in Iran fails.

BIBLIOGRAPHY

GENERAL WORKS

Peter N. Carroll, *It Seemed Like Nothing Happened: America in the 1970s* (1982).

Thomas Ferguson and Joel Rogers, *Right Turn: The Decline of the Democrats and the Future of American Politics* (1986).

Raymond Garthoff, *Détente and Confrontation: American-Soviet Relations from Nixon to Reagan* (1985).

Kim McQuaid, *The Anxious Years: America in the Vietnam-Watergate Era* (1989).

DOMESTIC ISSUES

Barry Bluestone and Bennett Harrison, *The Deindustrialization of America: Plant Closings, Community Abandonment, and the Dismantling of Basic Industry* (1982).

Vincent J. Burke and Vee Burke, *Nixon's Good Deed: Welfare Reform* (1974).

Paul R. Dommel, *The Politics of Revenue Sharing* (1974).

Daniel Patrick Moynihan, *The Politics of a Guaranteed National Income: The Nixon Administration and the Family Assistance Plan* (1973).

Herman Schwartz, ed., *The Burger Years: Rights and Wrongs in the Supreme Court* (1987).

Melvin Urofsky, *A Conflict of Rights: The Supreme Court and Affirmative Action* (1991).

ENERGY AND THE ENVIRONMENT

S. David Aviel, *The Politics of Nuclear Energy* (1982).

Thomas R. Dunlap, *DDT: Scientists, Citizens, and Public Policy* (1981).

Samuel P. Hays, *Beauty, Health, and Permanence: Environmental Politics in the United States, 1955–1985* (1987).

Michael J. Lacey, ed., *Government and Environmental Politics* (1991).

Martin V. Melosi, *Coping with Abundance: Energy and Environment in Industrial America* (1985).

Philip Shabecoff, *A Fierce Green Fire: The American Environmental Movement* (1993).

Franklin Tugwell, *The Energy Crisis and the American Political Economy: Politics and Markets in the Management of Natural Resources* (1988).

John C. Whitaker, *Striking a Balance: Environment and Natural Resources Policy in the Nixon-Ford Years* (1976).

Daniel Yergin, *The Prize: The Epic Quest for Oil, Money, and Power* (1990).

THE NIXON AND FORD ADMINISTRATIONS

Stephen E. Ambrose, *Nixon: The Triumph of a Politician, 1962–1972* (1989).

Gerald R. Ford, *A Time to Heal: The Autobiography of Gerald R. Ford* (1979).

Michael A. Genovese, *The Nixon Presidency: Power and Politics in Turbulent Times* (1990).

John Robert Greene, *The Limits of Power: The Nixon and Ford Administrations* (1992).

Joan Hoff, *Nixon Reconsidered* (1994).

Richard M. Nixon, *RN: The Memoirs of Richard Nixon* (1978).

Herbert S. Parmet, *Nixon and His America* (1989).

A. James Reichley, *Conservatives in an Age of Change: The Nixon and Ford Administrations* (1981).

Edward L. and Frederick H. Schapsmeier, *Gerald R. Ford's Date with Destiny: A Political Biography* (1989).

Tom Wicker, *One of Us: Richard Nixon and the American Dream* (1991).

WATERGATE

Carl Bernstein and Bob Woodward, *All the President's Men* (1974).

Fred J. Cook, *The Crimes of Watergate* (1981).

Leon Jaworski, *The Right and the Power: The Prosecution of Watergate* (1976).

Stanley I. Kutler, *The Wars of Watergate: The Last Crisis of Richard Nixon* (1990).

Gladys Engel Lang and Kurt Lang, *The Battle for Public Opinion: The President, the Press, and the Polls during Watergate* (1983).

Kathryn S. Olmsted, *Challenging the Secret Government: The Post-Watergate Investigations of the CIA and FBI* (1996).

Arthur M. Schlesinger, *The Imperial Presidency* (1973).

Michael Schudson, *Watergate in American Memory* (1992).

John J. Sirica, with John F. Stacks, *To Set the Record Straight: The Break-in, the Tapes, the Conspirators, the Pardon* (1979).

WOMEN'S MOVEMENTS

Mary Frances Berry, *Why ERA Failed* (1986).

Anne N. Costain, *Inviting Women's Rebellion* (1992).

Barbara Hinkson Craig and David M. O'Brien, *Abortion and American Politics* (1993).

Alice Echols, *Daring to Be Bad: Radical Feminism in America, 1967–1975* (1989).

Myra Marx Ferree and Beth B. Hess, *Controversy and Coalition: The New Feminist Movement* (1985).

Jo Freeman, *The Politics of Women's Liberation* (1985).

Joyce Gelb and Marion Lief Palley, *Women and Public Policies* (1987).

Susan M. Hartmann, *From Margin to Mainstream: American Women and Politics since 1960* (1989).

Jane J. Mansbridge, *Why We Lost the ERA* (1986).

Donald G. Mathews and Jane Sherron De Hart, *Sex, Gender, and the Politics of ERA* (1990).

Rosalind Pollack Petchesky, *Abortion and Woman's Choice: Private Morality and Public Policy* (1981).

Winifred D. Wandersee, *On the Move: American Women in the 1970s* (1988).

Guida West, *The National Welfare Rights Movement: The Social Protest of Poor Women* (1981).

Joan Hoff Wilson, *Rites of Passage: The Past and Future of the ERA* (1986).

THE CARTER ADMINISTRATION

M. Glenn Abernathy, Dilys M. Hill, and Phil Williams, eds., *The Carter Years: The President and Policymaking* (1984).

Peter G. Bourne, *Jimmy Carter: A Comprehensive Biography from Plains to Post-Presidency* (1997).

Jimmy Carter, *Keeping Faith: Memoirs of a President* (1982).

John Dumbrell, *The Carter Presidency: A Reevaluation* (1995).

Betty Glad, *Jimmy Carter: In Search of the Great White House* (1980).

Erwin C. Hargrove, *Jimmy Carter as President: Leadership and the Politics of the Public Good* (1988).

Charles O. Jones, *The Trusteeship Presidency: Jimmy Carter and the United States Congress* (1988).

Burton I. Kaufmann, *The Presidency of James Earl Carter* (1993).

Kenneth Earl Morris, *Jimmy Carter, American Moralist* (1996).

Herbert D. Rosenbaum and Alexej Ugrinsky, eds., *The Presidency and Domestic Policies of Jimmy Carter* (1993).

FOREIGN POLICY

James A. Bill, *The Eagle and the Lion: The Tragedy of American-Iranian Relations* (1988).

Seyom Brown, *The Crisis of Power: Foreign Policy in the Kissinger Years* (1979).

Zbigniew Brzezinski, *Power and Principle: Memoirs of the National Security Adviser, 1977–1981* (1983).

Raymond I. Garthoff, *Détente and Confrontation: American-Soviet Relations from Nixon to Reagan* (1994).

Mark J. Gasiorowski, *U.S. Foreign Policy and the Shah: Building a Client State in Iran* (1991).

Seymour Hersh, *The Price of Power: Kissinger in the Nixon White House* (1983).

J. Michael Hogan, *The Panama Canal in American Politics* (1986).

Keith I. Nelson, *The Making of Détente: Soviet-American Relations in the Shadow of Vietnam* (1995).

Gaddis Smith, *Morality, Reason, and Power: American Diplomacy in the Carter Years* (1986).

Terry Terriff, *The Nixon Administration and the Making of U.S. Nuclear Strategy* (1995).

Cyrus Vance, *Hard Choices: Critical Years in America's Foreign Policy* (1983).

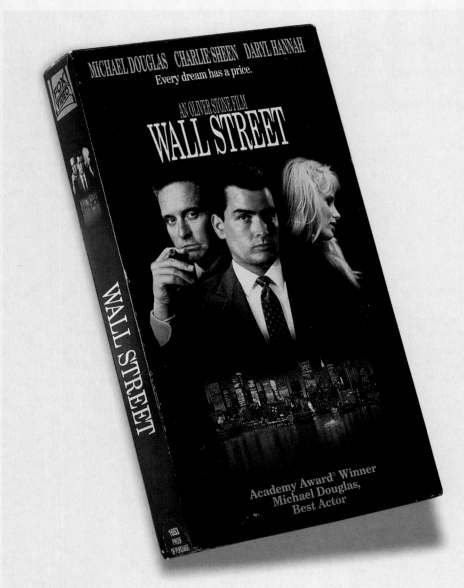

WALL STREET VIDEO

The popular 1987 movie Wall Street captured elements of the economy and society that led some observers to talk about the "money culture" and call the 1980s the decade of "greed." Wealth accumulation and lavish consumption were more visible than usual. One indication of the prosperity enjoyed by some was the growing presence of technology in the home, including computers, microwave ovens, compact disc players, and, especially, video cassette recorders. As the number of households with VCRs jumped from one million in 1980 to nearly 70 million in 1990, more and more people saw movies like "Wall Street" by renting videotapes for home viewing.

THE REAGAN-BUSH COUNTERREVOLUTION

31

1980–1991

"FRANKLIN DELANO REAGAN," headlined the *New York Times* editorial on Ronald Wilson Reagan's acceptance speech at the Republican convention in 1980. The presidential nominee had repeatedly quoted Roosevelt, all the while promising to reduce drastically the federal government's role in American life. Once in the White House, Reagan promptly rehung a portrait of President Calvin Coolidge—that staunch Republican believer in the virtues of big business—but he continued to grasp the mantle of Roosevelt even as his policies formed the antithesis of New Deal liberalism.

Reagan's invocation of Franklin Roosevelt made good politics, bolstering his appeal to traditional Democrats. It also served to reconcile Reagan's own history —he had once been an active Democrat and ardent Roosevelt supporter—with his present conservative Republicanism. He pulled off his identification with Roosevelt by quoting selectively and by emphasizing Roosevelt's early advocacy of government retrenchment and frugality. Reagan genuinely admired Roosevelt's dynamism and confidence in the nation's ability to rise to new challenges. He intended to exercise that same spirited leadership and to restore the United States to a global role as powerful as the one it held at the time of Roosevelt's death. He also aimed for a revolution in domestic policy as striking as Roosevelt's in extent, though not in kind, and a new national political alignment that would be as impressive as Roosevelt's New Deal coalition.

The frequent appeal by the most conservative president since Calvin Coolidge to the example of Franklin Roosevelt was not the only contradiction of the Reagan presidency. Reagan promised fiscal stringency and a balanced budget, but when he left office, the government owed the largest debt in the nation's history. He limited the role of the federal government through tax cuts and relaxation of regulations on business, but federal spending increased and the federal bureaucracy expanded during his eight years as president. Reagan appealed to Americans uncomfortable with the sexual permissiveness, new family structures, and other social changes of the 1960s and 1970s. Social conservatives liked his emphasis on "family values," but Reagan himself was divorced and estranged from some of his children. The darling of religious fundamentalists, the president rarely attended church.

Reagan set out to restore confidence in government, and he contributed mightily to a revival of national pride. Yet dozens of his aides were linked to government scandals, and many of his statements clouded the line between fact and fantasy. Although Reagan voiced the most hawkish rhetoric since the days of John Foster Dulles and promoted the largest military buildup in peacetime, when he left office the United States and the Soviet Union had moved closer together than at any time since World War II.

Unlike the era of Roosevelt, which had focused on the disadvantaged, the spotlight of the 1980s turned on the affluent. The Reagan administration conquered the inflation and unemployment that had bedeviled presidents in the 1970s, and the economy entered its longest boom in the nation's history. Better-off Americans enjoyed the greatest benefits. Resembling the 1920s rather than the 1930s in economic terms, the Reagan era saw wealth redistributed upward while prosperity bypassed large segments of the population.

Reagan's successor, George Bush, deviated only slightly from Reagan's antigovernment philosophy. He proposed few domestic policy initiatives and vetoed many passed by the Democrat-controlled Congress. Aside from new laws dealing with civil rights and environmental protection, domestic policy changed little from the Reagan years. With the president and Congress caught in gridlock, the economy slid into a recession in 1990.

In contrast to the domestic arena, which appeared stagnant, massive changes swept through the world, surprising even the most astute foreign policy observers. Eastern Europe broke free of Communist control in 1989, and the Soviet Union disintegrated in 1991. With the end of the cold war, which had been the obsession of U.S. foreign policy for forty-five years, Bush heralded a "new world order." Freed from having to worry about the Soviet Union's response to U.S. intervention, Bush responded quickly to a new crisis in the Middle East. When Iraq invaded Kuwait in 1990, the United States led an international coalition that expelled the invaders.

When Bush left the presidency in 1993, the United States had yet to articulate an overall strategy for a post-cold war era no longer defined by containment of communism. On the home front, Bush left the Reagan antigovernment legacy intact along with a continuing federal deficit and a declining economy.

The Rising Tide of Conservatism

Ronald Reagan's landslide election to the presidency in 1980 marked the most important turning point in politics since Franklin D. Roosevelt's victory in 1932. Eisenhower and Nixon had campaigned as middle-of-the-road Republicans, but Reagan's victory established conservatism's dominance in the Republican Party and enabled the right to shape the national political agenda during the decade to come. Since the 1930s, the Democratic Party had defined the major issues; in the 1980s, the Republicans assumed that initiative, while the Democrats moved toward the right in their search for an effective response.

Reagan's victory established conservatism's dominance in the Republican Party and enabled the right to shape the national political agenda during the decade to come.

An extraordinarily adept politician, Reagan appealed to a wide spectrum of conservative groups and sentiments. He won the allegiance of free-market conservatives, militant anti-Communists, fundamentalist and evangelical Christians, and white working-class Democrats who were disenchanted with Great Society programs. Above all, Reagan benefited from the economic disarray that had caused both inflation and unemployment rates to soar in the last years of the Carter administration. These conditions enabled Reagan to win votes from people who suffered economically but who otherwise would not have supported a conservative.

The Election of 1980

Ronald Reagan captured the 1980 Republican nomination from a large field of contenders, and his success was remarkable in several respects. The oldest candidate ever nominated for the presidency, Reagan was born in 1911 to a staunchly Democratic father who served as administrator of work relief in Dixon, Illinois, during the New Deal. After attending a small religious college in Illinois, Reagan worked as a sportscaster before becoming a movie actor.

In the 1940s, he became active in the Screen Actors Guild, a performers' union, ultimately becoming its president. When the Red scare reached Hollywood, Reagan worked energetically to rid the movie industry of alleged Communists and sympathizers. His conservatism developed further in the 1950s, when, after his acting career faded, General Electric Corporation (GE) hired him for public relations work. Speaking for GE all over the country, Reagan harped on the evils of big government.

In 1964, he campaigned for Barry Goldwater, his shift to conservatism complete.

Reagan's own political career took off when he was elected to the first of two terms as governor of California in 1966. Although he ran a conservative campaign, denouncing excessive government, welfare giveaways, and student protests at the state's universities, as governor he displayed considerable flexibility. He approved a major tax increase (blaming the need for it on the extravagance of the previous Democratic administration), a strong measure to control water pollution, and a liberal abortion bill.

Reagan displayed similar flexibility in his 1980 presidential campaign, softening, for example, his earlier attacks on the Panama Canal treaties and Social Security. As his running mate, he chose George Bush, a representative of the Republican center, who had attacked central features of the Reagan agenda when they were rivals in the primary races. (Once he became a member of Reagan's team, however, Bush displayed unswerving loyalty to the Reagan program.) Reagan's amiable personality helped him to avoid being cast as a rigid right winger, and his energetic campaign assuaged doubts that he was too old for the presidency.

Despite Reagan's move toward the center, some liberal Republicans balked at his nomination and at the party platform, which reflected the domination of the right wing. When the party adopted a plank reversing its forty-year support for the Equal Rights Amendment, moderate and liberal Republican women marched outside the convention hall to show their dismay. Some of these women, along with other liberal Republicans, found a more acceptable standard-bearer in John B. Anderson, representative of Illinois, who deserted his party to run as an independent candidate.

The poor state of the economy and the country's declining international stature provided ample weapons for Reagan's campaign. He kept reminding voters of the "misery index"—the combined rates of unemployment and inflation—and asked, "Are you better off now than you were four years ago?" Reagan also capitalized on the Soviet invasion of Afghanistan and the Iranian hostage crisis, accusing Jimmy Carter of weakening U.S. military strength and losing the confidence of the nation's allies and the respect of its enemies. "They say that the United States has had its day in the sun, that our nation has passed its zenith," Reagan scoffed. Staunchly rejecting that view, he insisted that more effective leadership and a determination to "take

THE REAGAN PRESIDENCY BEGINS
Ronald Reagan, one of the most popular presidents of the twentieth century, takes the oath of office in 1981 from Chief Justice Warren Burger. His wife, Nancy, looks on.
Dick Halstead/Time.

government off the backs of the people" would restore Americans' morale and other nations' respect.

Having lost confidence in Carter and his ability to contain inflation and unemployment, a narrow majority of voters responded to Reagan's upbeat message. Fifty-one percent of the electorate cast their votes for Reagan, while 41 percent favored Carter, 7 percent Anderson. Though his popular majority was slim, Reagan overwhelmed Carter 489 to 49 in electoral college votes. The Republicans also picked up thirty-three new seats in the House and won control of the Senate.

The returns appeared to reflect a rejection of Carter rather than an affirmation of Reagan. Only 52.3 percent of those eligible bothered to vote. One eighteen-year-old remarked, "I didn't want to be responsible for electing either one." Of those who did vote, more supported Reagan because "it was time for a change" than because they found his conservative principles compelling. Some analysts read the election results as signifying a major shift in popular attitudes, but others found persistent public support for a substantial government role in solving social and economic problems.

Reagan and the Spectrum of Conservatism

Whatever the election results signified, conservatism had gained greater ascendancy in American political culture than at any time since the 1920s. Reagan clearly benefited from a lingering backlash against the upheavals associated with the 1960s—the civil rights revolution, the reforms of the Johnson era, the antiwar movement, feminism, the new sexual permissiveness, and the liberalism of the Supreme Court.

Much of Reagan's support came from religious conservatives with an avid interest in social issues, who constituted a relatively new phenomenon known as the New Right. During the 1970s, evangelical Christianity not only claimed thousands of new adherents but also abandoned the customary political neutrality of fundamentalist religion. The New Right made adept use of powerful new techniques for mobilizing support, notably sophisticated mass-mailing techniques and the "electronic ministry." Evangelical ministers such as Jerry Falwell, Jim Bakker, and Pat Robertson preached to huge television audiences. Attacking feminism, abortion, homosexuality, and pornography, they called for restoration of old-fashioned "family values." They wanted prayer back in and sex education out of the schools.

Conservatives created or revitalized a raft of political organizations and journals. The religious right sought a specific Christian voice in government through the Moral Majority founded by Jerry Falwell in 1979 and subsequently through the Christian Coalition, which Pat Robertson created in 1989. Within a few years, the Christian Coalition claimed 1.6 million members and control of the Republican Party in more than a dozen states. The instruments of more traditional conservatives—those who advocated limited government at home and militant anticommunism abroad—likewise flourished. These included publications such as the *National Review*, edited by William Buckley, and think tanks (research foundations) such as the American Enterprise Institute and the Heritage Foundation, which supported experts who developed and publicized new policy approaches.

Reagan embraced the full spectrum of conservatism and avowed his agreement with the New

EVANGELIST JERRY FALWELL
One of the most popular televangelists, Baptist minister Jerry Falwell of Lynchburg, Virginia holds up the newsletter of the Moral Majority, the organization he founded in 1979. Established to promote "pro-God, pro-family policies in government," the Moral Majority and other groups of conservative Christians in the 1980s began to play a significant role in the Republican Party.
Eve Arnold/Magnum Photos, Inc.

Right on abortion, school prayer, and other social and moral issues. While these positions heartened social conservatives, they were not wholeheartedly embraced by the more traditional right, and few major policy changes came to fruition in these areas. Rather, Reagan's greatest success in promoting the conservative agenda lay in strengthening the nation's anti-Communist posture and reducing government restraints on free enterprise.

"In the present crisis," Reagan argued, "government is not the solution to our problem, government *is* the problem." Excessive government regulation and burdensome taxation crippled productivity, he claimed, while unbridled government spending was "mortgaging our future . . . for the temporary convenience of the present." Reagan asserted that the nation had prospered historically because "we unleashed the energy and individual genius of man to a greater extent than has ever been done before." A return to individualism would produce a booming economy once again.

Reagan also pledged to restore the nation's global power. Using the most bellicose rhetoric since the early years of the cold war, Reagan called the Soviet Union an "evil empire," one whose leaders "reserve unto themselves the right to commit any crime, to lie, to cheat." The United States, he insisted, must vastly increase its military might and demonstrate its resolve to confront communism anywhere in the world.

Enacting the Conservative Agenda

The United States underwent a huge military buildup during Reagan's first term. Yet despite the new aggressiveness—or, as some argued, because of it—throughout the 1980s, superpower conflict was confined to public rhetoric and the bargaining table. On the periphery of the cold war, however, the United States pursued a more activist role, intervening in the Middle East and the Caribbean.

While enlarging the nation's power and presence abroad, Reagan intended to cut back the government's power at home. On the domestic front, the Reagan administration left its most important mark on economic policies: victory over inflation, continued deregulation of industry, a moratorium on social spending, enormous tax cuts, and a staggering budget deficit. The deficit resulted in part from huge increases in military spending, which formed the basis of Reagan's efforts to reassert U.S. dominance abroad.

Militarization and Interventions Abroad

Reagan moved quickly to accelerate the arms buildup that Carter had begun, overseeing plans for new bombers and missiles, an enhanced nuclear force in Europe, an expanded navy, and a rapid-deployment force. The objectives were to enable the nation to fight three Vietnam-type wars at the same time and to close what the president claimed was a "window of vulnerability," through which U.S. missiles were exposed to a Soviet attack.

Despite the implications for the growing budget deficit, Congress approved most of the presi-

dent's defense programs, and military expenditures shot up by one-third in the first half of the 1980s. Throughout Reagan's presidency, defense spending averaged $216 billion a year, up from $158 billion in the Carter years and higher even than in the Vietnam era.

One justification for the arms buildup was to enable the United States to negotiate with the Soviets from a position of strength. Its unintended effect was to provoke an outburst of calls for a halt to the arms race. A rally demanding a freeze on nuclear weapons at current levels drew 700,000 people in New York City in 1982. Hundreds of thousands of Europeans demonstrated across the continent, stimulated by fears of new U.S. missiles that were scheduled for deployment in NATO countries in 1983.

Reagan startled many of his own advisers in March 1983 by announcing plans for research on a Strategic Defense Initiative (SDI). Immediately dubbed "Star Wars" by its critics, the project envisioned deploying lasers in space to destroy enemy missiles before they could reach their targets. Though SDI had a certain popular appeal because it was defensive and promised ultimate protection from nuclear weapons, most scientists scoffed at it as unrealistic.

While enlarging the nation's power and presence abroad, Reagan intended to cut back the government's power at home.

Star Wars represented a dramatic abandonment of the old system of mutual deterrence based on the threat of retaliation. Reagan conceded that it could be seen as "fostering an aggressive policy." Possessing an exclusive defense, the United States could fire first and not fear retaliation. The Soviets reacted angrily because SDI development violated the 1972 treaty restricting antiballistic missile systems and would require the Soviets to invest huge sums in their own Star Wars technology. For several years, Reagan's passionate attachment to SDI impeded superpower agreement on strategic arms control.

The U.S. military buildup placed the Soviets on the defensive, but it did not guarantee American dominance in the world. Iran released the American hostages at almost the exact hour of Reagan's inauguration, thanks to negotiations conducted during the Carter administration, but terrorism con-

THE NUCLEAR FREEZE CAMPAIGN
*An active movement in the United States and Europe worked to limit nuclear weapons and dimin-
ish the threat of nuclear destruction in the early 1980s. In 1982, half a million antinuclear protesters
marched and rallied in New York City.*
Corbis-Bettmann.

tinued to plague the United States. When its military personnel and civilians became victims of murder, kidnapping, and hijacking by various Middle
Eastern extremist groups, the United States responded with toughness. To bargain with terrorists,
Reagan insisted, would only encourage more assaults, and he pledged never to do so.

In 1982, Lebanon became the major crisis spot
in the Middle East. Ravaged by civil war between
Christians and Muslims, Lebanon was invaded by
Israeli troops, sent to crush Palestine Liberation Organization (PLO) forces that had settled there. Hoping to counter Soviet influence in the Middle East,
the United States sent 800 marines to Lebanon to
join a peacekeeping force with France and Italy. But
some Muslim factions saw the American presence
as an attempt to bolster their Christian enemies, and
in October 1983 an Islamic extremist drove a bomb-
filled truck into a marine barracks, killing 241 Americans. Although Middle Eastern hostilities continued to simmer, Reagan withdrew the marines early
the following year.

Closer to home, the U.S. military flexed its muscles. Just two days after the marine disaster, U.S.
troops invaded Grenada, a small British Commonwealth island nation in the Caribbean, in response
to a coup by left-wing forces. Ostensibly undertaken
to protect U.S. medical students on the island, the
intervention reflected administration fears that
Grenada would fall into the Cuban-Soviet orbit.
Margaret Thatcher, the conservative prime minister
of Great Britain, called the invasion a violation of
international law, but a majority of Americans exulted in the display of national power.

Elsewhere, the United States sought to contain
leftist movements privately and less aggressively. In
Asia, Afghan rebels fighting to dislodge the Soviet-
backed government received U.S. aid. In the African
nation of Angola, the United States armed rebel
forces against the Soviet- and Cuban-backed government. Siding with the racist South African government in the Angolan crisis did not trouble the
president. In one of his more colossal misrepresen-
tations, he told reporters—at a time when the South

African government was brutally suppressing black protest against apartheid—that South Africa had eliminated "the segregation that we once had in our own country." Congress had to force the administration to apply economic sanctions against South Africa, as most U.S. allies had already done, by overriding Reagan's veto of a sanctions bill in 1985.

Left-wing movements in Central America created the most alarm among administration officials. These movements, Reagan charged, were led by "professional guerrillas dedicated to the same philosophy that prevails in Nicaragua, Cuba, and . . . the Soviet Union." They threatened to "destabilize the entire region from the Panama Canal to Mexico." In response, the United States sent money and military advisers to prop up the conservative government of El Salvador that was threatened by a leftist uprising, even though that government had committed murderous human rights violations and opposed social reform.

In neighboring Nicaragua, Reagan aimed to unseat the Sandinistas, who had overthrown the repressive Somoza dictatorship and assumed power in 1979. Jimmy Carter had recognized and extended aid to the Sandinista government. But the Reagan administration threw itself into efforts to undercut the Nicaraguan government by aiding the Contras, a coalition of armed opposition to the Sandinistas that included many individuals from the ousted regime. Many Americans feared being drawn into another Vietnam and opposed aligning the United States with reactionary forces not supported by the majority of Nicaraguans. Holding its own against unrelenting administration efforts, Congress repeatedly instructed the president to cut off aid to the Contras or to limit it to nonmilitary purposes.

Deliberately violating congressional will, the administration secretly used economic pressure to destabilize the Sandinista government and provided weapons and training to the Contras, called "freedom fighters" by Reagan. The CIA itself directed assaults on economic targets and was involved in the covert mining of Nicaraguan harbors in 1984. Through legal and illegal means, the Reagan administration helped sustain the Contra opposition and wreck the Nicaraguan economy, thereby undermining support for the government. After nine years of civil war, Daniel Ortega, the Sandinista president, agreed to a political settlement that had been negotiated among the leaders of the five Central American states. When elections were held in 1990, a coalition of all the opposition groups defeated the Sandinistas, and Ortega stepped aside.

Unleashing Free Enterprise

Reagan's plan to reduce taxes in the face of inflation and huge budget deficits contradicted orthodox economics and traditional Republican doctrine, which stressed a balanced budget. His plan came from a few conservative economists who argued that tax cuts were compatible with deficit reduction and would actually increase federal revenues. Reagan made this thesis a key point in his campaign (a stand that drew from another Republican contender, his eventual vice president, George Bush, the derisive charge of "voodoo economics").

The new theory was called "supply-side economics," because it emphasized boosting production, or supply, which would in turn raise demand. In this view, high taxes had discouraged investment and weakened the economy; lower levies would enable businesses to expand and encourage individuals to work harder because they would keep more of their earnings. Savings, investment, and production all would rise. According to supply-siders, tax reduction would increase the amount of goods and services produced so dramatically that even with lower rates, more revenue would flow to the federal government.

Supply-side economics fit neatly with Reagan's emphasis on optimism and possibilities. In sharp contrast to Carter's talk of limitations and sacrifice, Reagan's agenda appeared to be pain-free. It fed on a popular resistance to the increasing tax load (though not to reduction of government services), exaggerated by inflation's tendency to push individual incomes into higher tax brackets. To sell his tax cut, however, Reagan had to allay worries about the budget deficit. So in addition to predicting an increase in revenues, he promised to cut federal expenditures, a position fully compatible with his antigovernment views.

In the summer of 1981, Congress passed the Economic Recovery Tax Act, the largest tax reduction in history. Individual income taxes were cut, the lowest rate falling from 14 percent to 11 percent and the highest from 70 percent to 50 percent. (The largest previous tax cut, in 1964, had reduced the lowest rate from 20 percent to 14 percent, and the highest from 91 percent to 70 percent.) Corporations also received tax breaks, and taxes on capital gains, gifts, and inheritances dropped. In contrast, Social Security contributions and other taxes that affected Americans across the board increased during the 1980s. The net effect was to make the entire tax structure more regressive—that is, affluent Americans saved far more on their tax bills than did the average taxpayer, further skewing the distribution of wealth in favor of the rich.

"Hack, chop, crunch!" was how *Time* magazine characterized the administration's efforts to liberate private enterprise from government restraints. Carter had initiated deregulation, but he had confined it to particular industries such as finance and transportation while promoting more regulation in areas such as health, safety, equal employment opportunity, and environmental protection. The Reagan administration, by contrast, pursued across-the-board deregulation.

Reagan presided over the most lax enforcement of the Sherman Antitrust Act—the law designed to reduce monopoly and promote competition—since its early history in the 1890s. The government's enforcement staff shrank by 40 percent, and in a decade of unprecedented business mergers and takeovers, the government opposed not a single one. The Reagan administration also loosened restraints on business imposed by employee health and safety measures and helped to weaken organized labor. When 13,000 members of the Professional Air Traffic Controllers Organization (PATCO) went on strike in 1981, in part to protest working conditions that compromised air traffic safety, Reagan fired them and destroyed their union.

Environmental regulatory laws were another target of deregulation. Blaming such laws for the nation's sluggish economic growth, Reagan set about reversing the tide. James Watt, his first secre-

TECHNOLOGY IN AMERICA
The Computer

Among the new technologies that profoundly shaped American society in the last half of the twentieth century, the computer was perhaps the most pervasive. With the ability to rapidly process enormous amounts of information and to control systems, computers have transformed work, medicine, communications, warfare, and even leisure. Computers have became so ubiquitous that few people even notice their use in such common activities as buying groceries, getting cash from a bank machine, making a telephone call, or riding in an airplane.

Engineers and scientists during World War II developed the first digital computers for the military. Later, Cold War military needs drove most computer research; computers were used in the design of the hydrogen bomb. By the late 1950s, most large corporations relied on computers. An important medical application was the invention of the computerized brain scanner in 1972. During the 1980s, personal computers, or PCs, became commonplace in offices, schools, and homes, with some 50 million installed by 1990. The 1990s also ushered in a communication revolution as the Internet and World Wide Web provided immediate access to immense amounts of information and put people in instant contact across the globe.

The chip, a thin piece of silicon or other semiconducting material, is the heart of the contemporary computer. It enables a tiny computer to perform vastly more functions than the 1945 MIT computer prototype, which required 200 miles of circuitry and rows of vacuum tubes.

1945 prototype: Eric Schaal/*Life* Magazine © Time, Inc.; Chip: © Chuck O'Rear/Westlight.

tary of the interior, declared, "We will mine more, drill more, cut more timber," and released federal lands to private exploitation. Similarly, the head of the Environmental Protection Agency reduced her staff and eased enforcement of air and water pollution measures. Environmental organizations experienced increasing membership rolls and fundraising as popular support for environmental protection blocked complete realization of the Reagan administration's deregulatory goals. Congress overrode vetoes of clean water legislation and a bill to promote cleanup of hazardous waste sites (the Superfund). Thus, the Reagan administration slowed environmental protections but failed to reverse either public sentiment or national policy on the environment.

Deregulation of the banking industry, begun under Carter and supported by Democrats and Republicans alike, created a crisis in the savings and loan industry and, ultimately, a burden for taxpayers. When deregulatory laws lifted interest rate ceilings and permitted savings and loan institutions (S&Ls) to lend money more freely, some S&Ls extended enormous loans to real estate developers and invested in other high-yield but risky ventures. The Reagan administration simultaneously slashed the number of federal regulators, and some officials yielded to pressure from both Republican and Democratic legislators to relax investigations. S&L owners reaped lavish profits during the early 1980s, and their depositors enjoyed high interest rates.

But when real estate values began to plunge in the mid-1980s, especially in California and the Southwest, hundreds of S&Ls went bankrupt. Depositors in bankrupt institutions were protected by federal insurance up to a limit of $100,000, and many institutional and wealthy depositors had covered their risks by investing in $100,000 units in multiple S&Ls. After Congress voted to bail out the S&L industry in 1989, the burden of the largest financial scandal in American history fell on American taxpayers, few of whom had profited from deregulation.

Budget Deficits, Inflation, and Unemployment

The S&L crisis deepened the federal budget deficit, which soared during the 1980s despite Reagan's pledge to pare federal spending. Although Reagan's budget director, David Stockman, doubted the rosy predictions of the supply-siders and urged draconian cuts in spending, cabinet officers were loath to

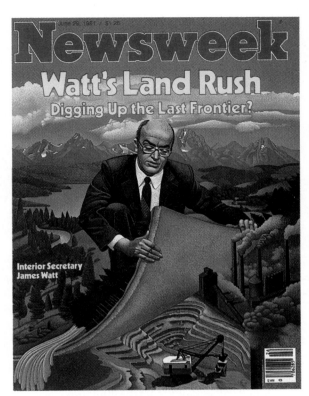

CONTROVERSY OVER THE ENVIRONMENT
Secretary of the Interior James Watt joined the Reagan cabinet committed to dismantling much of the environmental regulation of the previous two decades. His efforts drew considerable opposition. He failed to turn back the clock substantially, and in 1983 President Reagan appointed a more moderate replacement.
Illustration by Wilson McLean. Reprinted with permission of the artist and *Newsweek* Magazine.

see their own budgets slashed. Reagan himself drew back from politically risky cutbacks in entitlement programs such as Social Security and federal and military pensions. Since these consumed a substantial share of the budget, little room remained in which to make significant cuts.

The administration achieved some savings in entitlement programs under Social Security and Aid to Families with Dependent Children. But these programs were not gutted; the Reagan program represented an attack on the Great Society rather than the New Deal. Congress agreed to cut food stamps (14 percent), job training (39 percent), aid to low-income students (16 percent), and health services (33 percent). Hundreds of thousands of people lost eligibility or some of their benefits. Those with in-

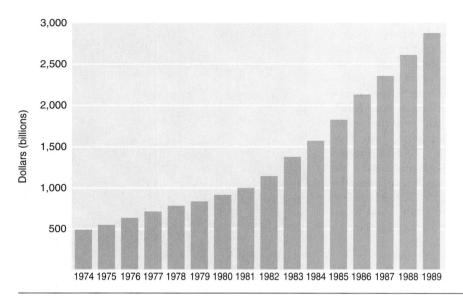

FIGURE 31.1
Rise in the National Debt, 1974–1989
Heavy military spending and large tax cuts contributed to the great leap in the national debt during the 1980s.

comes just around the poverty line took the hardest hits.

Even these cuts occupied too small a share of the total budget to make significant inroads in the deficit. Furthermore, they were counterbalanced by increases in defense spending, which overtook expenditures for human resources (excluding Social Security and Medicare). After a recession in 1981–1982, the economy entered an unprecedented period of growth. But the promises of the supply-siders proved empty. The budget deficit soared from $74 billion when Carter left office to a high of $220 billion in 1986, when interest on the national debt consumed one-seventh of all federal expenditures.

The problems of inflation and unemployment proved easier to control. Luck helped the administration's efforts to restrain inflation when a worldwide decline in the cost of oil pulled down domestic prices. Meanwhile, the Federal Reserve Board, with Reagan's support, tightened growth of the money supply. By 1983, the inflation rate was under 4 percent, down from a high of 12 percent in 1980. Control of inflation remained an enduring mark of the Reagan years.

It took the severest recession since the 1930s, however, to squeeze inflation out of the U.S. economy. Beginning in 1981, unemployment rose sharply, approaching 11 percent late in 1982. Record numbers of banks and businesses closed, thousands of families lost their farms, and twelve million workers could not find jobs. The threat of unemployment further undermined organized labor,

forcing unions to make concessions that management insisted were necessary for industry's survival. The economy recovered in 1983, and the number of jobs increased substantially, although unemployment never fell below 5 percent.

Liberalism on the Defensive

The recession hurt Republicans in the 1982 congressional elections, but by 1984 the economy was booming, with inflation and unemployment at their lowest points in a decade. Reagan delivered a humiliating defeat to the Democratic ticket in his 1984 reelection, although the Democrats retained control of the House of Representatives and picked up two Senate seats.

Liberal movements survived the Reagan triumph, but their accomplishments during the 1980s were largely defensive.

Liberal movements survived the Reagan triumph, but their accomplishments during the 1980s were largely defensive. Civil rights advocates fought off administration attacks in the courts, and, when that failed, they managed to find some help in Congress. Feminists discovered a few issues on which they could gain White House support and looked to the states and to electoral politics to advance other items on their agenda. The gay rights movement acquired members and visibility, making small inroads against intolerance of and discrimination against homosexuals.

Most alarming to many liberals was President Reagan's opportunity to reconstitute the federal courts, which had been a critical ally in their pursuit of social reform. With one notable exception, liberals found themselves helpless to block the nominations of conservative justices. By the end of his second term, Reagan had appointed half of the entire federal judiciary and three new Supreme Court justices.

The "Teflon President" and the Landslide of 1984

Even a candidate with considerably less ingrained optimism than Reagan would have approached the 1984 election with confidence. No serious international crises loomed, and the economy was booming. Since the easing of the 1981–1982 recession, public opinion stood strongly in the president's favor.

Political observers marveled at Reagan's popularity. He was liked even by Americans who opposed his policies and even when he made glaring mistakes. At one meeting, he failed to recognize his own secretary of housing and urban development, calling him "Mr. Mayor." On another occasion he proclaimed that vegetation caused 90 percent of all air pollution. He made so many misstatements to reporters that aides severely limited his press conferences and shielded him from reporters.

The Reagan administration also witnessed a striking number of scandals, and many insiders spoke of a president who was passive, incurious, and largely detached from policy formation. Reagan kept his cabinet officials at a distance, and he did not devote long hours to his duties. According to his first secretary of state, Alexander Haig, the White House was "as mysterious as a ghost ship; you heard the creak of the rigging . . . and sometimes even glimpsed the crew on deck. But which of the crew had the helm?"

Reagan associates and his wife, Nancy, managed the presidency of the former movie actor as if it were a Hollywood production. One aide reported that "every moment . . . was scheduled, every word was scripted, every place where Reagan was expected to stand was chalked with toe marks." Donald Regan, secretary of the treasury during Reagan's

first term and White House chief of staff during his second, even used an acting analogy to describe how Reagan formulated policy: "He listened, acquiesced, played his role, and waited for the next act to be written." Reagan's press secretary, Larry Speakes, admitted that he made up statements and then fed them to the press as Reagan's words.

Democratic Representative Patricia Schroeder tagged Reagan the "Teflon President" because none of his administration's mistakes, or even his own errors and falsehoods, seemed to stick to him. Reagan gave his own explanation when he was asked during the 1980 campaign what people saw in him: "Would you laugh if I told you that I think, maybe, they see themselves and that I'm one of them?" he replied. Near the end of his second term, he elaborated: "Well, I genuinely like people, and I think, perhaps, people can tell."

Reagan was at ease with himself—unlike Nixon—and supremely self-confident. He possessed an easygoing ability to laugh at himself that was unmatched by any president since Kennedy. Referring to reports of his leisurely business hours, Reagan remarked, "It's true that hard work never killed anybody, but I figure why take a chance at this late age." He also gained public sympathy after being shot by a would-be assassin in March 1981. Just before surgery for removal of a bullet in his chest, Reagan joked to physicians, "I hope you're Republicans." His rapid recovery calmed doubts about the health of the oldest president in history.

Democratic Representative Patricia Schroeder tagged Reagan the "Teflon President" because none of his administration's mistakes, or even his own errors and falsehoods, seemed to stick to him.

Even when he substituted fantasy for fact, Reagan came across as sincere. He often confused the facts of his own past with what he wanted to believe, talking, for example, about a role he had played in a World War II movie as if he had had genuine combat experience. Part of his popular appeal was his ability to ignore or recast the darker aspects of the nation's past and present a version of history that Americans could feel good about—just as he did with the facts of his own past.

"America is standing tall," the president exulted. In response his audience at the 1984 Repub-

THE DEMOCRATIC TICKET, 1984
Responding in part to feminist pressure, presidential nominee Walter F. Mondale electrified the Democratic Party convention when he announced his choice of Geraldine Ferraro for his running mate. An Italian-American Catholic mother of three, Ferraro represented Queens, New York, in the House of Representatives. Although Reagan's landslide swept away Mondale and Ferraro, her candidacy was an important breakthrough for women in politics.
Randy Taylor/Sygma.

lican National Convention chanted, "USA! USA!" Reagan's ability to revive national pride and confidence, to revitalize the myth of American superiority, reached beyond Republican loyalists. He defined the choice in the 1984 election as "two different versions of the future." The Democrats, he insisted, stressed America's limits and failures; his vision emphasized success and possibility.

Reagan's popular appeal and the prospering economy posed a formidable challenge for the Dem-

ocrats. Among the eight candidates for the 1984 presidential nomination was the Reverend Jesse Jackson, who had fought civil rights battles with Martin Luther King Jr. and who ran a vigorous campaign that concentrated on the needs of the disadvantaged. After a rocky start, however, Walter F. Mondale, who had been Carter's vice president, emerged as the Democratic nominee. Mondale electrified the Democratic National Convention by naming as his running mate New York Representative Geraldine A. Ferraro, the first woman nominated on a major party ticket.

The Mondale-Ferraro campaign emphasized the hardships that the unemployed, the poor, and victims of discrimination suffered under the Reagan presidency. Attacking the budget deficit, Mondale insisted that taxes would have to be raised and suggested that Reagan knew that to be true. Reagan simply turned that challenge around: Democrats, he claimed, "see an America where every day is April 15th [the due date for income tax returns] . . . we see an America where every day is the Fourth of July."

Voters responded to the president's vision and to the economic comeback. With 59 percent of the vote, Reagan's landslide was only slightly less over-

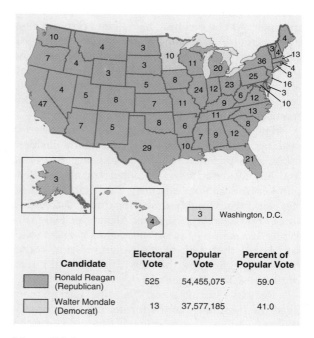

Candidate	Electoral Vote	Popular Vote	Percent of Popular Vote
Ronald Reagan (Republican)	525	54,455,075	59.0
Walter Mondale (Democrat)	13	37,577,185	41.0

MAP 31.1
The Election of 1984

whelming than those of Roosevelt in 1936, Johnson in 1964, and Nixon in 1972. Both the elderly and youth gave Reagan a healthy majority of their votes. And even though the president was not seen as a friend of labor, nearly half of all union members chose the Republican ticket.

What the president would do with his mandate was not clear. In contrast to his first campaign, he had said little about programmatic plans for a second term. The Democrats, for their part, pondered what it would take to stem the exodus of longtime loyalists—particularly southern white males—to the Republican Party. Stung by Republican charges that the Democratic Party was captive to "special interests" such as labor, women, and minorities, many Democratic leaders read the election results as a signal to shift further toward the right. Others urged rededication to the issues that had produced Democratic victories in the past.

Civil Rights on the Defensive

In keeping with its antigovernment philosophy, the Reagan administration made vigorous efforts to reverse federal protections of civil rights. Nixon's rhetoric had played upon the fears and prejudices of whites, but overall the Nixon administration had sustained and in some cases even advanced mechanisms for attacking discrimination. Reagan, however, was the first president to break sharply with the national commitment to equal opportunity undertaken in the 1960s.

Busing to achieve school integration and affirmative action were particularly repellent to the administration. Reagan's special counsel (and later attorney general) Edwin Meese, along with William Bradford Reynolds of the Justice Department's Civil Rights Division, worked to overturn busing and affirmative action agreements, even those that had been entered into voluntarily by school districts and public and private employers. When the Civil Rights Commission challenged administration positions, Reagan fired three of the commission's Carter appointees. A court ruled that action illegal, but Reagan eventually secured a majority on the commission, rendering it ineffective.

The administration also tried to overturn an Internal Revenue Service policy that denied tax-exempt status to segregationist private schools. In this instance, the Supreme Court sided with equal opportunity, holding that private schools practicing racial discrimination could not maintain their tax-exempt status. But the Court was more responsive to the administration regarding the use of federal funding decisions to promote equal opportunity. Agreeing with a Justice Department brief, the Court ruled in *Grove City College v. Bell* (1984) that an institution could practice discrimination in one of its programs, such as athletics, and still receive federal funds for scholarships and other programs that did not discriminate. This decision gutted Title IX of the Education Amendments Act of 1972, one of two major laws promoting equal opportunity in education.

Grove City allowed the Justice Department to abandon dozens of civil rights cases against schools and colleges. It also galvanized a coalition of civil rights organizations and groups representing women, the aged and disabled, and their allies. After four years of struggle and compromise, Congress passed the Civil Rights Restoration Act of 1988 and subsequently overturned a presidential veto. Not only was the administration's victory in *Grove City* reversed; the new law went even further. Not just schools and colleges but any organization that practiced discrimination on the basis of race, color, national origin, sex, handicap, or age was banned from receiving government funds.

Congress also renewed the Voting Rights Act for twenty-five more years, despite administration objections to provisions strengthening the measure and threats of a veto. After both houses passed the improved bill by overwhelming margins in 1982, Reagan not only signed it but took credit for enactment of "the crown jewel of American liberties." It was another example of the president's facility at adjusting facts to what he wanted to believe.

Reagan argued that minorities should look to his economic policies and their positive effects on inflation and employment as evidence of his commitment to equal opportunity. To be sure, his administration ended high inflation and high unemployment, which hit the poorest the hardest. Even so, the material status of most minority groups declined during the 1980s.

Congress and the courts deflected the administration's drive to shrink the government's support for civil rights, but the cause of equal opportunity languished in the absence of presidential leadership. Critics claimed that the administration established a national climate that made it no longer unfashionable to express prejudice and thus contributed to new outbreaks of racial violence in the late 1980s.

CONFRONTATIONS OVER ABORTION
Failing to win a constitutional amendment banning abortion, in the late 1970s and 1980s some groups in the right-to-life movement adopted more militant tactics, picketing abortion clinics, yelling at patients and employees, and trying to block entrance into clinics. In response, prochoice activists shown here, defend clinic access and the right to abortion.
Paul S. Howell/Gamma Liaison.

Shifting Strategies of the Women's Movement

Women, too, suffered from the Reagan administration's efforts to weaken antidiscrimination enforcement. In 1980, for the first time, the Republican Party took an explicitly antifeminist tone. Reversing previous positions, it opposed both the Equal Rights Amendment (ERA) and a woman's right to abortion, two principal goals of women's rights activists.

In the face of a hostile political environment, the women's movement in the 1980s shifted its strategies and goals. A renewed fight for the ERA occupied a low place on most feminists' agendas. Defense of abortion rights, antidiscrimination measures, and affirmative action remained high priorities. But activists increased their attention to women's economic and family problems, which eluded the grasp of antidiscrimination policies.

The new agenda reflected the increasing diversity of the women's movement and greater recognition of the needs of women of color, poor women, and working-class women. It also acknowledged the disproportionate representation of women and children among the poor, a development that some termed "the feminization of poverty." In addition, the shift in priorities evinced feminists' efforts to recapture the initiative from the New Right, which claimed to be the sole voice for the homemaker and the family.

The Reagan administration had its own concerns about women. Republican leaders worried about the "gender gap"—women's tendency, manifested in elections throughout the 1980s, to vote for liberal and Democratic candidates in larger numbers than men did, large enough in some cases to provide the margin of victory. Reagan appointed three women to cabinet posts and the first woman, Sandra Day O'Connor, to the Supreme Court. But these "showcase" actions accompanied a general decline in the number of women and minorities in high-level administrative and judicial posts. Moreover, the administration's assaults on antidiscrimination and affirmative action policies hurt women as they did racial minorities. And because poverty rates were higher among women than among men, women were hit hardest by budget cuts in social programs.

Feminists did find some common ground with the Reagan administration, however, producing two measures that addressed women's economic distress. The Child Support Enforcement Amendments made it easier to collect court-ordered child support payments from absent fathers, affording some relief to single and divorced mothers. The Retirement Equity Act of 1984 benefited older women by strengthening the claims of divorced and widowed women to their husbands' pensions and by enabling women to qualify more easily for private pensions. Feminists generally held their ground on the abortion issue, but they ran into a stone wall in their efforts to strengthen day care services, aid displaced homemakers, end discrimination in insurance, and promote pay equity—that is, equal pay for traditionally female jobs that were found to be comparable in worth to jobs performed primarily by men.

The Reagan administration's assaults on antidiscrimination and affirmative action policies hurt women as well as racial minorities. And because poverty rates were higher among women than among men, women were hit hardest by budget cuts in social programs.

Like other pressure groups, the women's movement pursued locally what it failed to achieve at the federal level. The pay equity movement took hold in several states, where new legislation mandated job evaluation studies that resulted in higher wages for jobs held primarily by women. Many states strengthened their laws against rape, and most passed legislation making it a crime for a man to force his wife to have sexual relations. States also increased funding for domestic violence programs and stepped up efforts to protect victims and prosecute abusers.

Using sophisticated fundraising and electioneering techniques, feminists made incremental gains in their efforts to elect more women to political office. By the end of the 1980s, women had made their marks as governors of Kentucky, Vermont, and Nebraska; and women served as mayors of several large cities, including Jane Byrne of Chicago, Dianne Feinstein of San Francisco, and Kathryn Whitmire of Houston. Women won three U.S. Senate races, and their share of congressional seats inched up to 5.6 percent from 2.8 percent in 1971. By the end of the decade, women claimed 17.2 percent of seats in state legislatures. Although Geraldine Ferraro had to endure media scrutiny of her appearance, her husband's business dealings, and other matters unrelated to her qualifications, she broke an important political barrier for women. When Democrat Patricia Schroeder and Republican Jeanne J. Kirkpatrick considered presidential races in 1988, the media took them seriously.

The Gay and Lesbian Rights Movement

An American organization for homosexual rights had existed as early as 1924, but not until the 1980s did a national mass movement play a significant role in U.S. politics. The contemporary movement emerged out of the social upheaval of the 1960s, its beginnings symbolized by the Stonewall riot of 1969, when gay men and lesbians fought back against a police raid on a gay bar in New York City's Greenwich Village. Influenced by the black freedom struggle, the New Left, the counterculture, and feminism, gays and lesbians began to claim equal rights for homosexuals and to express pride in their sexual identities.

In the 1970s, the gay and lesbian rights movement persuaded professional organizations of psychiatrists and social workers to stop considering homosexuality a disease. Although the Supreme Court in 1986 upheld the right of states to enforce sodomy laws, most states had repealed their laws against homosexuality by the end of the decade. The federal government lifted its ban against homosexuals in all areas except the military and intelligence agencies. Beginning with the election of Elaine Noble to the Massachusetts legislature in 1974, several openly gay politicians won election and reelection to offices from mayor to member of Congress. The Democrats began to include gay rights planks in their party platforms.

The acquired immune deficiency syndrome (AIDS) epidemic further mobilized the gay and lesbian rights movement in the 1980s, because at first male homosexuals accounted for the majority of AIDS cases. As the disease swept through and devastated communities of gay men in New York, San Francisco, and elsewhere, society responded with indifference—or worse: assertions by some right-wing politicians and religious leaders that AIDS represented just punishment for immoral behavior. Gay men and lesbians pressed for public education about AIDS and public funding for its treatment and prevention.

The gay and lesbian rights movement helped thousands of homosexuals experience the relief of being able to live openly. By "coming out" in great numbers, gay men and lesbians helped to make homosexuality more visible and somewhat more accepted in the larger population. Activists organized gay rights and gay pride marches throughout the country, bringing 500,000 demonstrators to Washington, D.C., in 1987. Gradually, the movement began to win local victories, gaining for lesbians and gay men protections that were enjoyed by heterosexual citizens. By the early 1990s, more than eighty-five cities banned job discrimination against homosexuals, and, beginning with Wisconsin in 1982, seven states expanded their civil rights laws to include sexual orientation as a protected category. (See Texts in Historical Context, page 1232.)

Yet these piecemeal victories left the majority of gay men and lesbians still vulnerable to discrimination. The New Right targeted gays and lesbians as symbols of national immorality and organized campaigns to overturn homosexual rights measures. In 1992, Cincinnati voters nullified an equal rights ordinance that the city council had enacted, and Colorado voters approved a measure prohibiting any laws that banned discrimination against homosexuals. Heartened by Oregon voters' defeat of a similar referendum, the gay and lesbian rights movement and its allies mounted a challenge to the Colorado measure. They achieved victory in 1996, when the Supreme Court declared the Colorado law unconstitutional (*Romer v. Evans*).

The Conservative Shift in the Federal Courts

Since the 1950s, proponents of reform had grown accustomed to counting on the federal judiciary as a powerful ally in their struggles for minority rights and social justice. Yet in the 1980s, liberals saw their critical allies slipping away as the Supreme Court and the lower federal courts became increasingly populated with conservative justices.

THE AIDS CRISIS
American pop artist Keith Haring made this AIDS awareness drawing before the disease killed him in 1990, citing the "growing burden that each of us carries as the AIDS crisis continues to escalate around the world." During the 1990s scientists made important advances in treatment, but the disease continued to elude a vaccine or a cure.
© The Estate of Keith Haring.

The changing composition of the federal judiciary reflected a determined strategy on the part of the Reagan administration. Given the opportunity to appoint half of the 761 federal court judges and three new Supreme Court justices, administration aides carefully selected candidates. They wanted to appoint individuals with strongly conservative views who would help reverse the liberal direction taken by the Supreme Court since the days of Earl Warren. Just 2 percent of Reagan appointees were black, in contrast to 14.3 percent under Carter. Women constituted 15.5 percent of Carter's appointments but only 8.2 percent of Reagan's.

The Supreme Court did not execute an abrupt about-face. It upheld important affirmative action and antidiscrimination policies (such as denying tax-exempt status to segregated private schools) and ruled that sexual harassment in the workplace constituted sex discrimination. But with Reagan's appointees, the tide began to turn in favor of the doctrine of strict construction—that is, strict interpretation of the original aims of the Constitution's authors, an approach that limits judicial power to protect individual rights.

After appointing the moderate conservative Sandra Day O'Connor in 1981, Reagan strengthened the strict constructionists by elevating William J. Rehnquist, a Nixon appointee, to chief justice when Warren Burger retired in 1986. His next nominee, Antonin Scalia, tipped the balance further to the right. But in 1987, when Reagan attempted to repeat that achievement by nominating Robert H. Bork, a court of appeals judge and former Yale law professor, he provoked a bitter national controversy over the role of the Supreme Court.

Opponents of Bork's nomination organized a diverse coalition of civil rights advocates, trade unionists, feminists, environmentalists, and senior citizens. They feared that Bork's passionate adherence to a strict interpretation of the Constitution would undermine civil rights and affirmative action, abortion rights, criminal rights, and a host of other reform initiatives. Bork's opponents testified before the Senate Judiciary Committee, took out newspaper ads, lobbied their senators, and mounted an unprecedented media assault on the nominee. Despite the president's steadfast support, the Senate rejected Bork. In the end, however, it was an empty victory for liberals. Anthony M. Kennedy, who was confirmed by the Senate, seemed more moderate than Bork, but subsequent decisions made clear that conservatives now constituted a slim majority on the highest court (Reagan's three appointees plus Rehnquist and Byron White).

The full impact of Reagan's appointments continued after he left office. The Court stopped short of overturning *Roe v. Wade,* which gave constitutional protection to the right to abortion, but it allowed states to impose severe restrictions that limited access to abortion for poor and uneducated women and those living in rural areas. Other rulings further weakened affirmative action efforts, limited the use of statistics to prove discrimination, and in some employment discrimination cases shifted the burden of proof from employers to plaintiffs. The Court also whittled away at legal protections for individuals who were under sentence of death and upheld the right to execute convicted murderers who were mentally retarded or as young as sixteen.

Disasters and Triumphs of Reagan's Second Term

In Reagan's second term (1985–1989) the costs of the administration's economic achievements became starkly clear. The federal budget deficit worsened through 1986 and then improved only slightly. The decline in the nation's global economic competitiveness continued, and the government, corporations, and individuals became ever more dependent on borrowing.

Reagan had achieved his counterrevolution in domestic affairs during his first term. Thereafter, Congress took control of the domestic agenda, reaching accord with the administration on major changes in the tax and welfare systems. Though hamstrung by the budget deficit, Congress enacted over presidential objections reforms in such areas as civil rights and the environment.

In Reagan's second term the costs of the administration's economic achievements became starkly clear.

Reagan's second term saw his worst disaster and his most impressive triumph in the realm of foreign policy. The Iran-Contra affair, which involved revelations of confused policy and illegal activities, seriously damaged the president's credibility. Yet he also responded favorably to new initiatives from the Soviet Union and presided over the most impressive improvement in superpower relations since the shattering of the World War II alliance.

The Debt-Based Economy

The gross national product increased by 25 percent during the Reagan years, and inflation remained in check. But along with this growth, evidence mounted of deep economic flaws. As it had in the nineteenth century, when it was still a developing country, the United States once again was importing more than it exported and depending heavily on foreign credit. The steel, automobile, and electronics industries failed to maintain a competitive edge over those of such countries as Germany and Japan, as Americans bought more and more Toyotas and Hondas and fewer Fords and Chevrolets. Because Americans purchased more foreign-made goods than domestic producers sold abroad, the

Protecting Gay and Lesbian Rights

*S*ince the 1970s, the gay and lesbian rights movement has worked for passage of laws and ordinances to protect homosexuals from discrimination. In 1982, Wisconsin became the first state to ban discrimination on the basis of sexual orientation, following the lead of several cities that passed gay rights ordinances in the 1970s. By the mid-1990s, nine states and more than eighty cities had such legislation on the books. These measures ignited controversy that continued to surround the issue through the 1990s.

*I*n 1974, the city council of Minneapolis amended its civil rights ordinance to cover discrimination based on sexual preference. The law provided a rationale for banning discrimination and, unlike some laws focusing exclusively on employment, encompassed a broad range of activities.

DOCUMENT 1. Ordinance of the City of Minneapolis, 1974

It is determined that discriminatory practices based on race, color, creed, religion, national origin, sex or affectional or sexual preference, with respect to employment, labor union membership, housing accommodations, property rights, education, public accommodations, and public services, or any of them, tend to create and intensify conditions of poverty, ill health, unrest, civil disobedience, lawlessness, and vice and adversely affect the public health, safety, order, convenience, and general welfare; such discriminatory practices threaten the rights, privileges and opportunities of all inhabitants of the city and such rights, privileges and opportunities are hereby to be declared civil rights, and the adoption of this Chapter is deemed to be an exercise of the policy power of the City to protect such rights.

*P*aul Moore, Episcopal bishop of New York, made a religious argument for gay rights in his letter to the editor of the New York Times.

DOCUMENT 2. Letter to the Editor from Paul Moore, November 23, 1981

I quote our diocesan resolution: "Whereas this Convention, without making any judgment on the morality of homosexuality, agrees that homosexuals are entitled to full civil rights. Now therefore be it resolved this Convention supports laws guaranteeing homosexuals all civil rights guaranteed to other citizens."

The Bible stands for justice and compassion for all of God's children. To deny civil rights to anyone for something he or she cannot help is against the clear commandment of justice and love, which is the message of the word of God.

As a New Yorker I find it incredible that this great city, populated by more gay persons than any other city in the world, still denies them basic human rights. They make an enormous contribution to the commercial, artistic, and religious life of our city.

*T*his statement from the Roman Catholic Church reflects the views of many religious groups that take positions against gay rights.

DOCUMENT 3. Vatican Congregation for the Doctrine of the Faith, August 6, 1992

"Sexual orientation" does not constitute a quality comparable to race, ethnic background, etc., in respect to nondiscrimination. Unlike these, homosexual orientation is an objective disorder and evokes moral concern.

There are areas in which it is not unjust discrimination to take sexual orientation into account, for example, in the placement of children for adoption or foster care, in employment of teachers or athletic coaches, and in military recruitment.

Although the U.S. Congress has never enacted legislation banning discrimination on the basis of sexual orientation, it has considered a number of bills for that purpose. Charles Cochrane Jr., an army veteran and police sergeant, testified on behalf of such a bill in 1982.

DOCUMENT 4. Testimony of Charles Cochrane Jr. before the House Subcommittee on Employment Opportunities of the Committee on Education and Labor, January 27, 1982

I am very proud of being a New York City policeman. And I am equally proud of being gay. I have always been gay.

I have been out of the closet for 4 years. November 6 was my anniversary. It took me 34 years to muster enough courage to declare myself openly.

We gays are loathed by some, pitied by others, and misunderstood by most. We are not cruel, wicked, cursed, sick, or possessed by demons. We are artists, business people, police officers, and clergymen. We are scientists, truck drivers, politicians; we work in every field. We are loving human beings who are in some ways different. . . .

During the early years of my association with the New York City Police Department a great deal of energy did go into guarding and concealing my innermost feelings. I believed that I would be subjected to ridicule and harassment were my colleagues to learn of my sexual orientation. Happily, when I actually began to integrate the various aspects of my total self, those who knew me did not reject me.

Then what need is there for such legislation as H.R. 1454? The crying need of others, still trapped in their closets, who must be protected, who must be reassured that honesty about themselves and their lives will not cost them their homes or their jobs. . . .

The bill before you will not act as a proselytizing agent in matters of sexual orientation or preference. It will not include affirmative action provisions. Passage of this bill will protect the inherent human rights of all people of the United States, while in no way diminishing the rights of those who do not see the need for such legislation. Finally, it will signify, quite clearly, recognition and compassion for a group which is often maligned without justification.

Carl Horowitz, a policy analyst at a conservative think tank, the Heritage Foundation, expresses arguments of those opposed to measures banning discrimination against homosexuals.

DOCUMENT 5. Carl F. Horowitz, "Homosexuality's Legal Revolution," May 1991

Homosexual activists have all but completed their campaign to persuade the nation's educational establishment that homosexuality is normal "alternative" behavior, and thus any adverse reaction to it is akin to a phobia, such as fear of heights, or an ethnic prejudice, such as anti-Semitism.

The movement now stands on the verge of fully realizing its use of law to . . . intimidate heterosexuals uncomfortable about coming into contact with it. . . .

The movement seeks to win sinecures through the state, and over any objections by "homophobic" opposition. With a cloud of a heavy fine or even a jail sentence hanging over a mortgage lender, a rental agent, or a job interviewer who might be discomforted by them, homosexuals under these laws can win employment, credit, housing, and other economic entitlements. Heterosexuals would have no right to discriminate against homosexuals, but apparently, not vice versa. . . .

These laws will create market bottlenecks. Heterosexuals and even "closeted" homosexuals will be at a competitive disadvantage for jobs and housing. . . .

The new legalism will increase heterosexual anger—and even violence—toward homosexuals.

Document 1. Norman Dorsen and Aryeh Neier, eds., *The Rights of Gay People: The Basic ACLU Guide to a Gay Person's Rights* (New York: E. P. Dutton, 1992), 251.

Document 2. Paul Moore, letter to the editor, *New York Times,* December 8, 1981.

Document 3. Vatican Congregation for the Doctrine of the Faith, *Origins,* August 6, 1992.

Document 4. Hearing on H.R. 1454, House Subcommittee on Employment Opportunities of the Committee on Education and Labor, 97th Cong., 2nd sess., 1982, 54–56.

Document 5. Carl F. Horowitz, "Homosexuality's Legal Revolution," *Freeman,* May 1991.

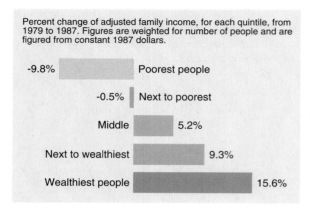

Percent change of adjusted family income, for each quintile, from 1979 to 1987. Figures are weighted for number of people and are figured from constant 1987 dollars.

-9.8%   Poorest people

-0.5%   Next to poorest

Middle   5.2%

Next to wealthiest   9.3%

Wealthiest people   15.6%

FIGURE 31.2

The Growth of Inequality: Changes in Family Income, 1979–1987

For most of the post-World War II period, income increased for all groups on the economic ladder; but after 1979, income of the poorest families actually declined, while it grew substantially for the richest 20 percent of the population.

nation's trade deficit (the difference between imports and exports) soared to $126 billion in 1988.

In response to heightened international competition, some older companies collapsed. Others moved their factories (and jobs) abroad to position themselves better to penetrate foreign markets or to benefit from the low wage standards of countries such as Mexico, the Philippines, and Korea. The growth of service industries created new jobs at home, but former blue-collar workers who were forced to make the shift found their wages substantially lower. David Ramos earned $12.75 an hour as a machine operator in a steel plant before being laid off in 1982. His new job as a security guard paid only $5 an hour, and his family of six had to rely on food stamps. Overall, the number of full-time workers earning wages below the poverty level ($12,195 for a family of four in 1990) rose sharply from 12 percent to 18 percent of all workers in the 1980s.

Labor unions called for the government to raise tariffs to protect American producers from foreign competition. One group of Detroit autoworkers summoned reporters and then demonstrated their frustration by taking sledgehammers to a Japanese-produced car. Committed to free trade and opposed to tariffs, the Reagan administration sought to make other countries more receptive to U.S. exports. It imposed some restrictions on imports but resisted extreme measures to keep out foreign products.

The trade gap necessitated a vast increase in borrowing from foreign investors. Once the largest creditor nation, the United States became the largest debtor nation in the space of a decade. Foreign investors from Japan, Western Europe, and the Middle East purchased American stocks and bonds, real estate, and corporations. Time-honored companies such as Firestone, Ralston Purina, Brooks Brothers, Sohio, 20th Century-Fox, and Capitol Records passed into foreign ownership. Local communities welcomed infusions of foreign capital, and several states went to great lengths to encourage Japanese companies to establish automobile plants within their boundaries.

Foreign investment in the U.S. economy helped compensate for a decline in domestic investment in the 1980s. Instead of putting their tax savings into new business enterprise or machinery that would boost productivity and create new jobs, as supply-siders had promised, entrepreneurs used them to take over other companies or to support lavish lifestyles. As savings and investment declined, indebtedness soared among the wealthy as well as ordinary Americans. Household debt, especially credit card spending, surpassed $3 trillion, and corporate debt reached $2 trillion, double the level of 1980.

The federal government made its own contribution to national indebtedness with an annual deficit that reached $220 billion in 1986. The president clung to his panacea—a constitutional amendment requiring a balanced budget. But he disclosed no new means for implementing such a requirement. Congress rejected Reagan's other solution—empowering the president to veto individual items in the budget, called the "line-item veto." In 1985, the president and Congress agreed to the Gramm-Rudman-Hollings deficit reduction law; it set deficit limits to be reached by certain dates in the near future and required automatic across-the-board cuts should the government fail to reach the targets. By the time Reagan left office, the deficit had fallen to $160 billion, but prospects for further reduction were poor. With the accumulating annual budget deficits, in eight years the government had increased the national debt from $834 billion to $2.3 trillion.

Reagan refused to rethink the wisdom of the 1981 tax cuts, but his willingness to undertake tax reform made it the most important domestic initiative of his second term. The Tax Reform Act of 1986 included both tax cuts and tax reforms. Conservatives won reductions in the maximum rate on individual incomes from 50 percent to 28 percent and on businesses from 48 percent to 34 percent. The law also eliminated income taxes for millions of low-income people, raised the capital gains tax, and reduced deductions and loopholes that overwhelmingly favored corporations and the wealthy.

The Initiative Shifts to Congress and the States

The Reagan administration exercised scant leadership in setting a domestic agenda after 1986. Having largely achieved the president's goal—getting the government off the back of free enterprise—Reagan was not about to reverse that trend with new programs. While his rhetoric continued to preach the aims of social conservatives, issues such as abortion were too politically charged to risk an all-out presidential effort.

Moreover, several developments crippled Reagan's domestic leadership. Disclosures of fraud and corruption among Reagan officials mounted. By the end of 1987, more than one hundred senior officials had been forced to resign, had been indicted, or had been accused of illegal or unethical conduct. Beset by internal conflicts, the administration also faced a more independent Congress after the Democrats recaptured the Senate in 1986.

In addition to defeating Bork's nomination, Congress overrode presidential vetoes of environmental protection legislation and highway and mass-transit programs and forced compromises with the executive branch on other issues. In 1987, Reagan reluctantly signed bills to aid the homeless. And in 1988, the two branches hammered out a $2.7 billion antidrug law, which included treatment programs for drug users and more severe penalties for dealers, including the death penalty for certain drug traffickers.

An overhaul of the welfare system in 1988 reflected give-and-take between those who believed that aid to the poor was inadequate and those who insisted that government handouts encouraged chronic "welfare dependency." The Family Support Act required all states to provide welfare benefits to impoverished families even when both parents were present. It also contained "workfare" provisions, which required at least one unemployed parent to work sixteen hours a week in unpaid community service jobs to remain eligible for welfare.

The Family Support Act sought to end welfare dependency by compelling single parents with children over the age of three to get jobs or to enroll in a new Job Opportunities and Basic Skills Program (JOBS). During a transitional period, they would receive Medicaid and help with transportation and day care costs. Critics argued that workfare ignored the fact that not enough jobs at decent wages existed for relatively untrained welfare recipients. The jobs that did exist would pay at or around the minimum wage, and losing access to Medicaid and other services would render people worse off than they had been on welfare.

Even the law's sponsors considered the five-year appropriation of $3.34 billion inadequate for the training and education that would be required to escape poverty. Efforts to alleviate poverty were held hostage—like many other initiatives—to the federal deficit. The revival of Democratic strength in Congress tempered the president's efforts to minimize federal activity, but advocates of new programs were stymied by the lack of resources to fund them.

"Our federal politics are gridlocked, and governors have become the ones who have to have the courage to put their necks out," said a spokesperson for state governors. In trying to compensate for the federal government's inaction and the paralyzing effect of the deficit, for the first time in decades state legislatures became more innovative than Washington. States passed legislation to block corporate takeovers, raise the minimum wage, establish parental leave policies, require equal pay for jobs of comparable worth in state and local governments, improve food labeling, protect the environment, and promote foreign trade. But by the end of the decade, the shifting of funding burdens from Washington to the states left state governments with their own financial crises.

The Iran-Contra Scandal

The most serious revelations of executive branch misconduct since Watergate surfaced during Reagan's second term. In the events that became known as the Iran-Contra scandal, administration officials engaged in secret and illegal activities, destroyed evidence of their undertakings, and lied to Congress. The president himself escaped criminal charges. But evidence that he had said one thing and done another and that he had failed to exercise control over his staff and policy shattered confidence in his leadership.

The Iran-Contra affair began in 1985 as a scheme invented by Robert C. McFarlane, head of the National Security Council (NSC), his successor

John Poindexter, NSC aide marine Lieutenant Colonel Oliver North, and CIA Director William Casey. They planned to sell arms to Iran, which was then at war with neighboring Iraq, in exchange for the Iranians' exertion of pressure on Muslim terrorists to bring about the release of seven American hostages who were being held in Lebanon. Funds from the arms sales were then diverted from the U.S. Treasury and channeled through Swiss bank accounts to aid the Nicaraguan Contras in their efforts to overthrow that country's leftist government. Over the objections of Secretary of State George Shultz and Defense Secretary Caspar Weinberger, Reagan approved the arms sales. He subsequently disclaimed knowledge of the diversion of funds to the Contras, as did his cabinet secretaries.

When news of the affair surfaced in November 1986, the administration faced a number of serious charges. First, the president had consistently pledged never to bargain with terrorists. Now it was revealed that the administration had in fact bargained with terrorists, aiding the virulently anti-American Iranian government of Ayatollah Khomeini and violating the United States' stated neutrality in the Iran-Iraq war. Even worse, the administration had defied Congress's express ban on military aid for the Contras.

Although North and others destroyed incriminating documents, enough evidence remained to demonstrate the culpability of seven individuals. Brought to trial by an independent prosecutor appointed by Reagan, all pleaded guilty or were convicted of lying to Congress and/or destroying evidence. North's felony conviction was later overturned on a technicality, and President George Bush pardoned six officials in December 1992. A joint congressional committee investigation found no evidence that Reagan knew of the diversion of funds to the Contras but criticized the president's lax management: He simply was not in charge.

Reagan's public statements confirmed the impression of a detached, fumbling leader who could not remember key events. He at first denied that the arms deal represented an exchange of weapons for hostages. Confronted with an official report to the contrary, Reagan responded that "my heart and my best intentions still tell me that is true [that he did not trade arms for hostages], but the facts and evidence tell me it is not." Public opinion polls reported that a substantial majority did not trust Reagan's assertions about his knowledge of the Iran-Contra affair. The independent prosecutor's final report, issued in 1994, found no evidence that Reagan had broken the law but concluded that both Reagan and Vice President Bush had known about the diversion of funds to the Contras and that Reagan had "knowingly participated or at least acquiesced" in covering up the scandal.

The United States delivered five shipments of arms to Iran, primarily antitank missiles. Two hostages were released, but terrorists killed a CIA official and took more hostages. By 1987, terrorists

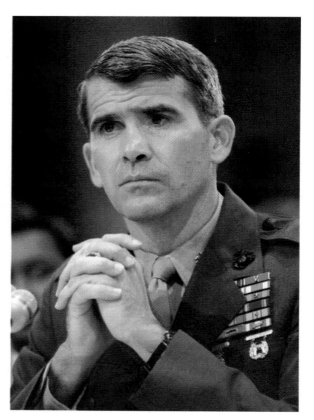

OLIVER NORTH

The central figure in the Iran-Contra affair, Lieutenant Colonel Oliver North, in his U.S. marine uniform, testified in July 1987 for six days before a congressional investigating committee. To many television viewers, North came across as a handsome young patriot whose lying to Congress, destroying public records, and other illegal actions were justified in the fight against Communism. In spite of his later conviction for a felony, which was overturned on a technicality, North maintained a strong following, especially among the right wing of the Republican Party, and nearly secured a Virginia Senate seat in 1994. Corbis-Bettmann.

held two more Americans than they had when the dealing began. The president ultimately accepted responsibility for what happened during his watch but never articulated his understanding of exactly what went wrong. Nor did he express outrage at the criminal acts of his aides. North remained for him "a hero" and Poindexter "an honorable man."

In the events that became known as the Iran-Contra scandal, administration officials engaged in secret and illegal activities, destroyed evidence of their undertakings, and lied to Congress.

The Iran-Contra scandal left the Reagan administration in disarray. Reagan ended his term with relatively high approval ratings, but his image as a confident leader was tarnished. More ominous for the nation, the Iran-Contra affair revealed that, despite all the efforts begun during the Nixon years to make the executive branch accountable to Congress and the public, abundant room remained for it to conduct a secret foreign policy outside the law.

A Thaw in Soviet-American Relations

Reagan weathered the Iran-Contra storm in part because he presided over a momentous thaw in the cold war, one all the more surprising because it occurred under an administration whose militant anti-communism exceeded that of any previous administration. Reagan's flexibility contributed to the Soviet-American accord, but it would not have happened without the innovative Soviet head of state who recognized that his country's domestic problems demanded a relaxation of cold war antagonism.

Mikhail Gorbachev assumed power in 1985 determined to revitalize a Soviet economy plagued with bureaucratic inefficiencies, a massive military budget, and an inability to deliver basic consumer goods and services. Hoping to stimulate production and streamline distribution, Gorbachev called for *perestroika* (economic restructuring), including the introduction of elements of free enterprise. He proclaimed a new era of *glasnost* (greater freedom of expression), eventually allowing such challenges to Communist rule as new political parties and contested elections.

Gorbachev recognized that economic revival depended on cutting the enormous costs of military production. Reagan, meanwhile, faced increasing congressional resistance to funding the arms race and popular support for arms reductions. Prodded too by Nancy Reagan, who had substantial influence on her husband, the president made disarmament a major goal in his last years in office. When Gorbachev took the initiative, Reagan was ready to respond.

A positive personal chemistry developed between Reagan and Gorbachev when the two met for the first time in Geneva in November 1985 and again at Reykjavik, Iceland, in 1986. Negotiations stalemated when Reagan refused to stop research and development on Star Wars, but eventually Gorbachev gave up that demand. By December 1987, negotiators had completed an intermediate-range nuclear weapons (INF) agreement, which eliminated all short- and medium-range missiles from Europe. These weapons amounted to a small portion of the entire nuclear arsenal, and other weapons would cover their targets. Nonetheless, the agreement provided for on-site inspection for the first time and raised expectations for strategic arms reduction talks (START).

When Gorbachev arrived in Washington in December 1987 to sign the INF treaty, Americans responded with a burst of "Gorbymania." Here was a new breed of Soviet leader—dynamic, witty, and sophisticated; he and his wife, Raisa, a professor of philosophy, made an engaging couple. Above all, here was a leader who could fulfill Americans' hopes for eliminating the anxieties of the cold war and stemming the flow of national resources into the war machine.

Reagan and Gorbachev did not realize their hopes to crown their accomplishments with a START treaty, but they enjoyed a fourth cordial meeting in Moscow in June 1988. When pressed by American reporters about the "evil empire," Reagan finally said, "I was talking about another empire." His remark articulated a major shift in his foreign policy. It also acknowledged genuine changes in Soviet internal affairs and global relations.

In 1988, Gorbachev announced a gradual withdrawal from Afghanistan, which had become the Soviet equivalent of America's Vietnam. In Africa, the Soviet Union, Cuba, and the United States agreed on a political settlement for the civil war in Angola. And in the Middle East, both superpowers supported a cease-fire and peace talks in the eight-

GORBYMANIA
Soviet leader Mikhail Gorbachev enjoyed great popularity with the American people on his trip to
the United States in December 1987. Bystanders on a street in Washington, D.C., press around him
to shake his hand. When President Reagan saw his appeal, he bantered, "I don't resent his popularity.
Good Lord, I co-starred with Errol Flynn once."
Wide World Photos, Inc.

year-old war between Iran and Iraq. Although the Soviet Union had seized the initiative, Reagan could justifiably claim a share of the credit for what he called "a satisfying new closeness with the Soviet Union"—a détente that far surpassed what Nixon and Kissinger had accomplished.

American Society in the 1980s

"More prosperous, more secure and happier than it was eight years ago." So Ronald Reagan described American society as he left the presidency in January 1989. And so it was for a majority of Americans, especially for those who had already been poised to profit from the economic revolution created by the Reagan administration. Great fortunes were made during the 1980s, and making money and displaying wealth were celebrated in popular culture.

At the same time, however, American society became more polarized along class lines. Increasing homelessness and growing poverty reversed the post–World War II trend toward greater economic equality. New immigration made the nation more culturally diverse, but African Americans, Hispanic Americans, and other minority groups fell disproportionately among those passed over by the surge of prosperity.

The Money Culture

Not since the 1920s had American culture so venerated free enterprise and the entrepreneur, and not since the Gilded Age had wealth been so extravagantly displayed. Books by businesspeople climbed onto best-seller lists. The press described lavish parties costing millions of dollars. Popular magazines featured articles entitled "High Life Afloat: Superduper Yachts" and "They're Like Us, Except

They're Rich." Evidence of immense fortunes and conspicuous consumption ranged from multimillion-dollar price tags on Manhattan apartments to specific area codes assigned to coastal waters to accommodate the proliferation of yachts.

Fascination with wealth and consumption drew vast audiences to prime-time TV serials such as *Dallas* and *Dynasty.* College students told poll takers that their primary ambition was to make money. Even fundamentalist ministers enjoyed homes with swimming pools and travel on private jets, though none lived as extravagantly as TV evangelist Jim Bakker, whose doghouses were air-conditioned and whose wife Tammy's shopping sprees were legendary.

Most Americans profited from the economic boom of the 1980s, but those already well off enjoyed the greatest gains. Family income for the richest one-fifth of the population increased by 11.1 percent between 1979 and 1987. The number of millionaires doubled during the decade, and the number of billionaires grew from thirteen to fifty-one. Greater concentration of wealth in fewer hands had been developing since the 1970s, but Reagan's tax and spending policies intensified the trend.

Participating conspicuously in the affluence of the 1980s were some members of the baby boom generation known popularly as "yuppies," short for "young urban professionals." These mostly white, well-educated young men and women tended to live in urban condominiums and to pursue fast-track careers; in their leisure time, they consumed lavishly—BMWs and other fancy sports cars, gourmet food, travel, electronic gadgets, and health clubs. Though constituting just a minority of their generation, they established consumption standards that were highly popularized and that others tried to emulate.

A striking feature of the new wealth of the 1980s was the extent to which it came from moving assets around rather than from producing goods. There were notable exceptions, of course, such as Steven Jobs, who invented the Apple computer in his garage, and Liz Claiborne, who in thirteen years turned a $250,000 investment into a billion-dollar fashion enterprise. But many others got rich—or richer—by manipulating debt and restructuring corporations. Called "paper entrepreneurs" by one expert, these were the investment bankers, bond brokers, and their lawyers and accountants who arranged corporate mergers and takeovers.

Large fortunes were made by "corporate raiders." These men generated the capital to take over a corporation by issuing junk bonds, so called because they were high-risk and high-yield. Once in control, the raiders reaped huge profits by selling off some of the corporation's valuable divisions. Corporate restructuring sometimes resulted in greater efficiency and productivity, but all too often the result was to line the financiers' pockets and leave the corporation deeply in debt.

Great fortunes were made during the 1980s. At the same time, however, American society became more polarized along class lines and increasing homelessness and growing poverty reversed the post–World War II trend toward greater economic equality.

"To say these guys are entrepreneurs is like saying Jesse James was an entrepreneur," opined Texas businessman Ross Perot, who defined entrepreneurship as making things rather than making money. While most financial entrepreneurs operated within the law, in some notable cases greed led to criminal convictions. The pioneer of junk bonds, Michael Milken, took home well over $50 million a year. But he and others ended up in jail for using insider information to maximize their financial manipulations.

The Other Side of the 1980s

Even yuppies and financiers had to be aware that the economic boom passed many Americans by. Affluent urbanites could see men and women sleeping in subway stations and on grates over steam vents, some within a mile of the White House. Experts debated the number of homeless Americans —estimates ranged from 350,000 upwards—but no one doubted that homelessness had increased. Women and children constituted the fastest-growing population without shelter: One-fourth of the homeless were families with children.

What accounted for the increasing numbers of homeless? The Reagan administration slashed new federal commitments for low-income housing from $33 billion to $8 billion, yet because of previous authorizations and congressional determination, federal spending on low-income housing actually increased during the 1980s, and the number of government-subsidized units grew as well. Nonetheless, hundreds of thousands still lacked affordable

HOMELESSNESS
The increased presence of homeless people in cities across the nation challenged the view of the
1980s as a decade of prosperity. Hundreds of homeless people could be found on the sidewalks of the
nation's capital every night. In November 1987, during the first snow of the season, a homeless man
sleeps in Lafayette Square across from the White House.
Corbis-Bettmann.

shelter. These included the victims of long-term unemployment, erosion of welfare benefits, and slum clearance as well as individuals suffering from mental illness, drug abuse, and alcoholism.

Homelessness was just one measure of the limited reach of economic expansion. Infant mortality was another. The United States fell behind other countries on this commonly used indicator of the general health of a nation. In fact, the United States ranked twentieth, below such countries as East Germany and Singapore.

Reagan insisted that a booming economy would benefit everyone. Average personal income did rise during his tenure, but the trend of income polarization that had begun in the 1970s sharpened in the 1980s, in part because of the new tax policies. The rich got richer, a portion of the middle class did well, and the poor got poorer. Personal income shot up sharply for the wealthiest 20 percent of Americans while it fell for the poorest by 9.8 percent between 1979 and 1987.

Poverty statistics, too, revealed a reversal of the trend toward greater equality. Between 1980 and 1988, poor people increased from 11.7 percent to

13.5 percent of the total U.S. population—the highest poverty rate in the industrialized world. A relatively low poverty rate among the elderly testified to the lasting success of New Deal and Great Society programs, especially Social Security and Medicare. Less fortunate were large segments of other groups that the economic boom had bypassed: racial minorities, female-headed families, and children. At the end of the decade, one in every five children lived in a household with income below the official poverty line.

Many nonpoor Americans struggled not to lose ground. The decline in manufacturing jobs and the weakening of organized labor eroded the position of blue-collar men with only high school educations. A second income was needed to stave off economic decline; in fact, families occupying the broad middle of the economic ladder achieved income gains only through female earnings. By 1990, nearly 60 percent of married women with young children worked outside the home, and women contributed nearly one-third of total family income. Yet even with the growth of two-income families, fewer young families could purchase their first home.

By 1990, employed women had narrowed the wage gap to the point that their median earnings were 72 percent those of men. However, this apparent achievement reflected a decline in male earnings as much as it did progress for women. It also mirrored the overall income redistribution in that the poorest women's income crept up scarcely at all while that of the top fifth grew by 35 percent. Moreover, the disparity between male and female earnings still amounted to an average of $10,000 a year, a vast difference to the nearly 20 percent of families that were headed by women. One mother of two, divorced from an abusive husband, found employment, but reported, "Jobs just don't pay good money." She managed to make ends meet by selling her blood and accepting help from her church.

Minorities' Struggles and Successes

Five million new immigrants sought to realize the American dream in the 1980s, surpassing the totals for every decade in the twentieth century but the first. The new wave of immigration was distinguished by a striking difference in country of origin. While 85 percent of the previous immigrants had come from Europe, almost half of the recent arrivals were Asians, and nearly 40 percent migrated from Latin America and the Caribbean.

The racial composition of the new immigration revived the century-old wariness of the native-born toward recent arrivals. Arguments for more restrictive policies included beliefs (generally unfounded) that immigrants took jobs from the native-born; anxiety about the tendency of highly motivated, hardworking immigrants to edge out U.S.-born students at prestigious universities; fears that immigrants would erode the dominant culture and language; and concern about population pressures on the environment. Many of the new immigrants "do not assimilate satisfactorily into our society," wrote Republican Senator Alan Simpson in 1985, worried about "the unity and political stability of our nation."

Americans expressed particular concern about immigrants who entered the country illegally. Primarily Latin Americans fleeing civil war and economic deprivation, they were estimated to number at least three million. To stem this tide, Congress passed the Immigration Reform and Control Act of 1986, which penalized employers who hired undocumented aliens, a step that critics feared would

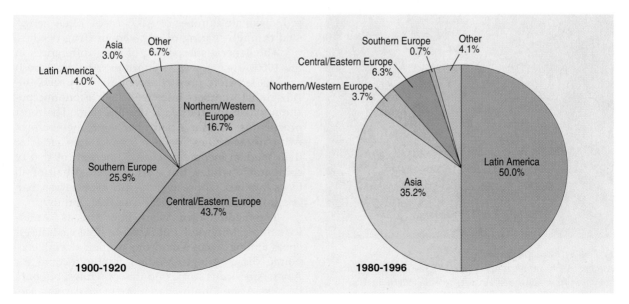

FIGURE 31.3
The Changing Profile of Immigration, 1900–1920 and 1980–1996
The United States received its largest number of immigrants during the opening and closing decades of the twentieth century, but the cultures and countries of origin of the new arrivals shifted dramatically between the two periods.

encourage discrimination against foreign-looking workers. One of the law's more benevolent provisions granted amnesty to undocumented immigrants who could prove residence before 1982. Around two million people took advantage of this provision.

The Immigration Reform and Control Act embodied both the generous and restrictive traditions in American policy, but two other laws were unequivocally open-hearted. In response to the plight of Vietnamese children fathered by U.S. servicemen and often treated as outcasts in Vietnam, the Amerasian Homecoming Act opened the door to these children and their immediate families.

Efforts to make amends for the past also extended to Japanese Americans. In 1983, a special

THE NEW IMMIGRATION
Among Asian immigrants in the 1980s, the largest number came from southeast Asia, where the Vietnam War and its aftermath created hundreds of thousands of refugees. Most of these refugees had little money and found adjustment difficult. Many like these Laotian Hmong immigrants in Providence, Rhode Island, came from rural, premodern societies.
Ira Wyman/Sygma.

commission declared the World War II internment of Japanese Americans to have been "a grave injustice," the result of "race prejudice, war hysteria, and a failure of political leadership." In 1988, Congress issued an official apology and granted $20,000 in reparations to each of the approximately 70,000 surviving internees.

Higher fertility rates among Hispanic Americans, Asian Americans, and African Americans, in combination with migration patterns, increased the racial and ethnic diversity in American society. While the total population increased by around 9 percent in the 1980s, the black population grew by 13 percent, the Hispanic population by 39 percent, and the Asian American population by nearly 50 percent. By 2010, the Census Bureau projected, people of color would account for nearly 30 percent of the nation's residents. In California and several other states, they would constitute a majority.

Minorities continued to occupy the lower rungs of the economic ladder, and their situation worsened with the upward flow of wealth. Median income for white families surpassed $32,000 in 1988, in contrast to $18,000 for African Americans and $20,300 for Hispanic Americans. Poverty afflicted one in three African Americans and 28 percent of all Hispanic Americans. With higher than average rates of drug use, these groups accounted for a disproportionate number of AIDS cases, often generated through sharing of intravenous drug needles.

The general sharpening of class differences in the 1980s also affected minorities. African Americans were barely present among the very rich, but substantial numbers improved their economic position, enlarging the black middle class. The most prosperous African Americans were members of two-parent families in which both parents had jobs; their median income reached 82 percent of that of comparable whites. But women headed half of all black families, whose average income was less than one-third that of the typical American family.

The media hailed Asian Americans as "America's Super Minority" but failed to note vast differences among Asian Americans or their overall economic disadvantage. Median family income for Asian Americans surpassed that of whites, but only because Asian families had more wage earners. Despite the greater educational achievement of Asian Americans (39 percent had completed college, in contrast to 22 percent of whites), they lagged behind whites in per capita income, and their poverty rates surpassed those of whites. Poor Chinese American women employed in the New York gar-

A NEW VOICE IN POLITICS

Jesse Jackson was among the civil rights activists who turned to electoral politics. A Baptist minister and dynamic speaker, Jackson mounted campaigns for the Democratic presidential nomination in 1984 and 1988, appealing to what he called a "Rainbow Coalition" of disadvantaged groups. Here he addresses students at Dartmouth College in January 1984.

Ira Wyman/Sygma.

ment industry endured wages, hours, and working conditions resembling those of the early-twentieth-century sweatshops.

Minorities edged slowly into the corridors of political power. At the end of the 1980s, more than seven thousand blacks held public office, an increase of nearly 50 percent from 1980. The most impressive gains occurred in city government, where black mayors presided over Atlanta, Chicago, Los Angeles, New Haven, Philadelphia, Seattle, and other large cities. The election of David Dinkins as mayor of New York City in 1989 epitomized the rise of black leaders even in cities with predominantly white electorates.

Jesse Jackson's campaigns for the presidency in 1984 and 1988 inspired African Americans and demonstrated that many whites were willing to support a minority candidate. In 1989, Democrat L. Douglas Wilder of Virginia became the first black governor since Reconstruction, joining the only Hispanic governor, Republican Bob Martinez of Florida. Access to the highest offices in the land

came slowly. In the 1992 elections, African Americans captured 38 seats in the 435-member House of Representatives, while Hispanics won 17 and Asian Americans 5. African American Carol Moseley Braun and Native American Ben Nighthorse Campbell won election to the Senate.

Domestic Gridlock and a New World Order

When Vice President George Bush announced his bid for the presidency in 1987, he declared, "We don't need radical new directions." Generally satisfied with the agenda set by Ronald Reagan, Bush displayed little interest in domestic affairs, and he faced a strong Democratic majority in Congress. Although the president and Congress reached agreement on a few important measures, overall stalemate marked the domestic record of the Bush presidency.

In foreign policy, too, Bush tended to react to events rather than to try to shape them. He acted aggressively in sending troops to overthrow the corrupt dictator of Panama. And the United States entered a full-scale war when Iraq threatened Middle Eastern stability by invading Kuwait in 1990. But the United States stood on the sidelines of the most momentous world events, which took place in Europe as one by one the Eastern bloc nations threw out their Communist rulers. After allowing the breakup of the system that had anchored its security since 1945, the Soviet Union itself disintegrated in 1991.

The Issueless Campaign of 1988

Explaining George Bush's campaign for the presidency in 1988, one of his aides remembered, "The biggest single factor was whether Ronald Reagan would turn the nation over in good shape. If he did that, Bush was home free." The vice president's campaign benefited from the country's continuing economic expansion and the warming relationship with the Soviet Union.

George Bush's election to the presidency capped a long career in politics and government. The son of a wealthy investment banker who had represented Connecticut in the U.S. Senate, George Herbert Walker Bush grew up in a privileged milieu that put a premium on public service. Bush interrupted his education to serve as a navy combat pilot in World War II; after earning his Yale degree, he settled in Texas to make his own way in the oil industry and politics.

Bush represented Texas in Congress during the 1960s and later served as head of the U.S. Liaison Office in China and director of the CIA during the Nixon-Ford years. When Ronald Reagan achieved a commanding lead in the 1980 primaries, Bush put his own aspirations on hold and accepted second place on the Republican ticket. His vice presidency was distinguished above all by absolute loyalty to Reagan. That, however, was not enough to secure his succession, and he won the Republican nomination only after bruising battles in the primaries.

The Democratic race was even more crowded. Jesse Jackson, whose Rainbow Coalition campaign centered on the needs of people who had been ignored by the political mainstream—blacks and other minorities, women, working-class families, and the poor—won several state primaries, gathering seven million votes, almost one-third of them from white voters. In the end, however, his race,

lack of experience in public office, and position on the left wing of the Democratic Party proved to be insuperable obstacles. Michael Dukakis, then serving his third term as governor of Massachusetts, won the nomination.

"The Trivial Pursuit of the Presidency," the subtitle of one account of the 1988 campaign, expressed the general view of political commentators. Neither Bush nor Dukakis presented a clear vision of how he wanted to use the power of the presidency, and the campaign was unprecedentedly issueless and vitriolic. Proving more adept at negative campaigning, Bush's staff distorted Dukakis's record and portrayed him as a dangerous liberal, soft on criminals, and out of step with traditional American values. Dukakis tried to present himself as a moderate, competent administrator, but he came across as arrogant and passionless, and his early lead slipped away.

Half of the eligible voters stayed home on election day. The lowest voter turnout since 1924 suggested the electorate's general disgust with an ugly, issueless campaign. Fifty-four percent of those who did vote were satisfied with the Republican record on peace and prosperity. But the Democrats gained seats in the House and Senate; for the first time since 1960, the strength of the presidential ticket did not translate into congressional gains for the party.

Domestic Stalemate

President Bush saw himself primarily as steward and guardian of the Reagan legacy. He promised "a kinder, gentler nation" and was more inclined than Reagan to approve government activity in the private sphere. But his most famous campaign pledge was "Read my lips: No new taxes." Boxed in by the budget deficit and his adamant refusal to seek new tax revenues, Bush opposed most proposals requiring federal funds to make the nation kinder and gentler for the poor, racial minorities, employed women, and other needy groups.

The president's aversion to new federal spending could not withstand the crisis in the savings and loan industry. In 1989, Bush signed legislation for the biggest federal bailout in history. The law authorized the government to sell off failing S&Ls at an estimated $159 billion cost to taxpayers over the next ten years. Bush also approved environmental protection legislation, the costs of which would be borne by industry and consumers. The Clean Air Act of 1990 was the strongest, most comprehensive environmental law in history, requiring power

PRESIDENTIAL RECREATION
President George Bush and Vice President Dan Quayle play golf near the Bush summer home in Kennebunkport, Maine. Although Bush was a hardworking president, after the economy slipped into recession in 1990, photos such as these contributed to his image as uncaring and unwilling to act to relieve ordinary Americans' economic distress.
Corbis-Bettmann.

plants to cut sulphur dioxide emissions by more than half by the year 2000 and oil companies to develop cleaner-burning gasoline.

Some 35 million to 43 million disabled Americans reaped the benefits of other regulatory legislation. Reflecting the growing power of the disability rights movement, the 1991 Americans with Disabilities Act banned job discrimination against the handicapped and required that private businesses, public accommodations, and transportation be made accessible to the disabled. Under pressure from legislators of both parties, Bush also signed the Civil Rights Act of 1991, which overcame Supreme Court rulings that made it harder for women and minorities to prove employment discrimination.

"If you're looking for George Bush's domestic program, and many people are, this is it: the veto pen," charged Democratic House majority leader

Richard Gephardt in 1991. Bush blocked congressional initiatives thirty-six times, vetoing bills that lifted abortion restrictions, extended unemployment benefits, raised taxes, mandated family and medical leave for workers, and reformed campaign financing. By the end of his term, press reports were filled with the words *stalemate, gridlock,* and *divided government.* To a Republican who preferred a more activist president, the Bush domestic policy was "all stop and no go."

The deadlock between president and Congress crippled the government's ability to deal with the budget deficit and the economic downswing that began in 1990. In June 1990, the worsening budget situation forced Bush to concede the fantasy of his "no new taxes" pledge. The next year's deficit was projected at a minimum of $160 billion, far above the Gramm-Rudman-Hollings limit of $64 billion. Failure to meet the target would trigger automatic cuts of 25 percent in military spending and 37 percent in most domestic programs.

The administration and Congress hammered out a compromise that set spending limits, increased taxes modestly for high-income Americans, and raised taxes on gasoline, cigarettes, alcoholic beverages, and luxury items. Although the budget agreement brought in new revenues and Congress stuck to the spending limits, three years later the deficit was even higher, boosted by rising costs in entitlement programs such as Social Security and Medicare-Medicaid as well as by spending on unforeseen emergencies of war and natural disasters. Conservative Republicans expressed so much outrage at Bush for going against his "no new taxes" pledge that in 1992 he conceded that the budget agreement had been a "mistake."

"If you're looking for George Bush's domestic program, and many people are, this is it: the veto pen," charged Democratic House majority leader Richard Gephardt in 1991.

Failure to control the deficit also resulted from an economic downswing that began in 1990. With higher unemployment and a drop in the economy's growth rate, federal revenues declined. Congress and the president found it even harder to agree on antirecession measures than they had on curbing the deficit. Bush signed a measure that would create jobs by funding $151 billion worth of highway and mass-transit construction over a six-year period. But Congress flatly refused to pass a capital gains tax cut that Bush claimed would stimulate economic growth; and Bush vetoed the Democrats' bill to cut taxes for the middle class. After vetoing aid to workers who had been thrown out of jobs by the recession in 1991, Bush reversed himself and approved legislation extending unemployment benefits in 1992.

Although the recession (as defined technically by economists) ended in 1991, the economy grew at a snail's pace. General Motors, Time Warner, Xerox, and other major corporations announced permanent reductions in their workforces. Economists characterized the sluggish economy as "jobless recovery" from the recession. As he faced his reelection campaign, Bush had to answer for an unemployment rate above 7 percent.

The president's greatest opportunity to influence policy in a lasting way came through Supreme Court appointments. Justice William Brennan's decision to retire in 1990 meant the departure of a justice who, even more than Earl Warren, had shaped the liberal direction of the Court. In selecting a successor, Bush avoided the turmoil and humiliation of the Bork nomination by naming David Souter, a federal court of appeals judge from New Hampshire who had left a scant written record and few clues about his views on judicial restraint or on specific issues. The Senate confirmed him easily.

In 1991, when Bush had to replace Justice Thurgood Marshall, the only African American on the Court, he set off a national controversy by nominating Clarence Thomas, a conservative black court of appeals judge. Thomas had opposed most affirmative action programs and busing as head of the Equal Employment Opportunity Commission under Reagan. Charging that Thomas would not protect minority rights, the NAACP and other civil rights organizations opposed the nomination. In spite of this opposition and Thomas's low rating by the American Bar Association, confirmation seemed certain until the media reported charges that Thomas had sexually harassed Anita Hill, a law professor, when she worked for him in the early 1980s. The Senate Judiciary Committee held three days of nationally televised hearings to investigate the charges. Thomas angrily and steadfastly denied the alleged incidents, and Hill's testimony failed to sway the Senate, which voted fifty-two to forty-eight to confirm him.

The hearings sensitized the public to sexual harassment and gave the women's movement a boost. Many women, including a dozen Congresswomen, expressed outrage at the shabby treatment that Hill received from senators who tried to discredit her. Feminists complained that men "still don't get it" and began preparing to put more women into office in the 1992 elections.

Toward a New World Order

"All the action is in Moscow and Berlin, not here," complained a former Reagan aide, referring to the Bush administration's distance from events unfolding in Europe. The administration possessed no grand strategies, and Bush articulated no commanding goal like Carter's emphasis on human rights or Reagan's drive to return the United States to global ascendency. Rather, the president and his secretary of state, James Baker, responded cautiously to initiatives produced by Gorbachev and European leaders.

In the most dramatic moment in the collapse of the postwar order, East Germany opened the border with West Germany. On November 12, 1989, ecstatic Germans danced on the Berlin Wall, using whatever was at hand to begin demolishing that dominant symbol of the cold war.

The forces of change that Gorbachev had helped to unleash in the Soviet Union spread in 1989 to Eastern Europe, where popular uprisings demanded an end to state repression, official corruption, and economic bureaucracies that failed to deliver an acceptable standard of living. Communist governments fell like dominoes, in most cases with little bloodshed. In Czechoslovakia, East Germany, Hungary, Poland, and Yugoslavia, citizens voted in multiparty elections for the first time since World War II. Non-Communist governments took office everywhere but in Albania and Bulgaria, and even those countries instituted reforms. In the most dramatic moment in the collapse of the postwar order, East Germany opened the border with West Germany. On November 12, 1989, ecstatic Germans danced on the Berlin Wall, using whatever was at hand to begin demolishing that dominant symbol of the cold war.

West German Chancellor Helmut Kohl's call for a united Germany immediately after the fall of the Berlin Wall shocked U.S. leaders. Nevertheless,

FALL OF THE BERLIN WALL
After 1961, the Berlin Wall symbolized the cold war and the iron grip of Communism over Eastern
Europe and the Soviet Union; more than four hundred easterners were killed trying to flee. After
Communist authorities opened the wall on November 9, 1989, permitting free travel between east
and west, Berliners from both sides gathered at the wall to celebrate.
Eric Bouvet/Gamma Liaison.

President Bush helped to persuade Gorbachev that the Soviet Union had nothing to fear from the unification of East and West Germany, a move that sped to completion in 1990. Germany would become a member of NATO, and though U.S. military forces would remain in Europe, the commanding role of the United States had been eclipsed. The same was true of its economic clout: Western Europe, including a unified Germany, would become a united economy in 1992. The destiny of Europe, to which the United States and the Soviet Union had held the key for forty-five years, now lay in European hands.

The superpowers continued to attune their relationship to the realities of a post-cold war world as well as to domestic economic needs. Gorbachev came to Washington in June 1990 and took home another breakthrough in arms reductions. More far-reaching than earlier accords, which had merely limited production of additional weapons, the strategic arms reduction treaty (START) actually eliminated existing nuclear weapons—about 30 percent of each superpower's nuclear arsenal. Bush and Gorbachev also pledged to scrap most of their poison gas weapons and to work to eliminate chemical weapons from the planet.

The Bush administration's approach to problems closer to home developed in distinct contrast to its cautious response to European developments. In fact, while the Soviet Union moved along a noninterventionist path, the United States sent military forces into Panama in 1989 to overthrow its dictator, General Manuel Noriega. Noriega had long fed off the CIA payroll, delivering information about Communist activities in Cuba and Central America and aiding the government's secret war against the Sandinistas. But he also passed information to Cuba's Castro while amassing a fortune through dealing in illegal drugs, torturing and killing his domestic opposition, and wrecking the Panamanian economy. In 1988, a Miami grand jury indicted Noriega for drug trafficking, and administration officials decided that he had to go.

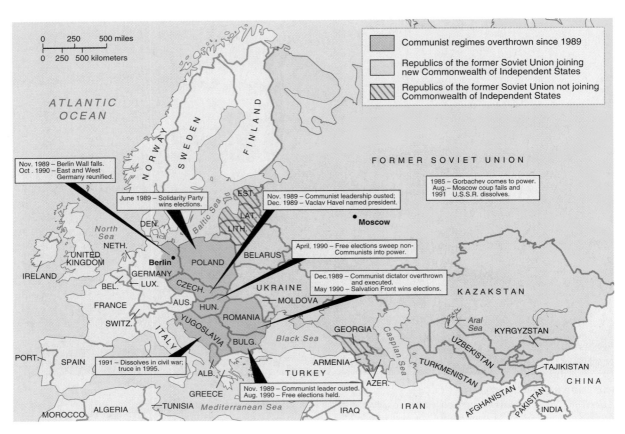

M A P 31.2
Events in Eastern Europe, 1989–1992
The overthrow of Communist governments throughout Eastern and Central Europe and the splinter-
ing of the Soviet Union into more than a dozen separate nations were the most momentous changes
in the world since World War II.

In December 1989, President Bush ordered 25,000 troops into Panama to capture the dictator. The invasion forces quickly overcame Noriega's troops, at the cost of 23 American lives and hundreds of Panamanian lives, many of them civilians. The administration called the invasion Operation Just Cause. But although most Panamanians and their Central American neighbors rejoiced to see the corrupt tyrant go, they were not sure that the end justified the means. "Good causes don't justify breaking good principles," insisted one Latin American diplomat. The resort to military intervention revived the image of "Yankee imperialism," a stark contrast to the principles of self-determination and nonintervention that held sway in Eastern Europe.

The administration deployed much greater force and it acted with allies when Iraq's army invaded and quickly took over the small, oil-rich country of Kuwait in August 1990. Iraqi President Saddam Hussein cited long-standing boundary disputes as grounds for the invasion, but his primary target was the Kuwaiti oil fields. Struggling with an enormous debt from the ten-year war against Iran, Hussein desperately needed revenues, and control of Kuwaiti oil would give him powerful leverage over prices. Within days of invading Kuwait, Iraqi troops moved toward the Saudi Arabian border, threatening the world's largest oil reserves.

In reacting to the invasion, President Bush invoked principles of national self-determination and international law, but oil primarily determined the U.S. response. As the largest oil importer, the United States consumed one-fourth of the world's supply. With the consent of Saudi Arabia, Bush ordered Operation Desert Shield, a massive mobilization of land, air, and naval forces to counter the Iraqi threat. At the same time, the administration began to assemble an international coalition—ultimately involving more than thirty nations—to repel the aggression.

Reflecting the end of superpower conflict in the Middle East, the Soviet Union and the United States issued a joint condemnation of Iraq, and the Soviets cut off Iraq's supply of arms. The United Nations instituted economic sanctions, and most of the world joined an embargo on oil from Iraq and Kuwait. In November, the United Nations authorized the use of force against Iraq if it did not withdraw from Kuwait by January 15, 1991. By early January, the United States had deployed 400,000 soldiers to Saudi Arabia, where 265,000 troops from European nations, Egypt, Syria, and several other Arab states joined them. Meanwhile, Bush asked Congress for authorization to use military force against Iraq. Considerable public and legislative sentiment favored waiting to see whether the embargo would force Hussein to back down. But after three days of solemn debate, Congress approved what amounted to a declaration of war by a margin of five votes in the Senate and sixty-seven in the House. Unlike Johnson in Vietnam, Bush would go to war with clear congressional authorization.

On January 17, 1991, Operation Desert Shield became Operation Desert Storm, when the U.S.-led coalition began a forty-day air war against Iraq. Bombs and missiles smashed not only military targets but also power plants, oil refineries, and transportation networks. Having severely crippled Iraq through air bombardment, the coalition launched an all-out ground assault against Iraqi troops on February 23. "These people threw down their arms and ran," said an American artillery officer. Allied forces quickly routed the Iraqi soldiers, and within one hundred hours, Hussein announced that he would withdraw from Kuwait.

"By God, we've kicked the Vietnam syndrome once and for all," said President Bush on March 1. Most Americans found no moral ambiguity in the Persian Gulf War and took pride in the display of military competence. The war's costs were relatively cheap: Germany and Japan (who sent no troops) and other coalition allies paid a substantial part of the bill, while 146 U.S. servicemen and -women were killed in action, and 124 died outside of combat. The United States stood at the apex of global leadership, steering a massive coalition in which, for the first time, Arab nations fought beside their former colonial rulers.

Yet victory did not bring stability to the Middle East. The position of Israel, which had endured

Iraqi missile attacks, was more secure, but the Israeli-Palestinian conflict continued to simmer. Despite considerable military losses, Saddam Hussein remained in power and turned the remains of his war machine on Iraqi Kurds and Shiite Muslims, whom the United States had encouraged to rebel. Two million rebels became refugees; other Iraqi citizens suffered malnutrition, disease, and death caused by the destruction of the nation's fuel, communications, and transportation systems.

After the Gulf War, the Bush administration reverted to a bystander role as the world continued to remake itself. By the end of 1991, changes initiated by Gorbachev had brought about his own demise. Inspired by the liberation of Eastern Europe, Soviet republics sought their own indepen-

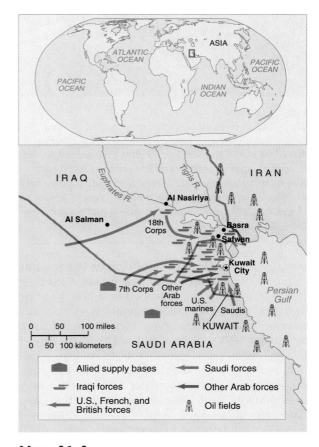

MAP 31.3
The Gulf War, February 1991
The heavy forty-day bombing of Iraq and the massive international mobilization on its borders enabled the U.S.-led United Nations force to defeat Iraq in just four days of ground war.

THE GULF WAR
These soldiers from the 24th Infantry arrived in Saudi Arabia in August 1990 as part of the U.S.-led effort to drive Iraq out of Kuwait. For the first time women served in combat-support positions with more than 33,000 stationed throughout the Gulf; eleven died and two were held as prisoners of war. Among their duties, women piloted planes and helicopters, directed artillery, and fought fires.
Corbis-Bettmann.

dence, while the Soviet Union's efforts at economic change brought widespread destitution. According to one Muscovite, "Gorbachev knew how to bring us freedom but he did not know how to make sausage." Gorbachev survived an attempted coup in August 1991, but he could not hold the Soviet Union together. In December, Boris Yeltsin, president of the Russian Republic, announced that Russia and eleven other republics had joined a new Commonwealth of Independent States. The three Baltic republics—Estonia, Latvia, and Lithuania—and Georgia became independent nations. With nothing left to govern, Gorbachev resigned.

The United States officially recognized Russia, but the breakup of the Soviet Union seemed as ominous as its existence had once appeared. "During the cold war, the threat was deliberate Soviet attack," declared Democratic Representative Les Aspin. "Now the bigger threat seems to be chaos in

a nation with 30,000 nuclear weapons." Russia and the three other republics possessing nuclear weapons—Ukraine, Belarus, and Kazakhstan—pledged to implement START, and Congress provided $400 million to help these nations store or destroy their nuclear weapons; but that process would take years. Meanwhile, the Russian economy deteriorated further, causing widespread destitution and despair, and Yeltsin maintained a precarious hold on the government. Civil wars broke out in several former Soviet republics, and power struggles among republics with nuclear weapons created a powderkeg.

Conclusion: Watersheds at Home and Abroad

During the Reagan-Bush years, the United States turned explicitly away from the assumptions that had shaped domestic policy since the New Deal of Franklin Roosevelt. To be sure, Republican Presidents Eisenhower and Nixon had attempted to curb the role of the federal government in addressing national problems. Moreover, since the late 1960s, growing numbers of Americans had questioned both the appropriateness and the effectiveness of government activism on behalf of economic stability and social justice. But no president before Ronald Reagan had applied the brakes so sharply to liberal reform or enjoyed such widespread popular support for those efforts.

The Reagan-Bush counterrevolution appealed to Americans whose real incomes declined in the 1970s as their tax bills increased and who believed that the federal government was sacrificing their well-being to the interests of poor and minority groups. Reagan cultivated these sentiments by winning enormous tax reductions and by portraying civil rights initiatives as favoritism or "reverse discrimination." The tax cuts, combined with hefty increases in defense spending, created a federal deficit crisis that justified cuts in spending for social welfare programs and made new federal initiatives unthinkable. Many Americans continued to look favorably on specific federal programs at the end of the Reagan-Bush years, but public sentiment about the government in general had undergone a U-turn from the Roosevelt era. To a large segment of the population, not only was the federal government ineffective at solving national problems, but government intervention often made things worse.

If Reagan and Bush could take credit for domestic change, the roots of global change were much more complex. Reagan and Bush claimed that the massive arms buildup they had undertaken in the 1980s had brought the Soviets to their knees and accounted for the worldwide fall of communism. Others pointed to the internal weaknesses of the Soviet economic system and the courageous risk taking of Mikhail Gorbachev. None could deny, however, that between 1988 and 1992 the world had experienced the most cataclysmic changes since the 1940s.

Containment of communism had shaped the American economy and politics for nearly fifty years and formed the linchpin of U.S. foreign policy. Its sudden collapse left policymakers unprepared to forge a new global strategy. When Iraq invaded Kuwait, the Bush administration reacted decisively. In its first substantial military engagement in forty-five years that was not directed against communism, the United States demonstrated that the end of the cold war did not mean a diminution of U.S. leadership in world affairs.

However, its leaders had yet to articulate what overarching vision would replace the containment of communism as the major foreign policy goal and define the American purpose in the world.

By 1992, however, domestic problems seemed most urgent. Part of the Reagan-Bush legacy was a host of economic problems that had been accumulating for more than a decade: the decline of industrial production and loss of good jobs, business instability and dependence on foreign investment, a worsening budget deficit, the end of the American dream of upward mobility for much of the middle class, and increasing poverty and growing economic disparity between the rich and poor and between whites and people of color. While public officials and the media trumpeted U.S. victory in the cold war, the nation had yet to come to grips with the economic casualties of that struggle. How the United States dealt with one part of the Reagan-Bush legacy—the economic problems—would depend on the strength and depth of the other part of that legacy—the turn against government as the guarantor of social and economic well-being.

CHRONOLOGY

1980 Ronald Reagan elected fortieth president of United States, defeating incumbent Jimmy Carter.

1981 Researchers identify cause of AIDS epidemic as virus.

Would-be assassin wounds Reagan in Washington, D.C.

Congress passes Economic Recovery Tax Act advocated by Reagan, largest tax cut in U.S. history.

Reagan appoints Sandra Day O'Connor, first female justice to sit on U.S. Supreme Court.

1982 Congress extends Voting Rights Act over Reagan administration's objections.

Banking industry deregulated.

United States invades Grenada and topples its Marxist government.

1983 U.S. involvement in Lebanon terminated after bombing of marine barracks and deaths of 241 U.S. troops.

Reagan announces plans for Strategic Defense Initiative ("Star Wars").

1984 Democrats nominate Walter F. Mondale for president and Geraldine Ferraro for vice president.

Ronald Reagan reelected president.

U.S. Supreme Court rules that schools can continue to receive federal funds even if they practice discrimination in some programs (*Grove City College v. Bell*).

1985 Congress passes Gramm-Rudman-Hollings deficit reduction law.

1986 Iran-Contra scandal shakes Reagan administration.

1987 Soviet leader Mikhail Gorbachev visits Washington to sign INF agreement.

Senate defeats nomination of Robert H. Bork for seat on U.S. Supreme Court.

1988   Reverend Jesse Jackson mounts strong campaign for Democratic presidential nomination.

Democrats nominate Michael Dukakis for president and Lloyd Bentsen for vice president.

Vice President George Bush elected forty-first president of United States.

1989   Communism collapses in Eastern Europe, and Berlin Wall falls.

United States invades Panama and ousts dictator Manuel Noriega, who is jailed in United States.

1990   Bush and Congress agree to tax increase because of mounting federal deficit.

1991   Bush's nominee Clarence Thomas becomes second African American to sit on U.S. Supreme Court.

United States commits more than 400,000 troops to oust Iraqi army from neighboring Kuwait in Persian Gulf War.

BIBLIOGRAPHY

GENERAL WORKS

Sidney Blumenthal and Thomas Byrne Edsall, eds., *The Reagan Legacy* (1988).

Kevin Phillips, *The Politics of Rich and Poor: Wealth and the American Electorate in the Reagan Aftermath* (1990).

Michael Schaller, *Reckoning with Reagan: America and Its President in the 1980s* (1992).

Gary Wills, *Reagan's America: Innocents at Home* (1987).

THE REAGAN WHITE HOUSE

Martin Anderson, *Revolution* (1988).

Lou Cannon, *President Reagan: The Role of a Lifetime* (1991).

Robert Dallek, *Ronald Reagan: The Politics of Symbolism* (1984).

Michael Deaver, *Behind the Scenes* (1987).

David C. Martin and John Walcott, *Best Laid Plans* (1988).

Donald Regan, *For the Record: From Wall Street to Washington* (1988).

Larry Speakes, with Robert Pack, *Speaking Out: Inside the Reagan White House* (1988).

DOMESTIC POLICIES

Jeffrey H. Birnbaum and Alan S. Murray, *Showdown at Gucci Gulch: Lawmakers, Lobbyists, and the Unlikely Triumph of Tax Reform* (1987).

Kathleen Day, *S&L Hell: The People and the Politics behind the $1 Trillion Savings and Loan Scandal* (1993).

Martha Derthick and Paul J. Quirk, *The Politics of Deregulation* (1985).

Benjamin Friedman, *Day of Reckoning: The Consequences of American Economic Policy under Reagan and After* (1988).

Lawrence Lindsey, *The Growth Experiment: How the New Tax Policy Is Transforming the U.S. Economy* (1990).

Martin Lowy, *High Rollers: Inside the Savings and Loan Debacle* (1994).

Richard P. Nathan and Fred C. Doolittle, *Reagan and the States* (1987).

Paul Craig Roberts, *The Supply-Side Revolution* (1984).

Murray Weidenbaum, *Rendezvous with Reality: The American Economy after Reagan* (1988).

POLITICS

Sidney Blumenthal, *The Rise of the Counter-Establishment: From Conservative Ideology to Political Power* (1986).

Steve Bruce, *The Rise and Fall of the New Christian Right: Conservative Protestant Politics in America, 1978–1988* (1988).

Thomas Byrd Edsall, with Mary D. Edsall, *Chain Reaction: The Impact of Race, Rights, and Taxes on American Politics* (1992).

Thomas Ferguson and Joel Rogers, *Right Turn: The Decline of the Democrats and the Future of American Politics* (1986).

Jack W. Germond and Jules Witcover, *Wake Us When It's Over: Presidential Politics of 1984* (1985).

Jack W. Germond and Jules Witcover, *Whose Broad Stripes and Bright Stars? The Trivial Pursuit of the Presidency, 1988* (1989).

Paul Gottfried and Thomas Fleming, *The Conservative Movement* (1988).

David Stockman, *The Triumph of Politics: How the Reagan Revolution Failed* (1986).

INDIVIDUAL RIGHTS AND THE SUPREME COURT

Barry D. Adam, *The Rise of a Gay and Lesbian Movement* (1987).

Norman C. Amaker, *Civil Rights and the Reagan Administration* (1988).

Robert H. Bork, *The Tempting of America: The Political Seduction of the Law* (1989).

Gerald David Jaynes and Robin M. Williams Jr., eds., *A Common Destiny: Blacks and American Society* (1989).

Michael Pertschuk and Wendy Schaetzel, *The People Rising: The Campaign against the Bork Nomination* (1989).

Herman Schwartz, *Packing the Courts: The Conservative Campaign to Rewrite the Constitution* (1988).

James F. Simon, *The Center Holds: The Power Struggle inside the Rehnquist Court* (1995).

FOREIGN POLICY AND ARMS CONTROL

Cynthia J. Arnson, *Crossroads: Congress, the Reagan Administration, and Central America* (1989).

Michael R. Beschloss and Strobe Talbott, *At the Highest Levels: The Inside Story of the End of the Cold War* (1993).

Thomas Carothers, *In the Name of Democracy: U.S. Policy toward Latin America in the Reagan Years* (1991).

John Dinges, *Our Man in Panama: How General Noriega Used the United States—and Made Millions in Drugs and Arms* (1990).

Theodore Draper, *A Very Thin Line: The Iran-Contra Affair* (1991).

Lawrence Freedman and Efraim Karsh, *The Gulf Conflict, 1990–1991: Diplomacy and War in the New World Order* (1993).

Raymond I. Garthoff, *The Great Transition: American-Soviet Relations and the End of the Cold War* (1994).

Michael J. Hogan, ed., *The End of the Cold War: Its Meanings and Implications* (1992).

Robert Kagan, *A Twilight Struggle: American Power and Nicaragua, 1977–1990* (1996).

Frederick Kempe, *Divorcing the Dictator: America's Bungled Affair with Noriega* (1990).

David E. Kyvig, ed., *Reagan and the World* (1990).

Sanford Lakoff and Herbert F. York, *A Shield in Space?* (1989).

Richard Ned Lebow and Janice Gross Stein, *We All Lost the Cold War* (1994).

William Pfaff, *Barbarian Sentiments: How the American Century Ends* (1989).

Peter Schweizer, *Victory: The Reagan Administration's Secret Strategy That Hastened the Collapse of the Soviet Union* (1995).

Elaine Sciolino, *The Outlaw State: Saddam Hussein's Quest for Power and the Gulf Crisis* (1991).

George P. Shultz, *Turmoil and Triumph: My Years as Secretary of State* (1993).

Strobe Talbott, *The Master of the Game: Paul Nitze and the Nuclear Peace* (1988).

Daniel Wirls, *Buildup: The Politics of Defense in the Reagan Era* (1992).

THE ECONOMY AND SOCIETY

Michael Bernstein, David E. Adler, and Robert Heilbroner, *Understanding American Economic Decline* (1994).

Joel Blau, *Homelessness in the United States* (1992).

George J. Borjas, *Friends and Strangers: The Impact of Immigrants on the U.S. Economy* (1990).

Kathryn Marie Dudley, *The End of the Line: Lost Jobs, New Lives in Postindustrial America* (1994).

L. H. Gann and Peter J. Duignan, *The Hispanics in the United States: A History* (1986).

David Gelsanliter, *Jump Start: Japan Comes to the Heartland* (1990).

Andrew Hacker, *Two Nations: Black and White, Separate, Hostile, Unequal* (1992).

Bennett Harrison and Barry Bluestone, *The Great U-Turn: Corporate Restructuring and the Polarizing of America* (1988).

Christopher Jencks, *The Homeless* (1994).

Sarah J. Mahler, *American Dreaming: Immigrant Life on the Margins* (1995).

David M. Reimers, *Still the Golden Door: The Third World Comes to America* (rev. ed., 1992).

Al Santoli, *New Americans: An Oral History* (1988).

John E. Schwarz and Thomas J. Volgy, *The Forgotten Americans* (1993).

Randy Shilts, *And the Band Played On: Politics, People, and the AIDS Epidemic* (1987).

David E. Simcox, *U.S. Immigration in the 1980s* (1988).

Peter Skerry, *Mexican Americans: The Ambivalent Minority* (1993).

Adam Smith, *The Roaring '80s* (1988).

Ronald Takaki, *Strangers from a Different Shore: A History of Asian Americans* (1989).

Sanford J. Ungar, *Fresh Blood: The New American Immigrants* (1995).

William Wei, *The Asian American Movement* (1993).

THE BUSH ADMINISTRATION

Ryan J. Barilleaux and Mary E. Stuckey, *Leadership and the Bush Presidency: Prudence or Drift in an Era of Change?* (1992).

Colin Campbell and Bert Rockman, *The Bush Presidency: First Appraisals* (1991).

Michael Duffy and Dan Goodgame, *Marching in Place: The Status Quo Presidency of George Bush* (1992).

David Mervin, *George Bush and the Guardianship Presidency* (1996).

**STATUE OF PRESIDENT
AS SAXOPHONIST**

*At a low point in his 1992 presidential
campaign, Bill Clinton went on the Arsenio
Hall television talk show, donned sunglasses, and
played the saxophone, prompting the African American
host to comment, "I'm glad to see a Democrat blow something besides an election." Clinton's
appearance on Arsenio Hall's show as well as on the cable Music Television channel, were efforts to appeal to younger voters. The instrument became Clinton's symbol, and after his victory saxophone pins were the hottest selling inaugural items. Bill Potts of Denver, Colorado
made this carving and presented it to the president in 1993.*

National Archives.

THE CLINTON ADMINISTRATION AND THE SEARCH FOR A POPULAR CENTER

32

1992–1997

I N 1992, THE DEMOCRATIC PARTY concluded its nominating convention as it had in years past, with the candidates, their families, and supporters celebrating on a massive podium above the cheering delegates. This year, however, the candidates represented something new. William Jefferson "Bill" Clinton and Albert Gore were both in their mid-forties, the first baby boomers to run on a major party ticket, the first candidates not to have experienced World War II. And the music, too, symbolized a new era. Instead of the traditional "Happy Days Are Here Again," the Democratic theme song since the 1930s, the band blared Fleetwood Mac's rock music. "Don't stop thinking about tomorrow," the lyrics sang. "Yesterday's gone."

Clinton and Gore symbolized the change that most voters seemed to want. "I was ready for a change," explained a Michigan grade school teacher who voted for Clinton that November. "I'm eager to see a fresh young face, and I'm eager to see new ideas. . . . What have we got to lose?" On the eve of Clinton's inauguration in January 1993, three of every four Americans responding to a poll expressed the need for "major changes in the way the federal government works."

Whether the new Clinton administration could deliver on its promise of change was another matter. "I think he promised a lot, and he may have promised too much," said a twenty-five-year-old voter just before Clinton's inauguration. Clinton voters had great expectations of the new administration but no consensus about what kinds of changes should occur. Some Americans worried about the growing federal debt, but most opposed higher taxes and did not want to give up the government benefits they enjoyed. As businesses tried to trim budgets and become more competitive, victims of corporate downsizing worried about finding new jobs while others were anxious about keeping theirs. Access to good health care and reducing crime constituted other major concerns, but seriously attacking those problems depended on more federal spending or more federal intrusion than most Americans seemed willing to accept.

The Clinton administration sought to reverse the disdain for government that Ronald Reagan had so successfully cultivated. Clinton wanted to restore confidence in government as a positive force for good. But he also inherited a national debt that had grown from less than $1 trillion in 1981 to $4.4 trillion in 1993—and the interest on that debt consumed one-fifth of the federal budget. Just as Clinton was

CLINTON THE CAMPAIGNER
Bill Clinton loved campaigning and was remarkably good at creating a rapport with audiences.
Here he dives into the crowd at Jackson, Mississippi as his presidential campaign entered the
homestretch in October 1992.
Ira Wyman/Sygma.

short on cash for using government in positive ways, he was also short on political capital. During his first two years in office, he had a slim Democratic majority in Congress, but thereafter he faced a legislature controlled by Republicans.

The end of the cold war also made governing more difficult. For decades the United States–Soviet rivalry had helped to unify the nation with a clear enemy against which Americans could rally. The cold war had given Americans a sense of national purpose and had encouraged domestic reform to strengthen the nation at home in order to combat communism abroad. Moreover, for better or worse, the cold war had provided a rationale by which officials made decisions about the international role of the nation. After the cold war no clear standards emerged to determine where and under what conditions the United States should act beyond its borders.

Clinton's personal qualities also complicated his presidency. Very smart, dedicated, and extraordinarily hardworking, Clinton suffered, particularly in his first years in office, from disorganization, failure to focus, overextending himself and his agenda, and indecisiveness. Moreover, his administration was distracted by a number of allegations

and scandals involving himself, his wife, and close aides. These problems and the president's inability to deliver on many of his promises helped the Republicans capture both the House and the Senate in 1994, the first time they had done so since the 1950s. Running against a weak candidate in 1996, Clinton hung on to the presidency, but voters evinced a lack of trust in either party, when they elected a Republican Congress.

A Mandate for Change: The 1992 Election

In March 1991, President Bush's chances for reelection in 1992 looked golden. Successful completion of the Gulf War sent his approval rating up to 88 percent, causing the most prominent Democrats to opt out of the presidential race. That, however, did not deter Bill Clinton, who at age forty-five had served as governor of Arkansas for twelve years. Clinton's childhood was far from the American dream: His father was killed in an auto accident before he was born, and his stepfather was an alco-

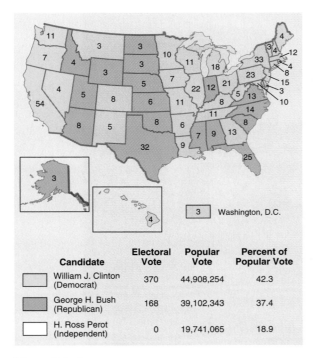

Candidate	Electoral Vote	Popular Vote	Percent of Popular Vote
William J. Clinton (Democrat)	370	44,908,254	42.3
George H. Bush (Republican)	168	39,102,343	37.4
H. Ross Perot (Independent)	0	19,741,065	18.9

MAP 32.1
The Election of 1992

holic. But Clinton's mother, who worked as a nurse most of her life, had endless faith in her son and nourished his political ambitions.

Clinton had attended Georgetown University and had won a prestigious Rhodes scholarship to Oxford University in England. He earned his law degree from Yale University, where he met his wife, Hillary Rodham, whose intelligence and ambition equaled his. While Clinton was governor of Arkansas, she pursued her own career in a prominent Little Rock law firm and at the same time served as one of her husband's most important advisers. The extent of her participation in her husband's career drew heavy criticism and was reflected in the derisive name Clinton-haters gave to the couple—"Billary."

Rejecting the traditional pattern of ticket balancing, Clinton chose Senator Albert Gore Jr. for his running mate. At forty-four, even younger than Clinton, Gore too hailed from the South. The son of a prominent U.S. senator, Gore had represented Tennessee in the House and Senate for a total of sixteen years. The youthfulness of the Democratic ticket reinforced Clinton's campaign theme of change.

Like Jimmy Carter in 1976 and Michael Dukakis in 1988, Clinton and Gore presented themselves as

"new Democrats." Both belonged to the Democratic Leadership Council, which Clinton had helped found in 1985 to rid the party of its liberal image. Clinton deliberately distanced himself from Jesse Jackson and his Rainbow Coalition and appealed to voters who believed that some Americans were getting a free ride at their expense. "We're going to put an end to welfare as we know it," Clinton claimed. Disavowing the "tax and spend" label that Republicans pinned on his party, Clinton promised a tax cut for the middle class.

Yet Clinton also advocated an active, positive role for the federal government, urging voters to put a Democrat in the White House to break the legislative-executive gridlock that had thwarted efforts to promote economic growth and deal with health care, crime, and other problems. Portraying President Bush as a do-nothing official even while unemployment neared 8 percent, Clinton promised to reinvigorate government and the economy.

The popularity of a third candidate revealed Americans' frustrations with government and thirst for change. In announcing his candidacy for president on a popular talk show, self-made Texas billionaire H. Ross Perot set the tone of his entire unconventional campaign. He used television extensively but gave no press conferences; he dropped out of the campaign in July, then dropped back in again in October; he chose an inexperienced running mate; and his promises were short on detail. But he had plenty of money and managed to attract a sizable grassroots movement with his down-to-earth personality and appeals to voters' disgust with Washington politics and politicians. Perot's candidacy hurt Bush more than it hurt Clinton, and it established the federal budget deficit as a key campaign issue.

In casting two-thirds of their votes for Clinton or Perot, voters in the 1992 election demonstrated a clear mandate for change but formed no majority around a particular direction that change should take.

The Bush campaign capitalized on revelations about Clinton's past and private life. Clinton had opposed the war in Vietnam and pulled strings to avoid being drafted; he confessed to having smoked marijuana; and, faced with allegations of extramarital affairs, he admitted "troubled" times in his marriage. Attempting to focus the election on personal

WOMEN SENATORS
The elections of 1996 sent nine women to the Senate, the greatest number in U.S. history. As the
105th Congress opened in January 1997, eight of them met to celebrate and to discuss opportuni-
ties to cooperate across party lines. Democrat Barbara Mikulski of Maryland, sixth from left, had
served in Congress for twenty years; and Democrat Carol Moseley-Braun of Illinois was the first
African American woman to serve in the U.S. Senate.
Joe Marquette/Wide World.

qualities rather than issues, Bush asked voters to choose experience, integrity, and character. But he failed to distract voters from their primary concerns —the economy and jobs, health care, and the deficit.

Americans reversed the thirty-year decline in voter turnout as 55 percent of those eligible went to the polls. They gave Clinton 43 percent of their votes, Bush 38 percent, and Perot 19 percent—the strongest third-party finish since Theodore Roosevelt's Progressive Party candidacy in 1912. In casting two-thirds of their votes for Clinton or Perot, voters demonstrated a clear mandate for change but formed no majority around a particular direction that change should take.

The Democrats barely maintained their majority in Congress, but the presence of women and minorities jumped significantly. Four Democratic women's victories in Senate races raised the female presence to six, while in the House the number of

seats held by women increased from twenty-eight to forty-seven. African Americans gained twelve seats in the House, bringing their total to thirty-eight, while the number of Hispanic representatives increased from ten to seventeen. Although the numbers did not jump so dramatically, the diversification of Congress continued through the 1990s.

Domestic Change and the Politics of Incrementalism

Clinton ran as a moderate, but he came to the White House with ambitious plans to spur economic growth, reform the health care system, improve public education, reduce taxes on the middle class, and more. Although he made good on many of his promises, the changes effected during his administration tended to be incremental rather than sweeping. Halfway through his first term, Clinton remarked, "Most everybody is for change in general and then against it in particular." Limiting what he accomplished were the budget deficit, Republican strength in Congress, lack of consensus among Democrats, and Clinton's desire to avoid the label of "liberal." Especially after the Republican victory in the 1994 congressional elections, Clinton forswore significant reforms in order to present himself as a centrist.

Right after the 1992 election, president-elect Clinton began to put together a cabinet "that looked like America." In keeping with his promise, he selected the most diverse group of department heads ever assembled.

After the election, president-elect Clinton began to put together a cabinet "that looked like America." In keeping with his promise, he selected the most diverse group of department heads ever assembled. Of twenty-three key appointments, six were women, three African Americans, and two Latinos. Janet Reno became the first female attorney general, and in his second term in office Clinton appointed the first female secretary of state, Madeleine K. Albright.

Clinton's judicial appointments had a similar cast. Of his first 129 appointments to federal courts, nearly one-third were women, 31 were black, and 11 were Hispanic. In June 1993, he appointed the second woman to the Supreme Court, Ruth Bader Ginsburg. Unlike the woman she joined, Reagan appointee Sandra Day O'Connor, Ginsburg was a self-identified feminist who had planned legal strategy and won key women's rights rulings from the Supreme Court before President Carter made her a federal appeals court judge in 1980.

Upon taking office in 1993, Clinton quickly used his executive powers to reverse policies of Presidents Reagan and Bush. He issued a series of executive orders easing restrictions on abortion counseling, allowing U.S. military hospitals abroad to perform privately funded abortions, and paving the way for importation of the French abortion pill, RU-486. But he failed to implement his campaign promise for an executive order to lift the ban on homosexuals in the military. Vehement opposition to allowing gays and lesbians openly to serve in the military from military leaders, enlisted men, and key legislators forced Clinton to back away from his promise. In June 1993, Clinton announced a compromise, called the "don't ask, don't tell" policy. It forbade officials from asking military personnel about their sexuality, but those who said they were gay or engaged in homosexual behavior could be dismissed.

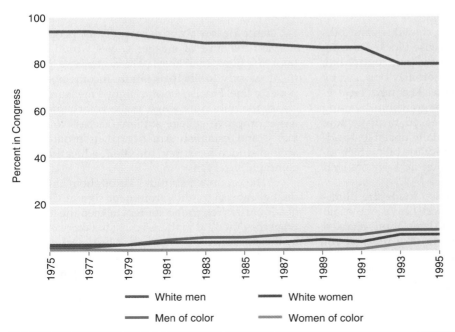

FIGURE 32.1
Towards a More Diverse Congress
In the last quarter of the twentieth century, women and minorities began to make their presence felt in the 535-member national legislature. White men continued to hold an overwhelming majority in Congress, but now some one hundred legislators were either white women or members of a minority group. Of the 57 women serving in the 105th Congress (1997–1998), more than one-fourth were women of color, including 12 African Americans, 3 Latinas, and an Asian American.

GAYS IN THE MILITARY

When Chairman of the Joint Chiefs of Staff Colin Powell spoke at Harvard University's commencement in June 1993, gay rights advocates protested the government's ban on homosexuals in the military. Many found it ironic that Powell, an African American, did not support President Clinton's effort to end discrimination against gay men and lesbians in military service.
Wide World.

More successfully, Clinton signed several bills that had been vetoed or otherwise blocked during the past twelve years. One was a gun control bill, first introduced in 1987 but vigorously opposed by the National Rifle Association. The new law required gun purchasers to undergo a short waiting period while records were checked to make sure they were not criminals or mentally unstable. In addition Clinton won a huge anticrime bill, which allocated $30 billion to prevention and prisons and banned assault weapons.

A Democratic president also made the difference for the Family and Medical Leave Act, a bill that Bush had vetoed. That legislation enabled workers in larger companies to take time off for childbirth, adoption, caring for aging parents, or medical emergencies affecting family members. To fulfill his campaign promise that no full-time worker should live in poverty, Clinton pushed through a substantial increase in the earned income

tax credit for low wage earners. Thus, people who worked full time at meager wages would receive tax reductions or, if they paid no taxes, a government subsidy to lift their family income above the poverty line. Finally, Clinton signed measures to increase the minimum wage, make voter registration easier, improve college students' access to federal loans, and establish Americorps, a program enabling students to pay for their education with community service.

"The economy, stupid." Throughout the presidential campaign, this prominent sign at Clinton's headquarters reminded staffers to keep the focus on what they thought mattered most to voters. Already by the election, the economy had begun to grow out of recession, but Clinton was as concerned with long-term growth as with short-term recovery. His economic program rested on the assumption that Americans could enjoy a higher standard of living only with substantial gains in productivity. Increasing an average of 2.9 percent a year during the 1950s and 1960s, rising productivity underwrote the tremendous material gains Americans had enjoyed in that era, but since 1974 productivity growth slumped to only about 1 percent a year. Clinton sought to boost output with greater public and private investment. He wanted government to invest more heavily in "infrastructure"—roads, harbors, communications systems, and the like—and in people, through education and training. And he wanted tax incentives to encourage private investment in new technology and equipment.

Clinton's investment program fell victim to the huge federal deficit, which Perot had spotlighted in his campaign and which gave legislators an excuse for rejecting new federal spending. Upon finding the projected deficit even larger than anticipated, Clinton abandoned his middle-class tax cut. Both Republicans and Democrats wanted to reduce the deficit, but Republicans wanted deeper cuts, their determination symbolized by a Republican member of the House Appropriations Committee who brought a machete and two knives to the first committee meeting of 1995.

Clinton and Congress battled so fiercely over budget bills that the Republicans shut down government twice near the end of 1995; but they did make a dent in the deficit. Between 1992 and 1996, the combination of budget cuts, tax increases that fell primarily on the wealthy, declining unemploy-

ment, and economic expansion reduced the deficit by about half. The government still operated at an annual deficit of about $150 billion; the national debt continued to rise, although more slowly; and no solution appeared to a fiscal crisis predicted for around 2010, when the baby boomers would begin to turn sixty-five and claim Social Security payments and Medicare. Nonetheless, the seemingly inexorable trend of increasing government debt had turned around.

In contrast, Clinton stumbled badly over health care reform. His plan had two key objectives: to help the 39 million Americans who lacked health insurance by providing universal coverage and to curb the steeply rising costs of medical care—an objective necessary for continued progress on deficit reduction. The goals in themselves stirred little opposition, but how to implement them stirred much.

The administration dealt its own blows to health care reform by presenting an extraordinarily complex bill that raised the specter of higher taxes and government interference in health care decisions. Elements of the health care industry ran TV ads encouraging such fears, and partisan Republicans ferociously attacked the Clinton plan. Concerns about cost and government interference also found expression among Democrats, whose disagreements among themselves helped to derail health reform. Yet, although comprehensive reform failed, private industry made significant progress in

"DILBERT" AND DOWNSIZING
This 1992 cartoon captures a prevalent feature of the economy of the 1990s, as corporations fired employees, or downsized, in order to reduce costs and become more competitive. Abandoning his own middle-management job to earn a fortune as a cartoonist, Scott Adams created the enormously popular strip "Dilbert" exposing idiocies in the workplace by poking fun at bosses, management fads, and other aspects of the business world.
Reprinted by permission of United Feature Syndicate.

**THE FIGHT OVER
HEALTH CARE REFORM**
*Featured in a series of TV com-
mercials, the middle-class couple
"Harry and Louise" criticize
President Clinton's health-care
plan. The Health Insurance
Association of America paid
$10 million for the ads, which
helped to defeat the bill and
cause the biggest failure of
Clinton's first term.*
Goddard-Clausen/First Tuesday.

curtailing costs, at patients' expense, some argued.
And Congress enacted incremental reform by making it easier for workers who changed jobs to retain
health insurance.

The 1996 Election and the Battle for Center Ground

When voters swept away the Democratic majorities
in both houses of Congress in 1994, Republicans assumed that control of the White House would follow in 1996. Democrats took the heat for voters' disgust with congressional infighting and stonewalling
and their disillusionment with the president. Clinton had delivered on some of his promises—an expanding economy, progress on deficit reduction, an
attack on crime—but had failed to achieve health
care reform, welfare reform, and a middle-class tax
cut. Moreover, scandals surrounding the Clintons'
financial dealings in Arkansas and charges of sexual harassment against the president while he was
governor shook the administration, contributing to
the image of a president with character and leadership defects.

Led by Representative Newt Gingrich of Georgia, Republicans considered the 1994 elections a
mandate for their "contract with America," a conservative platform that included drastic contraction
of the federal government, deep tax cuts, constitutional amendments to ban abortions and to require
a balanced federal budget, and term limits on members of Congress. Although Gingrich succeeded in
moving the debate to the right, Clinton vetoes and
opposition from Democrats and more moderate Republicans stymied most of the contract pledges.

A more extreme antigovernment movement operated far from Washington, in grassroots armed
militias claiming patriotism and the need to defend
themselves from government tyranny. Anticipating
government repression, they stockpiled, in the
words of one militia leader, "the four Bs: Bibles, bullets, beans, and bandages." The militias embraced
a wide variety of sentiments, including opposition
to taxes and the United Nations, anti-Semitism, and
white supremacy. Recruitment for militias rose after
gun control legislation passed and after government
agents stormed the headquarters of an armed religious cult in Waco, Texas, resulting in more than
eighty deaths. On the second anniversary of that
event, April 19, 1995, a bomb leveled a federal build-

ing in Oklahoma City, taking 169 lives—including 19 children—and constituting the worst terrorist attack in the nation's history. Authorities arrested two militia members as prime suspects.

Clinton's reassuring handling of the Oklahoma City bombing helped restore his presidential stature. In addition, he began, on the one hand, to stand up to the Republican Congress and, on the other, to compromise on certain measures. Looking toward the 1996 election, Clinton used his veto power and threats of vetoes against what he labeled "extreme" Republican measures. As he forced the shaping of legislation along more moderate lines, he himself moved toward the center and approved it. For example, he stood firm against deep Republican cuts in education, environment, and welfare programs, but he cooperated with Republicans to fashion a plan that would balance the budget in seven years.

Clinton's determination to cast himself as a centrist was nowhere more apparent than in his han-

dling of welfare reform. Since Lyndon Johnson's war on poverty in the 1960s, public sentiment had shifted. Instead of viewing poverty as the result of a shortage of adequate jobs and child care, poor education, and other circumstances beyond an individual's control, more people were inclined to blame the poor themselves and the government welfare program, Aid to Families with Dependent Children (AFDC), that, it was argued, kept poor people in cycles of dependency. Nearly everyone considered work better than welfare but disagreed about whether the nation's economy could provide sufficient jobs and how much government assistance poor people needed in the transition from work to welfare. Most estimates showed that it was cheaper to support a family on welfare than to provide the job training, child care, and other supports necessary for that transition.

Clinton allowed the Republicans to take the initiative in welfare reform. He vetoed two measures,

ARMING AGAINST THE GOVERNMENT
Organizing against what they called government tyranny, paramilitary groups, or militias, arose in more than twenty states in the 1990s. These groups stockpiled weapons and prepared to defend themselves against government efforts to take away their guns or otherwise encroach on what they considered their rights. Pictured here are members of the Michigan Militia at a training session in Wolverine, Michigan in 1995.
Valica Boudryl/*Detroit Free Press*/Corbis-Bettmann.

and then, having forced a less punitive bill, he signed the third as the 1996 election approached. The Personal Responsibility and Work Opportunity Reconciliation Act represented a dramatic reversal of social policy that had provided a safety net since the 1930s. It abolished AFDC and with it society's pledge to provide a minimum level of subsistence for all its children. In place of AFDC, the law established a system of grants to the states, with the requirement that most recipients be cut off welfare in two years whether they could find a job or not. The law set a lifetime limit of aid at five years; barred legal immigrants who had not become citizens from food stamps and supplemental security income for the elderly and disabled; and gave states the authority to stop Medicaid to legal immigrants.

A "moment of shame," cried Marian White Edelman, president of the Children's Defense Fund, when Clinton signed the bill. Liberal Senator Paul Simon called the measure "welfare denial," not welfare reform. State and local officials across the country scrambled to understand the law and then to figure out how to implement it while sustaining the most disadvantaged part of the population. "We certainly endorse the overall direction toward work," a Minnesota official said, while expressing grave concern about how the particular law would operate. "A child could very well have to go to foster care," predicted a social worker in Louisiana.

Clinton claimed that the new law meant that "welfare will no longer be a political issue," and his signature on it meant that the Republicans could not use the welfare issue against him in the 1996 election campaign. In an election distinguished by the electorate's lack of interest, the president ran as a moderate who would save the country from extremist Republicans.

In an election distinguished by the electorate's lack of interest, Clinton ran in 1996 as a moderate who would save the country from extremist Republicans.

In fact, the Republican Party also moved to the center, passing over a field of conservatives to nominate Kansan Robert Dole, former Senate majority leader who had served in Washington for more than two decades. The last candidate of the World War II generation and admired for his struggle to overcome grievous war wounds, the seventy-two-year-

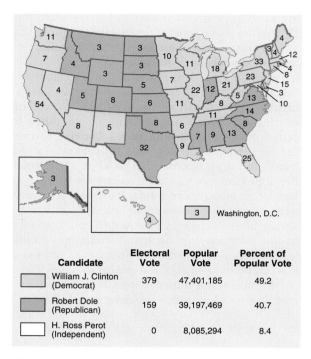

MAP 32.2
The Election of 1996

old Dole had spent most of his political life brokering compromises and was unable to articulate his own vision of what his presidency would bring.

Whether out of satisfaction with a favorable economy or out of boredom with the candidates, about half of all voters stayed home. Fifty percent of those who voted chose Clinton, while 41 percent favored Dole, and 9 percent Perot. The largest gender gap to date appeared in the election: Women awarded 54 percent of their votes to Clinton and 38 percent to Dole, while men split their votes between Dole and Clinton nearly evenly. Although Clinton won reelection with room to spare, voters sent a Republican majority back to Congress.

Creating Foreign Policy in a Post-Cold War World

With the cold war no longer monopolizing the foreign-policy agenda, global economic issues assumed a much larger place. Clinton built on progress made in the Reagan and Bush administrations and won bipartisan support for easing restrictions on international trade. In November 1993, Congress approved the North American Free Trade Agreement (NAFTA), a pact eliminating all tariffs and trade barriers among the United States, Canada, and Mexico. NAFTA ran into stiff opposition from organized labor and other groups—including Perot and his supporters—that feared loss of jobs and industries to Mexico where wages were substantially lower. Proponents argued that the United States would benefit from greater export opportunities, creation of more jobs in the long run, and the global clout the three trading partners would enjoy. With 360 million people and a $6 billion economy, the NAFTA trio constituted the largest trading bloc in the world.

A year later, the Senate took another step toward the elimination of trade barriers by ratifying the General Agreement on Tariffs and Trade (GATT), a treaty involving more than one hundred nations. GATT established a World Trade Organization to enforce provisions of the treaty, which included substantial tariff reductions and elimination of quotas on imports. Unlike NAFTA, GATT did not come close to achieving free trade, but the debates were similar in reflecting two visions of America's place in the world economy. Opponents of the agreements tied the nation's economic health to nurturing its established industries, keeping its traditional jobs at home, and maintaining labor and environmental standards. Those who ultimately prevailed envisioned American prosperity flowing from the greater export opportunities that would come with freer trade.

Clinton also inherited from the Bush administration the task of defining a clear and consistent role for the nation in a post-cold war world. Bush had acted decisively when Iraq invaded Kuwait in 1990, threatening the world's oil supply, and he rallied the nation behind him. But while the oil reserves in the Middle East made stability in that region of great concern to the United States, crises elsewhere in the world seemed less directly related to American self-interest. Both the Bush and Clinton administrations wrestled with decisions about whether and where to deploy American power in the world of some 190 nations.

In the case of the small African country of Somalia, where a famine was exacerbated by warring factions who disrupted the food supply, President Bush bowed to humanitarian pressures in December 1992 and dispatched U.S. troops to join a United Nations operation there. But in the summer of 1993,

Clinton allowed the humanitarian mission to turn into "nation building," an effort to restore national stability. Eighteen U.S. soldiers were killed, and an outcry at home suggested that most Americans were not prepared to sacrifice lives when they perceived no vital interests at stake.

As a consequence, the Clinton administration moved slowly in deciding to risk U.S. troops in Haiti, where the United States had maintained a military presence from 1915 to 1934. After American withdrawal, Haitians suffered under harsh dictatorships until December 1990, when the Reverend Jean-Bertrand Aristide won the Haitian presidency in the country's first free election. Nine months later, a military coup led by General Raoul Cedras overthrew the government.

The United States joined a United Nations embargo of oil and arms to Haiti, but Cedras maintained an iron grip, presiding over the killing of more than three thousand Haitians. Thousands of Haitians tried to escape the poverty and violence of the military dictatorship, many of them building flimsy boats and heading for Florida. With anti-immigrant sentiment already high in Florida and in the country as a whole, Clinton was pressed hard to stop the refugee flow. At the same time, the Black Congressional Caucus and others insisted that the nation had a moral responsibility to end the suffering and restore democracy in Haiti.

After winning UN authorization for the use of force, in September 1994 Clinton announced the dispatch of twenty thousand troops but also sent a last-minute mission to negotiate with Cedras. Hours before the U.S. invasion was to begin, the team led by former President Jimmy Carter reached an agreement under which the military leaders promised to step down. Consequently, when U.S. forces began landing on September 19 and then disarming Haitian troops, they did so peacefully and with tremendous gratitude from the Haitian people. Cedras resigned on October 10, and President Aristide returned to cheering crowds on October 15. Initially a huge success, U.S. Haitian policy would continue to be tested until the Aristide government met the grave challenges of economic and political reconstruction.

The situation in Yugoslavia appeared even more risky to officials in both the Bush and Clinton administrations. During the cold war, the Communist government in Yugoslavia had held ethnic tensions in check. But after the Communists were swept out, Yugoslavia disintegrated into the three

Still a Promised Land?

"THE UNITED STATES IS OUR LAND. . . . We intend to maintain it so. The day of unalloyed welcome to all peoples, the day of indiscriminate acceptance of all races, has definitely ended." So spoke Washington Senator Albert Johnson in 1924, just after Congress severely limited immigration with passage of the National Origins Act, which Johnson had sponsored. Thereafter immigration, which had forcefully shaped American society since its beginning, ebbed for several decades as the restrictive law combined with the Great Depression and World War II to discourage potential newcomers. In fact, during the worst years of the depression, more people left than migrated to the United States. Yet the immigration question had not been settled once and for all. By the 1980s, large numbers of immigrants once more entered the United States, reigniting old debates about whether Americans should share their political freedoms and economic opportunities with people from other lands.

What reopened the door to immigration after World War II? Economic considerations always loomed large in prompting migration to the United States and in determining how welcome immigrants would be: The twenty-five-year economic boom that followed World War II exerted a positive force on both ends. In fact, until 1964 the U.S. government actively encouraged the temporary migration of Mexicans by continuing the so-called *bracero* program that was begun during World War II to fill a shortage of agricultural workers. Hundreds of thousands of Mexicans established social networks in the United States and grew accustomed to crossing the border for jobs, even when the jobs were backbreaking and low-paying by U.S. standards. When the *bracero* program ended, many Mexicans continued to come north for work whether they could obtain legal authorization or not.

In addition to a prosperous economy, the United States also manifested a growing tolerance toward people of different races and ethnic groups in the decades following World War II. Like the key civil rights laws passed around the same time, the Immigration Act of 1965 reflected a more broad-minded climate of opinion based on the belief that people should be treated as human beings rather than as members of a particular group. The new immigration law ended the national quotas that were so insulting to non-Western European groups. It made possible a tremendous rise in the volume of immigration and facilitated a huge increase in newcomers from Asia and Latin America.

The new immigration law set an annual ceiling of 270,000, but the actual volume was much higher. Besides those who came illegally, hundreds of thousands of people fell into special categories that gained them legal admission above and beyond the ceiling. In 1986, for example, the United States admitted 335,000 immigrants over and above those entering under the ceiling: About two-thirds of these were children, spouses, or parents of U.S. citizens, and the rest were refugees and asylum seekers. Migration chains were thus established by which, once newcomers became citizens, their sisters, brothers, and adult children received special preference, while even closer relatives gained entry without regard to the limit.

The new waves of immigration also grew directly from U.S. foreign policy after World War II. The cold war spread U.S. military and other personnel throughout the world, enabling foreigners to learn about the United States and make personal contacts with Americans. Once the cold war identified communism as an unmitigated evil, the United States could hardly refuse asylum to its enemy's victims. In the twenty-five years following Fidel Castro's revolution, for example, more than 800,000 Cubans fled to the United States. The Vietnam War and its aftermath brought more than 600,000 Vietnamese, Laotians, and Cambodians to the United States in the decade following 1974.

Not all refugees entered the United States so easily, for American refugee policy bore a distinct anti-Communist bias. Haitians, Salvadorans, and others fleeing right-wing dictatorships were frequently turned back or, having reached the United States, were denied asylum and deported. "Why let Poles stay but not Salvadorans?" demanded one advocate for these refugees, pointing out the more favorable treatment given to immigrants from Communist countries.

Even though U.S. policy failed to accommodate all who wanted to immigrate, by the 1980s immigration was once more a major force in American society. During that decade the six million legal and an estimated two million undocumented immigrants

CUBAN REFUGEES
These Cubans are being towed by the U.S. Coast Guard into port at Miami, Florida. Their desire for the expected economic opportunity and political freedom of the United States is evinced in their willingness to flee Cuba on a crowded, makeshift vessel. Some "boat people" drowned in these risky ventures.
John Kral/*Miami Herald.*

accounted for more than one-third of total population growth. Seventy-five percent of the immigrants settled in just seven states, with California, New York, Texas, and Florida receiving the most. After the 1990 census, California won five additional seats in the House of Representatives solely on the basis of immigrant additions to the population. A 1983 *Time* magazine article called Los Angeles "the new Ellis Island" because of its large Asian and Hispanic populations. A decade later, one-third of Los Angeles area residents were foreign-born.

The higher volume of immigration, its third world sources, and the economy's recession combined to increase nativist sentiment in the 1980s. Increasingly, Americans saw immigrants as taking jobs from the native-born and acting as a drain on schools, health care, police, and other services. In the 1990s, anti-immigrant sentiment grew especially strong in California, then reeling from an economic slump owing to the downsizing of defense produc-

tion. That state took in more than one-third of the nation's immigrants in the 1980s and an estimated one-half of the undocumented ones.

Like people in the rest of the nation, Californians focused hostility on immigrants who entered without legal documentation, a phenomenon that the 1986 law penalizing employers of such people had not significantly curtailed. Some states, including California, Florida, and New Jersey, filed lawsuits charging the federal government with failure to stop the flow of illegal immigration and suing for the costs it added to state budgets.

Economic and political crises elsewhere and the continuing appeal of the U.S. meant that high levels of immigration—legal and illegal—persisted into the 1990s, as did the debate about how open U.S. policy should be. Even as anti-immigrant sentiment increased, however, the United States remained—as sociologist Nathan Glazer put it—a "permanently unfinished country."

THE FIRST WOMAN SECRETARY OF STATE
Madeleine K. Albright is sworn in as Secretary of State by Vice President Albert Gore, as her
three daughters and President Bill Clinton look on. Formerly a professor of international affairs
at Georgetown University, Albright served in the first Clinton cabinet as U.S. representative to
the United Nations.
Greg Gibson/Wide World.

states of Serbia, Croatia, and Bosnia and then fell into a brutal civil war. The Serbs' ruthless aggression against the Bosnian Muslims horrified much of the world, and people remembered how an event in Sarajevo had sparked World War I. For several years, the United States joined with its European allies in NATO and the United Nations in peace efforts, but both the United States and the European nations studiously avoided direct intervention.

As the terror, rape, and torture in Bosnia worsened, American leaders worried about the image of the most powerful nation unwilling to use its power to stop the violence. In November 1995, the United States brought the leaders of Serbia, Croatia, and Bosnia to Dayton, Ohio, where they hammered out a peace treaty. President Clinton then agreed to send twenty thousand American troops to Bosnia as part

of a NATO peacekeeping mission. The peace held through 1996, but Anthony Lake, the president's national security adviser, said, "We won't know for some years" whether the mission would succeed.

Promoting stability in the Middle East continued to be a goal of American foreign policy. Although the Clinton administration played a far less critical role than President Jimmy Carter had in the Egypt-Israel accord of 1979, U.S. officials encouraged negotiations that led to two dramatic breakthroughs. In September 1993, with President Clinton presiding over a ceremony on the White House lawn, Yasir Arafat, head of the Palestine Liberation Organization, and Yitzhak Rabin, Israeli prime minister, took a momentous step toward peace in the Middle East. They signed a declaration recognizing each other's existence for the first time and providing for Israeli withdrawal and self-government for Palestinians in the Gaza Strip and Jericho. Less than a year later, in July 1994, Clinton presided over another turning point as King Hussein of Jordan and Prime Minister Rabin of Israel signed a declaration of peace. Progress toward peace, however, suffered a severe setback when a right-wing Israeli murdered Rabin in November 1995, and a government came to power less trusting of Arab willingness to respect Israel's security.

"The post-cold war world is decidedly not postnuclear," said Clinton's first secretary of defense. Perhaps the biggest threat to American security lay in the proliferation of governments in possession of nuclear weapons.

"The post-cold war world is decidedly not postnuclear," said Clinton's first secretary of defense, Les Aspin. Perhaps the biggest threat to American security lay in the proliferation of governments in possession of nuclear weapons. The breakdown of the Soviet Union meant that four countries with nuclear weapons now stood in place of one—Russia, Ukraine, Belarus, and Kazakhstan—in addition to Britain, France, China, India, Israel, Pakistan, and possibly North Korea, still under a Communist dictatorship. Yet in 1996, the world took a small step away from the nuclear brink when the leaders of the nuclear powers signed a comprehensive test ban treaty at United Nations headquarters. Using the same pen with which John F. Kennedy had signed the limited test ban treaty in 1963, Clinton insisted, "Our children deserve to walk the earth in safety." He pledged continuing support for the UN "because our world is more interdependent than ever before."

Conclusion: Approaching the Twenty-First Century

With the largest economy in the world, the United States remained deeply embedded in the global economy as products and people crossed international borders with ever greater frequency. U.S. of-

ficials monitored developments across the globe and tried through diplomacy to promote order and democracy, expand economic opportunities for American business, reduce population growth, and curtail environmental destruction. But, in contrast to their counterparts at the end of the nineteenth century, Americans displayed little taste for foreign adventures as the twentieth century drew to a close. Nor did a majority want to see their tax dollars used for international purposes.

Instead, most Americans saw the main challenge as coming from within, and that challenge involved issues of economic justice, violence, and diversity that had engaged the nation for much of its history. A declining standard of living for a large portion of the middle class, a growing chasm between the educated and the unskilled, a rising income gap between the rich and the poor, and a poverty rate of 20 percent among children threatened the American promise of opportunity and security. Moreover, the persistent poverty in urban ghettos contributed to a stream of violence that undermined Americans' physical security. As the United States became even more heterogeneous, American identity and the extent to which the American promise should extend to diverse groups such as new immigrants, racial minorities, and homosexuals remained contested ground. (See Historical Question, page 1266.)

How to respond to the challenges of economic justice, physical security, and diversity often involved the question of the appropriate role of government. With a population derived to a great extent from people fleeing overweening governments, the United States had for more than two centuries experienced debates over what the government could or should do about the nation's aspirations and troubles and what was best left to private enterprise, churches, families, and other voluntary institutions. Far more than other democracies, the United States had taken the path of private rather than public obligation, individual rather than collective solutions. In the twentieth century especially, Americans had entrusted the federal government with significantly greater powers and responsibilities. But as the century wound down, the debate grew particularly intense again as Americans and their representatives struggled over both how to define and how to approach fulfillment of the American promise for the next century.

CHRONOLOGY

1992 Bill Clinton elected forty-second president of the United States.

1993 Janet Reno appointed first female attorney general in U.S. history.

Ruth Bader Ginsburg appointed second woman to U.S. Supreme Court.

Clinton announces "don't ask, don't tell" policy for gays in military.

Israeli Prime Minister Yitzhak Rabin and PLO leader Yasir Arafat sign peace accords.

Gun control and anticrime bills passed.

Eighteen U.S. soldiers killed on humanitarian mission in Somalia.

Congress approves North American Free Trade Agreement (NAFTA).

Clinton signs Family and Medical Leave Act, enabling many workers to take time off for childbirth, adoption, or family medical emergencies.

1994 U.S. troops oversee peaceful return of Haitian President Aristide to power.

Senate ratifies General Agreement on Tariffs and Trade (GATT).

Republicans recapture both House and Senate in congressional elections.

Representative Newt Gingrich declares 1994 elections a mandate for Republicans' conservative "contract with America."

1995 Bomb destroys federal building in Oklahoma City on April 19, claiming 169 lives; two militia members arrested as prime suspects.

U.S. leaders broker peace accords among Serbia, Croatia, and Bosnia in Dayton, Ohio, temporarily ending civil war in former Yugoslavia.

1996 Clinton signs Personal Responsibility and Work Opportunity Reconciliation Act, ending the federal welfare program begun in 1930s.

Clinton reelected president.

Leaders of nuclear powers sign comprehensive test ban treaty at United Nations.

BIBLIOGRAPHY

Dan Balz and Ronald Brownstein, *Storming the Gates: Protest Politics and the Republican Revival*, 1996.

Jennifer L. Hochschild, *Facing Up to the American Dream: Race, Class, and the Soul of the Nation*, 1995.

Haynes Johnson and David S. Broder, *The System: The American Way of Politics at the Breaking Point*, 1996.

Jacob S. Hacker, *The Road to Nowhere: The Genesis of President's Clinton's Plan for Health Security*, 1997.

David Maraniss, *First in His Class: A Biography of Bill Clinton*, 1995.

David Mixner, *Stranger among Friends*, 1996.

Roger Morris, *Partners in Power: The Clintons and Their America*, 1996.

Kevin Phillips, *Boiling Point: Democrats, Republicans and the Decline of Middle-Class Prosperity*, 1993.

Gerald Posner, *Citizen Perot: His Life and Times*, 1996.

Ralph Reed, *Active Faith: How Christians Are Changing the Soul of American Politics*, 1996.

Robert J. Samuelson, *The American Dream in the Age of Entitlement, 1945–1995*, 1996.

Martin Walker, *The President We Deserve: Bill Clinton, His Rise, Falls, and Comebacks*, 1996.

THE DECLARATION OF INDEPENDENCE

In Congress, July 4, 1776,

**THE UNANIMOUS DECLARATION OF THE
THIRTEEN UNITED STATES OF AMERICA**

When in the course of human events, it becomes necessary for one people to dissolve the political bands which have connected them with another, and to assume, among the powers of the earth, the separate and equal station to which the laws of nature and of nature's God entitle them, a decent respect to the opinions of mankind requires that they should declare the causes which impel them to the separation.

We hold these truths to be self-evident, that all men are created equal; that they are endowed by their Creator with certain unalienable rights; that among these, are life, liberty, and the pursuit of happiness. That, to secure these rights, governments are instituted among men, deriving their just powers from the consent of the governed; that, whenever any form of government becomes destructive of these ends, it is the right of the people to alter or to abolish it, and to institute a new government, laying its foundation on such principles, and organizing its powers in such form, as to them shall seem most likely to effect their safety and happiness. Prudence, indeed, will dictate that governments long established, should not be changed for light and transient causes; and, accordingly, all experience hath shown, that mankind are more disposed to suffer, while evils are sufferable, than to right themselves by abolishing the forms to which they are accustomed. But, when a long train of abuses and usurpations, pursuing invariably the same object, evinces a design to reduce them under absolute despotism, it is their right, it is their duty, to throw off such government and to provide new guards for their future security. Such has been the patient sufferance of these colonies, and such is now the necessity which constrains them to alter their former systems of government. The history of the present King of Great Britain is a history of repeated injuries and usurpations, all having, in direct object, the establishment of an absolute tyranny over these States. To prove this, let facts be submitted to a candid world:

He has refused his assent to laws the most wholesome and necessary for the public good.

He has forbidden his governors to pass laws of immediate and pressing importance, unless suspended in their operation till his assent should be obtained; and, when so suspended, he has utterly neglected to attend to them.

He has refused to pass other laws for the accommodation of large districts of people, unless those people would relinquish the right of representation in the legislature; a right inestimable to them, and formidable to tyrants only.

He has called together legislative bodies at places unusual, uncomfortable, and distant from the depository of their public records, for the sole purpose of fatiguing them into compliance with his measures.

He has dissolved representative houses repeatedly for opposing, with manly firmness, his invasions on the rights of the people.

He has refused, for a long time after such dissolutions, to cause others to be elected; whereby the legislative powers, incapable of annihilation, have returned to the people at large for their exercise; the state remaining in the mean-time exposed to all the danger of invasion from without, and convulsions within.

He has endeavoured to prevent the population of these States; for that purpose, obstructing the laws for naturalization of foreigners, refusing to pass others to encourage their migration hither, and raising the conditions of new appropriations of lands.

He has obstructed the administration of justice, by refusing his assent to laws for establishing judiciary powers.

He has made judges dependent on his will alone, for the tenure of their offices, and the amount and payment of their salaries.

He has erected a multitude of new offices, and sent hither swarms of officers to harass our people, and eat out their substance.

He has kept among us, in times of peace, standing armies, without the consent of our legislature.

He has affected to render the military independent of, and superior to, the civil power.

He has combined, with others, to subject us to a jurisdiction foreign to our Constitution, and unacknowledged by our laws; giving his assent to their acts of pretended legislation:

For quartering large bodies of armed troops among us:

For protecting them by a mock trial, from punishment, for any murders which they should commit on the inhabitants of these States:

For cutting off our trade with all parts of the world:

For imposing taxes on us without our consent:

For depriving us, in many cases, of the benefit of trial by jury:

For transporting us beyond seas to be tried for pretended offences:

For abolishing the free system of English laws in a neighboring province, establishing therein an arbitrary government, and enlarging its boundaries, so as to render it at once an example and fit instrument for introducing the same absolute rule into these colonies:

For taking away our charters, abolishing our most valuable laws, and altering, fundamentally, the powers of our governments:

For suspending our own legislatures, and declaring themselves invested with power to legislate for us in all cases whatsoever.

He has abdicated government here, by declaring us out of his protection, and waging war against us.

He has plundered our seas, ravaged our coasts, burnt our towns, and destroyed the lives of our people.

He is, at this time, transporting large armies of foreign mercenaries to complete the works of death, desolation, and tyranny, already begun, with circumstances of cruelty and perfidy scarcely paralleled in the most barbarous ages, and totally unworthy the head of a civilized nation.

He has constrained our fellow citizens, taken captive on the high seas, to bear arms against their country, to become the executioners of their friends, and brethren, or to fall themselves by their hands.

He has excited domestic insurrections amongst us, and has endeavored to bring on the inhabitants of our frontiers, the merciless Indian savages, whose known rule of warfare is an undistinguished destruction of all ages, sexes, and conditions.

In every stage of these oppressions, we have petitioned for redress; in the most humble terms; our repeated petitions have been answered only by repeated injury. A prince, whose character is thus marked by every act which may define a tyrant, is unfit to be the ruler of a free people.

Nor have we been wanting in attention to our British brethren. We have warned them, from time to time, of attempts made by their legislature to extend an unwarrantable jurisdiction over us. We have reminded them of the circumstances of our emigration and settlement here. We have appealed to their native justice and magnanimity, and we have conjured them, by the ties of our common kindred, to disavow these usurpations, which would inevitably interrupt our connections and correspondence. They, too, have been deaf to the voice of justice and consanguinity. We must, therefore, acquiesce in the necessity which denounces our separation, and hold them as we hold the rest of mankind, enemies in war, in peace, friends.

We, therefore, the representatives of the United States of America, in general Congress assembled, appealing to the Supreme Judge of the world for the rectitude of our intentions, do, in the name, and by authority of the good people of these colonies, solemnly publish and declare, that these united colonies are, and of right ought to be, free and independent states: that they are absolved from all allegiance to the British Crown, and that all political connection between them and the state of Great Britain is, and ought to be, totally dissolved; and that, as free and independent states, they have full power to levy war, conclude peace, contract alliances, establish commerce, and to do all other acts and things which independent states may of right do. And, for the support of this declaration, with a firm reliance on the protection of Divine Providence, we mutually pledge to each other our lives, our fortunes, and our sacred honor.

The foregoing Declaration was, by order of Congress, engrossed, and signed by the following members:

JOHN HANCOCK

New Hampshire
Josiah Bartlett
William Whipple
Matthew Thornton

New York
William Floyd
Phillip Livingston
Francis Lewis
Lewis Morris

Massachusetts Bay
Samuel Adams
John Adams
Robert Treat Paine
Elbridge Gerry

New Jersey
Richard Stockton
John Witherspoon
Francis Hopkinson
John Hart
Abraham Clark

Rhode Island
Stephen Hopkins
William Ellery

Connecticut
Roger Sherman
Samuel Huntington
William Williams
Oliver Wolcott

Delaware
Caesar Rodney
George Read
Thomas M'Kean

Pennsylvania
Robert Morris
Benjamin Rush
Benjamin Franklin
John Morton
George Clymer
James Smith
George Taylor
James Wilson
George Ross

North Carolina
William Hooper
Joseph Hewes
John Penn

Maryland
Samuel Chase
William Paca
Thomas Stone
Charles Carroll,
    of Carrollton

Virginia
George Wythe
Richard Henry Lee
Thomas Jefferson
Benjamin Harrison
Thomas Nelson, Jr.
Francis Lightfoot Lee
Carter Braxton

South Carolina
Edward Rutledge
Thomas Heyward, Jr.
Thomas Lynch, Jr.
Arthur Middleton

Georgia
Button Gwinnett
Lyman Hall
George Walton

Resolved, That copies of the Declaration be sent to the several assemblies, conventions, and committees, or councils of safety, and to the several commanding officers of the continental troops; that it be proclaimed in each of the United States, at the head of the army.

THE CONSTITUTION OF THE UNITED STATES*

Preamble

We the people of the United States, in order to form a more perfect union, establish justice, insure domestic tranquility, provide for the common defense, promote the general welfare, and secure the blessings of liberty to ourselves and our posterity, do ordain and establish this Constitution for the United States of America.

Article I

Section 1   All legislative powers herein granted shall be vested in a Congress of the United States, which shall consist of a Senate and a House of Representatives.

Section 2   The House of Representatives shall be composed of members chosen every second year by the people of the several States, and the electors in each State shall have the qualifications requisite for electors of the most numerous branch of the State Legislature.

No person shall be a Representative who shall not have attained to the age of twenty-five years, and been seven years a citizen of the United States, and who shall not, when elected, be an inhabitant of that State in which he shall be chosen.

Representatives and direct taxes shall be apportioned among the several States which may be included within this Union, according to their respective numbers, *which shall be determined by adding to the whole number of free persons, including those bound to service for a term of years and excluding Indians not taxed, three-fifths of all other persons.* The actual enumeration shall be made within three years after the first meeting of the Congress of the United States, and within every subsequent term of ten years, in such manner as they shall by law direct. The number of Representatives shall not exceed one for every thirty thousand, but each State shall have at least one Representative; *and until such enumeration shall be made, the State of New Hampshire shall be entitled to choose three, Massachusetts eight, Rhode Island and Providence Plantations one, Connecticut five, New York six, New Jersey four, Pennsylvania eight, Delaware one, Maryland six, Virginia ten, North Carolina five, South Carolina five, and Georgia three.*

When vacancies happen in the representation from any State, the Executive authority thereof shall issue writs of election to fill such vacancies.

The House of Representatives shall choose their Speaker and other officers; and shall have the sole power of impeachment.

Section 3   The Senate of the United States shall be composed of two Senators from each State, *chosen by the legislature thereof,* for six years; and each Senator shall have one vote.

Immediately after they shall be assembled in consequence of the first election, they shall be divided as equally as may be into three classes. The seats of the Senators of the first class shall be vacated at the expiration of the second year, of the second class at the expiration of the fourth year, and of the third class at the expiration of the sixth year, so that one-third may be chosen every second year; *and if vacancies happen by resignation or otherwise, during the recess of the legislature of any State, the Executive thereof may make temporary appointments until the next meeting of the legislature, which shall then fill such vacancies.*

No person shall be a Senator who shall not have attained to the age of thirty years, and been nine years a citizen of the United States, and who shall not, when elected, be an inhabitant of that State for which he shall be chosen.

The Vice-President of the United States shall be President of the Senate, but shall have no vote, unless they be equally divided.

The Senate shall choose their other officers, and also a President *pro tempore,* in the absence of the Vice-President, or when he shall exercise the office of President of the United States.

The Senate shall have the sole power to try all impeachments. When sitting for that purpose, they shall be on oath or affirmation. When the President of the United States is tried, the Chief Justice shall preside: and no person shall be convicted without the concurrence of two-thirds of the members present.

Judgment in cases of impeachment shall not extend further than to removal from the office, and disqualification to hold and enjoy any office of honor, trust or profit under the United States: but the party convicted shall nevertheless be liable and subject to indictment, trial, judgment and punishment, according to law.

Section 4   The times, places and manner of holding elections for Senators and Representatives shall be prescribed in each State by the legislature thereof; but the Congress may at any time by law make or alter such regulations, except as to the places of choosing Senators.

---

*Passages no longer in effect are in italic type.

The Congress shall assemble at least once in every year, and such meeting *shall be on the first Monday in December, unless they shall by law appoint a different day.*

Section 5   Each house shall be the judge of the elections, returns and qualifications of its own members, and a majority of each shall constitute a quorum to do business; but a smaller number may adjourn from day to day, and may be authorized to compel the attendance of absent members, in such manner, and under such penalties, as each house may provide.

Each house may determine the rules of its proceedings, punish its members for disorderly behavior, and with the concurrence of two-thirds, expel a member.

Each house shall keep a journal of its proceedings, and from time to time publish the same, excepting such parts as may in their judgment require secrecy; and the yeas and nays of the members of either house on any question shall, at the desire of one-fifth of those present, be entered on the journal.

Neither house, during the session of Congress, shall, without the consent of the other, adjourn for more than three days, nor to any other place than that in which the two houses shall be sitting.

Section 6   The Senators and Representatives shall receive a compensation for their services, to be ascertained by law and paid out of the treasury of the United States. They shall in all cases except treason, felony and breach of the peace, be privileged from arrest during their attendance at the session of their respective houses, and in going to and returning from the same; and for any speech or debate in either house, they shall not be questioned in any other place.

No Senator or Representative shall, during the time for which he was elected, be appointed to any civil office under the authority of the United States, which shall have been created, or the emoluments whereof shall have been increased, during such time; and no person holding any office under the United States shall be a member of either house during his continuance in office.

Section 7   All bills for raising revenue shall originate in the House of Representatives; but the Senate may propose or concur with amendments as on other bills.

Every bill which shall have passed the House of Representatives and the Senate, shall, before it become a law, be presented to the President of the United States; if he approve he shall sign it, but if not he shall return it with objections to that house in which it shall have originated, who shall enter the objections at large on their journal, and proceed to reconsider it. If after such reconsideration two-thirds of that house shall agree to pass the bill, it shall be sent, together with the objections, to the other house, by which it shall likewise be reconsidered, and, if approved by two-thirds of that house, it shall become a law. But in all such cases the votes of both houses shall be determined by yeas and nays, and the names of the persons voting for and against the bill shall be entered on the journal of each house respectively. If any bill shall not be returned by the President within ten days (Sundays excepted) after it shall have been presented to him, the same shall be a law, in like manner as if he had signed it, unless the Congress by their adjournment prevent its return, in which case it shall not be a law.

Every order, resolution, or vote to which the concurrence of the Senate and House of Representatives may be necessary (except on a question of adjournment) shall be presented to the President of the United States; and before the same shall take effect, shall be approved by him, or being disapproved by him, shall be repassed by two-thirds of the Senate and House of Representatives, according to the rules and limitations prescribed in the case of a bill.

Section 8   The Congress shall have power

To lay and collect taxes, duties, imposts, and excises, to pay the debts and provide for the common defense and general welfare of the United States; but all duties, imposts and excises shall be uniform throughout the United States;

To borrow money on the credit of the United States;

To regulate commerce with foreign nations, and among the several States, and with the Indian tribes;

To establish an uniform rule of naturalization, and uniform laws on the subject of bankruptcies throughout the United States;

To coin money, regulate the value thereof, and of foreign coin, and fix the standard of weights and measures;

To provide for the punishment of counterfeiting the securities and current coin of the United States;

To establish post offices and post roads;

To promote the progress of science and useful arts by securing for limited times to authors and inventors the exclusive right to their respective writings and discoveries;

To constitute tribunals inferior to the Supreme Court;

To define and punish piracies and felonies committed on the high seas and offences against the law of nations;

To declare war, grant letters of marque and reprisal, and make rules concerning captures on land and water;

To raise and support armies, but no appropriation of money to that use shall be for a longer term than two years;

To provide and maintain a navy;

To make rules for the government and regulation of the land and naval forces;

To provide for calling forth the militia to execute the laws of the Union, suppress insurrections and repel invasions;

To provide for organizing, arming, and disciplining the militia, and for governing such part of them as may be employed in the service of the United States, reserving to the States respectively the appointment of the officers, and the authority of training the militia according to the discipline prescribed by Congress;

To exercise exclusive legislation in all cases whatsoever, over such district (not exceeding ten miles square) as may, by cession of particular States, and the acceptance of Congress, become the seat of the government of the United States, and to exercise like authority over all places purchased by the consent of the legislature of the State, in which the same shall be, for erection of forts, magazines, arsenals, dock-yards, and other needful buildings;—and

To make all laws which shall be necessary and proper for carrying into execution the foregoing powers, and all other powers vested by this Constitution in the government of the United States, or in any department or officer thereof.

Section 9 *The migration or importation of such persons as any of the States now existing shall think proper to admit shall not be prohibited by the Congress prior to the year one thousand eight hundred and eight; but a tax or duty may be imposed on such importation, not exceeding ten dollars for each person.*

The privilege of the writ of habeas corpus shall not be suspended, unless when in cases of rebellion or invasion the public safety may require it.

No bill of attainder or ex post facto law shall be passed.

No capitation, or other direct, tax shall be laid, unless in proportion to the census or enumeration herein before directed to be taken.

No tax or duty shall be laid on articles exported from any State.

No preference shall be given by any regulation of commerce or revenue to the ports of one State over those of another; nor shall vessels bound to, or from, one State be obliged to enter, clear, or pay duties in another.

No money shall be drawn from the treasury, but in consequence of appropriations made by law; and a regular statement and account of the receipts and expenditures of all public money shall be published from time to time.

No title of nobility shall be granted by the United States: and no person holding any office of profit or trust under them, shall, without the consent of the Congress, accept of any present, emolument, office, or title, of any kind whatever, from any king, prince, or foreign state.

Section 10 No State shall enter into any treaty, alliance, or confederation; grant letters of marque and reprisal; coin money; emit bills of credit; make anything but gold and silver coin a tender in payment of debts; pass any bill of attainder, ex post facto law, or law impairing the obligation of contracts, or grant any title of nobility.

No State shall, without the consent of Congress, lay any imposts or duties on imports or exports, except what may be absolutely necessary for executing its inspection laws: and the net produce of all duties and imposts, laid by any State on imports or exports, shall be for the use of the treasury of the United States; and all such laws shall be subject to the revision and control of the Congress.

No State shall, without the consent of Congress, lay any duty of tonnage, keep troops, or ships of war in time of peace, enter into any agreement or compact with another State, or with a foreign power, or engage in war, unless actually invaded, or in such imminent danger as will not admit of delay.

Article II

Section 1 The executive power shall be vested in a President of the United States of America. He shall hold his office during the term of four years, and, together with the Vice-President, chosen for the same term, be elected as follows:

Each State shall appoint, in such manner as the legislature thereof may direct, a number of electors, equal to the whole number of Senators and Representatives to which the State may be entitled in the Congress; but no Senator or Representative, or person holding an office of trust or profit under the United States, shall be appointed an elector.

The electors shall meet in their respective States, and vote by ballot for two persons, of whom one at least shall not be an inhabitant of the same State with themselves. And they shall make a list of all the persons voted for, and of the number of votes for each; which list they shall sign and certify, and transmit sealed to the seat of government of the United States, directed to the President of the Senate. The President of the Senate shall, in the presence of the Senate and House of Representatives, open all the certificates, and the votes shall then be counted. The person having the greatest number of votes shall be the President, if such number be a majority of the whole number of electors appointed; and if there be more than one who have such majority, and have an equal number of votes, then the House of Representatives shall immediately choose by ballot one of them for President; and if no person have a majority, then from the five highest on the list said house shall in like manner choose the President. But in choosing the President the votes shall be taken by States, the representation from each State having one vote; a quorum for this purpose shall consist of a member or members from two-thirds of the States, and a majority of all the States shall be necessary to a choice. In every case, after the choice of the President, the person having the greatest number of votes of the electors shall be the Vice-President. But if there should remain two or more who have equal votes, the Senate shall choose from them by ballot the Vice-President.

The Congress may determine the time of choosing the electors, and the day on which they shall give their votes; which day shall be the same throughout the United States.

No person except a natural-born citizen, *or a citizen of the United States at the time of the adoption of this Constitution,* shall be eligible to the office of President; neither shall any person be eligible to that office who shall not have attained to the age of thirty-five years, and been fourteen years a resident within the United States.

In cases of the removal of the President from office or of his death, resignation, or inability to discharge the powers and duties of the said office, the same shall devolve on the Vice-President, and the Congress may by law provide for the case of removal, death, resignation, or inability, both of the President and Vice-President, declaring what officer shall then act as President, and such officer shall act accordingly, until the disability be removed, or a President shall be elected.

The President shall, at stated times, receive for his services a compensation, which shall neither be increased nor diminished during the period for which he shall have been elected, and he shall not receive within that period any other emolument from the United States, or any of them.

Before he enter on the execution of his office, he shall take the following oath or affirmation:—"I do solemnly swear (or affirm) that I will faithfully execute the office of the President of the United States, and will to the best of my ability preserve, protect and defend the Constitution of the United States."

Section 2 The President shall be commander in chief of the army and navy of the United States, and of the militia of the several States, when called into the actual service of the United States; he may require the opinion, in writing, of the principal officer in each of the executive departments, upon any subject relating to the duties of their respective offices, and he shall have power to grant reprieves and pardons for offenses against the United States, except in cases of impeachment.

He shall have power, by and with the advice and consent of the Senate, to make treaties, provided two-thirds of the Senators present concur; and he shall nominate, and by and with the advice and consent of the Senate, shall appoint ambassadors, other public ministers and consuls, judges of the Supreme Court, and all other officers of the United States, whose appointments are not herein otherwise provided for, and which shall be established by law: but Congress may by law vest the appointment of such inferior officers, as they think proper, in the President alone, in the courts of law, or in the heads of departments.

The President shall have power to fill up all vacancies that may happen during the recess of the Senate, by granting commissions which shall expire at the end of their next session.

Section 3 He shall from time to time give to the Congress information of the state of the Union, and recommend to their consideration such measures as he shall judge necessary and expedient; he may, on extraordinary occasions, convene both houses, or either of them, and in case of disagreement between them, with respect to the time of adjournment, he may adjourn them to such time as he shall think proper; he shall receive ambassadors and other public ministers; he shall take care that the laws be faithfully executed, and shall commission all the officers of the United States.

Section 4 The President, Vice-President and all civil officers of the United States shall be removed from office on impeachment for, and on conviction of, treason, bribery, or other high crimes and misdemeanors.

Article III

Section 1 The judicial power of the United States shall be vested in one Supreme Court, and in such inferior courts as the Congress may from time to time ordain and establish. The judges, both of the Supreme and inferior courts, shall hold their offices during good behavior, and shall, at stated times, receive for their services a compensation which shall not be diminished during their continuance in office.

Section 2 The judicial power shall extend to all cases, in law and equity, arising under this Constitution, the laws of the United States, and treaties made, or which shall be made, under their authority;—to all cases affecting ambassadors, other public ministers and consuls;—to all cases of admiralty and maritime jurisdiction;—to controversies to which the United States shall be a party;—to controversies between two or more States;—*between a State and citizens of another*

State;—between citizens of different States;—between citizens of the same State claiming lands under grants of different States, and between a State, or the citizens thereof, and foreign states, citizens or subjects.

In all cases affecting ambassadors, other public ministers and consuls, and those in which a State shall be party, the Supreme Court shall have original jurisdiction. In all the other cases before mentioned, the Supreme Court shall have appellate jurisdiction, both as to law and fact, with such exceptions, and under such regulations, as the Congress shall make.

The trial of all crimes, except in cases of impeachment, shall be by jury; and such trial shall be held in the State where said crimes shall have been committed; but when not committed within any State, the trial shall be at such place or places as the Congress may by Law have directed.

Section 3 Treason against the United States shall consist only in levying war against them, or in adhering to their enemies, giving them aid and comfort. No person shall be convicted of treason unless on the testimony of two witnesses to the same overt act, or on confession in open court.

The Congress shall have power to declare the punishment of treason, but no attainder of treason shall work corruption of blood, or forfeiture except during the life of the person attainted.

Article IV

Section 1 Full faith and credit shall be given in each State to the public acts, records, and judicial proceedings of every other State. And the Congress may by general laws prescribe the manner in which such acts, records, and proceedings shall be proved, and the effect thereof.

Section 2 The citizens of each State shall be entitled to all privileges and immunities of citizens in the several States.

A person charged in any State with treason, felony, or other crime, who shall flee from justice, and be found in another State, shall on demand of the executive authority of the State from which he fled, be delivered up, to be removed to the State having jurisdiction of the crime.

No Person held to service or labor in one State, under the laws thereof, escaping into another, shall, in consequence of any law or regulation therein, be discharged from such service or labor, but shall be delivered up on claim of the party to whom such service or labor may be due.

Section 3 New States may be admitted by the Congress into this Union; but no new State shall be formed or erected within the jurisdiction of any other State; nor any State be formed by the junction of two or more States, or parts of States, without the consent of the legislatures of the States concerned as well as of the Congress.

The Congress shall have power to dispose of and make all needful rules and regulations respecting the territory or other property belonging to the United States; and nothing in this Constitution shall be so construed as to prejudice any claims of the United States, or of any particular State.

Section 4 The United States shall guarantee to every State in this Union a republican form of government, and shall protect each of them against invasion; and on application of the legislature, or of the executive (when the legislature cannot be convened), against domestic violence.

Article V

The Congress, whenever two-thirds of both houses shall deem it necessary, shall propose amendments to this Constitution, or, on the application of the legislatures of two-thirds of the several States, shall call a convention for proposing amendments, which, in either case, shall be valid to all intents and purposes, as part of this Constitution, when ratified by the legislatures of three-fourths of the several States, or by conventions in three-fourths thereof, as the one or the other mode of ratification may be proposed by the Congress; provided *that no amendments which may be made prior to the year one thousand eight hundred and eight shall in any manner affect the first and fourth clauses in the ninth section of the first article*; and that no State, without its consent, shall be deprived of its equal suffrage in the Senate.

Article VI

All debts contracted and engagements entered into, before the adoption of this Constitution, shall be as valid against the United States under this Constitution, as under the Confederation.

This Constitution, and the laws of the United States which shall be made in pursuance thereof; and all treaties made, or which shall be made, under the authority of the United States, shall be the supreme law of the land; and the judges in every State shall be bound thereby, anything in the Constitution or laws of any State to the contrary notwithstanding.

The Senators and Representatives before mentioned, and the members of the several State legislatures, and all executive and judicial officers, both of the United States and of the several States, shall be bound by oath or affirmation to support this Constitution; but no religious test shall ever be required as a qualification to any office or public trust under the United States.

Article VII

The ratification of the conventions of nine States shall be sufficient for the establishment of this Constitution between the States so ratifying the same.

Done in convention by the unanimous consent of the States present, the seventeenth day of September in the year of our Lord one thousand seven hundred and eighty-seven and of the Independence of the United States of America the twelfth. In witness whereof we have hereunto subscribed our names.

GEORGE WASHINGTON
PRESIDENT AND DEPUTY FROM VIRGINIA

New Hampshire
John Langdon
Nicholas Gilman

Massachusetts
Nathaniel Gorham
Rufus King

Connecticut
William Samuel
   Johnson
Roger Sherman

New York
Alexander Hamilton

New Jersey
William Livingston
David Brearley
William Paterson
Jonathan Dayton

Pennsylvania
Benjamin Franklin
Thomas Mifflin
Robert Morris
George Clymer
Thomas FitzSimons
Jared Ingersoll
James Wilson
Gouverneur Morris

Delaware
George Read
Gunning Bedford, Jr.
John Dickinson
Richard Bassett
Jacob Broom

Maryland
James McHenry
Daniel of
   St. Thomas Jenifer
Daniel Carroll

Virginia
John Blair
James Madison, Jr.

North Carolina
William Blount
Richard Dobbs
   Spaight
Hugh Williamson

South Carolina
John Rutledge
Charles Cotesworth
   Pinckney
Charles Pinckney
Pierce Butler

Georgia
William Few
Abraham Baldwin

AMENDMENTS TO THE CONSTITUTION WITH ANNOTATIONS
(Including the six unratified amendments)

In their effort to gain Antifederalists' support for the Constitution, Federalists frequently pointed to the inclusion of Article 5, which provides an orderly method of amending the Constitution. In contrast, the Articles of Confederation, which were universally recognized as seriously flawed, offered no means of amendment. For their part, Antifederalists argued that the amendment process was so "intricate" that one might as easily roll "sixes an hundred times in succession" as change the Constitution.

The system for amendment laid out in the Constitution requires that two-thirds of both houses of Congress agree to a proposed amendment, which must then be ratified by three-quarters of the legislatures of the states. Alternatively, an amendment may be proposed by a convention called by the legislatures of two-thirds of the states. Since 1789, members of Congress have proposed thousands of amendments. Besides the seventeen amendments added since 1789, only the six "unratified" ones included here were approved by two-thirds of both houses and sent to the states for ratification, however.

Among the many amendments that never made it out of Congress have been proposals to declare dueling, divorce, and interracial marriage unconstitutional as well as proposals to establish a national university, to acknowledge the sovereignty of Jesus Christ, and to prohibit any person from possessing wealth in excess of ten million dollars.[1]

Among the issues facing Americans today that might lead to constitutional amendment are efforts to balance the federal budget, to limit the number of terms elected officials may serve, to limit access to or prohibit abortion, to establish English as the official language of the United States, and to prohibit flag burning. None of these proposed amendments has yet garnered enough support in Congress to be sent to the states for ratification.

Although the first ten amendments to the Constitution are commonly known as the Bill of Rights, only Amendments 1–8 actually provide guarantees of individual rights. Amendments 9 and 10 deal with the structure of power within the constitutional system. The Bill of Rights was promised to appease Antifederalists who refused to ratify the Constitution without guarantees of individual liberties and limitations to federal power. After studying more than two hundred amendments recommended by the ratifying conventions of the states, Federalist James Madison presented a list of seventeen to Congress, which used Madison's list as the foundation for the twelve amendments that were sent to the states for ratification. Ten of the twelve were adopted in 1791. The first on the list of twelve, known as the Reapportionment Amendment, was never adopted (see p. A-13). The second proposed amendment was adopted in 1992 as Amendment 27 (see p. A-23).

Amendment I

Congress shall make no law respecting an establishment of religion, or prohibiting the free exercise thereof; or abridging the freedom of speech, or of the press; or the right of the people peaceably to assemble, and to petition the government for a redress of grievances.

◆ ◆ ◆

The First Amendment is a potent symbol for many Americans. Most are well aware of their rights to free speech, freedom of the press, and freedom of religion and their rights to assemble and to petition, even if they cannot cite the exact words of this amendment.

The First Amendment guarantee of freedom of religion has two clauses: the "free exercise clause," which allows individuals to practice or not practice any religion, and the "establishment clause," which prevents the federal government from discriminating against or favoring any particular religion. This clause was designed to create what Thomas Jefferson referred to as "a wall of separation between church and state." In the 1960s, the Supreme Court ruled that the First Amendment prohibits prayer (see Engel v. Vitale, *p. A-46) and Bible reading in public schools.*

Although the rights to free speech and freedom of the press are established in the First Amendment, it was not until the twentieth century that the Supreme Court began to explore the full meaning of these guarantees. In 1919, the Court ruled in Schenck v. United States *(see p. A-45) that the government could suppress free expression only where it could cite a "clear and present danger." In a decision that continues to raise controversies, the Court ruled in 1990, in* Texas v. Johnson, *that flag burning is a form of symbolic speech protected by the First Amendment.*

---

[1]Richard B. Bernstein, *Amending America*, (New York: Times Books, 1993), 177–81.

Amendment II

A well-regulated militia being necessary to the security of a free State, the right of the people to keep and bear arms shall not be infringed.

Fear of a standing army under the control of a hostile government made the Second Amendment an important part of the Bill of Rights. Advocates of gun ownership claim that the amendment prevents the government from regulating firearms. Proponents of gun control argue that the amendment is designed only to protect the right of the states to maintain militia units.

In 1939, the Supreme Court ruled in United States v. Miller *that the Second Amendment did not protect the right of an individual to own a sawed-off shotgun, which it argued was not ordinary militia equipment. Since then, the Supreme Court has refused to hear Second Amendment cases, while lower courts have upheld firearms regulations. Several justices currently on the bench seem to favor a narrow interpretation of the Second Amendment, which would allow gun control legislation. The controversy over the impact of the Second Amendment on gun owners and gun control legislation will certainly continue.*

Amendment III

No soldier shall, in time of peace, be quartered in any house without the consent of the owner, nor in time of war, but in a manner to be prescribed by law.

The Third Amendment was extremely important to the framers of the Constitution, but today it is nearly forgotten. American colonists were especially outraged that they were forced to quarter British troops in the years before and during the American Revolution. The philosophy of the Third Amendment has been viewed by some justices and scholars as the foundation of the modern constitutional right to privacy. One example of this can be found in Justice William O. Douglas's opinion in Griswold v. Connecticut *(see p. A-47).*

Amendment IV

The right of the people to be secure in their persons, houses, papers, and effects, against unreasonable searches and seizures, shall not be violated, and no warrants shall issue but upon probable cause, supported by oath or affirmation, and particularly describing the place to be searched, and the persons or things to be seized.

In the years before the Revolution, the houses, barns, stores, and warehouses of American colonists were ransacked by British authorities under "writs of assistance" or general warrants. The British, thus empowered, searched for seditious material or smuggled goods that could then be used as evidence against colonists who were charged with a crime only after the items were found.

The first part of the Fourth Amendment protects citizens from "unreasonable" searches and seizures. The Supreme Court has interpreted this protection as well as the words search *and* seizure *in different ways at different times. At one time, the Court did not recognize electronic eavesdropping as a form of search and seizure, though it does today. At times, an "unreasonable" search has been almost any search carried out without a warrant, but in the two decades before 1969 the Court sometimes sanctioned warrantless searches that it considered reasonable based on "the total atmosphere of the case."*

The second part of the Fourth Amendment defines the procedure for issuing a search warrant and states the requirement of "Probable cause," which is generally viewed as evidence indicating that a suspect has committed an offense.

The Fourth Amendment has been controversial because the Court has sometimes excluded evidence that has been seized in violation of constitutional standards. The justification is that excluding such evidence deters violations of the amendment, but doing so may allow a guilty person to escape punishment.

Amendment V

No person shall be held to answer for a capital, or otherwise infamous crime, unless on a presentment or indictment of a grand jury, except in cases arising in the land or naval forces, or in the militia, when in actual service in time of war or public danger; nor shall any person be subject for the same offence to be twice put in jeopardy of life or limb; nor shall be compelled in any criminal case to be a witness against himself, nor be deprived of life, liberty, or property, without due process of law; nor shall private property be taken for public use without just compensation.

The Fifth Amendment protects people against government authority in the prosecution of criminal offenses. It prohibits the state, first, from charging a person with a serious crime without a grand jury hearing to decide whether there is sufficient evidence to support the charge and, second, from charging a person with the same crime twice. The best-known aspect of the Fifth Amendment is that it

prevents a person from being "compelled . . . to be a witness against himself." The last clause, the "takings clause," limits the power of the government to seize property.

Although invoking the Fifth Amendment is popularly viewed as a confession of guilt, a person may be innocent yet still fear prosecution. For example, during the Red-baiting era of the late 1940s and 1950s, many people who had participated in legal activities that were associated with the Communist Party claimed the Fifth Amendment privilege rather than testify before the House Un-American Activities Committee because the mood of the times cast those activities in a negative light. Since "taking the Fifth" was viewed as an admission of guilt, those people often lost their jobs or became unemployable. (See chapter 26.) Nonetheless, the right to protect oneself against self-incrimination plays an important role in guarding against the collective power of the state.

Amendment VI

In all criminal prosecutions, the accused shall enjoy the right to a speedy and public trial, by an impartial jury of the State and district wherein the crime shall have been committed, which district shall have been previously ascertained by law, and to be informed of the nature and cause of the accusation; to be confronted with the witnesses against him; to have compulsory process for obtaining witnesses in his favor, and to have the assistance of counsel for his defence.

◆◆◆

The original Constitution put few limits on the government's power to investigate, prosecute, and punish crime. This process was of great concern to the early Americans, however, and of the twenty-eight rights specified in the first eight amendments, fifteen have to do with it. Seven rights are specified in the Sixth Amendment. These include the right to a speedy trial, a public trial, a jury trial, a notice of accusation, confrontation by opposing witnesses, testimony by favorable witnesses, and the assistance of counsel.

Although this amendment originally guaranteed these rights only in cases involving the federal government, the adoption of the Fourteenth Amendment began a process of applying the protections of the Bill of Rights to the states through court cases such as Gideon v. Wainwright *(see p. A-46).*

Amendment VII

In suits at common law, where the value in controversy shall exceed twenty dollars, the right of trial by jury shall be preserved, and no fact tried by a jury shall be otherwise reexamined in any court of the United States, than according to the rules of the common law.

◆◆◆

This amendment guarantees people the same right to a trial by jury as was guaranteed by English common law in 1791. Under common law, in civil trials (those involving money damages) the role of the judge was to settle questions of law and that of the jury was to settle questions of fact. The amendment does not specify the size of the jury or its role in a trial, however. The Supreme Court has generally held that those issues be determined by English common law of 1791, which stated that a jury consists of twelve people, that a trial must be conducted before a judge who instructs the jury on the law and advises it on facts, and that a verdict must be unanimous.

Amendment VIII

Excessive bail shall not be required, nor excessive fines imposed, nor cruel and unusual punishments inflicted.

◆◆◆

The language used to guarantee the three rights in this amendment was inspired by the English Bill of Rights of 1689. The Supreme Court has not had a lot to say about "excessive fines." In recent years it has agreed that despite the provision against "excessive bail," persons who are believed to be dangerous to others can be held without bail even before they have been convicted.

Although opponents of the death penalty have not succeeded in using the Eighth Amendment to achieve the end of capital punishment, the clause regarding "cruel and unusual punishments" has been used to prohibit capital punishment in certain cases (see Furman v. Georgia, *p. A-47) and to require improved conditions in prisons.*

Amendment IX

The enumeration in the Constitution, of certain rights, shall not be construed to deny or disparage others retained by the people.

◆◆◆

Some Federalists feared that inclusion of the Bill of Rights in the Constitution would allow later generations of interpreters to claim that the people had surrendered any rights not specifically enumerated there. To guard against this, Madison added language that became the Ninth Amendment. Interest in this heretofore largely ignored amendment revived in 1965 when it was used in a concurring opinion in Griswold v. Connecticut *(see p. A-47). While Justice William O. Douglas called on the Third Amendment to support the right to privacy in deciding that case, Justice Arthur Goldberg, in the concurring opinion, argued that the right to privacy regarding contraception was an unenumerated right that was protected by the Ninth Amendment.*

In 1980, the Court ruled that the right of the press to attend a public trial was protected by the Ninth Amendment. While some scholars argue that modern judges cannot identify the unenumerated rights that the framers were trying to protect, others argue that the Ninth Amendment should be read as providing a constitutional "presumption of liberty" that allows people to act in any way that does not violate the rights of others.

Amendment X

The powers not delegated to the United States by the Constitution, nor prohibited by it to the States, are reserved to the States respectively, or to the people.

The Antifederalists were especially eager to see a "reserved powers clause" explicitly guaranteeing the states control over their internal affairs. Not surprisingly, the Tenth Amendment has been a frequent battleground in the struggle over states' rights and federal supremacy. Prior to the Civil War, the Democratic Republican Party and Jacksonian Democrats invoked the Tenth Amendment to prohibit the federal government from making decisions about whether people in individual states could own slaves. The Tenth Amendment was virtually suspended during Reconstruction following the Civil War. In 1883, however, the Supreme Court declared the Civil Rights Act of 1875 unconstitutional on the grounds that it violated the Tenth Amendment. Business interests also called on the amendment to block efforts at federal regulation.

The Court was inconsistent over the next several decades as it attempted to resolve the tension between the restrictions of the Tenth Amendment and the powers the Constitution granted to Congress to regulate interstate commerce and levy taxes. The Court upheld the Pure Food and Drug Act (1906), the Meat Inspection Acts (1906 and 1907), and the White Slave Traffic Act (1910), all of which affected the states, but struck down an act prohibiting interstate shipment of goods produced through child labor. Between 1934 and 1935, a number of New Deal programs created by Franklin D. Roosevelt were declared unconstitutional on the grounds that they violated the Tenth Amendment. (See chapter 24.) As Roosevelt appointees changed the composition of the Court, the Tenth Amendment was declared to have no substantive meaning. Generally, the amendment is held to protect the rights of states to regulate internal matters such as local government, education, commerce, labor, and business, as well as matters involving families such as marriage, divorce, and inheritance within the state.

Unratified Amendment

Reapportionment Amendment (proposed by Congress September 25, 1789, along with the Bill of Rights)

After the first enumeration required by the first article of the Constitution, there shall be one Representative for every thirty thousand, until the number shall amount to one hundred, after which the proportion shall be so regulated by Congress, that there shall be not less than one hundred Representatives, nor less than one Representative for every forty thousand persons, until the number of Representatives shall amount to two hundred; after which the proportion shall be so regulated by Congress, that there shall not be less than two hundred Representatives, nor more than one Representative for every fifty thousand persons.

If the Reapportionment Amendment had passed and remained in effect, the House of Representatives today would have more than 5,000 members rather than 435.

Amendment XI
[Adopted 1798]

The judicial power of the United States shall not be construed to extend to any suit in law or equity, commenced or prosecuted against one of the United States by citizens of another State, or by citizens or subjects of any foreign state.

In 1793, the Supreme Court ruled in favor of Alexander Chisholm, executor of the estate of a deceased South Carolina merchant. Chisholm was suing the state of Georgia because the merchant had never been paid for provisions he had supplied during the Revolution. Many regarded this Court decision as an error that violated the intent of the Constitution.

Antifederalists had long feared a federal court system with the power to overrule a state court. When the Constitution was being drafted, Federalists had assured worried Antifederalists that section 2 of Article 3, which allows federal courts to hear cases "between a State and citizens of another State," did not mean that the federal courts were authorized to hear suits against a state by citizens of another state or a foreign country. Antifederalists and many other Americans feared a powerful federal court system because they worried that it would become like the British courts of this period, which were accountable only to the monarch. Furthermore, Chisholm v. Georgia prompted a series of suits against state governments by creditors and suppliers who had made loans during the war.

In addition, State legislators and Congress feared that the shaky economies of the new states, as well as the country as a whole, would be destroyed, especially if Loyalists who had fled to other countries sought reimbursement for land and property that had been seized. The day after the Supreme Court announced its decision, a resolution proposing the Eleventh Amendment, which overturned the decision in Chisholm v. Georgia, *was introduced in the U.S. Senate.*

Amendment XII
[Adopted 1804]

The electors shall meet in their respective States, and vote by ballot for President and Vice-President, one of whom, at least, shall not be an inhabitant of the same State with themselves; they shall name in their ballots the person voted for as President, and in distinct ballots the person voted for as Vice-President, and they shall make distinct lists of all persons voted for as President, and of all persons voted for as Vice-President, and of the number of votes for each, which lists they shall sign and certify, and transmit sealed to the seat of government of the United States, directed to the President of the Senate;—the President of the Senate shall, in the presence of the Senate and House of Representatives, open all the certificates and the votes shall then be counted;—the person having the greatest number of votes for President shall be the President, if such number be a majority of the whole number of electors appointed; and if no person have such majority, then from the persons having the highest numbers not exceeding three on the list of those voted for as President, the House of Representatives shall choose immediately, by ballot, the President. But in choosing the President, the votes shall be taken by States, the representation from each State having one vote; a quorum for this purpose shall consist of a member or members from two-thirds of the States, and a majority of all the States shall be necessary to a choice. And if the House of Representatives shall not choose a President whenever the right of choice shall devolve upon them, before *the fourth day of March* next following, then the Vice-President shall act as President, as in the case of the death or other constitutional disability of the President.

The person having the greatest number of votes as Vice-President shall be the Vice-President, if such number be a majority of the whole number of electors appointed; and if no person have a majority, then from the two highest numbers on the list the Senate shall choose the Vice-President; a quorum for the purpose shall consist of two-thirds of the whole number of Senators, and a majority of the whole number shall be necessary to a choice. But no person constitutionally inel-

igible to the office of President shall be eligible to that of Vice-President of the United States.

The framers of the Constitution disliked political parties and assumed that none would ever form. Under the original system, electors chosen by the states would each vote for two candidates. The candidate who won the most votes would become president, while the person who won the second-highest number of votes would become vice president. Rivalries between Federalists and Antifederalists led to the formation of political parties, however, even before George Washington had left office. Though Washington was elected unanimously in 1789 and 1792, the elections of 1796 and 1800 were procedural disasters because of party maneuvering (see chapters 9 and 10). In 1796, Federalist John Adams was chosen as president, and his great rival, the Antifederalist Thomas Jefferson (whose party was called the Republican Party), became his vice president. In 1800, all the electors cast their two votes as one of two party blocs. Jefferson and his fellow Republican nominee, Aaron Burr, were tied with seventy-three votes each. The contest went to the House of Representatives, which finally elected Jefferson after thirty-six ballots. The Twelfth Amendment prevents these problems by requiring electors to vote separately for the president and vice president.

Unratified Amendment
Titles of Nobility Amendment (proposed by Congress May 1, 1810)

If any citizen of the United States shall accept, claim, receive or retain any title of nobility or honor or shall, without the consent of Congress, accept and retain any present, pension, office or emolument of any kind whatever, from any emperor, king, prince or foreign power, such person shall cease to be a citizen of the United States, and shall be incapable of holding any office of trust or profit under them, or either of them.

This amendment would have extended Article 1, section 9, clause 8 of the Constitution, which prevents the awarding of titles by the United States and the acceptance of such awards from foreign powers without congressional consent. Historians speculate that general nervousness about the power of the Emperor Napoleon, who was at that time extending France's empire throughout Europe, may have prompted the proposal. Though it fell one vote short of ratification, Congress and the American people thought the proposal had been

ratified and it was included in many nineteenth-century editions of the Constitution.

The Civil War and Reconstruction Amendments (Thirteenth, Fourteenth, and Fifteenth Amendments)

In the four months between the election of Abraham Lincoln and his inauguration, more than two hundred proposed constitutional amendments were presented to Congress as part of a desperate attempt to hold the rapidly dissolving Union together. Most of these were efforts to appease the southern states by protecting the right to own slaves or by disfranchising African Americans through constitutional amendment. None were able to win the votes required from Congress to send them to the states. The relatively innocuous Corwin Amendment seemed to be the only hope for preserving the Union by amending the Constitution.

The northern victors in the Civil War tried to restructure the Constitution just as the war had restructured the nation. Yet they were often divided in their goals. Some wanted to end slavery; others hoped for social and economic equality regardless of race; others hoped that extending the power of the ballot box to former slaves would help create a new political order. The debates over the Thirteenth, Fourteenth, and Fifteenth Amendments were bitter. Few of those who fought for these changes were satisfied with the amendments themselves; fewer still were satisfied with their interpretation. Although the amendments put an end to the legal status of slavery, it took nearly a hundred years after the amendments' passage before most of the descendants of former slaves could begin to experience the economic, social, and political equality the amendments had been intended to provide.

Unratified Amendment
Corwin Amendment (proposed by Congress March 2, 1861)

No amendment shall be made to the Constitution which will authorize or give to Congress the power to abolish or interfere, within any State, with the domestic institutions thereof, including that of persons held to labor or service by the laws of said State.

Following the election of Abraham Lincoln, Congress scrambled to try to prevent the secession of the slaveholding states. House member Thomas Corwin of Ohio proposed the "unamendable" amendment in the hope that by protecting slavery where it existed, Congress would keep

the southern states in the Union. Lincoln indicated his support for the proposed amendment in his first inaugural address. Only Ohio and Maryland ratified the Corwin Amendment before it was forgotten.

Amendment XIII
[Adopted 1865]

Section 1   Neither slavery nor involuntary servitude, except as a punishment for crime whereof the party shall have been duly convicted, shall exist within the United States, or any place subject to their jurisdiction.

Section 2   Congress shall have power to enforce this article by appropriate legislation.

Although President Lincoln had abolished slavery in the Confederacy with the Emancipation Proclamation of 1863, abolitionists wanted to rid the entire country of slavery. The Thirteenth Amendment did this in a clear and straightforward manner. In February 1865, when the proposal was approved by the House, the gallery of the House was newly opened to black Americans who had a chance at last to see their government at work. Passage of the proposal was greeted by wild cheers from the gallery as well as tears on the House floor, where congressional representatives openly embraced one another.

The problem of ratification remained, however. The Union position was that the Confederate states were part of the country of thirty-six states. Therefore, twenty-seven states were needed to ratify the amendment. When Kentucky and Delaware rejected it, backers realized that without approval from at least four former Confederate states, the amendment would fail. Lincoln's successor, President Andrew Johnson, made ratification of the Thirteenth Amendment a condition for southern states to rejoin the Union. Under those terms, all the former Confederate states except Mississippi accepted the Thirteenth Amendment, and by the end of 1865 the amendment had become part of the Constitution and slavery had been prohibited in the United States.

Amendment XIV
[Adopted 1868]

Section 1   All persons born or naturalized in the United States, and subject to the jurisdiction thereof, are citizens of the United States and of the State wherein they reside. No State shall make or enforce any law which shall abridge the privileges or immunities of citizens of the United States; nor shall any State deprive any person of life, liberty, or property, without due process of law; nor deny to any person within its jurisdiction the equal protection of the laws.

Section 2   Representatives shall be appointed among the several States according to their respective numbers, counting the whole number of persons in each State, excluding Indians not taxed. But when the right to vote at any election for the choice of Electors for President and Vice-President of the United States, Representatives in Congress, the executive and judicial officers of a State, or the members of the legislature thereof, is denied to any of the male inhabitants of such State, being twenty-one years of age and citizens of the United States, or in any way abridged, except for participation in rebellion, or other crime, the basis of representation therein shall be reduced in the proportion which the number of such male citizens shall bear to the whole number of male citizens twenty-one years of age in such State.

Section 3   No person shall be a Senator or Representative in Congress, or Elector of President and Vice-President, or hold any office, civil or military, under the United States, or under any State, who, having previously taken an oath, as a member of Congress, or as an officer of the United States, or as a member of any State legislature, or as an executive or judicial officer of any State, to support the Constitution of the United States, shall have engaged in insurrection or rebellion against the same, or given aid or comfort to the enemies thereof. Congress may, by a vote of two-thirds of each house, remove such disability.

Section 4   The validity of the public debt of the United States, authorized by law, including debts incurred for payment of pensions and bounties for services in suppressing insurrection or rebellion, shall not be questioned. But neither the United States nor any State shall assume or pay any debt or obligation incurred in aid of insurrection or rebellion against the United States, or any claim for the loss or emancipation of any slave; but all such debts, obligations, and claims shall be held illegal and void.

Section 5   The Congress shall have power to enforce, by appropriate legislation, the provisions of this article.

◆ ◆ ◆

Without Lincoln's leadership in the reconstruction of the nation following the Civil War, it soon became clear that the Thirteenth Amendment needed additional constitutional support. Less than a year after Lincoln's assassination, Andrew Johnson was ready to bring the former Confederate states back into the Union with few changes in their governments or politics. Anxious Republicans drafted the

Fourteenth Amendment to prevent that from happening. The most important provisions of this complex amendment made all native-born or naturalized persons American citizens and prohibited states from abridging the "privileges or immunities" of citizens; depriving them of "life, liberty, or property, without due process of law"; and denying them "equal protection of the laws." In essence, it made all ex-slaves citizens and protected the rights of all citizens against violation by their own state governments.

As occurred in the case of the Thirteenth Amendment, former Confederate states were forced to ratify the amendment as a condition of representation in the House and the Senate. The intentions of the Fourteenth Amendment, and how those intentions should be enforced, have been the most debated point of constitutional history. The terms due process *and* equal protection *have been especially troublesome. Was the amendment designed to outlaw racial segregation? Or was the goal simply to prevent the leaders of the rebellious South from gaining political power?*

The framers of the Fourteenth Amendment hoped Article 2 would produce black voters who would increase the power of the Republican Party. The federal government, however, never used its power to punish states for denying blacks their right to vote. Although the Fourteenth Amendment had an immediate impact in giving black Americans citizenship, it did nothing to protect blacks from the vengeance of whites once Reconstruction ended. In the late nineteenth and early twentieth centuries, section 1 of the Fourteenth Amendment was often used to protect business interests and strike down laws protecting workers on the grounds that the rights of "persons," that is, corporations, were protected by "due process." More recently, the Fourteenth Amendment has been used to justify school desegregation and affirmative action programs, as well as to dismantle such programs.

Amendment XV

[Adopted 1870]

Section 1   The right of citizens of the United States to vote shall not be denied or abridged by the United States or by any State on account of race, color, or previous condition of servitude.

Section 2   The Congress shall have power to enforce this article by appropriate legislation.

◆ ◆ ◆

The Fifteenth Amendment was the last major piece of Reconstruction legislation. While earlier Reconstruction acts had already required black suffrage in the South, the Fifteenth Amendment extended black voting rights to the entire nation. Some Republicans felt morally obligated to do away with the double standard between North and South since many northern states had stubbornly refused to enfranchise blacks. Others believed that the freedman's ballot required the extra protection of a constitutional amendment to shield it from white counterattack. But partisan advantage also played an important role in the amendment's passage, since Republicans hoped that by giving the ballot to northern blacks, they could lessen their political vulnerability.

Many women's rights advocates had fought for the amendment. They had felt betrayed by the inclusion of the word male *in section 2 of the Fourteenth Amendment and were further angered when the proposed Fifteenth Amendment failed to prohibit denial of the right to vote on the grounds of sex as well as "race, color, or previous condition of servitude." In this amendment, for the first time, the federal government claimed the power to regulate the franchise, or vote. It was also the first time the Constitution placed limits on the power of the states to regulate access to the franchise. Although ratified in 1870, however, the amendment was not enforced until the twentieth century.*

The Progressive Amendments (Sixteenth–Nineteenth Amendments)

No amendments were added to the Constitution between the Civil War and the Progressive Era. America was changing, however, in fundamental ways. The rapid industrialization of the United States after the Civil War led to many social and economic problems. Hundreds of amendments were proposed, but none received enough support in Congress to be sent to the states. Some scholars believe that regional differences and rivalries were so strong during this period that it was almost impossible to gain a consensus on a constitutional amendment. During the Progressive Era, however, the Constitution was amended four times in seven years.

Amendment XVI

[Adopted 1913]

The Congress shall have power to lay and collect taxes on incomes, from whatever source derived, without apportionment among the several States, and without regard to any census or enumeration.

Until passage of the Sixteenth Amendment, most of the money used to run the federal government came from customs duties and taxes on specific items, such as liquor. During the Civil War, the federal government taxed incomes as an emergency measure. Pressure to enact an in-

come tax came from those who were concerned about the growing gap between rich and poor in the United States. The Populist Party began campaigning for a graduated income tax in 1892, and support continued to grow. By 1909, thirty-three proposed income tax amendments had been presented in Congress, but lobbying by corporate and other special interests had defeated them all. In June 1909, the growing pressure for an income tax, which had been endorsed by Presidents Roosevelt and Taft, finally pushed an amendment through the Senate. The required thirty-six states had ratified the amendment by February 1913.

Amendment XVII

[Adopted 1913]

Section 1 The Senate of the United States shall be composed of two Senators from each State, elected by the people thereof, for six years; and each Senator shall have one vote. The electors in each State shall have the qualifications requisite for electors of [voters for] the most numerous branch of the State legislatures.

Section 2 When vacancies happen in the representation of any State in the Senate, the executive authority of such State shall issue writs of election to fill such vacancies: Provided, that the Legislature of any State may empower the executive thereof to make temporary appointments until the people fill the vacancies by election as the Legislature may direct.

Section 3 This amendment shall not be so construed as to affect the election or term of any Senator chosen before it becomes valid as part of the Constitution.

The framers of the Constitution saw the members of the House as the representatives of the people and the members of the Senate as the representatives of the states. Originally senators were to be chosen by the state legislators. According to reform advocates, however, the growth of private industry and transportation conglomerates during the Gilded Age had created a network of corruption in which wealth and power were exchanged for influence and votes in the Senate. Senator Nelson Aldrich, who represented Rhode Island in the late nineteenth and early twentieth centuries, for example, was known as "the senator from Standard Oil" because of his open support of special business interests.

Efforts to amend the Constitution to allow direct election of senators had begun in 1826, but since any proposal had to be approved by the Senate, reform seemed impossible. Progressives tried to gain influence in the Senate by instituting party caucuses and primary elections, which gave citizens the chance to express their choice of a senator who could then be officially elected by the state legislature. By 1910, fourteen of the country's thirty senators received popular votes through a state primary before the state legislature made its selection. Despairing of getting a proposal through the Senate, supporters of a direct-election amendment had begun in 1893 to seek a convention of representatives from two-thirds of the states to propose an amendment that could then be ratified. By 1905, thirty-one of forty-five states had endorsed such an amendment. Finally, in 1911, despite extraordinary opposition, a proposed amendment passed the Senate; by 1913, it had been ratified.

Amendment XVIII

[Adopted 1919; Repealed 1933 by Amendment XXI]

Section 1   After one year from the ratification of this article the manufacture, sale, or transportation of intoxicating liquors within, the importation thereof into, or the exportation thereof from the United States and all territory subject to the jurisdiction thereof, for beverage purposes, is hereby prohibited.

Section 2   The Congress and the several States shall have concurrent power to enforce this article by appropriate legislation.

Section 3   This article shall be inoperative unless it shall have been ratified as an amendment to the Constitution by the legislatures of the several States, as provided by the Constitution, within seven years from the date of the submission thereof to the States by the Congress.

◆ ◆ ◆

The Prohibition Party, formed in 1869, began calling for a constitutional amendment to outlaw alcoholic beverages in 1872. A prohibition amendment was first proposed in the Senate in 1876 and was revived eighteen times before 1913. Between 1913 and 1919, another thirty-nine attempts were made to prohibit liquor in the United States through a constitutional amendment. Prohibition became a key element of the Progressive agenda as reformers linked alcohol and drunkenness to numerous social problems, including the corruption of immigrant voters. While opponents of such an amendment argued that it was undemocratic, supporters claimed that their efforts had widespread public support. The admission of twelve "dry" western states to the Union in the early twentieth century and the spirit of sacrifice during World War I laid the groundwork for passage and ratification of the Eighteenth Amendment in 1919. Opponents added a time limit to the

amendment in the hope that they could thus block ratification, but this effort failed. (See also Amendment XXI.)

Amendment XIX

[Adopted 1920]

Section 1   The right of citizens of the United States to vote shall not be denied or abridged by the United States or by any State on account of sex.

Section 2   Congress shall have the power to enforce this article by appropriate legislation.

Advocates of women's rights tried and failed to link woman suffrage to the Fourteenth and Fifteenth Amendments. Nonetheless, the effort for woman suffrage continued. Between 1878 and 1912, at least one and sometimes as many as four proposed amendments were introduced in Congress each year to grant women the right to vote. While over time women won very limited voting rights in some states, at both the state and federal levels opposition to an amendment for woman suffrage remained very strong. President Woodrow Wilson and other officials felt that the federal government should not interfere with the power of the states in this matter. Others worried that granting suffrage to women would encourage ethnic minorities to exercise their own right to vote. And many were concerned that giving women the vote would result in their abandoning traditional gender roles. In 1919, following a protracted and often bitter campaign of protest in which women went on hunger strikes and chained themselves to fences, an amendment was introduced with the backing of President Wilson. It narrowly passed the Senate (after efforts to limit the suffrage to white women failed) and was adopted in 1920 after Tennessee became the thirty-sixth state to ratify it.

Unratified Amendment

Child Labor Amendment (proposed by Congress June 2, 1924)

Section 1   The Congress shall have power to limit, regulate, and prohibit the labor of persons under eighteen years of age.

Section 2   The power of the several States is unimpaired by this article except that the operation of State laws shall be suspended to the extent necessary to give effect to legislation enacted by Congress.

Throughout the late nineteenth and early twentieth centuries, alarm over the condition of child workers grew.

Opponents of child labor argued that children worked in dangerous and unhealthy conditions, that they took jobs from adult workers, that they depressed wages in certain industries, and that states that allowed child labor had an economic advantage over those that did not. Defenders of child labor claimed that children provided needed income in many families, that working at a young age developed character, and that the effort to prohibit the practice constituted an invasion of family privacy.

In 1916, Congress passed a law that made it illegal to sell goods made by children through interstate commerce. The Supreme Court, however, ruled that the law violated the limits on the power of Congress to regulate interstate commerce. Congress then tried to penalize industries that used child labor by taxing such goods. This measure was also thrown out by the courts. In response, reformers set out to amend the Constitution. The proposed amendment was ratified by twenty-eight states, but by 1925, thirteen states had rejected it. Passage of the Fair Labor Standards Act in 1938, which was upheld by the Supreme Court in 1941, made the amendment irrelevant.

Amendment XX

[Adopted 1933]

Section 1 The terms of the President and Vice President shall end at noon on the 20th day of January, and the terms of Senators and Representatives at noon on the 3rd day of January, of the years in which such terms would have ended if this article had not been ratified; and the terms of their successors shall then begin.

Section 2 The Congress shall assemble at least once in every year, and such meeting shall begin at noon on the 3d day of January, unless they shall by law appoint a different day.

Section 3 If, at the time fixed for the beginning of the term of the President, the President-elect shall have died, the Vice-President-elect shall become President. If a President shall not have been chosen before the time fixed for the beginning of his term, or if the President-elect shall have failed to qualify, then the Vice-President-elect shall act as President until a President shall have qualified; and the Congress may by law provide for the case wherein neither a President-elect nor a Vice-President-elect shall have qualified, declaring who shall then act as President, or the manner in which one who is to act shall be selected, and such person shall act accordingly until a President or Vice-President shall have qualified.

Section 4 The Congress may by law provide for the case of the death of any of the persons from whom the House of Representatives may choose a President whenever the right of choice shall have devolved upon them, and for the case of the death of any of the persons from whom the Senate may choose a Vice-President whenever the right of choice shall have devolved upon them.

Section 5 Sections 1 and 2 shall take effect on the 15th day of October following the ratification of this article.

Section 6 This article shall be inoperative unless it shall have been ratified as an amendment to the Constitution by the Legislatures of three-fourths of the several States within seven years from the date of its submission.

Until 1933, presidents took office on March 4. Since elections are held in early November and electoral votes are counted in mid-December, this meant that more than three months passed between the time a new president was elected and when he took office. Moving the inauguration to January shortened the transition period and allowed Congress to begin its term closer to the time of the president's inauguration. Although this seems like a minor change, an amendment was required because the Constitution specifies terms of office. This amendment also deals with questions of succession in the event that a president- or vice president-elect dies before assuming office. Section 3 also clarifies a method for resolving a deadlock in the electoral college.

Amendment XXI

[Adopted 1933]

Section 1 The eighteenth article of amendment to the Constitution of the United States is hereby repealed.

Section 2 The transportation or importation into any State, Territory, or Possession of the United States for delivery or use therein of intoxicating liquors, in violation of the laws thereof, is hereby prohibited.

Section 3 This article shall be inoperative unless it shall have been ratified as an amendment to the Constitution by conventions in the several States, as provided in the Constitution, within seven years from the date of the submission thereof to the States by the Congress.

Widespread violation of the Volstead Act, the law enacted to enforce prohibition, made the United States a nation of lawbreakers. Prohibition caused more problems than it solved by encouraging crime, bribery, and corruption.

Further, a coalition of liquor and beer manufacturers, personal liberty advocates, and constitutional scholars joined forces to challenge the amendment. By 1929, thirty proposed repeal amendments had been introduced in Congress, and the Democratic Party made repeal part of its platform in the 1932 presidential campaign. The Twenty-First Amendment was proposed in February 1933 and ratified less than a year later. The failure of the effort to enforce prohibition through a constitutional amendment has often been cited by opponents to subsequent efforts to shape public virtue and private morality.

Amendment XXII

[Adopted 1951]

Section 1   No person shall be elected to the office of the President more than twice, and no person who has held the office of President, or acted as President, for more than two years of a term to which some other person was elected President shall be elected to the office of President more than once. But this article shall not apply to any person holding the office of President when this Article was proposed by the Congress, and shall not prevent any person who may be holding the office of President, or acting as President, during the term within which this Article becomes operative from holding the office of President or acting as President during the remainder of such term.

Section 2   This article shall be inoperative unless it shall have been ratified as an amendment to the Constitution by the legislatures of three-fourths of the several States within seven years from the date of its submission to the States by the Congress.

◆ ◆ ◆

George Washington's refusal to seek a third term of office set a precedent that stood until 1912, when former President Theodore Roosevelt sought, without success, another term as an independent candidate. Democrat Franklin Roosevelt was the only president to seek and win a fourth term, though he did so amid great controversy. Roosevelt died in April 1945, a few months after the beginning of his fourth term. In 1946, Republicans won control of the House and the Senate, and early in 1947 a proposal for an amendment to limit future presidents to two four-year terms was offered to the states for ratification. Democratic critics of the Twenty-Second Amendment charged that it was a partisan posthumous jab at Roosevelt.

Since the Twenty-Second Amendment was adopted, however, the only presidents who might have been able to seek a third term, had it not existed, were Republicans Dwight Eisenhower and Ronald Reagan. Since 1826, Congress has entertained 160 proposed amendments to

limit the president to one six-year term. Such amendments have been backed by fifteen presidents, including Gerald Ford and Jimmy Carter.

Amendment XXIII

[Adopted 1961]

Section 1   The District constituting the seat of Government of the United States shall appoint in such manner as the Congress may direct: A number of electors of President and Vice-President equal to the whole number of Senators and Representatives in Congress to which the District would be entitled if it were a State, but in no event more than the least populous State; they shall be in addition to those appointed by the States, but they shall be considered for the purposes of the election of President and Vice-President, to be electors appointed by a State; and they shall meet in the District and perform such duties as provided by the twelfth article of amendment.

Section 2   The Congress shall have the power to enforce this article by appropriate legislation.

When Washington, D.C., was established as a federal district, no one expected that a significant number of people would make it their permanent and primary residence. A proposal to allow citizens of the district to vote in presidential elections was approved by Congress in June 1960 and was ratified on March 29, 1961.

Amendment XXIV

[Adopted 1964]

Section 1   The right of citizens of the United States to vote in any primary or other election for President or Vice-President, for electors for President or Vice-President, or for Senator or Representative in Congress, shall not be denied or abridged by the United States or any State by reason of failure to pay any poll tax or other tax.

Section 2   The Congress shall have the power to enforce this article by appropriate legislation.

In the colonial and Revolutionary eras, financial independence was seen as necessary to political independence, and the poll tax was used as a requirement for voting. By the twentieth century, however, the poll tax was used mostly

to bar poor people, especially southern blacks, from voting. While conservatives complained that the amendment interfered with states' rights, liberals thought that the amendment did not go far enough because it barred the poll tax only in national elections and not in state or local elections. The amendment was ratified in 1964, however, and two years later, the Supreme Court ruled that poll taxes in state and local elections also violated the equal protection clause of the Fourteenth Amendment.

Amendment XXV

[Adopted 1967]

Section 1 In case of the removal of the President from office or of his death or resignation, the Vice-President shall become President.

Section 2 Whenever there is a vacancy in the office of the Vice-President, the President shall nominate a Vice-President who shall take office upon confirmation by a majority vote of both Houses of Congress.

Section 3 Whenever the President transmits to the President pro tempore of the Senate and the Speaker of the House of Representatives his written declaration that he is unable to discharge the powers and duties of his office, and until he transmits to them a written declaration to the contrary, such powers and duties shall be discharged by the Vice-President as Acting President.

Section 4 Whenever the Vice-President and a majority of either the principal officers of the executive departments or of such other body as Congress may by law provide, transmit to the President pro tempore of the Senate and the Speaker of the House of Representatives their written declaration that the President is unable to discharge the powers and duties of his office, the Vice-President shall immediately assume the powers and duties of the office as Acting President.

Thereafter, when the President transmits to the President pro tempore of the Senate and the Speaker of the House of Representatives his written declaration that no inability exists, he shall resume the powers and duties of his office unless the Vice-President and a majority of either the principal officers of the executive department[s] or of such other body as Congress may by law provide, transmit within four days to the President pro tempore of the Senate and the Speaker of the House of Representatives their written declaration that the President is unable to discharge the powers and duties of his office. Thereupon Congress shall decide the issue, assembling within forty-eight hours for that purpose if not in session. If the Congress, within twenty-one days after receipt of the latter written declaration, or, if Congress is not in session, within twenty-one days after Congress is required to assemble, determines by two-thirds vote of both Houses that the President is unable to discharge the powers and duties of his office, the Vice-President shall continue to discharge the same as Acting President; otherwise, the President shall resume the powers and duties of his office.

The framers of the Constitution established the office of vice president because someone was needed to preside over the Senate. The first president to die in office was William Henry Harrison, in 1841. Vice President John Tyler had himself sworn in as president, setting a precedent that was followed when seven later presidents died in office. The assassination of President James A. Garfield in 1881 posed a new problem, however. After he was shot, the president was incapacitated for two months before he died; he was unable to lead the country, while his vice president, Chester A. Arthur, was unable to assume leadership. Efforts to resolve questions of succession in the event of a presidential disability thus began with the death of Garfield.

In 1963, the assassination of President John F. Kennedy galvanized Congress to action. Vice President Lyndon Johnson was a chain smoker with a history of heart trouble. According to the 1947 Presidential Succession Act, the two men who stood in line to succeed him were the seventy-two-year-old Speaker of the House and the eighty-six-year-old president of the Senate. There were serious concerns that any of these men might become incapacitated while serving as chief executive. The first time the Twenty-Fifth Amendment was used, however, was not in the case of presidential death or illness, but during the Watergate crisis. When Vice President Spiro T. Agnew was forced to resign following allegations of bribery and tax violations, President Richard M. Nixon appointed House Minority Leader Gerald R. Ford vice president. Ford became president following Nixon's resignation eight months later and named Nelson A. Rockefeller as his vice president. Thus, for more than two years, the two highest offices in the country were held by people who had not been elected to them.

Amendment XXVI

[Adopted 1971]

Section 1 The right of citizens of the United States, who are eighteen years of age or older, to vote shall not be denied or abridged by the United States or by any State on account of age.

Section 2 The Congress shall have power to enforce this article by appropriate legislation.

◆ ◆ ◆

Efforts to lower the voting age from twenty-one to eighteen began during World War II. Recognizing that those who were old enough to fight a war should have some say in the government policies that involved them in the war, Presidents Eisenhower, Johnson, and Nixon endorsed the idea. In 1970, the combined pressure of the antiwar movement and the demographic pressure of the baby boom generation led to a Voting Rights Act lowering the voting age in federal, state, and local elections.

In Oregon v. Mitchell (1970), the state of Oregon challenged the right of Congress to determine the age at which people could vote in state or local elections. The Supreme Court agreed with Oregon. Since the Voting Rights Act was ruled unconstitutional, the Constitution had to be amended to allow passage of a law that would lower the voting age. The amendment was ratified in a little more than three months, making it the most rapidly ratified amendment in U.S. history.

Unratified Amendment

Equal Rights Amendment (proposed by Congress March 22, 1972; seven-year deadline for ratification extended, June 30, 1982)

Section 1   Equality of rights under the law shall not be denied or abridged by the United States or by any State on account of sex.

Section 2   The Congress shall have the power to enforce, by appropriate legislation, the provisions of this article.

Section 3   This amendment shall take effect two years after the date of ratification.

◆ ◆ ◆

In 1923, soon after women had won the right to vote, Alice Paul, a leading activist in the woman suffrage movement, proposed an amendment requiring equal treatment of men and women. Opponents of the proposal argued that such an amendment would invalidate laws that protected women and would make women subject to the military draft. After the 1964 Civil Rights Act was adopted, protective workplace legislation was removed anyway.

The renewal of the women's movement, as a by-product of the civil rights and antiwar movements, led to a revival of the Equal Rights Amendment (ERA) in Congress. Disagreements over language held up congressional passage of the proposed amendment, but on March 22, 1972, the Senate approved the ERA by a vote of eighty-four to eight, and it was sent to the states. Six states ratified the

amendment within two days, and by the middle of 1973 the amendment seemed well on its way to adoption, with thirty of the needed thirty-eight states having ratified it. In the mid-1970s, however, a powerful "Stop ERA" campaign developed. The campaign portrayed the ERA as a threat to "family values" and traditional relationships between men and women. Although thirty-five states ultimately ratified the ERA, five of those state legislatures voted to rescind ratification, and the amendment was never adopted.

Unratified Amendment

D.C. Statehood Amendment (proposed by Congress August 22, 1978)

Section 1   For purposes of representation in the Congress, election of the President and Vice President, and article V of this Constitution, the District constituting the seat of government of the United States shall be treated as though it were a State.

Section 2   The exercise of the rights and powers conferred under this article shall be by the people of the District constituting the seat of government, and as shall be provided by Congress.

Section 3   The twenty-third article of amendment to the Constitution of the United States is hereby repealed.

Section 4   This article shall be inoperative, unless it shall have been ratified as an amendment to the Constitution by the legislatures of three-fourths of the several states within seven years from the date of its submission.

◆ ◆ ◆

The 1961 ratification of the Twenty-Third Amendment, giving residents of the District of Columbia the right to vote for a president and vice president, inspired an effort to give residents of the district full voting rights. In 1966, President Lyndon Johnson appointed a mayor and city council; in 1971, D.C. residents were allowed to name a nonvoting delegate to the House; and in 1981, residents were allowed to elect the mayor and city council. Congress retained the right to overrule laws that might affect commuters, the height of federal buildings, and selection of judges and prosecutors. The district's nonvoting delegate to Congress, Walter Fauntroy, lobbied fiercely for a congressional amendment granting statehood to the district. In 1978, a proposed amendment was approved and sent to the states. A number of states quickly ratified the amendment, but, like the ERA, the D.C. Statehood Amendment ran into trouble. Opponents argued that section 2 created a separate category of "nominal" statehood. They argued that the federal district should be eliminated and that the territory should be reabsorbed into the state of Maryland. Although these theoretical arguments were strong, some scholars believe that racist attitudes toward the predominantly black population of the city was also a factor leading to the defeat of the amendment.

AMENDMENT XXVII

[Adopted 1992]

No law, varying the compensation for the services of the Senators and Representatives, shall take effect, until an election of Representatives shall have intervened.

While the Twenty-Sixth Amendment was the most rapidly ratified amendment in U.S. history, the Twenty-Seventh Amendment had the longest journey to ratification. First proposed by James Madison in 1789 as part of the package that included the Bill of Rights, this amendment had been ratified by only six states by 1791. In 1873, however, it was ratified by Ohio to protest a massive retroactive salary increase by the federal government. Unlike later proposed amendments, this one came with no time limit on ratification. In the early 1980s, Gregory D. Watson, a University of Texas economics major, discovered the "lost" amendment and began a single-handed campaign to get state legislators to introduce it for ratification. In 1983, it was accepted by Maine. In 1984, it passed the Colorado legislature. Ratifications trickled in slowly until May 1992, when Michigan and New Jersey became the thirty-eighth and thirty-ninth states, respectively, to ratify. This amendment prevents members of Congress from raising their own salaries without giving voters a chance to vote them out of office before they can benefit from the raises.

APPENDIX II. FACTS AND FIGURES

U.S. POLITICS AND GOVERNMENT

PRESIDENTIAL ELECTIONS

Year	Candidates	Parties	Popular Vote	Percentage of Popular Vote	Electoral Vote	Percentage of Voter Participation
1789	**GEORGE WASHINGTON (Va.)***				69	
	John Adams				34	
	Others				35	
1792	**GEORGE WASHINGTON (Va.)**				132	
	John Adams				77	
	George Clinton				50	
	Others				5	
1796	**JOHN ADAMS (Mass.)**	Federalist			71	
	Thomas Jefferson	Democratic-Republican			68	
	Thomas Pinckney	Federalist			59	
	Aaron Burr	Dem.-Rep.			30	
	Others				48	
1800	**THOMAS JEFFERSON (Va.)**	Dem.-Rep.			73	
	Aaron Burr	Dem.-Rep.			73	
	John Adams	Federalist			65	
	C.C. Pinckney	Federalist			64	
	John Jay	Federalist			1	
1804	**THOMAS JEFFERSON (Va.)**	Dem.-Rep.			162	
	C. C. Pinckney	Federalist			14	
1808	**JAMES MADISON (Va.)**	Dem.-Rep.			122	
	C. C. Pinckney	Federalist			47	
	George Clinton	Dem.-Rep.			6	
1812	**JAMES MADISON (Va.)**	Dem.-Rep.			128	
	De Witt Clinton	Federalist			89	
1816	**JAMES MONROE (Va.)**	Dem.-Rep.			183	
	Rufus King	Federalist			34	
1820	**JAMES MONROE (Va.)**	Dem.-Rep.			231	
	John Quincy Adams	Dem.-Rep.			1	
1824	**JOHN Q. ADAMS (Mass.)**	Dem.-Rep.	108,740	30.5	84	26.9
	Andrew Jackson	Dem.-Rep.	153,544	43.1	99	
	William H. Crawford	Dem.-Rep.	46,618	13.1	41	
	Henry Clay	Dem.-Rep.	47,136	13.2	37	
1828	**ANDREW JACKSON (Tenn.)**	Democratic	647,286	56.0	178	57.6
	John Quincy Adams	National Republican	508,064	44.0	83	

*State of residence when elected president.

Year	Candidates	Parties	Popular Vote	Percentage of Popular Vote	Electoral Vote	Percentage of Voter Participation
1832	**ANDREW JACKSON (Tenn.)**	Democratic	687,502	55.0	219	55.4
	Henry Clay	National Republican	530,189	42.4	49	
	John Floyd	Independent			11	
	William Wirt	Anti-Mason	33,108	2.6	7	
1836	**MARTIN VAN BUREN (N.Y.)**	Democratic	765,483	50.9	170	57.8
	W. H. Harrison	Whig			73	
	Hugh L. White	Whig	739,795	49.1	26	
	Daniel Webster	Whig			14	
	W. P. Magnum	Independent			11	
1840	**WILLIAM H. HARRISON (Ohio)**	Whig	1,274,624	53.1	234	80.2
	Martin Van Buren	Democratic	1,127,781	46.9	60	
	J. G. Birney	Liberty	7,069		—	
1844	**JAMES K. POLK (Tenn.)**	Democratic	1,338,464	49.6	170	78.9
	Henry Clay	Whig	1,300,097	48.1	105	
	J. G. Birney	Liberty	62,300	2.3	—	
1848	**ZACHARY TAYLOR (La.)**	Whig	1,360,967	47.4	163	72.7
	Lewis Cass	Democratic	1,222,342	42.5	127	
	Martin Van Buren	Free-Soil	291,263	10.1	—	
1852	**FRANKLIN PIERCE (N.H.)**	Democratic	1,601,117	50.9	254	69.6
	Winfield Scott	Whig	1,385,453	44.1	42	
	John P. Hale	Free-Soil	155,825	5.0	—	
1856	**JAMES BUCHANAN (Pa.)**	Democratic	1,832,995	45.3	174	78.9
	John C. Frémont	Republican	1,339,932	33.1	114	
	Millard Fillmore	American	871,731	21.6	8	
1860	**ABRAHAM LINCOLN (Ill.)**	Republican	1,865,593	39.8	180	81.2
	Stephen A. Douglas	Democratic	1,382,713	29.5	12	
	John C. Breckinridge	Democratic	848,356	18.1	72	
	John Bell	Union	592,906	12.6	39	
1864	**ABRAHAM LINCOLN (Ill.)**	Republican	2,206,938	55.0	212	73.8
	George B. McClellan	Democratic	1,803,787	45.0	21	
1868	**ULYSSES S. GRANT (Ill)**	Republican	3,012,833	52.7	214	78.1
	Horatio Seymour	Democratic	2,703,249	47.3	80	
1872	**ULYSSES S. GRANT (Ill.)**	Republican	3,597,132	55.6	286	71.3
	Horace Greeley	Democratic; Liberal Republican	2,834,125	43.9	66	
1876	**RUTHERFORD B. HAYES (Ohio)**	Republican	4,036,572	48.0	185	81.8
	Samuel J. Tilden	Democratic	4,284,020	51.0	184	
1880	**JAMES A. GARFIELD (Ohio)**	Republican	4,454,416	48.5	214	79.4
	Winfield S. Hancock	Democratic	4,444,952	48.1	155	
1884	**GROVER CLEVELAND (N.Y.)**	Democratic	4,879,507	48.5	219	77.5
	James G. Blaine	Republican	4,850,293	48.2	182	
1888	**BENJAMIN HARRISON (Ind.)**	Republican	5,439,853	47.9	233	79.3
	Grover Cleveland	Democratic	5,540,309	48.6	168	
1892	**GROVER CLEVELAND (N.Y.)**	Democratic	5,555,426	46.1	277	74.7
	Benjamin Harrison	Republican	5,182,690	43.0	145	
	James B. Weaver	People's	1,029,846	8.5	22	

Year	Candidates	Parties	Popular Vote	Percentage of Popular Vote	Electoral Vote	Percentage of Voter Participation
1896	**WILLIAM McKINLEY (Ohio)**	Republican	7,104,779	51.1	271	79.3
	William J. Bryan	Democratic-People's	6,502,925	47.7	176	
1900	**WILLIAM McKINLEY (Ohio)**	Republican	7,207,923	51.7	292	73.2
	William J. Bryan	Dem.-Populist	6,358,133	45.5	155	
1904	**THEODORE ROOSEVELT (N.Y.)**	Republican	7,623,486	57.9	336	65.2
	Alton B. Parker	Democratic	5,077,911	37.6	140	
	Eugene V. Debs	Socialist	402,283	3.0	—	
1908	**WILLIAM H. TAFT (Ohio)**	Republican	7,678,908	51.6	321	65.4
	William J. Bryan	Democratic	6,409,104	43.1	162	
	Eugene V. Debs	Socialist	420,793	2.8	—	
1912	**WOODROW WILSON (N.J.)**	Democratic	6,293,454	41.9	435	58.8
	Theodore Roosevelt	Progressive	4,119,538	27.4	88	
	William H. Taft	Republican	3,484,980	23.2	8	
	Eugene V. Debs	Socialist	900,672	6.1	—	
1916	**WOODROW WILSON (N.J.)**	Democratic	9,129,606	49.4	277	61.6
	Charles E. Hughes	Republican	8,538,221	46.2	254	
	A. L. Benson	Socialist	585,113	3.2	—	
1920	**WARREN G. HARDING (Ohio)**	Republican	16,143,407	60.5	404	49.2
	James M. Cox	Democratic	9,130,328	34.2	127	
	Eugene V. Debs	Socialist	919,799	3.4	—	
1924	**CALVIN COOLIDGE (Mass.)**	Republican	15,725,016	54.0	382	48.9
	John W. Davis	Democratic	8,386,503	28.8	136	
	Robert M. LaFollette	Progressive	4,822,856	16.6	13	
1928	**HERBERT HOOVER (Calif.)**	Republican	21,391,381	58.2	444	56.9
	Alfred E. Smith	Democratic	15,016,443	40.9	87	
	Norman Thomas	Socialist	267,835	0.7	—	
1932	**FRANKLIN D. ROOSEVELT (N.Y.)**	Democratic	22,809,638	57.4	472	56.9
	Herbert Hoover	Republican	15,758,901	39.7	59	
	Norman Thomas	Socialist	881,951	2.2	—	
1936	**FRANKLIN D. ROOSEVELT (N.Y.)**	Democratic	27,751,597	60.8	523	61.0
	Alfred M. Landon	Republican	16,679,583	36.5	8	
	William Lemke	Union	882,479	1.9	—	
1940	**FRANKLIN D. ROOSEVELT (N.Y.)**	Democratic	27,244,160	54.8	449	62.5
	Wendell Willkie	Republican	22,305,198	44.8	82	
1944	**FRANKLIN D. ROOSEVELT (N.Y.)**	Democratic	25,602,504	53.5	432	55.9
	Thomas E. Dewey	Republican	22,006,285	46.0	99	
1948	**HARRY S. TRUMAN (Mo.)**	Democratic	24,105,695	49.5	303	53.0
	Thomas E. Dewey	Republican	21,969,170	45.1	189	
	J. Strom Thurmond	State-Rights Democratic	1,169,021	2.4	38	
	Henry A. Wallace	Progressive	1,156,103	2.4	—	
1952	**DWIGHT D. EISENHOWER (N.Y.)**	Republican	33,936,252	55.1	442	63.3
	Adlai Stevenson	Democratic	27,314,992	44.4	89	
1956	**DWIGHT D. EISENHOWER (N.Y.)**	Republican	35,575,420	57.6	457	60.6
	Adlai Stevenson	Democratic	26,033,066	42.1	73	
	Other	—	—		1	

Year	Candidates	Parties	Popular Vote	Percentage of Popular Vote	Electoral Vote	Percentage of Voter Participation
1960	**JOHN F. KENNEDY (Mass.)**	Democratic	34,227,096	49.9	303	62.8
	Richard M. Nixon	Republican	34,108,546	49.6	219	
	Other	—	—		15	
1964	**LYNDON B. JOHNSON (Tex.)**	Democratic	43,126,506	61.1	486	61.7
	Barry M. Goldwater	Republican	27,176,799	38.5	52	
1968	**RICHARD M. NIXON (N.Y.)**	Republican	31,770,237	43.4	301	60.6
	Hubert H. Humphrey	Democratic	31,270,533	42.7	191	
	George Wallace	American Indep.	9,906,141	13.5	46	
1972	**RICHARD M. NIXON (N.Y.)**	Republican	47,169,911	60.7	520	55.2
	George S. McGovern	Democratic	29,170,383	37.5	17	
	Other	—	—		1	
1976	**JIMMY CARTER (Ga.)**	Democratic	40,828,587	50.0	297	53.5
	Gerald R. Ford	Republican	39,147,613	47.9	241	
	Other	—	1,575,459	2.1	—	
1980	**RONALD REAGAN (Calif.)**	Republican	43,901,812	50.7	489	52.6
	Jimmy Carter	Democratic	35,483,820	41.0	49	
	John B. Anderson	Independent	5,719,722	6.6	—	
	Ed Clark	Libertarian	921,188	1.1	—	
1984	**RONALD REAGAN (Calif.)**	Republican	54,455,075	59.0	525	53.3
	Walter Mondale	Democratic	37,577,185	41.0	13	
1988	**GEORGE BUSH (Texas)**	Republican	47,946,422	54.0	426	50.2
	Michael S. Dukakis	Democratic	41,016,429	46.0	112	
1992	**WILLIAM J. CLINTON (Ark.)**	Democratic	44,908,254	42.3	370	55.2
	George Bush	Republican	39,102,282	37.4	168	
	H. Ross Perot	Independent	19,721,433	18.9	—	
1996	**WILLIAM J. CLINTON (Ark.)**	Democratic	47,401,185	49.2	379	49
	Robert Dole	Republican	39,197,469	40.7	159	
	H. Ross Perot	Independent	8,085,294	8.4	—	

PRESIDENTS, VICE PRESIDENTS, AND CABINETS

The Washington Administration (1789–1797)

Vice President	John Adams	1789–1797
Secretary of State	Thomas Jefferson	1789–1793
	Edmund Randolph	1794–1795
	Timothy Pickering	1795–1797
Secretary of Treasury	Alexander Hamilton	1789–1795
	Oliver Wolcott	1795–1797
Secretary of War	Henry Knox	1789–1794
	Timothy Pickering	1795–1796
	James McHenry	1796–1797
Attorney General	Edmund Randolph	1789–1793
	William Bradford	1794–1795
	Charles Lee	1795–1797
Postmaster General	Samuel Osgood	1789–1791
	Timothy Pickering	1791–1794
	Joseph Habersham	1795–1797

The John Adams Administration (1797–1801)

Vice President	Thomas Jefferson	1797–1801
Secretary of State	Timothy Pickering	1797–1800
	John Marshall	1800–1801
Secretary of Treasury	Oliver Wolcott	1797–1800
	Samuel Dexter	1800–1801
Secretary of War	James McHenry	1797–1800
	Samuel Dexter	1800–1801
Attorney General	Charles Lee	1797–1801
Postmaster General	Joseph Habersham	1797–1801
Secretary of Navy	Benjamin Stoddert	1798–1801

The Jefferson Administration (1801–1809)

Vice President	Aaron Burr	1801–1805
	George Clinton	1805–1809
Secretary of State	James Madison	1801–1809
Secretary of Treasury	Samuel Dexter	1801
	Albert Gallatin	1801–1809
Secretary of War	Henry Dearborn	1801–1809
Attorney General	Levi Lincoln	1801–1805
	Robert Smith	1805
	John Breckinridge	1805–1806
	Caesar Rodney	1807–1809
Postmaster General	Joseph Habersham	1801
	Gideon Granger	1801–1809
Secretary of Navy	Robert Smith	1801–1809

The Madison Administration (1809–1817)

Vice President	George Clinton	1809–1813
	Elbridge Gerry	1813–1817
Secretary of State	Robert Smith	1809–1811
	James Monroe	1811–1817
Secretary of Treasury	Albert Gallatin	1809–1813
	George Campbell	1814
	Alexander Dallas	1814–1816
	William Crawford	1816–1817
Secretary of War	William Eustis	1809–1812
	John Armstrong	1813–1814
	James Monroe	1814–1815
	William Crawford	1815–1817
Attorney General	Caesar Rodney	1809–1811
	William Pinkney	1811–1814
	Richard Rush	1814–1817
Postmaster General	Gideon Granger	1809–1814
	Return Meigs	1814–1817
Secretary of Navy	Paul Hamilton	1809–1813
	William Jones	1813–1814
	Benjamin Crowninshield	1814–1817

The Monroe Administration (1817–1825)

Vice President	Daniel Tompkins	1817–1825
Secretary of State	John Quincy Adams	1817–1825
Secretary of Treasury	William Crawford	1817–1825
Secretary of War	George Graham	1817
	John C. Calhoun	1817–1825
Attorney General	Richard Rush	1817
	William Wirt	1817–1825
Postmaster General	Return Meigs	1817–1823
	John McLean	1823–1825

Secretary of Navy	Benjamin Crowninshield	1817–1818
	Smith Thompson	1818–1823
	Samuel Southard	1823–1825

The John Quincy Adams Administration (1825–1829)

Vice President	John C. Calhoun	1825–1829
Secretary of State	Henry Clay	1825–1829
Secretary of Treasury	Richard Rush	1825–1829
Secretary of War	James Barbour	1825–1828
	Peter Porter	1828–1829
Attorney General	William Wirt	1825–1829
Postmaster General	John McLean	1825–1829
Secretary of Navy	Samuel Southard	1825–1829

The Jackson Administration (1829–1837)

Vice President	John C. Calhoun	1829–1833
	Martin Van Buren	1833–1837
Secretary of State	Martin Van Buren	1829–1831
	Edward Livingston	1831–1833
	Louis McLane	1833–1834
	John Forsyth	1834–1837
Secretary of Treasury	Samuel Ingham	1829–1831
	Louis McLane	1831–1833
	William Duane	1833
	Roger B. Taney	1833–1834
	Levi Woodbury	1834–1837
Secretary of War	John H. Eaton	1829–1831
	Lewis Cass	1831–1837
	Benjamin Butler	1837
Attorney General	John M. Berrien	1829–1831
	Roger B. Taney	1831–1833
	Benjamin Butler	1833–1837
Postmaster General	William Barry	1829–1835
	Amos Kendall	1835–1837
Secretary of Navy	John Branch	1829–1831
	Levi Woodbury	1831–1834
	Mahlon Dickerson	1834–1837

The Van Buren Administration (1837–1841)

Vice President	Richard M. Johnson	1837–1841
Secretary of State	John Forsyth	1837–1841
Secretary of Treasury	Levi Woodbury	1837–1841
Secretary of War	Joel Poinsett	1837–1841
Attorney General	Benjamin Butler	1837–1838
	Felix Grundy	1838–1840
	Henry D. Gilpin	1840–1841
Postmaster General	Amos Kendall	1837–1840
	John M. Niles	1840–1841
Secretary of Navy	Mahlon Dickerson	1837–1838
	James Paulding	1838–1841

The William Harrison Administration (1841)

Vice President	John Tyler	1841
Secretary of State	Daniel Webster	1841
Secretary of Treasury	Thomas Ewing	1841
Secretary of War	John Bell	1841
Attorney General	John J. Crittenden	1841
Postmaster General	Francis Granger	1841
Secretary of Navy	George Badger	1841

The Tyler Administration (1841–1845)

Vice President	None	
Secretary of State	Daniel Webster	1841–1843
	Hugh S. Legaré	1843
	Abel P. Upshur	1843–1844
	John C. Calhoun	1844–1845
Secretary of Treasury	Thomas Ewing	1841
	Walter Forward	1841–1843
	John C. Spencer	1843–1844
	George Bibb	1844–1845

Secretary of War	John Bell	1841
	John C. Spencer	1841–1843
	James M. Porter	1843–1844
	William Wilkins	1844–1845
Attorney General	John J. Crittenden	1841
	Hugh S. Legaré	1841–1843
	John Nelson	1843–1845
Postmaster General	Francis Granger	1841
	Charles Wickliffe	1841
Secretary of Navy	George Badger	1841
	Abel P. Upshur	1841
	David Henshaw	1843–1844
	Thomas Gilmer	1844
	John Y. Mason	1844–1845

The Polk Administration (1845–1849)

Vice President	George M. Dallas	1845–1849
Secretary of State	James Buchanan	1845–1849
Secretary of Treasury	Robert J. Walker	1845–1849
Secretary of War	William L. Marcy	1845–1849
Attorney General	John Y. Mason	1845–1846
	Nathan Clifford	1846–1848
	Isaac Toucey	1848–1849
Postmaster General	Cave Johnson	1845–1849
Secretary of Navy	George Bancroft	1845–1846
	John Y. Mason	1846–1849

The Taylor Administration (1849–1850)

Vice President	Millard Fillmore	1849–1850
Secretary of State	John M. Clayton	1849–1850
Secretary of Treasury	William Meredith	1849–1850
Secretary of War	George Crawford	1849–1850
Attorney General	Reverdy Johnson	1849–1850
Postmaster General	Jacob Collamer	1849–1850
Secretary of Navy	William Preston	1849–1850

Secretary of Interior	Thomas Ewing	1849–1850

The Fillmore Administration (1850–1853)

Vice President	None	
Secretary of State	Daniel Webster	1850–1852
	Edward Everett	1852–1853
Secretary of Treasury	Thomas Corwin	1850–1853
Secretary of War	Charles Conrad	1850–1853
Attorney General	John J. Crittenden	1850–1853
Postmaster General	Nathan Hall	1850–1852
	Sam D. Hubbard	1852–1853
Secretary of Navy	William A. Graham	1850–1852
	John P. Kennedy	1852–1853
Secretary of Interior	Thomas McKennan	1850
	Alexander Stuart	1850–1853

The Pierce Administration (1853–1857)

Vice President	William R. King	1853–1857
Secretary of State	William L. Marcy	1853–1857
Secretary of Treasury	James Guthrie	1853–1857
Secretary of War	Jefferson Davis	1853–1857
Attorney General	Caleb Cushing	1853–1857
Postmaster General	James Campbell	1853–1857
Secretary of Navy	James C. Dobbin	1853–1857
Secretary of Interior	Robert McClelland	1853–1857

The Buchanan Administration (1857–1861)

Vice President	John C. Breckinridge	1857–1861
Secretary of State	Lewis Cass	1857–1860
	Jeremiah S. Black	1860–1861

Secretary of Treasury	Howell Cobb	1857–1860
	Philip Thomas	1860–1861
	John A. Dix	1861
Secretary of War	John B. Floyd	1857–1861
	Joseph Holt	1861
Attorney General	Jeremiah S. Black	1857–1860
	Edwin M. Stanton	1860–1861
Postmaster General	Aaron V. Brown	1857–1859
	Joseph Holt	1859–1861
	Horatio King	1861
Secretary of Navy	Isaac Toucey	1857–1861
Secretary of Interior	Jacob Thompson	1857–1861

The Lincoln Administration (1861–1865)

Vice President	Hannibal Hamlin	1861–1865
	Andrew Johnson	1865
Secretary of State	William H. Seward	1861–1865
Secretary of Treasury	Samuel P. Chase	1861–1864
	William P. Fessenden	1864–1865
	Hugh McCulloch	1865
Secretary of War	Simon Cameron	1861–1862
	Edwin M. Stanton	1862–1865
Attorney General	Edward Bates	1861–1864
	James Speed	1864–1865
Postmaster General	Horatio King	1861
	Montgomery Blair	1861–1864
	William Dennison	1864–1865
Secretary of Navy	Gideon Welles	1861–1865
Secretary of Interior	Caleb B. Smith	1861–1863
	John P. Usher	1863–1865

The Andrew Johnson Administration (1865–1869)

Vice President	None	
Secretary of State	William H. Seward	1865–1869
Secretary of Treasury	Hugh McCulloch	1865–1869
Secretary of War	Edwin M. Stanton	1865–1867
	Ulysses S. Grant	1867–1868
	Lorenzo Thomas	1868
	John M. Schofield	1868–1869
Attorney General	James Speed	1865–1866
	Henry Stanbery	1866–1868
	William M. Evarts	1868–1869
Postmaster General	William Dennison	1865–1866
	Alexander Randall	1866–1869
Secretary of Navy	Gideon Welles	1865–1869
Secretary of Interior	John P. Usher	1865
	James Harlan	1865–1866
	Orville H. Browning	1866–1869

The Grant Administration (1869–1877)

Vice President	Schuyler Colfax	1869–1873
	Henry Wilson	1873–1877
Secretary of State	Elihu B. Washburne	1869
	Hamilton Fish	1869–1877
Secretary of Treasury	George S. Boutwell	1869–1873
	William Richardson	1873–1874
	Benjamin Bristow	1874–1876
	Lot M. Morrill	1876–1877
Secretary of War	John A. Rawlins	1869
	William T. Sherman	1869
	William W. Belknap	1869–1876
	Alphonso Taft	1876
	James D. Cameron	1876–1877
Attorney General	Ebenezer Hoar	1869–1870
	Amos T. Ackerman	1870–1871
	G. H. Williams	1871–1875
	Edwards Pierrepont	1875–1876
	Alphonso Taft	1876–1877
Postmaster General	John A. J. Creswell	1869–1874
	James W. Marshall	1874
	Marshall Jewell	1874–1876
	James N. Tyner	1876–1877
Secretary of Navy	Adolph E. Borie	1869
	George M. Robeson	1869–1877
Secretary of Interior	Jacob D. Cox	1869–1870
	Columbus Delano	1870–1875
	Zachariah Chandler	1875–1877

The Hayes Administration (1877–1881)

Vice President	William A. Wheeler	1877–1881
Secretary of State	William M. Evarts	1877–1881
Secretary of Treasury	John Sherman	1877–1881
Secretary of War	George W. McCrary	1877–1879
	Alex Ramsey	1879–1881
Attorney General	Charles Devens	1877–1881
Postmaster General	David M. Key	1877–1880
	Horace Maynard	1880–1881
Secretary of Navy	Richard W. Thompson	1877–1880
	Nathan Goff, Jr.	1881
Secretary of Interior	Carl Schurz	1877–1881

The Garfield Administration (1881)

Vice President	Chester A. Arthur	1881
Secretary of State	James G. Blaine	1881
Secretary of Treasury	William Windom	1881
Secretary of War	Robert T. Lincoln	1881
Attorney General	Wayne MacVeagh	1881
Postmaster General	Thomas L. James	1881
Secretary of Navy	William H. Hunt	1881
Secretary of Interior	Samuel J. Kirkwood	1881

The Arthur Administration (1881–1885)

Vice President	None	
Secretary of State	F. T. Frelinghuysen	1881–1885
Secretary of Treasury	Charles J. Folger	1881–1884
	Walter Q. Gresham	1884
	Hugh McCulloch	1884–1885
Secretary of War	Robert T. Lincoln	1881–1885
Attorney General	Benjamin H. Brewster	1881–1885
Postmaster General	Timothy O. Howe	1881–1883
	Walter Q. Gresham	1883–1884
	Frank Hatton	1884–1885
Secretary of Navy	William H. Hunt	1881–1882
	William E. Chandler	1882–1885
Secretary of Interior	Samuel J. Kirkwood	1881–1882
	Henry M. Teller	1882–1885

The Cleveland Administration (1885–1889)

Vice President	Thomas A. Hendricks	1885–1889
Secretary of State	Thomas F. Bayard	1885–1889
Secretary of Treasury	Daniel Manning	1885–1887
	Charles S. Fairchild	1887–1889
Secretary of War	William C. Endicott	1885–1889
Attorney General	Augustus H. Garland	1885–1889
Postmaster General	William F. Vilas	1885–1888
	Don M. Dickinson	1888–1889
Secretary of Navy	William C. Whitney	1885–1889
Secretary of Interior	Lucius Q. C. Lamar	1885–1888
	William F. Vilas	1888–1889
Secretary of Agriculture	Norman J. Colman	1889

The Benjamin Harrison Administration (1889–1893)

Vice President	Levi P. Morton	1889–1893
Secretary of State	James G. Blaine	1889–1892
	John W. Foster	1892–1893
Secretary of Treasury	William Windom	1889–1891
	Charles Foster	1891–1893
Secretary of War	Redfield Proctor	1889–1891
	Stephen B. Elkins	1891–1893

Attorney General	William H. H. Miller	1889–1893
Postmaster General	John Wanamaker	1889–1893
Secretary of Navy	Benjamin F. Tracy	1889–1893
Secretary of Interior	John W. Noble	1889–1893
Secretary of Agriculture	Jeremiah M. Rusk	1889–1893

The Cleveland Administration (1893–1897)

Vice President	Adlai E. Stevenson	1893–1897
Secretary of State	Walter Q. Gresham	1893–1895
	Richard Olney	1895–1897
Secretary of Treasury	John G. Carlisle	1893–1897
Secretary of War	Daniel S. Lamont	1893–1897
Attorney General	Richard Olney	1893–1895
	James Harmon	1895–1897
Postmaster General	Wilson S. Bissell	1893–1895
	William L. Wilson	1895–1897
Secretary of Navy	Hilary A. Herbert	1893–1897
Secretary of Interior	Hoke Smith	1893–1896
	David R. Francis	1896–1897
Secretary of Agriculture	Julius S. Morton	1893–1897

The McKinley Administration (1897–1901)

Vice President	Garret A. Hobart	1897–1901
	Theodore Roosevelt	1901
Secretary of State	John Sherman	1897–1898
	William R. Day	1898
	John Hay	1898–1901
Secretary of Treasury	Lyman J. Gage	1897–1901
Secretary of War	Russell A. Alger	1897–1899
	Elihu Root	1899–1901
Attorney General	Joseph McKenna	1897–1898
	John W. Griggs	1898–1901
	Philander C. Knox	1901

Postmaster General	James A. Gary	1897–1898
	Charles E. Smith	1898–1901
Secretary of Navy	John D. Long	1897–1901
Secretary of Interior	Cornelius N. Bliss	1897–1899
	Ethan A. Hitchcock	1899–1901
Secretary of Agriculture	James Wilson	1897–1901

The Theodore Roosevelt Administration (1901–1909)

Vice President	Charles Fairbanks	1905–1909
Secretary of State	John Hay	1901–1905
	Elihu Root	1905–1909
	Robert Bacon	1909
Secretary of Treasury	Lyman J. Gage	1901–1902
	Leslie M. Shaw	1902–1907
	George B. Cortelyou	1907–1909
Secretary of War	Elihu Root	1901–1904
	William H. Taft	1904–1908
	Luke E. Wright	1908–1909
Attorney General	Philander C. Knox	1901–1904
	William H. Moody	1904–1906
	Charles J. Bonaparte	1906–1909
Postmaster General	Charles E. Smith	1901–1902
	Henry C. Payne	1902–1904
	Robert J. Wynne	1904–1905
	George B. Cortelyou	1905–1907
	George von L. Meyer	1907–1909
Secretary of Navy	John D. Long	1901–1902
	William H. Moody	1902–1904
	Paul Morton	1904–1905
	Charles J. Bonaparte	1905–1906
	Victor H. Metcalf	1906–1908
	Truman H. Newberry	1908–1909
Secretary of Interior	Ethan A. Hitchcock	1901–1907
	James R. Garfield	1907–1909
Secretary of Agriculture	James Wilson	1901–1909
Secretary of Labor and Commerce	George B. Cortelyou	1903–1904
	Victor H. Metcalf	1904–1906
	Oscar S. Straus	1906–1909
	Charles Nagel	1909

The Taft Administration (1909 – 1913)

Vice President	James S. Sherman	1909–1913
Secretary of State	Philander C. Knox	1909–1913
Secretary of Treasury	Franklin MacVeagh	1909–1913
Secretary of War	Jacob M. Dickinson	1909–1911
	Henry L. Stimson	1911–1913
Attorney General	George W. Wickersham	1909–1913
Postmaster General	Frank H. Hitchcock	1909–1913
Secretary of Navy	George von L. Meyer	1909–1913
Secretary of Interior	Richard A. Ballinger	1909–1911
	Walter L. Fisher	1911–1913
Secretary of Agriculture	James Wilson	1909–1913
Secretary of Labor and Commerce	Charles Nagel	1909–1913

The Wilson Administration (1913–1921)

Vice President	Thomas R. Marshall	1913–1921
Secretary of State	William J. Bryan	1913–1915
	Robert Lansing	1915–1920
	Bainbridge Colby	1920–1921
Secretary of Treasury	William G. McAdoo	1913–1918
	Carter Glass	1918–1920
	David F. Houston	1920–1921
Secretary of War	Lindley M. Garrison	1913–1916
	Newton D. Baker	1916–1921
Attorney General	James C. McReynolds	1913–1914
	Thomas W. Gregory	1914–1919
	A. Mitchell Palmer	1919–1921
Postmaster General	Albert S. Burleson	1913–1921

Secretary of Navy	Josephus Daniels	1913–1921
Secretary of Interior	Franklin K. Lane	1913–1920
	John B. Payne	1920–1921
Secretary of Agriculture	David F. Houston	1913–1920
	Edwin T. Meredith	1920–1921
Secretary of Commerce	William C. Redfield	1913–1919
	Joshua W. Alexander	1919–1921
Secretary of Labor	William B. Wilson	1913–1921

The Harding Administration (1921–1923)

Vice President	Calvin Coolidge	1921–1923
Secretary of State	Charles E. Hughes	1921–1923
Secretary of Treasury	Andrew Mellon	1921–1923
Secretary of War	John W. Weeks	1921–1923
Attorney General	Harry M. Daugherty	1921–1923
Postmaster General	Will H. Hays	1921–1922
	Hubert Work	1922–1923
	Harry S. New	1923
Secretary of Navy	Edwin Denby	1921–1923
Secretary of Interior	Albert B. Fall	1921–1923
	Hubert Work	1923
Secretary of Agriculture	Henry C. Wallace	1921–1923
Secretary of Commerce	Herbert C. Hoover	1921–1923
Secretary of Labor	James J. Davis	1921–1923

The Coolidge Administration (1923–1929)

Vice President	Charles G. Dawes	1925–1929
Secretary of State	Charles E. Hughes	1923–1925
	Frank B. Kellogg	1925–1929
Secretary of Treasury	Andrew Mellon	1923–1929

Secretary of War	John W. Weeks	1923–1925
	Dwight F. Davis	1925–1929
Attorney General	Henry M. Daugherty	1923–1924
	Harlan F. Stone	1924–1925
	John G. Sargent	1925–1929
Postmaster General	Harry S. New	1923–1929
Secretary of Navy	Edwin Denby	1923–1924
	Curtis D. Wilbur	1924–1929
Secretary of Interior	Hubert Work	1923–1928
	Roy O. West	1928–1929
Secretary of Agriculture	Henry C. Wallace	1923–1924
	Howard M. Gore	1924–1925
	William M. Jardine	1925–1929
Secretary of Commerce	Herbert C. Hoover	1923–1928
	William F. Whiting	1928–1929
Secretary of Labor	James J. Davis	1923–1929

The Hoover Administration (1929–1933)

Vice President	Charles Curtis	1929–1933
Secretary of State	Henry L. Stimson	1929–1933
Secretary of Treasury	Andrew Mellon	1929–1932
	Ogden L. Mills	1932–1933
Secretary of War	James W. Good	1929
	Patrick J. Hurley	1929–1933
Attorney General	William D. Mitchell	1929–1933
Postmaster General	Walter F. Brown	1929–1933
Secretary of Navy	Charles F. Adams	1929–1933
Secretary of Interior	Ray L. Wilbur	1929–1933
Secretary of Agriculture	Arthur M. Hyde	1929–1933
Secretary of Commerce	Robert P. Lamont	1929–1932
	Roy D. Chapin	1932–1933
Secretary of Labor	James J. Davis	1929–1930
	William M. Doak	1930–1933

The Franklin D. Roosevelt Administration (1933–1945)

Vice President	John Nance Garner	1933–1941
	Henry A. Wallace	1941–1945
	Harry S. Truman	1945
Secretary of State	Cordell Hull	1933–1944
	Edward R. Stettinius, Jr.	1944–1945
Secretary of Treasury	William H. Woodin	1933–1934
	Henry Morgenthau, Jr.	1934–1945
Secretary of War	George H. Dern	1933–1936
	Henry A. Woodring	1936–1940
	Henry L. Stimson	1940–1945
Attorney General	Homer S. Cummings	1933–1939
	Frank Murphy	1939–1940
	Robert H. Jackson	1940–1941
	Francis Biddle	1941–1945
Postmaster General	James A. Farley	1933–1940
	Frank C. Walker	1940–1945
Secretary of Navy	Claude A. Swanson	1933–1940
	Charles Edison	1940
	Frank Knox	1940–1944
	James V. Forrestal	1944–1945
Secretary of Interior	Harold L. Ickes	1933–1945
Secretary of Agriculture	Henry A. Wallace	1933–1940
	Claude R. Wickard	1940–1945
Secretary of Commerce	Daniel C. Roper	1933–1939
	Harry L. Hopkins	1939–1940
	Jesse Jones	1940–1945
	Henry A. Wallace	1945
Secretary of Labor	Frances Perkins	1933–1945

The Truman Administration (1945–1953)

Vice President	Alben W. Barkley	1949–1953
Secretary of State	Edward R. Stettinius, Jr.	1945
	James F. Byrnes	1945–1947
	George C. Marshall	1947–1949
	Dean G. Acheson	1949–1953

Secretary of Treasury	Fred M. Vinson	1945–1946
	John W. Snyder	1946–1953
Secretary of War	Robert P. Patterson	1945–1947
	Kenneth C. Royall	1947
Attorney General	Tom C. Clark	1945–1949
	J. Howard McGrath	1949–1952
	James P. McGranery	1952–1953
Postmaster General	Frank C. Walker	1945
	Robert E. Hannegan	1945–1947
	Jesse M. Donaldson	1947–1953
Secretary of Navy	James V. Forrestal	1945–1947
Secretary of Interior	Harold L. Ickes	1945–1946
	Julius A. Krug	1946–1949
	Oscar L. Chapman	1949–1953
Secretary of Agriculture	Clinton P. Anderson	1945–1948
	Charles F. Brannan	1948–1953
Secretary of Commerce	Henry A. Wallace	1945–1946
	W. Averell Harriman	1946–1948
	Charles W. Sawyer	1948–1953
Secretary of Labor	Lewis B. Schwellenbach	1945–1948
	Maurice J. Tobin	1948–1953
Secretary of Defense	James V. Forrestal	1947–1949
	Louis A. Johnson	1949–1950
	George C. Marshall	1950–1951
	Robert A. Lovett	1951–1953

The Eisenhower Administration (1953–1961)

Vice President	Richard M. Nixon	1953–1961
Secretary of State	John Foster Dulles	1953–1959
	Christian A. Herter	1959–1961
Secretary of Treasury	George M. Humphrey	1953–1957
	Robert B. Anderson	1957–1961
Attorney General	Herbert Brownell, Jr.	1953–1958
	William P. Rogers	1958–1961
Postmaster General	Arthur E. Summerfield	1953–1961
Secretary of Interior	Douglas McKay	1953–1956
	Fred A. Seaton	1956–1961
Secretary of Agriculture	Ezra T. Benson	1953–1961
Secretary of Commerce	Sinclair Weeks	1953–1958
	Lewis L. Strauss	1958–1959
	Frederick H. Mueller	1959–1961
Secretary of Labor	Martin P. Durkin	1953
	James P. Mitchell	1953–1961
Secretary of Defense	Charles E. Wilson	1953–1957
	Neil H. McElroy	1957–1959
	Thomas S. Gates, Jr.	1959–1961
Secretary of Health, Education and Welfare	Oveta Culp Hobby	1953–1955
	Marion B. Folsom	1955–1958
	Arthur S. Flemming	1958–1961

The Kennedy Administration (1961–1963)

Vice President	Lyndon B. Johnson	1961–1963
Secretary of State	Dean Rusk	1961–1963
Secretary of Treasury	C. Douglas Dillon	1961–1963
Attorney General	Robert F. Kennedy	1961–1963
Postmaster General	J. Edward Day	1961–1963
	John A. Gronouski	1963
Secretary of Interior	Stewart L. Udall	1961–1963
Secretary of Agriculture	Orville L. Freeman	1961–1963
Secretary of Commerce	Luther H. Hodges	1961–1963
Secretary of Labor	Arthur J. Goldberg	1961–1962
	W. Willard Wirtz	1962–1963
Secretary of Defense	Robert S. McNamara	1961–1963
Secretary of Health, Education and Welfare	Abraham A. Ribicoff	1961–1962
	Anthony J. Celebrezze	1962–1963

The Lyndon Johnson Administration (1963 – 1969)

Vice President	Hubert H. Humphrey	1965–1969
Secretary of State	Dean Rusk	1963–1969
Secretary of Treasury	C. Douglas Dillon	1963–1965
	Henry H. Fowler	1965–1969
Attorney General	Robert F. Kennedy	1963–1964
	Nicholas Katzenbach	1965–1966
	Ramsey Clark	1967–1969
Postmaster General	John A. Gronouski	1963–1965
	Lawrence F. O'Brien	1965–1968
	Marvin Watson	1968–1969
Secretary of Interior	Stewart L. Udall	1963–1969
Secretary of Agriculture	Orville L. Freeman	1963–1969
Secretary of Commerce	Luther H. Hodges	1963–1964
	John T. Connor	1964–1967
	Alexander B. Trowbridge	1967–1968
	Cyrus R. Smith	1968–1969
Secretary of Labor	W. Willard Wirtz	1963–1969
Secretary of Defense	Robert F. McNamara	1963–1968
	Clark Clifford	1968–1969
Secretary of Health, Education and Welfare	Anthony J. Celebrezze	1963–1965
	John W. Gardner	1965–1968
	Wilbur J. Cohen	1968–1969
Secretary of Housing and Urban Development	Robert C. Weaver	1966–1969
	Robert C. Wood	1969
Secretary of Transportation	Alan S. Boyd	1967–1969

The Nixon Administration (1969 – 1974)

Vice President	Spiro T. Agnew	1969–1973
	Gerald R. Ford	1973–1974
Secretary of State	William P. Rogers	1969–1973
	Henry A. Kissinger	1973–1974
Secretary of Treasury	David M. Kennedy	1969–1970
	John B. Connally	1971–1972
	George P. Shultz	1972–1974
	William E. Simon	1974
Attorney General	John N. Mitchell	1969–1972
	Richard G. Kleindienst	1972–1973
	Elliot L. Richardson	1973
	William B. Saxbe	1973–1974
Postmaster General	Winton M. Blount	1969–1971
Secretary of Interior	Walter J. Hickel	1969–1970
	Rogers Morton	1971–1974
Secretary of Agriculture	Clifford M. Hardin	1969–1971
	Earl L. Butz	1971–1974
Secretary of Commerce	Maurice H. Stans	1969–1972
	Peter G. Peterson	1972–1973
	Frederick B. Dent	1973–1974
Secretary of Labor	George P. Shultz	1969–1970
	James D. Hodgson	1970–1973
	Peter J. Brennan	1973–1974
Secretary of Defense	Melvin R. Laird	1969–1973
	Elliot L. Richardson	1973
	James R. Schlesinger	1973–1974
Secretary of Health, Education and Welfare	Robert H. Finch	1969–1970
	Elliot L. Richardson	1970–1973
	Caspar W. Weinberger	1973–1974
Secretary of Housing and Urban Development	George Romney	1969–1973
	James T. Lynn	1973–1974
Secretary of Transportation	John A. Volpe	1969–1973
	Claude S. Brinegar	1973–1974

The Ford Administration (1974 – 1977)

Vice President	Nelson A. Rockefeller	1974–1977
Secretary of State	Henry A. Kissinger	1974–1977
Secretary of Treasury	William E. Simon	1974–1977

Attorney General	William Saxbe	1974–1975
	Edward Levi	1975–1977
Secretary of Interior	Rogers Morton	1974–1975
	Stanley K. Hathaway	1975
	Thomas Kleppe	1975–1977
Secretary of Agriculture	Earl L. Butz	1974–1976
	John A. Knebel	1976–1977
Secretary of Commerce	Frederick B. Dent	1974–1975
	Rogers Morton	1975–1976
	Elliot L. Richardson	1976–1977
Secretary of Labor	Peter J. Brennan	1974–1975
	John T. Dunlop	1975–1976
	W. J. Usery	1976–1977
Secretary of Defense	James R. Schlesinger	1974–1975
	Donald Rumsfeld	1975–1977
Secretary of Health, Education and Welfare	Caspar Weinberger	1974–1975
	Forrest D. Mathews	1975–1977
Secretary of Housing and Urban Development	James T. Lynn	1974–1975
	Carla A. Hills	1975–1977
Secretary of Transportation	Claude Brinegar	1974–1975
	William T. Coleman	1975–1977

The Carter Administration (1977 – 1981)

Vice President	Walter F. Mondale	1977–1981
Secretary of State	Cyrus R. Vance	1977–1980
	Edmund Muskie	1980–1981
Secretary of Treasury	W. Michael Blumenthal	1977–1979
	G. William Miller	1979–1981
Attorney General	Griffin Bell	1977–1979
	Benjamin R. Civiletti	1979–1981
Secretary of Interior	Cecil D. Andrus	1977–1981
Secretary of Agriculture	Robert Bergland	1977–1981
Secretary of Commerce	Juanita M. Kreps	1977–1979
	Philip M. Klutznick	1979–1981
Secretary of Labor	F. Ray Marshall	1977–1981
Secretary of Defense	Harold Brown	1977–1981

Secretary of Health, Education and Welfare	Joseph A. Califano	1977–1979
	Patricia R. Harris	1979
Secretary of Health and Human Services	Patricia R. Harris	1979–1981
Secretary of Education	Shirley M. Hufstedler	1979–1981
Secretary of Housing and Urban Development	Patricia R. Harris	1977–1979
	Moon Landrieu	1979–1981
Secretary of Transportation	Brock Adams	1977–1979
	Neil E. Goldschmidt	1979–1981
Secretary of Energy	James R. Schlesinger	1977–1979
	Charles W. Duncan	1979–1981

The Reagan Administration (1981 – 1989)

Vice President	George W. Bush	1981–1989
Secretary of State	Alexander M. Haig	1981–1982
	George P. Shultz	1982–1989
Secretary of Treasury	Donald Regan	1981–1985
	James A. Baker, III	1985–1988
	Nicholas Brady	1988–1989
Attorney General	William F. Smith	1981–1985
	Edwin A. Meese, III	1985–1988
	Richard Thornburgh	1988–1989
Secretary of Interior	James Watt	1981–1983
	William P. Clark, Jr.	1983–1985
	Donald P. Hodel	1985–1989
Secretary of Agriculture	John Block	1981–1986
	Richard E. Lyng	1986–1989
Secretary of Commerce	Malcolm Baldridge	1981–1987
	C. William Verity, Jr.	1987–1989
Secretary of Labor	Raymond Donovan	1981–1985
	William E. Brock	1985–1987
	Ann D. McLaughlin	1987–1989
Secretary of Defense	Caspar Weinberger	1981–1987
	Frank Carlucci	1987–1989

Secretary of Health and Human Services	Richard Schweiker	1981–1983
	Margaret Heckler	1983–1985
	Otis R. Bowen	1985–1989
Secretary of Education	Terrel H. Bell	1981–1985
	William J. Bennett	1985–1988
	Lauro F. Cavazos	1988–1989
Secretary of Housing and Urban Development	Samuel Pierce	1981–1989
Secretary of Transportation	Drew Lewis	1981–1983
	Elizabeth Dole	1983–1987
	James H. Burnley	1987–1989
Secretary of Energy	James Edwards	1981–1982
	Donald P. Hodel	1982–1985
	John S. Herrington	1985–1989

The Bush Administration (1989 – 1993)

Vice President	J. Danforth Quayle	1989–1993
Secretary of State	James A. Baker, III	1989–1992
Secretary of Treasury	Nicholas Brady	1989–1993
Attorney General	Richard Thornburgh	1989–1991
	William P. Barr	1991–1993
Secretary of Interior	Manuel Lujan	1989–1993
Secretary of Agriculture	Clayton K. Yeutter	1989–1991
	Edward Madigan	1991–1993
Secretary of Commerce	Robert Mosbacher	1989–1992
	Barbara Franklin	1992–1993
Secretary of Labor	Elizabeth Hanford Dole	1989–1991
	Lynn Martin	1991–1993
Secretary of Defense	Richard Cheney	1989–1993
Secretary of Health and Human Services	Louis W. Sullivan	1989–1993
Secretary of Education	Lauro F. Cavazos	1989–1991
	Lamar Alexander	1991–1993
Secretary of Housing and Urban Development	Jack F. Kemp	1989–1993

Secretary of Transportation	Samuel K. Skinner	1989–1992
	Andrew H. Card, Jr.	1992–1993
Secretary of Energy	James D. Watkins	1989–1993
Secretary of Veterans Affairs	Edward J. Derwinski	1989–1993

The Clinton Administration (1993 –   )

Vice President	Albert Gore	1993–
Secretary of State	Warren M. Christopher	1993–1997
	Madeleine K. Albright	1997–
Secretary of Treasury	Lloyd Bentsen	1993–1995
	Robert E. Rubin	1995–
Attorney General	Janet Reno	1993–
Secretary of Interior	Bruce Babbitt	1993–
Secretary of Agriculture	Mike Espy	1993–1995
	Dan Glickman	1995–
Secretary of Commerce	Ronald H. Brown	1993–1996
	Mickey Kantor	1996–1997
	William Daley	1997–
Secretary of Labor	Robert B. Reich	1993–1997
	Alexis Herman	1997–
Secretary of Defense	Les Aspin	1993–1994
	William J. Perry	1994–1997
	William Cohen	1997–
Secretary of Health and Human Services	Donna Shalala	1993–
Secretary of Housing and Urban Development	Henry G. Cisneros	1993–1997
	Andrew Cuomo	1997–
Secretary of Education	Richard W. Riley	1993–
Secretary of Transportation	Federico F. Peña	1993–1997
	Rodney Slater	1997–
Secretary of Energy	Hazel R. O'Leary	1993–1997
	Federico F. Peña	1997–
Secretary of Veterans Affairs	Jesse Brown	1993–

ADMISSION OF STATES TO THE UNION

State	Date of Admission
Delaware	December 7, 1787
Pennsylvania	December 12, 1787
New Jersey	December 18, 1787
Georgia	January 2, 1788
Connecticut	January 9, 1788
Massachusetts	February 6, 1788
Maryland	April 28, 1788
South Carolina	May 23, 1788
New Hampshire	June 21, 1788
Virginia	June 25, 1788
New York	July 26, 1788
North Carolina	November 21, 1789
Rhode Island	May 29, 1790
Vermont	March 4, 1791
Kentucky	June 1, 1792
Tennessee	June 1, 1796
Ohio	March 1, 1803
Louisiana	April 30, 1812
Indiana	December 11, 1816
Mississippi	December 10, 1817
Illinois	December 3, 1818
Alabama	December 14, 1819
Maine	March 15, 1820
Missouri	August 10, 1821
Arkansas	June 15, 1836

State	Date of Admission
Michigan	January 16, 1837
Florida	March 3, 1845
Texas	December 29, 1845
Iowa	December 28, 1846
Wisconsin	May 29, 1848
California	September 9, 1850
Minnesota	May 11, 1858
Oregon	February 14, 1859
Kansas	January 29, 1861
West Virginia	June 19, 1863
Nevada	October 31, 1864
Nebraska	March 1, 1867
Colorado	August 1, 1876
North Dakota	November 2, 1889
South Dakota	November 2, 1889
Montana	November 8, 1889
Washington	November 11, 1889
Idaho	July 3, 1890
Wyoming	July 10, 1890
Utah	January 4, 1896
Oklahoma	November 16, 1907
New Mexico	January 6, 1912
Arizona	February 14, 1912
Alaska	January 3, 1959
Hawaii	August 21, 1959

SUPREME COURT JUSTICES

Name	Service	Appointed by
John Jay*	1789–1795	Washington
James Wilson	1789–1798	Washington
John Blair	1789–1796	Washington
John Rutledge	1790–1791	Washington
William Cushing	1790–1810	Washington
James Iredell	1790–1799	Washington
Thomas Johnson	1791–1793	Washington
William Paterson	1793–1806	Washington
John Rutledge†	1795	Washington
Samuel Chase	1796–1811	Washington
Oliver Ellsworth	1796–1799	Washington
Bushrod Washington	1798–1829	J. Adams
Alfred Moore	1799–1804	J. Adams
John Marshall	1801–1835	J. Adams
William Johnson	1804–1834	Jefferson
Henry B. Livingston	1806–1823	Jefferson
Thomas Todd	1807–1826	Jefferson
Gabriel Duval	1811–1836	Madison
Joseph Story	1811–1845	Madison
Smith Thompson	1823–1843	Monroe
Robert Trimble	1826–1828	J. Q. Adams
John McLean	1829–1861	Jackson
Henry Baldwin	1830–1844	Jackson
James M. Wayne	1835–1867	Jackson
Roger B. Taney	1836–1864	Jackson
Philip P. Barbour	1836–1841	Jackson
John Catron	1837–1865	Van Buren
John McKinley	1837–1852	Van Buren
Peter V. Daniel	1841–1860	Van Buren
Samuel Nelson	1845–1872	Tyler
Levi Woodbury	1845–1851	Polk
Robert C. Grier	1846–1870	Polk
Benjamin R. Curtis	1851–1857	Fillmore
John A. Campbell	1853–1861	Pierce
Nathan Clifford	1858–1881	Buchanan
Noah H. Swayne	1862–1881	Lincoln
Samuel F. Miller	1862–1890	Lincoln

*Chief Justices appear in bold type.
†Acting Chief Justice; Senate refused to confirm appointment.

Name	Service	Appointed by
David Davis	1862–1877	Lincoln
Stephen J. Field	1863–1897	Lincoln
Salmon P. Chase	1864–1873	Lincoln
William Strong	1870–1880	Grant
Joseph P. Bradley	1870–1892	Grant
Ward Hunt	1873–1882	Grant
Morrison R. Waite	1874–1888	Grant
John M. Harlan	1877–1911	Hayes
William B. Woods	1880–1887	Hayes
Stanley Matthews	1881–1889	Garfield
Horace Gray	1882–1902	Arthur
Samuel Blatchford	1882–1893	Arthur
Lucious Q. C. Lamar	1888–1893	Cleveland
Melville W. Fuller	1888–1910	Cleveland
David J. Brewer	1889–1910	B. Harrison
Henry B. Brown	1890–1906	B. Harrison
George Shiras	1892–1903	B. Harrison
Howell E. Jackson	1893–1895	B. Harrison
Edward D. White	1894–1910	Cleveland
Rufus W. Peckham	1896–1909	Cleveland
Joseph McKenna	1898–1925	McKinley
Oliver W. Holmes	1902–1932	T. Roosevelt
William R. Day	1903–1922	T. Roosevelt
William H. Moody	1906–1910	T. Roosevelt
Horace H. Lurton	1910–1914	Taft
Charles E. Hughes	1910–1916	Taft
Willis Van Devanter	1910–1937	Taft
Joseph R. Lamar	1911–1916	Taft
Edward D. White	1910–1921	Taft
Mahlon Pitney	1912–1922	Taft
James C. McReynolds	1914–1941	Wilson
Louis D. Brandeis	1916–1939	Wilson
John H. Clarke	1916–1922	Wilson
William H. Taft	1921–1930	Harding
George Sutherland	1922–1938	Harding

Name	Service	Appointed by
Pierce Butler	1923–1939	Harding
Edward T. Sanford	1923–1930	Harding
Harlan F. Stone	1925–1941	Coolidge
Charles E. Hughes	1930–1941	Hoover
Owen J. Roberts	1930–1945	Hoover
Benjamin N. Cardozo	1932–1938	Hoover
Hugo L. Black	1937–1971	F. Roosevelt
Stanley F. Reed	1938–1957	F. Roosevelt
Felix Frankfurter	1939–1962	F. Roosevelt
William O. Douglas	1939–1975	F. Roosevelt
Frank Murphy	1940–1949	F. Roosevelt
Harlan F. Stone	1941–1946	F. Roosevelt
James F. Byrnes	1941–1942	F. Roosevelt
Robert H. Jackson	1941–1954	F. Roosevelt
Wiley B. Rutledge	1943–1949	F. Roosevelt
Harold H. Burton	1945–1958	Truman
Frederick M. Vinson	1946–1953	Truman
Tom C. Clark	1949–1967	Truman
Sherman Minton	1949–1956	Truman
Earl Warren	1953–1969	Eisenhower
John Marshall Harlan	1955–1971	Eisenhower
William J. Brennan Jr.	1956–1990	Eisenhower
Charles E. Whittaker	1957–1962	Eisenhower

Name	Service	Appointed by
Potter Stewart	1958–1981	Eisenhower
Byron R. White	1962–1993	Kennedy
Arthur J. Goldberg	1962–1965	Kennedy
Abe Fortas	1965–1969	Johnson
Thurgood Marshall	1967–1991	Johnson
Warren E. Burger	1969–1986	Nixon
Harry A. Blackmun	1970–1994	Nixon
Lewis F. Powell Jr.	1972–1988	Nixon
William H. Rehnquist	1972–1986	Nixon
John Paul Stevens	1975–	Ford
Sandra Day O'Connor	1981–	Reagan
William H. Rehnquist	1986–	Reagan
Antonin Scalia	1986–	Reagan
Anthony M. Kennedy	1988–	Reagan
David H. Souter	1990–	Bush
Clarence Thomas	1991–	Bush
Ruth Bader Ginsburg	1993–	Clinton
Stephen Breyer	1994–	Clinton

SIGNIFICANT SUPREME COURT CASES

Marbury v. Madison (1803)

This case established the right of the Supreme Court to review the constitutionality of laws. The decision involved judicial appointments made during the last hours of the administration of President John Adams. Some commissions, including that of William Marbury, had not yet been delivered when President Thomas Jefferson took office. Infuriated by the last-minute nature of Adams's Federalist appointments, Jefferson refused to send the undelivered commissions out, and Marbury decided to sue. The Supreme Court, presided over by John Marshall, a Federalist who had assisted Adams in the judicial appointments, ruled that although Marbury's commission was valid and the new president should have delivered it, the Court could not compel him to do so. The Court based its reasoning on a finding that the grounds of Marbury's suit, resting in the Judiciary Act of 1789, were in conflict with the Constitution.

For the first time, the Court had overturned a national law on the grounds that it was unconstitutional. John Marshall had quietly established the concept of judicial review: The Supreme Court had given itself the authority to nullify acts of the other branches of the federal government. Although the Constitution provides for judicial review, the Court had not exercised this power before and did not use it again until 1857. It seems likely that if the Court had waited until 1857 to use this power, it would have been difficult to establish.

McCulloch v. Maryland (1819)

In 1816, Congress authorized the creation of a national bank. To protect its own banks from competition with a branch of the national bank in Baltimore, the state legislature of Maryland placed a tax of 2 percent on all notes issued by any bank operating in Maryland that was not chartered by the state. McCulloch, cashier of the Baltimore branch of the Bank of the United States, was convicted for refusing to pay the tax. Under the leadership of Chief Justice John Marshall, the Court ruled that the federal government had the power to establish a bank, even though that specific authority was not mentioned in the Constitution.

Marshall maintained that the authority could be reasonably implied from Article 1, section 8, which gives Congress the power to make all laws that are nec-

essary and proper to execute the enumerated powers. Marshall also held that Maryland could not tax the national bank because in a conflict between federal and state laws, the federal law must take precedence. Thus he established the principles of implied powers and federal supremacy, both of which set a precedent for subsequent expansion of federal power at the expense of the states.

Scott v. Sanford (1857)

Dred Scott was a slave who sued for his own and his family's freedom on the grounds, that, with his master, he had traveled to and lived in free territory that did not allow slavery. When his case reached the Supreme Court, the justices saw an opportunity to settle once and for all the vexing question of slavery in the territories. The Court's decision in this case proved that it enjoyed no special immunity from the sectional and partisan passions of the time. Five of the nine justices were from the South and seven were Democrats.

Chief Justice Roger B. Taney hated Republicans and detested racial equality; his decision reflects those prejudices. He wrote an opinion not only declaring that Scott was still a slave but also claiming that the Constitution denied citizenship or rights to blacks, that Congress had no right to exclude slavery from the territories, and that the Missouri Compromise was unconstitutional. While southern Democrats gloated over this seven-to-two decision, sectional tensions were further inflamed and the young Republican Party's claim that a hostile "slave power" was conspiring to destroy northern liberties was given further credence. The decision brought the nation closer to civil war and is generally regarded as the worst decision ever rendered by the Supreme Court.

Butchers' Benevolent Association of New Orleans v. Crescent City Livestock Landing and Slaughterhouse Co. (1873)

The *Slaughterhouse* cases, as the cases docketed under the *Butchers'* title were known, were the first legal test of the Fourteenth Amendment. To cut down on cases of cholera believed to be caused by contaminated water, the state of Louisiana prohibited the slaughter of livestock in New Orleans except in one slaughterhouse, effectively giving that slaughterhouse a monopoly. Other New Orleans butchers claimed that the state had deprived them of their occupation without due process of law, thus violating the Fourteenth Amendment.

In a five-to-four decision, the Court upheld the Louisiana law, declaring that the Fourteenth Amendment protected only the rights of federal citizenship, like voting in federal elections and interstate travel. The federal government thus was not obliged to protect basic civil rights from violation by state governments. This decison would have significant implications for African Americans and their struggle for civil rights in the twentieth century.

United States v. E. C. Knight Co. (1895)

Also known as the *Sugar Trust* case, this was among the first cases to reveal the weakness of the Sherman Antitrust Act in the hands of a pro-business Supreme Court. In 1895, American Sugar Refining Company purchased four other sugar producers, including the E. C. Knight Company, and thus took control of more than 98 percent of the sugar refining in the United States. In an effort to limit monopoly, the government brought suit against all five of the companies for violating the Sherman Antitrust Act, which outlawed trusts and other business combinations in restraint of trade. The Court dismissed the suit, however, arguing that the law applied only to commerce and not to manufacturing, defining the latter as a local concern and not part of the interstate commerce that the government could regulate.

Plessy v. Ferguson (1896)

African American Homer Plessy challenged a Louisiana law that required segregation on trains passing through the state. After ensuring that the railroad and the conductor knew that he was of mixed race (Plessy appeared to be white but under the racial code of Louisiana was classified as "colored" because he was one-eighth black), he refused to move to the "colored only" section of the coach. The Court ruled against Plessy by a vote of seven to one, declaring that "separate but equal" facilities were permissible according to section 1 of the Fourteenth Amendment, which calls upon the states to provide "equal protection of the laws" to anyone within their jurisdiction. Although the case was viewed as relatively insignificant at the time, it cast a long shadow over several decades.

Initially, the decision was viewed as a victory for segregationists, but in the 1930s and 1940s civil rights advocates referred to the doctrine of "separate but equal" in their efforts to end segregation. They argued that segregated institutions and accommodations were often *not* equal to those available to whites, and finally succeeded in overturning *Plessy* in *Brown v. Board of Education* in 1954 (see p. A-46).

Lochner v. New York (1905)

In this case, the Court ruled against a New York state law that prohibited employees from working in bakeries more than ten hours a day or sixty hours a week. The purpose of the law was to protect the health of workers, but the Court ruled that it was unconstitutional because it violated "freedom of contract" implicitly protected by the due process clause of the Fourteenth Amendment. Most of the justices believed strongly in a laissez-faire economic system that favored survival of the fittest. They felt that government protection of workers interfered with this system. In a dissenting opinion, Justice Oliver Wendell Holmes accused the majority of distorting the Constitution and of deciding the case on "an economic theory which a large part of the country does not entertain."

Muller v. Oregon (1908)

In 1905, Curt Muller, owner of a Portland, Oregon, laundry, demanded that one of his employees, Mrs. Elmer Gotcher, work more than the ten hours allowed as a maximum workday for women under Oregon law. Muller argued that the law violated his "freedom of contract" as established in prior Supreme Court decisions.

Progressive lawyer Louis D. Brandeis defended the Oregon law by arguing that a state could be justified in abridging freedom of contract when the health, safety, and welfare of workers was at issue. His innovative strategy drew on ninety-five pages of excerpts from factory and medical reports to substantiate his argument that there was a direct connection between long hours and the health of women and thus the health of the nation. In a unanimous decision, the Court upheld the Oregon law, but later generations of women fighting for equality would question the strategy of arguing that women's reproductive role entitled them to special treatment.

Schenck v. United States (1919)

During World War I, Charles Schenck and other members of the Socialist Party printed and mailed out flyers urging young men who were subject to the draft to oppose the war in Europe. In upholding the conviction of Schenck for publishing a pamphlet urging draft resistance, Justice Oliver Wendell Holmes established the "clear and present danger" test for freedom of speech. Such utterances as Schenck's during a time of national peril, Holmes wrote, could be considered the equivalent of shouting "Fire!" in a crowded theater. Congress had the right to protect the public against such an incitement to panic, the Court ruled in a unanimous decision. But the analogy was a false one. Schenck's pamphlet had little power to provoke a public firmly opposed to its message. Although Holmes later modified his position to state that the danger must relate to an immediate evil and a specific action, the "clear and present danger" test laid the groundwork for those who later sought to limit First Amendment freedoms.

Schechter Poultry Corp. v. United States (1935)

During the Great Depression, the National Industrial Recovery Act (NIRA), which was passed under President Franklin D. Roosevelt, established fair competition codes that were designed to help businesses. The Schechter brothers of New York City, who sold chickens, were convicted of violating the codes. The Supreme Court ruled that the NIRA unconstitutionally conferred legislative power on an administrative agency and overstepped the limits of federal power to regulate interstate commerce. The decision was a significant blow to the New Deal recovery program, demonstrating both historic American resistance to economic planning and the refusal of the business community to yield its autonomy unless it was forced to do so.

Brown v. Board of Education (1954)

In 1950, the families of eight Topeka, Kansas, children sued the Topeka Board of Education. The children were blacks who lived within walking distance of a whites-only school. The segregated school system required them to take a time-consuming, inconvenient, and dangerous route to get to a black school, and their parents argued that there was no reason their children should not be allowed to attend the nearest school. By the time the case reached the Supreme Court, it had been joined with similar cases regarding segregated schools in other states and the District of Columbia. A team of lawyers from the National Association for the Advancement of Colored People (NAACP), led by Thurgood Marshall (who would later be appointed to the Supreme Court), urged the Court to overturn the fifty-eight-year-old precedent established in *Plessy v. Ferguson*, which had enshrined "separate but equal" as the law of the land. A unanimous Court, led by Chief Justice Earl Warren, declared that "Separate educa-

tional facilities are inherently unequal" and thus violate the Fourteenth Amendment. In 1955, the Court called for desegregation "with all deliberate speed" but established no deadline.

Roth v. United States (1957)

In 1957, New Yorker Samuel Roth was convicted of sending obscene materials through the mail in a case that ultimately reached the Supreme Court. With a six-to-three vote, the Court reaffirmed the historical view that obscenity is not protected by the First Amendment. Yet it broke new ground by declaring that a work could be judged obscene only if, "taken as a whole," it appealed to the "prurient interest" of "the average person."

Prior to this case, work could be judged obscene if portions were thought able to "deprave and corrupt" the most susceptible part of an audience (such as children). Thus, serious works of literature such as Theodore Dreiser's *An American Tragedy*, which was banned in Boston when first published, received no protection. Although this decision continued to pose problems of definition, it did help to protect most works that attempt to convey ideas, even if those ideas have to do with sex, from the threat of obscenity laws.

Engel v. Vitale (1962)

In 1959, five parents with ten children in the New Hyde Park, New York, school system sued the school board. The parents argued that the so-called Regents' Prayer that public school students in New York recited at the start of every school day violated the doctrine of separation of church and state outlined in the First Amendment. In 1962, the Supreme Court voted six to one in favor of banning the Regents' Prayer.

The decision threw the religious community into an uproar. Many religious leaders expressed dismay and even shock; others welcomed the decision. Several efforts to introduce an amendment allowing school prayer have failed. Subsequent Supreme Court decisions have banned reading of the Bible in public schools. The Court has also declared mandatory flag saluting to be an infringement of religious and personal freedoms.

Gideon v. Wainwright (1963)

When Clarence Earl Gideon was tried for breaking into a poolroom, the state of Florida rejected his demand for a court-appointed lawyer as guaranteed by the Sixth Amendment. In 1963, the Court upheld his demand in a unanimous decision that established the obligation of states to provide attorneys for indigent defendants in felony cases. Prior to this decision, the right to an attorney had applied only to federal cases, not state cases. In its ruling in *Gideon v. Wainwright*, the Supreme Court applied the Sixth through the Fourteenth Amendments to the states. In 1972, the Supreme Court extended the right to legal representation to all cases, not just felony cases, in its decision in *Argersinger v. Hamlin*.

Griswold v. Connecticut (1965)

With a vote of seven to two, the Supreme Court reversed an "uncommonly silly law" (in the words of Justice Potter Stewart) that made it a crime for anyone in the state of Connecticut to use any drug, article, or instrument to prevent conception. *Griswold* became a landmark case because here, for the first time, the Court explicitly invested with full constitutional status "fundamental personal rights," such as the right to privacy, that were not expressly enumerated in the Bill of Rights. The majority opinion in the case held that the law infringed on the constitutionally protected right to privacy of married persons.

Although the Court had previously recognized fundamental rights not expressly enumerated in the Bill of Rights (such as the right to procreate in *Skinner v. Oklahoma* in 1942), *Griswold* was a landmark case because it was the first time the Court had justified, at length, the practice of investing such unenumerated rights with full constitutional status. Writing for the majority, Justice William O. Douglas explained that the First, Third, Fourth, Fifth, and Ninth Amendments imply "zones of privacy" that are the foundation for the general right to privacy affirmed in this case.

Miranda v. Arizona (1966)

In 1966, the Supreme Court, by a vote of five to four, upheld the case of Ernesto Miranda, who appealed a murder conviction on the grounds that police had gotten him to confess without giving him access to an attorney. The *Miranda* case was the culmination of the Court's efforts to find a meaningful way of determining whether police had used due process in extracting confessions from people accused of crimes. The *Miranda* decision upholds the Fifth Amendment protection against self-incrimination outside the courtroom and requires that suspects be given what came to be known as the Miranda warning, which advises them of their right to remain silent and warns them that anything they say might be used against them in a court of law. Suspects must also be told that they have a right to counsel.

New York Times Co. v. United States (1971)

With a six-to-three vote, the Court upheld the right of the *New York Times* and the *Washington Post* to print materials from the so-called *Pentagon Papers*, a secret government study of U.S. policy in Vietnam, leaked by dissident Pentagon official Daniel Ellsberg. Since the papers revealed deception and secrecy in the conduct of the Vietnam War, the Nixon administration had quickly obtained a court injunction against their further publication, claiming that suppression was in the interests of national security. The Supreme Court's decision overturning the injunction strengthened the First Amendment protection of freedom of the press.

Furman v. Georgia (1972)

In this case, the Supreme Court ruled five to four that the death penalty for murder or rape violated the cruel and unusual punishment clause of the Eighth Amendment because the manner in which the death penalty was meted out was irregular, "arbitrary," and "cruel." In response, most states enacted new statutes that allow the death penalty to be imposed only after a postconviction hearing at which evidence must be presented to show that "aggravating" or "mitigating" circumstances were factors in the crime. If the postconviction hearing hands down a death sentence, the case is automatically reviewed by an appellate court.

In 1976, the Court ruled in *Gregg v. Georgia* that these statutes were not unconstitutional. In 1977, the Court ruled in *Coker v. Georgia* that the death penalty for rape was "disproportionate and excessive," thus allowing the death penalty only in murder cases. Between 1977 and 1991, some 150 people were executed in the United States. Public opinion polls indicate that about 70 percent of Americans favor the death penalty for murder. Capital punishment continues to generate controversy, however, as opponents argue that there is no evidence that the death penalty deters crime and that its use reflects racial and economic bias.

Roe v. Wade (1973)

In 1973, the Court found, by a vote of seven to two, that state laws restricting access to abortion violated a woman's right to privacy guaranteed by the due process clause of the Fourteenth Amendment. The decision was based on the cases of two women living in Texas and Georgia, both states with stringent anti-abortion laws. Upholding the individual rights of both women and physicians, the Court ruled that the Constitution protects the right to abortion and that states cannot prohibit abortions in the early stages of pregnancy.

The decision stimulated great debate among legal scholars as well as the general public. Critics argued that since abortion was never addressed in the Constitution, the Court could not claim that legislation violated fundamental values of the Constitution. They also argued that since abortion was a medical procedure with an acknowledged impact on a fetus, it was inappropriate to invoke the kind of "privacy" argument that was used in *Griswold v. Connecticut* (see p. A-47), which was about contraception. Defenders suggested that the case should be argued as a case of gender discrimination, which did violate the equal protection clause of the Fourteenth Amendment. Others said that the right to privacy in sexual matters was indeed a fundamental right.

Regents of the University of California v. Bakke (1978)

When Allan Bakke, a white man, was not accepted by the University of California Medical School at Davis, he filed a lawsuit alleging that the admissions program, which set up different standards for test scores and grades for members of certain minority groups, violated the Civil Rights Act of 1964, which outlawed racial or ethnic preferences in programs supported by federal funds. Bakke further argued that the university's practice of setting aside spaces for minority applicants denied him equal protection as guaranteed by the Fourteenth Amendment. In a five-to-four decision, the Court ordered that Bakke be admitted to the medical school, yet it sanctioned affirmative action programs to attack the results of past discrimination as long as strict quotas or racial classifications were not involved.

Webster v. Reproductive Health Services (1989)

By a vote of five to four, the Court upheld several restrictions on the availability of abortions as imposed by Missouri state law. It upheld restrictions on the use of state property, including public hospitals, for abortions. It also upheld a provision requiring physicians to perform tests to determine the viability of a fetus

that a doctor judged to be twenty weeks of age or older. Although the justices did not go so far as to overturn the decision in *Roe v. Wade* (see p. A-47), the ruling galvanized interest groups on both sides of the abortion issue. Opponents of abortion pressured state legislatures to place greater restrictions on abortions; those who favored availability of abortions tried to mobilize public action by presenting the decision as a major threat to the right to choose abortion.

Cipollone v. Liggett (1992)

In a seven-to-two decision, the Court ruled in favor of the family of Rose Cipollone, a woman who died of lung cancer after smoking for forty-two years. The Court rejected arguments that health warnings on cigarette packages protected tobacco manufacturers from personal injury suits filed by smokers who contract cancer and other serious illnesses.

Miller v. Johnson (1995)

In a five-to-four decision, the Supreme Court ruled that voting districts created to increase the voting power of racial minorities were unconstitutional. The decision threatens dozens of congressional, state, and local voting districts that were drawn to give minorities more representation as had been required by the Justice Department under the Voting Rights Act. If states are required to redraw voting districts, the number of black members of Congress could be sharply reduced.

Romer v. Evans (1996)

In a six-to-three decision, the Court struck down a Colorado amendment that forbade local governments from banning discrimination against homosexuals. Writing for the majority, Justice Anthony Kennedy said that forbidding communities from taking action to protect the rights of homosexuals and not of other groups unlawfully deprived gays and lesbians of opportunities that were available to others. Kennedy based the decision on the guarantee of equal protection under the law as provided by the Fourteenth Amendment.

THE AMERICAN ECONOMY

THESE FOUR "SNAPSHOTS" of the U.S. economy show significant changes over the past century and a half. In 1849, the agricultural sector was by far the largest contributor to the economy. By the turn of the century, with advances in technology and an abundance of cheap labor and raw materials, the country had experienced remarkable industrial expansion and the manufacturing industries dominated. By 1950, the service sector had increased significantly, fueled by the consumerism of the 1920s and the post-World War II years, and the economy was becoming more diversified. Note that by 1990, government's share in the economy was more than 10 percent and activity in both the trade and manufacturing sectors had declined, partly as a result of competition from Western Europe and Asia.

Main Sectors of the U.S. Economy: 1849, 1899, 1950, 1990

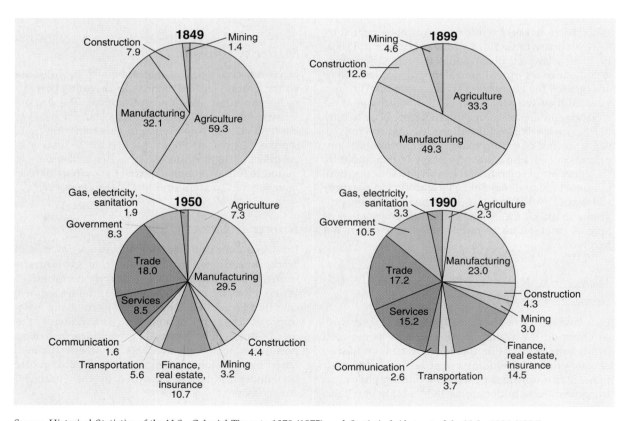

Source: Historical Statistics of the U.S., Colonial Times to 1970 (1975) and Statistical Abstract of the U.S., 1996 (1996).

Federal Spending and the Economy, 1790 – 1995

Year	Gross National Product (in billions)	Foreign Trade (in millions) Exports	Foreign Trade (in millions) Imports	Federal Budget (in billions)	Federal Surplus/Deficit (in billions)	Federal Debt (in billions)
1790	NA	20	23	0.004	0.00015	0.076
1800	NA	71	91	0.011	0.0006	0.083
1810	NA	67	85	0.008	0.0012	0.053
1820	NA	70	74	0.018	−0.0004	0.091
1830	NA	74	71	0.015	0.100	0.049
1840	NA	132	107	0.024	−0.005	0.004
1850	NA	152	178	0.040	0.004	0.064
1860	NA	400	362	0.063	−0.01	0.065
1870	7.4	451	462	0.310	0.10	2.4
1880	11.2	853	761	0.268	0.07	2.1
1890	13.1	910	823	0.318	0.09	1.2
1900	18.7	1,499	930	0.521	0.05	1.2
1910	35.3	1,919	1,646	0.694	−0.02	1.1
1920	91.5	8,664	5,784	6.357	0.3	24.3
1930	90.4	4,013	3,500	3.320	0.7	16.3
1940	99.7	4,030	7,433	9.6	−2.7	43.0
1950	284.8	10,816	9,125	43.1	−2.2	257.4
1960	503.7	19,600	15,046	92.2	0.3	286.3
1970	977.1	42,700	40,189	195.6	−2.8	371.0
1980	2,631.7	220,600	244,871	590.9	−73.8	907.7
1990	5,524.5	393,600	495,300	1,252.15	−221.1	3,233.3
1995	7,237.5	583,900	743,400	1,519.1	−163.9	4,921.0

Source: Historical Statistics of the U.S., Colonial Times to 1970 (1975) and Statistical Abstract of the U.S., 1996 (1996).

WHEN THE FEDERAL GOVERNMENT BEGAN OPERATING IN 1790, its size and expenditures were limited. Over time its functions increased, but its budget remained fairly small relative to the country's gross national product. The second half of the twentieth century witnessed a dramatic expansion in federal budget outlays. As the government's role increased and receipts could no longer offset growing expenditures, budget deficits mounted. In 1976, the federal deficit reached $65.6 billion and continued to rise, soaring as high as $290 billion in 1992, during the last year of George Bush's presidency. During the first Clinton administration, a combination of budget cuts, tax increases, declining unemployment, and economic expansion reduced the deficit by about half to approximately $145 billion.

The Federal Budget: Receipts, Outlays, and the Deficit, 1945 – 1995

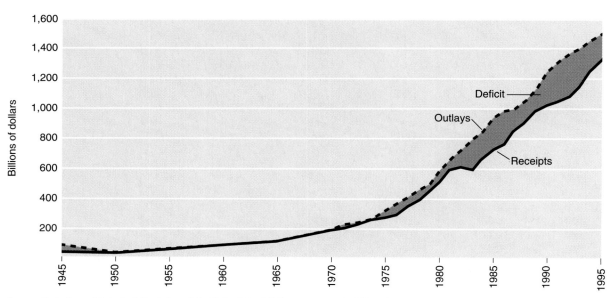

Source: Data from *Historical Statistics of the U.S., Colonial Times to 1970* (1975) and *Statistical Abstract of the U.S., 1996* (1996).

A DEMOGRAPHIC PROFILE OF THE UNITED STATES AND ITS PEOPLE

POPULATION

FROM AN ESTIMATED 4600 WHITE INHABITANTS IN 1630, the country's population grew to a total of just under 250 million in 1990. It is important to note that the U.S. census, first conducted in 1790 and the source of these figures, counted blacks, both free and slave, but did not include American Indians until 1860. The years 1790 to 1900 saw the most rapid population growth, with an average increase of 25 to 35 percent per decade. In addition to "natural" growth—birth rate exceeding death rate—immigration was also a factor in that rise, especially between 1840 and 1860, 1880 to 1890, and 1900 to 1910 (see table on page A-59). The twentieth century witnessed slower growth, partly a result of 1920s immigration restrictions, and a decline in the birth rate, especially during the Depression era and the 1960s and 1970s. The U.S. population is expected to reach almost 300 million by the year 2010.

Population Growth, 1630 – 2000

Year	Population	Percent Increase
1630	4,600	–––
1640	26,600	473.3
1650	50,400	89.1
1660	75,100	49.0
1670	111,900	49.1
1680	151,500	35.4
1690	210,400	38.9
1700	250,900	19.3
1710	331,700	32.2
1720	466,200	40.5
1730	629,400	35.0
1740	905,600	43.9
1750	1,170,800	30.0
1760	1,593,600	36.1
1770	2,148,100	34.8
1780	2,780,400	29.4
1790	3,929,214	41.3
1800	5,308,483	35.1
1810	7,239,881	36.4
1820	9,638,453	33.1
1830	12,866,020	33.5
1840	17,069,453	32.7
1850	23,191,876	35.9
1860	31,443,321	35.6
1870	39,818,449	26.6
1880	50,155,783	26.0
1890	62,947,714	25.5
1900	75,994,575	20.7
1910	91,972,266	21.0
1920	105,710,620	14.9
1930	122,775,046	16.1
1940	131,669,275	7.2
1950	150,697,361	14.5
1960	179,323,175	19.0
1970	203,302,031	13.4
1980	226,542,199	11.4
1990	248,718,301	9.8
2000	274,634,000*	11.0

*Projected

Source: Historical Statistics of the U.S. (1960), Historical Statistics of the U.S. from Colonial Times to 1970 (1975), and Statistical Abstract of the U.S., 1996 (1996).

A DEMOGRAPHIC PROFILE OF THE UNITED STATES AND ITS PEOPLE

The Ten Most Populous Cities, 1700 – 1994

Year	City	Population	Year	City	Population
1700	Boston	6,700	**1910**	New York	4,767,000
	New York	4,900		Chicago	2,185,000
	Philadelphia	4,400		Philadelphia	1,549,000
				St. Louis	687,000
1790	Philadelphia	42,500		Boston	670,600
	New York	33,100		Cleveland, Ohio	560,700
	Boston	18,000		Baltimore	558,500
	Charleston, S.C.	16,400		Pittsburgh	533,900
	Baltimore, Md.	13,500		Detroit, Mich.	465,800
	Salem, Mass.	7,900		Buffalo, N.Y.	423,700
	Newport, R.I.	6,700			
	Providence, R.I.	6,380	**1930**	New York	6,930,000
	Marblehead, Mass.	5,700		Chicago	3,376,000
	Portsmouth, N.H.	4,700		Philadelphia	1,951,000
				Detroit	1,569,000
1830	New York	197,100		Los Angeles	1,238,000
	Philadelphia	161,400		Cleveland	900,400
	Baltimore	80,600		St. Louis	822,000
	Boston	61,400		Baltimore	804,900
	Charleston	30,300		Boston	781,200
	New Orleans, La.	29,700		Pittsburgh	669,800
	Cincinnati, Oh.	24,800			
	Albany, N.Y.	24,200	**1950**	New York	7,892,000
	Brooklyn, N.Y.	20,500		Chicago	3,621,000
	Washington, D.C.	18,800		Philadelphia	2,072,000
				Los Angeles	1,970,000
1850	New York	515,500		Detroit	1,850,000
	Philadelphia	340,000		Baltimore	949,700
	Baltimore	169,000		Cleveland	914,800
	Boston	136,800		St. Louis	856,800
	New Orleans	116,400		Washington	802,200
	Cincinnati	115,400		Boston	801,500
	Brooklyn, N.Y.	96,800			
	St. Louis, Mo.	77,900	**1970**	New York	7,896,000
	Albany	50,800		Chicago	3,369,000
	Pittsburgh, Pa.	46,600		Los Angeles	2,812,000
				Philadelphia	1,950,000
1870	New York	942,300		Detroit	1,514,000
	Philadelphia	674,000		Houston	1,234,000
	Brooklyn	419,900		Baltimore	905,800
	St. Louis	310,900		Dallas	844,400
	Chicago, Il.	298,900		Washington	756,700
	Baltimore	267,300		Cleveland	750,900
	Boston	250,500			
	Cincinnati	216,200			
	New Orleans	191,400			
	San Francisco, Calif.	149,500		*(continues)*	

The Ten Most Populous Cities, 1700 – 1994 *(continued)*

Year	City	Population	Year	City	Population
1990	New York	7,323,000	**1994**	New York	7,333,000
	Los Angeles	3,485,000		Los Angeles	3,449,000
	Chicago	2,784,000		Chicago	2,732,000
	Houston	1,631,000		Houston	1,702,000
	Philadelphia	1,586,000		Philadelphia	1,524,000
	San Diego	1,111,000		San Diego	1,152,000
	Detroit	1,028,000		Phoenix	1,049,000
	Dallas	1,007,000		Dallas	1,023,000
	Phoenix	983,400		San Antonio	999,000
	San Antonio, Tex.	935,900		Detroit	992,000

U.S. Population, 1790 – 2010

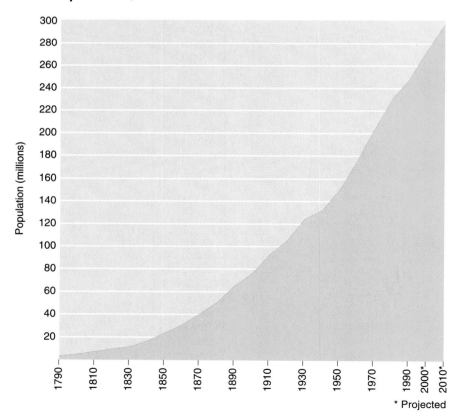

* Projected

VITAL STATISTICS

WITH SOME MINOR FLUCTUATIONS, the birth rate has been trending downward throughout the past century and a half, dipping especially low during the 1930s Depression years, when many economically hard-hit Americans postponed having children. A major exception to this decline was the steep but temporary rise nicknamed the "Baby Boom," which occurred during the relatively affluent post-World War II period. Improvements in health care and lifestyles have contributed to a decline in the death rate over the past century, which, in turn has increased life expectancy figures. Over time, as people lived longer and the birth rate declined, the median age of Americans has increased from approximately seventeen in 1820 to thirty-three in 1990, and continues to rise.

Birth Rate, 1820 – 2000

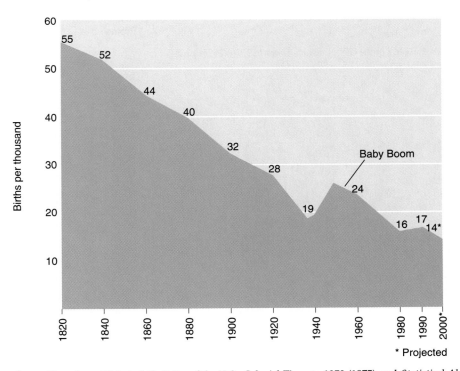

Source: Data from *Historical Statistics of the U.S., Colonial Times to 1970* (1975) and *Statistical Abstract of the U.S., 1996* (1996).

Death Rate, 1900 – 2000

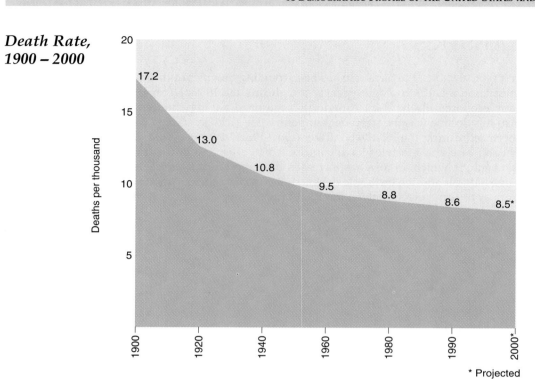

Source: *Historical Statistics of the U.S., Colonial Times to 1970* (1975) and
Statistical Abstract of the U.S., 1996 (1996).

Life Expectancy, 1900 – 2000

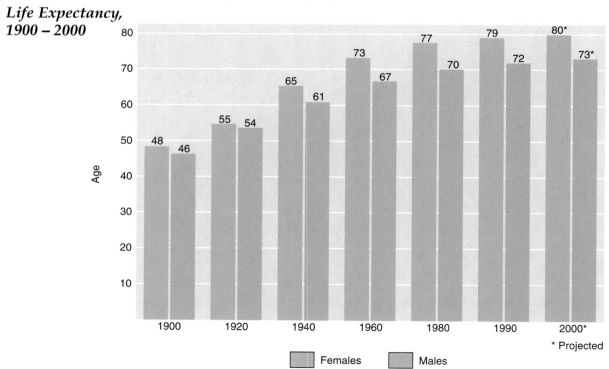

Source: *Historical Statistics of the U.S., Colonial Times to 1970* (1975) and
Statistical Abstract of the U.S., 1996 (1996).

MIGRATION AND IMMIGRATION

WE TEND TO ASSOCIATE INTERNAL MIGRATION with movement westward, yet equally significant has been the movement of the nation's population from the country to the city. In 1790, the first U.S. census recorded that approximately 95 percent of the population lived in rural areas. By 1990, that figure had fallen to less than 25 percent. The decline of the agricultural way of life, late nineteenth-century industrialization, and immigration have all contributed to increased urbanization. A more recent trend has been the migration, especially since the 1970s, of people to the "Sun Belt" states of the South and West, lured by factors as various as economic opportunities in the defense and high-tech industries and good weather. This migration has swelled the size of Sun Belt cities like Houston, Dallas, Tucson, Phoenix, and San Diego, all of which in recent years ranked among the top ten most populous U.S. cities (see the table on page A-53).

Rural and Urban Population, 1750 – 2000

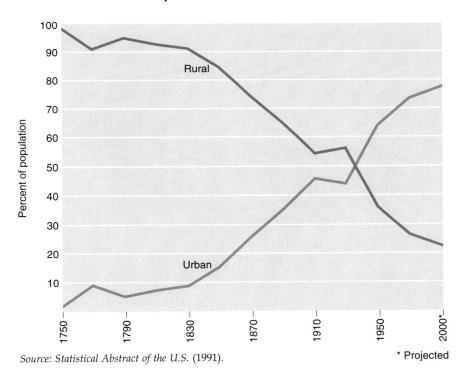

Source: Statistical Abstract of the U.S. (1991).   * Projected

Projected Change in State Populations by Percent, 1995 – 2010

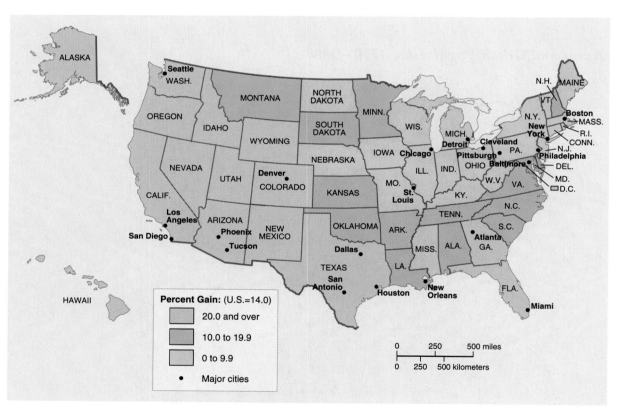

Source: Statistical Abstract of the U.S., 1996. (1996).

THE QUANTITY AND CHARACTER OF IMMIGRATION to the U.S. has varied greatly over time. During the first major influx, between 1840 and 1860, newcomers hailed primarily from Northern and Western Europe. From 1880 to 1915, when rates soared even more dramatically, the profile changed, with 80 percent of the so-called "new immigration" coming from Central, Eastern, and Southern Europe. Following World War I, strict quotas reduced the flow considerably. Note, also, the significant fall-off during the years of the Great Depression and World War II. The sources of immigration during the last half century have changed significantly, with the majority of people coming from Latin America, the Caribbean, and Asia. The latest surge during the 1980s brought more immigrants to the U.S. than in any decade except 1901–1910.

Rates of Immigration, 1820 – 1994

Year	Number	Percent of Total Population
1821–1830	151,824	1.6
1831–1840	599,125	4.6
1841–1850	1,713,521	10.0
1851–1860	2,598,214	11.2
1861–1870	2,314,824	7.4
1871–1880	2,812,191	7.1
1881–1890	5,246,613	10.5
1891–1900	3,687,546	5.8
1901–1910	8,795,386	11.6
1911–1920	5,735,811	6.2
1921–1930	4,107,209	3.9
1931–1940	528,431	0.4
1941–1950	1,035,039	0.7
1951–1960	2,515,479	1.6
1961–1970	3,321,677	1.8
1971–1980	4,493,300	2.2
1981–1990	7,338,100	3.0
1991	1,827,167	7.2
1992	973,977	3.8
1993	904,292	3.5
1994	804,416	3.0

Source: Historical Statistics of the U.S., Colonial Times to 1970 (1975), Statistical Abstract of the U.S., 1996 (1996).

Major Trends in Immigration, 1820 – 1990

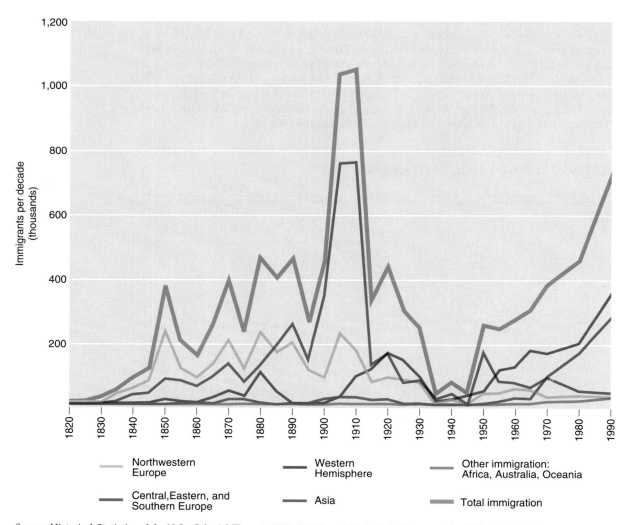

Source: Historical Statistics of the U.S., Colonial Times to 1970 (1975) and Statistical Abstract of the U.S., 1996 (1996).

LABOR

FOR MUCH OF THE NINETEENTH CENTURY, the United States was a nation of small farmers, with over half the population employed in agriculture. With the rise of industrialization, movement to the cities, and increasing takeover of farming by agribusiness (large-scale mechanized farming requiring little manpower), Americans increasingly moved from farming to work in manufacturing and other industries. In the twentieth century the number of people employed in services has increased; membership in labor unions peaked around 1970. Perhaps the most significant change in labor patterns has been the increase in the number of working women from approximately one sixth of the work force in 1890 to close to one half by 1994.

The Changing Nature of Work, 1810 – 1994

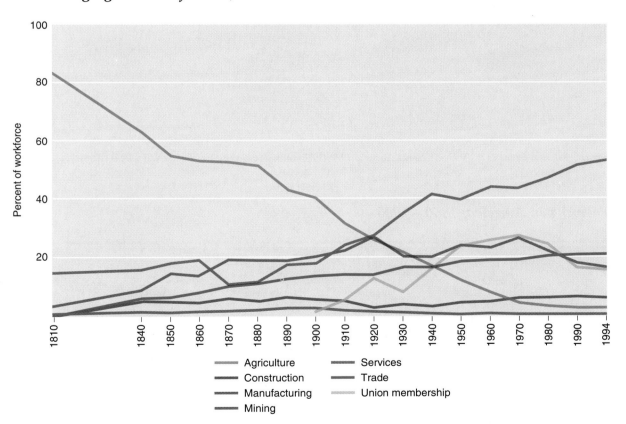

Source: *Historical Statistics of the U.S., Colonial Times to 1970* (1975) and *Statistical Abstract of the U.S., 1996* (1996).

Women in the Work Force, 1820 – 1994

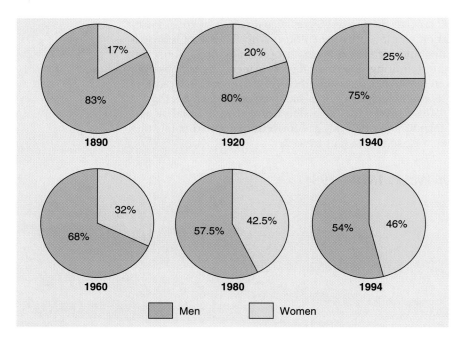

Source: Historical Statistics of the U.S., Colonial Times to 1970 (1975) and Statistical Abstract of the U.S., 1996 (1996).

Farming in America, 1850 – 1990

Year	Farm Population (in thousands)	Percent of Total Population	Number of Farms (in thousands)	Total Acres (in thousands)	Average Acreage Per Farm
1850	NA	NA	1,449	293,561	203
1860	NA	NA	2,044	407,213	199
1870	NA	NA	2,660	407,735	153
1880	21,973	43.8	4,009	536,082	134
1890	24,771	42.3	4,565	623,219	137
1900	29,875	41.9	5,740	841,202	147
1910	32,077	34.9	6,366	881,431	139
1920	31,974	30.1	6,454	958,677	149
1930	30,529	24.9	6,295	990,112	157
1940	30,547	23.2	6,102	1,065,114	175
1950	23,048	15.3	5,388	1,161,420	216
1960	15,635	8.7	3,962	1,176,946	297
1970	9,712	4.8	2,949	1,102,769	374
1980	6,051	2.7	2,440	1,039,000	426
1990	4,591	1.9	2,140	987,000	461

NA = Not available

Source: Historical Statistics of the U.S., Colonial Times to 1970 (1975) and Statistical Abstract of the U.S., 1996 (1996).

COMMUNICATIONS

THE TWENTIETH CENTURY WITNESSED the growing presence of communications technology in American homes. Especially revolutionary were radio and telephone, which connected people with the outside world in ways previously unimaginable. By 1994, telephones, radios, and televisions were standard in more than 90 percent of American homes, while more and more households had acquired cable television and video cassette recorders. The 1980s also saw the rise of the personal computer, which by 1993 could be found in nearly a quarter of American homes. As the graph shows, kids under seventeen make up a substantial percentage of computer users.

Households with Telephones, 1920 – 1994

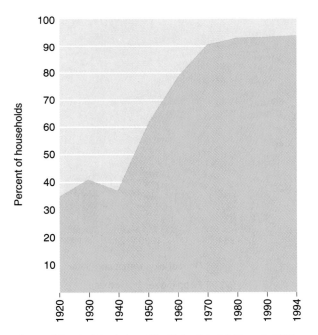

Source: *Historical Statistics of the U.S., Colonial Times to 1970* (1975) and *Statistical Abstract of the U.S., 1996* (1996).

Households with Radios and Television Sets, 1920 – 1970

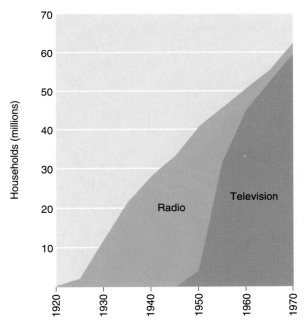

Source: *Historical Statistics of the U.S., Colonial Times to 1970* (1975) and *Statistical Abstract of the U.S., 1996* (1996).

Percent of Households with Radio, Television, Cable, and VCR, 1970 – 1994

Computer Use and Access, 1984 – 1993

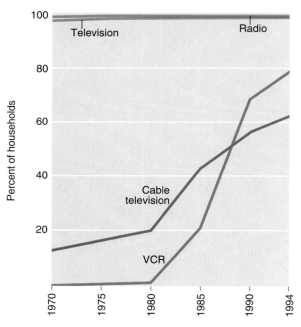

Source: Historical Statistics of the U.S., Colonial Times to 1970 (1975) and Statistical Abstract of the U.S., 1996 (1996).

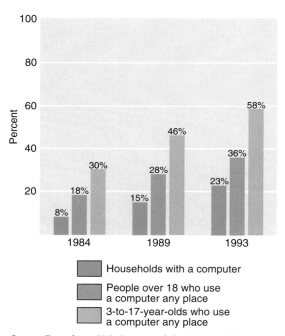

Source: Data from U.S. Bureau of the Census, Education and Social Stratification Branch, Population Division.

EDUCATION

DURING THE TWENTIETH CENTURY, there have been substantial increases in enrollments in secondary education and slower but still steady progress in degrees granted in higher education. In 1910, less than 14 percent of the population obtained high school diplomas; by 1995, that figure had risen to more than 80 percent. The number of people completing bachelor's degrees has grown steadily, from 400,000 in 1960 to just under 1.2 million in 1994, while the increasing professionalization of the workforce is reflected in the number of advanced degrees granted since 1960: Between 1960 and 1994, master's degrees awarded rose from almost 75,000 to almost 400,000, while doctoral degrees earned increased from 10,000 to 42,000.

Years of Schooling Completed, Ages 25 and Over, 1910 – 1995

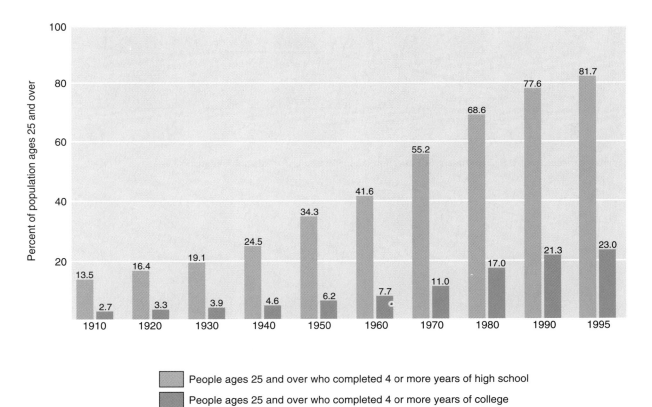

People ages 25 and over who completed 4 or more years of high school

People ages 25 and over who completed 4 or more years of college

Source: Statistics from U.S. Department of Commerce, Bureau of the Census.

Higher Education: Degrees Conferred, 1960 – 1994

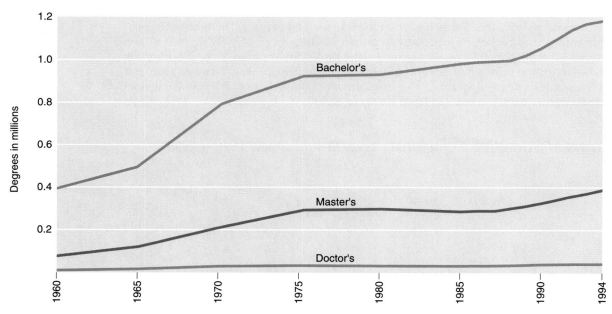

Source: Statistics from U.S. Department of Education, National Center for Education Statistics.

Appendix III. RESEARCH RESOURCES IN U.S. HISTORY

While doing research in history, you will use the library to track down primary and secondary sources and to answer questions that arise as you learn more about your topic. This appendix suggests helpful indexes, references, periodicals, and sources of primary documents. It also offers an overview of electronic resources available through the Internet. The materials listed here are not all carried at all libraries, but they will give you an idea of the range of sources available. Remember, too, that librarians are an extremely helpful resource. They can direct you to useful materials throughout your research process.

Bibliographies and Indexes

American Historical Association Guide to Historical Literature. 3rd ed. New York: Oxford University Press, 1995. Offers 27,000 citations to important historical literature, arranged in forty-eight sections covering theory, international history, and regional history. An indispensable guide recently updated to include current trends in historical research.

America History and Life. Santa Barbara: ABC-Clio, 1964–. Covers publications of all sorts on U.S. and Canadian history and culture in a chronological/regional format, with abstracts and alphabetical indexes. Available in computerized format. The most complete ongoing bibliography for American history.

Freidel, Frank Burt. *Harvard Guide to American History.* Cambridge: Harvard University Press, Belknap Press, 1974. Provides citations to books and articles on American history published before 1970. The first volume is arranged topically, the second chronologically. Though it does not cover current scholarship, it is a classic and remains useful for tracing older publications.

Prucha, Francis Paul. *Handbook for Research in American History: A Guide to Bibliographies and Other Reference Works.* 2nd rev. ed. Lincoln: University of Nebraska Press, 1994. Introduces a variety of research tools, including electronic ones. A good source to consult when planning an in-depth research project.

General Overviews

Dictionary of American Biography. New York: Scribner's, 1928–1937, with supplements. Gives substantial biographies of prominent Americans in history.

Dictionary of American History. New York: Scribner's, 1976. An encyclopedia of terms, places, and concepts in U.S. history; other more specialized sets include the *Encyclopedia of North American Colonies* and the *Encyclopedia of the Confederacy.*

Dictionary of Concepts in History. New York: Greenwood, 1986. Contains essays defining concepts in historiography and describing how the concepts were formed; excellent bibliographies.

Encyclopedia of American Social History. New York: Scribner's, 1993. Surveys topics such as religion, class, gender, race, popular culture, regionalism, and everyday life from pre-Columbian to modern times.

Encyclopedia of the United States in the Twentieth Century. New York: Scribner's, 1996. An ambitious overview of American cultural, social, and intellectual history in broad articles arranged topically. Each article is followed by a thorough and very useful bibliography for further research.

Specialized Information

Black Women in America: An Historical Encyclopedia. Brooklyn: Carlson, 1993. A scholarly compilation of biographical and topical articles that constitute a definitive history of African American women.

Carruth, Gordon. *The Encyclopedia of American Facts and Dates.* 9th ed. New York: HarperCollins, 1993. Covers American history chronologically from 986 to the present, offering information on treaties, battles, explorations, popular culture, philosophy, literature, and so on, mixing significant events with telling trivia. Tables allow for reviewing a year from a variety of angles. A thorough index helps pinpoint specific facts in time.

Cook, Chris. *Dictionary of Historical Terms.* 2nd ed. New York: Peter Bendrick, 1990. Covers a wide variety of terms—events, places, institutions, and topics—in history for all periods and places in a remarkably small package. A good place for quick identification of terms in the field.

Dictionary of Afro-American Slavery. New York: Greenwood, 1985. Surveys important people, events, and topics, with useful bibliographies; similar works include *Dictionary of the Vietnam War, Historical Dictionary of the New Deal,* and *Historical Dictionary of the Progressive Era.*

Knappman-Frost, Elizabeth. *The ABC-Clio Companion to Women's Progress in America.* Santa Barbara: ABC-Clio, 1994. Covers American women who were notable for their time as well as topics and organizations that have been significant in women's quest for equality. Each article is brief; there are a chronology and a bibliography at the back of the book.

United States. Bureau of the Census. *Historical Statistics of the United States, Colonial Times to 1970.* Washington, D.C.: Government Printing Office, 1975. Offers vital statistics, economic figures, and social data for the United States in time series. An index at the back helps locate tables by subject. For statistics since 1970, consult the annual *Statistical Abstract of the United States.*

Primary Sources

There are many routes to finding contemporary material for historical research. You may search your library catalog using the name of a prominent historical figure as an author; you may also find anthologies covering particular themes or periods in history. Consider also the following special materials for your research.

The Press

American Periodical Series, 1741–1900. Ann Arbor: University Microfilms, 1946–1979. Microfilm collection of periodicals from the colonial period to the turn of the century. An index identifies periodicals that focused on particular topics.

Herstory Microfilm Collection. Berkeley: Women's History Research Center, 1973. A microfilm collection of alternative feminist periodicals published between 1960 and 1980. Offers an interesting documentary history of the women's movement.

New York Times. New York: New York Times, 1851–. Many libraries have this newspaper on microfilm going back to its beginning in 1851. An index is available to locate specific dates and pages of news stories; it also provides detailed chronologies of events as they were reported in the news.

Readers' Guide to Periodical Literature. New York: Wilson, 1900–. This index to popular magazines started in 1900; an earlier index, *Poole's Index to Periodical Literature,* covers 1802–1906, though it does not provide such thorough indexing.

Diaries, Pamphlets, Books

The American Culture Series. Ann Arbor: University Microfilms, 1941–1974. A microfilm set, with a useful index, featuring books and pamphlets published between 1493 and 1875.

American Women's Diaries. New Canaan: Readex, 1984–. A collection of reproductions of women's diaries. There are different series for different regions of the country.

The March of America Facsimile Series. Ann Arbor: University Microfilms, 1966. A collection of more than ninety facsimiles of travel accounts to the New World published in English or English translation from the fifteenth through the nineteenth century.

Women in America from Colonial Times to the 20th Century. New York: Arno, 1974. A collection of reprints of dozens of books written by women describing women's lives and experiences in their own words.

Government Documents

Congressional Record. Washington D.C.: Government Printing Office, 1874–. Covers daily debates and proceedings of Congress. Earlier series were called *Debates and Proceedings in the Congress of the United States* and *The Congressional Globe.*

Foreign Relations of the United States. Washington D.C.: Department of State, 1861–. A collection of documents from 1861, including diplomatic papers, correspondence, and memoranda, that provides a documentary record of U.S. foreign policy.

Public Papers of the Presidents. Washington D.C.: Office of the Federal Register, 1957–. Includes major documents issued by the executive branch from the Hoover administration to the present.

Serial Set. Washington, D.C.: Government Printing Office, 1789–1969. A huge collection of congressional documents, available in many libraries on microfiche, with a useful index.

Local History Collections

State and county historical societies often house a wealth of historical documents; consider their resources when planning your research—you may find yourself working with material that no one else has analyzed before.

Internet Resources

The Internet has been a useful place for scholars to communicate and publish information in recent years. Electronic discussion lists, electronic journals, and primary texts are among the resources available for historians on the Internet. The following sources are good places to find historical information. You can also search for information on the World Wide Web using any of a number of search engines. However, bear in mind that there is no board of editors screening Internet sites for accuracy or usefulness, and the search engines generally rely on free-text searches rather than subject headings. Be critical of all of your sources, particularly those found on the Internet.

American Memory: Historical Collection from the National Digital Library Program. <http://rs6.loc.gov/amhome.html> An Internet site that features digitized primary source materials from the Library of Congress, among them African American pamphlets, civil war photographs, documents from the Continental Congress and the Constitutional Convention of 1774–1790, materials on woman suffrage, and oral histories.

Directory of Scholarly and Professional Electronic Conferences. <http://n2h2.com/KOVAKS/>. A good place to find out what electronic conversations are going on in a scholarly discipline. Includes a good search facility and instructions on how to connect to e-mail discussion lists, newsgroups, and interactive chat sites with academic content. Once identified, these conferences are good places to raise questions, find out what controversies are currently stirring the profession, and even find out about grants and jobs.

Historical Text Archive. <http://www.msstate.edu/Archives/History>. A Web interface for the oldest and largest Internet site for historical documents. Includes sections on Native American, African American, and U.S. history, in which can be found texts of the Declaration of Independence, the U.S. Constitution, the Constitution of Iroquois Nations, World War II surrender documents, photograph collections, and a great deal more. These can be used online or saved as files.

Index of Resources for Historians. <http://kuhttp.cc.ukans.edu/history/index.html>. A vast list of more than 1700 links to sites of interest to historians, arranged alphabetically by general topic. Some links are to sources for general reference information, but most are on historical topics. A good place to start an exploration of Internet resources.

MAPS, CHARTS, AND TABLES

Charts and Tables

SPECIAL FEATURES

ABOUT THE AUTHORS

James L. Roark

Born in Eunice, Louisiana, and raised in the West, James L. Roark received his B.A. from the University of California, Davis, in 1963 and his Ph.D. from Stanford University in 1973. His dissertation won the Allan Nevins Prize. He has taught at the University of Nigeria, Nsukka; the University of Nairobi, Kenya; the University of Missouri, St. Louis; and, since 1983, Emory University, where he is Samuel Candler Dobbs Professor of American History. In 1993, he received the Emory Williams Distinguished Teaching Award. He has written *Masters without Slaves: Southern Planters in the Civil War and Reconstruction* (1977). With Michael P. Johnson, he is author of *Black Masters: A Free Family of Color in the Old South* (1984) and editor of *No Chariot Let Down: Charleston's Free People of Color on the Eve of the Civil War* (1984). He has received research assistance from the American Philosophical Society and the National Endowment for the Humanities. Active in the Organization of American Historians and the Southern Historical Association, he is also a fellow of the Society of American Historians.

Michael P. Johnson

Born and raised in Ponca City, Oklahoma, Michael P. Johnson studied at Knox College, Illinois, where he received a B.A. in 1963, and at Stanford University, where he earned a Ph.D. in 1973. He is now professor of history at the Johns Hopkins University in Baltimore. His publications include *Toward a Patriarchal Republic: The Secession of Georgia* (1977); with James L. Roark *Black Masters: A Free Family of Color in the Old South* (1984) and *No Chariot Let Down: Charlestown's Free People of Color on the Eve of the Civil War* (1984); *Reading the American Past: Selected Historical Documents,* the documents reader for *The American Promise;* and articles that have appeared in the *William and Mary Quarterly,* the *Journal of Southern History, Labor History,* the *New York Review of Books,* the *New Republic,* the *Nation,* and other journals. Johnson has been awarded research fellowships by the American Council of Learned Societies and the National Endowment for the Humanities. He

has directed a National Endowment for the Humanities Summer Seminar for College Teachers and has been honored with university awards for outstanding teaching. He is an active member of the American Historical Association, the Organization of American Historians, and the Southern Historical Association.

Patricia Cline Cohen

Born in Ann Arbor, Michigan, and raised in Palo Alto, California, Patricia Cline Cohen earned a B.A. at the University of Chicago in 1968 and a Ph.D. at the University of California, Berkeley in 1977. In 1976, she joined the history faculty at the University of California at Santa Barbara. Cohen has written *A Calculating People: The Spread of Numeracy in Early America* (1982) and has published articles on numeracy, prostitution, sexual crime, and murder in journals including the *Journal of Women's History, Radical History Review,* the *William and Mary Quarterly,* and the *NWSA Journal.* Her scholarly work has received assistance from the National Endowment for the Humanities, the National Humanities Center, the American Antiquarian Society, the Schlesinger Library, and the Newberry Library. In the mid-1980s, she helped establish the Women's Studies Program on her campus, and she has been chair of the program since 1991.

Sarah Stage

Sarah Stage was born in Davenport, Iowa, and received a B.A. from the University of Iowa in 1966 and a Ph.D. in American studies from Yale University in 1975. She has taught twentieth-century U.S. history for more than twenty-five years at Williams College and the University of California, Riverside. Currently she is professor and chair of Women's Studies at Arizona State University West in Phoenix. Her books include *Female Complaints: Lydia Pinkham and the Business of Women's Medicine* (1979) and the forthcoming *Rethinking Women and Home Economics in the Twentieth Century.* Among the fellowships she has received are the Rockefeller Foundation Humanities Fellowship, the American Association of University Women dissertation fellowship, a fellowship from the Charles Warren Center for the Study of History at Harvard University, and the University of California President's Fellowship in the Humanities. She is at work on a book entitled *Women and the Progressive Impulse in American Politics, 1890–1914.*

Alan Lawson

Born in Providence, Rhode Island, Alan Lawson received his B.A. from Brown University in 1955 and his Ph.D. from the University of Michigan in 1967. Since winning the Allan Nevins Prize for his dissertation, Lawson has served on the faculties of the University of California, Irvine, Smith College, and, currently, Boston College. He has written *The Failure of Independent Liberalism* (1971) and coedited *From Revolution to Republic* (1976). While completing the forthcoming *The New Deal and the Mobilization of Progressive Experience,* he has published book chapters and essays on political economy and the cultural legacy of the New Deal. He has served as editor of the *Review of Education* and the *Intellectual History Newsletter* and contributed articles to those journals as well as to the *History Education Quarterly.* He has been active in the field of American studies as director of the Boston College American studies program and as a contributor to the *American Quarterly.* Under the auspices of the United States Information Agency, Lawson has been coordinator and lecturer for programs to instruct faculty from foreign nations in the state of American historical scholarship and teaching.

Susan M. Hartmann

Professor of history and women's studies at Ohio State University, Susan M. Hartmann grew up in St. Louis and received her B.A. from Washington University in 1961 and her Ph.D. from the University of Missouri in 1966. After specializing in the political economy of the post–World War II period and publishing *Truman and the 80th Congress* (1971), she expanded her interests to the field of women's history, publishing many articles and two books, *The Home Front and Beyond: American Women in the 1940s* (1982) and *From Margin to Mainstream: American Women and Politics since 1960* (1989). She has won research fellowships and grants from the Truman Library Institute, the Rockefeller Foundation, the National Endowment for the Humanities, and the American Council of Learned Societies. Hartmann has taught at the University of Missouri, St. Louis, and Boston University, and she has lectured on American history in Greece, France, Austria, Germany, Australia, and New Zealand. She has served on book and article award committees of the American Historical Association, the Organization of American Historians, the American Studies Association, and the National Women's Studies Association. At Ohio State she has served as director of women's studies, and in 1995 she won the Exemplary Faculty Award in the College of Humanities.

INDEX

Cuba *(Cont.):*
  refugees from, 1269(i)
  Spanish-American War (1898) and, 789–795, 791(m)
Cullen, Countee (1903–1946), 908
Cult of efficiency, 811–812
Culture
  Beat generation and, 1087–1088
  film heroes during the Great Depression and, 921–922
  Harlem Renaissance and, 908–909, 909(i)
  image of the West in, 660, 663–667
  Kennedy presidency and, 1102
  during the 1920s, 906–908
  popular music in the 1950s and, 1086–1087, 1086(i)
  Scopes trial and, 912
  success and "making it" in America and, 754–755
  television in the 1950s and, 1083–1084, 1084(i), 1085(f)
Currency
  Federal Reserve Act (1913) and, 829
  free silver fight (1880) and, 718–719
  sharecropper scrip as, 652(i)
Cushman, Belle, 740
Custer, George Armstrong (1839–1876)
  Little Bighorn River battle and, 662–663, 665
  reenactments of Last Stand of, 666, 666(i), 667
Czechoslovakia
  Communist government in, 1024, 1246
  German seizure of, 983, 983(i)

Dagenhart, Reuben, 835
Daley, Richard J., 1122, 1160
Da Nang, Vietnam, 1137, 1147
Darrow, Clarence (1857–1938), 912
Darwin, Charles (1809–1938), 706, 709, 912
Daughters of Bilitis, 1004
Daughters of the American Revolution (DAR), 961
Davis, Henry Winter, 608
Davis, James J., 734
Davis, John W., 896
Davis, Richard Harding, 792, 793
Dawes Act (1887), 663, 962
Daws, S. O., 768
D Day, in World War II, 1005, 1009(i)
Debs, Eugene V. (1855–1926), **774–776**, 827, 830–831, 831(i), 865, **887–888**
Debt
  Clinton presidency and, 1255
  crop lien system and, 651–652, 651(f), 767
  farmers and, 647, 648–649, 652(i), 657, 719, 766

free silver fight (1880) and, 718–719
Hoover presidency and, 915
Reagan presidency and, 1224, 1224(f)
Defense Department, 861, 1049
De Gaulle, Charles, 991, 1155
Deloria, Vine, 664
Democratic Party, 795
  city bosses in the nineteenth century and, 676–677, 677(i)
  Eisenhower presidency and, 1063–1064
  election of 1884 and, 715–716
  election of 1892 and, 779(i), 780, 780(m)
  election of 1896 and, 781–784, 782(i), 783(m)
  election of 1932 and, 935–938, 937(m), 938(m)
  election of 1936 and, 965–966
  election of 1960 and, 1099, 1100–1101, 1101(m)
  election of 1964 and, 1107–1110
  Franklin D. Roosevelt and, 934
  New Deal politics and, 950
  power of, after the Civil War, 711–712
  South and, 653, 711, 779, 781, 961, 1043, 1122–1123
  women's participation in, 959
Demonstrations. *See* Protests
Dempsey, Jack (1895–1983), 906
Denis, John Q. A., 612
Denmark, German invasion of, 984
Denver, Colorado, 661, 677
Department stores, workers in, 739–741, 740(i)
Depressions, 678, 682. *See also* Great Depression
  farming in during 1870s and 1890s and, 655, 656
  immigration in the nineteenth century and, 670
  impact on workers of, 725, 729(f)
  mergers among corporations and, 706
  politics in the 1890s and, 776–783, 786
De Soto, Hernando (c. 1500–1542), 665
Detention camps for Japanese Americans, in World War II, 1000–1001, 1002
Detroit, Michigan, 678, 681, 727, 859, 920, 937, 950, 998–999
Dewey, George (1837–1917), 791–794, 791(m)
Dewey, John (1859–1952), 811, 856, 1062
Dewey, Thomas E. (1903–1971), 995, 1043
DeWitt, John, 1000, 1002
Dewson, Molly, 959, 960

Diem, Ngo Dinh (1901–1963), 1067, 1068, 1145
Dime novels, 663–666
Diseases
  farmers and, 646
  penicillin and, 1010
  urban conditions and, 681
Dodge, Grace, 745–746
Doheny, Edward L., 894
Dole, Robert (1923–), 1264–1265
Domestic work, and women, 732(f), 741–742, 742(i)
Dominican Republic
  Lyndon Johnson's intervention in, 1149, 1149(i)
  Wilson's intervention in, 847
Donnelly, Ignatius, 778
Donovan, David, 1138
Doolittle, James H. (1896–1993), 990
Dos Passos, John (1896–1970), 894
Double V campaign, in World War II, 997(i), 999
Douglas, Aaron, 909, 909(i)
Douglas, Helen Gahagan, 1052–1053
Douglas, William O., 1025
Douglass, Frederick (1817–1895), 624, 764
Dreier, Mary, 805–806, 808
Dreiser, Theodore, 682
Dress. *See* Clothing
Du Bois, W. E. B. (1868–1963), 766, 837–838, 860, 909(i), 997
Dukakis, Michael, 1244
Duke, James ("Buck"), 654
Dulles, Allen (1893–1969), 1068, 1069
Dulles, John Foster (1888–1959), 1061
Dunne, Finley Peter, 795

Earth Day, 1186(i)
Eastern Europe
  Bush presidency and changes of government in, 1247–1248, 1248(m)
  Communist governments in, 1024
Eastern European Jewish immigrants, 669, 671–672, 676
Economic conditions
  bank failures and farm foreclosures (1932–1942) and, 944(f), 945
  Bush presidency and, 1244–1245
  Clinton presidency and, 1260–1261, 1261(i)
  consumer prices and farm income (1860–1913) and, 766, 768(f)
  crash of 1929 and, 915–916, 916(i), 922–923
  crop lien system and, 651–652, 651(f), 767
  economic regions of the world and, 727, 728(m)
  Eisenhower presidency and, 1064